FABRIC OF A NATION

A History with Skills and Sources

SECOND EDITION | FOR THE AP® U.S. HISTORY COURSE

Jason Stacy
Southern Illinois University, Edwardsville

Matthew Ellington
Ruben S. Ayala High School, Chino Hills, California

Adapted from *Exploring American Histories,* Third Edition
by Nancy A. Hewitt and Steven F. Lawson

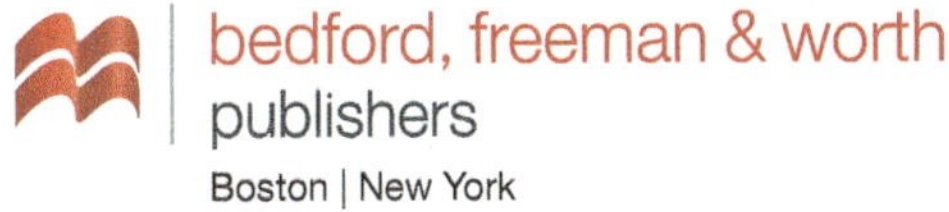

Program Director, High School: Yolanda Cossio
Program Manager, High School Humanities: Caitlin Kaufman
Media Manager, High School: Lisa Samols
Development Editor: Donald Gecewicz
Senior Media Editor: Justin Perry
Associate Media Editor: Michael Emig
Assistant Editor: Sophie Dora Tulchin
Director, High School Marketing: Janie Pierce-Bratcher
Senior Marketing Manager, High School: Claire Brantley
Marketing Assistant, High School: Brianna DiGeronimo
Senior Director, Content Management Enhancement: Tracey Kuehn
Executive Managing Editor: Michael Granger
Senior Manager, Publishing Services: Gregory Erb
Senior Workflow Project Manager: Lisa McDowell
Production Supervisor: Brianna Lester
Director of Design, Content Management: Diana Blume
Senior Design Manager: Natasha A. S. Wolfe
Interior Design: Jerilyn DiCarlo
Cover Design: William Boardman
Art Manager: Matthew McAdams
Cartographer: Mapping Specialists, Ltd. and Lumina Datamatics, Inc.
Senior Director, Rights and Permissions: Hilary Newman
Text Permissions Researcher: Elaine Kosta, Lumina Datamatics, Inc.
Senior Executive Permissions Editor: Cecilia Varas
Photo Researcher: Cheryl Dubois, Lumina Datamatics, Inc.
Senior Director of Digital Production: Keri deManigold
Lead Media Project Manager: Jodi Isman
Copyeditor: Matthew Van Atta, Lumina Datamatics, Inc.
Indexer: Sherri Dietrich, Lumina Datamatics, Inc.
Composition: Lumina Datamatics, Inc.
Printing and Binding: King Printing Co., Inc.

ISBN 978-1-319-48442-2 (Student Edition)

Library of Congress Control Number: 2023930489

Printed in the United States of America
3 4 5 6 28 27 26 25 24

Acknowledgments
Text acknowledgments and copyrights appear at the back of the book on page CR-1, which constitute an extension of the copyright page. Art acknowledgments and copyrights appear on the same page as the art selections they cover.

Bedford, Freeman & Worth Publishers
120 Broadway, New York, NY 10271
bfwpub.com/catalog

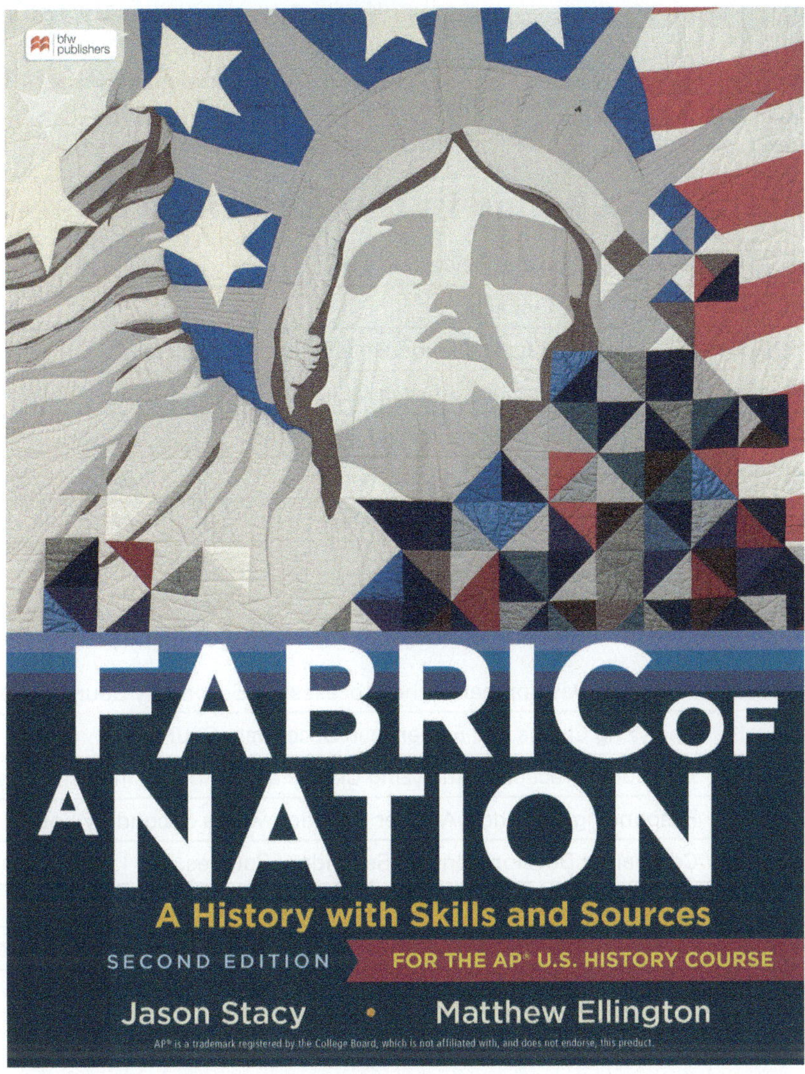

About the Cover Image

Freedom Is Fragile ★ Velda Newman, 1986

Velda Newman, quilt maker and fiber artist, has won the Quilts Japan Prize and was twice awarded the "Best in Show." Her quilt "HYDRANGEA" was selected as one of the 100 Best Quilts of the 20th Century. This powerful image of the Statue of Liberty posed in front of an enormous American flag was made in celebration of the hundredth anniversary of the dedication of the statue. More recently, it was featured in a 2013 exhibition *America the Beautiful* at the Texas Quilt Museum in La Grange. Newman lives in Nevada City, California. Her work can be found at www.veldanewman.com.

Find It Fast:
AP® SKILLS WORKSHOPS

PERIOD 1 Europeans Make Claims in the Americas (1491–1607)

PERIOD 2 Colonial America amid Global Change (1607–1754)

PERIOD 3 A Revolutionary Era (1754–1800)

PERIOD 4 Democracy, Industrialization, and Reform (1800–1848)

PERIOD 5 Expansion, Division, and Civil War (1844–1877)

PERIOD 6 A Gilded Age (1865–1898)

PERIOD 7 New Imperialism and Global Conflicts (1890–1945)

PERIOD 8 Cold War America (1945–1980)

PERIOD 9 Challenges in a Globalized World (1980–The Present)

Brief Contents

PERIOD 4 1800–1848

Democracy, Industrialization, and Reform *256*

PERIOD 5 1844–1877

Expansion, Division, and Civil War *382*

PERIOD 6 1865–1898

A Gilded Age *512*

New Imperialism and Global Conflicts 652

PERIOD 8 **1945–1980**

Cold War America 826

PERIOD 9 **1980–The Present**

Challenges in a Globalized World 972

Contents

PERIOD 3 1754–1800

A Revolutionary Era 144

PERIOD 4 1800–1848

Democracy, Industrialization, and Reform *256*

Expansion, Division, and Civil War *382*

About the Authors

Jason Stacy

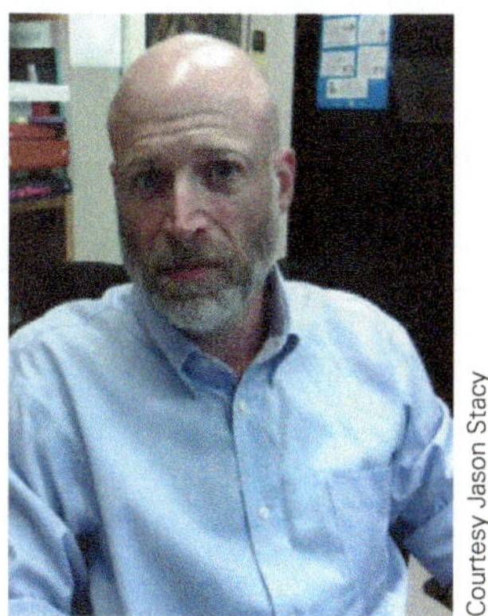

Courtesy Jason Stacy

Jason Stacy is Professor of U.S. History and Social Science Pedagogy at Southern Illinois University–Edwardsville. Before joining the history department at SIU-Edwardsville, Stacy taught AP® U.S. History for eight years at Adlai E. Stevenson High School in Lincolnshire, Illinois. Stacy has served as an AP® U.S. History reader, table leader, exam leader, consultant, senior auditor, and question author for the AP® U.S. History Exam. Author and editor of multiple books on authors like Walt Whitman and Edgar Lee Masters, his research has appeared in *Social Education*, the *Walt Whitman Quarterly Review*, and *American Educational History*. Stacy is also a contributing editor for the *Walt Whitman Archive*, where he edits Whitman's journalism. Recently, he published *Spoon River America: Edgar Lee Masters and the Myth of the American Small Town* with the University of Illinois Press. Stacy has served as the president of the Illinois Council for the Social Studies, the editor of *The Councilor: A Journal of the Social Studies*, and a reviewer for many academic journals and presses.

Matthew Ellington

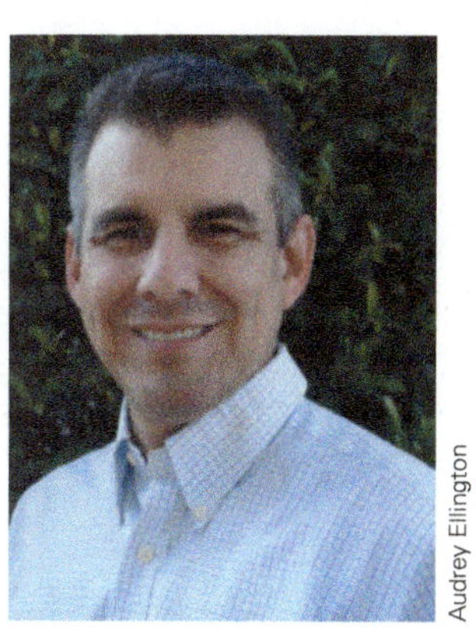

Audrey Ellington

Matthew Ellington has taught AP® U.S. History at Ruben S. Ayala High School in Chino Hills, California, since 1998, where he has also served as an instructional coach, induction mentor for new teachers, social science department chairperson, and a member of his school district's Teaching and Learning Taskforce. Ellington has been an active AP® U.S. History workshop consultant and exam reader for more than twenty years. He has also served as an AP® Mentor and as a member on the College Board's Consultant Advisory Panel. Ellington coauthored *The Survival Guide for AP® U.S. History* and contributed to *Teaching Ideas for AP® History: A Video Resource*.

Ellington and Stacy have been featured together on C-SPAN's AP® U.S. History televised annual review sessions since 2020.

To Our Fellow Teachers

The second edition of *Fabric of a Nation* extends our goal of creating a textbook that meets the needs of AP® U.S. History students in our classrooms and yours. As veteran AP® U.S. History teachers, exam readers, and workshop consultants, we have experienced firsthand the challenges in teaching this course, especially as the curriculum framework and preparation levels of our students have changed over the years.

This edition of *Fabric of a Nation* is carefully aligned to the College Board's Course and Exam Description. It unites historical knowledge, thinking and reasoning skills, and scaffolded pedagogy to maximize student success in the class and on the AP® U.S. History Exam. We have expanded the pedagogy from three to six units, incorporated new opportunities for primary-source analysis throughout the narrative, and included new Thinking Historically or Writing Historically skill activities in every module. Each period includes all-new AP® practice questions, and a new full-length AP® practice exam is provided at the back of the book. Unlike college textbooks that have been repackaged with some AP® add-ons, we designed and wrote *Fabric of a Nation* specifically for AP® students from the ground up. The narrative is shorter, and the embedded pedagogy focuses on essential content and skills appropriate for all high school AP® students.

Fabric of a Nation provides an accessible historical narrative that brings the College Board's curriculum framework to life. It's tightly aligned to the course curriculum, grounded in modern scholarship, and written to meet the diverse backgrounds of today's AP® U.S. History students. Unlike other textbooks, it seamlessly weaves primary sources directly into the narrative. The primary sources we have chosen represent a diverse range of voices and types of documents. They include analysis and comparison questions to broaden students' historical understanding and critical-thinking skills.

Fabric of a Nation's nine time periods align with the College Board's nine units of study, and each of the 105 modules matches the College Board's 105 unit topics. Every module opens with a Focus feature, drawing attention to the same historical reasoning process targeted in the corresponding unit topic, and closes with an AP® Skills Workshop exercise, providing students with instruction or practice in how to think or write historically. All modules can be taught in one to two days, aligning to the pacing recommended in the College Board's unit guides.

We've scaffolded the pedagogical instruction to provide students with step-by-step instructions and practice for how to think historically, analyze documents, and write short-answer, document-based, and long-essay questions. Using sample responses, graphic organizers, and a graduated approach, each module builds and reinforces the knowledge and skills students need to understand history and be successful on the AP® Exam.

Finally, *Fabric of a Nation* also includes AP®-style practice questions at the end of every period, consisting of stimulus-based multiple-choice, short-answer, document-based, and long-essay questions created by experienced item writers to give students solid practice with the kinds of questions they will encounter on the AP® Exam. Additionally, students are supported with a robust running glossary of key terms, helpful AP® Exam margin tips, and a full AP® practice exam.

Fabric of a Nation is the only textbook on the market made specifically for today's AP® U.S. History classroom by experienced AP® U.S. History teachers. We're confident your students will benefit from it, and we are proud to share it with you.

Jason Stacy — Matthew Ellington

Jason Stacy — *Matthew Ellington*

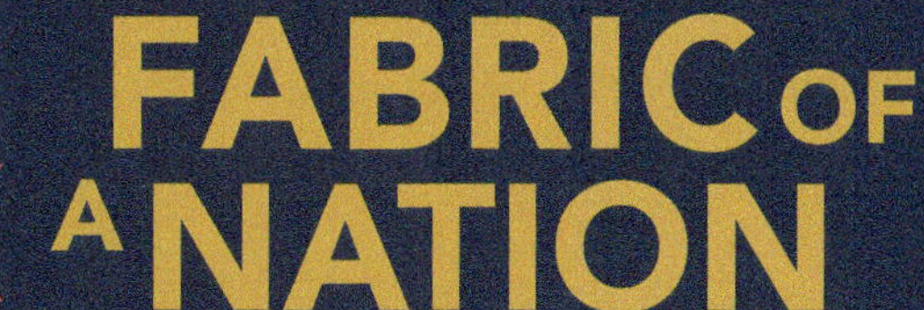

Back and Better Than Ever

The Only AP® U.S. History Book That Weaves Together Content, Skills, Sources, and AP® Exam Practice

AP® U.S. History is about so much more than just events on a timeline. The Course Framework is designed to develop crucial reading, reasoning, and writing skills that help students think like historians to interpret the world of the past—and understand how it relates to the world of today. And *Fabric of a Nation* is still the only textbook that covers *every* aspect of this course, seamlessly stitching together history, skills, sources, and AP® Exam practice. In this new edition, we make it easier than ever to cover all of the skills and topics in the AP® U.S. History Course and Exam Description by aligning our content to the Unit Topics and Historical Reasoning Processes of each Period.

An Accessible, Balanced Narrative

There's only so much time in a school year. To cover everything and leave enough time for skill development, you need more *focused* content, not just more content—and to be most effective, skills development should be accessible and placed just where it is needed. Within the narration are AP® Skills Workshops and AP® Working with Evidence features that support students as they learn the history and prepare to take the AP® Exam. *Fabric of a Nation* delivers a thorough, yet approachable historical narrative that perfectly aligns with all the essential content of the AP® course. An up-to-date historical survey based on current scholarship, this book is also easy to understand and fun to read, with plenty of interesting details and a crisp writing style that keeps things fresh.

Perfectly Aligned to the AP® Scope and Sequence

Fabric of a Nation has an easy-to-use organization that fully aligns with the College Board's Course and Exam Description for AP® U.S. History. Instead of long, meandering chapters, this book is divided into smaller, approachable modules that pull together content, skills, sources, and AP® Exam practice into brief one- to two-day lessons. Each module corresponds with a specific unit topic in the Course Framework, including the contextualization and reasoning process topics that bookend each time period. This approach takes the guesswork out of when to introduce which skills and how to blend sources with content—all at a manageable pace that mirrors the scope and sequence of the AP® Course Framework.

Seamlessly Integrated AP® Skills Workshops for Thinking and Writing Historically

Inspired by the authors' classroom experience and sound pedagogical principles, the instruction in *Fabric of a Nation* scaffolds learning throughout the course of the book. Every module offers an opportunity to either learn or practice new skills to prepare for each section of the AP® Exam in an AP® Skills Workshop. As the book progresses, the nature of these workshops moves from focused instruction early on, to guided practice in the middle of the book, and then finally, to independent practice near the end of the year.

- **Periods 1–3: Focused Instruction.** The first three periods of the textbook provide step-by-step support as they teach students how to think critically about historical developments and processes. Students put that thinking to work by learning to answer stimulus-based multiple-choice questions, short-answer questions with and without primary and secondary sources, construct thesis statements, and craft well-supported body paragraphs. This prepares students for the more complex set of skills taught in Periods 4–6.
- **Periods 4–6: Guided Practice.** In the second portion of the book, the instruction moves to guided writing practice as students deepen their understanding and apply new writing skills to outlining essays, answering Long-Essay and Document-Based Questions, and composing responses that demonstrate a complex and sophisticated historical understanding.
- **Period 7–9: Independent Practice.** The last third of the book shifts to independent practice in the run-up to the exam. In this part of the textbook, the workshops assess students' command of their historical understanding, newly developed skills, preparedness for the exam, and ability to produce college-level writing.

Fabric of a Nation was designed to provide you and your students everything needed to succeed in the AP® U.S. History course and on the exam. It's all there.

AP® Exam Practice: We Boast the Most Material

Every period culminates with AP® Practice questions providing students with a mini-AP® Exam with roughly 15 stimulus-based Multiple-Choice Questions, 4 Short-Answer Questions, 1 Document-Based Question, and 3 Long-Essay Questions. Further, a full-length practice exam is included at the end of the textbook. Because the periods in this book are divided into modules that align perfectly to the AP® U.S. History Course and Exam Description, it's also easy to pair *Fabric of a Nation* with the resources on AP® Classroom. Each textbook module can be used with the corresponding AP® Daily Videos and Topic Questions, while the AP® Exam Practice at the end of each period can be supplemented with the Personal Progress Checks from AP® Classroom.

Period-Opening Features Put History in Context

PERIOD 2
1607–1754
Colonial America amid Global Change

Each period begins with an inviting image about that period.

British Colonial Banner, 1745 This cotton banner was carried by the British at the siege of the French at Louisbourg (1745), Nova Scotia, during King George's War, also known as the War of Austrian Succession (1744–1748). King George's War was one of many colonial wars fought between the British and the French for control of North America in the eighteenth century. While the British soldiers and New England colonists who carried out the siege captured Louisbourg, the fort was later returned to the French as part of the Treaty of Aix-la-Chapelle, which ended the war in 1748.

© New York Historical Society/Bridgeman Images

Contextualizing Period 2

MODULE 2.1

England and France began to challenge Spanish dominance of the Western Hemisphere in the early seventeenth century. As these three kingdoms struggled with one another militarily, economically, and socially, each also consolidated power on the North American continent.

These nations engaged in shifting patterns of cooperation and competition with native populations in ways that reflected their cultural, social, religious, and economic interests. The French steadily established trade networks with native peoples in Canada. The Spanish in the Southwest sought to convert American Indians to Catholicism while at the same time exploiting their labor. The English colony at Jamestown tried to replicate the success of the Spanish, hoping to find easy profits in gold and silver mines, but the climate and geography of Virginia differed greatly from the Central American regions that the Spanish had begun to exploit nearly a hundred years before.

Thus, the early Jamestown settlers built a colony that differed from the ordered and authoritarian *encomienda* system of the Spanish, where native peoples worked under close Spanish supervision. Instead, a labor system in which English-born indentured servants traded several years of hard work in return for passage to the English colony provided much of the labor in the colony during the early seventeenth century. However, this arrangement gave way to a racial caste system in which enslaved Africans made up the bulk of the labor force on large cash-crop plantations in the southern colonies by the turn of the eighteenth century.

In the western backcountry regions of Virginia, the majority of the population was made up of independent farmers, many of whom were former indentured servants themselves. These backcountry settlers negotiated — and often violated — a shifting borderland of conflict and trade with American Indians.

As the seventeenth century progressed, growing European settlements in the New World led to the development of a transatlantic world in which Europeans, American Indians, and Africans traded, competed, and interacted with each other along networks that stretched from the foothills of the Appalachian Mountains to the cities of London, Paris, and Madrid to the villages of West Africa and back to the islands of the Caribbean.

Great Britain's colonies in North America formed an integral part of this transatlantic world. Beginning in the early 1650s, Britain pursued economic policies designed to monopolize trade with its colonies and protect British economic interests. This strategy proved successful. Starting in the late seventeenth century, the British fought a series of colonial wars with other European powers, most often the French, to establish English cultural, ideological, and economic dominance in the North Atlantic and the North American interior. While these wars were costly on many levels, repeated victories cemented Great Britain's dominance of the North American Atlantic seaboard from the late 1600s and well into the 1700s.

By the 1700s, colonists used European models to shape a distinctly British North American culture. For example, the Enlightenment, a European intellectual movement that emb… larity am… enthusias… touched c…

AP® EXAM TIP
Know how to compare and contrast European colonization efforts. Narrow your focus by concentrating on how cultural and economic factors affected the development of the French and Dutch colonies in the New World. Strong

NEW The **Period-Opening Modules,** aligned to the Contextualization Topic that starts off every unit in the AP® Course Framework, contextualize what a student will learn. Learning to place historical events and historical trends in context makes understanding easier.

NEW After each Contextualization module, you'll find a **What's Inside** table. This feature previews the modules ahead. Each module is introduced with its corresponding course theme and a quick summary of main ideas.

Period 2: What's Inside 1607–1754

MODULE	AP® THEMATIC FOCUS
2.1 Contextualizing Period 2	The first contact between Native Americans and Europeans in the fifteenth century and early sixteenth century caused enormous changes to both European and Native societies. The Columbian Exchange of the sixteenth century extended these changes and led to the beginnings of the African slave trade. The period 1607 to 1754 saw the consolidation of European colonial control in North America. This period also saw conflict between European colonial powers for control over the continent, which often divided native peoples among European rivals. Also during this period, transatlantic trade in enslaved African people become a source of labor for many of the European colonies. By the end of this time period, the British controlled much of the eastern seaboard of North America.
2.2 …opean …onization	**Migration and Settlement** Throughout the seventeenth and early eighteenth centuries, the English, French, and Dutch established colonies that challenged Spanish control in North America.
…3 …Regions of …ish Colonies	**Geography and the Environment** The earliest English colonies sought profit through agriculture and the cash crop tobacco, which became a valuable commodity in the Atlantic world. The first English settlers in New England, mostly Puritans, established an economy based on agriculture and commerce within a society of independent family farms and small towns. Distance from Great Britain led to self-governing towns that contained elements of democratic practice. These democratic elements included participatory town meetings and elected colonial legislatures. Starting in the 1660s, the English began to colonize the Middle Atlantic region in North America and build economies based on trade and societies built generally on religious and ethnic tolerance.

2.6 Slavery in the British Colonies	**Work, Exchange, and Technology ■ Social Structures** Slavery shaped the economy and society of British North America. While slavery was more prevalent in the southern colonies, its existence in the middle and northern colonies proved significant as well. Despite often harsh living conditions, enslaved Africans and African Americans found overt and covert ways to rebel against slavery and maintain their families and culture.
2.7 Colonial Society and Culture	**American and Regional Culture ■ American and National Identity** Inspired by religious movements and new political ideologies, British North Americans developed a sense of distinctness from England while, at the same time, experiencing fragmentation within the colonies themselves.
2.8 Comparison in Period 2	This time period offers opportunities for comparison between the different regions of British North America, between the various European powers that vied for control of North America, among native nations and European colonizers, and between Africans in the Western Hemisphere, both enslaved and free, and the European colonists.

Module Features Deepen Understanding and Encourage Historical Analysis

NEW The **Focus** feature is a brief introduction at the start of each module to help students approach the module's narrative the way a historian would. They are designed to promote active reading and prompt critical thinking about key AP® U.S. History developments. Each Focus feature also asks students to consider how the targeted historical reasoning process from the AP® Course Framework ties into the content of the module.

The Eighteenth-Century Atlantic Economy

MODULE 2.4

FOCUS

During the eighteenth century, the combined forces of global trade and international warfare altered the political and economic calculations of imperial powers. This was especially true for British North America, where colonists settled as families and created towns that provided key markets for Britain's commercial expansion. Over the course of the century, British colonists became increasingly avid consumers of products from around the world. Meanwhile, the king and Parliament sought greater control over these far-flung commercial networks.

As you read this module, think about the effects of the economic and political developments you encounter, and be sure to consider the reasons why they occurred. In other words, why did a particular development lead to the results that followed? Think about the ways important effects

In seaport cities, a frequent source of conflict was the **impressment** of colonial men who were seized and forcibly drafted into service in the Royal Navy. Impressment grew increasingly common as King William's War was followed by Queen Anne's War, only to be followed by King George's War. Impressment was viewed as a sign of the corrupt practices o... ...oups of colonists. Sailo... ...feared being pressed i... ...short-

impressment The forced enlistment of civilians into the army or navy. The impressment of residents of colonial seaports into the British navy was a major source of complaint in the eighteenth century.

A **running glossary** across the entire book helps track the most important concepts and events in each module, with definitions visible at a glance to help contextualize the book's historical narrative, illustrations, primary sources, and skill workshops. Even more terms are defined in a full glossary at the back of the book.

- How did Puritan society change between 1630 and 1700?
- What aspects of Puritan society remained the same between 1630 and 1700?

- How did Nathaniel Bacon justify his rebellion?
- What were the results of his rebellion?

Review Questions within the modules provide spots to pause and check understanding. They also offer opportunities to make connections and consider how to apply the thinking skills and reasoning processes of the AP® course to each short section of text.

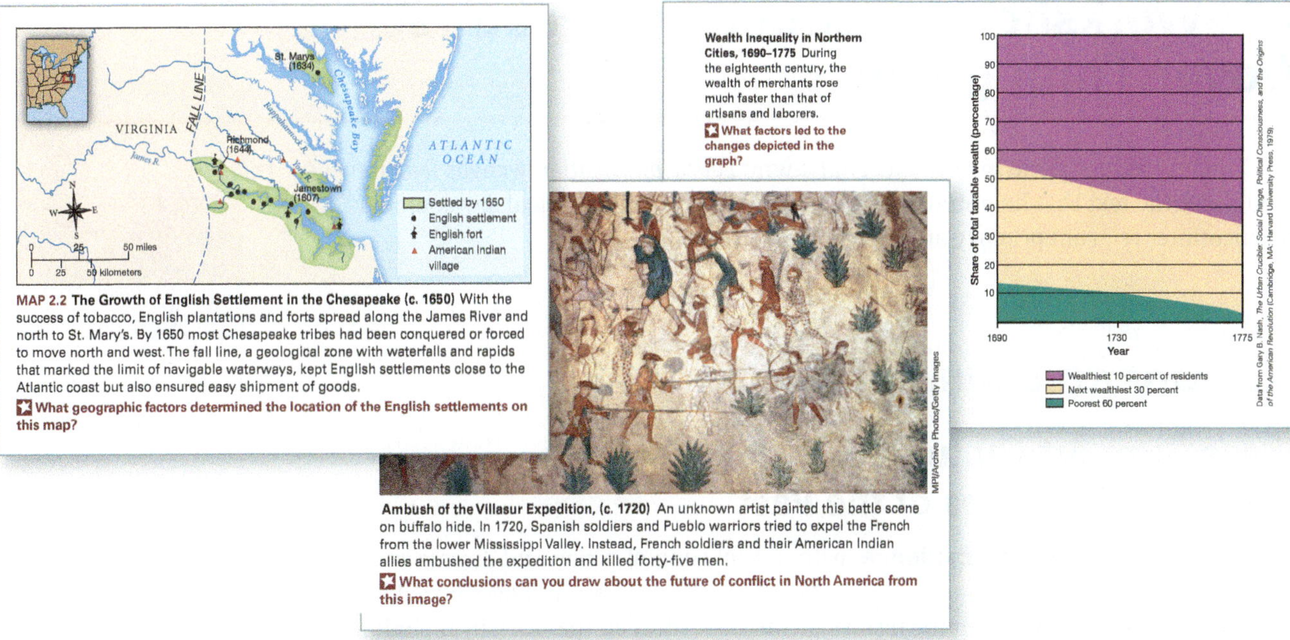

VIRGINIA
FALL LINE
St. Marys (1634)
Chesapeake Bay
Richmond (1644)
Jamestown (1607)
ATLANTIC OCEAN
Settled by 1650
English settlement
English fort
American Indian village
0 25 50 miles
0 25 50 kilometers
MAP 2.2 The Growth of English Settlement in the Chesapeake (c. 1650) With the success of tobacco, English plantations and forts spread along the James River and north to St. Mary's. By 1650 most Chesapeake tribes had been conquered or forced to move north and west. The fall line, a geological zone with waterfalls and rapids that marked the limit of navigable waterways, kept English settlements close to the Atlantic coast but also ensured easy shipment of goods.
What geographic factors determined the location of the English settlements on this map?
Wealth Inequality in Northern Cities, 1690–1775 During the eighteenth century, the wealth of merchants rose much faster than that of artisans and laborers.
What factors led to the changes depicted in the graph?
Share of total taxable wealth (percentage)
Year
1690 1730 1775
Wealthiest 10 percent of residents
Next wealthiest 30 percent
Poorest 60 percent
MPI/Archive Photos/Getty Images
Ambush of the Villasur Expedition, (c. 1720) An unknown artist painted this battle scene on buffalo hide. In 1720, Spanish soldiers and Pueblo warriors tried to expel the French from the lower Mississippi Valley. Instead, French soldiers and their American Indian allies ambushed the expedition and killed forty-five men.
What conclusions can you draw about the future of conflict in North America from this image?

Visuals for analysis: Learning history means examining sources in many forms. From stimulus-based multiple-choice questions to Short-Answer and Document-Based Questions, visual sources are an important part of the AP® U.S. History Exam, and a major challenge for students to analyze. To support learning and building skills, *Fabric of a Nation* provides a robust caption and an analytical question for every image in the book, asking students to draw on their historical knowledge to analyze and respond.

AP® EXAM TIP

The Pueblo Revolt is a specific event you should know for the AP® Exam. Explain how this historical example can be used to describe changes in the Spanish colonial system during the late seventeenth century.

AP® EXAM TIP

Mercantilism and the development of an Atlantic economy are required in the AP® Course and Exam Description. The concepts, which overlap, are often used as the main topics in long essay questions on the AP® Exam. Be able to give in-depth definitions for each, and try to describe how these two developments shaped each other.

AP® Exam Tips in the margins of the book offer a boost where it matters most, with the inside track on the major historical events and concepts you can expect to see on the exam. These tips also offer memorable and active on-the-spot advice for making connections between ideas.

AP® Workshops: Instructional Features Woven Throughout

Skill-building is best done in context. That's why *Fabric of a Nation* weaves features throughout the text that help students engage with important historical developments and encounter relevant primary and secondary sources.

WORKING with EVIDENCE

These Support Features Knit Together Stories and Sources of the Past

Look for **AP® Working with Evidence**, with its inclusion of a rich and diverse range of primary sources—texts, graphs, illustrations, photos, and more. These boxed features, placed at precise points in the historical narrative, deepen the story by including voices, images, and artifacts from the past. These documents appear just-in-time in the narrative to help students understand the necessity of primary sources within the historical record. Each exercise culminates with a scaffolded set of questions that guide students from the details of the source to an analysis of its significance in the history they've just read.

AP® **WORKING with EVIDENCE**

Source: Powhatan, Chief of Algonquian-Speaking Powhatan Confederation, Deerskin Cloak, c. 1608

Maidun Collection/Alamy

About the source: Chief Powhatan wore this deerskin cloak for tribe
The objects on this cloak are made from shells, which were considered
by the Powhatan people. The circles could represent regions under Po
trol, the animals most likely represent deer, and the individual in the cen
Chief Powhatan.

Questions for Analysis

1. Describe the arrangement of the images and materials that make up t
2. Explain what the arrangement of the images and materials that mak reveals about the Powhatan and the Algonquian-speaking peoples.
3. Explain the role Powhatan politics played in fostering conflict with Euro

AP® **WORKING with EVIDENCE**

Source: British Parliament, *Navigation Act*, 1660

"Be it enacted, etc., that no commodity of the growth, production, or manufacture of Europe, shall be imported into any . . . colony, territory, or place, to his Majesty belonging . . . in Asia, Africa, or America . . ., but which shall be . . . shipped in England . . . in English-built shipping . . .; and whereof . . . three fourths of the mariners, at least, are English, and which shall be carried directly thence to the said . . . colonies . . . and from no other place or places whatsoever; . . . under the penalty of the loss of all such commodities. . . ."

Questions for Analysis

1. Identify the rules that regulated exports to the colonies.
2. Describe the penalties for merchants who broke these rules.
3. Explain the reasons governing authorities in England could have used to justify the Navigation Acts.

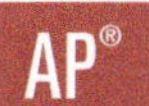

Skills Workshops: Thinking Historically

These Thinking Features Thread Reading and Writing Instruction into Every Module

The **AP® Skills Workshop: Thinking Historically** feature leads students in how to interpret historical developments and primary and secondary sources, as well as how to write about those developments and sources. These workshops appear at the end of most modules in Periods 1–6 to help develop the historical thinking skills and reasoning processes that are key to success in the AP® U.S. History course. Using the content examined in the module as examples, these workshops cover topics such as the interpretation of primary and secondary sources, comparison, and historical developments and processes. They also build the thinking skills that are the foundation of college-level historical writing.

Skills Workshop: Thinking Historically

Analyzing Developments and Processes in Secondary Sources

Historians call their written interpretations of the past **secondary sources**. This textbook, for example, is a secondary source because it includes information about the past written by historians. However, this textbook also includes **primary sources**, which are sources *from* the past. For example, the material in the Working with Evidence features includes primary sources.

In this U.S. history course, and on the AP® Exam, you will sometimes have to read a historian's argument and identify and explain a historical development or processes. By **development** we mean the rise or growth of a trend or historical change. By **processes** we mean the details of how a trend or change came about.

Let's say you wanted to identify the development of the Spanish colonies, described in Period 1. When you describe this development, you might say that these colonies began as a few scattered settlements on the islands of the Caribb... the mid-sixteenth century, they had expanded to the mainland and bega... atic conquest of the indigenous civilizations there.

If you were to explain the process of this development, you could ... the Spanish colonies were at first small settlements on islands, whic... economic and military centers for settlement and trade. These early ... allowed the Spanish to launch more ambitious exploration of the Car... Yucatán peninsula, and Central and South America. By the mid-six... tury, the Spanish had destroyed the Aztec empire and had begun to... Spain into a colony for larger settlements and greater exploitation of... people.

A historian might write a paragraph that describes this develo... explains the process like this:

> The Spanish colonies began as a few scattered settlements ... islands of the Caribbean in the early sixteenth century. By th... sixteenth century, these colonies expanded to the mainland and ... systematic conquest of the indigenous civilizations there. The first ... settlements in the Caribbean served as economic and military cen... settlement and trade. Settled a few decades after Columbus's arriva... settlements allowed the Spanish to launch more ambitious explor... the Caribbean, the Yucatán peninsula, and Central and South Ame... the mid-sixteenth century, the Spanish had destroyed the Aztec ... and begun to build New Spain into a colony of larger settleme... exploited more indigenous people. The *encomienda* system of forc... was one method of this exploitation.

ACTIVITY

On the next page is an excerpt about the French in North America ... seventeenth and eighteenth centuries. Read the excerpt and, in your ... **describe** the **development** of these French colonies according to the a... **explain** the **process** by which this development occurred.

(continued)

1609–1613

"Québec [the capital of New France] was used for little else than a warehouse. Champlain reported that sixteen people wintered there in 1609–1610 and seventeen the following winter. The Habitation [trading outpost] received only minimal maintenance and fell into disrepair.

1614–1620

The reinstated trade monopoly was now managed by Compagnie du Canada [which was the French company that controlled the fur trade in New France]. The company bought the Habitation. . . . Once the outpost changed hands, the number who overwintered in Québec increased sharply; from at least 1617 it rose to 50 or 60. More significant was the spread of settlement further away from the Habitation. . . . At the same time Champlain obliged the company to erect a fort on the height overlooking the Habitation. . . . It was a modest two-story structure in wood, probably surrounded by a simple wooden palisade.

1621–1632

This was a period of intense work. The rebuilding of all or part of the Habitation and Fort Saint-Louis was undertaken . . .; and the Jesuit convent . . . was erected on the opposite bank. In 1628, the development of the . . . colony was brought to a halt by war. The English fleet under the command of David Kirke took control of the river, preventing supplies from reaching Québec. . . .

[T]he efforts to protect the colony were in vain. On 20 July 1629 the keys to the Habitation and Fort Saint-Louis had to be handed over to [the English].

1632–1635

In 1632, France retook Québec . . . Champlain came back to Québec in 1633 and took up residence in Fort Saint-Louis . . . On Champlain's death on 25 December 1635, Québec had about 300 inhabitants."

Excerpt from Françoise Niellon, "Québec in the Time of Champlain," *Post-Medieval Archaeology*, vol. 43, no. 1, 2009: The Recent Archaeology of the Early Modern Period in Quebex City. Copyright © Society for Post-Medieval Archaeology 2009, reprinted by permission of Taylor & Francis Ltd, https://www.tandfonline.com on behalf of Society for Post-Medieval Archaeology.

Skills Workshops: Writing Historically

These Special Features Map Out How to Write for the AP® Exam

The **AP® Skills Workshop: Writing Historically** feature is a writing coach—teaching students how to craft their answers, whether brief or longer. Appearing twice per period in Periods 1–6, these essential exercises provide scaffolded, step-by-step instruction that takes students through how to approach each of the writing tasks on the AP® Exam: Short-Answer Questions, Long-Essay Questions, and Document-Based Questions. In Periods 7–9, these workshops appear at the end of each module to provide plenty of exam practice toward the end of the year.

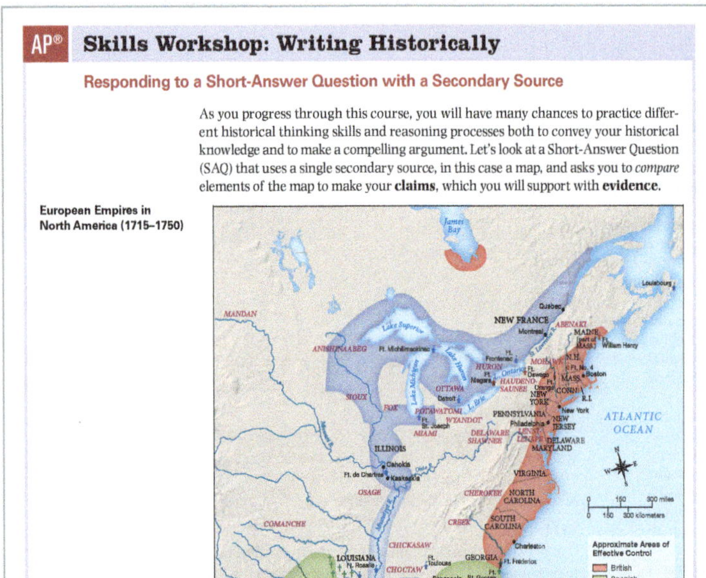

End-of-Period Features for Practice and Assessment

NEW Historical Reasoning Process Modules Aligned to the AP® Course Unit Topics

The final module of each time period is always an AP® Skills Workshop: Writing Historically activity focused on the same end-of-period historical reasoning process in the AP® U.S. History Unit Guide. In this way, *Fabric of a Nation* is precisely calibrated to the College Board's framework, making all of its instruction directly related to student success on the exam.

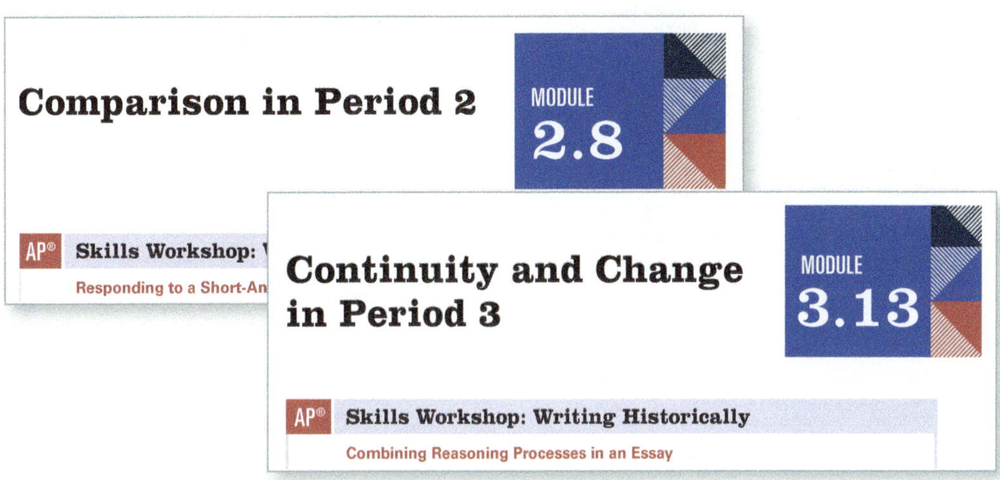

	AP® Course and Exam Description End-of-Period Topic	*Fabric of a Nation*, Second Edition End-of-Period Module
PERIOD 1 (1491–1607)	**Topic 1.7** Causation in Period 1	**Module 1.7** Causation in Period 1
PERIOD 2 (1607–1754)	**Topic 2.8** Comparison in Period 2	**Module 2.8** Comparison in Period 2
PERIOD 3 (1754–1800)	**Topic 3.13** Continuity and Change in Period 3	**Module 3.13** Continuity and Change in Period 3
PERIOD 4 (1800–1848)	**Topic 4.14** Causation in Period 4	**Module 4.14** Causation in Period 4
PERIOD 5 (1844–1877)	**Topic 5.12** Comparison in Period 5	**Module 5.12** Comparison in Period 5
PERIOD 6 (1865–1898)	**Topic 6.14** Continuity and Change in Period 6	**Module 6.14** Continuity and Change in Period 6
PERIOD 7 (1890–1945)	**Topic 7.15** Comparison in Period 7	**Module 7.15** Comparison in Period 7
PERIOD 8 (1945–1980)	**Topic 8.15** Continuity and Change in Period 8	**Module 8.15** Continuity and Change in Period 8
PERIOD 9 (1980–present)	**Topic 9.7** Causation in Period 9	**Module 9.7** Causation in Period 9

Period Review Sections Connect the Threads of History

Following the final module in each period, these short sections list the key concepts, events, and people of the era. Key concepts are defined in the glossary. A handy timeline helps organize the chronology of important events and historical turning points all in one place.

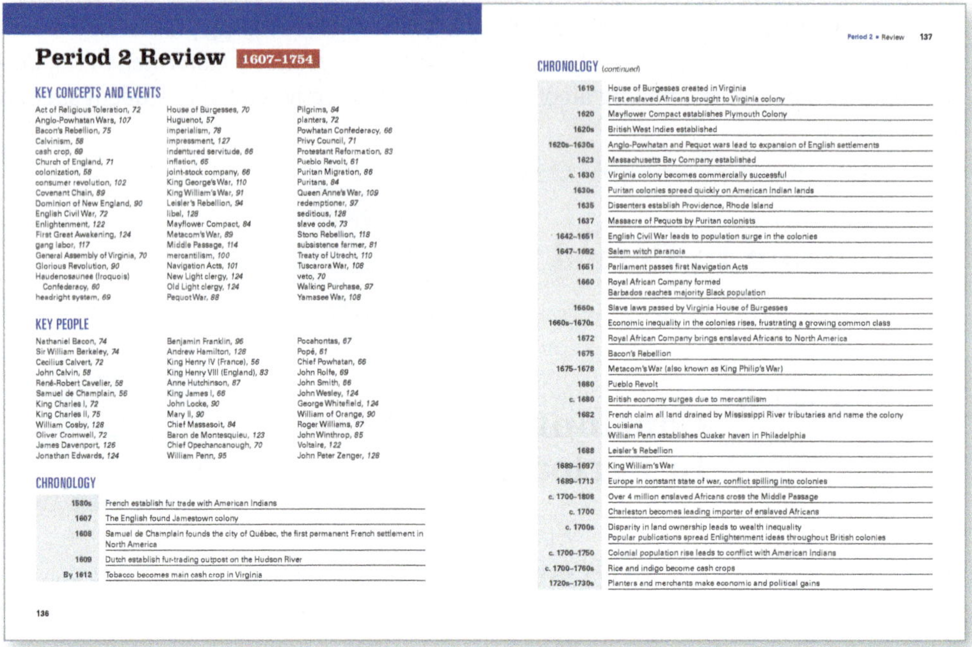

Period 2 Review 1607–1754

KEY CONCEPTS AND EVENTS

Act of Religious Toleration, *72*
Anglo-Powhatan Wars, *107*
Bacon's Rebellion, *75*
Calvinism, *58*
cash crop, *69*
Church of England, *71*
colonization, *58*
consumer revolution, *102*
Covenant Chain, *89*
Dominion of New England, *90*
English Civil War, *72*
Enlightenment, *122*
First Great Awakening, *124*
gang labor, *117*
General Assembly of Virginia, *70*
Glorious Revolution, *90*
Haudenosaunee (Iroquois) Confederacy, *60*
headright system, *69*
House of Burgesses, *70*
Huguenot, *57*
imperialism, *78*
impressment, *127*
indentured servitude, *66*
inflation, *65*
joint-stock company, *66*
King George's War, *110*
King William's War, *91*
Leisler's Rebellion, *94*
libel, *128*
Mayflower Compact, *84*
Metacom's War, *89*
Middle Passage, *114*
mercantilism, *100*
Navigation Acts, *101*
New Light clergy, *124*
Old Light clergy, *124*
Pequot War, *88*
Pilgrims, *84*
planters, *72*
Powhatan Confederacy, *66*
Privy Council, *71*
Protestant Reformation, *83*
Pueblo Revolt, *61*
Puritan Migration, *86*
Puritans, *84*
Queen Anne's War, *109*
redemptioner, *97*
seditious, *128*
slave code, *73*
Stono Rebellion, *118*
subsistence farmer, *81*
Treaty of Utrecht, *110*
Tuscarora War, *108*
veto, *70*
Walking Purchase, *97*
Yamasee War, *108*

KEY PEOPLE

Nathaniel Bacon, *74*
Sir William Berkeley, *74*
Cecilius Calvert, *72*
John Calvin, *58*
René-Robert Cavelier, *58*
Samuel de Champlain, *56*
King Charles I, *72*
King Charles II, *75*
William Cosby, *128*
Oliver Cromwell, *72*
James Davenport, *126*
Jonathan Edwards, *124*
Benjamin Franklin, *96*
Andrew Hamilton, *128*
King Henry IV (France), *56*
King Henry VIII (England), *83*
Anne Hutchinson, *87*
King James I, *66*
John Locke, *90*
Mary II, *90*
Chief Massasoit, *84*
Baron de Montesquieu, *123*
Chief Opechancanough, *70*
William Penn, *95*
Pocahontas, *67*
Popé, *61*
Chief Powhatan, *66*
John Rolfe, *69*
John Smith, *66*
John Wesley, *124*
George Whitefield, *124*
William of Orange, *90*
Roger Williams, *87*
John Winthrop, *85*
Voltaire, *122*
John Peter Zenger, *128*

CHRONOLOGY

1530s	French establish fur trade with American Indians
1607	The English found Jamestown colony
1608	Samuel de Champlain founds the city of Québec, the first permanent French settlement in North America
1609	Dutch establish fur-trading outpost on the Hudson River
By 1612	Tobacco becomes main cash crop in Virginia

136

Period 2 • Review 137

CHRONOLOGY *(continued)*

1619	House of Burgesses created in Virginia First enslaved Africans brought to Virginia colony
1620	Mayflower Compact establishes Plymouth Colony
1620s	British West Indies established
1620s–1630s	Anglo-Powhatan and Pequot wars lead to expansion of English settlements
1623	Massachusetts Bay Company established
c. 1630	Virginia colony becomes commercially successful
1630s	Puritan colonies spread quickly on American Indian lands
1635	Dissenters establish Providence, Rhode Island
1637	Massacre of Pequots by Puritan colonists
1642–1651	English Civil War leads to population surge in the colonies
1647–1692	Salem witch paranoia
1651	Parliament passes first Navigation Acts
1660	Royal African Company formed Barbados reaches majority Black population
1660s	Slave laws passed by Virginia House of Burgesses
1660s–1670s	Economic inequality in the colonies rises, frustrating a growing common class
1672	Royal African Company brings enslaved Africans to North America
1675	Bacon's Rebellion
1675–1678	Metacom's War (also known as King Philip's War)
1680	Pueblo Revolt
c. 1680	British economy surges due to mercantilism
1682	French claim all land drained by Mississippi River tributaries and name the colony Louisiana William Penn establishes Quaker haven in Philadelphia
1688	Leisler's Rebellion
1689–1697	King William's War
1689–1713	Europe in constant state of war, conflict spilling into colonies
c. 1700–1808	Over 4 million enslaved Africans cross the Middle Passage
c. 1700	Charleston becomes leading importer of enslaved Africans
c. 1700s	Disparity in land ownership leads to wealth inequality Popular publications spread Enlightenment ideas throughout British colonies
c. 1700–1750	Colonial population rise leads to conflict with American Indians
c. 1700–1760s	Rice and indigo become cash crops
1720s–1730s	Planters and merchants make economic and political gains

All New AP® Exam Practice for a New Edition

Fabric of a Nation gives students ample opportunity to practice their new AP® skills by presenting AP® Exam Practice at the end of every period and a full-length AP® Practice Exam at the back of the book. The AP® Exam Practice for every period and the end-of-book Practice Exam are completely new and exclusive to this edition.

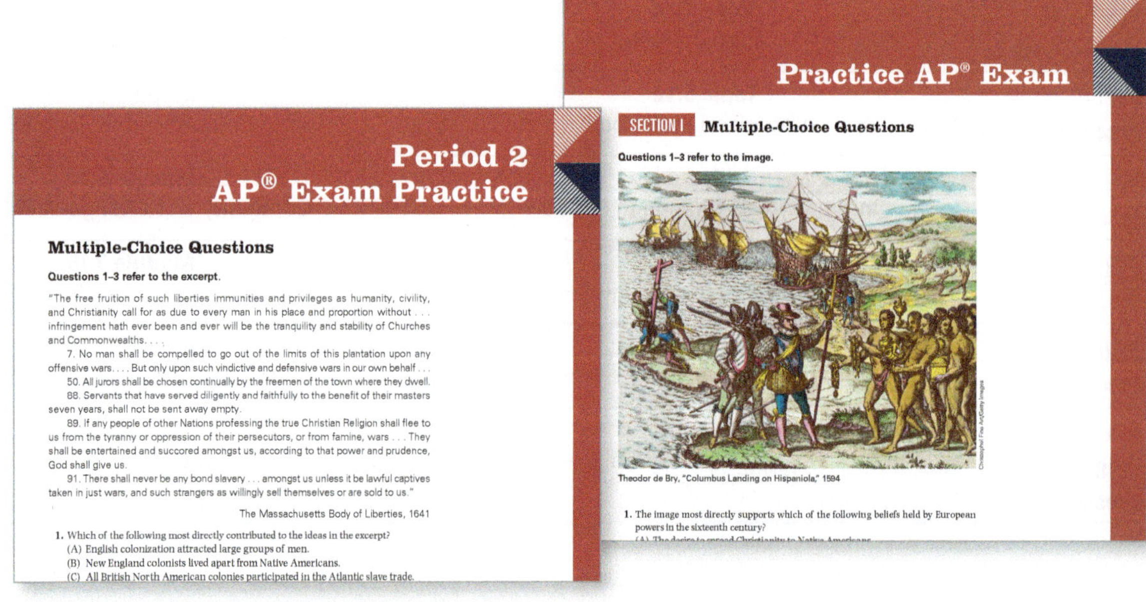

Period 2 AP® Exam Practice

Multiple-Choice Questions

Questions 1–3 refer to the excerpt.

"The free fruition of such liberties immunities and privileges as humanity, civility, and Christianity call for as due to every man in his place and proportion without . . . infringement hath ever been and ever will be the tranquility and stability of Churches and Commonwealths. . . .

7. No man shall be compelled to go out of the limits of this plantation upon any offensive wars. . . . But only upon such vindictive and defensive wars in our own behalf . . .

50. All jurors shall be chosen continually by the freemen of the town where they dwell.

88. Servants that have served diligently and faithfully to the benefit of their masters seven years, shall not be sent away empty.

89. If any people of other Nations professing the true Christian Religion shall flee to us from the tyranny or oppression of their persecutors, or from famine, wars . . . They shall be entertained and succored amongst us, according to that power and prudence, God shall give us.

91. There shall never be any bond slavery . . . amongst us unless it be lawful captives taken in just wars, and such strangers as willingly sell themselves or are sold to us."

The Massachusetts Body of Liberties, 1641

1. Which of the following most directly contributed to the ideas in the excerpt?
   (A) English colonization attracted large groups of men.
   (B) New England colonists lived apart from Native Americans.
   (C) All British North American colonies participated in the Atlantic slave trade.

Practice AP® Exam

SECTION I **Multiple-Choice Questions**

Questions 1–3 refer to the image.

Christophel Fine Art/Getty Images

Theodor de Bry, "Columbus Landing on Hispaniola," 1594

1. The image most directly supports which of the following beliefs held by European powers in the sixteenth century?

A Complete Package to Support AP® Teachers and Students

A Teacher's Edition | Written by Teachers for Teachers

The wraparound Teacher's Edition for *Fabric of a Nation* is an invaluable resource for both experienced and new AP® U.S. History instructors. Written by seasoned AP® instructors and workshop presenters, the Teacher's Edition includes thoughtful instruction for planning, pacing, differentiating, and enlivening your AP® U.S. History course.

Teacher's Resource Materials | Let You Build Your Course Your Way

The Teacher's Resource Materials accompany the Teacher's Edition and contain materials to effectively plan the course, including a detailed suggested pacing guide, handouts, suggested responses to AP® Working with Evidence questions and AP® Skills Workshops, activities, lecture presentation slides, videos, and so much more.

| More than Just an e-Book

Achieve is our new online courseware offering flexible assessment tools and content to support students of all levels. In Achieve, you have everything you need for a successful course at your fingertips. Teachers can access all of the Teacher's Resource Materials and the Teacher's Edition e-book. Students can stay organized and on schedule with a user-friendly interface that is as powerful as it is intuitive. This is a one-stop shop where students can easily:

- find their mobile-friendly and fully accessible e-book;
- increase their understanding with ready-made quizzes;
- complete online homework or assessments; and
- monitor their progress with the built-in gradebook.

Plus, all of this easily integrates with learning management systems for a seamless classroom experience.

LearningCurve | Game-Like Adaptive Quizzing

Embedded in the book's digital platform is the LearningCurve, an adaptive game-like assessment tool that helps students focus on the material they need the most help with. When they get a question wrong, feedback tells them why and links them to content review—and then they get a chance to try again.

Test Bank | Your Home for AP® Exam Prep

Get the most out of the course with ample practice for success on the AP® Exam! Our authors and editors analyzed hundreds of items from national assessments and AP® Exams to target key skills. They created a completely new Test Bank, exclusive to this edition. The Test Bank includes a full-length AP® U.S. History-style practice test with multiple-choice, short-answer, document-based, and long-essay questions for each unit. The Test Bank lets teachers quickly create paper and online tests in minutes. The platform is fully customizable, allowing teachers to enter their own questions, edit existing questions, set time limits, incorporate multimedia, and scramble answers and change the order of questions to prevent academic dishonesty. Detailed result reports feed into a gradebook or can be exported to Microsoft Excel.

Acknowledgments

We are fortunate to have had the assistance of some incredible people throughout this project, especially with the development of the Teacher's Edition and teacher resource materials. Our thanks to AP® U.S. History teachers Scott Birrell, Carlene Baurichter, Jose Gregory, Nicki Griffin, Jon Kinman, Bill Polasky, and Kyle Vanderwall.

We especially would like to thank Shannan Mason for her research assistance and ability to turn around quality work in record time. We would also like to thank the dedicated team at Bedford, Freeman, & Worth. We are grateful to Lee Benjamins for shepherding this edition's early stages, to Caitlin Kaufman for her indefatigable spirit and exceptional editing skills, to Don Gecewicz for his deft development of this edition, to Sophie Dora Tulchin for her superhuman organizational and troubleshooting skills, and to Greg Erb's expert guidance of the production process. Thanks also to Nathan Odell, who first proposed this project to us.

Jason Stacy also wishes to thank Michelle, Abigail, and Margaret Stacy, who make all good things possible for him.

Matthew Ellington also wishes to thank Jacqueline, Audrey, Daniel, and David Ellington for their consistent love and encouragement in all life's adventures.

Reviewers of *Fabric of a Nation*

These reviewers participated in many ways in shaping the content of the textbook. They reviewed modules; gave advice on content, AP® course alignment, pedagogy, and more; and participated in an early survey about the book and the AP® course that it serves.

Sarah Athey, *South Lyon East High School, Michigan*
Carlene Baurichter, *Bangor High School, Wisconsin*
Becky Berry, *Morgantown High School, West Virginia*
Drew Biri, *Colonia High School, New Jersey*
Jason A. Burns, *Hopkins Academy, Massachusetts*
Jayme Gafford, *West Valley High School, Alaska*
Christina Gallo, *Lake Forest High School, Delaware*
Glenn Leo Gapusan, *Pacific Law Academy, California*
Jose Gregory, *Marist School, Georgia*
Robin Grenz, *Hagerty High School, Florida*
Michelle Henry, *Danville Community High School, Indiana*
Constance Hines, *Wiregrass Ranch High School, Florida*
Pete Joseph, *RHAM High School, Connecticut*
Jared Kenish-Turnbull, *Wadleigh Secondary School for the Performing and Visual Arts, New York*
Jon Kinman, *Charlotte Mecklenburg Schools, North Carolina*
Barry Kirzner, *Kohelet Yeshiva High School, Pennsylvania*
Steve Klawiter, *Lafayette High School, Missouri*
Chris Madlena, *Life Christian Academy, Washington*
Joan O'Brien, *The MacDuffie School, Massachusetts*
Zack Olson, *Denmark High School, Wyoming*
Barbara Ramsey, *Asheville, North Carolina*
Kirstine Rivera, *Decatur High School, Washington*
Branden Roberson, *West Florence High School, South Carolina*
Elizabeth Roberts, *Taylor High School, Texas*
Rhonda Rush, *Homewood High School, Alabama*
John Santone, *Great Oak High School, California*
Kenny Savaglia, *Burlington High School, Wisconsin*
Dylan H. Scharf, *Great Oak High School, California*
Matt Scherbarth, *Mukwonago High School, Wisconsin*
Matt Tassinari, *Palmdale High School, California*
Bob Topping, *Palmetto Ridge High School, Florida*
Alan Vitale, *Northwest School of the Arts, North Carolina*
Susan Wascher-Jordan, *St. Philip Catholic Central High School, Michigan*
Russell Wellenstein, *Jefferson High School, Wisconsin*
Carol Yuen, *Kahuku High and Intermediate School, Hawaii*
James Zucker, *Loyola High School, California*
Chris Zuver, *Moses Lake High School, Washington*

We also thank the hundreds of teachers of AP® U.S. History who participated in surveys for both editions of this book. Your feedback was crucial in helping us craft this textbook program for the AP® course.

Reviewers of *Exploring American Histories*

Fabric of a Nation was originally adapted from *Exploring American Histories*, Third Edition, and a number of instructors helped to guide its development. Over the years, this book has had the privilege of being reviewed by hundreds of scholars. We appreciate the time and thoughts the following reviewers of *Exploring American Histories* put into their feedback for the third edition in particular, which helped authors Nancy A. Hewitt and Steven F. Lawson refine the textbook and ensure that the content is useful to both instructors and students.

Rob Alderson, *Perimeter College at Georgia State University*
Chad Gregory, *Tri-County Technical College*
Larry Grubbs, *Georgia State University*
Don Knox, *Wayland Baptist University*
Leslie Leighton, *Georgia State University*
Amani Marshall, *Georgia State University*
Ricky Moser, *Kilgore College*
David Soll, *University of Wisconsin, Eau Claire*
Ramon Veloso, *Palomar College*

PERIOD 1 1491–1607

Europeans Make Claims in the Americas

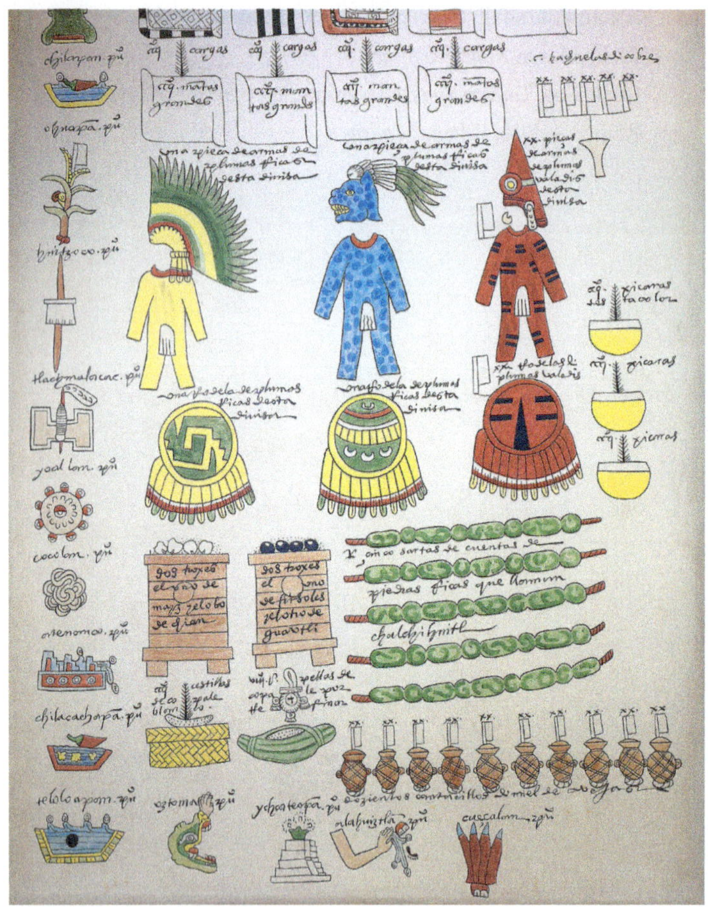

The Codex Mendoza, c. 1540 These images are taken from the *Codex Mendoza*, a collection of histories of Native American leaders in Central America and a catalog of tributes paid to the Spanish crown. The illustrations shown here are of ceremonial outfits and shields acquired by the Spanish as tribute.

Contextualizing Period 1

MODULE 1.1

Over 25,000 years ago, Asian peoples started migrating to the Americas by land and sea. Major migrations occurred 12,000–14,000 years ago. Over time, these peoples developed an astonishing array of cultures and societies, from small hunting-and-gathering bands to complex empires. By the fourteenth and fifteenth centuries of the Common Era, extensive commercial and political networks existed among the Mississippian Indians, the Aztecs, and the Incas, although only the latter two continued to thrive by the late 1400s.

In southern Europe, too, during the fifteenth century, economic, cultural, and political advances fueled interest in long-distance trade and exploration. Italy and Portugal led these efforts. Their firm control of trade routes across the Mediterranean and around Africa to Asia led Spain to look west in hopes of gaining access to China and the Indies (India, Indonesia, and Southeast Asia). In doing so, the Spanish unexpectedly came into contact with the Americas.

When Spanish explorers happened upon Caribbean islands and the nearby mainland of Central and South America they created contacts between European and American populations whose lives would be dramatically transformed in a matter of decades. While native residents of the Americas were sometimes eager to trade with the newcomers and form alliances against their traditional enemies, they fought against those they considered invaders.

Yet some of the most significant invaders—plants, pigs, and especially germs—were impossible to defend against. Even Europeans whose main goal was conversion to Christianity brought diseases that devastated local populations as well as plants and animals that transformed their landscape, diet, and traditional ways of life.

From the 1490s to the 1590s, the most dramatic and devastating changes for native peoples occurred in Mexico, the West Indies, Central America, and parts of South America. But events there also foreshadowed what would happen throughout the Americas. As Spanish conquerors and European competitors explored, they carried sufficient germs, seeds, and animals to transform native societies even before Europeans established permanent settlements in North America. As Native American populations died out in some regions and fended off conquest in others, the Spanish and Portuguese turned increasingly to the trade in enslaved Africans to provide the labor to produce enormously profitable items like sugar, coffee, and tobacco.

AP® EXAM TIP

It is important to understand that U.S. History is not the "beginning" of history on the North American continent. For the AP® Exam, be prepared to compare and contrast Native American life before and after European contact.

AP® Skills Workshop: Thinking Historically

Active Reading and Review

To fully understand, analyze, and interpret history—including everything from historical documents and artifacts to retellings of events to definitions of key historical concepts—it is essential to read and review actively. Although this may sound difficult and time-consuming, all that's required for active reading and review is to think about the meaning of what you read while you read it and to regularly revisit the reading or your notes on it. Sometimes, we are able to allow a piece of writing,

(continued)

usually fiction, to carry us away, and as the words fill your imagination, it can feel like you are watching a movie or television show. Unlike fiction, history requires that you think about the text as you read it, write down your observations or questions, and regularly review if you want to understand and recall important information.

Part of active reading is focusing on a text and creating an authentic, internal dialogue as you read. Mentally, you should be reacting to the reading by identifying main points and supporting details, connecting to what you have already read, and asking questions. Writing down these insights and questions in the margins, on sticky notes, or in a separate notebook as you read or right after you have read a section will help you clarify your thoughts and make meaning of the text.

Another useful active reading strategy is to skim a module before and after reading it closely. Reading the opening Focus feature and introductory paragraphs, noticing the headings, and looking at the images and captions can help your mind make connections to what you have already learned. Likewise, after you've read a module, reviewing the margin definitions, and thinking about the Review questions as well as the image caption and Working with Evidence questions can help you lock in the material.

Finally, it's important to look back over your reading notes, if possible, the next day and again a week later. Regular review will cement your understanding and help you build long-term recall.

ACTIVITY

As you read *Fabric of a Nation*, focus on creating a genuine, internal conversation with the text. Use your preferred method of annotation (highlighting and writing notes in the margin—if allowed, creating sticky notes, and/or writing in a notebook) to write down key points, connections, questions generated as you read, and/or answers to questions in the textbook. Make sure to review your notes a day later and then a week later.

Period 1: What's Inside 1491–1607

MODULE	AP® THEMATIC FOCUS
1.1 Contextualizing Period 1	Native peoples developed diverse and distinct societies across the Americas with extensive trade networks. By the 1400s, the Aztec empire dominated Mesoamerica, the Inca empire extended outward from Peru, and countless other Native American societies were spread across the Americas. As western Europe emerged from the devastation of the Black Death in the mid-1300s, the Renaissance, technological advancements, and a desire for foreign trade goods led Portugal and then Spain to embark on expeditions of exploration and conquest, in the mid- to late-1400s. Beginning with Christopher Columbus's first voyage to the New World in 1492, ongoing contact between Europe, Africa, and the Americas significantly changed the lives of peoples in all three parts of the world.
1.2 Native American Societies before European Contact	**Geography and the Environment** Geographic and environmental factors shaped the development of Native American societies, fostering diversity. The implementation of intensive agriculture and the cultivation of crops such as maize (corn) led to the formation of large and complex Native American societies in Central America and the Andes Mountain region. Societies in other regions were often smaller, resulting in a diverse fabric of indigenous cultures.
1.3 European Exploration in the Americas	**America in the World** Relying on technological innovations and driven by a desire for trade and economic competition, European countries began to fund voyages of exploration and conquest. Portugal secured trading posts in Africa as well as profitable ocean trade routes to the Middle East and Asia. Spain financed Columbus's voyages to the Americas, opening a New World for Europeans. Interactions between Columbus and Native American societies in the Caribbean established patterns for future relations.
1.4 Columbian Exchange, Spanish Exploration, and Conquest	**Geography and the Environment** The Columbian Exchange — of crops, animals, diseases, and more — shaped the development of both Native American and European societies. Crops transplanted from the Americas led to the growth of Europe's population, and the mineral wealth from the New World contributed to the transition from feudalism to capitalism in Europe. Yet for indigenous peoples in the Americas, the main effect of the Columbian Exchange was the introduction of European diseases, which eliminated much of the native population. The creation of an "Atlantic World" linking Europe, the Americas, and Africa in an economic system that relied on the forced labor of Native Americans and Africans also sped up as Britain, France, and the Netherlands began to colonize.
1.5 Labor, Slavery, and Caste in the Spanish Colonial System	**Social Structures** Spanish conquerors used local allies and technological superiority to overpower the Aztecs and other powerful Native American societies in Central and South America. As Spain built a large empire in the New World, it relied on the *encomienda* system to force Native Americans to labor on Spanish plantations and introduced a caste system, which created a social hierarchy based on race.
1.6 Cultural Interactions between Europeans, Native Americans, and Africans	**America in the World** The Atlantic World fused cultures through the contacts and migrations of people, both forced and free, from Europe and Africa to create new societies and social systems, while the harsh treatment of Native Americans fostered debate within Spanish society and contributed to establishment of the mission system.
1.7 Causation in Period 1	This period provides opportunities to consider the causes and effects of European exploration, conquest, and the Columbian Exchange on the lives of peoples living in the Americas, Africa, and Europe.
Support and Practice	• Practice thinking and writing historically in each module. • See the Period Review of key concepts, events, people, and dates after the last module. • Try the AP® Exam Practice at the end of the period.

MODULE 1.2

Native American Societies before European Contact

FOCUS

In everyday life, we often compare two or more things to understand each one better. For example, if you want to understand the weather today, it often helps to compare it to yesterday's weather. Likewise, if you want to understand what everyday life is like for people in rural communities, it's helpful to have a sense of what daily life is like for the average city dweller. Historians apply this same principle to their work, too: They use comparison to illuminate the similarities and differences between two or more historical events, individuals, groups, regions, developments, or concepts.

As you read this module, practice thinking comparatively about the relationships between and among the peoples, events, and concepts you encounter. Keep in mind that historical comparison is most effective when it takes into account both similarities *and* differences between two or more things. Your goal for this module is to compare things such as cultures, environments, and economies in relation to each other. As you read, keep track of what important aspects they share in common as well as where they diverge.

The first people in the Americas almost certainly arrived as migrants from northeast Asia. Although the timing of these migrations remains in doubt, they likely began at least 25,000 years ago. It is also difficult to estimate the population of the Americas before contact with Europeans — estimates of its peak range from 37 million to 100 million, the vast majority of whom lived within a few hundred miles of the equator. Only around 4 million to 7 million people lived in what would become the present-day United States. By the fifteenth century, the Americas were home to diverse societies, ranging from coastal fishing villages to nomadic hunter-gatherers to settled horticulturalists to large city-centered empires.

The complex societies that emerged in the Americas were made possible by an agricultural revolution that began about 10,000 years ago when these societies established crop systems, domesticated animals, and developed tools. Between 8000 and 2000 B.C.E., some communities in the Americas established agricultural systems that fostered more stable settlements and spurred population growth. **Horticulture** — a form of agriculture in which people work small plots of land with simple tools — became highly developed in the area of present-day Mexico.

horticulture
A form of agriculture in which people work small plots of land with simple tools.

Three Sisters
Native American agricultural practice of beneficially planting corn, beans, and squash together, resulting in higher yields and a healthy diet.

Maize (corn) was likely cultivated in present-day Mexico around 4000 B.C.E. and in the American Southwest as early as 2000 B.C.E. Over time, Native American tribes developed a system of companion planting known as the **Three Sisters**, in which corn, beans, and squash were farmed together. As the corn stalks grew tall, the vines from the bean plants would wrap around them and leafy squash would spread along the ground. While corn quickly depletes nitrogen from the soil, the beans replenish the ground with nitrates, and the squash thrives in their humid shade. Together, these three crops jewelry and decorative items, and thousands of laborers constructed elaborate palaces and temples. Like the Aztec priests, Incan priests sacrificed humans to the gods to stave off natural disasters and military defeat.

Incas Andean people who built a complex bureaucratic empire ruled by aristocrats in the centuries before the arrival of the Spaniards amid the fertile land of the Andes Mountains along the Pacific coast. The Inca relied on a variety of domesticated animals and diverse farming techniques to survive. They reached the height of their power in the fifteenth century, controlling some 16 million people.

REVIEW

- What similarities do you see among the Aztec, Incan, and Mayan civilizations?
- What differences do you note among these three peoples?

Skills Workshop: Thinking Historically

Working with Evidence

Although it might be tempting to think of history as a fixed set of events that everyone recognizes, the reality of how history is constructed is more complex. Just as there are many ways to tell a story, there are many ways to look at and understand history. For example, let's say you're at an extended family holiday dinner, and people are reminiscing about last year's gathering. While everyone may agree on some facts such as the location, who was present, and what food was served, other elements—for example, who did the most kitchen cleanup afterwards, who told the funniest story told last year, or why an invited person did not attend—may be in dispute. If you wanted to write an accurate account of what really happened and why, it would be best to draw on multiple voices and opinions and use them to form your own ideas about what happened, and why.

Likewise, historians construct history out of rich materials that have survived from the past; these materials are known as **primary sources**. These sources come in a variety of forms, including texts, material artifacts, architecture, and images. Historians examine these sources, sometimes considering them individually but usually in combination with others. Analyzing many primary sources from a particular time period, even if they conflict with each other, allows historians to draw broad conclusions about that time period, and thereby construct a historical narrative that says something useful about the past to readers in the present. Interpreting sources in this way is a historian's most fundamental task—in other words, how we think about these sources shapes our understanding of history. Because of this, analyzing primary sources is a crucial way to uncover meaning from the past.

Fabric of a Nation weaves primary sources throughout its narrative to provide you with additional historical information, unique perspectives, and interesting details. You will regularly encounter these sources as images (such as maps, photographs, or charts) and in the AP® Working with Evidence features. Each image source in the narrative includes a title, descriptive caption, and question that asks you to analyze an aspect of the source considering what you have just read in the narrative. Studying these images and connecting them to what you have read and are learning in the course can help you more fully understand and better remember specific historical developments. In the AP® Working with Evidence features, you will interact with one

(continued)

or two primary sources followed by a set of Questions for Analysis. These questions ask you to perform specific tasks.

- Identify: recognize, label, or indicate specific information.
- Describe: provide relevant characteristics of a topic.
- Compare: state the similarities and differences between two or more items.
- Explain: provide information about how or why an event or development occurred.
- Evaluate: determine the importance or significance of an event, development, or claim.

Analyzing and interpreting sources is an essential historical skill that you will have the opportunity to practice regularly. In fact, primary sources are a central component of the AP® U.S. History Exam and are tested in the multiple-choice, short answer, and document-based essay questions.

Let's take a look at how you might read and annotate a primary source that is a historical artifact. This means your "reading" of this source must be a close look at its details. Begin by reading the source line for the image. Here, it tells you that the maker of the artifact is unknown, that the objects in the images form a gold necklace of small, interlocking frogs, which have been arranged to show you how it might have been worn, that the necklace was produced under the Aztec empire, and that it was created during the fifteenth or sixteenth century (the 1400s or 1500s).

Source: Anonymous Mixtec artisan, Necklace with Gold Frog Ornaments, Aztec empire, fifteenth or sixteenth century. The Mixtec were a Mesoamerican people who paid tribute to the Aztecs.

About the source: Mixtec and Aztec peoples associated frogs with rain and fertility.

This source also includes an additional "About the source" line. These are sometimes included to provide you with additional information to help you interpret the source. In this case, the "About the source" line tells you that the religious beliefs held by Mixtec and Aztec peoples placed special significance in frogs.

Now consider the object itself. You can see that the golden frogs are uniform and well-detailed. This tells you that the maker of this necklace not only had access to precious materials (gold), but was highly skilled in metallurgy, a specialized craft that likely took years to learn. From this information, you can also make the educated guess, or inference, that the maker of this necklace had adequate time to make a detailed and valuable object.

(continued)

ACTIVITY

Throughout this book, you will encounter AP® Working with Evidence activities that will ask you to carefully examine and answer questions designed to foster critical thinking about a variety of historical sources. The following three questions ask about the frog necklace above. For the first two questions, you have been provided a partial sample response. Add at least one additional response of your own to each of these questions.

1. **Identify a feature of the Aztec economy, technology, culture, environment, or society revealed by this artifact.**
   - Technology: The image of the frog ornaments from a necklace shows that Aztec society was an advanced civilization supporting craft specialization of artists because the detail and quality of the work in gold are more than what amateurs or nonspecialists in less developed economies produced.
   - Environment: The large amount of gold used in making the Aztec frog ornaments for a single necklace suggests that the Aztec empire was rich and controlled, or had access to, large amounts of precious metals, including gold.
   - ***Your turn!***
2. **Describe an Aztec adaptation to the environment reflected in this artifact.**
   - Aztecs adapted to a swampy environment surrounding their capital by creating innovative floating gardens called chinampas.
   - ***Your turn!***
3. **Explain how the Spanish might have viewed this artifact.**
   - ***Your turn!***

Native Cultures to the North

To the north of these large civilizations, smaller societies also thrived. In present-day Arizona and New Mexico, the Hohokam established communities around 500 C.E. and developed extensive irrigation systems. In present-day Utah and Colorado, ancient villages supported settled populations by farming corn, which had spread to the region after domestication in Central America, as well as beans and squash, the Three Sisters.

As time went on, the **Pueblo** people gathered into villages built from adobe bricks made from clay and water and used advanced irrigation techniques to survive the arid climate of the Southwest. They built check dams and reservoirs to store water, dug canals and ditches to funnel water, planted in grid and waffle patterns to concentrate water on farmed lands, and planted with pumice and other natural mulch to preserve water. By around 750 C.E., they were building adobe and masonry homes cut into cliffs. Although the Pueblo people eventually migrated south and constructed large buildings that included administrative offices, religious centers, and craft shops, they returned to their cliff dwellings in the 1100s for protection from invaders. There, persistent drought eventually caused them to disperse into smaller settled groups.

Pueblo
Native American peoples in present-day New Mexico and Arizona who share common religious and agricultural practices. Pueblo, the Spanish word for village, was used to refer to Native Americans who built permanent multistory adobe dwellings in the Southwest.

Farther north, on plains that stretched from present-day Colorado into Canada, hunting societies developed around the herds of bison that roamed there. A weighted spear-throwing device, called an *atlatl*, allowed hunters to capture smaller game, while nets, hooks, and snares allowed them to catch birds, fish, and small animals. Societies in the Great Plains as well as the Great Basin (between the Rockies and the Sierra Nevada) generally remained small and widely scattered. Given the dry conditions in these regions, communities needed a large expanse of territory to ensure their survival

AP® WORKING with EVIDENCE

Source: Pueblo "Cliff Palace" at Mesa Verde, Colorado

Werner Forman/Getty Images

About the source: This Pueblo "cliff palace" was built around 1200 C.E. and inhabited for around 100 years. Residents grew corn, beans, and squash, traded goods, and competed with neighboring towns.

Questions for Analysis

1. Identify a Pueblo adaptation to the environment apparent in this image.
2. Describe the interactions of the Pueblo who lived in this structure with other nearby peoples, based on the evidence in this photograph.
3. Explain what this image reveals about the Pueblo people. Consider things like the economy, technology, environment, politics, and society in your response.

as they followed migrating animals or seasonal plant sources. Here, the adoption of the bow and arrow around 500 C.E. proved the most significant technological development.

The Ute peoples foraged and hunted nomadically in the Great Basin region. They held few possessions and lived in small, egalitarian kinship bands. The bands survived in the desolate desert by hunting and gathering. In the most barren areas, they survived on fish found in the few rivers in the area, small animals, and plant foods, including seeds from grasses and piñon nuts. Ute family bands traded with each other, as well as with other regional tribes, including Pueblo peoples, over an extensive network throughout the American Southwest.

Other Native American societies, like the Mandan, settled along rivers in the heart of the continent (present-day North and South Dakota). The rich soil along the riverbanks fostered farming, while forests and plains attracted a variety of animals for hunting. Around 1250 C.E., however, an extended drought forced these settlements to contract, and competition for resources increased among Mandan villages and with other groups in the region.

Hunting-and-gathering societies also emerged along the Pacific coast, where the abundance of fish, small game, and plant life provided the resources to develop permanent settlements. Although the Chumash Indians remained hunters and foragers, they settled in permanent villages near present-day Santa Barbara, California, where they harvested resources from the land and the ocean. Women gathered acorns and pine nuts, while men fished, using oceangoing canoes called *tomol*, and hunted. The Chumash, whose villages sometimes supported up to a thousand inhabitants without farming, participated in regional trade networks up and down the coast.

The Native Americans of the Pacific Northwest were composed of diverse peoples of different languages and cultures who lived in resource-rich regions near the Pacific Ocean. Ocean resources supported these hunters and gatherers after they gave up nomadic life and settled into village life. They depended on the sea and rivers for rich salmon harvests and on elk from the forests. They worshipped maritime and woodland deities, who were portrayed in detailed totem poles carved from the cedars of the dense forests of the region. Native Americans in the Pacific Northwest also built oceangoing canoes from cedar and often hauled in thousands of pounds of fish in a single harvest. The Chinook peoples in the Pacific Northwest used the cedars to build extensive plank houses, some hundreds of feet long, in which kinship groups with up to seventy family members lived under a single roof.

In the northeast regions of North America, the Haudenosaunee (Iroquois) people lived in villages of up to several hundred inhabitants and cultivated corn as well as vegetables like squash and beans. Because the Haudenosaunee lived in villages, they built large longhouses using timber from the rich forests of the Northeast, often living communally in extended groups that spanned multiple generations and families. Women exercised considerable power within village life, because descent and inheritance were traced through mothers' lines, and women selected male village leaders. The Haudenosaunee also depended upon deer hunting and fishing, which proved abundant

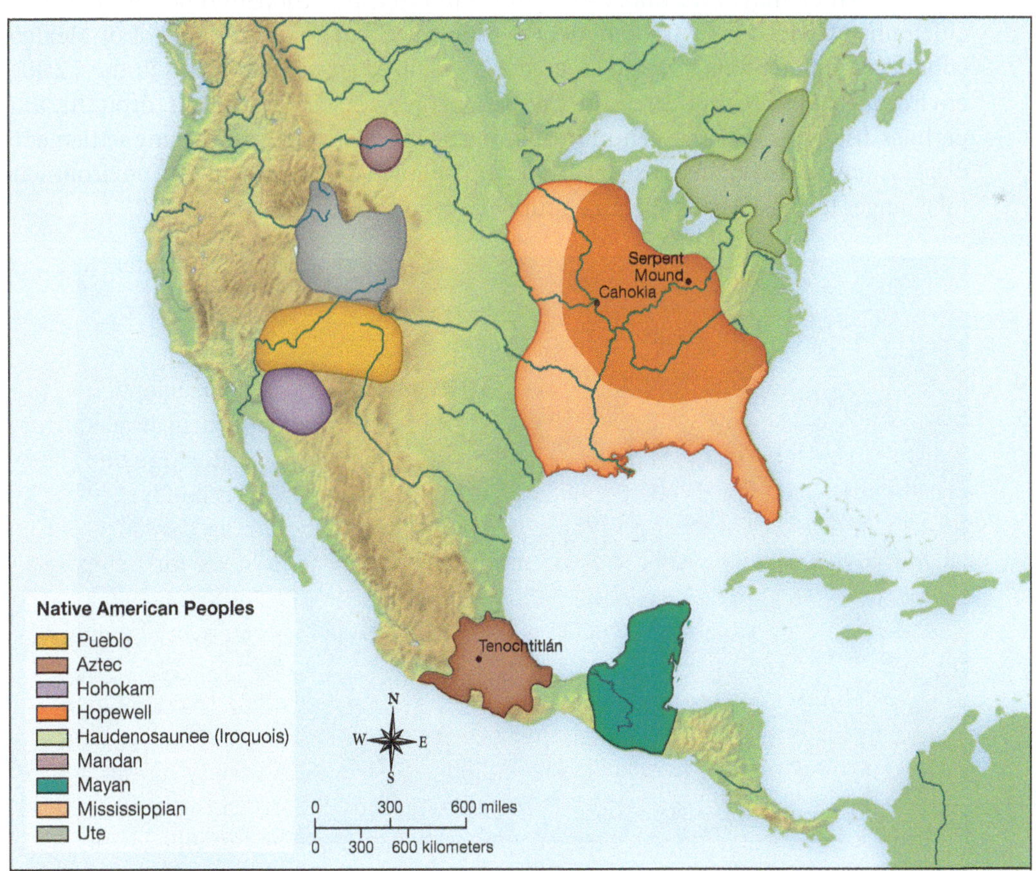

MAP 1.2 American Indian Peoples, c. 500–1500 C.E. Some Native Americans, like the Mississippian Indians, developed extensive trade networks over land or along rivers and coastlines. Others, such as the Aztecs, developed extensive agricultural economies based on Mayan precedents and practiced trade. Other groups, like the Pueblo, battled over scarce resources.

How did geographic location shape differences between Native American societies in North and Central America?

throughout the region. Haudenosaunee culture revolved around a warrior ethos that valued individual honor in battle, where ritual humiliation of an opponent was often more important than killing an opponent.

Even larger societies with more elaborate social, religious, and political systems developed near the Mississippi River. A group that came to be called the Hopewell people established a thriving culture in the early centuries C.E. The river and its surrounding lands provided fertile fields and easy access to distant communities. Centered in present-day southern Ohio and western Illinois, the Hopewell constructed towns of four thousand to six thousand people. Artifacts from their burial sites reflect extensive trading networks that stretched from the Missouri River to Lake Superior, and from the Rocky Mountains to the Appalachian region and Florida.

Beginning around 500 C.E., the Hopewell culture gave birth to larger and more complex societies that flourished in the Mississippi River valley and to the south and east. As bows and arrows spread into the region, people hunted more animals in the thick forests. But Mississippian groups also learned to cultivate corn. The development of corn as a staple crop allowed the population to expand dramatically, and more complex political and religious systems developed in which elite rulers gained greater control over the labor of farmers and hunters. Mississippian peoples created massive earthworks sculpted in the shape of serpents, birds, and other creatures. Some earthen sculptures stood higher than 70 feet and stretched longer than 1,300 feet. Mississippians also constructed huge temple mounds that could cover nearly 16 acres.

By about 1100 C.E., the Cahokia people established the largest Mississippian settlement, which may have housed ten thousand to thirty thousand people. Powerful chieftains extended their trade networks from the Great Lakes to the Gulf of Mexico, conquered smaller villages, and created a centralized government. But in the 1200s, environmental factors affected the Cahokia people, too. Deforestation, drought, and perhaps disease as well as overhunting diminished their strength, and many settlements dispersed. After 1400, increased warfare and political unrest joined with environmental changes to cause Mississippian culture as a whole to decline.

Mark Burnett/Alamy

Serpent Mound Memorial Mississippians constructed this mound, located in Locust Grove, Ohio, between 950 and 1200 C.E. Worshippers of the sun, Mississippians aligned the head of the serpent with the location of sunset on the summer solstice, June 20 or 21, the longest day of the year. Artifacts found at this site indicate that Mississippians extended Hopewell trade networks.

 **Based on this information, what can you conclude about Mississippian society during this period?**

REVIEW

- How did the societies of North America differ from those of the equatorial region and the Andes Mountain region?

European Exploration in the Americas

MODULE **1.3**

FOCUS

One reason people frequently look to the past is to understand the consequences of their decisions. This is because historical events have causes, and knowing what causes something often allows you to understand it better. For instance, staying up late to binge-watch your favorite TV show on a Sunday night will cause you to lose out on necessary sleep, and you will know why you're tired when your alarm for school goes off on Monday morning.

When historians seek to uncover why an event occurred, they use the historical pattern of thought called causation to establish why that development happened. Causation is more complicated, however, than one event leading into the next. For instance, the brief introduction that opens this module describes European exploration as the result of three causes: the value of Asian goods, blocked overland trade routes, and desires of monarchs to amass wealth. Important historical events result from—and are caused by—more than one factor. The three causes we describe at the beginning of this module are only a small slice of the story about what ushered in an era of European exploration.

As you read the rest of this module, take special note of the many additional causes that combined to lead the Portuguese and the Spanish to begin European colonization of the Americas.

Rising birthrates and productivity in early fifteenth-century Europe, aided by an improved climate and new approaches to farming that increased Europe's food supply overall, fueled a resurgence of trade with other parts of the world. The profits from agriculture and commerce allowed the wealthy and powerful to begin investing in the arts and purchasing luxury goods. Indeed, a cultural **Renaissance** (from the French word for "rebirth") flourished, first in the Italian city-states, and then spread throughout much of the rest of Europe. This cultural rebirth went hand in hand with political unification as more powerful rulers extended their control over smaller city-states and principalities, forming nation-states led by monarchs.

These factors combined to stabilize a continent that, only a few generations earlier, had been devastated by the bubonic plague. As trade thrived and European elites prospered, the wealthy developed tastes for fine Asian manufactured goods, as well as spices from India and China.

During this time, Portuguese and Spanish monarchs initiated efforts to explore the world, hoping to find new ways to gain access to valuable Asian goods. Powerful Italian city-states and merchants controlled the most important routes through the Mediterranean, while Muslims controlled more minor pathways, as well as the overland routes farther east to India and China.

Effectively blocked from access to existing eastward routes, and craving opportunity for greater wealth by conducting trade themselves, Portugal (and later, Spain) sought trade routes to Asia that could bypass those controlled by their Italian and Muslim rivals. These efforts were aided by explorers, **missionaries**, and merchants who traveled

Renaissance
A cultural and intellectual flowering that began in fifteenth-century Italy and then spread north throughout the late fifteenth and sixteenth centuries. During this time, European rulers pushed for greater political unification of their states. It contributed to dramatic changes in art, cultivated knowledge, and the questioning of old forms of authority.

missionary
A religious person who travels to foreign lands with the goal of converting those they meet to a new religion.

to Morocco, Turkey, India, and other distant lands. They brought back trade goods and knowledge of astronomy, shipbuilding, mapmaking, and navigation that allowed the Portuguese and Spanish to venture farther south along the Atlantic coast of Africa, and, eventually, west into the uncharted Atlantic Ocean.

Portugal and Spain Pursue Long-Distance Trade

Cut off from the Mediterranean by Italian city-states and Muslim rulers in North Africa, Portugal looked toward the Atlantic. Although a tiny nation, Portugal benefited from the leadership of its young prince, Henry, who launched explorations of the African coast in the 1420s, hoping to find a passage to India via the Atlantic Ocean. Prince Henry—known as Henry the Navigator—gathered information from astronomers, geographers, mapmakers, and craftsmen in the Arab world and recruited Italian cartographers and navigators along with Portuguese scholars, sailors, and captains. He then launched efforts aimed at exploration, observation, shipbuilding, and long-distance trade that revolutionized Europe and shaped developments in Africa and the Americas.

caravel

A narrow, small, and swift sailing ship invented by the Portuguese during the fifteenth century, particularly useful because it allowed sailors to sail into the wind much faster than traditional vessels.

astrolabe

A tool originally invented by Greek astronomers and sailors for navigation or astronomical calculations that allowed sailors to identify distance and time based on the location of the sun and stars in relation to the horizon.

Under Henry, the Portuguese developed ships known as **caravels**—vessels with narrow hulls and triangular sails that were especially effective for navigating the coast of West Africa. Innovative Portuguese navigators encouraged by Prince Henry created state-of-the-art oceanic charts, maps, and astronomical tables. They improved navigational instruments including the **astrolabe** and advanced ship designs, which featured the triangular lateen sail for sailing into the wind at an angle, originally an Arab invention, and a swiveling wooden rudder behind the stern (back) of the boat, both of which improved maneuverability. The Portuguese mastered the complex wind and sea currents along the African coast. Portuguese mariners' astrolabes allowed sailors to chart a straight line of latitude to keep ships on course when land was not in sight. Soon Portugal was trading in gold, ivory, and enslaved people from West Africa.

In 1482, the Portuguese built Elmina Castle, a trading post and fort on the Gold Coast, in present-day Ghana. Further expeditions were launched from the castle, and five years later, a fleet led by Bartolomeu Dias rounded the Cape of Good Hope, on the southernmost tip of Africa. This feat demonstrated the possibility of sailing directly from the Atlantic to the Indian Ocean. Vasco da Gama followed this route to India in 1497, returning to Portugal in 1499, his ships loaded with valuable cinnamon and pepper, scarce spices that were in high demand in Europe.

By the early sixteenth century, Portuguese traders started participating in Indian Ocean trade, bringing Asian goods to Europe. They established fortified trading posts at key locations on the Indian Ocean and extended their expeditions to Indonesia, China, and Japan. By the early sixteenth century, Portuguese traders had taken control of the India trade from Arab fleets. Within a decade, the Portuguese had become the European leaders in international trade.

Inquisition

A religious judicial institution established by Pope Gregory IX in 1232, designed to find and eliminate heretical beliefs that did not align with official Catholic practices. The Spanish Inquisition was first established in 1478.

Meanwhile, Portugal's neighbor, a newly reunited Spain, was also eager to explore the wider world. A vibrant and religiously tolerant culture had existed in Muslim Spain from the eighth to the tenth century, but that was followed by a long period of persecution of Christians. When Christians began reconquering Spain after 1200, Muslims and Jews alike became targets. Then in 1469, the marriage of Isabella of Castile and Ferdinand II of Aragon sealed the unification of Christian Spain. By 1492 their combined forces expelled the last Muslim conquerors from the Iberian peninsula.

Promoting Catholicism to create a more unified national identity, Isabella and Ferdinand launched an **Inquisition** in 1478 against supposed heretics and executed or

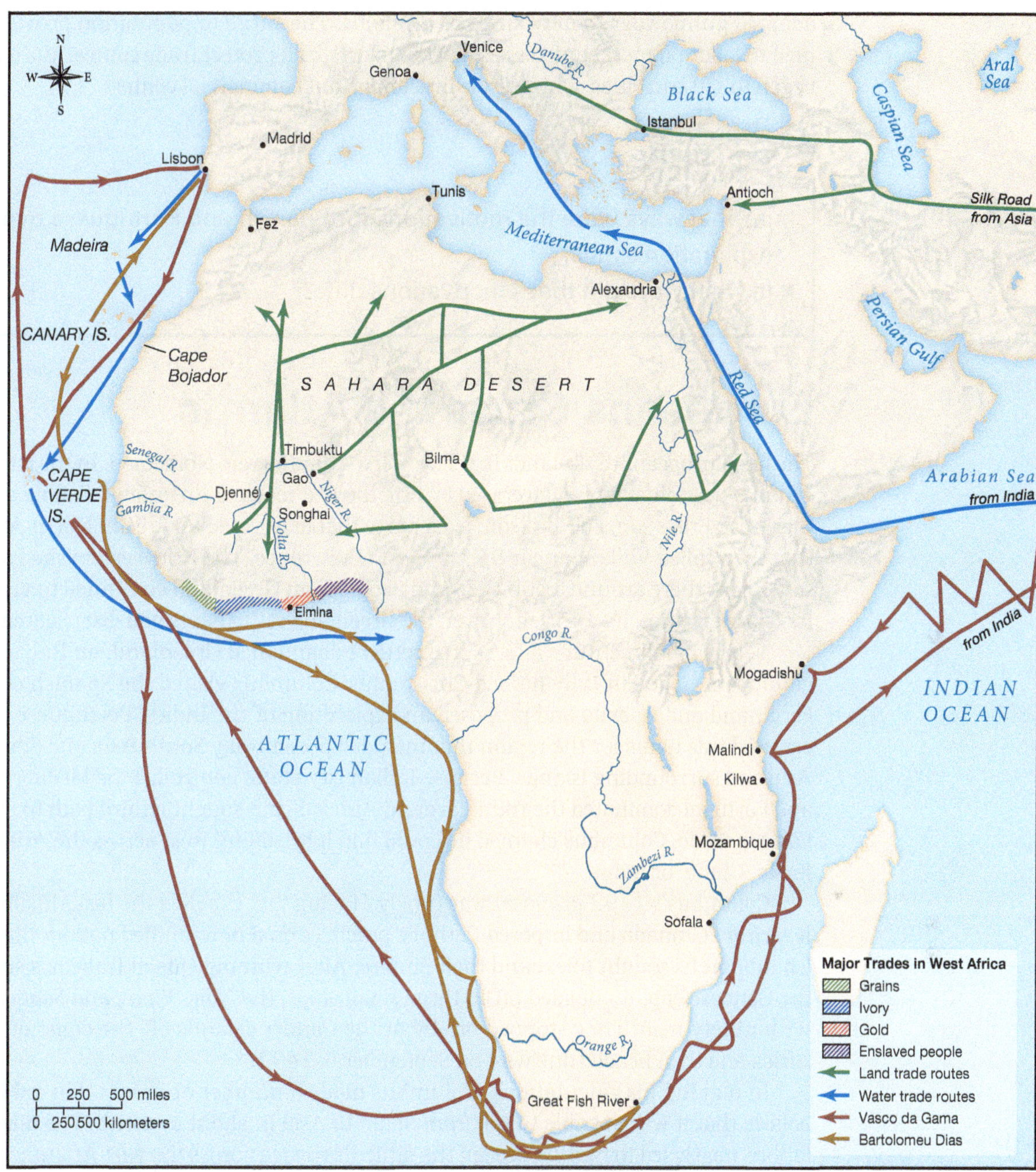

MAP 1.3 Fifteenth-Century Trade Routes in Africa and the Mediterranean While overland trade routes had long connected West Africa with the Mediterranean, by the 1430s, the Portuguese had opened a new trade route along the west coast of Africa, and, eventually, around the Cape of Good Hope at the southern tip of the continent, which gave the Portuguese access to the Indian Ocean.

What economic, political, and geographic factors made it possible for Portugal to open a new trade route along the west coast of Africa?

expelled some 200,000 Jews as well. After the reconquest and the Inquisition, Catholic Spain used its wealth and military power to expand its reach by forging its own trade networks with North Africa, India, and other Asian lands. The legacy of the reconquest of the Spanish peninsula and the Inquisition added an intense desire to spread Catholicism to Spain's motivations for exploration.

With expanding populations and greater agricultural productivity, Portugal and Spain developed more efficient systems of taxation, built larger military forces, and adapted gunpowder to new kinds of weapons. The surge in population provided the men to labor on merchant vessels, garrison forts, and protect trade routes. More people began to settle in cities, which grew into important commercial centers.

REVIEW

- In what ways were the motivations for Spanish and Portuguese overseas exploration similar?
- In what ways did these motivations differ?

Europeans Cross the Atlantic

The first Europeans to see lands in the western Atlantic were Norsemen. In the late tenth century, Scandinavian seafarers led by Erik the Red reached Greenland. Sailing still farther west, Erik's son, Leif Erikson, led a party that discovered an area in North America that they called Vinland, near the Gulf of St. Lawrence. The Norse established a small settlement there around 1000 C.E., and people from Greenland continued to visit Vinland for centuries. By 1450, however, the Greenland settlements had disappeared.

Nearly a half century after Norse settlers abandoned Greenland, an Italian navigator from Genoa in Italy named Christopher Columbus visited the Spanish court of Ferdinand and Isabella and proposed an exploration of the Indies. Portuguese explorers used this name for the region that included present-day South Asia and Southeast Asia and surrounding islands. Because Italian city-states controlled the Mediterranean and Portugal dominated the routes around Africa, Spain sought a third path to the rich Eastern trade. Columbus claimed he could find it by sailing west across the Atlantic to Japan, China, or India.

Columbus's 1492 proposal was timely. Having just expelled the last Muslims and Jews from Granada and imposed Catholic practices on a now-unified nation, the Spanish monarchs sought to expand their empire. After winning Queen Isabella's support, the Genoese captain headed off in three small ships, the *Niña*, *Pinta*, and *Santa Maria*, with ninety men. They stopped briefly at the Canary Islands off the coast of North Africa and then headed due west on September 6, 1492.

In making his calculations, Columbus made a number of errors that led him to believe that it was possible to sail from Spain to Asia in about a month. The miscalculations nearly led to mutiny during the difficult voyage across the vast Atlantic Ocean, but disaster was averted when a lookout finally spotted a small island on October 12. Columbus named the island San Salvador ("Holy Savior") and made contact with local residents, whom he named Indians in the belief that he had found the islands of the East Indies near Japan or China. Columbus was impressed with their warm welcome and considered the gold jewelry they wore as a sign of great riches in the region.

Although native inhabitants and Columbus's men did not speak a common language, the American inhabitants aided the Spanish in exploring the area, likely in hopes of encouraging trade. The crew then sailed on to an island they named Hispaniola. Leaving a small number of men behind, Columbus sailed back to Spain with samples of gold jewelry, captured and enslaved Native Americans, and tales of more wonders to come.

Columbus and his crew were welcomed as heroes when they returned to Spain in March 1493. The success of these voyages encouraged adventurous Spaniards to travel throughout the Caribbean, South America, and regions immediately to the north in search of trade routes to Asia, gold, silver, or other riches in the Americas. It also inspired the first expeditions by the Portuguese in South America, and later the French and English in North America.

AP® WORKING with EVIDENCE

Source: Christopher Columbus, Journal of the First Voyage, October 12, 1492

> "They are very well made with very handsome bodies, and very good countenances. Their hair is short and coarse, almost like the hairs of a horsetail. They wear the hairs brought down to the eyebrows except a few locks behind, which they wear long and never cut. They paint themselves black, and they are the color of the Canarians, neither black nor white. Some paint themselves white, others red, and others of what color they find. Some paint their faces, others the whole body, some only round the eyes, others only on the nose. They neither care nor know anything of arms, for I showed them swords, and they took them by the blade and cut themselves through ignorance. They have no iron, their darts being wands without iron, some of them having a fish's tooth at the end, and others being pointed in various ways. They are all of fair stature and size, with good faces, and well made. I saw some with marks of wounds on their bodies, and I made signs to ask what it was, and they gave me to understand that people from other adjacent islands came with the intention of seizing them, and that they defended themselves. I believed, and still believe, that they come here from the mainland to take them prisoners. They should be good servants and intelligent, for I observed that they quickly took in what was said to them, and I believe that they would easily be made Christians, as it appeared to me that they had no religion. I, our Lord being pleased, will take hence, at the time of my departure, six natives for your Highnesses, that they may learn to speak."

Questions for Analysis

1. Identify three significant details that Columbus communicates about his first meeting with Native Americans.
2. Describe how Columbus characterizes Native Americans in this excerpt.
3. Explain how Columbus's account shaped later Spanish interactions with Native Americans.

Sponsored by the Catholic Spanish monarchy, Columbus's discovery of islands seemingly unclaimed by any known or recognized power led the pope to confer Spanish sovereignty over all lands already claimed or to be claimed approximately five hundred miles west of the Cape Verde Islands, off the coast of West Africa. A protest by Catholic Portugal led to a treaty finalized in 1506 that moved the line dividing Spanish and Portuguese claims hundreds of miles farther west, granting Portugal control of territory that became Brazil and Spain control of the rest of what became known as South America. Thus, in the eyes of the Spanish and Portuguese monarchies and the Roman Catholic pope, Iberians, not other Europeans or the native inhabitants themselves, ruled the Americas.

Although it became clear within a decade that Columbus had not in fact discovered a route to the Indies, it took much longer for Europeans to understand the revolutionary nature of the process he had unleashed: a global system of exchange that came to be known as the Columbian Exchange (see Module 1.4).

AP® EXAM TIP

Be sure to understand the causes of European exploration in the New World. Formally, this includes a search for new sources of wealth, competition between nations, and a desire to spread Christianity. Informally, this is often referred to as the three Gs: Gold, God, and Glory.

REVIEW

- How did religious, economic, and political factors shape Portuguese and Spanish claims on the land in Central and South America?

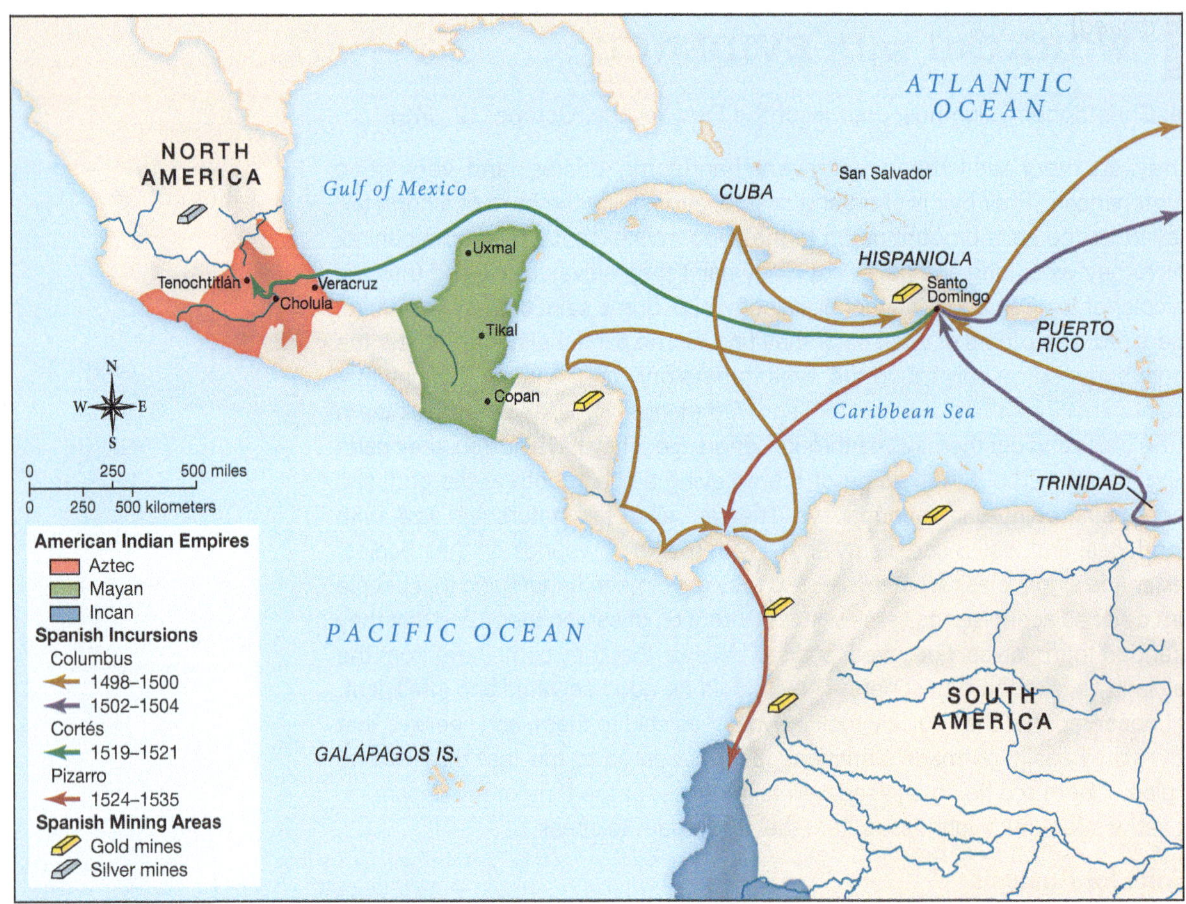

MAP 1.4 Spanish Incursions into American Empires Columbus first landed on the island he called San Salvador, and later sailed to an island he named Hispaniola. On a second voyage, he explored the coast of Central America and Cuba. Later conquerors made incursions farther inland, eventually overturning the Aztec and Incan empires.

Based on your knowledge of Columbus, what might explain his routes in these two voyages?

AP® Skills Workshop: Thinking Historically

Identifying Claims and Evidence in Primary Sources

One of the skills that historians and students of history must master is the ability to make **claims** and support those claims with historical **evidence**. While this may seem daunting, it is in fact something that most of us do regularly in our lives. A claim is simply an argument—something that you are trying to convince someone else of. Evidence is proof or support for your argument or position.

Let's look at an example: As history teachers, we (the authors of *Fabric of a Nation*) might naturally claim that U.S. history is the best subject in high school or college. To support that claim, we could cite evidence showing how studying history sharpens one's ability to think critically, write analytically, make more informed decisions when voting, better understand historical references and memes in popular culture, and so on. Of course, not everyone would agree. Some might accuse us of being biased because we are history teachers, while others could provide reasons why the study of English, math, or science is more worthwhile.

When reading and analyzing primary sources, it's important to remember that those writers are sometimes biased, too, and that they are often making an argument and providing examples to support their position. Before we practice making historical claims and supporting them with evidence, it's helpful to practice identifying claims

(continued)

and evidence in primary sources. The AP® U.S. History Exam will assess students' ability to identify claims and evidence in primary and secondary sources as well as to create historical claims and support them with specific and relevant evidence.

Earlier in the module, you read an excerpt from Christopher Columbus describing his initial encounter with Native Americans on October 12, 1492. If you carefully reread this excerpt, you will see that toward the end, he claims that the native inhabitants are well suited for use as servants ("They should be good servants and intelligent, for I observed that they quickly took in what was said to them"). To support that claim, Columbus argues that the natives are not militaristic ("They neither care nor know anything of arms"), they are physically strong ("They are all of fair stature and size"), they are used to enslavement ("they gave me to understand that people from other adjacent islands came . . . here from the mainland to take them prisoners"), and they could be easily converted to Spanish Catholicism ("they would easily be made Christians, as it appeared to me that they had no religion").

ACTIVITY

Now, it's your turn to practice identifying a claim and evidence. Read the following primary source. Identify one claim and at least three pieces of evidence used in the source to support that claim.

Source: *El Requerimiento*, 1513

About the source: Spanish conquistadors were supposed to read this document, written in Spanish, to Native Americans before any hostilities ensued.

> "On the part of the King . . . and . . . Queen, subduers of barbarous nations, we their servants notify and make known to you, . . . that the Lord our God, Living and Eternal, created the Heaven and the Earth, and one man and one woman, of whom you and we, and all the men in the world, were and are descendants, and all those who come after us. . . .
>
> Of all these nations God our Lord gave charge to one man, called St. Peter, that he should be Lord and Superior of all men in the world, that all should obey him, and that he should be the head of the whole human race, wherever men should live, and under whatever law, sect, or belief they should be; he gave him the world for his kingdom and jurisdiction.
>
> And he commanded him to place his seat in Rome, as the spot most fitting to rule the world from; but also permitted him to have his seat in any other part of the world, and to judge and govern all Christians, Moors, Jews, Gentiles, and all other sects. This man is called the Pope . . . Great Father and Governor of men.
>
> One of these Pontiffs [Popes] . . . made donation of these isles . . . to the . . . King and Queen [of Spain]. . . . So their Highnesses are kings and lords of these islands. . . . [A]nd . . . almost all those to whom this has been notified have received and served their Highnesses . . . and obeyed the priests their Highnesses sent to preach . . . to teach them our Holy Faith. . . . [Y]ou to[o] are held and obliged to do the same.
>
> If you do so, you will do well. . . . But if you do not do this, . . . I certify that, with the help of God, we shall powerfully enter into your country, and shall make war against you in all ways and manners we can, and shall subject you to the yoke and obedience of the Church and of their Highnesses; we shall take your wives and children, and shall make slaves of them, and as such shall sell and dispose of them as their Highnesses command; and we shall take away your goods, and shall do you all the . . . damage that we can, as to vassals who do not obey . . . their lord; . . . and . . . that the deaths and losses which shall accrue from this are your fault, and not that of their Highnesses."

MODULE 1.4

Columbian Exchange, Spanish Exploration, and Conquest

FOCUS

Historians use the historical pattern of thought called causation in explaining the relationship between an event and its effects. Put simply, this way of looking at history seeks to illustrate how one or more events leads to the next. It might be helpful to think of an effect as the outcome of a cause.

There are two major ways to use causation to consider the interplay of causes and effects. As we discussed in Module 1.3, when historians look to understand why a development occurred, they sometimes examine a cause, or multiple causes, that culminates in an effect. At other times, historians start with a major development and examine the effects that resulted from it. Historians taking this second approach are interested in how consequences can help us make predictions and guide better decision making in the future.

The effects described in the opening to this module—the beginnings of many continuing exchanges, changes to environments on four continents, and creation of the Atlantic World—are only the beginning of the story of the outcomes of European exploration.

As you read Module 1.4, be sure to keep track of the additional effects that followed from Columbus's journey and the Spanish colonization of the Americas.

Columbian Exchange
The biological exchange of people, plants, animals, and diseases between the Americas and the rest of the world between 1492 and the end of the sixteenth century. Although its initial impact was strongest in the Americas and Europe, it was soon felt globally.

Atlantic World
The social, intellectual, economic, and biological interactions among the peoples, plants, and animals bordering the Atlantic Ocean, mainly Africa, the Americas, and Western Europe, beginning in the late fifteenth century.

Continuing contact between Europe and the Americas, initiated by Columbus, started the process called the **Columbian Exchange**. This exchange—at times accidental and at other times purposeful—traded diseases, plants, animals, peoples, ideas, and resources among Africa, Europe, and the Americas. The numerous major and long-lasting effects this process unleashed transformed the economies and environments of all four continents. The lands bordering the Atlantic—Africa, the Americas, and Western Europe—were knit together by these exchanges into an **Atlantic World**, especially as the French, Dutch, and English followed the lead of the Portuguese and Spanish and began to establish their own colonies in the New World.

The Columbian Exchange Transforms Four Continents

The Spaniards were aided in their conquest of the Americas as much by germs as by guns or horses. Because native peoples in the Western Hemisphere had had almost no contact with the rest of the world for millennia, they lacked immunity to many germs carried by Europeans. This meant that Europeans' presence on their continents initiated demographic disasters, which native peoples called the Great Dying. These diseases, coupled with warfare and enslavement, first eradicated the Arawak and Taino on Hispaniola, wiping out some 300,000 people within a few decades. In the Incan empire, the population plummeted from about 9 million in 1530 to fewer than half a million by 1630. Among the Aztecs, the Maya, and their neighbors, the population collapsed from some 40 million people around 1500 to about 3 million a century and a half later. European germs spread northward as well, leading to catastrophic epidemics among the Pueblo peoples of the Southwest and the Mississippian cultures of the Southeast. Initially, the devastating decline in Native American populations ensured the victory of Spain and other European powers over American populations.

AP® EXAM TIP

Possibly one of the most significant events of this period, the Columbian Exchange, is almost guaranteed to be included on the AP® Exam. Make sure you can provide examples of diseases, plants, and animals that were part of this exchange. A refined written response about this topic would balance the positive and negative impacts of the exchange and how that impact also depended on the perspective of the people involved.

AP® WORKING with EVIDENCE

Source: Illustration by the Spanish missionary Bernardino de Sahagún of an Aztec woman with smallpox.

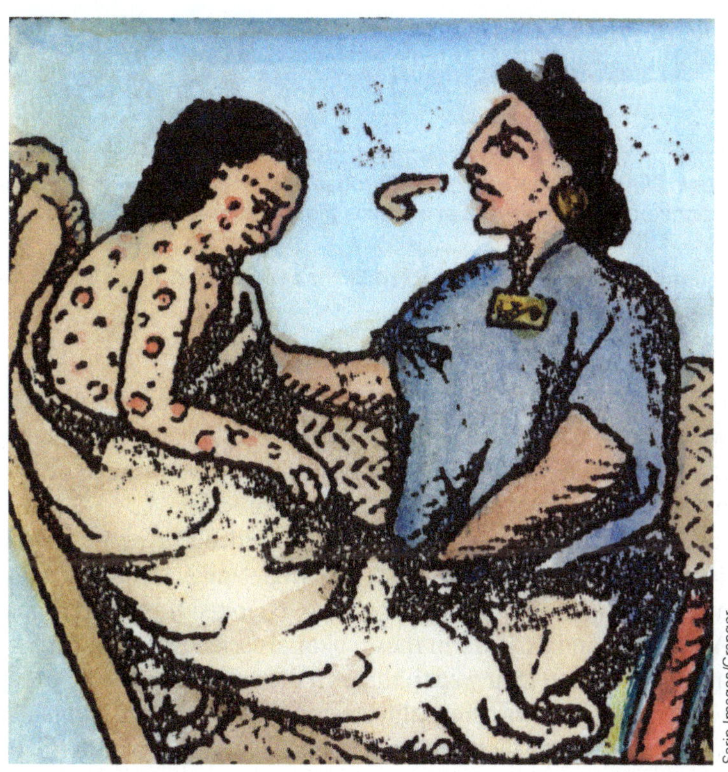

Sarin Images/Granger

Questions for Analysis

1. Identify details in the image that reflect the artist's European perspective.
2. Describe the impact of smallpox on Aztec and other Native American populations.
3. Evaluate the most significant negative effect and positive effect of the Columbian Exchange on native peoples.

In the Columbian Exchange, the Americas provided Europeans with high-yielding, nutrient-rich foods like corn, tomatoes, and potatoes, as well as new indulgences like tobacco and cacao. In exchange, Europe and Africa sent rice, wheat, rye, oats, lemons, and oranges to the Western Hemisphere (**Map 1.5** on page 24). These grain crops transformed the American landscape, particularly in North America, where wheat eventually became

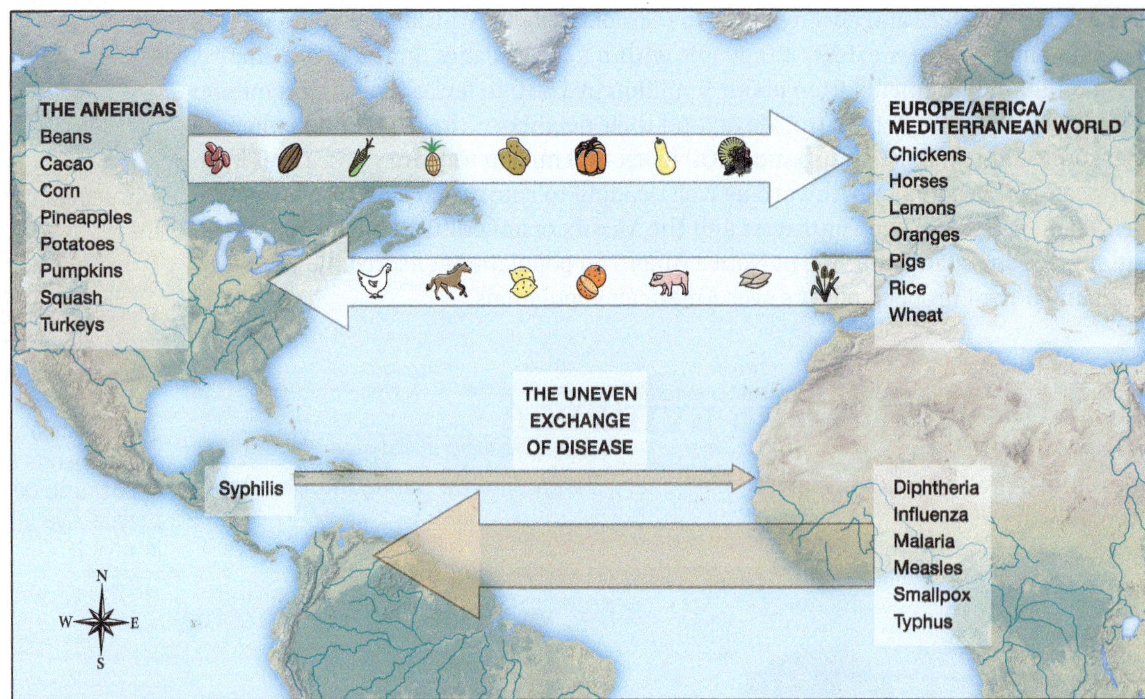

MAP 1.5 The Columbian Exchange, Sixteenth Century When Europeans made contact with Africa and the Americas, they initiated an exchange of plants, animals, and germs that transformed the food, labor, and mortality of all four continents.

What positive and negative ramifications of the Columbian Exchange on the Atlantic World are shown on this map?

a major food source. As a part of the Columbian Exchange, Europeans also brought animals unknown in the Americas, including cattle, horses, chickens, pigs, and honeybees. Cattle and pigs, in particular, changed native diets, while horses inspired new methods of farming, transportation, and warfare throughout the Americas.

The conquered Incan and Aztec empires also provided vast quantities of gold and silver to Spain, making it the treasure-house of Europe and ensuring its dominance on the continent for several decades. Elite Europeans exploited the labor of poor Europeans, Native Americans, and Africans in these colonial societies to extract these valuable resources, and also enhanced their wealth through the cultivation of staple crops such as sugar. In the Americas, sugar was first cultivated on the island of Hispaniola in the West Indies, but it became a source of enormous profits once it took root in the Portuguese colony of Brazil. Moreover, when mixed with cacao, sugar created an addictive candy or drink known as chocolate. Africans' partial immunity to malaria and yellow fever made them attractive to Europeans seeking enslaved labor to produce valuable exports of sugar and tobacco on Caribbean islands after the native population was eliminated.

The continued desire of European nations to acquire colonies in the Americas was a direct result of witnessing the enormous wealth garnered by Spain's conquests. Between 1500 and 1650, Spanish ships carried home more than 180 tons of gold and 16,000 tons of silver from Mexico and Bolivia. About one-fifth of this amount—and indeed, one-fifth of all other exports from Spanish colonies—was taken as taxes by the Spanish crown. The rest was dispersed among wealthy supporters of the expeditions, the families of **conquistadors** or landowners given rights over the labor of local peoples, or soldiers and sailors who returned from America.

conquistador
Spanish name for conqueror. This title was applied to Spanish and Portuguese military leaders who invaded and conquered the lands of Native Americans in Central and South America.

Indeed, the great wealth of the Americas transformed economies throughout Europe, and profits from colonialism and slavery played an important role in this transformation. Starting just after 1500, Western Europe experienced a globally unprecedented period of sustained growth resulting from capturing the land resources of the Americas. This influx of wealth from the Columbian Exchange accelerated the end of **feudalism**, a European social and economic system in which peasants lived and worked on a noble lord's land in exchange for military protection. The influx of wealth also triggered the rise of a new economic order, **capitalism**.

Not everyone, however, benefited from this influx of wealth. For example, in Spain, most of the benefits of the Columbian Exchange flowed to **aristocrats** and merchants. Very little of this wealth was invested in improving conditions at home because enriched European elites spent their wealth mainly on luxury goods imported from the Americas, Asia, or other European nations. Indeed, the rapid infusion of gold and silver fueled inflation, making it harder for ordinary people to afford the necessities of life.

At the same time, American riches generated in the Columbian Exchange increasingly flowed beyond Spain's borders. The Netherlands was a key beneficiary of this wealth, becoming a center for Spanish shipbuilding and trade. Still, the Dutch were never completely under Spanish control, and they traded gold, silver, and other items to France, England, and other European nations. Goods also followed older routes across the Mediterranean to the Ottoman empire, where traders could make huge profits on exotic items from the Americas. Thus, while some Europeans suffered under Spanish power, others benefited from the riches brought to the continent.

By the late sixteenth century, the desire for a greater share of those riches revitalized imperial dreams among the French and English as well as the Dutch. As a consequence, rulers of European nations of the Atlantic World began to fund expeditions to North America.

feudalism
A social and economic system organized by a hierarchy of hereditary classes, in which lower social orders owed loyalty to the social classes above them and, in return, those who worked the land, vassals, received from the nobility a guarantee of protection.

capitalism
An economic system based on private business, ownership of property, and the open exchange of goods between property holders.

aristocrat
Member of the highest class of society, typically nobility who inherited their ranks and titles.

REVIEW

- What were the short-term consequences of Columbus's voyages in both Europe and the Americas?
- Over the longer term, how did the Columbian Exchange transform both the Americas and Europe?

AP® Skills Workshop: Writing Historically

Responding to a Short-Answer Question

Short-answer questions (SAQs) are one of the types of writing that you will encounter on the AP® U.S. History Exam, and SAQs are the focus of the AP® Writing Historically features in Periods 1 and 2 in *Fabric of a Nation*. As the name suggests, SAQs require shorter, more direct responses than typical essay questions. Instead of a traditional essay prompt, on an SAQ you will respond, with evidence, to three distinct parts in just a few sentences per part.

You must answer three of the four SAQs on the AP® U.S. History Exam: one that includes a secondary source (usually a pair of historians with differing interpretations), one that includes a primary source (often, but not always an image), and one without an attached stimulus (primary or secondary source excerpt or image). In this exercise, we will examine how to answer an SAQ without a stimulus, but the same principles apply to answering any of the SAQ types.

(continued)

It may be helpful to think of SAQs as mini-essays where you get right to the point, provide some proof to back up what you are saying, and explain how or why your proof works. You will be doing something similar when responding to essays but on a larger scale, with multiple paragraphs and a lot more detail. In the Thinking Historically feature in Module 1.3, we practiced identifying **claims** and **evidence** in a primary source. After all, using claims and evidence is how authors convince an audience of their ideas.

Now, it's your turn to be the writer. For an SAQ, your job is to *create* a claim and *support* it with evidence and an *explanation*. We are going to call this approach **Claim**, **Support**, and **Explain**, or **CSE** for short. Remember this abbreviation and what it stands for. It will be your guide to good SAQ writing and a foundation for your answers to long-essay questions (LEQs) and document-based questions (DBQs).

Let's take a look at a sample short-answer question without a stimulus:

Directions: Answer **A**, **B**, and **C**.

(A) Briefly explain how ONE historical development led to European exploration between 1400 and 1600.

(B) Briefly explain ONE result of European exploration on European society between 1400 and 1600.

(C) Briefly explain ONE result of European exploration on Native Americans between 1400 and 1600.

After reading this question, you may be wondering where to begin and how to successfully answer all of the SAQs within the allotted time on the AP® U.S. History Exam. To help you do your best when writing SAQ responses, follow a three-step approach:

1. understand what the question is asking,
2. recall relevant information, and
3. write a focused response using CSE (Claim, Support, Explain).

Step 1 ▶ Read and annotate the question

A short-answer question is constructed with three parts, (A), (B), and (C), with directions to respond to each part. That's because each part is graded independently, so you should fashion a short, direct reply for each section. SAQs generally ask you to "briefly describe," or in this case to "briefly explain," which is a reminder to limit your overall answer length to just a few sentences per part.

Notice that the word ONE is written in all caps. There is no benefit to providing two or more of whatever is being asked. In other words, quality is more important than quantity when responding to an SAQ. So, provide and explain the best "one" of what is being asked.

When annotating SAQs, identify the topic, task, and time period. An annotation of the question will look something like this:

Task 1a — *Topic 1a*

(A) Briefly explain how ONE historical development led to European exploration

Time period 1a

between 1400 and 1600.

In annotating part (A), we can see that the topic is European exploration, and the task is to identify and explain how a historical development, some specific historical event or process, facilitated European exploration between 1400 and 1600. Those

(continued)

years are round numbers, with 1400 slightly predating the start of Portuguese exploration under Henry the Navigator, and 1600 being just before the settlement of the first permanent British colony in North America at Jamestown (discussed in Module 2.2).

Task 1b *Topic 1b*

(B) Briefly explain ONE result of European exploration on European society

Time period 1b

between 1400 and 1600.

Task 1c *Topic 1c*

(C) Briefly explain ONE result of European exploration on Native Americans

Time period 1c

between 1400 and 1600.

In annotating parts (B) and (C), we can see that they are identical except for the topic. The task in both is to identify and explain an *effect* of European exploration rather than a *cause*, as in part (A). The difference between (B) and (C) is the topic. While (B) asks for an effect on European society, (C) asks for an effect on Native Americans. The time period is also the same for all three parts, 1400 to 1600.

Step 2 ▶ Brainstorm evidence for each part of the question

To choose the best or strongest examples to use in a response, you may wish to create a simple chart to identify and categorize what you remember and can use in your answer. Here's what a sample could look like.

Causes of Exploration: Part A	Effects on European Society: Part B	Effects on Native Americans: Part C
- European desire for faster and cheaper trade routes to Asia - Support of rulers such as Prince Henry, Ferdinand and Isabella - New technological developments such as the astrolabe and caravel - Desire to spread Christianity to other peoples and lands	- Competition among European nations for New World trade and resources - Inflation caused by the influx of gold and silver - Wealth from New World trade accelerated the shift from feudalism to capitalism - Increased European lifespans from new crops such as potatoes and maize	- Population collapse due to lack of immunity to European diseases such as smallpox and malaria - Changed diets and farming methods from the introduction of new foods and animals - Forced labor on Spanish plantations through the *encomienda* system (see Module 1.5) - Efforts by the Spanish to force cultural and religious conversion on natives (see Module 1.6)

Step 3 ▶ Respond to each part using CSE (Claim, Support, Explain)

Now that we have generated a list of ideas, it's time to fashion a response using Claim, Support, Explain for each part of the SAQ. First, make a **claim** for each part by clearly stating one reason for European exploration for part (A), one way in which European exploration shaped European society for part (B), and one way in which European exploration affected Native Americans for part (C).

Second, provide **support** with specific evidence to validate each claim. In selecting which examples to include, remember that the best choices are the items you know the most about and are confident are in the time period, on topic, and aligned with the task.

(continued)

Third, **explain** how the evidence supports the claim and, if possible, explain their historical significance. Here's what a sample response to this SAQ could look like using the CSE approach and the second piece of evidence from each column of the graphic organizer above.

(A) Political and financial support from monarchs in Portugal and Spain allowed both countries to begin voyages of exploration and conquest in the 1400s **[claim]**. In Portugal, Prince Henry brought together sailors, mapmakers, and shipbuilders and encouraged explorations of the African coast, and in Spain, Ferdinand and Isabella sponsored Columbus's first transatlantic crossing in 1492 **[support]**. The early success of Portugal and Spain brought great wealth to both countries and encouraged other European countries to explore and conquer **[explain]**.

(B) One result of Spain's success in exploration and conquest was the inflation that it caused in the Spanish economy **[claim]**. The large amounts of gold and silver brought back on Spanish ships from the New World led to higher prices **[support]**. The decline of purchasing power in Spain mostly hurt ordinary people and contributed to growing economic inequality in the country **[explain]**.

(C) The Columbian Exchange introduced new foods and animals to the Americas, affecting the ways many Native Americans farmed, hunted, and ate **[claim]**. Over time, Old World crops such as wheat and rice and Old World animals such as cattle and chicken became major sources of food for many native peoples **[support]**. These crops and animals, as well as other Columbian Exchange imports, changed diets, farming habits, and ecosystems throughout the Americas **[explain]**.

ACTIVITY

Now it's your turn. Use CSE (Claim, Support, Explain) to respond to the same SAQ above. Aim for a minimum of three well-developed sentences per part, with nine or more sentences for the entire SAQ. Write at least one Claim sentence, one Support sentence, and one Explanation sentence for each part. While you may use the evidence discussed in the brainstorm chart, choose different evidence from what was modeled in the sample responses.

Labor, Slavery, and Caste in the Spanish Colonial System

MODULE 1.5

FOCUS

In everyday life, we often view cause and effect in a straightforward way. You might claim, for instance, that you did poorly on a test because you didn't study enough or, perhaps, because the test was too hard. Yet a closer look may reveal that several factors influenced each other, such as a misunderstanding of what was being tested or other commitments that limited the amount of time available for study. Likewise, historians can use the reasoning process of causation to more deeply probe beyond obvious causes and effects to investigate how and why historical events and developments influence each other.

As you read this module, consider both the causes and effects of labor systems in Spanish America. Consider how and why Native Americans and Africans were enslaved by the Spanish in the Americas. Note the impacts these labor systems had on Spanish colonial society.

Between 1492 and 1504, Columbus made a total of four voyages to the Caribbean to claim land for Spain, and he even tried to build a permanent Spanish settler colony that he could rule as governor. In his quest to create an orderly settlement, he tried to convince those who accompanied him from Spain to build houses, plant crops, and cut logs for forts; but they, too, had come for gold. When the American Indians stopped trading willingly, Spaniards used force to demand riches, coercing as much gold as possible from the indigenous peoples in the Caribbean.

On his final voyage, Columbus introduced the system of ***encomienda*** in the Caribbean, by which leading men, the *encomenderos*, received land and the unpaid labor from all Native Americans residing on it. The *encomienda* system spread widely and persisted as Spanish conquistadors made new efforts to locate gold and increase their wealth through whatever means they deemed necessary.

encomienda
System established by Christopher Columbus in the Caribbean by which Spanish leaders in the Americas received land and the labor of all resident Native Americans. For Native Americans, the *encomienda* system amounted to enslavement.

Requerimiento
A statement read by Spanish conquerors to native peoples claiming the religious authority of the Catholic Church and the secular authority of the Spanish Crown to rule in the name of the pope. This statement was typically read in Latin and threatened that Indians who did not embrace Spanish rule and Christian conversion faced enslavement and other harsh punishments.

Spanish Incursions in the Americas

By the time of Columbus's death in 1506, the islands he had discovered were dissolving into chaos as traders and adventurers fought with Native Americans and one another over the spoils of conquest. Once Spanish explorers overpowered tribes like the Arawak and Taino in the Caribbean, they headed toward the mainland. They justified the brutal subjugation of American people and lands through European concepts of law and religion.

As you read in the Thinking Historically exercise in Module 1.3, King Ferdinand and Queen Isabella of Spain issued a legal document in 1513 called the ***Requerimiento*** as the basis for Spanish interaction with American Indians.

Conquistadors began to spread its message to groups such as the Maya, Tlaxcala, and Aztecs: The pope had granted Spanish monarchs the authority to claim lands and protect priests preaching the faith in the Americas—and if anyone resisted, they forfeited the protection of the crown and could be "justly" enslaved or killed.

AP® EXAM TIP

The Spanish developed a caste system to maintain power and control based on racial categories. For the AP® Exam, understanding this precursor to racialized slavery in the United States will help you address any questions about slavery in terms of changes over time.

In 1519, as the Spanish invaded the mainland of present-day Mexico, a Native American girl named Malintzin was thrust into the center of this chaotic and violent world. She witnessed events that transformed not only her world but also the world at large. Malintzin, whose birth name is lost to history, lived in the rural area between the expanding kingdom of the Aztecs and the declining Mayan states of the Yucatán peninsula. Raised in a noble household, Malintzin was fluent in Nahuatl, the Aztec language. In 1515 or 1516, when she was between the ages of eight and twelve, she was either taken by or given to Aztec merchants, perhaps as a peace offering to stave off military attacks. She then entered a well-established slave trade, consisting mostly of women and girls, who were sent eastward to work in the expanding cotton fields or the households of slaveholders. During her captivity there, Malintzin learned the Mayan language. Although she could not have known it at the time, her circumstances would again change dramatically in just a few years' time.

In 1517, the Maya had driven Spanish adventurers from the banks of local rivers and were able to maintain control of their lands. But when the Spaniards returned in 1519, they defeated the Maya in battle. As a result, the Maya offered the Spaniards food, gold, and twenty enslaved women, including Malintzin. The Spanish leader, Hernán Cortés, baptized the enslaved women and assigned each of them Christian names, although the women did not consent to this ritual. Cortés then divided the women among his senior officers, giving Malintzin, named Doña Marina by Cortés, to the highest-ranking noble in his group.

Already fluent in Nahuatl and Mayan, Malintzin soon learned Spanish. Within a matter of months, she became the Spaniards' chief translator. When Diego de Velázquez, the Spanish governor of Cuba, granted Cortés the right to explore and trade along

Gianni Dagli Orti/Shutterstock

Hernán Cortés and Malintzin Meet Montezuma at Tenochtitlán, 1519 This image depicts Cortés and Malintzin meeting Montezuma in November 1519. It is a reproduction of an image created by Tlaxcalan artists and represents a Native American perspective on these events.

Identify Cortés, Malintzin, and Montezuma. What can you infer about the artists' attitude toward Cortés and Malintzin based on this image?

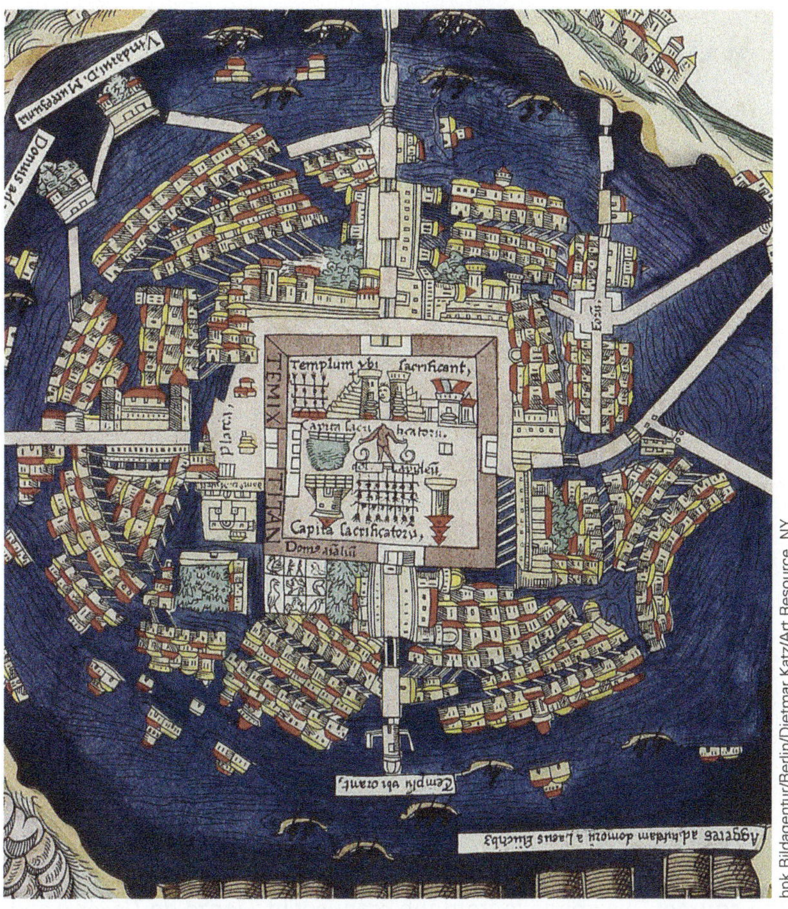

bpk Bildagentur/Berlin/Dietmar Katz/Art Resource, NY

The Aztec Capital City of Tenochtitlán German geographers drew this map of Tenochtitlán in 1524 based on Aztec sources. At its peak, the city had a population of 100,000 and contained a marketplace, schools, the emperor's palace, and a ball-game court. The Aztecs viewed Tenochtitlán as the intersection of the secular and divine worlds.

What does this map reveal about life in Tenochtitlán?

the coast of Central America, Malintzin had no choice but to go with him. Although Velázquez gave Cortés no direct authority to attack native peoples in the region or claim land for himself, the conquistador saw this expedition as an opportunity to amass great wealth. With Malintzin acting as a translator, Cortés forged alliances with local rulers willing to join in an attack against the Aztecs. From the perspective of local communities such as the Tlaxcala, Cortés's presence offered an opportunity to strike back against the brutal Aztec regime.

As Cortés moved into territories ruled by the Aztecs, his success depended on his ability to understand Aztec ways of thinking and to convince subjugated groups to fight against their oppressive rulers. Malintzin accompanied Cortés at every step, making diplomacy possible between the Spanish and leaders of native peoples ruled by the Aztec empire.

Despite their assumption of cultural superiority, many Spaniards who accompanied Cortés were astonished by Aztec cities, canals, and temples, which rivaled those in Europe. Seeing these architectural wonders may have given some soldiers pause about trying to conquer the kingdom. But when the Aztec chief, Montezuma, presented Cortés with large quantities of precious objects including gold-encrusted jewelry as a peace offering, he unwittingly confirmed that the Aztecs had the vast wealth that the Spanish had come for.

When Cortés and his men marched to Tenochtitlán in 1519, Montezuma was indecisive in his response. After an early effort to ambush the Spaniards failed, the Aztec leader allowed Cortés to march his men into the capital city, where they took Montezuma hostage. In response, Aztec warriors attacked the Spaniards, but Cortés and his men managed to fight their way out of Tenochtitlán. They suffered heavy losses and might have been crushed by their Aztec foes but for the alliances forged with native groups in the surrounding area. Given protection by Native American allies, the Spanish regrouped. The remaining Spanish soldiers and their allies returned to batter the Aztecs with a combination of cannons, steel weapons, horses, and trained dogs that won a final victory.

AP® WORKING with EVIDENCE

Source: Anonymous artists, Hernán Cortés assisted by the Tlaxcalan people of Mexico, 1560

The Picture Art Collection/Alamy

About the source: This image is from the manuscript *Lienzo de Tlaxcala* and shows a mural painted for Tlaxcalan nobles.

Questions for Analysis

1. Identify the groups portrayed in this image.
2. Identify who is depicted as the winner of this conflict.
3. Describe an apparent continuity between the pre-Columbian and post-Columbian Tlaxcalan culture revealed by this image.
4. Describe an apparent change between pre-Columbian and post-Columbian Tlaxcalan culture revealed by this image.

It is important to note that the germs the Spanish soldiers carried with them played a large role in their subjugation of the Aztecs. Smallpox swept through Tenochtitlán in 1521, killing thousands and leaving Montezuma's army dramatically weakened. This human catastrophe as much as military resources and strategies allowed Cortés to conquer the capital that year. He then claimed the entire region as New Spain and assigned soldiers to construct the Spanish capital of Mexico City at Tenochtitlán. Moreover, he extended Spanish rule over the native groups, including those that had allied with him.

As news of Cortés's victory spread, and as *encomenderos* grew extremely wealthy from the silver, gold, and other resources extracted from American lands through the forced labor of Native Americans and shipped across the Atlantic, other Spanish conquistadors sought glory in the Americas as well. Most importantly, in 1524 Francisco Pizarro conquered the vast Incan empire in present-day Peru. Once again, the Spaniards were helped by the spread of European diseases and non-Incan native peoples who had been ruled by the Incas. This victory ensured Spanish access to vast supplies of silver in Potosí (in present-day Bolivia) and the surrounding mountains. While the Spanish used enslaved Native Americans at Potosí, their conquests also ensured the spread of enslaved African labor from Caribbean plantations to mainland agriculture and mining projects. By 1535, Spain controlled the most densely populated regions of South America, which also contained the greatest mineral wealth.

REVIEW

- What factors shaped Spanish colonial society in the Western Hemisphere?

Spain Establishes Colonial Rule

The Spanish monarchs, Ferdinand and Isabella, sought to incorporate the Americas into their empire as an engine to generate wealth for the crown. To do this, they took for themselves the *quinto real* ("royal fifth")—that is, 20 percent of wealth produced in Spanish colonies. To secure this wealth, they divided colonial lands into viceroyalties, appointing governors called viceroys to ensure order. Moreover, they sent many political and military representatives, also royally appointed, to help govern locally. By the late sixteenth century, Spanish supremacy in the Americas and the wealth acquired there transformed the European economy.

In Spain, these economic transformations enriched nobles with access to wealth drained from the Americas but produced hard times for peasants. The influx of silver, for instance, caused inflation that raised prices and impoverished peasants. Threatened by poverty and starvation, peasants joined King Philip II's (reigned 1556–1598) military campaigns as soldiers and sailors. The king, a devout Catholic, claimed to be doing God's work as Spain subdued parts of Italy and conquered Portugal, including the Portuguese colonies in Africa.

Throughout the sixteenth century, Spain's colonial projects also established a new social order in the regions they ruled. In colonial societies, people were mixing in various ways that brought Spaniards, Native Americans, and Africans into frequent contact. In feudal tradition, the Spanish crown demanded more tax, tribute, and labor from those ranked lower in social class. Through the mechanisms of a variety of labor systems, people of Native American and African ancestry owed work or tribute to Spanish colonial elites. To account for who owed how much, the Spanish wrote guidelines for taxation based on ethnicity, influenced by other factors such as education, to define classes in colonial society. From these defined expectations, a system emerged, which later hardened and formalized into the **Spanish caste system**. Even after independence, this hierarchical system was largely maintained.

Spanish caste system
A system developed by the Spanish in the sixteenth century that defined the status of diverse populations based on a racial hierarchy that privileged Europeans.

This system categorized people by the degrees of their racial ancestry into a social hierarchy, which ultimately shaped the future of societies throughout the Western Hemisphere. An individual's place indicated how much labor or tax they owed. In theory, one's racial ancestry determined one's caste, but given the mixing of diverse people of the Atlantic World, both ancestry and skin color blurred. In practice, it also considered qualities such as education and wealth. For example, a darker-skinned educated landowner might be perceived as of higher class than a lighter-skinned landless craftsman.

Passing into a higher caste meant lower taxes or escaping forced labor in addition to other social benefits. The caste system in descending order of rank included: those born in Spain called *peninsulares* (named for the Iberian peninsula, which contained the kingdoms of Spain and Portugal), people born of Spanish parents in the colonies called *criollos* (or creoles), and those sharing Spanish and Native American parentage called *mestizos*. The Spanish ranked *mulattos*, persons of mixed Spanish and African parentage, below mestizos, but placed Africans, *negros*, above indigenous Native Americans they called *indios*. The Spanish considered the indios child-like wards of Spanish elites in need of parenting to enforce civilized behavior. Similarly, the Spanish enforced a lower status on Africans through laws prohibiting them from many government positions and the priesthood.

REVIEW

- What purpose did the Spanish caste system serve?

AP® Skills Workshop: Thinking Historically

Identifying Connections in Primary Sources

Making connections is a skill we routinely practice in life to help us organize information and make meaning from facts and observations. Let's say you were introduced to a new group of people. You might ask them questions, look for things you have in common, and focus on unique details they shared as you tried to learn their names and get to know them.

When analyzing historical events and developments, you can build on that approach by thinking and asking questions in the way a historian would. Here are three fundamental historical reasoning processes that you can use to make historical connections and analyze patterns: **Comparison** (examining similarities and differences), **Causation** (examining causes and effects), and **Continuity and Change over Time** (examining changes and what remains relatively the same during a time period).

Let's look at how you can use these ways of thinking to understand more fully a primary source image such as the one below.

Source: *Las Castas,* unknown artist, eighteenth century

Reading the panels left to right:

Panel 1: A child of a Spaniard and Indian is a Mestizo.
Panel 2: A child of a Mestizo and a Spaniard is a Castizo (¾ Spanish and ¼ Indian).
Panel 3: A child of a Castizo and a Spaniard is a Spaniard.
Panel 4: A child of a Spaniard and an African is a Mulatto.

(continued)

About the source: These portions of a Spanish oil painting depict the caste system in Spanish America. Each panel displays a specific racial combination of two parents and the resulting socioeconomic/racial caste of the child.

As we consider this painting, we can apply the historical reasoning processes both within the image and beyond the image to make historical connections.

Viewing it **comparatively**, we could explore similarities and differences within the painting by comparing individual panels, noting, for example, that each panel has a man, woman, and child. Perhaps you notice that the man's ethnicity is always listed before the woman's ethnicity.

When looking at the image through the lens of **causation**, we want to ask what events led to the formation of the Spanish caste system. These include the conquest of the native peoples of the Caribbean and the Americas, the enslavement of African people and their forced relocation to New Spain, and the resulting intermarriage of Spanish, Native Americans, and African people, which resulted in the marginalization of people based on racial categories that supported Spanish power.

For **continuity and change** (CCOT), the questions are what elements of the caste system persisted during this time period, such as race remaining a defining social characteristic, and what elements changed, such as the proliferation of different racial categories based on interaction among people in New Spain and the needs of those in power to retain their status.

Likewise, you can apply causation to CCOT and ask what led to or resulted from the similarities, differences, continuities, or changes you have identified.

ACTIVITY

Now, it's your turn to practice making historical connections using the same image. Identify and explain at least one specific similarity or difference between the castes as shown in the image. Then, explain one historical continuity or change regarding the caste system evident in the image. Finally, explain one cause or effect of the similarity, difference, continuity, or change you discussed. Be specific in your response and write at least two to three sentences for each reasoning process. Try to cite different examples from the ones that were provided to you.

MODULE 1.6

Cultural Interactions among Europeans, Native Americans, and Africans

FOCUS

Comparison is more than just noting the similarities and differences between two or more items. To compare things more fully, you can identify important characteristics of each object or event and then consider the ways in which those things interact over time. If, say, you are comparing high school teachers and students, some obvious differences show up, such as age (teenager vs. adult), education level (high school student vs. college graduate), and income (none or part-time vs. full-time with salary). Similarities also exist, such as they spend most of their day in a classroom, both usually have homework, and many students and teachers are involved in extracurricular activities. However, if you are trying to more deeply compare students and teachers, it's important to go beyond initial observations and ask how day-to-day and yearlong exchanges in and outside the classroom also shape the experiences of both groups.

As you read Module 1.6, practice thinking comparatively at a deeper level by noting key aspects of European, Native American, and African lives and culture, how their cross-cultural interactions shaped their experiences, and the ways and extent to which those experiences and changes were similar and different for each group.

At the height of the Roman empire in the early centuries C.E., dense global trade networks connected the peoples of Europe, Africa, and Asia. With the decline of Roman power in western Europe, those connections broke down, but commercial ties continued to thrive among diverse peoples surrounding the Mediterranean Sea. Because Portugal was denied access to Mediterranean trade, explorers there sought trade routes along the coast of Africa. Increased trade with African kingdoms by Portugal and other European societies included the purchase of slaves. This lucrative and devastating form of commerce would expand dramatically, with impacts on both sides of the Atlantic, as European nations colonized the Americas.

European Encounters with West Africa

Enslaved Africans were among the most lucrative "goods" traded by European merchants. Slavery had been practiced in Europe, the Americas, Africa, and other parts of the world for centuries. But in most times and places, enslaved people were captives of war or individuals sold in payment for deaths or injuries to conquering enemies. Under such circumstances, enslaved people generally retained some legal rights, and bondage was rarely permanent and almost never inheritable. With the advent of large-scale European participation in the African slave trade, however, the system of bondage began to change, transforming Europe and Africa and, in turn, the Americas.

In the fifteenth century, Europeans were most familiar with North Africa, a region deeply influenced by Islam and characterized by large kingdoms, well-developed cities, and an extensive network of trading centers. In northeast Africa, including Egypt, city-states flourished, with ties to India, the Middle East, and China. In northwest Africa, Timbuktu (in present-day Mali) linked North Africa to empires south of the Sahara as well as to Europe. Here, enslaved Africans labored for wealthier Africans in a system of bound labor long familiar to Europeans.

By the mid-sixteenth century, European nations established competing forts along the African coast from Senegambia in the north to the Gold Coast, the Bight of Biafra, and West Central Africa farther south. The enslaved men and women shipped from these forts to Europe generally came from communities that had been raided or conquered by more powerful coastal groups. African empires able to trade captives at the coast for European goods, most notably guns, gained power, which they used to expand and capture more humans for trade.

Enslaved Africans from the interior of West Africa arrived at the coast exhausted, hungry, dirty, and with few clothes. They worshiped gods unfamiliar to Europeans, and their cultural customs and social practices seemed, to the Europeans, strange and primitive. Over time, it was the image of the enslaved West Africans that came to dominate European visions of the entire continent.

As traders from Portugal, Spain, Holland, and England brought back more stories and more enslaved Africans, these negative portraits took deeper hold. Woodcuts and prints circulated in Europe showing half-naked Africans who were intentionally portrayed more like apes than humans.

Biblical stories also seemingly reinforced notions of Africans as naturally inferior to Europeans. In the Bible, Ham had sinned against his father, Noah. Noah then cursed Ham's son Canaan to a life of slavery. Increasingly, European Christians considered Africans the "sons of Ham," infidels who deserved a life of bondage. This self-serving idea was used to justify the enslavement of African men, women, and children.

These images of West Africa failed to reflect the diverse peoples who lived there and the diverse societies that developed in the area's tropical rain forests, plains, and savannas. As the slave and gun trades expanded in the sixteenth and seventeenth centuries, they destabilized large areas of western and central Africa, with smaller societies destroyed by raids and even the larger kingdoms damaged by the extensive buying and selling of human beings.

Men, women, and children were captured by Africans as well as Portuguese, Spanish, Dutch, and English traders. Still, Europeans had not yet instituted a system of perpetual slavery, in which enslavement was transmitted from one generation to the next. Instead, Africans formed another class of bound labor, alongside peasants, indentured servants, criminals, and apprentices.

Crucially, distinctions among bound laborers on the basis of race did not exist. Wealthy Englishmen, for instance, viewed both African and Irish laborers as ignorant and unruly heathens, although the Irish never experienced wholesale enslavement and exportation to foreign lands in the same fashion as enslaved Africans. As Europeans began to conquer and colonize the Americas and as demands for labor increased dramatically, however, ideas about race and slavery changed significantly.

REVIEW

- How and why did Europeans expand their connections with Africa and the Middle East in the fifteenth century?
- How did early European encounters with West Africans influence Europeans' ideas about African peoples and reshape existing systems of slavery?

Spain Debates the Human Costs of Colonization

Despite the obvious material benefits, the Spaniards were not blind to the enormous human costs of colonization. The conquest of the Americas sparked heated debates within Spain that raised critical questions about Spanish responsibilities to God and humanity. Catholic leaders believed that the conversion of native peoples to Christianity was critical to Spanish success in the Americas. However, most royal officials and colonial agents viewed the extraction of precious metals as far more important. They argued that cheap labor was essential to creating wealth. Yet the brutal conditions of enslaved labor led to the death of huge numbers of American Indians, and it was understandably difficult for those who survived to see any benefit in converting to the very religion the Spanish used to justify such brutal mistreatment.

By 1550, news of the widespread torture and enslavement of American Indians convinced the Spanish King Charles I (reigned 1519–1556), who was also Emperor Charles V of the Holy Roman Empire, to gather a group of theologians, jurists, and philosophers at Valladolid to discuss the moral and legal implications of conquest. Bartolomé de Las Casas took a leading role in defending the rights of American Indians. A former conquistador, Las Casas had become a Dominican friar and spent many years preaching to them in America. He asked, "And so what man of sound mind will approve a war against men who are harmless, ignorant, gentle, temperate, unarmed, and destitute of every human defense?" Las Casas reasoned that even if Spain defeated

Stefano Bianchetti/Bridgeman Images

Engraving of the Black Legend, 1598 In the late 1500s, Theodor de Bry and his sons created a series of detailed and graphic engravings of interactions between Spanish soldiers and Native Americans based on reports from explorers and missionaries. Some portrayed Spaniards torturing Native Americans, which they labeled the "Black Legend."

What details from this engraving support the myth of the "Black Legend"?

the American Indians, the souls of those killed would be lost to God, while among the survivors, "hatred and loathing of the Christian religion" would prevail. He even suggested replacing the labor of enslaved American Indians with that of enslaved Africans, apparently less concerned with the souls of African people.

Juan Ginés de Sepúlveda, a Catholic theologian with a position at the royal court, attacked Las Casas's arguments. Although he had never set foot in the Americas, he read reports of cannibalism and other violations of "natural law" among native peoples. He argued that since the American Indians were savages, the civilized Spaniards were obligated to "destroy barbarism and educate these people to a more humane and virtuous life." If they refused such help, Spanish rule "can be imposed upon them by force of arms." Although Sepúlveda spoke for the majority at Valladolid, Las Casas and his supporters continued to press their case as Spain expanded its reach into North America.

AP® EXAM TIP

Interactions among Native Americans, Europeans, and Africans led to cultural exchange as well as oppression. Be able to explain how changing ideas about religion, culture, and race led to various justifications for subjugation of Africans and Native Americans.

AP® WORKING with EVIDENCE

Source: Bartolomé de Las Casas, Catholic Dominican priest, *Brief Account of the Destruction of the Indies*, 1542

> "They are by nature the most humble, patient, and peaceable, holding no grudges, free from embroilments, neither excitable nor quarrelsome. . . . They are also poor people, for they not only possess little but have no desire to possess worldly goods. For this reason they are not arrogant, embittered, or greedy. . . . They are very clean in their persons, with alert, intelligent minds, docile and open to doctrine, very apt to receive our holy Catholic faith, to be endowed with virtuous customs, and to behave in a godly fashion. And once they begin to hear the tidings of the Faith, they are so insistent on knowing more and on taking the sacraments of the Church . . . that, truly, the missionaries who are here need to be endowed by God with great patience in order to cope with such eagerness. . . .
>
> Yet into this sheepfold, into this land of meek outcasts there came some Spaniards who immediately behaved like ravening wild beasts, wolves, tigers, or lions that had been starved for many days."

Source: Juan Ginés de Sepúlveda, Catholic priest and theologian, *Concerning the Just Causes of the War against the Indians*, 1547

> "[T]he Spanish have a perfect right to rule these barbarians of the New World and the adjacent islands, who in prudence, skill, virtues, and humanity are as inferior to the Spanish as children to adults, or women to men, for there exists between the two as great a difference as between savage and cruel races and the most merciful, between the most intemperate and the moderate and temperate and, I might even say, between apes and men. . . .
>
> Compare, then, these gifts of prudence, talent, magnanimity, temperance, humanity, and religion with those possessed by these half-men . . ., in whom you will barely find the vestiges of humanity, who not only do not possess any learning at all, but are not even literate or in possession of any monument to their history except for some obscure and vague reminiscences of several things put down in various paintings; nor do they have written laws, but barbarian institutions and customs. Well, then, if we are dealing with virtue, what temperance or mercy can you expect from men who are committed to all types of intemperance and base frivolity, and eat human flesh? . . . [B]efore the arrival of the Christians ... they waged continual and ferocious war upon one another with such fierceness that they did not consider a victory at all worthwhile unless they sated their monstrous hunger with the flesh of their enemies."

Questions for Analysis

1. Identify a specific similarity between Las Casas's and Sepúlveda's descriptions of the native people in the Western Hemisphere.
2. Identify a specific difference between Las Casas's and Sepúlveda's descriptions of the native people in the Western Hemisphere.
3. Describe a specific historical difference in the way Las Casas and Sepúlveda believed native people should be treated by the Spanish.

 REVIEW

- What consequences did Spain's acquisition of an American empire have in Europe?

Spain's Global Empire Declines

As religious conflicts escalated in Europe between Catholics and Protestants, the Spaniards in America continued to push north from Florida and Mexico in hopes of expanding their empire. The nature of Spanish expansion, however, changed. In 1573, Spanish authorities decided that missionaries, rather than soldiers, should direct all new settlements in what is known as the **mission system**.

mission system
Organizational system established by the Spanish in 1573 in which Catholic missionaries, rather than soldiers, directed all new settlements in the Americas.

Franciscan priests began founding missions on the margins of Pueblo villages north of Mexico. They named the area Nuevo México (New Mexico), and many learned American Indian languages. Over the following decades, as many as twenty thousand Pueblo Indians officially converted to Catholicism, although many still retained traditional beliefs and practices. Missionaries made a considerable effort to eradicate such beliefs and practices, including destroying Pueblo religious artifacts and flogging ceremonial leaders, but to little avail. Even years after "conversion" to Catholicism, Spanish authorities discovered Pueblo Indians performing traditional religious rituals in secret.

At the same time as they sought religious conversion, the Franciscans tried to force the Pueblo people to adopt European social and economic customs. They insisted that men rather than women farm the land and that the Pueblos speak, cook, and dress like the Spaniards. Yet the missionaries largely ignored Spanish laws intended to protect American Indians from coerced labor, demanding that the Pueblos build churches, provide the missions with food, and carry their goods to market. Wealthy landowners who followed the missionaries into New Mexico also demanded tribute in the form of goods and labor. Tribute payments that the Spanish enforced, violently, impoverished the Pueblo and diminished emergency stores of grains, leading to starvation during the fairly frequent droughts. The Spanish attempts to extract wealth ruined Pueblo societies' long-standing and delicate ecologically balanced agriculture, suited to the arid climate.

In 1598 Juan de Oñate, a member of a wealthy mining family, established a trading post and fort in the upper Rio Grande valley. The five hundred soldiers who accompanied him seized corn and clothing from Pueblo villages and murdered or raped those who resisted. Indians at the Acoma pueblo rebelled, killing eleven Spanish soldiers. The Spanish retaliated, slaughtering 500 men and 300 women and children. Fearing reprisals from outraged Pueblo Indians, most Spanish settlers withdrew from the region.

In 1610, the Spanish returned, founded Santa Fe, and established a network of missions and estates owned by *encomenderos*. This time, the Pueblo peoples largely accepted the new situation. In part, they feared military reprisals if they challenged Spanish authorities. But they were also facing drought, disease, and raids by hostile Apaches and Navajos. The Pueblo peoples hoped to gain protection from Spanish soldiers and priests. Yet their faith in the Franciscans' spiritual power soon began to fade when conditions did not improve.

Although Spain maintained a firm hold on Florida and its colonies in the West Indies, it had to exert ever-greater efforts to suppress growing resistance among the Pueblo peoples. Thus, as other European powers expanded their reach into North America, the Spaniards were left with few resources to protect their eastern frontier.

REVIEW

- In what ways did Spanish policy change toward native peoples after 1573?
- What effects did these changes have on the Pueblo people?

AP® Skills Workshop: Thinking Historically

Answering Multiple-Choice Questions with a Primary Source Stimulus

On the AP® U.S. History Exam you will encounter four different sections of questions: 55 stimulus-based multiple-choice questions (SBMCQs), 4 short-answer questions (SAQs), 1 document-based question (DBQ), and 3 long-essay questions (LEQs). We have already examined how to respond to an SAQ, and DBQs and LEQs will be discussed in later periods. Here we will take a look at the multiple-choice questions.

Stimulus-based multiple-choice are questions with a text excerpt or image attached to them. This stimulus can be a primary source from the time period or a secondary source constructed by a historian after the fact. These items typically appear in sets of two or three questions and require you to think critically and combine what you already know with information from the stimulus. Let's consider a stimulus-based set of questions based on the Las Casas excerpt from earlier in this module (see page 39).

The first step when approaching these types of questions is to carefully read the information provided about the source. Here you will usually discover the author, title, and time period of the stimulus. In this case, the excerpt is one you have already encountered: Bartolomé de Las Casas, Catholic Dominican priest, *Brief Account of the Destruction of the Indies*, 1542. Often, however, you will not have previously read the source and may not even be familiar with the author. Even so, you should still be able to connect source information to broader trends from the time period such as Spanish conquest and rule in the Americas and the efforts to extract wealth from the New World. You may remember that Las Casas was a Spanish priest who criticized the actions of conquistadors and argued for more humane treatment of Native Americans. Even if you didn't recall those specifics before reading the excerpt, you should realize from the title of his book that he wrote about the "Destruction of the Indies" and that it was published a few decades after the Spanish began their conquest, when there were still sizable populations of enslaved Native Americans and before widescale importation of enslaved Africans.

After considering the source information, it's time to closely read the excerpt. As you read it, try to identify the main point and ask yourself if the ideas in it reinforce

(continued)

your initial thoughts or if it introduces new information. Las Casas emphasizes the innocent, peaceful nature of the Native Americans and states that they are very receptive to Christian teachings. Clearly the content in this excerpt is consistent with what we know of Las Casas and supports his criticism of Spanish treatment of Native Americans.

The last step is to read the question and work through the answer choices, settling on the best answer. Here's a sample question based on the Las Casas excerpt.

1. Which of the following most directly resulted from concerns over the mistreatment of Native Americans by the Spanish?
   (A) An immediate ban on the use of all forced labor in Spanish colonies in America
   (B) A shift in how native labor was used by the Spanish from mining for gold to working on sugar plantations
   (C) The importation of African slaves to replace Native American labor in Spanish colonies
   (D) Formal debates within the Spanish kingdom over how Native Americans should be treated

This question asks us to identify a direct effect of the concerns of some, like Las Casas, about how Native Americans were treated by the Spanish. Let's have a look at which options are correct, and which are not:

Option A is not correct because it's false. Forced labor by Native Americans continued throughout the sixteenth century and beyond. As native populations dwindled due to disease and war, the absolute numbers may have fallen, but the practice did not end. Further, the use of "immediate" and "all" suggest an unlikely, complete shift in labor practices, making this answer choice easy to eliminate.

Option B is incorrect because even though a shift from mining to cash crops did happen, that change is not related to concerns about mistreatment and Las Casas's arguments. This is a reminder that true statements are not correct answers if they don't directly apply to the question asked.

Option C is incorrect both because the shift toward the use of enslaved African labor mostly happens later and because the change is for financial reasons not due to concern over the welfare of Native Americans. Chronological reasoning as well as remembering the European desire to profit from the New World can help us eliminate this answer.

Option D is the correct answer by process of elimination and because Las Casas's criticisms did lead to the formal debates at Valladolid sponsored by Charles V. Even if you didn't remember that fact, debates are a more realistic outcome of his criticism than the other options.

ACTIVITY

Now, it's your turn. Use your knowledge of the time period and information from the stimulus to select the best answer to the question.

1. The excerpt best serves as evidence of which of the following historical developments?
   (A) The development of the caste system
   (B) The Spanish desire to spread Christianity
   (C) The use of the *encomienda* system
   (D) The impact of the mission system

Causation in Period 1

MODULE 1.7

AP® Skills Workshop: Writing Historically

Responding to a Short-Answer Question with a Primary Source

Throughout Period 1, in the Focus sections at the beginning of each module and in the Writing Historically feature in Module 1.4, we have considered how to reason historically using the lenses of comparison, causation, and continuity and change over time (CCOT). Of those three reasoning processes, causation (cause and effect) is probably the most prominent in Period 1 and the focus of the SAQ in this exercise.

In the Writing Historically feature in Module 1.4, we also looked at how to write an SAQ without an accompanying stimulus. For that SAQ, we used a three-step approach: annotate the question, brainstorm outside information, and write the response using **CSE (Claim, Support, Explain)**.

Now, let's apply that same approach to an SAQ with a primary source image. On the AP® U.S. History Exam, you can expect to see an SAQ with a primary source, usually an image, as one of the three SAQs you will need to write.

Source: Unknown Spanish artist, sixteenth century

The Print Collector/Alamy

About the source: This drawing depicts Spanish conquistadors directing enslaved Native Americans to build Mexico City after the destruction of the Tenochtitlán, the Aztec capital.

(continued)

Directions: Answer **A**, **B**, and **C**.

(A) Briefly describe ONE historical perspective expressed in the image.
(B) Briefly explain how ONE specific event or development contributed to the process depicted in the image.
(C) Briefly explain ONE specific historical effect that resulted from the process depicted in the image.

Step 1 ▶ Annotate the image and the question

The first thing to do when examining a primary source of any type is to look at the sourcing provided with the document. In this case, we are given a good deal of information: the time period (1500s), the author's nationality (Spanish), identification of the two groups in the image (Spanish and Native Americans), the status of each group (conquistadors and enslaved, respectively), the main activity taking place (building Mexico City), and some immediate context (after the destruction of Tenochtitlán, the Aztec capital).

Now let's take a closer look at the picture itself. To make sense of an image such as this one, it is helpful to divide the image into parts, such as halves, thirds, quarters, or distinct components. In the top left of this painting, Spaniards are gathered around a table presumably planning the building of Mexico City, and in the top center, Spanish soldiers are massed, perhaps to enforce the orders given by those in charge. Across the bottom half of the panel, Spaniards are directing the labor of Native Americans carrying beams and stones, while the right side of the image shows Native American workers constructing a building, possibly a church.

After deconstructing the image, it's time to analyze the SAQ to make sure that each part of the response is correctly tailored to the task. In part (A), the task calls for a description of a historical perspective expressed in the image. In doing so, a good answer must discuss a point of view that can be reasonably inferred from the image, is supported by details from the image, and is consistent with basic historical understandings.

Note: Asking for "ONE" perspective rather than "the" perspective is a reminder that there are multiple valid interpretations of the image. For parts (B) and (C), the tasks are clearly centered on the causation reasoning process. Part (B) asks for an identification and explanation of a cause that led to the events in the image. Part (C) asks for an identification and explanation of an effect of the events in the image.

Step 2 ▶ Brainstorm and organize your information

As we have done before, making a chart can help organize information that can be used in an SAQ response. Here's what a sample could look like.

Historical Perspectives: Part A	Causes for the Process Depicted in Image: Part B	Effects of the Process Depicted in Image: Part C
- The artist supports the enslavement of Native Americans and the use of their labor to build Mexico City; the coordination and lack of resistance suggests Spanish rule over native peoples is part of the natural order.	- Deadlier military technology such as guns, caravels, and the use of horses helped the Spanish to conquer the Aztecs.	- Spanish conquest of the Aztecs led to widespread enslavement and even torture as conquistadors demanded gold and silver and the crown implemented a tribute system.

(continued)

- The finer clothes of the Spaniards, their weapons, and the European-style architecture suggest the artist believes in the superiority of European technology and culture. - The use of wood and stone building materials, the modest clothing worn by Native Americans, and the relative peacefulness of the scene despite their enslavement suggests the artist believes that natives have adapted to Spanish rule and culture.	- Diseases such as smallpox devastated Native American populations, making the Aztecs and other native peoples easier to conquer. - The Spanish allied with rival tribes, taking advantage of resentment toward the Aztecs and hesitation by Montezuma, the Aztec leader.	- The successful conquest of the Aztecs by Cortés and his men inspired others such as Francisco Pizarro, who led a conquest of the Incas and encouraged continued conquest in the 1500s. - Over time, the Spanish conquest of the Aztecs and other native peoples resulted in racial intermingling and the formation of a caste system in the Spanish colonies.

Step 3 ▶ Write the response for each part of the SAQ using *CSE (Claim, Support, Explain)*

The CSE approach calls for a claim (a direct answer to the question), a piece of historical evidence (specific, factual detail to support the claim), and an explanation (a description of the linkage or statement of the historical significance) connecting the claim and evidence. The sample response below uses the second item from each column of the chart to answer the question.

(A) One perspective seen in this image is the artist's belief in the superiority of European technology and culture **[claim]**. In the image, the artist depicts the Spanish as more finely dressed than the Native Americans, more powerful with their armed soldiers, and more sophisticated as they direct the construction of a building in European style **[support]**. The relatively peaceful atmosphere and sense of progress displayed in the image served as both justification for Spanish conquest and encouragement for continued attacks **[explain]**.

(B) Diseases brought over by the Spanish as part of the Columbian Exchange devastated the populations of the Aztecs and other Native Americans, making them easier to conquer and enslave **[claim]**. It's estimated that smallpox and other European diseases along with warfare ultimately reduced native populations by 90 percent **[support]**. Eventually, this population collapse and continued Spanish demand for New World riches led to the growing importation of African slaves **[explain]**.

(C) One effect of the conquest of the Aztecs and destruction of Tenochtitlán was that it inspired further attacks by Spanish conquistadors **[claim]**. A few years after Cortés, Francisco Pizarro used similar tactics to lead a small army to victory over the Incas in Peru **[support]**. The victories of Cortés, Pizarro, and others brought tremendous riches to Spain and accelerated Spanish conquest of Central and South America **[explain]**.

ACTIVITY

Respond to the SAQ using **CSE** for each part of the question. Strive to write three well-developed sentences for each part, for a total of nine or more sentences. Feel free to use your own examples or information from the chart above, but don't use the same evidence that was used in the model responses.

Period 1 Review 1491–1607

KEY CONCEPTS AND EVENTS

aristocrat, *25*
astrolabe, *16*
Atlantic World, *22*
Aztec, *8*
capitalism, *25*
caravel, *16*
Columbian Exchange, *22*
conquistador, *24*
encomienda, *29*
feudalism, *25*
horticulture, *6*
Incas, *9*
Inquisition, *16*
Maya, *8*
missionary, *15*
mission system, *40*
Pueblo, *11*
Renaissance, *15*
Requerimiento, *29*
Spanish caste system, *33*
Tenochtitlán, *8*
Three Sisters, *6*

KEY PEOPLE

King Charles I, *38*
Christopher Columbus, *18*
Hernán Cortés, *30*
Ferdinand II of Aragon, *16*
Isabella of Castile, *16*
Malintzin (Doña Marina), *30*
Montezuma, *31*
Francisco Pizarro, *32*

CHRONOLOGY

c. 27,000 B.C.E.	First peoples migrate from Asia to the Americas
c. 8000–2000 B.C.E.	Agriculture fostered stable settlements in the Western Hemisphere
c. 4000 B.C.E.	Maize cultivation appears in present-day Mexico
c. 2000 B.C.E.	Maize cultivation appears in American Southwest
c. 700–1100 C.E.	Complex irrigation systems increase food production and lead to complex native societies, including Maya, Pueblo, and Mississippian
c. 1000 C.E.	Norse reach North America
c. 1100 C.E.	Peak of population of Mississippian city, Cahokia
1200s	Droughts and competition contract some native societies, including the Cahokia and Mandan
1325	Aztec capital of Tenochtitlán built
1420s	Portugal explores coastal West Africa
1482	Portugal builds trading posts in West Africa
1492	Columbus's first voyage Columbian Exchange begins
1500	Portugal claims Brazil as a colony
c. 1500–1630	Epidemics ravage New World natives
1503	*Encomienda* system introduced
1513	*Requerimiento* statute established
1519	Attack on Tenochtitlán led by Cortés
1524	Pizarro conquers Incan empire
c. 1550	Sugar production begins in Brazil
1573	Mission system established in Spanish colonies

Period 1 AP® Exam Practice

Multiple-Choice Questions

Questions 1–3 refer to the following excerpt.

"They attacked the towns and spared neither the children nor the aged nor pregnant women nor women in childbed, not only stabbing them and dismembering them but cutting them to pieces as if dealing with sheep in the slaughter house. . . . Other infants they put to the sword along with their mothers and anyone else who happened to be nearby. They made some low wide gallows on which the hanged victim's feet almost touched the ground, stringing up their victims in lots of thirteen, in memory of Our Redeemer and His twelve Apostles, then set burning wood at their feet and thus burned them alive."

Bartolomé de Las Casas, *Brief Account of the Destruction of the Indies*, 1542

1. The description in the account by Las Casas is most similar to which of the following?
(A) The treatment of heretics during the Spanish Inquisition
(B) The movement of migrants from Asia to North America
(C) The system of slavery in Africa before 1500
(D) Disputes between rival European conquerors in the New World

2. Which Native American group invaded and conquered territory in the Western Hemisphere in a similar way to the account provided by Las Casas?
(A) Hopewell people near the Mississippi River
(B) Haudenosaunee (Iroquois) in the Northeast region of North America
(C) Aztecs in Central America
(D) Pueblo of the Southwest region of North America

3. Which of the following was a long-term result of Las Casas's account and other similar reports?
(A) The rise of the Black Legend
(B) The imposition of feudalism in the New World
(C) The spread of the Black Plague in the Americas
(D) The emergence of racial stereotypes of Native American inferiority

Questions 4–6 refer to the excerpt.

"There was then no sickness; they had no aching bones; they had then no high fever; . . . they had then no burning chest; they had then no abdominal pain; they had then no consumption; they had then no headache. At the time the course of humanity was orderly. The foreigners made it otherwise when they arrived here."

Native of Yucatán, *The Book of Chilam Balam of Chumayel,* mid-1500s

4. The account by the native of Yucatán is most likely written in response to European
(A) enslavement.
(B) religion.
(C) warfare.
(D) diseases.

5. What led the "foreigners" to move into the Yucatán area in the early 1500s?
   (A) Desire to reach Asia for the valuable spice trade
   (B) Desire to spread Christianity among residents of the Yucatán
   (C) Desire for natural resources available in the area
   (D) Desire to bring political stability to the Native American societies in the Yucatán area

6. The changes described in the excerpt resulted in which of the following?
   (A) The development of an elaborate Native American political structure
   (B) A rapid increase in Native American immunity to Old World diseases
   (C) The destruction and subjugation of Native American tribes to European dominance
   (D) A sophisticated trade relationship between European countries and Native Americans that mutually benefited both groups

Questions 7–9 refer to the excerpt.

"We saw your letter of July 15 of the year prior to 1540, in which we became aware of the state of things of that province and the things that you have worked on to bring peace to the natives of the land who remained in revolt . . . and of the good treatment of the natives that reside in the land . . . and that with your good management you place the land under my rule and bring its natives to the knowledge of my Holy Catholic faith and we do order you to, with all prudence and good order, work on making sure that the orders and provisions that have been ordered by us . . . provide what is beneficial to the service of my God."

Letter written by Francisco García de Loaysa, on behalf of King Charles V, to Francisco Vásquez de Coronado, new Governor and Captain General of the Province of Galicia of New Spain, 1540

7. What was the most likely purpose of the letter written on the king's behalf to Coronado?
   (A) Spain needed Western Hemisphere allies to combat mounting military threats in Europe.
   (B) Spain's main purpose was to save the Native Americans and convert them to Spain's official religion.
   (C) Spain needed political stability in the area, so they could transport immigrants to New Spain to reduce overpopulation in the home country.
   (D) Spain depended upon the Native Americans to provide valuable resources.

8. What long-term effect resulted from the actions described in the letter?
   (A) Catholicism became the dominant religion in Central and South America.
   (B) Monarchy became the dominant political structure in Central and South America.
   (C) Capitalism became the dominant economic structure of Central and South America.
   (D) Maize cultivation remained the dominant form of farming in Central and South America.

9. How did the accomplishment of the author's objectives affect international relationships in Europe?
   (A) Other European countries abandoned their efforts of colonization in the New World.
   (B) Spain established colonies throughout all of Europe.
   (C) Spain led the efforts toward the Protestant Reformation.
   (D) The natural resources from the New World turned Spain into the economic and military superpower of Europe.

Questions 10–12 refer to the map.

Library of Congress Geography and Map Division, Washington, D.C.

Map displaying the meridian established by the 1494 Treaty of Tordesillas to define the division of lands between Spain and Portugal, 1622.

10. Which of the following was most likely NOT a purpose of the treaty?
- (A) Preventing conflict with European rivals
- (B) Providing protections for native peoples from abuse
- (C) Dividing unknown territories between Catholic nations
- (D) Reinforcing the authority of the pope

11. The Treaty of Tordesillas was signed in the context of European nations seeking a faster route to
- (A) Central and South America.
- (B) India and Asia.
- (C) Australia and New Zealand.
- (D) the Pacific Islands.

12. Which group benefited the least from the treaty?
- (A) Spanish
- (B) Portuguese
- (C) Africans
- (D) British

Questions 13–16 refer to the image.

Theodor de Bry, engraving, late 1500s

13. The activities depicted in the image best represent which of the following?
(A) Advanced horticulture
(B) Feudalism
(C) The imposition of a caste system
(D) The *encomienda* system

14. Which group was most often used in the system of labor depicted in the image?
(A) European convicts
(B) African slaves
(C) Catholic missionaries
(D) Native Americans

15. What responsibility did Spanish landowners have toward their laborers in the system depicted in the image?
(A) Providing Natives with raw materials from Europe that they would then manufacture in the New World
(B) Converting them to Christianity and transforming them into civilized Spanish citizens
(C) Introducing them to capitalism to create a mutually beneficial trading system
(D) Maintaining that Spanish landowners had no responsibilities toward their laborers in the *encomienda* system

16. How did the process portrayed in the image expand the power of Spain in the New World?
(A) Conquistadors used the system to exploit the free labor of Natives for their personal benefit, and in the process spread the power and influence of Spain throughout the Western Hemisphere.
(B) Jesuits systematically pillaged the native populations of gold and silver. This wealth stayed in the New World to build elaborate cathedrals and spread Catholicism. This single facet brought about the downfall of the Native American religious and political infrastructure.
(C) Christianity used this system as a way to civilize Native Americans and prepare them to participate in European forms of political structure. This brought about the complete collapse of Native American societies, as Native Americans voluntarily copied the European format.
(D) The process led directly to the building of outdoor factories and the beginning of early industrialization in the Americas.

Short-Answer Questions

Theodor de Bry, engraving of the Native American village of Secoton, 1588

1. Using the image, which depicts a Native American village along the east coast of North America in the late 1500s, answer **A**, **B**, and **C**.

(A) Briefly describe ONE historical perspective expressed in the image regarding Native American societies.

(B) Briefly explain how ONE specific event or development in the period from 1492 to 1607 contributed to the historical situation depicted in the image.

(C) Briefly explain ONE specific effect in the period from 1492 to 1607 that resulted from the historical situation depicted in the image.

2. Answer **A**, **B**, and **C**.

(A) Briefly describe ONE specific historical similarity between the Aztec empire in Central America and the Inca empire in South America between 1492 and 1607.

(B) Briefly describe ONE specific historical difference between the Aztec empire in Central America and the Inca empire in South America between 1492 and 1607.

(C) Briefly explain ONE reason for either the similarity or difference between the Aztec empire in Central America and the Inca empire in South America between 1492 and 1607.

3. Answer **A**, **B**, and **C**.

(A) Briefly describe ONE specific effect of the Columbian Exchange on Native American societies between 1492 and 1607.

(B) Briefly describe ONE specific effect of the Columbian Exchange on European societies between 1492 and 1607.

(C) Briefly describe ONE specific effect of the Columbian Exchange on African societies between 1492 and 1607.

PERIOD 2 1607–1754

Colonial America amid Global Change

© New York Historical Society/Bridgeman Images

British Colonial Banner, 1745 This cotton banner was carried by the British at the siege of the French at Louisbourg (1745), Nova Scotia, during King George's War, also known as the War of Austrian Succession (1744–1748). King George's War was one of many colonial wars fought between the British and the French for control of North America in the eighteenth century. While the British soldiers and New England colonists who carried out the siege captured Louisbourg, the fort was later returned to the French as part of the Treaty of Aix-la-Chapelle, which ended the war in 1748.

Contextualizing Period 2

MODULE 2.1

England and France began to challenge Spanish dominance of the Western Hemisphere in the early seventeenth century. As these three kingdoms struggled with one another militarily, economically, and socially, each also consolidated power on the North American continent.

These nations engaged in shifting patterns of cooperation and competition with native populations in ways that reflected their cultural, social, religious, and economic interests. The French steadily established trade networks with native peoples in Canada. The Spanish in the Southwest sought to convert American Indians to Catholicism while at the same time exploiting their labor. The English colony at Jamestown tried to replicate the success of the Spanish, hoping to find easy profits in gold and silver mines, but the climate and geography of Virginia differed greatly from the Central American regions that the Spanish had begun to exploit nearly a hundred years before.

Thus, the early Jamestown settlers built a colony that differed from the ordered and authoritarian *encomienda* system of the Spanish, where native peoples worked under close Spanish supervision. Instead, a labor system in which English-born indentured servants traded several years of hard work in return for passage to the English colony provided much of the labor in the colony during the early seventeenth century. However, this arrangement gave way to a racial caste system in which enslaved Africans made up the bulk of the labor force on large cash-crop plantations in the southern colonies by the turn of the eighteenth century.

In the western backcountry regions of Virginia, the majority of the population was made up of independent farmers, many of whom were former indentured servants themselves. These backcountry settlers negotiated — and often violated — a shifting borderland of conflict and trade with American Indians.

As the seventeenth century progressed, growing European settlements in the New World led to the development of a transatlantic world in which Europeans, American Indians, and Africans traded, competed, and interacted with each other along networks that stretched from the foothills of the Appalachian Mountains to the cities of London, Paris, and Madrid to the villages of West Africa and back to the islands of the Caribbean.

Great Britain's colonies in North America formed an integral part of this transatlantic world. Beginning in the early 1650s, Britain pursued economic policies designed to monopolize trade with its colonies and protect British economic interests. This strategy proved successful. Starting in the late seventeenth century, the British fought a series of colonial wars with other European powers, most often the French, to establish English cultural, ideological, and economic dominance in the North Atlantic and the North American interior. While these wars were costly on many levels, repeated victories cemented Great Britain's dominance of the North American Atlantic seaboard from the late 1600s and well into the 1700s.

By the 1700s, colonists used European models to shape a distinctly British North American culture. For example, the Enlightenment, a European intellectual movement that embraced science and reason as the hallmarks of human progress, gained popularity among elites. Likewise, the First Great Awakening, a wave of renewed religious enthusiasm, swept North America during the 1740s with a spiritual intensity that touched colonists throughout the continent and challenged England's tradition of strict class differentiation.

AP® EXAM TIP

Know how to compare and contrast European colonization efforts. Narrow your focus by concentrating on how cultural and economic factors affected the development of the French and Dutch colonies in the New World. Strong comparisons move from broad categories such as cultural and economic to more specific historical evidence such as intermarriage and the fur trade.

Colonial society also underwent immense shifts as these religious and political awakenings transformed colonists' relationship to both spiritual and secular authorities. Over time, the colonial elite had developed a strong belief in the rights of the colonies to control their own destinies. As this belief grew more popular, local communities began to take steps to defend those rights, and many colonial assemblies grew accustomed to control over local government.

Yet even as aspects of a distinctly American identity began to emerge, the diversity and divisions among colonists increased as class, racial, religious, and regional differences multiplied across the colonies. Immigrants from Germany, Ireland, and Scotland created their own communities; economic inequality deepened in cities; conflicts between American Indians and settlers intensified along the frontier; and growing reliance on the labor of enslaved Africans reshaped economic and social relations in British North America, particularly in the southern colonies.

Period 2: What's Inside 1607–1754

MODULE	AP® THEMATIC FOCUS
2.1 Contextualizing Period 2	The first contact between Native Americans and Europeans in the fifteenth century and early sixteenth century caused enormous changes to both European and Native societies. The Columbian Exchange of the sixteenth century extended these changes and led to the beginnings of the African slave trade. The period 1607 to 1754 saw the consolidation of European colonial control in North America. This period also saw conflict between European colonial powers for control over the continent, which often divided native peoples among European rivals. Also during this period, transatlantic trade in enslaved African people become a source of labor for many of the European colonies. By the end of this time period, the British controlled much of the eastern seaboard of North America.
2.2 European Colonization	**Migration and Settlement** Throughout the seventeenth and early eighteenth centuries, the English, French, and Dutch established colonies that challenged Spanish control in North America.
2.3 The Regions of British Colonies	**Geography and the Environment** The earliest English colonies sought profit through agriculture and the cash crop tobacco, which became a valuable commodity in the Atlantic world. The first English settlers in New England, mostly Puritans, established an economy based on agriculture and commerce within a society of independent family farms and small towns. Distance from Great Britain led to self-governing towns that contained elements of democratic practice. These democratic elements included participatory town meetings and elected colonial legislatures. Starting in the 1660s, the English began to colonize the Middle Atlantic region in North America and build economies based on trade and societies built generally on religious and ethnic tolerance. Throughout the late seventeenth and early eighteenth centuries, the colonies of the southern Atlantic coast and the British West Indies developed plantation societies that depended on the labor of enslaved Africans to harvest crops such as rice and sugar for export.
2.4 Transatlantic Trade	**Work, Exchange, and Technology** During the eighteenth century, the Atlantic economy became increasingly complex, leading to increasing attempts by European powers to impose trade policies advantageous to home countries. These trade policies shaped the lives of colonial subjects in North America.
2.5 Interactions between American Indians and Europeans	**America in the World** Starting in the seventeenth century, British North American colonists were pulled into a series of conflicts with other European colonists and their Native American allies as European nations increasingly sought control over the Western Hemisphere.
2.6 Slavery in the British Colonies	**Work, Exchange, and Technology ■ Social Structures** Slavery shaped the economy and society of British North America. While slavery was more prevalent in the southern colonies, its existence in the middle and northern colonies proved significant as well. Despite often harsh living conditions, enslaved Africans and African Americans found overt and covert ways to rebel against slavery and maintain their families and culture.
2.7 Colonial Society and Culture	**American and Regional Culture ■ American and National Identity** Inspired by religious movements and new political ideologies, British North Americans developed a sense of distinctness from England while, at the same time, experiencing fragmentation within the colonies themselves.
2.8 Comparison in Period 2	This time period offers opportunities for comparison between the different regions of British North America, between the various European powers that vied for control of North America, among native nations and European colonizers, and between Africans in the Western Hemisphere, both enslaved and free, and the European colonists.
Support and Practice	• Practice thinking and writing historically in each module. • See the Period Review of key concepts, events, people, and dates after the last module. • Try the AP® Exam Practice at the end of the period.

MODULE 2.2

European Colonization

FOCUS

Historians think comparatively to identify, describe, and analyze similarities and differences among two or more historical events, individuals, groups, regions, developments, or concepts. Considering how these different aspects of history relate to each other is a critical step toward gaining a fuller understanding of the past. While comparison is a fundamental historical reasoning tool, it's also important to remember that it is just one aspect of historical analysis. One way historians strengthen comparative understanding is by examining the causes of the historical developments they compare. They do so because making meaningful historical comparisons isn't just recording observations—historians uncover reasons that help to explain similarities and differences. Making this connection to underlying causes is an important part of historical analysis.

As you read this module, think about the similarities and differences in the interactions between European colonizers and Native Americans before 1754. Make sure that, wherever you make these comparisons, you also ask the important question of *why*. If you see a similarity between two European colonies, for instance, ask yourself what factors help explain it. If, let's say, you discover a difference between the lives of women in two European colonies, ask yourself what caused it.

In the late sixteenth century, French, Dutch, and English investors became increasingly interested in establishing colonies in North America. But until Spain's grip on the Atlantic world was broken, other nations could not hope to compete for an American empire. Throughout the seventeenth century, the French, Dutch, and English established colonies in the Western Hemisphere, which led to conflict with both the Spanish and American Indians.

The French Expand into North America

Although French rulers shared Spain's Catholic faith, the two nations were rivals, and the defeat of its Armada by English naval forces in 1588 weakened Spain enough to allow the rest of Europe greater access to North America. Once in North America, the French adopted attitudes and policies that differed significantly from those of Spain. This was due in part to their greater interest in trade than in conquest. The French had fished the North Atlantic since the mid-sixteenth century, and in the 1580s they built stations along the Newfoundland coast for drying codfish. French traders then established relations with local American Indians, exchanging iron kettles and other European goods for valuable beaver skins.

By the early seventeenth century, France's King Henry IV (reigned 1589–1610) sought to profit more directly from the resources in North America, focusing on developing the increasingly lucrative trade in American fish and furs. In 1608, Samuel de Champlain founded Québec, the first permanent French settlement in North America.

Accompanied by several dozen men armed with guns, Champlain joined a Huron raid on the Haudenosaunee (Iroquois), who resided south of the Great Lakes. By ensuring a Huron victory, the French made the Huron people a powerful ally—but the battle also fueled lasting bitterness with the Haudenosaunee.

Trade relations flourished between the French and their American Indian allies during the seventeenth century. Fur traders, who journeyed throughout the St. Lawrence River valley in eastern Canada with the aid of the Huron, were critical to sustaining the French presence and warding off intrusion by the English—especially because relatively few French men and even fewer French women settled in North America during this period. French government policies discouraged mass migration, and peasants were concerned by reports of short growing seasons and severe winters in Canada.

Also, while French policy urged Catholic priests and nuns to migrate to the new world, French Protestants, known as **Huguenots**, were barred from doing the same. Thus, into the 1630s, what few permanent French settlements existed in North America were populated mostly by fishermen, fur traders, and Catholic missionaries.

Huguenot
A French Protestant who subscribed to the theology of John Calvin. Huguenots were persecuted by the French crown, which considered Catholicism the official faith of the kingdom.

In their ongoing search for new sources of furs, the French established a fortified trading post at Montreal in 1643, and over the next three decades they continued to push farther west into the Great Lakes. But in doing so, the French carried European diseases into new areas, ignited warfare among more native groups, and stretched their always-small population of settlers ever thinner.

MPI/Archive Photos/Getty Images

Ambush of the Villasur Expedition, (c. 1720) An unknown artist painted this battle scene on buffalo hide. In 1720, Spanish soldiers and Pueblo warriors tried to expel the French from the lower Mississippi Valley. Instead, French soldiers and their American Indian allies ambushed the expedition and killed forty-five men.

What conclusions can you draw about the future of conflict in North America from this image?

Some Frenchmen married American Indian women, who provided them with both domestic labor and kinship ties to powerful trading partners. Despite Catholic criticism of these marriages, they enhanced French traders' success and fostered alliances among the Ojibwe and Dakota nations to the west. These alliances, in turn, created a middle ground in which economic and cultural exchanges led to a remarkable degree of mutual adaptation. French traders benefited from American Indian women's skills in preparing beaver skins for market as well as from American Indian canoes, while natives adopted iron cooking pots and European cloth.

In 1682, French adventurers and their American Indian allies, led by René-Robert Cavelier (also known as "La Salle") journeyed from the Great Lakes down the Mississippi River in search of a southern outlet for furs. The party traveled to the Gulf of Mexico and claimed all the land drained by the river's tributaries for France, naming it Louisiana in honor of King Louis XIV (reigned 1643–1715). The newly claimed territory of Louisiana encompassed the vast lands between the Rockies, Appalachians, Great Lakes, and Gulf of Mexico and promised great wealth, but its development was hindered by a lack of permanent settlers and by underinvestment.

colonization
The process of settling and controlling an already inhabited area for the economic benefit of the settlers, or colonizers.

After repeated attempts at **colonization** in the early eighteenth century, French settlers solidified their grasp of Louisiana's Gulf coast by establishing forts at Biloxi and Mobile bays, where they traded with local Choctaw Indians. Recruiting settlers from Canada and France, the small outposts survived despite conflicts among settlers, pressure from the English and the Spanish, a wave of epidemics, and a lack of supplies from France. Still, Louisiana counted only three hundred French settlers by 1715.

Continuing to promote commercial relations with diverse American Indian nations, the French also built a string of missions and forts along the upper Mississippi and Illinois Rivers during the early eighteenth century. French outposts in the Mississippi River valley became multicultural communities of diverse American Indian groups, French fur traders, and Catholic Jesuit missionaries.

These small settlements in the continent's interior allowed France to challenge both English and Spanish claims to North America. In addition, extensive trade with a range of American Indian nations ensured that French power was far greater than the small number of French settlers suggests.

- What were the goals of the French in North America?
- What steps did they take to accomplish these goals?

The Dutch Expand into North America

Like the French, the Dutch sought North American colonies. As Spain's shipbuilding center, the Netherlands benefited from the wealth pouring in from Spain's American empire, and an affluent merchant class emerged. But the Dutch also embraced **Calvinism**, a form of Protestantism, and sought to separate themselves from Catholic Spain. In 1581, the Netherlands declared its independence from King Philip II (reigned 1556–1598), and their ships aided England in defeating the Spanish Armada in 1588. Although Spain refused to recognize their independence for several decades, the Netherlands by 1600 was both a Protestant haven and the trading hub of Europe, controlling trade routes to much of Asia and parts of Africa.

Calvinism
A branch of Protestantism developed by John Calvin that influenced Protestants in France, England, and Switzerland in the seventeenth and eighteenth centuries.

In 1609 the Dutch established a fur-trading center on the Hudson River in present-day New York. From the beginning, their goals were mainly economic, and the Protestant Dutch made no pretense of bringing religion to American Indians in the region.

MAP 2.1 European Empires in North America (1715–1750) European nations competed with one another and with many American Indian nations for control of vast areas of North America. Although wars continually reshaped areas under European and American Indian control, this map shows the general outlines of the empires claimed by each European nation, the key forts established to maintain those claims, and the major American Indian nations in each area.

Based on this map, what regions were most likely to experience the greatest conflict? What leads you to this conclusion?

The small number of Dutch traders who settled there developed friendly relations with the powerful Mohawk nation, and in 1614, their trading post was relocated to Fort Orange, near present-day Albany.

In 1624, to fend off French and English raids on ships sent downriver from Fort Orange, the Dutch established New Amsterdam on Manhattan Island, which they purchased from the Lenni-Lenape tribe. New Amsterdam was the centerpiece of the larger New Netherland colony and attracted a diverse community of traders, fishermen, and farmers. As the colony grew, it developed a representative government, provided greater equality for women, and became known for its religious toleration.

The European settlers of New Netherland may have tolerated one another, but the same could not be said for settlers and local American Indians. Wealthy Dutch settlers secured land in New Netherland in exchange for the import of approximately fifty families who were expected to work for the landowner. Tensions increased as Dutch colonists carved out farms north of New Amsterdam where large communities of Algonquian-speaking American Indians lived. In 1639, conflict escalated when the Dutch demanded an annual tribute in wampum beads or grain. Local Algonquins resisted, raiding farms on the frontier and killing at least two colonists. In 1643, the Dutch launched a surprise attack on an American Indian encampment on Manhattan Island, killing eighty people, mostly women and children. Outraged Algonquins burned and looted homes north of the city, slaughtered livestock, and killed settlers in response. For two years sporadic warfare continued, but eventually, the Algonquins were defeated.

At the same time, the Dutch eagerly traded for furs with Mohawk Indians along the upper Hudson River. The Mohawk Indians, rivals to the Algonquin, were a powerful tribe that had the backing of the even more powerful **Haudenosaunee (Iroquois) Confederacy**. Their ties to American Indian nations farther west allowed them to provide beaver skins to Dutch traders long after beavers had been overhunted in the Hudson valley. From this trade, the Mohawk and Haudenosaunee allies sought guns. They hoped to secure captives from other American Indian tribes to restore their population, which was reduced by European diseases. Moreover, they hoped to fend off economic competition from rival tribes. Still, the Mohawk people did not deceive themselves. As one treaty proposition declared in 1659, "The Dutch say we are brothers and that we are joined together with chains, but that lasts only so long as we have beavers."

Haudenosaunee (Iroquois) Confederacy
A group of allied American Indian nations that included the Mohawk, Oneida, Onondaga, Cayuga, Seneca, and later the Tuscarora. The Confederacy had largely dissolved by the final decade of the 1700s.

Meanwhile, reports of atrocities in the conflicts between the Dutch and Algonquin circulated in the Netherlands, damaging New Amsterdam's reputation and dramatically slowing migration to the colony. A series of wars between 1652 and 1674 with England further weakened Dutch power in North America. In 1664, England sent a naval convoy to take New Amsterdam. More focused on the profitable Asian trade and colonial projects in Southeast Asia, the Dutch had little choice but to surrender their lightly populated colony to the English.

REVIEW

- How did the economic relationship between the Dutch and American Indians compare to the French relationship with American Indians?

Spain's Fragile North American Empire

In the early decades of the sixteenth century, Spain continued to push north from Mexico in an attempt to expand its empire. As the French, Dutch, and English separately challenged Spain for North American colonies throughout the seventeenth century, the Spaniards were spread dangerously thin on the northern reaches of their American holdings. Even as they tried to maintain a firm hold on Florida and the West Indies, staving off growing resistance from the Pueblo people caused Spain to struggle to maintain its holdings in *Nuevo México*, now part of the American Southwest. Thus, as other European powers expanded their reach into North America, the Spaniards were left with few resources to protect their northern and eastern frontiers.

Spain's use of the mission system, directed by Franciscan priests, to extend its control into *Nuevo México* provoked resistance from the Pueblo nations (see Module 1.4). Following Pueblo resistance, which led to both the Acoma massacre and the flight of Spanish settlers, the Spanish crown developed a new plan for the region. In 1610, the Spanish returned with a larger military force, founded Santa Fe, and established a new network of missions and estates owned by *encomenderos*.

As the Spanish renewed their efforts to colonize *Nuevo México*, the Pueblo peoples largely accepted the situation. In part, they feared military reprisals if they challenged Spanish authorities. Moreover, they had been weakened by disease and untimely drought and were struggling to fend off raids by hostile Apache and Navajo tribes. In accepting Spanish rule, the Pueblo peoples hoped to gain protection by Spanish soldiers and priests.

However, the Pueblo peoples did not see their living conditions improve, and tensions between the Spanish and the Pueblo nations continued to simmer. Throughout the mid-seventeenth century, Spanish forces failed to protect the Pueblo Indians against new and devastating raids by Apache and Navajo warriors, and Catholic prayers proved unable to stop Pueblo deaths in a 1671 epidemic. Finally, relations worsened when another drought in the 1670s led to famine among many Pueblo Indians.

AP® WORKING with EVIDENCE

Source: King Philip IV of Spain, Letter to Don Luis Valdés, 1647

> "To my governor and captain-general of the province of Nueva Vizcaya: It has been learned in my royal Council of the Indies that that province adjoins the barbarous nations . . . who are now at war, though they are usually at peace; that while they were so at peace, there went among them to trade certain [magistrates] and religious instructors who carried off and sold their children to serve in the mines and elsewhere, disposing of them as slaves or giving them as presents, which amounts to the same thing. As a result they became disquieted, and the governor, Don Luis de Valdés, began to punish them immoderately and without regard for the public faith, for, after calling them to attend religious instruction, he seized and shot some of them. Thereupon they revolted, took up their arms and arrows, and made some raids; they broke into my treasury, and it has cost me over 50,000 pesos to pacify them, although they are not entirely quieted yet. It is very fitting to my service and to their peace to command strictly that the barbarous Indians shall not be made slaves nor sent as presents to anyone, nor made to serve anywhere against their will when they are at peace and are not taken in open war."

Questions for Analysis

1. Identify a cause of the developments that led Philip to send this letter.
2. Describe the underlying processes that led to this development.
3. Explain Philip's purpose in sending this letter.

When some Pueblo Indians openly returned to practicing their traditional religious customs, Spanish officials hanged three Pueblo leaders for idolatry as well as whipped and imprisoned forty-three others. Among those punished was Popé, who planned a broad-based revolt upon his release. On August 10, 1680, seventeen thousand Pueblo Indians initiated a coordinated assault on numerous Spanish missions and forts in what came to be known as the **Pueblo Revolt**. They destroyed buildings and farms, burned crops and houses, and demolished Catholic churches.

In response, the Spanish retreated to Mexico without launching any significant immediate counterattack. However, they returned in the 1690s and reconquered parts of *Nuevo México*, aided by growing internal conflict among the Pueblo and raids by the Apache. In 1696, the Pueblo resistance was finally crushed, and new lands were opened for Spanish settlement. At the same time, Franciscan missionaries improved relations with the Pueblo nations by allowing them to retain more indigenous practices.

Pueblo Revolt
An uprising of Pueblo Indians in 1680 against Spanish forces in New Mexico that led to the Spaniards' temporary retreat from the area. The uprising was sparked by mistreatment and the suppression of Pueblo culture and religion.

age fotostock/Superstock

San Esteban del Rey Mission Opened in 1644, this Spanish mission in present-day New Mexico taught Christianity and Hispanic customs to the Acoma (Pueblo) people. Spanish missionaries prohibited traditional Pueblo practices such as performing dances and wearing masks. The mission was one of the few to survive Pueblo revolts in the late seventeenth century.

In what ways was the San Esteban del Rey Mission representative of the Spanish relationship with the Pueblo peoples?

AP® EXAM TIP

The Pueblo Revolt is a specific event you should know for the AP® Exam. Explain how this historical example can be used to describe changes in the Spanish colonial system during the late seventeenth century.

Despite the Spanish reconquest, the Pueblo Revolt limited Spanish expansion in the long run by strengthening other indigenous peoples in the region. In the aftermath of the revolt, some Pueblo refugees moved north and taught the Navajo how to grow corn, raise sheep, and ride horses. Through trading with the Navajo and raiding Spanish settlements during the early eighteenth century, the Ute, Shoshone, and Comanche peoples also gained access to horses. By the 1730s, the Comanche launched mounted bison hunts and raids on other American Indian nations. They traded with the Spanish by exchanging American Indian captives for Spanish enslavement in return for more horses and guns. Thus, the Pueblo provided other indigenous nations with the means to support larger populations, wider commercial networks, and more warriors, allowing them to continue to contest Spanish rule.

In response to early eighteenth-century French settlements in the lower Mississippi valley, Spain also sought to reinforce its claims to Texas, named for the Tejas Indians, along the northeastern frontier of its North American empire. Here, Spain established missions and forts along the route from San Juan Bautista to the border of present-day Louisiana. Although small and scattered, these outposts were meant to ensure Spain's claim to Texas. But the presence of large and powerful American Indian nations, including the Caddo and the Apache, forced the small number of Spanish residents to accept many native customs to maintain their presence in the region.

REVIEW

- How did the French and Dutch colonies in North America differ from the Spanish colonies to the south?

AP® Skills Workshop: Thinking Historically

Analyzing Developments and Processes in Secondary Sources

Historians call their written interpretations of the past **secondary sources**. This textbook, for example, is a secondary source because it includes information about the past written by historians. However, this textbook also includes **primary sources**, which are sources *from* the past. For example, the material in the Working with Evidence features includes primary sources.

In this U.S. history course, and on the AP® Exam, you will sometimes have to read a historian's argument and identify and explain a historical development or processes. By **development** we mean the rise or growth of a trend or historical change. By **processes** we mean the details of how a trend or change came about.

Let's say you wanted to identify the development of the Spanish colonies, described in Period 1. When you describe this development, you might say that these colonies began as a few scattered settlements on the islands of the Caribbean, but by the mid-sixteenth century, they had expanded to the mainland and began a systematic conquest of the indigenous civilizations there.

If you were to explain the process of this development, you could explain that the Spanish colonies were at first small settlements on islands, which served as economic and military centers for settlement and trade. These early settlements allowed the Spanish to launch more ambitious exploration of the Caribbean, the Yucatán peninsula, and Central and South America. By the mid-sixteenth century, the Spanish had destroyed the Aztec empire and had begun to build New Spain into a colony for larger settlements and greater exploitation of indigenous people.

A historian might write a paragraph that describes this development and explains the process like this:

> The Spanish colonies began as a few scattered settlements on the islands of the Caribbean in the early sixteenth century. By the mid-sixteenth century, these colonies expanded to the mainland and began a systematic conquest of the indigenous civilizations there. The first Spanish settlements in the Caribbean served as economic and military centers for settlement and trade. Settled a few decades after Columbus's arrival, these settlements allowed the Spanish to launch more ambitious exploration of the Caribbean, the Yucatán peninsula, and Central and South America. By the mid-sixteenth century, the Spanish had destroyed the Aztec empire and begun to build New Spain into a colony of larger settlements that exploited more indigenous people. The *encomienda* system of forced labor was one method of this exploitation.

ACTIVITY

On the next page is an excerpt about the French in North America during the seventeenth and eighteenth centuries. Read the excerpt and, in your own words, **describe** the **development** of these French colonies according to the author. Then, **explain** the **process** by which this development occurred.

(continued)

1609–1613

"Québec [the capital of New France] was used for little else than a warehouse. Champlain reported that sixteen people wintered there in 1609–1610 and seventeen the following winter. The Habitation [trading outpost] received only minimal maintenance and fell into disrepair.

1614–1620

The reinstated trade monopoly was now managed by Compagnie du Canada [which was the French company that controlled the fur trade in New France]. The company bought the Habitation. . . . Once the outpost changed hands, the number who overwintered in Québec increased sharply; from at least 1617 it rose to 50 or 60. More significant was the spread of settlement further away from the Habitation. . . . At the same time Champlain obliged the company to erect a fort on the height overlooking the Habitation. . . . It was a modest two-story structure in wood, probably surrounded by a simple wooden palisade.

1621–1632

This was a period of intense work. The rebuilding of all or part of the Habitation and Fort Saint-Louis was undertaken . . .; and the Jesuit convent . . . was erected on the opposite bank. In 1628, the development of the . . . colony was brought to a halt by war. The English fleet under the command of David Kirke took control of the river, preventing supplies from reaching Québec. . . .

[T]he efforts to protect the colony were in vain. On 20 July 1629 the keys to the Habitation and Fort Saint-Louis had to be handed over to [the English].

1632–1635

In 1632, France retook Québec . . . Champlain came back to Québec in 1633 and took up residence in Fort Saint-Louis . . . On Champlain's death on 25 December 1635, Québec had about 300 inhabitants."

Excerpt from Françoise Niellon, "Québec in the Time of Champlain," *Post-Medieval Archaeology*, vol. 43, no. 1, 2009: The Recent Archaeology of the Early Modern Period in Quebex City.

The Regions of British Colonies: The South and the British West Indies

MODULE 2.3a

FOCUS

Module 1.7 discussed the ways historians understand events by studying and interpreting their effects. When historians examine events and developments through the lens of causation, they study the interplay of both causes and effects to come to a better understanding of their significance. This analysis can be deepened by explaining not only how one event led to other events, but also discussing reasons why later events were affected. With this approach to studying history, we can understand the relationships between historical developments as a chain reaction, each producing the next.

As you examine the ripple effects caused by historical developments, pay close attention to the beginning of this module, which explains how the financial success of early English plantation economies led to the founding of new colonies in North America, and note the ways the rapid expansion of these economies fostered conflicts with American Indian nations. Ultimately, varying settlement patterns, relations with native peoples, economies, and geography caused differences between southern British colonies in North America. Consider these factors while reading about this region.

Economic Causes of English Colonization

Changes in the English economy, which occurred throughout western Europe as a result of the Columbian Exchange, shaped British efforts to compete with Spain for North America during the early seventeenth century. As the sixteenth century came to a close, **inflation** posed a major challenge for the ruling class and a threat to the economic stability of England. Costly wars with France, the conquest of Ireland, and, most significantly, the influx of Spanish silver all contributed to the crippling increase in prices that in turn diminished nobles' traditional sources of wealth. Much of the nobility responded to these challenges by seeking new sources of wealth from colonies across the Atlantic Ocean.

inflation
When prices rise because of a decline in the value of money because of its overabundance.

The monarchy's and the nobility's efforts to seek new sources of wealth in the Western Hemisphere began with English colonial outposts, starting with Jamestown, located in modern Virginia, in 1607. This venture was fundamentally profit-seeking from the very beginning. Likewise, hard economic times created a large landless population available for colonial settlement. English elites took advantage of this situation

indented servitude

Condition of being contracted to work for a set period of time without pay.

by arresting many landless, unemployed people, convicting them as criminal vagrants and vagabonds, and forcing them into **indentured servitude**, a form of bound labor. Contracts of indenture allowed the purchase of a laborer for a set number of years, typically seven. Fearing arrest, many commoners chose to avoid imprisonment by indenturing themselves. Many early migrants to the English colonies indentured themselves in exchange for the price of passage to North America. In the first half of the seventeenth century, the vast majority of British colonial workers in North America was indentured servants. Once in the colonies, indentured servants were often treated harshly and had few legal protections.

REVIEW

- What were some of the causes of English colonization of North America?

The English Establish Jamestown

joint-stock company

A company in which large numbers of investors own stock. Such a company could quickly raise large amounts of money and share risk and reward equally among investors.

England's success in colonizing North America depended in part on a new economic model in which investors purchased shares in **joint-stock companies** that could raise large amounts of money quickly. If the venture succeeded, investors shared the profits. If they failed, no investor suffered the whole loss.

In 1606, a group of London merchants formed the Virginia Company, and King James I (reigned 1603–1625) granted them the right to settle a vast area of North America that stretched from present-day New York to North Carolina. Among the leaders of the group of 104 colonists who set out for the New World under the banner of the Virginia Company was John Smith. Born in 1580, Smith left England as a young man "to learne the life of a Souldier." After fighting and traveling throughout Europe, the Mediterranean, and North Africa for several years, Captain Smith returned to England around 1605, joining the Virginia Company when it was formed a year later.

Arriving on the coast of North America in the Chesapeake Bay in April 1607, the 104 colonists established Jamestown, named in honor of the king. Although the Virginia Company claimed the land for themselves and their country, the area was already controlled by a powerful American Indian leader, Chief Powhatan (proper name Wahunsonacock). He presided over a confederation of some 14,000 Algonquian-speaking peoples from twenty-five to thirty tribes, which surrounded the small Jamestown settlement. Indeed, the English chose the site of this settlement mainly for its easy defense, made necessary by the **Powhatan Confederacy**, which was far more powerful than the English settlers. For the first two years, the settlers depended on them to survive.

Powhatan Confederacy

Large and powerful confederation of Algonquian-speaking Native Americans in Virginia. The Jamestown settlers had a complicated and often combative relationship with the leaders of the Powhatan Confederacy.

Challenged by the swampy, mosquito-infested environment of Jamestown and struggling for survival, the colonists divided their energies between searching for gold and silver and building a military encampment. Despite the Englishmen's aggressive stance in building this military fort, Powhatan assisted the new settlers in hopes they could provide him with English cloth, iron hatchets, and even guns. His capture and eventual release of John Smith in 1607 suggests his interest in developing trade relations with the newcomers even as he sought to subordinate them.

AP® WORKING with EVIDENCE

Source: Powhatan, Chief of Algonquian-Speaking Powhatan Confederation, Deerskin Cloak, c. 1608

Maidun Collection/Alamy

About the source: Chief Powhatan wore this deerskin cloak for tribal ceremonies. The objects on this cloak are made from shells, which were considered items of value by the Powhatan people. The circles could represent regions under Powhatan's control, the animals most likely represent deer, and the individual in the center represents Chief Powhatan.

Questions for Analysis

1. Describe the arrangement of the images and materials that make up this cloak.
2. Explain what the arrangement of the images and materials that make up this cloak reveals about the Powhatan and the Algonquian-speaking peoples.
3. Explain the role Powhatan politics played in fostering conflict with European colonists.

When Powhatan Indians captured Smith and two other Virginia Company men in 1607, all but Smith were executed. Chief Powhatan then performed what was likely an adoption ceremony to bring Smith into his family and under his rule. The ceremony would have involved him sending out one of his daughters—in this case, Pocahontas, who was about twelve years old—to indicate that the captive was spared. In Chief Powhatan's culture, the capture, executions, ceremony, and release of an English leader established his dominance over Smith and the English.

Virginia Company leaders like Captain Smith considered Powhatan and his warriors a threat rather than an ally. During the first years of settlement, Jamestown colonists hoped to achieve wealth quickly, ideally by stealing or mining precious metals, as the Spanish had during the previous century. The search for gold led these early colonists to neglect establishing a steady source of food. Unable to feed themselves that first year, Jamestown residents raided Powhatan villages for corn and other food, making Powhatan increasingly distrustful of the colonists.

Art Resource, NY

Fort James at Jamestown, Virginia, 1607 This image, created by Jamestown colonist John Hull, portrays the earliest iteration of the settlement.

What does this image reveal about how the English perceived their colony in relation to the land, sea, and people they encountered?

On top of these rising tensions, a severe drought between 1606 and 1612 limited the Powhatan Indians' surpluses of food, and they became less willing to trade food to the English as a result. For their part, the English settlers' fear of their Powhatan neighbors led them to resist an exchange the Powhatan likely would have accepted: guns for food. The food shortage in Jamestown was worsened by several other factors: Some colonists refused to do manual labor; an injury forced John Smith to return to England in late 1609, thus severing the strongest link between the colony and Powhatan; nearby water was tainted by salt from the ocean; and diseases that festered in the low-lying area of Jamestown had killed more than half of the original settlers.

Meanwhile, the Virginia Company devised a new plan to stave off the collapse of its colony. It started selling seven-year joint-stock options to raise funds and recruited new settlers to produce staple crops, glassware, or other items for export. Interested individuals who could not afford to invest cash could sign a contract for indentured servitude in Virginia. After seven years, these indentured servants would gain their freedom and receive a hundred acres of land. In June 1609, a new contingent of colonists attracted by this plan—five hundred men and a hundred women—sailed for Jamestown.

The new arrivals, however, had not brought enough supplies to sustain the colony through the winter. Chief Powhatan did offer some aid, but American Indians, too, suffered from shortages in the winter of 1609–1610. A "starving time" settled on Jamestown. Some settlers resorted to cannibalism. By the spring of 1610, almost all settlers who had arrived in Jamestown since 1607 were dead.

That June, the sixty survivors decided to abandon the settlement and sail for home, but they changed their minds when they met three English ships in the harbor that were loaded with supplies and three hundred more settlers. Emboldened by fresh supplies and an enlarged population, Jamestown's new leaders adopted a more aggressive military strategy, attacking native villages, burning crops, killing many American Indians, and taking others captive. They believed that such brutality would convince neighboring tribes to obey English demands for food and labor.

REVIEW

- What factors shaped early English encounters with American Indians in Virginia?

Tobacco Fuels Growth in Virginia

It was not military aggression, however, but the discovery of a viable **cash crop** that saved the colony. Tobacco, grown in the West Indies and South America, had sold well in England and in other European markets addicted since the sixteenth-century Columbian Exchange. Virginia colonist John Rolfe began to experiment with its growth in 1612, just as the drought lifted. Production of the leaf soared as eager investors poured tobacco seeds, supplies, and labor into Jamestown. Exports multiplied rapidly, from 2,000 pounds in 1615 to 40,000 pounds five years later, and an incredible 1.5 million pounds by 1629.

cash crop
A crop produced for profit rather than for subsistence. Tobacco was the main cash crop in the Chesapeake region in the 1600s and 1700s, and sugar was most commonly grown in the Caribbean colonies.

Tobacco cultivation worsened tensions between the English and the American Indians. As production increased and prices declined, farmers could increase their profits only by obtaining more land and more laborers. That is why the Virginia Company was willing to offer land to indentured laborers who spent seven years clearing new fields and creating more plantations. In 1618, the Virginia Company developed a **headright system** (later used in other colonies) that rewarded those who imported laborers—at first indentured servants, and later enslaved Africans—with land. Wealthy Englishmen were generally granted fifty acres of land for each laborer they imported to Virginia. Yet in most cases, the land the Virginia Company granted was already settled by members of the Powhatan Confederacy. Thus, the rapid increase in tobacco cultivation intensified competition and hostility between English colonists and American Indians.

headright system
Created in Virginia in 1618, it rewarded those who imported indentured laborers and settlers with land.

In 1614, Chief Powhatan tried one last time to create an alliance between his confederacy and the English settlers. Perhaps, encouraged by the return of rain in 1612, he believed that increased productivity would ensure better trade relations with the English. In 1614, he agreed to allow his daughter Pocahontas to marry John Rolfe. Pocahontas converted to Christianity and traveled to England with Rolfe and their infant son in 1617. While there, she fell ill and died, and Rolfe returned to Virginia just as relations with the Powhatan Confederacy began to change.

Powhatan died in 1618, and his younger brother Opechancanough became chief. During this time, the Virginia Company, even using its new headright system, struggled

Library of Congress, Rare Book Division [LC-USZ62-8104]

Pocahontas (1616) Simon van de Passe created this portrait of Pocahontas during her visit to England in 1616. The engraving was commissioned by the Virginia Company to promote settlement in Jamestown. While van de Passe clothes her in English aristocratic style, he retains her dark complexion and direct gaze. Her name is listed both as Matoaka (her birth name) and Rebecca (the name she was given when she was baptized).

What does this portrayal of Pocahontas reveal about how the English viewed American Indians?

to import enough indentured servants to do the work required in Virginia to keep its cash-crop economy, based on tobacco cultivation, afloat. Too few English workers were willing to brave the risks to meet the company's demands for labor. Even landless and poor English commoners feared the prospects of death from starvation, disease, or conflicts with the Powhatan to volunteer.

General Assembly of Virginia
Local governing body in Virginia established by the English crown in 1619. Later, the assembly was known as the House of Burgesses.

House of Burgesses
Elected assembly within the General Assembly of Virginia formed in 1643 when the assembly was split into two houses. The second house in the assembly was called the Council of State and was appointed by British Crown.

veto
The right to block a decision made by a governing body.

Faced with unmet demand for more laborers, one Virginia Company solution was the purchase and transport of convicts from English prisons to Virginia as indentured servants. Another was to petition the crown for the right to establish a local governing body. The hope was that this would aid recruiting efforts by fostering the idea that the Company honored the traditional rights of Englishmen in the colony. In 1619, King James granted Virginia permission to create a **General Assembly of Virginia**, which was split later, in 1643, into two branches, the second of which was called the **House of Burgesses**. Its members could make laws and levy taxes, although the English governor or the company council in London held **veto** power. Lastly, the company set out to recruit more female settlers to increase the colony's population.

These tactics worked, and later that year, more young women and men arrived as indentured servants. Also in 1619, an English ship brought twenty Africans, first taken from present-day Angola by the Portuguese, to Jamestown. These Africans were the first to be enslaved in colonial Virginia.

Although the English colony still hugged the Atlantic coast, its expansion increased conflict with native inhabitants. In March 1622, after repeated English incursions on land cleared and farmed by American Indians, Chief Opechancanough and his allies launched a surprise attack that killed nearly a third of the colonists. In retaliation,

Map of Virginia (1612) John Smith published a remarkably accurate map of Virginia in 1612. It included major geographical features and the names of some 200 American Indian towns. Smith placed a sketch of a Susquehannock warrior in the upper right-hand corner. At his feet, Smith noted that the Susquehannock were "a Gyant-like people."

How does this map express the hopes and fears of early English colonists in Virginia?

Englishmen renewed their assaults on native villages, killing inhabitants, burning cornfields, and selling captive American Indians into slavery.

The English proclaimed victory over the American Indians in 1623, but hostilities continued. In 1624, in the midst of the crisis, King James repealed the Virginia Company charter and took control of the colony, seeking greater control and a larger share of the growing profits from the Chesapeake. For Virginia, he appointed the governor and a small advisory council, required that legislation passed by the General Assembly of Virginia in Jamestown be ratified by the **Privy Council**, or the King's council, in London, and demanded that property owners pay taxes to support the **Church of England**. These regulations became the model for royal colonies throughout North America.

Privy Council
Advisory council of the king of England, comprised typically of prominent aristocrats.

Church of England
National English Protestant faith with King Henry VIII as head of the church. Created after England split with the Catholic Church in 1534.

Royal proclamations could not halt American Indian opposition. In 1644, Opechancanough launched a second uprising against the English, killing hundreds of colonists. After two years of bitter warfare, however, he was finally captured and then killed. With the English population now too large to eradicate, the native peoples in the Chesapeake finally submitted to English authority in 1646.

AP® WORKING with EVIDENCE

Source: John Martin, Jamestown councilman, *The manner how to bring the Indians into subjugation*, 1622

> "The manner how to bring in the Indians into subjugation [under control of the English] . . .
>
> First, by disabling the main body of the enemy from having . . . [all necessities]. As namely corn and all manner of [food] of any worth.
>
> This is to be acted two manner of ways.—First by keeping them from setting corn at home and fishing. Secondly by keeping them from their accustomed trading for corn.
>
> For the first it is performed by having some 200 soldiers on foot, continually [harassing] and burning all their Towns in winter, and spoiling their wares. . . .
>
> For the second there must [be] provided some 10 ships, that in May, June, July and August may scour the bay and keep the rivers yet are belonging to [Opechancanough].
>
> By this arises two happy ends.—First the assured taking of great purchases in skins and prisoners. Secondly in keeping them from trading for corn on the Eastern shore."

Questions for Analysis

1. Identify the specific tactics Martin proposes to subjugate American Indians near Jamestown.
2. Describe the benefits that Martin believes his plan will bring to British colonists.
3. Explain what this document reveals about seventeenth-century English views of American Indians.

REVIEW

- How did the Virginia colony change between 1607 and the mid-1600s?
- What caused these changes?

The Second Chesapeake Colony: Maryland

By the 1630s, despite ongoing conflicts with American Indians, Virginia was well on its way to bringing England commercial success. In 1632, King Charles I (reigned 1625–1649) established the colony of Maryland. Taken together, Maryland and Virginia formed the Chesapeake region of the English empire during the seventeenth century. In the expanding tobacco economies that developed in the region, the most successful **planters** used indentured servants for labor, including some Africans as well as thousands of English and Irish immigrants. Between 1640 and 1670, some 40,000 to 50,000 of these migrants settled in Virginia and neighboring Maryland.

Act of Religious Toleration
Act passed in 1649 by the Maryland Assembly granting religious freedom to all Christians, including Catholics.

English Civil War
Conflict (1642–1651) between parliamentary forces and the king of England over Charles I's attempt to rule without Parliament. Culminated in the execution of Charles I and the establishment of the Commonwealth under Lord Protector Oliver Cromwell, leader of Parliament's forces. Cromwell ruled as lord protector until his death in 1658. Charles I's son, Charles II, was restored as king in 1660.

In founding Maryland, King Charles I granted most of the territory north of Chesapeake Bay to English nobleman Cecilius Calvert and appointed him Lord Baltimore, giving him and his descendants the power to govern the new colony. Calvert's family, unlike most English people, remained Catholic after the Church of England was founded in 1534. Because of the persecution he and fellow Catholics had endured in the century since, he planned to create Maryland as a refuge of (relative) religious toleration, where Catholics and Protestants could worship in peace.

Appointing his brother as governor, he carefully prepared for the first settlement by recruiting artisans and farmers (mainly Protestant) as well as wealthy merchants and aristocrats (mostly Catholic) to settle the colony. Although conflict continued to fester between members of the small set of Catholic elite and the Protestant majority, Governor Calvert convinced the Maryland assembly to pass the **Act of Religious Toleration** in 1649, granting religious freedom to all Christians.

The history of religious toleration in Maryland and its status as a haven for Catholics roughly mirrored the political and religious landscape back in England during the mid-seventeenth century. In 1642, disagreements over whether a king could rule without consent of his Parliament erupted in violence, and the **English Civil War** began. King Charles I was executed in 1649, and a parliamentary leader named Oliver Cromwell came to power as the war drew to its close in 1651, when Charles I's son, Charles

MAP 2.2 The Growth of English Settlement in the Chesapeake (c. 1650) With the success of tobacco, English plantations and forts spread along the James River and north to St. Mary's. By 1650 most Chesapeake tribes had been conquered or forced to move north and west. The fall line, a geological zone with waterfalls and rapids that marked the limit of navigable waterways, kept English settlements close to the Atlantic coast but also ensured easy shipment of goods.

What geographic factors determined the location of the English settlements on this map?

II, was exiled from England. Cromwell, who cemented his position of power as Lord Protector of the Commonwealth of England in 1653, was less accepting of Catholics than the king had been.

Thus, the Act of Religious Toleration was repealed in 1654, only five years after its initial passage. With aid from Maryland's Protestant colonists, new colonial governors appointed by Cromwell's Parliament then passed a new law prohibiting the open practice of Catholicism. However, the tide began to turn against Cromwell's rule as the decade wore on, and Calvert negotiated a return to his position as governor of Maryland. In 1657, the Act of Religious Toleration was again passed by the colonial assembly.

Over the course of the next sixty years, however, the act would be contested multiple times, and Catholics were eventually barred from voting in 1718. Despite the many challenges to its legitimacy, the Act of Religious Toleration set an important early precedent of religious freedom on the North American continent.

- How did religious conflict in Europe shape Maryland's shifting policies on religious tolerance?

Tobacco Economies, Class Rebellion, and the Emergence of Slavery

Throughout the seventeenth century, cash crops shaped the economies and societies of the southern colonies. When the English monarchy was restored to Charles II (reigned 1660–1685) in 1660, he established eight English noblemen as the leaders of a Carolina colony, a colony to the south of Virginia along the Atlantic coast. The northern region of the Carolina colony, in present-day North Carolina, came to rely on plantations focused mainly on producing tobacco. Thus, the new colony functioned in much the same way as the Chesapeake colonies. Although the political leaders of Carolina hoped to recreate a system of feudal manors in North America, they faced a labor shortage, as few migrants wished to brave the risks merely to remain peasants working the lands of different lords. The farmers and laborers who did migrate to northern Carolina would eventually rise up and force the ruling class to offer land at reasonable prices and a semblance of self-government.

Before 1650, neither the Chesapeake colonies nor northern Carolina had yet developed a legal code of slavery, but from that point on, legal matters began to change. Improved economic conditions in England meant fewer people were willing to gamble on a better life in North America, and as fewer people were arrested for crimes and vagrancy, the population of convicts who could be bought from English prisons dwindled.

To compensate for the shortage of white indentured servants, landowners in the Chesapeake and northern Carolina colonies increasingly came to rely on the labor of enslaved Africans to continue to produce the tobacco that generated wealth and fueled colonial growth. Thus, even though the number of enslaved African laborers remained small until late in the century, colonial leaders already began to take steps to increase their control over the African population. In 1660, the House of Burgesses passed an act that allowed Black laborers to be enslaved and, in 1662, defined slavery as an inherited status passed from mothers to children. In 1664, Maryland followed suit. In 1695, the Carolina colony, not yet divided into North and South Carolina, adopted a formal **slave code** that was based on Virginia's laws.

slave code
A law restricting enslaved persons' rights, largely due to slaveholders' fears of rebellion. Slave codes also defined slavery as a distinct status based on racial identity, which passed that status on through future generations.

While enslaved Africans became, in time, a crucial component of the tobacco labor force, indentured servants still continued to make up the majority of bound workers in Virginia, Maryland, and northern Carolina for most of the seventeenth century. Enslaved Africans labored under harsh conditions, and punishment for even minor infractions could be severe. Plantation owners beat, whipped, and branded enslaved people for a variety of behaviors.

During this time, some white indentured servants made common cause with Black laborers, both indentured servants and enslaved, who worked side by side with them on tobacco plantations. They ran away together, stole goods from slaveholders, and planned uprisings and rebellions. Contracted white laborers, however, had a far greater chance of gaining their freedom even before slavery was fully entrenched in colonial law.

AP® WORKING with EVIDENCE

Source: Virginia House of Burgesses, *Selected Statutes Passed 1662–1669*

1662

"Whereas some doubts have arisen whether children got by any Englishman upon a Negro woman should be slave or free, be it therefore enacted and declared by this present Grand Assembly, that all children born in this country shall be held bond or free only according to the condition of the mother . . .

October, 1669

[B]e it enacted and declared by this Grand Assembly if any slave resists his master (or other by his master's order correcting him) and by the extremity of the correction should chance to die, that his death shall not be accounted a felony, but the master (or that other person appointed by the master to punish him) be acquitted from molestation, since it cannot be presumed that premeditated malice (which alone makes murder a felony) should induce any man to destroy his own estate."

Questions for Analysis

1. Identify the main point of each law in this document.
2. Describe how the laws treat violence by slaveholders toward enslaved Africans differently from efforts of enslaved Africans to resist slaveholders.
3. Explain the factors that led the Virginia House of Burgesses to pass slave codes in the 1660s.

By the 1660s and 1670s, the population of former indentured servants who had become free formed a growing and increasingly unhappy class. Most were struggling economically, working as common laborers or tenants on large estates. Those who managed to move west and claim land on the frontier were confronted by hostile American Indians such as the Susquehannock nation.

Virginia governor Sir William Berkeley, who levied taxes to support nine forts on the frontier, had little patience with the complaints of these colonists. The labor demands of wealthy tobacco planters had to be met, and frontier settlers' call for an aggressive American Indian policy would hurt the profitable deerskin trade with the Algonquin.

In late 1675, conflict erupted when frontier settlers, many of whom were former indentured servants, attacked American Indians in the region. Rather than attacking only the Susquehannock nation, the settlers also assaulted communities allied with the English. When a large force of local Virginia militiamen surrounded a Susquehannock village, they ignored pleas for peace and murdered five chiefs. Susquehannock warriors retaliated with raids on frontier farms.

Despite the outbreak of open warfare, Governor Berkeley refused to send troops, so disgruntled farmers turned to Nathaniel Bacon. Bacon came from a wealthy family and

AP® EXAM TIP

Be able to explain how tobacco affected labor systems in Virginia and Maryland through indentured servitude and the enslavement of Africans. Avoid universal truisms, such as tobacco increased the use of enslaved laborers. Instead, illustrate your understanding by connecting tobacco, the headright system, and indentured servitude.

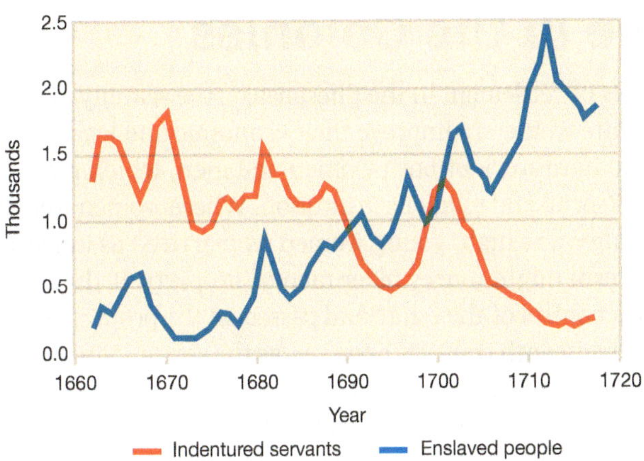

Indentured Servants and Enslaved People in Six Maryland Counties (1662–1717) Although based on a study of estate inventories from six Maryland counties, this chart illustrates a dramatic shift in the Chesapeake labor force between 1662 and 1717.

What does the trend shown here suggest about the nature and conditions of labor on Chesapeake farms?

was related to Berkeley by marriage, but that did not stop him from defying the governor's authority and raising an army to attack American Indians across the colony. **Bacon's Rebellion** had begun.

Bacon's Rebellion
An uprising in Virginia led by Nathaniel Bacon in 1676. Bacon and his followers were upset by the Virginia governor's unwillingness to send troops to intervene in conflicts between settlers and American Indians and by the lack of representation of western settlers in the House of Burgesses.

Frontier farmers formed an important part of Bacon's coalition, but affluent planters who had been left out of Berkeley's inner circle also joined Bacon in hopes of gaining access to power and profits, as did bound laborers, Black and white, who assumed that anyone who opposed the governor was on their side. Bacon's gathering forces included free, indentured, and enslaved Black people rebelling for greater freedoms and opportunities.

In the summer of 1676, Governor Berkeley declared Bacon guilty of treason. Rather than waiting to be captured, Bacon led his army toward Jamestown. Berkeley then arranged a hastily called election to undercut the rebellion. Even though Berkeley had barred men without property from voting, Bacon's supporters won control of the House of Burgesses, and his movement gained new followers. These included "news wives," lower-class women who spread information (and rumors) about oppressive conditions to aid the rebels. As Bacon and his followers marched across Virginia, his men plundered the plantations of Berkeley and his supporters. In September, they reached Jamestown after the governor and his administration fled across Chesapeake Bay. The rebels burned the capital to the ground, victory seemingly theirs.

Only a month later, however, Bacon died of dysentery, and the movement he formed unraveled. Governor Berkeley, using reinforcements brought by the English navy, quickly reclaimed power. He hanged twenty-three rebel leaders and urged his followers to plunder the estates of planters who had supported Bacon. But he could not undo the damage to American Indian relations on the Virginia frontier. Bacon's army had killed or enslaved hundreds of once-friendly American Indians and left behind a tragic, bitter legacy.

An even more important consequence of the rebellion was that wealthy planters and investors realized the depth of frustration among poor whites who were willing to make common cause with their Black counterparts. Having regained power, the planter elite worked to crush any such interracial alliance. Virginia legislators began to improve the conditions and rights of poor white settlers while imposing new restrictions on Black people. At nearly the same time, in an effort to meet the growing demand for labor in the West Indies and the Chesapeake, King Charles II chartered the Royal African Company in 1672 to transport enslaved Africans to North America. Thus, the march toward full-blown racial slavery in the English colonies began as enslaved labor quickly replaced indentured servitude in the plantation colonies.

REVIEW

- How did Nathaniel Bacon justify his rebellion?
- What were the results of his rebellion?

Daily Life in the Colonies

In the first decades of settlement in the Chesapeake, the scarcity of women and workers enabled many white women to improve their economic and legal status. Maintaining a farm required the hard work of both women and men, which made marriage an economic as well as a social and religious institution. Where women were in especially short supply and mortality was high, young women who arrived as indentured servants and completed their term might marry older men of property. If their husbands died first, widows often took control of the estate and passed on the property to their children.

By the late seventeenth century, however, as the sex ratio in the Chesapeake evened out, women lost the opportunity to marry "above their class" and widows lost control of family estates. Even though women still performed vital labor, the spread of indentured servitude and slavery lessened the recognition of their contributions. As a result, most white women in the colonies were assigned mainly domestic roles during this time period. They also found their legal and economic rights restricted in ways that mirrored those of their female counterparts in Great Britain.

The divisions between rich and poor, created and sustained by the Chesapeake and northern Carolina colonies' economic reliance on the cash crop of tobacco, became much more pronounced in the early decades of the eighteenth century. Tobacco was the most valuable product in the region, and the largest tobacco plantation owners lived in relative

MAP 2.3 Ethnic and Racial Diversity in British North America, 1750 In 1700, the English dominated most regions, while the Dutch controlled towns and estates in the Hudson River valley. By 1750, however, growing numbers of Africans and African Americans, Germans, Scots-Irish immigrants, and smaller communities of other ethnic groups predominated in various regions.

What accounts for the presence of these diverse populations in British North America?

Peter Newark American Pictures/Bridgeman Images

Enslaved People Working on a Tobacco Plantation (c. 1750) This wood engraving, created by nineteenth-century English author and engraver Frederick W. Fairholt, was based on a mid-eighteenth-century drawing. Fairholt depicts enslaved people packing tobacco leaves in large barrels and rolling them to waiting ships while whites oversee their work.

How do the items Fairholt included in this image compare with John Smith's map from over a century before (Module 2.3a)? What might explain the differences you see?

luxury. They developed trading contacts in seaport cities on the Atlantic coast and in the Caribbean and imported luxury goods from Europe. They also began using some enslaved people as domestic workers to relieve white women of the strain of household labor.

Small farmers could also purchase and maintain land based on the profits from tobacco. In 1750, two-thirds of white families farmed their own land in Virginia, a larger percentage than in northern colonies. An even higher percentage did so in North Carolina. Yet small farmers in the tobacco colonies became increasingly dependent on large landowners, who controlled markets, politics, and the courts. Many artisans in North Carolina, Virginia, and Maryland, too, depended on wealthy planters for their livelihood. Artisans worked directly for planters, or for the shipping companies and merchants that relied on plantation orders. And the growing number of tenant farmers in this region relied completely on large landowners for their sustenance.

However, some people in these colonies fared far worse during the mid-eighteenth century. One-fifth of all white southerners owned little more than the clothes on their backs. At the same time, free Black people found their opportunities for landownership and economic independence increasingly limited, while those who were enslaved had little hope of gaining their freedom and held almost no property of their own.

In the first half of the eighteenth century, the colonial population of Virginia, Maryland, and North Carolina surged. Some of the growth occurred from natural increase, but immigration of Germans and Scots-Irish to lands in the western parts of these colonies accounted for a significant portion. By the 1740s, German families created pockets of self-contained communities above the fall line in the backcountry of North Carolina and the Chesapeake colonies. They worshipped in German churches, read German newspapers, and preserved German traditions. Likewise, Scots-Irish immigrants established their own churches and communities in the areas where they settled.

REVIEW

- Describe the economic and ethnic diversity in the Chesapeake colonies during the middle of the eighteenth century.

The British West Indies and South Atlantic Colonies

Hoping to mimic Spanish successes with tobacco in the Caribbean, English investors turned their sights to Caribbean islands in the early seventeenth century. During the 1620s, the English developed permanent settlements on the islands of St. Christopher, Barbados, and Nevis, which came to be known as the British West Indies.

Barbados, with its highly profitable tobacco plantations, quickly emerged as the most attractive of the West Indies colonies. English migrants settled there in growing numbers, bringing in white indentured servants, many of whom were Irish and Scottish, to raise livestock in the early years, although cultivating tobacco and cotton soon took priority. English tobacco plantations throughout the West Indies quickly became the economic engine of English colonization and expansive **imperialism**. This economic expansion in turn led to demands for new forms of labor to ensure profitable returns on investment. Investors sent large numbers of the indentured servants across the Atlantic, and growing numbers of Africans were forced onto ships for sale in the Americas.

imperialism
A policy of expanding the border and increasing the global power of a nation, typically via military force.

In the 1630s, falling tobacco prices resulted in economic stagnation on Barbados. By that time, however, a few forward-looking planters were already considering another avenue to wealth: sugarcane. English and European consumers absorbed as much sugar as the market could provide, but producing sugar was difficult, expensive, and labor intensive. In addition, the sugar that was sent from North America needed further refinement in Europe before being sold to consumers. The Dutch had built the best refineries in Europe, but their small West Indies colonies could not supply sufficient raw sugar. By 1640, they formed a partnership with English planters, offering them the knowledge and financing to cultivate sugar on British-controlled Barbados, which was then refined in the Netherlands. That decision reshaped the economic and political landscape of North America and intensified competition for both land and labor. Thus, as the English developed an economy based on sugar in the West Indies, they also developed a harsh system of slavery.

Sarin Images/Granger – Historical Picture Archive

Sugar Manufacturing in the West Indies This seventeenth-century engraving depicts the use of enslaved labor in the production of sugar in the West Indies. The Dutch, English, and French used enslaved labor to plant sugarcane and then cut, press, and boil it to produce molasses. The molasses was turned into rum and refined sugar, both highly profitable exports. The top right corner of the image depicts sugarcane.

What activities are portrayed in this image? In what ways were the sugar and tobacco economies of the Western Hemisphere similar?

By 1660, Barbados had become the first English colony with a Black majority population. Twenty years later, there were seventeen enslaved people for every white indentured servant on Barbados. The growth of slavery on the island depended almost wholly on imports from Africa, because enslaved people in Barbados died faster than they could reproduce themselves. As an effect of high death rates, brutal working conditions, and the massive imports of ever-increasing numbers of enslaved workers, Barbados systematized its slave code, defining enslaved Africans as chattel — that is, as mere property more akin to livestock than to human beings. The booming sugar industry spurred the development of plantation slavery and gave rise in turn to the slave codes that legally enforced slavery in the British West Indies.

REVIEW

- How did the seventeenth-century Atlantic economy influence that of the West Indies?

The British West Indies Influence South Carolina

In return for their help in securing his rule after returning from exile and taking back the throne in 1660, and in hopes of creating financially rewarding colonies, Charles II granted the extensive lands that became the states of North and South Carolina to eight English nobles. Likewise, during the seventeenth century, planters from Barbados began to relocate to the Carolinas because of greater opportunities to acquire additional lands there.

In what is now South Carolina, English planters with West Indies connections quickly came to shape and dominate seventeenth-century society. They created a mainland version of Barbados by introducing enslaved Africans as laborers and carving out plantations. Early South Carolina plantations produced the labor-intensive cash crop of rice, which was then exported to the British West Indies, where it was used to feed enslaved Africans working on sugar plantations. Later in the century, South Carolina planters began themselves to produce sugar for export.

By the late seventeenth century, the enslaved labor needed to produce sugar and rice in South Carolina was controlled by a small, but enormously wealthy class of landholders who oversaw the politics and economy of the colony. The city of Charleston was one of the main ports receiving enslaved Africans by the early 1700s. The same trade in human cargo that brought misery to millions of Africans generated huge profits for traders, investors, and plantation owners and helped turn American seaport cities, like Charleston, into centers of culture and consumption. The necessity for a large labor force also created a population of enslaved Africans that by the early eighteenth century outnumbered white settlers in the colony.

REVIEW

- How did the economy of the West Indies affect the economy that developed in South Carolina during the late 1600s?

South Carolina: Origins and Daily Life

By the mid-eighteenth century, chances for economic autonomy among southern colonists were increasingly influenced by the spread of slavery. As hundreds and then thousands of Africans were imported into South Carolina in the 1720s and 1730s, economic and political power became more entrenched in the hands of planters and merchants. Increasingly, they controlled the markets, wrote the laws, and set the terms by which white as well as Black families lived. Farms along inland waterways and on the frontier were crucial in providing food and other items for urban residents and for planters with large labor forces. But farm families depended on commercial and planter elites to market their goods and help defend their communities against hostile American Indians or Spaniards.

During this time, more than two-thirds of white families in South Carolina owned no enslaved labor and farmed their own lands. As in the Chesapeake and North Carolina colonies, artisans in South Carolina depended on wealthy planters, who controlled markets, government, and the courts, for their livelihood. Artisans worked either for plantation owners directly or for the shipping companies and merchants that relied on plantation orders.

In 1745, some forty thousand Scots who had rebelled against the English in support of Stuart claims to the throne were shipped to the Carolinas after their rebellion

MAP 2.4 West Indies and Carolina in the Seventeenth Century Beginning in the 1630s, sugar cultivation transformed colonies in the West Indies. The British consumed sugar in large quantities, ensuring the economic success of Barbados and its neighbors and a vast increase in the enslaved population. In the 1660s, Barbados planters obtained a charter for Carolina and sent many early settlers — white planters and merchants as well as enslaved laborers — to this mainland colony.

Given where Barbados is located, what potential commercial rivalries could it cause between European powers during the seventeenth century?

was put down. They were mostly Presbyterian Protestants, although there was also a significant minority of Catholics who had fought for independence from Great Britain. They swelled the existing ranks of **subsistence farmers** in the South Carolina backcountry. These farmers purchased few goods manufactured by artisans, relying instead on home production. To complicate matters, these tenant farmers relied almost entirely on large landowners for access to land to earn their sustenance, whether by farming or hunting.

subsistence farmer
A farmer who grows crops that can supply only the needs of the family rather than being sold for profit.

Like other poor people in the colonies, some in South Carolina fared far worse than the few plantation owners who controlled its economy and politics. Twenty percent of white southerners lived in poverty. The very few free Black people in the colony had almost no opportunities for economic independence. Those who were enslaved faced harsh slave codes that policed their movement at all times. Thus, like their counterparts in North Carolina and the Chesapeake, they had little hope of gaining their freedom.

Economic changes driving expansion of existing plantations and the development of new plantation systems in the British American colonies did produce positive effects for some colonists. Large landholders able to secure bound labor generated great wealth that could be passed down to their families. The mechanization of cloth production in England during the eighteenth century also demanded vast amounts of labor and raw materials from both the English countryside and the colonies. It ensured, for example, the enormous profitability of indigo that was cultivated on southern plantations and used to dye English textiles in the mid-to-late eighteenth century. Thus, cash-crop indigo, tobacco, rice, and sugar plantations, each with profits built through the bound labor of hundreds of enslaved Black people, benefited white plantation families, who passed their profits and land to their children, creating a class of inherited wealth.

REVIEW

- What factors contributed to the rise of slavery in South Carolina?

AP® Skills Workshop: Thinking Historically

Analyzing Claims and Evidence in Secondary Sources

As you read in Period 1, historians make **claims**. Claims are arguments that attempt to convince a reader about a general truth about the past.

But historians aren't the only people who make claims. We make claims every day. For example, when my friend asks me, "How was your day?" I might reply that "I had an awful day." "I had an awful day" is an opinion about my day. It is a personal opinion based on my reflection on the facts. But a claim is more than just how I feel at the moment. Instead, a claim is based on my interpretation of specific factors that justify it, namely, the events that made my day so awful. These events are the **evidence** that I reflect upon to make my claim.

But my friend doesn't know about any of these events. So, to make my claim something that my friend can understand (and agree with), I should relate the evidence that made my day awful. Then, while my friend might not have experienced my awful day, they can review the evidence and decide whether to agree with me.

Let's say that I want to prove to my friend that "I had an awful day" by using evidence to support my claim. I might say, "Well, first my alarm didn't go off and I overslept. Then, I got fired from my job for being late. And finally, I crashed into a fire

(continued)

hydrant and totaled my car and got my groceries all wet." This is some strong evidence that I had an awful day! But the evidence I provide my friend is most important because it allows them to determine if they agree with my claim. My friend might say, "Wow! That's really awful. I've never had a day like that." This tells me that my evidence was compelling, which means that my friend was convinced to agree with my claim because of the power of my examples.

Yet someone else might say, "Oh come on! That kind of stuff happens to me every day!" This tells me that this person doesn't find my evidence as persuasive. Notice that they also offered a counterclaim ("This kind of stuff happens to me every day!"). I might find this an incredible claim and say, "What?! Prove it!" This requires them to provide evidence that they have my kind of day every day. And if I don't find their evidence compelling, I might try to provide my own evidence to disprove their claim.

Believe it or not, when historians argue, they follow the same steps: they claim, they cite evidence, and then they explain why their evidence supports their claim. This should remind you of the strategy of "Claim, Support, and Explain" (CSE) that you learned in Period 1.

ACTIVITY

Below is an excerpt from an article by Cara Anzilotti about women in colonial South Carolina. First, in a single sentence, and in your own words, summarize the **claim** that Anzilotti makes about women in colonial South Carolina. Then, write one to two sentences identifying three examples of evidence that Anzilotti uses to **support** her claim. Your evidence should be *specific historical information* that Anzilotti uses to prove her claim. Finally, in one to two sentences, **explain** how the evidence you collected from Anzilotti's article supports her claim.

> "[South Carolina's] great profits from the sale of cash crops, live-stock, and naval stores came at a high price for the settlers in the low-country around Charleston; adults there often died prematurely, and upon the death of their husbands, wives became heads of household and managers of their families' holdings. The death rate was alarmingly high. Throughout the colonial period, diseases, including malaria, dysentery, and yellow fever, contributed to a child mortality rate of 33 percent and an adult life expectancy of only forty-five years. . . . For the planter elite, who tried to maintain their position in a social environment plagued by demographic disruption, placing economic power in the hands of their wives and daughters became essential to the survival of the social order they had so carefully imported and erected. Women became the crucial links in the chain of inheritance among planter families, vital to the durability of Carolina's highly structured society, which relied upon a clearly defined, carefully implemented, locally adapted patriarchal system to ensure the social and political dominance of the men who had established it. These women, understanding both their own importance in this enterprise and the possibilities for independence presented to them, chose to take a conservative path and to forgo the opportunity to establish themselves as autonomous individuals. Instead, female planters shored up the patriarchal structure and thus helped their families remain wealthy and powerful."

Excerpt from Cara Anzilotti, "Autonomy and the Female Planter in Colonial South Carolina," *The Journal of Southern History*, vol. 63, no. 2, May 1997.

The Regions of British Colonies: New England and the Middle Colonies

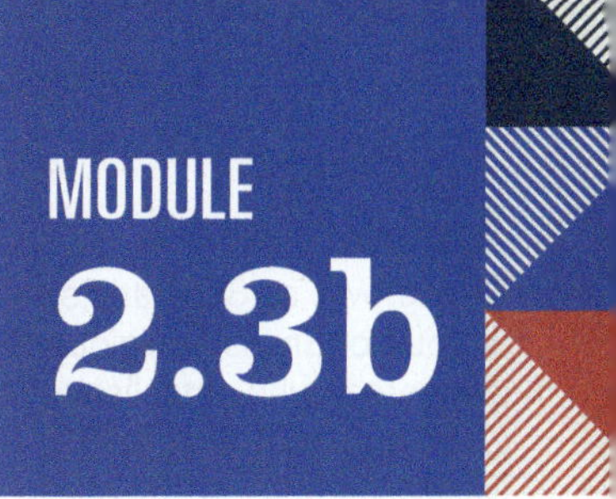

FOCUS

Historians look at historical change in very broad terms and describe patterns of continuity and change over time. Just as historians deepen their comparative analyses when they consider how causation factors into historical developments (see Module 1.7), they also deepen their understanding of continuity and change over time by incorporating explanations of causation. This is because uncovering the cause of a particular change or continuity fosters a fuller understanding of why these changes and continuities occur. Going beyond merely describing continuities and changes is also one way to examine why some aspects of a topic changed even as factors caused other aspects to persist unchanged across a timespan.

While reading this module, consider the ways in which religion, politics, economics, and geography shaped the northern and middle colonies at their inception, what historical realities changed throughout the seventeenth and early eighteenth centuries, and what remained the same.

The Protestant Reformation

The **Protestant Reformation**, from its beginning in 1517, transformed the religious and political landscape of Europe throughout the sixteenth century. The Catholic Church, in partnership with monarchs and the nobility, had long served as the dominant religion of Western Europe, but by the early sixteenth century, critiques of its practices began to multiply. Many saw the Catholic Church as corrupt and driven by the pope's involvement in conflicts among European monarchs.

Protestant Reformation
A European religious movement to break with the Catholic Church.

The formation of new denominations such as the Church of England during this time shattered the dominance of the Catholic Church and profoundly altered personal beliefs and royal alliances throughout Europe. The resulting conflicts had long-lasting effects that shaped the following century as well.

Protestant challenges and Catholic attempts to maintain authority led to intense conflicts. National competition for wealth and colonies in North America among the Spanish, French, Dutch, and English was complicated by the Protestant Reformation. Spanish and French Catholicism shaped their colonial efforts, as did Protestantism in the Netherlands and England.

Protestantism grew in England with support from the monarchy in the 1530s. When the pope refused to annul the marriage of King Henry VIII (reigned 1509–1547) and Catherine of Aragon, Henry publicly rejected papal authority and established the Church of England, with himself at its head as "defender of the faith." Despite the

Pilgrims
Also known as Separatists, a group of English religious dissenters who established a settlement at Plymouth, Massachusetts, in 1620.

Puritans
Radical English Protestants who hoped to reform the Church of England. The first Puritan settlers in the Americas arrived in Massachusetts in 1630.

king's conversion to Protestantism, the Church of England retained many Catholic practices, which is why groups such as the **Pilgrims** and, later, the **Puritans**—who would go on to colonize New England during the seventeenth century—also attracted followers.

REVIEW

- How did competition and conflict between European nations change as a result of the Protestant Reformation?

Pilgrims Arrive in Massachusetts

In Great Britain, critics of the Church of England formed a number of congregations in the early seventeenth century, and some sought refuge in Virginia. In the 1610s, to raise capital, the Virginia Company began offering legal charters to groups of private investors, who were promised their own tract of land in the Virginia colony with minimal company oversight. One such charter was purchased by a group of English Pilgrims (also known as Separatists) who wanted to form a separate church and community in a land untainted by other faiths. Unlike more mainstream Protestants, the Pilgrims aimed to cut all connections with the Church of England.

Setting sail on the *Mayflower* from England in September 1620, the Pilgrims never made it to Virginia. Blown off course by a storm, they landed far up the coast, north of the Dutch in New Amsterdam. Because a religious community wholly separate from the Church of England was more important to the Pilgrims than its specific location, they decided to remain on the Massachusetts coast, establishing a permanent settlement at Plymouth.

The Pilgrim Separatists who booked passage on the *Mayflower* in 1620 migrated as organized households, each headed by an elder male church member and accompanied by their families and servants. Finding themselves off course at Cape Cod in present-day Massachusetts, the male heads of households, led by William Bradford, signed a pact to form a "civill body politick" that followed the Separatist model of a self-governing religious congregation. In effect, the Pilgrims wrote and signed the first written constitution adopted in North America, the **Mayflower Compact**, before leaving the ship. They considered their agreement necessary because they settled in a region where they had no legal authority.

Mayflower Compact
Written agreement created by the Pilgrims upon their arrival in Plymouth. It was the first written constitution adopted in North America.

After several forays along the coast of Cape Cod, the Pilgrims eventually located an uninhabited village surrounded by cornfields, where they established Plymouth. Uncertain of native inhabitants' intentions, the Pilgrims were unsettled by sightings of American Indians. They did not realize that a smallpox epidemic in the area only two years earlier had killed nearly 90 percent of the local Wampanoag population. Indeed, fevers and other diseases proved far more deadly to the Pilgrim settlers than did the Wampanoag. By the spring of 1621, only half of the 102 English colonists from the *Mayflower* remained alive.

Desperate to find food, the survivors were stunned when two English-speaking American Indians—Samoset and Squanto—appeared at Plymouth that March. Both had been captured as young boys by English explorers, and they now negotiated a fragile peace between the Pilgrims and Chief Massasoit of the Wampanoag tribe. Although concerned by the power of English guns, Massasoit hoped to create an alliance that would assist him against his traditional native enemies, including the Massachusetts tribe. With Wampanoag assistance, the surviving Pilgrims soon regained their health.

In the summer of 1621, reinforcements arrived from England, and the next year the Pilgrims received a royal charter granting Separatists rights to Plymouth and a degree of self-government. Although some Pilgrims hoped to convert the American Indians, other leaders favored a more aggressive, military stance. In their eyes, the Massachusetts Indians posed an especially serious threat. In 1623, Captain Myles Standish kidnapped and killed the Massachusetts chief and his younger brother. Pilgrims led by Standish and allied Wampanoags then attacked a Massachusetts village. Standish's strategy, though controversial, ensured that Chief Massasoit of the Wampanoags achieved dominance in the region. Successful in war and diplomacy, the Pilgrims gradually expanded their colony during the 1620s.

REVIEW

- How did the Pilgrims maintain specific aspects of English society in Plymouth?
- How did the society the Pilgrims developed in Plymouth differ from specific aspects of English society?

Puritans Form Communities in New England

The Puritans, like the Pilgrims, followed the teachings of John Calvin, believing in an all-knowing God whose true word was presented in the Bible. Also similar to the Pilgrims, Puritans believed the church was a congregation formed by a group of believers who made a covenant with God. Only a small minority of people, known as Saints, were granted God's grace to receive salvation. However, unlike the Pilgrims, Puritans wanted to "purify" the Church of England, and transform the nation's religious practices to follow their beliefs.

The Puritans arrived in North America a decade after the Pilgrims in 1630, with plans to develop their own colony. By 1630, Puritans had come to believe that their country's church and government had grown corrupt and envisioned New England as a safe haven from God's wrath. Under Puritan lawyer John Winthrop's leadership, a group of affluent Puritans obtained a royal charter for the Massachusetts Bay Company in 1623. New England was, however, more than just a place of safety to the Puritans. By prospering spiritually and materially in America, they hoped to establish a model "city upon a hill" that would then inspire reform among residents of the mother country.

AP® WORKING with EVIDENCE

Source: John Winthrop, *A Model of Christian Charity*, 1630

> "Now the only way to . . . provide for our posterity . . . is to follow the counsel of Micah, to do justly, to love mercy, to walk humbly with our God. For this end, we must be knit together, in this work, as one man. . . . We must be willing to abridge ourselves of our superfluities, for the supply of others' necessities. We must uphold a familiar commerce together in all meekness, gentleness, patience and liberality. We must delight in each other; make others'

conditions our own; rejoice together, mourn together, labor and suffer together, always having before our eyes our commission and community in the work, as members of the same body. . . . For we must consider that we shall be as a city upon a hill. The eyes of all people are upon us."

Questions for Analysis

1. Describe the kind of society Winthrop envisions in this document.
2. Explain how this document reveals the ways in which seventeenth-century New England society continued English traditions.
3. Explain how this document reveals the ways in which seventeenth-century New England society broke from English traditions.
4. Explain how this document illustrates Puritan beliefs.

About one-third of all English Puritans chose to leave their homeland for North America, and a large proportion of those chose to sail with their entire families. They were better supplied, more prosperous, and more numerous than either their Pilgrim or Jamestown predecessors. The settlers, arriving on seventeen ships, included the households of ministers, merchants, craftsmen, farmers, and—significantly—their servants, many of whom served on contracts of indenture. Moreover, they settled in a cold climate that reduced the spread of disease. These demographic and geographic factors helped ensure the rapid growth of the colony.

The first Puritan settlers arrived on the coast north of Plymouth in 1630 and named their community Boston, after the port city in England from which they had departed. Established in the midst of growing conflicts leading to the English Civil War and growing fears of royally sanctioned persecution of Puritans, the Massachusetts Bay Company relocated its capital and records to New England. Through this process, the Puritans converted their commercial charter into the founding document of a self-governing colony. They also instituted a new political practice, in which adult male church members participated in the election of a governor, deputy governor, and legislature.

Although the Puritans suffered a difficult first winter in New England, they quickly recovered and soon cultivated sufficient crops to feed themselves and a steady stream of new migrants. During the 1630s, the time of the **Puritan Migration**, at least eighteen thousand people made their way to North America. Even without a cash crop like tobacco or sugar, the Puritan colony flourished.

Puritan Migration
The mass migration of Puritans from Europe to New England during the 1620s and 1630s.

Two factors aided Puritans in quickly forming and developing new communities throughout New England. Cleared agricultural lands, farmed very recently by American Indians, had been made more available by the effects of Columbian Exchange diseases, which severely reduced the native farming populations. Also, Puritan ideology idealized small, close-knit village communities as a means to achieve a religiously moral society. These small communities of faithful neighbors, led by male church members, could watch over each other's actions to ensure that the community remained within God's grace. Male church members acted as patriarchs of their households, responsible to each other, and for the dependents of the community—both family and servant.

Opposed to the elaborate rituals and hierarchy of the Church of England and believing that few Anglicans truly felt the grace of God, Puritans set out to establish a simpler form of worship in New England that focused on their inner lives and on the purity of their church and community.

Whether one was a Saint and thereby saved was predetermined by and known only to God. Still, some Puritans believed that the chosen were likely to lead a saintly life. Visible signs included individuals' passionate response to the preaching of God's Word, their sense of doubt and despair over their own soul, a sense of reassurance that came with God's "saving grace," and divine fortune manifested as land ownership and a higher economic status. Puritans believed God's hand in the world appeared in nature as well. Comets and eclipses were considered "remarkable providences." Puritans also celebrated as a sign of God's favor a smallpox epidemic that killed several thousand Massachusetts Indians in 1633–1634 and military victories over American Indians such as the massacre at a fort near Mystic River in 1637.

These shared religious beliefs helped forge a unified community where faith guided civil as well as spiritual decisions. Soon after the colony was established, Puritan ministers were discouraged from holding political office, although political leaders were devout Puritans who were expected to promote a godly society. These leaders determined who got land, how much, and where. They also served as judge and jury for those accused of crimes or sins. Their leadership was largely considered successful—even if colonists differed over who should get the most fertile strip of land, they agreed on basic principles.

Puritans assigned wives and daughters solely domestic roles with rare exceptions. By the eighteenth century, Puritan women, and indeed almost all women throughout the colonies, found their legal and economic rights similarly restricted as their female counterparts in Great Britain.

By the 1640s, Puritan settlers had turned their colony into a thriving commercial center. During the English Civil War (1642–1651), New England settlements spread due to both natural increase and migration. English communities stretched from Connecticut through Massachusetts and Rhode Island and into Maine and what became New Hampshire. They shipped codfish, lumber, grain, pork, and cheese to England in exchange for manufactured goods and to the West Indies in exchange for rum and molasses. This trade, along with the healthy climate, relatively egalitarian distribution of property among male church members, and more equal ratio of women to men, ensured a stable and prosperous colony. Meanwhile, the English king and Parliament, embroiled in war, paid little attention to events in North America, allowing these New England colonies to develop with little oversight.

REVIEW

- How did the Puritans maintain specific aspects of Pilgrim society in Massachusetts Bay?
- In what ways did the Puritans change society in Massachusetts Bay?

Challenges Arise in the New England Colonies

English men and women settled New England in the 1620s and 1630s seeking religious sanctuary and to support communities unified by common faith. Yet they, too, like the colony at Jamestown, suffered divisions in their ranks. Almost from the beginning, certain Puritans challenged some of the community's fundamental beliefs and, in the process, the community itself. Dissenters such as Roger Williams and Anne Hutchinson even led groups of discontented Puritans to establish new communities.

In the early 1630s, Roger Williams, a Salem minister, criticized Puritan leaders for not being sufficiently pure in their rejection of the Church of England and the English monarchy. He preached that not all the Puritan leaders were Saints and that some were bound for eternal damnation. Williams also criticized the confiscation of American

Indian lands. By 1635, he was forced out of Salem and moved south with his followers to found Providence in the area that became Rhode Island.

Believing that there were very few Saints in the world, Williams and his followers accepted that one must live among those who were not saved. Thus, unlike Massachusetts Bay, Providence welcomed Quakers, Baptists, and Jews to the community, and Williams's followers insisted on a strict separation of church and state. Williams also forged alliances with the Narragansett tribe, the most powerful American Indian nation in the region.

Remarkably, Anne Hutchinson, a wife and mother, led another such dissenting group. Born in Lincolnshire in 1591, she was well educated when she married William Hutchinson, a merchant, in 1612. The Hutchinsons and their children began attending Puritan sermons and by 1630 embraced the new faith. Four years later, they followed the Reverend John Cotton to Massachusetts Bay.

The Reverend Cotton soon urged Anne Hutchinson to use her exceptional knowledge of the Bible to hold prayer meetings in her home on Sundays for pregnant and nursing women who could not attend regular services. Hutchinson, like Cotton, preached that individuals must rely solely on God's grace rather than a saintly life or good works to ensure salvation.

Hutchinson began challenging Puritan ministers who opposed this position, charging that they posed a threat to their congregations. She soon attracted a loyal and growing following that included men as well as women. A year after Roger Williams's departure in 1637, Puritan leaders denounced Hutchinson's views and condemned her meetings. After she refused to recant, she was accused of sedition, or trying to overthrow the government by challenging colonial leaders, and put on trial. Hutchinson mounted a vigorous defense. An eloquent speaker, Hutchinson claimed that her authority to challenge the Puritan leadership came from "an immediate revelation" from God, "the voice of his own spirit to my soul." Unmoved, the Puritan judges convicted her of heresy and banished her from Massachusetts Bay.

Hutchinson was seen as a threat not only because of her religious beliefs but also because she was a woman. The Reverend Hugh Peter, for example, reprimanded her at trial: "You have stept out of your place, you have rather bine a Husband than a Wife and a preacher than a Hearer; and a Magistrate than a Subject." Many considered her challenge to Puritan authority especially serious because she also challenged traditional gender and social hierarchies. After being banished from Massachusetts Bay, Hutchinson, her family, and dozens of her followers joined Williams's Rhode Island colony. The likelihood of later radical women experiencing the success of Hutchinson diminished as the colonies developed larger populations and more elaborate formal institutions of politics, law, and culture.

As Anne Hutchinson and Roger Williams confronted religious leaders, Puritans and Pilgrims faced serious threats from their American Indian neighbors as well. The Pequot nation, which was among the most powerful tribes in New England, had been allies of the English for several years. Yet some Puritans feared that the Pequot people, who opposed the colonists' continued expansion, "would cause all the Indians in the country to join to root out all the English." Also, unlike the Spanish, who believed native peoples could be converted to Christianity, many Puritans believed that Native Americans were irredeemable in the eyes of God and destined to damnation.

Pequot War

A conflict between New England settlers and their Narragansett allies against the Pequot Indians in 1636–1637. The English perceived the Pequot tribe as both a threat and an obstacle to further English expansion.

Using the death of two Englishmen in 1636 to justify a military expedition against the Pequot nation, the colonists went on the attack. The Narragansett tribe, whom Roger Williams had befriended, allied with the English in the **Pequot War** (1636–1638). After months of bloody conflict, the English and their American Indian allies launched a brutal attack on a Pequot fort in May 1637 that killed more than four hundred men, women, and children. This massacre by the Puritans eliminated the Pequot tribe, and the American Indian population in the area never recovered. In New England, at most 16,000 native people remained by 1670, a loss of about 80 percent over fifty years. Meanwhile the English population had reached more than 50,000, with settlers claiming ever more land.

Relations between the New England colonists and American Indians grew even worse in 1671, when the English demanded that the Wampanoag Indians, who had been their allies since the 1620s, surrender their guns and be ruled by English law. Instead, many Wampanoags hid their weapons and, over the next several years, raided frontier farms and killed several settlers. English authorities responded by hanging three Wampanoag men.

By 1675, the Wampanoag chief Metacom, called King Philip by the English, came to believe that Europeans had to be forced out of New England if American Indians were going to survive. As conflict escalated between the English and the Wampanoags, Metacom gained the support of other tribes, and together, they formed a coalition that attacked white settlements, burning fields, killing male settlers, and taking women and children captive in what became known as **Metacom's War**.

Metacom's War Also known as King Philip's War, a conflict between English settlers and an alliance of Native Americans led by the Wampanoag tribe, in 1675–1676. The settlers were the eventual victors, but fighting was fierce and casualties on both sides were high.

Initially, the colonists believed they could win an easy victory over their foes. However, the war dragged on and became increasingly brutal on both sides. About a thousand English settlers were killed and dozens were taken captive during the conflict. Metacom's forces attacked Plymouth and Providence and marched within twenty miles of Boston.

AP® EXAM TIP

Metacom's War, or King Phillip's War, is a required historical development for the AP® Exam. In addition to knowing the importance of that event, think about ways you can illustrate continuity and/or change over time by comparing the historical context of the Pequot War with Metacom's War. When comparing, be specific as to issues surrounding land, religion, and the economic development of New England.

Meanwhile, the English attacked native villages, killing hundreds of American Indians and selling hundreds more into slavery in the West Indies, including Metacom's wife and son. Indian losses were catastrophic on both sides of the conflict, as food shortages and disease combined with military deaths to kill as many as 4,500 men, women, and children. About a quarter of the remaining Indian population of New England died in 1675–1676.

The war finally ended when Metacom's forces ran short of guns and powder and Mohawk allies of the English ambushed and killed Metacom in 1676. The remaining tribes allied with Metacom moved north and gradually intermarried with tribes allied with the French. As the carnage of the war spilled into New York, Haudenosaunee (Iroquois) leaders and colonists met at Albany in 1677 in hopes of salvaging their lucrative fur trade. There they formed an alliance, the **Covenant Chain**, to head off future conflict.

Covenant Chain Alliance between Haudenosaunee (Iroquois) and the northern colonies of British North America to maintain the fur trade and good relations in the aftermath of Metacom's War.

- How did conflicts in the Puritan colonies, both internally and with American Indians, reflect Puritan society in particular, and the English colonists in general?

Conflicts in England Echo in the Colonies

As Puritans formed new lives in North America, those who remained in England were soon engaged in armed conflict against their fellow countrymen. Differences over issues of religion, taxation, and royal authority had strained relations between Parliament and the crown for decades, as James I (reigned 1603–1625) and his son Charles I (reigned

1625–1649) sought to consolidate their own power at Parliament's expense, demanding conformity to the Church of England. By 1642, the relationship between Parliament and King Charles I broke down completely, and the country descended into a civil war that lasted until 1651. During this time, the Puritan migration to New England virtually halted.

Oliver Cromwell, a Puritan, emerged as the leader of the Protestant parliamentary forces against the crown, and, after several years of fighting, claimed victory. Charles I was executed in 1649, Parliament established a republican commonwealth, and bishops and elaborate rituals were banished from the Church of England. Cromwell ruled England as a military dictator until his death in 1658—when rival groups of nobles, members of the Church of England, commercial elites, and commoners overthrew Puritan rule and invited Charles I's son, Charles II (reigned 1660–1685), to return from exile, and restored the monarchy and the Church of England.

Shortly after he was restored to the English throne, Charles II came to terms with expanded Puritan settlements in New England. He formalized his rule in this region by granting the requests of Connecticut and Rhode Island for royal charters, accepting their authority to rule in local matters. Because the charters could be changed only with the agreement of both parties, Connecticut and Rhode Island maintained local autonomy throughout the colonial period. Before the end of his reign, the English could claim dominance—in population, trade, and politics—over the other European powers vying for empires along the northern Atlantic coast.

Charles's death in 1685 marked an abrupt shift in crown-colony relations. Charles's successor, King James II (reigned 1685–1688), instituted a more authoritarian rule both at home and abroad. In 1686, he combined British colonies in the Northeast and Middle Atlantic into the **Dominion of New England** and established tighter controls. Within the Dominion of New England, James II's officials banned town meetings, challenged land titles granted under the original colonial charters, and imposed new taxes.

Dominion of New England
The consolidation of northeastern colonies by King James II in 1686 to establish greater control over them, resulting in the banning of town meetings, new taxes, and other unpopular policies. The Dominion was dissolved during the Glorious Revolution.

Fortunately for the colonists, the Catholic James II alienated his subjects in England as well as in the colonies, inspiring a bloodless coup in 1688, the so-called **Glorious Revolution**. James left the country and was replaced by his Protestant daughter, Mary II (reigned 1689–1694) and her husband, William of Orange (reigned 1689–1702), who introduced more democratic systems of governance in England and the colonies. Soon after, John Locke, a physician and philosopher, published the widely circulated *Two Treatises of Government* supporting the initiatives of William and Mary by insisting that government depended on the consent of the governed.

AP® WORKING with EVIDENCE

Source: John Locke, English political philosopher, *Second Treatise on Civil Government*, 1690

> "If man in the state of nature be so free, as has been said; if he be absolute lord of his own person and possessions, equal to the greatest, and subject to no body, why will he part with his freedom? . . . To which 'tis obvious to answer, that though in the state of nature he hath such a right, yet the enjoyment of it is very uncertain, and constantly exposed to the invasion of others; for all being kings as much as he, every man his equal, and the greater part no strict observers of equity and justice; the enjoyment of the property he has in this state is very unsafe, very unsecure. This makes him willing to quit this condition, which however free, is full of fears and continual dangers: And 'tis not without

reason, that he seeks out, and is willing to join in society with others who are already united, or have a mind to unite for the mutual preservation of their lives, liberties and estates, which I call by the general name, property."

Questions for Analysis

1. Identify the reasons Locke provides for the existence of a government.
2. Describe the historical developments that contributed to the ideas Locke expresses in this document.
3. Explain how Locke's ideas could be used to undermine royal authority.

Eager to restore political order and create a commercially profitable empire, William and Mary established the new colony of Massachusetts with a charter in 1692 (which included Plymouth, Massachusetts Bay, and Maine) and restored town meetings and an elected assembly. The 1692 charter granted the English crown the right to appoint a royal governor and officials to enforce customs regulations. It ensured religious freedom to members of the Church of England and allowed all male property owners (not just Puritans) to be elected to the assembly. In Maryland, too, the crown imposed a royal governor and replaced the Catholic Church with the Church of England as the established religion. And in New York, wealthy English merchants won the backing of the newly appointed royal governor, who instituted a representative assembly for the colony, and supported a merchant-dominated ruling assembly for New York City, the colony's capital. Thus, taken as a whole, William and Mary's policies instituted a partnership between England and colonial elites by allowing colonists to retain long-standing local governmental institutions but also asserting royal authority to appoint governors and ensure the influence of the Church of England.

- How did conflict in England shape the North American English colonies during the late seventeenth and early eighteenth centuries?

Conflict and Daily Life in Puritan New England

In the late seventeenth century, Puritan ministers were divided over the issues of increasing merchant wealth and the concentration of power in the hands of Boston commercial elites. Some ministers denounced the materialism and accompanying irreligious behaviors, while other Puritan ministers created new theology that tried to meld the old and new.

The Glorious Revolution in England in 1688 offered Puritan ministers hope of regaining their customary authority. But the outbreak of **King William's War** in 1689 quickly ended any notion of an easy return to peace and prosperity. Instead, continued conflicts, burdensome local taxes to pay for colonial defense against the French and their American Indian allies, and renewed fears of American Indian attacks on rural settlements heightened the sense that Satan was at work in the region. Soon, accusations of witchcraft joined outcries against other forms of ungodly behavior. Even though the war ended with neither the French nor the English gaining substantial territory, the conflict left New Englanders with lingering

King William's War
A war from 1689 to 1697 that began as a conflict over competing French and English interests on the European continent but soon spread to the American frontier. Both sides pulled American Indian allies into the war.

anxiety about their relations with the French, American Indians, and even the English government.

Belief in witchcraft had been widespread in Europe and England for centuries. It was part of a general belief in supernatural causes for events that could not otherwise be explained—severe storms, a suspicious fire, a rash of deaths among livestock. When a community began to suspect witchcraft, they often pointed to individuals who challenged cultural norms.

Women who were difficult to get along with, eccentric, poor, or simply too independent, most especially those widows inheriting and controlling land, were easy to imagine as influenced by evil spirits and invisible demons. Some 160 individuals, mostly women, were accused of witchcraft in Massachusetts and Connecticut, and fifteen were put to death between 1647 and 1691.

At Salem, Massachusetts, potentially powerful females were targeted by residents in 1692. Within weeks of the initial accusations, more than one hundred individuals, 80 percent of them women, stood accused of witchcraft. Twenty-seven of the accused came to trial, and twenty were found guilty, with nineteen people hanged and one pressed to death under the weight of stones. Many of the accused were poor, childless, or disgruntled women, but widows who inherited property also came under suspicion, especially if they fought for control against distant male relatives and neighbors.

Shortages of land in established Puritan communities intensified social conflicts. In New England, the land available for farming shrank as the population soared. By 1700, a New England wife who married at age twenty and survived to forty-five bore an average of eight children, most of whom lived to adulthood. In the original Puritan New England colonies, the population rose from 100,000 in 1700 to 400,000 in 1750, and many parents were unable to provide their children with sufficient land for profitable farms.

Mrs. Elizabeth Freake and Baby Mary (1674) This portrait shows Elizabeth Freake, the wife of merchant John Freake, and their eighth child, Mary. Here Elizabeth and her daughter demonstrate Puritan simplicity in their white head coverings and aprons, yet they also display their family's wealth and John Freake's commercial ties through their silk gowns and embroidered cloth.

What does this painting reveal about Puritan values and society?

The shortage of land led many New England men to seek their fortune farther west, leaving young women with few eligible bachelors to choose from. Marriage prospects were affected as well by battles over inheritance. Still, for most Puritan women, daily rounds of labor shaped their lives more powerfully than legal statutes or inheritance rights. The result was increased migration to the frontier, where families were more dependent on their own labor and a small circle of neighbors. Husbands and wives depended on each other to support their families.

An ideology of marriage as a partnership took practical form in communities across the colonies, including New England. By the early eighteenth century, many colonial writers promoted the idea of marriage as a partnership, even if the wife remained the junior partner through common law.

This option was not accessible to all. Before 1700, servants who survived their indenture had a good chance of securing land, but by the mid-eighteenth century, only two of every ten were likely to become landowners.

In Puritan towns, and also commercial cities such as Boston and Salem, the wives of artisans learned aspects of their husband's craft and assisted their husbands in a variety of ways. Given the overlap between living spaces and workplaces in the eighteenth century, extended households of artisan women often cared for apprentices, journeymen, and laborers as well as their own children. Husbands, meanwhile, labored alongside their subordinates and represented their families' interests to the larger community. Both spouses were expected to model godliness and to encourage prayer and regular church attendance among household members.

The way of life of rural Puritans closely resembled the ways most land-owning, but not plantation-owning, farming families lived in all the colonies. On farms, where the majority of Puritans lived, women and men played crucial if distinct roles. In general, wives and daughters labored inside the home as well as in the surrounding yard with its kitchen garden, milk house, chicken coop, dairy, or washhouse. Husbands and sons worked the fields, kept the livestock, and managed the orchards. Some families in all the colonies supplemented their own family labor with that of indentured servants, hired field hands, or, even in New England, a small number of enslaved Africans or African Americans. Most families exchanged surplus crops and manufactured goods such as cloth or sausage with neighbors. Some sold at market, creating an economic network of small producers.

Indeed, in the late seventeenth and early eighteenth centuries, many farm families in long-settled areas participated in a household mode of production. Men lent each other tools and draft animals and shared grazing land, while women gathered to spin, sew, and quilt. Individuals with special skills like midwifery or blacksmithing assisted neighbors, adding farm produce or credit to the family ledger. One woman's cheese might be bartered for another woman's jam. A family that owned the necessary equipment might brew barley and malt into beer, while a neighbor with a loom would turn thread into cloth.

The system of exchange, managed largely through barter, allowed individual households to function even as they became more specialized in what they produced. Whatever cash was obtained could be used to buy sugar, tea, and other imported goods.

New England colonial mothers combined childbearing and child rearing with a great deal of other work. While some affluent families could afford wet nurses and nannies, most women fended for themselves or hired temporary help for particular tasks. Puritan mothers in New England with babies on the hip and children under foot hauled water, fed chickens, collected eggs, picked vegetables, prepared meals, spun thread, and manufactured soap and candles. In this way, they shared common experiences with the rural women of every other British North American colony.

REVIEW

- How did Puritan society change between 1630 and 1700?
- What aspects of Puritan society remained the same between 1630 and 1700?

The Middle Colonies

The most important developments of the middle colonies occurred in the context of the restoration of the English monarchy in 1660, when English kings began granting North American land to men loyal to the crown. These land grants served both as rewards for the nobles who had secured the monarchy for Charles II and also as part of a larger quest to build a North American empire that would produce vast wealth for the monarchy and English nation-state. During his reign, Charles II appointed English gentlemen as the proprietors of a string of colonies stretching from Carolina to New York.

The middle colonies grew in the coastal lands the British seized from the Netherlands in the 1660s, sandwiched between Maryland and the Puritan New England colonies. The English monarchy, first under the rule of Charles II and later under his brother King James II, aggressively conquered, chartered, populated, and developed the middle colonies in less than twenty years, setting in place patterns that persisted long after the Glorious Revolution halted James's reign in 1688.

Colonies Develop in New York and New Jersey

After the English grabbed control of New Amsterdam from the Dutch in 1664, they renamed it New York, appointing King Charles's brother James, whose title at the time was the Duke of York, to rule it. Later in 1664, the Duke of York divided the territory and granted a colony to Sir George Carteret, which eventually became the Middle Colony of New Jersey. English rule for the next twenty-four years imposed little change upon Dutch colonists in the Hudson River valley, who numbered fewer than 10,000.

Leisler's Rebellion

A class revolt in New York in 1689 led by merchant Jacob Leisler. Urban artisans and landless renters rebelled against new taxes and centralized rule.

The Glorious Revolution also resulted in a class revolt in New York called **Leisler's Rebellion**. When news arrived of the Glorious Revolution in 1689, a German-born merchant named Jacob Leisler led a faction that rallied against the centralized rule and taxes that had been levied under James II, overthrowing the royal authorities appointed to run New York by the deposed king. Once in power, Leisler favored middle- and lower-class colonists with government positions and often sided with tenants in disputes against their landlords.

Leisler's time in power was, however, brief. As royally appointed representatives of King William and Mary arrived to govern New York in 1691, they sided with the elites who had opposed Leisler. He was put on trial and executed later that year for leading a revolt against royal authority. The legacy of his rebellion, however, would live on. Class issues surrounding access to land would remain a critical issue in the middle colonies, and social unrest would persist into the 1740s, when protests echoing issues central to

Wealth Inequality in Northern Cities, 1690–1775 During the eighteenth century, the wealth of merchants rose much faster than that of artisans and laborers.

What factors led to the changes depicted in the graph?

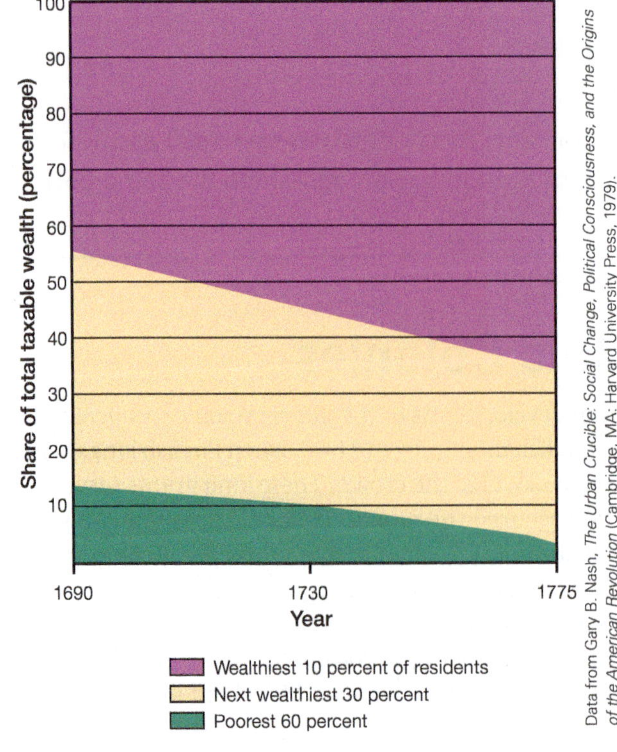

Leisler's Rebellion erupted on estates in New Jersey and along the Hudson River in New York.

In the 1690s, Dutch landholding families and wealthy English merchants in New York gained the backing of the newly appointed royal governor, who instituted representative assemblies through elections dominated by elite landlords. New York City already had a relatively diverse population, including small numbers of Jewish merchant families who had migrated when it was known as New Netherland, and it evolved as a center of commerce in the Atlantic economy. The colony would exert extensive economic, cultural, and social influence throughout the eighteenth century.

The emergence of an elite class of merchants in New York revealed growing colonial inequality. Wealthy urban merchants and professionals lived alongside a middle class of artisans and shopkeepers, as well as a growing underclass comprised of unskilled laborers, widows, orphans, the elderly, the disabled, and the unemployed.

The colony of New York was also a society with an enslaved population. By the 1710s, New York City hosted the second-largest slave market in the mainland colonies. While some enslaved people who passed through this market worked on agricultural estates in the Hudson River valley and New Jersey, even more labored as dockworkers, seamen, blacksmiths, and household servants in New York City. These enslaved laborers sometimes lived in slaveholders' homes, but more often they resided together in separate, impoverished communities. Black people accounted for about 14 percent of its inhabitants by the late 1770s. Symbolizing their lack of acceptance by the white population, Black people, both free and enslaved, were regularly taken outside the city limits for burial.

- How did international conflicts shape the colony of New York during the seventeenth and eighteenth centuries?

Penn's Goal of a Peaceable Kingdom

In 1681, King Charles II granted the lands that would become the colonies of Delaware and Pennsylvania to William Penn, a convert to a pacifist Protestant sect known as the Society of Friends, or Quakers. Quakers were considered radical and were severely persecuted in England, so Penn founded Pennsylvania as a safe place for Quakers to practice their religious beliefs in North America. As governor of the colony, Penn moved to Philadelphia in 1682, and, unlike other English colonial proprietors, personally governed it.

Penn provided a more inclusive model of colonial rule. He established friendly relations with the local Lenni-Lenape Indians and drew up a Frame of Government in 1682 that recognized religious freedom for all Christians and allowed all property-owning men to vote and hold office. Under Penn's leadership, Philadelphia grew into a bustling port city, while the rest of Pennsylvania attracted thousands of middle-class farm families, most of them Quakers, as well as artisans and merchants. During this time, Africans and African Americans formed only a small percentage of Pennsylvania's population, despite the notable concentration of enslaved Black dockworkers and porters in Philadelphia in the late seventeenth century.

In its first four decades, the population of Pennsylvania boomed as immigrants were drawn by Penn's tolerant policies. These colonists demanded more land and pushed westward to find unclaimed territory or purchase lands for sale. At the beginning of the eighteenth century, German and Scots-Irish immigrants joined Anglo-American

MAP 2.5 Frontier Settlements and American Indian Towns in Pennsylvania, 1700–1740 German and Scots-Irish immigrants to Pennsylvania mingled with American Indian settlements in the early eighteenth century. In the 1720s and 1730s, European migration escalated dramatically in the fertile river valleys. In response, once-independent American Indian tribes joined the Lenni-Lenape and Shawnee nations to strengthen their position against the influx of colonists. **What environmental factors contributed to the location of the European settlements on this map?**

settlers in rural areas of New Jersey, Pennsylvania, and Delaware. Many immigrants to Pennsylvania settled in areas that were dotted with Haudenosaunee (Iroquois), Lenni-Lenape, and Susquehannock towns. As a result of inheriting Penn's peaceable vision, and due to a lack of coordinated colonial military effort to dislodge American Indians, Pennsylvanian colonists mostly negotiated with them to purchase farmland.

At the same time, groups of Lenni-Lenape and Shawnee Indians, who had been pushed out of New Jersey into the Ohio River valley by pressure from settlers, also moved into Pennsylvania. They negotiated with colonists, the colonial government, and other American Indian tribes to establish new farming communities for themselves. All along the Pennsylvania frontier, the lines between American Indian and European immigrant settlements blurred. Many communities prospered in the region, with white settlers exchanging European and colonial goods for access to American Indian-controlled orchards, waterways, and lands.

Of the migrants attracted to Penn's colony in the early eighteenth century, Benjamin Franklin was the most notable. Franklin was apprenticed to his brother, a printer, an occupation that matched his interest in books, reading, and politics. At age sixteen, Benjamin published (anonymously) his first essays in his brother's paper, the *New England Courant*. At seventeen, Benjamin tried his luck in New York and then Philadelphia. His fortunes were fragile, but he combined hard work with a quick wit, good luck, and political connections, which together led to success. In 1729, Franklin purchased the *Pennsylvania Gazette* and became the colony's official printer.

- How did colonists' motivations for settlement in New York, New Jersey, and Pennsylvania during the late 1600s differ?

Expansion and Conflict in Pennsylvania

After William Penn died in 1718, his sons and closest advisers struggled to gain control over the colony. A surge of new laborers came to the British North American colonies in the 1720s, and many settled in the middle colonies. The population of the middle colonies swelled from 50,000 in 1700 to 250,000 in 1750.

The increase in population was due in part to wheat prices. Hoping to take advantage of this boom, Anglo-Americans, Germans, Scots-Irish, and other non-English groups settled western Pennsylvania and New York's Mohawk River valley, hoping to labor on or purchase grain farms in the middle colonies. Shipping agents offered many people seeking passage to America loans for their passage that were repaid when the immigrants found a colonial employer who would redeem (that is, repay) the agents. In turn, these **redemptioners**, who often traveled with families, labored for that employer for a set number of years, much like indentured servants. The redemption system was popular in the middle colonies, especially among German immigrants who hoped to establish farms on the Pennsylvania frontier. While many succeeded, their circumstances could be extremely difficult.

redemptioner
An immigrant who borrowed money from shipping agents to cover the costs of transport to America, loans that were repaid, or "redeemed," by colonial employers. A redemptioner worked for the "redeemer" for a set number of years.

In prosperous parts of the middle colonies, many landless laborers abandoned rural life and searched for urban opportunities during the first half of the eighteenth century. They moved to Philadelphia or other towns and cities in the region, seeking jobs as dockworkers, street vendors, or servants, or as apprentices in one of the skilled trades. But the surplus of redemptioners, and other immigrant laborers too poor to purchase land, meant there were far fewer jobs than job seekers.

Aside from German emigrants, in the 1720s and 1730s Scots-Irish settlers also flooded into Pennsylvania, fleeing bad harvests and high rents back home in the Irish province of Ulster. During this time, conflicts erupted regularly between the earlier British Quaker colonists and newer immigrant settlers, as well as between the various recent immigrant groups. Scots-Irish and German colonists took each other to court, sued land surveyors, and even burned down cabins built by their immigrant foes.

Some English Quakers viewed the actions of these newcomers as threats to their society. In 1728, James Logan, William Penn's longtime secretary, complained that the "[Germans] crowd in upon us and the Irish yet faster." For Logan, these difficulties were worsened by what he considered the "idle," "worthless," and "indigent" habits of Scots-Irish and other recent arrivals.

The new immigrants also overwhelmed Native American communities that had lived relatively peacefully with earlier settlers in Pennsylvania. American Indians were increasingly pushed to the margins as growing numbers of European settlers encroached on frontier territories.

Anglo-Americans had hardly set high standards when negotiating with American Indians. Even in Pennsylvania, where William Penn had previously established a reputation for (relatively) fair dealing, the desire for American Indian land led to dishonesty and trickery.

Conflicts among American Indian nations also aided colonial leaders in taking territory from them. Hoping to assert their authority over the independent-minded Delaware Indians, Haudenosaunee (Iroquois) chiefs insisted that they held rights to much of the Pennsylvania territory and therefore must be the ones to negotiate with colonial officials. Those colonial authorities, however, produced a questionable treaty supposedly drafted by Penn in 1686 that allowed them to claim large portions of the contested territory. James Logan "discovered" a copy of this treaty, which allowed the English to control an area that could be walked off in a day and a half. Seeking to maintain control of at least some territory, the Haudenosaunee finally agreed to this **Walking Purchase**. The Delaware tribe, far smaller, was then pressured into letting Pennsylvania officials walk off the boundaries. Through this and

Walking Purchase
A 1737 treaty that allowed Pennsylvania to expand its boundaries at the expense of the Delaware Indians. The treaty, likely a forgery, allowed the British to add territory that could be walked off in a day and a half.

other deceptions, colonists dispossessed the Haudenosaunee and Delaware of vast lands in Pennsylvania during the first half of the eighteenth century.

However, some religiously minded immigrants worked to improve relations with American Indians in Pennsylvania, at least temporarily. The tone had been set by William Penn's Quakers, who generally accepted American Indian land claims and tried to pursue honest and fair negotiations. German Moravians, who settled in eastern Pennsylvania in the 1740s, developed good relations with area tribes. On Pennsylvania's western frontier, Scots-Irish Presbyterians established alliances with Delaware and Shawnee groups. These alliances, however, were rooted less in religious principles than in the hope of profiting from the fur trade, as these tribes sought new commercial partners when their French allies became too demanding.

▪ What were the results of William Penn's interactions with American Indians?

AP® Skills Workshop: Thinking Historically

Additional Practice in Analyzing Claims and Evidence in Secondary Sources

Below is an excerpt from the article "The Devil, The Body, and the Feminine Soul in Puritan New England." First, in a single sentence, and in your own words, summarize the claim that Elizabeth Reis makes about women in colonial New England. Then, write one to two sentences identifying two examples of evidence that Reis uses to **support** her claim. Your evidence should be *specific historical information* that Reis uses to prove her claim. Finally, in one to two sentences, **explain** how the evidence you collected from Reis's article supports her **claim**.

> "The body, for its part, also entangled women. Puritans believed that Satan attacked the soul by assaulting the body, and that because women's bodies were weaker, the devil could reach women's souls more easily, breaching these 'weaker vessels' with greater frequency. Not only was the body the means toward possessing the soul, it was the very expression of the devil's attack. Among witches, the body clearly manifested the soul's acceptance of the diabolical covenant.
>
> Women were in a double bind during witchcraft episodes. Their souls, strictly speaking, were no more evil than those of men, but the representation of the vulnerable, unsatisfied, and yearning female soul, passively waiting for Christ but always ready to succumb to the devil, inadvertently implicated corporeal women themselves. The representation of the soul in terms of worldly gender arrangements, the understanding of women in terms of the characteristics of the feminine soul, in a circular fashion led Puritans to imagine that women were more likely than men to submit to Satan. A woman's feminine soul, jeopardized in a woman's feminine body, was frail, submissive, and passive—qualities that most New Englanders thought would allow her to become either a wife to Christ or a drudge to Satan."

Excerpt from Elizabeth Reis, "The Devil, the Body, and the Feminine Soul in Puritan New England," *Journal of American History*, vol. 82, no. 1, June 1995, pp. 15–36, https://doi.org/10.2307/2081913.

The Eighteenth-Century Atlantic Economy

MODULE 2.4

FOCUS

During the eighteenth century, the combined forces of global trade and international warfare altered the political and economic calculations of imperial powers. This was especially true for British North America, where colonists settled as families and created towns that provided key markets for Britain's commercial expansion. Over the course of the century, British colonists became increasingly avid consumers of products from around the world. Meanwhile, the king and Parliament sought greater control over these far-flung commercial networks.

As you read this module, think about the effects of the economic and political developments you encounter, and be sure to consider the reasons why they occurred. In other words, why did a particular development lead to the results that followed? Think about the ways important effects led, in turn, to subsequent effects.

Colonial Traders Join Global Networks

In the late seventeenth and early eighteenth centuries, trade became truly global. Not only did goods from China, India, the Middle East, Africa, and North America become desirable in England and the rest of Europe, but the tastes of European consumers also helped shape goods produced in other parts of the world. For instance, by the early eighteenth century, the Chinese manufactured porcelain teapots and bowls specifically for the English market. Similarly, European tastes shaped the trade in cloth, tea, tobacco, and sugar.

The exploitation of enslaved African laborers also contributed significantly to this global commerce. They were considered a crucial item of trade in their own right, and their labor in the Americas ensured steady supplies of sugar, rice, tobacco, and indigo for the world market.

By the early eighteenth century, both the volume and the diversity of goods multiplied. Silk, calico, porcelain, and other items were carried from the East to Europe and the American colonies. The colonies filled returning ships with cod, mackerel, shingles, pine boards, barrel staves, rum, sugar, rice, and tobacco. A lively trade also grew up within North America as New England fishermen, New York and Charleston merchants, and Caribbean planters met one another's needs. Salted cod and mackerel flowed to the Caribbean, and rum, molasses, and enslaved people flowed back to the mainland. This commerce required ships, barrels, docks, warehouses, and wharves, all of which ensured a lively trade in naval stores such as lumber, tar, pitch, rope, and rosin.

A flow of information was critical to the flow of goods and credit. During this time, coffeehouses flourished in port cities around the Atlantic, providing access to the latest news. Merchants, ship captains, and traders met in person to discuss new ventures and to learn of recent developments. British and American newspapers reported on parliamentary legislation, commodity prices in India and Great Britain, the state of trading

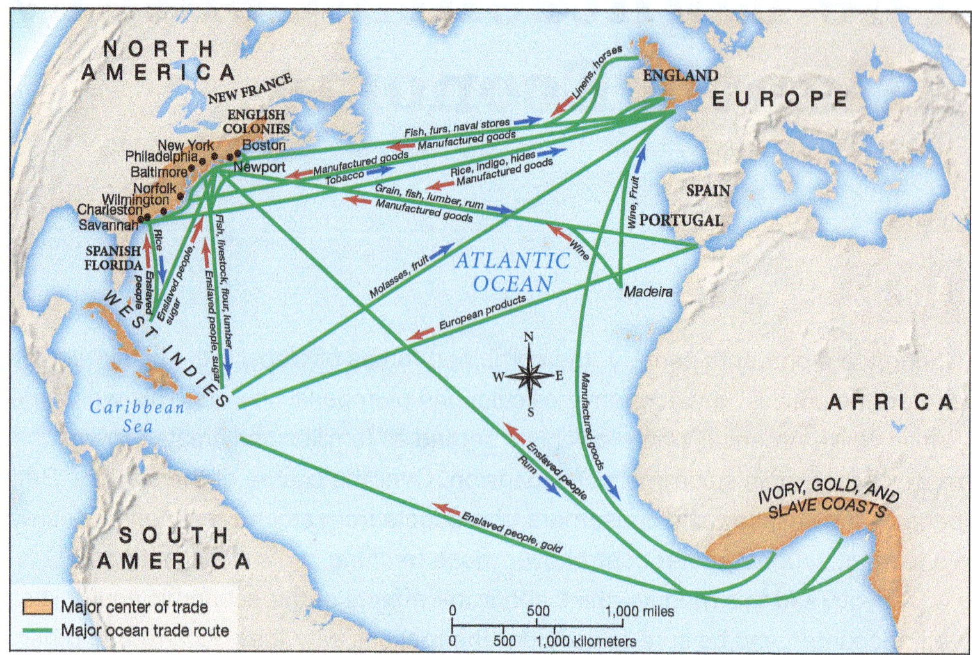

MAP 2.6 North Atlantic Trade in the Eighteenth Century North Atlantic trade provided various parts of the British empire with raw materials, manufactured goods, and labor. People and goods were exchanged among four key points: the West Indies, mainland North America, West Africa, and Great Britain.

Describe the effects of the North Atlantic trade on two of the regions shown on this map.

houses in China, the outbreak of disease in foreign ports, and investing opportunities in London. These markets were volatile. Speculative bubbles expanded all too often and burst, bankrupting thousands of overextended investors.

REVIEW

- How did the transatlantic trade network create a common British Atlantic culture?

Imperial Policies Focus on Profits

European rulers worked to ensure that this international trade and their colonial possessions benefited their own treasuries. Spain's royal monopolies and restrictions on trade were attempts to protect its domestic manufacturing and traditional arrangements of aristocratic power. Using this model, Spain initially extracted vast quantities of gold and silver from the Americas. When those natural resources were exhausted, though, these strategies were not able to maintain the Spanish empire's prosperity and stability.

mercantilism

An economic system centered on maintaining a favorable balance of trade for the home country, with more gold and silver flowing into that country than flowed out. Seventeenth- and eighteenth-century British colonial policy was largely shaped by mercantilism.

By the mid-seventeenth century, it was clear that a different approach to generating colonial wealth was necessary. Eventually, both French King Louis XIV and his English rivals embraced a system known as **mercantilism**, which centered on the maintenance of a favorable balance of trade, with more gold and silver flowing into the home country than flowed out. France refined the system. Beginning in the 1660s, Louis XIV taxed foreign imports while removing all barriers to trade within French territories. Colonies provided valuable raw materials that could be used to produce manufactured items for sale to foreign nations and to colonists.

While France's mercantile system was limited by the size of its empire, England benefited more fully from such policies. The English crown had access to a far wider array of natural resources from which to manufacture goods. In 1651, under Oliver Cromwell, Parliament passed the first Navigation Act, which King Charles II renewed in 1660 after the restoration.

Over the next three decades, Parliament passed a series of **Navigation Acts** that required merchants to conduct trade with English colonies in English-owned ships. In addition, certain items imported from foreign ports had to be carried in English ships or in ships with predominantly English crews. Finally, a list of "enumerated articles"—including tobacco, cotton, sugar, and indigo—had to be shipped from the colonies to England before being re-exported to foreign ports. Thus, the crown benefited directly and indirectly from nearly all commerce conducted by its colonies. While colonies were hurt by these limitations on their trade, they also sometimes benefited, such as when Parliament helped subsidize the development of indigo in South Carolina.

Navigation Acts
Acts passed by Parliament in the 1650s and 1660s that prohibited smuggling, established guidelines for legal commerce, and set duties on trade items.

WORKING with EVIDENCE

Source: British Parliament, *Navigation Act*, 1660

> "Be it enacted, etc., that no commodity of the growth, production, or manufacture of Europe, shall be imported into any . . . colony, territory, or place, to his Majesty belonging . . . in Asia, Africa, or America . . ., but which shall be . . . shipped in England . . . in English-built shipping . . .; and whereof . . . three fourths of the mariners, at least, are English, and which shall be carried directly thence to the said . . . colonies . . . and from no other place or places whatsoever; . . . under the penalty of the loss of all such commodities. . . ."

Questions for Analysis

1. Identify the rules that regulated exports to the colonies.
2. Describe the penalties for merchants who broke these rules.
3. Explain the reasons governing authorities in England could have used to justify the Navigation Acts.

In 1663, Parliament expanded its imperial reach through additional Navigation Acts, which required that goods sent from Europe to English colonies also pass through British ports. And a decade later, ship captains had to pay a duty or post bond before carrying enumerated articles between colonial ports. These acts ensured not only greater British control over shipping but also additional revenue for the crown, as captains paid duties in West Indies, mainland North American, and British ports. Beginning in 1673, England sent customs officials to the colonies to enforce the various parliamentary acts. By 1680, London, Bristol, and Liverpool all thrived as barrels of sugar and tobacco and stacks of deer and beaver skins were unloaded and bolts of dyed cloth and cases of metal tools and guns were put on board for the return voyage.

As mechanization and manufacturing expanded in England, Parliament sought to keep the profits at home by suppressing the growth of industry in the colonies. It thus prohibited the sale of products such as American-made textiles (1699), hats (1732), and iron goods (1750). In addition, Parliament worked to restrict trade among the North American colonies, especially between those on the mainland and in the West Indies.

AP® EXAM TIP
Mercantilism and the development of an Atlantic economy are required in the AP® Course and Exam Description. The concepts, which overlap, are often used as the main topics in long essay questions on the AP® Exam. Be able to give in-depth definitions for each, and try to describe how these two developments shaped each other.

A View of Charleston, South Carolina (c. 1760s) This eighteenth-century oil painting by English artist Thomas Mellish offers a view of Charleston harbor, c. 1760s. A ship flying an English flag sails in the foreground. The other ships and small boats along with the substantial buildings surrounding the harbor reflect Charleston's status as one of the main commercial centers of the North American colonies.

Based on this painting, how did the English view colonial cities?

REVIEW

- In what ways was mercantilism both a continuation of and a change in British policies toward its North American colonies?

Mercantilism Changes Colonial Societies

Despite the increasing regulation, American colonists could own British ships and transport goods produced in the colonies. Indeed, by the mid-eighteenth century, North American merchants oversaw 75 percent of the trade in manufactures sent from Bristol and London to the colonies and 95 percent of the trade with the West Indies. Ironically, then, a system established to benefit Great Britain ended up creating a mercantile elite in its North American colonies. Most of those merchants traded in goods, but some traded in human cargo.

The Atlantic slave trade generated enormous wealth for colonial elites like merchants, investors, and plantation owners. These funds helped turn North American seaport cities into thriving urban centers. North American seaports such as Charleston, with their elegant homes, fine shops, and lively social seasons, captured the most dynamic aspects of colonial life. Just as important, communities that were once largely rural—like Salem, Massachusetts, and Wilmington, Delaware—grew into thriving commercial centers in the late seventeenth century. Although cities like New York, Boston, Philadelphia, Baltimore, and Charleston contained less than 10 percent of the colonial population, they served as focal points of economic, political, social, and cultural activity during the eighteenth century.

consumer revolution

A process during the seventeenth and eighteenth centuries through which status in the colonies became more closely linked to financial success and a refined lifestyle rather than birth and family pedigree.

Affluent urban families created a **consumer revolution** in North America. Changing patterns of consumption challenged traditional definitions of status. Less tied to birth and family pedigree, status in the colonies became more closely linked to financial success and a refined lifestyle. Successful British men of humble origins and even those of Dutch, Scottish, French, and Jewish heritage might join the British-dominated colonial gentry.

While some certainly worried about the concentration of wealth in too few hands, most colonial elites in the early eighteenth century happily displayed their profits. Leading merchants in Boston, Salem, New York, and Philadelphia copied British styles and built fine dwellings that had separate rooms for sleeping, eating, and entertaining guests. Mercantile

Pictorial Press Ltd/Alamy

Industrious Americans in Boston, 1770 This English engraving appeared as a broadsheet (a kind of poster to spread news) in London. It depicts American colonists engaged in agricultural and artisanal labors on the outskirts of Boston.

Compare this image to the painting of the Charleston port on page 102. What similarities and differences do you notice? What accounts for both?

elites also redesigned the urban landscape, donating money for brick churches and stately town halls. They constructed new roads, wharves, and warehouses to facilitate trade, and they donated funds for the construction of bowling greens and public gardens.

The spread of international commerce created a lively cultural life and great affluence in colonial cities. The colonial elite replicated British fashions, including elaborate tea rituals. In Boston, the wives of merchants served fine teas imported from East Asia in cups and saucers from China, while decorated bowls held sugar from the West Indies.

However, a colonial elite emerged within view of growing inequality. Increasing income gaps and differences in property ownership accelerated in the eighteenth century. The frequent wars of the late seventeenth and early eighteenth centuries contributed to these economic and social divisions by boosting the profits of merchants, shipbuilders, and artisans. They temporarily improved the wages of seamen as well. But in their aftermath, rising prices, falling wages, and a lack of jobs led to the concentration of wealth in fewer hands.

Economic trends and migration to the British North American colonies produced growing numbers of young people seeking land and employment. Thus, many free laborers migrated from town to town and from country to city seeking work. They hoped to find farmers who needed extra hands for planting and harvesting, ship captains and contractors who would hire them to load or unload cargo or assist in the construction of homes and churches, or wealthy families who needed cooks, laundresses, or nursemaids.

Seasonal and temporary demands for labor created a mass of transient workers described as "the strolling poor." Many New England towns developed systems to "warn out" those who were not official residents. Modeled after the British system, warning-out was meant to ensure that strangers did not become public dependents. Still, being warned did not mean immediate removal. Sometimes, transients were simply warned that they were not eligible for aid given to the poor. At other times, local officials returned them to an earlier place of residence. In many ways, warning-out served as an early registration system, allowing authorities to encourage the flow of labor, keep residents under surveillance, and protect the town's finances. But it seldom aided those in need of work.

Residents who were eligible for public assistance might be given food and clothing or boarded with a local family. Many towns began appointing Overseers of the Poor to deal with the growing problem of poverty. By 1750, every seaport city had constructed an almshouse that sheltered residents without other means of support. In 1723, the Bridewell prison was added to Boston Almshouse, built in 1696. Then, in 1739, a workhouse was opened on the same site to employ the "able-bodied" poor in hopes that profits from it would help fund the almshouse and prison. Still, these efforts at relief fell far short of the need, especially in hard economic times.

Meanwhile, in the rural countryside, where the vast majority of colonial Americans lived, families remained the central unit of economic organization. Yet even farms were affected by the transatlantic circulation of goods and people. In areas along the Atlantic coast, rural families were drawn into commercial networks in a variety of ways. Towns and cities needed large supplies of vegetables, meat, butter, barley, wheat, and yarn. Farm families sold these goods to residents and bought sugar, tea, and other imported items that diversified their diet. Few rural families purchased ornamental or luxury items, but cloth or cheese bought in town saved hours of labor at home.

REVIEW

- What cultural changes did British North Americans experience in the early 1700s?

AP® Skills Workshop: Writing Historically

Responding to a Short-Answer Question with a Secondary Source

As you progress through this course, you will have many chances to practice different historical thinking skills and reasoning processes both to convey your historical knowledge and to make a compelling argument. Let's look at a Short-Answer Question (SAQ) that uses a single secondary source, in this case a map, and asks you to *compare* elements of the map to make your **claims**, which you will support with **evidence**.

European Empires in North America (1715–1750)

(continued)

Using the map, answer **A**, **B**, and **C**.

(A) Briefly explain ONE similarity between the settlement patterns of the British and the French in North America between 1715 and 1750.
(B) Briefly explain ONE difference between the settlement patterns of the British and the French in North America between 1715 and 1750.
(C) Briefly explain how the settlement patterns of the French OR the British shaped the economics of that empire in North America.

Step 1 ▶ Break down the prompts

Notice that each of the prompts in this question asks you to do ONE thing. In the first (A), you must identify one similarity between the settlement patterns of the British and the French. In the second (B), you must identify one difference. And in the third (C), you must explain how the settlement patterns of either the British or the French shaped the economics of that empire in North America. In A, B, and C, you need to make a **claim**, **support** that claim with evidence, and **explain** how your evidence supports your claim (**CSE**).

Step 2 ▶ List and categorize relevant information from the secondary source

As with all AP® questions that include a stimulus (a map, image, graph, chart, or written text), you will have to both understand the stimulus and apply your historical knowledge to answer the question. In the case of this SAQ, notice that the map shows you both *where* in North America the French and British settled, and around *what* geographic features both settled. This information will take you a long way to answering parts A and B, because comparing each requires only an understanding of the map. Your list of similarities and differences might look something like this:

Similarities	Differences
Both the British and the French settled around waterways **[claim]** like the Great Lakes, the Mississippi and St. Lawrence Rivers, and the Atlantic Ocean **[support with evidence]**. This settlement near water is a similarity between the British and the French **[explain]**.	The French settled mainly along rivers and lakes, whereas the British settled along the ocean **[claim]**. For example, most of the French colonists settled around the Great Lakes and the Mississippi and St. Lawrence Rivers, but the British colonized the coasts along the Atlantic Ocean **[support with evidence]**. This French settlement around lakes and rivers and the British settlement along the ocean represent a difference between their settlement patterns **[explain]**.
Both the British and the French settled large land areas in North America **[claim]**. The French took over much of what would become Canada and explored down the Mississippi River to the Gulf of Mexico, and the British colonies ranged from as far north as New England down to the borders of Spanish Florida **[support with evidence]**. The large land area of British and French settlement represents a similarity between them **[explain]**.	The French settled the northeastern and central portions of North America, whereas the British tended to settle along the eastern seaboard **[claim]**. Because of English settlement along the eastern seaboard, the French dominated the St. Lawrence River and most of Canada, whereas the British, who depended upon Atlantic trade and crop production, settled along the Atlantic Ocean **[support with evidence]**. The French settlements in the far north and the British settlements along the eastern seaboard represent a difference between the French and British settlement patterns **[explain]**.

(continued)

Both the British and the French had not settled the interior of North America by 1750 **[claim]**. The interior of North America was largely unexplored, mountainous, and controlled by many native nations **[support with evidence]**. Because of these factors, neither the British nor the French had settled in the interior portions of North America by 1750 **[explain]**.	French settlement patterns showed their dependence on rivers, like the St. Lawrence and Mississippi Rivers, whereas the British settlement pattern showed their dependence upon Atlantic trade **[claim]**. The French depended upon rivers for trade and access to the ocean to trade furs, whereas the British needed direct access to the Atlantic along the coast to sell cash crops grown in the North American interior **[support with evidence]**. The French dependence on the Mississippi and St. Lawrence Rivers and the British dependence on the Atlantic led to their different settlement patterns **[explain]**.

Now you're ready to answer A and B. When you do, be sure to present each answer with a **claim** that is supported by **evidence**. Let's use the second two examples from the chart above:

(A) Both the British and the French settled large land areas in North America **[claim]**. The French took over much of what would become Canada and explored down the Mississippi River to the Gulf of Mexico, while the British colonies ranged from as far north as New England down to the borders of Spanish Florida **[support with evidence]**. The large land area of British and French settlement represents a similarity between them **[explain]**.

(B) The French settled the northeastern and central portions of North America, whereas the British tended to settle along the eastern seaboard **[claim]**. Because of English settlement along the eastern seaboard, the French dominated the St. Lawrence River and most of Canada, whereas the British, dependent upon Atlantic trade and crop production, settled along the Atlantic Ocean **[support with evidence]**. The French settlements in the far north and the British settlements along the eastern seaboard represent a difference between the French and British settlement patterns **[explain]**.

Step 3 ▶ Explain historical information related to the economies of the French and British colonies in North America based on their settlement patterns

Now you're ready to tackle part C, which requires you to know something about one of these empire's economies, and to explain how that economic system was related to information in the map.

Let's use our second set of examples again from our list above. We already established that both the British and the French settled large areas, and each settled along different waterways. Let's choose the French for our explanation of how settlement patterns shaped that empire's economy in North America:

(C) The French depended on trade in furs, which were abundant in French North America **[claim]**. They transported these furs along the river systems of North America, which gave them access to overseas trade **[support with evidence]**. This fur trade shaped the French colonial economy in North America by creating a colony less dependent on trade in cash crops than the British **[explain]**.

ACTIVITY

Now, using the same map, answer A, B, and C on your own. Feel free to use the chart above to help you. For part C, explain how British settlement patterns shaped that empire's economy in North America. Be sure that each of your responses makes a claim and provides evidence to support that claim.

Interactions between American Indians and Europeans

MODULE
2.5

FOCUS

Throughout the early and mid-seventeenth century, English, Dutch, and French colonists profited from trade relations and military alliances with American Indian nations. Nonetheless, European demands for land fueled repeated conflicts with tribes. Already devastated by European-borne diseases, their very survival was at stake. Not all Europeans interacted with American Indians the same way. A comparison of the ways in which the English, Dutch, and French interacted with native peoples reveals important similarities and differences among them.

In the last Writing Historically exercise, you compared the ways in which the English and French interacted with native peoples differently. In this module, you will further explore the ways European colonizers interacted with American Indians before 1754. Each time you note similarities or differences, think critically about both the reasons for those similarities between different societies as well as the differences.

English colonists most often followed the example that the Spanish set before them, taking American Indian land by force. Most English colonists rebuffed American Indian efforts at trade in favor of theft and conflict from the very start—examples of this include the earliest years in Jamestown, when colonists preferred to beg, borrow, or steal American Indian goods rather than produce their own, and the atrocities committed by Pilgrim Captain Myles Standish in New England during the first half of the seventeenth century. Such aggressive policies created a frontier of exclusion in which American Indians were not welcome in English communities.

Continued intrusions on American Indians' lands led to the **Anglo-Powhatan Wars** in 1620s Virginia, and the Pequot War with New England Puritans in the 1630s (see Module 2.3). These wars, combined with the devastation of diseases brought to North America by the English, killed large percentages of American Indians in every colonial region and opened up lands to be colonized by the English through the 1640s.

Anglo-Powhatan Wars Series of conflicts in the 1620s between the Powhatan Confederacy and English settlers in Virginia and Maryland.

By contrast, colonization by the Dutch in New Amsterdam, and the French in the Great Lakes, succeeded mainly through trade with American Indians, although both European settlements also spread disease in their interactions with native peoples. These commercial alliances led to fewer violent conflicts in the first half of the seventeenth century. However, both of these nations sent far fewer colonists to North America, and as a result, they were significantly less motivated to invade American Indian land than the English.

A few English colonists followed a more peaceable route. For example, in New England, Roger Williams purchased the lands for his Rhode Island colony from local tribes. A small number of Puritans led by missionary John Eliot attempted to establish "praying towns," communities in which Puritan missionaries taught American Indians how to read the Bible, and a few American Indian students even attended Harvard College. Most "praying Indians," however, continued to embrace traditional rituals and beliefs alongside Christian practices. The efforts produced few lasting converts, and the lack of acceptance of American Indians within Puritan society at large persisted.

American Indians Resist European Intrusion

The European conflicts in North America put incredible pressure on American Indian peoples to choose sides. Although it was increasingly difficult for native peoples in colonized areas to remain autonomous, American Indian nations were not simply pawns of European powers. Some actively sought European allies against their native enemies, and nearly all desired European trade goods like cloth, guns, and horses. Moreover, struggles among English, French, and Spanish forces both reinforced conflicts among American Indian peoples that existed before European settlement and created new ones.

Colonial conflicts with American Indians started almost immediately in New England and continued with the Pequot War of 1636 to 1638. War broke out again in the 1670s, this time with the Wampanoag Indians, in Metacom's War (see Module 2.3). As the war dragged on, it became increasingly brutal on both sides, and about quarter of the remaining American Indian population of New England died between 1675 and 1676.

The trade in guns was especially significant in escalating conflicts among tribes during the late seventeenth century. By then, the English were willing to trade guns for American Indian captives sold as enslaved labor. American Indians had always taken captives in war, but some of those captives had been adopted into the victorious nation. This changed as the English in Carolina began exchanging guns for captives, shipping most to Caribbean plantations. As slave trading spread, more peaceful tribes were forced to acquire guns for self-protection, further escalating raiding by American Indian foes and enslavement. These raids also had the effect of forcing many American Indian nations off traditional lands.

These dynamics eventually led to two major early eighteenth-century conflicts in the Carolinas: the **Tuscarora War** (1711–1715), in which British, Dutch, and German colonists banded together against the Tuscarora Indians, and the **Yamasee War** (1715–1717), won by the English against a coalition of several American Indian nations. Although the English victories had high costs, in terms of both lives and money, they opened up the interior of North America for expanded English settlement, ensuring the growth of the plantation system.

Tuscarora War
A war launched by Tuscarora Indians from 1711 to 1715 against European settlers in North Carolina and their allies from the Yamasee, Catawba, and Cherokee nations.

Yamasee War
A war from 1715 to 1717 led by the Yamasee confederation, which intended, but failed, to oust the British from South Carolina.

In the aftermath of both wars, the Creek emerged as a powerful new confederation, and the Cherokee became the major trading partner of the British. The Yamasee nation was seriously weakened. The Tuscarora tribe lost their lands when they signed the peace treaty, and many then joined the Haudenosaunee (Iroquois) Confederacy to the north. Moreover, as the British gained a Cherokee alliance, their Creek and Caddo enemies reacted by strengthening their alliance with the French. American Indians, however, still continued raids into the Carolinas into the 1720s and 1730s.

REVIEW

- How were English and French interactions with American Indians during this era similar, and in what ways did they differ?

European Rivalry and American Indian Alliances

Developments in North America in the late seventeenth and early eighteenth centuries were driven as much by events in Europe as by those in the colonies. From 1689 until 1713, Europe was in an almost constant state of war, with continental conflicts spilling over into colonial possessions in North America. The result was increased tensions among colonists of different nationalities, American Indians and colonists, and colonists and their home countries.

France was at the center of much of the European warfare of the period, as Louis XIV hoped to expand France's borders and gain supremacy in Europe. To this end, he built a powerful professional army under state authority. Between 1689 and 1697, France and England fought their first sustained war in North America, King William's War (see Module 2.3). The war began over conflicting French and English interests on the European continent, but it soon spread to the American frontier when English and Haudenosaunee (Iroquois) forces attacked French and Huron settlements around Montreal and northern New York.

Although neither side had gained significant territory when peace was declared in 1697, the war had important consequences. Many colonists serving in the English army died of battle wounds, smallpox, and inadequate rations. Those who survived resented their treatment and the unnecessary deaths of so many comrades.

The Haudenosaunee fared even worse. Their fur trade was devastated, and hundreds of Mohawks and Oneidas were forced to flee from France's American Indian allies along the eastern Great Lakes. After a few more years of fighting against French-allied tribes, the Haudenosaunee agreed to remain neutral in all future European conflicts. Weary of further European entanglements, Haudenosaunee leaders focused on rebuilding their tattered confederacy.

A second lengthy conflict, known as the War of the Spanish Succession, or **Queen Anne's War** (1702–1713), had even more devastating effects on North America. The conflict erupted in Europe when the Spanish monarch died without an heir, launching a contest for the Spanish kingdom and its colonies. France and Spain squared off against England, the Netherlands, Austria, and Prussia. In North America, however, England alone faced France and Spain, with each nation hoping to gain additional territory. Both sides recruited American Indian allies.

AP® EXAM TIP

Be able to select an example of a Native American tribe, band, or confederacy resisting and accommodating British North American colonists. Identifying specific historical examples is a necessary aspect of detailing broader concepts such as resistance and accommodation.

Queen Anne's War

A war from 1702 to 1713 over control of Spain and its colonies; also known as the War of the Spanish Succession.

AP® WORKING with EVIDENCE

Source: Thomas Oliver, writing on behalf of the colonial government of Massachusetts, Letter to Queen Anne, 1708

> "[T]heir skill and dexterity for the making and Using of [canoes] is very extraordinary, which renders our Tiresome marches after them Ineffectual. These Rebels have no fixt Settlements, but are Ambulatory, & make frequent removes. . . . [T]hey are supported and Encouraged by the french, who make them yearly Presents . . . of Clothing, Armes and Ammunition, Besides the Supply they Afford them for the Beaver and Furrs, which they take in hunting, and Constantly keep their Priests & Emissaries among them, to steady them in their Interests, and the bigotries . . . [which] they have Instilled into them. [T]he most probable Method of doing Execution upon them & Reduceing them, is by men of their own Colour, way & manner of living. And if yor Majesty

> shall be Graciously pleased to Command the Service of the Mohawks, and other Nations of the Western Indians that are in friendship . . . with your . . . [Majesty's] Several Governments, [t]hey would with the Blessing of God in Short time [destroy] or Reclaim them, and prevent the Incursions made upon us from Canada or the East."

Questions for Analysis

1. Identify Oliver's proposed solution to American Indian raids in Massachusetts.
2. Describe the tactics employed by American Indians and their French allies in this excerpt.
3. Explain how this document reveals the connection between mercantilism and conflicts in the Americas during the late 1600s and early 1700s.

After more than a decade of savage fighting, Queen Anne's War ended in 1713 with the **Treaty of Utrecht**, which aimed to secure a lasting peace by balancing the interests of the great powers in Europe and their colonial possessions. Although the Treaty of Utrecht was intended to bring peace by establishing a balance of power, imperial conflict continued to escalate. England benefited the most in North America as France surrendered Newfoundland, Nova Scotia, and the Hudson Bay territory to England, while Spain granted control of St. Kitts in the West Indies, Gibraltar, and Minorca as well as the right to sell African slaves in its American colonies.

Yet neither the treaty nor Britain's gains prevented further conflict. Indeed, Spain, France, and Britain all strengthened fortifications along their North American borders.

REVIEW

- How were King William's War and Queen Anne's War similar, and in what ways did they differ?

Imperial Conflicts on the Southern Frontier

King George's War
A war from 1739 to 1748 between France, Spain, and England fought in North America. King George's War secured Georgia for the English, although Louisbourg was ceded to the French in return.

From 1739 to 1748, England and Spain fought yet another war—**King George's War**—in North America. It started with Spanish anger at the founding in 1732 of the English colony of Georgia by King George II (reigned 1727–1760). Tensions between the two nations grew, and in August 1739, they erupted into violence. The Spanish navy captured English ship captain Robert Jenkins, who was trading illegally in the Spanish West Indies, and punished him by cutting off one of his ears. In response, Great Britain attacked the Spanish colony of St. Augustine (in present-day Florida) and Cartagena (in present-day Colombia). In 1742 Spain sent troops into Georgia, but the colonial militia pushed back the attack.

This American war, also known as the War of Jenkins's Ear, became part of a more general European conflict, the War of Austrian Succession. Once again, France and Spain joined forces. By the time the war ended in 1748, the British had successfully defended the future of Georgia and reaffirmed their military superiority. The British victory cost the lives of many colonial settlers and soldiers, however, and some colonists began to wonder whether their interests and those of the crown were truly the same.

King William's War (1689–1697), Queen Anne's War (1702–1713), and King George's War (1739–1748) had all failed to settle the contest for supremacy in North

America. Europeans and their American Indian allies resumed fighting a mere six years later in a new conflict: the French and Indian War (1754–1763), also known in Europe as the Seven Years' War (because it started there two years later). Early in the war, a young British officer from the colony of Virginia named George Washington led troops against the French in the Ohio River valley.

Yet another in the series of imperial contests for North America, this war too had high costs in lives and treasure. Moreover, it intensified some colonists' questioning of British colonial rule. Unlike King William's War, Queen Anne's War, and King George's War, the Seven Years' War decisively changed the balance of power in North America, setting the stage for outright conflict between British colonists and the British government.

REVIEW

- What were two of the common causes of Britain's colonial wars between 1689 and 1754?
- What were two common effects of those wars?

AP® Skills Workshop: Thinking Historically

Comparing Developments in Secondary Sources

ACTIVITY

In Module 2.2, you identified **developments** in a secondary source. Below are two secondary sources about the origins of the Yamasee War (1715–1717). In two sentences, identify the developments that led to the Yamasee War according to each historian.

Then, review the Writing Historically exercise in Module 2.4. In one to two sentences, write down one **similarity** between each historian's description of the origins of the Yamasee War and one **difference**.

> "During the first decade and a half of the 18th century, the hunting of whitetail deer, the expansion of cattle and pig raising, the rapid development of rice cultivation, and the elimination of Spanish mission Indians of Florida and Georgia combined to exhaust the Yamasee's trade resources. It was this depletion which forced the Yamasee deeper into debt and eventually into a position where war was the only alternative."

Richard L. Haan, "The 'Trade Do's Not Flourish as Formerly': The Ecological Origins of the Yamassee War of 1715," in *Ethnohistory*, vol. 28, no. 4, pp. 341–358.

> "[The Yamasee, among other indigenous people in the British American south east,] formed a coherent zone of settlement along Carolina's oldest and most lucrative trade route, extending south and southwest from Charles Town into central Georgia. . . . [T]hose [native] nations had fewer options for European trade open to them than others. They had done much

(continued)

themselves, in fact, to limit their access to alternative sources of European goods between 1680 and 1704 by assisting in the destruction of the Spanish mission system in Florida. Having thus entered into . . . [an exclusive trading] relationship with Charles Town by the first decade of the eighteenth century, one in which there is only a single buyer of goods, Yamasees . . . may have found it necessary to engage English officials more aggressively in order to affect the terms of exchange. Even so, their prominence in the historical record should not be read simply as evidence of greater victimization. In many cases, their protests suggest they were active, intelligent participants in exchange, attempting purposefully to influence and direct the process for their own advantage."

Excerpt from William L. Ramsey, "Something Cloudy in Their Looks": The Origins of the Yamasee War Reconsidered, *Journal of American History*, vol. 90, no. 1, June 2003, pp. 44–75, https://doi.org/10.2307/3659791.

Slavery in the British Colonies

MODULE 2.6

FOCUS

Slavery shaped the economy and society of British North America. While it was more prevalent in the southern colonies, its existence in the middle and northern colonies proved significant as well. Enslaved Africans and African Americans found overt and covert ways to rebel against slavery and maintain their families and distinct cultures.

As you read this module, prepare to explain causation by writing down your observations about major historical developments and the chain reaction effect of their causes. One way to help keep all of this at the forefront of your mind as you read is to periodically ask yourself why developments occurred. The overarching question you should keep in mind as you read this module is: Why did some English colonies develop economies that relied on enslaved labor?

The Human Cost of the Atlantic Slave Trade

As part of an expansion of England's role in the Atlantic slave trade, Parliament chartered the Royal African Company to bring enslaved Africans to British colonies in 1660 and then re-chartered the company after financial difficulties in 1672. Between 1700 and 1808, some three million captive Africans were carried on British and Anglo-American ships, about 40 percent of the total of those sold in the Americas in this period. Half a million Africans died on the voyage across the Atlantic. Huge numbers also died in Africa while being marched to the coast or held in forts waiting to be forced aboard ships. Yet despite this astounding death rate, the slave trade yielded enormous profits and had far-reaching consequences. In effect, the Africans whom British traders bought and sold transformed labor systems in the colonies, fueled international trade, and enriched merchants, planters, and their families and communities.

European traders worked closely with African merchants to procure their human cargo, trading muskets, metalware, and linen for men, women, and children. Originally many of those sold into slavery were war captives. African groups securing trade with Europeans rose in wealth and power, building empires and defeating rivals to conquer vast interior lands. Many Africans who traded in enslaved labor feared the consequences if their rivals secured the lucrative trade with Europeans for their guns. Over time, African traders moved farther inland to fill the demand, devastating large areas of Africa, particularly the Congo-Angola region in the southwest, which supplied some 40 percent of all enslaved people who crossed the Atlantic.

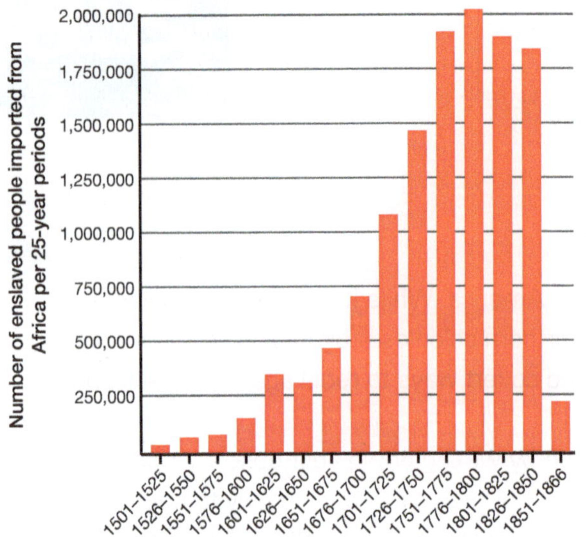

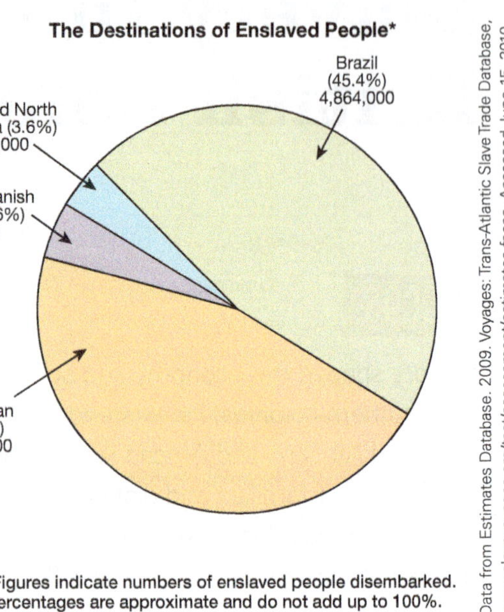

Data from Estimates Database. 2009. Voyages: Trans-Atlantic Slave Trade Database, www.slavevoyages.org/tast/assessment/estimates.faces. Accessed June 15, 2010.

The Slave Trade in Numbers, 1501–1866 Extraordinary numbers of enslaved Africans were shipped to other parts of the world from the sixteenth to the nineteenth century. The slave trade transformed mainland North America, Brazil, and the West Indies.

What broad conclusions about the transatlantic slave trade can you draw from these data?

Middle Passage

The brutal transatlantic portion of the forced journey of enslaved Africans from Africa to the Americas. Historians estimate that millions of enslaved Africans died before they arrived in the Americas.

The trip across the Atlantic, known as the **Middle Passage**, was a brutal and often deadly experience for enslaved Africans. Exhausted and undernourished by the time they boarded the large oceangoing vessels, the captives were placed in dark and crowded holds. Most had been poked and prodded by slave traders, and some had been branded to ensure that a trader received the exact individuals he had purchased. Once in the hold, they might wait for weeks before the ship finally set sail. By that time, the foul-smelling and crowded hold became a nightmare of disease and despair. There was never sufficient food or fresh water for the captives, and women especially were subject to sexual abuse by crew members. Many captives could not communicate with each other because they spoke different languages, and none of them knew exactly where they were going or what would happen when they arrived.

Those who survived the voyage were most likely to find themselves in the slave markets of Barbados or Jamaica, where they were put on display for potential buyers. Once purchased, enslaved people went through a period known as seasoning as they regained their strength, became accustomed to their new environment, learned commands in a new language, and became experts at the labor they would be forced to perform. Some did not survive seasoning, falling prey to malnutrition and disease or committing suicide. Others adapted to the new circumstances and adopted enough European or British ways to survive even as they sought means to resist the shocking and oppressive conditions.

WORKING with EVIDENCE

Source: King Charles II, *Royal African Company Charter*, 1672

"The Royal African [Company's] Limits for Trade granted them by His [Majesty's] Charter. . . .

In the River Gambia, upon James Island, the [Company] have built a Fort, where seventy men, at least, are kept. And there is a Factory from whence Elephants' Teeth, Bees-wax, and Cowhides are exported in very considerable quantities. The River Gambia is very large, and runs up very high (much higher than any discovery hath bin made) and it is supposed the Gold comes most from places, at the head of this River. . . .

The Slaves they [purchased] are sent, for a Supply of Servants, to all His [Majesty's] American Plantations which cannot subsist without them. The Gold and Elephants' Teeth, and other Commodities, which are procured in Africa, are all brought into England. The Gold is always coined in His [Majesty's] Mint. And the Elephants Teeth, and all other goods, which the Company receives, either from Africa or the Plantations, in returne for their Negros, are always sold publicly."

Questions for Analysis

1. Identify the goods the Royal African Company acquired along the coast of West Africa.
2. Describe a cause stated in this charter for the founding of the Royal African Company.
3. Explain how this document reveals the developments that led to the founding of the Royal African Company.

REVIEW

- How did the transatlantic slave trade affect the societies of both British North America and West Africa?

The Rise of Slavery Reshapes Southern Colonial Society

Societies with cash-crop plantation economies that relied in part on enslaved labor during the mid-seventeenth century transformed into societies shaped by slavery itself during the late seventeenth and early eighteenth centuries. Southern Carolina was, from the start, heavily influenced by the economies of the British West Indies, and developed from its founding as a slave society. Enslaved labor allowed plantation owners to expand cultivation of cash crops like tobacco, rice, and indigo, which promised high profits for planters as well as merchants.

These developments made southern elites more dependent on the global market and limited opportunities for poorer white people and all Black people, both free and enslaved. They also ensured that American Indians and many white colonists were pushed farther west as planters sought more land for their ventures.

In the 1660s, Virginia legislators followed a model established in Barbados by passing laws legalizing human bondage and codifying a slave society (see Module 2.2). A series of laws passed by the House of Burgesses during this time transformed the colony into a society almost completely reliant on a system of chattel slavery in which enslavement was defined as a distinct status based on racial identity and passed on through future generations. The enactment of these slave codes was driven largely by the desires for profits through a more numerous and controlled labor force, which neither the population of enslaved American Indians nor that of indentured servants was large enough to fill.

As time went on, these laws became harsher. For example, one law granted slaveholders the right to kill enslaved people who defied their authority. In 1680 it was declared illegal for "any negro or other slave to carry or arme himself with any club, staffe, gunn, sword, or any other weapon of defence or offence." Nor could enslaved people leave slaveholders' premises without a certificate of permission, a legally enforced document that regulated an enslaved person's movements. By the late seventeenth century, an enslaved mother passed on her legal status to her children, and it was illegal to free enslaved people even if they had converted to Christianity, thereby establishing enslavement as hereditary and racial.

Illustration of a Slave Trader's Ship This image, which was created during the eighteenth century, portrays people being captured in Africa alongside a ship transporting them to enslavement in the Western Hemisphere.

What is the perspective on slavery portrayed in this image?

Increasingly harsh laws in Virginia, Maryland, and North Carolina were enacted as tobacco cultivation spread across the Chesapeake and the numbers of imported enslaved Africans increased. By 1668, one-third of all Africans and African Americans in Virginia and Maryland were still free, but the percentages dwindled year by year. Once the Royal African Company started supplying the Chesapeake with enslaved people directly from Africa in the 1680s, the pace of change quickened. By 1750, out of 150,000 Black people residing in the Chesapeake, only about 5 percent remained free.

Direct importation from Africa had other negative consequences for the enslaved. Far more men than women were imported, skewing the sex ratio and making it more challenging for them to form families and communities. Enslaved women, like men, performed heavy field work. When these conditions, along with brutal work regimens, sparked resistance by the enslaved, fearful whites imposed even stricter regulations, further distinguishing between white indentured servants and enslaved Black people.

While slavery in the Carolinas was influenced by developments in the Chesapeake, it was shaped even more directly by practices in the British West Indies. During the late seventeenth century, many wealthy families from Barbados, Antigua, and other sugar islands also established plantations in the Carolinas. At first, they brought enslaved people from the West Indies to oversee cattle and pigs and assist in the slaughter of livestock and curing of meat for shipment back to the West Indies. Some enslaved laborers grew rice, using techniques learned in West Africa, to supplement their diet. Slaveholders soon realized that rice might prove very profitable. Although not widely eaten in northern Europe, it could provide cheap and nutritious food for sailors, orphans, convicts, and peasants. Thus, relying initially on enslaved Africans' knowledge, planters began cultivating rice for export.

As rice cultivation expanded, slavery in the southern Carolinas turned more brutal, just as slavery in Virginia had. Harsher and harsher slave codes were enacted to ensure control of the growing labor force. No longer could enslaved people carry guns, join militias, meet in groups, or travel without a pass. Colonial authorities initiated military patrols by whites to enforce laws and labor practices. Some plantations along the Carolina coast turned into camps where thousands of enslaved people worked under harsh conditions of the "**gang labor**" system, in which large groups of enslaved people were forced to work at a rapid pace under the direction of an overseer to ensure extensive cultivation of a cash crop. Gang labor proved to be particularly harsh.

gang labor
A system to produce cash crops based on dividing a work force into "gangs" who work at a consistent pace at a designated task. This labor system was used to produce cash crops in the eighteenth century mainly in the southern colonies, where enslaved people were forced to work long hours in harsh conditions in a highly regulated manner.

By 1720, Black people outnumbered white people in the Carolinas, and fears of slave rebellions inspired South Carolina officials to impose even harsher laws and more brutal enforcement measures. When indigo was introduced as a cash crop in the 1740s, the demand for enslaved labor increased further. Although far fewer enslaved people—about 40,000—resided in South Carolina than in the Chesapeake, they already constituted more than 60 percent of the colony's total population by 1750.

During the mid-eighteenth century, Africans and African Americans formed only a small percentage of the northern population: just 5 percent of the combined populations of the middle colonies and New England. Some enslaved Black people worked on agricultural estates in the Hudson River valley and New Jersey, and even more labored as household servants, dockworkers, seamen, and blacksmiths in New York City alongside British colonists and European immigrants.

Fertility rates among enslaved Africans and African Americans were much lower than those among whites in the early eighteenth century, and fewer infants survived to adulthood. It was not until the 1740s that the majority of enslaved people was born in the colonies rather than imported, as some southern slaveholders began to realize that encouraging reproduction gave them economic benefits. Still, enslaved women, most of whom worked in the fields, gained only minimal relief from assigned work during pregnancy.

- How did economic trends shape slave laws in the southern colonies?

Africans Resist Enslavement

Enslaved laborers in British North America resisted their subjugation in a variety of ways. They secretly tried to retain customs, belief systems, languages, and naming practices from their homelands. They also secretly broke tools, burned down buildings, ruined stored seeds with moisture, stole livestock and food, and faked illness. Some even poisoned slaveholders. They openly resisted, too, challenging slaveholders and overseers by refusing to work or running away. Some fought back physically in the face of punishment for disrupting whites' authority. A few planned revolts.

The consequences for resisting were severe, from whipping, mutilation, and branding to summary execution. Southern white people, living amid large numbers of Black people, were deeply concerned about resistance and rebellion and often punished people falsely accused of planning revolts. As more enslaved people were imported directly from Africa, both the fear and the reality of rebellion increased.

AP® EXAM TIP

The AP® Course and Exam Description calls for you to be able to explain how enslaved people reacted to enslavement. These reactions ranged from resisting enslavement through overt and covert means to creating new cultures and negotiating the terms of their labor. Be able to create explanations for each of these reactions and try to add more specific information in your response.

Stono Rebellion

A 1739 uprising by enslaved Africans and African Americans in South Carolina, which intensified white fear of slave revolts.

In New York City in 1712, several dozen enslaved Africans and American Indians set fire to a building. When white people rushed to the scene, the insurgents attacked them with clubs, pistols, axes, and staves, killing eight and injuring many more. The rebels were soon defeated by the militia. Authorities executed eighteen insurgents, burning several at the stake as a warning to others, while six of those imprisoned committed suicide.

In 1741, a series of suspicious fires in the city led to accusations against a white couple who owned an alehouse where Black people gathered to drink. To protect herself from prosecution, an Irish indentured servant testified that she had overheard discussions of an elaborate plot involving Black and white conspirators. Frightened of any hint that the poor might band together regardless of race, authorities immediately arrested suspects and eventually executed thirty-four people, including four white people. They also banished seventy-two Black people from the city.

The most serious slave revolt, however, erupted in South Carolina, where a group of enslaved Africans led the **Stono Rebellion** in 1739. On Sunday, September 9, a group of enslaved men who had recently arrived stole weapons from a country store and killed the owners. They then marched south, along the Stono River, beating drums and recruiting others to join them. Torching plantations and killing whites along the route, they had gathered more than fifty insurgents when armed whites overtook them. In the ensuing battle, dozens of rebels died. The militia, along with American Indians hired to assist them, killed another twenty over the next two days and then captured a group of forty, who were executed without trial.

AP® WORKING with EVIDENCE

Source: George Cato, great-great-grandson of Stono Rebellion leader Cato, *Account of the Stono Rebellion, 1739*, recording, 1937

"How it all start? Dat what I ask but nobody ever tell me how 100 slaves between de Combahee and Edisto rivers come to meet in de woods not far from de Stono River on September 9, 1739. And how they elect a leader, my kinsman, Cato, and late dat day march to Stono town, break in a warehouse, kill two white men in charge, and take all de guns and ammunition they wants. But they do it. Wid dis start, they turn south and march on.

They work fast, coverin' 15 miles, passin' many fine plantations, and in every single case, stop, and break in de house and kill men, women, and children. Then they take what they want, 'cludin' arms, clothes, liquor and food.

Governor Bull and some planters . . . ride fast and spread de alarm and it wasn't long 'til de militiamen was on de trail in pursuit of de slave army. When found, many of de slaves was singin' and dancin' and Cap. Cato and some of de other leaders was cussin' at them sumpin awful. From dat day to dis, no Cato has tasted whiskey, 'less he go 'gainst his daddy's warnin'. Dis war last less than two days but it sho' was pow'ful hot while it last.

I reckons it was hot, 'cause in less than two days, 21 white men, women, and chillun, and 44 Negroes, was slain. My granddaddy say dat in de woods and at Stono, where de war start, dere was more than 100 Negroes in line. When de militia come in sight of them at Combahee swamp, de drinkin' dancin' Negroes scatter in de brush and only 44 stand deir ground.

Commander Cato speak for de crowd. He say: "We don't lak slavery. We start to [join] de Spanish in Florida. We surrender but we not whipped yet and we 'is not converted.'" De other 43 say: "Amen." They was taken, unarmed, and hanged by de militia. . . . He die but he die for doin' de right, as he see it."

Questions for Analysis

1. Identify three actions that the Stono rebels undertook as part of their rebellion.
2. Explain the goals of the Stono Rebellion, using the actions of the Stono rebels described in this document as evidence.
3. Explain how this document reveals the causes that led to the Stono Rebellion.

This revolt echoed widely in a colony where Black people outnumbered white people nearly two to one, direct importation from Africa was at an all-time high, and Spanish authorities in Florida promised freedom to enslaved people who had fled. In 1738, the Spanish governor had formed a Black militia company, and he allowed thirty-eight fugitive families to settle north of St. Augustine and build Fort Mose for their protection. When warfare erupted between Spain and Britain over commercial rivalries in 1739, the enslaved people who participated in the Stono Rebellion may have seen their chance to gain freedom as a group. But as with other rebellions, this one failed, and the price of failure was death.

REVIEW

- How did enslaved Africans and African Americans use the economic interests of slaveholders to rebel against their enslavement?

AP® Skills Workshop: Thinking Historically

Making Connections in Secondary Sources

When historians **make connections** they identify and explain how developments or processes are connected to other historical developments or processes. For a review of identifying and explaining developments and processes in secondary sources, see Module 2.2.

Identifying historical connections between developments or processes requires historians to identify common ties between two seemingly separate events or trends. These ties could have been made through a common origin, or they could be ties established through common interests or motivations.

We make connections like this all the time. For example, you and your classmates might be anxious about the AP® U.S. History Exam. While the exam might be the *cause* of your anxiety, the facts that *connect* you and your classmates are varied. You might all be in the same class together. You are all likely in the same grade. You all perhaps have the same teacher, who is also anxious about the test, and thereby making all of you a little anxious. You all will likely take the test on the same day, so watching this date get closer adds to your common anxiety. These are the factors that connect all of you in this circumstance.

ACTIVITY

Below, historian Mark Smith, writing about the Stono Rebellion (1739) in South Carolina, identifies some interesting connections between enslaved peoples' revolts in the British colony of South Carolina and the Portuguese colonies in Brazil. In three to five sentences, identify the connections that Smith makes between them.

(continued)

"[T]he evidence presented here clarifies the . . . context and content of that very bloody but spiritually meaningful rebellion. Recent work on the role of Catholicism in shaping the form and timing of slave resistance in Brazil suggests that the Stono rebels were hardly exceptional . . . in this regard. . . . Portuguese Catholicism . . . and the appearance of 'Saint Mary Our Lady, Mother of God' among the Indians conspired to promote . . . rebellion among Brazilian slaves. The rebels' . . . religion rested on a 'reinterpretation of Christianity,' and, like the Kongolese, Brazilian slaves were taught 'to say Mass in the Morning on saints days' and enjoined 'to encourage the establishment of the confraternity of Our Lady of the Rosary.' Brazilian slaves also incorporated key elements of Catholicism into their own religious beliefs. . . . Worsening social and economic conditions, an African millenarian tradition, and . . . revolutionary religious beliefs of the enslaved led to the uprising. Despite the tendency for some earlier scholars to 'reject the relevance of the U.S. South to Brazil because the slave religions of the United States came out of a Protestant tradition,' and notwithstanding the scholarly emphasis on the revolutionary theology of Afro-Protestantism, the arguments presented here . . . suggest that Afro-Catholicism was an important influence on organized resistance in both regions. Slaves in Brazil and South Carolina both used a syncretic [combining of various religious traditions] version of Catholicism—one anchored to varying degrees in the image Virgin Mary—to shape . . . their resistance."

Excerpt from Mark M. Smith, "Remembering Mary, Shaping Revolt: Reconsidering the Stono Rebellion." *The Journal of Southern History*, vol. 67, no. 3, August 2001, p. 513.

Colonial Society and Culture

MODULE

2.7

FOCUS

During the early eighteenth century, challenges to the culture of traditional patriarchy and religion in the colonies sparked a religious response. Young people experienced increased independence from their parents and developed tighter bonds with siblings, cousins, and neighbors their own age. Colonial people in general had greater mobility, moving more often in the dynamic economy. Further, towns and cities developed clearer hierarchies by class and status, which at times protected wealthier individuals from punishment for misdeeds and undermined social confidence in the patriarchal order.

The practices of traditional religion faced challenges as well: generally reduced religious enthusiasm during the later seventeenth century led some to believe that new approaches to religion were needed to correct society's ills. The combined contexts of a more open, less patriarchal society, and the failure of traditional religion to inspire devout Christian followers unleashed powerful religious forces—later called the First Great Awakening—that swept through the colonies in the early eighteenth century.

As you read this module, pay careful attention to historical developments, including simultaneous historical events, that help explain the era discussed in this module. Remember also to consider how context shapes the most important events you read about and to periodically ask yourself why important developments occurred. The overarching question you should keep in mind as you read this module is: What aspects of the Enlightenment and First Great Awakening led to fragmentation in colonial society, and why?

Colonial Family Life and the Limits of Patriarchal Order

By the early eighteenth century, many colonial writers promoted the idea of marriage as a partnership, even if the wife remained the junior partner. This concept took practical form in communities across the colonies. In towns, the wives of artisans often learned aspects of their husband's craft and helped oversee as well as care for apprentices, journeymen, and laborers.

Colonial mothers likewise combined childbearing and child rearing with a great deal of other work. Infants were the most vulnerable to disease, and childbirth was also a dangerous ordeal for colonial women. In 1700, roughly one out of thirty births ended in the mother's death. Women who bore six to eight children thus regularly faced death. When a mother died while her children were still young, her husband was likely to remarry soon afterward to maintain the family and his livelihood. Even though fathers held legal guardianship over their children, child care undoubtedly was women's work.

While most families accepted the idea of female subordination in return for patriarchal protection, signs of change emerged in the early eighteenth century. Ads for runaway spouses, servants, and enslaved people; reports of domestic violence; poems about bossy wives; petitions for divorce; and legal suits charging rape, seduction, or breach of contract make clear that ideals of patriarchal authority did not always match the reality. A variety of evidence points to increasing tensions around issues of control—by husbands over wives, fathers over children, and men over women.

In New England, colonial law allowed divorce, but few were granted, and almost none to women, before 1750. In other colonies, divorce could be obtained only by an act of the colonial assembly and was therefore confined to the wealthy and powerful. In the rare instances when women sought a divorce, they had to bring multiple charges against their husbands. Domestic violence, adultery, or abandonment alone were not enough to secure a divorce. Indeed, ministers and relatives were likely to counsel abused wives to change their behavior or suffer in silence. If a divorce was granted, custody of any children was usually awarded to fathers who had the economic means to support them, although infants or young girls might be assigned to live with the mother.

A quicker and cheaper means of ending an unsatisfactory marriage was to abandon one's spouse. Colonial divorce petitions citing desertion and newspaper ads for runaway spouses suggest that husbands fled in at least two-thirds of such cases.

REVIEW

- What were the effects of social changes in colonial society during the early eighteenth century?

Enlightenment and Awakening

Enlightenment
A European cultural movement spanning the late seventeenth century to the end of the eighteenth century, emphasizing rational and scientific thinking over traditional religion and superstition.

By the eighteenth century, the **Enlightenment**, a European cultural movement that emphasized rational and scientific thinking over traditional religion and superstition, had taken root in the colonies, particularly among elites. The development of a lively transatlantic print culture spread the ideas of Enlightenment thinkers like the English philosopher John Locke and the French intellectuals Montesquieu and Voltaire. These thinkers argued that through reason, humans could discover the laws that governed the universe and thereby improve society.

Benjamin Franklin, a leading printer in Philadelphia, was one of the foremost advocates of Enlightenment ideas in the colonies. His experiments with electricity reflected his faith in rational thought, and his publication of *Poor Richard's Almanack* spread such ideas throughout the colonies in the 1720s and 1730s.

WORKING with EVIDENCE

Source: Benjamin Franklin, *Poor Richard's Almanack*, 1739

"Kind Reader,

Encouraged by thy former Generosity, I once more present thee with an Almanack, which is the 7th of my Publication. While thou art putting Pence in my Pocket, and furnishing my Cottage with necessaries, Poor Dick is not unmindful to do something for thy Benefit. . . .

Ignorant Men wonder how we Astrologers foretell the Weather so exactly, unless we deal with the old black Devil. Alas! . . . For Instance; The Stargazer peeps at the Heavens thro' a long Glass: . . . He spies perhaps VIRGO (or the Virgin;) she turns her Head round as it were to see if any body observ'd her; then crouching down gently, with her Hands on her Knees, she looks wistfully for a while right forward. He judges rightly what she's about: And having calculated the Distance and allow'd Time for its Falling, finds that next Spring we shall have a fine April shower. . . . O the wonderful Knowledge to be found in the Stars! Even the smallest Things are written there, if you had but Skill to read. . . .

Besides the usual Things expected in an Almanack, I hope the profess'd Teachers of Mankind will excuse my scattering here and there some instructive Hints in Matters of Morality and Religion. And be not thou disturbed, O grave and sober Reader, if among the many serious Sentences in my Book, thou findest me trifling now and then, and talking idly. In all the Dishes I have hitherto cook'd for thee, there is solid Meat enough for thy Money. There are Scraps from the Table of Wisdom, that will if well digested, yield strong Nourishment to thy Mind. . . .

When I first begun to publish, the Printer made a fair Agreement with me for my Copies, by Virtue of which he runs away with the greatest Part of the Profit.—However, much good may't do him; I do not grudge it him; he is a Man I have a great Regard for, and I wish his Profit ten times greater than it is. For I am, dear Reader, his, as well as thy

Affectionate Friend,
R. SAUNDERS."

Questions for Analysis

1. Describe Franklin's tone, citing examples from the text to support your characterization.
2. Explain the causes of the popularity of *Poor Richard's Almanack.*
3. Explain how this excerpt from *Poor Richard's Almanack* undermines a traditional source of social authority.

Opposed to the religious concept that people were born sinful, Enlightenment thinkers generally believed that human beings were born neither necessarily good nor evil, but instead open to the world around them, and were innately capable of understanding the logic behind natural laws and the construction of governments that protected their individual rights as human beings. From this stemmed a general belief that governments were created for the benefit of people, rather than as a means of keeping them under control.

John Locke led the way in the late seventeenth century, with his argument that human beings created government to bring people out of a state of nature, where individuals had to protect their own rights, into a civilized state where government represented the people's interest and instituted laws for the general good. The French "philosophe" Baron de Montesquieu refined this idea in the mid-eighteenth century by arguing that good government was divided into executive, legislative, and judicial branches that prevented any one individual or group of individuals from acquiring too much power to the detriment of the people. Likewise, another French philosopher, Voltaire, advocated free speech based on his belief that truth and justice were born of rational discourse rather than the dictates of all-powerful monarchs or priests wielding divine power.

The Enlightenment provided colonists with a worldview with more room for acceptance of religious diversity than had previously existed. Enlightenment ideas also undermined what many likely saw as the religious vitality of the colonies. While many

Enlightenment thinkers believed in a Christian God, they rejected the revelations and rituals that defined traditional church practices and challenged the claims of many ministers that God was directly engaged in the daily workings of the world.

There were, however, opposing forces. Many Protestant ministers, possibly afraid that material concerns increasingly overshadowed spiritual devotion or that growing religious diversity was undermining the power of the church, lamented the state of faith in eighteenth-century America. Ministers eager to address this crisis of faith—known as **New Light clergy**—worked together to reenergize the faithful and were initially welcomed, or at least tolerated, by more traditional **Old Light clergy**.

New Light clergy
Colonial religious leaders who called for religious revivals and emphasized the emotional aspects of spiritual commitment. The New Lights were leaders in the First Great Awakening.

Old Light clergy
Colonial religious leaders from established churches who supported the religious status quo in the early eighteenth century.

Some New Lights took inspiration from German Pietist (a Protestant sect) ideas criticizing the power of established churches and urged individuals to follow their hearts rather than their heads in spiritual matters. Pietist ideas influenced John Wesley, the founder of Methodism (an English Protestant denomination) and a professor of theology at Oxford University, where he taught some of its central ideas to his students, including George Whitefield. Like the Pietists, Whitefield considered the North American colonies a perfect place to restore intensity and emotion to religious worship.

Ministers in the British North American colonies also questioned the status of religion, challenging the religiosity of urban churches that maintained class distinctions, with wealthier members paying high rents to seat their families in the front pews. Farmers and shopkeepers rented the cheaper pews in the middle of the church, while the poorest sat on free benches at the very back or in the gallery. One such clergyman was Jonathan Edwards, a Congregational minister in New England. A brilliant scholar who studied natural philosophy and science as well as theology, Edwards viewed the natural world as powerful evidence of God's design. He came to view the idea that God elected some individuals for salvation and others for damnation as a source of mystical joy. His sermons of 1733 to 1735 joined Enlightenment ideas with religious fervor, and they initiated a revival that reached hundreds of parishioners.

At around the same time, the English clergyman George Whitefield was perfectly situated to extend the series of revivals in North America that scholars later called the **First Great Awakening**. Gifted with a powerful voice, he understood that the expanding networks of communication and travel—developed to promote commerce—could also be used to promote religion. Advertising in newspapers and broadsides and traveling by ship, coach, and horseback, Whitefield made seven trips to the North American colonies beginning in 1738 as part of a fifteen-month preaching tour that reached tens of thousands of colonists, from Georgia to New England to the Pennsylvania backcountry, and inspired other ministers in the colonies.

First Great Awakening
Series of religious revivals in colonial America that began in 1720 and lasted until about 1750.

Like Edwards, he asked individuals to invest less in material goods and more in spiritual devotion. If they admitted their depraved and sinful state and truly repented, God would hear their prayers. Whitefield's preaching style was larger than life: He shouted and raged, and gestured dramatically, drawing huge crowds everywhere he went. He attracted 20,000 people to individual events, at a time when the entire city of Boston counted just 17,000 residents.

New Light ministers carried on Whitefield's work throughout the 1740s, refining their methods and appeal. Less concerned with what church their followers belonged to than with their core beliefs, New Lights denounced sophisticated and educated clergy, used spontaneous speeches and outdoor venues to attract crowds, and invited colonists from all walks of life to build a common Christian community. Some became traveling preachers, preferring to carry their message throughout the colonies than to be limited to a single church.

AP® EXAM TIP
The AP® Exam calls for you to understand the social effects of the First Great Awakening. Be sure you can detail one cause and one effect of the Great Awakening on British North American colonial society.

New Light clergy brought young people to religion by the thousands. In addition, thousands of colonists who were already church members were "born again," recommitting themselves to their faith. Poor women and men who felt little connection to

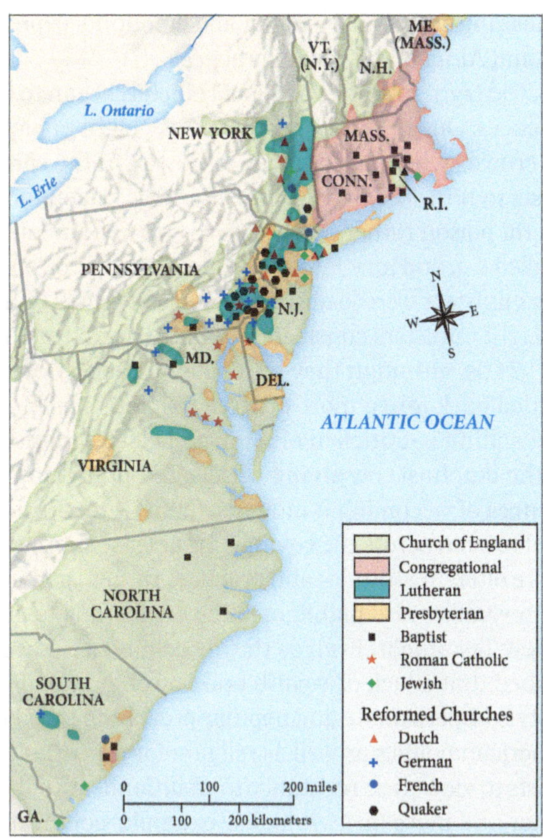

MAP 2.7 Religious Diversity in 1750 The appeal of Whitefield and other New Light ministers led to increased religious diversity by 1750. Baptist churches multiplied in New England, where Congregationalists had long held sway. Presbyterian and Lutheran churches emerged in the South where the Church of England was the official church. Other houses of worship, such as Quaker meeting houses and Jewish synagogues, also gradually increased in number.

Explain two historical trends before 1750 that caused the religious diversity shown on this map.

preaching when they sat on the back benches eagerly joined the crowds at outdoor revivals, where they could stand as close to the pulpit as a rich merchant.

REVIEW

- How did the ideologies that shaped both the First Great Awakening and the Enlightenment undermine imperial authority in the British North American colonies?

Dissent and Resistance Rise

At first, the Great Awakening drew support from large numbers of ministers from traditional churches because it increased religious enthusiasm and church attendance. The early embrace by Old Light clergy diminished, however, as revivals spread farther afield, as critiques of educated clergy became more pointed, and as worshippers left established congregations for new churches.

As the First Great Awakening peaked in the early 1740s, ministers and other colonial leaders increasingly feared that revivalists provided lower-class whites, free Black people, women, and even the enslaved with compelling critiques of those in power. A backlash developed among more settled ministers and their congregations.

Itinerant preachers traveling across the South seemed especially threatening because they invited Blacks and whites to attend revivals together and proclaimed their equality before God. Although New Light clergy rarely attacked slavery directly, they implicitly challenged racial hierarchies. Revivalists also attracted African Americans and Indians by emphasizing communal singing and emotional expressions of the spirit, which echoed traditional African and Indian practices.

In the North, too, Old Light ministers and local officials began to question New Light techniques and influences. One of the most radical New Light preachers, James Davenport, attracted huge crowds when he preached in Boston in the early 1740s. Drawing thousands of colonists to Boston Common day after day, Davenport declared that the people "should drink rat poison rather than listen to corrupt, unconverted clergy." Boston officials finally called a grand jury into session to silence him "on the charge of having said that Boston's ministers were leading the people blindfold to hell."

Even some New Light ministers considered Davenport extreme. Yet revivals continued throughout the 1740s, although they lessened in intensity over time as churches and parishioners settled back into a more ordered religious life. Moreover, the central ideas of revivalist preaching—criticism of educated clergy, ministers traveling from place to place, and the emphasis on giving unscripted preaching—worked against the movement's chances of becoming a more permanent institution. The First Great Awakening continued to echo across the colonies for at least another generation, but its influence was felt more often in attitudes and practices rather than in institutions.

In various ways, revivalists also highlighted the democratic tendencies in the Bible, particularly in the New Testament. Even as they proclaimed God's wrath against sinners, they also preached that a lack of wealth and power did not diminish a person in God's eyes. And the style of passionate and popular preaching they brought to the colonies would shape American politics as well as religion for centuries to come. New Light clergy allowed colonists to view their resistance to traditional authorities as part of their effort to create a better and more just world. For example, colonists soon mobilized to resist what they saw as tyrannical actions by the wealthy colonial officials and others in authority. Thus, the effects of eighteenth-century religious awakenings rippled out from churches and revivals to influence social and political relations.

At the same time, the environment of the colonies contributed to changes in their attitudes toward colonial authorities. The settlements of the seventeenth century could be regulated with a small number of officials. With eighteenth-century geographical expansion, population growth, and commercial development, colonial authorities—whether appointed by the crown or selected by local residents—found themselves confronted with a more complex, and more contentious, situation.

In New England, most colonies developed participatory town meetings, which elected members to their colonial legislatures. In the South, wealthy planters exercised greater authority locally and colony-wide, but they still embraced ideals of self-governance and political liberty.

Throughout the British American colonies, officials were usually educated men who held property and had family ties to other colonial elites. Although ultimate political authority—or sovereignty—rested with the king and Parliament, many decisions were made by local officials because English officials were often too distant to have a hand in daily colonial life.

Another factor that weakened the power of royal officials was the tradition of town meetings and representative bodies, like the Virginia House of Burgesses, that gave colonists a stake in their own governance. Officials in England and the colonies assumed that most people would defer to those in authority, and they minimized resistance by holding public elections in which freemen cast ballots by voice vote. Not surprisingly, those with wealth and power continued to win office.

Still, evidence from throughout the colonial period indicates that deference to authority was not always enough to maintain order. Roger Williams and Anne Hutchinson, Bacon's Rebellion, the Stono Rebellion, the Salem witchcraft trials, and both New York class rebellions, one led by Jacob Leisler in 1689 and the other a series of tenant revolts in the 1740s, all demonstrate the frequency and range of colonial conflict and protest. These episodes of dissent and protest were widely scattered across time and place. But as the ideas circulated by New Light clergy and Enlightenment thinkers converged with changing political relations, resistance to established authority became more frequent and more collective.

Protests against colonial elites multiplied after the 1730s. A lack of access to reasonably priced food, especially bread, inspired regular protests in the eighteenth century. During the 1730s, the price of bread—a staple in colonial diets—rose despite falling wheat prices and a recession in seaport cities. Bread rioters attacked grain warehouses, bakeries, and shops, demanding more bread at lower prices. In New England, such uprisings were often led by women, who were responsible for putting bread on the table. When grievances involved domestic or consumer issues, women felt they had the right to make their voices heard, a right reinforced by New Light clergy's insistence on their moral obligations to society.

Public markets were another site where struggles over food led to collective protests. In 1737, for instance, Boston officials decided to construct a public market and charge fees to farmers who sold their goods there. Many Bostonians opposed the move because it would lessen competition and raise prices for consumers, many farmers could not afford the fee, and those that could would raise prices to offset the extra expense. After their petitions were ignored by city officials, protesters demolished the market building and stalls in the middle of the night. Local authorities could find no witnesses to the crime.

Access to land was also a critical issue in the colonies. Beginning in the 1740s, protests erupted on estates in New Jersey and along the Hudson River in New York over the leasing policies of landlords as well as the amount of land controlled by speculators. Here, again, when tenants and squatters petitioned colonial officials and received no response, they took collective action. They formed associations, targeted specific landlords, and then burned barns, attacked livestock, and emptied houses and farm buildings of furniture and tools. Embracing Enlightenment ideas of "natural law," they also established regional committees to hear grievances and formed "popular" militia companies and courts to dispense justice to uncooperative land owners.

In seaport cities, a frequent source of conflict was the **impressment** of colonial men who were seized and forcibly drafted into service in the Royal Navy. Impressment grew increasingly common as King William's War was followed by Queen Anne's War, only to be followed by King George's War. Impressment was viewed as a sign of the corrupt practices of imperial authorities, and resistance to it energized diverse groups of colonists. Sailors, dockworkers, and men drinking at taverns along the shore feared being pressed into military service, while colonial officials worried about labor shortages. Those officials petitioned the British government to stop impressment, but workingmen who faced the navy's high mortality rates, bad food, rampant disease, and harsh discipline also took action on their own behalf. Asserting their growing sense of political liberty, they fought back against both colonial and British authorities.

impressment
The forced enlistment of civilians into the army or navy. The impressment of residents of colonial seaports into the British navy was a major source of complaint in the eighteenth century.

In 1747 in Boston, a general impressment during King George's War led to three days of rioting. An observer noted that "Negros, servants, and hundreds of seamen seized a naval lieutenant, assaulted a sheriff, and put his deputy in stocks, surrounded the governor's house, and stormed the Town House (city hall)." Such riots did not end the system of impressment, but they showed that many colonists now refused to be deprived of what they considered their natural rights.

The religious upheavals and economic uncertainties of the 1730s and 1740s led colonists to challenge colonial and British officials more often than in earlier decades and to justify their actions in evangelical or Enlightenment terms. Still, most protests also accentuated class lines as small farmers, craftsmen, and the poor fought against merchants, landowners, and local officials. However, the resistance to impressment proved that colonists could mobilize across economic differences when British policies affected diverse groups of colonial subjects.

In the mid-eighteenth century, colonists protested with increasing force against many aspects of colonial life that they found unsatisfying. The issues repeatedly raised, the political responses that failed to fully address them, and resultant further protest show a pattern of dissent and discontent with deep roots.

Beginning in the 1730s, conflicts among the elite led astute political leaders in cities like New York and Philadelphia to seek support from a wider constituency, channeling the "popular" will for their own ends. In 1731, for instance, a new royal charter confirmed New York City's existence as a "corporation" and stipulated the rights of freemen (residents who could vote in local elections after paying a small fee) and freeholders (individuals, whether residents or not, who held property worth £40 and could vote on that basis). A large number of artisans, shopkeepers, and laborers had the financial means to vote, and shopkeepers and master craftsmen now sat alongside wealthier men on the Common Council. Yet most laboring men did not participate actively in elections until 1733, when local elites aimed to mobilize the mass of voters against royal officials, like New York Governor William Cosby, who had been appointed in London.

Opponents took their case to the people, who were in the midst of a serious economic depression. They launched an opposition newspaper, published by a man named John Peter Zenger, to mobilize artisans, shopkeepers, and laborers around an agenda to stimulate the economy and elect men supportive of workers to the Common Council. In his *New-York Weekly Journal*, Zenger boldly accused Governor Cosby and his cronies of corruption, incompetence, election fraud, and tyranny, leading to Zenger's indictment for **seditious** libel and his imprisonment in November 1734.

seditious
Describing behavior or language aimed at starting a rebellion against a government.

libel
A false written statement designed to damage the reputation of its subject.

At the time, **libel** related only to whether published material undermined government authority, not whether it was true or false. Zenger's lead attorney, Andrew Hamilton of Philadelphia, argued that truth must be recognized as a defense against charges of libel. Appealing to the jury, Hamilton proclaimed, "It is not the cause of a poor printer, nor of New York alone, which you are now trying. . . . It is the best cause. It is the cause of liberty." In response, jurors ignored the law as written and found Zenger not guilty.

Although the decision in Zenger's case did not lead to a change in British libel laws, it did signal the willingness of colonial juries to side with fellow colonists against the king and Parliament in at least some situations. Zenger's journalistic challenge to ruling power, and the ability of the political movement he championed to inspire ordinary freemen to participate in elections, foreshadowed political developments near the end of the eighteenth century.

For the time being, however, even as freemen gained a greater voice in urban politics and newspapers readily attacked corrupt officials whose actions posed threats to the liberties of the British colonists, challenges to the powerful could succeed only when the elite were divided.

The rising inequality of wealth was especially apparent in the largest cities of British North America—New York, Philadelphia, Boston, and Charleston—but economic distinctions were also growing in smaller cities and towns. As the price of some goods, such as sugar and tobacco, fell in the 1750s, more colonists were able to afford them. At the same time, the expansion of transatlantic trade ensured that wealthier colonists had growing access to silver plates, clocks, tea services, bed and table linens, and other luxury goods. With British exporters extending more credit to colonial merchants and affluent white consumers, the division between rich and poor became increasingly visible to colonists of all backgrounds.

REVIEW

- How did politics and religion bring colonists together across economic lines in the first half of the eighteenth century?
- How did religion and politics highlight and reinforce class divisions during this era?

AP®

Skills Workshop: Thinking Historically

Answering Multiple-Choice Questions with a Secondary Source Stimulus

The AP® Exam will assess your knowledge of U.S. history with essays, short-answer questions, and multiple-choice questions. In Module 1.6, we learned that the multiple-choice questions on the exam are called "stimulus-based" multiple-choice questions. "Stimulus" means that every multiple-choice question is preceded by a document, image, chart, or graph that you will use to answer the question.

But that is not all that you will use to answer the question. Stimulus-based multiple-choice questions require you to do more than understand the stimulus. You must also apply your historical knowledge to interpret the stimulus and answer the question. You will need to unite the information you know and your ability to understand the stimulus before you can successfully answer the question.

As you recall from Module 1.6, the stimuli for multiple-choice questions are sometimes primary sources. Other times, they are secondary sources, either in prose or as graphs or charts. Let's look at a graph from Module 2.3a.

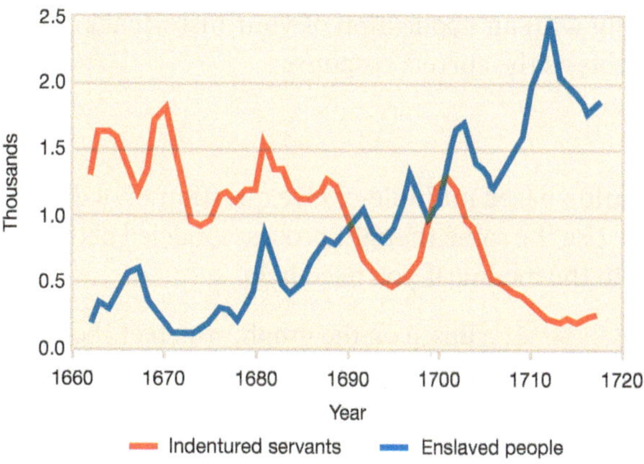

It's important that you understand the stimulus before you look at the multiple-choice question(s). As you can see in this graph, indentured servitude generally declined as a labor source between 1662 and 1717, while enslaved labor grew throughout this period. Also, notice that the graph shows data from only one colony, Maryland. Once you've understood the stimulus, you should recall information from the chapter not explicitly in the stimulus itself. For example:

- Maryland was a colony in Chesapeake Bay.
- Maryland depended on the cash crop tobacco for much of its exports and used both indentured servants and enslaved labor to produce this crop.
- Starting in the late seventeenth century, colonies dependent on cash crops, especially colonies like Maryland, Virginia, and the Carolinas, shifted from indentured labor to enslaved labor.

Now that you've understood the stimulus and recalled relevant historical information about the stimulus, you're ready to move on to the multiple-choice question:

1. Based on the graph, which of the following best describes developments in labor in the South during the late seventeenth and early eighteenth centuries?
   (A) As indentured servants left the colonies, enslaved people increasingly arrived.
   (B) Enslaved and indentured labor proved to be equally used throughout the period by large landholders.
   (C) Yeoman farmers in the South were often former indentured servants, while Africans forcibly brought to the British colonies were permanently enslaved.
   (D) Throughout the late seventeenth and early eighteenth centuries, indentured servitude declined, while enslaved labor grew.

Let's talk briefly about each option. Option A is incorrect, because we know that indentured servants didn't typically *leave* the colonies. While their use as laborers declined, there was no large-scale departure from British North America

(continued)

by indentured servants. Here, your knowledge of the history is very important, because you might choose this option without that knowledge. Even if you were unsure about whether indentured servants left the colonies, you could reason that option A is probably not correct because the overall trend during this time was that colonies' populations were growing, making this option unlikely.

Option B is incorrect because it misreads the graph. While there was a point when indentured and enslaved labor reached parity, this option says "throughout the period," and therefore, this option can't be correct.

Option C is incorrect, because while the information it contains is generally true, it does not relate to a "development," which is a key part of the question. Specifically, option C is a good example of an answer that is factual but not correct. These kinds of wrong answers often appear in multiple-choice questions. If you narrowed down your choices to C and D because both are true, ask yourself which one can be *proven* by the graph. If you do that, you will notice that the graph contains no information about who the indentured or enslaved were.

Option D is the correct answer because it reflects the developments seen in the graph. Literally, there are two lines in the graph. The red line shows a decreasing number of indentured servants over time, while the blue line shows the increase in numbers of enslaved people during the same period. With an accurate understanding of the graph along with an application of your historical knowledge, you should be able to identify this as the correct response.

ACTIVITY

Now, try to answer a stimulus-based multiple-choice question on a different graph from earlier in the module. Use the same thought process modeled above. Feel free to review the content earlier in the module if you need help.

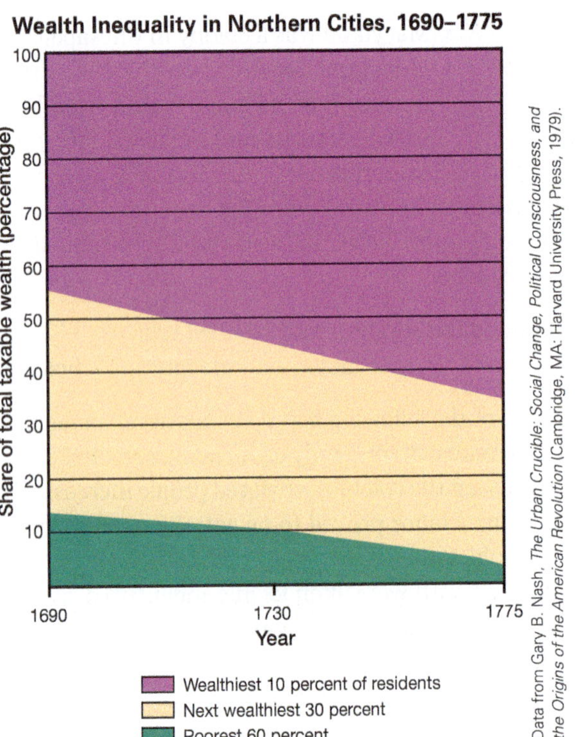

Data from Gary B. Nash, *The Urban Crucible: Social Change, Political Consciousness, and the Origins of the American Revolution* (Cambridge, MA: Harvard University Press, 1979).

1. Based on the graph, which of the following best accounts for developments in wealth inequality in northern cities between 1690–1775:
   (A) Planters increasingly controlled the trade of cash crops between British North America and Great Britain.
   (B) Merchants increasingly profited from the trade between British North America and Great Britain.
   (C) Middle-class consumers increasingly purchased more luxury goods from Great Britain than the poorest 60 percent of consumers.
   (D) Yeoman farmers increasingly sold their crops in colonial cities for export to Great Britain.

Comparison in Period 2

MODULE

2.8

AP® Skills Workshop: Writing Historically

Responding to a Short-Answer Question with Two Secondary Sources

Responding to a Short-Answer Question with Secondary Sources

As you learned in Period 1, the AP® U.S. History Exam has three different types of short-answer questions:

- secondary-source interpretation questions, which require you to understand the claims that historians make about a specific time period, and how evidence from specific events or developments during that time period can be used to support those claims;
- primary-source interpretation questions, which give you a source — typically an image — and ask you to draw connections between that source, often using the historical reasoning process of causation, and larger historical developments; and
- questions without primary or secondary sources that require you to use your knowledge of a time period and historical reasoning, which you encountered in Module 1.3.

As you learned in Module 2.2, a *secondary source* is a secondhand account of a historical event or development created after the fact by someone who was not there, often a historian. Books and scholarly articles about history, written by historians, are the most common form of secondary source you will be asked to read and write about in this course. In fact, these types of short-answer questions will generally provide you with two short secondary sources that discuss the same topic. Most often, you will be asked to compare two arguments in some meaningful way and cite a piece of evidence to support each of their claims.

Let's take a look at a typical short-answer question on a pair of secondary sources:

> Using the excerpts, answer **A**, **B**, and **C**.
>
> "Small tokens of gentility [refinement] can be found scattered through all of American society in the eighteenth century, like pottery shards in an excavated house lot. Estate inventories of many middling people show a teacup, a silver spoon, knives and forks, and a book or two among the household possessions. Over the course of the century, probably a majority of the population adopted some of the amenities associated with genteel living. But it would be an error to conclude that by [1776] most Americans were genteel. Gentility flecked lives without coloring them. Gentility was the proper style of the gentry alone in the eighteenth century."
>
> Richard Bushman, *The Refinement of America: Persons, Houses, Cities*, 1993

(continued)

"Within a few decades during the middle of the eighteenth century, imported goods transformed monochrome spaces into Technicolor. . . . Imported goods reflected cosmopolitan tastes and manners, so that an American who managed to purchase a porcelain teacup or a modest pewter bowl could fancy that he or she partook of a polite society centered in faraway places such as London or Bath. These wonderful objects arouse suspicion today that however much local ministers may have once railed against the corrupting influence of luxury, they did not really discourage the members of their congregations from buying goods that yielded so much personal satisfaction."

T. H. Breen, *The Marketplace of the Revolution: How Consumer Politics Shaped American Independence*, 2005

(A) Briefly describe ONE major difference between Bushman's and Breen's historical interpretations of colonial society.
(B) Briefly explain how ONE specific historical event or development from 1650 to 1754 that is not explicitly mentioned in the excerpts could be used to support Bushman's interpretation.
(C) Briefly explain how ONE specific historical event or development from 1650 to 1754 that is not explicitly mentioned in the excerpts could be used to support Breen's argument.

In this particular question, part A calls for you to think historically using comparison, while parts B and C assess your content knowledge and your skill in using evidence to support an argument. In the following steps, we'll walk through how to approach each one.

Step 1 ▶ Read both excerpts and summarize their viewpoints

Read each secondary source carefully, and take a moment to clarify the general topic or development that both historians are writing about. It may be helpful to annotate the prompt so that you can keep it in mind as you think about each source individually. For example, notice that both historians discuss the existence of consumable goods, even luxuries, in the homes of average colonial Americans. Note also that both historians talk about relatively small objects such as eating utensils, bowls, and teacups.

Now that you have focused on the general topic under discussion by both historians, jot down a quick summary of what each one has to say about that subject. Remember, you are looking for one major difference in the historians' interpretations, although the historians will have points in common as well. Rarely will two sources express polar-opposite views of a given historical development. Your summary of each historian's claims, like the example that follows, should address the differences so that you maintain a focus on the specific task at hand. For example, while both historians agree generally:

Richard Bushman argues that small luxury goods ("tokens of gentility") were found in the homes of most Americans. T. H. Breen also argues that items of gentility were found in the homes of average British colonists **[points in common]**.

(continued)

There is an important point of difference between them:

> Bushman claims it would be a mistake to assume that most Americans were "genteel." Breen, on the other hand, argues that these items allowed average British colonists to imagine themselves as part of a broader genteel culture, making gentility a more important part of their identity than Bushman claims **[points of difference]**.

Part A asks you for the major difference between their interpretations. While Bushman and Breen agree about the existence of a few luxury items in American homes, Bushman claims that it is a mistake to assume the few luxury items in colonial homes made Americans genteel, but Breen implies that these few items allowed colonists to connect with faraway gentility in Europe, thereby making these items an important part of average colonists' identity.

Step 2 ▶ Use *Claim, Support, Explain* to answer each part of the prompt

The next step is to apply the **CSE** strategy (claim, support, explain) to part A:

Briefly describe ONE major difference between Bushman's and Breen's historical interpretations of colonial society.

Start by writing a **claim** that states a difference between Bushman's and Breen's interpretations. You may find it helpful to use words such as *but, although, whereas, while, on the other hand,* or *however*. For example, "While Bushman argues X, Breen claims Y."

However, it is not enough to merely state a claim about the difference between the two historians' interpretations. You must prove to your reader that your claim is valid, and to do this, you will need to **support** your claim with evidence from both passages. Finally, you should **explain** how the evidence you connected to your claim proves it.

So your CSE for part A might look like this:

> While Bushman argues that colonists owned a few luxury goods and therefore could not be called "genteel," Breen argues that access to trade goods shaped colonists' identity and allowed them to feel connected to European gentility **[claim]**. For example, Bushman notes that while many colonies had teacups and utensils for eating, true gentility was reserved for the gentry, who were much wealthier. However, Breen argues that because colonists could afford simple luxuries like pewter bowls, they could imagine themselves part of a larger genteel culture in faraway places in England **[support with evidence from the secondary sources]**. Bushman understands these small luxury goods only in terms of their economic value, which therefore lack enough worth to offer any hope of gentility for colonists. On the other hand, Breen claims that with these few luxury goods, colonists imagined themselves part of a larger genteel culture, and therefore believed themselves to be genteel despite their lowly economic status **[explain]**.

Now you're ready to move on to part B of the question:

Briefly explain how ONE specific historical event or development from 1650 to 1754 that is not explicitly mentioned in the excerpts could be used to support Bushman's interpretation.

(continued)

Start by brainstorming evidence from your knowledge of history that you can use to support Bushman's argument. Select the best historical example you can think of to showcase that knowledge. One strategy for doing this is to consider the context that shaped the topic under discussion by both historians. For example, for this part of the question, we can think of a few pieces of evidence that come from this module:

- The majority of colonists was agriculturalists and relatively poor compared to elites in the colonies.
- Most goods that were consumed in average colonial homes, like clothing, were made at home.
- Throughout the eighteenth century, colonial elites increasingly held a larger portion of the colonies' wealth.

As you did with part A, apply **CSE** to part B. Make a **claim** that answers the prompt—that is, present a historical event or development that supports Bushman's interpretation. Then, using your knowledge of history, **support** your claim with evidence that demonstrates your claim. Lastly, **explain** how the evidence you chose to include proves your claim. The following example is a strong answer to part B:

> Bushman's argument can be supported by noting the few luxury goods average colonists owned **[claim]**. While luxury goods increasingly became accessible to some colonists after 1650, for the majority of British Americans the everyday goods they used, like clothing, were overwhelmingly made at home **[support]**. This shows that for most Americans, a genteel lifestyle was still very far from their everyday lives **[explain]**.

Notice how this response supports Bushman's argument that while some genteel items found their way into the homes of colonial Americans, the bulk of their goods were made at home. This piece of historical evidence best supports Bushman's contention that even though average colonists might have had a few luxury items, the items that they lived in (their clothes) were still homespun and far from genteel.

Now let's try part C using **CSE**:

> Breen's argument can be supported by noting that luxury goods became increasingly accessible in the colonies after 1650, even though many colonists remained relatively poor **[claim]**. Rising access to simple luxurious items that were produced in England and shipped to the colonies over the Atlantic in exchange for raw materials proved popular among even subsistence farmers, though they likely could have survived without them **[support]**. This shows that colonists, even those who weren't wealthy, invested in goods that made them feel able to partake in the genteel culture they imagined in colonial cities and the faraway dining tables of London **[explain]**.

You will find opportunities to practice this type of Short-Answer Question in each Period of this textbook. As you practice, remember to systematically **CSE** each of the three parts.

(continued)

ACTIVITY

Carefully read the following pair of secondary sources and answer the accompanying Short-Answer Question.

Using the excerpts, answer **A**, **B**, and **C**.

> "By 1763 the American colonies were reconciled to the English mercantilist policy. . . . Mercantilism as a theory of statecraft . . . was dominant in Europe during the entire colonial period. . . . Mercantilism had for its primary purpose the creation of a strong state. . . . Governments extended their control over commerce and industry on the theory that the economic activity of the individual should be subordinated to the welfare of the nation. The state must become a self-sufficient unit, independent from other competing nations."
>
> E. A. J. Johnson, "Some Evidence of Mercantilism in Massachusetts Bay," *The New England Quarterly*, 1928

> "The nature of wealth and the role of colonies formed only part of the debates that raged over trade, markets, money, consumption, . . . morality, and the proper role of government in commerce. Free-trade ideas circulated as early as the late sixteenth century and gained traction in the early seventeenth century. . . . [T]he Navigation Acts, although devastating to some colonial economies in the short term, opened a huge English free-trade zone . . . which benefited the northern colonies enormously. . . . [T]hey were free to trade directly with non-English nations—that is, until the 1760s, when authorities expanded the enumerated list to include many heretofore-unregulated exports and imports."
>
> Ellen Newell, "Putting the 'Political' Back in Political Economy (This Is Not Your Parents' Mercantilism)," *The William and Mary Quarterly*, 2012

(A) Briefly describe ONE major difference between Johnson's and Newell's historical interpretations of British mercantilist policy.

(B) Briefly explain how ONE specific historical event or development from the period 1607 to 1754 that is not explicitly mentioned in the excerpts could be used to support Johnson's argument.

(C) Briefly explain how ONE specific historical event or development from the period 1607 to 1754 that is not explicitly mentioned in the excerpts could be used to support Newell's argument.

Period 2 Review 1607–1754

KEY CONCEPTS AND EVENTS

KEY PEOPLE

CHRONOLOGY

1580s	French establish fur trade with American Indians
1607	The English found Jamestown colony
1608	Samuel de Champlain founds the city of Québec, the first permanent French settlement in North America
1609	Dutch establish fur-trading outpost on the Hudson River
By 1612	Tobacco becomes main cash crop in Virginia

CHRONOLOGY *(continued)*

1619	House of Burgesses created in Virginia First enslaved Africans brought to Virginia colony
1620	Mayflower Compact establishes Plymouth Colony
1620s	British West Indies established
1620s–1630s	Anglo-Powhatan and Pequot wars lead to expansion of English settlements
1623	Massachusetts Bay Company established
c. 1630	Virginia colony becomes commercially successful
1630s	Puritan colonies spread quickly on American Indian lands
1635	Dissenters establish Providence, Rhode Island
1637	Massacre of Pequots by Puritan colonists
1642–1651	English Civil War leads to population surge in the colonies
1647–1692	Salem witch paranoia
1651	Parliament passes first Navigation Acts
1660	Royal African Company formed Barbados reaches majority Black population
1660s	Slave laws passed by Virginia House of Burgesses
1660s–1670s	Economic inequality in the colonies rises, frustrating a growing common class
1672	Royal African Company brings enslaved Africans to North America
1675	Bacon's Rebellion
1675–1678	Metacom's War (also known as King Philip's War)
1680	Pueblo Revolt
c. 1680	British economy surges due to mercantilism
1682	French claim all land drained by Mississippi River tributaries and name the colony Louisiana William Penn establishes Quaker haven in Philadelphia
1688	Leisler's Rebellion
1689–1697	King William's War
1689–1713	Europe in constant state of war, conflict spilling into colonies
c. 1700–1808	Over 4 million enslaved Africans cross the Middle Passage
c. 1700	Charleston becomes leading importer of enslaved Africans
c. 1700s	Disparity in land ownership leads to wealth inequality Popular publications spread Enlightenment ideas throughout British colonies
c. 1700–1750	Colonial population rise leads to conflict with American Indians
c. 1700–1760s	Rice and indigo become cash crops
1720s–1730s	Planters and merchants make economic and political gains

CHRONOLOGY *(continued)*

1730s	Economic recession triggers protests against elites
1730s–1740s	First Great Awakening
1739	Stono Rebellion
1739–1748	War between England and Spain reaches into North America
1740s	Number of enslaved African Americans born in colonies outnumbers imports of enslaved Africans
1742	First Great Awakening peaks
1747	Impressment leads to riots in Boston
1754–1763	French and Indian War (also known as Seven Years' War)

Period 2 AP® Exam Practice

Multiple-Choice Questions

Questions 1–3 refer to the excerpt.

"The free fruition of such liberties immunities and privileges as humanity, civility, and Christianity call for as due to every man in his place and proportion without . . . infringement hath ever been and ever will be the tranquility and stability of Churches and Commonwealths. . . .

7. No man shall be compelled to go out of the limits of this plantation upon any offensive wars. . . . But only upon such vindictive and defensive wars in our own behalf . . .

50. All jurors shall be chosen continually by the freemen of the town where they dwell.

88. Servants that have served diligently and faithfully to the benefit of their masters seven years, shall not be sent away empty.

89. If any people of other Nations professing the true Christian Religion shall flee to us from the tyranny or oppression of their persecutors, or from famine, wars . . . They shall be entertained and succored amongst us, according to that power and prudence, God shall give us.

91. There shall never be any bond slavery . . . amongst us unless it be lawful captives taken in just wars, and such strangers as willingly sell themselves or are sold to us."

The Massachusetts Body of Liberties, 1641

1. Which of the following most directly contributed to the ideas in the excerpt?
(A) English colonization attracted large groups of men.
(B) New England colonists lived apart from Native Americans.
(C) All British North American colonies participated in the Atlantic slave trade.
(D) Communities in New England developed around small towns.

2. The excerpt is most clearly an example of which of the following developments in New England during the early seventeenth century?
(A) The creation of self-governing political institutions
(B) A decline in trade networks throughout the Atlantic world
(C) An increase in the number of villages dependent on the labor of enslaved Africans
(D) An increase in the number of towns led by a planter elite

3. The ideas expressed in the excerpt most directly reflect which of the following characteristics of the British North American colonies during the seventeenth century?
(A) European conflicts led to increased Anglicization over time.
(B) Regional differences in culture led to the creation of different economic and political systems.
(C) Competition over natural resources led to fewer conflicts with Native Americans.
(D) Wars with European rivals created a sense of colonial unity.

Questions 4–6 refer to the excerpt.

"The concept of discovery functioned as the expression of an ideology by which Europeans divided the world between civilized and savage peoples. Civilized peoples lived within sovereign societies of their own making. Savage peoples lived as part of the natural world rather than as members of a society. Virtually all Europeans who produced a written record of their encounters with the Native peoples of North America understood their contact with the indigenous Other through the lens of discovery.

Of course, in reality discovery unfolded as a mutual process where the peoples of the Eastern and Western Hemispheres came to know each other.

On the ground, however, the reality of European conquest varied."

Michael Witgen, *An Infinity of Nations: How the Native New World Shaped Early North America*, 2012.

4. Which of the following factors most directly contributed to the ideas expressed by Witgen?
   (A) Europeans created a unified vision of economic systems in the New World.
   (B) Europeans produced very similar migration patterns.
   (C) British colonists lived among and sought to accommodate Native Americans.
   (D) Native Americans allied with and fought Europeans to maintain land.

5. Which of the following groups were least likely to displace Native Americans in the process of colonization?
   (A) English colonists
   (B) French colonists
   (C) Spanish colonists
   (D) Portuguese colonists

6. Which of the following is an important consequence of the historical developments described in the excerpt above?
   (A) Competition over resources decreased tensions between European colonial empires.
   (B) A growing acceptance of cultural pluralism improved relations between British colonists and Native Americans.
   (C) A decrease in the number of military confrontations with British colonists.
   (D) Epidemic diseases radically changed demographics in the New World.

Questions 7–9 refer to the map.

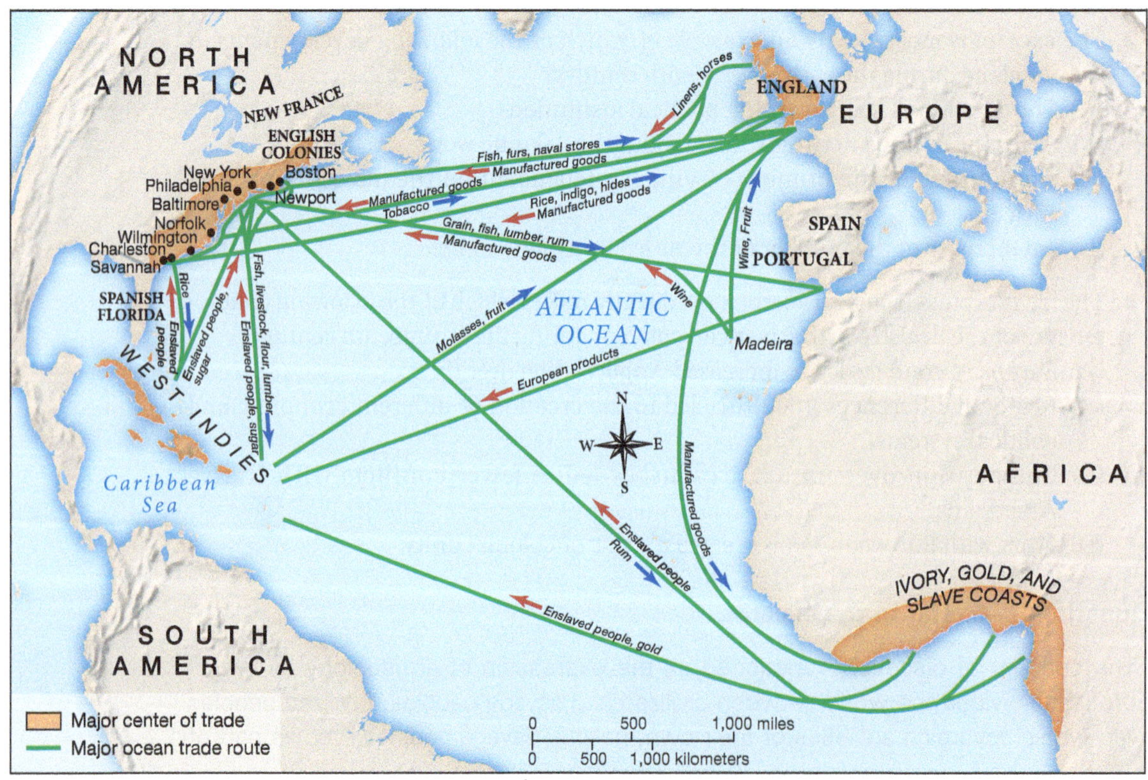

North Atlantic Trade in the Eighteenth Century

7. The patterns depicted on the map most directly account for which of the following developments?
   (A) Increased direct trade between the British North American colonies and France, Spain, and Portugal
   (B) An embrace of cultural pluralism throughout the New World
   (C) Regional economic differences due to environmental factors
   (D) A decrease on the reliance of enslaved labor in the New World

8. Which of the following best explains the long-term effects of trade routes depicted on the map?
   (A) Great Britain imposing an imperial economic system on its North American colonies.
   (B) Less mercantilist competition among European powers
   (C) A decline in the number of ethnic groups that migrated to the British North American colonies
   (D) Increased accommodation of Native American land claims by Great Britain

9. The trade routes depicted on the map affected Native American communities because:
   (A) a reliance on Native enslavement developed among colonists in the West Indies.
   (B) their ability to maintain alliances with Europeans improved.
   (C) new sources of cultural exchange occurred in the British North American colonies.
   (D) economic growth led to less frequent confrontations with British colonists.

Questions 10–12 refer to the excerpt.

"In 1739 arriv'd among us from England the Rev. Mr. Whitefield, who had made himself remarkable there as an itinerant Preacher. . . . The Multitudes of all Sects and Denominations that attended his Sermons were enormous and it was [a] matter of Speculation to me who was one of the Number, to observe the extraordinary Influence of his Oratory on his Hearers and how much they admir'd and respected him, notwithstanding his common Abuse of them, by assuring them they were naturally half Beasts and half Devils. It was wonderful to see the Change soon made in the Manners of our Inhabitants; from being thoughtless or indifferent about Religion, it seeme'd as if all the world were growing Religious . . ."

Benjamin Franklin,
On George Whitefield, the Great Revivalist, 1739

10. The ideas expressed in the excerpt emerged in the context of which of the following?
    (A) A decline in Anglicization in the British North American colonies
    (B) A rejection of the mercantilist system
    (C) A new focus on the international slave trade for cash crops
    (D) Cultural pluralism in the British North American colonies

11. The sentiments expressed in the excerpt reflect which of the following conditions in the British North American colonies?
    (A) An economy based mainly on exporting staple crops
    (B) The migration of various European religious groups
    (C) European desire to settle more swiftly on Native American lands
    (D) The presence of competing European empires

12. Which of the following developments most likely resulted from the ideas expressed in the excerpt?
    (A) An acceptance of Protestant evangelicalism
    (B) Continued reliance on enslaved labor
    (C) Colonial political interdependence
    (D) An enforcement of imperial policies

Questions 13–15 refer to the excerpt.

"Slaves are the Negroes . . . following the condition of the Mother, . . . They are called Slaves, in respect of the time of their Servitude, because it is for Life.

Servants, are those which serve for only a few years according to the time of the Indenture, or the Custom of the Country. . . .

The Male-Servants, and Slaves of both Sexes, are employed together in Tilling and Manuring the Ground, in Sowing and Planting Tobacco, Corn, etc. Some Distinction indeed is made between them in the Clothes, and Food; but the Work of both, is no other than what the Overseers, the Freemen, and the Planters themselves do."

Robert Beverley, *The History and Present State of Virginia*, 1705

13. Which of the following pieces of evidence best supports the descriptions from the source?
- (A) European migrants found economic opportunity in the middle colonies.
- (B) Enslaved workers labored on plantations to cultivate cash crops.
- (C) An Atlantic slave trade continued throughout the eighteenth century.
- (D) Enslaved workers in the Northeast worked mainly in port cities.

14. Laws regarding enslaved people reflect which of the following historical developments?
- (A) A continuity in the use of British indentured servants in the eighteenth century
- (B) An increase in the use of Native Americans as indentured servants
- (C) A movement away from the use of enslaved Africans in the West Indies
- (D) A more severe racialized system over time

15. Which of the following would be most likely to benefit from the descriptions in the excerpt?
- (A) An owner of a rice plantation in South Carolina
- (B) A wheat farmer in Pennsylvania
- (C) A tenant farmer in New Jersey
- (D) A fur trader in New York

Short-Answer Questions

"As Europeans vied with one another for claims to North America, the familiar tale goes, they destabilized and enmeshed Native groups in an ongoing cycle of trade, dependence, and warfare. . . . Though historians have made much of the creation of 'middle grounds' between some Native groups and European powers—places and processes that neither Natives nor newcomers could dominate completely and where new worlds were created—the end result was often the same in the eastern half of North America: Native Americans were eventually defeated, dispossessed, and usually removed from the line of European settlement. In this tale, Europeans drive the story of early America. . . .Yet European posts did not mean European dominance. Quite the contrary. For most of the colonial period, Europeans at Michilimackinac were dependent on the Odawa and other Algonquian nations for their very subsistence."

Michael A. McDonnell, *Masters of Empire: Great Lakes Indians and the Making of America*, 2015

"The middle ground is the place in between: in between cultures, peoples, and in between empires and the nonstate world of villages. It is a place where many of the North American subjects and allies of empires lived. It is the area between the historical foreground of European invasion and occupation and the background of Indian defeat and retreat. On the middle ground diverse peoples adjust their differences through what amounts to a process of creative, and often expedient, misunderstandings. . . .

They often misinterpret and distort both the values and the practices of those they deal with, but from these misunderstandings arise new meanings and through them new practices—the shared meaning and practices of the middle ground. . . . The world of the *pays d'en haut*, then, is not a traditional world either seeking to maintain itself unchanged or eroding under the pressure of whites. It is a joint Indian-white creation."

Richard White, *The Middle Ground: Indians, Empires, and Republics in the Great Lakes Region, 1650–1815*, 1991

1. Using the excerpts, answer **A**, **B**, and **C**.
   (A) Briefly describe one major difference between McDonnell's and White's historical interpretations of the relations between Native Americans and Europeans.
   (B) Briefly explain how one historical event or development that is not explicitly mentioned in the excerpts could support McDonnell's interpretation.
   (C) Briefly explain how one historical event or development that is not explicitly mentioned in the excerpts could support White's interpretation.

"The day after, I went to visit the governour at his house, and among other discourse I told him I tooke notice of several ships that were arrived at Boston, some since my being there, from Spain, France, Streights, Canaries and other parts of Europe, contrary to your Majesties lawes for encouraging navigation, and regulating the trade of the plantations. He freely declared to me that the lawes made by your Majestie and your parliament obligeth them in nothing but what consists with the interest of that colony, that the legislative power is and abides in them soley to act and make lawes by virtue of a charter from your Majesties royall father, and that all matters indifference are to be concluded by their final determination, without any appeal to your majestie, and that your Majestie ought not to retrench their liberties, but may enlarge them if your Majestie please . . . yet they did believe your Majestie to be their very good friend, for that your Majestie had several letters expressed by your kindnesse to them . . ."

Letter from Edward Randolph to the King of England, 1676

2. Using the excerpt, answer **A**, **B**, and **C**.
   (A) Briefly describe the historical situation described in the excerpt.
   (B) Briefly explain how one specific historical event or development between 1607 and 1676 led to the historical situation depicted in the excerpt.
   (C) Briefly explain how one specific historical event or development between 1676 and 1754 resulted from the historical situation depicted in the excerpt.

3. Answer **A**, **B**, and **C**.
   (A) Briefly describe one specific historical change in relations between Native Americans and British North American colonists in the period 1607 to 1754.
   (B) Briefly describe one specific historical continuity in relations between Native Americans and British North American colonists in the period 1607 to 1754.
   (C) Briefly explain one way in which Native Americans resisted British colonization in the period from 1676 to 1754.

4. Answer **A**, **B**, and **C**.
   (A) Briefly explain one example of how enslavement changed over time in the British North American colonies from 1619 to 1754.
   (B) Briefly explain one similarity in enslavement between two regions of the British North American colonies from 1619 to 1754.
   (C) Briefly explain one difference in enslavement between two regions of the British North American colonies from 1619 to 1754.

PERIOD 3 1754–1800

A Revolutionary Era

© New York Historical Society/Bridgeman Images

Banner of the Pewter Artisans, 1788 This painted silk banner was carried by the Society of Pewterers of the City of New York at a parade to celebrate the ratification of the U.S. Constitution in 1788. Pewter is a tin alloy used to make inexpensive utensils and kitchenware. Skilled artisans used images like this banner to make clear that their work was woven into the fabric of the new republic.

Contextualizing Period 3

MODULE **3.1**

Following King William's War (1689–1697), Queen Anne's War (1702–1713), and King George's War (1744–1748), the Seven Years' War (1756–1763)—which began in 1754 in North America and was known as the French and Indian War—was Britain's largest victory in the ongoing imperial contest for North America. Expelling the French from North America came at a high price, however. This latest war had left Britain in massive debt, and the new policies the crown created to raise money to pay it off were unpopular with North American colonists.

The British Parliament's efforts to impose greater control over its North American colonies sparked a strong reaction. Impressment and quartering, the Proclamation of 1763, and the Sugar Act in 1764 were just some of the policies that drew protest from colonists. These protests became more effective as colonists developed organizations and systems of communication that allowed them to spread their ideas far and wide. This also helped unite colonists across classes, because many British laws—such as those that placed limits on westward expansion—were unpopular with everyone.

AP® EXAM TIP

Debt from the French and Indian War, as well as managing a global empire, caused Britain to look for more ways to increase revenue. Make sure you understand Britain's economic and political purposes for taxing the American colonies. Also, what ideological and constitutional arguments did the colonists assert to denounce Britain's attempts at taxation? What methods did American colonies use to resist Britain's abandonment of "salutary neglect"? Finally, how did this change Britain's relationship with her American colonies?

Although many colonists were displeased with British policies by 1774, many others still supported them. Indeed, the majority of colonists did not participate in any protest activities. For the most part, the aim of those who did protest continued to be resistance to particular acts, not independence from Britain—that is, colonists sought greater liberty within the empire.

Colonists moved reluctantly from resistance to revolution. When faced with threats from British troops, a sufficient number of colonists took up arms and made war a reality. This surge of violent conflict finally gave the advantage to those few radical political leaders urging independence.

The patriots' eventual victory over Great Britain after seven years of war won them independence, but the new country faced many difficult problems in its aftermath. The nation owed a huge debt to private citizens and state and foreign governments, and difficult economic times followed. Continental soldiers had not been paid, and they demanded to be given what they were owed so that they could return home and reestablish their former lives. This was just one of many economic issues that devastated many war veterans and their families during the remainder of the eighteenth century.

These problems affected American Indians and Black Americans as well as whites. Warfare between settlers and American Indians west of the Appalachian Mountains, from the Ohio River valley to Georgia, continued for decades. At the same time, enslavers seeking more fertile fields also expanded into the trans-Appalachian region.

AP® EXAM TIP

Understand the political, economic, and social relationships that Britain had with its American colonies. How did various European countries view North America and its inhabitants? How did European attitudes toward North America affect the events that took place there from 1754–1800?

In the 1780s and 1790s, the United States faced many obstacles to securing the nation. Financial hardship, enormous debts, conflicts with American Indians, and European diplomacy had to be addressed by a federal government that, under the Articles of Confederation, was weak. By 1787 concerns about national security, fueled by backcountry conflicts that sometimes erupted into outright rebellion, persuaded some political leaders to embrace a new governmental structure. While it required many compromises among groups with competing ideas and interests, the Constitution was drafted and, after fierce debates, narrowly approved.

George Washington took office as the first president of the United States at the head of a more powerful federal government. His administration sought to enhance U.S. power at home and abroad. Secretary of the Treasury Alexander Hamilton proposed a series of measures to stabilize the American economy, pay off Revolutionary War debts, and promote trade and industry. However, these Federalist policies drew opposition from leaders such as Thomas Jefferson and James Madison, whose positions aligned with many ordinary farmers and frontiersmen.

By 1796, Jefferson and Madison had formed a separate political party, the Democratic-Republicans, and in 1800, they gained control of Congress and won the presidency for their candidate, Jefferson. Power transitioned peacefully from one political party to another, a promising sign for the future of the young United States.

Period 3: What's Inside 1754–1800

MODULE	AP® THEMATIC FOCUS
3.1 Contextualizing Period 3	The explosive growth of the British colonies in North America and conflicts with Native Americans and rival European powers led to the French and Indian War (Seven Years' War). After the British victory, attempts to assert greater imperial control in the colonies and increase tax revenue sparked the American Revolution, in which thirteen colonies won their independence after a seven-year conflict. Debates over the challenges facing the new nation and the proper role of government shaped the formation of the Articles of Confederation, and its replacement, the Constitution, and led to the formation of the first political party system in the United States.
3.2 The Seven Years' War (The French and Indian War)	**America in the World** By 1764, the British had fought a number of colonial wars with European powers over control of North America. The Seven Years' War proved to be the costliest and most consequential of these wars. British victory left Great Britain in control of much of North America, but also deeply in debt. The policies Great Britain introduced in the aftermath of the war raised tensions with British colonists.
3.3 Taxation without Representation	**America in the World** In the aftermath of the Seven Years' War, British North Americans increasingly believed that British colonial policies benefited Britain at their expense. In reaction to colonial rebellion, British officials tried a number of different responses, including compromising and exercising greater control over the colonies. All of these strategies had limited success.
3.4 Philosophical Foundations of the American Revolution	**American and National Identity** By 1774, many British colonists began to see themselves as members of a society separate from Great Britain. In response to the harsh Coercive Acts, a series of armed conflicts, and the publication of Thomas Paine's *Common Sense*, the Second Continental Congress issued a Declaration of Independence, using Enlightenment principles to argue that the British government had violated colonists' natural rights and that therefore the colonists had a right to create their own republican form of government.
3.5 The American Revolution	**America in the World** During the American Revolution, the former British colonies defined themselves as an independent nation and formed crucial alliances with France and Spain in their conflict with Great Britain, broadening the conflict beyond North America. Victory in the Revolutionary War brought official diplomatic recognition and expanded the new nation's western border to the Mississippi River.
3.6 The Influence of Revolutionary Ideals	**Social Structures** During and immediately after the American Revolution, Americans faced financial hardships that generated debate over economic policy. The events and ideas that underpinned the American Revolution also challenged traditional ethnic and gender structures during the conflict and gave rise to a movement to educate young Americans for future republican citizenship.
3.7 The Articles of Confederation	**Politics and Power** In the aftermath of the American Revolution, Americans debated the proper role of a national government and faced internal conflicts that challenged the ideals of the American Revolution itself.
3.8 The Constitutional Convention and Debates over Ratification	**Politics and Power** By the mid-1780s, it had become increasingly clear that the government structured by the Articles of Confederation could not maintain control over the new republic. During this period, Americans debated how best to strengthen the federal government without undermining the rights gained in the Revolution. During the debates over the new constitution, various regional interests vied for influence over the new federal government.
3.9 The Constitution	**Politics and Power** During the Constitutional Convention, delegates from the states created a new, stronger federal government with executive, legislative, and judicial branches. This federalist system, with a separation of powers, checks and balances, and eventually a bill of rights, replaced the Articles of Confederation and has endured as the nation's governing document.

MODULE	AP® THEMATIC FOCUS
3.10 Shaping a New Republic	**America in the World** Even as George Washington led the new government and strengthened federal authority, growing debates over economic and foreign policy led to the emergence of competing political factions. The French Revolution and conflicts in Europe further divided Americans as the nation faced challenges to its sovereignty on its borderlands and abroad.
3.11 Developing an American Identity	**American and National Identity** During this time, a distinctly American identity began to emerge through the work of writers, artists, and intellectuals as well as the shared experience of the American Revolution. However, conflicts over western lands, the persistence of slavery, and a legacy of racism limited the inclusion of American Indians and Black Americans.
3.12 Movement in the Early Republic	**Migration and Settlement** Westward migration during the mid-1700s led to the creation of new communities and heightened ethnic tensions as well as regional conflicts. American Indians grappled with the impacts of migration and settlement as they adjusted alliances and sought to maintain their access to resources and control of land.
3.13 Continuity and Change in Period 3	Period 3 offers opportunities to trace the ways in which the British North American colonies changed as a result of the Seven-Years War, and the extent to which economic, social, cultural, and political trends continued from before the war.
Support and Practice	• Practice thinking and writing historically in each module. • See the Period Review of key concepts, events, people, and dates after the last module. • Try the AP® Exam Practice at the end of the period.

The Seven Years' War (The French and Indian War)

MODULE 3.2

FOCUS

Examining history through the lens of cause and effect is a valuable skill and one of the basic tools of historical analysis. To help identify possible causes or effects of a historical development, you may wish to think about categories. What were the political, economic, or social factors that led to or resulted from a historical development or process? In addition to those common categories, you should also consider other potential categories such as geographic, diplomatic, cultural, military, or technological. Thinking broadly about the different types of causes and effects will help you synthesize information and create an effective argument.

As you read about the French and Indian War (also known as the Seven Years' War) in this module, keep the process of cause and effect at the front of your mind. Ask yourself the following questions: What causes led to the conflict? What factors enabled the British to prevail? What effects resulted from war? Remember to consider the different categories of cause and effect mentioned in the paragraph above as you think about these questions.

The war that erupted in the Ohio River Valley in 1754 caused an enormous shift in political and economic relations across colonial North America. What began as a small-scale regional conflict expanded into a brutal and lengthy war with battles around the world. Known as the French and Indian War in North America and the Seven Years' War in Great Britain and Europe, where battles broke out in 1756, the extended conflict led to a dramatic expansion of British territory in North America and increasing demands from American colonists for more control over their own lives.

In the long run, imperial wars led to growing discord between Great Britain and its colonies. American colonists grew increasingly tired of spending their lives and money on seemingly endless conflicts with origins across the Atlantic Ocean. During King William's War (1689–1697), Queen Anne's War (1702–1713), and King George's War (1739–1748), North America was just one theater in a larger global conflict—and the same proved true of the Seven Years' War, known in North America as the French and Indian War.

French and Indian War (Seven Years' War)
A global conflict from 1754–1763 among European nations, mainly Britain and France, that began in North America over disputed territorial rights to the Ohio River Valley in 1754, with further conflict erupting in Europe in 1756. France ultimately ceded all its North American territories to Britain and Spain, but the enormous cost of the war also severely damaged the British and French economies.

A New Colonial War

One of the young colonial officers who would lead troops during the **French and Indian War** was George Washington. Born in 1732 to a prosperous planter family in eastern Virginia, Washington had a comfortable upbringing. By the time he was twenty years old, he had invested in western properties and inherited the large estate at Mount Vernon, Virginia. Following his inheritance, he set about expanding its boundaries and its enslaved workforce.

Washington was soon appointed lieutenant colonel in the Virginia militia, and in the fall of 1753, Virginia's governor sent him to warn the French against advancing on British territory in the Ohio River Valley. Despite warnings, the French commander disregarded Washington and, within six months, gained control of a British post near present-day Pittsburgh, Pennsylvania, naming it Fort Duquesne. With help from American Indians hostile to the French, Washington's surprise attack on Fort Duquesne in May 1754 led the governors of Virginia and North Carolina to provide the newly promoted Colonel Washington with more troops to strengthen colonial claims to the disputed area. The French then responded with a much larger force and forced Washington to surrender just two months later, in July 1754. These skirmishes later became the opening shots of the French and Indian War (1754–1763).

Even before Washington and his troops were defeated, the British attempted to protect the colonies against threats from the French and American Indians. To limit such threats, the British tried to form an alliance with the powerful Haudenosaunee (Iroquois) Confederacy, composed of six northeastern tribes. The British invited an official delegation from the Haudenosaunee to a meeting in the summer of 1754 in Albany, New York, with representatives from several colonies. Benjamin Franklin used the meeting to introduce an **Albany Plan of Union** that would establish a council of representatives from the various colonial assemblies to debate issues of borderlands defense, trade, and territorial expansion and to recommend terms agreeable to both colonists and American Indians. Their deliberations were to be overseen by a president-general appointed and supported by the British crown. Despite the British government's goal of improving relations with the Haudenosaunee, Franklin's plan excluded American Indian representatives from participation.

Albany Plan of Union
A plan put together in 1754 by Benjamin Franklin to create a more centralized colonial government that would establish policies regarding defense, trade, and territorial expansion, as well as aim to facilitate better relations between colonists and American Indians.

This meeting created new bonds among a small circle of colonial leaders, but it failed to establish a stronger alliance with the Haudenosaunee or resolve problems of colonial governance. British officials opposed Franklin's plan, fearing it would undermine the authority of the royal government. It was rejected outright by the individual

Granger – Historical Picture Archive

Colonel George Washington This 1772 oil painting by Charles Willson Peale portrays George Washington as a colonel in the Virginia militia. Washington commanded this militia during the French and Indian War following the death of General Braddock. After the war, Washington prospered as a planter and land speculator.

How does this portrayal of Washington reflect the expansion of British power in North America?

Library of Congress, LC-USZC4-5315

The First Political Cartoon Benjamin Franklin created the first political cartoon in American history to accompany an editorial he wrote in the *Pennsylvania Gazette* in 1754. Franklin's cartoon urged the mainland British colonies to unite politically during the French and Indian War. Legend had it that a snake could come back to life if its severed sections were attached before dusk. **How does the symbolism in Franklin's image support his argument for colonial unity?**

colonies, unwilling to give up any of their independence in military, trade, and political matters. Meanwhile, Haudenosaunee delegates, angered by their exclusion from participating in the council of representatives, left the Congress and broke off talks with the British. Despite the threat posed by the French and their American Indian allies, the Albany Plan of Union was never implemented.

For most American Indian nations, contests among European nations for land and power afforded them the best chance of survival in the eighteenth century, and the French and Indian War was no exception. They had leverage as long as various European imperial powers needed their trade items, military support, and political alliances—but this leverage would vanish if one European nation controlled most of North America.

Still, American Indians adopted different strategies during the French and Indian War. The Delaware, Huron, Miami, and Shawnee nations, for example, allied themselves with the French, hoping that a French victory would stop the far more numerous British colonists from invading their settlements in the Ohio River Valley. Nations of the Haudenosaunee (Iroquois) Confederacy, on the other hand, tried to play one power against the other, hoping to win concessions from the British in return for their military support. The Creek, Choctaw, and Cherokee also tried to prolong the existing standoff between different European powers by bargaining alternately with the British in Georgia and the Carolinas, the French in Louisiana, and the Spaniards in Florida. Faced with invasion of their lands, some American Indian tribes, like the Abenaki in northern New England, launched attacks on colonial settlements. They also seized British ships amid the chaos of war, seeking to enrich themselves and establish themselves as a power in the Atlantic Ocean.

The British government soon decided to send additional troops to defend its American colonies against attacks from American Indians and intrusions from the French. General Edward Braddock and two regiments arrived in 1755 to expel the French from Fort Duquesne. At the same time, colonial militia units were sent to battle the French and their American Indian allies along the New York and New England borders. Colonel Washington joined Braddock as his personal aide-de-camp. Within months, however, Braddock's forces were ambushed, badly beaten by French and American Indian forces, and Braddock was killed. Other British forces did little better during the next three years.

guerilla tactics Tactics deployed by irregular forces in a conflict, usually dependent on surprise attack, raids on supply lines, assassinations, and attacks on civilian supporters of an enemy.

Despite having far fewer colonists in North America than the British, the French had established extensive trade networks and alliances with powerful American Indian nations that helped outweigh their military disadvantages. Alternating **guerrilla tactics** with conventional warfare, the French and allied American Indian nations captured several important forts, built a new one on Lake Champlain, and moved troops deep into British territory. The ineffectiveness of the British and colonial armies also encouraged tribes along the New England and Appalachian border areas to reclaim land from colonists. Bloody raids devastated many outlying settlements, leading to the death and capture of hundreds of Britain's colonial subjects.

As the British faced defeat after defeat in North America, European nations began to contest imperial claims elsewhere in the world. In 1756, France and Great Britain officially declared war against each other. Eventually Austria, Russia, Sweden, most of the German states, and Spain allied with France, while Portugal and Prussia sided with Great Britain. As the French and Indian War expanded into a global conflict fought on multiple continents, it became known as the Seven Years' War (1756–1763). With the approach of winter in 1757, a French victory in this newly global conflict appeared all but certain.

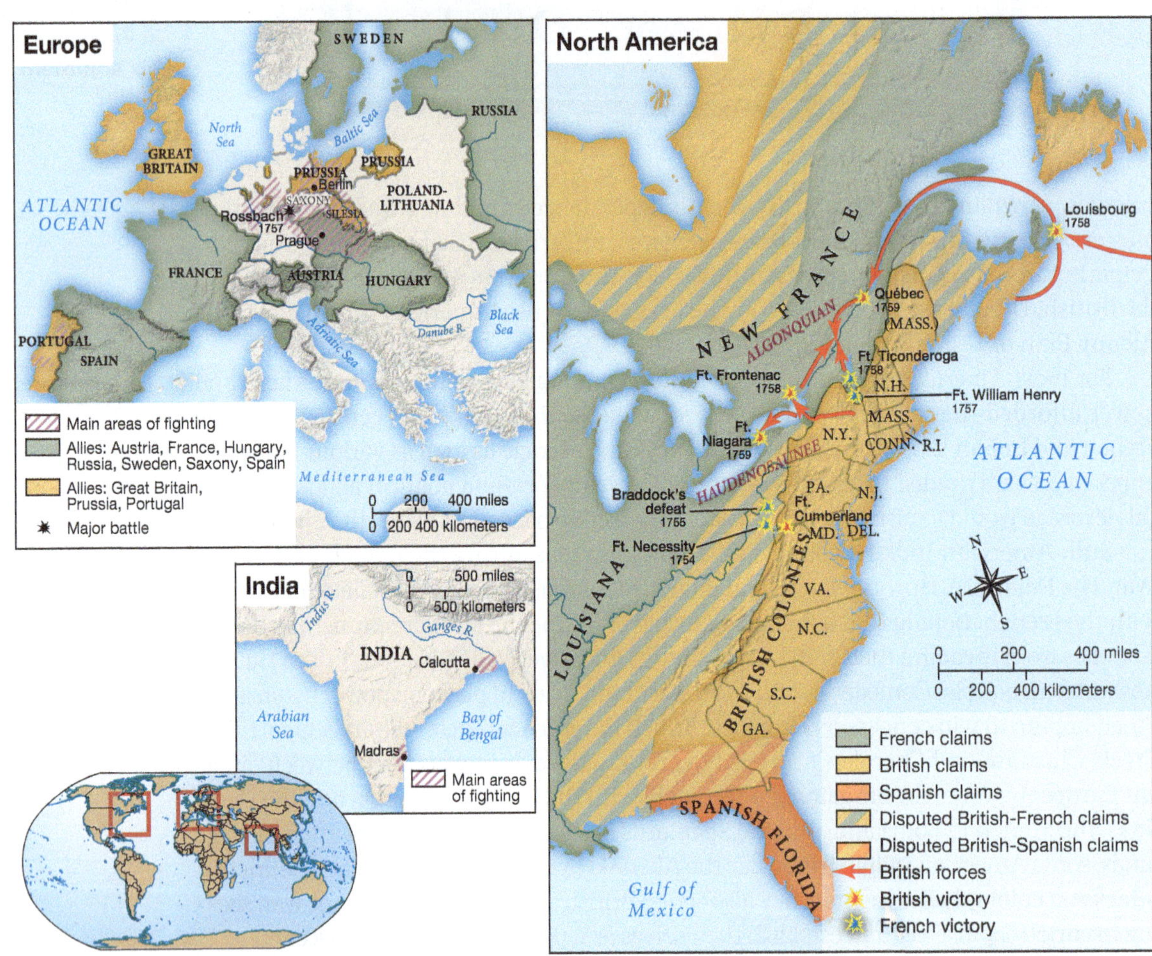

MAP 3.1 The French and Indian War, 1754–1763 Clashes between colonial militia units and the allied French and American Indian forces erupted in North America in 1754. The conflict sparked a wider war that engulfed Europe as well as the West Indies and India. In the aftermath of this first global war, Britain gained control of present-day Canada and India, but France retained its West Indies colonies.

Based on this map, what territorial disputes were most significant in North America during the French and Indian War?

REVIEW

- How did British interests shape colonial involvement in the French and Indian War?

The Costs of Victory

As the French and Indian War grew into a global military conflict, Britain implemented increasingly unpopular policies to meet its demands. For instance, the English desperately needed sailors to fight for Britain as naval warfare erupted in the Mediterranean Sea and the Atlantic and Indian Oceans. Battles raged not only in North America and Europe, but in far-flung places such as the West Indies, India, and the Philippines.

Britain's solution to its shortage of sailors was brutal: The Royal Navy forced young colonial men living in port cities into military service via impressment. Seamen and dockworkers had good reason to fight off impressment agents. Men in the Royal Navy faced low wages, bad food, harsh punishment, rampant disease, and a high possibility of death. The efforts to capture new "recruits" often met violent resistance from merchants and common folk alike, especially in the North American colonies where several hundred men might be impressed at one time. In such circumstances, whole communities joined in the battle for resistance.

American employers and politicians who opposed impressment learned that they gained important advantages in directing the anger of colonists away from themselves and toward British policies. Even after the war's conclusion, impressment riots occurred in places such as Boston and New York City because the British continued the practice.

Throughout the war, British military officers also quartered their troops in homes of colonists, because there were not enough public buildings to seize, and harsh winters made camping in tents intolerable. Thus, colonial towns and cities were required to house and support the British military with food, supplies, and other goods that were generally in short supply during the war because of piracy and seizures of ships by the French and Spanish navies. British officers were put up in luxurious mansions while their troops stayed in modest homes. Any colonists who objected to the use of their homes, food, or supplies were threatened with violence. Like impressment, the practice

Chronicle/Alamy

Impressment by the British This eighteenth-century engraving depicts the harsh impressment of men into the British navy. Set in England, this illustration shows that impressment was widely practiced at home. The British government did not single out the colonists for special mistreatment.

How did the differing views toward impressment shape colonial relations with the British?

AP® WORKING with EVIDENCE

Source: European Land Claims in North America, 1754–1763

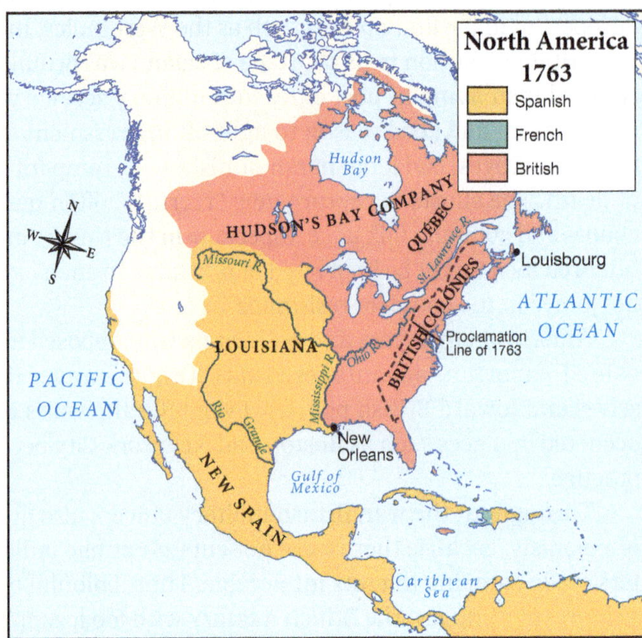

Questions for Analysis

1. Identify the changes in territorial holdings shown on these two maps.
2. Describe why some territorial holdings increased while others decreased.
3. Explain how the changing territorial holdings could influence European colonists' relationships with American Indians.

of quartering troops in private homes also united colonists across social classes in protest against British practices.

Despite growing unrest due to British wartime policies, the tide of the French and Indian War began to turn in their favor by the summer of 1758. As Prussian troops held the line on the European front, Britain poured more soldiers and arms into its North American campaign. With the aid of colonial troops, British forces recaptured the fort at Louisburg on Cape Breton Island, a key to France's defense of Canada. Then British troops, with Washington's aid, once again seized Fort Duquesne and renamed it Fort Pitt. Other British forces took control of Fort Frontenac along the St. Lawrence River as well as Forts Ticonderoga and Crown Point on Lake Champlain. French efforts in North America suffered as Prussia defeated France and its allies in Europe and Britain gained key victories in India. The British won Québec and control of Canada, albeit at the cost of many lives, by 1759.

Despite these key victories, the war dragged on in North America, Europe, India, and the West Indies for three more years. Finally, King George III (reigned 1760–1820) grew concerned enough with the expense of imperial conflict to open peace negotiations with France in 1762. He agreed to give up a number of conquered territories to finalize the **Peace of Paris** in 1763. Spain ceded Florida to Great Britain to regain control of its Cuban and Philippine colonies. While France was expelled from North America, it rewarded Spanish support by granting Spain Louisiana and all French-claimed lands west of the Mississippi River. The British empire reigned supreme, however, as it established its control over India, North America east of the Mississippi, all of Canada, and a number of Caribbean islands. Although the Peace of Paris had successfully negotiated international relationships, many internal conflicts in the British Empire were still unresolved, including those with American Indian nations in North America.

Peace of Paris
A 1763 peace treaty ending the French and Indian War (Seven Years' War). Under its terms, France gave up all of its North American territorial rights and Britain gained control of present-day Canada and of North America east of the Mississippi River. Spain gained all of French-controlled Louisiana, including the Port of New Orleans.

REVIEW

- What were some of the early signs of conflict between Great Britain and British North Americans?
- What gains did Great Britain make in the aftermath of the French and Indian War?

Unresolved Issues in the Colonies

The war reshaped European empires and transformed patterns of global trade. Yet the Peace of Paris did not resolve many of the problems that had plagued the colonies before the war, and it created new ones as well. British victory encouraged thousands of colonists to move farther west, into lands once controlled by France and currently occupied by American Indian nations, inflaming already strained relations. To make matters worse, British traders often either deceived American Indians outright or ignored American Indian trading practices such as gift giving and restrictions against trading with enemies.

The harsh realities of the British regime led some American Indians to seek a return to ways of life that preceded the arrival of white men. A visionary named Neolin preached that American Indians had been corrupted by contact with Europeans and urged them to purify themselves by returning to their ancient traditions, abandoning white ways, and reclaiming their lands. Neolin was a prophet, not a warrior, but his message inspired others, including an Ottawa leader named Pontiac.

When news arrived in early 1763 that France was about to cede all of its North American lands to Britain and Spain, Pontiac convened a council of more than four hundred Ottawa, Potawatomi, and Huron leaders near Fort Detroit. Drawing on Neolin's vision, he proclaimed, "It is important my brothers, that we should exterminate from our land [Britain], whose only object is our death. You must all be sensible," he continued, "that we can no longer supply our wants the way we were accustomed to do with our Fathers the French." Pontiac then mobilized support to drive out the British. In May 1763, Pontiac's forces laid siege to Detroit and soon gained the support of eighteen American Indian nations. They then attacked Fort Pitt and other British border outposts as well as white settlements along the Virginia and Pennsylvania borderlands.

Accounts of violent encounters with Native Americans in the backcountry circulated throughout the colonies and sparked resentment among settlers as well as British troops. Many colonists did not distinguish between friendly and hostile American Indians. In December 1763, a group of men from Paxton Creek, Pennsylvania, raided families of peaceful, Christian Conestoga Indians near Lancaster, killing thirty. Protests from eastern colonists infuriated these Paxton Boys, who then marched on Philadelphia demanding protection from inland "savages."

Benjamin Franklin negotiated a truce between the Paxton Boys and the Pennsylvania authorities, but it did not settle the fundamental issues over protection of western settlers.

Native American diplomatic efforts fell short of gaining French support for renewed conflict, and Pontiac and his followers failed to push the British back. Hoping to avoid further costly clashes and to improve trade relations with American Indians, the British crown issued a proclamation in October 1763 forbidding colonial settlement west of a line running down the Appalachian Mountains to create a buffer between American Indians and colonists.

Proclamation Line of 1763
Act of Parliament following the end of the French and Indian War that restricted colonial settlement west of the Appalachian Mountains, generating widespread resentment in the colonies.

speculator
An investor who buys large quantities of a commodity at a low price in hopes that prices will rise and produce a profit when sold. Speculation in a product tends to drive up its price.

The **Proclamation Line of 1763** denied colonists the right to settle west of the Appalachian Mountains. Imposed by the British government following the Peace of Paris, the Proclamation Line frustrated colonists who sought the right to economic benefits they believed were won by participation in a long and bloody war.

Small farmers, backcountry settlers, and squatters who had hoped to improve their lot by acquiring rich farmlands were told to stay put. Meanwhile, George Washington and other wealthy **speculators** bought additional western lands, certain that the Proclamation was merely "a temporary expedient to quiet the Minds of the Indians."

MAP 3.2 British Conflicts with American Indians, 1758–1763 The entrance of British troops into former French territory in the Ohio River Valley during and following the Seven Years' War fueled conflicts with American Indian nations. Colonists in Pennsylvania and the Carolinas also battled with American Indians, including tribes who had formerly been neutral, or even allies. In 1763, at the war's conclusion, Parliament established the Proclamation Line to limit westward expansion and thereby diminish such hostilities.

How did the Proclamation Line of 1763 reveal differing priorities between British officials and North American colonists?

The Peace of Paris ignored the claims of American Indian tribes to territories they occupied, even as it left unresolved disputes between the colonies over lands in the Ohio River Valley and elsewhere along British North America's new borderlands.

Moreover, it raised tensions between colonists and Britain. Victory had come at an enormous cost: Over the course of the war, the national debt of Great Britain more than doubled. At the same time, as the North American colonies grew and conflicts with American Indians along their border areas intensified in response to that growth, the costs of running these colonies increased fivefold. With an empire that now stretched around the globe, the British crown and Parliament needed more funds than ever to pay off war debts, administer far-flung territories, and keep sufficient currency in circulation for expanding international trade. As you will read in later modules, the methods they undertook to raise these funds provoked growing resistance from American colonists.

AP® EXAM TIP

The competition between France and Great Britain for dominance in the area west of the Appalachian Mountains, along with profitable alliances with American Indians in the region, led to the Seven Years' War. Great Britain emerged victorious, but at a great cost. Make sure you understand the cause and effects of the French and Indian War and how it changed Britain's relationships in North America with her colonies, American Indians, and other European nations.

AP® Skills Workshop: Thinking Historically

Creating a Thesis Statement

History is often seen as a documentation of past events to create a historical record. And while historians regularly engage in research to uncover new details and better understand past events, the job of a historian is not simply to collect information. Instead, historians make meaning of what happened by asking questions and engaging in debates with other historians.

Through this process, historians create a narrative to explain past events, and continually revise that narrative as new information and arguments come to light. *Fabric of a Nation* is itself a narrative history, and a product of hundreds of historians doing research, making arguments, debating each other, and coming to conclusions about the past. The authors of this book have also made their own interpretations and conclusions about the past, and they have written them into this book. While you will probably never attempt to write a large, detailed account of American history, you will be expected in your class and on the AP® Exam to create sound historical arguments in response to specific questions, just like historians do.

In Modules 1.3 and 2.3, you were introduced to how primary-source authors make claims and use evidence to support those claims in primary sources as well as how historians make and support claims in secondary sources. Recall that a claim is an argument or position being taken, and evidence is the proof or support used to back up that claim. Then, you had the opportunity to make your own claims, support those claims with specific evidence, and explain how the evidence proved your claims using **CSE** to respond to various types of Short-Answer Questions (SAQs) in Modules 1.4, 1.7, 2.4, and 2.8.

Now we are going to move beyond SAQs and look at how to construct a larger argument in response to an essay prompt by building on CSE. For an SAQ, we advised writing a **Claim, Support, Explain** answer of two to four sentences for each part of the question. Similarly, for an essay, you should address the prompt with a multi-sentence answer that states an overall claim and provides two to four clear areas of

(continued)

support. This is known as a **thesis statement**, and it's an important element of an essay's introduction.

Let's take a look at a sample essay question and how to create a thesis statement for it. We will use a three-step process similar to the one we previously practiced for SAQs:

1. Understand the question,
2. Brainstorm information, and
3. Write a thesis statement that makes a claim and provides an outline of the reasoning used to support your argument.

Explain the factors that contributed to British victory in the French and Indian War.

Step 1 ▶ **Closely examine the prompt**

The first step is to carefully analyze the prompt by identifying the topic, time frame, and historical reasoning process (causation, comparison, or continuity and change over time). This essay question refers specifically to the French and Indian War, the subject of this module. While the years are not specified, we can infer that the prompt covers the years of the conflict, 1754–1763 and possibly a few years before its start. Finally, "factors that contributed" is a clear indication that the reasoning process involved is causation. That's important because the thesis statement and the overall essay should be framed as a set of reasons (causes) for British victory.

Step 2 ▶ **Brainstorm relevant historical information**

The second step is to recall relevant information, otherwise known as brainstorming. Think of how and why the British and their colonists triumphed. As you sort through your ideas, try to distinguish larger, more significant events or processes from more minor details. These minor details will be useful later in your body paragraphs as support for your broader points. One way to do this is to think broadly about the question using the analytical categories discussed in this module's Focus opener (see page 149). Here's an example of what a thesis brainstorming chart for this essay prompt could look like.

General Categories	Main Points	Supporting Details
Military	Key battlefield victories abroad and in the colonies	- Prussian military success in Europe - British military success in India - Capture of strategic French forts in the colonies such as Louisburg and Montreal
Economic	Commitment of large number of troops and mobilization of extensive colonial and British resources	- Colonial population advantage - Large military expenditures and British debt - Impressment of colonial sailors and quartering of British troops in colonial homes
Political	Compromises and successful negotiations during 1763 Treaty of Paris	- British trading overseas territories for North American gains - British gaining lands east of Mississippi River and Canada - France ceding Louisiana territory to Spain

Notice that the chart is organized left to right from broad topic (general category) to a brief description of the cause (main point) to examples of specific developments that demonstrate the main point (supporting details). The purpose of the General Categories column is to help you to think broadly about different types of causes. Information from the Main Points column should be used in your

(continued)

thesis statement and then later as the basis of the topic sentences for your body paragraphs. The Supporting Details in the third column provide the evidence you can discuss and analyze in the body paragraphs.

Step 3 ▶ Write a thesis with a claim and line of reasoning

The third step is to write an effective thesis statement that directly answers the question and sets up the overall essay. A good thesis statement makes a **historically defensible claim** and establishes a **line of reasoning** to support that claim. It's often easiest to write a **two-sentence thesis statement** that makes the claim in the first sentence and lays out the line of reasoning in the second sentence. Fortunately, all the information we need is in the completed brainstorming chart. The most important column for the thesis statement is the "Main Points" column. That's what you should use to construct your line of reasoning after making a more general claim in response to the question. Here's an example of a good two-sentence thesis statement for this prompt:

> While the British and their colonists initially fared poorly in the French and Indian War, over time they turned the tide and ultimately prevailed [**claim**]. Important battlefield victories abroad and in North America, the large commitment of troops and resources, and skillful negotiations at the 1763 Treaty of Paris were the main factors that enabled the British to triumph [**line of reasoning**].

ACTIVITY

Now it's your turn to write an effective thesis statement. Use the same three-step process as modeled above to analyze and deconstruct the prompt, brainstorm and categorize information, and write a strong thesis by making a historically defensible claim and providing a line of reasoning.

> Explain the short-term effects of the French and Indian War.

MODULE 3.3

Taxation without Representation

FOCUS

Often, historical events have clear and distinct causes or effects. However, that's not always true. Sometimes, those causes and effects are interwoven into a chain of causation tying multiple developments together as people and institutions react to each other, leading to further events.

As you read Module 3.3, pay attention to this dynamic. Notice how specific British policies generated colonial reactions that then, in turn, led to additional British actions and colonial reactions to those actions. Consider how and why this pattern produced a breakdown of relations between the colonists and the British government in the decade after the French and Indian War in 1763.

Between the end of the Glorious Revolution in 1689 and the beginning of the French and Indian War in 1754, British officials and their colonial subjects coexisted in relative harmony. Economic growth in the British empire led Britain to ignore much of the smuggling and domestic manufacturing that took place in the colonies, since these activities did not disrupt Britain's mercantile goals. Similarly, although the king and Parliament held ultimate political sovereignty, or final authority, over the American colonies, it was easier to allow some local control over political decisions, given the communication challenges created by distance. This pattern of **salutary (benign) neglect** led some American colonists to view themselves as more independent of British control than the crown and Parliament believed them to be. Many colonists came to see free trade (or smuggling, from the British perspective), domestic manufacturing, and local self-governance as rights rather than privileges.

salutary neglect
British colonial policy from around 1700 to 1760 that relaxed supervision of internal colonial affairs as long as the North American colonies produced sufficient raw materials and revenue.

Over the long term, the policy had the unintended effect of increasing colonial claims of self-governance. Thus, when British officials decided to assert greater control, many colonists protested. Between 1764 and 1774, as Parliament sought to extend its political and economic control over the American colonies, colonists periodically resisted. With each instance of resistance, Parliament demanded further submission to royal authority. With each demand for submission, colonists responded with greater assertions of their rights. Still, no one imagined that a revolution was in the making.

Intensifying Conflict and Resistance, 1763–1766

To King George III and to Parliament, asserting control over the colonies was both right and necessary. In 1763, King George appointed George Grenville to lead the British government. Faced with an economic depression in England, he believed that regaining political and economic control in the colonies could help resolve this financial crisis.

Eighteenth-century wars, especially the French and Indian War, cost a fortune. British subjects in England paid taxes to help offset the nation's debts, even though few of them benefited as directly from the British victory in 1763 as did their counterparts in North America. The colonies would cost the British treasury more if the crown could not control colonists' movement into American Indian territories, limit smuggling and domestic manufacturing, and house British troops in the colonies cheaply.

To reassert control, the Parliament led by Grenville launched a three-pronged program. First, it sought stricter enforcement of existing laws, such as the seventeenth-century Navigation Acts (see Module 2.4), which prohibited trade with English rivals, established guidelines for legal commerce, and set duties (taxes) on trade goods. Second, Parliament extended wartime policies into peacetime. For example, the **Quartering Act** of 1765 ensured that British troops would remain in the colonies to carry out imperial policies, including enforcing impressment and cracking down on smuggling. Colonial governments were expected to support them by allowing them to use vacant buildings and providing them with food and supplies. Predictably, tensions between colonists and British officials rose, as wealthier local leaders joined forces with ordinary colonists in protest. This was one of the first steps in a conflict that would escalate over the next ten years.

The third part of Grenville's colonial program was the most important. It called for the passage of new laws to raise funds and reestablish British authority. The first revenue act passed by Parliament was the **Sugar Act** in 1764. It imposed import duties on coffee, wine, and other luxury items. The act reduced the import tax on foreign molasses, which was regularly smuggled into the colonies from the West Indies, but required that the tax be collected. The crackdown on smuggling increased the power of customs officers and established the first vice-admiralty courts in North America to prosecute smugglers and ensure that the Sugar Act raised money for the crown. Over time, colonial protests against the act escalated as smugglers' livelihoods were threatened and New England distilleries' costs rose.

Also in 1764, Parliament passed the **Currency Act**, which prohibited colonial assemblies from printing their own paper money. Taken together, these provisions meant that colonists would pay more money into the British treasury even as the supply of money (and illegal goods) diminished in the colonies.

Some colonial leaders protested the Sugar Act through speeches, pamphlets, and petitions, and by forming **committees of correspondence** to circulate concerns to leaders in other colonies. Although dissent remained largely disorganized and ineffective in the 1760s, the passage of the Sugar, Currency, and Quartering Acts caused anxiety among many colonists.

Quartering Act
A 1765 act requiring colonial governments to provide food and housing for British troops in the colonies. Many colonists resented subsidizing the presence of British troops and eventually viewed those troops as occupiers rather than protectors.

Sugar Act
A 1764 act of Parliament designed to increase revenue and encourage the importation of molasses from the British West Indies by cracking down on the smuggling of French molasses into the colonies even as the tax on it was cut in half.

Currency Act
A 1764 act of Parliament preventing colonial assemblies from printing paper money. This limited colonial economic growth because the colonies exported lower-cost raw materials and imported higher-cost finished goods, resulting in a shortage of currency.

committee of correspondence
Correspondence network designed to rapidly circulate concerns and reports of protest and other political events to leaders and colonial assemblies in the aftermath of the Sugar Act. By 1774, each of the thirteen colonies except Pennsylvania had established an intercolonial committee of correspondence.

REVIEW

- How did British colonial officials attempt to raise funds in the aftermath of the French and Indian War?

The Colonies Forge New Ties

The ties forged between poorer and wealthier colonists over issues of westward expansion, impressment, new taxes, and quartering of British troops grew stronger in the 1760s, but they tended to be localized in seaport cities or in specific areas of the backcountry. Creating bonds across the colonies required considerably more effort in a period when communication and transportation beyond local areas were limited. Means had to be found to spread information and create a sense of common purpose if the colonists were going to persuade Parliament to take their complaints seriously. One important model for such intercolonial communication was the Great Awakening (see Module 2.7).

Even though the Great Awakening had faded in most parts of North America by the 1760s, the techniques of mass communication and critiques of excessive wealth and corruption it initiated provided emotional and practical ways of creating common beliefs among widely dispersed colonists. Many evangelical preachers had condemned the luxurious lifestyles of colonial elites and the spiritual corruption of local officials. Now, in the context of conflicts with Great Britain, colonial leaders used such rhetoric to paint Parliament and British officials as corrupt aristocrats with little faith and less compassion. Political protesters also adopted the tactics and style of New Light sermons, and these mass gatherings offered public spectacles designed to inspire unified action against British imperial policies.

Stamp Act

A 1765 act of Parliament that imposed a duty on all transactions involving paper items such as newspapers and wills. The Stamp Act prompted widespread, coordinated protests by colonists who insisted it was a direct attempt to raise revenue, and that only their representatives had the right to tax them. It was repealed in 1766.

virtual representation

The British claim that every member of Parliament represented the interests of all British subjects, so that colonists did not need the right to vote for members of Parliament.

Sons of Liberty

A loosely organized society throughout the colonies whose goal was to assure colonial support for resistance to British taxation. The Sons of Liberty often used intimidation tactics against merchants and businesses as well as the crown's representatives.

Daughters of Liberty

The Daughters of Liberty worked with the Sons of Liberty to assure colonial resistance to British taxation, usually through fund-raising efforts and campaigns to encourage colonists to avoid purchasing goods produced by Great Britain.

Virginia Resolves

A series of statements by the Virginia legislature dedicated to resistance to British taxation without representation in Parliament or colonial control over taxation.

Even as colonial resistance to new British policies mounted, Grenville decided to impose a stamp tax on the colonies similar to that long used in England, announcing his plans in 1764. The stamp tax required that a revenue stamp be attached to all transactions involving paper items, from newspapers and contracts to playing cards and diplomas. In the spring of 1765, Parliament enacted the **Stamp Act**. The tax was to be collected by colonists appointed for the purpose, and the money was to be spent within the colonies at the direction of Parliament for "defending, protecting, and securing the colonies." To the British government, the Stamp Act seemed completely fair. After all, Englishmen paid on average 26 shillings in tax annually, while Bostonians averaged just 1 shilling. Moreover, Parliament believed the act was purposely written to benefit the American colonies.

The colonists saw it in a more threatening light. The Stamp Act differed from earlier parliamentary laws in three important ways. First, by the time it passed, the colonies were experiencing rising unemployment, falling wages, and a downturn in trade made worse by the Sugar and Currency Acts passed the previous year. Second, critics viewed the Stamp Act as an attempt to control the *internal* affairs of the colonies. It was not an indirect tax on trade, paid by importers and exporters as part of the long-established global mercantilist system, but a direct tax on daily business. Third, such a direct interference with economic affairs in the colonies unleashed concerns of both local officials and ordinary residents that Parliament was taxing colonists who had no representation in its debates and decisions.

The question of representation became a mainstay of colonial protests. The North American colonies had developed a system of representation based on locality. According to colonial leaders, only elected officials could truly represent their interests. In rejecting their complaint that taxation without representation was tyranny, the British claimed the colonists had "**virtual representation**" in Parliament, no different from nonvoting citizens in Britain.

In New York City, Boston, and other cities, merchants, traders, and artisans formed groups—such as the **Sons of Liberty** and **Daughters of Liberty**—dedicated to the repeal of the Stamp Act. Even before it was implemented, angry mobs throughout the colonies attacked stamp distributors. Some were beaten, others tarred and feathered, and all were forced to take an oath never to sell stamps again.

Colonists lodged more formal protests with the British government as well. The Virginia House of Burgesses, led by Patrick Henry, passed five resolutions, known as the **Virginia Resolves**, denouncing taxation without representation. Colonial newspapers reprinted them, and orators performing to eager audiences in Massachusetts and elsewhere recited them from memory. The Massachusetts House also created a circular letter—a written protest circulated to the other colonial assemblies—calling for a congress (convention) to be held in New York City in October 1765 to consider the threat posed by the Stamp Act.

AP® WORKING with EVIDENCE

Source: Patrick Henry, *Virginia Resolves*, 1765

"Whereas, the honorable House of Commons in England have of late drawn into question how far the General Assembly of this colony hath power to enact laws for laying of taxes and imposing duties, payable by the people of this, his majesty's most ancient colony: for settling and ascertaining the same to all future times, the House of Burgesses of this present General Assembly have come to the following resolves: . . .

Resolved

That the first adventurers and settlers of this, his majesty's colony and dominion, brought with them and transmitted to their posterity, and all other his majesty's subjects, since inhabiting in this, his majesty's colony, all the privileges, franchises, and immunities that have at any time been held, enjoyed, and possessed, by the people of Great Britain. . . .

That his majesty's liege [loyal] people of this most ancient colony have uninterruptedly enjoyed the right of being thus governed by their own Assembly in the article of their taxes and internal police, and that the same hath never been forfeited, or any other way given up, but hath been constantly recognized by the kings and people of Great Britain. . . .

Therefore, That the General Assembly of this colony have the only and sole exclusive right and power to lay taxes and impositions upon the inhabitants of this colony; and that every attempt to vest such power in any person or persons whatsoever, other than the General Assembly aforesaid, has a manifest tendency to destroy British as well as American freedom."

Questions for Analysis

1. Identify the problem Henry outlines in the Virginia Resolves.
2. Describe the solution Henry proposes in the Virginia Resolves.
3. Identify an intended audience of the Virginia Resolves in British politics and explain the way a section of it is directed to this audience.

These protests revealed the growing power of the written word, printed images, political rhetoric, and public spectacle in spreading new ideas among colonists. Broadsides (large posters with political statements printed on them), political cartoons, handbills (flyers), newspapers, and pamphlets circulated widely, reinforcing discussions and proclamations at taverns, rallies, demonstrations, and more formal political assemblies.

As the protests turned violent in Boston, Sons of Liberty leaders like Samuel Adams gave intense and emotional political speeches, in the style of the traveling preachers of the Great Awakening, to inspire mass demonstrations. Activists also used more threatening and dramatic tactics to convey their ideas to the public. At dawn on August 14, 1765, the Boston Sons of Liberty hung an effigy (likeness) of stamp distributor Andrew Oliver on a tree and called for his resignation. A mock funeral procession, joined by farmers, artisans, apprentices, and the poor, marched to Boston Common. In this public spectacle, the crowd, led by shoemaker and French and Indian War veteran Ebenezer Mackintosh, carried the fake corpse of Oliver to the Boston stamp office and then destroyed the building.

Regardless of the specific strategy they adopted, colonial protesters carefully chose their targets: stamp agents, sheriffs, judges, and colonial officials. Even when violence

The Mansion of a Patriot Merchant Jeremiah Lee, the wealthiest merchant in Massachusetts, moved his family into a newly built Marblehead mansion in 1768. It was decorated with hand-carved bannisters, furniture made by colonial craftsmen, and hand-painted wallpaper from England. Despite his strong ties to British commercial circles, he was a committed patriot and friend of Samuel Adams and used his wealth to promote the colonists' cause.

What accounts for colonial merchants' resistance to British trade policy in the mid-to-late 1700s?

erupted, it remained focused, with most crowds destroying stamps and stamp offices first and then turning to the private property of tax collectors or politically connected Stamp Act supporters. Such actions also revealed growing autonomy on the part of middle- and working-class colonists, who attacked men of wealth and power and sometimes chose men from the ranks of artisans rather than the wealthy as their leaders. However, colonial elites still considered themselves the leaders of the movement against the stamp tax, and they refused to support actions they considered too radical. By and large, they preferred attempts to inspire others through the power of their written political arguments and public speeches.

It was these more affluent protesters who dominated the **Stamp Act Congress** that met in New York City in October 1765, where twenty-seven delegates from nine colonies petitioned Parliament to repeal the Stamp Act. Taxation without representation, they argued, was tyranny. Delegates then urged colonists to boycott British goods and refuse to pay the stamp tax. Yet they still proclaimed their loyalty to king and country. Even as delegates at the Stamp Act Congress declared themselves loyal, albeit dissatisfied, British subjects, they participated in the process of developing a common identity in the American colonies.

The battle against the Stamp Act continued to unfold across the colonies, with riots, beatings, and resignations reported from Newport, Rhode Island, to New Brunswick, New Jersey, to Charleston, South Carolina. By the time the Stamp Act officially took effect on November 1, 1765, every stamp agent in the colonies had resigned, undermining the entire system of selling stamps and collecting taxes.

Eventually the British Parliament responded to colonial protests and even more to rising complaints from English merchants and traders whose businesses had been damaged by the colonists' boycott. Parliament repealed the Stamp Act in March and the Sugar Act in April 1766.

Celebrating their victories, American colonists paid little attention to Parliament's simultaneous passage of the **Declaratory Act**, which announced Parliament's authority to pass any law "to bind the colonies and peoples of North America" closer to Britain. No new tax or policy was established. Parliament simply wanted to assert Great Britain's political supremacy over its colonies in the aftermath of the successful Stamp Act protests.

Declaratory Act

A 1766 act stating Parliament's authority to pass any law, including direct taxes, on its North American colonies. The declaration was passed following the repeal of the Stamp Act to demonstrate that the repeal had not lessened the imperial authority of Britain.

From the colonists' perspective, the crisis triggered by the Stamp Act showed the limits of parliamentary control. Colonists had organized effectively and forced Parliament to roll back the hated legislation. Individual leaders, like Patrick Henry of Virginia and Samuel Adams of Massachusetts, became more widely known through their fiery speeches and their success in appealing to the masses. The protests that raged across the colonies—and attracted support from a wide range of colonists—demonstrated the growing influence of ordinary citizens, and the effectiveness of their attacks on stamp agents and the homes of British officials.

For all the success of the Stamp Act protests, however, American colonists still could not imagine in 1765 that protest would ever lead to open revolt against

British rule. Disagreements over who should hold political power over the colonies would continue for the next decade. More well-to-do colonists were concerned that a revolution against British authority might fuel a dual revolution in which small farmers, laborers, tenants, servants, and enslaved people would rise up against the political and economic elites in the colonies. Even most middle- and working-class protesters believed that the best solution to the colonies' problems was to gain greater economic and political rights within the British empire, not to break from it.

REVIEW

- What were the colonists' primary grievances with Great Britain after 1763?

Ongoing Tension, 1767–1773

After the passage of the Declaratory Act in 1766, relative harmony prevailed in the colonies for about a year. Then, in June 1767, Charles Townshend rose to power as the new chancellor of the exchequer in Britain. He persuaded Parliament to return to the indirect taxation model of the Sugar Act of 1764 as he sought to address the continuing revenue shortfall facing Great Britain. The **Townshend Acts**, like the Sugar Act, established an import tax on a range of items sent to the colonies, including glass, lead, paint, paper, and tea.

Townshend Acts
A series of acts of Parliament in 1767 that instituted an import tax on a broad range of items including glass, lead, paint, paper, and tea. The taxes prompted a boycott of British goods, because of a lack of colonial representation in the Parliament and the desire of the colonists to avoid increased taxes and led to increased violence between British soldiers and colonists.

This time, even an external tax led to immediate, highly organized protests and calls for a boycott of taxed items. In 1767 and 1768, John Dickinson, a prominent Pennsylvania attorney and Quaker, published a series of letters attacking the Townshend Acts. He presented himself as an ordinary colonist in his "Letters from a Farmer in Pennsylvania." Arguing that any duty on goods was a tax, he insisted, "We are taxed without our own consent given by ourselves, or our representatives. We are therefore—I speak it with grief—I speak it with indignation—we are slaves." Clearly, colonists thought boycotts and protests necessary and effective to demonstrate and secure their rights as British subjects.

In February 1768, Samuel Adams wrote a circular letter reminding colonists of the importance of the boycott, and the Massachusetts Assembly made sure it reached other colonial assemblies. In response, Parliament stationed two more British army regiments in Boston and New York City to enforce the law. Angry colonists did not retreat when confronted by this show of military force. Instead, a group of outspoken colonial leaders demanded that colonists expand the boycotts by refusing to import any goods from Britain.

This success of such boycotts depended especially on the support of women, who were often in charge of the day-to-day buying of household items. Women were expected to boycott a wide array of British goods. To provide substitutes for boycotted goods, they produced their own shirts and dresses and brewed herbal teas to replace British products. Despite the hardships, many embraced nonimportation. Among other efforts, some women organized spinning bees in which dozens of participants produced yards of homespun cloth. Textiles woven from homespun came to symbolize female commitment to the cause of liberty, and the wearing of such homespun clothing publicly announced that commitment.

Refusing to drink British tea offered another way for women to protest parliamentary taxation. In February 1770, more than "300 Mistresses of Families, in which number the Ladies of the Highest Rank and Influence," signed a petition in Boston, pledging

Library of Congress, LC-USZ62-12711

The Edenton Proclamation, 1774 In Edenton, North Carolina, a group of women published a proclamation in 1774 stating their allegiance to the cause of liberty by refusing to serve or drink British tea. Their public statement received much attention in the American and the British press. This political cartoon, which ridicules the women who signed the declaration, appeared in several London newspapers.

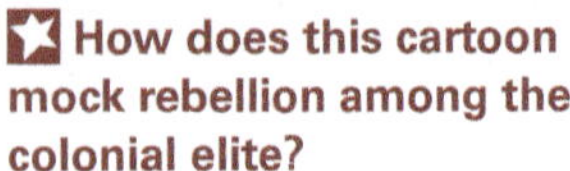

How does this cartoon mock rebellion among the colonial elite?

to stop drinking tea. Dozens of women from less prosperous families signed their own nonimportation agreement.

Angry over Parliament's taxation policies, Boston men also considered the soldiers, who moonlighted for extra pay, as economic competitors. Throughout the winter of 1769–1770, boys and young men harassed the growing number of British soldiers stationed in the city. On the evening of March 5, 1770, young men began throwing snowballs at the lone soldier guarding the Boston Customs House. An angry crowd began to form, now joined by a group of sailors led by Crispus Attucks, a freedman of mixed African and American Indian ancestry. The guard called for help, and Captain Thomas Preston arrived at the scene with seven British soldiers. He appealed to the "gentlemen" present to leave. Instead, the taunts of the crowd continued, and snowballs, stones, and other projectiles flew in greater numbers. After a shot was fired, likely by a scared soldier, the remaining soldiers immediately opened fire. Eleven men in the crowd were hit and five were killed, including Attucks.

Boston Massacre

A clash in Boston in March 1770 between colonial protesters and British soldiers that led to the death of five colonists. The bloody incident was used as evidence of English aggressions and to promote the patriot cause. In contrast, the British referred to the event as a "riot."

Despite confusion about who, if anyone, gave the order to fire, colonists expressed outrage at the shooting of ordinary men on the streets of Boston. Samuel Adams and other Sons of Liberty recognized the great potential for anti-British propaganda. Adams organized a mass funeral for those killed, and thousands watched the coffins being paraded through the city. Newspaper editors and broadsides printed by the Sons of Liberty labeled the shooting a "massacre." But when the accused soldiers were tried in Boston for the so-called **Boston Massacre**, the jury acquitted six of the eight of any crime. Still, ordinary colonists as well as colonial leaders were growing more convinced that British rule had become tyrannical and that such tyranny must be opposed.

To ensure that colonists throughout North America learned about the Boston Massacre, once again committees of correspondence formed to spread the news—including an engraving by Bostonian Paul Revere that suggested the soldiers shot at a peaceful and notably respectable-looking crowd with few lower-class participants. These committees became important pipelines for sending information about plans and protests across the colonies.

Parliament was already considering the repeal of the Townshend duties, and in the aftermath of the shootings, public pressure increased to do so. Merchants in England and North America insisted that parliamentary policies had resulted in economic losses on both sides of the Atlantic and failed to generate significant tax revenue. In response, Parliament repealed all of the Townshend duties except the import tax on tea, which it kept in place to demonstrate its political authority to tax the colonies.

- What factors contributed to rising tensions between Britain and its North American colonies between 1764 and 1770?

Widening Resistance, 1773–1774

For a brief period after the Boston Massacre and the repeal of the Townshend duties, the tea tax was collected. Tea tax funds ensured that British officials in the colonies were less dependent on local assemblies for financial support to carry out their duties, and general prosperity seemed to lessen the antagonism between colonists and royal authorities.

This lull in hostility ended in May 1773 when Parliament passed a new **Tea Act** that granted the financially struggling East India Company a monopoly on shipping and selling tea in the colonies. This eliminated the role of colonial merchants, who often dealt in smuggled Dutch tea. Although the act did not add any new tax or raise the price of tea, it did fuel a new round of protests as merchants now joined with radicals to assert their rights.

Tea Act
An act of Parliament in 1773 that aimed to reduce the financial debts of Britain and the British East India Company by providing the company with a tea monopoly in the British American colonies leading to widespread colonial protests.

Committees of correspondence quickly organized another colony-wide boycott. In some cities, like Charleston, South Carolina, tea was unloaded from East India Company ships but never sold. In others, like New York, the ships were turned back at the port. In Boston, ships loaded with tea sat anchored in the harbor. On the night of December 16, 1773, the Sons of Liberty organized what came to be known as the **Boston Tea Party**. After a large rally against British policy, a group of about fifty men disguised as American Indians boarded the British ships and dumped into the harbor forty-five tons of tea worth millions of dollars today.

Boston Tea Party
A protest against British tax policy organized by the Sons of Liberty on December 16, 1773, consisting of about fifty men disguised as American Indians who boarded British ships and dumped about forty-five tons of monopolized tea belonging to the British East India Company into Boston Harbor.

WORKING with EVIDENCE

Source: "Account of the Boston Tea Party," *Massachusetts Gazette*, 1773

"Just before the dissolution of the meeting [discussing the new Tea Act], . . . a number of brave and resolute men, dressed in the Indian manner, approached near the door of the assembly, gave the war-whoop, which rang through the house, and was answered by some in the galleries, but silence was commanded, and a peaceable deportment enjoined until the dissolution.

The Indians, as they were then called, repaired to the wharf, where the ships lay that had the tea on board, and were followed by hundreds of people, to see the event of the transactions of those who made so grotesque an appearance. The Indians immediately repaired on board Captain Hall's ship, where they hoisted out the chests of tea, and when on deck stove the chests and emptied the tea overboard. Having cleared this ship, they proceeded to Captain Bruce's, and then to Captain Coffin's brig. They applied themselves so dexterously to the destruction of this commodity, that in the space of three hours they broke up three hundred and forty-two chests, which was the whole number in these vessels, and discharged the contents into the dock. When the tide rose it floated the broken chests and the tea insomuch that the surface of the water was filled therewith a considerable way from the south part of the town to Dorchester Neck, and lodged on the shores. There was the greatest care taken to prevent the tea from being purloined by the populace; one or two being detected in endeavoring to pocket a small quantity were stripped of their acquisitions and very roughly handled."

Questions for Analysis

1. Describe the events of the Boston Tea Party, according to this document.
2. Explain why colonists dressed as American Indians during the Boston Tea Party.
3. Explain how the actions taken by the Sons of Liberty during the Boston Tea Party were a reaction against specific British policies.

Although hundreds of spectators knew who had boarded the ship, witnesses refused to provide names or other information to British investigators. The Boston Tea Party was a direct challenge to British authority and resulted in large-scale destruction of valuable property.

Parliament responded immediately with a show of force. The **Coercive Acts**, passed in 1774, were intended to punish Massachusetts and to strongly discourage similar protests in other colonies. These acts closed the port of Boston until residents paid for the tea, moved Massachusetts court cases against royal officials back to England, and revoked the colony's charter to strengthen the authority of royal officials and weaken that of the colonial assembly. The British government also approved a new Quartering Act, which forced Boston residents to accommodate more soldiers in their own homes or build more barracks. Parliament also passed the **Québec Act**, which extended the boundary of Québec to areas of the Ohio River Valley that American colonists wanted to settle, set up a colonial government without a local representative assembly, and permitted Roman Catholicism. Colonists viewed all of these acts as part of a larger pattern in British policy, one they believed aimed to strip them of their rights and liberties. Taken together, this legislation, which colonists called the **Intolerable Acts**, spurred a militant reaction.

Coercive Acts
Acts of Parliament passed in 1774 in response to the Boston Tea Party. The acts closed the port of Boston until residents paid for the damaged property and moved Massachusetts court cases against royal officials back to England in a bid to weaken colonial authority. Colonists referred to these acts as the Intolerable Acts.

Québec Act
A 1774 act of Parliament extending the boundary of Québec to areas of the Ohio River valley that American colonists wanted to settle, thus revoking the Proclamation of 1763 and placing rule between the Ohio and Mississippi Rivers under the control of a royal governor. This act also set up a colonial government without a local representative assembly in Québec and legalized Catholicism in the territory.

By passing the punitive Coercive Acts, Parliament hoped to stamp out the long-smoldering conflict with the colonies. Instead, tensions exploded, with radical leaders committing themselves to the use of violence, moderate merchants and shopkeepers making common cause with radicals, and ordinary women and men embracing a boycott of all British goods.

REVIEW

- What attempts did British officials make to prevent colonial rebellion?
- Why did these attempts to prevent rebellion fail?

AP® Skills Workshop: Thinking Historically

Additional Practice in Creating a Thesis Statement

Additional Practice features in *Fabric of a Nation* provide you with an opportunity to reinforce a previously learned skill by practicing it with new information. For this exercise, review the AP® Thinking Historically section in Module 3.2. Then create a thesis for the prompt below. Make sure to follow the same three-step process as outlined in Module 3.2.

1. Carefully analyze the prompt. Identify the topic, time period, and historical reasoning process (causation, comparison, or continuity and change over time).
2. Brainstorm and categorize information. Complete the chart below to organize your information. Remember, the "Main Points" column is a description of the cause/effect, similarity/difference, or continuity/change.
3. Write a two-sentence thesis statement that answers the question (your claim) and outlines your essay (your line of reasoning). Use the "Main Points" column of your completed chart for the second sentence in your thesis statement.

Analyze the factors that led to rebellion in the American colonies by 1774.

General Categories	Main Points	Supporting Details
-	-	- - -
-	-	- - -
-	-	- - -

MODULE 3.4

Philosophical Foundations of the American Revolution

FOCUS

The years between 1763, the end of the French and Indian War, and 1776, the signing of the Declaration of Independence, witnessed an enormous change in how many colonists viewed the British government and its actions in the colonies. Although protests against imperial taxes and acts began in the mid-1760s with the passage of the Sugar and Stamp Acts, over time an ideology of independence evolved as patriot authors fused Enlightenment ideas with criticisms of British policies and fears over higher taxes and less autonomy.

As you read Module 3.4, try to identify the continuities and changes in thought and attitudes that led to a war between the thirteen colonies and Great Britain. Which factors were most important and why? Why were the commonalities and shared heritage of the British and the colonists not enough to prevent conflict?

patriots
American colonists who favored the movement for independence during the 1770s.

AP® EXAM TIP
Events such as British attempts to tax Americans, influential colonial leaders, Lexington and Concord, the Continental Congress, Bunker Hill, and *Common Sense* caused Americans eventually to declare independence from Britain. Each person or social group had to decide for themselves which side they would support. Make sure you understand the similarities and differences between the patriots and loyalists.

Continental Congress
An assembly convened in Philadelphia in 1774 in response to the Intolerable Acts. The delegates launched a boycott against British goods and called for a halt of all colonial exports to Great Britain.

In the aftermath of the passage of the widely hated Intolerable Acts in 1774, committees of correspondence spread news of the fate of Boston and of Massachusetts. Colonial leaders, who increasingly identified themselves as **patriots**, soon formed committees of safety—armed groups of colonists who gathered weapons and vowed to protect themselves against British assaults on their rights and institutions. Other colonies sent support, both political and material, to Massachusetts and instituted a boycott of British goods. As with previous boycotts, all ranks of people throughout the colonies joined in.

That spring, a group of patriots meeting in Virginia called for colonies to send representatives to a Continental Congress to meet later that year to discuss relations between the North American colonies and Great Britain.

The Continental Congress Convenes

When the **Continental Congress** convened in Philadelphia in September 1774, fifty-six delegates represented every colony but Georgia. Many of these men—no women or people of color were included in its ranks—had met before. Some had worked together in the Stamp Act Congress in 1765. Others had joined forces in the intervening years on committees of correspondence or in petitions to Parliament. The men who participated were white, relatively wealthy, and—at least in the eyes of many of their contemporaries—radical activists. Many participants were enslavers, although some were abolitionists.

The representatives held a wide range of views on the subject of colonial relations with Britain. Some were radical, like Samuel Adams and Patrick Henry. Others held moderate views, including George Washington and John Dickinson of Pennsylvania. And a few, like John Jay of New York, voiced conservative positions.

Despite their ideological differences, all of the delegates were able to agree that the colonies must resist further parliamentary violations of their liberties. They talked not of independence, but rather of reestablishing the freedoms that colonists had enjoyed in an earlier period.

Washington voiced the sentiments of many. Although opposed to the idea of independence, he echoed John Locke by refusing to submit "to the loss of those valuable rights and privileges, which are essential to the happiness of every free State, and without which life, liberty, and property are rendered totally insecure."

To demonstrate their unified resistance to the Intolerable Acts, delegates called on colonists to continue the boycott of British goods and to end all colonial exports to Great Britain. Committees were established in all of the colonies to plan and carry out these actions. Delegates also insisted that Americans were "entitled to a free and exclusive power of legislation in their several provincial legislatures." By 1774 a growing number of colonists supported these measures and the ideas on which they were based.

The delegates at the Continental Congress showed no interest in challenging race and class relations within the colonies themselves. Nonetheless, it was a significant event because the congress drew power away from individual colonies and local organizations and instead placed emphasis on plans and actions across all of the colonies.

To some extent, the delegates shifted leadership of the protests away from more radical artisans and put planning in the hands of men of wealth and standing. Moreover, even as they denounced Parliament, many representatives felt a special loyalty to the king and wanted him to step in and repair the damage done to British–colonial relations.

The Continental Congress adjourned in October 1774 with plans to reconvene in May 1775. During the intervening months, patriots refined their arguments for resisting British tyranny, and committees of correspondence continued to circulate the latest news. While some patriots called for nonviolent resistance, the eruption of armed clashes between British soldiers and local farmers created a strong push for independence. It also led the Second Continental Congress to establish a national army in June 1775. A year later, in July 1776, the congress declared independence.

REVIEW

- How did the actions of the Continental Congress represent continuities with traditional British–colonial relations?
- In what ways did its tactics differ from colonial protests in the 1760s?

Armed Conflict Erupts

As debates over liberty intensified under the Intolerable Acts, patriots along the Atlantic coast expanded their efforts. The Sons of Liberty and other patriot groups spread propaganda against the British, gathered and stored weapons, and organized and trained local militia companies. In addition to boycotting British goods, female patriots manufactured bandages and bullets. Some northern colonists freed enslaved Black Americans who agreed to enlist in the militia. Others kept close watch on the movements of British troops.

On April 18, 1775, Boston patriots observed British movement in the harbor. British soldiers were headed to Lexington, intending to confiscate guns and ammunition hidden there and in neighboring Concord and perhaps to arrest patriot leaders. To warn his fellow patriots, Paul Revere raced to Lexington on horseback but was stopped on the road to Concord by the British. By that time, however, a network of riders was spreading the alarm to Concord.

Early on the morning of April 19, the first shots rang out on the village green of Lexington. After a brief exchange between British soldiers and local militiamen—known as **minutemen** for the speed with which they assembled—eight colonists lay dead. The British troops then marched on Concord, where they burned the few colonial supplies they found because most had already been moved.

minuteman
A member of a colonial militia group, consisting mainly of farmers, trained for local defense in case of British attack. A "minuteman" supposedly could be ready on a minute's notice.

Meanwhile, patriots in nearby towns were ready and waiting. Borrowing guerrilla tactics from American Indians, colonists hid behind trees, walls, and barns while shooting at the British as they marched back to Boston, killing 73 and wounding 200.

Word of the conflict traveled quickly. Outraged Bostonians attacked British troops and forced them to retreat to ships in the harbor. The victory was short-lived, however, and the British soon regained control of Boston. But colonial forces entrenched themselves on hills just north of the city. Then, in May, militias from Connecticut and Massachusetts captured the British garrison at Fort Ticonderoga, New York. The battle for North America had begun.

Second Continental Congress
An assembly of colonial representatives that served as a national government beginning in May 1775 and lasting the duration of the American Revolution. Despite limited formal powers, the Second Continental Congress coordinated the war effort, printed currency, and conducted negotiations with outside powers.

When the **Second Continental Congress** convened in Philadelphia on May 10, 1775, the most critical question for some delegates, like Pennsylvania patriot John Dickinson, was how to ensure time for discussion and negotiation. Armed conflict had erupted, but should, or must, revolution follow? Other delegates, including Patrick Henry, insisted that independence was the only appropriate response to armed attacks on colonial residents.

Just over a month later, on June 16, British forces under General William Howe attacked patriot fortifications on Breed's Hill and Bunker Hill, north of Boston. Patriot commander William Prescott is reported to have ordered his men, "Don't fire until you see the whites of their eyes!" The British won the **Battle of Bunker Hill** when patriots ran out of ammunition. But the redcoats—so called because of their bright red uniforms—suffered twice as many casualties as the patriots. The victory allowed the British to maintain control of Boston for nine more months, but the heavy losses emboldened patriot militiamen.

Continental Army
Army created by the Second Continental Congress after the battles of Lexington and Concord began the Revolutionary War in 1775. George Washington was appointed as its commander in chief.

The Battle of Bunker Hill convinced the Second Continental Congress to establish the **Continental Army** to defend the colonies. They appointed forty-three-year-old George Washington as commander in chief, and he headed to Massachusetts to take command of militia companies already engaged in battle.

akg-images/Newscom

The Battle of Bunker Hill
On June 16, 1775, 2,500 British infantry sought to dislodge 1,500 Patriot volunteers from Breeds Hill, 600 yards below strategic Bunker Hill on Charlestown Peninsula. Although the British managed to expel the patriots on their third attempt, more than a thousand British soldiers were wounded or killed.

How do the details from this image and the historical situation of the battle reveal the future difficulties the British would encounter during the war?

Because the congress had not yet proclaimed itself a national government, Washington depended largely on the willingness of local militias to accept his command and of individual colonies to supply soldiers, arms, and ammunition. Throughout the summer of 1775, Washington wrote many letters to patriot political leaders detailing the army's urgent need for men and supplies. He also sought to remove incompetent officers and improve order among the troops, who spent too much time drinking and socializing.

As he worked to build a disciplined army, Washington and his officers developed a military strategy with two immediate goals in mind: driving the British out of Boston and securing the colonies from attack by British forces and their American Indian allies in New York and Canada. They had mixed success. Although American troops captured Montréal in November 1775, the cold weather and the spread of smallpox destroyed the reinforcements sent to aid the campaign, and the Continental Army failed to dislodge the British from Québec.

Despite the reversal in Canada, the patriots also achieved important victories during the winter of 1775–1776. In March 1776, Washington surprised the British with a bombardment that drove them from Boston and forced them to retreat to Nova Scotia.

When the British retreated from Boston, the war had already spread into Virginia. In spring 1775, local militias forced Lord Dunmore, Virginia's royal governor, to take refuge on British ships in Norfolk harbor. Dunmore encouraged white servants and enslaved Black people to join him there, and hundreds of Black men fought with British troops when the governor led his army back into Virginia in November 1775. Dunmore reclaimed the governor's mansion and issued an official proclamation that declared "all [indentured] Servants, Negroes or others (appertaining to Rebels)" to be free if they were "able and willing to bear Arms" for the British.

Dunmore's Proclamation, offering freedom to enslaved people and indentured servants who fought for the crown, heightened concerns among patriot leaders about the consequences of declaring independence. They feared movements rejecting British authority might also reinforce other challenges to the social hierarchies that granted them elite status and rule.

Dunmore's Proclamation
A proclamation issued by the royal governor of Virginia, Lord Dunmore, in 1775, which offered freedom to all enslaved Black Americans and indentured servants held by patriots in exchange for joining the British army. Between 800 and 2,000 enslaved people joined Dunmore's army.

Challenges to social hierarchies existed before the conflict as well throughout the Anglo-American world. During the 1760s, Baptist preachers had rejected class and racial distinctions. Even in the South, they invited poor white people and enslaved Black people to their services. By 1775, 15 percent of whites in Virginia and hundreds of Black Americans had joined Baptist churches.

In England itself, a group of radicals drew on anti-authoritarian ideas developed during the English Civil War (1642–1651) to criticize British rule over its expanding empire. Through pamphlets and newspapers, their ideas circulated widely in the colonies. In addition, Enlightenment thinkers generally emphasized individual talent over inherited privilege.

Thus, many delegates at the Continental Congress, which included large-scale planters, successful merchants, and professional men, still hesitated to act. They held out hope for a negotiated settlement that would increase the colonies' political liberty without disrupting social and economic hierarchies.

The king and Parliament, however, refused to compromise in any way with colonies they considered in rebellion. Instead, in December 1775, the king prohibited any negotiation or trade with the colonies, increasing the leverage of radicals who argued it was time for the colonies to announce their independence.

The January 1776 publication of *Common Sense*, by Thomas Paine, bolstered their case. A recent transplant to the colonies, Paine had been a government employee in England, where he was repeatedly hired and dismissed from various jobs, before Benjamin Franklin persuaded him to try his luck in America, where he came to work for

Pennsylvania Magazine in late 1774. In *Common Sense,* Paine used both biblical references and Enlightenment ideas to provide a rationale for independence and an emotional plea for creating a new democratic republic that would ensure liberty and equality for all Americans. He urged colonists to fully separate from Britain. *Common Sense* was a best-seller, widely read throughout the colonies, impressing everyone from patriot leaders to ordinary farmers and artisans, who debated his ideas at taverns and coffeehouses.

AP® WORKING with EVIDENCE

Source: Thomas Paine, *Common Sense*, 1776

> "But there is another and greater distinction, for which no truly natural or religious reason can be assigned, and that is, the distinction of men into KINGS and SUBJECTS. Male and female are the distinctions of nature, good and bad, the distinction of heaven; but how a race of men came into the world so exalted above the rest, and distinguished like some new species, is worth enquiring into, and whether they are the means of happiness or of misery to mankind.
>
> In the early ages of the world, according to the scripture chronology, there were no kings; the consequence of which was, there were no wars: it is the pride of kings which throws mankind into confusion. Holland without a king hath enjoyed more peace for this last century than any of the monarchical governments in Europe. . . .
>
> Government by kings was first introduced into the world by the Heathens, from whom the children of Israel copied the custom. It was the most prosperous invention the Devil ever set on foot for the promotion of idolatry. The Heathens paid divine honors to their deceased kings, and the Christian world hath improved on the plan, by doing the same to their living ones. How impious is the title of sacred majesty applied to a worm who in the midst of his splendor is crumbling into dust!"

Questions for Analysis

1. Identify the subject of this excerpt from *Common Sense.*
2. Describe Paine's main argument in this excerpt.
3. Explain how Paine appeals to his audience in this excerpt.

Source: Charles Inglis, Anglican minister of Trinity Church in New York City, *The true interest of America impartially stated, in certain [strictures] on a pamphlet [entitled] Common sense*, 1776

> "I find no Common Sense in this pamphlet but much uncommon phrenzy. It is an outrageous insult on the common sense of Americans; an insidious attempt to poison their minds and seduce them from their loyalty and truest interest. The principles of government laid down in it, are not only false, but too absurd to have ever entered the head of a crazy politician before. . . .
>
> It is probable that this pamphlet like others will soon sink in oblivion—that the destructive plan it holds out will speedily be forgotten, and vanish like the baseless fabric of a vision; yet while any honest man is in danger of being seduced by it . . . I think it a duty which I owe to God, to my King and Country, to counteract in this manner, the poison it contains. . . .
>
> [I]t will be proper to bestow a few minutes in examining what is here alledged concerning monarchy in general; against which this republican marshals a formidable host of arguments. The reader will remember, that monarchy may

be either absolute; or mixed and combined with the other simple forms of government. Our author makes no distinction between these; and although all he says, and a thousand times more that might be said, were true with respect to the former; yet all this would not militate in the least against the mild and tempered monarchy of Great-Britain."

Questions for Analysis

1. Identify Inglis's intended audience.
2. Describe Inglis's response to *Common Sense*.
3. Explain how Inglis appeals to his audience in this excerpt.

Questions for Comparison

1. Identify the main differences between Paine's and Inglis's arguments.
2. Describe the biases that each author brings to his argument.
3. Explain who in the colonies would find each argument most appealing, and why.

By the spring of 1776, a growing number of patriots believed that independence was necessary. Patriots began to take control of their legislatures and instruct their delegates to the Continental Congress to support independence. Meanwhile, the congress requested economic and military assistance from France. In May, the congress advised colonies that had not yet done so to establish independent governments. Still, many colonists opposed the idea of breaking free from Britain—among them, Charles Inglis, the rector at Trinity Church in New York City, who insisted that "limited monarchy is the form of government which is most favorable to liberty."

- How did the eruption of armed conflict and the publication of *Common Sense* accelerate the colonial movement toward independence?

The Colonies Declare Independence

As colonists argued back and forth, Richard Henry Lee of Virginia introduced a motion to the Continental Congress in early June 1776 resolving that "these United Colonies are, and of right ought to be, Free and Independent States." A heated debate followed in which Lee and John Adams argued passionately for independence. Eventually, even more cautious delegates, like Robert Livingston of New York, were convinced. Livingston concluded that "they should yield to the torrent if they hoped to direct it." He then joined Adams, Thomas Jefferson, Benjamin Franklin, and Roger Sherman on a committee to draft a formal statement justifying independence.

The thirty-three-year-old Jefferson took the lead in preparing the declaration, building on ideas expressed by Paine, Adams, and Lee. He also drew on language used in dozens of "declarations" written by town meetings, county officials, and colonial assemblies, particularly the Virginia Declaration of Rights drafted by George Mason in May 1776. Several of these documents insisted on religious freedom, since the official religion of Great Britain, the Church of England, was often tied to British political and economic elites.

Another principle central to these documents was the contract theory of government, proposed by the seventeenth-century British philosopher John Locke. Locke argued that sovereignty resided in the people, who submitted voluntarily to laws and authorities in exchange for protection of their life, liberty, and property. The people could therefore reconstitute or overthrow a government that abused its powers. Jefferson summarized this argument and then listed the abuses and crimes perpetrated by King George III against the colonies, which justified patriots' decision to break their contract with British authorities.

Declaration of Independence A document listing colonial grievances and outlining the philosophical foundations for declaring the independence of the colonies from Great Britain. Drafted by Thomas Jefferson, then debated and revised by the Second Continental Congress, the Declaration was made public on July 4, 1776.

Once prepared, the **Declaration of Independence** was debated and revised. In the final version, all references to slavery were removed. But delegates agreed to list among the abuses suffered by the colonies the fact that the king "excited domestic insurrections amongst us," referring to the threat posed by Dunmore's Proclamation. On July 4, 1776, independence was publicly proclaimed by the Second Continental Congress when the Declaration was published as a broadside to be circulated throughout the colonies.

Probably no more than half of American colonists actively supported the patriots. Perhaps a fifth actively supported the British. The rest tried to stay neutral or were largely indifferent unless the war came to their doorstep. Both sides included men and women from all classes and races and from both rural and urban areas.

AP® WORKING with EVIDENCE

Source: Thomas Jefferson, *Declaration of Independence*, 1776

> "When, in the course of human events, it becomes necessary for one people to dissolve the political bands which have connected them with another, and to assume, among the powers of the Earth, the separate and equal station to which the laws of nature and of nature's God entitle them, a decent respect to the opinions of mankind requires that they should declare the causes which impel them to the separation.
>
> We hold these truths to be self-evident; that all men are created equal; that they are endowed, by their Creator, with certain unalienable rights; that among these are life, liberty, and the pursuit of happiness.—That to secure these rights, governments are instituted among men, deriving their just powers from the consent of the governed; that whenever any form of government becomes destructive of these ends, it is the right of the people to alter or to abolish it, and to institute new government, laying its foundation on such principles, and organizing its powers in such form, as to them shall seem most likely to effect their safety and happiness. Prudence, indeed, will dictate, that governments long established, should not be changed for light and transient causes; and accordingly all experience hath shewn, that mankind are more disposed to suffer, while evils are sufferable, than to right themselves by abolishing the forms to which they are accustomed. But when a long train of abuses and usurpations, pursuing invariably the same object, evinces a design to reduce them under absolute despotism, it is their right, it is their duty, to throw off such government, and to provide new guards for their future security."

Questions for Analysis

1. Identify the origin of the authority to rule, according to Jefferson.
2. Describe the responsibilities of people with regard to government, according to Jefferson.
3. Explain the relationship that this document illustrates between government and human beings' inalienable rights.

REVIEW

- How did the Declaration of Independence go beyond merely declaring colonial independence from Great Britain?

Choosing Sides

Once independence was declared, there was far more pressure to choose sides. The stance of political and military leaders and soldiers was clear. But to win a war against Great Britain required the support of a large portion of the civilian population as well.

As battle lines shifted back and forth across New England, the Middle Atlantic region, and the South, civilians caught up in the fighting were faced with difficult decisions. Men who took up arms against the British before independence was declared and the women who supported them clearly demonstrated their commitment to the patriot cause. In some colonies, patriots organized local committees, courts, and assemblies to assume governance should British officials lose their authority. At the same time, white servants and enslaved Black people in Virginia who fled to British ships or marched with Lord Dunmore made their loyalties known as well.

Andrew M. Mellon Collection. Courtesy National Gallery of Art, Washington

Colonel Guy Johnson and Karonghyontye (Captain David Hill), 1776 Benjamin West painted this portrait of Colonel Johnson, British superintendent of Indian affairs, with the Mohawk chief Karonghyontye. Johnson directed joint Mohawk and British attacks against patriots during the Revolution. His red coat and musket are combined with moccasins, a wampum belt, and an American Indian blanket, while Karonghyontye holds a peace pipe, representing the Mohawk–British alliance before and during the war.

What does this painting reveal about the relations between American Indians and the British during the American Revolution?

Both Britain and the colonists sought American Indian allies. The Continental Congress, recognizing the importance of American Indians to the outcome of any colonial war, appointed commissioners from the "United Colonies" to meet with representatives of the Haudenosaunee (Iroquois) Confederacy in August 1775.

Early in the war, many American Indian nations proclaimed their neutrality, but neither the colonists nor the British respected such declarations, each pressuring native peoples to join their efforts. Colonial troops killed the Shawnee chief Cornstalk under a flag of truce in 1777, leading that nation to ally, finally, with the British—as did the majority of American Indians during the conflict, viewing a British victory as their best hope of limiting further encroachments on their territory.

Native American help enabled British success early in the conflict. In May 1775, Colonel Guy Johnson, the British superintendent for American Indian affairs, left Albany, New York, and sought refuge in Canada. He was accompanied by 120 British loyalists and 90 Mohawk warriors led by their mission-educated chief, Joseph Brant (Thayendanegea). While Brant's group of Mohawk warriors was already committed to the British, some Oneida Indians, influenced by missionaries and patriot sympathizers, wanted to support the colonists. Others, however, urged neutrality, including Oneida's chief warriors, who declared that the English and patriots were "two brothers of one blood."

As the war continued, British forces and their American Indian allies fought bitter battles against patriot militias and Continental forces all along the interior. Each side destroyed property, ruined crops, and killed civilians. In the summer and fall of 1778, American Indian and American civilians suffered

Black Americans in New York City amid the Upheavals of 1776 On July 9, the day New York's Provincial Congress approved the Declaration of Independence, a rowdy crowd of soldiers and civilians toppled a statue of King George III. However, an etching of the event presents it as the work of Black Americans, with most whites simply observing.

What does this portrayal suggest about the artist's sympathies?

through a series of brutal attacks in Wyoming, Pennsylvania; Onoquaga, New York; and Cherry Valley, New York. Patriots and American Indians also battled along the Virginia backcountry after pioneer and militia leader Daniel Boone established a fort there in 1775. In the South, 6,000 patriot troops laid waste to Cherokee villages in the Appalachian Mountains in retaliation for the killing of white intruders along the Watauga River.

Meanwhile, many colonists who remained loyal to the king found safe haven in cities like New York, Newport, and Charleston, which remained under British control throughout much of the war. Although the British army welcomed **loyalists**, those who made their loyalist sympathies clear still risked a good deal. When British troops were forced out of cities or towns they had temporarily occupied, many loyalists faced harsh reprisals. Patriots had no qualms about invading the homes of loyalists, punishing women and children, and destroying or confiscating property.

loyalist

A colonial supporter of the British during the American Revolution.

Although many loyalists were members of the economic and political elite, others came from ordinary backgrounds. Tenants, small farmers, and enslaved people joined the loyalist cause in defiance of the patriot elite, which included landlords and wealthy plantation owners. Many poorer loyalists lived in New York's Hudson valley, their sympathy for the British heightened by the patriot commitments of the powerful men who controlled the region's local politics. When the fighting moved south, many backcountry farmers in North Carolina also supported the British, who challenged the domination of patriot leaders among the colony's eastern elite.

Colonists who sought to remain neutral during the war also faced hostility. Some 80,000 Quakers, Mennonites, Amish, Shakers, and Moravians considered war immoral and refused to bear arms, hire substitutes, or pay taxes to new state governments. Both sides treated the pacifists poorly. In the areas they controlled, British authorities harassed Quakers, and patriots routinely fined and imprisoned Quakers for refusing to support the revolution. In June 1778, Pennsylvania authorities jailed nine Mennonite farmers who refused to take an oath of allegiance to the revolutionary government and then sold their property, leaving their wives and children destitute. Meanwhile, Quaker meetings regularly disciplined members who offered aid to either side. Betsy Ross was among those disowned Quakers when her husband joined the patriot forces, and she sewed flags for the Continental troops.

After July 4, 1776, the decision to support independence took on new meaning. If the United States failed to win the war, all those who actively supported the cause would be considered traitors. The families of Continental soldiers faced especially difficult decisions as the conflict spread and soldiers moved farther and farther from home. Men too old or too young to fight proved their patriotism by gathering arms and ammunition and patrolling local communities.

Some female patriots accompanied their husbands, fiancés, or partners as camp followers, cooking, washing clothes, nursing, and providing other services for soldiers. Most patriot women remained at home, however, and demonstrated their commitment by raising funds, gathering information, and sending clothes, bedding, and other goods to soldiers at the front. The Continental Army suffered desperate shortages of supplies from the beginning of the war. Patriot leaders urged northern women to increase cloth production, while calling on southern women to harvest crops for hungry troops. The response was overwhelming. Women in Hartford, Connecticut, produced 1,000 coats and vests and 1,600 shirts in 1776 alone. Across the colonies, women collected clothing door-to-door and opened their homes to sick and wounded soldiers.

AP® EXAM TIP

While the Continental Army waged war against the British army, other American groups provided much-needed support. These included religious denominations, laborers, artisans, farmers, and women. Make sure you understand how these groups helped maintain the patriotic movement, even as the alliance with France turned a civil war into an international conflict.

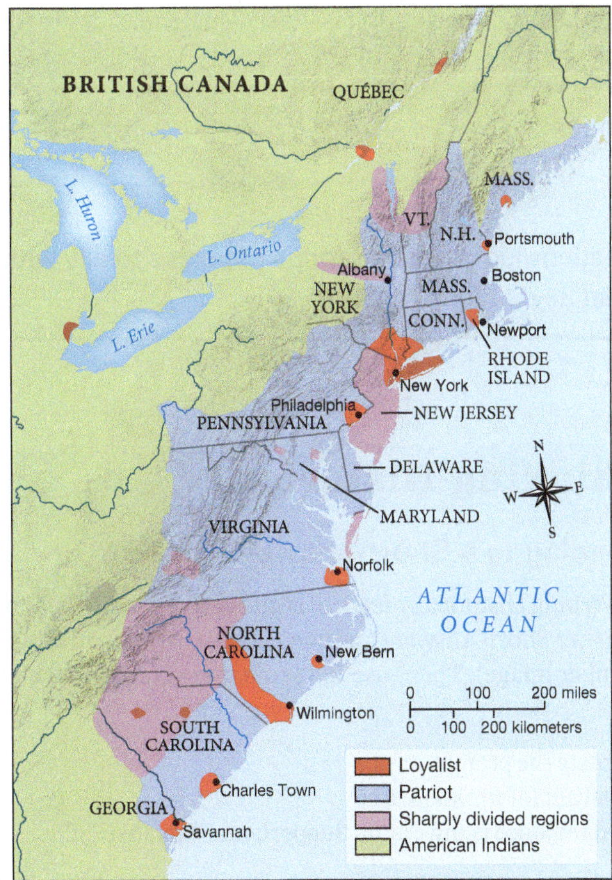

MAP 3.3 Choosing Sides in the American Revolution This map portrays the conflicted loyalties of British North Americans during the American Revolution.

What commonalities do you see between loyalist strongholds? What accounts for these commonalities?

A small number of Black Americans also sided with the patriots. In Boston, a formerly enslaved woman named Phillis Wheatley believed in the movement for independence. Born in Gambia around 1753, she was sold into slavery and brought to Boston in 1761, where she was bought by the Wheatley family. Although they were enslavers, the Wheatleys were nevertheless considered progressive: Phillis received a thorough education that included subjects such as Greek and Latin. Freed in 1773, Phillis Wheatley wrote a collection of poetry in 1776 and sent a copy to General Washington, who was himself a slaveholder. In her book, she urged readers to recognize Black people as children of God.

AP® WORKING with EVIDENCE

Source: Phillis Wheatley, "On Being Brought from Africa to America" (poem), 1770

" 'Twas mercy brought me from my *Pagan* land,
Taught my benighted [pitiable] soul to understand
That there's a God, that there's a *Saviour* too;
Once I redemption neither sought nor knew.
Some view our sable [black] race with scornful eye,
"Their colour is a diabolic dye."
Remember, *Christians*, negroes, black as *Cain*,
May be refin'd, and join th' angelic train."

Questions for Analysis

1. Identify the role of God in relation to the poet in this poem.
2. Explain how the speaker of this poem conveys her attitude toward her captivity.
3. Explain how Wheatley's poem asserts Black Americans' desire for independence during this time period.

REVIEW

- What motivations led different groups of people to ally with each side in the American Revolution?

AP® Skills Workshop: Thinking Historically

Additional Practice in Responding to a Short-Answer Question

Review the AP® Writing Historically feature at the end of Module 1.4 for a reminder on how to best answer Short-Answer Questions (SAQs) without an attached stimulus (document excerpt or image). Then, use the same three-step approach to formulate your response:

1. Read and annotate the prompt,
2. Brainstorm relevant information, and
3. Write a focused response using Claim, Support, and Explain (CSE).

(continued)

Notice how this approach resembles the process we practiced for creating Thesis Statements in Modules 3.2 and 3.3. The main differences are that thesis brainstorming is longer because it helps to create an outline for an entire essay, yet the thesis statement itself is shorter than an SAQ response because it's the summary of a longer argument.

Answer **A**, **B**, and **C**.

(A) Briefly describe ONE specific historical continuity in relations between the British government and American colonists in the period from 1763 to 1776.

(B) Briefly describe ONE specific historical change in relations between the British government and American colonists in the period from 1763 to 1776.

(C) Briefly explain how ONE historical development in the period from 1763 to 1776 arose from earlier changes in relations between the British government and American colonists.

MODULE 3.5

The American Revolution

FOCUS

As you read this module, take special note of the many events that contributed to the Continental Army's eventual victory in the American Revolution. Consider the importance of the effects of these events. Which ones played a greater role? Which ones were less important? As you answer these questions for yourself, think about how you could support an argument asserting which causes had the most influential effects.

After July 4, 1776, battles between British and colonial troops intensified, but it was not until December that the patriots would celebrate another major military victory. Over the course of the eighteenth century, Great Britain had developed the world's most powerful military force, including a huge navy. Moreover, by declaring independence, the colonists had lost their main trading partner, and finding ways to sustain their economy while funding a war was a tough challenge. To succeed, the patriots needed support from men and women on the home front as well as the battlefront and assistance from Europeans experienced in fighting the British.

Critical Years of Warfare, 1776–1777

The Continental Army did not win a single military victory between July and December 1776. In the summer of 1776, General Washington tried to lead his army out of Boston to confront British troops set to invade New York City, but many soldiers deserted—they believed New Yorkers should defend New York. Washington arrived in New York with 19,000 men, many of whom were poorly armed and poorly trained and some of whom were forced into service by local committees of safety.

Meanwhile, British ships sailed into New York harbor or anchored off the coast of Long Island. General William Howe, hoping to overwhelm the colonists, ordered 10,000 troops to march into the city in the weeks immediately after the Declaration of Independence was signed. Still, the Continental Congress rejected Howe's offer of peace and a royal pardon. Howe then prepared to take New York City by force and thereafter isolate New York and New England from the other colonies. On August 27, 1776, British forces killed or wounded more than 1,500 patriots in the fiercely fought Battle of Long Island.

By November, the British had captured Fort Lee in New Jersey and made headway north of New York City. Meanwhile, Washington led his weary troops into Pennsylvania as the Continental Congress, fearing a British attack on Philadelphia, fled to Baltimore. Although General Howe might have ended the war there and then through an aggressive campaign, he wanted to wear down the Continental Army and force the colonies to sue for peace.

Washington did not have the troops or the arms to launch a major assault, but he hoped the British would accept American independence once they saw how difficult it would be to defeat the colonies. So the war continued.

Fortunately for Washington, Howe followed the European tradition of suspending battle during the winter months. This allowed the patriots to regroup, repair weapons and wagons, and recruit soldiers. Camped in eastern Pennsylvania, Washington learned that Hessian troops (Germans paid to fight for the British) had been sent to occupy the city of Trenton, New Jersey, just across the Delaware River. On Christmas Eve, Washington's troops crossed the river to attack Trenton in an icy rain and quickly won. They then marched on Princeton and emerged victorious once more on January 3, 1777. The British army soon retreated to New York City. These early victories boosted patriot morale after a difficult start to the war.

By mid-January 1777, the tide began to turn in favor of the Continental Army, but victory was far from certain. British forces remained strong, and Washington's troops were devastated by smallpox throughout the remainder of winter. His army numbered fewer than 5,000 men when General Howe resumed battle in the spring, planning to capture Philadelphia to force a patriot surrender. Washington's force was too small to defeat Howe's army but delayed his advance by guerrilla attacks. On the way, Howe learned that he was expected to reinforce General John Burgoyne's soldiers, who were advancing south from Canada. Instead, he continued inching toward Philadelphia. Meanwhile, Burgoyne and his 7,200 troops regained control of Fort Ticonderoga on July 7.

Howe managed to capture Philadelphia in September 1777. But in so doing, he had withheld his troops from reinforcing General Burgoyne, who was pressing southward. In mid-September Burgoyne faced a brutal onslaught from patriot militia forces at Freeman's Farm, outside Saratoga, New York. The patriots defeated the British, with the British suffering twice the casualties of the Continentals. In early October, Burgoyne lost a second battle for the strategic site. The defeat proved decisive. Ten days later, he surrendered his remaining army of 5,800 men to General Horatio Gates at Saratoga.

The **Battle of Saratoga** gave an important victory to the Continental Army and stunned the British. It undercut the significance of Howe's victory at Philadelphia and indicated the general's misunderstanding of the nature of the war he was fighting. Meanwhile, the patriot victory energized Washington and his troops as they dug in at **Valley Forge** for a long winter. It gave Benjamin Franklin, the envoy sent by the Continental Congress to Paris, greater leverage in convincing French officials to support American independence.

AP® EXAM TIP

While the AP® Exam generally de-emphasizes military history, military strategy (such as Washington hoping to outlast the British) and key turning points (such as the patriot victory at Saratoga) are important to know.

Battle of Saratoga

Key Revolutionary War battle fought at Saratoga, New York, resulting in the surrender of British General John Burgoyne's forces. The Patriot victory at Saratoga in October 1777 provided hope that the colonists could triumph and increased the chances that the French would formally join the patriot side.

- How did the patriot forces fare in 1776?
- How and why did the tide of war turn in 1777?

Women Contribute to the Revolution

Whether black or white, enslaved or free, women and children faced hardship and uncertainty as a result of the war. Even those who did not directly engage enemy troops took on enormous burdens: Farm wives plowed and planted and carried on their domestic duties, while in cities, women worked ceaselessly to find sufficient food, wood, candles, and cloth to care for themselves and their children. As the war intensified, Continental and British forces slaughtered cattle and hogs for food, stole corn and other crops or burned them to keep the enemy from obtaining supplies, looted houses and shops, and kidnapped or liberated enslaved people and servants.

To survive these desperate circumstances, many women asserted themselves. When merchants hoarded goods to make greater profits when prices rose, housewives raided stores and warehouses and took the supplies they needed. Others learned as much as they could about finances, submitting reports to local officials when their family properties were damaged or looted. Growing numbers of women banded together to assist one another, help more impoverished families, and supply troops with badly needed clothes, food, bandages, and bullets—as did the wives of patriot leaders, who formed voluntary associations, like the Ladies Association of Philadelphia, to provide critical resources for the army.

While most women worked tirelessly on the home front, some cast their fate with the army as camp followers, who provided critical services to the military and suffered, as the troops did, from scarce supplies and harsh weather. Families living in regions surrounding battlefields were especially vulnerable to the shifting fortunes of war, but some women made the most of it, serving as spies and couriers for British or Continental forces. Lydia Darragh, a wealthy Philadelphian, eavesdropped on conversations among the British officers who occupied her house and carried detailed reports to Washington hidden in the folds of her dress. Others, like Nancy Hart Morgan of Georgia, took more direct action. Morgan lulled half a dozen British soldiers into a sense of security at dinner, hid their guns, and shot two before neighbors came to hang the rest.

Some patriot women took up arms on the battlefield. A few, such as Margaret Corbin, accompanied their husbands to the front lines. When her husband was killed in battle in 1776, Corbin took his place loading and firing cannons. In addition, a small number of women, like Deborah Sampson, disguised themselves as men and enlisted as soldiers. A former indentured servant who had become a teacher after her term of service ended in 1778, Sampson disguised herself as a man and enlisted in the Continental Army. Under the name Robert Shurtliff, Sampson marched, fought, and lived with her Massachusetts regiment for a year. Her ability to carry off the deception was helped by the era's standards of hygiene: Soldiers rarely undressed fully to bathe, and most slept in their uniforms.

As in all wars, women faced fear and hardship during the American Revolution, but also embraced new opportunities in the public sphere. Women contributed significantly to the patriot cause, but they also faced serious challenges—and although many were glad of women's political and practical contributions to the war effort, patriot leaders failed to treat them as equal partners in the revolution.

REVIEW

- How did the American Revolution affect the status of women in the colonies?

France Allies with the Patriots

Despite significant Continental victories in the fall of 1777, the following winter proved especially difficult. The quarters at Valley Forge were marred by bitter cold, poor food, inadequate clothing, and scarce supplies. A French volunteer arrived to see "a few militia men, poorly clad, and for the most part without shoes; many of them badly armed." Many recent recruits were also poorly trained.

The Continental Army continued to be plagued by problems of recruitment, discipline, wages, and supplies. Critical assistance from foreign volunteers arrived with Baron Friedrich von Steuben, a Prussian officer recruited by Benjamin Franklin, who took charge of drilling soldiers. Other officers experienced in European warfare also joined the patriot cause that winter.

Despite these contributions and the strong leadership of Washington and his officers, the Continental Congress considered an alliance with France critical to patriot success. In December 1776, the congress had sent Benjamin Franklin to Paris to serve as its unofficial liaison. Franklin was enormously successful, securing supplies and becoming a favorite among the French aristocracy and ordinary citizens alike. France's long rivalry with Britain made it a likely ally, and the French government had secretly provided funds to the patriots early in the war.

The French initially resisted a formal compact with the upstart patriots. Only after the patriot victory at Saratoga in October 1777 did the French king agree to an alliance. In February 1778, Franklin secured an agreement that approved trading rights between the United States and all French possessions. France then recognized the United States as an independent nation, gave up French territorial claims on mainland North America, and sent troops to reinforce the Continental Army. In return, the United States promised to defend French holdings in the Caribbean. A year later, Spain allied itself with France to protect its own North American holdings.

Archives Charmet/Bridgeman Images

The Marquis de Lafayette with an Aide-de-Camp This eighteenth-century portrait of the Marquis de Lafayette was painted by a Frenchman during the Revolution. It shows him with his aide-de-camp, probably from the French West Indies. Lafayette joined the Continental Army in September 1777, led patriot forces in numerous battles, camped at Valley Forge, and trapped British forces under General Cornwallis at the decisive Battle of Yorktown.

In what ways does this image portray the American Revolution as a conflict with international effects?

AP® WORKING with EVIDENCE

Source: Treaty of Alliance between the United States and France, 1778

"The most Christian king and the United States of North-America, . . . having resolved . . . to join their councils and efforts against the enterprizes of their common enemy, . . . have, after the most mature deliberation, concluded and determined on the following articles:

Art. 1. If war should break out between France and Great-Britain, during the continuance of the present war between the United States and England, his majesty and the said United States, shall make it a common cause, and aid each other mutually with their good offices, their counsels and their forces, . . . as becomes good and faithful allies.

Art. 2. The essential and direct end of the present defensive alliance, is, to maintain effectually the liberty, sovereignty and independence, absolute and unlimited, of the said United States, as well in matters of government as of commerce.

Art. 3. The two contracting parties shall, each on its own part, and in the manner it may judge most proper, make all the efforts in its power against their common enemy, in order to attain the end proposed."

Questions for Analysis

1. Describe the causes motivating the French to ally with the United States.
2. Explain the effects that France's recognition of the U.S. government had on other nations.
3. Evaluate the relative importance of political, economic, and military motivations behind a French alliance with the United States.

British leaders responded by declaring war on France. Yet doing so ensured that military conflicts would spread well beyond North America and military expenditures would skyrocket. French forces attacked British outposts in Gibraltar in the Mediterranean, the Bay of Bengal in Southeast Asia, Senegal in West Africa, and Grenada in the West Indies. At the same time, the French supplied the United States with military officers, weapons, funds, and critical naval support. Faced with this new alliance, Britain's Prime Minister Lord North (1770–1782) decided to concentrate British forces in New York City. For the remainder of the war, New York City was the sole British stronghold in the North, serving as a supply center and prisoner-of-war camp.

The French alliance did create one unintended problem for the Continental Army. When Americans heard that France was sending troops, fewer men volunteered for military service. As the war dragged on, fewer and fewer men volunteered to fight. Bonuses paid to enlistees produced ever-declining results. Local officials had the authority to draft men into the army or to accept substitutes for draftees. In the late 1770s, some draftees forced enslaved men to take their place. Others hired landless laborers, the disabled, or the mentally unfit as substitutes.

As the war spread south and west in 1778–1779, Continental forces were stretched thin, and enlistments continued to decline. Soldiers faced injuries, disease, and shortages of food and ammunition. They also risked capture by the British, one of the worst fates to befall a Continental. Considered traitors by the British, most captives were held on ships in New York harbor. They faced filthy accommodations, a horrid stench, inadequate water, and widespread disease and abuse. Altogether, between 8,000 and 11,500 patriots died in British prisons in New York—more than died in battle.

MAP 3.4 The War in the North, 1775–1778 After early battles in Massachusetts, patriots invaded Canada but failed to capture Québec. The British army captured New York City in 1776 and Philadelphia in 1777, but New Jersey remained a battle zone through 1778. Meanwhile, General Burgoyne secured Canada for Britain and then headed south, but his forces were defeated by patriots at the crucial Battle of Saratoga.

Why did the British focus on capturing port cities during the early battles of the American Revolution? What were the effects of this strategy?

The Continental Congress faced enormous financial problems. With no authority to impose taxes on citizens, the congress resorted to borrowing money from wealthy patriots, accepting loans from France and the Netherlands, and printing money of its own—some \$200 million by 1780. However, money printed by the states was used far more widely than Continental dollars. "Continentals" depreciated so quickly that by late 1780 it took one hundred continentals to buy one silver dollar's worth of goods.

By 1779, the cost of goods skyrocketed in the chaotic wartime economy. Housewives, sailors, and artisans in Philadelphia and other cities attacked merchants who were hoarding goods, forcing officials to distribute food to the poor. The congress finally improved its financial standing slightly by using a \$6 million loan from France to back certificates issued to wealthy patriots. Meanwhile, states raised money through taxes to provide funds for government operations, backing for paper money, and other expenses.

Most residents found such taxes burdensome given wartime inflation, and even the most patriotic began to protest increased taxation. Thus, the financial status of the new nation remained precarious.

■ In what ways did the American Revolution become an international conflict by 1780?

Patriots Achieve Victory

From 1778 to 1781, the battlefront in the Revolution moved south, because King George III believed that southern colonists' sympathies were more loyalist than patriot. British troops captured Savannah, Georgia, in 1778 and soon extended their control over the entire state. In May 1780, General Charles Cornwallis reclaimed Charleston, South Carolina. He then evicted patriots from the city, purged them from the state government, gained military control of the state, and imposed loyalty oaths on all Carolinians able to fight.

To aid Cornwallis's efforts, local loyalists organized militias to battle patriots in the interior. British officer Banastre Tarleton led one especially vicious company of loyalists in slaughtering civilians and murdering many patriots who surrendered. In retaliation, patriot planter Thomas Sumter organized 800 men who showed a similar disregard for regular army procedures, raiding largely defenseless loyalist settlements.

By 1780, British chances for victory seemed more hopeful. Cornwallis was in control of Georgia and South Carolina, and local loyalists were eager to gain control of the southern countryside. Meanwhile Continental soldiers in the North mutinied in early 1780 over enlistment terms and pay. Patriot morale was low, funds were scarce, and civilians were growing weary of the war.

Yet the patriots prevailed in the end through a combination of luck, strong leadership, and French support. In October 1780, when Continental hopes looked especially bleak, a group of 800 backcountry patriots routed loyalist troops at King's Mountain in South Carolina, keeping Cornwallis from advancing into North Carolina. Continental forces supplemented by local patriot militias then checked Cornwallis in South Carolina, winning key victories at Cowpens and Guilford Court House. Inflicting enormous losses on British troops gave the Continentals an opportunity to regroup.

In August 1781, frustrated at the large amount of local support patriots received in the South, Cornwallis hunkered down in Yorktown on the Virginia coast and waited for reinforcements from New York. In response, Washington coordinated strategy with French allies to cut off Cornwallis's escape. The Comte de Rochambeau, a French general, marched 5,000 troops south from Rhode Island to Virginia as General Lafayette led his troops south along Virginia's eastern shore. At the same time, French naval ships headed north from the West Indies. One French naval unit cut off a British fleet trying to resupply Cornwallis by sea, while another joined up with Americans to bombard Cornwallis's forces. By mid-October, British supplies had run out, and it was clear that reinforcements would not be forthcoming. On October 19, 1781, at the **Battle of Yorktown**, Cornwallis and the British army admitted defeat.

Battle of Yorktown
Decisive battle in which French naval forces forced the surrender of British forces on October 19, 1781, at Yorktown, Virginia. The joint French and American victory led to the withdrawal of the British in the American Revolution.

The Continental Army had managed the impossible. It had defeated the British army and won the colonies' independence. Yet even with the surrender after the Battle of Yorktown, the war continued here and there as British forces challenged Continental troops in and around New York City.

Peace negotiations in Paris dragged on as French, Spanish, British, and American representatives sought to settle a host of issues. Patriot representatives in Paris—Benjamin Franklin, John Adams, and John Jay—continued to negotiate peace terms, but the French foreign minister opposed the Americans' republican principles. Given the importance of the French to the American victory, the Continental Congress had instructed its delegates to defer to French wishes. This blocked the American representatives from signing a separate peace with the British.

Eventually, U.S. delegates finalized a treaty that secured substantial benefits for the young nation. Its terms granted the United States control of all lands south of Canada and north of Louisiana and Florida stretching to the Mississippi River. In addition, the treaty recognized the United States to be "free Sovereign and independent states." Spain signed a separate treaty with Great Britain in which it regained control of Florida. Despite their role in the war, none of the American Indian nations that occupied the lands under negotiation were consulted. On September 2, 1783, delegates of the United States and Britain signed the **Treaty (Peace) of Paris**, formally ending the American Revolutionary War.

Treaty (Peace) of Paris
The 1783 treaty that ended the Revolutionary War, recognized American independence, and established U.S. territory as the lands between the Mississippi River in the west, Florida in the south, and Canada to the north.

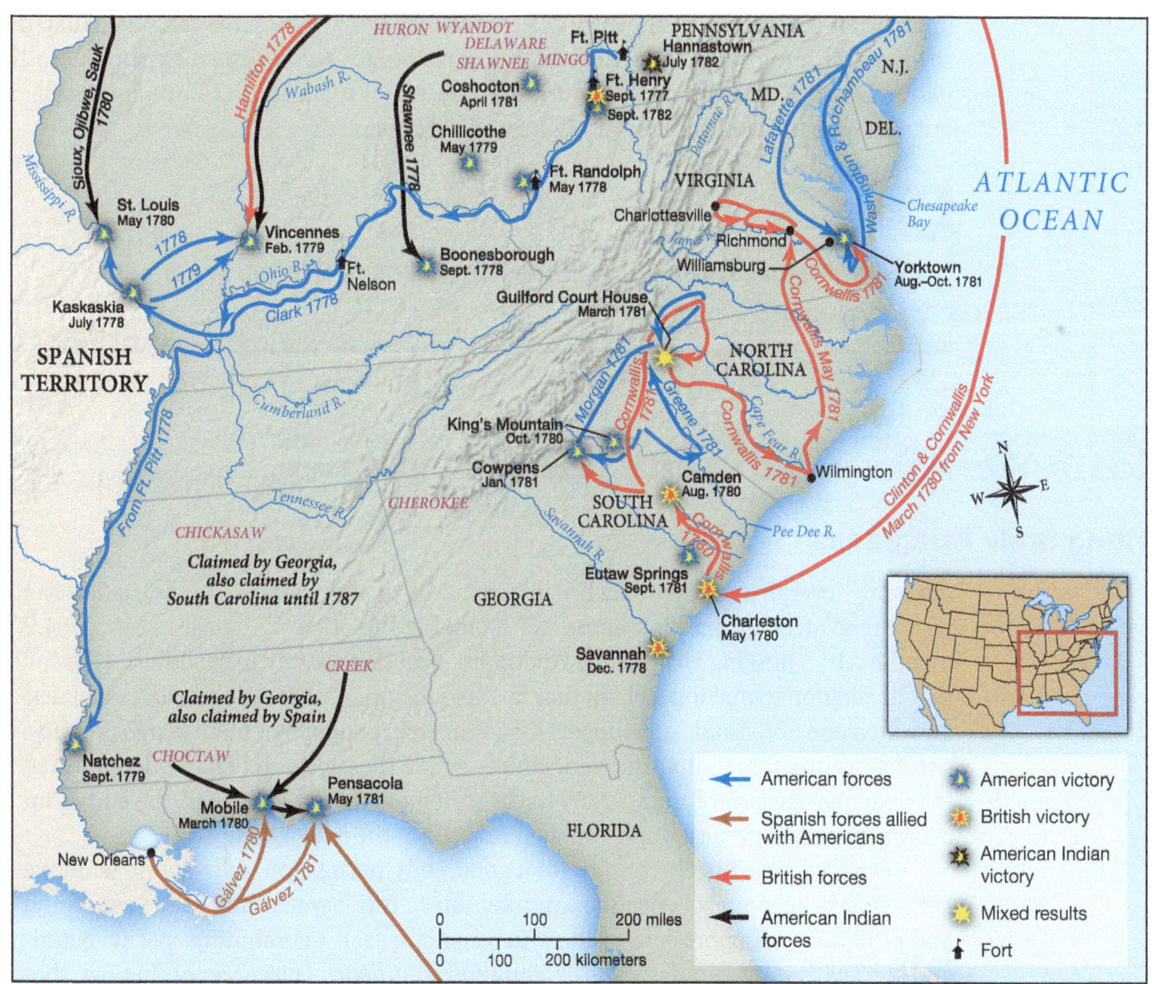

MAP 3.5 The War in the West and the South, 1777–1782 Between 1780 and 1781, major battles between Continental and British troops took place in Virginia and the Carolinas, and the British general Cornwallis finally surrendered at Yorktown, Virginia in October 1781. But patriot forces also battled British troops and their American Indian allies from 1777 to 1782 in the Ohio River valley, the lower Mississippi River, and the Gulf coast.

How do the battles shown on this map differ from those in the Northeast?

Americans had managed to defeat one of the most powerful military forces in the world. That victory resulted from the convergence of many circumstances. Certainly, Americans benefited from fighting on their own soil. Their knowledge of the land and its resources as well as earlier experiences fighting against American Indians and the French helped prepare them for battles against the British.

Just as important, British troops and officers were far removed from centers of decision making and supplies. Even supplies housed in Canada could not be easily transported the relatively short distance into New York.

British commanders were often hesitant to make decisions independently. Awaiting instructions from England proved costly on several occasions, especially since strategists in London often had little sense of conditions in America.

Both sides depended on outsiders for assistance, but here, too, Americans gained the advantage. The British army relied heavily on German mercenaries, American Indian allies, and freed people to bolster its regular troops. In victory, these supplementary forces were relatively reliable, but in defeat, many of them chose to look out for their own interests. The patriots marched with French and Spanish armies well prepared to challenge British troops and motivated to gain advantages for France and Spain if Britain was defeated.

Perhaps most important, a British victory was nearly impossible without conquering new American states one by one. Mobilized by Enlightenment ideals articulated in the Declaration of Independence, a large percentage of colonists now supported the patriot cause. British troops would have to contend not only with Continental soldiers, but also with an aroused citizenry fighting for independence.

- What major factors allowed the Americans to win the American Revolution?

AP® Skills Workshop: Thinking Historically

Writing Body Paragraphs

An essay's overall argument is called its thesis. You examined how to create a thesis in response to an essay question in the AP® Thinking Historically exercise in Module 3.2 and the AP® Thinking Historically Additional Practice activity in Module 3.3. Recall that in addition to making a claim that answers the question, the thesis statement also lays out a line of reasoning to support its claim. This road map of main points previews smaller arguments or sub-arguments that support the thesis and will be developed in the body paragraphs of an essay. A thesis statement is best located at the end of an essay's introductory paragraph and then restated at the end of the essay.

Before we dive into how to write a good body paragraph, let's define what we are trying to accomplish. Written argumentation is the systematic use of reasoning and evidence to support conclusions. In other words, it's combining specific details and facts with sound analysis and explanation to support a larger point. In turn, that main point supports the overall argument, the thesis. Ideally, the evidence, analysis, and main points will form a tightly connected whole just as puzzle pieces fit together to show a larger picture.

(continued)

Fortunately, you already have an approach that will help you create well-structured body paragraphs—**Claim, Support, Explain.** While you used a shortened version of CSE to create two-sentence thesis statements in Modules 3.2 and 3.3, we will now use an expanded version of CSE to write strong, tightly argued paragraphs.

The first sentence in a good body paragraph should state the sub-argument that was briefly mentioned in the thesis statement (this is sometimes called a topic sentence). The next three sentences should make a claim, support that claim with evidence or details, and explain how the evidence supports the claim as well as its significance. The next few sentences should repeat Claim, Support, Explain with additional material. Then the final sentence should summarize and restate the paragraph's sub-argument.

Let's take a look at a sample prompt, a completed thesis organizer for the prompt, and a thesis statement.

Explain the factors that led to a patriot victory in the Revolutionary War.

General Categories	Main Points	Supporting Details
- Military	- Despite its experience and resources, the British military made a series of costly errors.	- The British not fighting in winter of 1776–1777 gave the Continental Army time to regroup. - Howe's invading Philadelphia instead of reinforcing Burgoyne led to the defeat at Saratoga. - Slow and poor decision making due to distance and hesitancy.
- Social	- Many women also contributed to war effort by taking on men's role on the home front or even more directly helping the war effort.	- Women often took on husbands' role to provide food and shelter as men fought in the war. - Some women supported the patriot cause as spies or camp followers. - A few women even took up arms such as Deborah Sampson and Margaret Corbin.
- Diplomatic	- France and other countries provided invaluable military assistance and supplies.	- The Treaty of Alliance brought French diplomatic recognition, aid, troops, and the French navy. - French attacks against British colonies across the globe expanded the conflict and raised the stakes for Britain. - French troops and ships played a crucial role at Yorktown, helping to win the war.

(continued)

Thesis: "Despite long odds and tremendous hardships, the patriots outlasted the British and won their independence in the Revolutionary War **[claim]**. Errors in British military strategy, the strong support of patriot women for the war effort, and the assistance of France and other allies all contributed to the surprising American victory **[line of reasoning]**."

The second sentence of the thesis identifies the three main sub-arguments in the essay: British military mistakes, the involvement of patriot women, and support from France. The sample below illustrates a body paragraph using CSE and the information from the first row of the graphic organizer.

"Even though the British military was battle hardened and well supplied, poor decisions undermined the war effort and contributed to the surprising loss in the Revolutionary War **[sub-argument]**. For example, by following the European tradition of not fighting during winter, the British allowed the Continental Army to regroup during the winter of 1776–1777 and prolong the war **[claim]**. The pause in the British offensive at the end of the first year not only gave the Continentals time to rearm and recruit new soldiers, but it also allowed Washington to launch successful attacks at Trenton and Princeton **[support]**. Instead of possibly ending the war with a decisive victory against Washington's depleted forces in late 1776, the unexpected patriot victories led the British army to retreat to New York City and ensured the conflict would continue much longer **[explain]**. Further, the decision by General Howe in 1777 to invade and hold Philadelphia instead of marching north to support General Burgoyne's forces led to the devastating British defeat at Saratoga **[claim]**. Despite having orders to reinforce Burgoyne, Howe chose to attack Philadelphia, the patriot capital and home of the Continental Congress, in hopes of ending the war by occupying the largest city in the colonies **[support]**. Lacking additional support, Burgoyne's forces were overwhelmed by patriot militias forcing the surrender of his large army and encouraging France to join the conflict against the British **[explain]**. Despite their obvious military advantages, especially at the outset of the war, poor decision making by the British military allowed the patriots to extend the war and turn the tide of the conflict in their favor **[summary of sub-argument]**."

ACTIVITY

Now it's your turn. Write a complete body paragraph for the same essay prompt using one of the other two areas of support mentioned in the thesis statement: the role of women in supporting the Revolutionary War or the ways French assistance contributed to the patriot victory. Feel free to include information from the graphic organizer, although you may supplement it with additional details. Make sure to start your paragraph with a statement of the sub-argument, use CSE in the heart of the paragraph, and end the paragraph with a restatement of the sub-argument.

The Influence of Revolutionary Ideals

MODULE 3.6

FOCUS

The ideals of the Declaration of Independence forced many Americans to confront inequalities at home. Throughout the last twenty years of the eighteenth century, Americans whose voices were previously oppressed sought to define themselves within the new egalitarian rhetoric. However, others were ambivalent about expanding the ideal of equality to embrace all Americans.

While reading this module, compare the effects of the changes in American society on farmers who fought in the war, women, and Black Americans in the aftermath of the American Revolution. In what ways did their lives change, and in what ways did they remain the same?

The victory over Great Britain won independence but left the United States confronting difficult problems. When the Treaty of Paris was finally signed in 1783, thousands of British troops and their loyalist supporters left the colonies for Canada, the West Indies, or England.

Most soldiers simply wanted to return home and resume their former lives. But the government's inability to pay back wages and the huge debt the nation owed to private citizens and state and foreign governments hinted at difficult economic times ahead. Poor and middling veterans and small farmers suffered economically in the postwar period, but they were not alone. Women faced challenges as they sought to enhance their role in the nation. Black Americans, too, whose hopes for freedom had been raised by the Revolution, continued to fight for full citizenship and an end to slavery.

Veteran Farmers Struggle in a Postwar Economy

Many Revolutionary War veterans, most often would-be farmers, found the adjustment to postwar life difficult. Many men waited more than twenty years to receive any compensation for fighting in the American Revolution. In the meantime, they struggled to establish or reestablish farms and businesses and pay off debts accrued while engaged in the war for independence.

Disputes over western lands were deeply intertwined with the economic difficulties that plagued the new nation. Victory in the Revolution was followed by years of economic depression and growing debt. While the war fueled the demand for domestic goods and ensured high employment, both the demand and the jobs declined in peacetime. International trade was also slow to recover from a decade of disruption. Meanwhile, the nation owed a huge war debt.

Individuals, the states, and the federal government all viewed western lands as a solution to their problems. Farm families could start over on "unclaimed" land; states could distribute land instead of cash to veterans or creditors; and congress could sell land to fund its debts. Yet there was never enough land to meet these conflicting needs, nor did the United States, given American Indian nations' land claims and occupation of the trans-Appalachian west, hold secure title to the territory.

Some national leaders, including Alexander Hamilton, focused on other ways of repaying the war debt. Fearing that wealthy creditors would lose faith in a nation that could not repay its debts, they urged states to grant the federal government a percentage of import duties as a way to increase its revenue.

The states had their own problems. Legislators in Massachusetts and other states passed hard-money laws that required debts to be repaid in gold or silver rather than in paper currency. Affluent creditors favored these measures to ensure repayment in full. But small farmers, including Revolutionary War veterans, who had borrowed paper money during the war, now had to repay those loans in hard currency as the money supply shrank. Taxes, too, were rising as states sought to cover the interest on wartime bonds held by wealthy investors.

- What challenges did veterans face after the American Revolution?

Revolutionary Women Seek Wider Roles

Women's diverse contributions to the American Revolution played vital roles in securing the patriot victory. While their influence was praised in the post-Revolutionary era, state laws seldom expanded their rights. All states limited women's economic independence, although a few did allow married women to enter into business. Many states legalized divorce, but in practice it was still available only to the wealthy and well connected. Meanwhile, states excluded women from juries, legal training, and, with one exception, voting rights.

Abigail Adams had written her husband John in 1776, "Remember the Ladies . . . [I]f perticuliar care and attention is not paid to the Laidies we are determined to foment a Rebelion." While she and other elite women sought a greater public role, only New Jersey granted women — widowed or single and property owning — the right to vote, a right that the state rescinded less than three decades later. The vast majority of women could only hope to shape political decisions by influencing their male relatives and friends.

Many leaders of the early republic viewed wives and mothers as necessary to the development of a strong nation, leading to a push for women's education. In 1787, Benjamin Rush, in his *Essay on Female Education*, developed a notion of **republican motherhood**. He claimed that women could best shape political ideas and relations by "instructing their sons in principles of liberty and government." To prepare young women for this role, Rush suggested educating them in literature, music, composition, geography, history, and bookkeeping.

republican motherhood
A concept proposed by some American political leaders in the 1790s, which supported women's education so that they could in turn instruct their sons in principles of republican government.

Judith Sargent Murray offered a more radical approach to women's education, arguing that "girls should be enabled to procure for themselves the necessaries of life; independence should be placed within their grasp." A few American women in the late eighteenth century did receive broad educations. Some ran successful businesses; wrote plays, poems, and histories; and established urban salons where women and men

Terra Foundation for American Art, Chicago/Art Resource, NY

Judith Sargent Stevens, later Murray, c. 1772 Born into a wealthy Massachusetts family, Judith Sargent was allowed to study alongside her brother until she married John Stevens at age eighteen. In the 1770s, she wrote well-received essays on social and political topics and later promoted women's education and independence. Widowed at thirty-five, she soon married Universalist minister John Murray and continued to publish into her sixties.

How does the artist of this portrait display the confidence of Judith Sargent Stevens? How does the artist maintain popular perceptions of women during the period?

discussed the issues of the day. Notably, Quaker women testified against slavery in the 1780s, writing statements on the topic in separate women's meetings. Almost no other religious groups, however, offered women such spiritual autonomy.

In 1789, Massachusetts became the first state to institute free elementary education for all children, and female academies also multiplied in this period. While schooling for affluent girls was often focused on preparing them for domesticity, the daughters of artisans and farmers learned practical skills so they could assist in the family enterprise. Gains for these women fell short of the revolutionary political rights granted to voting citizens, but this expanded education nevertheless built a foundation upon which later generations of women pushed for equal rights.

Black American and American Indian women lived under much more severe constraints than white women. Most Black women were enslaved by whites, and those who were free could usually find jobs only as domestic servants or agricultural workers. Among American Indian nations, years of warfare enhanced men's role as warriors and diplomats while reducing matrilineal traditions and women's political influence. U.S. government officials and Protestant missionaries encouraged American Indians to embrace gender roles that mirrored those of Anglo-American culture, further diminishing women's roles. American Indian women forced to move west also lost authority tied to their traditional control of land, crops, and households.

AP® EXAM TIP

The impact of major developments such as the American Revolution is a frequent topic on the AP® Exam. Be sure to know how the Revolution affected various groups of people and the extent to which it did and did not change the lives of Americans.

REVIEW

- To what extent did the American Revolution provide new opportunities for women?

Slavery in the Revolutionary Era

Although the earliest state constitutions offered revolutionary change in many respects, few of them addressed the issue of slavery. As you will read in Module 3.7, only Vermont (which technically remained outside of the United States until 1791) abolished slavery in its 1777 constitution, and legislators in Pennsylvania provided for a very gradual abolition.

In southern states like Virginia, the Carolinas, and Georgia, however, life for enslaved people grew increasingly harsh during the war. Because British forces promised freedom to Black people who fought with them, enslavers and patriot armies in the South took extreme measures attempting to keep enslaved Black people from reaching British lines. When the British retreated, some generals, like Lord Dunmore and Sir Henry Clinton, took Black volunteers with them. Others left behind thousands to fend for themselves.

Nonetheless, the ideals of the American Revolution dealt a blow to human bondage in the northern states. For many Black people, revolutionary ideals required the end of slavery. In Massachusetts, two enslaved people sued for their freedom in county courts in 1780–1781. Quock Walker, who had been promised his emancipation by a former enslaver, sued his current enslaver to gain his freedom. About the same time, an enslaved woman, Mum Bett, who was the widow of a Revolutionary soldier, initiated a similar case, which she won. When Walker won his case as well, his former enslaver appealed the local court's decision, and the Massachusetts Supreme Court cited Mum Bett's case in its ruling that slavery conflicted with the state constitution.

Northern free Black communities grew rapidly during the war, especially in seaport cities. In the South, too, thousands of enslaved people gained freedom, either by joining the British army or by fleeing in the midst of battlefield chaos. As many as one-quarter of those enslaved in South Carolina had emancipated themselves by the end of the Revolution.

AP® WORKING with EVIDENCE

Source: Petition of Enslaved Black Americans to the Massachusetts Legislature, 1777

> "The petition of a great number of blacks detained in a state of slavery in the bowels of a free and Christian country. . . . Your petitioners apprehend that they have in common with all other men a natural and unalienable right to that freedom which the Great Parent of the Universe has bestowed equally on all mankind and which they have never forfeited by any compact or agreement whatever, but . . . were unjustly dragged by the hand of cruel power . . . to be sold like beasts of burden and like them condemned to slavery for life. . . . [Y]our petitioners . . . express their astonishment that it has never been considered that every principle from which America has acted in the course of their unhappy difficulties with Great Britain pleads stronger than a thousand arguments in favor of your petitioners. They therefore humbly beseech your honors . . . to cause an act of the legislature to be passed whereby they may be restored to the enjoyments of that which is the natural right of all men."

Questions for Analysis

1. Identify the grievances presented in this petition.
2. Describe the context that shaped this petition.
3. Evaluate the extent to which the sentiments expressed in this document reflect the ideas of the American Revolution.

Source: Thomas Cole, Peter Bassnett Matthewes, and Matthew Webb, free Black Americans, Petition to the South Carolina Senate, 1791

> "That in the enumeration of free citizens by the Constitution of the United States for the purpose of representation of the Southern states in Congress your [petitioners] have been considered under that description as part of the citizens of this state.
>
> Although by the . . . 1740 . . . Negro Act, now in force, your [petitioners] are deprived of the rights and privileges of citizens by not having it in their power to give testimony on oath in prosecutions on behalf of the state; from which cause many culprits have escaped the punishment due to their atrocious crimes, nor can they give their testimony in recovering debts due to them, or in establishing agreements made by them . . . except in cases where persons of color are concerned, whereby they are subject to great losses and repeated injuries without any means of redress.
>
> That by . . . said Act, they are debarred of the rights of free citizens by being subject to a trial without the benefit of a jury. . . .
>
> Your [petitioners] show that they have at all times since the independence of the United States contributed and do now contribute to the support of the government by cheerfully paying their taxes proportionable to their property with others who have been during such period, and now are, in full enjoyment of the rights and immunities of citizens, inhabitants of a free independent state."

Questions for Analysis

1. Identify the grievances presented in this petition.
2. Describe the rights Cole, Matthewes, and Webb claim for free Black Americans.
3. Explain how the effects of the American Revolution led to this petition.

Questions for Comparison

1. Describe the similarities the two documents share.
2. Describe how the two documents differ.
3. Explain how specific historical developments and their context shaped those differences.

The evacuation of the British at the end of the war also led to the exodus of thousands of Black Americans who had fought against the patriots. Before leaving North America, British officials granted certificates of manumission (freedom) to more than 1,300 men, 900 women, and 700 children. Most of these freed Black people settled in Nova Scotia, where they received small allotments of land from the British, but they generally lacked the resources to make these homesteads profitable. Despite these obstacles, some created a small Afro-Canadian community in Nova Scotia. Others starving in "Nova Scarcity" migrated internationally to areas considered more hospitable, such as Sierra Leone along the western coast of Africa.

Some Protestant churches were also challenged from within by free Black people who sought a greater role in how churches were run. In 1794, Richard Allen, who had been born into slavery, founded the first Black church in the United States, the African Methodist Episcopal Church (AME) in Philadelphia. At first, this church remained within the larger white Protestant fold, but by the early 1800s, Allen's church served as the basis for the first independent Black Protestant denomination in the nation.

It was no accident that the first independent Black church was founded in Philadelphia, which attracted large numbers of free Black people after the state adopted a gradual emancipation law in 1780. At the same time, the limits on emancipation in the South nurtured the growth of free Black communities in the North. Many Black Americans migrated to seaport cities like Philadelphia, New York, and New Bedford where they focused on finding jobs, supporting families, and securing the freedom of enslaved relatives. Others, like Richard Allen, sought to establish churches, schools, and voluntary societies and claim a political voice.

Some white people aided Black people in their struggles for freedom. Quakers, the only religious group to oppose slavery in the colonial period, became more outspoken. By the 1790s, nearly all Quakers had freed the people they had enslaved and withdrawn from the slave trade. Anthony Benezet, a writer and educator, worked tirelessly for the abolition of slavery. In 1770, he founded, and thereafter directed, the Negro School of Philadelphia, which was one of several such schools founded by Quakers.

Some northern states, such as New Jersey, granted property-owning Black people the right to vote. Others, such as Pennsylvania, did not specifically exclude them. Although the northern states with the largest enslaved populations, New York and New Jersey, did not pass gradual abolition laws until 1799 and 1804, respectively, the free Black population increased throughout the region.

Southern states, by contrast, maintained their laws protecting slavery in the years immediately following the Revolution, although some changes did occur. A few enslavers took revolutionary ideals to heart and emancipated the people they had enslaved following the war. Others granted emancipation in their wills. In addition, several states prohibited the importation of enslaved people from Africa during or immediately following the Revolution. They all stopped far short, however, of ending slavery.

- How did the American Revolution affect Black Americans?

AP® Skills Workshop: Writing Historically

Creating an Evaluative Thesis Statement

In the AP® Thinking Historically feature in Module 3.2, we explained that a **thesis statement** is the summary of a well-conceived argument in response to a historical question. An effective thesis statement makes a historically defensible claim and backs that claim with a line of reasoning that presents a road map of the main points which will be developed in the essay. To create a good thesis, we followed a three-step approach:

1. Understand the question,
2. Brainstorm and categorize relevant information, and
3. Write a thesis statement that makes an argument and provides reasoned areas of support.

(continued)

If necessary, review the thesis instruction in Module 3.2 before proceeding.

We are going to again discuss and practice how to create an effective thesis, but this time, we will use a prompt that more closely aligns to the wording and expectations you might see on the AP® Exam. We will then use the same process as before to work through the prompt and write a strong thesis statement. Here's the essay question.

> Evaluate the extent of difference in the effects of the French and Indian War (1754–1763) and the Revolutionary War (1776–1783) on the lives of people living in the new nation in the period 1754 to 1800.

Step 1 ▶ Carefully analyze the essay question

Break down the prompt so you can understand what the question is asking, how you should structure your response, and what parameters or limits are in place. In our previous look at essay questions, we noted the importance of identifying the topic, time frame, and historical reasoning process.

Here, you have more information to digest. Instead of one topic, you have two related topics—effects of the French and Indian War *and* effects of the Revolutionary War. Notice that the years are stated for both wars, which is often the case on the AP® Exam, because there's no emphasis on memorizing dates. The compound topic is important because the reasoning process assessed here is comparison, specifically the differences in the effects of both conflicts on Americans. A time frame is also provided, 1754 (the start of the French and Indian War) to 1800 (the end of the century and the year of Jefferson's election to the presidency). This span of years also matches the years of this period in the textbook.

This essay prompt is worded a little differently from the one in Module 3.2. Instead of "explain," the task is to "evaluate." (Review pages 9–10 in Module 1.2 for definitions of commonly used history task verbs.) The key difference here is that "evaluate" includes everything that "explain" does but also requires an appraisal. To evaluate is to weigh the significance, and including "the extent" clarifies that the question is how much or to what degree. So, this question isn't just asking for an examination of key differences; it's also asking you to consider the relative importance of those differences in the lives of Americans from 1754 to 1800.

Step 2 ▶ Brainstorm relevant historical information and organize it into an outline

Jot down what you remember and then develop an outline for the essay that you can summarize in the introduction. As before, the best way to do that is to create a graphic organizer with broad topics (left column), descriptions of the differences or similarities (center column), and specific examples of those differences or similarities (right column).

Now you may wonder why we are including similarities in the chart. That's because the reasoning process of comparison includes examining differences and/or similarities. While the prompt only mentions differences, the best essays will often also include similarities. We will discuss the importance of incorporating both sides of a historical reasoning process in greater depth in Period 6. Here's an example of what a completed brainstorming chart could look like for this essay question.

(continued)

General Categories of Difference or Similarity	Main Points of Differences or Similarities	Supporting Details
- Political (difference)	- Stronger government without direct representation vs. weaker, republican government	- British Acts: Stamp, Declaratory, Townshend, Coercive - Virtual representation vs. republican government - Articles of Confederation government lacked ability to tax, executive branch, or a federal judiciary
- Social (difference)	- No significant change for women after French and Indian War vs. a wider role for women in society after Revolutionary War	- Republican motherhood - Greater educational opportunities for women - Changes in divorce laws
- Westward Settlement (similarity)	- Victories in each war accelerated western migration of Americans	- Both conflicts expanded western borders to the Mississippi River - Disagreements between settlers and the government over "unclaimed" land occurred after each war. - Westward settlement after each war led to continued conflicts with American Indians

Step 3 Write a thesis statement with a claim and a line of reasoning

Remember that a good thesis statement accomplishes two tasks—making a historically defensible claim and establishing a line of reasoning. Your first thesis statement sentence should make a claim by directly answering the question and, if possible, establishing "the extent" of impact. The second sentence describes the support for your argument and, in this case, can be drawn from the "main points" column of the graphic organizer. Effective thesis statements can, of course, be longer or shorter than two sentences, but it's a good rule of thumb. Here's a sample thesis statement for this prompt.

> "Although the French and Indian War and the Revolutionary War both encouraged continued western migration, more significantly, the conflicts had differing impacts on American politics and the role of women in society **[claim]**. The French and Indian War led to a stronger exercise of British government power in the colonies while having little effect on women's lives, while the Revolutionary War opened new opportunities for women and led to the creation of a weak, republican government with limited federal powers **[line of reasoning]**."

ACTIVITY

Now it's your turn. Use the same three-step process to carefully analyze the prompt, brainstorm and categorize your information, and write an effective thesis statement that makes a historically defensible claim and establishes a line of reasoning for the prompt below.

> Evaluate the extent to which the American Revolution impacted the lives of veterans, women, and Black Americans differently in the period 1775 to 1800.

The Articles of Confederation

MODULE **3.7**

FOCUS

In the study of history, causes are events or developments that bring about or lead to other events or developments. While a basic concept, causation can sometimes be oversimplified. Oftentimes, a cause does not lead to a singular outcome or even multiple outcomes. Instead, causes work by degree and regularly interact with each other. That's why historians will often talk about causes as "contributing" or "shaping" rather than simply as causing. It's a reminder that causation is nuanced.

As you read this module, think about how and why states formed new governments during and after the American Revolution. What factors influenced the creation of their new constitutions? Also consider how state experiments and the experiences of the colonists shaped the Articles of Confederation.

Amid the constant upheavals of war, patriot leaders established new governments. At the national level, responsibilities ranged from coordinating and funding military operations to developing diplomatic relations with foreign countries and American Indian nations. At the state level, they wrote and ratified constitutions, enforced laws, and attempted to raise men, funds, and material support for military efforts both local and continental. Whether state or national, new governments tried to assure their followers that they were not simply replacing old forms of oppression with new ones.

States Form Their Own Governments, 1776–1786

Without a formal central government, state governments played crucial roles throughout the American Revolution. Even before the Continental Congress declared American independence, some colonies had forced royal officials to flee and established new state governments. Some states followed the regulations in their colonial charters or English common law. Others created new governments based on a written constitution.

These constitutions reflected the colonial history of opposition to centralized power fueled by the struggle against British tyranny. In Pennsylvania, patriots developed one of the most democratic constitutions. They replaced the governor with an executive council. The legislature consisted of a single house annually elected by popular vote. Legislators could serve only four of any seven-year period to discourage the formation of a political aristocracy. Although Pennsylvania's constitution was among the most radical, all states limited centralized power in some way.

As a check against tyranny, most states adopted Virginia's model, including a bill of rights in their constitutions that ensured citizens' fundamental rights and freedoms: freedom of the press, freedom of elections, the right to speedy trials by one's peers, the right to humane punishments, and the right to form militias. Some states also insisted on people's freedom of speech and assembly, the right to petition and to bear arms, and

AP® EXAM TIP

Following the Revolutionary War, why did Americans place greater power within the legislative branches of the state governments, while making the Articles of Confederation—national power—intentionally weak? Identify the successes and failures of the Articles of Confederation, along with the eventual decision to revise the Articles.

equal protection of the laws. Almost all state constitutions prohibited titles of nobility and any symbols of inherited aristocracy, such as family crests and shields.

The New Jersey constitution of 1776 gave all free inhabitants who met the property qualifications the right to vote in elections, thus allowing some propertied single and widowed women and free Black people to vote—until New Jersey passed a law specifically limiting the franchise (right to vote) to men in 1807. Most new state constitutions, however, allowed only white men with property to vote. Nearly all granted significant power to the legislative branch, where white men of property dominated.

During the Revolution, few legislatures moved in any way to eliminate the most oppressive institution, slavery. The exception was Vermont. Already containing only a few enslaved people, Vermont abolished slavery in its 1777 constitution. The new Pennsylvania state legislature also passed a gradual abolition law in 1780—under it, all Black American children born enslaved could claim freedom at the age of twenty-eight.

The creation of new state constitutions also generally marked the end of direct government sponsorship of churches. In many states, freedom of religion became a guaranteed right. In other states, legislatures made laws in the 1780s that reduced or eliminated government funds for religion. The Church of England had long benefited from British support by taxing residents to support its ministries before the Revolution. These taxes in effect privileged one Christian religious denomination over others and were ended as state constitutions started separating church and state, resulting in new guarantees of free worship.

Statute of Religious Freedom
A 1786 law passed by the Virginia Assembly that ensured the separation of church and state and largely guaranteed freedom of religion. Enactment of the statute established a legal precedent followed by other states and was later included in the Bill of Rights to the U.S. Constitution.

But more than wartime tactics, what prompted the biggest change in how the states approached religious practices was the fact that white Americans no longer generally joined the Church of England. Denominations that had dominated the various colonies now faced greater competition, especially in inland areas, where groups like the Baptists and Methodists gained thousands of converts. The Society of Friends (Quakers) and the Presbyterians also gained new followers during the latter half of the eighteenth century, while Catholics and Jews experienced greater tolerance than in the colonial era as a result of a growing ethos of religious freedom that uncoupled religious practice from secular government. This ensured that no single religious perspective dominated the new nation. Instead, Christian churches competed for members, money, and political influence. After the Revolution, in 1786, the Virginia Assembly approved the **Statute of Religious Freedom**, which made church attendance and support voluntary. Many other states followed Virginia's lead.

REVIEW

- What similarities did the new state governments share between 1776 and 1786?
- What accounted for the differences among these governments?

A Revolutionary National Government, 1777–1781

Articles of Confederation
Plan for national government with limited powers proposed by the Continental Congress of 1777 and ratified in March 1781. The Articles were replaced by the Constitution in 1789.

For most of the American Revolution, the Continental Congress acted in place of a national government while the delegates worked to devise a more permanent structure. In 1777, they drafted the **Articles of Confederation**, which established a confederation of equal states but granted the national government limited powers, reflecting widespread fear of centralized authority. The Continental Congress submitted the articles to the states for approval. Eight of the thirteen ratified the plan by mid-1778, yet some states delayed while delegates to the Continental Congress worked to resolve conflicting land claims in the trans-Appalachian west. Nearly three more years passed before the last state, Maryland, approved the Articles of Confederation.

Many patriot leaders made it clear that independence would mean further expansion and had little regard for American Indians, much of whose land had already been claimed when the states were still colonies. States like Connecticut, Georgia, New York, Massachusetts, and Virginia hoped to use western lands to reward soldiers and expand their settlements. States without such claims, like Maryland, argued that if such lands were "wrested from the common enemy by the blood and treasure of the thirteen States," they should be considered "common property, subject to be parceled out by Congress into free and independent governments." In 1780, New York State ceded its western claims to the Continental Congress, and others followed suit.

With land disputes settled, Maryland ratified the Articles of Confederation in March 1781. A new national government was finally formed, unifying the rebellious states just as it appeared they would gain their independence. Still, the Continental Congress's guarantee that western lands would be "disposed of for the common benefit of the United States" ensured continued conflicts with American Indians as the Confederation government took charge.

AP® WORKING with EVIDENCE

Source: Articles of Confederation, 1781

> "ART. 2. Each state retains its sovereignty, freedom, and independence, and every power, jurisdiction, and right which is not by this Confederation expressly delegated to the United States in Congress assembled.
>
> ART. 3. The said states hereby severally enter into a firm league of friendship with each other for their common defence, the security of their liberties, and their mutual and general welfare; binding themselves to assist each other against all force offered to or attacks made upon them on account of religion, sovereignty, trade, or any other pretence whatever. . . .
>
> ART. 9. . . . The United States in Congress assembled shall never engage in a war nor grant letters of marque [an authorization to commit piracy] or reprisal in time of peace, nor enter into any treaties or alliances, nor coin money nor regulate the value thereof, nor ascertain the sums and expenses necessary for the defence and welfare of the United States, or any of them; nor emit bills, nor borrow money on the credit of the United States, nor appropriate money, nor agree upon the number of vessels of war to be built or purchased, or the number of land or sea forces to be raised, nor appoint a commander-in-chief of the army or navy, unless nine states assent to the same; nor shall a question on any other point, except for adjourning from day to day, be determined, unless by the votes of a majority of the United States in Congress assembled. . . .
>
> ART. 13. Every state shall abide by the determinations of the United States in Congress assembled on all questions which by this Confederation are submitted to them. And the Articles of this Confederation shall be inviolably observed by every state, and the Union shall be perpetual; nor shall any alteration at any time hereafter be made in any of them; unless such alteration be agreed to in a Congress of the United States, and be afterwards confirmed by the legislatures of every state."

Questions for Analysis

1. Identify the powers these articles give the new national government.
2. Identify the powers these articles give state governments.
3. Explain how the Articles of Confederation were designed to prevent laws like the British parliamentary acts of the 1760s and 1770s that so angered the colonists.

REVIEW

- How did the Articles of Confederation government's policies on western expansion compare to those of the British crown before the American Revolution?

New Economic Challenges, 1780–1783

The United States faced serious financial instability in its early years. As the Revolutionary War ground to an end, issues of military pay sparked conflict and threatened the new nation. Some Continental soldiers continued to fight, but others focused on the long-festering issue of overdue wages. Uprisings by ordinary soldiers were common but successfully suppressed by Washington, who maintained a uniquely well-fed and loyal unit for such purposes.

When the Continental Congress decided in June 1783 to discharge the remaining troops without providing back pay, a near-mutiny erupted in Pennsylvania, where nearly four hundred soldiers marched on the congress in Philadelphia. Washington sent troops to put down the revolt, but bloodshed was avoided when the Pennsylvania soldiers agreed to accept half pay and certificates for the remainder. Despite this compromise, the issue of back pay would continue to plague the nation.

Complaints from Continental Army officers about payment, however, posed a greater problem. In 1780, officers extracted a promise from the Continental Congress for half pay for life but had received no pay at all in the last years of the war. Officers encamped at Newburgh, New York, awaiting a peace treaty, petitioned the confederation government in December 1782 for back pay for themselves and their soldiers, again with no success. By March 1783, most soldiers had returned home without pay, but some five hundred officers remained at Newburgh. Quietly encouraged by political supporters, dissident officers circulated veiled threats of a military takeover. However, on March 15, the officers were confronted by General George Washington. In an emotional speech, he urged them to respect civilian control of the government.

Congressional leaders promised the officers full pay for five years. However, lacking sufficient funds, they could provide only "commutation certificates," promising future payment.

Many confederation leaders, such as Alexander Hamilton, were sympathetic to the officers' plight and hoped to use pressure from this formidable group to enhance the powers of the congress. Hamilton had been pressing state governments to grant the confederation congress a new duty of 5 percent on imported goods to provide the federal government with an independent source of revenue. The threat posed by an uprising of Continental Army officers proved useful in his efforts to convince states like New York to agree to his plan.

Despite such efforts at creating revenue, the economy declined further as postwar American diplomacy failed to open up international trade. In 1783, the British Parliament denied the United States the right to trade with the British West Indies. The following year, Spain, seeking leverage against the United States in disputes over western territories, prohibited American ships from accessing the port of New Orleans. Spain and Great Britain also threatened U.S. sovereignty by conspiring with American citizens on the borderlands, promising them protection from American Indians. To arrange that protection, they offered American Indians valuable trade, including guns. At the same time, British troops remained in forts on America's western borderlands and urged American Indians to harass settlers there. Off the coast of North Africa, Barbary pirates attacked U.S. merchant ships. These international obstacles to U.S. trade after the Revolution slowed the economic growth necessary to stabilize the new nation.

Almost immediately after achieving independence, financial distress among small farmers and tensions with American Indians on the western borderlands intensified concerns that the confederation government was not up to ensuring order and prosperity for its citizens. While some patriots demanded a new political compact to strengthen the national government, others feared reproducing British tyranny.

- What financial challenges did the new national government face during and immediately after the American Revolution?

The Northwest Ordinances of 1785 and 1787

To regulate the vast territory of the Ohio River valley and the Great Lakes region granted to the United States in the Treaty of Paris at the conclusion of the Revolutionary War, Thomas Jefferson drafted the **Northwest Ordinance** in 1785. It provided that the territory be surveyed and divided into adjoining townships. He hoped to carve nine small states out of the region to enhance the representation of western farmers and thus ensure the dominance of their views in the national government. The congress revised his proposal, however, specifying that only three to five states be created and thereby limiting the future influence of western settlers in the federal government. The ordinance also set aside lands for public schools in each future township. The population of the territory grew rapidly, with speculators buying up huge tracts of land and selling smaller parcels to eager settlers. In response, congressional leaders modified the Northwest Ordinance in 1787, clarifying the process by which territories could become states. The congress appointed territorial officials and guaranteed residents the basic rights of U.S. citizens. After a territory's population reached 5,000, residents could choose an assembly, but the territorial governor retained the power to veto legislation. When a would-be state reached a population of 60,000, it could apply for admission to the United States. Thus, the congress established an orderly system by which territories became states in the Union.

Northwest Ordinances of 1785 and 1787
The 1785 act of the confederation congress provided for the survey, sale, and eventual division into states of the Northwest Territory and set aside land for public schools. A 1787 act then clarified the process by which settled territories could become states and banned slavery across the Northwest Territory.

The 1787 ordinance also addressed concerns about American Indians and the question of slavery in the territories. It encouraged fair treatment of American Indian nations but did not include any means of enforcing such treatment and failed to resolve the land claims of American Indian nations. It abolished slavery throughout the Northwest Territory but mandated the return of fugitives from slavery to prevent a flood of runaways and satisfy the interests of slavery-supporting politicians.

The 1787 legislation did not address territory south of the Ohio River. Enslavers, seeking more fertile fields, had brought tens of thousands of enslaved Black people into Kentucky, Tennessee, and the Mississippi territories. Moreover, as Americans streamed westward south of the Ohio River, they confronted Creek, Choctaw, and Chickasaw tribes, well supplied with weapons by Spanish traders, as well as armed Cherokee who had sided with the British during the Revolution. Conflicts there were largely ignored by the national government for the next quarter century.

- What dilemmas did the Northwest Ordinances seek to resolve?
- How did the Northwest Ordinances represent a continuation of pre-American Revolution policy, and how did they represent a change?

Indebted Farmers Fuel Political Crises, 1783–1787

Farmers enlisted and fought in the American Revolution, hoping to expand their political rights and roles in the new nation. Such efforts initially seemed to bear fruit. Most state constitutions written during the Revolution specifically allowed men with little or even no property, such as small-scale farmers, to vote and hold office.

One such farmer was Daniel Shays. One of six children born to Irish parents in Hopkinton, Massachusetts, Shays received little formal education. In 1772, at age twenty-five, he married, had a child, and settled into farming. By June 1775, he was among the patriots defending Bunker Hill. After distinguishing himself in the Continental Army, Shays purchased a farm in 1780 and hoped to return to a normal life. Instead, economic turmoil rocked the region as it did the nation in the years following the Revolution.

Many farmers had fallen into debt while fighting for independence. They returned to an economic recession and increased taxes as state governments struggled to repay wealthy creditors and fund their portion of the federal budget. Therefore, the economic interests of small farmers and workers diverged sharply from those of wealthy merchants and large landowners.

As conflicts between debtors and creditors escalated between 1783 and 1787, state governments came down firmly on the side of the wealthy. But indebted farmers did not give up. They continued their revolutionary efforts by voting, petitioning, and protesting to gain more favorable policies.

In western Massachusetts, where many farmer-veterans faced eviction, Shays kept his farm and represented his town at county conventions that petitioned the state government for economic relief. However, the legislature largely ignored the farmers' concerns.

For the time being, national political elites worried far more about international threats to prosperity and the independence of the new nation. The continued efforts of Great Britain and Spain to undercut U.S. sovereignty and ongoing struggles with American Indian nations posed especially serious dangers. George Washington, James Madison, Alexander Hamilton, and others questioned whether the Articles of Confederation held enough power to deal with international threats to the new nation. When Madison and Hamilton attended the 1786 convention in Annapolis to address problems related to interstate commerce, they discovered that their concerns about the weakness of the confederation were shared by many large landowners, planters, and merchants. Despite these elite concerns, state political leaders resisted giving up some of the powers they had been granted under the Articles of Confederation.

Meanwhile, when farmers' efforts to petition the government failed, tense conflicts ensued. Debt-ridden farmers in New Hampshire marched on the state capital in September 1786, demanding reform. But they were confronted by cavalry units, who quickly seized and imprisoned their leaders.

The internal discord in congress also inspired radicals to more coordinated action. In 1786, angered by the state's failure to act, armed groups of farmers attacked courthouses throughout western Massachusetts. Although a reluctant leader, Daniel Shays headed the largest band of more than a thousand farmer-veteran-soldiers. In January 1787, this group headed to the federal arsenal at Springfield, Massachusetts, to seize guns and ammunition. Shays's rebels, however, were routed by state militia and pursued by Massachusetts Governor James Bowdoin's army. Many rebel leaders were captured; others, including Shays, escaped to Vermont and New York. Four were convicted and two were hanged before Bowdoin granted amnesty to the others in hopes of avoiding further conflict.

This uprising, known as **Shays's Rebellion**, alarmed many state and national leaders, who feared such insurgencies might break out elsewhere. On December 26, 1786, Washington wrote to a fellow politician to express his concerns about the rebellion: "If the powers [of the central government] are inadequate, amend or alter them; but do not let us sink into the lowest states of humiliation and contempt." Hamilton agreed, claiming that Shays's Rebellion "marked almost the last stage of national humiliation." Congress thus decided to convene a convention in Philadelphia in 1787 to revise and thereby strengthen the Articles of Confederation.

Shays's Rebellion
A rebellion in 1786–1787 by western Massachusetts farmers, many of whom were war veterans, caused mainly by economic hardships and taxation policies they saw as benefitting an eastern elite in the aftermath of the American Revolution. The rebellion encouraged political leaders to consider strengthening the Articles of Confederation.

AP® WORKING with EVIDENCE

Source: Image of Daniel Shays and Job Shattuck, *Boston Almanac,* 1787.

National Portrait Gallery, Smithsonian Institution

The verse on the left of the image reads: "Thro' drifted Storms let SHAYS the Court Assail, And SHATTUCK rise, illustrious [respected] from the Jail, In coward Hands let legal Powers expire [end], And give new Subjects to my sounding Lyre [a type of guitar often accompanying singing]"

Questions for Analysis

1. Identify the two individuals in this image.
2. Describe how these two individuals are depicted in this image.
3. Explain the sympathies of the maker of the image and the short poem that accompanies it.

- What economic struggles did farmers face in the aftermath of the American Revolution?
- How did political leaders contribute to these struggles?

Skills Workshop: Thinking Historically

Additional Practice in Creating an Evaluative Thesis Statement

Review the AP® Writing Historically exercise in Module 3.6. Use the same three-step method to create your thesis.

1. Understand the prompt by identifying the topic, years, and reasoning process.
2. Brainstorm relevant historical information and organize it into an outline (use a graphic organizer such as the one below).
3. Write a robust, two-sentence thesis statement that makes a historically defensible claim and establishes a line of reasoning (use the second column from the chart for the line of reasoning).

> Evaluate the extent to which the experiences of colonists in the years before the American Revolution influenced the development of the Articles of Confederation.

General Categories	Main Points	Supporting Details
-	-	- - -
-	-	- - -
-	-	- - -

The Constitutional Convention and Debates over Ratification & The Constitution

MODULES 3.8 3.9

FOCUS

As you read these modules, think about how and why the Constitution replaced the Articles of Confederation as the new nation's governing document. Compare the two documents and their contexts. In what ways were the concerns of Americans and the events surrounding the creation of each document similar, and in what ways were they different?

In the decade following the Revolution, Americans of all stripes engaged in heated disagreements over the best means to unify and stabilize the United States. Many, especially those in positions of economic and political influence, had come to question the strength of the government under the Articles of Confederation—even if they hardly agreed on where to go from there. As financial distress among patriotic small farmers and tensions with American Indians on the western borderlands continued to escalate, the worry that revising the Articles would lead to the very tyranny that tens of thousands of patriots had just fought a war to escape began to be outweighed by the necessity of changes to steady the course for the new nation.

AP® EXAM TIP

Identify the key features of the Constitutional Convention. What compromises happened to bring about the proposed Constitution? You have to be able to compare the arguments of those who supported (Federalists) with those who opposed (Antifederalists) ratification of the Constitution.

Making a Constitution

The fifty-five delegates who met at the **Constitutional Convention** in Philadelphia in May 1787 were white, educated men of property, mainly lawyers, merchants, and planters. Only eight had signed the Declaration of Independence eleven years earlier. The elite status of the delegates and the absence of many leading patriots raised concern among those who saw the convention as a threat to the rights of states and of citizens. Not wanting to alarm the public, delegates agreed to meet in secret until they had hammered out a new framework of government.

Constitutional Convention The meeting in Philadelphia from May to September 1787 at which delegates drafted the Constitution to replace the Articles of Confederation.

On May 25, the convention opened, and delegates quickly turned to the key question: Revise the Articles of Confederation, or draft an entirely new document? The majority of men came to Philadelphia with the intention of strengthening the existing government by amending the Articles, including James Monroe of Virginia.

A core group who sought a more powerful central government—including James Madison—had met before the convention and drafted a plan to replace the Articles. This **Virginia Plan** proposed a strong centralized state, including a bicameral (two-house) legislature in which representation was to be based on population. Members of the two houses would select the national executive and the national judiciary, and would settle

Virginia Plan A plan put forth at the beginning of the Constitutional Convention that proposed a strong central government and a system of representation based on population.

disputes between states. Although most delegates opposed the Virginia Plan, it launched discussions in which strengthening the central government was assumed to be the goal.

Discussions of the Virginia Plan raised an issue that nearly paralyzed the convention: the question of representation. Heated debates pitted large states such as Virginia against small states. In mid-June, William Patterson introduced the **New Jersey Plan**, which highlighted the needs of smaller states. In this plan, Congress would consist of only one house, with each state having equal representation.

New Jersey Plan
A proposal at the Constitutional Convention endorsed by small states for a one-house legislature with each state having an equal vote.

The convention finally appointed a special committee to solve the problem of representation so all delegates could agree to a new constitution to replace the Articles. This committee helped the convention reach what later became known as the "Great Compromise," in which representation in the House of Representatives would be determined by population — counted every ten years in a national census — while in the Senate, each state, regardless of size, would have equal representation. Although the Senate was granted more authority than the House in certain areas, only the House could introduce funding bills. Members of the House of Representatives were to be elected by voters in each state, whereas members of the Senate would be appointed by state legislatures.

Along with this agreement, one of the few direct considerations of slavery at the Philadelphia convention emerged. With little apparent debate, the committee decided that representation in the House of Representatives was to be based on a record of the entire free population and three-fifths of "all other persons" — that is, enslaved Black Americans. If delegates had moral reservations about this **three-fifths compromise**, most found them outweighed by the urgency of settling the troublesome question of representation.

three-fifths compromise
The compromise between northern and southern delegates at the 1787 Constitutional Convention to count enslaved persons as three-fifths of a free person in deciding the proportion of representation in the House of Representatives and taxation by the federal government. It had the long-term effect of granting slaveholding states a larger amount of voting power.

Still, slavery was on the minds of delegates. In the same week that the Philadelphia convention accepted the institution of slavery as shown by the three-fifths compromise, the confederation congress meeting in New York City outlawed slavery in the Northwest Territory. News of that decision likely inspired representatives from Georgia and South Carolina to insist that the new constitution protect the slave trade. Delegates in Philadelphia agreed that the importation of enslaved people would not be interfered with for at least twenty years. Another provision demonstrating federal support for slavery guaranteed the return of fugitives from slavery to enslavers. At the same time, northern delegates insisted that the three-fifths formula be used in assessing taxation as well as representation, ensuring that the states with enslaved people paid for the increased size of their congressional delegations with increased taxes.

Two other issues provoked considerable debate in the following weeks. All delegates supported federalism, a system in which states and the central government shared power, but they disagreed over the balance of power between them. They also disagreed over the degree of popular participation in selecting national leaders.

The new Constitution increased the powers of the central government significantly. For instance, Congress would now have the power to raise revenue by levying and collecting taxes and tariffs and coining money; to raise armies; to regulate interstate commerce; to settle disputes between the states; to establish uniform rules for the **naturalization** of immigrants; and to make treaties with foreign nations and American Indians. But Congress could rescind state laws only when those laws challenged "the supreme law of the land," and states retained all rights that were not specifically granted to the federal government.

Unlike the Articles of Confederation, which set up a "firm league of friendship" between the states, the Constitution established a stronger national government to bind the states more closely into a single union. But, to allay concerns that the new government might replicate the abuses of the British against the colonists, the Constitution created a **separation of powers** between the three branches of the new government. The legislative branch, consisting of the House and Senate, would pass laws and, in the case of the Senate, declare wars. The Senate also ratified treaties and approved key presidential appointments to the courts and cabinet. The president, head of the executive branch, would execute laws, act as commander-in-chief of the military, and oversee the federal bureaucracy. The judicial branch, overseen by the Supreme Court, would interpret legislation and executive actions and rule on the constitutionality of federal and state laws, though that power was not clarified until some time later.

separation of powers A system of government advocated by Baron de Montesquieu dividing powers across multiple branches of government. In the U.S. Constitution, federal powers are distributed among legislative, executive, and judicial branches.

A system of **checks and balances** also allowed each branch to limit some of the actions of the other two branches. For example, even today, a president appoints a justice to the Supreme Court, but that candidate has to be confirmed by the Senate. Although the Senate and House pass legislation, the president has discretion in choosing how to implement laws and can even veto bills, although any vetoes can be overridden by a two-thirds vote in each chamber. Finally, the Supreme Court serves as the highest court in the nation and, later, acquired the power to rule on the meaning and constitutionality of legislation and executive actions. In all these ways and more, the framers sought to create a self-correcting system of government that would be able to exercise power effectively without the threat of tyranny.

checks and balances The specific ways a branch of government can limit or modify the behavior of other branches. The system of checks and balances in the U.S. Constitution was designed to keep any one branch from exercising too much power.

One of the important powers retained by the states was the right to determine who was eligible to vote, but the Constitution regulated the influence that eligible voters would have in national elections. Unlike the Articles of Confederation, which had no nationally elected office, members of the House of Representatives were to be elected directly by popular vote for two-year terms. Senators — two from each state — were to be selected by state legislatures for a term of six years.

Selection of the president was even further removed from voters. The president would be selected every four years by an **electoral college**, with each state granted the number of electors equal to its members in the House and Senate. State legislatures would decide how to choose their electors. The electoral college was a compromise between determining the president via a direct popular vote or via congressional vote.

electoral college A group of electors whose vote is the formal election of the president and vice president after the general election votes are tallied. States decide how to choose their electors, and most instituted a system requiring their electors to vote in accordance with a state's popular vote, resulting in a state's vote winner receiving all of the state's electoral votes.

Finally, the federal judicial system was to be wholly removed from popular influence. Once ratified, justices on the Supreme Court served for life to protect their judgments from the pressure of popular opinion.

WORKING with EVIDENCE

Source: The Preamble to the Constitution of the United States, 1787

> "We the People of the United States, in Order to form a more perfect Union, establish Justice, insure domestic Tranquility, provide for the common defence, promote the general Welfare, and secure the Blessings of Liberty to ourselves and our Posterity, do ordain and establish this Constitution for the United States of America."

Questions for Analysis

1. Identify the purposes for the new government listed in the preamble.
2. Explain how the preamble was a response to concerns about the Articles of Confederation.
3. Evaluate the extent to which the newly written U.S. Constitution fulfilled its preamble.

With the final debates concluded, delegates agreed that approval by nine states, rather than all thirteen, would make the Constitution the law of the land despite the Articles of Confederation requiring unanimous consent to be amended. Some delegates sought formal reassurance that the powers granted to the federal government would not be abused and urged the inclusion of a bill of rights, like the Virginia Declaration of Rights. But the weary delegates, eager to finish their business, voted down the proposal. On September 17, 1787, the Constitution was approved and sent to the states for ratification.

AP® EXAM TIP

How did the U.S. Constitution resolve the weaknesses of the Articles of Confederation? Often, the AP® Exam asks for a comparison or contrast between these two foundational documents.

REVIEW

- How did the various proposals at the Constitutional Convention reflect regional interests?

Americans Debate Ratification

The confederation congress sent the Constitution to state legislatures and asked them to call conventions to consider ratification. These conventions could not modify the document, but only accept or reject it. Thousands of copies of the Constitution were circulated in newspapers and as broadsides. Pamphleteers, civic leaders, and ministers proclaimed their opinions publicly, while ordinary citizens in homes, shops, and taverns debated the wisdom of establishing a stronger central government.

Fairly quickly, two sides emerged. The **Federalists**, who supported ratification, came mainly from urban and commercial backgrounds and lived in towns, cities, or large plantations along the Atlantic coast that produced staple crops. They viewed a stronger central government as necessary to the economic and political stability of the nation. Their opponents were generally more rural, less wealthy, and more likely to live in interior or border regions. Labeled **Antifederalists**, they feared the potential of overreaching powers of a strong central government and demanded the addition of a Bill of Rights to the Constitution to protect individual liberties.

Federalist

A supporter of ratification of the Constitution of 1787, many of whom came from urban and commercial backgrounds. Federalists supported a strong central government with vigorous powers.

Antifederalist

An opponent of ratification of the Constitution of 1787. Antifederalists were generally from more rural and less wealthy backgrounds than the Federalists and opposed increasing the powers of the central government.

AP® WORKING with EVIDENCE

Source: Alexander Hamilton, Federalist Argument at the New York State Convention, June 1788

> "I will not agree with gentlemen who trifle with the weaknesses of our country; and suppose, that they are enumerated to answer a party purpose, and to terrify with ideal dangers. No; I believe these weaknesses to be real, and pregnant with destruction. Yet, however weak our country may be, I hope we never shall sacrifice our liberties. . . .
>
> Sir, it appears to me extraordinary, that, while gentlemen in one breath acknowledge that the old confederation requires many material amendments, they should in the next deny, that its defects have been the cause of our political weakness, and the consequent calamities of our country. . . . [T]he states have almost uniformly weighed the requisitions by their own local interests; and have only executed them so far as answered their particular conveniency or advantage. Hence there have ever been thirteen different bodies to judge of the measures of Congress, and the operations of government have been distracted by their taking different courses. . . .
>
> Shall we take the old Confederation, as the basis of a new system? . . . certainly not. Will any man who entertains a wish for the safety of his country,

trust the sword and the purse with a single Assembly organized on principles so defective—so rotten? Though we might give to such a government certain powers with safety, yet to give them the full and unlimited powers of taxation and the national forces would be to establish a despotism; the definition of which is, a government in which all power is concentrated in a single body. . . . These considerations show clearly, that a government totally different must be instituted. . . . [T]he convention . . . therefore formed two branches, and divided the powers, that each might be a check upon the other. . . .

Sir, the natural situation of this country seems to divide its interests into different classes. . . . It became necessary, therefore, to compromise; or the Convention must have dissolved without effecting any thing. . . .

The first thing objected to is that clause which allows a representation for three fifths of the negroes. . . . It is the unfortunate situation of the Southern States to have a great part of their population, as well as property, in blacks. The regulation complained of was one result of the spirit of accommodation, which governed the Convention; and without this indulgence, no union could possibly have been formed. But, Sir, considering some peculiar advantages which we derive from them, it is entirely just that they should be gratified. The Southern States possess certain staples, tobacco, rice, indigo, &c. which must be capital objects in treaties of commerce with foreign nations; and the advantages which they necessarily procure in these treaties, will be felt throughout all the States. . . . [Moreover,] representation and taxation go together, and one uniform rule ought to apply to both. Would it be just to compute these slaves in the assessment of taxes; and discard them from the estimate in the apportionment of representatives?"

Questions for Analysis

1. Identify the claims that Hamilton makes in this excerpt.
2. Explain how Hamilton supports the claims he makes in this excerpt.
3. Evaluate the extent to which the ideals of the American Revolution shaped the dissent offered by some delegates to the Constitutional Convention.

The pro-Constitution position was presented in a series of editorials that appeared in New York newspapers from 1787 to 1788 and were published collectively as **the *Federalist Papers***. The authors—James Madison, John Jay, and Alexander Hamilton—articulated broad principles embraced by most supporters of the Constitution.

The *Federalist Papers* A series of eighty-five essays by Federalists Alexander Hamilton, James Madison, and John Jay. Published in newspapers throughout the country, the *Federalist Papers* promoted the ratification of the Constitution.

Most notably, in *Federalist* No. 10, Madison countered the common wisdom that small governmental structures were most effective in representing the interests of their citizens and avoiding the development of political parties. He argued that in large units, groups with competing interests had to collaborate and compromise, providing the surest check on the "tyranny of the majority."

Hamilton, a young New York politician, played a particularly important role in the Federalist effort, authoring fifty-one of the eighty-five *Federalist Papers*. Born in poverty in the British West Indies and orphaned at eleven, he was apprenticed to a firm of merchants that sent him to the American colonies. There Hamilton was attracted to the activities of radical patriots and joined the Continental Army in 1776, where Washington noticed his abilities and kept him close by to manage the war as his chief of staff from 1777 to 1781.

After the war, Hamilton established himself as a lawyer and financier in New York City, eventually winning election to the New York state legislature in 1786, where he focused on improving the state's finances. Although Hamilton played only a small role in the Constitutional Convention of 1787, he worked tirelessly with his fellow *Federalist Papers* authors for ratification of the Constitution.

Still, Antifederalists worried that a large and powerful central government could lead to tyranny. Small farmers claimed that a strong congress filled with merchants, lawyers, and planters was likely to place the interests of creditors above those of ordinary (and indebted) Americans. Even some wealthy patriots, like Mercy Otis Warren of Boston, feared that the Constitution would empower a few individuals who cared little for the "true interests of the people." Further, the absence of a bill of rights concerned many Americans.

Federalists worked in each state to overcome criticism of the Constitution through persuasive arguments and the promise of a bill of rights once the Constitution was ratified. They gained strength from the quick ratification of the Constitution by Delaware, Pennsylvania, New Jersey, Georgia, and Connecticut by January 1788. Federalists also gained the support of influential newspapers based in eastern cities and tied to commercial interests.

Still, the contest in many states was heated. In Massachusetts, Antifederalists, including leaders of Shays's Rebellion (see Module 3.7), gained the majority among convention delegates. Federalists worked hard to overcome the objections of their opponents, even drafting a preliminary bill of rights. On February 6, Massachusetts delegates voted 187 to 168 in favor of ratification. Maryland and South Carolina followed in April and May. A month later, New Hampshire Federalists won a close vote, making it the ninth state to ratify the Constitution.

However, two of the most populous and powerful states—New York and Virginia—had not yet ratified. Passionate debates erupted in both ratifying conventions, and Federalists decided it was better to wait until these states acted before declaring victory. After promising that a bill of rights would be added quickly, Virginia Federalists finally won ratification by a few votes. A month later, New York approved the Constitution by a narrow margin. The divided nature of the votes, and the fact that two states (North Carolina and Rhode Island) had still not ratified, meant that the new government would have to prove itself quickly.

State	Date	For	Against
Delaware	December 1787	30	0
Pennsylvania	December 1787	46	23
New Jersey	December 1787	38	0
Georgia	January 1788	26	0
Connecticut	January 1788	128	40
Massachusetts	February 1788	187	168
Maryland	April 1788	63	11
South Carolina	May 1788	149	73
New Hampshire	June 1788	57	47
Virginia	June 1788	89	79
New York	July 1788	30	27
North Carolina	November 1788	194	77
Rhode Island	May 1790	34	32

Votes of State Ratifying Conventions This table shows the votes in the various state conventions for ratifying the new constitution.

Choose three of the state-convention vote tallies and explain what might account for each tally.

REVIEW

- Why were the Federalists able to win ratification of the Constitution?

Skills Workshop: Thinking Historically

Incorporating Claims and Evidence from Sources into Body Paragraphs

Claims and evidence are at the heart of historical inquiry and analysis. They have been the focus of our skill instruction in Period 3. You've made larger claims and supported those claims with main points and specific evidence when you constructed arguments and crafted thesis statements in Modules 3.2, 3.3, and 3.6. You practiced **Claim, Support, Explain** as you responded to a Short-Answer Question in Module 3.4. Then, you built on CSE when you wrote full-body paragraphs for an essay's sub-arguments in Modules 3.5 and 3.7. Now, we will look at how to use a source's claims and evidence in body paragraphs using CSE.

Here's an essay prompt and thesis statement on the ratification debates.

> Evaluate the extent of difference between the arguments of the Federalists and the Antifederalists in the debates over ratifying the Constitution.

> **Thesis:** Although the Federalists and Antifederalists clearly disagreed on whether to ratify the Constitution, they shared many of the same concerns about the ineffectiveness of the Articles of Confederation and the need for a government that did not abuse its power **[claim]**. Both sides appealed to Enlightenment ideals and the need for a representative, effective government even as they differed on the best ways to accomplish those goals **[line of reasoning]**.

While an essay response can be written without referring to specific documents or borrowing the claims and evidence those authors use, historians will sometimes incorporate those items to support their arguments. Additionally, on the AP® U.S. History Exam, you will be asked to use evidence from primary sources in responding to an SAQ and a document-based question (DBQ).

Here's the first of two opposing excerpts from the 1788 ratification debate in New York that we will use as we practice this skill.

Source: Melancton Smith, Antifederalist Delegate at the New York State Convention, June 1788

> "In the discussion of this question, he [Smith] was disposed to make every reasonable concession, and, indeed, to sacrifice every thing for a union, except the liberties of his country. . . .
>
> The defects of the Old Confederation needed as little proof as the necessity of an Union. But there was no proof in all this that the proposed Constitution was a good one. Defective as the Old Confederation is, . . . no one could deny but it was possible we might have a worse government. . . .
>
> He would agree with the honorable gentlemen [Hamilton] that perfection in any system of government was not to be looked for. . . . But he would observe, that this observation applied with equal force against changing any systems, especially against material and radical changes. Fickleness and inconstancy, he said, were characteristic of a free people; and in framing a Constitution for them, it was, perhaps the most difficult thing to correct this spirit, and guard against the evil effects of it. . . .
>
> He would now proceed to state his objections to the clause just read, (section 2, of article 1, clause 3). . . . In the first place, the rule of apportionment of the representatives is to be according to the whole number of the white

(continued)

inhabitants, with three fifths of all others, that is in plain English, each state is to send Representatives in proportion to the number of freemen, and three fifths of the slaves it contains. He could not see any rule by which slaves were to be included in the ratio of representation. The principle of a representation, being that every free agent should be concerned in governing himself, it was absurd to give that power to a man who could not exercise it. . . . The very operation of it was to give certain privileges to those people who were so wicked as to keep slaves. He knew it would be admitted that this rule of apportionment was founded on unjust principles, but that it was the result of accommodation; which, he supposed, we should be under the necessity of admitting, . . . though utterly repugnant to his feelings. . . .

[And] how was the will of the community to be expressed? . . . [W]e may approach a great way towards perfection by increasing the representation and limiting the powers of Congress. He considered that the great interests and liberties of the people could only be secured by the State Governments. He admitted, that if the new government was only confined to great national objects, it would be less exceptionable; but it extended to every thing dear to human nature. . . . [F]or that power which had both the purse and the sword had the government of the whole country, and might extend its powers to any and to every object."

Here's an example of how Melancton Smith's antifederalist speech can be used to build the first half of a body paragraph supporting our thesis sub-argument that each side shared the same goals of creating an effective, representative government.

Even as Federalists and Antifederalists fought over replacing the Articles of Confederation with the Constitution, both sides were united in their beliefs that that the new nation's government should fairly represent its populace and effectively exercise legitimate power **[sub-argument]**. In opposing ratification at the New York convention, Melancton Smith agreed with Hamilton that the Articles were flawed and that a perfect government was not possible, yet he warned that that change could be dangerous, and that the Constitution was worse than the Articles **[claim]**. Smith cited the three-fifths compromise as an example of how the Constitution unjustly provided greater political representation to enslavers while the enslaved were denied basic rights **[support]**. Therefore, even as Antifederalists opposed ratification, Smith argued that the answer was greater representation, not less **[explain]**.

ACTIVITY

Now it's your turn to finish the above paragraph using Alexander Hamilton's reply to Smith, which was an AP® Working with Evidence document earlier in this module (pages 212–213). Start with a transition word such as "Similarly" and then write **Claim, Support, Explain** sentences like the ones using Smith's document to build the remainder of the paragraph. Make sure to end the paragraph with a summary sentence restating the sub-argument. When you're done, the combined paragraph should have approximately eight robust sentences.

Shaping a New Republic

MODULE
3.10

FOCUS

While reading this module, think about the connections between the debates over the ratification of the Constitution and the political disagreements of the 1790s. What caused the sharp differences that ultimately led to the formation of the country's first political parties? How did the emergence of political parties change American politics?

Most political leaders hoped that the partisanship of the ratification battle would fade away with the Constitution approved. The electoral college's unanimous decision to name George Washington the first president and John Adams as vice president helped calm the political turmoil after the contentious ratification debates. The two took office in April 1789, and by 1792, Treasury Secretary Hamilton had succeeded in implementing an ambitious plan for U.S. economic development.

Yet as Washington began his second term in the spring of 1793, signs of strain appeared throughout the nation. The United States faced new challenges to foreign trade and diplomacy. Migration to the interior increased, which intensified conflicts between American Indians and white settlers and increased hostilities between the United States and Great Britain. Yellow fever swept through Philadelphia and other cities, causing fear and disrupting political and economic life. Finally, the excise tax on whiskey fueled armed protests among backcountry farmers. This cluster of crises split the Federalists into warring factions during Washington's second term, giving rise to the first form of the two-party system in American politics. By the time the election of 1796 took place, Federalist Party candidates faced opposition from members of a new party, the Democratic-Republicans.

Organizing the Federal Government

To bring order to his administration, newly elected President George Washington quickly established four departments—State, War, Treasury, and Justice—by appointing respected leaders to fill the posts. Washington named Thomas Jefferson secretary of state; Henry Knox, secretary of war; Alexander Hamilton, secretary of the treasury; and Edmund Randolph, attorney general at the head of the Department of Justice.

Congress, meanwhile, worked to establish a judicial system. The Constitution called for a Supreme Court but provided no specific guidelines. The Judiciary Act of 1789 established a Supreme Court composed of six justices along with thirteen district courts and three circuit courts to hear cases appealed from the states.

Congress also quickly produced a bill of rights. Representative James Madison gathered more than two hundred resolutions passed by state ratifying conventions and honed them into twelve amendments, which Congress approved and submitted to the states for ratification. In 1791, ten of the amendments were ratified, and these became the **Bill of Rights**. It guaranteed the rights of individuals and states in the face of

Bill of Rights
The first ten amendments to the Constitution explicitly guaranteeing all Americans basic rights. These amendments, promised by Federalists during the ratification debates, helped reassure Americans who feared that the federal government established under the Constitution would infringe on the rights of individuals and states.

Granger – Historical Picture Archive

Federal Hall This drawing shows Federal Hall, located on Wall Street in New York City. The building housed the Stamp Act Congress in 1765 and the confederation congress from 1785 to 1788. In 1789, it became the seat of Congress under the new constitution and the site of President Washington's first inauguration. The nation's capital was moved to Philadelphia in December 1790 and then to Washington, D.C., in 1800.

How does this image represent the egalitarian ideals of the American Revolution? How does it also differentiate Federal Hall as more significant than the other buildings in the image?

a powerful central government, including freedom of speech, the press, religion, and the right to petition.

REVIEW

- How did Washington's administration reflect Federalist goals and principles?
- In what ways did the Bill of Rights achieve the goals of the Antifederalists?

Hamilton Forges a Financial Plan

Hamilton played a leading role in supporting and establishing the new national government, particularly by seeking to stabilize and strengthen the national economy. The new government's leaders recognized that without a stable economy, even the best political structure could falter.

Therefore, Hamilton's appointment as secretary of the treasury was especially significant. In formulating his economic policy, Hamilton's main goal was to establish the nation's credit. He believed paying down the debt and establishing a national bank would strengthen the United States in the eyes of the world and tie wealthy Americans more firmly to the federal government. Hamilton advocated funding the complete national debt with interest (face value) and taking on the remaining state debts as part of the national debt. To pay for this policy, he planned to raise revenue through government bonds and new taxes.

Hamilton also called for the establishment of a central bank to carry out the financial operations of the United States. In three major reports to Congress—on public credit and a national bank in 1790 and on manufactures in 1791—he laid out a system of federally assisted economic development.

Hamilton's proposal to repay the full value of the millions of dollars in securities issued by the United States under the Articles of Confederation was very controversial. Thousands of soldiers, farmers, and shopkeepers had been paid with these securities during the war, but needing money in its aftermath, most sold them to speculators for a fraction of their face value believing that the new government might not ever be able to pay them back fully. These speculators would make enormous profits if the securities were paid off at face value.

One of the policy's most vocal critics, Patrick Henry, claimed that Hamilton's policy was intended "to erect, and concentrate, and perpetuate a large monied interest" that would prove "fatal to the existence of American liberty." Despite such passionate opponents, Hamilton gained the support of Washington and other key national leaders as they believed this plan would restore the young nation's credit.

The federal government's assumption of the remaining state war debts also faced fierce opposition, especially from southern states like Virginia that had already paid off their debt. Hamilton again won his case, though this time by agreeing to reimburse states that had repaid their debts. To secure the necessary votes, Hamilton and his supporters agreed to move the nation's capital from Philadelphia to a more central location along the Potomac River. Jefferson hoped the move, by shifting the capital away from a commercial center, would reduce the growing influences of merchants and monied interests in the new nation's politics.

Funding the national debt, assuming the remaining state debts, and redeeming state debts already paid would cost \$75.6 million (about \$1.5 billion today). But Hamilton believed maintaining some debt was useful. He thus proposed establishing a **Bank of the United States**, funded by \$10 million in stock to be sold to private stockholders and the national government. The bank would serve as a storage place for federal revenues, and it would grant loans and sell bills of credit to merchants and investors, thereby creating a permanent national debt. This, he argued, would bind investors to the United States, turning the national debt into a "national blessing."

Bank of the United States A national bank established in 1791. The bank was responsible for holding large portions of federal funds, distributing loans and currency, and funding the national debt.

Not everyone agreed. Jefferson and Madison argued vehemently against the Bank of the United States, noting that there was no constitutional provision for a federal bank. Hamilton fought back by citing a clause in the Constitution (later known as the "elastic clause") that Congress had the right to make "all Laws which shall be necessary and proper" for carrying out the provisions of the Constitution. Once again, he prevailed. Congress chartered the bank for a period of twenty years, and Washington signed the legislation into law. The chartering of the bank was divisive and continued to be a key split between political parties, eventually leading to the bank's dissolution in 1811.

The final piece of Hamilton's plan focused on raising revenue. Congress quickly agreed to pass tariffs on a range of imported goods, which generated some \$4 million to \$5 million annually. Some congressmen viewed these tariffs as a way to protect new industries in the United States, from furniture to shoes. Excise taxes placed on a variety of consumer goods, most notably whiskey, generated another \$1 million each year.

Hamilton's financial policies, supported by Washington, proved enormously successful in stabilizing the American economy, repaying outstanding debts, and tying men of wealth to the new government. The federal bank effectively collected and distributed the nation's resources. Commerce flourished, revenues rose, and confidence revived among foreign and domestic investors. And while the United States remained an agricultural nation, Hamilton's 1791 "Report on the Subject of Manufactures" foreshadowed the growing significance of industry, which gradually lessened U.S. dependence on European nations.

- How did Hamilton's policies stabilize the national economy?
- Why did these policies draw political opposition?

Foreign Trade and Foreign Wars

Jefferson and Madison led the opposition to Hamilton's policies during the 1780s and 1790s. They drew notable support from farmers who envisioned the country's future rooted in agriculture, not the commerce and industry supported by Hamilton and his allies.

Jefferson agreed with the Scottish economist Adam Smith that an international division of labor could best provide for the world's people. According to this view, Americans could supply Europe with food and raw materials in exchange for manufactured goods. Jefferson thought that his views were confirmed when wars in Europe, including a revolution in France, disrupted European agriculture in the 1790s and increased demands for the goods produced by American farms and plantations.

Although trade with Europe remained the most important source of goods and wealth for the United States, some merchants expanded into other parts of the globe. In the mid-1780s, the first American ships reached China, where they traded ginseng root and sea otter pelts for silk, tea, and fine porcelain. Still, events in Europe exerted far greater influences on the United States at the time than those in the Pacific world.

The **French Revolution** (1789–1799) was especially significant for U.S. politics. The ideals of freedom of speech, assembly, and religion declared in the American Declaration of Independence resonated with French men and women who opposed the tyrannical rule of King Louis XVI (reigned 1774–1792). The resulting uprising disrupted French agriculture, increasing demand for American wheat, while the efforts of French revolutionaries to institute an egalitarian republic gained support from many Americans. The followers of Jefferson and Madison formed Republican societies, and members adopted the French term *citizen* when addressing each other. At the same time, the importance of workers and farmers among France's revolutionary forces reinforced critiques of the "monied power" that drove the Federalist policies promoted by Hamilton and Washington.

In late 1792, as French revolutionary leaders began executing thousands of their opponents in the Reign of Terror, wealthy Federalists grew more anxious. The beheading of King Louis XVI horrified them, as did the revolution's condemnation of Christianity. When France declared war against Prussia, Austria, and then Great Britain, merchants worried about the impact on trade. In response, President Washington proclaimed U.S. neutrality in April 1793, prohibiting Americans from providing support or war materials to any warring nations—including France and Great Britain.

Alfredo Dagli Orti/Shutterstock

Americans Trade with China This painting by an unknown artist from around 1800 shows the *hongs* at Canton, trading posts with warehouses where ships from foreign countries arrived to unload and load goods. The foreign ships were limited to this small area outside the city walls of Canton (now called Guangzhou). There, each nation established a trading post identified by its national flag and overseen by a Chinese merchant.

How does this image of a Chinese port represent Hamilton's vision for American trade?

While the **Neutrality Proclamation** limited the shipment of certain items to Europe, Americans simultaneously increased trade with colonies in the British and French West Indies. Indeed, U.S. ships took over much of the lucrative sugar trade. Britain, however, ignored U.S. neutrality. The Royal Navy stopped U.S. ships carrying French sugar and seized more than 250 vessels. At the same time, farmers in the Chesapeake and Middle Atlantic regions filled the growing demand for wheat in Europe, causing their profits to soar.

These benefits did not bring about a political reconciliation. Although Jefferson condemned the French Reign of Terror, he protested the Neutrality Proclamation by resigning his cabinet post. Tensions escalated when the French envoy to the United States, Edmond Genêt, sought to enlist Americans in the European war. Republican clubs poured out to hear him speak and donated generously to the French cause. In response, the British took more aggressive action, supplying American Indians in the Ohio River valley with guns and encouraged them to raid U.S. settlements.

Concerned with the potential harm of Britain's meddling in the American West, President Washington sent John Jay to England to resolve concerns over trade with the British West Indies, compensation for seized American ships, the continued British occupation of borderlands forts, and southerners' ongoing demands for reimbursement of enslaved people evacuated by the British during the Revolution. Jay returned from England in 1794 with what became known as the **Jay Treaty**, but it was widely criticized in Congress and the popular press. While securing limited U.S. trading rights in the West Indies, the treaty failed to address British reimbursement for captured cargoes or enslaved people and granted Britain eighteen months to leave borderlands forts.

Neutrality Proclamation
A 1793 proclamation declaring U.S. neutrality in any conflicts between other nations, including France and Great Britain, despite French aid in the Revolutionary War effort. The proclamation also warned American citizens against favoring either party. Britain largely ignored U.S. neutrality and seized American merchant vessels heading for France.

Jay Treaty
Controversial 1796 treaty between the United States and Great Britain negotiated by John Jay that required British forces to withdraw from U.S. soil, required American repayment of debts to British firms, limited U.S. trade with the British West Indies, and permitted Britain to continue to stop neutral vessels.

It also demanded that U.S. planters repay British firms for debts accrued during the Revolutionary War. In June 1795, the Senate approved the treaty by a single vote, and it remained a source of political dispute.

REVIEW

- How did Washington's foreign policies cause political debates in the United States?

The Whiskey Rebellion

Despite these foreign crises, it was the effect of Hamilton's policies on the American interior that crystallized opposing factions into distinctly opposed parties. In the early 1790s, Republican societies from Maine to Georgia demanded the removal of British and Spanish troops from border areas, while backcountry farmers lashed out at enforcement of the excise tax on whiskey. Many inland farmers grew corn and rye and turned them into whiskey to make it easier to transport over poorly constructed dirt roads and more profitable to sell. The whiskey tax hurt these farmers, hundreds of whom petitioned the federal government for relief.

Western Pennsylvania farmers were particularly angry and rallied in 1792 and 1793 to protest the tax and those who enforced it. Adopting tactics from Stamp Act protests and Shays's Rebellion, farmers blocked roads, burned sheriffs in effigy, marched on courthouses, assaulted tax collectors, and disguised themselves with blackface paint and Native American clothing. When a yellow fever epidemic largely paralyzed government operations in Philadelphia from August to November 1793, the lack of response only fueled the rebels' anger. By 1794, an all-out rebellion had erupted.

Whiskey Rebellion
An uprising beginning in 1791 by western Pennsylvania farmers who led protests against the excise tax on whiskey. The federal government used military force to crush the rebellion, demonstrating the increased federal powers under the new Constitution in contrast to the confederation congress's inability to respond to Shays's Rebellion in 1786.

Washington, Hamilton, and their Federalist supporters worried that the rebellion could spread and might encourage greater efforts from American Indians to fight against intrusions on their lands. Since Spanish and British soldiers were eager to stir trouble along the borderlands, the **Whiskey Rebellion** might spark their intervention as well. Federalists also suspected that pro-French immigrants from Scotland and Ireland helped fuel the insurgency.

Unlike 1786, however, when the federal government had little power to intervene in Shays's Rebellion, the Constitution offered more powerful federal options. Washington federalized militias from four states, calling up nearly thirteen thousand soldiers to put down the uprising. The army that marched into western Pennsylvania in September 1794 vastly outnumbered and easily suppressed the "whiskey rebels." Having gained

Let us tar and feather the rascal.
AN EXCISEMAN. Carrying off two Kegs of Whiskey, is pursued by two farmers, intending to tar and feather him. he runs for 'Squire Vultures to divide with him; but is met on the way by his evil genius who claps an hook in his nose, leads him off to a Gallows, where he is immediately hanged. the

Fotosearch/Archive Photos/Getty Images

"An Exciseman," c. 1791 This early cartoon depicts an excise agent, carrying two casks of whiskey to "Squire Vultures," with whom he intends to divide his take. He is pursued by two farmers opposed to the whiskey tax, who yell, "let us tar and feather the rascal." The exciseman is eventually hung over a barrel of whiskey, which is set on fire and explodes.

Explain the context of this image.

victory, the federal government prosecuted only two of the leaders, who, although convicted, were later pardoned by Washington.

Washington proved that the Constitution provided the necessary powers to put down internal threats. Yet in doing so, the administration horrified many Americans who condemned the force used against the farmers as excessive. Jefferson and Madison gave voice to popular outrage from within the government. The Revolutionary generation had managed to compromise on many issues, from representation and slavery to the balance between federal and state authority. But now Hamilton's economic policies had led to a backcountry uprising, and Washington had used a federal army to destroy popular dissent.

REVIEW

- How did the Constitution allow the federal government to respond differently to the Whiskey Rebellion than it did to Shays's Rebellion under the Articles of Confederation?

A Two-Party System Forms

In September 1796, when President Washington decided not to run again, he offered a Farewell Address in which he warned the nation against the "spirit of party." "It agitates the community with ill-founded jealousies and false alarms," he claimed, and "kindles the animosity of one part against another." By then, deep disagreements over Hamilton's economic policies, Washington's assault on the whiskey rebels, and Jay's Treaty led to the coalescing of two distinct political parties, Federalists led by Adams and Hamilton and Democratic-Republicans led by Jefferson and Madison.

AP® EXAM TIP

Compare the significant domestic and international events that took place during George Washington's administration to those of John Adams's administration. How did these shape U.S. foreign policy? Likewise, how did they influence the creation of the first party system (Federalists and Democratic-Republicans)? Make sure you know the significance of these events, because the challenges facing the new nation are regularly asked on the AP® Exam.

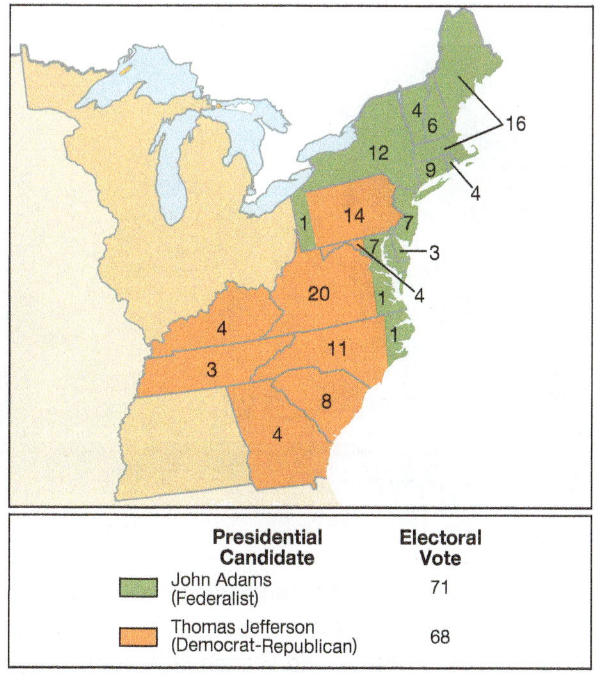

MAP 3.6 The Election of 1796 In the presidential election of 1796, the nation split regionally between supporters of Adams's Federalists and Jefferson's Democratic-Republicans.

What economic factors account for the regional divisions between Federalists and Democratic-Republicans?

The election of 1796 was the first to be contested by candidates identified with opposing parties, a scenario not envisioned during the Constitution's drafting. The document made no provision for political parties. Federalists supported John Adams for president and Thomas Pinckney for vice president. The **Democratic-Republicans** chose Thomas Jefferson and Aaron Burr of New York to represent their interests. The electoral college, hoping to bring the warring sides together, chose Federalist John Adams as president and Thomas Jefferson as vice president. The two disagreed fundamentally on a wide range of issues, and events soon heightened these divisions. The effects of an administration divided against itself were nearly disastrous, and opposing interests became more thoroughly entrenched.

Democratic-Republicans
A political party that emerged out of opposition to Federalist policies in the 1790s. The Democratic-Republicans chose Thomas Jefferson as their presidential candidate in 1796, 1800, and 1804.

Adams and Jefferson had disagreed on almost every major policy issue when they served together in Washington's administration. Not surprisingly, President Adams seldom took advice from his vice president. At the same time, Adams retained most of Washington's appointees, who often sought advice from Hamilton, undercutting Adams's authority. Worse still, the new president had poor political instincts and faced many challenges.

AP® WORKING with EVIDENCE

Source: Anonymous, The Providential Detection, 1797

Universal History Archive/Universal Images Group/Getty Images

About the source: In this image, the American eagle takes the Constitution away from Jefferson before he can burn it on the "Altar to Gallic [French] Despotism." Fueling the flames are the works of Thomas Paine and French philosophers, whom Federalists saw as threats to order. In Jefferson's right hand is a letter from Jefferson to the Philip Mazzei, a friend who was also a supporter of the French Revolution. The letter supposedly criticized George Washington.

Questions for Analysis

1. Identify the figure in the lower right corner of the image.
2. Describe the way the image portrays Providence.
3. Explain why the cartoonist might pair Providence and the figure in the lower right corner of the image.
4. Explain the significance of the eagle.
5. Explain the message the artist conveys about Thomas Jefferson.

At first, foreign disputes enhanced the authority of the Adams administration. The Federalists remained pro-British, and French seizures of U.S. ships threatened to provoke war. In 1798, Adams tried to negotiate compensation for the losses suffered by merchants. When an American delegation arrived in Paris, however, three French agents demanded a bribe to initiate talks.

Adams made public secret correspondence from the French agents, whose names were listed only as X, Y, and Z. Americans, including Democratic-Republicans, expressed outrage at this French insult to U.S. integrity, which became known as the **XYZ Affair**. Congress quickly approved an embargo act that prohibited trade with France and permitted privately owned American ships to attack French merchant ships. For the next two years, the United States fought the Quasi-War, an undeclared war, with France.

Despite praise for his handling of the XYZ Affair, Adams feared criticism from opponents at home and abroad. Consequently, the Federalist majority in Congress passed a series of security acts in 1798 referred to collectively as the **Alien and Sedition Acts**. The Alien Act allowed the president to order the imprisonment or deportation of noncitizens and was directed mainly at Irish and Scottish dissenters who criticized the government's pro-British policies. The Sedition Act outlawed "false, scandalous, or malicious" statements against the president or Congress. In the following months, nearly

Alien and Sedition Acts
Two security acts passed in 1798 by the Federalist-controlled Congress. The Alien Act allowed the president, then John Adams, to imprison or deport noncitizens. The Sedition Act outlawed certain public criticisms of the federal government.

Congressional Pugilists
He in a trice struck Lyon thrice
Upon his head, enrag'd sir,
Who seiz'd the tongs to ease his wrongs,
And Griswold thus engag'd, sir.
Congress Hall,
in Philad. Feb. 15.1798.

Congressional Pugilists
This cartoon depicts a fight on the floor of the House of Representatives on January 30, 1798. Connecticut Representative Roger Griswold, a Federalist, is waving a cane. Vermont Representative Matthew Lyon, a Democratic-Republican brandishing tongs, was a newspaper editor and critic of the Alien and Sedition Acts. Lyon was later convicted of sedition but won reelection while in jail. The caption reads: "He in a trice struck Lyon thrice / Upon his head, enrag'd sir, / Who seiz'd the tongs to ease his wrongs, / And Griswold thus engag'd, sir."

What factors not addressed in the U.S. Constitution caused this kind of conflict?

two dozen Democratic-Republican editors and legislators were arrested for sedition, and some were fined and imprisoned.

Naturalization Act
An act passed in 1798 by the Federalist-controlled Congress that raised the residency requirement for citizenship from five to fourteen years. It was designed to delay the naturalization of immigrants who largely voted Democratic-Republican. The act included only free white persons, meaning that it excluded indentured servants, American Indians, free Black persons, and enslaved persons from gaining citizenship.

The Federalist majority in Congress also approved the **Naturalization Act**. This act raised the residency requirement for citizenship from five to fourteen years in an attempt to delay immigrants, who tended to support Democratic-Republicans, from voting by postponing their citizenship.

WORKING with EVIDENCE

Source: Sedition Act, 1798

> "SECTION 2. *And be it further enacted,* That if any person shall write, print, utter, or publish, or shall cause or procure to be written, printed, uttered, or published, or shall knowingly and willingly assist or aid in writing, printing, uttering, or publishing any false, scandalous and malicious writing or writings against the government of the United States, with intent to defame the said government, or either house of the said Congress, or the said President, or to bring them or either of them into disrepute; or to excite against them, or either, or any of them, the hatred of the good people of the United States, or to stir up sedition within the United States, or to excite any unlawful combinations therein, for opposing or resisting any law of the United States, or any act of the President of the United States, and one in pursuance of any such law, or of the powers in him vested by the Constitution of the United States, or to resist, oppose or defeat any such law or act, or to aid, encourage or abet any hostile designs of any foreign nation against the United States, their people or government, then such person, being thereof convicted before any court of the United States having jurisdiction thereof, shall be punished by a fine not exceeding ten thousand dollars, and by imprisonment not exceeding two years."

Questions for Analysis

1. Identify the dangers expressed by the authors of this document.
2. Describe the political debates in the United States during the 1790s that shaped this legislation.
3. Explain what conflict this legislation aimed to resolve.

Democratic-Republicans were infuriated by the Alien and Sedition Acts. They considered the near tripling of residency requirements an attempt to limit the votes of farmers, artisans, and frontiersmen, who formed the core of their supporters. The Sedition Act threatened Democratic-Republican critics of Federalist policies by weakening the First Amendment's guarantee of free speech.

Virginia and Kentucky Resolutions
Resolutions passed by legislatures in Virginia and Kentucky in protest of the Alien and Sedition Acts. The resolutions claimed the acts passed by the Federalists were unconstitutional and politically motivated, thus "void and of no force" in their states.

In response, Jefferson and Madison encouraged states to pass resolutions that would counter this violation of the Bill of Rights. Using language drafted by the two Democratic-Republican leaders, legislators passed the **Virginia and Kentucky Resolutions**, which declared the Alien and Sedition Acts "void and of no force." They protested against the "alarming infractions of the Constitution," particularly the freedom of speech that "has been justly deemed, the only effectual guardian of every other right." Virginia even claimed that states had a right to nullify any powers exercised by the federal government that were not explicitly granted to it.

AP® WORKING with EVIDENCE

Source: Kentucky Resolution, 1799

> "*Resolved,* . . . That the several states who formed [the Constitution], being sovereign and independent, have the unquestionable right to judge of its infraction, and *that a nullification by those sovereignties, of all unauthorized acts done under color of that instrument, is the rightful remedy:* That this Commonwealth does, upon the most deliberate reconsideration, declare that the said Alien and Sedition Laws are, in their opinion, palpable violations of the said Constitution; and, however cheerfully it may be disposed to surrender its opinion to a majority of its sister states in matters of ordinary or doubtful policy, yet, in momentous regulations like the present, which so vitally wound the best rights of the citizen, it would consider a silent acquiescence as highly criminal: That although this Commonwealth, as a party to the Federal Compact, will bow to the laws of the Union, yet it does at the same time declare that it will not now, nor ever hereafter, cease to oppose in a constitutional manner, every attempt, from what quarter soever offered, to violate that compact."

Questions for Analysis

1. Identify the proper role of government, according to this document.
2. Explain how the Kentucky Resolution sought to prevent an overly powerful federal government.
3. Explain how the Kentucky Resolution sought to balance federal and state power.

Although the Alien and Sedition Acts curbed public expressions of dissent in the short run, they reinforced popular concerns about the power wielded by the Federalists. Combined with the ongoing war with France, continuing disputes over taxes, and relentless partisan attacks in the press, these acts set the stage for the presidential election of 1800.

REVIEW

- How did the Adams administration justify the Alien and Sedition Acts?
- How did the Democratic-Republicans challenge this justification?

The Election of 1800

By 1800, Adams had negotiated a peaceful settlement of the undeclared war between the United States and France, considering it one of the greatest achievements of his administration. However, other Federalists, including Hamilton, disagreed and wanted open warfare and an all-out victory. Therefore, the Federalists faced the election of 1800 deeply divided. Democratic-Republicans, meanwhile, united behind Jefferson and portrayed the Federalists as the new "British" tyrants.

For the first time, the presidential candidates were chosen by congressional leaders from their respective parties. The Federalists agreed on Adams and Charles Pinckney of South Carolina. The Democratic-Republicans again chose Jefferson and Burr as their candidates. The campaign was marked by bitter mudslinging, with Adams accused of being a monarchist and Jefferson alleged to be an atheist and a coward.

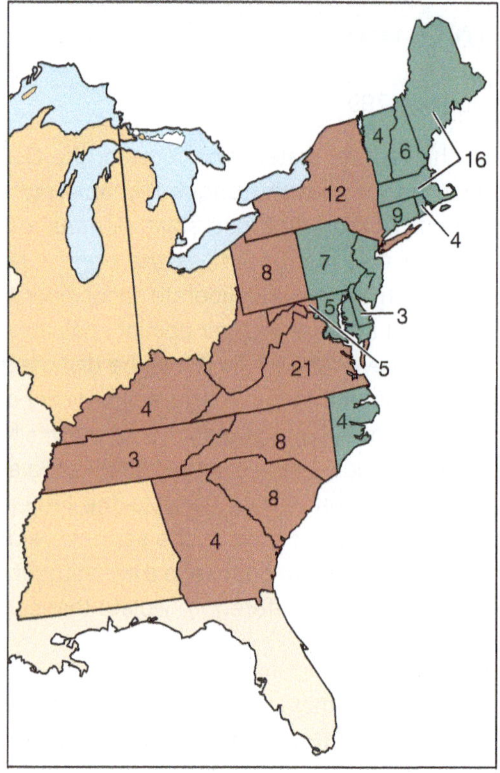

Party

Democratic-Republican		Federalist	
Presidential Candidate	**Electoral Vote**	**Presidential Candidate**	**Electoral Vote**
Thomas Jefferson	73	John Adams	65
Aaron Burr	73	Charles Pinckney	64
		John Jay	1

MAP 3.7 The Election of 1800 The presidential election of 1800 represented the first peaceful transfer of political power from one faction to another in American history. The results of the election tended to divide along regional lines, reflecting Federalist support from merchants, creditors, and yeoman farmers in New England and along the Middle Atlantic coast, and Democratic-Republican support from immigrants, plantation owners, settlers in the interior, new western states, and the South.

What political changes since 1796 are reflected in this map? What continuities do you see?

Because it was the first highly contested presidential election, the different methods states used to record voters' preferences gained more attention. Only five states determined members of the electoral college by popular vote. In the rest, state legislatures appointed electors.

Created at a time when political parties were considered harmful to good government, the electoral college was not prepared for the situation it faced in January 1801. Federalist and Democratic-Republican caucuses nominated one candidate for president and one for vice president on party tickets. As a result, Jefferson and Burr received exactly the same number of electoral college votes, requiring the House of Representatives to break the tie. There, Burr sought to gain the presidency with the help of Federalist representatives ardently opposed to Jefferson. But Alexander Hamilton stepped in and warned against Burr's leadership. This helped Jefferson to emerge victorious, but it also inflamed animosity between Burr and Hamilton that eventually led Burr to kill Hamilton in a duel in 1804.

President Jefferson labeled his election the Revolution of 1800, achieved not "by the sword" but by "the suffrage [voting rights] of the people." The election was hardly a popular revolution, given the restrictions on suffrage and the methods of selecting the electoral college. Still, between 1796 and 1800, partisan factions had been transformed into opposing parties, and the United States had managed a peaceful transition from one party to another.

REVIEW

- What main issues divided the Federalists and the Democratic-Republicans?
- What do the Alien and Sedition Acts and the election of 1800 reveal about the political partisanship in America during the late 1700s?

AP® Skills Workshop: Thinking Historically

Additional Practice in Incorporating Claims and Evidence from Sources into Body Paragraphs

In Modules 3.8 and 3.9, we examined how to use claims and evidence from primary sources in an essay's body paragraph to support part of an argument. Now, we will practice it again, this time using information from the Sedition Act and the Kentucky Resolution that you read earlier in this module (pages 226 and 227).

Below is an essay question and sample thesis statement. Write a strong body paragraph that supports the underlined summary of the sub-argument. Start with a clear, expanded statement of the sub-argument. Then use **Claim, Support, Explain** to incorporate the documents into the heart of the paragraph. Finish the paragraph with a summary sentence that restates the sub-argument.

Review the AP® Thinking Historically exercise in Modules 3.8 and 3.9 if you need more help before you begin.

> Evaluate the relative importance of causes of the emergence of a two-party political system in the 1790s.

Thesis: Even though the Founding Fathers made no provisions for political parties in the Constitution, during the 1790s, distinct political factions began to emerge **[claim]**. Federalists and Democratic-Republicans represented different visions for the new nation disagreeing over economic programs, foreign policy, and the legitimate exercise of federal power **[line of reasoning]**.

MODULE 3.11

Developing an American Identity

FOCUS

As you read this module, pay attention to the changes in American culture that helped form a more cohesive American identity while also noting the continuities that remained, especially for American Indians and Black Americans.

In the quarter century after declaring independence from Britain, Americans strove to create a uniquely American culture. Young people were expected to be steeped in virtue by a nation of Republican mothers, while a growing system of public education taught character values alongside subjects such as math and reading. As literacy rates increased, Americans consumed a growing array of publications, further creating common ties. In addition, the construction of a new capital city to house the federal government offered a powerful symbol of nationhood.

These developments also illuminated political and racial dilemmas in the young nation. The decision to move the U.S. capital south from Philadelphia was prompted by concerns among southern politicians about the power of northern economic and political elites. The very construction of the capital, in which enslaved and free workers labored side by side, highlighted racial and class differences. Forging a singular notion of American identity in a country where differences of race, class, and sex loomed so large would prove to be an enduring challenge.

Developing a Distinct American Culture

The widespread desire to define and promote a specifically American culture began as soon as the Revolution ended. In 1783, Noah Webster, a schoolmaster, declared that "America must be as independent in literature as she is in politics, as famous for arts as for arms."

Before the Revolution, public education for children was widely available in New England and the Middle Atlantic region. In the South, only those whose parents could afford private schooling—perhaps 25 percent of the boys and 10 percent of the girls—received any formal instruction. Few young people enrolled in high school in any part of the colonies.

Following the Revolution, state and national leaders proposed ambitious plans for public education. In 1789, Massachusetts became the first state to demand that each town provide free schools for local children, though attendance policies were decided by the towns.

The American colonies boasted nine colleges that provided higher education for young men, including Harvard, Yale, King's College (Columbia), Queen's College (Rutgers), and the College of William and Mary. After independence, many Americans worried that these institutions were tainted by British and aristocratic influences. They pushed for the founding of new colleges based on republican ideals.

Artists, too, devoted considerable attention to historical themes, although in the late eighteenth century, they tended more to Enlightenment perspectives. Charles Willson Peale painted Revolutionary generals while serving in the Continental Army

AP® EXAM TIP

With the formation of the new United States of America came the creation of a new national culture. To what extent did Americans develop elements of sectionalism (unique features or characteristics of geographic regions), as well as a national culture with art and literature?

The Library Company of Philadelphia

Samuel Jennings, Liberty Displaying the Arts and Sciences, 1792 Samuel Jennings painted this image for the newly established Library Company of Philadelphia, many of whose directors were Quakers who opposed slavery. The directors requested that he include Lady Liberty with her liberty cap on the end of a staff.

How does this image characterize the ideals of the American Revolution?

and became best known for his portraits of George Washington. Samuel Jennings offered a more radical perspective on the nation's character by incorporating women and Black Americans into works like *Liberty Displaying the Arts and Sciences* (1792) but highlighted the importance of learning and rationality. So, too, did William Bartram, the son of a botanist. He journeyed through the southeastern United States and Florida and published beautiful, and scientifically accurate, engravings of plants and animals in his *Travels* (1791). His less expensive engravings circulated more widely than more expensive paintings. Bartram's inexpensive and popular engravings highlighted national symbols like flags, eagles, and Lady Liberty.

In 1780, the Massachusetts legislature established the American Academy of Arts and Sciences to promote American literature and science. Six years later, Philadelphia's American Philosophical Society created the first national prize for scientific endeavor. Philadelphia was also home to the nation's first medical college, founded at the University of Pennsylvania. As in the arts, American scientists built on developments in continental Europe and Britain but prided themselves on contributing their own expertise.

REVIEW

- How did changes in education during the late 1700s reflect the ideas and principles of the American Revolution?

The Racial Limits of an American Culture

White Americans in the early republic often used native names and symbols as they set about creating a distinct national identity. Some working-class Americans followed in the tradition of the Boston Tea Party, dressing as American Indians to protest economic and political tyranny (see the "Whiskey Rebellion" in Module 3.10). More affluent white people also embraced American Indian names and symbols. Tammany societies, which promoted patriotism and republicanism in the late eighteenth century, were named after a mythical Delaware chief called Tammend. They attracted large numbers of lawyers, merchants, and skilled artisans.

Poets, too, focused on American Indians. In his 1787 poem "Indian Burying Ground," for instance, Philip Freneau offered a sentimental portrait that highlighted the lost heritage of a nearly extinct native culture in New England. The theme of lost cultures and heroic (if still "savage") American Indians became even more pronounced in American poetry in the following decades. Such sentimental portraits were less popular along the nation's borderlands, where American Indians continued to fight for their lands and rights. Cultural representations most often emphasized American Indians' supposed savagery and deceit.

Whether their depictions were realistic, sentimental, or derogatory, American Indians were almost always presented to the American public through the eyes of whites. Cultural leaders among American Indians gained little recognition from U.S. society, working mainly within their own nations either to maintain their languages and customs or to introduce their people to European American ideas and beliefs they found useful.

Most white Americans believed that American Indians were untamed and uncivilized, but not innately different from Europeans. As U.S. borders expanded, white Americans considered ways to "civilize" American Indians and incorporate them into the nation. The improved educational opportunities available to white Americans generally excluded American Indians, and government officials left the schooling of American Indians to religious groups. Several denominations sent missionaries, ministers, and teachers to the American Indians, and a few American Indian students themselves went on to American colleges to be trained as ministers or teachers for their own people.

Outside of missionaries, few whites bothered to learn American Indian languages. And even these attempts to bring American Indians into early republican society still failed to recognize the legitimacy of American Indian cultures. Moreover, however well-intentioned educators were, these sentiments never outweighed most white Americans' desire simply to colonize American Indian land.

In the emergent new national culture, sympathetic depictions of Africans and Black Americans by white artists and authors were as uncommon as those of American Indians. Most depictions of Black people were produced in the North and were intended for the rare patrons who opposed slavery. These portrayals were, however, far from flattering: They exaggerated Black people's perceived physical and intellectual differences from whites, to imply inferiority. Whether their depictions were intended to be "realistic," sentimental, or derogatory, Africans and Black Americans, like American Indians, were almost unfailingly rendered through the eyes of white people.

Because the new nation had failed to end slavery, its role in America's national culture made it more difficult for white people to imagine Black Americans as anything more than lowly laborers, despite free Black people who clearly demonstrated otherwise. Thus, most white people in America either believed or assumed Black people were inferior—and that no amount of education could change that.

AP® EXAM TIP

Throughout the National period (1789 to 1817), persistent social questions continued to dominate political and economic conditions in the young country. These questions included the policy that the United States should pursue toward American Indians, along with the continuation and expansion of slavery.

In the North, states did not generally incorporate Black children into their plans for public education. Moreover, most southern planters had little desire to teach enslaved people to read and write. Black Americans in cities with large free Black populations often took matters into their own hands and funded schools. Reverend Richard Allen opened a Sunday school for children in 1795 at his church in Philadelphia, and other free Black people formed literary and debating societies during this era. Still, only a small percentage of Black Americans received an education equivalent to that available to white people in the early republic.

AP® WORKING with EVIDENCE

Source: Thomas Jefferson, *Notes on the State of Virginia*, 1782

> "Many millions of them [enslaved Black people] have been brought to, and born in America. Most of them indeed have been confined to tillage, to their own homes, and their own society: yet many have been so situated, that they might have availed themselves of the conversation of their masters; many have been brought up to the handicraft arts, and from that circumstance have always been associated with the whites. Some have been liberally educated, and all have lived in countries where the arts and sciences are cultivated to a considerable degree, and have had before their eyes samples of the best works from abroad.
>
> The Indians, with no advantages of this kind, will often carve figures on their pipes not destitute of design and merit. They will crayon out an animal, a plant, or a country, so as to prove the existence of a germ in their minds which only wants cultivation. They astonish you with strokes of the most sublime oratory; such as prove their reason and sentiment strong, their imagination glowing and elevated. But never yet could I find that a black had uttered a thought above the level of plain narration; never saw even an elementary trait of painting or sculpture. In music they are more generally gifted than the whites with accurate ears for tune and time, and they have been found capable of imagining a small catch [piece of music]. Whether they will be equal to the composition of a more extensive run of melody, or of complicated harmony, is yet to be proved. Misery is often the parent of the most affecting touches in poetry. Among the blacks is misery enough, God knows, but no poetry. . . . The improvement of the blacks in body and mind, in the first instance of their mixture with the whites, has been observed by every one, and proves that their inferiority is not the effect merely of their condition of life."

Questions for Analysis

1. Identify how Jefferson justifies his arguments for the superiority of white Americans over American Indians and enslaved Black people.
2. Identify the areas in which Jefferson stated that American Indians and enslaved Black people were equal to or superior to white Americans.
3. Describe how Jefferson viewed American Indians and enslaved Black people differently.
4. Explain how the opinions Jefferson expressed toward American Indians and enslaved Black people justified American treatment of American Indians and Blacks in the late 1700s.

- Describe white Americans' attitudes toward American Indian and Black American cultures during the late eighteenth century.

A New Capital for a New Nation

The construction of Washington City, the new capital, provided an opportunity to highlight the nation's distinctive culture and identity. But here, again, slavery emerged as a crucial part of that identity. Jefferson's plan, accepted by Washington and Hamilton, situated the capital between Virginia and Maryland, two states where more than 300,000 enslaved workers lived.

To construct the capital, between 1792 and 1809, the government hired hundreds of enslaved men and a few women, paying enslavers $5 per month for each individual's labor. Enslaved men cleared trees and stumps, built roads, dug trenches, baked bricks, and cut and laid sandstone while enslaved women cooked, did laundry, and nursed the sick and injured. A small number performed skilled labor as carpenters or assistants to stonemasons and surveyors. Some four hundred enslaved laborers worked on the Capitol building alone, more than half the workforce.

Free Black people also participated in the development of Washington. Many worked alongside enslaved laborers, but a few held important positions. Benjamin Banneker, for example, a self-taught clock maker, astronomer, and surveyor, was hired as an assistant to the surveyor Major Andrew Ellicott. In 1791, Banneker had helped to plot the 100-square-mile site on which the capital was to be built.

WORKING with EVIDENCE

Source: Benjamin Banneker, Letter to Thomas Jefferson, 1791

> "I am fully sensible of the greatness of that freedom which I take with you on the present occasion; a liberty which seemed to me scarcely allowable, when I reflected on that distinguished, and dignifyed station in which you Stand. . . . Sir I freely and Chearfully acknowledge, that I am of the African race. . . . Sir, Suffer me to recall to your mind that time in which the Arms and tyranny of the British Crown were exerted with every powerful effort in order to reduce you to a State of Servitude, look back I intreat you on the variety of dangers to which you were exposed, reflect on that time in which every human aid appeared unavailable. . . . This Sir, was a time in which you clearly saw into the injustice of a State of Slavery, and in which you had just apprehensions of the horrors of its condition, it was now Sir, that your abhorrence thereof was so excited, that you publickly held forth this true and invaluable doctrine, which is worthy to be recorded and remember'd in all Succeeding ages. 'We hold these truths to be Self evident, that all men are created equal, and that they are endowed by their creator with certain unalienable rights, that among these are life, liberty, and the pursuit of happyness.' . . . [A]s Job proposed to his friends 'Put your Souls in their Souls stead,' thus shall your hearts be enlarged with kindness and benevolence toward them, and thus shall you need neither the direction of myself or others in what manner to proceed herein. . . .
>
> And now, Sir, altho my Sympathy and affection for my brethren hath caused my enlargement thus far, I ardently hope that your candour and generosity

will plead with you in my behalf, when I make known to you, that it was not originally my design; but that having taken up my pen in order to direct to you as a present, a copy of an Almanack which I have calculated for the Succeeding year. . . . And altho I had almost declined to make my calculation for the ensuing year, in consequence of that time which I had allotted therefor being taking up at the Federal Territory by the request of Mr. Andrew Ellicott, yet finding myself under Several engagements to printers of this state to whom I had communicated my design, on my return to my place of residence, I industriously apply'd myself thereto, which I hope I have accomplished with correctness and accuracy, a copy of which I have taken the liberty to direct to you."

Questions for Analysis

1. Identify the comparison Banneker makes between the colonies under British rule and enslaved African Americans.
2. Explain the purpose of Banneker's comparison.
3. Explain how this letter reflects the historical situation in which it was written.

Black Americans often worked alongside Irish immigrants, whose wages were kept in check by the availability of enslaved labor. Most workers, regardless of race, faced poor housing, sparse meals, malarial fevers, and limited medical care. Despite these obstacles, in less than a decade, a system of roads was laid out and cleared, the Executive Mansion was built, and the north wing of the Capitol was completed.

More prosperous immigrants and foreign professionals were also involved in creating the U.S. capital. Irish-born James Hoban designed the Executive Mansion. A French engineer developed the plan for the city's streets. A West Indian physician turned architect drew the blueprints for the Capitol building, the construction of which was directed by Englishman Benjamin Latrobe. Perhaps what was most "American" about the new capital was the diverse nationalities and races of those who designed and built it.

The founders of Washington envisioned the city as a beacon to the world, proclaiming the advantages of the nation's republican principles. But its location on a

The United States Capitol, 1800 This watercolor by William Russell Birch presents a view of the Capitol in Washington, D.C., in 1800. Birch had emigrated from England in 1794 and lived in Philadelphia. As this painting suggests, neither the Capitol nor the city was as yet a vibrant center of republican achievements.

Compare this image to Federal Hall (Module 3.10, p. 216). What similarities and differences are apparent in each? What accounts for these similarities and differences?

slow-moving river and its clay soil left the area hot, humid, and dusty in the summer and muddy and damp in the winter and spring.

When the federal government officially moved to Washington in June 1800, they considered themselves on the frontiers of civilization. The tree stumps that remained on the mile-long road from the Capitol to the Executive Mansion made it nearly impossible to navigate in a carriage. On rainy days, when roads proved impassable, officials walked or rode horses to work. Many early residents painted Washington in harsh tones. New Hampshire congressional representative Ebenezer Matroon wrote a friend, "If I wished to punish a culprit, I would send him to do penance in this place . . . this swamp—this lonesome dreary swamp, secluded from every delightful or pleasing thing."

Despite its critics, Washington was the center of federal power and thus played an important role in the social and political worlds of American elites. From January through March, the height of the social season, the wives of congressmen, judges, and other officials created a lively schedule of teas, parties, and balls in the capital city. When Thomas Jefferson became president in 1801, he regularly opened the White House to visitors. Yet for all his republican principles, when Jefferson moved into the Executive Mansion, he brought several enslaved people with him.

In decades to come, Washington City would become Washington, D.C., a city with broad boulevards decorated with beautiful monuments to the American political experiment. And the Executive Mansion would become the White House, a proud symbol of republican government. Yet the nation's capital was always characterized by wide disparities in wealth, status, and power, which were especially visible when enslaved people labored in the Executive Mansion's kitchen, laundry, and yard.

- What roles did different groups of people have in constructing the new nation's capital city?

AP® Skills Workshop: Thinking Historically

Additional Practice in Responding to a Short-Answer Question with a Primary Source

On the AP® Exam, you will be asked to respond to three Short-Answer Questions (SAQs) including one with a primary source, usually an image. In Module 1.7, we learned how to apply the three-step SAQ process of (1) carefully analyzing the image, source information, and question; (2) brainstorming and organizing information we could use in our answer; and (3) writing three-sentence responses to each part of the SAQ using **Claim, Support, Explain**.

Review Module 1.7, if you need more help, and then complete the activity.

Using the Samuel Jennings painting on page 231 of this module, answer **A**, **B**, and **C**.

(A) Briefly describe ONE historical perspective expressed in the image.

(B) Briefly explain how ONE specific event or development contributed to the process depicted in the image.

(C) Briefly explain ONE specific historical effect that resulted from the process depicted in the image.

Movement in the Early Republic

MODULE 3.12

FOCUS

As you read this module, consider the ways life on the western borderlands and in cities both changed and remained the same. As American settlers moved west, think about how interactions with American Indians affected both groups. Also, consider the changes that resulted from the growth of existing cities and the rise of new western cities.

During the American Revolution and into the republic's early years, the American government struggled to settle western land claims and had an uphill climb to build alliances with American Indian nations. The two issues were intertwined, and both were difficult to resolve.

Most American Indian nations had long-standing complaints against colonists who intruded on their lands. Regardless of American Indian rights, new states claimed western lands, and after a 1777 proposal under the Articles of Confederation to use lands in the trans-Appalachian west for the benefit of the new nation passed in the Continental Congress, most American Indian nations saw little hope that their territories would be respected. With the patriot victory in the Revolutionary War and subsequent granting of lands between the Appalachians and the Mississippi to the United States by the Treaty of Paris in 1783, conflicts between settlers moving west and American Indians intensified.

Conflicts over Western Lands

Violence between settlers and American Indians west of the Appalachian Mountains, from the Ohio River valley to Georgia, continued for decades. Despite the continued presence of British and Spanish troops in the Ohio River valley, the United States hoped to convince American Indian nations that it controlled the territory.

During the Revolution, Americans had moved west, occupying American Indian lands. After the war, vast numbers of squatters, mainly white men and women, continued to live on land to which they had no legal claim. In the fall of 1784, George Washington traveled west to survey nearly thirty thousand acres of territory he had been granted as a reward for leading the Continental Army. He found much of it occupied by squatters who refused to acknowledge his ownership. Such flaunting of property rights deepened Washington's concerns about the weaknesses of the confederation government.

The confederation congress was less concerned about individual property rights, however, and more occupied with the ongoing refusal of some states to give up the American Indian lands they claimed to federal control. Between 1783 and 1785, the congress finally persuaded the two last states with the largest claims, Virginia and Massachusetts, to give up the remainder of their territories north of the Ohio River.

MAP 3.8 Cessions of Western Land, 1782–1802 Beginning under the Articles of Confederation, political leaders sought to resolve competing state claims to western territory based on colonial charters. The confederation congress and, after ratification of the Constitution, the U.S. Congress gradually persuaded states to cede their claims and create a "national domain," part of which was then organized as the Northwest Territory.

Using this map, determine how regional cultures along the Atlantic seaboard could be reflected in these newly ceded territories.

American Indians did not just stand by and watch as white Americans argued over who had the rights to these lands. As eastern American Indians were increasingly pushed into the Ohio River valley, they crowded onto lands already claimed by other nations. Initially, these migrations increased conflict among nations, but eventually some leaders used this forced intimacy to launch united tribal movements against further American expansion onto their land.

In 1784, some two hundred American Indian leaders from the Haudenosaunee (Iroquois), Shawnee, Creek, Cherokee, and other nations gathered in St. Louis, where they complained to the Spanish governor that the Americans were "extending themselves like a plague of locusts." Nevertheless, the United States continued to push its boundaries.

The New York Historical Society/Contributor/Archive Photos/Getty Images

Cornplanter, Seneca Chief Cornplanter, son of a white father and Seneca mother, fought alongside the British during the Revolution. Afterward, however, he argued that American Indians must adapt to American control. He helped negotiate three treaties that ceded large tracts of American Indian land to the U.S. government, arousing opposition from more militant leaders.

What elements of this portrait portray the influence of European culture on Cornplanter?

In October 1784, U.S. commissioners met with Haudenosaunee delegates at Fort Stanwix, New York, and demanded they surrender land in western New York and the Ohio River valley. When the Seneca chief Cornplanter and other leaders refused, the commissioners insisted that "you are a subdued people" and must submit. An exchange of gifts and captives taken during the Revolution finally ensured the deal.

American Indian leaders not at the meeting disavowed the Treaty of Fort Stanwix. But the confederation government insisted it was legal, and New York State began surveying and selling the land. With a similar mix of negotiation and coercion, U.S. commissioners signed treaties at Fort McIntosh, Pennsylvania (1785), and Fort Finney, Ohio (1786), claiming lands held by the Wyandot, Delaware, Shawnee, and others.

AP® WORKING with EVIDENCE

Source: United Indian Nations Council, Message to Congress, 1786

To the Congress of the United States of America:

"Brethren of the United States of America: It is now more than three years since peace was made between the King of Great Britain and you, but we, the Indians, were disappointed, finding ourselves not included in that peace, according to our expectations: for we thought that its conclusion would have promoted a friendship between the United States and Indians, and that we might enjoy that happiness that formerly subsisted between us and our elder brethren. . . . In the course of our councils, we imagined we hit upon an expedient that would promote a lasting peace between us.

Brothers: We are still of the same opinion as to the means which may tend to reconcile us to each other; and we are sorry to find, although we had the best thoughts in our minds, during the beforementioned period, mischief has, nevertheless, happened between you and us. We are still anxious of putting our plan of accommodation into execution, and we shall briefly inform you of the means that seem most probable to us of effecting a firm and lasting peace and reconciliation: the first step towards which should, in our opinion, be, that all treaties carried on with the United States, on our parts, should be with the general voice of the whole confederacy, and carried on in the most open manner, without any restraint on either side; and especially as landed matters are often the subject of our councils with you, a matter of the greatest importance and of general concern to us, in this case we hold it indispensably necessary that any cession of our lands should be made in the most public manner, and by the united voice of the confederacy; holding all partial treaties as void and of no effect."

Questions for Analysis

1. Identify the main complaint and proposed remedy in excerpt.
2. Describe the kinds of "mischief" the Council is referring to.
3. Explain how the tone of the message reflects the author's purpose and audience.

Ratification of the Constitution of the United States changed little in relations between American Indians and the new nation. In 1790, Congress passed the **Indian Trade and Intercourse Act** to regulate relations on the borderlands and to ensure fair and equitable dealings. White Americans, however, widely ignored the act. Migration to the borderlands increased, which, yet again, intensified conflicts between American Indians and white settlers and increased hostilities between the United States and Great Britain. The British continued supplying American Indians in the Ohio River valley with guns and encouraging them to raid U.S. settlements.

The government's failure to halt the flood of settlers into the Ohio and Mississippi River valleys proved costly. In 1790, Little Turtle, a war chief of the Miami nation, gathered a large force of Shawnee, Delaware, Ottawa, Ojibwe, Sauk, Fox, and other American Indians. This alliance of tribes successfully attacked federal troops in the Ohio River valley that fall. A year later, the allied American Indian warriors defeated a large U.S. force, killing or wounding approximately nine hundred soldiers and support personnel. The stunning defeat shocked Americans and led to the creation of a more disciplined, standing army comprised of professional soldiers rather than state militias. In the meantime, Spanish authorities negotiated with Creeks and Cherokees, encouraging and arming their attacks on U.S. settlements on the southern borderlands.

At the same time, the events of the Whiskey Rebellion added to the chaos and fear for the viability of the new nation. Washington decided to deal with American Indians in the Northwest Territory first, sending 2,000 men in the new army under the command of General Anthony Wayne into the Ohio borderland. In August 1794, Wayne's forces attacked 1,500 to 2,000 American Indians gathered at a British fort. In the **Battle of Fallen Timbers**, an alliance of American Indian nations, led by Little Turtle, suffered a devastating defeat. As a result, a year later, the warring American Indians in the Northwest Territory signed the **Treaty of Greenville**, granting the United States vast tracts of land in the future states of Ohio, Indiana, Illinois, and Michigan.

Treaty of Greenville
A 1795 treaty signed following the Battle of Fallen Timbers. The treaty ended the Northwest Indian War and ceded vast tracts of lands claimed by American Indians in the Northwest Territory to the United States.

Amid this turmoil, in November 1794, John Jay signed his controversial treaty with Great Britain. With Britain agreeing to withdraw its forces from the U.S. borderlands by 1796, the treaty may have helped persuade American Indian nations to accept U.S. peace terms at Greenville.

Before the Jay Treaty took effect, Spain agreed to negotiate an end to hostilities on the southern borderlands of the United States. Envoy Thomas Pinckney negotiated the more popular **Pinckney Treaty**, which was supported by many Americans—particularly from the west and south—who had opposed the Jay Treaty. Ratified in 1796, it recognized the thirty-first parallel as the boundary between U.S. and Spanish territory in the South and opened the Mississippi River and the port of New Orleans to U.S. shipping. As Britain and Spain both stopped contesting U.S. control of its western lands, American Indians found it increasingly difficult to hold back the continued influx of settlers.

Pinckney Treaty
A treaty between Spain and the United States ratified in 1796 that defined the boundary between U.S. and Spanish territory in the South and opened the Mississippi River and New Orleans to U.S. shipping. It allowed the free movement of goods from the far interior to the Atlantic via the Mississippi.

REVIEW

- What led to armed conflicts between the U.S. government and American Indians in the 1780s and 1790s?
- What resulted from those conflicts?

U.S. Population Growth and Migration

Migration to the West and the growth of cities were fueled by an increased population, combined with the exhaustion of farmland along the eastern seaboard. These developments heightened conflicts with American Indians and over slavery, but they also encouraged innovations in transportation and communication and improvements in agriculture and manufacturing.

As white Americans encroached more deeply on lands long settled by native peoples, American Indian tribes were forced ever westward. As early as 1800, groups like the Shoshone nation, who originally inhabited the Great Plains, had been forced into the Rocky Mountains by eastern American Indians who had been forced onto the plains from their original homes, the Mississippi and Ohio River valleys (Map 3.9). These trends accelerated in the following decades as removal became federal policy, increasing pressure on the Shoshone and other nations as white migration escalated.

Although the vast majority of Americans continued to live in rural areas, a growing number moved to cities as farming technology improved. At the same time, eastern farmland lost its fertility, reducing the need for rural laborers. Consequently, young people sought job opportunities in manufacturing, skilled trades, and service work.

Cities were defined at the time as places with 8,000 or more inhabitants, but New York City and Philadelphia both counted more than 60,000 residents by 1800. In New York City, the number of Black Americans increased to more than 6,000. At the same time, immigrants, most of them Irish, made up a rapidly growing part of the population. The percentage of foreign-born New York City residents rose to 25 percent by 1825.

Cities began to emerge along the nation's borderlands as well. After the Louisiana Purchase in 1803, New Orleans became a key commercial center, while western migration fueled cities like Cincinnati. Even smaller borderland towns, like Alton, Illinois, served important functions for migrants traveling west.

Trading posts appeared across the Mississippi valley, which eased the migration of thousands headed farther west. They served as sites of exchange between American Indians and white Americans and created the foundations for later cities.

Most Americans who headed west hoped to benefit from the increasingly liberal terms for land offered by the federal government, as the minimum acreage for sale, percentage of sale price due at closing, and the inflation-adjusted price per acre all

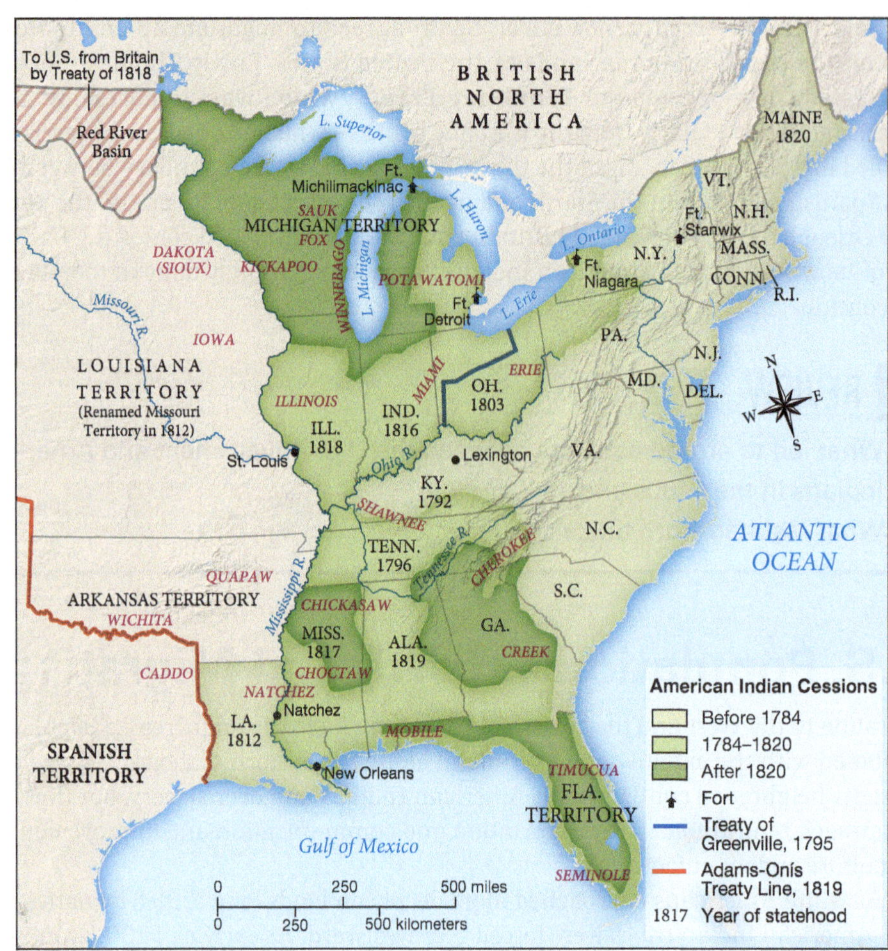

MAP 3.9 American Indian Land Cessions, 1790–1820 With the ratification of the Constitution, the federal government gained greater control over American Indian relations, including land cessions. At the same time, large numbers of white settlers poured into regions west of the Appalachian Mountains. The U.S. government gained most American Indian land by purchase or treaty, but these agreements were often the consequence of military victories by the U.S. army, as well as steady encroachment on native lands by white settlement.

What does the map's portrayal of cessions of lands by Native American peoples reveal about the pace and direction of white settlement during this era?

declined over the first few decades after the United States won its independence. Small farmers sought sufficient acreage to feed their families and grow some crops for sale. They were eager to settle in western sections of the original thirteen states and in the Ohio River valley. In the South, these small farmers had to compete with enslaving planters who headed west in the early nineteenth century. Migrants to the Mississippi valley also had to contend with a sizable population of Spanish and French residents, as well as Chickasaw and Creek Indians in the South and Shawnee, Ojibwe, Sauk, and Fox communities farther north.

The development of roads and turnpikes hastened the movement of people and the transportation of goods. Borderlands farmers wanted to get their produce to eastern markets quickly and cheaply. In 1795, construction of the privately funded sixty-two-mile Lancaster Turnpike connecting Philadelphia and Lancaster, Pennsylvania, was completed. Considered the nation's first engineered road, its use greatly reduced the price to carry wheat overland—which had previously cost the same as to ship it by sea from Philadelphia to London. With the admission of Kentucky (1792), Tennessee (1796), and Ohio (1803) to the Union, demands for congressional support for building transportation routes grew louder.

Between 1776 and early 1800, the United States had won its independence from Britain, replaced its original frame of government with the Constitution, and managed a peaceful, democratic transfer of presidential power. Yet, in the coming years, the new republic would be challenged at home and abroad. Great Britain, France, and the Barbary States of North Africa regularly challenged U.S. sovereignty, while internal debates over slavery and conflicts over American Indian lands multiplied. Moreover, as federal power expanded over time, some Americans continued to worry about protecting the rights of states and of individuals. The American identities forged in the early republic would be continually tested as new disagreements emerged and older conflicts intensified in the following decades.

REVIEW

- Why did Americans move to cities and to the West in the late 1700s?

Skills Workshop: Thinking Historically

Combining Reasoning Processes in an Evaluative Thesis Statement

As we saw in the AP® Thinking Historically feature in Module 1.5, historians make connections by examining the past through the use of reasoning processes including **causation** (causes and effects), **comparison** (similarities and differences), and **continuity and change over time** (elements that remain the same and those that do not).

In Modules 3.2 and 3.6, we revisited the historical reasoning processes as we created thesis statements in response to essay questions. We practiced framing our arguments as a set of causes and effects, similarities and differences, or continuities and changes.

It turns out that while these ways of thinking about the past appear separate, they can and sometimes do overlap. In examining causes or effects, we could investigate how those causes or effects led to changes or contributed continuities. Also, we could compare those causes, effects, continuities, and changes. Further, we could even explore the causes or effects of specific similarities or differences and compare how those similarities or differences represent important historical changes or continuities. If you are feeling a little confused by all this, don't worry. The key point is that these reasoning processes can be combined in a variety of ways. As long as you use relevant historical evidence from the time period to construct a sound argument, you can incorporate whichever elements naturally fit your thesis.

Let's take a look at a typical essay prompt that could be answered using a combination of historical reasoning processes.

> Evaluate the extent to which internal migration fostered change in the United States from 1776 to 1800.

The first step always is to make sure you understand the question by identifying the topic, time period, and the reasoning process you want to focus on. The subject is clearly internal migration, the movement of peoples within the United States. The years covered are from 1776 (when the United States declared its independence) to 1800 (the election of Jefferson to the presidency).

However, the historical reasoning process is a little less clear. The prompt uses the word "change," making continuity and change the process most directly aligned to the question. A closer look reveals that the prompt is asking us to analyze the extent to which internal migration *fostered change*. Since "caused" could be easily substituted for "fostered," a response could be centered around the ways internal migration caused change. While comparison doesn't appear to apply to the prompt as naturally as the other two reasoning processes, we could still compare internal migration with other causes that changed American society or compare the changes that occurred within the United States.

(continued)

Here's a potential thesis statement that combines both continuity and change as well as causation in its answer. Remember, good thesis statements should both make a claim and provide a line of reasoning.

> The movement of peoples within the United States significantly changed the country because it accelerated the growth of American cities as exhausted farmlands encouraged the relocation of young adults, while conflicts over land and taxation demonstrated the need for a stronger central government **[claim]**. Despite these changes, violence with American Indians on the borderlands remained a constant as settlers continued moving west lured by transportation improvements that made it easier to ship farmed goods to market **[line of reasoning]**.

In this example, the first sentence makes a claim and describes two significant *changes*—the growth of cities and the strengthening of the federal government—while the second sentence describes a *continuity*—continued conflict with American Indians over land. These two changes and one continuity are the sub-arguments in the thesis and could form the basis for the three main body paragraphs in an essay response.

Notice, however, that each continuity or change is explained as the result of a particular cause. Exhausted farmlands *caused* the migration that led to urban growth. A stronger government was *caused* in part by the need to address borderland conflicts, and settlers still moving west *caused* the continuity of conflicts with American Indians on the borderlands. This is one way to combine continuity and change with causation in a thesis.

ACTIVITY

Now, it's your turn to weave these reasoning processes together as you practice structuring an argument. Create your own multi-sentence thesis statement for the same prompt. Make sure to include at least two of the three historical reasoning processes: causation, comparison, and continuity and change over time. While you may use some of the same ideas from the sample thesis, try to include some different main points and write the thesis statement in your own words.

Continuity and Change in Period 3

MODULE 3.13

Skills Workshop: Writing Historically

Combining Reasoning Processes in an Essay

Continuity and change over time (CCOT) is a historical reasoning process that examines whether significant developments change in a meaningful way or remain fundamentally the same during a time period. One way to consider continuity and change is to describe the state of an item at the beginning of a time period and then at the end of a time period.

For example, in a physical education class, you might be asked to record various measures of your physical fitness such as your percentage of body fat, speed running a mile, and how many push-ups you can do in a minute during the first week of class and then again during the last week of the class. Comparing those measurements over the span of a school year will give you an indication of how much change or continuity there was in your physical fitness. Likewise, if we compared the percentage of white men who were able to vote in local elections in 1754 versus 1800, we would have an idea of the extent of continuity or change in white male local voting rights during the era.

Here's a broad continuity and change essay prompt that covers the period we have been studying.

> Evaluate the extent to which the American Revolution fostered change in American society from 1754 to 1800.

You may notice that this question is very similar to the essay question from the AP® Thinking Historically exercise in Module 3.12 in that both that ask us "evaluate the extent to which" a historical process or development "fostered change." As we noted in that feature, the use of the word "change" makes a focus on the reasoning process of continuity and change a natural fit, but causation and even comparison also work.

In the partially completed graphic organizer that follows, we will use causation to support our first main point of change over time. We will also distinguish our continuity evidence as "before" versus "after" to demonstrate the nature and extent of the change.

General Categories: Continuity or Change	Main Points: Continuities or Changes	Supporting Details: Including Causation or Comparison
Political (change)	The Revolution replaced a monarchy and unrepresentative Parliament with state and federal governments that increased white-male, democratic participation.	- Cause: the spread of Enlightenment ideals such as Locke's natural rights - Before the Revolution: virtual representation in Parliament, British monarchy, and taxation without representation - After the Revolution: New Jersey allowed all free men and women to vote, the Articles of Confederation created a weak federal system with most powers retained by the states, and a Bill of Rights was added to the U.S. Constitution

(continued)

General Categories: Continuity or Change	Main Points: Continuities or Changes	Supporting Details: Including Causation or Comparison
(change)		- - -
(continuity)		- - -

Here's a written body paragraph using **Claim**, **Support**, and **Explain** for the first sub-argument from the graphic organizer.

The American Revolution created significant political change in the United States as a ruling foreign constitutional monarchy without direct representation was replaced by state and federal constitutions granting many white men a direct voice in the new nation's government **[sub-argument]**. Before the American Revolution, the colonies were ruled over by the British crown, a hereditary institution with few limits on its power, and a Parliament that no American colonists could vote for or hold office in **[claim]**. Colonial protests against tax measures such as the Stamp Act and Townshend Act were answered by claims of virtual representation in Parliament **[support]**. The rebellion against foreign rule was fueled by the growing acceptance of Enlightenment ideals including John Locke's theory of natural rights, which colonists used as the basis for their Declaration of Independence **[explain]**. During and after the Revolutionary War, states and eventually the federal government adopted constitutions that allowed white males to directly participate in the political process **[claim]**. For instance, New Jersey allowed all free men and women to vote, while the Articles of Confederation and later the Constitution limited the powers of the federal government **[support]**. To further protect against federal overreach, a Bill of Rights was added to the Constitution securing basic rights that the British had violated such as freedom of speech, assembly, and the right to a jury trial **[explain]**. In sum, one of the most important changes fostered by the American Revolution was the creation of a political democracy and the protection of basic rights **[summary of sub-argument]**.

ACTIVITY

Now, it's your turn. Complete the graphic organizer, making sure to include an element of causation or comparison for your continuity and for your change. Then, write a multi-sentence thesis statement that also includes the political sub-argument already provided in the graphic organizer. Finally, write the two remaining body paragraphs for this essay using **Claim**, **Support**, and **Explain**. Refer to the skill instruction in AP® Thinking Historically and AP® Writing Historically exercises if you need to review how to complete the graphic organizer (Modules 3.2, 3.6), write the thesis statement (Modules 3.2, 3.6), or compose the body paragraphs (Module 3.5).

Period 3 Review 1754–1800

KEY CONCEPTS AND EVENTS

Albany Plan of Union, *150*
Alien and Sedition Acts, *225*
Antifederalist, *212*
Articles of Confederation, *202*
Bank of the United States, *219*
Battle of Bunker Hill, *172*
Battle of Fallen Timbers, *240*
Battle of Saratoga, *183*
Battle of Yorktown, *188*
Bill of Rights, *217*
Boston Massacre, *166*
Boston Tea Party, *167*
checks and balances, *211*
Coercive Acts, *168*
committee of correspondence, *161*
Continental Army, *172*
Continental Congress, *170*
Constitutional Convention, *209*
Currency Act, *161*
Daughters of Liberty, *162*
Declaration of Independence, *176*
Declaratory Act, *164*
Democratic-Republican, *224*
Dunmore's Proclamation, *173*
electoral college, *211*
The *Federalist Papers*, *213*
Federalist, *212*
French and Indian War (Seven Years' War), *149*
French Revolution, *220*
guerrilla tactics, *151*
Indian Trade and Intercourse Act, *240*
Intolerable Acts, *168*
Jay Treaty, *221*
loyalist, *178*
minuteman, *172*
naturalization, *210*
Naturalization Act, *226*
Neutrality Proclamation, *221*
New Jersey Plan, *210*
Northwest Ordinances of 1785 and 1787, *205*
patriot, *170*
Peace of Paris, *155*
Pinckney Treaty, *241*
Proclamation Line of 1763, *156*
Quartering Act, *161*
Québec Act, *168*
republican motherhood, *194*
salutary (benign) neglect, *160*
Second Continental Congress, *172*
separation of powers, *211*
Shays's Rebellion, *207*
Sons of Liberty, *162*
speculator, *156*
Stamp Act, *162*
Stamp Act Congress, *164*
Statute of Religious Freedom, *202*
Sugar Act, *161*
Tea Act, *167*
three-fifths compromise, *210*
Townshend Acts, *165*
Treaty of Greenville, *240*
Treaty (Peace) of Paris, *189*
Valley Forge, *183*
Virginia and Kentucky Resolutions, *226*
Virginia Plan, *209*
Virginia Resolves, *162*
virtual representation, *162*
Whiskey Rebellion, *222*
XYZ Affair, *225*

KEY PEOPLE

Abigail Adams, *194*
John Adams, *175*
Samuel Adams, *163*
Richard Allen, *197*
Crispus Attucks, *166*
Benjamin Banneker, *234*
William Bartram, *231*
Mum Bett, *196*
Daniel Boone, *178*
Edward Braddock, *151*
Joseph Brant (Thayendanegea), *177*
John Burgoyne, *183*
Charles Cornwallis, *188*
John Dickinson, *165*
Lord Dunmore, *173*
Philip Freneau, *232*
Edmond Genêt, *221*
King George III, *154*
George Grenville, *160*
Alexander Hamilton, *145*
Patrick Henry, *162*
Sir William Howe, *172*
John Jay, *170*
Thomas Jefferson, *146*
Samuel Jennings, *231*
Henry Knox, *217*
Marquis de Lafayette, *185*
Richard Henry Lee, *175*
Little Turtle, *240*
King Louis XVI, *220*
James Madison, *146*
George Mason, *175*
James Monroe, *209*
Judith Sargent Murray, *194*
Neolin, *155*
Lord North, *186*
Andrew Oliver, *163*
Thomas Paine, *173*
Charles Willson Peale, *230*
Charles Pinckney, *227*
Thomas Pinckney, *241*
Pontiac, *155*
Edmund Randolph, *217*
Paul Revere, *167*
Comte de Rochambeau, *188*
Betsy Ross, *179*
Benjamin Rush, *194*
Deborah Sampson, *184*
Daniel Shays, *206*
Adam Smith, *220*
Baron Friedrich von Steuben, *185*
Thomas Sumter, *188*
Banastre Tarleton, *188*
Charles Townshend, *165*
Mercy Otis Warren, *214*
George Washington, *149*
Anthony Wayne, *240*
Noah Webster, *230*
Phillis Wheatley, *180*

CHRONOLOGY

1700–1760	Salutary (benign) neglect spurs independent thought in colonies
1754	Washington attacks Fort Duquesne Introduction of Albany Plan of the Union
1754–1763	Seven Years' War reshapes political and trade boundaries
1760	British alienation of American Indian groups amplifies tensions
1763	Peace of Paris ends the French and Indian War Proclamation of 1763 antagonizes colonists
1764–1765	Stamp Act gives rise to colonial opposition until repeal in 1766
1765	Expansion of Quartering Act sparks united colonial resistance
1767	Townshend Acts result in colonial protests
1770	Colonial boycotts of British goods multiply Boston Massacre
1772	Massachusetts Committee of Correspondence created
1773	Boston Tea Party
1774	Parliament passes the Intolerable Acts to punish colonies for the Boston Tea Party First Continental Congress convenes
1775	British forces attack at Lexington and Concord Second Continental Congress convenes Costly British victory at Battle of Bunker Hill
1776	Thomas Paine publishes *Common Sense* General Washington forces British retreat from Boston Thomas Jefferson and other members of the Continental Congress draft the Declaration of Independence General Howe's troops occupy New York City Benjamin Franklin serves as unofficial liaison in Paris
1777	Continental Army victory at Battle of Saratoga secures French alliance Articles of Confederation drafted Slavery abolished in Vermont
1778–1779	American Revolution spreads south and west
1780	British sustain heavy battle losses
1780s	Quaker men and women fight for abolition of slavery
1781	Continental victory at Battle of Yorktown leads to peace negotiations Last state, Maryland, ratifies Articles of Confederation
1783	Treaty of Paris officially ends the Revolutionary War British deny U.S. shipping trade access to West Indies Noah Webster advocates universal education
1785	Northwest Ordinance of 1785
1786–1787	Shays's Rebellion spurs revision of Articles of Confederation

CHRONOLOGY *(continued)*

1787	Northwest Ordinance of 1787 Constitutional Convention
1787–1788	Publication of *The Federalist Papers*
1787–1790	Ratification of the Constitution
1789	Massachusetts creates free public schools Judiciary Act of 1789 passed
1789–1791	Ratification of the Bill of Rights
1790	Indian Trade and Intercourse Act passed
1790s	Free Black literary and debate societies emerge
1791	Hamilton releases "Report on the Subject of Manufactures"
1792	American farmers protest taxes
1792–1809	Construction of Washington, D.C.
1793	Washington issues Neutrality Proclamation
1794	Whiskey Rebellion First independent African American church founded
1795	Jay Treaty ratified Treaty of Greenville secures large land gains from American Indian nations for United States
1796	Democratic-Republican Party emerges Pinckney Treaty opens Mississippi River to the United States.
1797	XYZ Affair leads to a Quasi-War with France
1798	Alien and Sedition Acts restrict expressions of dissent
c. 1800	Cotton planting expands slavery westward
1800	Federal government relocates to Washington, D.C. Jefferson elected president, resulting in the first transition of power between political parties

Period 3 AP® Exam Practice

Multiple-Choice Questions

Questions 1–3 refer to the excerpt.

"Q: What was the temper of America towards Great Britain before the year 1763?
A: The best in the world. They submitted willingly to the government of the Crown, and paid, in all their courts, obedience to the acts of Parliament . . . They had not only respect, but affection, for Great Britain, for its laws, its customs and manners, and even a fondness for its fashions, that greatly increased the commerce . . .

Q: What is your opinion of a future tax, imposed on the same principle with that of the Stamp Act? How would Americans receive it?
A: Just as they do this. They would not pay it. . . .

Q: What used to be the pride of the Americans?
A: To indulge in the fashions and manufactures of Great Britain.

Q: What is now their pride?
A: To wear their old clothes over again, till they can make new ones."

Testimony of Benjamin Franklin before the House of Commons of the British Parliament, January 1766

1. Which of the following most directly contributed to the situation described in the excerpt?

(A) The intensified colonial rivalry between Britain and France in the mid-eighteenth century
(B) The increased awareness of the inequalities in colonial society
(C) The mobilization of large numbers of men and women providing support to the patriot movement
(D) Imperial efforts to raise revenue and consolidate control over the colonies

2. Which of the following colonial actions was the most immediate result of the ideas discussed in the excerpt?

(A) The creation of nonimportation agreements
(B) The Boston Tea Party
(C) The publication of *Common Sense*
(D) The formation of the Continental Army

3. Which of the following most likely accounts for the concerns of colonists as expressed in the excerpt?

(A) Local traditions of self-rule
(B) British military occupation of some regions
(C) The expenses incurred by the British in defeating the French in the French and Indian War
(D) Considerable loyalist opposition to the patriot cause

Questions 4–6 refer to the excerpt.

"[W]ith the deepest regret do I announce to you that during your recess some of the citizens of the United States have been found capable of insurrection. During the session of the year 1790 it was expedient to exercise the legislative power granted by the Constitution of the United States 'to lay and collect excises.' In a majority of the States scarcely an objection was heard to this mode of taxation. In the four western counties of Pennsylvania a prejudice . . . produced symptoms of riot and violence. . . . I sought and weighted what might best subdue the crisis. On the one hand the judiciary was pronounced to be stripped of its capacity to enforce the laws; crimes which reached the very existence of social order were perpetrated without control; the friends of Government were insulted, abused, and overawed into silence or an apparent acquiescence; and to yield to the treasonable fury of so small a portion of the United States would be to violate the fundamental principle of our Constitution, which enjoins [commands] that the will of the majority shall prevail."

President George Washington, Sixth Annual Message to Congress, November 19, 1794

4. The excerpt best supports the conclusion that in the 1790s, the U.S. government
   (A) found its powers reduced relative to those of the states.
   (B) was imbalanced due to a lack of checks and balances.
   (C) was denied the authority to levy taxes.
   (D) asserted its powers to maintain law and order.

5. Washington's concerns as expressed in the excerpt emerged most directly from the context of
   (A) the Articles of Confederation.
   (B) the Revolutionary War.
   (C) his Farewell Address.
   (D) ideas of the Enlightenment.

6. Those who did not share Washington's perspective most likely supported which of the following developments in the United States?
   (A) The formation of the Federalist Party
   (B) Shays's Rebellion
   (C) The Constitutional Convention
   (D) The economic policies of Alexander Hamilton

Questions 7–9 refer to the excerpt.

"The army . . . marched for the Valley Forge in order to take up our winter quarters. We were now in a truly forlorn condition—no clothing, no provisions, and as disheartened as need be. We arrived, however, at our destination a few days before Christmas. Our prospect was indeed dreary. In our miserable condition, to go into the wild woods and build us habitations to stay (not to live) in, in such a weak, starved, and naked condition, was appalling in the highest degree . . . However, there was no remedy, no alternative but this or dispersion; but dispersion, I believe was not thought of . . . We had engaged in the defense of our injured country and were willing, nay, we were determined to persevere as long as such hardships were not altogether intolerable . . . had the enemy, strong and well provided as he then was, thought fit to pursue us, our poor emaciated carcasses must have "strewed the plain." But a kind and holy Providence took more notice and better care of us than did the country in whose service we were wearing away our lives by piecemeal."

Joseph Plumb Martin, *A Narrative of Some of the Adventures, Dangers, and Sufferings of a Revolutionary Soldier*, 1830

7. The ideas expressed in the excerpt best serve as evidence of
(A) the colonists' ideological commitment and resilience.
(B) American emphasis upon individual talent over hereditary privilege.
(C) the considerable loyalist opposition to the Revolution.
(D) the inability of the patriot movement to acquire European allies.

8. The excerpt is best understood in the context of
(A) Great Britain's apparently overwhelming military advantages.
(B) an increased awareness of the inequalities in society.
(C) the American Revolution's inspiring of future independence movements.
(D) the failure of men and women to mobilize to support the patriot movement.

9. Which of the following historical events in the 1780s most directly followed from the developments described in the excerpt?
(A) The abolition of slavery
(B) The disbanding of the colonial militias
(C) The establishment of a strong central government
(D) The success of the patriot cause

Questions 10–12 refer to the excerpt.

"Ambition must be made to counteract ambition . . . It may be a reflection on human nature, that such devices should be necessary to control the abuses of government. But what is government itself, but the greatest of all reflections on human nature? If men were angels, no government would be necessary. If angels were to govern men, neither external nor internal controls on government would be necessary. In framing a government which is to be administered by men over men, the great difficulty lies in this: you must first enable the government to control the governed; and in the next place oblige it to control itself."

James Madison, *Federalist* No. 51, 1788

10. Madison's excerpt was written in the context of
(A) the foreign policy challenges faced by the United States due to war between Britain and France.
(B) the ambiguous relationship between the federal government and American Indian tribes.
(C) the shortcomings of the Articles of Confederation.
(D) the expression of ideas about national identity.

11. The ideas expressed in the excerpt arose most directly in reaction to which of the following?
   (A) The passage of the Northwest Ordinance
   (B) The debate over ratifying the Constitution
   (C) The writing of many state constitutions in the post–Revolutionary War period
   (D) The French Revolution

12. To create a government, and then to "oblige it to control itself," was best accomplished by which of the following?
   (A) The addition of a Bill of Rights
   (B) The imposition of a federal system of governance
   (C) The separation of powers among its three branches
   (D) The debates between the Federalists and the Antifederalists

Questions 13–15 refer to the excerpt.

"**SECTION 1.** *Be it enacted by the Senate and House of Representatives of the United States of America, in Congress assembled,* That it shall be lawful for the President of the United States, at any time during the continuance of this act, to *order* all such *aliens* as he shall judge dangerous to the peace and safety of the United States . . . to depart out of the territory of the United States . . . And in case any alien, so ordered to depart, shall be found at large within the United States after the time limited in such order for his departure, and not having obtained a *license* from the President to reside therein . . . every such alien shall, on conviction thereof, be imprisoned for a term not exceeding three years, and shall never after be admitted to become a citizen of the United States: *Provided always, and be it further enacted,* That if any alien so ordered to depart shall prove, to the satisfaction of the President, by evidence . . . that no injury or danger to the United States will arise from suffering such alien to reside therein, the President may grant a ***license*** to such alien to remain within the United States. . . . And the President may also require of such alien to enter into a bond to the United States, in such penal sum as he may direct . . . conditioned for the good behavior of such alien during his residence in the United States, and not violating his license, which license the President may revoke whenever he shall think proper."

The Alien Act, 1798

13. Who would have been most supportive of the ideas expressed in the excerpt?
   (A) James Madison
   (B) John Adams
   (C) Thomas Jefferson
   (D) Thomas Paine

14. Opposition to ideas such as those expressed in the excerpt most directly resulted in the writing of which of the following documents?
   (A) The Northwest Ordinance
   (B) The Bill of Rights
   (C) The Kentucky and Virginia Resolutions
   (D) The *Federalist Papers*

15. The excerpt most directly reflects which of the following continuities in debates over the governing of the United States?

(A) Concerns over the dangers of political factions

(B) Controversies over the appropriate balance between liberty and order

(C) Questions on the relationship of the national government to the states

(D) Differences regarding the appropriate relationship among the three branches of government

Short-Answer Questions

"One of the striking, and to many readers, surprising aspects of the debate over the Constitution is the conservative posture of the opposition. The Anti-Federalists did not deny the need for some change, but they were on the whole defenders of the status quo. . . . They shook their heads at "the frenzy of innovation" sweeping the country . . . Some expressed the primitive conservative view that whatever is old is good. . . . In the main, they saw in the Framers' easy thrusting aside of old forms and principles threats to four cherished values: to law, to political stability, to the principles of the Declaration of Independence, and to federalism."

Herbert J. Storing, *What the Anti-Federalists Were For*, 1981

"Federalists had made their point about the power of the new government . . . It was a signal victory for the self-styled "friends of order" . . . It is remarkable how little changed in the nature of conflict and the parameters of political discourse during three decades of Revolutionary upheaval . . . Some readers may also be surprised that heroes of the American Revolution espoused during the 1790's the very ideas that, we are told as children, they had once risked their lives and fortunes to oppose."

Thomas P. Slaughter, *The Whiskey Rebellion*, 1986

1. Using the excerpts, answer **A**, **B**, and **C**.

(A) Briefly describe ONE major difference between Storing's and Slaughter's historical interpretations of American political ideologies between 1775 and 1800.

(B) Briefly explain how ONE historical event or development from 1775 to 1800 that is not explicitly mentioned in the excerpts could support Storing's interpretation.

(C) Briefly explain how ONE historical event or development from 1775 to 1800 that is not explicitly mentioned in the excerpts could support Slaughter's interpretation.

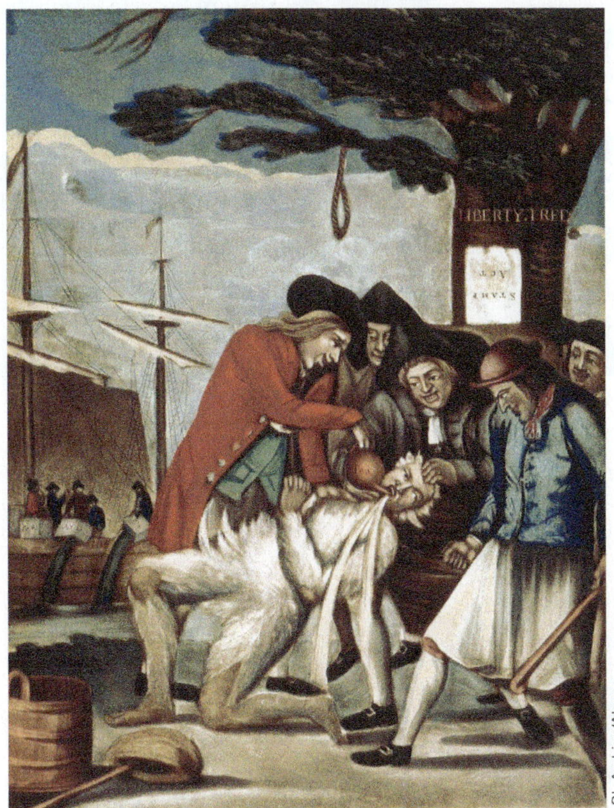

GL Archive/Alamy

"The Bostonians paying the excise-man, or tarring and feathering," 1774

2. Using the image, answer **A**, **B**, and **C**.
   (A) Briefly describe ONE historical perspective expressed in the image.
   (B) Briefly explain how ONE specific event or development in the period from 1754 to 1774 contributed to the events depicted in the image.
   (C) Briefly explain ONE specific historical effect in the period from 1774 to 1800 that resulted from the events depicted in the image.

3. Answer **A**, **B**, and **C**.
   (A) Briefly explain how ONE specific historical event or development contributed to colonial victory in the Revolutionary War (1776–1783).
   (B) Briefly explain how ANOTHER specific historical event or development contributed to colonial victory in the Revolutionary War (1776–1783).
   (C) Briefly explain ONE specific historical event or development from 1783 to 1800 that resulted from colonial victory in the Revolutionary War (1776–1783).

Long-Essay Questions

1. Evaluate the extent of change in the concept of American national identity brought about by the French and Indian War, analyzing what changed and what stayed the same from the period before the war to the period after it.

2. Evaluate the extent to which the American Revolution affected the lives of women and Black Americans.

3. Evaluate the extent of difference between the competing ideologies of the Federalists and Antifederalists regarding the role of the national government between 1787 and 1800.

PERIOD 4 1800–1848

Democracy, Industrialization, and Reform

Universal Images Group/Getty Images

Spinning Cotton in a New England Mill, c. 1835
Industrialization created new and sometimes dangerous job opportunities for men, women, and children in factories that knit the economic production of the North and South together. In this photograph, self-acting mules, powered by a water wheel or steam engine through belt-and-shafting, spun cotton fibers into cloth as the machines automatically wound the yarn onto spindles. A child was employed to crawl under the threads and sweep up under the mule minded by the woman on the left.

Contextualizing Period 4

MODULE 4.1

Debates regarding the rightful powers of the federal government over the state government and of the state over the individual continued in the first half of the nineteenth century. In the early 1800s, Federalists and Democratic-Republicans argued over a range of issues, including tariffs, foreign policy, and how to interpret the meaning of the Constitution. The steady expansion of voting rights for white men increased political participation and led to the creation of new parties, the Democrats and Whigs, which fought a series of closely contested elections in the 1830s and 1840s.

While U.S. politics was being remade, innovations in technology and infrastructure transformed the growing economy of the United States. These changes allowed goods to be produced more efficiently and traded more easily among the various regions of the United States and between the nation and the world. The newly resulting regional specialization led to greater economic integration through trade but also to clearer economic and social differences among the different regions. A "market revolution" affected where and how Americans worked and lived, reshaped regional and national identities, and influenced how citizens interacted with each other at home, in the marketplace, and at work.

Throughout the first half of the nineteenth century, policymakers sought to extend U.S. power internally and abroad in hopes of expanding markets and opportunities to exploit land and resources west of the Mississippi River. As westward expansion continued, the debate over the fate of enslaved Americans and whether slavery should be allowed in new territories and states became increasingly heated. Compromises over the expansion of slavery proved successful in the first half of the nineteenth century but became increasingly difficult toward the middle of the century.

Throughout this period, Americans debated the legacy of the American Revolution, whether the expansion of slavery was part of or harmful to that legacy, whether voting rights could be limited to landholders and to men, and whether federal policies threatened states' rights. By the end of this time period, Americans had resolved some of these debates, while others continued to cause tension in the United States.

AP® EXAM TIP

At the start of the nineteenth century, the U.S. population resided mainly along the eastern seaboard. During this period, the United States expanded economically, politically, and socially. International conflicts, technological discoveries, economic innovation, debates regarding federalism, and religious and social movements based on new ideas about human nature shaped this period. Make sure you understand the key contextual concepts that brought about change from 1800 to 1848.

Period 4: What's Inside 1800–1848

MODULE	AP® THEMATIC FOCUS
4.1 Contextualizing Period 4	By the end of the eighteenth century the United States looked back on a generation of war, revolution, and political conflict. With Thomas Jefferson's election in 1800, political leaders imagined a future of expansion and agricultural settlement for white Americans. However, the years between 1800 and 1844 also saw the rise of industry in the United States, which transformed the ways Americans worked, produced, and exchanged goods. Technological and transportation innovations fueled these changes. Likewise, during this period, political opportunities expanded for some Americans while remaining closed to others. Reform and religious movements arose in reaction to these many changes.
4.2 The Rise of Political Parties and the Era of Jefferson	**Politics and Power** With the election of 1800, Democratic-Republicans took control of Congress and the presidency, while the Supreme Court remained under Federalist influence. Westward settlement and expansion, armed conflicts with American Indians, foreign policy challenges from Great Britain and France, and Supreme Court rulings all contributed to an expansion of the federal government's power during the early 1800s.
4.3 Politics and Regional Interests	**Politics and Power** During the early 1800s, the United States faced external threats and internal conflicts. During the Democratic-Republican administrations of Thomas Jefferson, James Madison, and James Monroe, the nation engaged in conflicts with Great Britain. Domestically, northern, southern, and newly admitted western states competed for influence over federal policy. Proposals like the "American System" attempted to create a national economic plan for development, but caused tensions with regional interests. Likewise, the expansion of states to the west raised tensions over the expansion of slavery. While compromises among northern, southern, and western interests delayed conflict over these issues, the debates they inspired foreshadowed later conflicts.
4.4 America on the World Stage	**America in the World** U.S. participation in the War of 1812 and conflicts with American Indian nations solidified U.S. control of its western lands at the same time as the Monroe Doctrine and efforts to promote foreign trade expanded America's global presence. Tensions and war with Great Britain, the emergence of distinct, regional economies, and disagreements over the expansion of slavery also led to growing political debates because regional interests often outweighed national concerns.
4.5 Market Revolution: Industrialization	**Work, Exchange, and Technology** As the United States industrialized through the factory production of textiles, the regions became increasingly interconnected economically. Agricultural production in the West increasingly produced surpluses for urban consumption, while southern agriculture depended on a system of enslaved labor to produce raw cotton for export and for textile production in the Northeast. Technological developments including the steam engine, mass production of interchangeable parts, and the cotton gin propelled American manufacturing in the North, the spread of slavery in the South, and an improved transportation network throughout the nation. These technological advances, combined with the expansion of the federal government's power, spurred the industrialization of the American economy.
4.6 Market Revolution: Society and Culture	**Social Structures** The market revolution boosted urbanization by drawing international and rural migrants to industrializing cities in the Northeast and fast-growing towns in the Midwest. It also increased class distinctions, as rising prosperity benefited the business elite and led to the growth of both the middle class and the working poor. Middle- and upper-class women's roles changed, with a growing societal emphasis on domesticity.
4.7 Expanding Democracy	**Politics and Power** By the 1820s, states expanded voting rights to all white men by ending property requirements while simultaneously restricting voting rights for women, Black Americans, and American Indians. As a more popularly oriented style of campaigning emerged, Andrew Jackson's presidential election victory in 1828 confirmed the staying power of the new Democratic Party and signaled the end of a political system dominated by eastern elites.

MODULE	AP® THEMATIC FOCUS
4.8 Jackson and Federal Power	**Politics and Power** Debates about the use of federal power — including its ability to impose tariffs, the continued existence of the Bank of the United States, and American Indian policy — contributed to sectional crises over developments such as state nullification of federal tariffs, the forced relocation of thousands of American Indians, the Panic of 1837, and the formation of the Whig Party.
4.9 The Development of an American Culture	**American and Regional Culture** During the early nineteenth century, a new American culture began to emerge that combined European influences and regional cultures. These trends shaped American literature through novels and poetry, as well as ideas about human nature itself.
4.10 The Second Great Awakening	**American and Regional Culture** Democratic politics and a reaction against a focus on reason in religion fostered religious revivals across the United States that emphasized a personal relationship with the divine and salvation, along with an impulse for reform.
4.11 An Age of Reform	**American and Regional Culture** A new reform impulse combining European and American elements took shape in the early 1800s with the spread of public education and printed materials. Many of these reform movements were inspired by the Second Great Awakening and transcendentalism and sparked an array of social-reform efforts, further transforming American culture. The pursuit of the abolition of slavery proved to be one of the more influential of these reform movements, while Black Americans resisted their oppression through community and political activism.
4.12 African Americans in the Early Republic	**Social Structures** Antislavery movements in the North steadily grew from the 1820s until the Civil War (1860–1865) as reformers split over banning the expansion of slavery into new territories or abolishing slavery throughout the United States. Despite brutality and the prevalence of slave codes, a vibrant Black culture emerged on plantations and among free Black people in the South.
4.13 The Society of the South in the Early Republic	**Geography and the Environment** The expansion of cotton planting generated wealth for the planter elite, triggered the forced internal migration of enslaved people, and limited the growth of industry and cities in the South. Enslaved laborers regularly resisted in various ways, while many free Black people worked to improve their status.
4.14 Causation in Period 4	Period 4 allows opportunities to determine the causes of the economic changes during this time period, and, in turn, to consider the ways in which those changes transformed the lives of white Americans, Black Americans, and American Indians.
Support and Practice	• Practice thinking and writing historically in each module. • See the Period Review of key concepts, events, people, and dates after the last module. • Try the AP® Exam Practice at the end of the period.

MODULE 4.2

Political and Economic Transformations

FOCUS

As you read this module, consider the short- and long-term effects of the political changes that occurred in the White House and Congress under the control of the Democratic-Republicans during the early nineteenth century. At the same time, take note of both short- and long-term effects of significant technological advances on how Americans worked and lived between the late eighteenth century and the early nineteenth century.

Thomas Jefferson, like other Democratic-Republicans, envisioned the United States as a republic composed of small, independent farmers who had little need or desire for extensive federal powers. Despite Jefferson's early efforts to impose this agrarian vision on the government, developments in international affairs soon converged with Supreme Court rulings to expand federal power.

Jefferson, too, contributed to this expansion. Imagining the nation's extensive frontiers as a boon to its development, he purchased the Louisiana Territory from France in 1803. The purchase and development of this vast territory increased federal authority. It also raised new questions about the place of American Indians and Black people in a republican society.

Technological advances enabled the geographical expansion of United States. The spread of U.S. settlements into new territories necessitated improved forms and networks of transportation and communication and increased demands for muskets and other weapons to protect the nation's frontier. The growing population also fueled improvements in agriculture and manufacturing to meet demands for clothing, food, and farm equipment. Continued conflicts with Great Britain and France also highlighted the need to develop the nation's natural resources and technological capabilities.

Yet even though American ingenuity was widely praised, the daily lives of most Americans changed slowly. And for some, especially enslaved women and men, technological advances merely added to their burdens.

A New Administration Faces Challenges

In 1801, Democratic-Republicans worked quickly to implement their vision of limited federal power. Holding the majority in Congress, they repealed the whiskey tax and let the Alien and Sedition Acts expire. Jefferson significantly reduced government expenditures and immediately set about slashing the national debt, cutting it nearly in half by the end of his second term. Democratic-Republicans also worked to curb the powers granted to the Bank of the United States and the federal court system.

Soon, however, international upheavals forced Jefferson to make fuller use of his presidential powers. The U.S. government had paid tribute to the **Barbary States** of

North Africa during the 1790s to gain protection for American merchant ships. The new president opposed this practice and, in 1801, refused to continue the payments. In response, the Barbary pirates quickly resumed their attacks, and Jefferson sent the U.S. Navy and Marine Corps to retaliate. Although a combined American and Arab force did not achieve the objective of capturing Tripoli, the Ottoman viceroy agreed to negotiate a new agreement with the United States. Seeking to avoid all-out war, Congress accepted a treaty with the Barbary States, one that reduced the tribute payment.

Jefferson also followed the developing crisis in the West Indies during the 1790s. In 1791, enslaved people in the sugar-rich colony of Saint Domingue (later known as Haiti) launched a revolt against French rule. Inspired in part by the American Declaration of Independence, the **Haitian Revolution** escalated into a complicated conflict in which free people of color, white slaveholders, and enslaved people formed competing alliances with British and Spanish forces as well as with leaders of the French Revolution. Finally, in December 1799, Toussaint L'Ouverture, a military leader and freedperson, claimed the presidency of the new Republic of Haiti. But Napoleon Bonaparte seized power in France that same year and sent thousands of troops to reclaim the island. Toussaint was captured and shipped off to France, where he died in prison. Many Haitians fled to the United States, but other Haitian rebels continued the fight.

Haitian Revolution
Revolt against a racialized social hierarchy and French rule by free and enslaved Black people between 1791 and 1804 in the French colony of Saint Domingue on the island of Hispaniola. The revolution led to the establishment of the Republic of Haiti, the first independent Black-led nation in the Americas, in 1803.

In the United States, reactions to the revolution were mixed, but southern whites feared that it might incite rebellions among the enslaved. Adding to their fears, Gabriel, an enslaved blacksmith in Richmond, Virginia, plotted such a rebellion in 1800. Inspired by both the American and Haitian revolutions, supporters rallied around the demand for "Death or Liberty." Gabriel's conspiracy failed when informants betrayed him to authorities, resulting in the hanging of twenty-six enslaved people, including Gabriel. News of the plot traveled across the South and terrified white residents. Their anxieties were heightened when, in November 1803, prolonged fighting, yellow fever, and the loss of sixty thousand soldiers forced Napoleon to admit defeat in Haiti. Haiti became the first independent Black-led nation in the Americas.

AP® EXAM TIP

You should be able to articulate the factors that shaped the United States during this period. As the country began to accumulate more territory, beginning with the Louisiana Purchase (1803), divisive issues intensified. These issues included the role of the federal government, the implementation of tariffs, and the nation's international policy.

REVIEW

- How did the Haitian Revolution affect politics in the United States?

Acquiring the Louisiana Territory

In France's defeat, Jefferson saw an opportunity to gain navigation rights on the Mississippi River, which the French controlled. This was a matter of crucial concern to Americans living west of the Appalachian Mountains. Jefferson sent James Monroe to France to offer Napoleon $2 million to ensure Americans the right of navigation and deposit (offloading cargo from ships) on the Mississippi. To Jefferson's surprise, a fiscally strained Napoleon offered instead to sell the entire Louisiana Territory for $15 million.

The president agonized over the constitutionality of this **Louisiana Purchase**. Because the Constitution contained no provisions for buying land from foreign nations, a strict interpretation would prohibit the purchase. In the end, though, the opportunity proved too tempting, and the president finally agreed to buy the Louisiana Territory. Jefferson justified his decision by arguing that the territory would allow for the removal of more American Indians from east of the Mississippi River, end European influence in the region, and expand U.S. trade networks.

Louisiana Purchase
The U.S. government's 1803 purchase from France of the vast territory stretching from the Mississippi River to the Rocky Mountains and from New Orleans to present-day Montana, doubling the size of the nation.

Opponents viewed the purchase as benefiting mainly agrarian interests. They also suspected Jefferson of trying to offset Federalist power in the Northeast. Neither party seemed especially concerned about the French, Spanish, or native peoples living in the region. They came under U.S. control when the Senate approved the purchase in October 1803. The purchase ultimately proved popular among ordinary Americans, most of whom focused on the opportunities it offered rather than the expansion of federal power it ensured.

At Jefferson's request, Congress had already appropriated funds for an expedition known as the **Corps of Discovery** to explore territory along the Missouri River. That expedition could now explore much of the Louisiana Territory. The president's personal secretary, Meriwether Lewis, headed the venture and invited a fellow Virginian, William Clark, to serve as co-captain. The two set off with about forty-five men on May 14, 1804. For two years, they traveled thousands of miles up the Missouri River, through the northern plains, over the Rocky Mountains, and beyond the Louisiana Territory to the Pacific coast. A young Shoshone woman, Sacagawea, and her husband joined them in April 1805 as they headed into the Rocky Mountains.

Although Sacagawea was born in a Shoshone village in what is now Idaho, as a young girl of twelve she was taken captive by members of the Hidatsa tribe and marched hundreds of miles to a Hidatsa-Mandan village on the Missouri River. Later, Sacagawea was sold to a French trader, Toussaint Charbonneau, along with another young Shoshone woman, and both became his wives. In November 1804, Lewis and Clark set up winter camp near the Hidatsa village where Sacagawea lived. Charbonneau, who spoke French and Hidatsa, and Sacagawea, who spoke several Indian languages, joined the expedition as interpreters. Sacagawea's extensive knowledge of the terrain and fluency in American Indian languages proved essential to the success of the mission.

Throughout the expedition, members meticulously recorded observations about local plants and animals as well as American Indian residents, providing valuable evidence for scientists and fascinating information for ordinary Americans. Further, this information would be useful for economic and political expansion of the United States into lands occupied by native peoples, French, and Spanish settlers.

Sacagawea was the only American Indian to travel as a permanent member of the expedition, but many other native women and men assisted the Corps when it journeyed near their villages. They provided food and lodging for the Corps, hauled baggage up steep mountain trails, and traded food, horses, and other items. The one Black American on the expedition, an enslaved man named York, also helped negotiate trade with local American Indians. York, who realized his value as a trader, hunter, and scout, asked his enslaver, William Clark, for his freedom when the expedition ended in 1806. York eventually became a free man, but it is unclear whether it was by Clark's choice or York's escape.

WORKING with EVIDENCE

Source: William Clark, *Journal Entry*, October 12, 1804

> "After breakfast, we went on shore to the house of the chief of the second village named Lassel, where we found his chiefs and warriors. They made us a present of about seven bushels of corn, a pair of leggings, a twist of their tobacco, and the seeds of two different species of tobacco. The chief then delivered a speech expressive of his gratitude for the presents and the good counsels which we had given him; his intention of visiting [the president of the United States] but for fear of the Sioux; and requested us to take one of the Ricara [Arikara] chiefs up to the Mandans and negociate a peace between the two nations. . . . After we had answered and explained the magnitude and power of the United States, the three chiefs came with us to the boat. We gave

them some sugar, a little salt, and a sun-glass. Two of them left us, and the chief of the third [village] . . . accompanied us to the Mandans. . . .

[The Arikara] express a disposition to keep at peace with all nations, but they are well armed with [muskets], and being much under the influence of the Sioux, who exchanged the goods which they got from the British for Ricara corn, their minds are sometimes poisoned and they cannot always be depended on."

Questions for Analysis

1. Describe Clark's characterization of the Arikara Indians.
2. Describe the attitude of the Arikara Indians toward American explorers and other American Indian nations, according to Clark.
3. Explain how this document illustrates the influence the Corps of Discovery had on relations between American Indian nations.

Other expeditions followed Lewis and Clark's venture. In 1806, Lieutenant Zebulon Pike led a group to explore the southern portion of the Louisiana Territory (Map 4.1). After traveling from St. Louis to the Rocky Mountains, the expedition entered Mexican territory. In early 1807, Pike and his men were captured by Mexican forces. They were returned to the United States at the Louisiana border that July. Throughout his travels, Pike learned a great deal about lands that would eventually become part of the

MAP 4.1 Lewis and Clark and Zebulon Pike Expeditions, 1804–1807 The expeditions led by Meriwether Lewis, William Clark, and Zebulon Pike illustrate the vast regions explored in just four years after the U.S. purchase of the Louisiana Territory. Journeying through and beyond the borders of that territory, the explorers gathered information about American Indian nations, plants, animals, and the natural terrain even as Comanche and Shoshone nations, with access to horses, transformed the region.

According to this map, what were the competing territorial claims to North America in the early 1800s?

United States and about Mexican desires to overthrow Spanish rule, information that proved valuable over the next two decades.

Early in this series of expeditions, in November 1804, Jefferson easily won reelection as president. His popularity among farmers, already high, increased when Congress reduced the minimum allotment for federal land sales from 320 to 160 acres. This act allowed more small and independent farmers to purchase land on their own rather than via speculators, who sought high returns, thus increasing the cost of land. Yet, despite continued popularity among his core of supporters, Jefferson's original vision of limiting federal power had already been undermined by his own actions—and those of the Supreme Court. The expansion of federal and executive powers would continue through Jefferson's second term.

REVIEW

- How did Jefferson reconcile his support for the Louisiana Purchase with his limited view of federal power?
- Why did Federalists oppose the Louisiana Purchase even though they believed the Constitution permitted it?

The Supreme Court Defines Its Powers

In 1801, just before the Federalist-dominated Congress turned over power to the Democratic-Republicans, it passed a new **Judiciary Act**. The act created six additional circuit courts and sixteen new judgeships, which President Adams filled with Federalist "midnight appointments" before he left office. Jefferson accused the Federalists of having "retired into the judiciary" and worried that "from that battery all the works of Republicanism are to be beaten down and destroyed." Meanwhile, John Marshall, chief justice of the United States Supreme Court (1801–1835), insisted that the powers of the Supreme Court must be equal to and balance those of the executive and legislative branches.

Marbury v. Madison
A Supreme Court decision in 1803 penned by Chief Justice John Marshall that established the authority of the Supreme Court to rule on the constitutionality of federal laws, also known as judicial review.

McCulloch v. Maryland
A Supreme Court decision in 1819 that reinforced the federal government's ability to employ an expansive understanding of the implied powers clause of the Constitution. The court ruled that the state of Maryland was unable to tax the Second Bank of the United States, allowing the federal government the right to establish a federal bank while rejecting the ability of states to tax it.

One of the first cases to test the Court's authority involved a dispute over President Adams's midnight appointments. Jefferson's secretary of state, James Madison, refused to deliver the appointment papers to several of the appointees, including William Marbury. Marbury and three others sued Madison to receive their commissions.

In ***Marbury v. Madison*** (1803), the Supreme Court ruled that it was not empowered to force the executive branch to give Marbury his commission. But in his decision, Chief Justice Marshall declared that the Supreme Court did have the duty "to say what the law is." He thus asserted a fundamental constitutional power: that the Supreme Court had the authority to decide which federal laws were constitutional. The following year, the Court also claimed the right to rule on the constitutionality of state laws. In doing so, the justices rejected Democratic-Republicans' claim that state legislatures had the power to nullify federal law. Instead, the Supreme Court declared that federal laws took precedence over state laws.

Over the next dozen years, the Supreme Court continued to assert Federalist principles. In 1810, it insisted that it was the proper and sole arena for determining matters of constitutional interpretation.

In 1819, the highest court embraced a loose interpretation of the Constitution's implied powers clause in ***McCulloch v. Maryland***. This clause gave the federal government the right to "make all laws which shall be necessary and proper" for carrying out the explicit powers granted to it by the Constitution. By loosely rather than strictly interpreting that clause, the Court reasoned that Congress had broad powers to enact legislation not explicitly denied it in the Constitution. Despite Democratic-Republicans' earlier opposition to a national bank, Congress had chartered the Second Bank of the United States in 1816, and its branch banks issued notes that circulated widely in local communities. Legislators in Maryland, believing that branch banks had gained excessive power, approved a tax on their operations. Marshall's Court ruled that the establishment of the bank was "necessary and proper" for the functioning of the national government, and therefore fit under Article I of the Constitution, which establishes Congress's powers. Marshall thereby rejected Maryland's right to tax the branch bank, claiming that "the power to tax involves the power to destroy."

By the 1820s, the Supreme Court, under the forceful direction of John Marshall, had established the power of **judicial review**—the authority of the nation's highest court to rule on cases involving states as well as the national government. It also strengthened property rights and reinforced the supremacy of national laws over state laws. From the Court's perspective, the judiciary was as important an institution in framing and preserving a national agenda as Congress or the president.

judicial review
The Supreme Court's ability to rule on the constitutionality of cases at both the federal and state levels. The policy had the effect of solidifying a more federalist interpretation of the constitution and the powers of the government.

 REVIEW

- How did the Supreme Court's rulings in the cases of *Marbury* and *McCulloch* strengthen the power of the federal government?

Democratic-Republicans Expand Federal Powers

Although Democratic-Republicans generally opposed Marshall's rulings, they, too, continued to expand federal power. Once again, international developments drove the Jefferson administration's political agenda. By 1805, the security of the United States was threatened by continued conflicts between France and Great Britain. Both sought alliances with the young nation, while ignoring U.S. claims of neutrality. Indeed, each nation sought to punish Americans for trading with the other. Britain's Royal Navy began stopping American ships carrying sugar and molasses from the French West Indies. Between 1802 and 1811, the British impressed more than eight thousand sailors from such ships, including many U.S. citizens, and seized American goods. France claimed a similar right to stop U.S. ships that continued to trade with Great Britain.

Unable to convince foreign powers to recognize U.S. neutrality, Jefferson and Madison pushed for congressional passage of an embargo they hoped would, like colonial boycotts, force Great Britain's hand. In 1807, Congress passed the **Embargo Act**, which prohibited U.S. ships from leaving their home ports until Britain and France repealed their restrictions on American trade. Although the act kept the United States out of war, it devastated national commerce by banning virtually all foreign trade.

Embargo Act
An act passed in 1807 that prohibited American ships from leaving their home ports until Britain and France repealed restrictions on U.S. trade and ceased British impressment of American sailors. While the act was intended to assert U.S. neutrality between British and French trading partners, it had a devastating impact on American commerce.

Following the passage of the Embargo Act, New England merchants immediately voiced their outrage, and some began sending goods to Europe via Canada. In response, Congress passed the Force Act, granting extraordinary powers to customs officials to end such smuggling. The economic pain caused by the rapid decline in trade spread well beyond the merchant class. The effects of the embargo were widespread, as farmers and

Opposition to the Embargo Act Although Congress repealed the Embargo Act in 1809, lawmakers still barred the United States from trading with Great Britain and France. Both countries had attacked American shipping in violation of U.S. neutrality. This political cartoon by Alexander Anderson criticizes the embargo, which proved costly to merchants, sailors, and dockworkers. Here, a merchant carrying a barrel of goods curses the snapping turtle "Ograbme," which is *embargo* spelled backward. **Who during this time period would most agree with the perspective expressed in this image? Who would most disagree with it?**

urban workers, as well as southern planters, directly suffered. Exports nearly stopped, and sailors and dockworkers faced escalating unemployment.

Within a deepening recession, American concerns about the expansion of federal power reemerged. Congress and the president had not simply regulated international trade. They had brought it to a halt.

Still, despite the effects of the Embargo Act, many Americans viewed Jefferson favorably. He had devoted his adult life to the creation of the United States. With the purchase of the Louisiana Territory, vast lands were now open to American exploration and development. This internal geographical boon encouraged inventors and artisans to pursue ideas that would help the early republic take full advantage of its resources and recover from its current economic plight. Some might have wondered, however, how a Democratic-Republican president had so significantly expanded the power of the federal government.

Democratic-Republicans also began to expand federal power by increasingly using the federal government to shape a national transportation network. Secretary of the Treasury Albert Gallatin urged Congress to fund roads and canals to enhance the economic development of the nation. He advocated a "great turnpike road" along the Atlantic seaboard from Maine to Georgia as well as roads to connect the four main rivers that flowed from the Appalachians to the Atlantic Ocean. Although such projects traditionally were funded by the states, Congress in 1815 approved funds for a **National Road** from western Maryland through southwestern Pennsylvania to Wheeling, West Virginia. This so-called Cumberland Road was completed in 1818 and later extended into Ohio and Illinois.

National Road
A road built using federal funds that ran from western Maryland through southwestern Pennsylvania to Wheeling, West Virginia, also called the Cumberland Road. Completed in 1818, it was part of a larger effort to improve infrastructure. The road bridged the Potomac and Ohio Rivers and accelerated western settlement and commercial expansion.

Carrying people and goods by water was even faster and cheaper than transporting them over land, but rivers ran mainly north and south. In addition, although loads moved quickly downstream, the return voyage was long and slow. While both local and national politicians advocated the construction of canals along east–west routes to link river systems, inventors and mechanics focused on building boats powered by steam to overcome the problems of sending goods upriver.

Granger – Historical Picture Archive

Robert Fulton's *Clermont*, c. 1813 This painting of the *Clermont* by an unknown artist was published as a lithograph in France around 1830, suggesting Europeans' interest in American innovations. As the illustration shows, early steamboats included paddle wheels and sails to guide their travels. Here, the *Clermont* plies the Hudson River alongside sailboats as it passes a cluster of houses on the far shore.

What does this painting suggest about the state of technological development in the early 1800s?

In 1804, Oliver Evans, a machinist in Philadelphia, invented a high-pressure steam engine attached to a dredge that cleaned the silt around the docks in Philadelphia harbor. He had insufficient funds, however, to pursue work on a steam-powered boat. Robert Fulton, a New Yorker, improved on Evans's efforts, using the low-pressure steam engine developed in England. In 1807, Fulton launched the first successful steamboat, the *Clermont*, which traveled up the Hudson River from New York City to Albany in only thirty-two hours.

The powerful Mississippi River proved a greater challenge, but by combining Evans's high-pressure steam engine with a flat-bottom hull that avoided the river's sandbars, mechanics who worked along the frontier improved Fulton's design and launched the steamboat era in the West.

Item	Price	Item	Price
Ax	$6.00	Large copper kettle	$30.00
Beaver trap	$8.00	Lead	$0.20 per pound
Black silk handkerchief	$2.00	Lead shot for guns	$1.00 per 5 pounds
Breechcloth	$3.00	Medium copper kettle	$10.00
Bridles	$2.00–$10.00	Muskrat spear	$2.00
Chain for staking down traps	$0.75 per 6 feet	Muskrat trap	$5.00
Combs	$1.00 per pair	Muslin or calico shirt	$3.00
File (for sharpening axes)	$2.00	Ordinary butcher knife	$0.50
Flannel	$1.00 per yard	Sheet iron kettle	$10.00
Flannel mantle	$3.00	Small copper kettle	$3.00
Gunflints	$1.00 per 15	Spurs	$6.00 per pair
Hand-size mirrors	$0.25	Tin kettle	$14.00
Heavy wool cloth	$10.00 per yard	Tomahawk	$1.50
Hoe	$2.00	Trade gun	$20.00–$25.00
Horn of gunpowder	$1.50	Wool blanket	$4.00
Horses	$35.00–$50.00	Wool mantle (short cloak or shawl)	$4.00

Prices at George Davenport's Trading Post, Rock Island, Illinois, c. 1820

What do the items listed for sale reveal about the daily lives of people living or traveling near the trading post?

Data from Will Leinicke, Marion Lardner, and Ferrel Anderson, *Two Nations, One Land* (Rock Island, IL: Citizens to Preserve Black Hawk Park, 1981).

REVIEW

- In what ways did the Democratic-Republicans embrace a loose interpretation of the Constitution between 1801 and 1820?

AP® Skills Workshop: Thinking Historically

Additional Practice in Writing Body Paragraphs

Below are an essay question and sample thesis statement. Write a strong paragraph that supports the underlined summary of the sub-argument. Start with a clear, expanded statement of the sub-argument. Then use **Claim, Support, Explain** to prove the sub-argument. Finish the paragraph with a summary sentence that restates the sub-argument. Review the AP® Thinking Historically exercise in Modules 3.8 and 3.9 if you need more help before you begin.

> **Prompt:** Evaluate the extent to which Democratic-Republican administrations between 1801 and 1820 focused on westward expansion instead of overseas trade.

Thesis: While the ideology of Thomas Jefferson's Democratic-Republicans promoted westward expansion over Atlantic trade, Democratic-Republican administrations also were sometimes forced to turn their attention to trade issues overseas. **[claim]** During the Jefferson, Madison, and Monroe administrations, exploration and transportation to the West were paramount, but conflict in the Atlantic and Mediterranean regions often distracted Democratic-Republican administrations from their western focus. **[line of reasoning]**

Politics, Economics, and Regional Interests

MODULE 4.3

FOCUS

The expansion of the American economy into a national network of agricultural and industrial production was fueled by a growing transportation network along rivers and roads. Nevertheless, this growth stimulated tensions among the various regions of the United States. National economic policies, such as the American System, and the expansion of settlement west of the Mississippi River, revived the argument over the future of the national economy and the expansion of slavery, leading to compromises that temporarily soothed conflict.

As you read this module, compare different regional interests, North, South, and West, in the midst of economic change and expansion.

More secure borders and state and federal investments in transportation fueled overseas trade and the development of increasingly distinct regional economies. Regional economies ensured economic interdependence, but also political differences.

For instance, when an economic panic and severe recession hit in 1819, many southern planters and midwestern farmers blamed it on the banks. In reality, falling prices for cotton and wheat abroad as well as an overextension of credit by U.S. banks contributed to the recession. Whatever the cause, the interdependence of regional economies ensured that everyone suffered.

At the same time, these economies were built on distinct forms of labor, with the South becoming more dependent on slavery and the North less so. When Missouri, situated between the old Northwest Territory and expanding southern cotton lands, applied for statehood in 1819, these regional differences set off a furious national debate over the continued westward extension of slavery.

Governments Fuel Economic Growth

In 1800, Thomas Jefferson captured the presidency by advocating a reduction in federal powers and a renewed emphasis on the needs of small farmers and workingmen. Once in power, however, Jefferson and his Democratic-Republican supporters faced a series of economic and political developments that led many to embrace a loose interpretation of the U.S. Constitution and support federal efforts to aid economic growth. Population growth and commercial expansion encouraged these federal efforts.

In 1811, the first steamboat traveled down the Mississippi from the Ohio River to New Orleans. Over the next decade, steamboat traffic expanded. This development helped western and southern residents but hurt trade across overland routes between northeastern seaports and the Ohio River valley. The federal government began construction of the Cumberland Road in 1811 to reestablish this regional connection by linking Maryland and Ohio. The Democratic-Republican Congress passed additional bills to fund ambitious federal transportation projects, but President Madison vetoed much of this legislation, believing it overstepped even a loose interpretation of the Constitution.

After the War of 1812 (see Module 4.4), British merchants resumed the sale of textiles and manufactured goods to the American market. Eager to reduce their large inventories built up over the years since Jefferson's Embargo Act, British importers began selling their wares below market prices as a way to outcompete domestically made textiles in the United States. In response, Congress passed the **Tariff of 1816**, the first tariff legislation with the goal of protecting American manufacturers rather than simply raising federal revenue. Unlike future tariffs during this era, the 1816 tariff received some southern support as a temporary measure to stem British efforts to undermine the American economy.

Within a few years, Kentucky representative Henry Clay formulated a plan to promote U.S. economic growth and advance commercial ties throughout the country. Ultimately called the **American System**, it combined federally funded internal improvements, such as roads and canals, to aid both farmers and merchants, along with federal tariffs to protect U.S. manufacturing. The American System also proposed a national bank to oversee economic development.

American System
A national economic plan proposed by Henry Clay in the 1810s and 1820s to promote the U.S. economy by combining federally funded internal improvements to aid farmers while protecting American manufacturers by placing high tariffs on imported goods.

These proposals proved popular among many Americans in the West because they encouraged internal improvements and an incorporation of the region into the national economy through a transportation network, especially as the white population west of the Appalachian Mountains more than doubled between 1810 and 1820, from 1,080,000 to 2,234,000. Population growth was swift following the War of 1812, as many veterans settled there after receiving 160-acre parcels of land in the region as payment for wartime service. In response to this population growth, Congress admitted four new states to the Union in just four years: Indiana (1816), Mississippi (1817), Illinois (1818), and Alabama (1819).

Congress also negotiated with American Indian nations to secure trade routes farther west. In the 1810s, Americans began trading along an ancient trail from Missouri to Santa Fe, a town in northern Mexico, even though the trail cut across Osage Indian territory. In 1825, Congress approved a treaty with the Osage to guarantee a right of way for U.S. merchants. The Santa Fe Trail soon became a critical overland route for commerce between the United States and Mexico.

akg-images/Newscom

"Erie-Canal, Lockport," c. 1850
This steel engraving, based on an 1839 painting, depicts one of five locks that lifted boats sixty feet over a limestone ridge near the western end of the canal. The remarkable engineering feat required 1,200 laborers to blast the ridge, clear the rocks, and build the locks. The village of Lockport, which emerged at the site, grew rapidly after 1825.

How does this image portray the changes the Erie Canal brought to local towns?

Unlike the West, state governments east of the Appalachian Mountains funded most internal improvement projects because a rudimentary transportation network, access to overseas trade, and a thriving economy already existed there. The most significant of these was New York's **Erie Canal**, a 363-mile waterway stretching from the Mohawk River to Buffalo, completed in 1825 and connecting the Great Lakes to the Hudson River in New York, allowing the upper Midwest access to eastern markets, and vice versa. Self-taught men directed this extraordinary engineering feat by which thousands of workers carved a swath forty feet wide and four feet deep through limestone cliffs, mountains, forests, and swamps. The canal, which rises 566 feet along its route, required the construction of 35 locks to lift and lower boats.

Erie Canal Completed in 1825, the Erie Canal was an important internal improvement that spanned 363 miles from Lake Erie to the Hudson River, thereby providing access, via the Great Lakes, through the canal, and down the Hudson, to trade between the Midwest and the Northeast.

The arduous and dangerous work was carried out mainly by Irish, Welsh, and German immigrants, many of whom settled along its route. Tolls on the Erie Canal quickly repaid the tremendous financial cost of its construction. Freight charges quickly declined by 90 percent and shipping times plunged. By linking western farmers to the Hudson River, the Erie Canal ensured that New York City became the nation's leading seaport (Map 4.2).

The Erie Canal's success inspired hundreds of similar projects in other states. Canals carried manufactured goods from New England and the Middle Atlantic states to rural households in the Ohio River valley. Western farmers, in turn, shipped agricultural

MAP 4.2 Roads and Canals to 1837 During the 1820s and 1830s, state and local governments, as well as private companies, built roads and canals to foster migration and commercial development. The Erie Canal, completed in 1825, was the most significant of these projects. Many other states, particularly in the Northeast and the old Northwest, sought to duplicate that canal's success over the following decade.

Compare the system of roads and canals in the Northeast, old Northwest, and South. What conclusions can you draw about each region based on this map?

products back east. Canals linked smaller cities within Pennsylvania and Ohio, facilitating the rise of commercial and manufacturing centers like Harrisburg, Pittsburgh, and Cincinnati. Canals also allowed vast quantities of coal to be transported out of the Allegheny Mountains, fueling industrial development throughout the Northeast.

- How were the National Road and Erie Canal both a result of economic change and a cause of further economic change?

Regional Economic Development

The roads, rivers, canals, and steamboats that connected a growing nation meant that people in one region could more easily exchange the goods they produced for those they needed. This development fostered the emergence of distinct, regional economies. In the South, for instance, vast American Indian land cessions and the acquisition of Florida in 1819 ensured the expansion of cotton cultivation. At the same time, overcultivation in older regions of the Southeast forced many planters to relocate farther west and south. In the process, they extended slavery into new lands to produce cash crops like sugar, rice, and most predominately cotton. Farmers often planted as much cotton as they could and used profits from this cash crop to buy grain and other food items from the West and manufactured shoes and cloth from the North.

Plantation homes in long-settled areas like Montpelier in Virginia became more fashionable, as they increasingly consumed luxury goods imported from China and Europe. But, after decades of overcultivation, the soil in the Chesapeake region became depleted, limiting the profits from tobacco and making a shift to cotton impossible. As agricultural production declined, some Virginia planters made money by selling enslaved people to planters farther south and west while others diversified their crops by growing wheat and other agricultural products.

Many white Americans benefited from the expansion of southern agriculture west of the Appalachians. Southern farmers and planters who cultivated cotton made substantial profits in the 1810s. So did western farmers, who shipped vast quantities of agricultural produce to the South. Towns like Cincinnati, located across the Ohio River from Kentucky, sprang up as regional centers of commerce. Americans living in the Northeast increased their commercial connections with the South as well. Northern merchants became more deeply engaged in the southern cotton trade, opening warehouses in cities like Savannah and Charleston and sending agents into the countryside to bargain for cotton to be spun into thread in mills powered by water.

The southern cotton boom thus fueled northern industrial growth, the improvement of roads, the expansion of canals, and the building of larger and faster ships. Factory owners and merchants in New England could ship growing quantities of yarn, thread, and cloth along with shoes, tools, and leather goods to the South. Meanwhile, merchants in Philadelphia and Pittsburgh built ties to western farmers, exchanging manufactured goods for agricultural products. Over time, regional economies became not only more distinctive but also increasingly interdependent.

- How did the economies of the North and South benefit from the westward expansion of southern agriculture?

The Panic of 1819

In 1818, the directors of the **Second Bank of the United States**, fearing a continued expansion of the money supply, tightened the credit they provided to branch banks. This sudden effort to curtail credit led to economic panic. Some branch banks failed immediately. Others survived by calling in loans to companies and individuals, who in turn demanded repayment from those to whom they had extended credit. The chain of indebtedness pushed many people to the brink of economic ruin just as factory owners cut their workforce and merchants decreased orders for new goods. Individuals and businesses faced bankruptcy and foreclosure, and property values fell sharply.

The rising interconnectedness of the U.S. economy also led to a greater national risk of widespread economic crises. In effect, an economic weakness in one sector of the economy often led to a cycle of falling prices and bankruptcy nationwide in a phenomenon often called an economic "panic." The earliest of these, the **Panic of 1819**, resulted mainly from irresponsible banking practices in the United States and was deepened by the declining overseas demand for American goods, especially cotton.

Panic of 1819
The nation's first severe economic depression, due largely to irresponsible banking practices and a decline in American exports such as cotton. The panic lasted four years, slowed previously rapid westward expansion, and resulted in widespread bankruptcies and mass unemployment, generating the loss of millions of acres of land and businesses in nationwide bankruptcies, and resulting in massive popular protests.

Beginning in 1816, American banks, including the newly chartered Second Bank of the United States, had lent huge sums to settlers seeking land on the frontier and merchants and manufacturers expanding their businesses. Loans were often not backed by sufficient collateral because many banks assumed continued economic growth would ensure repayment. Then, as agricultural production in Europe revived with the end of the Napoleonic Wars, the demand for American foodstuffs dropped sharply. Farm income plummeted by roughly one-third in the late 1810s.

Auction in Chatham Street, New York, 1820 Widespread unemployment between 1819 and 1823 resulted in evictions of thousands of families. Public auctions of the furniture, dishes, and other household goods of evicted families were held regularly in cities across the country. This depiction of an 1820 auction in New York's Chatham Square was painted by E. Didier in 1843, during the next major economic panic.

What details in this image convey the hardships created by the Panic of 1819?

Bankruptcies, foreclosures, unemployment, and poverty spread across the country. Cotton farmers were especially hard hit by declining exports and falling prices. Planters who had gone into debt to purchase land in Alabama and Mississippi were unable to pay their mortgages. Many western residents, who had invested all they had in new farms, lost their land or simply stopped paying their mortgages. This further strained state banks, some of which collapsed, leaving the national bank holding mortgages on vast amounts of western territory.

Many Americans viewed banks as the cause of the panic. Some states defied the Constitution and the Supreme Court by trying to tax branches of the Second Bank of the United States or printing state banknotes with no hard currency (gold or silver) to back them, which led to rising inflation. Some Americans called for government relief, but there was no system to provide the kinds of assistance needed.

When Congress debated how to reignite the nation's economy, regional differences quickly appeared. Northern manufacturers called for even higher tariffs to protect them from foreign competition, but southern planters argued that high tariffs raised the price of manufactured goods while agricultural profits declined. Meanwhile, workingmen and small farmers feared that their economic needs were being ignored by politicians tied to bankers, planters, manufacturers, and merchants.

By 1823, the panic had largely dissipated, but the prolonged economic crisis shook national confidence, and citizens became more skeptical of federal authority and more suspicious of banks, particularly the Second Bank of the United States. From 1819 until the Civil War, one of the greatest limitations on national growth remained the cycle of economic expansion and contraction punctuated by economic panics that periodically shook the national economy.

- What were the causes and consequences of the Panic of 1819?

Slavery in Missouri

AP® EXAM TIP

The issues of slavery and the path that the United States should pursue for its economic foundation—agriculture or industry—continued to define the country's growing sectionalism. Know how compromises regarding slavery such as the Missouri Compromise temporarily resolved that issue, while economic proposals such as the American System intensified the economic debate.

A second national crisis highlighted regional systems of labor. In February 1819, the Missouri Territory applied for statehood. New York congressman James Tallmadge Jr. proposed that Missouri be admitted only if it banned further importation of enslaved people and passed a gradual emancipation law. Southern congressmen blocked Tallmadge's proposals, but the northern majority in the House of Representatives then rejected Missouri's admission.

Southern politicians were outraged, claiming that since the Missouri Territory allowed slavery, so should the state of Missouri. With cotton production moving ever westward, southern congressmen wanted to ensure the availability of new lands. They also wanted to ensure the South's power in Congress. Because the northern population had grown more rapidly than in the South, by 1819 northern politicians controlled the House of Representatives.

The Senate, however, was evenly divided. According to southern policymakers, if northern senators could block the admission of slave states like Missouri while allowing the admission of free states, the balance of power in the Senate would tip in the North's favor, threatening the legal status of slavery itself.

AP® WORKING with EVIDENCE

Source: Senator Rufus King (New York), *Speech to Congress on the Admission of Missouri to the United States*, 1819

> "The question respecting slavery in the old thirteen States had been decided and settled before the adoption of the constitution, which grants no power to Congress to interfere with, or to change what had been previously settled—the slave States, therefore, are free to continue or to abolish slavery. Since the year 1808 Congress have possessed power to prohibit and have prohibited the further migration or importation of slaves into any of the old thirteen States, and at all times, under the constitution, have had power to prohibit such migration or importation into any of the new States or territories of the United States. The constitution contains no express provision respecting slavery in a new State that may be admitted into the Union; every regulation upon the subject belongs to the power whose consent is necessary to the formation and admission of new States into the Union. Congress may, therefore, make it a condition of the admission of a new State, that slavery shall be for ever prohibited within the same."

Questions for Analysis

1. Identify King's arguments about the power of Congress to regulate slavery in the new states.
2. Identify the evidence from the Constitution that King uses to support his argument.
3. Explain the connection between King's argument and the prevailing economic system in the North.

Source: Senator Freeman Walker (Georgia), *Speech to Congress on the Admission of Missouri to the United States*, 1820

> "I cannot but remark, sir, to what lengths arguments might be carried, predicated upon the supposition of the existence of the power, on the part of congress, to impose conditions and restrictions.
>
> If you have the authority to impose the one now sought to be imposed, may you not impose any other? If you have the right to inhibit the introduction of slaves into the new state, you have a right to inhibit the introduction of any other species of property. And you may go a step further, and prescribe the manner in which the soil shall be cultivated. In fine, there is no restriction or condition whatever, which may not, with equal propriety, be imposed."

Questions for Analysis

1. Identify Walker's arguments about the power of Congress to regulate slavery in the new states.
2. Explain the connection between Walker's argument and the prevailing economic system in the South.

Questions for Comparison

1. Identify King's and Walker's respective arguments about the power of Congress to regulate slavery in new states.
2. Explain the causes underlying the differences between King's and Walker's arguments.
3. Evaluate the extent to which the Missouri Compromise reconciled the debate over slavery in the territories.

MAP 4.3 The Missouri Compromise and Westward Expansion, 1820s The debate over the Missouri Compromise occurred as the United States began expanding farther westward. Within a few years of its adoption, the growth of U.S. settlements in eastern Texas and increased trade with a newly independent Mexico suggested the importance of drawing a clear boundary between slave and free states.

In what ways did the Missouri Compromise line lessen sectional tensions, and in what ways did it fuel them?

For southern planters, the decision regarding Missouri defined the future of slavery. With the importation of enslaved people banned in 1808, planters relied on natural increase and selling enslaved people from older to newer areas of cultivation to meet the demand for labor. Moreover, free Black people packed the congressional galleries in Washington to listen to congressmen debate Missouri statehood, leading supporters of slavery to worry that any signs of weakness would fuel resistance to slavery. Recent attacks on Georgia plantations by a coalition of formerly enslaved Black people who had escaped bondage and Seminole Indians lent power to such fears.

Missouri Compromise

A compromise generated to maintain the balance of power between slave and free states in the U.S. Senate. The 1820 act established the southern border of Missouri as the boundary between future slave and free states admitted from the Louisiana Territory.

In 1820, Representative Henry Clay of Kentucky forged a compromise that resolved the immediate issues and promised a long-term solution. Maine was to be admitted as a free state and Missouri as a slave state, thereby maintaining the balance between North and South in the U.S. Senate (Map 4.3). At the same time, Congress agreed that the status of any future states from the Louisiana Territory would be based on the 36°30′ line of latitude. States above the line would be admitted without slavery, while states below the line would enter the union allowing slavery.

The **Missouri Compromise** ended the crisis for the moment. Still, the debates made clear how quickly a disagreement over slavery could escalate into clashes that threatened the survival of the nation.

REVIEW

- Why was the issue of slavery in Missouri so controversial?

AP® Skills Workshop: Thinking Historically

Sourcing and Situating Primary Sources

Historians build historical arguments out of primary sources. As you recall from the Thinking Historically exercises in Period 1 (Modules 1.2, 1.3, 1.5), primary sources are one of the most important kinds of evidence historians use when providing **support** for their **claims**. As you also recall from learning to apply **CSE** in Period 1, an essential part of the process of making **claims** and providing **support** for those claims is **explaining** to a reader how the support for a claim provides support. One skill that helps historians explain their support for a claim from a primary source is **sourcing**.

Sourcing is a process in which a historian uses certain information *beyond the source* to better understand the source's meaning. We do this all the time when we try to understand what someone means when they say something. For example, here is a statement:

"I really should not have eaten that."

This statement likely calls all sorts of scenarios to mind for you. In fact, if you ask a friend what they think is the background of this statement, they might tell you something very different from what you thought was behind the statement. When we read a statement like this, we immediately begin to fill in information outside of the statement to give it meaning. Who is speaking? Who is this person speaking to? What is the context in which this statement is made? What is the purpose of this statement? What did they eat? You could come up with various possibilities to answer these questions. However, if we add a little information, you immediately begin to "see" the situation where this comment was made. Like this:

Source: Marcus, after a large meal of mussels and linguine, to his friend, Katelyn, the chef, 7:00 p.m.: "I really should not have eaten that."

Now, our ideas about different scenarios should have shrunk to only a few options. These are two friends, one of whom has made a large meal, likely a dinner (notice the time!), and Marcus regrets having eaten it, probably because it was too much.

These conclusions are a result of **sourcing**, where you evaluate the statement, "I really should not have eaten that," in light of information about the source. These conclusions fall within certain sourcing categories useful to you on the AP® U.S. History Exam:

Intended Audience: The source statement tells us that Marcus is speaking to his friend, who made the meal.

Point of View (POV): The source statement, along with the primary source itself (Marcus's quote), tells us that, from Marcus's point of view, he has just eaten a large meal and now regrets it.

Purpose: This one is trickier. We don't want to speculate. About the best we can say is that Marcus's purpose is to express regret over what he's done, and he's expressing this regret to the friend who made the meal.

Let's try sourcing two historical documents from this module. Reread the section in this module called "Slavery in Missouri." Here are the two primary sources from that section:

(continued)

Source: Senator Rufus King (New York), *Speech to Congress on the Admission of Missouri to the United States*, 1819

> "The question respecting slavery in the old thirteen States had been decided and settled before the adoption of the constitution, which grants no power to Congress to interfere with, or to change what had been previously settled—the slave States, therefore, are free to continue or to abolish slavery. Since the year 1808 Congress have possessed power to prohibit and have prohibited the further migration or importation of slaves into any of the old thirteen States, and at all times, under the constitution, have had power to prohibit such migration or importation into any of the new States or territories of the United States. The constitution contains no express provision respecting slavery in a new State that may be admitted into the Union; every regulation upon the subject belongs to the power whose consent is necessary to the formation and admission of new States into the Union. Congress may, therefore, make it a condition of the admission of a new State, that slavery shall be for ever prohibited within the same."

Source: Senator Freeman Walker (Georgia), *Speech to Congress on the Admission of Missouri to the United States*, 1820

> "I cannot but remark, sir, to what lengths arguments might be carried, predicated upon the supposition of the existence of the power, on the part of congress, to impose conditions and restrictions.
>
> If you have the authority to impose the one now sought to be imposed, may you not impose any other? If you have the right to inhibit the introduction of slaves into the new state, you have a right to inhibit the introduction of any other species of property. And you may go a step further, and prescribe the manner in which the soil shall be cultivated. In fine, there is no restriction or condition whatever, which may not, with equal propriety, be imposed."

We've already sourced Senator King's statement for you below. Try sourcing Senator Walker's statement in terms of the **Intended Audience**, **Point of View**, and **Purpose** in a similar way. Keep in mind that a number of factors will help with your sourcing: (1) the document itself, (2) the source line for each document, and (3) the information in the section entitled "Slavery in Missouri," as well as your knowledge of the growing debate over the expansion of slavery during this period.

	Senator Rufus King	Senator Freeman Walker
Intended Audience	King is speaking to Congress, during the debate over whether Missouri should be admitted as a free or slave state. His audience is fellow senators whose votes will determine Missouri's status.	
Point of View	King is from a northern state (New York). His point of view is likely influenced by the fact that slavery is disappearing as an institution in this region, and most northern states have already abolished slavery.	
Purpose	King is arguing that the federal government has the power to regulate the expansion of slavery in territories like Missouri because he likely supports preventing Missouri from becoming a slave state and wants senators to vote accordingly.	

America on the World Stage

MODULE 4.4

FOCUS

As you read this module, consider the causes and effects of U.S. expansion before and after the War of 1812, as well as growing conflict with American Indians as the United States expanded into traditional native lands. Compare U.S. conflicts internationally and domestically, and consider the similarities and differences among them.

In March 1809, Thomas Jefferson was succeeded in the presidency by his friend and ally James Madison. Both men sought to end foreign interference in American affairs and to resolve conflicts between American Indians and white residents on the nation's frontier. By 1815, the United States had weathered a series of domestic and foreign crises. Even though Jefferson and Madison both believed in a national government with limited powers, each found himself expanding federal authority, especially in response to the tensions with Great Britain and the War of 1812.

After the war, Democratic-Republicans in Congress sought to use federal authority to settle boundary disputes in the West, make investments in transportation, and reestablish a national bank. Federal power was again asserted to settle disputes with Britain and Spain over U.S. borders in the north and the south.

AP® EXAM TIP

U.S. efforts to expand economically came into direct conflict with European wars, which eventually shifted to America with the War of 1812. After successfully defending itself against the British, the United States became more aggressive in securing its position in North America through treaties such as Adams–Onís; the Indian Removal Act; and asserting its rising status in the Western Hemisphere through the Monroe Doctrine.

Tensions at Sea and on the Borderlands

When President Madison took office, Great Britain and France remained deeply involved in the Napoleonic Wars in Europe and refused to modify their policies toward American shipping or to recognize U.S. neutrality. Both nations seized American ships, and British authorities continued to impress "deserters" into the Royal Navy.

Just before Madison's inauguration in March 1809, Congress replaced the Embargo Act with the **Non-Intercourse Act**, which restricted trade only with France and Britain and their colonies. Although the continued embargo against Britain encouraged U.S. manufacturing and the act allowed trade with other European nations, many Americans still opposed Congress using its power to restrict their right to trade.

Non-Intercourse Act

An act passed by Congress in 1809 allowing Americans to trade with every nation except France and Britain in an effort to spur a sagging economy following the Embargo Act of 1807. The act failed to stop the seizure of American ships or to improve the economy.

In the midst of these crises, Madison also faced difficulties in the Northwest Territory. In 1794, General Anthony Wayne had won a decisive victory against a multi-tribe coalition at the Battle of Fallen Timbers. But this victory inspired two forceful native leaders to create an alliance of the American Indian peoples throughout the Ohio River valley. The Shawnee prophet Tenskwatawa and his brother Tecumseh, a warrior, encouraged native peoples to resist white encroachments on their territory and to give up all aspects of white society and culture, including liquor and other popular trade goods. They imagined a vast American Indian nation that stretched from the Canadian border to the Gulf of Mexico.

Although powerful Creek and Choctaw nations in the lower Mississippi valley refused to join the alliance, American Indians in the upper Midwest rallied around the brothers. In 1808, Tenskwatawa and Tecumseh established Prophet Town along the Tippecanoe River in Indiana Territory. The next year, William Henry Harrison, the territorial governor, tricked several American Indian leaders into signing a treaty selling three million acres of land to the United States for only $7,600. An enraged Tecumseh dismissed the treaty, claiming the land belonged collectively to all the American Indians.

AP® WORKING with EVIDENCE

Source: Chief Tecumseh, *Address to Governor William Henry Harrison*, 1810

> "*Brother.* Since the peace was made you have kill'd some of the Shawanese, Winebagoes, Delawares, and Miamies and you have taken our lands from us, and I do not see how we can remain at peace with you if you continue to do so.
>
> You endeavor to make distinctions, you wish to prevent the Indians to do as we wish them: to unite and let them consider their land as the common property of the whole.
>
> You take tribes aside and advise them not to come into this [coalition] and untill our design is accomplished we do not wish to accept of your invitation to go and visit the President.
>
> The reason I tell you this is you want by your distinctions of Indian tribes in allotting to each a particular track of land to make them to war with each other. You never see an Indian come and endeavour to make the white people do so. You are continually driving the red people when at last you will drive them into the great Lake where they can't either stand or work."

Questions for Analysis

1. Identify the main elements of Tecumseh's complaint.
2. Describe how prior events created the context for Tecumseh's speech.
3. Explain how differing views of land ownership contributed to conflict between American Indian nations and the United States during the early nineteenth century.

In November 1811, fearing the growing power of the Shawnee leaders, President Madison ordered Harrison to attack Prophet Town. With more troops and superior weapons, the U.S. army defeated the allied American Indian forces at the Battle of Tippecanoe and burned Prophet Town to the ground. The rout damaged Tenskwatawa's stature as a prophet, and he and his supporters fled to Canada, where skirmishes continued along the U.S.–Canadian border.

REVIEW

- How did the federal government respond to the challenges posed by both Great Britain and American Indians between 1800 and 1812?

War Erupts with Britain

Convinced that British officials in Canada fueled American Indian resistance, many Democratic-Republicans demanded an end to British intervention on the western frontier and transatlantic trade. Some called for the United States to declare war. Yet merchants in the Northeast, who hoped to renew trade with Great Britain and the

British West Indies, feared the commercial disruptions that war would bring. Thus, New England Federalists strongly opposed a declaration of war.

For months, Madison avoided taking a clear stand on the issue. On June 1, 1812, however, with diplomatic efforts exhausted, Madison sent a secret message to Congress outlining U.S. grievances against Great Britain. Within weeks, Congress declared war, although the vote counts in the House of Representatives and the Senate revealed sharp divisions on the matter.

Supporters of the **War of 1812** claimed that a victory over Great Britain would end threats to U.S. sovereignty and raise America's stature in Europe. However, the nation was ill-prepared to launch a major offensive against such an imposing foe given cuts in federal spending, falling tax revenues, and diminished military resources. The U.S. navy, for example, established under President Adams, had been reduced to only six small gunboats by President Jefferson.

War of 1812
War between the United States and Great Britain from 1812 to 1815. The war was one consequence of ongoing conflict between Great Britain and France, as each nation sought to forcibly restrict U.S. trade with the other. While the war resulted in little territorial gains by either side, it solidified foreign recognition of the United States as a power and pushed the United States to create a stronger military and national economic foundation in the event of future wars.

Democratic-Republicans had also failed to recharter the Bank of the United States when it expired in 1811, so the nation lacked a vital source of credit. Nonetheless, many in Congress believed Britain would be too engaged by the ongoing conflict with France to attack the United States.

Meanwhile, U.S. commanders devised plans to attack Canada, but the U.S. army and navy proved no match for Great Britain and its American Indian allies. Tecumseh, who was appointed a brigadier general in the British army, helped capture Detroit. Joint British and American Indian forces also launched successful attacks on Fort Dearborn, Fort Mackinac, and other points along the U.S.–Canadian border.

Even as U.S. forces faced many defeats in the summer and fall of 1812, American voters reelected James Madison as president. While Madison won most western and southern states, where the war was most popular, he lost in New England and New York, where Federalist opponents held sway.

After a year of fighting, U.S. forces drove the British back into Canada (Map 4.4). A naval victory on Lake Erie led by Commodore Oliver Perry proved crucial to U.S. success. Soon after, Tecumseh was killed in battle, and U.S. forces burned York (present-day Toronto). Yet just as U.S. prospects in the war improved, New England Federalists demanded an end to the fighting. The war devastated the New England maritime trade as the British naval blockade crippled American shipping, causing economic hardship throughout the region. In 1813, state legislatures in New England withdrew their support for any invasion of "foreign British soil," and Federalists in Congress sought to block funding for the war and the deployment of local militia units into the U.S. army.

But the New England Federalists were not powerful enough to change national policy, particularly after news arrived in March 1814 that Andrew Jackson and Tennessee militiamen had defeated a force of Creek Indians, important British allies. Cherokee warriors, longtime foes of the Creek, joined the fight. At the **Battle of Horseshoe Bend**, in present-day Alabama, the combined U.S.–Cherokee forces slaughtered eight hundred Creek warriors, leaving some Americans appalled at the death toll. In the resulting treaty, the Creek nation lost two-thirds of its tribal domain to the United States and its Cherokee allies.

Despite some wartime successes, the United States was no closer to winning the war when the British defeated Napoleon in June 1814. Emboldened by that major victory, in August 1814, the British sailed up the Chesapeake directly to Washington, D.C. As American troops retreated, First Lady Dolley Madison and Peter Jennings, an enslaved man, gathered up government papers and valuable belongings before fleeing the White House. The redcoats then burned and sacked Washington, destroying the White House and the Capitol in the process. U.S. troops quickly rallied, defeating the British in Maryland and expelling them from Washington and New York. But later in 1814, the

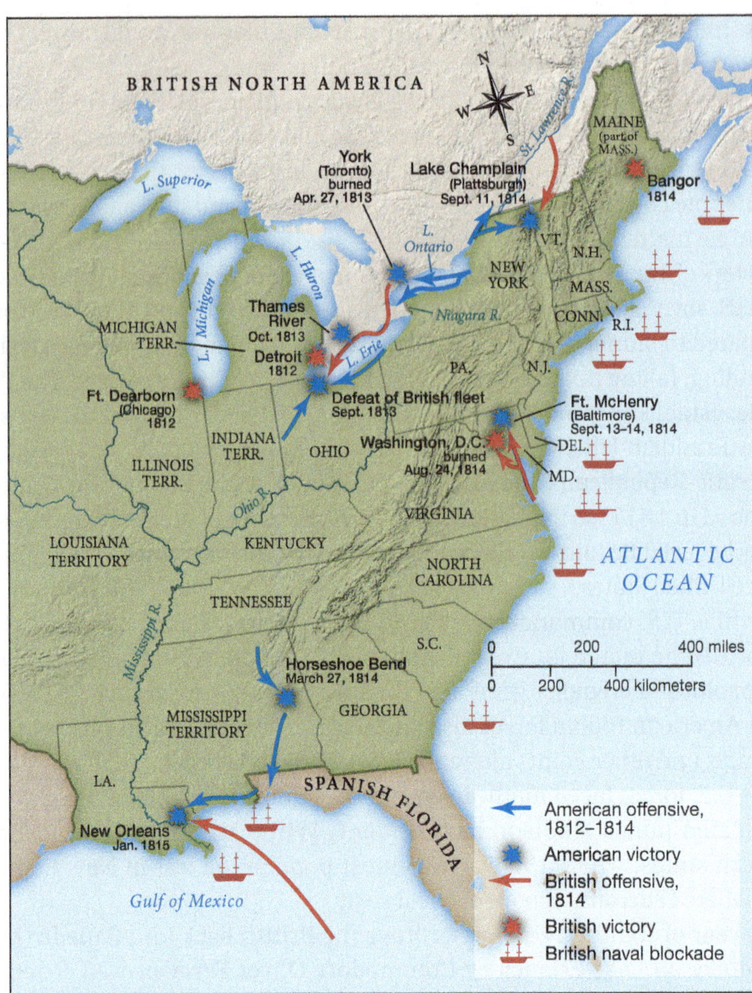

MAP 4.4 The War of 1812 Most conflicts in this war occurred in the Great Lakes region or around Washington, D.C. Yet two crucial victories occurred in the South. At Horseshoe Bend, troops under General Andrew Jackson and aided by Cherokee warriors defeated Creek allies of the British. At New Orleans, Jackson beat British forces shortly after a peace agreement was signed in Europe.

How does this map illustrate the economic challenges faced by New England during the War of 1812?

Hartford Convention

A secret convention in 1814 of Federalists opposed to the War of 1812. Delegates to the convention considered a number of constitutional amendments, as well as the possibility of secession. After news of the convention spread, public sentiment turned against the Federalists, and the party never fully recovered.

Treaty of Ghent

The accord signed in December 1814 that ended the War of 1812 and reestablished the pre-war status quo regarding land claims between the United States and Britain.

British, seemingly undaunted, blockaded major ports and landed thousands of troops at New Orleans.

In the midst of the protracted conflict, New England Federalists revived their efforts to end the war. They took the unusual step of calling a secret meeting at Hartford, Connecticut, in December 1814 to "deliberate upon the alarming state of public affairs." Some participants at the **Hartford Convention** called for New England's secession from the United States. Most supported amendments to the U.S. Constitution that would restrict federal power by limiting presidents to a single term and ensuring they were elected from diverse states (ending Virginia's domination of the office). Other amendments would require a two-thirds majority in Congress to declare war or prohibit trade.

However, despite outward appearances, Great Britain was losing steam as well, as its treasury and national mood were depleted by a decade of warfare. At the end of 1814, representatives of the two countries met in Ghent, in modern Belgium, to negotiate a peace settlement. On Christmas Eve, the **Treaty of Ghent** was signed, returning to each nation the lands it controlled before the war. The issue of British impressment

A CORRECT VIEW of the BATTLE Near the City of NEW ORLEANS, on the
Eighth of January 1815, Under the Command of Genl. Andw. Jackson, Over 10,000 British Troops, in
which 3 of their most distinguished Generals were killed & several wounded and upwards of 3000 of their choicest
Soldiers were killed, wounded, and made Prisoners, &c

Sarin Images/Granger – Historical Picture Archive

The Battle of New Orleans On January 8, 1815, General Andrew Jackson's troops launched grapeshot and canister bombs against British forces in New Orleans in this final battle of the War of 1812. Jackson's troops included American Indian allies, backcountry immigrants, and French-speaking Black soldiers. This engraving by Francisco Scacki shows the slain British commander, Major General Sir Edward Pakenham, in the center foreground.

What details in this image indicate the decisive defeat of the British army? How might a British artist have presented this battle differently?

was not resolved and American Indian allies to the British lost large swaths of land, opening much of the Northwest to American settlement.

News of the treaty had not yet reached North America in January 1815, when U.S. troops under General Andrew Jackson attacked and routed the British army at the **Battle of New Orleans**. The victory cheered Americans, who were unaware that peace had already been achieved, and they made Jackson a national hero. The victory also made New England Federalists look foolish, and potentially subversive, in the eyes of many Americans. The party would never fully recover its reputation.

Battle of New Orleans Battle in the War of 1812 that ended a British attempt to invade the United States through the city of New Orleans. While the Battle of New Orleans took place after the Treaty of Ghent officially ended the war, the British and U.S. forces in the American southwest had not yet received word of the cessation of hostilities. General Andrew Jackson's victory in the Battle of New Orleans led to a rush of nationalism in the United States and launched his political career.

Although the War of 1812 achieved no formal territorial gains, it did represent an important defense of U.S. sovereignty and garnered international prestige for the young nation. In addition, American Indians on the western frontier lost a powerful ally when British representatives at Ghent failed to act as advocates for their allies. In practical terms, the U.S. government gained greater control over vast expanses of land in the Ohio and Mississippi River valleys.

REVIEW

- Why did Congress declare war on Great Britain in 1812?
- What changed as a result of the War of 1812, and what remained the same?

Americans Expand the Nation's Borders

In 1816, in the midst of an economic resurgence, James Monroe, a Democratic-Republican from Virginia and Madison's secretary of war, won an easy victory in the presidential election over Senator Rufus King, a New York Federalist. To improve relations with Britain and resolve problems on the borderlands of the United States, Monroe sent John Quincy Adams to London. He negotiated treaties that limited U.S. and British naval forces on the Great Lakes, set the U.S.–Canadian border at the forty-ninth parallel, and established joint British–U.S. occupation of the Oregon Territory. In 1817 and 1818, the Senate approved these treaties, which further restricted American Indian rights and power.

President Monroe harbored grave concerns about the nation's southern boundary as well. He sought to limit Spain's power in North America and stop Seminole Indians in Florida and Alabama from claiming lands that the defeated Creeks had ceded to the United States. Shifting from diplomacy to military force, in 1817, the president sent General Andrew Jackson to force the Seminoles back into central Florida. Yet he ordered Jackson to avoid direct conflict with Spanish forces for fear of igniting another war. However, in spring 1818, Jackson attacked two Spanish forts, hanged two Seminole chiefs, and executed two British citizens.

Jackson's attacks spurred outrage among Spanish and British officials and many members of Congress. The threat of conflict with Britain, Spain, and the Seminole prompted President Monroe to establish the nation's first peacetime army. In the end, the British chose to ignore the execution of citizens engaged in "unauthorized" activities, while Spain decided to sell the Florida Territory to the United States in return for setting the border at the Sabine River in Texas, which established the boundary between Louisiana and Spanish territory in the west. Indeed, in the **Adams–Onís Treaty** (1819), negotiated by John Quincy Adams, Spain ceded all its lands east of the Mississippi to the United States in hopes of maintaining this western border.

Monroe Doctrine
The assertion by President James Monroe in 1823 that the Western Hemisphere was part of the U.S. sphere of influence and off limits to future European colonization. Although the United States lacked the power to back up this claim, it signaled an intention to challenge Europeans for authority in the Americas.

Success in acquiring Florida encouraged the administration to look for other opportunities to limit European influence in the Western Hemisphere. By 1822, Argentina, Chile, Peru, Colombia, and Mexico had all overthrown Spanish rule. That March, President Monroe recognized the independence of these southern neighbors, and Congress quickly established diplomatic relations with the new nations. The following year, President Monroe claimed the entire Western Hemisphere as part of the U.S. sphere of influence, stating the Americas are "not to be considered as subjects for further colonization by any European powers" while also promising the United States would not interfere in Europe. Although the United States did not have sufficient power to enforce what later became known as the **Monroe Doctrine**, it had declared its intention to challenge Europeans for authority in the Americas, thereby challenging traditional European claims on the Western Hemisphere.

WORKING with EVIDENCE

Source: President James Monroe, Annual Address to Congress, later called the *Monroe Doctrine*, 1823

> "[T]he American continents, by the free and independent condition which they have assumed and maintain, are henceforth not to be considered as subjects for future colonization by any European powers. . . .
>
> In the wars of the European powers in matters relating to themselves we have never taken any part, nor does it comport with our policy so to do. It is only when our rights are invaded or seriously menaced that we resent injuries or make preparation for our defence. With the movements in this hemisphere we are, of necessity, more immediately connected, and by causes which must be obvious to all enlightened and impartial observers. The political system of the allied powers is essentially different in this respect from that of America. This

difference proceeds from that which exists in their respective Governments. And to the defence of our own, which has been achieved by the loss of so much blood and treasure, and matured by the wisdom of their most enlightened citizens, and under which we have enjoyed unexampled felicity, this whole nation is devoted. We owe it, therefore, to candor, and to the amicable relations existing between the United States and those powers, to declare that we should consider any attempt on their part to extend their system to any portion of this hemisphere as dangerous to our peace and safety."

Questions for Analysis

1. Identify the reasons why the Monroe Doctrine was issued, based on this excerpt.
2. Explain how the Monroe Doctrine represented a continuation of the expansion of federal power.
3. Evaluate the extent to which economic considerations shaped the creation of the Monroe Doctrine.
4. Evaluate the extent to which the Monroe Doctrine was a result of the War of 1812.

By the late 1820s, U.S. residents were moving to and trading with newly independent Mexican territories. Southern whites began settling on Mexican lands in eastern Texas, while traders traveled the Santa Fe Trail. Meanwhile, New England manufacturers and merchants began sending goods via clipper ships (fast, three-masted vessels used for trade) to another Mexican territory, Alta California.

Some Americans looked even farther afield. In the early nineteenth century, U.S. ships carried otter pelts and merchandise across the Pacific, returning with Chinese porcelains and silks. Eventually, the Alta California and China trades converged, expanding the reach of U.S. merchants. Some Americans then set their sights on Pacific islands, especially Hawaii and Samoa.

Expanded trade routes along with wartime disruptions of European imports fueled the expansion of U.S. manufacturing, which improved opportunities for entrepreneurs and workers. By 1813, the area around Providence, Rhode Island, boasted seventy-six spinning mills. In 1815, Philadelphia claimed pride of place as the nation's top industrial city, turning out glass, chemicals, metalwork, and leather goods.

- How did the United States use diplomacy and military force to expand its borders during the early nineteenth century?

AP® Skills Workshop: Thinking Historically

Additional Practice in Sourcing and Situating Primary Sources

Review the AP® Thinking Historically exercise in Module 4.3 and determine the **Intended Audience**, **Point of View**, and **Purpose** of the document below. Use the table following the primary source to help you organize your thoughts.

(continued)

Source: Chief Tecumseh, *Address to Governor William Henry Harrison*, 1810

"*Brother.* Since the peace was made you have kill'd some of the Shawanese, Winebagoes, Delawares, and Miamies and you have taken our lands from us, and I do not see how we can remain at peace with you if you continue to do so.

You endeavor to make distinctions, you wish to prevent the Indians to do as we wish them: to unite and let them consider their land as the common property of the whole.

You take tribes aside and advise them not to come into this [coalition] and untill our design is accomplished we do not wish to accept of your invitation to go and visit the President.

The reason I tell you this is you want by your distinctions of Indian tribes in allotting to each a particular track of land to make them to war with each other. You never see an Indian come and endeavour to make the white people do so. You are continually driving the red people when at last you will drive them into the great Lake where they can't either stand or work."

	Chief Tecumseh, *Address to Governor William Henry Harrison*, 1810
Intended Audience	
Point of View	
Purpose	

Now that you have determined the Audience, Point of View, and Purpose of the document, you can use the **CSE** (Claim, Support, Explain) strategy to provide evidence for a complete answer to the following question.

To what extent were conflicts between native peoples a product of U.S. government policy?

If you were writing a whole essay to answer this question, your CSE statement would likely be part of a body paragraph, which will begin with a sub-argument aligned to a portion of your thesis. So, let's say your sub-argument for this paragraph is:

The federal government sought to pit native peoples against one another to prevent alliances against the U.S. government.

Now, write a **CSE** statement that takes into account intended audience, point of view, and purpose. If you were to write a full body paragraph, you would repeat CSE multiple times, and perhaps interpret the audience, point of view, and purpose of different primary sources.

Market Revolution: Industrialization

MODULE 4.5

FOCUS

The title of this module really describes two "revolutions" that took place during the first half of the nineteenth century: a technological and an economic revolution. Both brought profound and unexpected changes. The market revolution boosted urbanization by drawing international and rural migrants to industrializing cities in the Northeast and fast-growing towns in the Midwest. The economic revolution transformed the way many people worked day to day.

Keeping causation and comparison in mind as you read will help you remember not only to compare the effects of these major changes, but to examine how and why these effects differed. As you read this module, identify the major changes resulting from these revolutions and compare the ways those changes affected different groups of people and different regions in the United States.

Commercial and industrial development, immigration from Europe, and migration from rural areas led to the rapid growth of cities in the northern United States from 1820 on. Such growth both built on and furthered the expansion of roads and canals, which were funded by federal and state governments in the 1810s and 1820s. By linking northern industries with western farms and southern plantations, these innovations in transportation fueled a **market revolution**, as the manufacture of goods became better organized and innovations in industry, agriculture, and communication increased efficiency and productivity. These changes fostered urbanization, which, in turn, reinforced economic growth and innovation.

Industrial enterprises in the Northeast transformed the nation's economy even though they employed less than 10 percent of the U.S. labor force. In the 1830s and 1840s, factories grew considerably in size, and some investors, especially in textiles, constructed factory towns. New England textile mills relied increasingly on the labor of girls and young women, while urban workshops hired children, young women and men, and older adults.

Although men still dominated the skilled trades, making chairs, clocks, shoes, hats, and fine clothing, employment in these trades slowly declined as industrial jobs expanded. An economic panic in 1837 intensified this trend and increased tensions that made it more difficult for workers to organize across differences of skill, ethnicity, race, and sex.

market revolution
Innovations in agriculture, industry, communication, and transportation in the early 1800s that increased efficiency and productivity and linked local producers to distant markets. It also solidified the connections of northern industry with western farms and southern plantations and eliminated independent shops and artisans in favor of factory mass production.

AP® EXAM TIP

Following the War of 1812, America experienced both the first industrial revolution and vast improvements in transport. What caused these interdependent revolutions to occur during the antebellum period, and what effect did they have on the United States economically, politically, and socially? Make sure you understand the impact of these two revolutions on the unique sectional development as well, since the AP® Exam often asks for comparisons among regions of the country.

Creating an Urban Landscape

Across the North, urban populations boomed. As commercial centers, seaports like New York and Philadelphia were the most populous cities in the early nineteenth century. Between 1800 and 1850, the number of cities with 100,000 inhabitants increased from zero to six; five were seaports. The sixth was the river port of Cincinnati, Ohio. Smaller boomtowns like Rochester, New York, emerged along inland waterways as the completion of the Erie Canal in 1825 spurred agriculture and industry.

Development along the Erie Canal illustrates the ways advances in transportation transformed the surrounding landscape and ecology. As soon as the first stretch was complete in 1819, its economic benefits became clear. As the forty-foot-wide canal was extended across central and western New York State, settlers rushed to establish farms, mills, and ports. They chopped down millions of trees to construct homes and businesses and to open land for cattle, sheep, wheat, and orchards. As bear and deer fled to still-forested areas, farmers shipped grain, cattle, and hogs to eastern markets or to emerging cities like Rochester. There, flour millers and butchers turned wheat, cattle, and hogs into flour, beef, and pork, products that were now easier and cheaper to ship east and south.

As the population in western New York and along the Great Lakes as well as access to goods increased, residents demanded more and more manufactured goods. This demand fueled the growth of factories, especially in New England. Cotton, lumber, and flour mills were constructed near waterfalls for power, transforming isolated villages into mill towns while endangering the natural habitats of fish and wildlife. As thousands of newcomers cleared more land in Ohio and Michigan, they expanded trade between the areas served by the Erie Canal and the Great Lakes and the older towns from New England to New York City. Moreover, midwesterners could ship food south via the Ohio and Mississippi Rivers in exchange for southern cotton, rice, and sugar.

Business and political leaders in Philadelphia and Baltimore, seeing the economic benefits created by the Erie Canal, demanded state funding for canals linking them to the Midwest. Where state funding proved insufficient, they persuaded English bankers and merchants to invest in American canals as well as railroads, which were just beginning to compete with waterways as a method to transport people and goods.

- What economic and environmental changes did the construction of the Erie Canal cause?

Technology Reshapes Agriculture and Industry

Advances in agricultural and industrial technology paralleled the development of roads and steamboats. Key inventions such as the steam engine spurred others, inducing a **multiplier effect** that led to additional dramatic changes. Two inventions—the cotton gin and the spinning machine—were especially notable in transforming southern agriculture and northern industry, transformations that were deeply intertwined.

American developments were also closely tied to the earlier rise of industry in Great Britain. By the 1770s, British manufacturers had built spinning mills in which steam-powered machines spun raw cotton into yarn. Eager to maintain their monopoly on industrial technology, the British made it illegal for engineers to emigrate. However, they could not stop everyone who worked in a cotton mill from leaving.

At age fourteen, Samuel Slater was hired as an apprentice in an English mill that used a yarn-spinning machine designed by Richard Arkwright. Slater was promoted to supervisor of the factory, but at age twenty-one he disguised himself as a poor farmer and emigrated to America. While working in New York City, he learned that Moses Brown, a wealthy Rhode Island merchant, was eager to develop a machine like Arkwright's. Funded by Rhode Island investors and assisted by local craftsmen, Slater designed and built a spinning mill in Pawtucket.

The mill opened in December 1790 and began producing yarn, which was then woven into cloth in private shops and homes, a process known as "putting out." By 1815, a series of cotton mills dotted the Pawtucket River. These factories offered workers, most of whom were the wives and children of farmers, a steady income, and they ensured employment for weavers in the countryside. They also increased the demand for cotton in New England just as British manufacturers sought new sources of the crop as well.

Ensuring a steady supply of cotton required another technological innovation, this one created by Eli Whitney. After graduating from Yale, Whitney agreed to serve as a private tutor for a planter family in South Carolina. On the ship carrying him south, Whitney met the widow Catherine Greene, who invited him to stay at her Mulberry Plantation near Savannah, Georgia. There, local planters complained to him about the difficulty of making a profit on cotton. Long-staple cotton, grown in the Sea Islands, yielded enormous profits, but the soil in most of the South could sustain only the short-staple variety, which required hours of intensive labor to separate its sticky green seeds from the cotton fiber.

In 1793, in as little as ten days, Whitney built a machine that could speed the process of removing seeds from short-staple cotton. Using mesh screens, rollers, and wire brushes, Whitney's **cotton gin** could clean as much cotton fiber in one hour as several workers could clean in a day. Recognizing the gin's value, Whitney received a U.S. patent, but because the machine was easy to duplicate, he never profited from his invention.

cotton gin
A machine invented by Eli Whitney in 1793 to remove seeds from short-staple cotton. The cotton gin dramatically reduced the time and labor involved in deseeding, facilitating the expansion of cotton production in the South and West.

However, Whitney had other ideas that proved more profitable. In June 1798, amid U.S. fears of a war with France, the U.S. government granted him an extraordinary contract to produce 4,000 rifles in eighteen months. Expanding on the work of Honoré Blanc, a French gunsmith who had devised a musket with interchangeable parts, Whitney demonstrated the potential for using machines to produce various parts of a musket, which could then be assembled in large quantities. With Jefferson's enthusiastic support, the federal government extended Whitney's contract, and by 1809 his New Haven factory was turning out 7,500 guns annually.

Whitney's factory became a model for the **American system of manufacturing**, in which water-powered machinery and the division of production into several small tasks allowed less skilled workers to produce large quantities of a particular item. Moreover, the factories developed by Whitney and Slater became training grounds for younger mechanics and inventors who devised improvements in machinery or set out to solve new technological puzzles. Their efforts also transformed the lives of generations of workers—enslaved and free—who planted and picked the cotton, spun the yarn, wove the cloth, and sewed the clothes that cotton gins and spinning mills made possible.

American system of manufacturing
Manufacturing methods that emphasized mechanization, waterpower, division of labor, and the use of interchangeable parts. The introduction of the American system in the early nineteenth century greatly reduced the number of artisans and small shops but, through standardization, increased the productivity of American manufacturing.

REVIEW

- How did Eli Whitney's cotton gin and factory production of interchangeable parts affect the early nineteenth-century American economy?

Transforming Domestic Production

Slater and Whitney were among the most influential American inventors, but both required the assistance and collaboration of other inventors, machinists, and artisans to implement their ideas. The achievement of these enterprising individuals was seen by many Americans as part of a larger spirit of inventiveness and technological ingenuity that characterized Americans. Although many Americans built on foreign ideas and models, a cascade of inventions appeared in the United States during the early nineteenth century.

Cotton gins and steam engines, steamboats and interchangeable parts, gristmills and spinning mills, clocks and woodworking lathes—each of these items and processes was improved over time and led to myriad other inventions. For instance, in 1811, Francis Cabot invented a power loom for weaving, a necessary step once spinning mills began producing more yarn than hand weavers could handle. Eventually, clocks would be used to routinize the labor of workers in those mills so that they all arrived, ate lunch, and left at the same times.

Despite these rapid technological advances, the changes that occurred in the early nineteenth century were more evolutionary than revolutionary. Most political leaders and social commentators viewed gradual improvement as a blessing. For many Americans, the ideal situation consisted of either small mills scattered through the countryside or household enterprises that could supply neighbors with finer cloth, wool cards, sturdier chairs, or other items that improved household comfort and productivity.

The importance of domestic manufacturing increased after the passage of the Embargo Act, as imports of cloth and other items fell dramatically. Small factories, like those along the Pawtucket River, increased their output, and so did women, often wives and daughters in farming families, who undertook this work to supplement family income. Blacksmiths, carpenters, and wheelwrights busily repaired and improved the spindles, looms, and other equipment that allowed family members to produce more and better cloth from wool, flax, and cotton.

These developments allowed some Americans, especially in towns and cities, to achieve a middling status between poorer laborers and wealthier elites. In this middling sector of society, new ideas about companionate marriage, which emphasized mutual obligations, may have encouraged husbands and wives to work more closely in domestic enterprises. While husbands generally carried out the heavier parts of home manufacturing, wives and daughters spun yarn and sewed together sections of cloth into finished goods. In this way, women remained critical to the production of household items. For example, in early nineteenth-century Hallowell, Maine, Martha Ballard labored alongside her daughters and a niece, producing cloth and food for domestic consumption, while she supplemented her husband's income as a surveyor by working as a midwife.

In wealthy households north and south, servants and enslaved people took on a greater share of domestic labor in the late eighteenth and early nineteenth centuries. Most female servants in the North were young and unmarried. Some arrived with children in tow or became pregnant while on the job.

Planters' wives in the South had fewer worries in this regard because if enslaved women became pregnant, their children added to the slaveholder's labor supply. Moreover, on larger plantations, slaveholders increasingly assigned a few enslaved women to spin, cook, wash clothes, make candles, and wait tables. Wives of male plantation owners might also hire the wives of small farmers and landless laborers to spin cotton into yarn, weave yarn into cloth, and sew clothing for members of the household, both enslaved and free. While mistresses, the wives of the head of household, in both regions still engaged in household production, they expanded their roles as domestic managers.

However, most Americans at the turn of the nineteenth century continued to live on family farms, producing or trading locally to meet their needs, using techniques handed down for generations. Yet by 1820, their lives, like those of wealthier Americans, were transformed by the expanding economy. Gradually, more and more families would sew clothes with machine-spun thread made from cotton ginned in the American South, work their fields with newly invented cast-iron plows, and vary their diet by adding items shipped from other regions by steamboat.

- How did technological advances in the early 1800s affect the lives of Americans?
- How did those effects differ for Americans of different races and social classes?

Technology, Cotton, and Enslavement

Some of the most dramatic technological changes occurred in agriculture. None was more significant than the cotton gin, which had led to vast expansion of agricultural production and slavery in the South. This in turn fueled regional specialization, with each area specializing in farm commodities or manufactured goods in which they held a cost advantage. As a result, residents in one area of the nation—the North, South, or West—depended on those in other areas. Southern planters relied on a growing demand for cotton from northern merchants and manufacturers. At the same time, planters, merchants, manufacturers, and factory workers became more dependent on western farmers to produce grain and livestock to feed the nation.

As cotton gins spread across the South, cotton and slavery expanded into the interior of many southern states as well as into the lower Mississippi valley. While rice and sugar were also produced in the South, cotton quickly became the most important crop. By 1800, southern farms and plantations produced about 73,000 bales of cotton per year, each weighing about 300 pounds. By 1820, with the aid of the cotton gin, the South produced more than 330,000 bales annually.

For southern Black people, increased production meant increased burdens. Because seeds could be separated from raw cotton with much greater efficiency, farmers could plant substantially larger quantities of the crop. Although family members, neighbors, and hired hands performed this work on small farms with only a few or no enslaved people, wealthy planters, with perhaps a dozen enslaved laborers, took advantage of rising cotton prices in the early eighteenth century to purchase more enslaved labor.

The dramatic increase in the amount of cotton planted and harvested each year was paralleled by a jump in the numbers of the enslaved population. Thus, even as northern states began to abolish the institution, southern plantation owners significantly increased the number of enslaved people they held. In 1800, there were roughly 900,000 enslaved people in the United States. By 1850, there were nearly 3.2 million. Despite this population increase, growing competition for field hands drove up the price of enslaved people, which roughly doubled between 1795 and 1805.

Year	Production in Bales	Year	Production in Bales
1790	3,135	1815	208,986
1795	16,719	1820	334,378
1800	73,145	1825	532,915
1805	146,290	1830	731,452
1810	177,638		

Growth of Cotton Production in the United States, 1790–1830

What technological advancements in the North and South led to the changes in U.S. cotton production shown in this table?

Data from Lewis Cecil Gray, *History of Agriculture in the Southern United States to 1860*, vol. 2 (Gloucester, MA: Peter Smith, 1958).

Although the international slave trade was banned in the United States in 1808, some planters smuggled in women and men from Africa and the Caribbean. Most planters, however, depended on enslaved women to bear more children, increasing the size of their labor force through natural reproduction. In addition, planters in the Deep South—from Georgia and the Carolinas west to Louisiana—began buying enslaved people from farmers in Maryland and Virginia, where cotton and slavery were less profitable. Expanding slave markets in New Orleans and Charleston showed the continued importance of this domestic or internal slave trade as cotton moved west.

In the early nineteenth century, most white Southerners believed there was enough land to go around. The rising price of cotton allowed small farmers to imagine they would someday be planters.

Certain southern American Indians also placed their hopes in cotton. Cherokee and Creek Indians cultivated the crop, even purchasing enslaved Blacks to increase production. Some villages now welcomed ministers to their communities, hoping that embracing white culture might allow them to retain their current lands. Yet other native residents foresaw the increased pressure for land that cotton cultivation produced and organized to defend themselves from the further loss of territory. Regardless of the policies adopted by American Indians, cotton and slavery expanded rapidly into Cherokee- and Creek-controlled lands in the interior of Georgia and South Carolina.

The admission of the states of Louisiana, Mississippi, and Alabama between 1812 and 1819 marked the rapid spread of southern agriculture farther west. Enslaved men and women played critical roles in the South's geographical expansion. Without their labor, neither cotton nor sugar could have become mainstays of the South's economy. The heavy work of clearing the land for new plantations led most planters to select young enslaved men and women to move west, breaking apart families in the process. Some enslaved people resisted their removal and, if forced to go, used their role in the labor process to limit slaveholders' control by working slowly, covertly breaking tools, and feigning illness or injury. Other enslaved women and men hid out temporarily as a respite from brutal work regimes or harsh punishments. Still others fled to areas controlled by American Indians, hoping for better treatment, or to regions where slavery was no longer legal.

AP® WORKING with EVIDENCE

Source: Harriet Jacobs, *Incidents in the Life of a Slave Girl*, 1861

"But I now entered on my fifteenth year [1828]—a sad epoch in the life of a slave girl. My master began to whisper foul words in my ear. Young as I was, I could not remain ignorant of their import. I tried to treat them with indifference or contempt. . . . I turned from him with disgust and hatred. But he was my master. I was compelled to live under the same roof with him—where I saw a man forty years my senior daily violating the most sacred commandments of nature. He told me I was his property; that I must be subject to his will in all things. My soul revolted against the mean tyranny. But where could I turn for protection? . . . [T]here is no shadow of law to protect . . . from insult, from violence, or even from death; all these are inflicted by fiends who bear the shape of men. The mistress, who ought to protect the helpless victim, has no other feelings towards her but those of jealousy and rage. . . .

Even the little child . . . before she is twelve years old . . . will become prematurely knowing in evil things. Soon she will learn to tremble when she hears her master's footfall. She will be compelled to realize that she is no longer a child. If God has bestowed beauty upon her, it will prove her greatest curse. That which commands admiration in the white woman only hastens the degradation of the female slave."

Questions for Analysis

1. Describe the perils faced by young enslaved women such as Harriet Jacobs.
2. Explain how this document reflects the ways in which slavery negatively affected southern society.
3. Explain how the expansion of American slavery during the early nineteenth century contributed to the dynamic Jacobs describes in this document.

Given the power and resources wielded by whites, most enslaved people had to find ways to improve their lives within the system of bondage. The end of the international slave trade helped Black people in this regard because planters had to depend more on natural reproduction to increase their labor supply. To ensure that enslaved people lived longer and healthier lives, planters were forced to provide better food, shelter, and clothing. Some enslaved people gained the leverage to fish, hunt, or maintain small gardens to improve their diet.

With the birth of more children, southern Black people also developed more extensive kinship networks, which often allowed other family members to care for children if their parents were compelled to move west. Enslavement was still brutal, but enslaved people made small gains that improved their chances of survival.

To find release from the oppressive burdens of daily life, enslaved people not only joined camp meetings and religious revivals that swept the South in the late eighteenth and early nineteenth centuries, but they also established their own religious ceremonies. These were often held in the woods or swamps at night, away from the prying eyes of planters and overseers.

Evangelical religion, combined with revolutionary ideals promoted in the United States and Haiti, proved a potent mix. Planters rarely lost sight of the potential dangers this posed to the system of bondage. Outright rebellions occurred only rarely, yet the Haitian Revolution and Gabriel's conspiracy in Virginia reminded enslaved people and slaveholders alike that uprisings were possible. Clearly, the power of new American identities could not be separated from the dangers embedded in the nation's oppressive racial history.

- What led to the spread of slavery in the South?
- How did enslaved people resist enslavement?

Factory Towns and Women Workers

In the late 1820s, investors and manufacturers joined forces to create factory towns in the New England countryside. The most famous mill town, Lowell, Massachusetts, was based on an earlier experiment in nearby Waltham. In the Waltham system, every step of the production process was mechanized; and planned communities included factories, boardinghouses, government offices, and churches. Agents for the Waltham system recruited the daughters of New England farm families as workers, assuring parents that they would be watched over by managers and foremen as well as landladies.

The young women were required to attend church and observe curfews, and their labor was regulated by clocks and bells to ensure discipline and productivity.

Farm families needed more cash because of the growing market economy, and daughters in the mills could contribute to family finances and save money for the clothes and linens required for married life. Factory jobs also provided an alternative to marriage, as young New England men moved west and left a surplus of women behind. Boardinghouses provided a relatively safe, all-female environment for the young mill workers, and sisters and neighbors often lived together. Despite nearly constant supervision, many rural women viewed factory work as an adventure. They could set aside a bit of money for themselves, attend lectures and concerts, meet new people, and acquire a wider view of the world.

During the 1830s, however, working conditions began to deteriorate. Factory owners cut wages, lengthened hours, and sped up machines. Boardinghouses became overcrowded, and company officials regulated both rents and expenses so that higher prices for lodging did not necessarily mean better food or furnishings.

Factory workers launched numerous strikes in the 1830s against longer hours, wage cuts, and speedups in factory production. The solidarity required to sustain these strikes was forged in boardinghouses and at church socials as well as on the factory floor. At age twelve, Harriet Robinson led a walkout at the Lowell mills in 1836. In her memoir, written in 1898, she noted, "As I looked back at the long line that followed me, I was more proud than I have ever been since at any success I have achieved."

AP® WORKING with EVIDENCE

Source: Harriet H. Robinson, *Loom and Spindle or Life among the Early Mill Girls*, 1898

"In 1831 Lowell was little more than a factory village. Several corporations were started, and the cotton-mills belonging to them were building. Help was in great demand; and stories were told all over the country of the new factory town, and the high wages that were offered to all classes of work-people,—stories that reached the ears of mechanics' and farmers' sons, and gave new life to lonely and dependent women in distant towns and farmhouses. . . .

Troops of young girls came by stages and baggage-wagons, men often being employed to go to other States and to Canada, to collect them at so much a head, and deliver them at the factories. . . .

I worked first in the spinning-room as a 'doffer.' The doffers were the very youngest girls, whose work was to doff, or take off, the full bobbins, and replace them with the empty ones. . . .

These mites had to be very swift in their movements, so as not to keep the spinning-frames stopped long, and they worked only about fifteen minutes in every hour. The rest of the time was their own, and when the overseer was kind they were allowed to read, knit, or go outside the mill-yard to play. . . .

The working-hours of all the girls extended from five o'clock in the morning until seven in the evening, with one-half hour for breakfast and dinner. Even the doffers were forced to be on duty nearly fourteen hours a day, and this was the greatest hardship in the lives of these children. For it was not until 1842 that the hours of labor for children under twelve years of age were limited to ten per day; but the 'ten-hour law' itself was not passed until long after some of these little doffers were old enough to appear before the legislative committee on the subject, and plead, by their presence, for a reduction of the hours of labor."

Questions for Analysis

1. Describe the effect the Lowell mills had on the surrounding community, according to Robinson.
2. Describe Robinson's attitude toward the experience of working in the mills.
3. Explain how the Lowell mills exploited female labor.

Despite mill workers' solidarity, it was difficult to overcome the economic power wielded by manufacturers. Working women's efforts at collective action were generally short-lived, lasting only until a strike was settled. Then employees returned to their jobs until the next crisis hit. As competition increasingly cut into profits, owners resisted mill workers' demands more vehemently. When the Panic of 1837 intensified fears of job loss, women's organizing activities were doomed until the economy recovered.

REVIEW

- What aspects of the Waltham–Lowell system did farm families and young women initially find attractive?
- How did the Waltham–Lowell system exploit the workers in its factories?

The Decline of Craft Work

While the construction of factory towns expanded economic opportunities for young women, the gradual decline of time-honored crafts narrowed the prospects for workingmen. Craft workshops gradually increased in size yet hired fewer skilled workers and more men who performed single tasks, like attaching soles to shoes. Many tasks also became mechanized during the nineteenth century. The final product was less distinctive than an entire item crafted by a skilled artisan, but it was less expensive and available in large quantities.

The shift from craft work to factory work threatened to undermine workingmen's skills, pay, and labor conditions. Masters began hiring foremen to regulate the workforce and installing bells and clocks to regulate the workday. As this process of **deskilling** transformed shoemaking, printing, tailoring, and other trades, laboring men fought to maintain their status.

Some workers formed **mutual-aid societies** to provide assistance in times of illness, injury, or unemployment. Others participated in religious revivals or joined fraternal orders to find the camaraderie they once enjoyed at work.

The expansion of voting rights in the 1820s offered another avenue for action. The first workingmen's political party was founded in Philadelphia in 1827, and working-class men in the North joined forces to support politicians sympathetic to their needs. Most workingmen's parties focused on practical proposals: government distribution of free land in the West, ending compulsory militia service and imprisonment for debt, public funding for education, and regulations on banks and corporations. Although the electoral success of these parties was modest, the major political parties of the 1830s—the Democrats and the Whigs—adopted many of their proposals.

Workingmen also formed **unions** to demand better wages and working conditions. In the 1820s and 1830s, skilled journeymen held mass meetings to protest employers' efforts to lengthen the workday, merge smaller workshops into larger factories, and cut wages. In New York City in 1834, labor activists formed a citywide federation, the General Trades Union, which provided support for striking workers. The National

deskilling
The replacement of skilled labor with unskilled labor and machines.

mutual-aid society
An organization formed by laborers to care for members who were unemployed, ill, or injured and unable to work. Such organizations required dues from their members, and these dues were used to care for those who could no longer work and for their families. Before unemployment insurance and health care, mutual-aid societies helped workers survive changes in the new industrial economy.

union
A group of organized allied workers seeking rights and benefits from their employers through collective efforts. By collectively bargaining, workers may negotiate with employers with more strength than the individual worker.

Trades Union was established later that year, with delegates representing more than 25,000 workers across the North. These organizations aided skilled workers but refused admission to women and unskilled men.

It proved difficult to establish broader labor organizations, however. Most skilled workers considered unskilled workers as competitors, not allies. Many workingmen feared women workers would undercut their wages and so refused to organize alongside them. Anti-immigrant and racist beliefs among many native-born Protestant workers interfered with organizing across racial and ethnic lines. With the onset of the Panic of 1837, the common plight of workers became clearer. Yet the economic crisis made unified action nearly impossible, as individuals sought to hold on to what little they had.

REVIEW

- How did workingmen respond to the decline of craft work, and what limited the success of their responses?
- What factors limited the success of workers' unions during the early 1800s?

The Panic of 1837

Panic of 1837

The Panic of 1837 started in the South and was rooted in a collapsing land and cotton market, as American cotton prices plummeted. The panic resulted in mass unemployment, bankruptcy, deflation, and discontent.

boom–bust cycle

An economic cycle where strong national economic growth is often ended by a sudden fall in prices, often called a "panic," and followed by a long economic contraction and high unemployment. Boom–bust cycles continued throughout the nineteenth and twentieth centuries in the United States.

The **Panic of 1837** began in the South but hit northern cotton merchants hard (see "Van Buren and the Panic of 1837" in Module 4.8). As a result, cotton shipments were sharply curtailed by planters, textile factories drastically cut production, unemployment rose, and merchants and investors went broke. This panic, after a number of years of prosperity, begin a cycle of economic "busts," or recessions, that often followed an extended period of "booms," or economic expansion and prosperity. This **boom–bust cycle** continued throughout the nineteenth and twentieth centuries in the United States. After the Panic of 1837, those still employed saw their wages cut in half. Petty crime, prostitution, and violence also rose as men and women struggled to make ends meet.

In factories across the country, hours increased and wages fell. Just as important, the process of deskilling intensified. Factory owners considered mechanization one way to improve their economic situation. A cascade of inventions, including power looms, steam boilers, and the steam press, transformed industrial occupations and led factory owners to invest more of their limited resources in machines. At the same time, the rising tide of immigrants provided a ready supply of relatively cheap labor. Artisans tried to maintain their traditional skills and status, but in many trades, they were fighting a losing battle.

By the early 1840s, when the panic subsided, new technologies did spur new jobs. Factories demanded more workers to handle machines that ran at a faster pace. In printing, the steam press allowed publication of more newspapers and magazines, creating positions for editors, publishers, printers, engravers, reporters, and sales agents. Similarly, mechanical reapers sped the harvest of wheat and led to changes in flour milling that required engineers to design machines and mechanics to build and repair them.

These changing circumstances fueled new labor organizations as well. Many of these unions comprised a particular trade or ethnic group, and almost all continued to address mainly the needs of skilled male workers. Textile operatives remained the one important group of organized female workers. In the 1840s, workingwomen joined with workingmen in New England to fight for a ten-hour day. Slowly, however, farmers' daughters left the mills as desperate Irish immigrants flooded in and accepted lower wages.

For most women in need, charitable organizations offered more support than unions. Organizations like Philadelphia's Female Association for the Relief of Women and Children in Reduced Circumstances provided a safety net for many poor families because public monies for such purposes were limited. Although most northern towns and cities now provided some form of public assistance, they never had sufficient resources to meet local needs in good times, much less the extraordinary demands posed by the panic.

REVIEW

- What were the immediate and longer-term effects of the Panic of 1837 on the North?

AP® Skills Workshop: Thinking Historically

Using Outside Evidence to Create a Body Paragraph

As you learned in Period 3, body paragraphs are the core of a good AP® U.S. History essay. Module 3.5 showed you that good body paragraphs make **arguments**, while Modules 3.8/3.9 and 3.13 discussed how **claims in sources** and **making connections** are key elements of your body paragraphs. Review those AP® Thinking Historically and Writing Historically exercises to refresh your memory of these hallmarks of body paragraphs.

Now we're going to build a body paragraph that makes an argument by using sources and makes connections, all while applying the **CSE** (Claim, Support, Explain) approach.

Even though every body paragraph makes an argument, each body paragraph is part of an essay's overall argument, the thesis. So, to write a proper body paragraph, you must first know your essay's overall thesis. (For a review of thesis writing, see the AP® Thinking Historically exercise at the end of Module 3.2 and the AP® Writing Historically exercise at the end of Module 3.6.)

Let's start with a question, and then look at a sample thesis:

> Evaluate the extent to which the market revolution lead to better working lives for laborers in the United States between 1820 and 1840.

A decent thesis that responds to this question could look like this:

> The market revolution improved the lives of workers by providing jobs with wages, even for women **[claim]**. However, the market revolution's most lasting effects were the difficult working conditions endured in factories and the acceleration of a cycle of prosperity and recession, a boom-bust cycle, that led to high unemployment and depressed wages during economic downturns **[line of reasoning]**.

This thesis contains three **sub-arguments**:

(A) The market revolution provided jobs with wages, including for women.
(B) The market revolution created difficult working conditions.
(C) The market revolution accelerated the boom–bust economic cycle.

Each body paragraph in an essay should focus on **one** of these sub-arguments and prove it by making connections between primary source evidence and factual support using the **CSE** approach.

(continued)

Let's say you wanted to create a body paragraph using the first sub-argument of the thesis,

The market revolution provided jobs with wages, including for women.

To build a body paragraph to prove this sub-argument, you would follow these steps:

1. Start the body paragraph by restating the sub-argument in a more focused fashion (see the example below).
2. Claim that two to three pieces of evidence, from sources or the historical record, prove this sub-argument. **CSE** each of these pieces of evidence separately so the reader knows how each claim is supported by evidence. Each of these pieces of evidence can be separated with a transition word (connecting word or phrase) such as "For example . . ." "Furthermore . . ." "Additionally . . ." etc.
3. Summarize the paragraph by explaining how it proves the sub-argument.

Here's an example of a body paragraph for the sub-argument, "The market revolution provided jobs with wages, including for women."

The market revolution created jobs that paid wages, and this provided income for laborers, including women, who were often excluded from wage work before this period **[sub-argument].** For example **[transition word]**, starting in the 1820s, the textile factories in Lowell, Massachusetts, typically hired women to work for wages **[claim]**. While these wages were not substantial enough for these women to achieve financial independence, they did provide some economic freedom **[support]**. These women likely would not have had the opportunity to work for wages before the market revolution **[explain]**. Furthermore **[transition word]**, Harriet Robinson recalled that the relatively high wages paid to the working women and girls in Lowell were known throughout the countryside **[claim]**. The spread of this information encouraged farm families to send their daughters to work in the mills for additional wages, which supplemented family income **[support]**. In this way **[transition word]**, wage work also transformed the life of laborers in the countryside who had daughters who went to work in the mills, thus enhancing the income of agricultural laborers who did not traditionally earn wages **[explain]**. In sum **[transition word]**, the wage work stimulated by the market revolution transformed the economic lives of both the women who worked in the textile mills, and their agricultural families back home **[summary that explains how the claims prove the sub-argument]**.

Notice how this body paragraph uses both facts from the historical record (textile factories, Lowell, women earning wages) and a primary source (Harriet Robinson). Also notice how you should apply the **CSE** approach when analyzing both historical facts and primary sources to prove your sub-argument.

ACTIVITY

Now write a body paragraph on your own using a different **sub-argument** from the thesis above. Remember, your body paragraph should start with a more focused statement of the sub-argument you choose. Then, your body paragraph should **CSE** two to three pieces of historical information to prove that **sub-argument**. And then the body paragraph should conclude with a summary sentence that explains how the paragraph proves the sub-argument.

Here are the other two **sub-arguments** from the thesis above:

1. The market revolution created difficult working conditions.
2. The market revolution accelerated the boom–bust economic cycle.

Market Revolution: Society and Culture

MODULE 4.6

FOCUS

The shift to industrialization and an integrated national economy during the market revolution fostered urbanization, which, in turn, reinforced economic growth and innovation. However, it also created social upheaval. Cultural divisions intensified in urban areas where Catholics and Protestants, workers and the well-to-do, immigrants, Blacks, and native-born whites lived side by side. Class dynamics also changed with the development of a defined middle class of shopkeepers, professionals, and clerks.

While reading this module, consider the causes of increased class distinctions as rising prosperity benefited the business elite and led to the growth of both the middle class and the working poor. Also note how middle- and upper-class women's roles changed, with a growing societal emphasis on domesticity. Compare how the market revolution shaped class, ethnic, and religious groups in similar and different ways.

The Lure of Urban Life

As transportation improved and the economy expanded, cities across the North increased not only in size but also in diversity. During the 1820s, some 150,000 European immigrants entered the United States; during the 1830s, nearly 600,000; and during the 1840s, more than 1,700,000. This surge of immigrants included more Irish and German settlers than ever before, as well as large numbers of Scandinavians.

Many settled along the eastern seaboard. Others migrated west, including thousands of Irish immigrants who labored in difficult and dangerous conditions to build the Erie Canal. Many Irish workers eventually settled in local communities along the canal's route. Others added to the growth of western cities such as Cincinnati, St. Louis, and Chicago.

Late-eighteenth-century Irish immigrants, many of whom were Protestants, were joined by hundreds of thousands more in the 1830s and 1840s, when Irish Catholics poured into the United States. The Irish countryside was then plagued by bad weather, a potato blight, and harsh economic policies imposed by the British government. From 1845 to 1846, a famine forced hundreds of thousands more Irish Catholic families to emigrate. Young Irish women, who could easily find work as domestics or seamstresses, emigrated in especially large numbers.

Mass immigration was not limited to the Irish, however, as poor harvests, droughts, failed revolutions, and repressive landlords convinced large numbers of Germans, including Catholics, Lutherans, and Jews, as well as Scandinavians, to flee their homelands as well. By 1850, the Irish made up about 40 percent of immigrants to the United States, and Germans nearly a quarter.

These immigrants provided an expanding pool of cheap labor as well as skilled artisans who further fueled northern commerce and industry. This period also saw

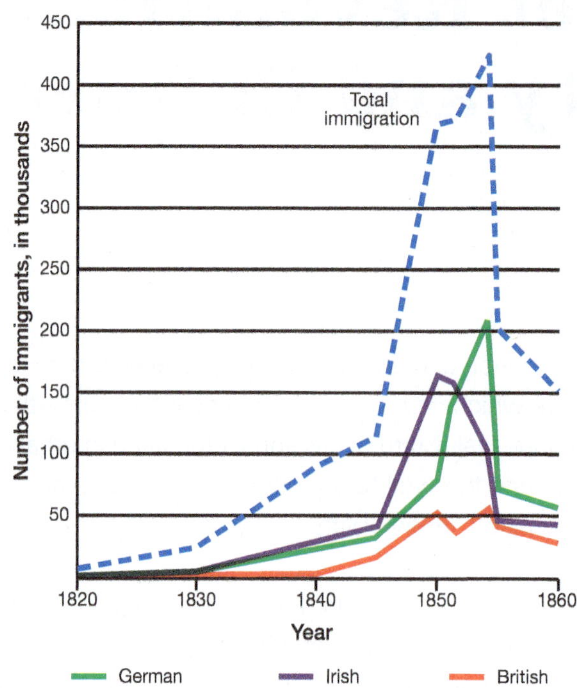

Immigration to the United States, 1820–1860
Famine, economic upheaval, and political persecution led masses of people from Ireland, Germany, and Britain to migrate to the United States from the 1820s through the 1850s. The vast majority settled in cities and factory towns in the North or farms in the Midwest. An economic recession in the late 1850s finally slowed immigration, though only temporarily.

How did the changes in German and Irish immigration shown in this graph change urban life in nineteenth-century America?

AP® EXAM TIP

In conjunction with the first industrial revolution and building of roads and canals, large numbers of immigrants—mostly Irish and Germans—arrived. The Irish provided cheap labor in the factories, while the Germans generally moved to western regions often to practice agriculture. Class structures (laboring poor, larger middle, and wealthy elite) developed during the antebellum decades. Be able to describe the effects of the market revolution on both society and the family, because the AP® Exam often asks how these changed over the first half of the nineteenth century.

the expansion of banks, mercantile houses, and dry-goods stores, which sold tools and household necessities that had a long shelf life. Urban industrial enterprises included both traditional workshops and mechanized factories. Credit and insurance agencies emerged to aid entrepreneurs in their ventures.

The increase in business also drove the demand for ships, commercial newspapers, warehouses, and other commercial necessities, which created a surge in jobs for many urban residents. Instead of depending upon semi-subsistence farming as many Americans before them had, these workers earned wages producing goods for export to the rest of the nation and the world, and used these wages to supply their daily needs.

Businesses focused on leisure also flourished. In the 1830s, theater became affordable to working-class families, who often attended comedies, musical revues, and morality plays. They also joined middle- and upper-class audiences at productions of Shakespeare and contemporary dramas. Minstrel shows mocked self-important capitalists but also portrayed Black people in crude caricatures. One of the most popular characters was Jim Crow, who appeared originally in a Black American song. In the 1820s, he was incorporated into a song-and-dance routine by Thomas Rice, a white performer who blacked his face with burnt cork.

The lures of urban life were especially attractive to the young. Single men and women and newly married couples flocked to cities. By 1850, half the residents of New York, Philadelphia, and other seaport cities were under sixteen years of age. Young men sought work in factories, construction, and the maritime trades or in banks and commercial houses, while young women competed for jobs as seamstresses and domestic servants.

REVIEW

- How did increased immigration to the United States during the first half of the nineteenth century change city life?

Immigrants in the Cities

While immigrant labor stimulated northern economic growth, immigrant families transformed the urban landscape. They crowded into houses and apartments and built ethnic institutions, including synagogues and convents—visible indicators of the growing diversity of northern cities.

While most native-born Protestants applauded economic growth, cultural diversity aroused anxieties. Anti-Catholicism and antisemitism flourished in the 1830s and 1840s. Crude stereotypes portrayed Jews as manipulative moneylenders and Catholic nuns and priests as sexually depraved. Ethnic groups also battled stereotypes. Irishmen, for example, were often pictured as habitual drunkards.

Still, rising immigration did not deter rural Americans from seeking economic opportunities in the city. Native-born white men often set out on their own, but most white women settled in cities under the supervision of a husband, landlady, or employer. Blacks, too, sought greater opportunities in urban areas. In the 1830s, Philadelphia's vibrant Black community grew, as people were attracted by its churches, schools, and mutual-aid societies. New Bedford, Massachusetts, a thriving center for whaling, recruited Black workers and thus attracted enslaved people who had fled the South as well.

Yet even as cities welcomed many migrants and immigrants, newcomers also faced dangers. Racial and ethnic minorities regularly faced discrimination and hostility. Physical battles erupted between immigrant and native-born residents, Protestant and Catholic gangs, and white and Black workers. Criminal activity flourished as well, and disease spread quickly through densely populated neighborhoods. When innovations in transportation made it possible for more affluent residents to distance themselves from crowded inner cities, they moved to less congested neighborhoods on the outer edge of cities. Horse-drawn streetcar lines, first built in New York City in 1832, hastened this development.

By the 1840s, economic competition intensified, fueling violence among those driven to the margins. Racism and resentment from native-born white employers and workers pushed Irish immigrants to the bottom of the economic ladder, where they competed with Black Americans. Yet Irish workers insisted that their whiteness gave them a higher status than even the most skilled Black laborers. When Black reformers protested against alcohol consumption and organized a parade in Philadelphia in August 1842, white onlookers—mostly Irish laborers—attacked the marchers, and the conflict escalated into a riot.

Americans who lived in small towns and rural areas regularly read news of urban violence and vice. Improvements in printing created vastly more and cheaper newspapers, while the construction of the first telegraph in 1844 ensured that news could travel more quickly from town to town. The penny press, mass-produced newspapers sold cheaply on the street, lured readers with sensational stories of crime, sex, and scandal. Even more respectable newspapers reported on urban mayhem, and religious periodicals warned churchgoers against urban immorality. In response to both a real and a perceived increase in crime, cities replaced voluntary night watchmen with paid police forces.

- What challenges did urban residents in the United States face during the first half of the nineteenth century?

The New Middle Class

Members of the emerging middle class, which developed first in the North, included ambitious businessmen, successful shopkeepers, doctors, and lawyers as well as teachers, journalists, ministers, and other salaried employees. At the top rungs, successful entrepreneurs and professionals adopted affluent lifestyles. At the lower rungs, a growing cohort of salaried clerks and managers hoped that their hard work, honesty, and thrift would be rewarded with upward mobility.

Education, religious affiliation, and sobriety were important indicators of middle-class status. A well-read man who attended a well-established church and drank in strict moderation was marked as belonging to this new rank. He was also expected to own a comfortable home, marry a pious woman, and raise well-behaved children. The rise of the middle class inspired a flood of advice books, ladies' magazines, religious periodicals, and novels advocating new ideals of womanhood. These publications emphasized the centrality of child rearing and homemaking to women's identities. This **cult of domesticity** ideally restricted wives to home and hearth, where they provided their husbands with a break from the cares and corruptions of the world.

cult of domesticity
New ideals of womanhood that emerged alongside the middle class in the 1830s and 1840s that called for women to remain within the domestic sphere and devote themselves to the care of children, the home, and hardworking husbands in part to promote the moral and spiritual development of their children.

In reality, however, entrance to the middle class required the efforts of wives as well as husbands. While men of the upper middle class were expected to provide financial security, women helped cement social and economic bonds by entertaining the wives of business associates, serving in charitable and reform societies, and organizing Sabbath schools, which met on Sundays, often after church services, and taught young children the reading, writing, and math skills often necessary for admission into primary schools. Families struggling to enter the middle class might take in boarders or extended family members to help secure their financial status.

The adoption of new marital ideals of affection and companionship also made the boundaries between public and domestic life more fluid. Nevertheless, spaces became increasingly separated by gender in middle-class lives during this period, a phenomenon called **separate spheres** by historians.

separate spheres
Widespread belief in the nineteenth century that men and women had separate roles and should occupy separate places in society. According to this belief, men should occupy the social public sphere, while women belonged in the domestic private sphere.

In the middle-class home, for example, the study was often considered the preserve of a husband and father, whereas the parlor and kitchen were the realm of wives and mothers. Likewise, although men increasingly took part in the activities of the household, domestic duties were generally considered a feminine sphere. On the other hand, work and business were perceived as the realm of men. In this light, women's supposedly domestic nature tasked them overwhelmingly with the responsibility of raising children, founded on the assumption that women were naturally more sentimental and inclined to moral uprightness. The worlds of business and politics, where competition reigned, were assumed to be naturally spaces for men.

In many middle-class families, both husbands and wives participated in church, civic, and reform activities, yet many of these activities were divided by gender. Although husbands joined in domestic activities in the evening, presiding over dinner or reading to children, the interaction with the youngest children was often assumed to be the preserve of women.

The ideal of separate spheres of work and home had even less relevance to the millions of women who toiled on farms and factories or as domestic servants, providing goods and services for middle-class, and elite, families. In turn, those middle-class families played a crucial role in the growing market economy and the jobs it created. Wives and daughters were responsible for much of the family's consumption. They purchased cloth, rugs, chairs, clocks, housewares, and, if wealthy enough, European crystal and Chinese porcelain figures. Middling housewives bought goods once made at home, such as butter and candles, and arranged music lessons and other educational opportunities for their children.

Shoe Shopping from *Godey's Lady's Book* In the 1830s and 1840s, women's magazines appeared to promote new ideals of middle-class womanhood and to guide them as consumers. This 1848 image of women shopping for shoes from *Godey's Lady's Book* encouraged female outings to elegant shops. The elaborate and aspirational engravings created by *Godey's* quickly made it the best-selling women's magazine in the United States.

How does this image reflect the social and economic changes that took place during the mid-1800s?

Middle-class women also performed significant domestic labors. While many could afford servants, they often joined their domestic workers and daughters in household tasks. Except for those in the upper-middle class, most women still cut and sewed garments, cultivated gardens, canned fruits and vegetables, cooked at least some meals, and entertained guests. As houses expanded in size and clothes became fancier, domestic servants shouldered the most laborious and time-consuming chores, but many mothers and daughters still performed domestic labor as well. However, such work was increasingly focused inwardly on the family rather than outwardly as part of the market economy.

Middle-class men contributed to the consumer economy by creating and investing in industrial and commercial ventures. Moreover, in carrying out business and professional obligations, many enjoyed restaurants, the theater, or sporting events. Men attended plays and lectures with their wives and visited museums and circuses with their children. They also purchased hats, suits, mustache wax, and other symbols of middle-class masculinity.

AP® WORKING with EVIDENCE

Source: 1850 U.S. Census of the Isaac and Amy Post Household

About the source: In 1850, for the first time, the federal census listed each member of the household by name as well as by age, sex, race (then labeled "color"), and place of birth. Some census takers noted the relationship of each household member to the family head. This census taker did not, nor did he note color. That information appears in brackets and comes from other genealogical records.

Names of Residents in Household	Relation to Head of Household	Age/Sex/Color*	Occupation for Males over 15 Years	Place of Birth
Isaac Post	[head]	50 / male / [white]	Druggist	New York
Amy Post	[wife]	45** / female / [white]		New York
Jacob K. Post	[son]	20 / male / [white]	Clerk	New York
Joseph Post	[son]	16 / male / [white]	Clerk	New York
Willet Post	[son]	3 / male / [white]		New York
Sarah Hallowell	[sister-in-law]	30 / female / [white]		New York
Ansel Bowen	[boarder]	28 / male / [white]	Teacher	New York
Elizabeth Bowen	[boarder]	28 / female / [white]		New York
Bridget Head	[servant]	23 / female / [white]		Ireland
Mary Ann Pitkin	[boarder]	10 / female / [Black]		New York

Data from Seventh U.S. Federal Census, 1st Ward, Rochester, NY, 2 August 1850.

*The options for "color" in the 1850 Census were white, Black, and "mulatto." The bracketed information is from the 1855 New York State Census and Rochester city directories.

**Amy Post was 47 in summer 1850, not 45.

Questions for Analysis

1. Identify the occupations of the men and the number of families represented in this household.
2. Describe the relationships among the women in this household and the work they likely performed.
3. Evaluate the extent to which the families represented in this household conformed to ideals of the middle-class American family during the mid-1800s.

REVIEW

- What values and beliefs did the new middle class embrace?
- What factors shaped the lives of mid-1800s middle-class men and women, and how did their experiences differ?

AP® Skills Workshop: Thinking Historically

Linking Primary Sources to Create a Body Paragraph

Historians often take different primary sources and **link** them to support broader arguments. This can be useful when trying to establish a development or process over time (for a review of developments and processes, see Module 2.2).

Consider the two primary sources:

Source: 1850 U.S. Census of the Isaac and Amy Post Household

(continued)

Names of Residents in Household	Relation to Head of Household	Age/Sex/Color*	Occupation for Males over 15 Years	Place of Birth
Isaac Post	[Head]	50 / male / [white]	Druggist	New York
Amy Post	[wife]	45**/ female / [white]		New York
Jacob K. Post	[son]	20 / male / [white]	Clerk	New York
Joseph Post	[son]	16 / male / [white]	Clerk	New York
Willet Post	[son]	3 / male / [white]		New York
Sarah Hallowell	[sister-in-law]	30 / female / [white]		New York
Ansel Bowen	[boarder]	28 / male / [white]	Teacher	New York
Elizabeth Bowen	[boarder]	28 / female / [white]		New York
Bridget Head	[servant]	23 / female / [white]		Ireland
Mary Ann Pitkin	[boarder]	10 / female / [Black]		New York

Data from Seventh U.S. Federal Census, 1st Ward, Rochester, NY, 2 August 1850.

*The options for "color" in the 1850 Census were white, Black, and "mulatto." The bracketed information is from the 1855 New York State Census and Rochester city directories.

**Amy Post was 47 in summer 1850, not 45.

Source: Shoe Shopping from *Godey's Lady's Book* 1848

Archive Photos/Stringer/Getty Images

Both of these primary sources should be familiar to you from this module. The first is from the census records of the Post household in 1850. The second is from *Godey's Lady's Book* (1848), and shows women shoe shopping, likely in an American city. While these sources are two years apart, historians would consider them part of the same era, and, therefore, representative of similar trends during this era.

(continued)

A historian can **link** these two sources to prove a more general **sub-argument** (Module 4.5) using the **CSE** approach. First, the historian needs a thesis (Module 3.2). Here's one that answers a question about the market revolution:

> Evaluate the extent to which the market revolution shaped urban life in the United States between 1800 and 1848.

Thesis: During the early nineteenth century, the market revolution transformed urban life by creating more distinct social classes **[claim]**. While a wage-earning working class often lived on the edge of subsistence, a relatively affluent middle class had enough wealth to purchase small luxuries, and a very wealthy upper class owned much of the means of production **[line of reasoning]**.

You can see here that there are three **sub-arguments** to this thesis, the first about a working class, the second about a middle class, and the third about a wealthy upper class.

Let's take a look at the way in which the historian might create a body paragraph that proves the second sub-argument by linking two primary sources.

> By the second quarter of the nineteenth century, various professions had grown in U.S. cities, which gave rise to a thriving middle class that had enough wealth to buy consumable goods and small luxuries **[sub-argument showing development]**. Many of these middle-class workers had large households supported by professional work and boarders who rented rooms in their large homes **[claim]**. For example **[transition word]**, according to the 1850 census **[citation of source]**, the Post family consisted of a father who was a working professional, in this case a druggist (or pharmacist), his wife, three sons, and a large set of others who lived in the household, including a sister-in-law, three boarders, and a servant **[support]**. Mr. Post clearly had enough income to reside in a large house that could accommodate all of these people, even though three were boarders, who might have paid rent **[explain]**. This new middle-class affluence also allowed family members to consume goods that were made available through new industrial production **[claim]**. For instance **[transition word]**, new publications like *Godey's Lady's Book* were produced on industrial printing presses and purchased by subscription for home delivery. They advertised consumable goods likely also produced by industrial means, as seen in the advertisement for shoe shopping in 1848 **[support and citation of source]**. This kind of consumption would have been available to Mr. and Mrs. Post, her sister, Sarah, who lived with the Posts, and the Posts' three sons, though likely not to the servant or boarders who lived in the Post residence, since they didn't earn middle-class wages **[explain]**. In this regard **[transition word]**, class status during this period shaped the consumption choices and living standards in the Post household, a period when the middle class had increasing purchasing power **[summary of sub-argument]**.

Notice how this paragraph **links** the two primary sources to make a sub-argument about middle-class purchasing power during the market revolution. In this example, the body paragraph links both sources to make a larger point about the development of this class as well as who could consume new, industrially produced luxuries and who could not.

(continued)

ACTIVITY

Create a body paragraph on your own that proves the first sub-argument of the thesis above. Link the two primary sources below to prove the sub-argument. Below is a partially completed graphic organizer to get you started.

The market revolution transformed urban life by

(A) **[sub-argument]** creating a wage-earning working class that often lived on the edge of subsistence

Source: Portion of "Five Points," George Catlin (1827)

About the source: The Five Points District in New York City was a working-class neighborhood that was known for its poverty and crime in the nineteenth century.

Library Company of Philadelphia

Source: *The Rights of Man to Property!* Thomas Skidmore (1829)

> "One thing must be obvious to the plainest understanding; that as long as property is unequal; or rather, as long as it is so enormously unequal, as we see it at present, that those who possess it, *will* live on the labor of others, and themselves perform none . . . or a very disproportionate share[;] they have no *just* right to preserve or retain that existence, even for a single hour."

Sub-argument:	**Primary Source:** Portion of "Five Points," George Catlin (1827)	**Primary Source:** *The Rights of Man to Property!* Thomas Skidmore (1829)
The market revolution transformed urban life by a. **[sub-argument]** creating a wage-earning working class that often lived on the edge of subsistence.	- The Five Points District was working class. - It is crowded, dirty, and full of conflict. - The shops are all basic, offering groceries and other necessities. - There don't appear to be any luxuries sold there.	

MODULE 4.7

Expanding Democracy

FOCUS

This module examines the emergence of America's second political party system—the Democrats and National Republicans, later replaced by the Whigs—during the 1820s and early 1830s.

As you read this module, consider the extent to which the federal policies of the Jeffersonian Era (1790s–1810s) shaped the expansion of democracy during the ensuing decades. What aspects of the first decades of the new Republic's existence shaped the 1820s and 1830s?

With the Panic of 1819 and the debates over Missouri shaking many Americans' faith in their economic and political leaders and the borderlands moving ever westward, the nation was ripe for change. Workingmen, small farmers, and frontier settlers, who had long been locked out of the electoral system by property qualifications and eastern elites, demanded the right to vote. The resulting political movement ensured voting rights for nearly all white men during the 1820s.

Yet Black Americans lost political and civil rights in the same period, and American Indians fared poorly under the federal administrations brought to power by this expanded electorate. While some white women gained greater political influence as a result of the voting rights gained by fathers and husbands, they did not achieve independent political rights. Finally, as a wave of new voters entered the political fray, ongoing conflicts over slavery, tariffs, and the rights of American Indian nations transformed political party alignments.

Voting Rights Expand

Between 1788 and 1820, the U.S. presidency was dominated by Virginia elites and after 1800 by Democratic-Republicans. With little serious political opposition at the national level, few people bothered to vote in presidential elections. Far more people engaged in political activities at the state and local levels. Many towns attracted large audiences to public celebrations on the Fourth of July and election days. Female participants sewed symbols of their partisan loyalties on their clothes and joined in parades and feasts organized by men.

The Panic of 1819 stimulated even more political activity, as laboring men, who were especially vulnerable to economic downturns, demanded the right to vote so they could hold politicians accountable. In New York State, Martin Van Buren, a rising star in the Democratic-Republican Party, led the fight to eliminate property qualifications for voting. At the state constitutional convention of 1821, the committee on suffrage argued that the only qualification for voting should be "the virtue and morality of the people." By the word *people*, Van Buren and the committee meant white men.

Art Collection 3/Alamy

Election Day in Philadelphia, 1815 This engraving, based on a painting by German immigrant John Lewis Krimmel, depicts an election-day celebration in Philadelphia in 1815. The image highlights the widespread popular participation of men, women, and children in political events even before the expansion of voting rights for white men in the 1820s. **What do the bustling scene and presence of American flags in this engraving suggest about popular sentiment toward elections?**

Despite opposition from powerful and wealthy men, by 1825 most states along the Atlantic seaboard had lowered or eliminated property qualifications on white male voters. Meanwhile, states along the borderlands that had joined the Union in the 1810s established universal white male suffrage from the beginning. And by 1824, three-quarters of the states (18 of 24) allowed voters, rather than state legislatures, to elect members of the electoral college in presidential elections.

Yet as white workingmen gained political rights in the 1820s, democracy did not spread to other groups. American Indian nations were considered sovereign entities, so American Indians voted in their own nations, not in U.S. elections. Women were excluded from voting because of their perceived dependence on men. Black men faced increasing restrictions on their political rights. No southern legislature had ever granted Black people the right to vote, and northern states began disfranchising them as well in the 1820s. In many cases, expanded voting rights for white men went hand in hand with new restrictions on Black men. In New York State, for example, the constitution of 1821, which eliminated property qualifications for white men, raised property qualifications for Black voters.

When Black men protested their disfranchisement, some whites spoke out on their behalf. They claimed that denying rights to men who had in no way abused the privilege of voting set "an ominous and dangerous precedent." In response, opponents of Black suffrage offered explicitly racist justifications. Some argued that Black voting would lead to interracial socializing, even marriage. Others feared that Black voters might hold the balance of power in close elections, forcing white civic leaders to give in to their demands. Gradually, racist arguments won the day, and by 1840, 93 percent of free Black people in the North were excluded from voting.

REVIEW

- How and why did voting rights change for white men, women, and Black people in the 1820s?

Racial Restrictions and Antiblack Violence

CLASS No. 1.

Comprises those prisoners who were found guilty and executed.

Prisoners Names.	*Owners' Names.*	*Time of Commit.*	*How Disposed of.*
Peter	James Poyas	June 18	
Ned	Gov. T. Bennett,	do.	Hanged on Tuesday
Rolla	do.	do	the 2d July, 1822,
Batteau	do.	do.	on Blake's lands,
Denmark Vesey	A free black man	22	near Charleston.
Jessy	Thos. Blackwood	23	
John	Elias Horry	July 5	Do. on the Lines near
Gullah Jack	Paul Pritchard	do.	Ch.; Friday July 12.
Mingo	Wm. Harth	June 21	
Lot	Forrester	27	
Joe	P. L. Jore	July 6	
Julius	Thos. Forrest	8	
Tom	Mrs. Russell	10	
Smart	Robt. Anderson	do.	
John	John Robertson	11	
Robert	do.	do.	
Adam	do.	do.	
Polydore	Mrs. Faber	do.	Hanged on the Lines
Bacchus	Benj. Hammet	do.	near Charleston,
Dick	Wm. Sims	13	on Friday, 26th
Pharaoh	— Thompson	do.	July.
Jemmy	Mrs. Clement	18	
Mauidore	Mordecai Cohen	19	
Dean	— Mitchell	do.	
Jack	Mrs. Purcell	12	
Bellisle	Est. of Jos. Yates	18	
Naphur	do.	do.	
Adam	do.	do.	
Jacob	John S. Glen	16	
Charles	John Billings	18	
Jack	N. McNeill	22	
Cæsar	Miss Smith	do.	
Jacob Stagg	Jacob Lankester	23	Do. Tues. July 30.
Tom	Wm. M. Scott	24	
William	Mrs. Garner	Aug. 2	Do. Friday, Aug. 9.

Record of Thirty-Five Men Executed for Conspiring to Revolt against Slaveholders This official record of executions related to an alleged 1822 conspiracy of several enslaved people lists the name of Denmark Vesey, the only free Black man accused, fifth. The enslaved men are listed next to slaveholders' names, including the governor of South Carolina, twenty-one other men, and six women. There were no appeals of their convictions, and the hangings took place quickly.

In what ways does this record reflect the treatment of Black people during this time period?

Restrictions on voting followed other constraints on Black men and women. As early as 1790, Congress limited naturalization (the process of becoming a citizen) to white immigrants. It also excluded Blacks from enrolling in federal militias. In 1820, Congress authorized city officials in Washington, D.C., to adopt a separate legal code governing free and enslaved Black people. This federal legislation encouraged states, in both the North and the South, to add their own restrictions, including the separation of white and Black students in public schools, transportation, and accommodations. Some northern legislatures even denied Black people the right to settle in their state.

In addition, Black people faced mob and state-sanctioned violence across the country. In 1822, officials in Charleston, South Carolina, accused Denmark Vesey, a free Black man, of following the revolutionary leader Toussaint L'Ouverture's lead and plotting a conspiracy to free the city's enslaved inhabitants. Vesey had helped to organize churches, mutual-aid societies, and other Black institutions. His accomplishments were considered threatening to the future of slavery by challenging assumptions about Black inferiority. Vesey may have organized a plan to free enslaved people in the city, but it is also possible that white officials concocted the plot to terrorize Blacks. Despite scant evidence, Vesey and thirty-four of his alleged co-conspirators were found guilty and hanged. The African Methodist Episcopal Church where they supposedly planned the insurrection was demolished.

Black people in the North also suffered from violent attacks by whites. For example, white residents of Cincinnati attacked Black neighborhoods in 1829, and more than half of the city's Black residents fled. Many of them resettled in Ontario, Canada. They were soon joined by Black Philadelphians who had been attacked by groups of white residents in 1832. Such attacks continued in northern cities throughout the 1830s and 1840s.

REVIEW

- In what ways were the rights of Black people restricted and their safety threatened during the first half of the nineteenth century?

Political Realignments

Restrictions on Black political and civil rights converged with the continued decline of the Federalists. Federalist majorities in New York State had approved the gradual abolition law of 1799. In 1821, New York Federalists advocated equal rights for Black and white voters as long as property qualifications limited suffrage to respectable citizens. But Federalists were losing power, and the concerns of Black Americans were low on the Democratic-Republican agenda.

Struggles within the Democratic-Republican Party now turned to a large extent on the limits of federal power. Many Democratic-Republicans had come to embrace a more expansive view of federal authority and a looser interpretation of the U.S. Constitution. Others argued forcefully for a return to limited federal power and a strict construction of the Constitution. At the same time, rising young politicians—like Martin Van Buren and Andrew Jackson—and newly enfranchised voters sought to seize control of the party from its longtime leaders.

AP® EXAM TIP

In the early 1800s, political participation expanded to all white men, while continuing to restrict political access for women, Black men and women, and American Indians. The national political unity associated with the Era of Good Feelings collapsed in the 1820s, bringing about the events that led to the second party system. What caused the perceived unity in society to unravel?

The election of 1824 brought these conflicts to a head, splitting the Democratic-Republicans into rival factions that by 1828 coalesced into two distinct entities: the **Democrats** and the **National Republicans**. Unable to agree on a single presidential candidate in 1824, the Democratic-Republican congressional caucus fractured into four camps backing separate candidates: John Quincy Adams, Andrew Jackson, Henry Clay, and Secretary of the Treasury William Crawford.

Democratic Party

One of two parties that resulted from the split of the Democratic-Republicans in the early 1820s. Andrew Jackson and Martin Van Buren emerged as leaders of the Democrats.

National Republican Party

One of two parties that resulted from the split of the Democratic-Republicans in the early 1820s. Henry Clay and John Quincy Adams emerged as leaders of the National Republicans.

As the race developed, Adams and Jackson emerged as the two strongest candidates. John Quincy Adams's stature rested on his diplomatic achievements and the reputation of his father, former president John Adams. He favored internal improvements and protective tariffs that would bolster northern industry and commerce. Andrew Jackson, on the other hand, relied largely on his fame as a war hero and American Indian fighter to inspire popular support. He advocated limited federal power.

As a candidate who appealed to ordinary voters, Jackson held a decided edge. Outgoing and boisterous, Jackson took his case to the people. Emphasizing his humble origins, he appealed to small farmers and northern workers. Just as important, Jackson gained the support of Van Buren, who also wanted to expand the political clout of the "common [white] man" and limit the reach of a central government that was becoming too powerful.

The four presidential candidates created a truly competitive race, and turnout at the polls increased significantly. Jackson won the popular vote by carrying Pennsylvania, New Jersey, the Carolinas, and much of the West and led in the electoral college with 99 electors. Adams finished in second place and claimed 84 electors. But with no candidate gaining an absolute majority in the electoral college, the Constitution called for the House of Representatives to choose the president from the three leading contenders—Jackson, Adams, and Crawford.

Clay, who came in fourth and was then Speaker of the House, asked his supporters to back Adams, ensuring his election. Once in office, President Adams appointed Clay secretary of state. Jackson claimed that the two had engineered a **"corrupt bargain,"** but as National Republicans, Adams and Clay shared various positions.

"corrupt bargain"

An allegation by Andrew Jackson of a secret agreement between Henry Clay and John Quincy Adams in the 1824 presidential election that Clay would urge his supporters in the House of Representatives to support Adams over Jackson in exchange for an appointment in Adams's cabinet. Andrew Jackson's supporters expressed outrage over the perceived deal, while Adams and Clay denied the exchange.

President Adams ran into vigorous opposition in Congress, led by Van Buren. John C. Calhoun, who had been elected vice president, also opposed Adams's policies. Van Buren argued against federal funding for internal improvements because New York State had financed the Erie Canal with its own monies. Calhoun, meanwhile, joined other southern politicians in opposing any expansion of federal power for fear it would then be used to restrict the spread of slavery.

The most serious battle in Congress, however, involved tariffs. The Tariff of 1816 had excluded most cheap English cotton cloth from the United States to aid New England manufacturing. In 1824, the tariff was extended to more expensive cotton and woolen cloth and to iron goods. During the presidential campaign, Adams and Clay appealed to northern voters by advocating even higher duties on these items. When Adams introduced tariff legislation that extended duties to raw materials like wool, hemp, and molasses, he gained support from both Jackson and Van Buren, who considered these tariffs beneficial to farmers on the frontier. Despite the opposition of Vice President Calhoun and congressmen from southeastern states, the **Tariff of 1828** (also known as the **Tariff of Abominations**) was approved, raising duties on imports to an average of 62 percent.

Tariff of 1828 (Tariff of Abominations)
A protective tariff that substantially raised tariff rates and extended duties to include raw materials such as wool, hemp, and molasses. It was passed despite opposition from southeastern states.

The Tariff of 1828, however, was Adams's only notable legislative victory. His foreign policy was also stymied by a hostile Congress. Adams entered the 1828 election campaign with little to show in the way of domestic or foreign achievements, and Jackson and his supporters took full advantage of the president's political vulnerability.

REVIEW

- What factors led Jackson to call Adams's victory in the presidential election of 1824 "corrupt"?

The Presidential Election of 1828

The election of 1828 completed the split between the two major factions in the Democratic-Republican Party. President Adams followed the traditional approach of "standing" for office. He told supporters, "If my country wants my services, she must ask for them." Jackson and his supporters chose instead to "run" for office. They took their case directly to the voters, introducing innovative techniques to create enthusiasm among the electorate.

Van Buren managed the first truly national political campaign in U.S. history, seeking to re-create the original Democratic-Republican coalition of farmers, northern artisans, and southern planters while adding a sizable constituency of frontier voters. He was aided in the effort by Calhoun, who again ran for vice president and supported the Tennessee war hero despite their disagreement over tariffs. Jackson's supporters organized state nominating conventions rather than relying on the congressional caucus. They established local Jackson committees in critical states like Virginia and New York. They organized newspaper campaigns and developed a logo, the hickory leaf, based on the candidate's nickname, "Old Hickory," and transformed elections by engaging in direct campaigning, where candidates spoke publicly during a campaign to convince potential voters.

Jackson traveled the country to build loyalty to himself as well as to his party. His Tennessee background, rise to great wealth, and reputation as an American Indian fighter ensured his popularity among southern and western voters. He also reassured Southerners that he advocated "judicious" duties on imports, suggesting that he might try to lower the 1828 rates. At the same time, his support of the Tariff of 1828 and his military credentials created enthusiasm among northern workingmen and frontier farmers.

President Adams's supporters demeaned the "dissolute" and "rowdy" men who attended Jackson rallies. They also launched personal attacks on the candidate and his wife, Rachel. They questioned the timing of her divorce from her first husband and remarriage to Jackson. A Cincinnati newspaper headline asked: "Ought a convicted adulteress and her paramour husband be placed in the highest offices of this free and Christian land?"

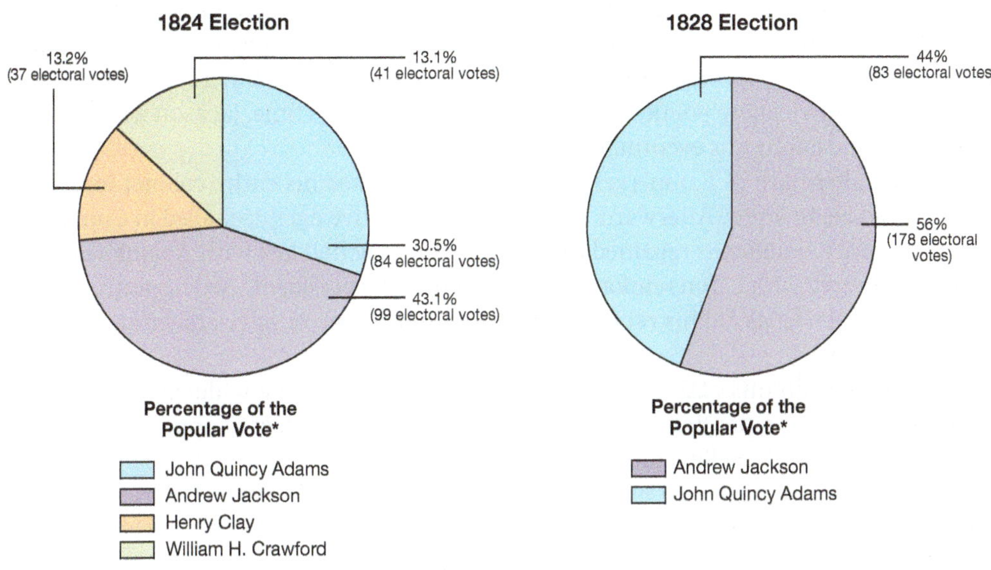

The Elections of 1824 and 1828 Andrew Jackson lost the 1824 election to John Quincy Adams when the decision was thrown into the House of Representatives. In 1828, Jackson launched the first popular campaign for president, mobilizing working-class white men who were newly enfranchised. Three times as many men—more than one million voters—cast ballots in 1828 as in 1824, ensuring Jackson's election as president.

What changed and what remained the same between the 1824 and 1828 electoral results? What factors account for those changes and continuities?

Unlike Jackson, Adams distanced himself from his own campaign. He sought to demonstrate his statesmanlike gentility by letting others speak for him. This strategy worked well when only men of wealth and property could vote. But with an enlarged electorate and an astonishing turnout of more than 50 percent of eligible voters, Adams's approach failed, and Jackson became president.

The election of 1828 formalized a new party alignment. During the campaign, Jackson and his supporters referred to themselves as "the Democracy" and forged a new national Democratic Party. In response, Adams's supporters called themselves National Republicans. The competition between Democrats and National Republicans heightened interest in national politics among ordinary voters and ensured that the innovative techniques introduced by Jackson would be widely adopted in future campaigns.

A Democratic Spirit?

On March 4, 1829, crowds of ordinary citizens came to see Jackson's inauguration. Jackson's wife, Rachel, had died of heart failure shortly after his election, leaving her husband devastated. Now Jackson, dressed in a plain black suit, walked alone to the Capitol as vast throngs of supporters waved and cheered. A somber Jackson read a brief inaugural address, took the oath of office, and then rode his horse through the crowds to the White House.

The size and enthusiasm of the crowds soon shattered the decorum of the inauguration. Author Margaret Bayard Smith reported mobs "scrambling, fighting, [and] romping" through the White House reception. Jackson was nearly crushed to death by "rabble" eager to shake his hand. Tubs of punch laced with rum, brandy, and champagne were finally placed on the lawn to draw the crowds outdoors.

While Jackson and his supporters viewed the event as a symbol of a new democratic spirit, others were less optimistic. Bayard Smith and other conservative political leaders saw echoes of the French Revolution in the unruly behavior of the masses. Supreme Court justice Joseph Story, too, feared "the reign of King 'Mob.'"

Tensions between the president and the capital's traditional leaders intensified when Jackson appointed Tennessee senator John Eaton as secretary of war. Eaton had

had an affair with a woman thought to be of questionable character and later married her. When Jackson announced his plans to appoint Eaton to his cabinet, congressional leaders urged him to reconsider. When the president appointed Eaton anyway, the wives of Washington's leading politicians snubbed Mrs. Eaton. This time, Jackson was outmaneuvered, and Eaton was eventually forced from office.

In the aftermath of Eaton's resignation, Jackson asked his entire cabinet to resign so he could begin anew. Afterward, however, his legislative agenda stalled in Congress, and National Republicans regained the momentum they had lost with Adams's defeat. The controversy with Eaton reinforced concerns that the president used his authority to reward his friends, as did his reliance on an informal group of advisers, known as the Kitchen Cabinet.

spoils system
Also known as the "patronage system," introduced by Andrew Jackson, in which federal offices or "spoils" were awarded based on political loyalty. While supporters claimed it encouraged robust political participation, opponents claimed it encouraged corruption. The system remained in place until the late nineteenth century.

While his administration opened up government posts to a wider range of individuals, ensuring more democratic access, Jackson often selected appointees based on personal ties. He believed that "to the victor goes the spoils," and the resulting **spoils system** — continued by future administrations — assigned federal posts as gifts for partisan loyalty rather than as jobs that required experience or expertise.

AP® WORKING with EVIDENCE

Source: Alexis de Tocqueville, *Letter to Louis de Kergorlay*, 1831

> "My American informants tell me that there was no aristocracy but, instead a class of great landowners leading a simple, rather intellectual life characterized by its air of good breeding, its manners, and a strong sense of family pride. . . .
>
> The aristocratic bias that marked the republic's early years was replaced by a democratic thrust of irresistible force. . . . I've seen several members of these old families. . . . They regret the loss of everything aristocratic: patronage, family pride, high tone. . . .
>
> What I see in America leaves me doubting that government by the multitude, even under the most favorable circumstances — and they exist here — is a good thing. There is general agreement that in the early days of the republic, statesmen and members of the two legislative houses were much more distinguished than they are today. They almost all belonged to that class of landowners I mentioned above. The populace no longer chooses with such a sure hand. It generally favors those who flatter its passions and descend to its level."

Questions for Analysis

1. Describe how Tocqueville's letter characterizes American political democracy.
2. Explain how a specific historical development in the early 1800s changed American political democracy in the ways Tocqueville describes in his letter.
3. Explain how the 1828 presidential election and events in Jackson's first term created a context for Tocqueville's argument.

REVIEW

- In what ways did President Jackson break from traditional political norms during his first term in office?

AP®

Skills Workshop: Thinking Historically

Connecting Developments Across Primary Sources to Create a Body Paragraph

As you recall from Module 2.6, historians review primary source evidence and the historical record to identify patterns. These patterns become apparent when historians draw connections between particular events and recognize long-term trends.

Historians also draw connections between multiple developments or processes and analyze how they relate to one another. This means seeing connections between different long-term developments that might not be readily apparent but, when related to each other, reveal something new about a time period.

A good everyday example might help here. Here are two simple developments:

1. Lately, Francis has been staying increasingly late to help the marching band pack up the percussion section after practice. In the past, there had been no opportunity to stay late on Tuesday night, since that night Francis's father made dinner, and he had to pick Francis up from practice one hour before dinnertime. Lately, however, Francis has been able to stay later.
2. Also, Francis has increasingly been going out with friends. Sometimes they go out after marching band practice, or on a weekend to the big box store out near the highway. This development makes Francis very happy, since the newfound freedom with friends is very satisfying.

While these two developments are seemingly disconnected, once we discover that Francis has recently acquired a driver's license, we now see how the two developments relate to one another. First, Francis is able to stay later after practice because Dad is home making dinner and doesn't need to be a chauffeur. Second, Francis is able to spend more time with friends because a driver's license offers all sorts of new opportunities for socializing away from home. An even broader trend that can be discerned from these two developments is that Francis is growing into an independent and responsible person.

Below are two primary sources. Analyze each, and don't forget to have a close look at their source line. Then, determine what development each represents. After you have determined the development that each represents, generate a working argument as to how they relate to each other. Take a close look at the historical information in this module to make this working argument. (Hint: Have a look at the sections "Voting Rights Expand" and "Racial Restrictions and Antiblack Violence.")

Source: Pennsylvania State Constitution (1838), Article III, Sec. I

> "In elections . . . every white freeman of the age of twenty-one years . . . shall enjoy the rights of an elector. But a citizen of the United States who had previously been a qualified voter of this State, and removed therefrom and returned . . . shall be entitled to vote after residing in the State six months. . . . That white freemen . . . shall be entitled to vote, although they shall not have paid taxes."

Source: The *Liberator*, an abolitionist newspaper, August 12, 1842, p. 2, col. 1

> "The Philadelphia Riots: Riot and Bloodshed.
>
> The Mayor proceeded at once to increase his establishment, by swearing a large number of police men, and sending them, with proper badges, to the place of disturbance. Meantime the rioters were assaulting the houses of the

(continued)

blacks in the vicinity of Lombard Street, between Fifth and Eighth, where are a number of small alleys and courts, and in which a vast number of colored people reside. Their windows were beaten in, doors knocked to pieces, and other injuries committed."

Characterize a development apparent in the first document:

Characterize a development apparent in the second document:

Determine how these two developments relate to one another:

ACTIVITY

In a paragraph using the documents above, answer the following question in a body paragraph. Be sure to begin with what could be a **sub-argument** if this were part of a full essay. **CSE** the evidence that you use to support your **sub-argument**. And use **transition words** to link your evidence.

In what ways did race shape U.S. society and politics in the 1830s and 1840s?

Jackson and Federal Power

MODULE
4.8

FOCUS

As you read this module, consider how battles over tariff rates, the re-chartering of the Bank of the United States, and the land claims of American Indians all shaped the events leading into the 1830s. Be sure to take note of the ways in which the political and economic challenges in the 1830s changed American politics, affected the lives of American Indians, and deepened sectional divisions between the North and South. Consider also the extent to which many of these challenges and divisions reflected older, continuous patterns in U.S. history.

President Andrew Jackson hoped to make government more responsive to the needs of white workers and frontier farmers. But Jackson's notion of democracy did not extend to American Indians or Black Americans. During his presidency, American Indian nations actively resisted his efforts to take more of their land, and Black people continued to resist their enslavement.

Of more immediate importance, once President Jackson had to take clear positions on tariffs and other controversial issues, he could not please all of his constituents. Jackson also confronted experienced adversaries like Henry Clay, Daniel Webster, and former president John Quincy Adams, who was elected to the House of Representatives from Massachusetts in 1830. President Jackson faced considerable difficulty in translating popular support into public policy.

Confrontations over Tariffs and the Bank

The Democratic Party that emerged in the late 1820s was built on an unstable foundation. The coalition that formed around Jackson included northern workers who benefited from high tariffs as well as southern farmers and planters who did not. It brought together western voters who sought federal support for internal improvements and strict constructionists who believed such expenditures were unconstitutional. In nearly every legislative battle, then, decisiveness aroused conflict. In 1830, Congress passed four internal improvement bills with strong support from National Republicans. Jackson vetoed each one, which pleased his southern constituency but not his frontier supporters.

Southern congressmen, however, were more interested in his stand on tariffs. This interest veiled a more long-standing issue, namely, whether the federal government had the power to regulate the institution of slavery. Because the tariff was a national economic policy that had regional effects, debates about the tariff mirrored debates about slavery itself, and whether the federal government could use its power over interstate transit to regulate economic policy in such a way that could threaten slavery itself.

The Tariff of 1828 (see Module 4.7) enraged many southern planters and politicians, but most believed that once Jackson reached the White House, he would reverse course and reduce this so-called Tariff of Abominations. Instead, he avoided the issue, and southern agriculture continued to suffer. Agricultural productivity in Virginia and other states of the Old South was declining from soil exhaustion, while prices for cotton and rice had not fully recovered after the Panic of 1819. At the same time, higher duties on manufactured items raised prices for Southerners on many goods.

Even as Calhoun campaigned with Jackson in 1828, the South Carolinian developed a philosophical argument to block the effects of high tariffs on his state. In *The South Carolina Exposition and Protest*, published anonymously in 1828, Calhoun argued that states should have final power to determine the constitutionality of laws passed by Congress. When Jackson, after taking office, realized that his vice president advocated **nullification**—the right of individual states to declare individual laws void within their borders—it damaged their relationship.

nullification
The legal doctrine that individual states maintained their sovereignty despite union, because the federal union was created by the states, thus maintaining the right to declare federal laws unconstitutional and, therefore, void within their borders. South Carolina attempted to invoke the doctrine of nullification in response to the Tariff of 1832.

When Congress debated the tariff issue in 1830, South Carolina senator Robert Hayne defended nullification. Claiming that the North intended to crush the South economically, he argued that only the right of states to nullify federal legislation could protect southern society. In response, Massachusetts senator Daniel Webster denounced nullification and the states' rights doctrine on which it was built. Jackson further antagonized southern political leaders by supporting Webster's position.

Matters worsened in 1832, when Congress confirmed the high duties set four years earlier with passage of the Tariff of 1832. In response, South Carolina held a special convention that approved the **Ordinance of Nullification**. It stated that duties on imports would not be collected in the state after February 1, 1833, and threatened secession if federal authorities tried to collect them.

Ordinance of Nullification
A law passed in 1832 by South Carolina proclaiming several congressional tariff acts null and void within the state and threatening secession if the federal government tried to enforce the tariffs.

The tariff crisis escalated in the fall of 1832 just as Jackson faced reelection. The tariff debates had angered many Southerners, and Calhoun refused to run again as his vice president. Fortunately for Jackson, opponents in Congress had provided him with another issue that could unite his supporters and highlight his commitment to ordinary citizens: the renewal of the charter of the Second Bank of the United States.

Clay and Webster persuaded Nicholas Biddle, head of the bank, to request an early re-chartering of the bank. Jackson's opponents in Congress knew they had the votes to pass a new charter in the summer of 1832, and they hoped Jackson would veto the bill and thereby split the Democratic Party just before the fall elections.

The Second Bank was nothing short of a political mess. The bank had stabilized the economy during the 1820s by regularly demanding gold or silver payments from state-chartered banks. This kept those banks from issuing too much paper money and thereby prevented inflation and higher prices. This tight-money policy also kept banks from expanding too rapidly in the western states. Most financial elites applauded the bank's efforts, but its policies created hostility among the wider public. When state-chartered banks closed because of a lack of gold or silver payments, ordinary Americans were often stuck with worthless paper money. Tight-money policies also made it more difficult for individuals to get credit to purchase land, homes, or farm equipment.

As the president's opponents had hoped, Congress approved the new charter. Jackson vetoed it. Yet rather than dividing the Democrats, Jackson's veto gained enormous support from voters across the country. In justifying his action, the president cast the Second Bank as a "monster" that was "dangerous to the liberties of the people"—particularly farmers, mechanics, and laborers—while promoting "the advancement of the few." Finally, Jackson noted that because wealthy Britons owned substantial shares of the bank's stock, national pride demanded ending the Second Bank's reign over the U.S. economy.

Jackson rode the enthusiasm for his bank veto to reelection over National Republican candidate Henry Clay. Within a year, the Second Bank was dead, deprived of government deposits by Jackson, who moved the government's money to other banks, nicknamed "pet banks" by his opponents.

Soon after his reelection, however, the president faced a grave political crisis related to the tariff issue. Jackson now supported lower tariffs, but he was adamant in his opposition to nullification. In early 1833, he persuaded Congress to pass the **Force Bill**, which gave him authority to use the military to enforce national laws in South Carolina. At the same time, Jackson made clear that he would work with Congress to reduce tariffs. The resulting compromise Tariff of 1833, negotiated by Henry Clay, gradually lowered import duties over the next decade, allowing South Carolina to rescind its nullification ordinance without losing face. However, in a symbolic act of resistance, South Carolina nullified the Force Bill. Open conflict was avoided, but the question of nullification remained unresolved.

Force Bill
A bill passed by Congress in 1833 in response to South Carolina's Ordinance of Nullification. It gave the president the authority to use military force to enforce national laws—in particular the Tariff of 1832.

- Why did issues involving tariff rates and the Bank of the United States cause political discord during the 1820s and 1830s?

The Battle for Texas

As southern agriculture expanded westward during the early nineteenth century, some looked toward Texas for fresh land. White Southerners had begun moving into eastern Texas in the early nineteenth century, but the Adams–Onís Treaty of 1819 (see Module 4.4) guaranteed Spanish control of the territory. Then, in 1821, Mexicans overthrew Spanish rule and claimed Texas as part of the new Republic of Mexico. But Mexicans faced serious competition from Comanche Indians, who controlled vast areas in northern Mexico and launched frequent raids into Mexico's Texas territory.

Eager to increase settlement in the area and to create a human buffer against the Comanche nation, the Mexican government granted U.S. migrants some of the best land in eastern Texas. It hoped these settlers would eventually spread into the interior, where Comanche raids had devastated Mexican communities. To entice more Southerners, the Mexican government negotiated a special exemption for U.S. planters when it outlawed slavery in 1829. But rather than spreading into the interior, American migrants stayed east of the Colorado River, which flows through central Texas, out of reach of Comanche raids and close to U.S. markets in Louisiana.

Moreover, U.S. settlers resisted assimilation into Mexican society. Instead, they continued to worship as Protestants, speak English, send their children to separate schools, and trade mainly with the United States. By 1835, the 27,000 white Southerners and 3,000 enslaved people far outnumbered the 3,000 Mexicans living in eastern Texas.

Forming a majority of the eastern Texas population and eager to expand their plantations and trade networks, growing numbers of U.S. settlers demanded independence. Then, in 1836, Mexicans elected a strong nationalist leader, General Antonio López de Santa Anna, as president. He sought to calm **Tejanos** (Mexican Texans) angered by their vulnerability to Comanche attacks and to curb U.S. settlers seeking further concessions. However, when Santa Anna appointed a military commander to rule Texas, U.S. migrants organized a rebellion and, on March 2, declared their independence. Some elite Tejanos, long neglected by authorities in Mexico City, sided with the rebels. But the rebellion appeared to be short-lived. On March 6, 1836, General Santa Anna crushed

Alamo
A Texas fort captured by General Santa Anna from rebel defenders on March 6, 1836. Sensationalist accounts of the siege of the Alamo increased popular support in the United States for Texas independence.

settlers defending the **Alamo** in San Antonio. Soon thereafter, he captured the U.S. settlement at Goliad.

At this point, Santa Anna was convinced that the uprising was over. But the U.S. government, despite its claims of neutrality, aided the rebels with funds and army officers. American newspapers picked up the story of the Alamo and published accounts of the battle, describing the Mexican fighters as brutal butchers bent on saving Texas for the pope. These stories, some more fable than fact, increased popular support for the war at a time when many Americans were increasingly hostile to Catholic immigrants in the United States.

As hundreds of armed volunteers headed to Texas, General Sam Houston led rebel forces in a critical victory at San Jacinto in April 1836. While the Mexican government refused to recognize rebel claims, it did not try to regain the lost territory. Few of the U.S. volunteers arrived in time to participate in the fighting, but some settled in the newly liberated region. The Comanche nation quickly recognized the Republic of Texas and developed trade relations with residents to gain access to the vast U.S. market. Still, Santa Anna's failure to recognize Texas independence kept the U.S. government from granting the territory statehood for fear it would lead to war with Mexico.

gag rule
A rule passed by the House of Representatives in 1836 to postpone action on all antislavery petitions without hearing them read to prevent congressional debate over slavery. It was renewed annually until 1844.

President Jackson also worried that admitting a new slave state might split the national Democratic Party before the fall elections. To limit debate on the issue, Congress passed a **gag rule** in March 1836 that tabled all antislavery petitions without being read. Nevertheless, thousands of antislavery activists still flooded the House of Representatives with petitions opposing the annexation of Texas.

REVIEW

- What factors led to conflict between Americans in Texas and the Republic of Mexico?

American Indians Resist Removal

Under Jackson, the United States also faced continued challenges from American Indian nations. The acquisition of American Indian land was another long-standing issue that earned Jackson the support of white Southerners and most frontier settlers. Yet not all Americans agreed with his effort to force American Indians off their lands.

In the 1820s, nations like the Cherokee gained the support of Protestant missionaries who hoped to "civilize" American Indians by converting them to Christianity and "American" ways. Congress had previously granted these groups federal funds to advance these goals. Jackson, however, was unsupportive of such efforts and sided with political leaders who sought to force eastern American Indians to accept homelands west of the Mississippi River.

In 1825, three years before Jackson was elected president, Creek Indians in Georgia and Alabama were forcibly removed to the Unorganized Territory (previously part of Arkansas Territory and later called the Indian Territory) based on a fraudulent treaty. Jackson supported this policy. When he became president, politicians and settlers in Georgia, Florida, the Carolinas, and Illinois demanded federal assistance to force American Indian communities out of their states.

The largest American Indian nations vehemently protested their removal. The Cherokee, who had fought alongside Jackson at Horseshoe Bend, adopted a republican form of government in 1827 based on the U.S. Constitution. John Ross served as the president of the Cherokee constitutional convention and a year later was elected principal chief. He and the other chiefs then declared themselves a sovereign nation within the borders of the United States. The Georgia legislature rejected Cherokee claims of independence and argued that American Indians were simply guests of the state, a position that gained added significance when gold was discovered in Cherokee territory in 1829.

Ross appealed to Jackson to recognize Cherokee sovereignty, but the president was offended by what he saw as a challenge to his authority. He urged Congress to pass the **Indian Removal Act** in 1830, by which the Cherokee and other American Indian nations would be forced to exchange their lands in the Southeast for a "clear title forever" on territory west of the Mississippi River. The majority of Cherokees refused to accept these terms.

Indian Removal Act
An 1830 act, supported by President Andrew Jackson, by which American Indian peoples in the East were forced to exchange their lands for territory west of the Mississippi River. The act also voided all prior land treaties.

AP® WORKING with EVIDENCE

Source: Indian Removal Act, 1830

> "AN ACT to provide for an exchange of lands with the Indians residing in any of the States or Territories, and for their removal west of the river Mississippi.
>
> *Be it enacted, & c.,* That it shall and may be lawful for . . . any territory belonging to the United States, west of the river Mississippi, not included in any State or organized Territory . . . to be divided into a suitable number of districts, for the reception of such tribes or nations of Indians as may choose to exchange the lands where they now reside, and remove there . . .
>
> Sec. 2. *And be it further enacted,* That it shall and may be lawful for the President to exchange any or all of such districts . . . with any tribe or nation of Indians . . . with which the United States have existing treaties, for the whole or any part or portion of the territory claimed and occupied by such tribe or nation . . . where the land claimed and occupied by the Indians, is owned by the United States, or the United States are bound to the State within which it lies to extinguish the Indian claim thereto.
>
> Sec. 3. *And be it further enacted,* That . . . it shall and may be lawful for the President solemnly to assure the tribe or nation with which the exchange is made, that the United States will forever secure and guaranty to them, and their heirs or successors, the country so exchanged with them . . . *Provided always,* That such lands shall revert to the United States, if the Indians become extinct, or abandon the same. . . .
>
> Sec. 8. *And be it further enacted,* That for the purpose of giving effect to the provisions of this act, the sum of five hundred thousand dollars is hereby appropriated."

Questions for Analysis

1. Identify the main provisions of this excerpt from the Indian Removal Act.
2. Explain the factors that led to passage of the Indian Removal Act.
3. Evaluate the extent to which the Indian Removal Act represented a continuity in U.S. government relations with American Indians.

As the dispute between the Cherokee nation and Georgia unfolded, Jackson made clear his intention to implement the Indian Removal Act. In 1832, he sent federal troops into western Illinois to force the Sauk and Fox peoples to move farther west. Instead, whole villages, led by Chief Black Hawk, fled to the Wisconsin Territory. Black Hawk

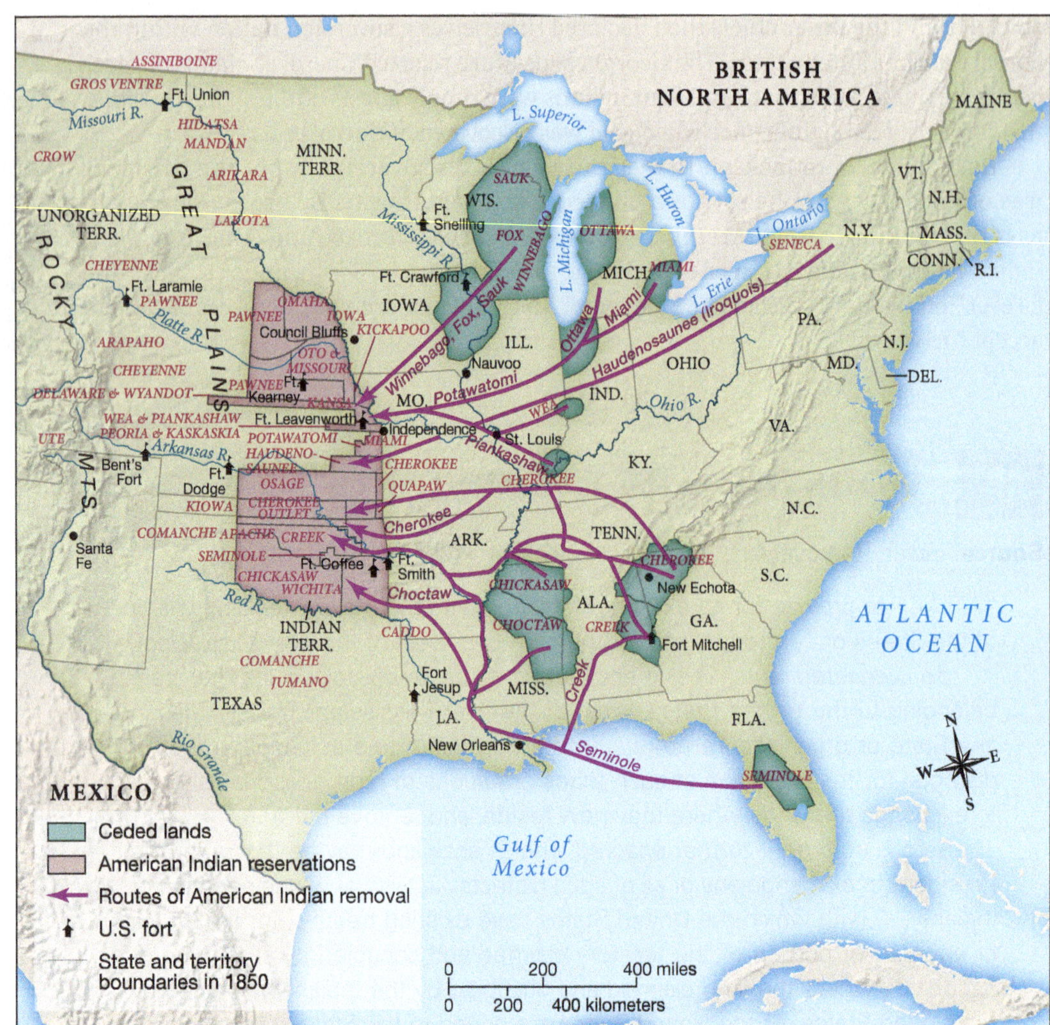

MAP 4.5 American Indian Removals and Relocations, 1820s–1840s In the 1820s and 1830s, the federal government used a variety of tactics, including military force, to expel American Indian nations residing east of the Mississippi River. As these tribes resettled in the West, white migration along the Oregon and other trails began to increase. The result, by 1850, was the forced relocation of many western American Indian nations as well.

Compare this map with Map 3.9 (Module 3.12). What do these maps reveal about the impact of American expansionism on American Indians?

Second Seminole War

A war between the Seminole nation, including enslaved Blacks who had escaped captivity and joined the tribe, and the U.S. government from 1835 to 1842 over whether the Seminole people would be forced to leave Florida and settle west of the Mississippi River. Despite substantial investments of men, money, and resources, it took seven years for the United States to achieve victory.

and a thousand warriors confronted U.S. troops at Bad Axe, in the Wisconsin Territory, but the Sauk and Fox warriors were massacred in a brutal daylong battle. The survivors were forced to move west.

Meanwhile, the Seminole Indians prepared to go to war to protect their territory. Between 1832 and 1835, federal authorities forcibly removed the majority of Florida Seminoles to Indian Territory, although a minority fought back. Jackson and his military commanders expected that this **Second Seminole War** would be short-lived. However, they misjudged the Seminoles' strength; the power of their charismatic leader, Osceola; and the resistance of Black fugitives living among the Seminole people.

The conflict continued long after Jackson left the presidency. During the seven-year guerrilla war, 1,600 U.S. troops died. U.S. military forces defeated the Seminoles in 1842 only by luring Osceola into an army camp with false promises of a peace settlement. Instead, officers took him captive, finally breaking the back of the resistance. Still,

Sarin Images/Granger

Cherokee Removal, 1838 This woodcut appeared in a U.S. geography textbook around 1850. The title "Indian Emigrants" and the image of Cherokee disembarking from a steamboat falsely suggest that the emigration was voluntary and the means of travel relatively easy. The U.S. fort on the hill symbolizes the role of the federal government in forcing the Cherokee people to move west of the Mississippi.

Based on the title of this image and its portrayal of the Cherokees, what was the purpose of this woodcut? Explain your reasoning.

to end the conflict, the U.S. government had to allow enslaved Blacks who had escaped and were living among the Seminoles to accompany the tribe to Indian Territory.

Unlike the Seminole nation, members of the Cherokee nation challenged removal by peaceful means, believing that their prolonged efforts to coexist with white society would ensure their success. American Indian leaders like John Ross had urged Cherokees to embrace Christianity, white gender roles, and a republican form of government as the best means to ensure control of their communities. Large numbers had done so, but in 1829 and 1830, Georgia officials sought to impose new regulations on the Cherokee living within the state's borders. Tribal leaders took them to court, demanding recognition as a separate nation and using evidence of their Americanization to claim their rights.

In 1831, ***Cherokee Nation v. Georgia*** reached the Supreme Court, which denied a central part of the Cherokee claim. It ruled that all American Indians were "domestic dependent nations" rather than fully sovereign governments. Yet the following year, in *Worcester v. Georgia*, the Court declared that the state of Georgia could not impose *state* laws on the Cherokee, for they had "territorial boundaries, within which their authority is exclusive," and that both their land and their rights were protected by the federal government.

Cherokee Nation v. Georgia A Supreme Court ruling in 1831 that denied the Cherokee claim to be a separate sovereign and independent nation, ruling that all American Indian nations were "domestic dependent nations" rather than fully sovereign governments.

President Jackson, who sought Cherokee removal, argued that only the tribe's displacement west of the Mississippi River could ensure its "physical comfort," "political advancement," and "moral improvement." Most southern whites, seeking to mine gold and expand cotton production in Cherokee territory, agreed. But Protestant women and men in the North launched a large petition campaign in 1830 supporting the Cherokees' right to their land. The Cherokee people themselves stalled any action during Jackson's second term.

In December 1835, however, U.S. officials convinced a small group of Cherokee men—without tribal authorization—to sign the **Treaty of New Echota**. It proposed the exchange of 100 million acres of Cherokee land in the Southeast for $68 million and 32 million acres in Indian Territory. Outraged Cherokee leaders like John Ross lobbied Congress to reject the treaty. But in May 1836, Congress approved the treaty by a single vote and set the date for final removal two years later (Map 4.5).

Treaty of New Echota A treaty made in 1836 in which a small group of Cherokee men agreed to exchange their land in the Southeast for money and land in Indian Territory. Although the treaty was obtained without tribal approval, it was approved by the U.S. Congress.

In 1838, the U.S. army forcibly removed Cherokees who had not yet resettled in Indian Territory. That June, General Winfield Scott, assisted by 7,000 U.S. soldiers, forced some 15,000 Cherokees into forts and military camps. American Indian families spent the next several months without sufficient food, water, sanitation, or medicine. In October, when the Cherokees finally began the march west, torrential rains were followed by snow. Although the U.S. army planned for a trip of less than three months, the journey took five months. As supplies ran short, thousands of American Indians died. The remaining Cherokees completed this **Trail of Tears**, as it became known, in March 1839. But thousands more remained near starvation a year later.

Trail of Tears

The forced march following passage of the Indian Removal Act of some 15,000 Cherokees from Georgia to areas west of the Mississippi River that were designated as Indian Territory, beginning in 1831. Inadequate planning, food, water, sanitation, and medicine led to the deaths of thousands of Cherokees.

Following the Trail of Tears, Seneca Indians petitioned the federal government to stop their removal from western New York. Federal agents had negotiated the Treaty of Buffalo Creek with several Haudenosaunee (Iroquois) leaders in 1838. But some Seneca chiefs claimed the negotiation was marred by bribery and fraud. With the aid of Quaker allies, the Seneca petitioned Congress and the president for redress. Perhaps reluctant to repeat the Cherokee and Seminole debacles, Congress approved a new treaty in 1842 that allowed the Seneca to retain two of their four reservations in western New York. The contest for American Indian lands continued well past Jackson's presidency, but the president's desire to force indigenous nations westward would prevail.

REVIEW

- How did American Indian nations challenge attempts to forcibly relocate them?
- Compare the experiences of the Seminole, Cherokee, and Seneca Indians as each group faced forcible relocation.

Van Buren and the Panic of 1837

Although Jackson proposed the Indian Removal Act, it was President Martin Van Buren who confronted ongoing challenges from American Indian nations. When Van Buren ran for president in 1836, the newly formed **Whig Party**, made up of former National Republicans and so named as a retort to Jackson's perceived "kinglike" conduct, hoped to defeat him by bringing together diverse supporters: evangelical Protestants who objected to Jackson's American Indian policy, financiers and commercial farmers who advocated internal improvements and protective tariffs, merchants and manufacturers who favored a national bank, and Southerners who were antagonized by the president's heavy-handed use of federal authority.

Whig Party

Named for the British political faction that overthrew King James II in the Glorious Revolution, the Whig political party formed in the 1830s to challenge the power of the Democratic Party generally, and Andrew Jackson in particular. The Whigs attempted to forge a diverse coalition from around the country by promoting commercial interests and moral reforms.

But the Whigs could not agree on a single candidate, and this lack of unity allowed Democrats to prevail. Although Van Buren won the popular vote by only a small margin (50.9 percent), he secured an easy majority in the electoral college.

Inaugurated on March 4, 1837, President Van Buren soon faced a major financial crisis. The Panic of 1837 started in the South and was rooted in the changing fortunes of American cotton in Great Britain. During the 1820s and 1830s, British banks lent large sums to states such as New York to fund internal improvements, which drove the market revolution but also fueled inflation. The British also invested heavily in cotton plantations, and southern planters used the funds to expand production and improve shipping facilities.

In late 1836, the Bank of England, faced with bad harvests at home and a declining demand for textiles, tightened credit to limit the flow of money out of the country. This forced British investors to call in their loans, which drove up interest rates in the United States just as cotton prices started to fall. Some large American cotton merchants were forced to declare bankruptcy. The banks where they held accounts, many in the South, then failed—ninety-eight of them in March and April 1837 alone.

The economic crisis hit the South hard. Cotton prices continued to fall, cut by nearly half in less than a year. Land values declined dramatically, port cities came to a standstill, and cotton communities on the southern frontier collapsed.

Because regional economies were increasingly intertwined, the panic radiated throughout the United States. Northern brokers, shippers, and merchants were devastated by losses in the cotton trade, and northern banks were hit by unpaid debts incurred for canals and other internal improvements. In turn, entrepreneurs who borrowed money to expand their businesses defaulted in large numbers, and shopkeepers, artisans, factory workers, and farmers in the North and Midwest suffered unemployment and foreclosures.

AP® EXAM TIP

Slavery, tariff policy, American Indian removal, and the American system divided the United States during these years along political, economic, and section lines. Make sure you can describe the causes and effects of these issues and divisions.

In the North and West, many Americans blamed Jackson's war against the Bank of the United States for precipitating the panic. Americans everywhere were outraged at Van Buren's refusal to intervene in the crisis by supporting works projects or public assistance. While it is unlikely that any federal policy could have resolved the nation's economic problems, the president's apparent lack of interest in the suffering of Americans inspired harsh criticisms from ordinary citizens as well as political opponents. Worse, despite brief signs of recovery in 1838, the depression deepened in 1839 and continued for four more years.

REVIEW

- What were the causes and consequences of the Panic of 1837?

The Whigs Win the White House

Eager to exploit the weakness of Van Buren and the Democrats, the Whig Party organized its first national convention in fall 1840 and united behind military hero William Henry Harrison, the party's largest vote-getter in the previous election. Harrison was born to a wealthy planter family in Virginia, but he was portrayed as a self-made man who lived in a simple log cabin and drank hard cider. His running mate, John Tyler, another Virginia gentleman and a onetime Democrat, joined the Whigs because of his opposition to Jackson's stand on nullification. Whig leaders hoped he would attract southern votes.

Taking their cue from the Democrats, the Whigs organized rallies, barbecues, parades, and mass meetings. They turned the tables on their foe by portraying Van Buren as an aristocrat and Harrison as a war hero and friend of the common man. Whigs celebrated American innovation and the entrepreneurial spirit, proclaimed farmers and skilled workers the backbone of the country, and insisted on their moral and religious superiority to Democrats. At the same time, eager to remind voters that Harrison had defeated Tenskwatawa at the 1811 Battle of Tippecanoe, the Whigs adopted the slogan "Tippecanoe and Tyler Too."

The Whigs also welcomed women into the campaign. By 1840, thousands of women had circulated petitions against Cherokee removal, organized antislavery societies, promoted religious revivals, and joined charitable associations. They embodied the kind of moral force that the Whig Party claimed to represent. In October 1840, Whig senator Daniel Webster spoke to a gathering of 1,200 women, calling on them to encourage their brothers and husbands to vote for Harrison.

The Whig strategy paid off handsomely on election day. Harrison won easily, and the Whigs gained a majority in Congress. Yet the election's promise was shattered when Harrison died of pneumonia a month after his inauguration. Whigs in Congress now had to deal with John Tyler, whose sentiments were largely southern and Democratic. Vetoing legislation to increase tariffs and re-charter the Bank of the United States, President Tyler infuriated Whigs, who eventually kicked him out of the party. Tyler's actions allowed the Democratic Party to regroup and set the stage for close elections in 1844 and 1848.

REVIEW

- What tactics did Whigs use to win the election of 1840?
- How did these tactics reflect changes in campaigning since the election of 1824?

AP® Skills Workshop: Writing Historically

Creating Historical Context in an Essay Introduction

You've probably heard the saying, "Context is everything." Context is what helps you fully understand the world around you and the people in it. Let's think about a simple example of why context matters and how it shapes our perceptions.

Let's say it's freezing outside and snowing—you put on a heavy jacket and gloves before heading out the door, and everyone you see outside is dressed similarly. Given the context of the weather, your outfit makes sense—but deciding to wear that same outfit in Hawaii in August would no doubt raise a few eyebrows. Context (the climate in this case) shapes the way you dress.

When thinking about context, think big. Context includes not only your friends and family and your town and state, but also the political, economic, and cultural trends in your country, and even the world at large. Consider the way in which these things shape each other, right down to the everyday. Culturally, you might not like the music your dad listens to, and he might not like yours, but both of you form your opinions within a specific musical context that also shapes the kind of music people listen to all over the country. Or politics: your dad might not like the politics of your neighbor, but both sets of political opinions exist within a context where those opinions are formed.

It's impossible to exist outside of context. Your opinions, your beliefs, your hopes, your fears, and even your dreams happen within a historical context.

Historians are always talking about "context." Context is the historical atmosphere in which all events happen and the sum total of all of those events. Context shaped the way people in the past understood themselves and their world.

(*continued*)

Introductions

Since historians believe everything happens in context, it's important for you to incorporate **contextualization** in your AP® U.S. History essays. One of the best places to "contextualize" is in the first paragraph of an essay. The AP® Exam doesn't require you to contextualize anywhere in particular, but because you'll be busy proving your thesis in your body paragraphs, one of the best places to contextualize is in your introduction.

Choosing the right context for your thesis will help focus your reader's attention and open the door to your main argument. This is why, regardless of the details of a given prompt, or what type of essay prompt you encounter, you should always start your essay by presenting context in direct response to the prompt. Remember, context broadly shapes a given situation. Starting off with a meaningful context helps to set up the parameters of your response by illustrating how important background influences helped shaped the topic at hand. In other words, it sets the scene for the argument you're about to make.

The following essay prompt asks you to draw on what you have learned in this module:

> Evaluate the extent to which political and economic changes between 1820 and 1840 contributed to sectional divisions and social conflicts.

Step 1 ▶ Break down the prompt and pre-write your response

The first thing you should do is what you've been doing so far in response to essay questions: break down the prompt and pre-write to organize your thoughts on its topic—in this case, the effects of political and economic changes on section divisions and social conflicts.

Step 2 ▶ Set the context

From there, quickly scan your pre-writing for events and developments that form an **immediate context** that explains the surrounding background of the topic. For example, the period between 1820 and 1840 saw the development of the market economy, the expansion of white male suffrage, the transformation of campaigning from a gentlemen's affair to the rough-and-tumble "common man" politics of Andrew Jackson's Democrats, the rise of industrial production, and the expansion of the cotton economy.

But keep in mind that sometimes your pre-writing observations will not easily lend themselves to picking out details of context from within the prompt's time range (in this case, 1820–1840). When this happens, you should look for a **preceding context**—that is, an event or development from a time period immediately before the one named in the prompt. A good example of an event from the preceding context of this time period might be the purchase of the Louisiana Territory in 1803, which paved the way for further expansion of the U.S. economy. Another example might be the "common man" rhetoric of Thomas Jefferson's supporters during his administration that paved the way for Jackson's style of politics. All of these provide context that *precedes* 1820, yet is *related* to the period 1820–1840. In fact, incorporating preceding context has an additional benefit. By using specific information from *before* the prompt's time period, you can save the relevant outside information you recall from within the time period from your pre-write to use as support in the body paragraphs.

(continued)

Step 3 ▶ Claim, Support, and Explain the Context

Next, you should think about how to prove that the context you've chosen exists—and how you'll explain why its influence on the topic of the prompt is important. One way to quickly do this is to create a table using **CSE**. The following examples show both an immediate context and a preceding context.

Immediate Context Claim	Immediate Context Support	Immediate Context Explanation
After 1820, politics and the economy developed in ways radically different from what Americans had experienced in previous generations.	The market revolution transformed the way goods like cotton were produced and consumed, and "common man" politics as seen in Andrew Jackson's campaigns transformed the way Americans thought about politics and power.	These changes created a context in which Americans found themselves increasingly in conflict over different sectional interests, and over who was rightly considered an American.

You can also use preceding context to introduce a response to the prompt above.

Preceding Context Claim	Preceding Context Support	Preceding Context Explanation
In the decades before 1820, the United States appeared to be on the cusp of an economic and political transformation.	Early transportation networks like roads and canals made it easier to move goods and commodities throughout the nation.	Yet a more integrated economy led to rising conflicts, both between regions and between individual Americans, after 1820.

Step 4 ▶ Connect the context to your thesis

Now you're ready write your contextualization statement. A full contextualization statement should be three sentences or longer. Remember, you're not just stating the context—you are also proving its existence by citing historical evidence *and* offering an explanation of its influence on the topic of the prompt. In other words, you're not only asserting its relevance, but describing how it is relevant.

Here is an example of an immediate context statement for the prompt above:

After 1820, politics and the economy developed in ways radically different from what Americans had experienced in previous generations **[immediate context claim]**. The market revolution transformed the way goods like cotton were produced and consumed, and "common man" politics as seen in Andrew Jackson's campaigns transformed the way Americans thought about politics and power **[immediate context support]**. These changes created a context in which Americans found themselves increasingly in conflict over different sectional interests, and over who was rightly considered an American. **[immediate context explanation]**.

Here is an example of a preceding context statement for this prompt:

In the decades before 1820, the United States appeared to be on the cusp of an economic and political transformation **[preceding context claim]**. Early transportation networks like roads and canals made it easier to move goods and commodities throughout the nation **[preceding context support]**. Yet a more integrated economy led to rising conflicts, both between regions and between individual Americans, after 1820 **[preceding context explanation]**.

(continued)

Notice how each of these context-setting statements use the **CSE** method. First, each makes a claim; second, each supports that claim with evidence; and third, each explains how the evidence that supports the claim sets the **context** for the prompt about how political and economic changes between 1820 and 1840 deepened sectional divisions and social conflicts.

A context statement sets up your **thesis statement** (Module 3.6)—it's a bridge between the larger topic of the prompt and the argument you are about to make in response to it. So, if we were to use the immediate context statement above and attach it to a thesis statement, our introductory paragraph could look like this:

> After 1820, politics and the economy developed in ways radically different from what Americans had experienced in previous generations **[immediate context claim]**. The market revolution transformed the way goods like cotton were produced and consumed, and "common man" politics as seen in Andrew Jackson's campaigns transformed the way Americans thought about politics and power **[immediate context support]**. These changes created a context in which Americans found themselves increasingly in conflict over different sectional interests, and over who was rightly considered an American **[immediate context explanation]**. Between 1820 and 1840, significant political and economic changes in the United States increased sectionalism and largely worsened the plight of marginalized social groups **[thesis claim]**. Westward expansion, industrialization, and the advent of white male suffrage led to tensions among the North, South, and West over competing economic interests, and conflicts between White male Americans and disenfranchised people like Blacks, women, and native peoples **[thesis line of reasoning]**.

ACTIVITY

Here is a prompt from material in Period 4. Write an introduction with either immediate or long-term context. Make sure to include your thesis in the introduction.

> Evaluate the extent to which sectional interests shaped national politics between 1820 and 1840.

MODULE 4.9

Development of an American Culture

FOCUS

In his inaugural address in March 1801, President Thomas Jefferson argued that the vast distance between Europe and the United States was a blessing, allowing Americans to develop their own unique culture and institutions. For many Americans, education offered one means of ensuring a distinctive national identity. Public schools could train American children in republican values, while the wealthiest among them could attend private academies and colleges. Newspapers, sermons, books, magazines, and other printed works could also help forge a common identity among the nation's far-flung citizens. Even the presence of American Indians and Black people contributed to art and literature that were uniquely American. Yet educational opportunities differed by race and class as well as by sex.

While this module focuses mostly on the effects of cultural and religious developments, remember to take the context of those developments into account as you read. In particular, consider how the emergence of a distinctly American culture grew from the political and economic changes that were also taking place at the same time.

Building a National Culture

At the turn of the nineteenth century, many Americans sought to create a new and distinct culture to complement the country's newly established political independence. To promote his vision of a distinctly American literature, Noah Webster published the *American Spelling Book* (1810) and the *American Dictionary of the English Language* (1828). Webster's books were widely used in the nation's expanding network of schools and academies and led to more standardized spelling and pronunciation of commonly used words.

WORKING with EVIDENCE

Source: Horace Mann, "The Necessity of Education in a Republican Government" (1839)

> "My proposition, therefore, is simply this:—If republican institutions do wake up unexampled energies in the whole mass of a people, and give them implements of unexampled power wherewith to work out their will; then these same institutions ought also to confer upon that people unexampled wisdom and rectitude. If these institutions give greater scope and impulse to the lower order of faculties belonging to the human mind, then, they must also give more authoritative control, and more skilful [*sic*] guidance to the higher ones. If they multiply temptations, they must fortify against them. If they quicken the activity and enlarge the sphere of the appetites and passions, they must, at least in an equal ratio, establish the authority and extend the jurisdiction of reason and conscience. In a word, we must not add to the impulsive, without also adding to the regulating forces."

Questions for Analysis

1. Identify what Mann is concerned about when he notes the awakened "energies," "powers," faculties," "temptations," and "appetites" that republican institutions awaken for people.
2. Describe what Mann believes schools should do in light of these awakened energies, powers, faculties, etc.
3. Explain the changes in politics and economics during this period that gave rise to Mann's anxieties about awakened energies, powers, etc., in the United States.

At the same time, developments in Europe, particularly liberal social ideas and **Romantic-era** beliefs in human perfectibility, shaped American art, literature, philosophy, and architecture in the early nineteenth century. European Romantics, like the English poet William Wordsworth, the German philosopher Immanuel Kant, and the French painter Eugène Delacroix, challenged Enlightenment ideas of rationality by insisting on the importance of human passion, the mysteries of nature, and the virtues of common folk.

Romantic era The early nineteenth-century artistic and philosophical movement that challenged Enlightenment ideas of rationality, materialism, and classicism by asserting the prominence of the subjective and emotional national world. The movement originated in Europe in the late eighteenth century and was widely expressed in the arts as the triumph of senses over rationalism.

American novelists in the early republic drew on these ideas as they sought to educate readers about virtue. Advances in printing and the manufacture of paper increased the circulation of novels, a literary genre developed in Britain and continental Europe at the turn of the eighteenth century. Improvements in girls' education then produced a growing audience for novels among women. American authors like Susanna Rowson placed ordinary women and men in moments of high drama that tested their moral character. Novelists also emphasized new marital ideals, by which husbands and wives became affectionate partners and companions in creating a home and family.

Washington Irving was one of the most well-known literary figures in the early republic. He wrote a series of popular folktales, including "The Legend of Sleepy Hollow" and "Rip Van Winkle," that were published in his *Sketchbook* in 1820. They drew on the Dutch culture of the Hudson valley region and often poked fun at more celebratory tales

Granger – Historical Picture Archive

Marmaduke Multiply's Merry Method of Making Minor Mathematics, c. 1815 After Noah Webster introduced his *American Spelling Book* in 1810, math instructors introduced books for young people like the one shown here. The book uses rhymes and colorful illustrations to teach students multiplication tables.

What does the publication of educational books such as this one suggest about the value Americans placed on public schooling during the early 1800s?

of early American history. In one serious essay, Irving challenged popular accounts of colonial wars that ignored courageous actions by American Indians while applauding white atrocities.

Still, books that glorified the nation's past were also enormously popular. Just as European Romantics emphasized individual, especially heroic, action, so too did America's earliest historical writers. Among the most influential were Mason Weems, author of the *Life of Washington* (1806), a celebratory if fanciful biography, and Mercy Otis Warren, who wrote a three-volume *History of the Revolution* (1805). The influence of American authors increased as residents in both urban and rural areas purchased growing numbers of books.

- How did Romanticism contribute to the development of a national identity?

Thinking Historically

Sourcing, Situating, and Evaluating the Significance of Primary Sources

Not only do historians analyze primary sources, but they also judge their significance. Think of all the future primary sources that are being produced right now: emails, social media posts, television shows, movies, government documents, videos, artwork, doodles in your APUSH book—all of these are potential primary sources. But not all of these are significant to historians at all times.

The significance of primary sources is determined not by the source, but by the topic of a historian's analysis. Depending on what questions a historian asks, *anything* produced by people could be a significant primary source. So, it's important to know the subject of an analysis before determining the significance of a primary source.

Consider the Horace Mann primary source from this module:

Source: Horace Mann, Massachusetts Secretary of Education, "The Necessity of Education in a Republican Government" (1839)

> "My proposition, therefore, is simply this:—If republican institutions do wake up unexampled energies in the whole mass of a people, and give them implements of unexampled power wherewith to work out their will; then these same institutions ought also to confer upon that people unexampled wisdom and rectitude. If these institutions give greater scope and impulse to the lower order of faculties belonging to the human mind, then, they must also give more authoritative control, and more skilful [*sic*] guidance to the higher ones. If they multiply temptations, they must fortify against them. If they quicken the activity and enlarge the sphere of the appetites and passions, they must, at least in an equal ratio, establish the authority and extend the jurisdiction of reason and conscience. In a word, we must not add to the impulsive, without also adding to the regulating forces."

(continued)

If you're undertaking historical analysis on the breeding of horses in the 1830s, this source is not particularly significant. But if you're studying the origins of public education in the 1830s and 1840s, this is a very important source.

Have a look at your responses to the "AP® Working with Evidence" questions for this document, especially question 3:

> Explain the changes in politics and economics during this period that gave rise to Mann's anxieties about awakened energies, powers, etc., in the United States.

While this question doesn't ask *directly* about education, it assumes public education is a *response* to certain anxieties during the period. Therefore, Mann's speech could be a significant primary source for exploring the anxieties of some Americans during this period.

Let's think about how the sourcing categories of **point of view**, **purpose**, and **historical situation** can be used to understand this source within the context of the 1830s and trends that would cause American anxiety during this period.

Historical situation might be new to you as a term, but it is not new as a concept. In short, the historical situation forms the backdrop of a source, like the scene behind an actor on a stage. In the case of the primary source above, Horace Mann is giving a speech as the government official tasked with education of the children of Massachusetts, a state whose economy had been transformed by the rise of industrial textile production during the 1820s and 1830s.

Complete the following table based on the excerpt from Mann's speech. For "historical situation," consider changes in politics and elections during this era. The first category has been done for you:

Point of View	Purpose	Historical Situation
Mann believes that American political freedoms have unleashed certain "energies," "powers," faculties," "temptations," "energies," and "appetites" in the American people.		

ACTIVITY

Write a body paragraph that begins with a claim statement about Mann's source that incorporates **purpose** and **historical situation** as part of your explanation. Use the **CSE** approach with information from your completed graphic organizer to construct your claim statement for the following sub-argument of this thesis:

> **Prompt:** Evaluate the extent to which economic and political changes shaped American society in the 1830s.

Thesis: Large-scale changes during the 1830s caused great anxiety for many Americans **[claim]**. Popular culture was transformed by the spread of print media, the market revolution revolutionized production and upended the way people worked, and the idea of the "common man" led to fears of a coarser style of politics no longer controlled by traditional elites **[line of reasoning]**.

Sub-argument: By the 1830s, many Americans were concerned that the "common man" politics had become too unruly, and proposed various ways to control political enthusiasm.

MODULE 4.10 The Second Great Awakening

FOCUS

The development of a common American identity continued as men and women of all classes and races embraced the Protestant religious revival known as the Second Great Awakening to express deeply held beliefs and reclaim a sense of the nation's godly mission. Yet evangelical Protestantism was not the only religious tradition to thrive in this period. Catholic churches and Jewish synagogues multiplied with immigration, and in the North, Quaker meetings and Unitarian congregations flourished as well. New religious groups also attracted thousands of followers, while transcendentalists sought deeper engagements with nature as another path to spiritual renewal.

As you read this module, consider the causes of this religious movement, as well as the effects, many of which were not themselves explicitly religious in character.

Second Great Awakening
A series of Protestant revivals, larger in number than the first Great Awakening, from the 1790s to the 1830s that spurred social-reform movements in response to the changes brought about by the market revolution. Prominent leaders of this movement were Charles Grandison Finney and Lyman Beecher.

The Roots of the Second Great Awakening

Amid the wave of scientific discoveries of the late eighteenth and early nineteenth centuries, religious leaders sought to renew American spirituality. However, like the first Great Awakening (see Module 2.7), the spiritual renewal of the **Second Great Awakening** was rooted less in established churches and educated ministers than in new religious organizations and popular preachers. Methodist and Baptist churches were especially vital to this development. In 1780, only fifty Methodist churches existed in the United States. By 1820, it was the largest denomination in the nation, followed closely by Baptists. Believing that everyone could gain salvation, the two denominations appealed to small farmers, workers, and the poor as well as to women and Blacks.

In some cases, women and Black people joined this popular ministry, and a few attracted followings independent of any church. Jemima Wilkinson, a white woman who called herself "the Publick Universal Friend," developed a gender-neutral persona. Proclaiming herself the "Spirit of Light," she preached throughout the Northeast.

In rural and frontier areas, Baptists, Methodists, and Presbyterians organized camp meetings, where a dozen or more preachers, many without formal training, tapped into deep wells of spirituality. The first camp meeting, held in Cane Ridge, Kentucky, in 1801, attracted some 10,000 men and women. White and Black people, enslaved and free, attended these meetings and were encouraged to dance, shout, sing, and pray. For the next two decades, camp meetings continued to attract large crowds across the South and West.

AP® EXAM TIP

The Second Great Awakening was a major religious revival that lasted for decades and spread throughout every region of the country. You need to understand the ideology and events of the Second Great Awakening. Be able to explain how the Second Great Awakening affected American society.

Although diverse religious traditions flourished in the United States, evangelical Protestantism proved the most powerful in the 1820s and 1830s, spreading northward from its southern and western roots. Evangelical churches hosted revivals, celebrated conversions, and organized prayer and missionary societies. The Second Great Awakening transformed Protestant churches and the social fabric of northern life.

Ministers like Charles Grandison Finney and Lyman Beecher adopted techniques first used by southern Methodists and Baptists: plain speaking, powerful images, and mass meetings. But Finney molded these techniques for a more affluent audience and held his "camp meetings" in established churches.

By the late 1820s, boomtown growth along the Erie Canal aroused deep concerns among religious leaders about the rising tide of sin. In response, the Reverend Finney arrived in Rochester in September 1830. He began preaching in local Presbyterian churches, leading crowded prayer meetings that lasted late into the night. Individual worshippers walked to special benches designated for anxious sinners, who were prayed over in public. Female parishioners played crucial roles, encouraging their husbands, sons, friends, and neighbors to submit to God.

Thousands of Rochester residents joined in the evangelical experience as Finney's powerful message engulfed other denominations. The significance of these revivals went far beyond an increase in church membership. Finney converted "the great mass of the most influential people" in the city: merchants, lawyers, doctors, master craftsmen, and shopkeepers. Equally important, he proclaimed that if Christians were "united all over the world," the return of Jesus Christ "might be brought about in three months." Preachers in Rochester and the surrounding towns took up his call, and converts committed themselves to preparing the world for Christ's arrival.

AP® WORKING with EVIDENCE

Source: Charles G. Finney, *An Influential Woman Converts*, 1830

> "The wife of a prominent lawyer . . . was one of the first converts. She was a woman of high standing, a lady of culture and extensive influence. . . .
>
> Mrs. M. had been a [happy], worldly woman, and very fond of society. She afterward told me that when I first came there, she greatly regretted it, and feared [that] . . . a revival would greatly interfere with the pleasures and amusements that she had promised herself that winter. On conversing with her I found that the Spirit of the Lord was indeed dealing with her. . . . She was bowed down with great conviction of sin. . . . I pressed her earnestly to renounce sin, and the world, and self, and everything for Christ. . . . [W]e knelt down to pray; and my mind being full of the subject of the pride of her heart . . . I very soon introduced the text: 'Except ye be converted and become as little children, ye shall in no wise enter into the kingdom of heaven.' . . . [A]lmost immediately I heard Mrs M. . . . repeating that text:
>
> 'Except ye be converted and become as little children—as little children—Except ye be converted and become as little children.' I observed that her mind was taken with that, and the Spirit of God was pressing it upon her heart. I therefore continued to pray, holding that subject before her mind. . . .
>
> [H]er heart broke down, her sensibility gushed forth, and before we rose . . . , she was indeed a little child."

Questions for Analysis

1. Describe Finney's depiction of Mrs. M.
2. Describe the context surrounding Finney's revival efforts.
3. Explain why Finney targeted wealthy and influential individuals such as Mrs. M. for conversion.

Developments in Rochester were replicated in cities across the North. Presbyterian, Congregational, and Episcopalian churches overflowed with middle-class and wealthy Americans, while Baptists and Methodists ministered more to laboring women and men. Black Baptists and Methodists evangelized in their own communities, combining powerful preaching with rousing spirituals. In Philadelphia, Black people built fifteen churches between 1799 and 1830. A few Black women joined men in evangelizing their fellow Black Americans.

Tens of thousands of Black and white converts embraced evangelicals' message of moral outreach. No reform movement gained greater impetus from the revivals than **temperance**, whose advocates sought to moderate and then ban the sale and consumption of alcohol. In the 1820s, Americans fifteen years and older consumed six to seven gallons of distilled alcohol per person per year (about double the amount consumed today). Middle-class evangelicals, who once accepted moderate drinking as healthful, now insisted on eliminating alcohol consumption altogether.

temperance
The movement to moderate and then ban the sale and consumption of alcohol that emerged in the early nineteenth century as part of the larger push, mainly by middle-class reformers, to improve society.

REVIEW

- How did the Second Great Awakening change American society during the mid-nineteenth century?

New Visions of Faith and Reform

Although enthusiasm for temperance and other reforms faded during the Panic of 1837 and many churches lost members, the Second Great Awakening continued in its aftermath. But now evangelical ministers competed for souls with a variety of other religious groups, many of which supported good works and social reform.

The Society of Friends (Quakers), the first religious group to refuse fellowship to slaveholders, expanded throughout the early nineteenth century, but largely in the North and Midwest. As the Society of Friends continued to grow so, too, did its influence in reform movements, as activists like Amy Post carried Quaker testimonies against alcohol, war, and slavery into the wider society.

Unitarians also combined religious worship with social reform. They differed from other Christians by believing in a single unified higher spirit rather than the Trinity. Emerging mainly in New England in the early nineteenth century, Unitarian societies slowly spread west and south in the 1830s. Opposed to evangelical revivalism and dedicated to a rational approach to understanding the divine, Unitarians attracted prominent literary figures and intellectuals.

Other denominations grew as a result of immigration. Dozens of Catholic churches were established to meet the needs of Irish and some German immigrants. With the rapid increase in Catholic churches, Irish priests multiplied in the 1840s and 1850s, and women's religious orders became increasingly Irish as well.

At the same time, synagogues, Hebrew schools, and Jewish mutual-aid societies signaled the growing presence of Jewish immigrants, chiefly from Germany, in the United States. These religious groups were less active in social reform and more focused on assisting their own congregants in securing a foothold in their new home.

Entirely new religious groups also flourished in the 1840s. One of the most important was the Church of Jesus Christ of Latter-Day Saints, or Mormons, founded by Joseph Smith. Smith claimed he had received visions from God at age fifteen and was directed to dig up gold plates inscribed with instructions for redeeming the Lost Tribes of Israel. *The Book of Mormon* (1830), supposedly based on these inscriptions, served, along with the

Bible, as the scriptural foundation of the Church of Jesus Christ of Latter-Day Saints, which Smith led as the Prophet.

Smith founded not only a church but a theocracy (a community governed by religious leaders). In the mid-1830s, Mormons established a settlement at Nauvoo, Illinois, and recruited followers—Black and white—from the eastern United States and England. When Smith voiced antislavery views, some local residents expressed outrage. But it was his claim to revelations permitting polygamy that led local authorities to arrest him and his brother. When a mob then lynched the Smith brothers, Brigham Young, a successful missionary, took over as Prophet. In 1846, he led 12,000 followers west, 5,000 of whom settled near the Great Salt Lake, in what would soon become the Utah Territory. Isolated from anti-Mormon mobs, Young established a thriving theocracy. In this settlement, leaders practiced polygamy and denied Black members the right to become priests.

New religious groups also formed by separating from established denominations. William Miller, a prosperous farmer and Baptist preacher, claimed that the Bible proved that the Second Coming of Jesus Christ would occur in 1843. Thousands of Americans joined the Millerites. When various dates for Christ's Second Coming passed without incident, however, Millerites developed competing interpretations for the failure and divided into distinct groups. The most influential group formed the Seventh-Day Adventist Church in the 1840s.

- What religious changes took place in America during the 1830s and 1840s?

Transcendentalism

Another important movement for spiritual renewal was rooted in the transcendent power of nature. The founder of this **transcendentalist** school of thought was Ralph Waldo Emerson. Raised a Unitarian, Emerson began challenging the church's ideas. His 1836 essay entitled "Nature" expounded his newfound belief in a Universal Being. This Being existed as an ideal reality beyond the material world and was accessible through nature. Emerson's view of the natural world was distinctly American and suggested that moral perfection could be achieved in the United States. Emerson expressed his ideas in widely read essays and books and in popular lectures.

transcendentalism
A Romantic-era movement founded in the 1830s, proposing that individuals look inside themselves and to nature for spiritual and moral guidance rather than to formal religion or organizations.

Emerson's hometown of Concord, Massachusetts, served as a haven for writers, poets, intellectuals, and reformers who were drawn to transcendentalism. In 1840, Margaret Fuller, a close friend of Emerson, became the first editor of *The Dial*, a journal dedicated to transcendental thought. In 1844, she moved to New York City, where Horace Greeley hired her as a critic at the *New York Tribune*. She soon published a book, *Woman in the Nineteenth Century* (1845), which combined transcendental ideas with arguments for women's rights.

Henry David Thoreau also followed the transcendentalist path. He grew up in Concord and read "Nature" while a student at Harvard in the mid-1830s. In July 1845, Thoreau moved to a cabin near Walden Pond and launched an experiment in simple living. A year later, he was imprisoned overnight for refusing to pay his taxes as a protest against slavery and the Mexican-American War. In the anonymous *Civil Disobedience* (1846), Thoreau argued that individuals of conscience had the right to resist government policies they believed to be immoral. Five years later, he published *Walden*, which highlighted the interplay among a simple lifestyle, natural harmony, and social justice.

AP® EXAM TIP
You should know the significant individuals in the transcendentalist movement, along with their philosophies about humanity, their methods to spread their message, and their effect on U.S. society.

Thomas Cole, View of the Round-Top in the Catskill Mountains, 1827 Thomas Cole was born in England in 1801, migrated to America in 1818, and lived for many years in Catskill, New York, with his wife and children until his death in 1848. Many of his paintings captured a romantic view of nature that combined a hint of wildness with the beauty of mountain mists and sunlit rivers shown here.

How does the portrayal of nature in this painting reflect transcendentalist ideas of the time?

Like Emerson, many American artists embraced the power of nature. Led by Thomas Cole, members of the **Hudson River School** painted romanticized landscapes from New York's Catskill and Adirondack Mountains. Some northern artists also traveled to the West, painting the region's grand vistas. Pennsylvanian George Catlin portrayed the dramatic scenery of western mountains, gorges, and waterfalls and also painted moving portraits of Plains Indians.

REVIEW

- In what ways were the transcendentalist movement and Second Great Awakening similar, and in what ways did they differ?

AP® Skills Workshop: Thinking Historically

Creating Historical Context in an Essay Conclusion

Ideally, every essay should end with a conclusion. A good conclusion convinces your reader of your essay's thesis, leaves them with a feeling that the essay is thoroughly argued, and gives a sense of how the topic influenced U.S. history after the time period of the question. In this way, a conclusion is more than just a final statement to finish your essay. It is also a place where you can summarize your essay's argument and once again express your knowledge of the context of your historical analysis. An essay conclusion that includes meaningful context helps finish your argument by signaling to your reader the ways in which your topic shaped the future.

(continued)

Let's think about how you might craft a conclusion for the following prompt and thesis:

Prompt: Evaluate the extent to which change in U.S. society shaped religious and social reforms between 1800 and 1840.

Thesis: The industrial revolution and the growth of the middle class transformed American society between 1800 and 1840 **[claim]**. The expansion of the slave economy and the advent of separate spheres between men and women shaped a Second Great Awakening and later reform movements, which sought reform of racial and gender norms during this era **[line of reasoning]**.

Generally, a good rule of thumb for concluding context is to take a "step forward" in the historical narrative by discussing the **immediate concluding context** (a context that is present during the essay's time frame and continues afterward), or to take a larger step forward and discuss the **long-term concluding context** (a related context that occurs in a later time period) of your essay's topic. And, like your introduction, your context statement needs support and an explanation. If this sounds familiar, that's because it's the **CSE** approach.

You should keep in mind that when you take the AP® Exam, you will have the knowledge to make claims that extend past the time period in the prompt. For the purpose of this example, we've provided a model that includes historical developments you have not yet encountered in this textbook. You will learn more about these developments throughout the rest of the school year. For now, you should focus on how the examples provided can be used to build strong concluding context statements.

Let's start by exploring the immediate context of the prompt above. You might build a strong set of concluding statements by creating a table like this one:

Immediate Concluding Context Claim	Immediate Concluding Context Support	Explanation of Immediate Concluding Context
After 1840, reform movements continued to challenge prescribed gender roles and the enslavement of Black people in the South.	In 1845, Frederick Douglass published the first edition of his autobiography, boosting the message of the abolitionist movement. At the Seneca Falls Convention in 1848, Elizabeth Cady Stanton and other reformers demanded voting rights for women.	Agitation by reformers helped bring liberation for Black people in 1865, although women would be disappointed in their quest for suffrage until the early twentieth century.

You can also apply the same strategy to long-term contexts:

Long-Term Concluding Context Claim	Long-Term Concluding Context Support	Explanation of Long-Term Concluding Context
After 1840, racial and gender conflicts continued to simmer in the United States.	Jim Crow laws, which created a race-based legal system, continued to exist officially in the South, and unofficially throughout much of the rest of the nation, while women would not acquire the right to vote until 1920.	In this way, the conflicts and reform movements that arose between 1820 and 1840 continued to shape U.S. history, even well into the twentieth century.

(continued)

Your concluding paragraph that uses immediate concluding context could look like this:

> The women's rights movement and abolitionism were all shaped by social changes between 1820 and 1840, specifically the expansion of the slave system, and the invention of "separate spheres" between genders **[reiteration of thesis]**. After 1840, reform movements continued to challenge prescribed gender roles and the enslavement of Black people **[immediate concluding context claim]**. In 1845, Frederick Douglass published the first edition of his autobiography, spreading the message of the abolitionist movement. At the Seneca Falls Convention in 1848, Elizabeth Cady Stanton and other reformers demanded voting rights for women **[immediate concluding context support]**. Agitation by reformers helped bring liberation for Black people in 1865, although women would be disappointed in their quest for suffrage until the early twentieth century **[explanation of immediate concluding context]**.

And a concluding paragraph that uses long-term concluding context might look like this:

> The women's rights movement and abolitionism were all shaped by social changes between 1820 and 1840, specifically the expansion of the slave system, and the invention of "separate spheres" between genders **[reiteration of thesis]**. Unfortunately, after 1840, racial and gender conflicts continued to simmer in the United States **[long-term concluding context claim]**. Jim Crow laws, which created a race-based legal system, continued to exist officially in the South, and unofficially throughout much of the rest of the nation during the late nineteenth century, while women would not acquire the right to vote until 1920 **[long-term concluding context support]**. In this way, the conflicts and reform movements that arose between 1820 and 1840 continued to shape U.S. history, even well into the twentieth century **[explanation of long-term concluding context]**.

ACTIVITY

Here is a prompt from material in Period 4. Write a conclusion paragraph with either immediate or long-term concluding context. Make sure to include your thesis in the introduction and restate it in the conclusion. For your conclusion, use your knowledge of Period 4 so far.

> Evaluate the extent to which economic change drove reform in the United States between 1815 and 1848.

An Age of Reform

MODULE 4.11

FOCUS

Both religious commitments and secular problems spurred social activism in the 1830s and 1840s. In cities, small towns, and rural communities, Northerners founded organizations, launched campaigns, and established institutions to better the world around them. Yet even Americans who agreed that society should be reformed still often disagreed over priorities and solutions. Moreover, while some activists employed moral arguments to persuade Americans to follow their lead, others insisted that laws that imposed reform were the only effective means of change. Antislavery movements in the North steadily grew from the 1820s until the Civil War (1860–1865), as reformers split over banning the expansion of slavery into new territories or abolishing slavery throughout the United States. A women's rights movement also emerged, fueled in part by the backlash many women experienced from their participation in abolitionist organizations.

As you read this module, compare the reform movements that arose to address economic and social changes during this period. In what ways did these reform movements seek similar goals through similar means, and in what ways did they attempt reforms differently for different ends?

Varieties of Reform

Middle-class Protestants formed the core of many reform movements in the North during the mid-nineteenth century. They had more time and money to devote to social reform than did their working-class counterparts and were less tied to traditional ways than their wealthy neighbors. Nonetheless, workers and farmers, Black people and immigrants, Catholics, and Jews also participated in efforts to improve society.

Reformers used different techniques to pursue their goals. Because women could not vote, for example, they were excluded from direct political participation. Instead, they established charitable associations, distributed food and medicine, constructed asylums for the mentally ill or physically infirm, circulated petitions, organized boycotts, arranged meetings and lectures, and published newspapers and pamphlets. Other groups with limited political rights—Black Americans and immigrants, for instance—embraced similar modes of action and also formed mutual-aid societies. Native-born white men participated in these forms of activism and, in addition, organized political campaigns and lobbied legislators.

The reform techniques chosen were also affected by the goals of a particular movement. Moral persuasion worked best with families, churches, and local communities, while legislation was more likely to succeed if the goal involved transforming people's behavior across a whole state or region.

Reformers often used a variety of tactics to support a single cause, and many changed their approach over time. For instance, reformers who sought to eradicate prostitution in the 1830s prayed in front of urban brothels and attempted to rescue "fallen" women. They soon launched *The Advocate of Moral Reform*, a monthly journal

AP® EXAM TIP

Develop a clear understanding of the key issues of reform efforts, what they hoped to accomplish, and their eventual outcomes. The AP® Exam often asks questions regarding the cause and effect of these reforms. The AP® Exam also often asks for comparison responses between reform movements, such as feminism and abolitionism, or comparison between antebellum reforms and reforms in later time periods.

filled with morality tales, advice to mothers, and lists of men who visited brothels. In small towns, moral reformers sought to alert young women and men to the dangers of city life. By the 1840s, urban reformers opened Homes for Virtuous and Friendless Females to provide safe havens for vulnerable women. And across the country, moral reformers began petitioning state legislators to make punishments for men who hired prostitutes as harsh as those for prostitutes themselves.

REVIEW

■ What strategies did reformers employ during the mid-1800s?

The Problem of Poverty

Poverty had existed since the colonial era, but the Panic of 1837 aroused greater public concern. Leaders of both government and private charitable groups increasingly tied relief to the moral character of those in need. Affluent Americans had long debated whether the poor would learn to work hard and live responsibly if they were simply provided assistance without working for it. The debate was deeply gendered. Women and children were considered the most deserving of aid, and middle- and upper-class women the ideal dispensers of that aid. Successful men, meanwhile, often viewed poverty as weakness and considered giving pennies to a beggar an unmanly act that indulged the worst traits of the poor.

While towns and cities had long abandoned the poorest residents to almshouses or workhouses, charitable societies in the early nineteenth century sought to change the conditions that produced poverty. As the number of poor people increased with urban growth, women in the North involved in charitable work began visiting poor neighborhoods, offering blankets, clothing, food, and medicine to needy residents. Many charitable organizations began building orphanages, hospitals, and homes for working women to provide deserving but vulnerable individuals with resources to improve their life chances.

The "undeserving" poor faced less appealing choices. They generally received assistance only through the workhouse or the local jail. By the 1830s, images of rowdy men who drank or gambled away what little they earned, prostitutes who tempted respectable men into vice, and immigrants who preferred idle poverty to virtuous labor became stereotypical figures in debates over the causes of and responses to poverty.

At the same time, young poor women — at least if they were white and Protestant — were increasingly portrayed as the victims of immoral men or unfortunate circumstance. In fictional tales, naive girls were seduced and abandoned by manipulative men. One of the first mass-produced books in the United States, Nathaniel Hawthorne's *The Scarlet Letter* (1850), was set in Puritan New England but addressed contemporary concerns about the seduction of innocent young women. It illustrated the social ostracism and poverty suffered by a woman who bore a child outside of marriage.

nativist

An anti-immigrant American involved in public campaigns against foreigners in the 1840s. Nativism emerged as a response to increased immigration to the United States in the 1830s and 1840s, particularly the large influx of Catholic immigrants.

Other fictional tales placed the blame for fallen women on foreigners, especially Catholics. Such works drew vivid portraits of young nuns raped by priests and then thrown out pregnant and penniless. These stories heightened anti-Catholic sentiment, which periodically boiled over into attacks on Catholic homes, schools, churches, and convents.

At the same time, economic competition intensified conflicts between immigrants and native-born Americans. By the 1840s, Americans who opposed immigration took the name **nativists** and launched public political campaigns that blamed foreigners for poverty and crime. Samuel F. B. Morse, the inventor of the telegraph, was among the most popular anti-immigrant spokesmen.

Irish Catholics were often targeted in attacks against immigrants. In May 1844, working-class nativists clashed with Irishmen in Philadelphia after shots were fired from a firehouse. A dozen nativists and one Irishman were killed the first day. The next night, nativists looted and burned Irish businesses and Catholic churches.

Many nativists blamed poverty among immigrants on their drinking habits. Others considered alcohol abuse, whether by native-born or immigrant Americans, the root cause not only of poverty but of many social evils.

REVIEW

- What economic and social factors help explain the rise of nativism in the mid-1800s?

The Temperance Movement

Temperance advocates first organized officially in 1826 with the founding of the American Temperance Society. This all-male organization was led by clergy and businessmen but focused on alcohol abuse among working-class men. Religious revivals inspired the establishment of some 5,000 local chapters, and Black and white men founded other temperance organizations as well.

Over time, the temperance movement changed its goal from moderation to total abstinence, targeted middle-class and elite as well as working-class men, and also welcomed women's support. Wives and mothers were expected to persuade male relatives to stop drinking and sign a temperance pledge. Women founded dozens of temperance societies in the 1830s, which funded the circulation of cautionary tales, woodcuts, and etchings about the dangers of "demon rum."

From The National Temperance Offering, and Sons and Daughters of Temperance Gift, Clifton Waller Barrett Library of American Literature, Albert and Shirley Small Special Collections Library, University of Virginia

Drunkard's Home, 1850
Temperance societies undertook a variety of activities to publicize the dangers of alcohol. This engraved illustration is from *The National Temperance Offering*, published by the Sons of Temperance, one of the oldest temperance organizations in the United States.

How does this image reinforce the arguments made by temperance advocates and moral reformers during the mid-1800s?

Some workingmen viewed temperance as a way to gain dignity and respect. For Protestants, in particular, embracing temperance distinguished them from Irish Catholic workers. A few working-class temperance advocates criticized liquor dealers, whom they claimed directed "the vilest, meanest, most earth-cursing and hell-filling business ever followed." More turned to self-improvement. In the 1840s, small groups of laboring men formed Washingtonian societies—named in honor of the nation's founder—to help each other stop excessive drinking. Martha Washington societies appeared shortly thereafter, composed of the wives, mothers, and sisters of male alcoholics.

Despite the rapid growth of temperance organizations, appeals to morality failed to reduce alcohol consumption significantly. As a result, many temperance advocates turned to legal reform. In 1851, Maine was the first state to legally prohibit the sale of alcoholic beverages. By 1855, twelve more states had restricted the manufacture or sale of alcohol. Yet these stringent measures inspired a backlash. Hostile to the imposition of middle-class Protestant standards on the population at large, Irish workers in Maine organized the Portland Rum Riot in 1855. It led to the Maine law's repeal the next year. Still, the diverse strategies used by temperance advocates gradually reduced, but did not eliminate, the consumption of beer, wine, and spirits across the United States.

REVIEW

- How did the efforts of temperance advocates compare to those of anti-poverty reformers of the mid-nineteenth century?

Utopian Communities

utopian society
A community formed in the first half of the nineteenth century to embody alternative social and economic visions and to create models for society at large to follow.

While most reformers attempted to change the wider society, some activists established self-contained communities to serve as models for others. The architects of these **utopian societies**, most commonly formed in the North and Midwest, gained inspiration from European intellectuals and reformers as well as American religious and republican ideals.

In the 1820s, Scottish and Welsh labor radicals such as Frances Wright, Robert Owen, and his son Robert Dale Owen established several utopian communities in the United States. They believed the nation was open to experiments in communal labor, gender equality, and (in Wright's case) racial justice. Their efforts eventually failed, but they did generate impassioned debate.

Then in 1841, former Unitarian minister George Ripley established a transcendentalist community at Brook Farm in Massachusetts. Four years later, Brook Farm was reorganized according to the principles of the French socialist Charles Fourier. Fourier believed that cooperation across classes was necessary to lessen the conflicts inherent in capitalist society. He developed a plan for communities, where residents chose jobs based on individual interest but were paid according to the contribution of each job to the community's well-being. Fourier also advocated equality for women. More than forty Fourierist communities were founded in the northern United States during the 1840s.

A uniquely American experiment, the Oneida community, was established in central New York by John Humphrey Noyes in 1848. He and his followers believed that Christ's Second Coming had already occurred and embraced the communalism of the early Christian church. Noyes required members to turn over their private property to the community and to embrace the notion of "complex marriage," in which women and men were free to have sexual intercourse with any consenting adult. He also introduced a form of birth control that sought to ensure women's freedom from constant childbearing and instituted communal child-rearing practices. Despite the public outrage provoked by Oneida's economic and sexual practices, the community recruited several hundred residents and thrived for more than three decades.

REVIEW

- How did mid-nineteenth-century utopian societies compare with more mainstream reform movements?

Abolitionism

Free Black people were the earliest advocates of abolition, but their role in the movement against slavery generated conflict as more white people joined in the 1830s. For a small percentage of Northerners, slavery was the most extreme injustice. While most Northerners considered it sufficient to rid their own region of human bondage, antislavery advocates argued that the North remained complicit because Northerners still benefited from slavery. After all, enslaved people labored under brutal conditions to provide cotton for New England factories, sugar and molasses for northern tables, and profits for urban traders.

In the 1820s, Black Americans increasingly led the fight to abolish slavery. They published pamphlets, lectured to small audiences, and helped enslaved people reach freedom when they fled from slaveholders. In 1829, David Walker wrote the militant antislavery statement, *Walker's Appeal . . . to the Coloured Citizens of the World.* The free son of an enslaved father, Walker left his North Carolina home for Boston in the 1820s and became a writer for *Freedom's Journal*, the country's first newspaper published by Black people. In his *Appeal*, Walker warned that enslaved people would claim their freedom by force if white people did not agree to emancipate them.

Some northern Black people feared Walker's radical *Appeal* would unleash a white backlash, while Quaker **abolitionists** like Benjamin Lundy, editor of the *Genius of Universal Emancipation*, admired Walker's courage but rejected his call for violence. Nonetheless, the *Appeal* circulated widely among free and enslaved Black people, with copies spreading from northern cities to Charleston, Savannah, New Orleans, and Norfolk.

Maria Stewart, a free Black widow in Boston, began to speak out against slavery in 1831 and 1832. She lectured to mixed-sex and interracial audiences, demanding that northern Black people take more responsibility for ending slavery and fighting racial discrimination. In 1833, free Black and white Quaker women formed an interracial organization, the Philadelphia Female Anti-Slavery Society, which advocated the boycott of cotton, sugar, and other goods produced using enslaved labor.

William Lloyd Garrison, a white Bostonian, was inspired by radical stances like Walker's and Stewart's. In 1831, he launched his own abolitionist newspaper, the ***Liberator***, and urged white antislavery activists to embrace the goal of immediate emancipation without compensation to slaveholders, a position first advocated by the English Quaker Elizabeth Heyrick.

The *Liberator* demanded that white people take an absolute stand against slavery but use moral persuasion rather than armed force to halt its spread. With like-minded Black and white activists in Boston, Philadelphia, and New York City, Garrison organized the **American Anti-Slavery Society (AASS)** in 1833. By the end of the decade, the AASS boasted branches in dozens of towns and cities across the North. Members supported lecturers and petition drives, criticized churches that refused to denounce slavery,

American Anti-Slavery Society (AASS)
An abolitionist society founded by William Lloyd Garrison in 1833 that became the most important northern abolitionist organization of the period. The society featured prominent orators and activists such as Frederick Douglass. Members argued slavery was neither economically nor morally viable. The group often met with violence.

and proclaimed the U.S. Constitution a proslavery document. Some Garrisonians also participated in the work of the Underground Railroad, a secret network of activists who assisted fugitives fleeing enslavement.

In 1835, Sarah Grimké and her sister, Angelina Grimké, joined the AASS and soon began lecturing for the organization. Daughters of a prominent South Carolina planter, they had moved to Philadelphia and converted to Quakerism. As white Southerners, their denunciations of slavery carried particular weight. Because they were women, their public presence aroused fierce opposition. In 1837, Congregationalist ministers in Massachusetts decried their presence in front of "promiscuous" audiences of men and women, but 1,500 female millworkers still turned out to hear them at Lowell's city hall.

The abolitionist movement quickly expanded to the west, where debates over slave and free territory were especially intense. In 1836, Ohio claimed more antislavery groups than any other state, and Ohio women initiated a petition drive to abolish slavery in the District of Columbia. The petition campaign, which spread across the North, inspired the first national meeting of women abolitionists in 1837. Other antislavery organizations, like the AASS, recruited male and female abolitionists, Black and white. And still others remained all-white, all-Black, or single-sex.

- What roles did Black people and women play in the abolitionist movement in the 1830s?

Abolition Gains Ground, Faces Conflict, and Inspires Women

The growth of the abolitionist movement shocked many Northerners, and in the late 1830s, violence often erupted in response to antislavery agitation. Northern manufacturers and merchants were generally hostile, fearing abolitionists' effect on the profitable trade in cotton, sugar, cloth, and rum. And white workingmen feared increased competition for jobs from Black men if slavery were abolished. In the 1830s, mobs routinely attacked antislavery meetings, lecturers, and printing presses. At the 1838 Antislavery Convention of American Women at Philadelphia's Pennsylvania Hall, mobs forced Black and white women to flee and then burned the hall to the ground.

Major antislavery petition campaigns in 1836 and 1837 generated opposition in and between the North and South. Thousands of abolitionists signed petitions to ban slavery in the nation's capital (the District of Columbia), end the internal slave trade, and limit further expansion of slavery.

Some evangelical women considered such efforts part of their Christian duty, but most ministers (including Charles Finney) condemned antislavery work as outside women's sphere. Many female evangelicals retreated in the face of clerical disapproval, but others continued their efforts alongside their non-evangelical sisters. Meanwhile, southern politicians, incensed by antislavery petitions, persuaded Congress to pass the gag rule in 1836 (see Module 4.8).

But gag rules did not silence abolitionists. Indeed, new groups of activists, especially enslaved people who had successfully fled to reach freedom in the North, offered powerful personal tales of the horrors of bondage. The most famous fugitive abolitionist was Frederick Douglass, a Maryland-born enslaved man who in 1838 escaped to New Bedford, Massachusetts. He met Garrison in 1841, joined the AASS, and four years later published his life story, *Narrative of the Life of Frederick Douglass, as Told by Himself.* Having revealed his identity as a formerly enslaved man, Douglass sailed for England, where he launched a successful two-year lecture tour. While he was abroad, British abolitionists purchased Douglass's freedom, and Douglass returned to the United States a free man. In 1847, he decided to launch his own antislavery newspaper, the ***North Star***, a decision that Garrison and other white AASS leaders opposed. Douglass moved to Rochester, where he had earlier found free Black and white Quaker allies.

AP® WORKING with EVIDENCE

Source: Frederick Douglass, *Narrative of the Life of Frederick Douglass, an American Slave, Written by Himself*, 1845

> "Very soon after I went to live with Mr. and Mrs. Auld, she very kindly commenced to teach me the A, B, C. After I had learned this, she assisted me in learning to spell words of three or four letters. Just at this point of my progress, Mr. Auld found out what was going on, and at once forbade Mrs. Auld to instruct me further, telling her, among other things, that it was unlawful, as well as unsafe, to teach a slave to read. To use his own words, '. . . He would at once become unmanageable, and of no value to his master.' . . . From that moment, I understood the pathway from slavery to freedom. . . . Though conscious of the difficulty of learning without a teacher, I set out with high hope, and a fixed purpose, at whatever cost of trouble, to learn how to read. The very decided manner with which he spoke, and strove to impress his wife with the evil consequences of giving me instruction, served to convince me that he was deeply sensible of the truths he was uttering. . . . In learning to read, I owe almost as much to the bitter opposition of my master, as to the kindly aid of my mistress."

Questions for Analysis

1. Identify what Douglass believed allowed white people to keep those they enslaved in bondage.
2. Explain how Douglass sought to prove that enslaved Black people deserved freedom and equal rights.
3. Explain how Douglass's point of view shaped his account.

While eager to have formerly enslaved people tell their dramatic stories, many white abolitionists did not show vigorous support of Black people who asserted an independent voice. Some abolitionists opposed slavery but still believed that Black people were racially inferior. Others supported racial equality but assumed that Black abolitionists would defer to white leaders. Thus, several affiliates of the AASS refused to accept Black members. Yet the independent efforts of Douglass and other Black activists expanded the antislavery movement, even as they made clear the limits of white abolitionist ideals.

Conflicts also arose over the responsibility of churches to challenge slavery. The major Protestant denominations included southern as well as northern branches.

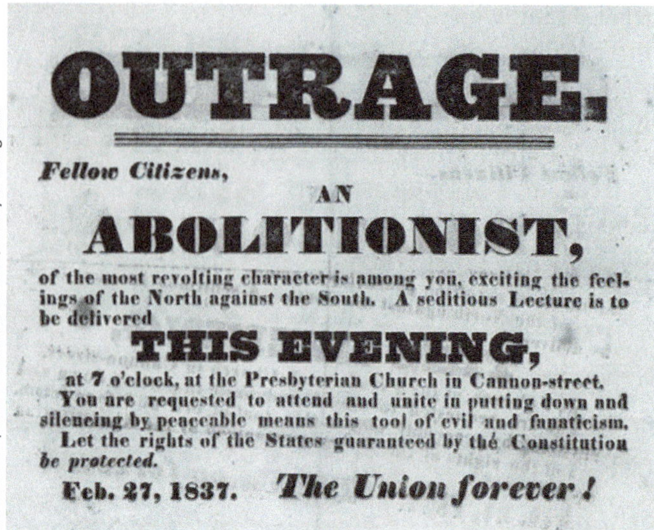

Antiabolitionist Poster, 1837 Opponents of abolitionism, fearful of social upheaval resulting from growing antislavery sentiment in the North, often resorted to violence against abolitionists. This 1837 poster encourages "Fellow Citizens" to protest an abolitionist meeting, albeit through ostensibly "peaceable means."

How does the language used in this image promote fear and anger toward abolitionism?

If mainstream churches — Presbyterians, Baptists, Methodists — refused communion to slaveholders, their southern branches would secede. Still, from the 1830s on, abolitionists pressured churches to take Christian obligations seriously and denounce human bondage. Individual congregations responded, but aside from the Society of Friends (Quakers), larger denominations failed to follow suit.

In response, abolitionists urged parishioners to break with churches that admitted slaveholders as members. Antislavery preachers pushed the issue, and some worshippers "came out" from mainstream churches to form antislavery congregations. White Wesleyan Methodists and Free Will Baptists joined Black Methodists and Baptists in insisting that their members oppose slavery. Although these denominations remained small, they served as a living challenge to mainstream denominations.

Women were increasingly active in the AASS and the **"come outer" movement**, but their growing participation aroused opposition even among abolitionists. By 1836–1837, female societies formed the backbone of many antislavery petition campaigns. More women also joined the lecture circuit, including Abby Kelley, a fiery orator who demanded that women be granted an equal role in the movement. But when Garrison and his supporters appointed Kelley to the AASS business committee in May 1839, angry debates erupted over the propriety of women participating "in closed meetings with men." Of the 1,000 abolitionists in attendance, some 300 walked out in protest. The dissidents, including many evangelical men, soon formed a new organization, the American and Foreign Anti-Slavery Society, which excluded women from public lecturing and office holding but encouraged them to support men's efforts.

"come outer" movement
A protest movement whose members would often abstain from political office, activity, or voting to protest the government and other organizations' complicity in slavery.

Those who remained in the AASS then continued to expand the roles of women. In 1840, local chapters appointed a handful of female delegates, including Lucretia Mott of Philadelphia, to the World Anti-Slavery Convention in London. The majority of men at the meeting, however, rejected the female delegates' credentials. Women were then forced to watch the proceedings from a separate section of the hall, confirming for some that women could be effective in campaigns against slavery only if they gained more rights for themselves.

Finally, in July 1848, a small circle of women, including Lucretia Mott and a young American she met in London, Elizabeth Cady Stanton, organized the first convention focused explicitly on women's rights. Held in Stanton's hometown in New York State, the Seneca Falls convention attracted three hundred women and men. James Mott, husband of Lucretia, presided over the convention, and Frederick Douglass spoke, but women dominated the proceedings. One hundred participants signed the **Declaration of Sentiments**, which called for women's equality in everything from education and employment to legal rights and voting. Two weeks later, a second convention convened in Rochester, where participants took the radical action of electing a woman, Abigail Bush, to preside. Here, too, Douglass spoke alongside other Black abolitionists and local working women.

Declaration of Sentiments
Penned by Elizabeth Cady Stanton, it was a call for women's rights in marriage, family, religion, politics, and law, first issued at the 1848 Seneca Falls convention. The document mirrored the language of the Declaration of Independence.

AP® WORKING with EVIDENCE

Source: Elizabeth Cady Stanton, *Declaration of Sentiments*, 1848

"We hold these truths to be self-evident: that all men and women are created equal; that they are endowed by their Creator with certain inalienable rights; that among these are life, liberty, and the pursuit of happiness. . . .

But when a long train of abuses and usurpations . . . reduce them under absolute despotism, it is their duty to throw off such government. . . .

The history of mankind is a history of repeated injuries and usurpations on the part of man toward woman, having in direct object the establishment of an absolute tyranny over her. . . .

He has never permitted her to exercise her inalienable right to the elective franchise.

He has compelled her to submit to laws, in the formation of which she had no voice. . . .

He has taken from her all right in property, even to the wages she earns.

He has made her . . . promise obedience to her husband, he becoming, to all intents and purposes, her master—the law giving him power to deprive her of her liberty, and to administer [punishment].

He has so framed the laws of divorce, as to what shall be the proper causes, and in case of separation, to whom the guardianship of the children shall be given . . . going upon the false supposition of the supremacy of man, and giving all power into his hands. . . .

He has monopolized nearly all the profitable employments, and from those she is permitted to follow, she receives but a scanty remuneration."

Questions for Analysis

1. Identify the main points of this excerpt from the *Declaration of Sentiments*.
2. Explain how women's experiences in the abolitionist movement and other social factors provide context for this document.

Questions for Comparison

Thomas Jefferson, Declaration of Independence, 1776 (see Module 3.4)

1. Evaluate the extent of similarity in the stated complaints listed in both documents.
2. Evaluate the extent of similarity between the context surrounding this document and the Declaration of Independence.

Although abolitionism provided much of the momentum for the women's rights movement, other movements also contributed. Strikes by seamstresses and mill workers in the 1830s and 1840s highlighted women's economic needs. Utopian communities experimented with gender equality, and temperance reformers focused attention on domestic violence and sought changes in divorce laws. A diverse coalition also advocated for married women's property rights in the mid-1840s.

Women's rights were debated among New York's Seneca Indians as well. Like the Cherokee, Seneca women had lost traditional rights over land and tribal policy as their nation adopted Anglo-American ways. In the summer of 1848, the creation of a written constitution threatened to enshrine these losses in writing. The Seneca constitution did strip women of their dominant role in selecting chiefs but protected their right to vote on the sale of tribal lands.

Earlier in 1848, revolutions had erupted against repressive regimes in France and elsewhere in Europe. Antislavery newspapers like the *North Star* covered developments in detail, including European women's demands for political and civil recognition. The meetings in Seneca Falls and Rochester drew on these ideas and influences even as they focused primarily on the rights of white American women.

REVIEW

- How did the changes to the American Anti-Slavery Society during the 1840s differentiate it from earlier abolitionist organizations?
- What prejudices did women face from within the movement?

The Rise of Antislavery Parties

As women's rights advocates demanded female suffrage, debates over the role of partisan politics in the antislavery campaign intensified. Keeping slavery out of western territories depended on the actions of Congress, as did abolishing slavery in the nation's capital and ending the internal slave trade. Moral arguments had seemingly done little to change minds in Congress or in the South.

Liberty Party

An antislavery political party formed in 1840. The Liberty Party, along with the Free-Soil Party, helped place slavery at the center of national political debates.

To force abolition onto the national political agenda, the **Liberty Party** was formed in 1840. Many Garrisonians were appalled at the idea of participating in national elections when the federal government supported slavery in numerous ways, from the three-fifths compromise to allowing slavery in newly acquired territories. Still, the Liberty Party gained significant support among abolitionists in New York, the Middle Atlantic states, and the Midwest.

The Whigs and Democrats generally avoided the antislavery issue to keep their southern and northern wings intact, but that strategy became more difficult once the Liberty Party entered campaigns. In 1840, the party won less than 1 percent of the popular vote but organized rallies that attracted large crowds. In 1844, the party more than doubled its votes, which was sufficient to deny Henry Clay a victory in New York State and thus, ironically, the election of slaveholder James K. Polk (see Module 5.2).

When President Polk led the United States into war with Mexico, interest in an antislavery political party surged. In 1848, the Liberty Party gained the support of antislavery Whigs, also called Conscience Whigs; northern Democrats who opposed the extension of slavery into the territories; and Black leaders like Frederick Douglass, who broke with Garrison on the usefulness of electoral politics.

Free-Soil Party

A party founded by political abolitionists in 1848 to expand the appeal of the Liberty Party by focusing less on the moral wrongs of slavery and more on the benefits of providing economic opportunities for northern white people in western territories.

Seeing a political opportunity, more practically minded political abolitionists founded the **Free-Soil Party**, which quickly subsumed the Liberty Party. Free-Soilers focused less on the moral wrongs of slavery than on the benefits of keeping western territories free for northern white people seeking economic opportunity. The Free-Soil Party nominated former Democratic president Martin Van Buren in 1848 and won 10 percent of the popular vote. But once again, the result was to send a slaveholder to the White House—Zachary Taylor. Nonetheless, the Free-Soil Party had expanded beyond the Liberty Party, raising fears in the South and in the two major parties that the battle over slavery could no longer be contained.

REVIEW

- What challenges did abolitionists face during the 1830s and 1840s?
- How did the Liberty Party and Free-Soil Party change American politics in the 1840s?

Skills Workshop: Thinking Historically

Using Claims and Evidence in Sources to Create a Body Paragraph

You've already had a lot of practice with **claims** and **evidence** using the **CSE** method. And, of course, you've already done a lot of thinking about **primary sources**. As you recall, historians build their arguments on primary sources. But sometimes, historians also consider the claims and evidence that sources *themselves* contain.

Consider, for example, this quote from the *Declaration of Sentiments* (1848) that you read in this module:

Source: Elizabeth Cady Stanton, *Declaration of Sentiments*, 1848

> "We hold these truths to be self-evident: that all men and women are created equal; that they are endowed by their Creator with certain inalienable rights; that among these are life, liberty, and the pursuit of happiness. . . .
>
> But when a long train of abuses and usurpations . . . reduce them under absolute despotism, it is their duty to throw off such government. . . .
>
> The history of mankind is a history of repeated injuries and usurpations on the part of man toward woman, having in direct object the establishment of an absolute tyranny over her. . . .
>
> He has never permitted her to exercise her inalienable right to the elective franchise.
>
> He has compelled her to submit to laws, in the formation of which she had no voice. . . .
>
> He has taken from her all right in property, even to the wages she earns.
>
> He has made her . . . promise obedience to her husband, he becoming, to all intents and purposes, her master—the law giving him power to deprive her of her liberty, and to administer [punishment]."

It's clear what the **claim** is in this source, as well as its **evidence.** You could summarize the source's claim like this:

> Stanton believes that women have suffered a long history of abuse and need remedy.

You could summarize an example of the source's evidence like this:

> One example of the abuse described by Stanton is the fact that men have not allowed women to vote, to exercise the "elective franchise."

A **CSE** statement that follows a sub-argument and uses Stanton's claims and evidence might look like this:

> Women faced political oppression as white male citizens experienced greater political rights, including suffrage **[sub-argument]**. For example, in the *Declaration of Sentiments* (1848), Elizabeth Cady Stanton argued that women had suffered a long history of abuse and need remedy **[claim]**. One of these abuses, according to Stanton, was the fact that men had not allowed women to vote, or, as she said, to exercise the "elective franchise" **[support]**. In this way, Stanton went to the heart of the way in which women continued to be oppressed politically: They could not vote for the government that represented them **[explain]**.

(continued)

Now have a look this source from the same time period. Put the source's **claim** in your own words, and then list three pieces of **evidence** the source provides:

Source: Matthew Carey, *Appeal to the Wealthy of the Land,* 1833

> "Let us now turn to the appalling case of seamstresses, . . . [who are] Beset . . . by poverty and wretchedness, with scanty and poor fare, miserable lodgings, clothing inferior in quality. . . . [W]ithout the most distant hope of amelioration of condition. . . .
>
> It is frequently asked—what remedy can be found for the enormous and cruel oppression experienced by females employed as seamstresses . . . I venture, to suggest a few [reforms]. . . .
>
> Let the employments of females be multiplied as much as possible . . . especially in shop-keeping in retail stores. . . .
>
> Let schools be opened for instructing poor women in cooking. . . .
>
> In the towns in the interior of the state, and in those in western states, there is generally a want of females as domestics, seamstresses, etc. . . . [The rich should] provide for sending some of the superabundant poor females of our cities to those places."

Claim:

Evidence:

ACTIVITY

Now, write a body paragraph for the following thesis. Use the underlined portion of the line of reasoning in the thesis to form the **sub-argument** of your body paragraph. Don't forget to **CSE** both the Stanton and Carey sources when you use them for evidence. When you make *your* **claims**, be sure to discuss each source's **claim** and **evidence** when you **support** and **explain** how each supports your **sub-argument**.

> **Prompt:** Evaluate the extent to which reform efforts fostered change in the lives of women in the period 1820 to 1840.

Thesis: Inspired by the Second Great Awakening, women played a significant role in the reform movements of the 1820s and 1830s **[claim]**. Although women were instrumental in the temperance and abolition movements and found new ways to participate in boisterous politics of the era, women continued to face political and economic oppression as white male citizens experienced greater political rights including suffrage **[line of reasoning]**.

African Americans & The Society of the South in the Early Republic

MODULES 4.12 4.13

FOCUS

As you read these two modules, consider how the South's geography shaped its dependence on a system of enslaved labor and caused its economy and society to develop differently from those of the North. Be sure to take note of the social tensions that developed within the South as a result. Also consider how enslaved people resisted their status in covert (secret) and occasionally overt (open) ways. How did enslaved and free Black people in the South contribute to the development of a distinctly Black American culture during the first half of the nineteenth century?

The cotton gin, developed in the 1790s, ensured the growth of southern agriculture into the 1840s. As the cotton kingdom spread west, planters, those who owned the largest plantations, forged a distinctive culture around the institution of slavery. But this agricultural economy based on slavery limited the development of cities, technology, and educational institutions, leaving the South increasingly dependent on the North and West for many of its needs.

As the cotton economy spread, Black people continued to maintain relationships, identities, and cultural practices in the harshest of circumstances. Many found small ways to resist their enslavement every day. Others resisted more openly, and a small number organized rebellions against those holding them in bondage.

White slaveholders' fears of rebellion led to stricter regulations of Black life, and any uprisings temporarily reinforced white solidarity. While yeomen farmers, poor white people, and middle-class professionals all voiced some doubts about the ways in which slavery affected southern society, the increasing dependence of the southern economy on enslaved labor undermined these doubts.

AP® EXAM TIP

Even after the importation of enslaved people was banned in 1808, the population of enslaved persons continued to grow through natural reproduction. In this repressive environment, enslaved people developed a distinct culture, along with communities based on religion and kinship networks. To what extent did these developments help Black people survive the horrific conditions? The AP® Exam regularly asks questions regarding effects of the institution of slavery on American society.

Amid hard work and harsh treatment, enslaved people created social bonds and a rich culture of their own. Thus, Black people continued for generations to employ African names, like Cuffee and Binah. Even if slaveholders gave them English names, they might use African names in the slave quarters to sustain family memories and community networks. Elements of West African and Caribbean languages, agricultural techniques, medical practices, forms of dress, folktales, songs and musical instruments, dances, and courtship rituals demonstrated the continued importance of these cultures to African Americans.

This hybrid culture spread as enslaved people hauled cotton to market, forged families across plantation boundaries, or were sold farther south. It was also passed across generations through storytelling, music, rituals, and health care. Most enslaved women's births were attended by Black midwives, and Black healers sought southern equivalents to herbal cures used in West Africa.

Religious practices offer an important example of this blended culture among enslaved people. Africans from Muslim communities often continued to follow Muslim

MPI/Getty Images

"A Slave Wedding," c. 1800 This rare watercolor painting of a Black wedding probably dates from the turn of the nineteenth century. The distance between the slave quarters and the plantation house suggests this may be a South Carolina scene. The enslaved women and men are dressed in their finest clothing, and the musicians appear to be playing African-style instruments made from gourds.

 **How does this painting depict the blending of African and American cultures?**

religious practices even if they were also required to attend Protestant churches, while Black Protestant preachers developed rituals that combined African and American elements. In the early nineteenth century, many enslaved people eagerly embraced the evangelical teachings offered by Baptist and Methodist preachers, which echoed some of the expressive spiritual forms in West Africa. On Sundays, those who listened in the morning to white ministers proclaim slavery as God's will might gather in the evening to hear their own preachers declare God's love and the possibilities of liberation, at least in the hereafter. Enslaved people often incorporated drums, dancing, or other West African elements into these worship services.

Although most Black preachers were men, a few enslaved women gained a spiritual following. Many enslaved women embraced religion enthusiastically, hoping that Christian baptism might substitute for West African rituals that protected newborn babies. These women sometimes called on church authorities to intervene when white slaveholders, overseers, or even enslaved men abused them. They also considered the church one means of recognizing marriages between enslaved people that were not acknowledged legally.

REVIEW

- How and why did enslaved people blend elements of African and American culture?

A Plantation Society Develops in the South

Plantation slavery existed throughout the Americas in the early nineteenth century. Extensive plantations worked by large numbers of enslaved people existed in the West Indies and South America. In the U.S. South, however, the unstable cotton market and a scarcity of fertile land kept most plantations relatively small before 1830. Over the next two decades, though, territorial expansion and the profits from cotton, rice, and sugar allowed successful southern planters to build grand houses and purchase a variety of luxury goods.

As plantations grew, a wealthy aristocracy sought to ensure productivity by employing harsh methods of discipline. For instance, although plantation owner James Henry Hammond, a South Carolina politician, imagined himself a progressive slaveholder, he used the whip often, hoping thereby to ensure that his estate generated sufficient profits to support a lavish lifestyle.

The wives of wealthy southern men, meanwhile, managed their own families and the enslaved household workers as well as the feeding, clothing, and medical care of the entire enslaved labor force. Plantation mistresses also organized social events, hosted relatives and friends for extended stays, and sometimes directed the plantation in their husbands' absence. Still, enslaved women, not plantation mistresses, completed most of the manual labor as they cooked, cleaned, and washed for the family, cared for the children, and even nursed the babies.

Wealthy white women benefited from the best education, the greatest access to music and literature, and the finest clothes and furnishings. Yet the pedestal on which plantation mistresses stood was shaky, built on a patriarchal system in which husbands and fathers held substantial power. For example, most plantation wives tried to ignore the frequent sexual relations that husbands initiated with enslaved women. A few, such as Catherine Hammond, the wife of James Henry Hammond, did not. She moved to Charleston with her two youngest daughters when she discovered James's sexual abuse of an enslaved mother and daughter. Other women, however, took out their anger and frustration on enslaved women already victimized by their husbands. Moreover, some mistresses were slaveholders themselves, gave enslaved people as gifts to family members and friends, and traded them on the open market.

Not all slaveholders were wealthy planters like the Hammonds, with an enslaved labor force of fifty or more people and extensive landholdings. Far more planters in the 1830s and 1840s held between twenty and fifty enslaved people, and an even larger number of farmers kept just three to six people in bondage. However, the majority of white Southerners was not slaveholders. As Hammond wrote a friend in 1847, "The planters here are essentially what the nobility are in other countries. They stand at the head of society & politics."

- What was the lifestyle of plantation owners and their families during the mid-nineteenth century?

Urban Life in the Slaveholding South

The social supremacy of slaveholders had broad repercussions. The richest men in the South invested in slavery, land, and household goods, with little left to develop industry, technology, or urban institutions. The largest factory in the South, the Tredegar Iron Works in Richmond, Virginia, employed several hundred free and enslaved Black people by 1850. Most southern industrialists, however, like South Carolina textile manufacturer William Gregg, employed poor white women and children. But neither Tredegar nor a scattering of textile mills fundamentally reshaped the region's economy, leaving it much less industrialized than the North's.

The South also fell behind in urban development. The main exception was port cities. Yet even in Baltimore, Charleston, and Savannah, commerce was often directed by northern agents, especially cotton brokers. In addition, nearly one-third of southern whites had no access to cash and instead bartered goods and services, further restricting the urban economy.

Southern cities did attract many free Black people. The growing demand for cheap domestic labor in urban areas and planters' greater willingness to emancipate less valuable single enslaved women meant that free Black women generally outnumbered men in southern cities. These women worked mainly as washerwomen, cooks, and general domestic laborers, while free Black men typically became skilled artisans, dockworkers, or sailors. Free Black people competed for these jobs with enslaved people and growing numbers of European immigrants who flocked to southern cities in the 1840s and 1850s. The presence of immigrants and free Black people, as well as the reputation of ports as escape hatches for enslaved people fleeing the South, ensured the suspicion of many Southerners that cities represented a potential threat to their way of life.

The scarcity of cities and industry in the South also limited the development of transportation. State governments invested little in roads, canals, and railroads. Most small farmers traded goods locally, and most planters used the South's extensive river system to ship goods to commercial hubs. Only Virginia and Maryland, with their proximity to the nation's capital, developed extensive road and rail networks.

- What major factors affected mid-nineteenth-century industrialization, urbanization, and transportation developments in the South?

The Consequences of Slavery's Expansion

Outside the South, industry and agriculture increasingly benefited from technological innovation. Planters, however, continued to rely on intensive manual labor. Even reform-minded planters focused on fertilizer and crop rotation rather than machines to enhance productivity. The limited use of new technologies — such as iron plows or seed drills — resulted from a lack of investment capital and planters' refusal to purchase expensive equipment that they feared might be broken or purposely sabotaged by enslaved people. Instead, they relied on continually expanding the acreage under cultivation.

One result of these practices was that a declining percentage of white Southerners came to control vast estates with large numbers of enslaved laborers. Between 1830 and 1850, the absolute number of both enslaved people and slaveholders grew. But slaveholders became a smaller proportion of all white Southerners, dropping to under a third by 1850, because the white population grew faster than the number of slaveholders. At the same time, distinctions among wealthy planters, small slaveholders, and white people who were not slaveholders also increased.

The concern with productivity and profits and the concentration of more enslaved people on large plantations did have some limited benefits for Black women and men. The end of the international slave trade in 1808 forced planters to rely more heavily on natural reproduction to increase their labor force. Thus, many planters thought more carefully about how they treated those they enslaved, who were increasingly viewed as "valuable property." It was no longer good business to work enslaved people to death or cripple them by severe punishments. In fact, planters often hired poorly paid Irish dayworkers to perform dangerous tasks rather than using their enslaved laborers.

Nonetheless, slaveholders continued to whip and sexually exploit enslaved people and made minimal investments in their diet and health care. Most enslaved people lived in small houses with dirt floors and little furniture and clothing. They ate a diet high in calories, especially fats and carbohydrates, but with little meat, fish, fresh vegetables, or fruits. The high mortality rate among enslaved infants and children—more than twice that of white children to age five—reflected this limited care.

The spread of slavery into Mississippi, Louisiana, Alabama, Missouri, and eventually Texas affected both white and Black families, though again not equally. The younger sons of wealthy planters were often forced to move to the borderlands, and their families generally lived in rough quarters on isolated plantations. A woman traveler noted that the men "think only of making money, and their houses are hardly fit to live in." A planter's wife complained, "Mississippi and Alabama are a dreary waste."

Such moves were far more difficult for enslaved people, however. Between 1830 and 1850, more than 440,000 enslaved people were forced to move from the Upper South to the Lower South, often tearing them away from their families. They endured especially harsh conditions on the southern borderlands as they cleared and cultivated new lands.

By the 1830s, slave markets emerged in key cities across the South. Solomon Northup was held in one in Washington, D.C., where a woman named Eliza watched as her son Randall was "won" by a planter from Baton Rouge. She promised "to be the most faithful slave that ever lived" if he would also buy her and her daughter. The slave trader threatened the desperate mother with a hundred lashes, and her tears could not change the outcome. As slavery spread westward, such scenes were repeated thousands of times.

AP® EXAM TIP

Crops cultivated by enslaved persons became the foundation of the U.S. economy before the Civil War, but they were destructive to the nutrients in the soil. Consequently, slavery continued to expand as new western lands (such as Texas) opened to occupation and settlement. Be sure to understand the impact of slavery on the economy in both the North and the South, as well as why non-slaveholding southern whites supported the institution of slavery.

REVIEW

- How did the 1808 ban on the importation of enslaved people and the westward spread of slavery affect the lives of enslaved Black Americans?

Enslaved Labor Fuels the Southern Economy

The labor of enslaved Black people drove the nation's economy as well as the South's. In 1820, the South produced some 500,000 bales of cotton, much of it exported to England. By 1850 the region produced nearly three million bales, feeding textile mills in New England and abroad (Map 4.6). A decade later, cotton accounted for nearly two-thirds of the U.S. export trade and added nearly $200 million a year to the American economy.

Enslaved laborers, of course, saw very little of this wealth. Enslaved carpenters, blacksmiths, and other skilled laborers were sometimes hired out and allowed to keep

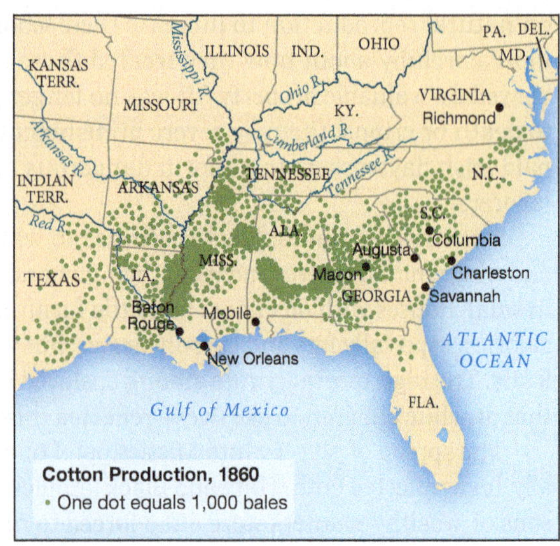

MAP 4.6 The Spread of Cotton Production, 1820–1860 While tobacco, rice, and sugar remained important crops in a few states, cotton became the South's and the nation's major export. The need to find more fertile fields led planters to migrate to Alabama, Mississippi, and Louisiana. As a result of cotton's success, the number of enslaved people increased dramatically, the internal slave trade expanded, and labor demands intensified.

How do the changes in cotton production shown on this map reflect the economic and social changes occurring simultaneously in the region?

a small amount of the money they earned. They traveled to nearby households, compared their circumstances to those on other plantations, and sometimes made contact with free Black people. Some of them also learned to read and write and had access to tools and knowledge denied to field hands. Still, they were constantly hounded by whites who demanded travel passes and deference, and they were often suspected of involvement in rebellions.

Enslaved household workers sometimes received old clothes and bedding or leftover food from slaveholders. Yet they were under the constant surveillance of whites, and women especially were vulnerable to sexual abuse. Moreover, the work they performed was physically demanding.

James Curry, an enslaved man who escaped bondage, recalled that his mother, a cook in North Carolina, rose early each morning to milk cows, bake bread, and churn butter. She was responsible for meals for her fellow enslaved people and their slaveholders. In summer, she cooked her last meal around eight o'clock, after which she milked the cows again. Then she returned to her quarters, put her children to bed, and often fell asleep while mending clothes.

Once enslaved children reached the age of ten to twelve, they were put to work full time, usually in the fields. Although field labor was defined by its relentless pace and drudgery, it also brought together large numbers of enslaved people for the entire day and thus helped forge bonds among laborers on the same plantation. Songs provided a rhythm for their work and offered them the chance to communicate their frustrations or hopes.

Field labor was generally organized by task or by gang. Under the task system, typical on rice plantations, enslaved people could return to their quarters once the day's task was completed. This left time for them to cultivate gardens, fish, or mend clothes. In the gang system, widely used on cotton plantations, men and women worked in groups under the supervision of a driver. Often working from sunup to sundown, they swept across fields hoeing, planting, or picking.

AP® WORKING with EVIDENCE

Source: Solomon Northup, *Twelve Years a Slave*, 1853

"The hands are required to be in the cotton field as soon as it is light in the morning, and, with the exception of ten or fifteen minutes, which is given them at noon to swallow their allowance of cold bacon, they are not permitted to be a moment idle until it is too dark to see, and when the moon is full, they often times labor till the middle of the night. They do not dare to stop even at dinner time, nor return to the quarters, however late it be, until the order to halt is given by the driver.

The day's work over in the field, the baskets are . . . carried to the gin-house, where the cotton is weighed. No matter how fatigued and weary he may be—no matter how much he longs for sleep and rest—a slave never approaches the gin-house with his basket of cotton but with fear. If it falls short in weight—if he has not performed the full task appointed him, he knows that he must suffer. And if he has exceeded it by ten or twenty pounds, in all probability his master will measure the next day's task accordingly. . . . Most frequently they have too little, and therefore it is they are not anxious to leave the field. After weighing, follow the whippings; and then the baskets are carried to the cotton house, and their contents stored away like hay, all hands being sent in to tramp it down. . . .

Finally, at a late hour, they reach the quarters, sleepy and overcome with the long day's toil. Then a fire must be kindled in the cabin, the corn ground in the small hand-mill, and supper, and dinner for the next day in the field, prepared. All that is allowed them is corn and bacon, which is given out at the corncrib and smoke-house every Sunday morning. . . .

An hour before day light the horn is blown. . . . Then the fears and labors of another day begin."

Questions for Analysis

1. Describe how Northup characterizes the daily challenges and fears faced by enslaved men on cotton plantations.
2. Describe the economic context that contributed to the working conditions Northup describes.
3. Explain how the publication of accounts such as Northup's affected the debate over slavery.

Questions for Comparison

Harriet Jacobs, *Incidents in the Life of a Slave Girl*, 1861 (Module 4.5)

1. Explain how Northup's and Jacobs's accounts highlight the differing experiences of enslaved men and women.
2. Evaluate the extent of similarity between the factors that contributed to Northup's and Jacobs's accounts.

REVIEW

- What factors shaped daily life for enslaved Black people during the first half of the nineteenth century?

Resistance and Rebellion

Many slaveholders worried that Black preachers and West African folktales inspired Black people to resist enslavement. Fearing defiance, planters went to great lengths to control the people they held in bondage. Although they were largely successful in quelling open revolts, they were unable to eliminate more subtle forms of opposition, like slowing the pace of work, feigning illness, and damaging equipment. More overt forms of resistance such as truancy and running away, which disrupted work and lowered profits, also proved impossible to stamp out.

The forms of everyday resistance enslaved people employed varied in part on their location and resources. Skilled artisans, mostly men, could do more substantial damage because they used more expensive tools, but they were less able to protect themselves through pleas of ignorance. Field laborers could often damage only hoes, but they could do so regularly without exciting suspicion. Enslaved household workers could burn dinners, scorch shirts, break china, and even poison slaveholders. Often considered the most loyal to slaveholders, they were also among the most feared because of their intimate contact with white families. Enslaved single men were the most likely to run away, planning their escape to get as far away as possible before their absence was noticed. Women who fled plantations were more likely to hide out for short periods in the local area. Eventually, isolation, hunger, or concern for children led most of these runaways to return if slave patrols did not find them first.

Despite their rarity, efforts to organize slave uprisings, such as the one supposedly hatched by Denmark Vesey in 1822, continued to haunt southern whites. Rebellions in the West Indies, especially the one in Haiti, also echoed through the early nineteenth century. Then in 1831, an enslaved man named Nat Turner—who previously seemed obedient—organized a revolt in rural Virginia that stunned whites across the South.

Turner was a religious visionary who believed God had given him a mission. On the night of August 21, he and his followers killed his enslavers, the Travis family, and then headed to nearby plantations in Southampton County. The insurrection led to the deaths of fifty-seven white men, women, and children and liberated more than fifty enslaved people. By the next day, outraged white militiamen captured the Black rebels. Turner managed to hide for two months but was eventually caught, tried, and hanged. Virginia executed fifty-five other Black people suspected of assisting Turner.

Nat Turner's rebellion

A slave uprising in Virginia led by Nat Turner in 1831. Turner's rebellion generated panic among white Southerners, leading to tighter control of Black people through the passage of stricter slave codes in southern states.

Nat Turner's rebellion incited panic among white Virginians, who beat and killed some 200 Black people with no connection to the uprising. White Southerners worried they might be killed in their sleep by seemingly submissive enslaved people. News of the rebellion traveled through enslaved communities as well, inspiring both pride and anxiety. The execution of Turner and his followers reminded Blacks how far whites would go to protect the institution of slavery.

A mutiny on the Spanish slave ship ***Amistad*** in 1839 reinforced white Southerners' fears of rebellion. When Africans being transported for sale in the West Indies seized control of the ship near Cuba, the U.S. navy captured the vessel and imprisoned the enslaved rebels. But international treaties outlawing the Atlantic slave trade and pressure applied by abolitionists led to a court case in which former president John Quincy Adams defended the right of the Africans to their freedom. The widely publicized case reached the U.S. Supreme Court in 1841, and the Court freed the rebels. While the ruling was cheered by abolitionists, who supported ending slavery, white Southerners were shocked that the justices would liberate enslaved men.

Slave revolts led many southern states to impose harsher controls. Nat Turner's rebellion, however, led some white Virginians to question slavery itself. In December 1831, the state assembly established a special committee to consider the crisis.

Representatives from western counties, where slavery was never profitable, argued for gradual abolition laws and the relocation of the state's Black population to colonies in Africa. Hundreds of women in the region sent petitions to the Virginia legislature supporting these positions.

While advocates of colonization gained significant support, eastern planters strongly opposed abolition or colonization, and leading intellectuals argued for the benefits of slavery. Professor Thomas Dew, president of the College of William and Mary, insisted that slaveholders performed godly work in raising Africans and Black Americans from the status of brute beast to civilized Christian. "Every one acquainted with southern slaves," he claimed, "knows that the slave rejoices in the elevation and prosperity of his master." In the fall of 1832, the Virginia legislature embraced Dew's proslavery argument, rejected gradual emancipation, and imposed new restrictions on enslaved and free Black people.

From the 1820s to the 1840s, more stringent slave codes were enacted across the South. Most southern legislatures prohibited slaveholders from manumitting (freeing) the people they kept enslaved, made it illegal to teach enslaved people to read or write, placed new limits on independent Black churches, ended enslaved people's already-limited access to the courts, prohibited marriage between enslaved people, banned antislavery literature, defined rape as a crime only against white women, and outlawed gatherings of more than three Black people without a white person present.

States also regulated the lives of free Black people. Some states banned free Black people from residing within their boundaries. Other states required free Black people to post large bonds to ensure good behavior, which could be claimed for perceived infractions by community authorities. Most states forbade those who left the state from returning. The homes of free Black people could be raided at any time, and the children of free Black women were subject to stringent apprenticeship laws that kept many in virtual slavery.

Such measures proved largely successful in controlling enslaved people and significantly worsened the lives of Black people in the South. White people paid a much smaller price. Restricting education and mobility for Black people often hindered schooling and transportation for poor whites as well. Moreover, characterizing the region's main labor force as savage and lazy discouraged investment in industry and other forms of economic development. Further, the regulations increased tensions between poorer whites, who were often responsible for enforcement, and wealthy whites, who benefited most clearly from the strict slave codes.

REVIEW

- What were the most common methods enslaved people used to rebel?
- What restrictions were placed on enslaved and free Black people after Nat Turner's rebellion?

White Southerners Who Were Not Slaveholders

Yeomen farmers, independent owners of small plots who were generally not slaveholders, had a complex relationship with the South's plantation economy. Many were related to slaveholders, and they often depended on planters to ship their crops to market. Some made extra money by hiring themselves out to planters.

yeomen farmer
Non-slaveholding independent landowner. Although southern yeomen farmers had connections to the plantation economy, many realized that their interests were not always identical to those of the planter elite.

Yet yeomen farmers also recognized that their economic interests and daily experiences often diverged from those of planters. This divergence was particularly clear on slavery's frontier, where many yeomen farmers had to carve fields out of forests without the benefit of enslaved labor. They joined with friends and neighbors for barn raisings, corn shuckings, quilting bees, and other collective tasks that combined labor with sociability. Church services and church socials also brought small farm families together.

While most yeomen farmers supported slavery, they sometimes challenged planters' authority and assumptions. In the Virginia slavery debates, for example, small farmers from western districts advocated gradual abolition. As growing numbers gained the right to vote in the 1830s and 1840s, they voiced their concerns in county and state legislatures. They advocated more liberal policies toward debtors and demanded greater representation in state legislatures. They also protested planters' obstruction of common lands and waterways, such as building dams upriver that deprived farmers downriver of fishing rights.

Yeomen farmers questioned certain ideals embraced by elites. Although plantation mistresses considered manual labor beneath them, the wives and daughters of many small farmers worked in the fields, hauled water, and chopped wood. Still, yeomen farmers' ability to diminish planter control was limited by the continued importance of cotton to the southern economy.

White Southerners who owned no property at all had fewer means of challenging planters' power. These poor whites depended on hunting and fishing in borderlands areas, performing day labor on farms and plantations, or working on docks or as servants in southern cities. Poor white people competed with free and enslaved Black people for employment and often harbored resentments against them as a result.

Some poor whites remained in the same community for decades, establishing themselves on the margins of society. They attended church regularly, performed day labor for affluent families, and taught their children to defer to those higher on the social ladder. Other poor whites moved often and survived by combining legal and illegal ventures. They might perform day labor while also stealing food from local farmers. These men and women often had few ties to local communities and little religious instruction or education. Although poor white people unnerved southern elites by flouting the law and sometimes befriending poor Black people, they could not mount any significant challenge to planter control.

The South's small but growing middle class distanced themselves from poorer whites in pursuit of stability and respectability. They worked as doctors, lawyers, teachers, and shopkeepers and often looked to the North for models to emulate. Many were educated in northern schools and developed ties with commercial or professional counterparts in that region. They were avid readers of newspapers, religious pamphlets, and literary periodicals published in the North. And, like middle-class Northerners, southern businessmen often depended on their wives' social and financial skills to succeed.

Nonetheless, middle-class southern men shared many slaveholders' social attitudes and political priorities. They participated alongside planters in charitable, literary, and temperance societies and agricultural reform organizations. Most middle-class Southerners also adamantly supported slavery. In fact, some suggested that bound labor might be useful to industry. Despite the emergence of a small middle class, however, the gap between rich and poor continued to expand in the South.

- How did slavery shape the lives of white Southerners who were not slaveholders?

Planters Seek to Unify White Southerners

Planters faced another challenge as nations in Europe and South America began to abolish slavery. Antislavery views, first widely expressed by Quakers, gained growing support among evangelical Protestants in Great Britain and the United States and among political radicals in Europe. Slave rebellions in Haiti and the British West Indies in the early nineteenth century intensified these efforts.

In 1807, the British Parliament forbade the sale of enslaved people within its empire and, in 1834, emancipated all those who remained enslaved. France followed suit in 1848. As Spanish colonies such as Mexico and Nicaragua gained their independence in the 1820s and 1830s, they, too, eradicated slavery. Meanwhile, gradual abolition laws in the northern United States slowly eliminated slavery there. Although slavery continued in Brazil and in Spanish colonies such as Cuba, and serfdom remained in Russia, international attitudes toward human bondage were shifting.

In response, planters used their political and economic power to forge tighter bonds among white Southerners. According to the three-fifths compromise in the U.S. Constitution, areas with large enslaved populations gained more representatives in Congress than those without. The policy also applied to state elections, giving such areas disproportionate power in state politics, thus allowing planters a greater say in southern politics. In addition, planters used their resources to provide credit for

WORKING with EVIDENCE

Source: John C. Calhoun, *Slavery a Positive Good,* 1837

> "I hold that in the present state of civilization, where two races of different origin, and distinguished by color, and other physical differences, as well as intellectual, are brought together, the relation now existing in the slave-holding States between the two, is, instead of an evil, a good—a positive good. . . . [T]here never has yet existed a wealthy and civilized society in which one portion of the community did not, in point of fact, live on the labor of the other. . . . [L]ook at the sick, and the old and infirm slave, on one hand, in the midst of his family and friends, under the kind superintending care of his master and mistress, and compare it with the forlorn and wretched condition of the pauper in the poor house. . . . I fearlessly assert that the existing relation between the two races in the South, against which these blind fanatics are waging war, forms the most solid and durable foundation on which to rear free and stable political institutions. It is useless to disguise the fact. There is and always has been in an advanced stage of wealth and civilization, a conflict between labor and capital. The condition of society in the South exempts us from the disorders and dangers resulting from this conflict; and which explains why it is that the political condition of the slave-holding States has been so much more stable and quiet than those of the North."

Questions for Analysis

1. Identify the moral and economic justifications for slavery that Calhoun uses in this speech.
2. Describe the political and social contexts surrounding Calhoun's speech.
3. Explain how Calhoun's argument reflects an ideology of white supremacy.

those in need, offer seasonal employment for poorer whites, transport crops to market for yeomen farmers, and help out in times of crisis. Few whites could afford to anger wealthy plantation owners.

While planters continued to insist that the U.S. Constitution protected slavery and the right of states to enforce their own labor systems, they did not take white solidarity for granted. From the 1830s on, they relied on the ideology of **white supremacy** to cement the belief that all white people, regardless of class or education, were superior to all Black people.

Following on Thomas Dew, southern elites argued with growing intensity that the moral and intellectual failings of Black people meant that slavery was not just a necessary evil but a positive good. At the same time, they insisted that Black people harbored deep animosity toward whites, which could be controlled only by regulating every aspect of their lives. Combining racial fear and racial pride, planters forged bonds with poor and middle-class whites to guarantee their continued dominance. They continued to seek support from state and national legislators as well.

REVIEW

- How were planters able to maintain southern support for slavery after it was ended in the North and in other countries?

AP® Skills Workshop: Thinking Historically

Additional Practice in Using Claims and Evidence in Sources to Create a Body Paragraph

Review the AP® Thinking Historically exercise about determining claims and evidence in sources (Module 4.11), and then read the two primary sources below. Next, write a body paragraph that includes a **sub-argument** and uses the **claims** and **evidence** from these sources to prove it. Build your sub-argument from the gender portion of this thesis, which is underlined, and be sure to **CSE** each primary source to prove your sub-argument.

> **Prompt:** Evaluate the extent of difference in the abolitionist movement of the 1830s and 1840s.

Thesis: The antislavery movement during the 1830s and 1840s grew in size and significance as the issue of slavery was pushed to the forefront by outspoken abolitionists **[claim]**. Although the movement attracted men and women, women were often treated as second-class citizens in the movement, and abolitionist appeals were often framed according to the gender of the audience appealed to **[line of reasoning]**.

Source: David Walker, *Walker's Appeal . . . to the Coloured Citizens of the World*, 1830

> "Men of colour, who are also of sense, for you particularly is my APPEAL designed. Our more ignorant brethren are not able to penetrate its value. I call upon you therefore to cast your eyes upon the wretchedness of your brethren, and to do your utmost to enlighten them . . . Let the Lord see you doing what you can to rescue them and yourselves from degradation. Do any of you say that you and your family are free and happy, and what have you

(continued)

to do with the wretched slaves and other people? . . . Look into our freedom and happiness, and see of what kind they are composed!! They are of the very lowest kind—they are the very *dregs*!—they are the most servile and abject kind, that ever a people was in possession of! If any of you wish to know how FREE you are, let one of you start and go through the southern and western States of this country, and unless you travel as a slave to a White man . . . or have your free papers . . . if they do not take you up and put you in jail, and if you cannot give good evidence of your freedom, sell you into eternal slavery, I am not a living man."

Source: Elizabeth Emery and Mary P. Abbott, *Letter to the* Liberator, 1836

"The call of our female friends . . . above all, the sighs, the groans, the deathlike struggles of scourged sisters in the South—these have moved our hearts, our hands. We feel that woman has a place in this Godlike work, for woman's woes, and woman's wrongs, are borne to us on every breeze that flows from the South; woman has a place, for she forms a part in God's created intelligent instrumentality to reform the world. . . . We believe God gave woman a heart to feel—an eye to weep—a hand to work—a tongue to speak. Now let her use that tongue to speak on slavery. Is it not a curse—a heaven-daring abomination? Let her employ that hand, to labor for the slave. Does not her sister in bonds, labor night and day without reward? Let her heart grieve, and her eye fill with tears, in view of a female's body dishonored—a female's mind debased—a female's soul forever ruined!"

MODULE 4.14

Causation in Period 4

AP® Skills Workshop: Writing Historically

Outlining an Essay

You now have all the pieces to outline an AP® U.S. History essay. You've learned how to:

1. introduce and conclude an essay with a **thesis** and **context**.
2. compose body paragraphs with a **sub-argument**, which you prove with **CSE**, and
3. interpret primary sources for their **Historical Situation**, **Intended Audience**, **Purpose**, and/or **Point of View**.

Let's see how we can use all of this to outline an essay:

Step 1 ▶ Break down the prompt

All APUSH essay questions begin with a prompt. Here's one based on the material in Period 4:

> Evaluate the extent to which the market revolution led to greater opportunity for Americans in terms of race, class, and gender between 1830 and 1855.

You'll notice that the question asks "to what extent" and, therefore, wants you to evaluate the degree to which something is true or false. Whenever you see a prompt begin like this, you know your thesis is not going to be all one way, or all another.

Also, the prompt frames the context and the time period of your response. First, you'll focus your response on the topic of the "market revolution," the great changes you read about in Modules 4.5 and 4.6. The question also sets chronological parameters between 1830 and 1855, so you will confine your response to those years.

The last portion of the prompt tells you what you will evaluate. In effect, the prompt wants you to evaluate whether "greater opportunity" was more or less caused by the "market revolution" for different kinds of Americans in terms of their "race, class, and gender."

Here, then, you have a question about causation, and you will determine the extent to which the "market revolution" caused "opportunity" for certain people.

Step 2 ▶ Source the documents

We've also talked about how primary source documents can serve as evidence for your claims. On the AP® Exam, you will have one prompt that specifically asks you to incorporate a series of primary sources into your response. This is called "Document-Based Question," and it includes seven primary sources.

We're going to start off with just three primary sources. All of these can be used as evidence in your response. They should also look familiar, because you already read them in this unit. Review each source while keeping the prompt in mind.

(continued)

Source: Harriet H. Robinson, *Loom and Spindle or Life among the Early Mill Girls,* 1898

"In 1831 Lowell was little more than a factory village. . . . Help was in great demand; and stories were told all over the country of the new factory town, and the high wages that were offered to all classes of work-people,—stories that reached the ears of mechanics' and farmers' sons, and gave new life to lonely and dependent women in distant towns and farmhouses. . . .

Troops of young girls came by stages and baggage-wagons. . . .

I worked first in the spinning-room as a 'doffer.' The doffers were the very youngest girls, whose work was to doff, or take off, the full bobbins, and replace them with the empty ones. . . .

These mites had to be very swift in their movements, so as not to keep the spinning- frames stopped long, and they worked only about fifteen minutes in every hour. The rest of the time was their own, and when the overseer was kind they were allowed to read, knit, or go outside the mill-yard to play. . . .

The working-hours of all the girls extended from five o'clock in the morning until seven in the evening, with one-half hour for breakfast and dinner. Even the doffers were forced to be on duty nearly fourteen hours a day, and this was the greatest hardship in the lives of these children. For it was not until 1842 that the hours of labor for children under twelve years of age were limited to ten per day; but the 'ten-hour law' itself was not passed until long after some of these little doffers were old enough to appear before the legislative committee on the subject, and plead, by their presence, for a reduction of the hours of labor."

Source: 1850 U.S. Census of the Isaac and Amy Post Household

About the source: In 1850, for the first time, the federal census listed each member of the household by name as well as by age, sex, race (then labeled "color"), and place of birth. Some census takers noted the relationship of each household member to the family head. This census taker did not, nor did he note color. That information appears in brackets and comes from other genealogical records.

Names of Residents in Household	Relation to Head of Household	Age/Sex/Color*	Occupation for Males over 15 Years	Place of Birth
Isaac Post	[head]	50 / male / [white]	Druggist	New York
Amy Post	[wife]	45**/ female / [white]		New York
Jacob K. Post	[son]	20 / male / [white]	Clerk	New York
Joseph Post	[son]	16 / male / [white]	Clerk	New York
Willet Post	[son]	3 / male / [white]		New York
Sarah Hallowell	[sister-in-law]	30 / female / [white]		New York
Ansel Bowen	[boarder]	28 / male / [white]	Teacher	New York
Elizabeth Bowen	[boarder]	28 / female / [white]		New York
Bridget Head	[servant]	23 / female / [white]		Ireland
Mary Ann Pitkin	[boarder]	10 / female / [Black]		New York

Data from Seventh U.S. Federal Census, 1st Ward, Rochester, NY, 2 August 1850.

*The options for "color" in the 1850 Census were white, Black, and "mulatto." The bracketed information is from the 1855 New York State Census and Rochester city directories.

**Amy Post was 47 in summer 1850, not 45.

(continued)

Source: Solomon Northup, *Twelve Years a Slave,* 1853

"The hands are required to be in the cotton field as soon as it is light in the morning, and, with the exception of ten or fifteen minutes, which is given them at noon to swallow their allowance of cold bacon, they are not permitted to be a moment idle until it is too dark to see, and when the moon is full, they often times labor till the middle of the night. They do not dare to stop even at dinner time, nor return to the quarters, however late it be, until the order to halt is given by the driver.

The day's work over in the field, the baskets are . . . carried to the gin-house, where the cotton is weighed. No matter how fatigued and weary he may be—no matter how much he longs for sleep and rest—a slave never approaches the gin-house with his basket of cotton but with fear. If it falls short in weight—if he has not performed the full task appointed him, he knows that he must suffer. . . . After weighing, follow the whippings; and then the baskets are carried to the cotton house, and their contents stored away like hay, all hands being sent in to tramp it down. . . .

Finally, at a late hour, they reach the quarters, sleepy and overcome with the long day's toil. Then a fire must be kindled in the cabin, the corn ground in the small hand-mill, and supper, and dinner for the next day in the field, prepared. All that is allowed them is corn and bacon, which is given out at the corncrib and smoke-house every Sunday morning. . . .

An hour before day light the horn is blown. . . . Then the fears and labors of another day begin."

How are all of these primary sources shaped by the market revolution? To what extent did each experience opportunity? How did their race, class, and/or gender play a role in these effects? What other facts from the time period do these primary sources bring to mind? Jot down notes that answer all of these questions.

Step 3 ▶ Create the outline

Your essay's outline will have the following sections and subsections.

1. Introduction Paragraph
   a. Immediate or Preceding Context Claim
   b. Immediate or Preceding Context Support
   c. Immediate or Preceding Context Explanation
   d. Thesis Statement
2. Body Paragraph 1
   a. Sub-Argument 1
      i. Claim 1, Support 1, Explanation 1
      ii. Claim 2, Support 2, Explanation 2
3. Body Paragraph 2
   a. Sub-Argument 2
      i. Claim 1, Support 1, Explanation 1
      ii. Claim 2, Support 2, Explanation 2
4. Body Paragraph 3
   a. Sub-Argument 3
      i. Claim 1, Support 1, Explanation 1
      ii. Claim 2, Support 2, Explanation 2
5. Conclusion Paragraph
   a. Rephrase of Thesis Statement
   b. Immediate or Long-Term Concluding Claim
   c. Immediate or Long-Term Concluding Support
   d. Immediate or Long-Term Concluding Explanation

(continued)

Let's see how an outline for the prompt above might look.

1. Introduction
   a. During the early nineteenth century, changes in technology, trade, and production transformed the American economy. **[Immediate Context Claim]**
   b. Innovations like water-powered factories, steamboats, and the mass production of cotton and textiles changed the ways Americans lived. **[Immediate Context Support]**
   c. These innovations made life easier for some, and made life difficult for others, often depending on their race, class, or gender. **[Immediate Context Explanation]**
   d. The market revolution led to significantly greater opportunities for Americans though the impacts differed based on race, class, and gender. Between 1830 and 1855, some American women experienced benefits from the market economy, while many working-class American men saw their skilled crafts transformed into wage labor and Black people saw their lives grow even more difficult than before the market revolution. **[Thesis Statement]**
2. Body Paragraph 1
   a. White women in New England experienced some economic opportunities during the market economy. **[Sub-Argument 1]**
      i. Most of the benefits from the market economy came to working-class white women in the textile factories. **[Claim 1]**
      ii. For example, Harriet Robinson recalled earning wages for her work, though the work was long and difficult. **[Support 1]**
      iii. These wages allowed her a small degree of economic freedom and provided some income for her family back home. **[Explanation 1]**
      iv. Likewise, these working women were able to secure some leisure for themselves. **[Claim 2]**
      v. The publication Lowell Offering by female textile workers in Lowell, Massachusetts, during these years was one of the first publications in the nation by women for women. **[Support 2]**
      vi. This publication symbolized a degree of freedom to explore ideas and culture for these young women in the market economy. **[Explanation 2]**
3. Body Paragraph 2
   a. Working-class men, on the other hand, saw their skilled labor transformed into unskilled factory work. **[Sub-Argument 2]**
      i. For example, the shoe industry during this time period changed from production in small workshops to production in large factories. **[Claim]**
      ii. This meant that an artisan went from owning his own shop and the tools of the trade to working as an employee for wages. **[Support 1]**
      iii. This meant that the shoemaker was no longer an independent artisan, but had only his time and labor to sell to a factory owner, a decrease in his opportunity to own property of his own. **[Explanation 1]**
      iv. However, during this same time period, opportunities for middle-class workers expanded. **[Claim 2]**
      v. Isaac Post, a druggist, had a large household and likely a thriving business because his skill had not been mechanized like the shoemaker. **[Support 2]**
      vi. Post's affluence in the market economy represents a growing gulf between working-class and middle-class Americans. **[Explanation 2]**

(continued)

4. Body Paragraph 3
   a. Enslaved Black people experienced the least opportunity during the market economy. **[Sub-Argument 3]**
      i. For example, with the growth of the cotton economy and textile production, enslaved Black people found themselves subject to the gang system of labor. **[Claim 1]**
      ii. Solomon Northup described the back-breaking work and constant fear that enslaved Black people faced on the large cotton plantations under this work system. **[Support]**
      iii. These large plantations and their harsh conditions were a direct result of the need for cotton and the mass production of textiles in the market economy. **[Explanation 1]**
      iv. Also, enslaved Black people were increasingly forced by the market economy into the dissolution of their families. **[Claim 2]**
      v. As the cotton economy advanced to the west, Black people who were enslaved were often forcibly separated from family members when they were sold to enslavers who advanced into states like Mississippi. **[Support 2]**
      vi. These forced separations were a result of the market economy because the hunger for more cotton-producing land stimulated expansion, thereby undermining the opportunity for enslaved people to enjoy kinship and family life. **[Explanation 2]**
5. Conclusion
   a. Overall, the market economy caused opportunities for some white women, and for few white men, and worsened conditions for enslaved Black people. **[Rephrase of Thesis Statement]**
   b. In the coming years, the effects of the market economy only grew stronger. **[Immediate Concluding Claim]**
   c. The Civil War was won by the North with the power of industry, and after the Civil War, industrial corporations dominated the American economy. **[Immediate Concluding Support]**
   d. In this regard, the effects of the market revolution continued to shape the nation for the rest of the century. **[Immediate Concluding Explanation]**

ACTIVITY

Here's a new prompt on the same time period. Outline your own detailed response using the steps above. Use the sample outline as a model for your own outline. You can use the same three documents above.

> Evaluate the extent to which sectional tensions between the North, South, and West were shaped by changes in the economy between 1830 and 1855.

Period 4 Review 1800–1848

KEY CONCEPTS AND EVENTS

abolitionist, 345
Adams–Onís Treaty, 284
Alamo, 320
American Anti-Slavery Society (AASS), 345
American System, 270
American system of manufacturing, 289
Amistad mutiny, 360
Barbary States, 260
Battle of Horseshoe Bend, 281
Battle of New Orleans, 283
boom–bust cycle, 296
Cherokee Nation v. Georgia, 323
"come outer" movement, 348
Corps of Discovery, 262
"corrupt bargain," 311
cotton gin, 289
cult of domesticity, 302
Declaration of Sentiments, 348
Democratic Party, 311
deskilling, 295
Embargo Act, 265
Erie Canal, 271
Free-Soil Party, 350
Force Bill, 319
gag rule, 320
Haitian Revolution, 261
Hartford Convention, 282
Hudson River School, 338
Indian Removal Act, 321
judicial review, 265
Judiciary Act, 264
The *Liberator*, 345
Liberty Party, 350
Louisiana Purchase, 261
Marbury v. Madison, 264
market revolution, 287
McCulloch v. Maryland, 264
Missouri Compromise, 276
Monroe Doctrine, 284
multiplier effect, 288
mutual-aid society, 295
Nat Turner's rebellion, 360
National Republican Party, 311
National Road, 266
nativist, 342
Non-Intercourse Act, 279
North Star, 347
nullification, 318
Ordinance of Nullification, 318
Panic of 1819, 273
Panic of 1837, 296
Romantic era, 331
Second Bank of the United States, 273
Second Great Awakening, 334
Second Seminole War, 322
separate spheres, 302
spoils system, 314
Tariff of Abominations, 312
Tariff of 1816, 270
Tariff of 1828, 312
Tejano, 319
temperance, 336
Trail of Tears, 324
transcendentalism, 337
Treaty of Ghent, 282
Treaty of New Echota, 323
union, 295
utopian society, 344
War of 1812, 281
Whig Party, 324
white supremacy, 364
yeoman farmer, 361

KEY PEOPLE

John Quincy Adams, 284
Napoleon Bonaparte, 261
John C. Calhoun, 311
William Clark, 262
Henry Clay, 270
Thomas Cole, 338
Frederick Douglass, 347
Ralph Waldo Emerson, 337
Charles Grandison Finney, 335
Margaret Fuller, 337
William Lloyd Garrison, 345
Angelina Grimké, 346
Sarah Grimké, 346
William Henry Harrison, 280
Sam Houston, 320
Washington Irving, 331
Andrew Jackson, 281
Thomas Jefferson, 269
Meriwether Lewis, 262
Toussaint L'Ouverture, 261
William Marbury, 264
John Marshall, 264
William Miller, 337
James Monroe, 283
Samuel F. B. Morse, 343
Solomon Northup, 357
James K. Polk, 350
Sacagawea, 262
Antonio López de Santa Anna, 319
Winfield Scott, 324
Samuel Slater, 288
Joseph Smith, 336
Elizabeth Cady Stanton, 348
Zachary Taylor, 350
Tecumseh, 279
Tenskwatawa, 279
Henry David Thoreau, 337
Nat Turner, 360
John Tyler, 325
Martin Van Buren, 308
David Walker, 345
Mercy Otis Warren, 332
Mason Weems, 332
Eli Whitney, 289
Jemima Wilkinson, 334
Brigham Young, 337

CHRONOLOGY

1791	Haitian Revolution
1793	Invention of cotton gin makes enslaved labor more profitable
1798	Development of American system of manufacturing
1803	Louisiana Purchase
1804–1806	Corps of Discovery expedition
1807	Embargo Act limits foreign trade
1812–1814	War of 1812 ends with Treaty of Ghent in 1814
1814	Hartford Convention expresses Federalist dissent
1815	Battle of New Orleans Approval of National Road project
1819	Panic of 1819 Adams–Onís Treaty
By 1820	Market economy well established
1820s	Emergence of Lowell mills and factory towns in New England countryside
1820s–1830s	Second Great Awakening
1820	Missouri Compromise temporarily eases national tensions over the extension of slavery
1821	Federalists advocate Black and white male suffrage Mexico wins independence and claims Texas territory
1823	Monroe Doctrine announced
1824	Election of President John Quincy Adams (Democratic-Republican) via "corrupt bargain"
By 1825	Elimination of voter qualifications for white males in most states
1825	Completion of Erie Canal
1827	Establishment of first workingmen's party
1828	Election of President Andrew Jackson (Democrat) Cherokee people declare themselves an independent sovereign nation
1830s	Emergence of cultural norms emphasizing domesticity and separate spheres for women Abolitionist movement grows substantially
1830s–1840s	Rapid spread of industrialization, immigration, urbanization, and nativism High point of founding of utopian communities
1830s–1850s	Forced migration of large numbers of enslaved people to lower South
1830	Passage of Indian Removal Act
1831	Nat Turner's rebellion The *Liberator* started by William Lloyd Garrison
1832	South Carolina approves Ordinance of Nullification, resulting in the federal Force Bill
1833	Establishment of American Anti-Slavery Society (AASS)
1836	Texas applies for statehood Passage of gag rule in the U.S. House of Representatives

CHRONOLOGY *(continued)*

1836–1837	Widespread antislavery campaigns
1837	Panic of 1837 First national meeting of women abolitionists
1838–1839	Forced removal of American Indians via the Trail of Tears
1839	Mutiny on the *Amistad*
By 1840s	Restrictions on Black male voting rights in place nationwide
1844	First telegraph message sent
1845	Publication of *Narrative of the Life of Frederick Douglass*
1846	Brigham Young and followers settle near Great Salt Lake
1847	*North Star* started by Frederick Douglass
1848	Free-Soil Party established Election of President Zachary Taylor (Whig) Seneca Falls convention on the status of women
By 1850	One-third of Southerners are slaveholders

Period 4 AP® Exam Practice

Multiple-Choice Questions

Questions 1–3 refer to this 1807 image.

OGRABME, or, The American Snapping Turtle

1. The ideas addressed in the image most directly relate to
  (A) imperial efforts to raise revenue and consolidate control over the colonies.
  (B) plans to further unify the U.S. economy, such as the American System.
  (C) struggles of the United States to create an independent global presence.
  (D) regional interests superseding national concerns as the basis for economic policy.

2. Which of the following most directly led to the circumstances illustrated by the image?
  (A) Disagreements over the powers of the federal government
  (B) Debates between national political parties regarding U.S. relations with major European powers
  (C) Efforts of the U.S. government to influence and control North America after the Louisiana Purchase
  (D) Resistance by the New England states to the Monroe Doctrine

3. The developments referenced by the image most directly contributed to U.S. involvement in
  (A) American Indian removal.
  (B) the War of 1812.
  (C) efforts to stop France from providing arms and support to American Indians on the western border areas.
  (D) establishing regional and national markets for the production and consumption of goods.

Questions 4–6 refer to the excerpt.

"Regulations to be observed by all persons employed in the factories of the Hamilton Manufacturing Company. The overseers are to be always in their rooms at the starting of the mill . . . They are to see that all those employed in their rooms, are in their places . . . and keep a correct account of their time and work. . . .

All persons in the employ of the Hamilton Manufacturing Company . . . are not to be absent from their work without the consent of their overseer, except in cases of sickness . . . They are to board in one of the houses of the company, and . . . are to observe the regulations of their boarding-house . . .

The company will not employ any one who is habitually absent from public worship on the Sabbath, or known to be guilty of immorality. . . .

Payment will be made monthly, including board and wages. The accounts will be made up to the last Saturday but one in every month, and paid in the course of the following week.

These regulations are considered part of the contract, with which all persons entering into the employment of the Hamilton Manufacturing Company, engage to comply."

Regulations to Be Observed,
Hamilton Manufacturing Company, 1848

4. Regulations like those expressed in the excerpt best serve as evidence of which of the following long-term trends?
   (A) A decrease in the number of Americans who relied on semi-subsistence agriculture
   (B) The contraction of the American middle class
   (C) An increase in the use of slavery in manufacturing production
   (D) An acceleration in the settlement of small family farms in the North

5. The excerpt is best understood in the context of
   (A) westward expansion.
   (B) declines in immigration.
   (C) the market revolution.
   (D) the fracturing of American commerce into more localized spheres.

6. Which of the following most accounted for the establishment of regulations such as those expressed in the excerpt?
   (A) Innovations such as textile machinery and steam engines
   (B) Changes in gender and family roles
   (C) The growth of definitions of domestic ideals separating public and private spheres
   (D) The movement of many Americans away from industrializing cities

Questions 7–9 refer to the excerpt.

"With regard to Mr. Van Buren's policy respecting the annexation of Texas I conceive it to be simply as follows[.] He would like to get Texas, but he is afraid of the consequences . . . For by coming out as an open advocate of the measure, he would lose the North en masse . . . and dash his party into chaos. He would have to change his ground altogether and commence an entirely new system of operations . . . The question is one of tremendous import, for it involves the destiny of North America for fifty years to come . . . I doubt not that Mr. Van Buren is fully alive to all the momentous bearings of the question upon the future welfare of the Union, and that he dreads the approach of the debate in Congress . . . Yet it was not the less necessary that the proposition should be made. It has been made, declined, and it now rests with the Congress of the United States to determine whether Texas shall add another star to the cluster of the Union or—commence the conquest of the whole of Mexico. But the negotiation may be regarded as closed for the present."

Letter from Fairfax Catlett, member of the Republic of Texas delegation to the United States, to Sam Houston, President of the Republic of Texas, September 5, 1837

7. The ideas expressed in the excerpt best serve as evidence of
(A) the nation's transition to a more participatory democracy.
(B) the growth of political parties.
(C) congressional attempts at political compromise.
(D) western settlers championing expansion efforts.

8. The excerpt is best understood in the context of
(A) the Missouri Compromise.
(B) the American System.
(C) federal efforts to control and relocate American Indian populations.
(D) the rise of Henry Clay to political power.

9. Who would have been most supportive of the sentiments expressed by Catlett in the excerpt?
(A) A plantation owner in Mississippi
(B) A member of the Whig Party
(C) An Irish immigrant in New York City
(D) William Lloyd Garrison

Questions 10–12 refer to the excerpt.

"No sin has fewer apologies than intemperance . . . The prospect of a destitute old age, or a suffering family, no longer troubles the vicious portion of our community. They drink up their daily earnings, and bless God for the poor-house, and begin to look upon it as, of right, the drunkard's home . . . What then is [the] universal, natural, and national remedy for intemperance?

IT IS THE BANISHMENT OF ARDENT SPIRITS FROM THE LIST OF LAWFUL ARTICLES OF COMMERCE, BY A CORRECT AND EFFICIENT PUBLIC SENTIMENT."

Lyman Beecher, *Six Sermons on the Nature, Occasions, Signs, Evils, and Remedy of Intemperance*, 1827

10. The concerns Beecher raises in the excerpt were most directly a result of which of the following?
(A) The expression of new ideas about national identity
(B) Changes to society caused by the market revolution
(C) The formation of voluntary organizations that aimed to improve society
(D) A decline in the establishment of utopian communities

11. Which of the following would have been LEAST likely to support the sentiments expressed by Beecher in the excerpt?
(A) Revivalist preachers
(B) Recent immigrants from Germany and Ireland
(C) New England abolitionists
(D) Women's rights supporters

12. Which of the following most contributed to the rise of the temperance movement?
(A) The Know-Nothing (American) Party
(B) The Second Great Awakening
(C) The Democratic Party
(D) The doctrine of nullification

Questions 13–15 refer to the excerpt.

"No mind can look back upon the history of this region for the last twenty years, and not feel convinced that the labor bestowed in cotton growing during that period has been a total loss to this part of the country . . . No country has ever acquired permanent wealth by exporting its unmanufactured products . . .

This is the great evil under which the southwest labors. She is yearly wearing out her soil in the production of one great staple, which has become ruinously low in price by reason of great supply: she parts with this staple at prime cost, and purchases almost all her necessary appliances of comfort from abroad, not a prime cost, but burdened with the profits of merchants, the costs of transportation, duties, commissions, exchange, and numerous other charges, all of which go to support and enrich others at her expense."

James D. B. DeBow, *Domestic Manufactures in the South and West*, 1847

13. Which of the following most contributed to the process described in the excerpt?
(A) The development of interchangeable parts
(B) Transportation networks that linked the North and Midwest more closely than the South
(C) The development of national and international commercial ties
(D) The establishment of a small but wealthy business elite

14. The concerns DeBow raises in the excerpt were most directly a result of which of the following?
(A) Enslaved and free Blacks joining political efforts to change their status
(B) The inability of the majority of Southerners to own slaves
(C) The enactment of the American System
(D) The growth of a distinctive southern regional identity

15. DeBow's ideas would have been most strongly challenged by which of the following?
(A) Arguments that slavery was an essential part of the southern way of life
(B) The emergence of a large and growing population of urban laboring poor
(C) Unsuccessful slave rebellions in the South
(D) The relocation of plantations to lands west of the Appalachians

Short-Answer Questions

"Dedicated as they were to particularism and diversity . . . Democrats found doctrines of little government congenial. The natural rights philosophy of the Jacksonians asserted the individual's claims to be protected against interference from reformers. . . . Thus, in the place of the Puritan and evangelical religious tradition that the Whigs drew upon, the Democrats invoked the political ideas of the Enlightenment. . . . The freedom such people prized was 'freedom from'; the goal of the Whigs was 'freedom to.'"

Daniel Walker Howe, "The Evangelical Movement and Political Culture in the North during the Second Party System," *Journal of American History*, 1991

"The first major alteration of executive power came with the administration of Andrew Jackson. He redefined the presidency both in its relationship to Congress and to the people. He claimed primacy in government. . . . He represented the concept of a strong president who takes charge of the government, defines the issues, and leads Congress and the nation in achieving successful resolution of those issues . . . It was a new departure in the structure and operation of government. It represented the political beginnings of modern America."

Robert V. Remini,
The Revolutionary Age of Andrew Jackson, 1976

1. Using the excerpts, answer **A**, **B**, and **C**.
   (A) Briefly describe one major difference between Howe's and Remini's historical interpretations of the Jacksonian Democracy movement between 1820 and 1840.
   (B) Briefly explain how one historical event or development from 1820 to 1840 that is not explicitly mentioned in the excerpts could support Howe's interpretation.
   (C) Briefly explain how one historical event or development from 1820 to 1840 that is not explicitly mentioned in the excerpts could support Remini's interpretation.

North Wind Picture Archives/Alamy

George B. Cheever, *The True History of Deacon Giles' Distillery*, 1844

2. Using the image, answer **A**, **B**, and **C**.
   (A) Briefly describe ONE historical perspective expressed in the image.
   (B) Briefly explain how ONE specific event or development in the period from 1820 to 1850 contributed to the events depicted in the image.
   (C) Briefly explain ONE specific historical effect in the period from 1820 to 1850 that resulted from the events depicted in the image.

3. Answer **A**, **B**, and **C**.
   (A) Briefly explain how ONE specific historical event or development contributed to economic development in the United States from 1800 to 1850.
   (B) Briefly explain how ANOTHER specific historical event or development contributed to economic development in the United States from 1800 to 1850.
   (C) Briefly explain ONE specific historical event or development from 1830 to 1860 that resulted from economic growth from 1800 to 1830.

4. Answer **A**, **B**, and **C**.
   (A) Briefly explain how ONE specific historical event of development contributed to political tensions in the United States in the period 1800 to 1825.
   (B) Briefly explain how ANOTHER specific historical event or development contributed to political tensions in the United States in the period 1800 to 1825
   (C) Briefly explain ONE specific historical event or development from 1825 to 1845 that resulted from increased political tensions between 1800 and 1825.

Document-Based Question

This question is based on the accompanying documents. The documents have been edited for the purpose of this exercise.

> Evaluate the extent to which the presidency of Thomas Jefferson (1801–1808) pursued and enacted policies consistent with the ideals of republicanism.

Document 1

Source: Thomas Jefferson, First Inaugural Address, March 1, 1801

"About to enter, fellow-citizens, on the exercise of duties which comprehend everything dear and valuable to you, it is proper you should understand what I deem the essential principles of our Government, and consequently those which ought to shape its Administration. . . . Equal and exact justice to all men, of whatever state or persuasion, religious or political; peace, commerce, and honest friendship with all nations, entangling alliances with none; the support of the State governments in all their rights, as the most competent administrations for our domestic concerns and the surest bulwarks against antirepublican tendencies; the preservation of the General Government in its whole constitutional vigor, as the sheet anchor of our peace at home and safety abroad; a jealous care of the right of election by the people . . . absolute acquiescence in the decisions of the majority . . . the supremacy of the civil over the military authority; economy in the public expense, that labor may be lightly burthened; the honest payment of our debts and sacred preservation of the public faith; encouragement of agriculture, and of commerce as its handmaid . . . freedom of religion; freedom of the press, and freedom of person under the protection of the habeas corpus, and trial by juries impartially selected. . . . The wisdom of our sages and blood of our heroes have been devoted to their attainment. They should be the creed of our political faith, the text of civic instruction . . . and should we wander from them in moments of error or of alarm, let us hasten to retrace our steps and to regain the road which alone leads to peace, liberty, and safety."

Document 2

Source: U.S. Congress, *An Act to Repeal the Internal Taxes,* April 8, 1802

"Be it enacted, That, from and after the thirtieth day of June next, the internal duties on stills, and domestic distilled spirits, on refined sugars, licenses to retailers . . .

shall be discontinued, and all acts and parts of acts relative thereto, shall, from and after the said thirtieth day of June next, be repealed . . . that the office of collectors of internal duties shall continue in each collection district . . . no longer, unless sooner discontinued by the President of the United States, who shall be and is hereby empowered . . . to discontinue any of the said collectors . . . [and] any of the said offices . . . and the Office of Commissioner of the Revenue shall cease and be discontinued, whenever the collection of the [current] said duties and tax shall have been so far completed."

Document 3

Source: Robert Wilkinson, *Map of North America,* published August 12, 1804.

David Rumsey Map Collection, David Rumsey Map Center, Stanford Libraries

Long-Essay Questions

1. Evaluate the effectiveness of political compromises in addressing national problems in the United States from 1800 to 1850.

2. Evaluate the extent to which reform movements between 1800 and 1850 changed American society.

3. Evaluate the extent of difference in the philosophies and policies of the Democratic and National Republican Parties between 1824 and 1840.

PERIOD 5 1844–1877

Expansion, Division, and Civil War

The Robin Stanford Collection

Knox Plantation, South Carolina, c. 1865 In this image, formerly enslaved Black American women sit outside a cotton gin surrounded by raw cotton. Throughout the nineteenth century, southern cotton supplied the factories of the northern states and England with the raw material necessary to make textile mills profitable. In this way, both enslaved Black Americans and free white factory workers, Southerners and Northerners, and the rich and the poor on both sides of the Atlantic Ocean were all interwoven into the early industrial economy of textile production.

Contextualizing Period 5

MODULE 5.1

By the mid-nineteenth century, most Americans considered western expansion critical to sustaining the nation's economic growth. Southern planters, in turn, considered it necessary to slavery's success. While most white Northerners were willing to leave slavery alone where it already existed, many hoped to keep it out of newly acquired territories.

The simultaneous growth of antislavery sentiment in the North and proslavery beliefs in the South fueled a series of political realignments in the decades before the Civil War. By 1860, debates over territorial expansion, regional economic interests, and demographic changes all revolved around the issue of slavery. It was the one enduring issue that consistently divided the nation along sectional lines.

When the election of 1860 took place, many Americans who lived in slaveholding states believed that the constitutionally elected president, Abraham Lincoln, was a threat to the rights guaranteed to American citizens in the Constitution. As a result, by March 1861, when Lincoln was inaugurated, seven southern states had declared their independence from the United States. Four more states would secede shortly thereafter.

Both North and South mobilized their economies and societies during the Civil War (1861–1865). Early on, the South achieved many victories despite its smaller population and largely agricultural economy. In 1862, President Lincoln issued the Emancipation Proclamation, shifting the North's goal from maintaining the Union to assuring freedom for enslaved Black Americans in the South. Ultimately, the North achieved victory through its military and economic advantages over the agrarian South.

The Thirteenth Amendment to the Constitution, which abolished slavery, proved to be both the most far-reaching and immediate result of the war. This sweeping reform was followed by the Fourteenth Amendment, which guaranteed that the federal government would protect civil rights, and the Fifteenth Amendment, which removed racial barriers to voting.

Although these three amendments led to temporary political successes for formerly enslaved Black Americans throughout the 1870s, northern support for Reconstruction—the remaking of the South according to northern conceptions of racial equality and economic justice—faltered as southern resistance to reforms, often in the form of violent attacks on Black Americans and their northern and southern supporters, almost entirely reversed the progress made in the first years after the war.

Period 5: What's Inside 1844–1877

MODULE	AP® THEMATIC FOCUS
5.1 Contextualizing Period 5	The expansion of the United States in the 1840s to the Pacific Ocean led to renewed debates on slavery in the territories. As sectional tensions increased in the 1850s, political compromise became more difficult, and the second two-party system broke down. After Lincoln's presidential victory in 1860, eleven southern states seceded from the Union, leading to a bloody four-year war in which the Union prevailed against the Confederacy. During Reconstruction, Republicans in Congress used legislation, military force, and constitutional amendments to remake the South and protect the rights of freed Blacks but were met with fierce and sometimes violent resistance. In 1877, Reconstruction ended due to a political compromise that gave Republicans the presidency in a disputed election in return for the removal of the remaining federal troops from the South.
5.2 Manifest Destiny	**Geography and the Environment** The lure of fertile lands in Oregon and the discovery of gold in California led to a surge of migration to the West. Also, a growing belief in the manifest destiny of the United States to expand to the Pacific Ocean fueled westward settlement and led the country to annex Texas and settle claims with Britain for Oregon.
5.3 The Mexican-American War	**America in the World** U.S. victory in the Mexican-American War resulted in diplomatic recognition of the annexation of Texas and the transfer of the California and New Mexico territories to the United States. Expanding the nation's borders led to renewed conflicts with American Indian peoples.
5.4 The Compromise of 1850	**American and National Identity** The acquisition of new lands from Mexico reopened the contentious debate between Northerners and Southerners over the westward expansion of slavery. Although the Compromise of 1850 allowed California's admission as a free state and addressed other related concerns, the newly strengthened Fugitive Slave Act fueled abolitionist sentiment in the North and southern anger over efforts to undermine the law.
5.5 Sectional Conflict: Regional Differences	**American and Regional Culture** Disagreements over slavery worsened during the 1850s exposing and magnifying the growing rift between North and South on the issue of slavery. Abolitionist efforts to undermine enforcement of the Fugitive Slave Act, support for the Underground Railroad, and blocking the Pierce administration's attempts to acquire new southern territory to expand slavery angered many Southerners and convinced them that their way of life was at stake.
5.6 Failure of Compromise	**Politics and Power** Compromise over the expansion of slavery became increasingly difficult during the 1850s and attempts such as the Kansas-Nebraska Act and the *Dred Scott* case only worsened tensions. At the same time, increased immigration from both Europe and Asia led to the temporary rise of anti-immigrant parties throughout the North. These two factors contributed greatly to the breakdown of the Second Party System.
5.7 Election of 1860 and Secession	**Politics and Power** Republican Abraham Lincoln won the presidential election of 1860 as northern and southern Democrats fractured over the issue of slavery and nominated separate candidates. His victory and later battle of Fort Sumter led eleven southern states to secede even as Lincoln used extraordinary measures to keep the remaining four slaveholding border states in the Union.
5.8 Military Conflict in the Civil War	**America in the World** During the Civil War, the Union and the Confederacy increasingly depended on commitment from their citizens, even as both faced internal opposition. At the onset of the war, the South won a number of battles. However, the lack of significant foreign intervention and key battlefield victories, as well as a change in tactics, allowed the Union to turn the tide of the conflict by 1863.

MODULE	AP® THEMATIC FOCUS
5.9 Government Policies during the Civil War	**American and National Identity** Over the course of the Civil War, Lincoln shifted from a strategy aimed at preserving the Union to one that promoted the emancipation of enslaved people. As Union troops invaded the South, this new strategy devastated the southern economy, which relied almost entirely upon slavery. It also led to the recruitment of Black troops, and allowed Lincoln to reframe the war as a "new birth of freedom." These factors, along with the North's superior industrial production and larger population, led to victory for the Union.
5.10 Reconstruction	**Politics and Power** In the aftermath of the Civil War, Presidents Lincoln and Johnson and moderates and radical Republicans in Congress all proposed competing plans to restore the South. In spite of disagreements and southern resistance, Republican efforts to ensure civil rights for freedpeople led to short-term successes, including the election of Black Americans to local and federal offices and long-term changes, including three constitutional amendments. However, women, Black and white, were denied the right to vote, leading to a split in the women's suffrage movement.
5.11 Failure of Reconstruction	**American and National Identity** White Southerners used both legal and criminal tactics to maintain white supremacy and prevent Black Americans from achieving equality. Public fatigue in the North, economic fallout from the Panic of 1873, and political setbacks led the federal government to narrow its protections for Black Americans' rights. While the electoral compromise of 1877 effectively ended Reconstruction, leaving important civil rights issues unresolved, the Reconstruction amendments and glimpse of what was possible laid the foundation for the civil rights movement in the twentieth century.
5.12 Comparison in Period 5	The Mexican-American War, Civil War, and Reconstruction all profoundly changed the nation though the impacts varied across geographies and demographics as Americans debated differing visions of national identity.
Support and Practice	• Practice thinking and writing historically in each module. • See the Period Review of key concepts, events, people, and dates after the last module. • Try the AP® Exam Practice at the end of the period.

MODULE

5.2

Manifest Destiny

FOCUS

Remember that historians use causation as a way to analyze both the causes of events and their effects. One way to think of historical developments is to imagine them as links in a long chain of events—a particular event can be both an effect of earlier developments, whether immediate and distant, *and* a cause of events that have yet to unfold.

As you read this module, consider not only particular causes and effects, but the ways in which multiple causes played a role in the settlement of the West and how that settlement affected local and national developments during the mid-nineteenth century.

During the 1830s and 1840s, national debates over slavery intensified. The most important battles now centered on western territories gained through victory in the war with Mexico. Before 1848, government-sponsored expeditions had opened up vast new lands for American pioneers seeking opportunity, and migrants moved west in growing numbers. Then, following the Mexican-American War and the discovery of gold in California, tens of thousands of men and women rushed to the Pacific coast seeking riches. But the West was already home to a diverse population that included American Indians, Mexicans, Mormons, and missionaries. The new settlers converged, and often clashed, with these groups.

Traveling the Overland Trails

In the 1830s, a growing number of migrants followed **overland trails** to the far West. The panic of 1837 further prompted families to head west. Thousands of U.S. migrants and European immigrants sought better economic prospects in Oregon Territory, the Rocky Mountain region, and the Great Plains, while Mormons continued to settle in Salt Lake City. Some pioneers opened trading posts where American Indians exchanged goods with Anglo-American settlers or with merchants back east. Small settlements developed around these posts and near the expanding system of U.S. forts that dotted the region.

Oregon Trail
The route west from the Missouri River to the Oregon Territory. By 1860, some 350,000 Americans had made the three- to six-month journey along the trail.

For many pioneers, the journey on the **Oregon Trail** began at St. Louis. From there, they traveled by wagon train across the Great Plains and the Rocky Mountains to Oregon's Willamette Valley. By 1860, some 350,000 Americans had made the journey, claimed land from the Mississippi River to the Pacific, and transformed the United States into an expanding empire.

Because the journey west required funds for wagons and supplies, most pioneers were of middling economic status. The majority of pioneers made the three- to six-month journey with family members, to help share the labor and risks associated with travel. Men, mainly farmers, comprised some 60 percent of these migrants westward, but women and children traveled in significant numbers, often alongside relatives or neighbors from back east. Some courageous families headed west alone, but most traveled in wagon trains—from a few wagons to a few dozen—that provided support and security.

Despite attempts to create community and establish security along the trail, traditional gender roles often broke down on the trail, and even conventional domestic tasks posed novel problems. Women had to cook unfamiliar food over open fires in all kinds of weather and with only a few pots and utensils. They washed laundry in rivers or streams and on the plains hauled water from great distances. Wood, too, was scarce on the plains, and women and children gathered buffalo dung (called "chips") for fuel. Men often had to gather food rather than hunt and fish, or they had to learn to catch strange (and sometimes dangerous) animals, such as jack rabbits and rattlesnakes. Few men were prepared for the dangerous work of floating wagons across rivers. Nor were many of them expert in shoeing horses or fixing wagon wheels, tasks generally performed by skilled artisans at home.

Expectations changed dramatically when men took ill or died. Then wives often drove the wagon, gathered or hunted for food, and learned to repair axles and other wagon parts. When large numbers of men were injured or ill, women might serve as scouts and guides or pick up guns to defend wagons under attack by American Indians or wild animals. Yet despite their growing burdens, pioneer women gained little power over decision making. Moreover, the addition of men's jobs to women's responsibilities was seldom reciprocated. Few men cooked, did laundry, or cared for children on the trail.

In one area, however, relative equality reigned. Men and women were equally susceptible to disease, injury, and death during the journey. Accidents, gunshot wounds, drownings, broken bones, and infections affected people on every wagon train. Some groups were struck as well by deadly epidemics of measles or cholera. In addition, about 20 percent of women on the overland trail became pregnant, which posed even greater dangers than usual given the lack of medical services and sanitation. About the same percentage of women lost children or spouses to death on the trip west. Overall, about one in ten to fifteen migrants died on the western journey.

REVIEW

- In what ways did traveling the overland trails both support and challenge traditional gender roles during the mid-nineteenth century?

The Gold Rush

Despite the hazards, more and more Americans traveled overland to the Pacific coast, although only a few thousand Americans initially settled in California. Some were agents sent there by eastern merchants to purchase fine leather made from the hides of Spanish cattle. Several agents married into families of elite Mexican ranchers, known as **Californios**, and adopted their culture, even converting to Catholicism.

However, the Anglo-American presence in California changed dramatically after 1848 when gold was discovered at Sutter's Mill in northeastern California. Beginning in 1849, news of the discovery brought tens of thousands of settlers from the eastern United States, South America, Europe, and Asia. In the **California gold rush**, "forty-niners" raced to claim riches in California, and men vastly outnumbered women.

The rapid influx of gold seekers heightened tensions between newly arrived whites, local American Indians, and Californios. Forty-niners confiscated land owned by Californios, shattered the fragile ecosystem in the California mountains, and forced

Californio
A Spanish or Mexican resident of California. Before the nineteenth century, Californios made up California's economic and political elite. Their position, however, deteriorated after California became a part of the United States in 1848.

California gold rush
The rapid influx of migrants from across the world into California seeking riches after the discovery of gold in 1848.

Granger – Historical Picture Archive

Gold Rush Miners, 1849
These prospectors were two of some 80,000 who traveled to California after gold was discovered. While many Chinese miners were run off their claims, these two men, dressed in a mix of Chinese and American attire, panned for gold with the tools of their trade – pickax, hoe, and pan. A shed in the background may have served as their home.

Based on this image, how would you characterize forty-niners' interaction with their environment?

Mexican and American Indian men to labor for low wages or a promised share in uncertain profits. New conflicts erupted when migrants from Asia and South America joined the search for wealth in California. Forty-niners from the United States generally viewed foreign-born miners as competitors and often stole from and assaulted them.

The gold rush also led to the increased exploitation of women, as thousands of male migrants demanded food, shelter, laundry, and medical care. While some California women earned a good living by renting rooms, cooking meals, washing clothes, or working as prostitutes, many faced exploitation and abuse. American Indian and Mexican women were especially vulnerable to sexual harassment and rape, while Chinese women were imported specifically to provide sexual services for male miners.

Chinese men were also victims of abuse by whites, who ran them off their claims. Despite these aggressions, some Chinese men used the skills traditionally assigned them in their homeland—cooking and washing clothes—to earn a far steadier income than prospecting for gold could provide. Other men also took advantage of the demand for goods and services. Levi Strauss, a German Jewish immigrant, moved from New York to San Francisco to open a dry-goods store in 1853. He soon made his fortune producing canvas and then denim pants for miners that could withstand harsh weather and long wear.

REVIEW

- What impact did the gold rush have on different peoples living in California?

The Politics of Expansion

After the Whig victory in 1840, southern planters still held considerable influence in Washington, D.C., because of the importance of cotton to the U.S. economy. In turn, Southerners needed federal support to expand into more fertile areas. With the financial panic of 1837 now ended, the presidential election of 1844 turned on this issue, with Democratic candidate James K. Polk demanding continued expansion into Oregon and Mexico.

Once Polk was in office, his claims were contested not only by Britain and Mexico but also by the Comanche, whose territory spanned much of the Southwest, including territory in the future states of Texas, New Mexico, Kansas, and Oklahoma. After 1848, conflicts with American Indians and debates over slavery only intensified.

Southerners eager to expand the plantation economy were at the forefront of the push for territorial expansion. Yet expansion was not merely a southern strategy. Northerners demanded that the United States reject British claims to the Oregon Territory, and some northern politicians and businessmen advocated acquiring distant lands like Hawaii and Samoa to benefit U.S. trade.

In 1844, the Democratic Party built on these expansionist dreams to recapture the White House. The Democrats nominated a Tennessee congressman and governor, James K. Polk. The Whigs, unwilling to nominate John Tyler for a second term as president, chose Kentucky senator Henry Clay. Polk declared himself in favor of the annexation of Texas. Clay, meanwhile, waffled on the issue. This proved his undoing when the **Liberty Party**, a small antislavery party founded in 1840, denounced annexation. Liberty Party candidate James G. Birney captured just enough votes in New York State to throw the state and the election to Polk.

In February 1845, a month before Polk took office, Congress passed a joint resolution annexing the Republic of Texas. That summer, John L. O'Sullivan's journal, the *Democratic Review*, captured the American mood by declaring that nothing must

AP® EXAM TIP

Economic factors such as access to natural and mineral resources created an atmosphere of support for expansion westward. Yet political parties disagreed over the extent to which they advocated new territories. Be able to explain both the reasons for support and opposition to expansion in the context of the election of 1844.

AP® EXAM TIP

The causes of the belief in manifest destiny are well-known historical topics. Privilege the consequences of manifest destiny as it relates to violent conflicts with American Indian groups such as the Comanche.

American Progress This painting by John Gast in 1872 depicts Columbia with the "Star of Empire" on her head. She is moving from east to west holding a schoolbook in her right hand and stringing telegraph wire with her left hand. The stagecoach in the background is labeled "overland mail." This image was commissioned to accompany a popular set of western travel guidebooks in the 1870s.

How do the details in this painting support the concept of manifest destiny?

manifest destiny

The term coined by John L. O'Sullivan in 1845 to describe what he saw as the nation's God-given right to expand its borders across the North American continent. Throughout the nineteenth century, the concept of manifest destiny was used to justify U.S. territorial and cultural expansion.

interfere with "the fulfillment of our manifest destiny to overspread the continent allotted by Providence." This vision of **manifest destiny**—of the nation's God-given right to expand its borders—defined Polk's presidency.

With the Texas question seemingly resolved, President Polk turned his attention to Oregon, which stretched from the forty-second parallel to latitude 54°40′ and was jointly occupied by Great Britain and the United States. In 1842, three years before Polk took office, glowing reports of the mild climate and fertile soil around Puget Sound had inspired thousands of farmers and traders to flood into the Oregon Territory. Alarmed by this "Oregon fever," the British tried to confine Americans to areas south of the Columbia River. But U.S. settlers demanded access to the entire territory. President Polk encouraged migration into Oregon but was unwilling to risk war with Great Britain. Instead, diplomats negotiated a treaty in 1846 that extended the border with British Canada (the forty-ninth parallel) to the Pacific Ocean. Over the next two years, Congress admitted Iowa and Wisconsin to statehood, reassuring northern residents that expansion benefited all regions of the nation.

The United States also looked to expand its influence and reach into Asia. Trade with China had declined in the 1840s, but the United States had begun commercial negotiations with Japan in 1846. These came to fruition in 1854, when U.S. emissary Commodore Matthew C. Perry, a renowned naval officer and founder of the U.S. Navy's engineer corps, obtained the first formal trade agreement with Japan by coercion, threatening war if Japan would not accept its terms. Within four years, the United States had expanded commercial ties and enhanced diplomatic relations with Japan, in large part by supporting the island nation against its traditional enemies in China, Russia, and Europe.

WORKING with EVIDENCE

Source: *New York Daily Times*, "Commodore Perry at the Loo Choo Isles," 1853

> "At last accounts Commodore Perry and Squadron had sailed from the Loo-Choo Islands, the southernmost group of the Japan Empire. Private letters from one of the officers of his Flag-ship give some interesting particulars not published in the Journals. Under date of July 1, this gentleman writes that: 'On the 6th of June we marched to Shudi, the capital of the Loo-Choo Islands, with all the officers, marines and sailors, with artillery, &c. It was a march of some three or four miles, over a magnificent paved road, through a rich and highly cultivated country. The clumps of trees and other ornamental embellishments of the way astonished us much less than our heavy cloth uniforms and accoutrements astonished the timid natives, who gathered along our road to gape at us with wonder and poorly concealed disquietude. They cannot tell what to make of this ambiguous demonstration. Poor devils! Their Japanese masters will find out one of these days. The object of this visit was to be received by the Regent of these Islands at his Royal Palace. The honor of the visit may have rebounded to his tawny Excellence, but it is certain the pleasure, such as it was, was all on our side. They are suspicious, and very ill at ease. Commodore Perry was carried in a sedan chair. The rest of us gave the natives a specimen of how Yankees . . . can march under a scorching sun on foot. If the Japanese give us a friendly reception, all will be smooth. If not, we will have a far more effective squadron here, one of these days, and teach them conformity to Christian manners. . . .
>
> The land is inviting, and is, I think, destined to become a flourishing American colony."

Questions for Analysis

1. Describe the reception that Perry received in Japan, as reported in this excerpt.
2. Describe the ways in which the author of this document characterizes Japan in relation to the United States.
3. Explain how this document reveals the ways in which America's domestic economy shaped its trade relations with Asia during the mid-1800s.

REVIEW

▪ What were the causes and effects of manifest destiny?

AP® Skills Workshop: Thinking Historically

Using AP® Course Themes to Brainstorm and Organize an Essay

The focus of the AP® Skills Workshop features in Periods 5 and 6 will be on preparing you to successfully write timed essays in your class and on the AP® Exam. Fortunately, you have already practiced many of the skills you will need. In this segment, you will be introduced to a set of themes and learn how you can use them to help you organize a brainstorm and outline an essay.

There are eight main **themes** that are woven throughout the historical narrative in this textbook and on the AP® Exam. Think of these themes as broad categories that provide you an opportunity to examine topics from different angles or perspectives. These AP® course themes are listed below with a brief definition of each theme. Notice that they have been arranged to create an easy-to-remember anagram: **A PASSAGE.**

American and National Identity: how and why definitions of American and national identity and values have developed among the diverse and changing population of North America as well as on related topics, such as citizenship, constitutionalism, foreign policy, assimilation, and American exceptionalism.

Politics and Power: how different social and political groups have influenced society and government in the United States as well as how political beliefs and institutions have changed over time.

America in the World: the interactions between nations that affected North American history in the colonial period and on the influence of the United States on the modern world.

Settlement and Migration: why and how the various people who moved to and within the United States both adapted to and transformed their new social and physical environments.

Social Structures: how and why systems of social organization develop and change as well as the impact that these systems have on the broader society.

American and Regional Culture: how and why national, regional, and group cultures developed and changed as well as how culture has shaped government policy and the economy.

Geography and the Environment: the role of geography and both the natural and human-made environments in the social and political developments in what would become the United States.

(continued)

Exchange, Work, and Technology: the factors behind the development of systems of economic exchange, particularly the role of technology, economic markets, and government.

The first step in answering a question is to carefully analyze the prompt. You want to identify the topic, the time period, and the historical reasoning process. The second step is to brainstorm information you can use in your essay. That historical information is commonly called **outside evidence** because it's not provided in the prompt (or documents if you are writing a response to an SAQ with stimulus or to a DBQ). Outside evidence is defined as the use of specific, relevant historical details and examples that support an argument. The best outside evidence includes items such as people, events, laws, court cases, wars, books, inventions, historical terms, and more. Sometimes referred to as "proper nouns," outside evidence strengthens an argument by providing detailed support for the claims you are making.

Consider that there are two ways to brainstorm: from the bottom up (inductively), or from the top down (deductively). Inductive brainstorming is when you try to think of historical examples that you can use in an essay and then categorize them to outline an argument. Deductive brainstorming starts with identifying possible categories and then trying to brainstorm evidence to support them. In reality, in a pressured, timed situation, you may end up doing a bit of both as you gather your thoughts together.

Here is an example of an inductive and deductive brainstorm using the theme American and National Identity:

Inductive Brainstorm (Start with the facts and think of a general category under which they fit.)	**Deductive Brainstorm** (Start with a general category and brainstorm facts that you know fit under it.)
Gold rush (1849) Oregon Trail (mid-to-late 1840s) Polk's 1844 presidential campaign (1844) John O'Sullivan's coining of U.S. "manifest destiny" (1845)	American and National Identity
American and National Identity	Gold rush (1849) Oregon Trail (mid-to-late 1840s) Polk's 1844 presidential campaign (1844) John O'Sullivan's coining of U.S. "manifest destiny" (1845)

Remembering and applying the relevant course themes can be helpful when organizing your essay ideas. Think back to the Period 3 essay graphic organizer, first introduced in Module 3.2, that you regularly encountered in the AP® Skills Workshop exercises. It consisted of three columns: General Categories, Main Points, and Supporting Details. The themes can help you identify potential general categories. When brainstorming, you can jot down the themes and then match your outside information to those themes. Or you can ask yourself if you know and can use any

(continued)

information from each of those thematic areas. Think of the themes as both a premade list of categories that you can choose from and a good double check to make sure you didn't leave something important out of your outline.

ACTIVITY

Now, it's time to practice using the themes to help you organize an essay response. Complete the graphic organizer and write a thesis statement with a claim and line of reasoning for the prompt below. See Modules 3.2 and 3.6 if you need a refresher. Make sure that at least one or two of your general categories directly align with an identified course theme (A PASSAGE).

Evaluate the relative causes of manifest destiny in the 1830s and 1840s.

Here's a partial brainstorm of potential outside information you might use to answer this question to get you started:

Settlers traversing the Oregon Trail, forty-niners, and the gold rush, the annexation of Texas, Polk's presidential campaign, the belief in Anglo-Saxon cultural superiority, Southerners wishing to expand the geographic extent of slavery, access to natural resources in the West, and a desire to trade and gain access to markets in Asia.

Think about how you can connect some of that evidence with whatever examples you add to the themes in your outline. Don't forget to use the main points from the organizer in your thesis statement.

General Categories	Main Points	Supporting Details
-	-	- - -
-	-	- - -
-	-	- - -

MODULE 5.3

The Mexican-American War

FOCUS

There are many ways to analyze the causes and effects of a historical development such as considering short-term versus long-term causes or effects or the links between various causes or effects. Another way to think about causation is to compare the intended versus the unintended effects (or even causes) of a major historical event.

As you read this module, think about why the United States went to war with Mexico. What developments, both intentional and unplanned, led to the conflict? How did the effects of the war, including the lands gained, change the United States in predictable and unexpected ways?

Some Americans hoped to gain even more territory than Texas and Oregon by pushing Mexicans out of northern Mexico and California. Polk entered the presidency in 1844 with an expansionist agenda that included the annexation of Texas, resolving the dispute over Oregon with Britain, and acquiring California. With Texas and Oregon under U.S. control by 1846, Polk set about wresting control of California from Mexico.

Pursuing War with Mexico

Spanish missions and forts, built in the late eighteenth century, dotted the Pacific coast from San Diego to San Francisco. Mexico achieved independence from Spain in 1821 and took control of this expansive missionary and military network. Diseases carried by the Spanish and forced labor in their missions and forts had devastated some American Indian tribes in the region. As Mexican soldiers took control over former Spanish territories, some married into American Indian families, gaining land and social status and nurturing compound cultures. More often, however, diseases, guns, thefts of food and animals, sexual assault, and forced labor continued to plague native peoples.

American Indians in the lands newly claimed by the U.S. government faced some of these same dangers. In addition, as the U.S. government forced eastern tribes to move west of the Mississippi, tensions increased among various American Indian nations. When the Cherokee and other southeastern tribes were removed to Indian Territory, for example, they confronted tribes such as the Osage. Pushed into the Southwest, the Osage came into conflict with the Comanche, who had earlier fought the Apache for control of the southern plains. Other American Indian nations were pushed onto the northern plains from the Old Northwest. When tribes like the Mandan were devastated by smallpox in the 1830s, the Sioux took advantage of the power vacuum and came to dominate the region.

The flood of U.S. migrants into Texas and the southern plains transformed relations among American Indian nations as well as between American Indians and Mexico. In the face of Spanish and then Mexican claims on their lands, for example, the Comanche nation forged alliances with former foes like the Wichita and the Osage nations.

The Comanche also developed commercial ties with tribes in Indian Territory and with both Mexican and Anglo-American traders. They thereby hoped to benefit from the imperial ambitions of the United States and Mexico while strengthening bonds among American Indians in the region.

Comanche expansion caused greater problems for Mexico. The young nation did not have enough resources to sustain the level of gift giving that Spanish authorities had used to maintain peace. As a result, Comanche warriors launched continual raids against Tejano settlements in Texas. But the Comanche also developed commercial relations with residents of New Mexico, who flouted trade regulations created in Mexico City. By 1846, Comanche trade and diplomatic relations with New Mexican settlements had seriously weakened the hold of Mexican authorities on their northern provinces.

At the same time, with Texas now a state, Mexico faced growing tensions with the United States. Conflicts centered on Texas's western border. Mexico insisted on the Nueces River as the boundary line, while Americans claimed all the land south to the Rio Grande. In January 1846, Polk secretly sent emissary John Slidell to negotiate a border treaty with Mexico. But Polk also sent U.S. troops under General Zachary Taylor across the Nueces River. Mexican officials refused to see Slidell and instead sent their own troops across the Rio Grande. Meanwhile, U.S. naval commanders prepared to seize San Francisco Bay from the Mexicans if war was declared. The Mexican government responded by sending more troops into the disputed Texas territory.

When fighting erupted near the Rio Grande in May 1846, Polk claimed that "American blood had been shed on American soil" and declared that a state of war was now in existence with Mexico. Many Whigs in Congress opposed Polk's declaration, arguing that the president had provoked the conflict. However, antiwar Whigs, like Representative Abraham Lincoln of Illinois, failed to convince the Democratic majority, and Congress voted to formally declare and finance the **Mexican-American War**. Generals Zachary Taylor and Winfield Scott, who commanded U.S. forces, were themselves Whigs and later built political careers on their military successes. Although northern abolitionists protested the war, most Americans — North and South — considered westward expansion a blessing.

AP® EXAM TIP

Be able to detail how the Mexican-American War led to a variety of debates over citizenship and freedom in the newly acquired territories. Specifically, look to understand the effects on slavery, American Indians, and Mexicans. Consider using citizenship and freedom as categories of analysis.

Mexican-American War
The 1846–1848 war between the United States and Mexico, resulting in the transfer of approximately one million square miles of land to the United States, including the present-day states of California, Nevada, New Mexico, Arizona, Utah, and Texas. Debates over the status of slavery in these territories reignited the national debate about the expansion of slavery.

AP® WORKING with EVIDENCE

Source: President James K. Polk, *War Message*, 1846

"The Mexican Government . . . , after a long-continued series of menaces, have at last invaded our territory, and shed the blood of our fellow-citizens on our own soil. . . .

It became, therefore, of urgent necessity to provide for the defence of that portion of our country. Accordingly, on the 13th of January last, instructions were issued to the general in command of these troops to occupy the left bank of the Del Norte [Rio Grande]. This river which is the southwestern boundary of the state of Texas, is an exposed frontier. . . .

The movement of the troops to the Del Norte was made by the commanding general, under positive instructions to abstain from all aggressive acts toward Mexico or Mexican citizens, and to regard the relations between that republic and the United States as peaceful, unless she should declare war, or commit acts of hostility indicative of a state of war. . . .

The Mexican forces at Matamoras assumed a belligerent attitude, and, on the 12th of April, General Ampudia, then in command, notified General Taylor to break up his camp within twenty-four hours, and to retire beyond the Nueces river; and, in the event of his failure to comply with these demands, announced that arms, and arms alone, must decide the question. . . . A party of dragoons, of sixty-three men and officers, were on the same day dispatched from the American camp up the Rio del Norte, on its left bank, to ascertain whether the Mexican troops had crossed or were preparing to cross the river, 'became engaged with a large body of these troops, and after a short affair, in which some sixteen were killed and wounded, appear to have been surrounded and compelled to surrender.'

The grievous wrongs perpetrated by Mexico upon our citizens throughout a long period of years remain unredressed; and solemn treaties, pledging her public faith for this redress, have been disregarded. A government either unable or unwilling to enforce the execution of such treaties, fails to perform one of its plainest duties."

Questions for Analysis

1. Identify the immediate cause that Polk provides for engaging in hostilities with Mexico.
2. Explain at least two distant causes of Polk's declaration of war.
3. Evaluate the extent to which Polk's declaration was caused by events beyond his control.

Source: Abraham Lincoln, Illinois Whig Representative, *Spot Resolutions*, 1847

"*Resolved by the House of Representatives*, That the President of the United States be respectfully requested to inform this House—

1st. Whether the spot on which the blood of our citizens was shed, as in his messages declared, was or was not within the territory of Spain, at least after the treaty of 1819, until the Mexican revolution.

2nd. Whether that spot is or is not within the territory which was wrested from Spain by the revolutionary Government of Mexico.

3rd. Whether that spot is or is not within a settlement of people, which settlement has existed ever since long before the Texas revolution, and until its inhabitants fled before the approach of the United States army. . . .

5th. Whether the people of that settlement, or a majority of them, or any of them, have ever submitted themselves to the government or laws of Texas or the United States, by consent or compulsion, either by accepting office, or voting at elections, or paying tax, or serving on juries, or having process served upon them, or in any other way.

6th. Whether the people of that settlement did or did not flee from the approach of the United States army, leaving unprotected their homes and their growing crops, *before* the blood was shed, as in the messages stated; and whether the first blood so shed, was or was not shed within the enclosure of one of the people who had thus fled from it.

7th. Whether our *citizens*, whose blood was shed, as in his messages declared, were or were not, at that time, armed officers and soldiers, sent into that settlement by the military order of the President, through the Secretary of War."

Questions for Analysis

1. Identify the questions Lincoln poses in this excerpt.
2. Describe three causes that Lincoln implies are responsible for the conflict with Mexico.

Questions for Comparison

1. Explain how Lincoln's attitude toward the concept of America's "manifest destiny" compares to that of Polk.
2. Explain how the developments that Lincoln implies caused the war with Mexico differ from those that Polk addresses in his War Message.

Once the war began, battles erupted in a variety of locations. In May 1846, U.S. troops defeated Mexican forces in Palo Alto and Resaca de la Palma. A month later, the U.S. army captured Sonoma, California, with the aid of local settlers. John Frémont then led U.S. forces to Monterey, where the navy launched a successful attack and declared the California territory part of the United States. That fall, U.S. troops gained important victories at Monterrey, Mexico, just west of the Rio Grande, and Tampico, along the Gulf coast.

MAP 5.1 The Mexican-American War, 1846–1848 Although a dispute over territory between the Nueces River and the Rio Grande initiated the Mexican-American War, most of the fighting occurred between the Rio Grande and Mexico City. In addition, U.S. forces in California launched battles to claim independence for that region.

What do the locations of battles depicted on the map reveal about the goals of the United States in the war?

Herbert Orth/Contributor/The LIFE Images Collection/Getty Images

"Hanging of the Patricios," 1847 In 1846–1847, more than two hundred immigrants, most of them Irish Catholics who defected from U.S. army units, joined the Mexican army. They formed the *Batallón de San Patricio*, which fought fiercely in many battles. When dozens were captured after the Battle of Chapultepec, the soldiers were convicted of desertion. Samuel Chamberlain painted one of two mass hangings that followed.

In what way could religion and nativist sentiment have played a role in the creation and punishment of the Batallón de San Patricio?

Despite major U.S. victories, Santa Anna, who reclaimed the presidency of Mexico during the war, refused to give up. In February 1847, his troops attacked U.S. forces at Buena Vista and nearly secured a victory. Polk then sent General Winfield Scott to Veracruz with 14,000 soldiers. Capturing the port in March, Scott's army marched on to Mexico City. After a crushing defeat of Santa Anna at Cerro Gordo, the president-general was removed from power and the new Mexican government sought peace.

Treaty of Guadalupe Hidalgo
The 1848 treaty ending the Mexican-American War. In exchange for $15 million and a settlement of $3 million in U.S. citizens' claims against the Mexican government, the prior U.S. annexation of Texas was officially recognized, and the California and the New Mexico territories were ceded to the United States.

With victory ensured, U.S. officials faced a difficult decision: How much Mexican territory should they claim? The U.S. army in central Mexico faced continued guerrilla attacks. Meanwhile, Whigs and some northern Democrats denounced the war as a southern conspiracy to expand slavery. In this context, Polk agreed to limit U.S. claims to the northern regions of Mexico. The president signed the **Treaty of Guadalupe Hidalgo** in February 1848, committing the United States to pay Mexico $15 million in return for control over Texas north and east of the Rio Grande plus California and the New Mexico territory.

- How and why was the United States able to win the Mexican-American War?

A Crowded Land

While U.S. promoters of migration continued to depict the West as open territory, it was in fact the site of competing national ambitions in the late 1840s. Despite granting statehood to Texas in 1845 and winning the war against Mexico in 1848, the United States had to battle for control of the Great Plains with powerful American Indian nations, like the Sioux and Cheyenne.

Although attacks on wagon trains were rare, American Indians did threaten frontier settlements throughout the 1840s and 1850s. Settlers often retaliated, and U.S. army troops joined them in efforts to push American Indians back from areas newly claimed by whites.

In many parts of the West, American Indians were as powerful as whites, and they did not cede territory without a fight. The Reverend Marcus Whitman and his wife, Narcissa, became victims of their success in promoting western settlement when new pioneers brought a deadly measles epidemic to the region — an epidemic that quickly spread from white settlers to local indigenous populations, resulting in the deaths of thousands of Cayuse and Nez Percé Indians. In 1847, convinced that whites brought disease but no useful medicine, a group of Cayuse Indians killed the Whitmans and ten other white settlers.

Yet violence against whites could not stop the flood of migrants into the Oregon Territory. Indeed, attacks by one American Indian tribe were often used to justify assaults on any American Indian tribe. Thus, John Frémont and Kit Carson, whose party was attacked by Modoc Indians in Oregon in 1846, retaliated by destroying a Klamath Indian village and killing its inhabitants.

The defeat of Mexico and the discovery of gold in California only intensified such conflicts. Although American Indians and white Americans were the main players in many battles, American Indian nations also competed with each other. In the southern plains, drought and disease worsened those conflicts in the late 1840s and dramatically changed the balance of power there. In 1845, the southern plains were struck by a dry spell, which lasted on and off until the mid-1860s. In 1848, smallpox ravaged Comanche villages, and a virulent strain of cholera was introduced into the region the next year by forty-niners traveling to California. In the late 1840s, the Comanche nation was the largest American Indian group, with about twenty thousand members; by the mid-1850s, less than half that number remained.

Yet the collapse of the Comanche empire was not simply the result of outside forces. As the Comanche expanded their trade networks and incorporated smaller American Indian nations into their orbit, they overextended their reach. Most important, they allowed too many bison to be killed to meet the needs of their American Indian allies and the demand of Anglo-American and European traders. The Comanche also herded growing numbers of horses, which required extensive grazing lands and winter havens in the river valleys and forced the bison onto more marginal lands. Opening the Santa Fe Trail to commerce multiplied the problems by destroying vegetation and polluting springs, thereby diminishing resources in more of the region. The prolonged drought completed the depopulation of the bison on the southern plains.

Without bison, the Comanche lost a trade item critical to sustaining their commercial and political control. As the Comanche empire collapsed, former American Indian allies sought to advance their own interests. These developments reignited American Indian wars on the southern plains as tens of thousands of settlers poured through the region.

Black Americans also participated in these western struggles. Many were held in slavery by southeastern tribes forced into Indian Territory, while others were freed and married Seminole or Cherokee spouses. The Creek people proved harsh enslavers, prompting some of those enslaved to escape north to free states or south to Mexican or Comanche territory. Yet as southern officers in the U.S. army moved to frontier outposts, they carried more enslaved people into the region. Many changed posts often, taking enslaved workers into both slaveholding and free territories. Still, it was white planters who brought the greatest numbers of Black Americans into Texas, Missouri,

MAP 5.2 Western Trails and American Indian Nations, c. 1850 As wagon trains and traders journeyed west in rapidly growing numbers during the 1830s and 1840s, the United States established forts along the most well-traveled routes. At the same time, American Indians claimed or were forced into new areas through the pressure of forced removals, white settlement, and the demands of hunting, trade, and agriculture.

What historical developments best explain the specific destinations for the wagon trains shown here?

and Kansas, pushing the frontier of slavery ever westward. At the same time, some free Blacks joined the migration voluntarily in hopes of finding better economic opportunities and less overt racism in the West.

- What groups competed for land and resources in the West?
- How did disease, drought, and violence shape this competition?

Skills Workshop: Thinking Historically

Additional Practice in Using AP® Course Themes to Brainstorm and Organize an Essay

In Module 5.2, you were introduced to the course themes and how you can use them to help brainstorm outside evidence and organize an essay. Those themes are listed below and are arranged in an easy-to-remember anagram: "A PASSAGE."

American and National Identity

Politics and Power

America in the World

Settlement and Migration

Social Structures

American and Regional Culture

Geography and the Environment

Exchange, Work, and Technology

Complete the graphic organizer and write a thesis statement for the following prompt. Make sure to think about the themes during your brainstorm and consider using them for some or all of the general categories. Review the AP® Skills Workshop exercise in Module 5.2, if you need more help, before completing this activity.

Evaluate the relative causes of the Mexican-American War.

General Categories	Main Points	Supporting Details
-	-	- - -
-	-	- - -
-	-	- - -

MODULE 5.4

The Compromise of 1850

FOCUS

Comparison requires more than just a look at similarities and differences between two different places, societies, historical events, or processes. Sometimes, historians examine similarities and differences *within* the broader categories they are analyzing. The issue of slavery in both the northern and southern United States provides an opportunity for this kind of complex comparison.

While reading this module, compare the reactions to the debate over slavery throughout the North and South in the aftermath of the Mexican-American War. Be sure to consider the extent to which this issue also produced divisions *within* each region.

While many Americans supported the idea of manifest destiny and the Mexican-American War, westward expansion caused conflict between native peoples and American settlers, as well as between Americans themselves. The issue of slavery proved especially divisive because the Treaty of Guadalupe Hidalgo left unclear the status of slavery in the territories gained in the war.

The conflict over slavery spread from the plains of the West to the halls of Congress, and it threatened to split both the Whigs and the Democrats. While Congress had established a compromise on the issue of Missouri in 1820 that lasted for thirty years, the Compromise of 1850, in the aftermath of the Mexican-American War, proved unsatisfying to all sides.

Debates over Slavery Intensify

News of the U.S. victory in the Mexican-American War traveled quickly across the United States. In the South, planters imagined slavery spreading into the lands acquired from Mexico. Northerners, too, applauded the expansion of U.S. territory but focused on California as a center for agriculture and commerce.

The acquisition of new territory heightened sectional conflicts. Debates over slavery had erupted during the war, fueled by abolitionist outrage, and a few northern Democrats joined Whigs in denouncing "the power of SLAVERY" (referred to as the "Slave Power" at the time) to "govern the country, its Constitutions and laws."

Wilmot Proviso
An 1846 proposal by Democratic congressman David Wilmot of Pennsylvania to outlaw slavery in all territory acquired from Mexico. The proposal was defeated, but the fight over its adoption foreshadowed the sectional conflicts of the 1850s, especially regarding the legality of slavery in the territories.

In August 1846, Democratic congressman David Wilmot of Pennsylvania proposed outlawing slavery in all territory acquired from Mexico so that the South could not profit from the war. While the **Wilmot Proviso** passed in the House, southern and proslavery northern Democrats defeated it in the Senate. Nevertheless, Wilmot gave voice to a powerful northern antislavery bloc known as "free-soilers," who were less concerned with the plight of Black Americans, and more worried about the effect the spread of slavery to the West would have on the economic viability of small farmers and urban workers. Free-soil ideas added to the debate and extended antipathy toward slavery as farmers and workers, who were not necessarily sympathetic to abolitionist moral arguments, supported free-soiler concerns that expanding slavery into newly acquired western lands would undermine the republican ideal of a society of independent farmers.

The presidential election of 1848 opened with the unresolved question of whether to allow slavery in the territories acquired from Mexico. With Polk declining to run for a second term, Democrats nominated Lewis Cass, a Michigan senator and ardent expansionist who had supported annexing Mexico's Yucatán Peninsula and purchasing Cuba. Hoping to keep northern antislavery Democrats in the party, Cass argued for "popular sovereignty"—that residents in each territory should decide whether to make the region free or slave. This strategy put the slavery question on hold but satisfied almost no one.

The Whigs, too, hoped to avoid the slavery issue for fear of losing southern votes. They nominated Mexican-American War hero General Zachary Taylor, a Louisiana slaveholder who had no declared position on slavery in the western territories. But they sought to reassure their northern wing by nominating Millard Fillmore of Buffalo, New York for vice president. As a member of Congress in the 1830s, Fillmore had opposed the annexation of Texas.

The Liberty Party, disappointed in the Whig ticket, decided to run its own candidate for president. Its leaders hoped to expand their support by reconstituting themselves as the Free-Soil Party. This party, following the arguments of David Wilmot's proviso in 1846, focused more on excluding enslaved people from western territories than on the moral injustice of slavery. The party nominated former Democratic president Martin Van Buren and appealed to small farmers.

Once again, the presence of a third party affected the outcome of the election. While Whigs and Democrats tried to avoid the slavery issue, Free-Soilers demanded attention to it. By focusing on the exclusion of slavery in western territories rather than its abolition, the party won more adherents in northern states. Indeed, Van Buren won enough northern Democrats so that Cass lost New York State and the 1848 election. Zachary Taylor and the Whigs won, but only by placing a southern slaveholder and war hero in the White House.

- What arguments did members of the Liberty Party make about the expansion of slavery?
- How do those arguments compare to the Free-Soil Party's perspective on expanding slavery?

California and the Compromise of 1850

As the lure of getting rich quick drew migrants from across to the world to California's gold rush, its non-American Indian population exploded, with 80,000 new inhabitants arriving in 1849 alone. That winter, just before President Zachary Taylor's March inauguration, California applied for admission to the Union as a free state, skipping the traditional step of first becoming an organized territory. Some California political leaders opposed slavery on principle. Others wanted to "save" the state for whites by outlawing slavery, discouraging free Black migration, and restricting the rights of Mexican, American Indian, and Chinese residents.

Yet the internal debates among Californians were not uppermost in the minds of politicians. Southerners were concerned about the impact of California's free-state

U.S. Senate Collection

The United States Senate, A.D. 1850 This print captures seventy-three-year-old Henry Clay presenting his Compromise of 1850 to colleagues in the Old Senate Chamber. An aged John C. Calhoun, seated to the left of the Speaker's chair, denounced the compromise, as did antislavery Whigs and Free-Soilers. Daniel Webster, sitting to the left of Clay, offered a passionate defense but failed to gain the passage of the compromise.

What traditional regional interests do Clay, Calhoun, and Webster represent in this picture?

status on the sectional balance in Congress, while northern Whigs were shocked when President Taylor suggested that California should be quickly admitted by the U.S. Senate.

Fugitive Slave Act of 1793
An Act that allowed enslavers to capture enslaved people who had fled from a slave state by mandating that local governments, even in free states, seize and return them. However, the act was largely ignored by Northerners.

Other debates continued in Congress at the same time. Many Northerners were horrified by the spectacle of slavery and slave trading in the nation's capital and argued that it damaged America's international reputation. Southerners, meanwhile, complained that the **Fugitive Slave Act of 1793** was being widely ignored in the North. Further, a boundary dispute between Texas and New Mexico irritated western legislators, and Texas continued to claim that debts it accrued while an independent republic and during the Mexican-American War should be assumed by the federal government.

Compromise of 1850
A series of acts admitting California as a free state, banning the slave trade in the District of Columbia, referring the decision of slavery in Utah and New Mexico to popular sovereignty, strengthening the Fugitive Slave Law, and resolving Texas's border and debt.

Senator Henry Clay of Kentucky, the Whig leader who had hammered out the Missouri Compromise in 1820, again tried to resolve the many conflicts that stalled congressional action. He offered what became known as the **Compromise of 1850** with the following major proposals. California would be admitted as a free state. The remaining land acquired from Mexico would be divided into two territories—New Mexico and Utah—and slavery there would be decided by popular sovereignty. The border dispute between New Mexico and Texas would be decided in favor of New Mexico, but the federal government would assume Texas's war debts. The slave trade (but not slavery) would be abolished in the District of Columbia. A new and more effective fugitive slave law would be approved. Although Clay's compromise offered something to everyone, his colleagues did not immediately embrace it.

By March 1850, after months of passionate debate, the sides remained sharply divided, as did their respective leaders. John C. Calhoun, a proslavery senator from South Carolina, refused to support any compromise that allowed Congress to decide the fate of slavery in the western territories. William H. Seward, an antislavery Whig senator from New York, proclaimed he could not support a compromise that forced Northerners to help hunt down freedom-seeking fugitives from slavery. Daniel Webster, a Massachusetts Whig, urged fellow senators to support the compromise to preserve the Union. Yet Congress adjourned with the fate of California still undecided.

Before the Senate reconvened in September 1850, however, the political landscape changed in unexpected ways. Henry Clay retired the previous spring, leaving the Capitol with his last great legislative effort unfinished. On March 31, 1850, Calhoun died, and his absence from the Senate made compromise more likely. Then in July, President Taylor died unexpectedly, and his vice president, Millard Fillmore, became president. Fillmore then appointed Webster as secretary of state, removing him from the Senate as well.

AP® EXAM TIP

There are five specific elements to the Compromise of 1850. Select the three you think are most consequential to the debates over enslavement and rank their level of importance. This type of exercise is useful when writing free-response questions on the AP® Exam.

AP® WORKING with EVIDENCE

Source: John C. Calhoun, *The Clay Compromise Measures*, 1850

> "[H]ow can the Union be saved? To this I answer, there is but one way by which it can be, and that is, by adopting such measures as will satisfy the States belonging to the southern section that they can remain in the Union consistently with their honor and their safety. There is, again, only one way by which that can be effected, and that is, by removing the causes by which this belief has been produced. Do *that*, and discontent will cease, harmony and kind feelings between the sections be restored, and every apprehension of danger to the Union removed. The question then is, By what can this be done? . . . There is but one way by which it can with any certainty; and that is, by a full and final settlement, on the principle of justice, of all the questions at issue between the two sections. . . .
>
> But can this be done? Yes, easily; not by the weaker party, for it can of itself do nothing—not even protect itself—but by the stronger. The North has only to will it to accomplish it—to do justice by conceding to the South an equal right in the acquired territory, and to do her duty by causing the stipulations relative to fugitive slaves to be faithfully fulfilled—to cease the agitation of the slave question, and to provide for the insertion of a provision in the Constitution, by an amendment, which will restore to the South in substance the power she possessed of protecting herself, before the equilibrium between the sections was destroyed by the action of this Government. There will be no difficulty in devising such a provision—one that will protect the South, and which at the same time will improve and strengthen the Government, instead of impairing and weakening it."

Questions for Analysis

1. Identify Calhoun's main argument.
2. Explain what Calhoun means by "equilibrium between the sections" in the second paragraph of this excerpt.
3. Evaluate the extent to which the return of fugitives from slavery to the South was the main reason for Calhoun's argument.

In fall 1850, with President Fillmore's support, a younger group of senators and representatives steered the Compromise of 1850 through Congress, one clause at a time. This tactic allowed legislators to support only those parts of the compromise they found acceptable. In the end, all the provisions passed, and Fillmore quickly signed the bills into law.

The Compromise of 1850, like the Missouri Compromise thirty years earlier, fended off a sectional crisis but signaled future problems. Would popular sovereignty prevail when later territories sought admission to the Union, and would Northerners abide by a fugitive slave law that called on them to aid directly in the capture of freedom seekers who had escaped slavery and fled to the North?

REVIEW

- What steps did legislators take in the 1840s and early 1850s to address the issue of the expansion of slavery?

AP® Skills Workshop: Thinking Historically

Writing an Essay Introduction, Revisited

In Module 4.8, you learned the importance of contextualizing an essay response. You also learned how context can be incorporated into your introduction to provide essential background information to set up your argument. Let's briefly review how and why you should aim to craft a preceding contextualization statement in your introduction and link it to your thesis.

In your introduction, context sets the scene. Imagine if you started watching a weekly television drama in the middle of its first season. If you had never seen it before, you wouldn't immediately understand what was happening and why characters were behaving in certain ways. To address that, these types of shows often start with scenes from the last episode (or last several episodes) to provide context for what is going to happen.

In a similar way, your **preceding contextualization statement** should provide a connection to a previous event or process that can give the reader some insight into developments that you will examine in your essay.

The preceding context statement should come *before* your thesis. Remember, context and thesis are essential components of an essay. While you can get credit if your thesis is only in the conclusion and the location of your context is completely flexible, it is best practice to locate both in the introduction.

When writing a preceding context statement, the key is to identify a larger, more significant historical event just before (or at the beginning of the prompt's time period) and develop it using **CSE**. You may find it helpful to brainstorm and write your thesis first and then work backwards to identify and write your preceding contextualization statement.

Remember, too, when writing on the AP® Exam, a piece of evidence used to fulfill a specific requirement such as context, thesis, outside evidence, or sourcing cannot also be used to meet another requirement. In other words, since you can't double-dip, you will need multiple pieces of evidence, and you should organize how you are going to use that evidence before you start writing.

(continued)

Let's practice writing an introduction. We will start with the thesis first and then write the opening paragraph with preceding context and the thesis.

Prompt: Evaluate the extent of difference in American political attitudes before and after the Mexican War.

Thesis: U.S. involvement in the Mexican War marked a turning point in American politics and set in motion a decade of political disagreements that led to the Civil War. **[claim]** Although debates over the extension of slavery into western territories were not a new phenomenon, the war reopened the contentious issue, sparked the growth of a free-soil movement in the North, and set a precedent of popular sovereignty, which raised the possibility of more proslavery representation in the federal government. **[line of reasoning]**

For context, there are a variety of events in the years before the time period that you could choose to develop, such as manifest destiny, the Missouri Compromise, annexation of Texas, Polk's policies, Oregon fever, earlier western settlement, or the Slave Power. We will model the first example, manifest destiny, as preceding context in the introductory paragraph below.

In the years before the Mexican-American War, manifest destiny had swept the country, leading many Americans to believe that expansion to the Pacific Ocean was preordained by God. **[preceding context claim]** The Treaty of Guadalupe Hidalgo, which ceded the lands between Texas and the Pacific Ocean to the United States, represented a fulfillment of this ideology. **[preceding context support]** Differing positions between Northerners and Southerners over the status of slavery in the newly conquered territory created a context for growing political disagreements in the 1850s. **[preceding context explanation]** U.S. involvement in the Mexican-American War marked a turning point in American politics and set in motion a decade of political disagreements that led to the Civil War. **[thesis claim]** Although debates over the extension of slavery into western territories were not a new phenomenon, the Mexican War reopened the contentious issue, sparked the growth of a free-soil movement in the North, and set a precedent of popular sovereignty, which raised the possibility of more proslavery representation in the federal government. **[thesis line of reasoning]**

ACTIVITY

Now it's your turn. Write an essay introduction with preceding contextualization using CSE and a thesis statement with a claim and line of reasoning for the prompt below. Make sure to choose something besides manifest destiny for your context. Your finished paragraph should be five to six sentences in length.

Evaluate the extent to which debates over the expansion of slavery changed between 1845 and 1850.

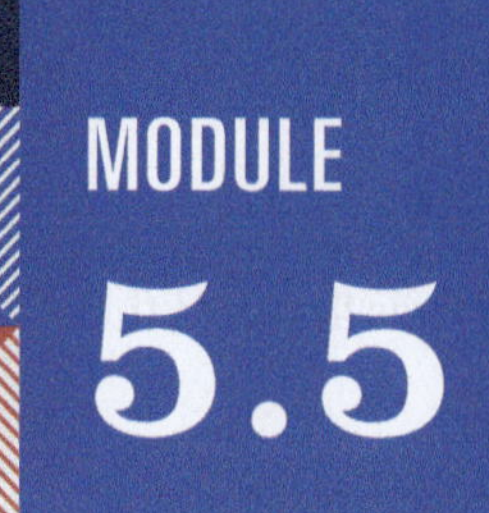

Sectional Conflict: Regional Differences

FOCUS

As you read, compare the reactions of Northerners and Southerners to the historical developments discussed in this module. Why were the Fugitive Slave Act, the Underground Railroad, the expansionist efforts of President Pierce, and the publication of abolitionist literature received so differently by various groups of Americans? In what ways were their reactions similar?

AP® EXAM TIP

Opposition to slavery increased over time during the antebellum period. Identify at least three ways to explain the importance of the abolitionist movement. Analyzing broad movements such as abolitionism with more specific examples such as the Underground Railroad or speeches such as "What to the Slave Is the Fourth of July?" by Frederick Douglass can buttress strong historical arguments.

Fugitive Slave Act of 1850

An act that strengthened earlier fugitive slave laws, passed as part of the Compromise of 1850. The act required northern citizens to help catch runaways and made it difficult for alleged runaways to receive a fair trial. The act provoked widespread anger in the North, and the backlash against it enraged Southerners.

Underground Railroad

A secret network of routes and safe houses from southern plantation areas to northern free states and Canada along which abolitionist supporters, known as conductors, provided hiding places, transportation, and resources to enslaved people seeking freedom in the North and Canada.

The place of slavery in the West aroused intense political debates and shaped the election of 1848. After the Compromise of 1850, granting California admission as a free state and enacting a stricter Fugitive Slave Act, those debates only intensified. Abolitionists inspired Northerners to resist helping slavecatchers while also supporting efforts to smuggle enslaved Blacks out of the South. President Franklin Pierce (1853–1857), a proslavery Democrat, encouraged further territorial expansion to extend slavery's reach, heightening tensions over slavery even more.

The Fugitive Slave Act Inspires Northern Protest

The fugitive slave laws of 1793 and 1824 mandated that all states aid in apprehending and returning escapees from slavery to their enslavers. The **Fugitive Slave Act of 1850** was different in several important respects. It eliminated jury trials for alleged runaways and barred the accused from even being able to testify on their own behalf. Commissioners who decided the cases were paid $10 for each alleged escapee they sent back to slavery in the South, but only $5 for each they freed. The law also required individual citizens, not just state officials, to help return freedom seekers under threat of heavy fines and significant jail time. As a result, the act angered many Northerners who believed that the federal government had gone too far in protecting the rights of enslavers and aroused sympathy for the abolitionist cause.

Following passage of the Fugitive Slave Act, the number of enslavers and hired slave catchers pursuing runaways increased dramatically. So, too, did the number of northern abolitionists helping fugitives escape. Once enslaved people seeking freedom crossed into free territory, most contacted free Black Americans or sought out Quaker, Baptist, or Methodist meetinghouses whose members might be sympathetic to their cause. They then began the journey along the **Underground Railroad**, from house to house or barn to barn, until they found safe haven.

Thousands of enslaved people, out of a total enslaved Black population of over three million in the 1850s, were led north by a network of abolitionists and others sympathetic to their plight. Harriet Tubman, a formerly enslaved woman, returned to the South repeatedly to free dozens of family members and other enslaved men and women. Abolitionists also purchased the freedom of some, including sisters Mary and Emily Edmondson who had been sold to slave traders after a failed escape attempt in 1848. Most freedom seekers followed disparate paths, depending on "conductors" to get them from one stop to the next. Despite its limits, the Underground Railroad was an important resource for runaways seeking refuge in Canada or hoping to blend into free Black communities stateside.

Before 1850, free Black people led the effort to aid freedom seekers, including David Ruggles in New York City; William Still in Philadelphia; and, after his own successful escape, Frederick Douglass. Among their most dependable allies were white Quakers and political abolitionists. However, free Black people were endangered by the claim that enslaved people hid themselves in their midst. In Chester County, Pennsylvania, on the Maryland border, newspapers reported on at least a dozen free Black people who were kidnapped or arrested as runaways in the first three months of 1851.

Digital image courtesy of the Getty's Open Content Program

Anti-Fugitive Slave Law Convention, Cazenovia, New York, 1850 This rare daguerreotype captures abolitionists, outraged over the 1850 Fugitive Slave Law, at a large protest meeting. Some two thousand participants met in an apple orchard. Frederick Douglass sits at the left side of the table. Mary and Emily Edmondson, in plaid shawls, were among fifty formerly enslaved people who attended the meeting.

What does this photograph reveal about the abolitionist movement?

At the same time, a growing number of Northerners challenged the federal government's right to enforce the law. Black and white people organized protest meetings throughout the free states. At a meeting in Boston in 1851, William Lloyd Garrison denounced the law: "We execrate it, we spit upon it, we trample it under our feet." On July 5, 1852, Frederick Douglass asked a mixed-race audience, "What to the American slave, is your 4th of July? I answer, a day that reveals to him . . . the gross injustice and cruelty to which he is the constant victim." He then declared, "There is not a nation on the earth guilty of practices more shocking and bloody than are the people of these United States at this very hour."

Some abolitionists established vigilance committees to rescue fugitives who had been arrested. In Syracuse in October 1851, Jermaine Loguen, Samuel Ward, and the Reverend Samuel J. May, three prominent Black abolitionists, led a well-organized crowd that broke into a Syracuse courthouse and rescued a runaway known as Jerry. They successfully hid him from authorities before smuggling him to Canada.

Meanwhile, Americans continued to debate the law's effects. John Frémont, one of the first two senators from California, helped defeat a federal bill that would have imposed harsher penalties on those who assisted runaways. Congress felt growing pressure to calm the situation, including from foreign officials who were horrified by the violence required to sustain slavery in the United States. Meanwhile, some northern states passed a new wave of personal liberty laws banning state officials from aiding in the capture and return of accused runaways and providing the right for a jury trial in state courts.

Black abolitionists also denounced the Fugitive Slave Act across Canada, Ireland, and England, intensifying foreign concern over the law. Great Britain and France had abolished slavery in their West Indian colonies and could not support what they saw as extreme policies to keep the institution alive in the United States. Yet southern slaveholders refused to compromise further, as did northern abolitionists.

AP® WORKING with EVIDENCE

Source: William C. Nell, *Meeting of Colored Citizens of Boston*, 1850

"The Chairman [Lewis Hayden] announced, as a prominent feature in calling the present meeting—Congress having passed the infamous Fugitive Slave Bill—the adoption of ways and means for the protection of those in Boston liable to be seized by the prowling man-thief. He said that safety was to be obtained only by an united and persevering resistance of this ungodly, anti-republican law. . . .

The following resolutions were submitted, as a platform for vigilant action in the trial hour:—

Resolved, That the Fugitive Slave Bill, recently adopted by the United States Congress, puts in imminent jeopardy the lives and liberties of ourselves and our children; it deprives us of trial by jury, when seized by the infernal slave-catcher, and by high penalties forbids the assistance of those who would otherwise obey their heart-promptings in our behalf; in making it obligatory upon marshals to become bloodhounds in pursuit of human prey; leaving us no alternative . . . but to be prepared in the emergency for self-defense; therefore, assured that God has no attribute which can take sides with oppressors, we have counted the cost, and as we prefer *liberty* to *life*, we mutually pledge to defend ourselves and each other in resisting this God-defying and inhuman law, at any and every sacrifice, invoking Heaven's defense of the right.

Resolved, That . . . eternal vigilance is the price of liberty, and that they who would be free, themselves must strike the first blow."

Questions for Analysis

1. Identify the rights Nell asserts are violated by the Fugitive Slave Act.
2. Describe what Nell claims he is prepared to do to defend these rights.
3. Evaluate the extent to which Nell draws on the rhetoric of America's founding documents.

Source: President Millard Fillmore, *Proclamation 56 Calling on Citizens to Assist in the Recapture of a Fugitive Slave*, 1851

"Whereas information has been received that sundry [various] lawless persons, principally persons of color, combined and confederated together for the purpose of opposing by force the execution of the laws of the United States, did, at Boston, in Massachusetts, on the 15th of this month, make a violent assault on the marshal or deputy marshals of the United States for the district of Massachusetts, in the court-house, and did overcome the said officers, and did by force rescue from their custody a person arrested as a fugitive slave, and then and there a prisoner lawfully [held] by the said marshal or deputy marshals of the United States, and other scandalous outrages did commit in violation of law:

Now, therefore, to the end that the authority of the laws may be maintained and those concerned in violating them brought to immediate and condign punishment, I have issued this my proclamation, calling on all well-disposed citizens to rally to the support of the laws of their country, and requiring and commanding all officers, civil and military, and all other persons, civil or military, who shall be found within the vicinity of this outrage, to be aiding and assisting by all means in their power in quelling this and other such combinations and assisting the marshal and his deputies in recapturing the above-mentioned prisoner; and I do especially direct that prosecutions be commenced against all persons who shall have made themselves aiders or abettors in or to this . . . offense."

Questions for Analysis

1. Identify the consequences President Fillmore proposes for disregarding the Fugitive Slave Act.
2. Describe how Fillmore views the Boston abolitionists who opposed the act.

Questions for Comparison

1. Explain how those present at the meeting Nell describes would likely have responded to Fillmore's Proclamation.
2. Explain the ways in which conflicts over the Fugitive Slave Act in Boston reveal rising tensions across the nation during this time period.

- Why did the Fugitive Slave Act of 1850 prompt protest from Northerners?

Further Expansion under President Pierce

In the presidential election of 1852, the Whigs and the Democrats tried once again to appeal to voters across the North-South divide by running candidates who either skirted the slavery issue or voiced ambiguous views.

The Democrats nominated Franklin Pierce of New Hampshire. A northern opponent of abolition, Pierce had served in Congress from 1833 to 1842 and in the U.S. army during the Mexican-American War. The Whigs rejected President Millard Fillmore, who angered many by supporting popular sovereignty and a vigorous enforcement of the Fugitive Slave Act. They turned instead to General Winfield Scott of Virginia. General Scott had never expressed any proslavery views and had served with distinction in the war against Mexico. The Whigs thus hoped to gain southern support while maintaining their northern base. The Free-Soil Party, too, hoped to expand its appeal by nominating John Hale, a New Hampshire Democrat.

AP® EXAM TIP

Know the multi-prong antislavery movement that developed during the antebellum years. For instance, free labor as espoused by the Free-Soil Party and, later, the Republican Party is a strong example that is required content. Compare free labor with how slaveholders defended slavery.

Franklin Pierce's eventual victory, however, left the Whigs and the Free-Soilers in disarray. Seeking a truly proslavery party, a third of southern Whigs threw their support to the Democrats in the election. But despite the Democratic triumph, that party also remained fragile. The nation now faced some of its gravest challenges under a president with limited political experience, no firm base of support, and a cabinet that included men of widely differing views. When confronted with difficult decisions, Pierce received contradictory advice from cabinet members and generally pursued his own expansionist vision.

Early in his administration, Pierce focused on expanding U.S. trade and extending the "civilizing" power of the nation to other parts of the world. In addition to signing the first formal trade agreement with Japan shortly after taking office, Pierce was willing to consider conquests in the Caribbean and Central America.

For decades, U.S. politicians, particularly Southerners, had looked to gain control of Cuba, Mexico, and Nicaragua. A "Young America" movement within the Democratic

Party imagined manifest destiny reaching southward as well as westward. In hopes of stirring up rebellious Cubans against Spanish rule, some Democrats joined with private adventurers to send three unauthorized expeditions, known as **filibusters**, to invade Cuba. In 1854, the capture of one of the filibustering ships led to an international incident. Spanish officials confiscated the ship, and southern Democrats urged Pierce to seek an apology and compensation from Spain. But many northern Democrats rejected any effort to obtain another slave state, and Pierce was forced to renounce the filibusters.

Other politicians still pressured Spain to sell Cuba to the United States. These included Pierce's secretary of state, William Marcy, and the U.S. ambassador to Great Britain, James Buchanan, as well as the ministers to France and Spain. In October 1854, these ministers met in Ostend, Belgium, and sent a letter to Pierce urging the conquest of Cuba. When the **Ostend Manifesto** was leaked to the press, Northerners were outraged. They viewed the episode as "a dirty plot" to gain more slave territory and forced Pierce to give up plans to obtain Cuba.

Ostend Manifesto

A letter from U.S. ambassadors and the secretary of state to President Franklin Pierce written in 1854 urging him to purchase Cuba from Spain and, if Spain refused the sale, to conquer Cuba for U.S. territorial expansion. When it was leaked to the press, Northerners voiced outrage at what they saw as a plot to use the power of the federal government to expand slave territories.

In 1855, a private adventurer named William Walker, who had organized four filibusters to Nicaragua, invaded that country and set himself up as ruler. He then invited southern planters to come to Nicaragua and establish plantations. Pierce and many Democrats endorsed his plan, but neighboring Hondurans forced Walker from power in 1857 and executed him three years later. Although Pierce's expansionist dreams failed, his efforts succeeded in heightening sectional tensions.

REVIEW

- In what ways were slavery and American expansionism linked during the 1850s?

Popularizing the Antislavery Movement

The Fugitive Slave Act forced Northerners to reconsider their role in sustaining the institution of slavery. In 1852, just months before Franklin Pierce was elected president, their concerns were heightened by the publication of the novel ***Uncle Tom's Cabin*** by Harriet Beecher Stowe. Stowe's father, Lyman Beecher, and brother Henry were among the nation's leading evangelical clergy, and her sister Catharine had opposed Cherokee removal and promoted women's education. Stowe was inspired to write *Uncle Tom's Cabin* in 1850, after the passage of the Fugitive Slave Act. Published in both serial and book forms, the novel created a national sensation.

Uncle Tom's Cabin

A novel by abolitionist Harriet Beecher Stowe, published in 1852. Meant to publicize the evils of slavery, the novel struck an emotional chord in the North, expanding calls for the abolition of slavery, and was an international bestseller.

Uncle Tom's Cabin was built on accounts by formerly enslaved people as well as tales gathered by abolitionist lecturers and writers, which gained growing attention in the North. The autobiographies of Frederick Douglass (1845), Josiah Henson (1849), and Henry Bibb (1849) set the stage for Stowe's novel. So, too, did the expansion of the antislavery press, which by the 1850s included dozens of newspapers. Antislavery poems and songs also circulated widely and were performed at abolitionist conventions and fund-raising fairs.

Still, nothing captured the public's attention as did *Uncle Tom's Cabin*. Read by millions in the United States and England and translated into French and German, the book reached a mass audience. Its sentimental portrait of saintly slaves and its vivid depiction of cruel masters and overseers offered white Northerners a way to identify with enslaved Black people. While some Black Americans expressed frustration that a white woman's fictional account gained far more readers than their factual narratives, most recognized the book's important contribution to the antislavery cause.

Yet the real-life stories of fugitives from slavery could often surpass their fictional counterparts for drama. In May 1854, abolitionists sought to free Anthony Burns from a Boston courthouse, where an enslaver was attempting to reclaim him. They failed to secure his release, and Burns was soon marched to the docks to be shipped south. Twenty-two companies of state militia held back tens of thousands of angry Bostonians who lined the streets. A year later, supporters purchased Burns's freedom, but the incident raised painful questions among local residents. In a city that was home to so many intellectual, religious, and antislavery leaders, Bostonians wondered how they had come so far in aiding and abetting slavery.

REVIEW

- What factors increased the popularity of antislavery sentiment in the North?

AP® Skills Workshop: Thinking Historically

Sourcing a Document's Historical Situation, Revisited

Throughout this course, you have worked regularly with primary-source documents. On the AP® Exam, you will also be expected to analyze documents like a historian through a process called sourcing. In the AP® Skills Workshop in Module 4.8, you were introduced to a new way to source documents by examining their **historical situation**.

Let's take a closer look at how to identify and explain a document's historical situation and how that differs from contextualization.

Think of a scene in a play. This scene needs a physical backdrop to set the scene, perhaps a chair for a character to sit in, a door through which another character will enter, or even the false front of a house with a window for a character to lean out and talk to the other characters.

You can think of historical situation like the backdrop of a document. Items within a historical situation are specific historical factors that directly influenced the creation, perception, or reaction to the document. Ask yourself if there was a specific event or development that led to the document. Perhaps the document reminds you of something else related to it that took place during that time. Maybe the document could be used as evidence or an example of a historical trend or process. To demonstrate your understanding of a document's historical situation in an essay, you need to connect the document to a *specific* and *relevant* piece of historical information that you can link to your argument.

While there are some similarities between historical situation and **preceding contextualization/immediate contextualization** (Modules 4.3, 4.9, and 5.4), there are also some important differences. First, preceding contextualization should appear in the introduction, preferably before the thesis, whereas historical situation is explained in a body paragraph when analyzing a specific document. Second, preceding context usually predates the essay's time period, and ideally, it should represent a larger event or process such as a major war, movement, ideology, or economic change. And while immediate context takes place within the essay's time frame, it also tends to be a larger-scale development or process. Historical situation, on the other hand, introduces events, facts, or very specific trends that relate directly to the primary source you are analyzing. Think of the example of the scene in a play again. If an actor is the primary source, the chair she sits on is the historical situation.

(continued)

We will practice analyzing a document's historical situation by taking a deeper look at two documents you already encountered in this module.

Source: Anti-Fugitive Slave Law Convention, Cazenovia, New York, 1850

Digital image courtesy of the Getty's Open Content Program

The completed table below consists of the types of questions you need to consider when thinking about a document's historical situation. If you can answer *one* of those questions with the type of specific information modeled for you, then you have much of the information you need to demonstrate your understanding of a document's historical situation. Note that the specific outside information in each sample answer has been underlined.

Historical Situation Question	Sample Response with Outside Evidence
What *led to* the Anti-Fugitive Slave Law convention (or these types of meetings)?	Anger over specific provisions of the Fugitive Slave Act such as paying commissioners twice as much if runaways were found guilty led to a growing abolitionist movement in the North.
How does the activity depicted in the photograph *relate to* another event during the time period?	The mixed-race audience depicted in the photo is evidence that the abolitionist movement was led by both free Blacks such as Frederick Douglass and white allies like William Lloyd Garrison.
What *resulted from* the protests against the Fugitive Slave Act?	Northern states began to pass personal liberty laws to protect the rights of accused escapees by banning state officials from helping slavecatchers and guaranteeing the right to a jury trial in state court.
Does the image *remind you* of anything else from the time period?	Those opposed to the act and slavery did more than protest. For example, Uncle Tom's Cabin was widely read in the North and similarly stimulated anti-slavery sentiment.

(continued)

ACTIVITY

Now it's your turn. Reread the following document from earlier in the module and complete the chart for it below. Make sure to note specific, outside information in your response to each historical situation question.

Source: William C. Nell, *Meeting of Colored Citizens of Boston*, 1850

> "The Chairman [Lewis Hayden] announced, as a prominent feature in calling the present meeting—Congress having passed the infamous Fugitive Slave Bill—the adoption of ways and means for the protection of those in Boston liable to be seized by the prowling man-thief. He said that safety was to be obtained only by an united and persevering resistance of this ungodly, anti-republican law. . . .
>
> The following resolutions were submitted, as a platform for vigilant action in the trial hour:—
>
> Resolved, That the Fugitive Slave Bill, recently adopted by the United States Congress, puts in imminent jeopardy the lives and liberties of ourselves and our children; it deprives us of trial by jury, when seized by the infernal slave-catcher, and by high penalties forbids the assistance of those who would otherwise obey their heart-promptings in our behalf; in making it obligatory upon marshals to become bloodhounds in pursuit of human prey; leaving us no alternative . . . but to be prepared in the emergency for self-defense; therefore, assured that God has no attribute which can take sides with oppressors, we have counted the cost, and as we prefer *liberty* to *life*, we mutually pledge to defend ourselves and each other in resisting this God-defying and inhuman law, at any and every sacrifice, invoking Heaven's defense of the right.
>
> Resolved, That . . . eternal vigilance is the price of liberty, and that they who would be free, themselves must strike the first blow."

Historical Situation Question	Sample Response with Outside Evidence
What *led* to the document?	
How does the document *relate* to another event during the time period?	
What *resulted* from the document?	
Does the document *remind* you of anything else from the time period?	

MODULE

5.6 Failure of Compromise

FOCUS

While reading this module, consider the various reasons why developments in the 1850s continued to divide the country and why efforts at compromise over the issue of the extension of slavery into territories failed despite the success of previous compromises.

The political crises of the early 1850s bred social turmoil, which in turn further pushed American politics from one crisis to the next. While the decade started out with hope for compromise, passion over the expansion of slavery, both for and against, caused upheaval from the plains of Kansas, to the halls of Congress, and to the Supreme Court. The weakness and fragmentation of the existing political parties gave rise to the Republican Party in 1854, which soon absorbed enough Free-Soilers, Whigs, and northern Democrats to become a major political force. The events that drove these cultural and political developments included continued challenges to the Fugitive Slave Act, a battle over the admission of Kansas to the Union, a Supreme Court ruling in the *Dred Scott* case, and John Brown's raid at Harper's Ferry.

The Kansas-Nebraska Act Stirs Dissent

transcontinental railroad
A railroad linking the East and West Coasts of North America. Completed in 1869, the transcontinental railroad facilitated the flow of migrants and the development of economic connections between the West and the East and symbolized American industrial and economic achievement.

Kansas-Nebraska Act
A 1854 act creating the territories of Kansas and Nebraska out of what was then American Indian land. The act repealed the Missouri Compromise and allowed the issue of slavery to be settled by a popular referendum in each territory. Its passage led to widespread violence in Kansas and the demise of the Whig Party.

Kansas provided the first test of the effects of *Uncle Tom's Cabin* on northern sentiments toward slavery's expansion. As white Americans displaced American Indian nations from their homelands, diverse groups of American Indians settled in the northern half of the Louisiana Territory. This unorganized region had once been considered beyond the reach of white settlement, but Democratic senator Stephen Douglas of Illinois was eager to have a **transcontinental railroad** run through his home state. To do so, the federal government would have to gain control of land along the route he proposed, so Douglas argued for the establishment of a vast Nebraska Territory. But to support his plan, Douglas also had to convince southern congressmen, who sought a route through their own region.

According to the Missouri Compromise, slavery was barred from any territory and future state in the remainder of the Louisiana Purchase above the southern border of Missouri. To gain southern support for his scheme, Douglas was willing to reopen the question of slavery in the territories. In January 1854, Douglas introduced the **Kansas-Nebraska Act** to Congress. The act extinguished American Indians' long-held treaty rights in the region and repealed the Missouri Compromise. Two new territories—Kansas and Nebraska—would be carved out of the unorganized lands, and voters in each territory would determine whether to enter the nation as a slave or a free state (Map 5.3). The act spurred intense opposition from most Whigs and some northern Democrats who wanted to retain the Missouri Compromise line. Months of fierce debate followed, but the bill was voted into law.

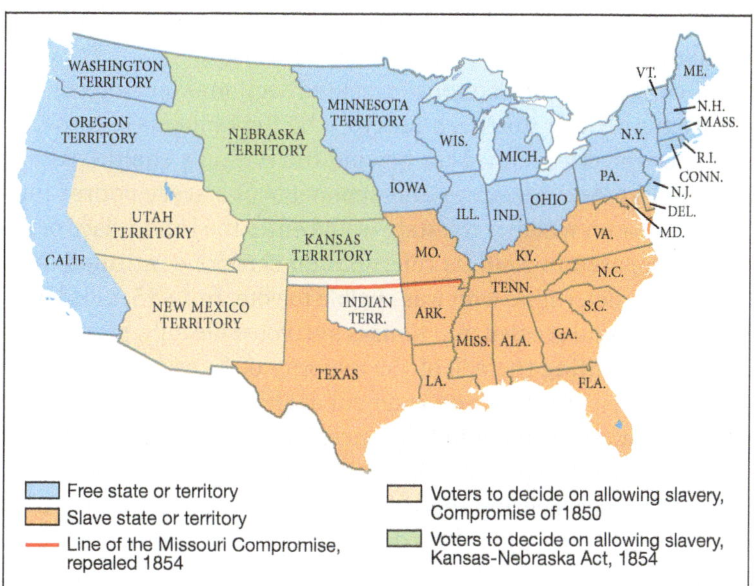

MAP 5.3 Kansas-Nebraska Territory From 1820 on, Congress tried to limit sectional conflict. But the Missouri Compromise (1820) and the Compromise of 1850 failed to resolve disagreements over slavery's expansion.

How did the Kansas-Nebraska Act attempt to ease tensions that arose over slavery? To what extent did the act worsen these tensions?

Passage of the Kansas-Nebraska Act enraged many Northerners who considered the dismantling of the Missouri Compromise a sign of the rising power of the South. They were infuriated that the South—or what some now called the *Slave Power*—had again taken advantage of northern politicians' willingness to compromise.

Although few of these opponents considered the impact of the law on American Indians, the act also shattered treaty provisions that had protected the Arapaho, Cheyenne, Ponca, Pawnee, and Sioux nations. These Plains Indians lost half the land they had held by treaty as thousands of settlers swarmed into the newly organized territories. In the fall of 1855, conflicts between white settlers and American Indians erupted across the Great Plains. The U.S. army then sent six hundred troops to retaliate against a Sioux village, killing eighty-five residents of Blue Water in the Nebraska Territory and triggering continued violence throughout the region.

As tensions escalated across the nation, Americans faced the 1854 congressional elections. The Democrats, increasingly viewed as supporting the priorities of enslavers, lost badly in the North. But the Whig Party also proved weak, having failed to stop the Slave Power from extending its influence over federal policies. A third party, the **American Party** (also known as the Know-Nothing Party), was founded in the early 1850s and attracted native-born workers and Protestant farmers who were drawn to its anti-immigrant and anti-Catholic message. They sought limits on immigrants' political power and cultural influence.

Responding to these political realignments, another new party, led by antislavery Whigs and Free-Soilers—the **Republican Party**—was founded in the spring of 1854. Among its early members was a Whig politician from Illinois, Abraham Lincoln.

Although established only months before the fall 1854 elections, the Republican Party gained significant support in the Midwest, particularly in state and local campaigns. Meanwhile, the American Party gained control of the Massachusetts legislature and nearly captured New York.

These victories marked the demise of the Whigs and the Second Party System. Unlike the Whig Party with its national constituency, the Republican Party was rooted solely in the North. Like Free-Soilers, the Republicans argued that slavery should not be extended into new territories. But the Republicans also advocated a program of commercial and internal improvements to attract a broader base than earlier antislavery parties. The Republican Party attracted both abolitionists and those whose main

American Party
Also known as the Know-Nothing Party, a political party that arose in the Northeast during the 1840s. The party was anti-Catholic and anti-immigration. It also supported workers' rights against business owners, who were perceived to support immigration as a way to keep wages low.

Republican Party
A political party formed in 1854 that was committed to stopping the expansion of slavery and that advocated economic development and internal improvements. Although their appeal was limited to the North, the Republicans quickly became a major political force.

AP® EXAM TIP

Knowing the formation of the Republican Party is required for the AP® Exam. Use the information in this section to detail the various causes of the Republican Party's formation in northern states over time. Be specific in your analysis, drawing on examples such as anti-immigration, free soil, and economic development in the West to strengthen your response.

concern was keeping western territories open to free white men. This latter group was more than willing to accept slavery where it already existed.

The 1854 congressional elections increased sectional tensions by bringing representatives from a strictly northern party — the Republicans — into Congress. But the conflicts over slavery reached far beyond the nation's capital. After passage of the Kansas-Nebraska Act, advocates and opponents of slavery poured into Kansas in anticipation of a vote on whether the state would enter the Union slave or free.

As Kansas prepared to hold its referendum, settlers continued to arrive daily, making it difficult to determine who was eligible to vote. In 1855, aided by "border ruffians" from Missouri who crossed into Kansas and voted illegally, proslavery forces stole the election, circumventing the will of the majority of Kansans who favored free soil. The winners installed a proslavery government at Shawnee Mission, while abolitionists established a shadow government in Lawrence. Violence erupted when proslavery settlers invaded Lawrence, killing one resident, demolishing newspaper offices, and plundering shops and homes. Fearing that southern settlers in Kansas were better armed than antislavery Northerners in the territory, eastern abolitionists raised funds to ship rifles to Kansas.

In 1856, longtime abolitionist John Brown carried his own rifles to Kansas. Four of his sons already lived in the territory. To retaliate for proslavery attacks on Lawrence, the Browns and two friends kidnapped five proslavery advocates from their homes along Pottawatomie Creek and hacked them to death. The so-called Pottawatomie Massacre infuriated southern settlers, and the illegitimately elected government then drew up the Lecompton Constitution, which declared Kansas a slave state. President Pierce made his support of the proslavery government clear, but Congress remained divided. While Congress deliberated, armed battles raged in Kansas. In the first six months of 1856, more than fifty settlers — on both sides of the conflict — were killed in what became known as **Bleeding Kansas**.

Bleeding Kansas The nickname given to the Kansas Territory as a result of a series of violent conflicts over the fate of slavery in Kansas in the mid-1850s. Violence continued in Kansas until the Civil War.

Fighting was not limited to the plains of Kansas. It also broke out on the floor of Congress. Republican senator Charles Sumner of Massachusetts delivered an impassioned speech against the continued expansion of the Slave Power on May 20, 1856.

Peter Newark American Pictures/Bridgeman Images

John Doy and His Rescue Party, Kansas, 1859 John Doy and his son Charles were captured in Kansas in January 1859 while aiding thirteen enslaved people in an attempted escape. Taken to Missouri, Charles was set free, but his father was sentenced to five years in prison for abducting enslaved people. John Doy (seated) was freed when his armed abolitionist friends successfully stormed the jail. The group posed for this picture when they reached Lawrence, Kansas.

Who would be the intended audience(s) for this photograph, and what message does it send?

He launched scathing attacks on planter politicians like South Carolina senator Andrew Butler. Butler's nephew, Preston Brooks, a Democratic member of the House of Representatives, decided to defend his family's honor. Two days later, he assaulted Sumner in the Senate chamber, severely beating him with a cane. Sumner, who never fully recovered from his injuries, was considered a martyr in the North. The Massachusetts legislature reelected Sumner in 1857 even though he wasn't physically able to serve until 1859, leaving his seat vacant as a silent protest. Meanwhile, Brooks was celebrated throughout South Carolina. Supporters mailed him new canes, and he was promptly reelected after resigning his House seat.

The presidential election of 1856 began amid an atmosphere poisoned by violence and recrimination. The Democratic Party nominated James Buchanan of Pennsylvania, a proslavery advocate. He had the advantage of being out of the country as the ambassador to England, and his lack of involvement in the recent slavery controversies made him acceptable to various factions within the Democratic Party. John C. Frémont, a free-soiler celebrated for aiding the conquest of California during the Mexican-American War, headed the Republican Party ticket. The American Party, in its final presidential contest, selected former Whig president Millard Fillmore as its candidate. The strength of the party was diminishing, however, and Fillmore would win only the state of Maryland.

Frémont drew cheering crowds as he traveled across the nation and appealed to many northern nativists with his calls for immigration restrictions. Large numbers of women turned out to see Jessie Frémont, the first presidential candidate's wife to play a significant role in a campaign. On election day, Frémont carried most of the North and the West. Buchanan captured the South along with Pennsylvania, Indiana, and Illinois. Although Buchanan won only 45 percent of the popular vote, he received a comfortable majority in the electoral college, securing his victory. The electoral results showed the nation was becoming increasingly divided along sectional lines, and President Buchanan would do little to resolve these differences.

AP® WORKING with EVIDENCE

Source: *American (Know-Nothing) Party Platform*, 1856

"*Resolved*, That the American democracy place their trust in the intelligence, the patriotism, and the discriminating justice of the American people. . . .

3. *Americans must rule America*; and to this end *native*-born citizens should be selected for all state, federal, and municipal offices of government employment, in preference to all others. *Nevertheless*,

4. Persons born of American parents residing temporarily abroad, should be entitled to all the rights of native-born citizens. . . .

7. The recognition of the right of native-born and naturalized citizens of the United States, permanently residing in any territory thereof, to frame their constitution and laws, and to regulate their domestic and social affairs in their own mode, subject only to the provisions of the federal constitution, with the privilege of admission into the Union whenever they have the requisite population for one Representative in Congress: *Provided, always*, that none but those who are citizens of the United States under the constitution and laws thereof, and who have a fixed residence in any such territory, ought to participate in the formation of the constitution or in the enactment of laws for said territory or state. . . .

13. Opposition to the reckless and unwise policy of the present administration in the general management of our national affairs, and more especially as shown in removing 'Americans' (by designation) and conservatives in principle, from office, and placing foreigners and [abolitionists] in their places . . . as shown in reopening sectional agitation, by the repeal of the Missouri Compromise; as shown in granting to unnaturalized foreigners the right of suffrage in Kansas and Nebraska; as shown in its vacillating course on the Kansas and Nebraska question; as shown in the corruptions which pervade some of the departments of the government; as shown in disgracing meritorious naval officers through prejudice or caprice; and as shown in the blundering mismanagement of our foreign relations."

Questions for Analysis

1. Identify an element of the American Party's platform that addresses the debate over slavery.
2. Describe the American Party's position on immigration in this excerpt.
3. Explain the contexts that shaped the American Party platform.

Source: *Republican Campaign Song,* 1856

"FREMONT AND VICTORY.

A Rallying Song — Tune of Marseilles Hymn*

Behold! the furious storm is rolling,
Which border fiends, confederates, raise,
The dogs of war, let loose, are [howling],
And lo! our infant cities blaze,
And shall we calmly view the ruin,
While lawless force with giant stride,
Spreads desolation far and wide,
In guiltless blood his hands imbruing?
Arise, arise, ye brave!
And let our war cry be,
FREE SPEECH, FREE PRESS, FREE SOIL, FREE MEN,
FRE-MONT AND LIBERTY! . . .

Hurrah, hurrah, from hill and valley;
Hurrah from prairie wide and free!
Around our glorious chieftain rally,
For Kansas and for liberty!
Let him who first her wilds exploring,
Her virgin beauty gave to fame,
Now save her from the curse and shame
Which slavery o'er her soil is pouring.
Our standard bearer then,
The brave path finder be!
FREE SPEECH, FREE PRESS, FREE SOIL, FREE MEN,
FRE-MONT AND LIBERTY."

---

*"La Marseillaise" was first written and popularized during the French Revolution and adopted by the French Republic as its national anthem in 1795. For Americans of the 1850s, the Marseillaise immediately called to mind the ideals of liberty and equality. The American national anthem, "The Star-Spangled Banner," was not adopted by the United States until the twentieth century. — Eds.

Questions for Analysis

1. Identify the "furious storm" in the first line of the song.
2. Explain how this campaign song provides both a moral and a legal call to action.

Questions for Comparison

1. Identify the intended audiences for each document.
2. Explain how each document attempts to appeal to its intended audience.
3. Explain how the perspective toward slavery in the territories expressed in the American Party platform compares to that of the Republican campaign song.

REVIEW

- How did the violence in Kansas reflect and intensify growing sectional divisions in the United States?

The *Dred Scott* Decision

Just two days after Buchanan's inauguration, the Supreme Court finally announced its decision in the ***Dred Scott* case**. Dred Scott was an enslaved person who sued for his freedom on the basis of having lived with his enslaver for the previous five years in free areas of Illinois and Wisconsin Territory. Led by Chief Justice Roger Taney, a proslavery Southerner, the majority ruled that an enslaved person was not a citizen and therefore could not sue in court. Indeed, Taney claimed that Black men had no rights that a white man was bound to respect. The ruling annulled Scott's suit and meant that he and his wife remained enslaved. But the ruling went further. The *Dred Scott* decision declared that Congress had no constitutional authority to exclude slavery from any territory, thereby declaring the Missouri Compromise, the earlier Northwest Ordinance, and any future effort to restrict slavery's expansion unconstitutional.

Dred Scott v. Sandford
Dred Scott v. Sandford, a Supreme Court decision, centered on the status of Dred Scott and his family. In its 1857 ruling, the Court denied the claim that Black men had any rights, ruled that the Missouri Compromise had been unconstitutional, and blocked Congress from excluding slavery from any territory.

Taney's opinion stated slavery could be banned only by territorial legislatures when they wrote their constitutions. The ruling outraged many Northerners, who were now convinced that a Slave Power conspiracy had taken hold of the federal government, including the judiciary.

In 1858, when Illinois Democratic senator Stephen Douglas, the architect of the Kansas-Nebraska Act, faced reelection, the Republican Party nominated Abraham Lincoln, a successful lawyer from Springfield, Illinois, to oppose him. The candidates participated in seven debates in which they explained their positions on slavery in the wake of the *Dred Scott* decision.

Pointing to the landmark ruling, Lincoln asked Douglas how he could favor popular sovereignty, which allowed residents to keep slavery out of a territory, and yet support the *Dred Scott* decision, which protected slavery in all territories. Douglas claimed that if residents did not adopt local legislation to protect enslavers' property, for all practical purposes, slavery would not exist in the territory. At the same time, he accused Lincoln of advocating "Negro equality," a position that went well beyond Lincoln's views. Lincoln did support economic opportunity for free Black people, but not political or social equality. Still, Lincoln warned that the proslavery Supreme Court might eventually rule that free states could not prohibit slavery. He also cautioned that "this government cannot endure permanently half slave and half free. . . . It will become all one thing or all the other."

AP® EXAM TIP

Know how to rank the various attempts to resolve the disputes over the future of slavery in the western territories. The AP® Exam expects you to know events such as the Kansas-Nebraska Act and the *Dred Scott* decision. Think about adding developments such as the failure of the Second Party System and events such as Harpers Ferry to improve your analysis.

Lincoln-Douglas debates
A series of debates between Abraham Lincoln and Stephen Douglas during the 1859 Illinois Senate race that mainly focused on the expansion of slavery in the territories.

The **Lincoln-Douglas debates** attracted national attention, but the Illinois legislature selected the state's senator. Narrowly controlled by Democrats, it returned Douglas to Washington.

Although Douglas retained his seat, he was concerned by how far the Democratic Party had tilted toward the South. When President Buchanan tried to push the Lecompton Constitution through Congress, legitimating the proslavery government in Kansas, Douglas opposed him. The two struggled over control of the party, with Douglas eventually winning a symbolic victory in January 1861 when Kansas was admitted as a free state. By then, however, the Democratic Party had split into southern and northern wings, and the nation was on the verge of civil war.

AP® WORKING with EVIDENCE

Source: Abraham Lincoln, *Speech at Edwardsville, Illinois*, 1858

> "The difference between the Republican and the Democratic parties on the leading issue of this contest, as I understand it, is, that the former consider slavery a moral, social and political wrong, while the latter *do not* consider it either a moral, social or political wrong; and the action of each, as respects the growth of the country and the expansion of our population, is squared to meet these views. . . . Every measure of the Democratic party of late years, bearing directly or indirectly on the slavery question, has corresponded with this notion of utter indifference whether slavery or freedom shall outrun in the race of empire across the Pacific—every measure, I say, up to the Dred Scott decision, where, it seems to me, the idea is boldly suggested that slavery is *better* than freedom. The Republican party, on the contrary, hold that this government was instituted to secure the blessings of freedom, and that slavery is an unqualified evil to the negro, to the white man, to the soil, and to the State. Regarding it an evil, they will not molest it in the States where it exists; they will not overlook the constitutional guards which our forefathers have placed around it; they will do nothing which can give proper offence to those who hold slaves by legal sanction; but they will use every constitutional method to prevent the evil from becoming larger and involving more negroes, more white men, more soil, and more States in its deplorable consequences. . . . All, or very nearly all, of Judge Douglas' arguments about 'Popular Sovereignty,' as he calls it, are logical if you admit that slavery is as good and as right as freedom; and not one of them is worth a rush if you deny it. This is the difference, as I understand it, between the Republican and the Democratic parties."

Questions for Analysis

1. Identify Lincoln's main argument.
2. Describe how Lincoln supports his argument.
3. Explain how Lincoln appeals to his intended audience in this speech.

Questions for Comparison

Source: *Republican Campaign Song*, 1856 (See page 420.)

1. Describe the similarities and differences between Lincoln's characterization of Republican Party goals and that of the campaign song.
2. Explain how specific historical developments account for the differences between Lincoln's argument and that of the campaign song.

■ What historical developments led to the *Dred Scott* decision?
■ How did the *Dred Scott* decision reflect and intensify growing sectional divisions within the United States?

From Crisis to Secession

During the 1850s, an abundance of abolitionist lectures, conventions, and literature swelled antislavery sentiment in the North. Mainstream newspapers regularly covered rescues of fugitives, the *Dred Scott* case, and the bloody crisis in Kansas. Republican candidates in state and local elections also kept concerns about slavery's expansion and southern Slave Power alive. Nothing, however, riveted the nation's attention as much as **John Brown's raid** on the federal arsenal at Harpers Ferry, Virginia, in 1859.

John Brown's raid An attack on the federal arsenal at Harper's Ferry, Virginia, in 1859 led by John Brown, who hoped to inspire a slave uprising and arm enslaved Black Americans with the weapons taken from the arsenal. No uprising happened, and Brown was captured and eventually executed for treason.

John Brown was committed not only to the abolition of slavery but also to complete equality between white and Black people. A militant abolitionist and deeply religious man, Brown held views quite similar to those of David Walker, whose 1829 *Appeal* warned that enslaved people would eventually rise up and claim their freedom by force. Following the bloody battles in Bleeding Kansas, Brown was convinced that direct action was the only answer. After the Pottawatomie killings, he went into hiding and reappeared back east, where he hoped to initiate an uprising to overthrow slavery.

Brown focused his efforts on the federal arsenal in Harpers Ferry. With eighteen followers—five Black Americans and thirteen whites, including three of his sons—Brown planned to capture the arsenal and distribute arms to enslaved people in the surrounding area. He hoped this action would ignite a rebellion that would destroy the plantation system. He tried to convince Frederick Douglass to join the venture, but Douglass considered it a foolhardy plan. However, Brown did manage to persuade a small circle of white abolitionists to bankroll the effort.

On the night of October 16, 1859, Brown and his men successfully kidnapped some leading townsmen and seized the arsenal. Local residents were stunned but managed to alert authorities, and state militia swarmed into Harpers Ferry. The next day, federal troops arrived, led by Colonel Robert E. Lee. With troops flooding into the town, Brown and his men were soon under siege, trapped in the arsenal. Fourteen rebels were killed, including two of Brown's sons. On October 18, Brown and three others were captured.

As word of the shocking raid spread, Brown was hailed as a hero by many devoted abolitionists and depicted as a madman by southern planters. Southern whites were sure the raid was part of a widespread conspiracy led by power-hungry abolitionists. In response, federal authorities moved quickly to quell enslavers' fears and end the episode. Brown rejected his lawyer's advice to plead insanity, and a local jury found him guilty of murder, criminal conspiracy, and treason. He was hanged on December 2, 1859.

John Brown's execution unleashed an enormous outpouring of grief, anger, and uncertainty across the North. Abolitionists organized parades, demonstrations, bonfires, and tributes to the newest abolitionist martyr. Even many Quakers and other pacifists viewed Brown as a hero for giving his life in the cause of emancipation. But most northern politicians and editors condemned the raid as a reckless act that could only intensify sectional tensions.

Among southern whites, fear and panic greeted the attack on Harpers Ferry, and the execution of John Brown did little to quiet their outrage. By this time, southern intellectuals had developed a sophisticated proslavery argument that, to them, demonstrated the benefits of bondage for Black Americans and its superiority to the northern system of wage labor. They argued that enslavers provided care and guidance for Black Americans from birth to death. Considering Black people too childlike to fend for themselves, proslavery advocates saw no problem with the enslaved providing labor and obedience in return for their care. Such arguments failed to convince abolitionists, who highlighted the brutality, sexual abuse, and shattered families that marked the system of bondage. In this context, Americans on both sides of the sectional divide considered the 1860 presidential election critical to the nation's future.

- How did John Brown's raid and execution further inflame tensions between North and South?

Skills Workshop: Thinking Historically

Additional Practice in Writing Body Paragraphs for a Long-Essay Question

In Modules 3.5 and 4.5, you learned how to use **CSE** to write a body paragraph with evidence. Review those AP® Skills Workshops, if needed, and then compose three main body paragraphs for the prompt below. Each paragraph should start with a sub-argument, use CSE twice, and end with a summary of the sub-argument. To help you, a completed graphic organizer and introductory paragraph have been provided.

Evaluate the extent to which political disagreements between 1844 and 1860 led to the Civil War.

General Categories	Main Points	Supporting Details
- Exchange, Work, and Technology	- Lack of industrialization hindered the South's economic development and urban growth.	- Lowell mills and most textile factories were built in the North. - Erie Canal and railroads mostly constructed in the Northeast and Midwest. - European immigration was mainly to the North, leading to its greater population and ethnic diversity. - New York City and other northern cities boomed, while the South remained more rural.
- Politics and Power	- Debates resumed over the extension of slavery into new territories.	- Wilmot Proviso would have banned slavery in the lands gained from Mexico, angering Southerners. - Compromise of 1850 tipped the balance in the Senate toward free states and left slavery in New Mexico and Utah to popular sovereignty. - Kansas-Nebraska Act angered many Northerners and wrecked the Whig Party by repealing the Missouri Compromise. - Bleeding Kansas violence resulted from popular sovereignty and a fraudulent election in Kansas.

(continued)

General Categories	Main Points	Supporting Details
- American and National Identity	- Northern and Southern attitudes toward slavery increasingly hardened the actions of radicals on both sides.	- Caning of Senator Sumner and reactions to it demonstrated growing anger and resolve in both the North and South. - Filibustering efforts showed the lengths pro-southern political leaders were willing to take to expand slavery. - The Underground Railroad infuriated many enslavers despite its limited impact and showed the willingness of some abolitionists to risk their lives for their cause. - Harpers Ferry raid convinced many Southerners that slavery was under siege, especially because some Northerners viewed John Brown as a martyr.

Political disagreements between the North and South over the expansion of slavery began well before 1844. **[preceding context claim]** For example, the Tallmadge Amendment of 1819, which would have greatly restricted slavery in Missouri, led to months of heated debate and the Missouri Compromise, which confined slavery in the remainder of Louisiana Purchase territory at the 36°30′ line. **[preceding context support]** Although the Missouri Compromise settled the issue of slavery in the remaining western territory, it left unresolved the fate of slavery in any newly acquired lands, which again became an issue in the 1840s. **[preceding context explanation]** After successfully going to war with Mexico and adding Texas, California, and the lands in between to the United States, growing political disagreements tore the nation apart by 1860. **[thesis claim]** While the lack of industrialization had hindered the South's economic development and urban growth resulting in growing differences between the South and the rest of the nation, the debates over the extension of slavery into the new territories and the increasingly hardened attitudes on both sides of the slavery issue made the Civil War inescapable. **[thesis line of reasoning]**

MODULE 5.7

Election of 1860 and Secession

FOCUS

While reading this module, consider the reasons Lincoln won the presidential election in 1860 and how his victory prompted southern states to secede from the Union. What were the effects of Lincoln's positions and actions? How did the choices made on both sides lead to the Civil War?

Although Democrats held the White House from 1852 to 1860, the Democratic Party was split into northern and southern factions. The Democratic fracture helped Republican candidate Abraham Lincoln win the presidency in the election of 1860 without support from any southern states. When Lincoln took office in March 1861, seven states in the Lower South had already formed the Confederate States of America, and more states threatened to secede. Lincoln had promised not to interfere with slavery where it existed, but many southern whites doubted such assurances. Still, not all slave states were yet willing to cut their ties to the nation. Northerners, too, disagreed about the appropriate response to secession. Once fighting erupted, however, preparations for war became the main focus in both the Union and the Confederacy, and four more states seceded.

Lincoln Wins the Presidency in 1860

John Brown's raid set the tone for the 1860 presidential campaign. The Republicans met in Chicago five months after Brown's execution and distanced themselves from the more radical wing of the abolitionist movement. The party platform condemned both John Brown and southern "Border Ruffians," who initiated the violence in Kansas. The Republican platform accepted slavery where it already existed, but continued to demand its exclusion from western territories. The platform also supported federally funded internal improvements and protective tariffs.

After considering higher-profile politicians such as New York senator William Seward and Ohio governor Salmon Chase, the Republicans nominated Abraham Lincoln as their candidate for president. Lincoln's reputation as a political moderate and his appeal to various factions within the party led delegates to believe he had the best chance of winning the general election. Recognizing the impossibility of gaining significant votes in the South, the party focused instead on winning as many states as possible in the Northeast and Midwest.

The Democrats met in Charleston, South Carolina. Although Stephen Douglas was the leading candidate, southern delegates were still angry with him over the admission of Kansas as a free state. When Mississippi senator Jefferson Davis introduced a resolution to protect slavery in the territories, Douglas's northern supporters rejected it. President Buchanan also came out against Douglas, and the Democratic convention ended without choosing a candidate. Instead, various factions met separately. A group of largely northern Democrats met in Baltimore and nominated Douglas. Southern Democrats selected John Breckinridge, the vice president, a slaveholder, and an advocate of annexing Cuba. The new Constitutional Union Party, comprised mainly of former southern Whigs, nominated Senator John Bell of Tennessee, claiming "no political principle other than the Constitution of the country, the union of the states, and the enforcement of the laws."

Although Lincoln won just less than 40 percent of the popular vote, he carried a clear majority in the electoral college. With the admission of Minnesota and Oregon to the Union in 1858 and 1859, free states outnumbered slave states eighteen to fifteen, and Lincoln won all but one of them. Because free states were more populous than slave states, they therefore controlled a large number of electoral votes. Lincoln did not win a single southern electoral vote. Douglas ran second to Lincoln in the popular vote, but Bell and Breckinridge captured more electoral votes than Douglas did because of their success in the South. Despite a deeply divided electorate, Lincoln became president.

Although many abolitionists were wary of the Republicans, who were willing to leave slavery alone where it existed, most were nonetheless relieved at Lincoln's victory and hoped he would become more sympathetic to their views once in office. Meanwhile, southern whites, especially those in the deep South, were furious that a Republican had won the White House without carrying a single southern state.

On December 20, 1860, six weeks after Lincoln's election, the legislature of South Carolina announced that because "a sectional party" had engineered "the election of a man to the high office of President of the United States whose opinions and purposes are hostile to slavery," the people of South Carolina dissolve their union with "the other states of North America." In early 1861, Mississippi, Florida, Alabama, Georgia, Louisiana, and Texas followed suit.

Representatives from these states met on February 8 in Montgomery, Alabama, where they adopted a provisional constitution, elected Jefferson Davis as their president, and established the **Confederate States of America**, also known as the Confederacy.

AP® EXAM TIP

Strong analyses on the free-response questions take something such as secession, a well-known historical topic, and create a layered approach. For instance, think about how the Lower South, Middle South, and border South each responded to Lincoln's election. You can also take something such as the split in the Democratic Party and explain the reasons for its demise.

Confederate States of America

The name of the government that seceded from the Union after the election of President Lincoln in 1860. Originally consisting of seven states, the Confederacy quickly grew to eleven states and located its capital in Richmond, Virginia.

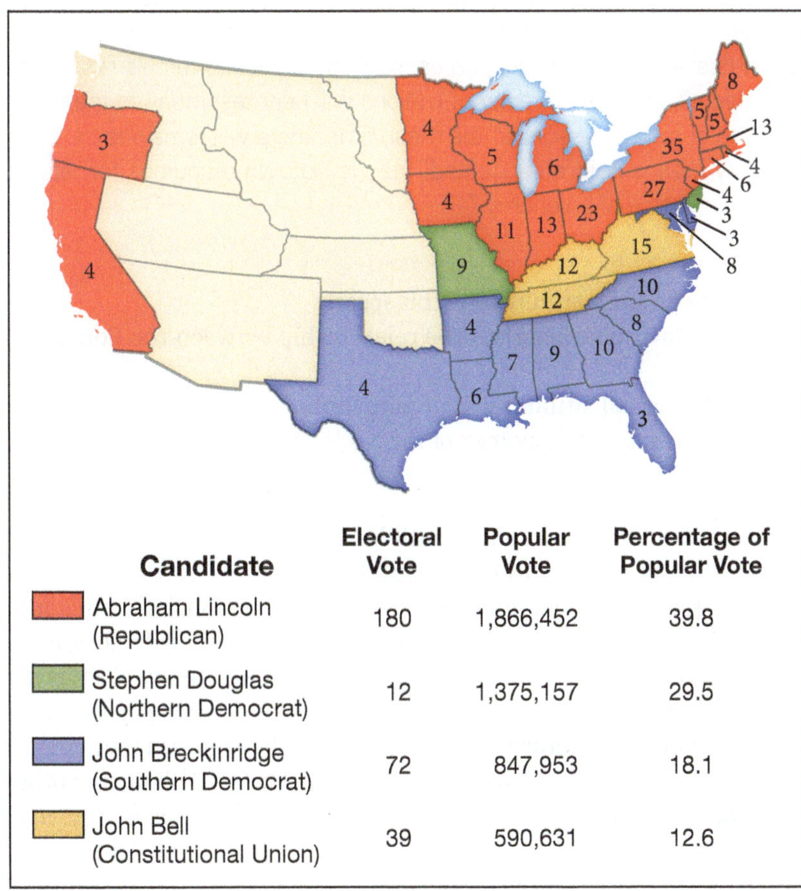

Candidate	Electoral Vote	Popular Vote	Percentage of Popular Vote
Abraham Lincoln (Republican)	180	1,866,452	39.8
Stephen Douglas (Northern Democrat)	12	1,375,157	29.5
John Breckinridge (Southern Democrat)	72	847,953	18.1
John Bell (Constitutional Union)	39	590,631	12.6

MAP 5.4 The Election of 1860 Four candidates vied for the presidency in 1860, and voters split along clearly sectional lines. Although Stephen Douglas gained the second-highest popular vote total, he won a plurality only in Missouri. Lincoln triumphed in the North, Upper Midwest, and far West. Bell captured the Upper South while Breckinridge won the other southern states.

What developments help explain why Stephen Douglas won so much of the popular vote but so few electoral votes?

WORKING with EVIDENCE

Source: Jefferson Davis, *Inaugural Address*, 1861

"[W]e have entered upon the career of independence, and it must be inflexibly pursued. Through many years of controversy, with our late associates, the Northern States, we have vainly endeavored to secure tranquillity, and to obtain respect for the rights to which we were entitled. As a necessity, not a choice, we have resorted to the remedy of separation; and henceforth, our energies must be directed to the conduct of our own affairs, and the perpetuity of the Confederacy which we have formed. If a just perception of mutual interest shall permit us, peaceably, to pursue our separate political career, my most earnest desire will have been fulfilled. But, if this be denied to us, and the integrity of our territory and jurisdiction be assailed, it will but remain for us, with firm resolve, to appeal to arms, and invoke the blessing of Providence on a just cause. . . .

Actuated solely by the desire to preserve our own rights and promote our own welfare, the separation of the Confederate States has been marked by no aggression upon others, and followed by no domestic convulsion. Our industrial pursuits have received no check—the cultivation of our fields has progressed as heretofore—and even should we be involved in war, there would be no considerable diminution in the production of the staples which have constituted our exports, and in which the commercial world has an interest scarcely less than our own. This common interest of the producer and consumer, can only be interrupted by exterior force, which should obstruct its transmission [of our staples] to foreign markets—a course of conduct which would be as unjust toward us as it would be detrimental to manufacturing and commercial interests abroad. Should reason guide the action of the Government from which we have separated, a policy so detrimental to the civilized world, the Northern States included, could not be dictated by even the strongest desire to inflict injury upon us; but if otherwise, a terrible responsibility will rest upon it, and the suffering of millions will bear testimony to the folly and wickedness of our aggressors. In the mean time, there will remain to us, besides the ordinary means before suggested, the well-known resources for retaliation upon the commerce of an enemy."

Questions for Analysis

1. Identify Davis's primary argument in this speech.
2. Describe how Davis characterizes the relationship between the Confederacy and the Union.
3. Explain the historical situation that contributed to Davis's claim that war will ultimately undermine the economies of the North and of "civilized" nations "abroad."

President Buchanan, still in office until Lincoln's inauguration in March 1861, did nothing to stop the secessionist movement. His cabinet included three secessionists and two unionists, one of whom resigned in frustration over Buchanan's failure to act. Washington, D.C., located in the Upper South, was filled with Confederate sympathizers, who urged caution on an already timid president. Although many Northerners were shocked by the decision of South Carolina and its allies, some supported their right to leave or believed they would return to the Union when they realized they could not survive economically on their own. Moreover, Virginia, North Carolina, and other Upper South slave states remained part of the nation, so the secessionist movement seemed unlikely to succeed.

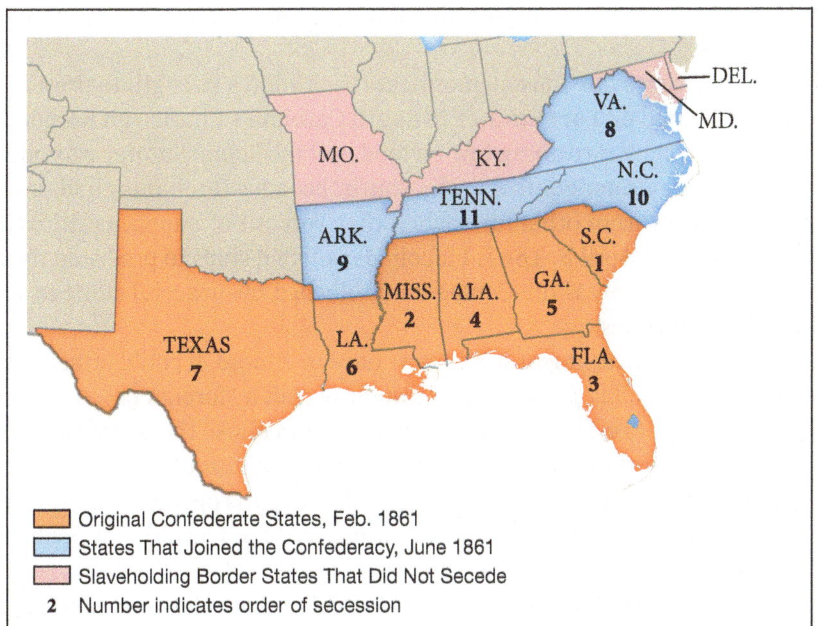

MAP 5.5 The Confederacy Seven states in the Lower South seceded from the United States and formed the Confederate States of America in February 1861. After fighting began, an additional four states joined the Confederacy. Four other slaveholding border states remained in the Union.

What factors best explain the regional differences in southern states seceding from the Union?

In the midst of the crisis, Kentucky senator John Crittenden proposed a compromise that gained significant support. Indeed, Congress approved the first part of the **Crittenden Plan**, which called for a constitutional amendment to protect slavery from federal interference in any state where it already existed. But the second part of his plan failed to win Republican votes. It would have extended the Missouri Compromise line (latitude 36°30′) to the California border and barred slavery north of that line. South of that line, however, slavery would be protected, including in any territories "acquired hereafter." Fearing that passage would encourage southern planters to again seek territory in Cuba, Mexico, or Central America, Republicans in Congress with the strong support of President-elect Lincoln rejected the proposal. Despite the hopes of the Buchanan administration, it was becoming apparent that compromise was impossible.

Crittenden Plan
A proposed political compromise which would have protected slavery in states where it already existed with a constitutional amendment and extended the Missouri Compromise line to the California border. Slavery would be protected in any existing or new territories below the line. Republicans rejected the compromise.

REVIEW

- Why did many Southerners believe that the election of Abraham Lincoln was cause for secession?

The South Chooses Secession

Confederate president Jefferson Davis joined other planters in arguing that Lincoln's victory jeopardized the future of slavery and that secession was therefore a necessity. Advocates of secession contended that the federal government had failed to implement fully the Fugitive Slave Act of 1850 and the *Dred Scott* decision. They were convinced that a Republican administration would do even less to support southern interests. White Southerners also feared that Republicans might inspire a vast uprising of enslaved people, and secession would allow whites to maintain control over the South's Black population.

When Lincoln was sworn into office, some legislators in the Upper South still hoped a compromise could be reached and that the new president wished to bring the Confederates back into the Union without using military force. Most northern merchants,

AP® EXAM TIP

Lincoln's policies regarding slavery are required content for the AP® Exam. Think about how Lincoln explained his free-soil position from the Lincoln-Douglas debates to his first inaugural. If asked on the AP® Exam, it will be helpful to detail the reasons for his free-soil position rather than only being able to state the fact.

manufacturers, and bankers approved, wanting to maintain their economic ties to southern planters.

Lincoln also believed he must demonstrate the Union's strength to prevent further secessions. He focused on **Fort Sumter** in South Carolina's Charleston harbor, where a small Union garrison was running low on food and medicine. Sumter was one of only two forts still under Union control in the South, because Buchanan had ordered the military to withdraw from other forts when they ran out of supplies rather than risk an armed conflict. On April 8, 1861, Lincoln dispatched ships to provision the fort but promised to use force only if the Confederates blocked his peaceful effort to send food and other needed supplies.

Fort Sumter

The Union fort that guarded the harbor in Charleston, South Carolina. The Confederacy's decision to fire on the fort and block resupply in April 1861 marked the beginning of the Civil War.

The Confederate government would now have to choose. It could attack Union vessels and bear responsibility for starting a war, or permit a "foreign power" to maintain a fort in its territory. President Davis and his advisers chose the aggressive course of action, demanding Fort Sumter's immediate and unconditional surrender. The commanding officer refused, and on April 12, Confederate guns opened fire. Two days later, Fort Sumter surrendered. On April 15, Lincoln called for 75,000 new soldiers to put down the southern insurrection.

These hostilities led whites in the Upper South to reconsider secession. Some small farmers and landless whites were drawn to Republican promises of free labor and free soil and remained suspicious of the goals and power of secessionist planters. Yet the vast majority of southern whites, rich and poor, defined their liberty in relation to bondage of Black people. They feared that Republicans would free enslaved people and introduce miscegenation, the mixing of white and Black people, in the South.

Four slave states—North Carolina, Virginia, Tennessee, and Arkansas—quickly seceded after the fighting at Fort Sumter. Virginia, with its strategic location near the nation's capital, was by far the most significant. Richmond, which would soon become the capital of the Confederacy, was also home to the South's largest iron manufacturer, which could produce weapons and munitions.

Fearing more secessions, Lincoln used extraordinary powers to keep the border states that allowed slavery—Maryland, Delaware, Missouri, and Kentucky—in the Union. He suspended the constitutional right of habeas corpus (which protects citizens against arbitrary arrest and detention), jailed secessionists without trials, arrested Confederate-sympathizing state legislators, and limited freedom of the press. These actions were unprecedented, but Lincoln claimed expansive wartime authority as commander in chief.

While Northerners differed over how to respond when the first seven states seceded, the firing on Fort Sumter prompted most people in the North to align with Lincoln's call for war. Manufacturers and merchants, once intent on maintaining commercial links with the South, now rushed to support the president, while northern workers, including immigrants, responded to Lincoln's call for army volunteers. They assumed that the Union, with its greater resources and manpower, could quickly set the nation right. New York editor Horace Greeley proclaimed, "Jeff Davis and Co. will be swingin' [hanging] from the battlements at Washington at least by the 4th of July."

REVIEW

- How did northern public opinion about southern secession change after the firing on Fort Sumter?

AP® Skills Workshop: Thinking Historically

Writing Essay Conclusions, Revisited

Just as any good story deserves an ending, essays should end with a strong conclusion—although if you are running out of time, you may have to make finishing your last body paragraph the priority if you can't do both. However, unlike some Hollywood movies or television shows that deliver a surprise plot twist at the end, an essay conclusion is a place where you should summarize and extend your argument, not surprise the reader.

In your conclusion, you want to accomplish two tasks: **restating the thesis** (both the claim and line of reasoning) and extending an element of your argument forward by **providing an immediate concluding context** (see Module 4.8). In a way, the conclusion is a mirror of the introduction. Both contain the thesis and context. However, the conclusion should start with the thesis and then contextualize forward, while the introduction starts with preceding context and then states the thesis.

Immediate concluding context should be approached the same way as preceding context. Both should be developed using **CSE**, both should include a specific and significant piece of outside information, and both should not stray too far from the time period; forty years or less is a good rule of thumb, although every essay is unique.

Because contextualizing forward requires you to have studied historical information beyond the time frame of the essay prompt, we are going to practice writing our conclusion using the sample essay prompt and thesis from Module 5.4. That way, we can use material from this module and the previous modules as well for our concluding context.

> **Prompt:** Evaluate the extent of difference in American political attitudes before and after the Mexican-American War.

> **Thesis:** U.S. involvement in the Mexican-American War marked a turning point in American politics and set in motion a decade of political disagreements that led to the Civil War. **[claim]** Although debates over the extension of slavery into western territories were not a new phenomenon, the war reopened the contentious issue, sparked the growth of a free-soil movement in the North, and set a precedent of popular sovereignty, seemingly moving the debate over slavery from the federal government to local leaders in the territories. **[line of reasoning]**

Now, let's brainstorm significant developments in the years *after* the essay's time frame so we can develop into an immediate concluding context. Because our thesis, and presumably the essay, is mostly limited to events that happened by 1850, we have many options to choose from. Here are just a few of many possibilities for concluding context: the Kansas-Nebraska Act, personal liberty laws, the formation of the Republican Party, the *Dred Scott* decision, the secession of southern states, and Fort Sumter.

ACTIVITY

Read the sample conclusion below that restates the original thesis and develops personal liberty laws as its concluding context. Then, create your own conclusion for the same essay prompt. Make sure to rewrite the thesis in your own words and choose a different piece of relevant outside information to develop using **CSE** for your **immediate concluding context**.

(continued)

In conclusion, the events and controversy regarding the Mexican War significantly changed political attitudes and set in motion a chain of events that led to the Civil War. **[thesis claim]** Not only did the Mexican-American War forcibly reopen the issue of expanding slavery into western lands, but it also led to a new free-soil movement seen by Southerners as a threat to slavery and introduced the doctrine of popular sovereignty to move the debate from the federal arena to the local level. **[thesis line of reasoning]** Political disagreements continued in the 1850s as northern states passed new personal liberty laws to counteract the Fugitive Slave Act, a key pro-southern law passed as part of the Compromise of 1850. **[immediate concluding context claim]** These personal liberty laws banned local law enforcement from helping slavecatchers in an effort to undermine the effectiveness of the Fugitive Slave Act. **[immediate concluding context support]** While the personal liberty laws signaled a growing willingness of many Northerners to resist the system of slavery, Southerners viewed them as proof that slavery was increasingly threatened. The discord generated over the issue of runaways continued to push both sides apart during the 1850s. **[immediate concluding context explanation]**

Military Conflict in the Civil War

MODULE 5.8

FOCUS

Comparison is a useful tool when studying a significant topic with two distinct sides such as the Union and Confederacy during the Civil War.

As you read this module, compare the motivations, advantages, and strategies of both the Union and the Confederacy during the early years of the war. Think about how those differences contributed to the Union's victory.

After Confederate troops attacked Fort Sumter, four of the eight slave states not already in the Confederacy seceded as the Civil War began in earnest. The Union and the Confederacy faced very different tasks in the war. The South had to defend its territory and force the federal government to halt military action.

The North had a more complicated challenge. Initially, northern political leaders believed that secession was driven mainly by enslavers and that high death rates and destruction of property would only alienate southern white people who favored reconciliation. But such a policy depended on early Union victories. With early defeats, it was clear the North would have to invade the South and isolate it from potential allies abroad. At the same time, most northern politicians believed that the nation could be reunited without abolishing slavery even as abolitionists argued that only emancipation could resolve the problems that led to war. Meanwhile, enslaved Black Americans immediately looked for ways to loosen their bonds.

AP® EXAM TIP

The AP® Exam does not focus on the military history of the war, yet you have to be able to explain how the course of the war affected policies and mobilization efforts. For instance, think about specific answers to how the Union and Confederacy mobilized for war on the home front. Be specific about factors such as confiscation, monetary policy, or the strength of central governments.

Both Sides Prepare for War

At the onset of the war, the Union held a significant advantage in resources and population. More than 60 percent of the U.S. population lived in Union states, and the Confederate population included several million enslaved people who would not be armed for combat. The Union also far outstripped the Confederacy in manufacturing and even led the South in agricultural production. The North's many miles of railroad track ensured greater ease in moving troops and supplies. The Union could also launch far more ships to blockade southern ports.

Yet Union forces were less prepared for war than the Confederates, who had been organizing troops and gathering munitions for months. To match their efforts, Winfield Scott, commanding general of the U.S. army, told Lincoln he would need at least 300,000 men committed to serve for two or three years. Scott believed that massing such huge numbers of soldiers would force the Confederacy to negotiate a peace. But fearing to unnerve Northerners, the president asked for only 75,000 volunteers for three months. Moreover, rather than forming a powerful national army led by seasoned officers, Lincoln left recruitment, organization, and training largely to the states. The result was disorganization and the appointment of officers based more on political connections than on military expertise.

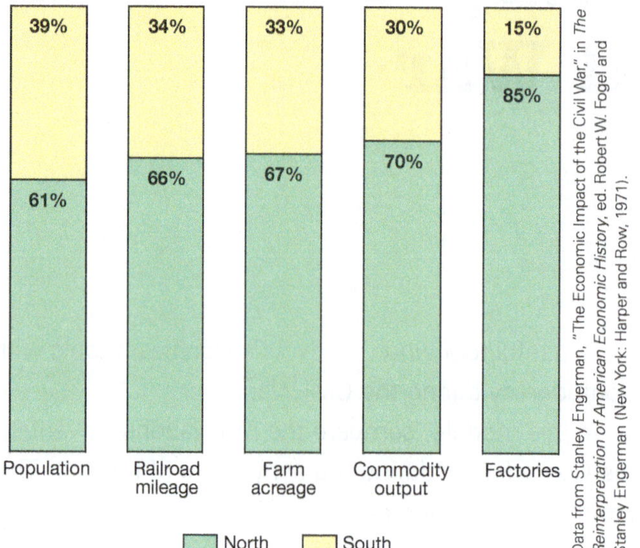

Economies of the North and South, 1860 This figure shows the enormous advantages in resources the North held over states with slavery on the eve of the Civil War. The North led slave states in population, farm acreage, and railroad mileage as well as factories and commodity output.

Over four years of war, how might the differences in each area of this graph affect the ability of the Union and the Confederacy to pursue their objectives?

Confederate leaders also relied at first on state militia units and volunteers, but they prepared for a prolonged war from the start. Before the firing on Fort Sumter, President Davis signed up 100,000 volunteers for a year's service. The labor provided by enslaved people allowed a large proportion of white working-age men to volunteer for military service. Southerners also knew they were likely to be fighting mainly on home territory, where they had expert knowledge of the terrain. When the final four states joined the Confederacy, the southern army also gained important military leadership. It recruited 280 West Point graduates, including Robert E. Lee, Thomas "Stonewall" Jackson, James Longstreet, and others who had proven themselves in the Mexican-American War.

The South's advantages were apparent in the first major battle of the war. Confederate troops were also aided by information on Union plans sent by Rose Greenhow, a Washington, D.C., socialite who spied for the Confederacy during the war. When 30,000 Union troops marched on northern Virginia on July 21, 1861, Confederate forces were

Library of Congress, LC-DIG-pga-01861

Battle of Wilson's Creek This colored lithograph depicts the First Iowa Regiment, led by General Nathaniel Lyon, charging Confederate forces at the Battle of Wilson's Creek, Missouri, on August 10, 1861. The Confederates won the battle, and Lyon, on the ground here, became the first Union general to die in the war. The lithograph was created in 1893 based on a wartime sketch.

What does this image reveal about popular notions of war early in the conflict?

ready. At the **First Battle of Bull Run** (or **First Manassas**), 22,000 Confederates repelled the Union attack and forced the Union troops to hastily retreat. Civilians from Washington who traveled to the battle site to view the combat had to flee for their lives to escape Confederate artillery.

First Battle of Bull Run (First Manassas)
The first major battle of the Civil War, at which Confederate troops defeated Union forces in July 1861.

Despite Union defeats at Bull Run and then at Wilson's Creek, Missouri, in August 1861, the Confederate army did not launch major strikes against Union forces. Meanwhile, the Union navy began blockading the South's deepwater ports. By the time the armies settled into winter camps in 1861–1862, both sides had come to realize that the war was likely to be a long and costly struggle.

- What advantages and disadvantages did each side have at the onset of the Civil War?

Wartime Roles of Black Americans and American Indians

The outbreak of war intensified debates over abolition. Some 225,000 Black Americans lived in the free states, and many offered their services in an effort to end slavery. Black American leaders in Cleveland proclaimed, "Today, as in the times of '76, we are ready to go forth and do battle in the common cause of our country." But Secretary of War Simon Cameron had no intention of calling up Black soldiers.

Northern optimism about a quick victory contributed to the rejection of Black American volunteers. Union leaders feared that white men would not enlist if they had to serve alongside Black Americans. In addition, Lincoln and his advisers were initially wary of letting a war to preserve the Union become a war against slavery, and they feared that any further threat to slavery might drive the four slave states that remained in the Union into the Confederacy. This political strategy, however, depended on quick and overwhelming victories; and with U.S. soldiers posted mainly on the western frontier and a third of officers joining the Confederacy, victories were few. Nonetheless, a rush of volunteers allowed Union troops to push into Virginia while the Union navy captured crucial islands along the Confederate coast.

Wherever Union forces appeared in the South, enslaved people began considering freedom as a possibility. Enslaved people living near battle sites circulated information on Union troop movements. Then, as planters in Virginia began sending enslaved men to more distant plantations for fear of losing them, some managed to flee and headed to Union camps. Many enslavers tracked runaways behind Union lines and demanded their return. Some Union commanders denied enslaved people entrance or returned them to their enslavers.

A few Union officers recognized these freedom seekers' value: They knew the local geography well, could dig trenches and provide other services, and their continued and growing presence drained the Confederate labor supply. At the Union outpost at Fort Monroe, Virginia, in May 1861, General Benjamin Butler offered military protection to people fleeing from enslavement. He claimed them as **contraband** of war: property forfeited by the act of rebellion.

contraband
A term first used by Union general Benjamin Butler in May 1861 to describe enslaved people who during the Civil War had fled to Union lines to obtain freedom. By designating enslaved people as property forfeited by the act of rebellion, the Union was able to strike at slavery by allowing self-emancipated people to remain free without proclaiming a general emancipation.

Lincoln endorsed Butler's policy because it allowed the Union to strike at the institution of slavery without proclaiming a general emancipation that might prompt border states where slavery remained legal to secede. Congress expanded Butler's

Confiscation Acts

Laws passed by Congress in 1861 and 1862 during the Civil War that authorized the emancipation of enslaved people as the confiscation of Confederate property. Under the first Confiscation Act, any enslaved people who were forced to work for the Confederate army would no longer be bound to their enslavers. The second act permanently freed any people enslaved by civilian or military Confederate officials.

policy by passing the first **Confiscation Act** in August 1861. It proclaimed that any enslaved persons who were forced to work for the Confederate army would no longer be bound to their enslavers. Although it was far from a clear-cut declaration of freedom, the act spurred the hopes of northern abolitionists and many enslaved people in the South.

While Northerners continued to debate Black Americans' role in the war effort, the Union army recruited a wide array of other ethnic and racial groups, including American Indians. Ely Parker, a Seneca sachem and engineer, became a lieutenant colonel in the Union army, serving with General Ulysses S. Grant.

Unlike Black people, however, American Indians did not necessarily all support the Union. The Comanche nation negotiated with both Union and Confederate agents while raiding the Texas frontier for horses and cattle. The Confederacy gained significant support from American Indian enslavers who had earlier been removed from the Southeast. The Cherokee nation split over the war, just as they had over removal. General Stand Watie led a pan-Indian force into battle for the Confederates. Initially, John Ross joined the Confederates as well, but later he led a group of Cherokees into Union army ranks alongside the Osage, Delaware, Seneca, and other American Indian nations.

Likewise, American Indians played crucial roles in a number of important early battles, particularly on the Confederate side. Cherokee and Seminole warriors fought alongside Confederates at the Battle of Pea Ridge in Tennessee in March 1862 but were defeated by a smaller but better-supplied Union force. In late summer that same year, American Indians contributed to the Confederate efforts in a series of major battles in Virginia and Maryland. The Confederate army recruited Mexican American soldiers as well, hoping to gain control of the West's gold and silver mines. But a Union victory gained by a troop of Colorado soldiers at Glorieta Pass near Santa Fe, New Mexico, ended that Confederate dream.

A series of Union military defeats in 1862 helped transform the attitudes of northern whites about slavery and about the place of Black Americans in the war effort. That spring, Confederate general Stonewall Jackson won stunning victories against three Union armies in Virginia's Shenandoah Valley. That June and July, General Robert E. Lee fought a much better-equipped Union army under General George B. McClellan to a standstill in the Seven Days Battle near Richmond. Then in August, Lee, Jackson, and General James Longstreet joined forces to defeat Union troops at the **Second Battle of Bull Run (Second Manassas)**.

As the war turned against the North, the North turned against slavery. In April 1862, Congress approved a measure to abolish slavery in the District of Columbia, symbolizing a significant shift in Union sentiment. During that bloody summer, Congress passed a second Confiscation Act, declaring that the people held in slavery by anyone who supported the Confederacy should be "forever free of their servitude, and not again held as slaves." In July, Congress also approved a militia act that allowed Black Americans to serve in "any military or naval service for which they may be found competent."

Support for the 1862 Militia Act built on Union victories as well as defeats. In April 1862, a Union blockade led to the capture of New Orleans, while the **Battle of Shiloh** in Tennessee provided the army entry to the Mississippi valley. There, Union troops came face-to-face with slavery. Few of these soldiers were abolitionists, but many were shocked by what they saw, including instruments used to torture enslaved people. Southern Black people also provided important intelligence to northern officers, making clear their value to the Union war effort.

MAP 5.6 Early Civil War Battles, 1861–1862 In 1861 and 1862, the Confederate army stunned Union forces with a series of dramatic victories in Virginia and Missouri. However, the Union army won a crucial victory at Antietam (Sharpsburg); gained control of Confederate territory in Tennessee, Arkansas, and Mississippi; fended off Confederate efforts to gain New Mexico Territory; and established a successful naval blockade of Confederate ports.

What advantages did Union forces have during this period, even as they were losing battles?

Whether in victory or defeat, rising death tolls increased northern support for Black American enlistment. The bloodshed of the Battle of Shiloh, the deadliest battle in American history to that point, shocked both North and South. Earlier battles had resulted in a few hundred or perhaps a few thousand casualties; at Shiloh, the toll was more than 23,000. As the war continued, such brutal battles became routine. The Union army would need every available man—white, Black, and American Indian—to sustain its effort against the Confederates.

American Indian regiments had already proven themselves in battle, and Black Americans soon followed suit. In October 1862, a group of Black soldiers in the First Kansas Colored Volunteers repulsed Confederates at a battle in Missouri. In the South, white abolitionists serving as Union officers organized former enslaved men into units like the First South Carolina Volunteers in January 1863. A few months later, another Black regiment—the Massachusetts Fifty-fourth—attracted recruits from across the North, including Frederick Douglass's three sons. For the next two years, tens of thousands of Black American soldiers fought valiantly in dozens of battles.

You should know how "key victories" led to Union victory. Detail how the Battles of Antietam, Gettysburg, and Vicksburg represented turning points in the course of the war.

REVIEW

- In what ways did white Americans' treatment of American Indians and Black Americans change over the course of the Civil War?
- In what ways did this treatment remain the same?

Union Politicians and Emancipation

By the fall of 1862, Black Americans and abolitionists had gained widespread support for emancipation as a necessary goal of the war. Lincoln and his cabinet realized that embracing abolition as a war aim would likely prevent international recognition of southern independence. As Massachusetts senator Charles Sumner proclaimed, "You will observe that I propose no crusade for abolition. [Emancipation] is to be presented strictly as a measure of military necessity." Still, some Union politicians feared that emancipation might arouse deep animosity in the slaveholding border states and drive them from the Union.

From the Confederate perspective, international recognition was critical. Support from European nations might persuade the North to accept southern independence. More immediately, recognition would ensure markets for southern agriculture and access to manufactured goods and war materiel. Confederate officials were especially focused on Britain, the leading market for cotton and a leading producer of industrial products.

Fearing that the British might openly side with the Confederacy, abolitionist lecturers toured Britain, reminding residents of their early leadership in the antislavery cause. The Union's formal commitment to emancipation would certainly increase British support for its position and prevent diplomatic recognition of the Confederacy. By the summer of 1862, Lincoln was convinced, but he wanted to wait for a military victory before making a formal announcement regarding emancipation to avoid any appearance that freeing the enslaved was an act of desperation.

Battle of Antietam
The fiercely fought battle at Sharpsburg, Maryland, in September 1862, resulting in more than 22,000 deaths, the single bloodiest day in U.S. military history. After repelling the Confederate invasion of Maryland, Lincoln declared it a great victory and announced a preliminary Emancipation Proclamation.

Emancipation Proclamation
The proclamation by President Lincoln on January 1, 1863, that declared all enslaved people in areas still in rebellion "forever free" based on his legal authority as commander in chief during wartime. While the Emancipation Proclamation did not free enslaved people in the border states, it reframed the purpose of the war from simply preserving the Union to abolishing slavery.

Instead, the Union suffered a series of defeats that summer, and Lee marched his army into Union territory in Maryland. On September 17, Longstreet joined Lee in a fierce battle along Antietam Creek as Union troops brought the Confederate advance to a standstill near the town of Sharpsburg. Union forces suffered more than 12,000 casualties, despite having discovered Lee's battle plans before the engagement, and the Confederates more than 10,000, the bloodiest single day of battle in U.S. history. Yet because Lee and his army were forced to retreat, Lincoln claimed the **Battle of Antietam** as a great victory. Five days later, the president announced his preliminary **Emancipation Proclamation** to the assembled cabinet, promising to free all enslaved people in states still in rebellion by January 1863.

On January 1, 1863, Lincoln signed the final edict, proclaiming that enslaved people in areas still in rebellion were "forever free" and inviting them to enlist in the Union army. Over the next two years, tens of thousands of enslaved men fled southern plantations and fought in the Union army alongside equal numbers of free Black men who volunteered to ensure the Confederacy's defeat.

Still, the proclamation was a moderate document in many ways. Its provisions exempted from emancipation the 452,000 enslaved people in the loyal border states, as well as more than 300,000 enslaved people in Union-occupied areas

Library of Congress, LC-DIG-pga-02502

President Lincoln Presenting the Emancipation Proclamation to His Cabinet In this engraving, Lincoln reads the draft of his Emancipation Proclamation to his cabinet in September 1862. On the left are Secretary of War Edwin Stanton (seated) and Secretary of the Treasury Salmon P. Chase, the two strongest supporters of the proclamation. Postmaster General Montgomery Blair and Attorney General Edward Bates (seated), who opposed the plan, are on the right. **What point might the artist of this engraving have made by arranging its subjects in this way?**

of Tennessee, Louisiana, and Virginia. The proclamation also justified the abolition of southern slavery on military, not moral, grounds. Despite its limits, the Emancipation Proclamation inspired joyous celebrations among free Black people and white abolitionists, who viewed it as the first step toward final eradication of slavery.

AP® EXAM TIP

Although emancipation is a well-known historical topic, think about how you can explain this in a way many other students will not. Rather than making blanket statements about the importance of emancipation, write about the limitations of the proclamation. You can focus on Lincoln's border-state strategy, where the proclamation had no immediate effect.

AP® WORKING with EVIDENCE

Source: The *Charleston Mercury*, "President Lincoln and His Scheme of Emancipation," 1862

> "[T]he Constitution of a country ought to be, in the relations of this world, as sacred as the Bible is in those of the next. Yet Abolitionism teaches a man that there is a higher law than the Constitution of the country, or the Bible itself. Hence, their [unethical] aggressions upon the slave institution of the South, in spite of the Constitution, and even the plain dictates of interest itself. Hence President LINCOLN['s] Proclamation for the abolition of slavery in the Confederate States, without a particle of constitutional authority. . . . The truth is, his Proclamation is declarative for emancipation to all the slaves of the South. That is what . . . [it] signifies, and that is what he means by it. President LINCOLN is not such a fool as not to know that the emancipation of all the slaves in the South, belonging to the citizens of the Confederate States, is also an emancipation of all the slaves belonging to the few traitors who affect allegiance to the United States. . . . The fellow is a rogue. He wishes to disguise the scope and atrocity of his unconstitutional and fiendish policy. . . . If he can deprive White men in the United States of their liberties, whenever he pleases, why can he not liberate black men?"

Questions for Analysis

1. Identify the author's intended audience.
2. Describe the evidence the author uses to support his position on the Emancipation Proclamation.
3. Evaluate the extent to which the author considers the Emancipation Proclamation a continuation of Lincoln's previous policies.

REVIEW

- What events led to the Emancipation Proclamation?

The Front and the Home Front

Few soldiers entered the conflict knowing what to expect. A young private wrote that his idea of combat had been that the soldiers "would all be in line, all standing in a nice level field fighting, a number of ladies taking care of the wounded, etc., etc., but it isn't so."

Improved weaponry turned battles into scenes of bloody carnage. The shift from smoothbore muskets to rifles, which had grooves that spun the bullet, made weapons far more effective at longer distances. The use of Minié balls—small bullets with a deep cavity that expanded upon firing—increased fatalities as well. By 1863, Union army sharpshooters acquired new repeating rifles with metal cartridges. With more accurate rifles and deadlier bullets, the rival armies increasingly relied on heavy fortifications, elaborate trenches, and distant mortar and artillery fire when they could. Still, casualties continued to rise, especially since the trenches served as breeding grounds for disease.

The hardships and discomforts of war extended beyond combat itself. As General Lee complained before Antietam, many soldiers fought in ragged uniforms and without shoes. Rations, too, ran short. Food was dispensed sporadically and was often spoiled. Many Union troops survived on an unleavened biscuit called hardtack as well as small amounts of meat and beans and enormous quantities of coffee. Their diet improved over the course of the war, however, as the Union supply system grew more efficient, while Confederate troops increasingly subsisted on cornmeal and fatty meat. As early as 1862, Confederate soldiers began gathering food from the haversacks of Union dead.

For every soldier who died as a result of combat, three died of disease. Measles, dysentery, typhoid, and malaria killed thousands who drank contaminated water, ate tainted food, and were exposed to the elements. And infected soldiers on both sides carried yellow fever and malaria into towns where they built fortifications. Prisoner-of-war camps, like Andersonville in Georgia, were especially deadly locales. In a camp near Danville, Virginia, debilitating fevers spread to the town, killing civilians as well as soldiers.

The sufferings of Black American troops were particularly severe. The death rate from disease for Black Union soldiers was nearly three times greater than that for white Union soldiers, reflecting their poorer health upon enlistment, the hard labor they performed, and the minimal medical care they received in the field. Southern Black men who began their army careers in contraband camps fared even worse. A camp near Nashville lost a quarter of its residents to death in just three months in 1864.

For all soldiers, medical assistance was primitive. Antibiotics did not exist, antiseptics were still unknown, and anesthetics were scarce. Union medical care improved with the U.S. Sanitary Commission, which was established by the federal government in June 1861 to promote and coordinate better medical treatment for soldiers. Nonetheless, a commentator accurately described most field hospitals as "dirty dens of butchery and horror," where amputations often occurred with whiskey as the only anesthetic.

AP® WORKING with EVIDENCE

Sources: Photographer unknown, Union soldiers gathered in camp, 1861–1865 (upper). Alexander Gardner, Bodies of Confederate artillerymen after Battle of Antietam, 1862 (lower).

About the sources: The development of battlefield photography in the 1860s offered civilians new perspectives on warfare. Popular photographers such as Mathew Brady were able to take and widely disseminate still photographs, though any movement resulted in a blurred image. Photographs were exhibited in photographers' studios and reproduced as engravings in newspapers across the country.

Library of Congress, LC-DIG-ppmsca-34191

Library of Congress, LC-DIG-ppmsca-32887

Questions for Analysis

1. Describe the details in each image that create a stark emotional difference between them.
2. Explain how limitations in photography at the time shaped the point of view expressed in each image.
3. Evaluate the extent to which images like these might affect attitudes toward the war in the North and South.

As the horrors of war sank in, large numbers of soldiers deserted or refused to reenlist. With volunteers declining and deserters increasing, both the Confederate and the Union governments were forced to institute laws to draft men into service. In 1863, the Union passed its first binding draft law.

In 1862, the Confederate Congress had passed the first mandatory draft law in American history. The three conscription acts enacted by the Confederacy between 1862 and 1864 required all white adult males (eventually from ages 17 to 50) to serve in the military, though some exceptions were made for certain occupations, and men could hire a substitute if they had enough money.

Most controversially, the acts exempted white males from military service who enslaved twenty or more people. Thus, large planters, many of whom served in the Confederate legislature, had effectively spared themselves from fighting.

As the war dragged on, the North's economic advantages became more apparent. At first, the effects of the war on northern industry had been disastrous. Raw cotton for textiles disappeared, southern planters stopped ordering shoes, and trade fell off precipitously. By 1863, however, the northern economy was in high gear and could provide more arms, food, shoes, and clothing to its troops as well as for those back home. As cotton production declined, woolen manufacturing doubled; and northern iron and coal production increased 25 to 30 percent during the war. Northern factories turned out weapons and ammunition, while shipyards built the fleets that blockaded southern ports.

These economic improvements were linked to a vast expansion in the federal government's activities. War Department orders fueled the industrial surge. It also created the U.S. Military Railroads unit to construct tracks in newly occupied southern territories and granted large contracts to northern railroads to carry troops and supplies. With southern Democrats out of federal office, Congress raised tariffs on imported goods to protect northern industries. In addition, the government hired thousands of "sewing women," who were contracted to make uniforms for Union soldiers. Other women joined the federal labor force as clerical workers to sustain the expanding bureaucracy and the enormous amounts of government-generated paperwork.

That paperwork multiplied exponentially when the federal government created a national currency and a national banking system. Before the Civil War, private banks (chartered by the states) issued their own banknotes, which were used in most economic transactions. During the war, Congress revolutionized this system, giving the federal government the power to create currency, issue federal charters to banks, and take on national debt. The government then flooded the nation with treasury bills, commonly called greenbacks. The federal budget ballooned as well—from $63 million in 1860 to nearly $1.3 billion in 1865. By the end of the war, the federal bureaucracy had become the nation's largest single employer.

Northern manufacturers faced a major problem: a shortage of labor. Over half a million workers left their jobs to serve in the Union army, and others were hired by the expanding federal bureaucracy. Manufacturers responded by mechanizing more tasks and by hiring more native-born and immigrant women and children. Combining the lower wages paid to these workers with production speedups, manufacturers improved their profits while advancing the Union war effort.

In the South, industry and cities grew as well. Although Southerners had gone to war to protect an essentially rural lifestyle, the war encouraged the growth of cities and industry. The creation of a large governmental and military bureaucracy brought thousands of Southerners to the Confederate capital of Richmond. As the war expanded, refugees also flooded into Atlanta, Savannah, Columbia, and Mobile.

Industrialization also contributed to urban growth. With the South unable to buy manufactured goods from the North and limited in its trade with Europe, military necessity spurred southern industry. Clothing and shoe factories had "sprung up almost like magic" in Natchez and Jackson, Mississippi. The Tredegar Iron Works in Richmond expanded significantly as well, employing more than 2,502 men, Black and white. More than 10,000 people labored in war industries in Selma, Alabama, where one factory produced cannons. With labor in short supply, widows and orphans, enslaved Black people, and white men too old or injured to fight were recruited for industrial work in many cities.

Women of all classes contributed to the war effort, North and South. Thousands filled jobs in agriculture, industry, and the government that were traditionally held by men, while others assisted the military effort more directly. Most Union and Confederate officials initially opposed women's direct engagement in the war. Yet it was women's voluntary organization of relief efforts that inspired the federal government to establish the U.S. Sanitary Commission.

By 1862, tens of thousands of women donated money and their time through hundreds of local groups across the North. They hosted fundraising fairs, coordinated sewing and knitting circles, rolled bandages, and sent supplies to the front lines. With critical shortages of medical staff, some female nurses and doctors eventually gained acceptance in northern hospitals and field camps. Led by such memorable figures as Clara Barton, who tended to thousands of injured soldiers and later founded the American Red Cross, northern women almost entirely replaced men as military nurses by the end of the war.

In the South, too, much of the medical care was performed by women. But without government support, nursing was never recognized as a legitimate profession for women, and most nurses worked out of their own homes. As a result, a Confederate soldier's chances of dying from wounds or disease were greater than those of his Union counterpart. Southern women also worked tirelessly to supply soldiers with clothes, blankets, munitions, and food. But this work, too, was often performed locally and by individuals rather than as part of a coordinated Confederate effort.

Some Union and Confederate women played more unusual roles in the war. Some women gathered information for military and political leaders as spies. One of the most effective spies on the Union side was the formerly enslaved Underground Railroad conductor Harriet Tubman, who gathered intelligence in South Carolina, including from many enslaved people, between 1862 and 1864. Even more women served as couriers, carrying messages across battle lines to alert officers of critical changes in military orders or in the opponent's position. In addition, at least four hundred women, from the North and South, disguised themselves as men and fought as soldiers.

Union women also sought to influence wartime policies. Following the Emancipation Proclamation, Elizabeth Cady Stanton, Susan B. Anthony, and Lucy Stone founded the **Women's National Loyal League** and launched a large petition drive to broaden Lincoln's policy. Collecting 260,000 signatures, two-thirds of them from women, the League demanded a congressional act "emancipating all persons of African descent" everywhere in the nation.

For soldiers and civilians seeking to survive the upheaval of war, political pronouncements seldom lessened the dangers they faced. The war's extraordinary death tolls shocked Americans on both sides. On the home front, the prolonged conflict created labor shortages and severe inflation in both North and South. The war initially disrupted industrial and agricultural production as men were called to service, but the North recovered quickly by building on its prewar industrial base and technological know-how.

In the South, manufacturing increased, with enslaved laborers pressed into service as industrial workers, but this created shortages on plantations. The changed circumstances of the war required women to take on new responsibilities as well. Yet these dramatic transformations also inspired dissent and protest as rising death tolls and rising prices made the costs of war ever clearer.

In 1863 and 1864, frustration spread across the North and the South generally with increasing casualties, declining numbers of volunteers, and rising inflation. As the war dragged on, many white Northerners began to wonder whether defeating the Confederacy was worth the cost, and many white Southerners whether saving slavery was.

Dissent posed issues in some border states as well. From 1861 on, battles raged among residents in the border state of Missouri, with Confederate sympathizers refusing to accept living in a Union state. Pro-southern residents formed militias and staged guerrilla attacks on Union supporters. The militia attacks, supported by Confederate officials, claimed thousands of lives during the war and forced the Union army to station troops in the area.

By 1863, dissent broadened to include Northerners who had earlier embraced the Union cause. Some white Northerners had always opposed emancipation, based on racial prejudice or fear that a flood of newly freed Black migrants would increase competition for jobs. Then, just two months after the Emancipation Proclamation went into effect, a new law deepened concerns among many working-class Northerners. The **Enrollment Act**, passed by Congress in March 1863, established a draft system to ensure sufficient soldiers for the Union army. While draftees were to be selected by an impartial lottery, the law allowed a person with $300 to pay the government in place of serving or to hire another man as a substitute. Many workers deeply resented the draft's profound inequality.

Enrollment Act

A March 1863 Union draft law that provided for draftees to be selected by an impartial lottery. A loophole in the law allowing wealthy Americans to avoid military service by paying $300 or hiring a substitute created widespread resentment.

Dissent turned to violence in July 1863 when the new law went into effect. Riots broke out in cities across the North. In New York City, where inflation caused tremendous suffering and a large immigrant population solidly supported the Democratic Party, implementation of the draft triggered four days of the worst rioting Americans had ever seen. Women and men—including many Irish and German immigrants—attacked Republican draft officials, wealthy businessmen, and the free Black community. Between July 13 and 16, rioters lynched at least a dozen Black Americans and looted and burned the city's Colored Orphan Asylum. The violence ended only when Union troops put down the riots by force. By then, more than one hundred New Yorkers, most of them Black, lay dead.

By 1864, inflation also fueled protests in the North as rising prices reduced the purchasing power of rural and urban residents. Women, children, and old men took over much of the field labor in the Midwest, trying to feed their families and the army while struggling to pay their bills.

Factory workers, servants, and day laborers felt the pinch as well. With federal greenbacks flooding the market and military production a priority, the price of consumer goods climbed about 20 percent faster than wages. Although industrialists collected huge profits, workers suffered. A group of Cincinnati seamstresses complained to President Lincoln in 1864 about employers "who fatten on their contracts by grinding immense profits out of the labor of their operatives." At the same time, employers persuaded some state legislatures to prohibit strikes in wartime. The federal government, too, supported business over labor. When workers at the Parrott arms factory in Cold Spring, New York, struck for higher wages in 1864, the government declared **martial law** and arrested the strike leaders.

martial law

The temporary suspension of civil law in favor of military rule during a war, rebellion, or major emergency.

Sarin Images/Granger – Historical Picture Archive

New York City Draft Riots, July 1863 On July 13, the draft riots in New York City began with an attack on the Colored Orphan Asylum on Fifth Avenue. As the matron led 233 Black children to safety, mobs of white men and women looted the building and set it ablaze. This wood engraving appeared in illustrated weeklies from New York to London.

Why would an anti-draft riot target an orphanage for Black children?

Northern Democrats saw the widening unrest as a political opportunity. Although some Democratic leaders supported the war effort, many others—whom opponents called **Copperheads**, after the venomous snake—rallied behind Ohio politician Clement L. Vallandigham in opposing the war. Presenting themselves as the "peace party," these Democrats enjoyed considerable success in eastern cities where inflation was rampant and immigrant workers were caught between low wages and military service. The Copperheads were also strong in parts of the Midwest, like Missouri, where sympathy for the southern cause and antipathy to Black Americans ran deep.

Copperhead
A northern Democrat who did not support the Union war effort. Such Democrats enjoyed considerable support in eastern cities and parts of the Midwest, especially across the Ohio River valley. Originally a pejorative term, the name was later embraced by antiwar northern Democrats.

In the South, too, some whites expressed growing dissatisfaction with the war. Small farmers were hard hit by policies that allowed the Confederate army to take whatever supplies it needed. The army's forced acquisition of farm produce intensified food shortages that had been building since early in the war. Moreover, the lack of an extensive railroad or canal system in the South limited the distribution of what food was available.

Food shortages drove up prices on basic items like bread and corn, while the Union blockade and the focus on military needs dramatically increased prices on other consumer goods. As the Confederate government issued ever more treasury notes to finance the war, inflation soared 2,600 percent in less than three years. In spring 1863, food riots led by working-class women erupted in cities across the South, including the Confederate capital of Richmond.

Some state legislatures then tried to control food prices, but Richmond workers continued to voice their resentment. In fall 1863, a group proclaimed, "From the fact that he consumes all and produces nothing, we know that without [our] labor and production the man with money could not exist."

The devastation of the war added to all these grievances. Since most battles were fought in the Upper South or along the Confederacy's western frontier, small farmers in these regions saw their crops, animals, and fields devastated. A phrase that had seemed cynical in 1862—"A rich man's war and a poor man's fight"—became the rallying cry of the southern peace movement in 1864. Secret peace societies flourished mainly among small farmers and in regions, like the Appalachian Mountains, where plantation slavery did not develop. A secret organization centered in North Carolina provided Union forces with information on southern troop movements and encouraged desertion by Confederates. In mountainous areas, southern draft evaders and deserters formed guerrilla groups that attacked draft officials and actively impeded the war effort. Women joined these efforts, hiding deserters, raiding grain depots, and burning the property of Confederate officials.

When enslavers led the South out of the Union in 1861, they had assumed the loyalty of yeomen farmers, the deference of southern ladies, and the privileges of the southern way of life. Far from preserving social harmony and social order, however, the war undermined ties between elite and poor Southerners, between planters and small farmers, and between women and men. Although most white Southerners still supported the Confederacy in 1864 and internal dissent alone did not lead to defeat, it did weaken the ties that bound soldiers to their posts in the final two years of the war.

■ How did social divisions fuel dissent and protest in the North and the South during the Civil War?

AP® Skills Workshop: Writing Historically

Responding to a Long-Essay Question

In the opening Focus section, you were asked to keep in mind some of the similarities and differences between the North and South as you read this module. In this exercise, you will have the opportunity to apply the historical thinking and writing skills we have been practicing to your understanding of this time period as you respond to a Long-Essay Question.

Recall that on the AP® Exam, you will encounter three different writing assessments: Short-Answer Questions (SAQs), a Document-Based Essay (DBQ), and Long-Essay Questions (LEQs). Unlike two of the three SAQs and the DBQ, an LEQ is a question without a stimulus or documents. On the exam, you will be able

(continued)

to choose which one of the three LEQ prompts to answer, and it will be worth 15 percent of the total score. It is suggested that for the 100-minute free-response section of the exam, students allocate 60 minutes to the DBQ and 40 minutes to the LEQ.

As you plan and write your LEQ, keep in mind that it will be scored based on the following criteria:

- Thesis (making a historically defensible claim with a line of reasoning)
- Contextualization (connecting to a relevant and broader historical context)
- Evidence (supporting an argument by using multiple pieces of relevant information)
- Historical Reasoning (using causation, comparison, or continuity and change over time to frame an argument)
- Complexity (demonstrating a sophisticated historical understanding of the topic—this category will be examined in AP® Skills Workshops in Period 6)

Consider the following Long-Essay Question that asks to reflect on what you have learned in this module:

> Evaluate the extent of difference between the Union and the Confederacy at the outset of the Civil War.

Step 1 ▶ Break down the prompt

When reading an essay question, you have to identify the topic, time period, and historical reasoning process you want to address in your essay. On the surface, this essay is a straightforward comparison of the differences and, possibly, similarities between the Union and the Confederacy at the beginning of the Civil War. However, with any essay in this course, you should consider whether any of the other reasoning processes (causation or continuity and change over time) could also be incorporated in your response. For this topic, analyzing *why* certain differences existed and *how* those differences impacted the conflict can provide additional depth to your response. Also, because the prompt asks you to "evaluate the *extent* of difference," don't forget to weigh the significance of the differences (and any similarities) in your essay.

Step 2 ▶ List and categorize your historical knowledge

The next step is to brainstorm and organize information you might include in your response. You can start your brainstorm *inductively* by jotting down specific information that comes to mind such as population or economic differences. Or you could approach the brainstorm *deductively* by first identifying relevant course themes such as social structures or American and national identity, or another set of broad categories, and then considering if relevant differences or similarities exist in those areas between North and South. (See the AP® Skills Workshop in Module 5.2 for a review of this approach.)

Here's one possible table you could use to organize your information. Feel free, however, to create whatever type of organizer works best for you. We've completed the first row for you as an example.

(continued)

Difference or Similarity	Description of the Main Point	Supporting Evidence	Cause or Effect
Military draft (mostly a similarity)	Believing the war would be short, both sides initially relied on volunteers but later instituted the first binding drafts in U.S. history.	- Southern draft acts starting in 1862. - Enrollment Act of 1863 (North). - Exemptions for $300 (both sides); owning twenty or more enslaved people (South).	- High casualties led to a draft (both sides). - South's smaller population led them to draft sooner. - Union draft led to New York City riots.

Remember, your list does not have to be exhaustive. You just need enough information to make and support a strong argument. Essays are never scored for what they don't include. Instead, they receive points for what they do include. If you develop a historically sound argument backed by relevant and specific evidence, and meet the criteria listed earlier, you will have written a successful essay.

Step 3 ▶ Set the context and write a thesis

Once you've completed your brainstorm and have organized the information, you are ready to craft your thesis statement. Be sure to include both a **claim** where you respond to the *extent* of difference and a **line of reasoning** that describes the specific sub-arguments that you will use to support your overall claim.

If you use the graphic organizer from above, you can borrow information from the second column for your line of reasoning. Don't include any specific supporting evidence in your thesis, because those items belong in the body paragraphs.

After you've written your thesis, it's time to develop a context. While you can choose a preceding context in the introduction, an immediate context in the body, and/or a concluding context in the conclusion, it's generally easier to set the stage for your thesis with a well-developed **preceding context** in the introduction. That context should make a relevant connection between a prior development and a part of your argument. The market revolution, transportation revolution, immigration, and urbanization are just a few examples of broader historical developments that you could develop into your context by using **Claim, Support, Explain (CSE).**

(continued)

Step 4 ▶ Write the full essay

Each body paragraph should be devoted to one of the main points in your essay that supports your thesis. The first sentence should fully state the **sub-argument** (topic sentence). The bulk of the paragraph should use **CSE** to provide and connect relevant outside information to your argument. And the final sentence should summarize your sub-argument.

As you write your paragraphs, keep the targeted **historical reasoning process** (comparison, causation, and/or continuity and change over time) in mind. Frame your argument to the reasoning process by explaining *how* or *why* your evidence your evidence proves the difference, effect, and so on, that you are examining.

ACTIVITY

Following the steps provided, write a complete essay consisting of five to six fully developed paragraphs in response to the prompt. You may use the following outline to guide your response.

I. Introductory Paragraph (approximately five or six sentences)
   (A) Preceding Contextualization Using CSE
   (B) Thesis Claim and Line of Reasoning
II. Body Paragraphs (approximately seven to nine sentences each)
   (A) Sub-Argument
   (B) Claim, Support, Explain
   (C) Claim, Support, Explain
   (D) Summary of Sub-Argument
III. Conclusion (approximately five sentences)
   (A) Restatement of Thesis Claim and Line of Reasoning
   (B) Forward Contextualization Using CSE

MODULE

5.9 Government Policies during the Civil War

FOCUS

When examining a period of rapid transformation like the Civil War, historians often characterize change (or lack of change) by comparing one era to another. In this module, which discusses Lincoln's actions and the war's end, you will examine the extent of change in the conflict, both at home and on the battlefield, during this period.

As you read this module, note in what ways and how much the conflict changed in the last years of the Civil War, both at home and on the battlefield. Be sure to consider how the earliest tactics by both the North and South evolved in the last two years of the war.

In spring 1863, amid turmoil on the home front, General Robert E. Lee's army defeated a Union force twice its size at Chancellorsville, Virginia. The victory set the stage for a Confederate thrust into Pennsylvania, but Lee's decision to go on the offensive proved the Confederacy's undoing.

In July 1863, the Union won two decisive military victories: at Gettysburg, Pennsylvania, and Vicksburg, Mississippi. At the same time, the flood of Black Americans, including former enslaved people, into the Union army transformed the very meaning of the war. By 1864, with the momentum favoring the Union, General Ulysses S. Grant implemented a strategy that forced the Confederacy to surrender a year later.

Key Victories for the Union

In mid-1863, Confederate commanders believed the tide was turning in their favor. Following major victories in Virginia at Fredericksburg and Chancellorsville, General Lee launched an invasion of northern territory at the end of June. The demoralized Union army had maneuvered to protect Washington, D.C., and its new commander, General George A. Meade, was untested. He immediately faced a momentous engagement at the Battle of Gettysburg in Pennsylvania. If Confederates won a victory there, European countries might finally recognize the southern nation and provide the assistance necessary to help the Confederacy win its independence.

Neither Lee nor Meade set out to launch the **Battle of Gettysburg** in this small Pennsylvania town. But Lee was afraid of outrunning his supply lines, and Meade wanted to keep Confederates from gaining control of the roads that crossed at Gettysburg. Between July 1 and July 3, 1863, the opposing armies fought a desperate battle, with Union troops occupying the high ground and Confederate forces launching fierce assaults from below. Gettysburg proved a disaster for the South: More than 4,700 Confederates were killed, including a large number of officers; another 18,000 were wounded, captured, or missing. Although the Union suffered similar casualties, it had more men to lose, and it could claim victory.

Battle of Gettysburg
A three-day battle in July 1863, the deadliest of the entire war, that halted the invasion of Pennsylvania by Lee's forces. The Confederate defeat, combined with the near-simultaneous Union victory at Vicksburg, turned the tide of the war and ended the threat of European intervention.

As Lee retreated to Virginia, the South suffered another devastating defeat. Troops under General Grant had been pounding Vicksburg, Mississippi, since May 1863.

The **Siege of Vicksburg** ended with the surrender of Confederate forces on July 4. This victory was even more important strategically than Gettysburg. Combined with a victory five days later at Port Hudson, Louisiana, the Union army now controlled the entire Mississippi valley, the richest plantation region in the South. This series of victories also effectively cut Louisiana, Arkansas, and Texas off from the rest of the Confederacy, ensuring Union control of the West.

In November 1863, Grant's troops achieved another major victory at Chattanooga, opening up much of the South's remaining territory to invasion. Thousands of enslaved people deserted their plantations, and many joined the Union war effort.

That same month, November 1863, President Lincoln spoke at the official dedication ceremony for the National Cemetery at Gettysburg, Pennsylvania. In his **Gettysburg Address**, Lincoln tied the war against slavery to the fulfillment of the nation's founding ideal, "that all men are created equal." He insisted that the United States "shall have a new birth of freedom—and that government of the people, by the people, and for the people, shall not perish from the earth." Only in this way, he declared, could Americans ensure that the "honored dead" had not "died in vain."

Siege of Vicksburg
After a prolonged siege, Union troops forced Confederate forces to surrender at Vicksburg, Mississippi, leading to Union control of the Mississippi River valley and cutting off Louisiana, Arkansas, and Texas from the rest of the Confederacy.

Gettysburg Address
A speech given by President Lincoln to inaugurate the federal cemetery at Gettysburg, Pennsylvania, in November 1863. In this speech, Lincoln expressed his belief that the war was a struggle for a "new birth of freedom" and likened the Union efforts in the Civil War to the principles of the American Revolution.

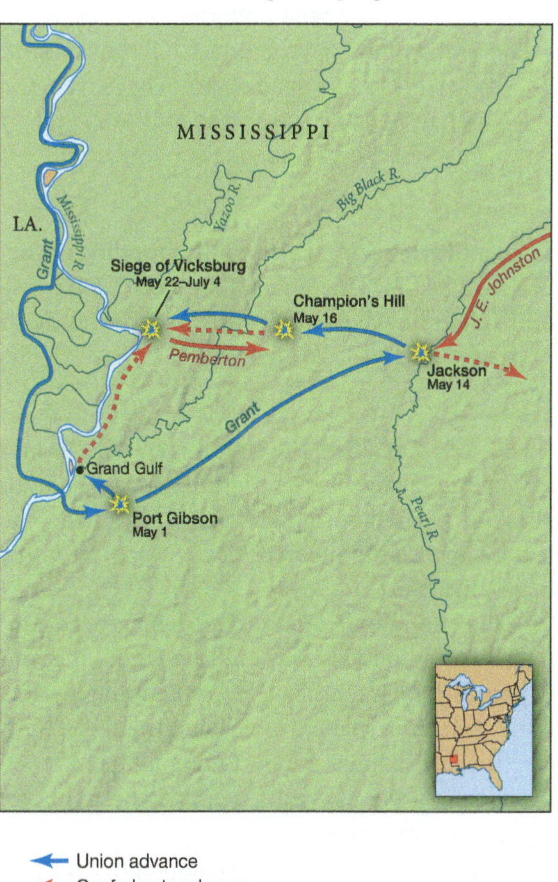

MAP 5.7 Battles of Gettysburg and Vicksburg, 1863 The three-day Battle of Gettysburg and the six-week siege of Vicksburg led to critical victories for the Union. Together, these victories forced General Lee's troops back into Confederate territory and gave the Union control of the Mississippi River. Still, the war was far from over. Confederate troops controlled the southern heartland, and Northerners wearied of the ever-increasing casualties.

What was the military and political significance of northern victory in these two locations?

AP® EXAM TIP

The Gettysburg Address is a specific piece of historical information you need to know for the AP® Exam. Think about connecting language from the speech such as "dedicated to the great task remaining before us," "increased devotion," and "we here highly resolve" to explain how Lincoln tried to define the "new birth of freedom" of democratic ideals.

WORKING with EVIDENCE

Source: Abraham Lincoln, Gettysburg Address, November 19, 1863

> "Four score and seven years ago our fathers brought forth on this continent a new nation, conceived in Liberty, and dedicated to the proposition that all men are created equal.
>
> Now we are engaged in a great civil war, testing whether that nation, or any nation so conceived and so dedicated, can long endure. We are met on a great battle-field of that war. We have come to dedicate a portion of that field, as a final resting-place for those who here gave their lives that that nation might live. It is altogether fitting and proper that we should do this.
>
> But, in a larger sense, we cannot dedicate—we cannot consecrate—we cannot hallow—this ground. The brave men, living and dead, who struggled here, have consecrated it, far above our poor power to add or detract. The world will little note, nor long remember what we say here, but it can never forget what they did here. It is for us the living, rather, to be dedicated here to the unfinished work which they who fought here have thus far so nobly advanced. It is rather for us to be here dedicated to the great task remaining before us—that from these honored dead we take increased devotion to that cause for which they gave the last full measure of devotion—that we here highly resolve that these dead shall not have died in vain—that this nation, under God, shall have a new birth of freedom—and that government of the people, by the people, for the people, shall not perish from the earth."

Questions for Analysis

1. Identify three references to the founding of the United States in this document.
2. Describe how Lincoln uses the word "dedicated" differently throughout his speech.
3. Explain how both the context surrounding the speech and Lincoln's words in the speech changed the Civil War.

As 1864 dawned, the Union had twice as many forces in the field as the Confederacy, whose soldiers were suffering from low morale, high mortality, and dwindling supplies. Although more difficult battles lay ahead, the war of attrition (in which the larger, better-supplied Union forces slowly wore down their Confederate opponents) had begun to pay dividends.

The changing Union fortunes increased support for Lincoln and his congressional allies. Union victories and the Emancipation Proclamation also convinced Great Britain not to recognize the Confederacy as an independent nation. The heroics of Black American soldiers, who engaged in direct and often brutal combat against southern troops, expanded support for emancipation. Republicans, who now fully embraced abolition as a war aim, were nearly assured the presidency and a congressional majority in the 1864 elections.

Northern Democrats still campaigned for peace and the readmission of Confederate states with slavery intact. They nominated George B. McClellan, the onetime Union commander, for president. McClellan attracted working-class and immigrant voters who traditionally supported the Democrats and bore the heaviest burdens of the war. But Democratic hopes for victory in November were crushed when Union general William Tecumseh Sherman captured Atlanta, Georgia, just two months before the election. Lincoln and the Republicans won the election easily, giving the party a clear mandate to continue the war to its conclusion.

REVIEW

▪ What factors contributed to northern victories after 1863?

Black Americans Contribute to Victory

Lincoln's election secured the eventual downfall of slavery. Yet the president and Congress did not eradicate human bondage on their own. From the fall of 1862 on, Black Americans enlisted in the Union army and helped ensure that nothing short of universal emancipation would be the outcome of the war. As Private Thomas Long, a former enslaved male serving with the First South Carolina Volunteers, explained: "If we hadn't become sojers, all might have gone back as it was before. . . . But now tings can neber go back, because we have showed our energy and our courage and our naturally manhood."

In the border states, which were exempt from the Emancipation Proclamation, enslaved men were adamant about enlisting because those who served in the Union army were granted their freedom. Because of this provision, enslavers in these states did everything in their power to prevent enslaved people from joining the army. Despite these efforts, military-age enslaved men in the four border states escaped and joined the Union army. By the end of the war, nearly 200,000 Black men had served officially in the army and navy, and some 37,000 Black men had given their lives for the Union.

Yet despite their courage and commitment, Black soldiers felt the sting of racism. They were segregated in camps, given the most menial jobs, and often treated as inferiors by white soldiers and officers. Particularly galling was the Union policy of paying Black soldiers less than whites. Black soldiers openly protested this discrimination even after a Black sergeant who voiced his views was charged with mutiny and executed by firing squad in February 1864. The War Department finally equalized wages four months later.

AP® EXAM TIP

Know how to explain the role of Black Americans in U.S. military efforts during the Civil War. This can be explained through immediate connections to military victories or the effects of enslaved Black Americans escaping enslavers and moving to Union states.

Library of Congress, LC-DIG-ppmsca-36454

Portrait of a Black Union Soldier and Family, c. 1863–1865 Taken after Black Americans were allowed to join the Union army, this daguerreotype captures a Union soldier with his wife and two daughters. He was likely a member of one of the seven Union regiments raised in Maryland, where the picture was discovered. The dresses and hats worn by the wife and daughters suggest the family was free.

How could this image elicit sympathy for equal rights for Black Americans among white Northerners?

A main concern of Black soldiers was to liberate enslaved people as Union armies moved deeper into the South. At the same time, thousands of southern enslaved people headed for Union lines. Even those forced to remain on plantations learned when Union troops were nearby and talked openly of emancipation. "Now they gradually threw off the mask," a freedperson remembered, "and were not afraid to let it be known that the 'freedom' in their songs meant freedom of the body in this world."

REVIEW

- What practical and idealistic reasons led Black Americans to volunteer to fight for the Union?

The Final Battles of a Hard War

hard war
The strategy promoted by General Ulysses S. Grant in which Union forces destroyed civilian crops, livestock, fields, property, and infrastructure to undermine Confederate morale and supply chains.

In the spring of 1864, the war in the East entered its final stage. That March, Lincoln placed General Grant in charge of all Union forces. Grant embarked on a strategy of **hard war**, in which soldiers not only attacked military targets but also destroyed civilian crops, livestock, fields, and property to undermine morale and supply chains.

Grant was also willing to accept huge casualties to achieve victory. Over the next year, he led his troops overland through western Virginia in an effort to take Richmond. Meanwhile, General Philip Sheridan devastated the "Breadbasket of the Confederacy" in Virginia's Shenandoah Valley, and General Sherman laid waste to the remnants of the plantation system in Georgia and the Carolinas.

Grant's troops headed toward Richmond, where Lee's army controlled strong defensive positions. The Confederates narrowly won a series of bloody victories, but Grant continued to push forward. Although Lee lost fewer men, they were losses he could not afford, given the Confederacy's much smaller population. Because of high casualties and deserters, Lee's army was melting away with each engagement. Although soldiers and civilians—North and South—called Grant "the butcher" for his seeming lack of regard for human life, the Union general was undeterred.

In the fall of 1864, implementing tactics of hard war, Sheridan rendered the Shenandoah Valley in western Virginia a "barren waste." Called "the burning" by local residents, Sheridan's soldiers torched fields, barns, and homes and destroyed thousands of bushels of grain along with livestock, shops, and mills. His campaign demoralized civilians in the region and denied Confederate troops crucial supplies.

Sherman's March to the Sea
A Union military campaign lasting thirty-seven days led by General Sherman across Georgia from Atlanta on November 15, 1864, to Savannah. Employing hard-war tactics and abandoning their supply lines to speed up their progress, Union troops intentionally blazed a wide path of destruction as they tried to break the morale of Confederate troops.

In the preceding months, Sherman had laid siege to Atlanta, but on September 2, his forces swept around the city and destroyed the roads and rails that connected it to the rest of the Confederacy. When General John B. Hood and his Confederate troops abandoned the city for fear of being encircled, Sherman telegraphed Lincoln: "Atlanta is ours, and fairly won." That victory cut the eastern half of the Confederacy in two, but Sherman continued on after his troops burned over 40 percent of the city.

Sherman's March to the Sea introduced hard-war tactics to Southerners along the three-hundred-mile route from Atlanta to Savannah, on the Atlantic coast. His troops cut a path of destruction fifty to sixty miles wide. They confiscated or destroyed millions of pounds of cotton, corn, wheat, and other agricultural items and tore up thousands of miles of railroad tracks. After reaching the coast, Sherman turned north, marched his forces through the Carolinas, and burned Columbia, the South Carolina capital. As Eleanor Cohen Seixas, whose family had earlier fled to

Columbia for safety, recorded in her journal, "The fires raged fearfully all night" and the "vile Yankees took from us clothing, food, jewels, all our cows, horses, carriages, etc." Despite later claims that Sherman's men ravished white women, instances of such behavior were rare, although Union soldiers did ransack homes and confiscate food and clothing.

Enslaved Black people hoped that Sherman's arrival marked their emancipation. During his ferocious march, nearly 18,000 enslaved men, women, and children fled ruined plantations and sought to join the victorious troops. To their dismay, soldiers refused to take them along. Union soldiers realized that they could not care for this vast number of people and carry out their military operations. Some Union soldiers went further, abusing Black men, raping Black women, or stealing their few possessions. Angry Confederates captured many Black people who were turned away, killing some and returning others to slavery.

These actions caused a scandal in Washington. In January 1865, Lincoln dispatched Secretary of War Edwin Stanton to Georgia to investigate the charges. At an extraordinary meeting in Savannah, Stanton and Sherman met with Black ministers to hear their complaints and hopes. The ministers spoke movingly of the war lifting "the yoke of bondage." Freedpeople, they argued, "could reap the fruit of their own labor" and, if given land, "take care of ourselves, and assist the Government in maintaining our freedom."

In response, Sherman issued **Field Order Number 15**, setting aside more than 402,000 acres of captured Confederate land to be divided into small plots for former enslaved people. The order proved highly controversial, but it offered Black people some hope of significant change. However, in the fall of 1865, a few months after the war ended, the order was rescinded by President Johnson and the land returned to former Confederates.

If many Black Americans were disappointed by the actions of Union soldiers in the East, American Indians were even more devastated by developments in the West. Despite American Indian nations' substantial aid to Union armies, any hope of being rewarded for their efforts vanished by 1864. Tens of thousands of whites migrated west of the Mississippi during the Civil War, and congressional passage of an 1864 act providing free 160-acre homesteads increased the numbers. At the same time, the U.S. army grew exponentially during the war, using its increased power to assault western American Indian nations even as the fighting during the Civil War raged on.

Attacks on American Indians were not an extension of hard-war policies, but rather a government-sanctioned effort to conquer and subdue native communities. Beginning in 1862, Dakota Sioux went to war with the United States over broken treaties. After being defeated, four hundred warriors were arrested by military officials, and just over three hundred were sentenced to death by a military commission. After personally reviewing all of the capital cases, President Lincoln approved the hanging of thirty-eight Sioux men, the largest mass execution in U.S. history.

In 1863, California Volunteers slaughtered more than two hundred men, women, and children in a Shoshone-Bannock village in Idaho. Meanwhile, thousands of white settlers had been flooding into Colorado after gold was discovered in 1858, forcing Cheyenne and Arapaho Indians off their land. In 1864, they were promised refuge at Sand Creek by officers at nearby Fort Lyon. Despite flying a white flag of truce, Colonel John M. Chivington led his Third Colorado Cavalry in a rampage that slaughtered at least 150 American Indians, mostly women and children. The **Sand Creek Massacre** united Plains Indians in the belief that U.S. government promises were worthless and peace with whites was not possible, thus ensuring

Sand Creek Massacre
A massacre and mutilation of more than 150 Cheyenne and Arapaho Indians, mostly women and children, by U.S. soldiers in southeastern Colorado Territory in November 1864. The atrocity led to decades of continued warfare on the Great Plains.

AP® EXAM TIP

While the Civil War drew to a close in 1865, wars against American Indians in the West persisted. Explaining how one war ended while another began and what the historical implications were can advance a more complex understanding of the Civil War.

Thirteenth Amendment

Amendment to the Constitution abolishing slavery except as a form of criminal punishment. The first of three Reconstruction-era amendments, it was passed in January 1865.

decades of continued conflict in the region. At the same time, in the Southwest, the Navajo were defeated by U.S. troops and their Ute allies and forced into a four-hundred-mile trek to a reservation in New Mexico.

U.S. army officers considered "winning the West" one way to restore national unity once the Civil War ended. For American Indian nations, the increased migration, expanded military presence, and sheer brutality they experienced in 1863 and 1864 boded ill for their future, whichever side won the Civil War.

As the defeat of the Confederacy loomed, the U.S. Congress finally considered abolishing slavery throughout the nation. With intense pressure by abolitionists, petitioning by the Women's National Loyal League, and President Lincoln's lobbying of wavering senators, Congress passed the **Thirteenth Amendment** to the U.S. Constitution on January 31, 1865. The amendment prohibited slavery and involuntary servitude anywhere in the United States, except as a form of punishment for convicted criminals.

Some northern and western states had already enacted laws to ease racial inequities. Ohio, California, and Illinois repealed statutes barring Black Americans from testifying in court and serving on juries. Then, in May 1865, Massachusetts passed the first comprehensive public-accommodations law in U.S. history, ensuring equal treatment in stores, schools, theaters, and other social spaces. Cities from San Francisco to Cincinnati and New York also desegregated their streetcars.

Still hoping to stave off defeat, southern leaders also began rethinking their racial policies. The Confederate House passed a law to recruit enslaved men into the army in February 1865, but the Senate defeated the measure. It was too late to make a difference anyway.

Richmond in Ruins, April 1865 This photograph shows the Richmond and Petersburg Railroad Depot following the capture of the Confederate capital by General Grant and his troops in April 1865. The Black man sitting amid the devastation no doubt realized that Richmond's fall marked the defeat of the South.

How does this image reflect the ways that Union war tactics changed during the second half of the Civil War?

Library of Congress, LC-DIG-cwpb-02709

AP® WORKING with EVIDENCE

Source: Abraham Lincoln, Second Inaugural Address, March 4, 1865

"*FELLOW-COUNTRYMEN . . .*

On the occasion corresponding to this, four years ago, all thoughts were anxiously directed to an impending civil war. All dreaded it; all sought to avert it. While the inaugural address was being delivered from this place, devoted altogether to *saving* the Union without war, insurgent agents were in the city seeking to *destroy* it without war—seeking to dissolve the Union and divide effects by negotiation. Both parties deprecated war; but one of them would *make* war rather than let the nation survive, and the other would *accept* war rather than let it perish. And the war came.

One-eighth of the whole population were colored slaves, not distributed generally over the Union, but localized in the southern part of it. These slaves constituted a peculiar and powerful interest. All knew that this interest was somehow the cause of the war. To strengthen, perpetuate, and extend this interest was the object for which the insurgents would rend the Union even by war, while the Government claimed no right to do more than to restrict the territorial enlargement of it. Neither party expected for the war the magnitude or the duration which it has already attained. Neither anticipated that the *cause* of the conflict might cease with or even before the conflict itself should cease. Each looked for an easier triumph, and a result less fundamental and astounding. Both read the same Bible and pray to the same God, and each invokes His aid against the other. It may seem strange that any men should dare to ask a just God's assistance in wringing their bread from the sweat of other men's faces, but let us judge not, that we be not judged. The prayers of both could not be answered. That of neither has been answered fully. The Almighty has His own purposes. 'Woe unto the world because of offenses; for it must needs be that offenses come, but woe to that man by whom the offense cometh.' If we shall suppose that American slavery is one of those offenses which, in the providence of God, must needs come, but which, having continued through His appointed time, He now wills to remove, and that He gives to both North and South this terrible war as the woe due to those by whom the offense came, shall we discern therein any departure from those divine attributes which the believers in a living God always ascribe to Him? Fondly do we hope, fervently do we pray, that this mighty scourge of war may speedily pass away. Yet, if God wills that it continue until all the wealth piled by the bondsman's two hundred and fifty years of unrequited toil shall be sunk, and until every drop of blood drawn with the lash shall be paid by another drawn with the sword, as was said three thousand years ago, so still it must be said 'the judgments of the Lord are true and righteous altogether.'

With malice toward none, with charity for all, with firmness in the right as God gives us to see the right, let us strive on to finish the work we are in, to bind up the nation's wounds, to care for him who shall have borne the battle and for his widow and his orphan, to do all which may achieve and cherish a just and lasting peace among ourselves and with all nations."

Questions for Analysis

1. Identify the points of contrast and similarity Lincoln draws between the North and South at the outset of the war.
2. Explain how Lincoln quotes the Bible and refers to God to support his point of view.
3. Evaluate the extent to which Northerners and Southerners would have been receptive to Lincoln's pleas in the last paragraph at the time of his speech.

In early April 1865, with Sherman heading toward Raleigh, North Carolina, Grant captured Petersburg, Virginia, and then drove Lee and his forces out of Richmond. Seasoned Black American troops led the final assault on the city and were among the first Union soldiers to enter the Confederate capital.

On April 9, after a brief engagement at Appomattox Court House, Virginia, Lee surrendered his worn-out army to Grant. Within hours, Lee's troops began heading home. While sporadic fighting continued — Cherokee Stand Watie was the last Confederate general to surrender in June 1865 — the back of the Confederate army had been broken, and the Civil War was effectively over.

With Lee's surrender, many Northerners hoped that the reunited nation would be stronger and more just. Jubilation in the North was short-lived, however. On April 14, Abraham Lincoln was shot at Ford's Theatre by a Confederate fanatic named John Wilkes Booth. The president died the next day, leading to great uncertainty about how peace and national unity would be achieved.

- What role did Black Americans play in the defeat of the Confederacy?
- How did the Union win the war against the Confederacy while also conquering American Indians in the West?

AP® Skills Workshop: Thinking Historically

Sourcing Document-Based Questions Using the *Claim, Support, Explain* Approach

In this exercise, we are going to learn how to "source" a document and then look at how to integrate sourcing into our existing CSE for a complete document analysis on a Document-Based Question (DBQ). Recall that "sourcing" means approaching a primary source critically, as a historian would. You have been introduced to this skill and had the opportunity to practice it in the AP® Skills Workshops in Modules 4.3, 4.9, and 5.5. Now it's time to review the different ways to source a document when responding to a DBQ.

Always "source" a document by examining the source information provided, which usually states the author, title, and year of the document. Consider what you already know about those items. Even if you are unfamiliar with an author or the work, you likely know something about the era. Once you've activated your prior knowledge, closely read the document. Compare what you read to what you expected based on your background knowledge and what you gathered from the source line.

There are four categories of analysis that we have used with primary source documents: Historical Situation, Intended Audience, Purpose, and Point of View (POV). Let's briefly review each one.

- **Historical Situation:** This is the immediate context surrounding the document. Ask yourself what led to, explains, or resulted from the document. Try to connect the document to a specific piece of relevant, outside information.
- **Intended Audience:** The audience is the group the document was originally meant for. Sometimes there is both an immediate and a larger, secondary audience. Either way, know that identifying an audience isn't enough. You have to explain

(continued)

why the audience matters. Ask yourself how the document is tailored to a specific audience and how the author is trying to influence that audience.

- **Purpose:** This is the goal or action the document seeks to achieve. It is not a summary of the contents of the document. If you have trouble distinguishing between a summary and the purpose, remember that a summary is the "what" of a document and the purpose is the "action" that should be taken. Ask yourself what the author wants to happen or what "verb" describes what the author is trying to accomplish.
- **Point of View:** POV is the perspective or bias of the author reflected in the document. When considering point of view, think about such factors as the author's background, life experience, gender, age, region, education level, religion, political affiliation, and race. Ask yourself how the life experience or the group represented by the author is reflected in the content of the document.

Reread Lincoln's Gettysburg Address from earlier in the module and the completed sourcing chart below it. Note that the first row in the graphic organizer asks for a brief summary of the document. While we've previously established that summarizing is not sourcing, it's still a related and essential task. In a DBQ, you are expected to demonstrate an understanding of the contents of a document and how it connects to your argument, as well as being able to source it.

Source: Abraham Lincoln, Gettysburg Address, November 19, 1863

> "Four score and seven years ago our fathers brought forth on this continent a new nation, conceived in Liberty, and dedicated to the proposition that all men are created equal.
>
> Now we are engaged in a great civil war, testing whether that nation, or any nation so conceived and so dedicated, can long endure. We are met on a great battle-field of that war. We have come to dedicate a portion of that field, as a final resting-place for those who here gave their lives that that nation might live. It is altogether fitting and proper that we should do this.
>
> But, in a larger sense, we cannot dedicate—we cannot consecrate—we cannot hallow—this ground. The brave men, living and dead, who struggled here, have consecrated it, far above our poor power to add or detract. The world will little note, nor long remember what we say here, but it can never forget what they did here. It is for us the living, rather, to be dedicated here to the unfinished work which they who fought here have thus far so nobly advanced. It is rather for us to be here dedicated to the great task remaining before us—that from these honored dead we take increased devotion to that cause for which they gave the last full measure of devotion—that we here highly resolve that these dead shall not have died in vain—that this nation, under God, shall have a new birth of freedom—and that government of the people, by the people, for the people, shall not perish from the earth."

Sourcing Category and Question	Sample Response
Document Summary: What information is provided in the document?	The Gettysburg Address was a speech given by President Lincoln in November 1863 commemorating the deaths of Union soldiers in the bloodiest battle of the Civil War. The speech also defines the war as for a "new birth of freedom" to fulfill the ideals of the Declaration of Independence ("Four score and seven years ago . . .").

(continued)

Sourcing Category and Question	Sample Response
Historical Situation: What event or development led to, is related to, or resulted from the Gettysburg Address?	The victories at Gettysburg and Vicksburg in July 1863 ended southern incursions into the North and cut the Confederacy in half at the Mississippi River. These battles took place six months after Lincoln's Emancipation Proclamation took effect, which changed the nature of the war from simply preserving the Union to abolishing slavery, too.
Intended Audience: Who was Lincoln speaking to, and how was he trying to influence them?	Lincoln's speech was intended not just for those present but also the larger public, especially those whose support for the war had wavered during 1862–1863.
Purpose: What does Lincoln want to accomplish with his speech?	In addition to honoring the sacrifice of those who died, Lincoln is trying to rally public opinion as he urges people to continue supporting the Union cause. He is also mindful of the presidential election one year in the future and hopes to maintain support for his reelection.
Point of View: How does Lincoln's background and perspective influence his address?	Lincoln was a Republican who believed slavery was immoral and as president believed the South did not have the right to secede. As such, he defends the war and links the sacrifice of lives to a higher purpose. In effect, Lincoln links the Civil War to the larger cause of freedom, arguing that democracy itself is at stake.

Now that we have sourced the document, it's time to practice how to incorporate sourcing into an essay response. To accomplish this, we are going to use a modified version of **Claim, Support, Explain** to accomplish the three main document tasks in a DBQ: **summarizing** the document, **connecting** the document to our argument (the underlined sub-argument of the thesis), and **sourcing** the document.

For DBQ essays, think of the **Claim** sentence as a statement of what the document is saying—in other words, a short summation of the document that shows you understand the document and lays the groundwork for your document analysis. The **Support** sentence is where you use the document to propel your argument forward by showing how it proves the point you are making. Finally, the **Explain** sentence is where you "source" the document by explaining how or why its **historical situation**, **intended audience**, **purpose**, or **point of view** is connected to your argument.

Prompt: Evaluate the extent to which the actions of President Lincoln impacted American ideals during the Civil War.

Thesis: As president and commander in chief during the Civil War, Lincoln had a significant impact on American ideals of freedom and democratic rule. **[claim]** <u>Lincoln's rhetoric broadened the meaning of freedom to include formerly enslaved people</u>, while his Emancipation Proclamation and the expansion of federal power extended civil rights and changed the relationship between the U.S. government and its citizens. **[line of reasoning]**

Document Sourcing Statement: In his Gettysburg Address, Lincoln honored the Union soldiers who died on the bloodiest battlefield of the Civil War. **[Claim: document summary]** In the speech, Lincoln reminds the audience that the nation was founded on the principle that "all men are created equal" and then argues that the Civil War is a test of that principle. Since the war is now being fought to

(continued)

end slavery, Lincoln is clearly expanding the meaning the freedom beyond how the founders had envisioned it. **[Support: connection to the argument]** Lincoln's perspective as a Republican who believes slavery is immoral and as his actions as president to preserve the Union, are evident as he links the war to preserving a government of, by, and for the people. **[Explain: point of view]**

ACTIVITY

Now it's your turn to practice with a different document you encountered earlier in the module. Reread Lincoln's Second Inaugural Address, complete the sourcing chart, and then use **CSE** to write a complete document sourcing statement by explaining the content, how it advances your argument, and the significance of its historical situation, intended audience, purpose, or point of view. Remember, when sourcing a document, you need to explain *how* or *why* one of the sourcing categories relates to your argument. Don't simply identify or summarize when sourcing.

Source: Abraham Lincoln, Second Inaugural Address, March 4, 1865

"*FELLOW-COUNTRYMEN . . .*

On the occasion corresponding to this four years ago all thoughts were anxiously directed to an impending civil war. All dreaded it, all sought to avert it. While the inaugural address was being delivered from this place, devoted altogether to *saving* the Union without war, insurgent agents were in the city seeking to *destroy* it without war—seeking to dissolve the Union and divide effects by negotiation. Both parties deprecated war, but one of them would *make* war rather than let the nation survive, and the other would *accept* war rather than let it perish, and the war came.

One-eighth of the whole population were colored slaves, not distributed generally over the Union, but localized in the southern part of it. These slaves constituted a peculiar and powerful interest. All knew that this interest was somehow the cause of the war. To strengthen, perpetuate, and extend this interest was the object for which the insurgents would rend the Union even by war, while the Government claimed no right to do more than to restrict the territorial enlargement of it. Neither party expected for the war the magnitude or the duration which it has already attained. Neither anticipated that the *cause* of the conflict might cease with or even before the conflict itself should cease. Each looked for an easier triumph, and a result less fundamental and astounding. Both read the same Bible and pray to the same God, and each invokes His aid against the other. It may seem strange that any men should dare to ask a just God's assistance in wringing their bread from the sweat of other men's faces, but let us judge not, that we be not judged. The prayers of both could not be answered. That of neither has been answered fully. The Almighty has His own purposes. 'Woe unto the world because of offenses; for it must needs be that offenses come, but woe to that man by whom the offense cometh.' If we shall suppose that American slavery is one of those offenses which, in the providence of God, must needs come, but which, having continued through His appointed time, He now wills to remove, and that He gives to both North and South this terrible war as the woe due to those by whom the offense came, shall we discern therein any departure from those divine attributes which the believers in a

(continued)

living God always ascribe to Him? Fondly do we hope, fervently do we pray, that this mighty scourge of war may speedily pass away. Yet, if God wills that it continue until all the wealth piled by the bondsman's two hundred and fifty years of unrequited toil shall be sunk, and until every drop of blood drawn with the lash shall be paid by another drawn with the sword, as was said three thousand years ago, so still it must be said 'the judgments of the Lord are true and righteous altogether.'

With malice toward none, with charity for all, with firmness in the right as God gives us to see the right, let us strive on to finish the work we are in, to bind up the nation's wounds, to care for him who shall have borne the battle and for his widow and his orphan, to do all which may achieve and cherish a just and lasting peace among ourselves and with all nations."

Sourcing Category and Question	Sample Response
Document Summary: What information is provided in the document?	
Historical Situation: What event or development led to, is related to, or resulted from Lincoln's Second Inaugural Address?	
Intended Audience: Who was Lincoln speaking to, and how is he trying to influence them?	
Purpose: What does Lincoln want to accomplish or happen as a result of his speech?	
Point of View: How do Lincoln's background and perspective influence his address?	

Reconstruction

FOCUS

Reconstruction was the culmination of a long process of emancipation of Black Americans, but American politicians could not agree on how to approach rebuilding the nation in the aftermath of the Civil War. While leaders in Washington, D.C., debated various models of reconstruction, the expansion of suffrage to Black Americans opened new debates about the rights of women and divided activists who sought justice for all Americans.

As you read this module, consider the ways in which the many social changes in the immediate aftermath of the war were a product of multiple causes with roots in developments that began in the years before the war, as well as during the war itself. Be sure to also consider the causes and effects of various approaches to Reconstruction and the ways in which expanding the rights of Black Americans led to further conflict about civil rights for other groups.

Even before the war came to a close, **Reconstruction** had begun on a small scale. During the Civil War, Black Americans remaining in Union-occupied areas, such as the South Carolina Sea Islands, gained some experience with freedom. When Union troops arrived, most southern whites fled, but enslaved workers chose to stay on the land. Some farmed for themselves, but most worked for northern whites who moved south to demonstrate the profitability of free Black labor. After the war, however, former plantation owners returned. Rather than work for these whites, freedpeople preferred to establish their own farms. If forced to hire themselves out, they insisted on negotiating the terms of their employment. Wives and mothers often refused to labor for whites at all in favor of caring for their own families.

Reconstruction
The period from 1865 to 1877, during which the eleven ex-Confederate states were subject to federal legislative and constitutional efforts to remake their societies as they were readmitted to the Union.

These conflicts reflected the priorities that would shape the actions of freedpeople across the South in the immediate aftermath of the war. For freedom to be meaningful, it had to include economic independence, the power to make family decisions, and the right to control some community decisions.

On a national level, Presidents Abraham Lincoln and Andrew Johnson viewed Reconstruction as a process of national reconciliation. They sketched out terms by which the former Confederate states could reclaim their political representation in Congress without serious penalties.

Congressional Republicans, however, had a more thoroughgoing reconstruction in mind. Like many Black Americans, Republican congressional leaders expected the South to extend constitutional rights to the freedmen and to provide them with the political and economic resources to sustain their freedom. Over the next decade, these competing visions of Reconstruction played out in a tumultuous battle over the meaning of the South's defeat and the emancipation of Black people.

AP® EXAM TIP

One of the keys to success when studying Reconstruction is to consider it as a historical process with multiple perspectives. The perspectives of Blacks as many moved from slavery to freedom are particularly important. Be able to explain how debates over citizenship—as it relates to Black Americans—became a crucial part of Reconstruction.

Black Americans Embrace Freedom

When U.S. troops arrived in Richmond, Virginia in April 1865, the city's enslaved population knew that freedom was, finally, theirs. Four days after Union troops arrived, 1,502 Black Americans, including a large number of soldiers, packed First African Baptist, the largest of the city's Black churches. During the singing of the hymn "Jesus My All to Heaven Is Gone," they raised their voices at the line "This is the way I long have sought." As news of the Confederacy's defeat spread, newly freed Black Americans across the South experienced similar emotions. Many years later, Houston H. Holloway, a freedman from Georgia who had been sold three times before he was twenty years old, recalled the day of emancipation: "I felt like a bird out a cage. Amen. Amen, Amen. I could hardly ask to feel any better than I did that day."

For southern whites, however, the end of the war brought fear, humiliation, and uncertainty. From their perspective, the jubilation of former enslaved people poured salt in their wounds. In many areas, Black Americans celebrated their freedom under the protection of Union soldiers. When the army moved out, freedpeople suffered deeply for their enthusiasm. White people beat, whipped, raped, and shot Black people who they felt had been too joyous in their celebration or too helpful to the Yankee invaders. As one North Carolina freedman testified, the Yankees "tol' us we were free," but once the army left, the planters "would get cruel to the slaves if they acted like they were free."

Newly freed persons also faced less visible dangers. During the 1860s, disease swept through the South and through the contraband camps that housed many freedpeople. Widespread malnutrition and poor housing heightened the problem. A smallpox epidemic that spread south from Washington, D.C., killed more than sixty thousand freedpeople.

Despite the dangers, southern Black Americans eagerly embraced emancipation. They moved; they married; they attended school; they demanded wages; they refused to work for whites; they gathered together their families; they created Black churches and civic associations; they held political meetings. Sometimes, Black women and men acted on their own, pooling their resources to advance their freedom. At other times, they received help from private organizations—particularly northern missionary and educational associations—staffed mostly by former abolitionists, free Black people, and evangelical Christians.

Freedpeople also called on federal agencies for assistance and support. The most important of these agencies was the newly formed Bureau of Refugees, Freedmen, and Abandoned Lands, popularly known as the **Freedmen's Bureau**. Created by Congress in 1865 and signed into law by President Lincoln, the bureau provided formerly enslaved people with economic and legal resources. The Freedmen's Bureau also aided many in achieving one of their primary goals: obtaining land.

Freedmen's Bureau
Federal agency created in 1865 to provide freedpeople with economic, educational, and legal resources. The Freedmen's Bureau played an active role in shaping Black life in the postwar South through the 1870s.

A South Carolina freedman summed up the feeling of the newly emancipated. "Give us our own land and we take care of ourselves," he remarked. "But without land, the old masters can hire or starve us, as they please." During the last years of the war, the federal government had distributed to the freedpeople around 402,000 acres of abandoned land from the South Carolina Sea Islands to Florida. Immediately after hostilities ceased, the Freedmen's Bureau made available hundreds of thousands of additional acres to the men and women who had been recently emancipated.

The first priority for many newly freed persons was to reunite families torn apart by slavery. Men and women traveled across the South to find family members. Well into the 1870s and 1880s, parents ran advertisements in newly established Black newspapers, providing what information they knew about their children's whereabouts and asking for assistance in finding them. Milly Johnson wrote to the Freedmen's Bureau in March 1867, after failing to locate the five children she had lost under slavery. She finally

The Freedmen's Bureau In this image from the prominent northern magazine *Harper's Weekly*, a Union soldier, representing the Freedman's Bureau, holds back an angry southern mob from attacking an equally outraged mob of freed Black Americans.

In what ways do the hand gestures of the Union soldier represent the attitude of northern readers toward both former rebels and freedpeople?

Library of Congress, LC-USZ62-105555

located three of them, but any chance of discovering the whereabouts of the other two disappeared because the records of the slave trader who purchased them burned during the war. Despite such obstacles, thousands of formerly enslaved children were reunited with their parents in the 1870s.

Husbands and wives, or those who considered themselves as such despite the absence of legal marriage under slavery, also searched for each other. Those who lived on nearby plantations could now live together for the first time. Those whose spouse had been sold to distant plantations had a more difficult time. They wrote (or had letters written on their behalf) to relatives and friends who had been sold with their mate; sought assistance from government officials, churches, and even their former enslavers; and traveled to areas where they thought their spouse might reside.

These searches were complicated by long years of separation and the lack of any legal standing for marriages of enslaved people. In 1866, Philip Grey, a Virginia freedman, located his wife, Willie Ann, and their daughter Maria, who had been sold away to Kentucky years before. Willie Ann was eager to reunite with her husband, but in the years since being sold, she had remarried and had three children. Her second husband had joined the Union army and was killed in battle. When Willie Ann wrote to Philip in April 1866, she explained her new circumstances, concluding: "If you love me you will love my children and you will have to promise me that you will provide for them all as well as if they were your own. . . . I know that I have lived with you and loved you then and love you still."

Most black spouses who found each other sought to legalize their relationship. A superintendent for marriages for the Freedmen's Bureau in northern Virginia reported that he gave out seventy-nine marriage certificates on a single day in May 1866. In another case, four couples went right from the fields to a local schoolhouse, still dressed in their work clothes, where the parson married them.

Of course, some freedpeople hoped that freedom would allow them to leave unhappy relationships. Having never been married under the law, those couples could simply separate and move on. Complications arose, however, if they had children. In Lake City, Florida, in 1866, a Freedmen's Bureau agent asked his superiors for advice

Gift of William T. Evans/Smithsonian American Art Museum

Winslow Homer, A Visit from the Old Mistress, 1876 Civil War correspondent and artist Winslow Homer visited Virginia in the mid-1870s and visually captured the tensions existing between freedpeople and former enslavers. Here, a former mistress visits the home of three black women. Although the house is humble, one woman refuses to stand for the "old mistress" and the other two, one holding a free-born child, eye her warily.

To what extent does this painting portray a change from pre–Civil War society in the South?

on how to deal with Madison Day and Maria Richards. They refused to legalize the relationship forced on them under slavery, but both sought custody of their three children. As with white couples in the mid-nineteenth century, the father was granted custody on the assumption that he had the best chance of providing for the children financially.

Seeking land and reuniting families were only two of the many ways that southern Black people proclaimed their freedom. Learning to read and write was another. The desire to learn was all but universal. Enslaved people had been forbidden to read and write, and with emancipation they pursued what had been denied them. A newly liberated father in Mississippi proclaimed, "If I nebber does nothing more while I live, I shall give my children a chance to go to school, for I considers education [the] next best ting to liberty."

A variety of organizations opened schools for freedpeople during the 1860s and 1870s. By 1870, nearly a quarter million Black Americans were attending one of the 4,300 schools established by the Freedmen's Bureau. Black and white churches and missionary societies sent hundreds of teachers, Black and white, into the South to establish schools in former plantation areas. Their attitudes were often paternalistic and the schools were segregated, but the institutions they founded offered important educational resources for Black Americans.

AP® WORKING with EVIDENCE

Source: Colonel Eliphalet Whittlesey, *Report on the Freedmen's Bureau*, 1865

> "All officers of the bureau are instructed—
>
> To aid the destitute, yet in such a way as not to encourage dependence.
> To protect freedmen from injustice.
> To assist freedmen in obtaining employment and fair wages for their labor.
> To encourage education, intellectual and moral. . . .

[W]e have in our camps at Roanoke Island and Newbern, many women and children, families of soldiers who have died in the service, and refugees from the interior during the war, for whom permanent provision must be made. . . . The reports prepared by Surgeon Hogan will show the condition of freedmen hospitals. In the early part of the summer much suffering and mortality occurred for want of medical attendance and supplies. This evil is now being remedied by the employment of surgeons by contract. . . .

Contrary to the fears and predictions of many, the great mass of colored people have remained quietly at work upon the plantations of their former masters during the entire summer. The crowds seen about the towns in the early part of the season had followed in the wake of the Union army, to escape from slavery. After hostilities ceased these refugees returned to their homes, so that but few vagrants can now be found. In truth, a much larger amount of vagrancy exists among the whites than among the blacks. It is the almost uniform report of officers of the bureau that freedmen are industrious.

The report is confirmed by the fact that out of a colored population of nearly 350,000 in the State, only about 5,000 are now receiving support from the government. Probably some others are receiving aid from kind-hearted men who have enjoyed the benefit of their services from childhood. To the general quiet and industry of this people there can be no doubt that the efforts of the bureau have contributed greatly."

Questions for Analysis

1. Identify the likely audience for Whittlesey's report.
2. Describe Whittlesey's perspective on both freedpeople and white Southerners.
3. Explain how Whittlesey measures the success of the Freedmen's Bureau.

Freedmen's Bureau School, 1860s This photograph of a one-room Freedmen's Bureau school in North Carolina in the late 1860s shows the large number and diverse ages of students who sought to obtain an education following emancipation. The teachers included white and Black northern women sent by missionary and reform organizations as well as southern Black women who had already received some education.

Why was education an important step toward ensuring rights for freedpeople?

Parents worked hard to keep their children in school during the day. As children gained the basics of an education, they passed on their knowledge to parents and older siblings whose jobs prevented them from attending school. In addition, many adult freedpeople also sought an education for themselves. In New Bern, North Carolina, where many Black people labored until eight o'clock at night, a teacher reported that they then spent at least an hour "in earnest application to study."

Freedmen and freedwomen sought education for a variety of reasons. Some viewed it as a sign of liberation. Others knew that they must be able to read the labor contracts they signed if they were ever to challenge exploitation by whites. Some freedpeople were eager to correspond with relatives, others to read the Bible. Growing numbers hoped to participate in politics, particularly the public meetings organized by Black people in cities across the South. When such gatherings set priorities for the future, the establishment of public schools was high on the list.

Despite the enthusiasm of Black Americans and the efforts of the federal government and private agencies, schooling remained severely limited throughout the South. A shortage of teachers and funds kept enrollments low among Black and white people alike. The isolation of Black farm families and the difficulties in eking out a living limited the resources available for education. By 1880, only about a quarter of Black Americans were literate.

One of the constant concerns freedpeople expressed was the desire to read the Bible and interpret it for themselves. A few Black congregations had existed under slavery, but most enslaved people had been forced to listen to white preachers who claimed that God created slavery.

From the moment of emancipation, freedpeople gathered at churches to celebrate community events. Black Methodist and Baptist congregations spread rapidly across the South following the Civil War. In these churches, Black Americans were no longer forced to sit in the back benches or punished for moral infractions defined by white enslavers. Now Black people invested community resources in their own religious institutions where they filled the pews, hired the preachers, and selected boards of deacons and elders.

Churches were the largest structures available to freedpeople in many communities and thus were used by a variety of community organizations. They often served as schools and hosted picnics, dances, weddings, funerals, festivals, and other events that brought Black people together. Church leaders also often served as arbiters of community standards of morality.

In the early years of emancipation, Black churches also served as important sites for political organizing. Some Black ministers worried that political concerns would overwhelm spiritual devotions. Others agreed with the Reverend Charles H. Pearce of Florida, who declared, "A man in this State cannot do his whole duty as a minister except he looks out for the political interests of his people." Whatever the views of ministers, Black churches were among the few places where Black Americans could express their political views free from white interference.

- How did freedpeople define freedom?
- What steps did freedpeople take to make freedom real for themselves and their children?

Lincoln and Johnson's Reconstruction Plans

In December 1863, President Lincoln issued the **Proclamation of Amnesty and Reconstruction**, which offered relatively generous terms to seceded states if they rejoined the Union in an effort to shorten the war. Lincoln declared that defeated states would have to accept the abolition of slavery, but then new governments could be formed when 10 percent of those eligible to vote in 1860 (which in practice meant white, but not Black, southern men) swore an oath of allegiance to the United States. Lincoln's plan granted amnesty to all but the highest-ranking Confederate officials. The restored voters in each state would elect members to a constitutional convention and representatives to take their seats in Congress. In the next year and a half, Arkansas, Louisiana, and Tennessee reestablished their governments under Lincoln's "Ten Percent Plan."

Republicans in Congress had other ideas. **Radical Republicans** argued that the Confederate states should be treated as "conquered provinces" subject to congressional supervision. In 1864, Congress passed the **Wade-Davis bill**, which established much higher barriers for readmission to the Union than did Lincoln's plan. For instance, the Wade-Davis bill substituted 50 percent of voters for the president's 10 percent requirement. Lincoln put a stop to this harsher proposal by using a pocket veto—refusing to sign it within ten days of Congress's adjournment.

Although Lincoln and congressional Republicans disagreed about many aspects of postwar policy, Lincoln was flexible, and his actions mirrored his desire both to heal the Union and to help southern Black people. For example, the president supported the Thirteenth Amendment, abolishing slavery, which passed Congress in January 1865 and was sent to the states for ratification. In March 1865, Lincoln signed the law to create the Freedmen's Bureau. That same month, the president expressed his sincere wish for reconciliation between the North and the South. "With malice toward none, with charity for all," Lincoln declared in his second inaugural address, "let us strive on to finish the work . . . to bind up the nation's wounds."

Lincoln would not, however, have the opportunity to implement his approach to Reconstruction. When he was assassinated in April 1865, it fell to Vice President Andrew Johnson, a very different sort of politician, to lead the country through the process of reintegration.

The nation needed a president who could transmit northern desires to the South with clarity and conviction and ensure that they were carried out. Instead, the nation got a president who substituted his own aims for those of the North, refused to engage in meaningful compromise, and misled the South into believing that he could achieve restoration quickly. In the 1864 election, Lincoln chose Johnson, a pro-Union southern Democrat, as his running mate in an effort to attract border-state voters. The vice presidency was normally an inconsequential role, so it mattered little to Lincoln that Johnson was out of step with many Republican Party positions.

As president, however, Johnson's views took on profound importance. Born into rural poverty, Johnson had no sympathy for the southern aristocracy. Yet he had been an enslaver, so his political opposition to slavery was not rooted in moral convictions. Instead, it sprang from the belief that slavery gave plantation owners inordinate power and wealth, which came at the expense of the majority of white Southerners, who were not enslavers. Johnson saw emancipation as a means to "break down an odious and dangerous [planter] aristocracy," not to empower Black people. Consequently, he was unconcerned with the fate of Black Americans in the postwar South.

AP® EXAM TIP

In addition to understanding the perspectives of Blacks during Reconstruction, the AP® Exam expects you to explain how Radical Republicans, Southern Democrats, the Supreme Court, and the executive branch affected policy decisions. Think about creating a chart to keep track of each perspective.

Radical Republican

A Republican politician who actively supported abolition before the Civil War and sought tighter controls over the South in the aftermath of the war. Radical Republicans repeatedly clashed with President Johnson over Reconstruction policy.

Six months after taking office, President Johnson rescinded the wartime order to distribute confiscated land to freedpeople in the Sea Islands. He saw no reason to punish the Confederacy's leaders, because he believed that the end of slavery would doom the southern aristocracy. He hoped to bring the South back into the Union as quickly as possible and then let Southerners take care of their own affairs.

Johnson's views, combined with a lack of political savvy and skill, ensured his inability to work constructively with congressional Republicans, even the moderates who constituted the majority. Moderate Republicans shared the prevalent belief of their time that Black people were inferior to white people, but they argued that the federal government needed to protect newly emancipated people. Senator Lyman Trumbull of Illinois, for example, warned that without national legislation, freedpeople would "be tyrannized over, abused, and virtually reenslaved." The moderates expected southern states, where 90 percent of Black Americans lived, to extend basic civil rights to the freedpeople, including equal protection, due process of law, and the right to work and hold property.

Nearly all Republicans shared these positions, but the Radical wing of the party wanted to go further. Led by Senator Charles Sumner of Massachusetts and Congressman Thaddeus Stevens of Pennsylvania, this small but influential group advocated suffrage, or voting rights, for Black American men as well as the redistribution of southern plantation lands to freedpeople. Stevens called on the federal government to provide freedpeople "a homestead of forty acres of land," which would give them some measure of autonomy. These efforts failed, and the Republican Party proved unable to pass a comprehensive land distribution program that enabled freedpeople to gain economic independence.

Whatever the disagreements between Radicals and moderates, all Republicans believed that Congress should have a strong voice in determining the fate of the former Confederate states. From May to December 1865, with Congress out of session, they waited to see what Johnson's restoration plan would produce, ready to assert themselves if his policies deviated too much from their own.

At first, it seemed as if Johnson would proceed as they hoped. He appointed provisional governors to convene new state constitutional conventions and urged these

Virginia Military Institute Archives

Mourning at Stonewall Jackson's Gravesite, 1866 Many Northerners were concerned that the defeat of the Confederacy did not lessen white Southerners' devotion to the "Lost Cause" or the heroism of soldiers who fought to maintain a society based on the domination of Black Americans. Women, who led the efforts to memorialize Confederate soldiers, are shown at the gravesite of General Stonewall Jackson in Lexington, Virginia.

What details in this picture support Northerners' fear of Southerners' devotion to the "Lost Cause"?

conventions to ratify the Thirteenth Amendment, abolishing slavery, and revoke the states' ordinances of secession. He also allowed the majority of white Southerners to obtain amnesty and a pardon by swearing their loyalty to the U.S. Constitution, but he required those who had held more than $20,000 of taxable property—the members of the southern aristocracy—to personally petition him for a special pardon to restore their rights. Republicans expected him to be harsh in dealing with his former political foes. Instead, Johnson relished the reversal of roles that put members of the southern elite at his mercy. As the once-prominent petitioners paraded before him, the president granted almost all of their requests for pardons.

By the time Congress convened in December 1865, Johnson was satisfied that the southern states had fulfilled his requirements for restoration. Moderate and Radical Republicans disagreed, seeing few signs of change or even regret in the South. Mississippi, for example, rejected ratification of the Thirteenth Amendment. As a result of Johnson's liberal pardon policy, many former leaders of the Confederacy won election to state constitutional conventions and to Congress. Indeed, the Georgia legislature elected Confederate vice president Alexander H. Stephens to the U.S. Senate.

AP® EXAM TIP

On the AP® Exam, you should be able to describe southern resistance to Reconstruction. When you describe how southerners resisted Reconstruction, keep track of chronological reasoning so you are better able to show moments of historical inflection.

Far from providing freedpeople with basic civil rights, the southern states passed a variety of **Black codes** intended to reduce Black Americans to a condition as close to slavery as possible. Some laws prohibited Black people from bearing arms. Others outlawed intermarriage and excluded them from serving on juries. The codes also made it difficult for Black people to leave plantations unless they proved they could support themselves financially. Laws like this were designed to ensure that white landowners had a supply of cheap Black labor despite slavery's abolition.

Black codes
Racial laws passed by southern legislatures in the immediate aftermath of the Civil War that aimed to keep freedpeople in a condition as close to slavery as possible.

Northerners viewed this situation with alarm. In their eyes, the postwar South looked much like the Old South, with a few cosmetic adjustments. If the Black codes prevailed, one Republican proclaimed, "then I demand to know of what practical value is the amendment abolishing slavery." Others wondered what their wartime sacrifices meant if the South admitted no mistakes, was led by the same people, and continued to oppress its Black inhabitants.

REVIEW

- What historical developments best explain President Lincoln's plans for Reconstruction?
- What was President Johnson's plan for Reconstruction, and how did his views compare to those of most Republican politicians?

Congressional Reconstruction and Resistance

Faced with growing opposition in the North, Johnson stubbornly held his ground. He insisted that the southern states had followed his plan and were entitled to resume their representation in Congress. Republicans objected, and in December 1865, they barred the admission of southern lawmakers.

Johnson refused to compromise. In January 1866, the president rejected a bill passed by Congress to extend the life of the Freedmen's Bureau for two years. A few months later, he vetoed the Civil Rights Act, which Congress had passed to protect freedpeople from the restrictions placed on them by the Black codes. These bills represented a consensus among moderate and Radical Republicans on the federal government's responsibility toward formerly enslaved people.

AP® EXAM TIP

You have to know the Reconstruction Amendments and how states and the federal government interpreted these amendments over time. Keep track of how the three amendments led to significant changes and how those changes were challenged. You are trying to see the continuities and changes to the interpretations of the Reconstruction Amendments.

Johnson justified his vetoes on both constitutional and personal grounds. He and other Democrats contended that so long as Congress refused to admit southern representatives, it could not legally pass laws affecting the South. The president also condemned the Freedmen's Bureau bill because it infringed on the right of states to handle internal affairs such as education and economic policies. Johnson's vetoes exposed his racism and his lifelong belief that the evil of slavery lay in the harm it did to poor white people, not to enslaved Black people. Johnson argued that the bills he vetoed discriminated against whites, who would receive no benefits under them, and thus put whites at a disadvantage with Black people who received government assistance. Johnson's private secretary reported in his diary, "The president has at times exhibited a morbid distress and feeling against the Negroes."

Johnson's actions united moderates and Radicals against him. In April 1866, Congress repassed both the Freedmen's Bureau extension and Civil Rights Act over the president's vetoes. In June, lawmakers adopted the **Fourteenth Amendment**, which incorporated many of the provisions of the Civil Rights Act, and submitted it to the states for ratification. Reflecting its confrontational dealings with the president, Congress wanted to ensure more permanent protection for Black Americans than simple legislation could provide.

Fourteenth Amendment A constitutional amendment ratified in 1868 granting citizenship, due process, and equal protection under the law to all persons born in the United States. This amendment overturned the *Dred Scott* ruling and was aimed at protecting the rights of freedpeople.

Lawmakers also wanted to act quickly, as the situation in the South seemed to be deteriorating rapidly. In May 1866, a race riot had broken out in Memphis, Tennessee. For a day and a half, white mobs, encouraged by local police, went on a rampage, during which they terrorized Black people. Forty-six Black people were killed, many of them Union army veterans, and over one hundred Black homes, schools, and churches were burned.

The Fourteenth Amendment defined citizenship to include Black Americans, thereby nullifying the ruling in the *Dred Scott* case of 1857, which declared that Black people were not citizens. It extended equal protection and due process of law to all persons, not only citizens. The amendment repudiated Confederate debts, which some state governments had refused to do, and it barred Confederate officeholders from holding elective office unless Congress removed this provision by a two-thirds vote. Although

Memphis Race Riot A skirmish between white policemen and Black Union veterans on May 1, 1866, resulted in three days of rioting by white mobs that attacked the Black community of Memphis, Tennessee. Before federal troops restored peace, many women had been raped, and forty-six Blacks and two whites had been killed. This illustration from *Harper's Weekly* depicts the carnage.

What does this image reveal about the resistance to Reconstruction in the South?

Granger – Historical Picture Archive

most Republicans were upset with Johnson's behavior, at this point they were not willing to embrace the Radical Republican position entirely. Rather than granting the right to vote to black adult males, the Fourteenth Amendment gave the states the option of excluding Black people and accepting a reduction in congressional representation if they did so.

Johnson remained inflexible. Instead of counseling the southern states to accept the Fourteenth Amendment, which would have sped up their readmission to the Union, he encouraged them to reject it. In the fall of 1866, Johnson decided to take his case directly to northern voters before the midterm congressional elections. Campaigning for candidates who shared his views, he embarked on a swing through the Midwest. Out of touch with northern opinion, Johnson attacked Republican lawmakers and engaged in shouting matches with audiences. On election day, Republicans increased their majorities in Congress and now controlled two-thirds of the seats, providing them with greater power to override presidential vetoes.

When the Fortieth Congress convened in 1867, Republican lawmakers charted a new course for Reconstruction. With moderates and Radicals united against the president, Congress intended to force the former Confederate states to protect the basic civil rights of Black Americans as well as to grant them the vote. Moderates now agreed with Radicals that unless Black people had access to the ballot, they would not be able to sustain their freedom. Extending the suffrage to Black Americans also aided the fortunes of the Republican Party in the South by adding significant numbers of new voters.

By the end of March 1867, Congress enacted three **Military Reconstruction Acts**. Together they divided ten southern states into five military districts, each under the supervision of a Union general. The male voters of each state, regardless of race, were to elect delegates to a constitutional convention; only former Confederate officials were disfranchised. The conventions were required to draft constitutions that guaranteed Black suffrage and ratified the Fourteenth Amendment. Within a year, North Carolina, South Carolina, Florida, Alabama, Louisiana, and Arkansas had fulfilled these obligations and reentered the Union.

Military Reconstruction Acts
Three acts passed in 1867 dividing southern states into military districts and requiring those states to grant Black male suffrage and ratify the Fourteenth Amendment.

Having imposed their version of Reconstruction in the South, Republican lawmakers turned their attention to disciplining the president. Johnson continued to resist their policies and used his power as commander in chief to order generals in the military districts to soften the intent of congressional Reconstruction. In response, Congress passed the Command of the Army Act in 1867, which required the president to issue all orders to army commanders in the field through the General of the Army in Washington, D.C., Ulysses S. Grant. The Radicals knew they could count on Grant to carry out their policies.

Even more threatening to presidential power, Congress passed the **Tenure of Office Act**, which prevented Johnson from firing cabinet officers sympathetic to congressional Reconstruction. This measure barred the chief executive from removing from office any appointee that the Senate had ratified previously without returning to the Senate for approval.

Tenure of Office Act
A law passed by Congress in 1867 to prevent the president from firing appointed officials confirmed by the Senate without Senate approval. President Johnson was impeached, but not convicted, for violating the act.

Convinced that the new law was unconstitutional and outraged at the effort to limit his power, the quick-tempered Johnson chose to confront the Radical Republicans directly rather than seek a way around a congressional showdown. In February 1868, Johnson fired Secretary of War Edwin Stanton, a Lincoln appointee and a Radical Republican sympathizer, without Senate approval. In response, congressional Republicans prepared articles of impeachment.

In late February, the House voted 126 to 47 to impeach Johnson, the first president ever to be impeached, or charged with unlawful activity. The case then went to trial in the Senate, where the chief justice of the United States presided and a two-thirds

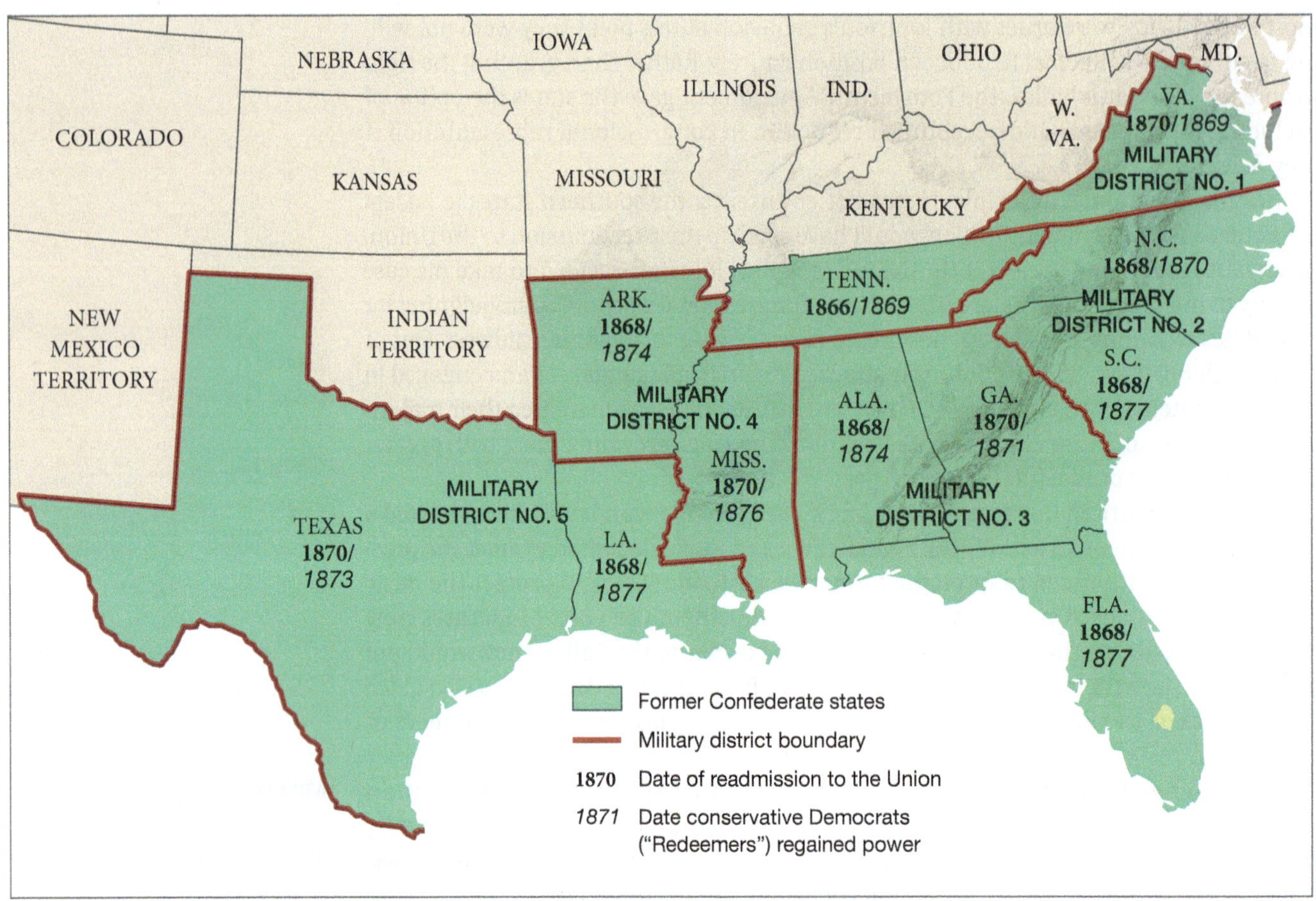

MAP 5.8 Reconstruction in the South In 1867, Congress enacted legislation dividing the former Confederate states into five military districts. All the states were readmitted to the Union by 1870, and white conservative Democrats (Redeemers) had replaced Republicans in most states by 1875. Only in Florida, Louisiana, and South Carolina did federal troops remain until 1877.

In what ways were these military districts a product of Radical Republican policy?

AP® EXAM TIP

You can frame your explanations about Reconstruction through the idea that a revolution in civil rights ended with a violent counterrevolution. Categorize at least two specific historical events or developments to frame your understanding of the revolution and counterrevolution during Reconstruction.

vote was necessary for conviction and removal from office. After a six-week hearing, the Senate fell one vote short of convicting Johnson. Most crucial for Johnson's fate were the votes of seven moderate Republicans who refused to find the president guilty of violating his oath to uphold the Constitution. They were convinced that Johnson's actions were insufficient to merit the enormous step of removing a president from office. Although Johnson remained in office, Congress effectively ended his power to shape Reconstruction policy.

The Republicans had restrained Johnson, and in 1868 they won back the presidency. Ulysses S. Grant, the popular Civil War general, ran against Horatio Seymour, the Democratic governor of New York. Although an ally of the Radical Republicans, Grant called for reconciliation with the South. He easily defeated Seymour, winning nearly 53 percent of the popular vote and 73 percent of the electoral vote.

REVIEW

- What caused congressional resistance to President Johnson's Reconstruction plan?
- What priorities were reflected in congressional Reconstruction legislation?

The Struggle for Universal Suffrage

In February 1869, Congress passed the **Fifteenth Amendment** to protect Black male suffrage, which had initially been guaranteed by the Military Reconstruction Acts. A compromise between moderate and Radical Republicans, the amendment prohibited voting discrimination based on race, but it did not deny states the power to impose qualifications based on literacy, payment of taxes, moral character, or any other standard that did not directly relate to race. Subsequently, the wording of the amendment provided loopholes for white leaders to disfranchise Black Americans. The amendment did, however, cover the entire nation, including the North, where states like Connecticut, Kansas, Michigan, New York, Ohio, and Wisconsin still excluded Black people from voting.

Fifteenth Amendment
An amendment to the Constitution ratified in 1870 that forbids state voting restrictions based on "race, color, or previous condition of servitude." After Reconstruction ended, southern states devised many tactics for disenfranchising Black voters.

The Fifteenth Amendment sparked serious conflicts not only within the South but also among old abolitionist allies. The American Anti-Slavery Society disbanded with emancipation, but many members believed that important work remained to be done to guarantee the rights of freedpeople. They formed the **American Equal Rights Association** immediately following the war, but members divided over the Fifteenth Amendment.

American Equal Rights Association
A group of Black and white women and men formed in 1866 to promote gender and racial equality. The organization split in 1869 over divided support for the Fifteenth Amendment. Prominent members included Frederick Douglass, Susan B. Anthony, and Elizabeth Cady Stanton.

Some women's rights advocates, including Elizabeth Cady Stanton and Susan B. Anthony, had earlier objected to the Fourteenth Amendment because it inserted the word *male* into the Constitution for the first time when describing citizens. Although they had supported abolition before the war, Stanton and Anthony worried that postwar policies intended to enhance the rights of southern Black men would further limit the rights of women. While most Black American activists embraced the Fifteenth Amendment, a few voiced concern. At a meeting of the American Equal Rights Association in 1867, Sojourner Truth noted, "There is quite a stir about colored men getting their rights, but not a word about colored women."

AP® EXAM TIP
Explaining concepts such as how Reconstruction led to significant constitutional changes for Black Americans even as women did not experience similar reform efforts can create more complex interpretations in essay questions. Narrow the focus to a concept such as suffrage to allow for a more thorough explanation.

At the 1869 meeting of the American Equal Rights Association, differences over the measure erupted into open conflict. Stanton and Anthony denounced suffrage for Black men only, and Stanton now supported her position on racial grounds. She claimed that the "dregs of China, Germany, England, Ireland, and Africa" were degrading the U.S. polity and argued that white, educated women should certainly have the same rights as immigrant and Black American men.

Black and white supporters of the Fifteenth Amendment, including Frances Ellen Watkins Harper, Wendell Phillips, Abby Kelley, and Frederick Douglass, denounced Stanton's bigotry. Believing that southern Black men urgently needed suffrage to protect their newly won freedom, they argued that ratification of the Fifteenth Amendment would speed progress toward the enfranchisement of women, Black and white.

This dispute led to the formation of competing organizations committed to women's suffrage. The **National Woman Suffrage Association**, established by Stanton and Anthony, allowed only women as members and opposed ratification of the Fifteenth Amendment. The American Woman Suffrage Association, which attracted the support of women and men, white and Black, supported ratification. Less than a year later, in the spring of 1870, the Fifteenth Amendment was ratified and went into effect.

Because the amendment did not grant the vote to either white or Black women, women suffragists attempted to use the Fourteenth Amendment to achieve their goal. In 1875, Virginia Minor, who had been denied the ballot in Missouri, argued that the right to vote was one of the "privileges and immunities" granted to all citizens under the Fourteenth Amendment. In *Minor v. Happersett*, the Supreme Court ruled against her, and most women continued to be denied national suffrage for decades thereafter.

AP® WORKING with EVIDENCE

Source: Elizabeth Cady Stanton, *Speech to the American Equal Rights Association*, 1869

> "If the civilization of the age calls for an extension of the suffrage, surely the government of the most virtuous, education men and women would better represent the whole, and protect the interests of all than could the representation of either sex alone. But government gains no new element of strength in admitting all men to the ballot-box, for we have too much of the man-power already. We see this in every department of legislation, and it is a common remark, that unless some new virtue is infused into our public life the nation is doomed to destruction. Will the foreign element, the dregs of China, Germany, England, Ireland, and Africa supply this needed force, or the nobler types of American womanhood who have taught our presidents, senators, and congressmen the rudiments of all they know?"

Questions for Analysis

1. Identify Stanton's main objective in this excerpt.
2. Explain how historical situation shaped Stanton's statement.
3. Explain the intended political effect of Stanton's statement.

REVIEW

- To what extent did Reconstruction change the lives of Black Americans in the South?

AP® Skills Workshop: Thinking Historically

Writing Body Paragraphs for Document-Based Questions

Throughout this course, you've practiced various elements of argumentation in previous AP® Skills Workshops. Now it's time to weave together those pieces to construct a fully developed DBQ body paragraph.

For this exercise, you have been provided completed graphic organizers and an annotated sample body paragraph that incorporates two primary sources from earlier in this module and an additional piece of outside information to support an argument. Read through the documents, charts, and sample body paragraph, and note how each item is integrated into a coherent response to the essay's prompt.

Source: Colonel Eliphalet Whittlesey, *Report on the Freedmen's Bureau*, 1865

> "All officers of the bureau are instructed—
> To aid the destitute, yet in such a way as not to encourage dependence.
> To protect freedmen from injustice.
> To assist freedmen in obtaining employment and fair wages for their labor.
> To encourage education, intellectual and moral. . . .

(continued)

[W]e have in our camps at Roanoke Island and Newbern, many women and children, families of soldiers who have died in the service, and refugees from the interior during the war, for whom permanent provision must be made. . . . The reports prepared by Surgeon Hogan will show the condition of freedmen hospitals. In the early part of the summer much suffering and mortality occurred for want of medical attendance and supplies. This evil is now being remedied by the employment of surgeons by contract. . . .

Contrary to the fears and predictions of many, the great mass of colored people have remained quietly at work upon the plantations of their former masters during the entire summer. The crowds seen about the towns in the early part of the season had followed in the wake of the Union army, to escape from slavery. After hostilities ceased these refugees returned to their homes, so that but few vagrants can now be found. In truth, a much larger amount of vagrancy exists among the Whites than among the blacks. It is the almost uniform report of officers of the bureau that freedmen are industrious.

The report is confirmed by the fact that out of a colored population of nearly 350,000 in the State, only about 5,000 are now receiving support from the government. Probably some others are receiving aid from kind-hearted men who have enjoyed the benefit of their services from childhood. To the general quiet and industry of this people there can be no doubt that the efforts of the bureau have contributed greatly."

Source: Photograph at the Site of Confederate General Stonewall Jackson's Grave, 1866

Virginia Military Institute Archives

Prompt: Evaluate the relative effects of federal Reconstruction policy during the period 1865 to 1877.

Sub-Argument: *Even as the federal government took unprecedented steps to begin the process of Reconstruction shortly after the Civil War ended, southern whites began to resist those efforts and started to mythologize the "Lost Cause" of the Confederacy.*

(continued)

Document Title	Summary of Document	Connection to Argument	Sourcing Category and Description
Report on the Freedman's Bureau by Colonel Whittlesey, 1865	Official report summarizing the role of the Freedmen's Bureau and assessing the situation of whites and freed Blacks in the reporting area.	Author claims Freedmen's Bureau is having great success in helping freed Blacks and notes higher vagrancy among whites.	Point of View: Author was a Union military soldier and associated with the Bureau, possibly influencing elements of his official report.
Photograph of mourning at Stonewall Jackson's gravesite, 1866	The picture depicts women mourners posing at Stonewall Jackson's gravesite in 1866.	Wreath and formal pose convey respect toward a celebrated Confederate war hero.	Purpose: Staged photograph is meant to generate feelings of pride and nostalgia to promote the idea of a "Lost Cause."

Outside Evidence	Claim	Support	Explanation
Fourteenth Amendment	Expansion of federal efforts to protect formerly enslaved peoples in the South.	Granted citizenship to all people born in the United States and equal protection under the law.	Made expansion of civil rights permanent and set stage for additional actions.

DBQ Body Paragraph: Even as the federal government took unprecedented steps to begin the process of Reconstruction shortly after the Civil War ended, southern whites began to resist those efforts and started to mythologize the "Lost Cause" of the Confederacy. **[sub-argument]** In 1865 Congress created the Freedmen's Bureau to assist freed Blacks in the South with economic and legal aid as Whittlesey stated in the opening of his *Report on the Freedmen's Bureau*. **[document 1 claim by summarizing]** In the report he claims that the Freedmen's Bureau had greatly aided freed Blacks, even noting that vagrancy was much more of a problem among whites. **[document 1 support by connection to argument]** From his perspective as a Union army colonel and presumably part of the Freedmen's Bureau, Whittlesey clearly supports Republican policies such as the work of the Freedmen's Bureau and wants it to continue. **[document 1 explanation by sourcing for point of view]** The following year, Congress expanded the federal commitment to reconstructing the South by adopting the Fourteenth Amendment. **[outside evidence claim]** The Fourteenth Amendment granted citizenship to all persons born in the United States and equal protection to all under the law. **[outside evidence support]** By amending the Constitution, Congress made these newly extended rights to freed Blacks permanent and set the stage for further federal actions. **[outside evidence explanation]** Yet, many southerners resisted Reconstruction efforts as seen by the photograph of a group of women at the gravesite of Stonewall Jackson in 1866.

(continued)

[document 2 claim by summarizing] In the image, the young women have laid a wreath at the tomb and are seen looking respectfully at the ground to honor a famous Confederate war general. **[document 2 support by connection to the argument]** The reverential and posed nature of the photograph is clearly meant to encourage feelings of pride in white Southerners and promote the ideology of the "Lost Cause." **[document 2 explanation by sourcing for purpose]** The battle over southern Reconstruction began soon after the war ended and only grew more heated as Reconstruction progressed. **[sub-argument restatement and transition]**

ACTIVITY

Now it's your turn. Reread the two documents below from earlier in the module, complete the sourcing and outside information charts, and then write a full body paragraph for the same DBQ prompt using both documents and the additional piece of outside information from your chart. Start and end your paragraph with your sub-argument. Use **CSE** for your outside evidence and for both documents. For each document, make a **Claim** by summarizing the content of the document, **Support** your argument with evidence by showing the connection between the document and your sub-argument, and **Explain** the sourcing by explaining how or why the historical situation, intended audience, purpose, or point of view are relevant to a part of your argument.

Source: Freedmen's Bureau School, North Carolina, late 1860s

Granger – Historical Picture Archive

(continued)

Source: Elizabeth Cady Stanton, *Speech to the American Equal Rights Association*, 1869

"If the civilization of the age calls for an extension of the suffrage, surely the government of the most virtuous, education men and women would better represent the whole, and protect the interests of all than could the representation of either sex alone. But government gains no new element of strength in admitting all men to the ballot-box, for we have too much of the man-power already. We see this in every department of legislation, and it is a common remark, that unless some new virtue is infused into our public life the nation is doomed to destruction. Will the foreign element, the dregs of China, Germany, England, Ireland, and Africa supply this needed force, or the nobler types of American womanhood who have taught our presidents, senators, and congressmen the rudiments of all they know?"

Document	Summary	Connection	Sourcing
Photograph of Freedmen's Bureau School, late 1860s			
Speech to the American Equal Rights Association by Elizabeth Cady Stanton, 1869			

Outside Evidence	Claim	Support	Explanation

The Failure of Reconstruction

MODULE

5.11

FOCUS

By 1877, the nation had undergone enormous social change. However, many questions from before the Civil War remained unanswered: How could the government ensure equal rights for all Americans? To what extent did economic inequality undermine political equality? What was the relationship of the federal government to the newly reconstructed states? How would national political parties respond to the recent sectional divisions?

As you read this module, consider the extent of change in the South during Reconstruction as well as what remained the same.

With President Johnson's power effectively curtailed, reconstruction of the South moved quickly. New state legislatures, ruled by a coalition of southern white and Black people as well as white northern migrants, enacted political, economic, and social reforms that improved the overall quality of life in the South. Despite these changes, many Black and white Southerners barely eked out a living under the planter-dominated sharecropping system. Moreover, the biracial Reconstruction governments lasted a relatively short time, as conservative whites used a variety of tactics, including terror and race baiting, to defeat their opponents at the polls.

While Reconstruction promised to remake the South into a more just society, white Southerners mounted an aggressive resistance to Reconstruction-era policies. As a result, many of the reforms enacted between 1863 and 1877 were gradually undone.

The continued resistance of southern whites does not, however, fully explain the unraveling of Reconstruction. By the early 1870s, most white Northerners had come to believe that they had done more than enough for Black Southerners, and it was time to focus on other issues. Growing economic problems intensified this feeling, as the Panic of 1873 devastated the nation's economy and led to calls to decrease government spending on Reconstruction. Allegations of widespread corruption in funds earmarked for Reconstruction and Supreme Court rulings limiting the exercise of federal power in the South further undermined public support for the effort to remake the South. By the end of the 1870s, most white Americans, in the North and South, shared the belief that it was time to move on, abandoning the issue of civil rights for Blacks in the South until the mid-twentieth century.

AP® EXAM TIP

Several factors contributed to the failure of Reconstruction, including violence, the Supreme Court, and the diminishing commitment of Northerners to the ideas of Radical Republicans. Be able to explain these concepts with specific references, many of which can be found in Modules 5.10 and 5.11.

Early Reconstruction in the South

During the first years of congressional Reconstruction, two groups of whites occupied the majority of elective offices in the South. A significant number of native-born Southerners joined Republicans in forging postwar constitutions and governments. Before the war, some had belonged to the Whig Party and opposed secession from the Union. Western sections of Alabama, Georgia, North Carolina, and Tennessee had demonstrated a fiercely independent strain, and many residents had remained loyal to the Union. Small merchants and farmers who detested large plantation owners also threw in their lot with the Republicans. Even a few ex-Confederates, such as General James A. Longstreet, decided that the South must change and allied with the Republicans. The majority of whites who continued to support the Democratic Party viewed these whites as traitors. They showed their distaste by calling them **scalawags**, an unflattering term meaning "scoundrels."

scalawag
A derogatory term in the South for white Southerners who supported Reconstruction.

At the same time, some Northerners came south to support Republican Reconstruction. They had varied reasons for making the journey, but most viewed Reconstruction as an opportunity to remake the South culturally, politically, and economically. Some—white and Black—had served in the Union army during the war, liked what they saw of the region, and decided to settle there. Some of both races came to provide education and assist freedpeople in adjusting to their new lives.

As a relatively underdeveloped area, the South also beckoned fortune seekers and adventurers who saw opportunities to get rich. Southern Democrats denounced northern migrants, particularly whites, as **carpetbaggers**, suggesting that they invaded the region with all their possessions in a bag, seeking to plunder it and then leave. While Northerners did seek economic opportunity, they were acting as Americans always had in settling new frontiers and pursuing dreams of success. In fact, much of the animosity directed toward them resulted less from their presence, but more from their efforts to ally with Black Americans in reshaping the South.

carpetbagger
A derogatory term in the South for white Northerners who moved to the South in the years following the Civil War. Many white Southerners believed such migrants were intent on exploiting their suffering.

Still, the main targets of southern white hostility were Black Americans who attempted to exercise their hard-won freedom. Black people constituted a majority of voters in five states—Alabama, Florida, South Carolina, Mississippi, and Louisiana. They did not use their ballots to impose Black rule on the South, as many white Southerners feared. Only in South Carolina did Black Americans control the state legislature, and in no state did they manage to elect a governor. Nevertheless, for the first time in American history, Black men won a wide variety of elected positions. Between 1865 and 1877, more than six hundred Black men served in state legislatures; another sixteen held seats in the U.S. House of Representatives; and two from Mississippi were chosen to serve in the U.S. Senate.

Freedpeople showed enthusiasm for politics in other ways, too. Black Americans considered politics a community responsibility, and in addition to casting ballots, they held rallies and mass meetings to discuss issues and choose candidates. Although they could not vote, women attended these gatherings and helped influence their outcome. Covering a Republican convention in Richmond in October 1867, held in the First African Baptist Church, the *New York Times* reported that "the entire colored population of Richmond" attended. In addition, freedpeople formed mutual-aid associations to promote education, economic advancement, and social welfare programs, all of which they saw as deeply intertwined with politics.

Southern Black people also bolstered their freedom by building alliances with sympathetic whites. These interracial political coalitions produced considerable reform in the South. They created the first public school systems; provided funds for social services, such as poor relief and state hospitals; upgraded prisons; and rebuilt the South's transportation system.

Moreover, the state constitutions that the Republicans wrote brought a greater measure of political democracy and equality to the South by extending suffrage to poor white men as well as Black men. Some states allowed married women greater control over their property and liberalized the criminal justice system. In effect, these Reconstruction governments brought the South into the nineteenth century.

Obtaining political representation was one way in which Black Americans defined freedom. Economic independence constituted a second. Without government-sponsored land redistribution, however, the options for Black Southerners remained limited. Lacking capital to purchase farms, most entered into various forms of tenant contracts with large landowners. **Sharecropping** proved the most common arrangement. Black and poor white people became sharecroppers for much the same reasons. They received tools and supplies from landowners and farmed their own plots of land on the plantation. In exchange, sharecroppers turned over a portion of their harvest to the owner and kept the rest for themselves.

Sharecropping proved less beneficial to Black farmers in practice than in theory. To tide themselves over during the growing season, sharecroppers had to purchase household provisions on credit from a local merchant, who was often also their landlord. At the mercy of store owners who kept the books and charged high interest rates, tenants usually found themselves in considerable debt at the end of the year. To satisfy the debt, merchants devised a crop-lien system in which tenants pledged a portion of their yearly crop to satisfy what they owed. Falling prices for agricultural crops in this period ensured that most indebted tenants did not receive sufficient return on their produce to get out of debt and thus remained bound to their landlords.

sharecropping

A widespread form of agricultural labor in the South after the Civil War in which sharecroppers, often poor Blacks and whites, rented tools and supplies from landowners in exchange for a share of the eventual harvest. Corrupt practices and laws allowing creditors to take part of the harvest for nonpayment often left sharecroppers in permanent debt and resulted in a system of forced labor.

AP® EXAM TIP

Sharecropping is a topic that necessitates a detailed explanation. When writing about something such as sharecropping in essay questions on the AP® Exam, take your time by defining the concept and connecting it to other historical issues. For example, after you define sharecropping, connect it to economic class structures after the Civil War.

AP® WORKING with EVIDENCE

Source: Sharecropping Agreement, 1870

> "Contract made the 3rd day of January in the year 1870 between us the free people who have signed this paper of one part, and our employer, Willis P. Bocock, of the other part. . . . We are to furnish the necessary labor . . . and are to have all proper work done, ditching, fencing, repairing, etc., as well as cultivating and saving the crops of all kinds, so as to put and keep the land we occupy and tend in good order for cropping, and to make a good crop ourselves; and to do our fair share of job work about the place. . . . We are to be responsible for the good conduct of ourselves, our hands, and families, and agree that all shall be respectful to employer, owners, and manager, honest, industrious, and careful about every thing . . . and then our employer agrees that he and his manager shall treat us kindly, and help us to study our interest and do our duty. If any hand or family proves to be of bad character, or dishonest, or lazy, or disobedient, or any way unsuitable our employer or manager has the right, and we have the right, to have such turned off. . . .
>
> For the labor and services of ourselves and hands rendered as above stated, we are to have one third part of all the crops, or their net-proceeds, made and secured, or prepared for market by our force. . . .
>
> We are to be furnished by our employer through his manager with provisions if we call for them . . . to be charged to us at fair market prices.
>
> And whatever may be due by us, or our hands to our employer for provisions or any thing else, during the year, is to be a lien on our share of the crops, and is to be retained by him out of the same before we receive our part."

Questions for Analysis

1. Identify five details of a sharecropper's job description in this contract.
2. Explain the relationship this contract creates between the sharecropper and the landowner.
3. Explain the economic effects of this contract on the Black Americans who signed it.

For many Black Americans, sharecropping turned into a form of virtual slavery. The picture for Black farmers was not all bleak, however. Through careful management and extremely hard work, Black families planted gardens for household consumption, raised chickens for eggs and meat, and raised pigs. Despite its pitfalls, sharecropping provided a limited measure of labor independence and allowed some Black people to accumulate small amounts of cash. About 20 percent of Black farmers managed to buy their own land, in spite of the grinding racism they faced.

Following the war's devastation, many of the South's white small farmers, known as yeomen, also fell into sharecropping. Meanwhile, many planters' sons abandoned farming and became lawyers, bankers, and merchants. Despite these changes, one thing remained the same: White elites ruled over Black and poor white people, and they kept these two economically exploited groups from uniting by fanning the flames of racial prejudice.

Exodusters
Black Americans who migrated from the South to Kansas in 1879 seeking land, economic opportunity, and a better way of life.

Economic hardship and racial bigotry drove many Black people to leave the South. In 1879 formerly enslaved people, known as **Exodusters**, pooled their resources to create land companies and purchase property in Kansas on which to settle. They encouraged an exodus of some 25,000 Black Americans from the South. Kansas was ruled by the Republican Party and had been home to the great antislavery martyr John Brown. As one hopeful freedman from Louisiana wrote to the Kansas governor in 1879, "I am anxious to reach your state . . . because of the sacredness of her soil washed in the blood of humanitarians for the cause of black freedom." Poor-quality land and unpredictable weather often made farming on the Great Plains hard and unrewarding. Nevertheless, for many migrants, the chance to own their own land and escape the oppression of the South was worth the hardships. In 1880 the census counted 40,000 people living in Kansas.

REVIEW

- What role did sharecropping play in reshaping the southern economy during Reconstruction?
- What role did Black Americans play in remaking southern society during Reconstruction?

White Resistance

Despite the Republican record of accomplishment during Reconstruction, white Southerners did not accept its legitimacy. They accused interracial governments of conducting a spending spree that raised taxes and encouraged corruption. Indeed, taxes did rise significantly, but mainly because legislatures funded much-needed educational and social services. Corruption on building projects and railroad construction was common during this time. Still, it is unfair to single out Reconstruction governments and especially legislators as inherently depraved, as their Democratic opponents acted the same way when given the opportunity.

Economic scandals were part of American life after the Civil War. As enormous business opportunities arose in the postwar years, many economic and political leaders made unlawful deals to enrich themselves.

Furthermore, southern opponents of Reconstruction exaggerated its harshness. In contrast to revolutions and civil wars in other countries, only one rebel was executed for war crimes (the commandant of Andersonville Prison in Georgia); only one high-ranking official went to prison (Jefferson Davis); no official was forced into exile, though some fled voluntarily; and most rebels regained voting rights and the ability to hold office within seven years of the rebellion's end.

Most important, these Reconstruction governments had only limited opportunities to transform the South. By the end of 1870, civilian rule had returned to all of the former Confederate states, and they had reentered the Union. Republican rule did not continue past 1870 in Virginia, North Carolina, and Tennessee and did not extend beyond 1871 in Georgia and 1873 in Texas. In 1874, Democrats deposed Republicans in Arkansas and Alabama; two years later, Democrats triumphed in Mississippi. In only three states—Louisiana, Florida, and South Carolina—did Reconstruction last until 1877.

The Democrats who replaced Republicans trumpeted their victories as bringing "redemption" to the South. Of course, these so-called **Redeemers** were referring to the white South. For Republicans and their white allies, redemption meant defeat. Democratic victories came at the ballot boxes, but violence, intimidation, and fraud paved the way.

In 1865, Tennessee veterans formed the **Knights of the Ku Klux Klan (KKK)**, and made the former Confederate general Nathan Bedford Forrest its first "Grand Wizard," or supreme leader, in 1868. Spreading throughout the South, its followers donned robes and masks to hide their identities and terrify their victims. Gun-wielding Ku Kluxers rode on horseback to the homes and churches of Black and white Republicans to keep them from voting. When threats did not work, they beat and murdered their victims. In 1871, for example, 150 Black Americans were killed in Jackson County in the Florida Panhandle. A clergyman lamented, "That is where Satan has his seat." There and elsewhere, many of the individuals targeted had managed to buy property, gain political leadership, or in other ways defy white stereotypes of Black American inferiority. Other white supremacist organizations joined the Klan in waging a reign of terror. During the 1875 election in Mississippi, which toppled the Republican government, armed terrorists killed hundreds of Republicans and scared many more away from the polls.

Redeemers
White, conservative Democrats who challenged and overthrew Republican rule in the South during Reconstruction hoping to restore pre-Civil War racial norms.

Knights of the Ku Klux Klan (KKK)
A secret organization formed in 1865 by Confederate general Nathan Bedford Forrest to restore white supremacy in the South. KKK members used threats and violence to terrorize freed Black people and their white allies in the South.

AP® WORKING with EVIDENCE

Source: Abram Colby, a formerly enslaved Black person and Georgia state legislator, *Testimony Taken by the Joint Select Committee to Inquire into the Condition of Affairs in the Late Insurrectionary States,* 1872

> "Colby: On the 29th of October 1869, [the Klansmen] broke my door open, took me out of bed, took me to the woods and whipped me three hours or more and left me for dead. They said to me, 'Do you think you will ever vote another damned Radical [Republican] ticket?' . . . I said, 'If there was an election tomorrow, I would vote the Radical ticket.' They set in and whipped me a thousand licks more . . .
>
> Question: What is the character of those men who were engaged in whipping you?
>
> Colby: Some are first-class men in our town. One is a lawyer, one a doctor, and some are farmers. . . . They had their pistols and they took me in my night-clothes and carried me from home. They hit me five thousand blows. . . . About two days before they whipped me they offered me $5,000 to go with them and said they would pay me $2,500 in cash if I would let another man go to the legislature in my place. I told them that I would not do it if they would give me all the county was worth.

The worst thing was . . . my mother, wife and daughter were in the room when they came. . . . My little daughter begged them not to carry me away. They drew up a gun and actually frightened her to death. She never got over it until she died.

Question: How long before you recovered from the effects of this treatment?

Colby: I have never got over it yet. They broke something inside of me. I cannot do any work now, though I always made my living before in the barber-shop, hauling wood, etc.

Question: You spoke about being elected to the next legislature?

Colby: . . . Yes, sir, but they run me off during the election. . . . They got after me, and swore they would kill me if I stayed there. . . . The Saturday night before the election I went to church. . . . [W]hen I got home my dogs out in the yard began barking. . . . I took my gun and ran up stairs, and I thought I could shoot through the window. They heard me going up stairs, and they just peppered . . . the house with shot and bullets.

Question: . . . Did you make a general canvas there last fall?

Colby: No, sir. I was not allowed to. . . . No man can make a free speech in my county. I do not believe it can be done anywhere in Georgia. . . .

Question: You say no man can do it; do you mean no republican, or no man of your color?

Colby: I mean no Republican, either white or colored."

Questions for Analysis

1. Identify the various tactics used by Klansmen to intimidate and pressure Colby.
2. Describe how Colby responded to the efforts of the Klansman.
3. Explain the impact of incidents such as the ones described in the excerpt on Reconstruction in the South.

Force Acts

Three acts passed by Congress in 1870 and 1871 in response to vigilante attacks on southern people. The acts were designed to protect political rights and end violence by the Ku Klux Klan and similar organizations.

To combat the terror unleashed by the Klan and its allies, Congress passed three **Force Acts** in 1870 and 1871. These measures empowered the president to dispatch officials into the South to supervise elections and prevent voting interference. Directed specifically at the KKK, one law barred secret organizations from using force to violate equal protection of the laws.

In 1872, Congress established a joint committee to probe Klan tactics, and its investigations produced thirteen volumes of gripping testimony about the horrors perpetrated by the Klan. Elias Hill, a freedman from South Carolina who had become a Baptist preacher and teacher, was one of those who appeared before Congress. Klansmen dragged Hill out of his house and beat, whipped, and threatened to kill him. On the basis of such testimony, the federal government prosecuted some 3,000 Klansmen. Only 600 were convicted, however. When the Klan officially disbanded in the wake of federal prosecutions, other vigilante organizations arose to take its place.

- How did white Southerners fight back against Reconstruction?
- What role did terrorism play in this effort?

The Retreat from Reconstruction

Most northern whites shared the racial prejudices of their counterparts in the South. Although they had supported protection of Black civil rights and suffrage, they still believed that Black Americans were inferior to whites and were horrified by the idea of social integration. They began to sympathize with southern whites' racist complaints that Black people were not capable of governing honestly and effectively.

In 1872, a group calling themselves Liberal Republicans challenged the reelection of President Ulysses S. Grant. Financial scandals had racked the Grant administration. This high-level corruption reflected other get-rich-quick schemes connected to economic speculation and development following the Civil War. Outraged by the rising level of dishonest behavior in government and business, Liberal Republicans nominated Horace Greeley, editor of the *New York Tribune*, to run against Grant. They linked government corruption to the expansion of federal power that accompanied Reconstruction and called for the removal of troops from the South and amnesty for all former Confederates. They also campaigned for civil service reform, which would base government employment on a merit system and abolish the "spoils system"—in which the party in power rewarded loyal supporters with political appointments—that had been introduced by Andrew Jackson in the 1820s.

The Democratic Party believed that Liberal Republicans offered the best chance to defeat Grant, and it endorsed Greeley. Despite the scandals that surrounded him, Grant remained popular. Moreover, Republicans "waved the bloody shirt," reminding northern voters that a ballot cast for the opposition tarnished the memory of brave Union soldiers killed during the war. The president won reelection with an even greater margin than he had four years earlier. Nevertheless, the attacks against Grant foreshadowed the Republican retreat on Reconstruction.

Among the Democrats sniping at Grant was ex-President Andrew Johnson. Johnson had returned to Tennessee, and in 1874, the state legislature chose the former president to serve in the U.S. Senate. He continued to speak out against the presence of federal troops in the South until his death in 1875.

By the time Grant began his second term, Congress was already considering bills to restore officeholding rights to former Confederates who had not yet sworn allegiance to the Union. Black representatives, including Georgia congressman Jefferson Long, as well as some white lawmakers, remained opposed to such measures, but in 1872, Congress removed the penalties placed on former Confederates by the Fourteenth Amendment and permitted nearly all rebel leaders the right to vote and hold office. Two years later, for the first time since the start of the Civil War, the Democrats gained a majority in the House of Representatives and prepared to remove the remaining troops from the South.

Republican leaders also rethought their top priority, as economic concerns increasingly replaced racial considerations. The **Panic of 1873**, caused largely by the collapse of the Northern Pacific Railroad, triggered a severe economic depression lasting late into the decade. Tens of thousands of unemployed workers across the country worried more about finding jobs than they did about Black civil rights. Businessmen, too, were plagued with widespread bankruptcy.

Panic of 1873
A severe economic depression largely triggered by the collapse of the Northern Pacific Railroad.

Strikes erupted across the country in 1877, most notably the **Great Railway Strike**. When more than half a million workers walked off the job, employers asked the U.S. government to remove troops from the South and dispatch them against strikers across the North and West.

While white Northerners sought ways to extricate themselves from Reconstruction, the Supreme Court weakened enforcement of the civil rights acts. In 1873, the **Slaughterhouse Cases** defined the rights that Black Americans were entitled to under

AP® EXAM TIP

Fewer students cite examples such as the Panic of 1873, the Slaughterhouse Cases, or *United States. v. Cruikshank* as reasons for the demise of Reconstruction. Select one or more of these topics to help you create a more complex understanding of the end of Reconstruction.

the Fourteenth Amendment very narrowly. Reflecting the shift from moral to economic concerns, the justices interpreted the amendment as extending greater protection to corporations in conducting business than to people. As a result, people had to depend on southern state governments to protect their civil rights—the same state authorities that had deprived them of their rights in the first place. In ***United States v. Cruikshank*** (1876), the high court narrowed the Fourteenth Amendment further, ruling that it protected people against abuses only by state officials and agencies, not by private groups such as the Ku Klux Klan. Seven years later, the Court struck down the **Civil Rights Act of 1875**, which had extended "full and equal treatment" in public accommodations for persons of all races.

Civil Rights Act of 1875

An act extending "full and equal treatment" for all races in public accommodations, jury service, and public transportation. However, in 1883, the Supreme Court ruled that the act was unconstitutional.

REVIEW

▪ Why did northern interest in Reconstruction fade during the 1870s?

The Presidential Compromise of 1876

The presidential election of 1876 set in motion events that officially brought Reconstruction to an end. The Republicans nominated the governor of Ohio, Rutherford B. Hayes, who was chosen partly because he was untainted by the corruption that plagued the Grant administration. The Democrats selected their own anticorruption crusader, Governor Samuel J. Tilden of New York.

The outcome of the election depended on twenty disputed electoral votes, nineteen from the South and one from Oregon. Tilden won 51 percent of the popular vote, but Reconstruction political battles in Florida, Louisiana, and South Carolina put the election up for grabs. In each of these states, the outgoing Republican administration certified Hayes as the winner, while the incoming Democratic regime declared for Tilden.

The Constitution assigns Congress the task of counting and certifying the electoral votes submitted by the states. Normally, this is a mere formality, but 1876 was different. Democrats controlled the House, Republicans controlled the Senate, and neither branch would budge on which votes to count. Hayes needed all twenty for victory; Tilden needed only one. To break the logjam, Congress created a fifteen-member Joint Electoral Commission, composed of seven Democrats, seven Republicans, and one independent. Ultimately, a majority voted to count all twenty votes for the Republican Hayes, making him president (Map 5.9).

Still, Congress had to ratify this count, and disgruntled southern Democrats in the Senate threatened a filibuster—unlimited debate—to block certification of Hayes. With the March 4, 1877, date for the presidential inauguration creeping perilously close and no winner officially declared, behind-the-scenes negotiations finally settled the controversy.

Compromise of 1877

The compromise between Republicans and southern Democrats that resulted in the election of Rutherford B. Hayes. Southern Democrats agreed to support Hayes in the disputed presidential election in exchange for his promise to end Reconstruction.

A series of meetings between Hayes supporters and southern Democrats led to a bargain. According to the agreement, Democrats would support Hayes in exchange for the president appointing a Southerner to his cabinet, withdrawing the last federal troops from the South, and endorsing construction of a transcontinental railroad through the South. This **Compromise of 1877** averted a crisis over presidential succession, underscored increased southern Democratic influence within Congress, and marked the end of strong federal protections for Black Americans in the South.

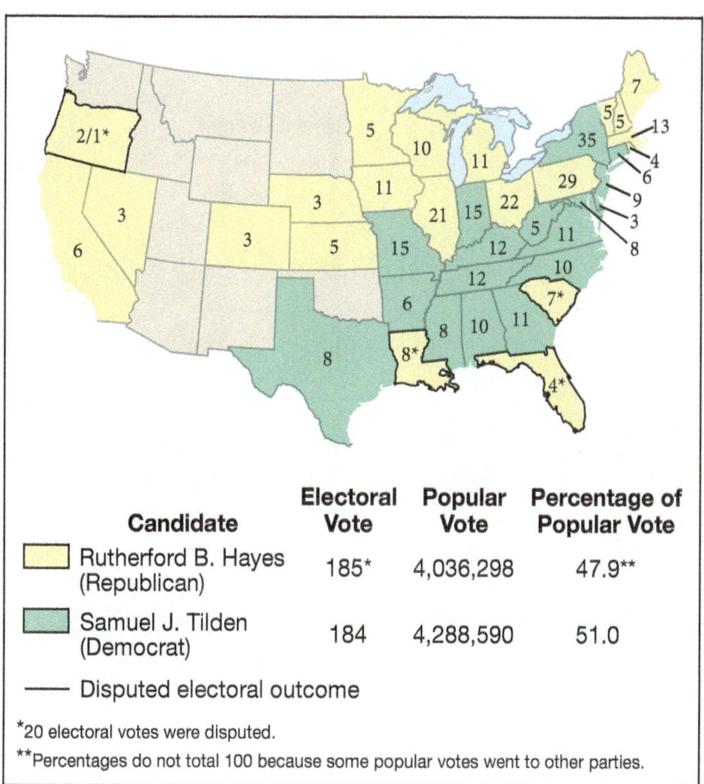

Candidate	Electoral Vote	Popular Vote	Percentage of Popular Vote
Rutherford B. Hayes (Republican)	185*	4,036,298	47.9**
Samuel J. Tilden (Democrat)	184	4,288,590	51.0

—— Disputed electoral outcome

*20 electoral votes were disputed.

**Percentages do not total 100 because some popular votes went to other parties.

MAP 5.9 The Election of 1876 The presidential election of 1876 got swept up in Reconstruction politics. Democrats defeated Republicans in Florida, Louisiana, and South Carolina, but both parties claimed the electoral votes for their candidates. A federal electoral commission set up to investigate the twenty disputed votes, including one from Oregon, awarded the votes and the election to the Republican, Rutherford B. Hayes.

How does this map reveal the extent to which sectionalism persisted in national politics after the end of the Civil War?

REVIEW

- What common values and beliefs held by white Americans were reflected in the Compromise of 1877?

The Legacies of Reconstruction

Reconstruction was, in many ways, severely limited. Notwithstanding the efforts of the Freedmen's Bureau, Black Americans did not receive the landownership that would have offered economic independence and bolstered their freedom from the racist assaults of white Southerners. The civil and political rights that the federal government granted did not withstand the efforts of former Confederates to deprive the freedpeople of equal rights, particularly the right to vote. The Republican Party shifted its priorities, and Democrats gained enough political power nationally to curtail federal intervention, even as many problems remained unresolved in the South. Northern support for racial equality did not run very deep, so white Northerners, who shared many of the prejudices of white Southerners, were happy to avoid further intervention in southern racial matters. Nor was there sufficient support to give women, white or Black, the right to vote. Finally, federal courts, with growing concerns over economic rather than social issues, supported Northerners' retreat by providing constitutional legitimacy for abandoning Black Southerners and rejecting women's suffrage in court decisions that narrowed the interpretation of the Fourteenth and Fifteenth Amendments.

Despite all of these setbacks, Reconstruction did transform the country. As a result of Reconstruction, slavery was abolished, and the legal basis for freedom was

A Prospective Scene in the "City of Oaks," 4th of March, 1869.

K.K.K.

OHIO

"Hang, curs, hang! * * * * * *Their* complexion is perfect gallows. Stand fast, good fate, to *their* hanging! * * * * * If they be not born to be hanged, our case is miserable."

The above cut represents the fate in store for those great pests of Southern society—the carpet-bagger and scallawag—if found in Dixie's Land after the break of day on the 4th of March next.

Fotosearch/Getty Images

"A Prospective Scene in the 'City of Oaks,' 4th of March, 1869" This cartoon was published in the Tuscaloosa, Alabama [then commonly called the City of Oaks] *Independent Monitor.* Depicted in the image are the Reverend Arad Lankin from Ohio, who had just been made president of the University of Alabama, and Dr. Noah Cloud, the newly elected Superintendent of Public Instruction. The smaller text directly beneath this image reads, "Hang, curs, hang! ***** *Their* complexion is perfect gallows. Stand fast, good fate, to *their* hanging! ***** If they be not born to be hanged, our case is miserable."

What details in this image demonstrate southern resistance to Reconstruction?

enshrined in the Constitution. Indeed, Black people exercised a measure of political and economic freedom during Reconstruction that never entirely disappeared over the decades to come. In many areas, freedpeople, exemplified by Congressman Jefferson Franklin Long and many others, asserted what they never could have during slavery — control over their lives, their churches, their labor, their education, and their families. What they could not practice during their own time, their descendants would one day revive through the promises codified in the Fourteenth and Fifteenth Amendments.

Black Americans transformed not only themselves; they transformed the nation. The Constitution became much more democratic and egalitarian through inclusion of the Reconstruction amendments. Reconstruction lawmakers took an important step toward making the United States the "more perfect union" that the nation's Founders had pledged to create. Reconstruction established a model for expanding the power of the federal government to resolve domestic crises that lay beyond the abilities of states and ordinary citizens. It remained a powerful legacy for elected officials who dared to invoke it.

AP® EXAM TIP

To prepare yourself for an essay question on Reconstruction, think about how you can explain the concept that Reconstruction led to significant changes and continuities in American life. You can focus your answer on either a specific group such as Black Americans or a concept such as citizenship.

Reconstruction also transformed the South. It modernized state constitutions, expanded educational and social welfare systems, and unleashed the repressed potential for industrialization and economic development that the preservation of slavery had restrained. Ironically, Reconstruction did as much for white Southerners as it did for Black Southerners in liberating them from the past.

REVIEW

- To what extent was southern society changed by Reconstruction?

AP® Skills Workshop: Thinking Historically

Additional Practice in Responding to a Short-Answer Question with Secondary Sources

The nature and effectiveness of Reconstruction are topics that historians are still debating, as you will see from the two excerpts below. This exercise will provide you with the opportunity to grapple with different understandings of Reconstruction and use your understanding of the time period to respond to those interpretations.

Read the two passages and then use **CSE** to answer each part of the question. For part A, make sure you draw a clear distinction between the two interpretations. Contrasting a summary of each document might be helpful in that regard. For parts B and C, be sure to include a concrete piece of outside information (a "proper noun," if possible) and explain *how* it supports the historian's argument. If you need more help, review the content in Modules 5.10 and 5.11 and the AP® Skills Workshop in Module 2.8.

> "If blacks failed to achieve the economic independence envisioned in the aftermath of the Civil War, Reconstruction closed off even more oppressive alternatives than the Redeemers' New South. The post-Reconstruction labor system embodied neither a return to the closely supervised gang labor of the antebellum days, nor the complete dispossession and immobilization of the black labor force and coercive apprenticeship systems envisioned by white Southerners in 1865 and 1866. . . . As illustrated by the small but growing number of black landowners, businessmen, and professionals, the doors of economic opportunity that had opened could never be completely closed. Without Reconstruction, moreover, it is difficult to imagine the establishment of a framework of legal rights enshrined in the Constitution that, while flagrantly violated after 1877, created a vehicle for future federal intervention in Southern affairs. As a result of this unprecedented redefinition of the American body politic, the South's racial system remained regional rather than national, an outcome of great importance when economic opportunities at last opened in the North."
>
> Eric Foner, *Reconstruction: America's Unfinished Revolution, 1863–1877*, 1998

(continued)

"This Greater Reconstruction [of the whole nation] was even more morally ambiguous than the lesser one [in the South]. It included not one war but three—the Mexican War, Civil War, and War against Indian America—and while it saw the emancipation of one non-white people, it was equally concerned with dominating others. It included the Civil Rights Acts and the 13th, 14th, and 15th Amendments, but it began with U.S. soldiers clashing with a Mexican patrol on disputed terrain along the Rio Grande in 1846. . . . Always the Greater Reconstruction was as much about control as liberation, as much about unity and power as about equality. Indians were given roles they mostly didn't want, and freedmen were offered roles they mostly did, but both were being told that these were the roles they *would* play, like it or not."

Elliott West, "Reconstructing Race,"
Western Historical Quarterly 34, Spring 2003

Using the excerpts, answer **A**, **B**, and **C**.

(A) Briefly describe ONE major difference between Foner's and West's historical interpretations of Reconstruction.

(B) Briefly explain how ONE historical event or development from the period 1865 to 1877 that is not explicitly mentioned in the excerpts could be used to support Foner's argument.

(C) Briefly explain how ONE historical event or development from the period 1865 to 1877 that is not explicitly mentioned in the excerpts could be used to support West's argument.

Comparison in Period 5

MODULE 5.12

AP® Skills Workshop: Writing Historically

Responding to a Document-Based Question

The Document-Based Question (DBQ) is an essay that asks you to combine your historical knowledge, understanding of the supplied documents, and ability to think historically. On the AP® Exam, a DBQ will contain excerpts from seven primary source documents, although occasionally one of the documents may instead be a visual representation of data such as a graph, chart, or electoral map. The DBQ represents 25 percent of the total exam score, and you will be advised to spend about 60 minutes on it.

As you plan and write your DBQ, keep in mind that it will be scored based on the following criteria:

- Thesis (making a historically defensible claim with a line of reasoning)
- Contextualization (connecting to a relevant and broader historical context)
- Document Content (addressing the prompt with information from three or more documents)
- Document Evidence (supporting an argument by using four or more of the documents)
- Outside Evidence (advancing an argument by using relevant information beyond the documents)
- Sourcing (explaining *how* or *why* historical situation, intended audience, purpose, or point of view from two or more of the documents are relevant to an argument)
- Complexity (demonstrating a sophisticated historical understanding of the topic—this category will be examined in AP® Skills Workshops in Period 6)

The following prompt requires you to draw on what you have learned about Reconstruction as well as the seven accompanying documents.

> Evaluate the extent of change in regional attitudes regarding civil rights between 1855 and 1877.

Step 1 ▶ Break down the prompt

Just as with an LEQ, the first task with a DBQ is to identify the topic, time period, and historical reasoning process you want to target in your argument. The topic here is the degree to which regional attitudes changed in the North and South toward civil rights for Black people.

The use of the word "change" in the prompt immediately suggests that **continuity and change over time** should be the focus of this essay. For this prompt, however, **comparison** should also be embedded in your response as you examine both North and South. Additionally, **causation** could be included if you explore what led to or resulted from the changes in attitudes. While you may not be able to address all three reasoning processes in your essay, you should consider them during your prewrite.

Finally, notice that the time frame, 1855 to 1877, spans several modules and part or all of the three main chronological blocks in this unit of study: before the Civil War (1855–1860), during the Civil War (1861–1865), and Reconstruction (1865–1877).

(continued)

This range of years suggests that the changes will be significant and is a reminder to think about how the Civil War and Reconstruction affected views toward civil rights.

Step 2 ▶ Initial brainstorm

When you encounter a DBQ, your first impulse might be to read the prompt and then quickly scan the documents. While that's understandable and not wrong, we suggest a different approach—brainstorm some facts after you read the prompt, but before you review the documents. Quickly think about and jot down any relevant outside information and even categories of analysis, in this case continuities or changes in regional attitudes toward civil rights, *before* reading the documents.

It's easy to focus so much on the documents that you'll forget that you are answering a specific essay question and that you need to include information beyond the documents for outside evidence, context, and sourcing. Here's a trick: when you read the prompt (and before you read the documents), think of the DBQ like an LEQ. This should help you think more broadly about the topic and write a more complete essay. Of course, be prepared to adjust or modify your brainstorm once you start reading the documents.

Step 3 ▶ Read and annotate the documents

Once you've completed your initial brainstorm, it's time to read and mark up the documents. As with any other primary source, you should start by reading the source information and considering what you know, if anything, about the author or work. Make sure to jot down anything that comes to mind before reading the document itself. Then, as you read each document, consider the following questions:

- What is the document about? How would you summarize its content?
- Does the content in the document suggest a topic you could use in your essay? How can you connect it to the prompt? If you've already generated some organizational categories, how can it be used as evidence in your essay?
- Can you analyze the sourcing of this document by examining its historical situation, intended audience, purpose, or point of view?
- Are you reminded of any other relevant information from the time period as you read the document?

Here's a sample of a graphic organizer you could use as your read and analyze the primary source documents in the following DBQ. The first document has been analyzed for you as an example. The "Additional Information" column is a list of any outside information that you are reminded of when reading the document.

Document Name	Document Summary	Connection to the Prompt	Sourcing Analysis	Additional Information
1. Lincoln speech at Edwardsville, 1858	Lincoln argued that Democrats do not care about slavery, but Republicans considered it wrong and wanted to block its expansion, though they would leave it alone in the South.	This document can be used to illustrate political differences in the North and South over slavery before the Civil War.	Historical Situation: Lincoln ran for the U.S. Senate against Douglas in 1858. This speech was shortly after the controversial *Dred Scott* decision stating that slavery could be allowed in any territory.	- Free-soil movement - *Uncle Tom's Cabin* - Popular sovereignty - Kansas-Nebraska Act

(continued)

Document 1

Source: Abraham Lincoln, *Speech at Edwardsville, Illinois*, 1858

"The difference between the Republican and the Democratic parties on the leading issue of this contest, as I understand it, is, that the former consider slavery a moral, social and political wrong, while the latter do not consider it either a moral, social or political wrong. . . . Every measure of the Democratic party of late years, bearing directly or indirectly on the slavery question, has corresponded with this notion of utter indifference whether slavery or freedom shall outrun in the race of empire across the Pacific . . . The Republican party, on the contrary, hold that this government was instituted to secure the blessings of freedom, and that slavery is an unqualified evil to the negro, to the white man, to the soil, and to the State. Regarding it an evil, they will not molest it in the States where it exists . . . but they will use every constitutional method to prevent the evil from becoming larger and involving more negroes, more white men, more soil, and more States in its deplorable consequences."

Document 2

Source: *A Declaration of the Immediate Causes which Induce and Justify the Secession of the State of Mississippi from the Federal Union*, 1861

"Our position is thoroughly identified with the institution of slavery—the greatest material interest of the world. Its labor supplies the product which constitutes by far the largest and most important portions of commerce of the earth. These products are peculiar to the climate verging on the tropical regions, and by an imperious law of nature, none but the black race can bear exposure to the tropical sun. These products have become necessities of the world, and a blow at slavery is a blow at commerce and civilization. That blow has been long aimed at the institution, and was at the point of reaching its consummation. There was no choice left us but submission to the mandates of abolition, or a dissolution of the Union, whose principles had been subverted to work out our ruin."

Document 3

Source: *New York Herald*, "What to Do with the Slaves When Emancipated," 1862

"What is to be done with the slaves when emancipated? It would not do to let them work or not, as they may think proper. If they were as willing to work as the white man there would be no slavery now in any Southern State. The proposed change would involve the necessity of transferring from the master to the State the superintendence of negro labor, and vagrant laws should be passed compelling negroes to work—laws which exist in many parts of Europe in reference to the white population, but infinitely more necessary for blacks, whose idea of paradise is to have nothing to do. The wages should be regulated by law, and be sufficient not only to procure food and clothing, but to enable the negro to lay up something for sickness and old age."

(*continued*)

Document 4

Source: Civil Rights Act, 1866

"Be it enacted by the Senate and House of Representatives of the United States of America in Congress assembled, That all persons born in the United States and not subject to any foreign power, excluding Indians not taxed, are hereby declared to be citizens of the United States; and such citizens, of every race and color, without regard to any previous condition of slavery or involuntary servitude, except as a punishment for crime whereof the party shall have been duly convicted, shall have the same right, in every State and Territory in the United States, to make and enforce contracts, to sue, be parties, and give evidence, to inherit, purchase, lease, sell, hold, and convey real and personal property, and to full and equal benefit of all laws and proceedings for the security of person and property, as is enjoyed by white citizens, and shall be subject to like punishment, pains, and penalties, and to none other, any law, statute, ordinance, regulation, or custom, to the contrary notwithstanding."

Document 5

Source: Elizabeth Cady Stanton and Susan B. Anthony, *American Equal Rights Association: Stanton-Anthony Resolutions*, 1869

"Resolved, That the American Equal Rights Association, in loyalty to its comprehensive demands for the political equality of all American citizens, without distinction of race or sex, hails the extension of suffrage to any heretofore disfranchised, as a cheering part of the triumph of our whole idea.

Resolved, therefore, That we gratefully welcome the pending fifteenth amendment, prohibiting disfranchisement on account of race, and earnestly solicit the State Legislatures to pass it without delay.

Resolved, furthermore, That in view of this promised and speedy culmination of one-half of our demands, we are stimulated to redouble our energy to secure the further amendment guaranteeing the same sacred rights without limitation to sex.

Resolved, That until the constitution shall know neither black nor white, neither male nor female, but only the equal rights of all classes, we renew our solemn indictment against that instrument as defective, unworthy, and an oppressive charter for the self-government of a free people."

Document 6

Source: Senator Hiram Revels (Mississippi), *On Readmission of Georgia to the Union*, 1870

"I maintain that the past record of my race is a true index of the feelings which today animate them. They bear toward their former masters no revengeful thoughts, no hatred, no animosities. They aim not to elevate themselves by sacrificing one single interest of their white fellow-citizens. They ask but the rights which are theirs by God's universal law, and which are the natural outgrowth, the logical sequence of the condition in which the legislative enactments of the nation have placed on them. They appeal to you and to me to see that they receive that protection which alone will

(continued)

enable them to pursue their daily avocations with success and enjoy the liberties of citizenship on the same footing with their white neighbors and friends. I do not desire to simply defend my own race from unjust and unmerited charges, but I also desire to place upon record an express of my full and entire confidence in the integrity of purpose with which I believe the president, Congress, and the Republican party will meet these questions . . . not only to my own people, but to the whole South."

Document 7

Source: Thomas Nast, *This Is a White Man's Government*, 1874

About the source: The text at the bottom of the image reads, "We regard the Reconstruction Acts (so called) of Congress as usurpations, and unconstitutional, revolutionary, and void"—*Democratic platform.* The man in the center of the cartoon is wearing a belt with a buckle labeled "CSA," and holds a knife labeled "the lost cause." The man on the left is an Irish man, who holds a club labeled "a vote." The man on the right is wearing a button labeled "5 Avenue" and holding a wallet labeled "capital for votes." All three men have a foot on the back of an Black Union soldier, who is lying on the ground. In the background of the cartoon, a "colored orphan asylum" and a "southern school" are burning down, and Black children have been lynched nearby.

Library of Congress, LC-USZ62-121735

(continued)

Step 4 ▶ Update your brainstorm and organize your essay

After you have read and annotated the documents, it's time to combine information from the documents and your initial brainstorming into an organized plan for your essay. You've been provided a partially completed chart below that structures the essay by making sub-arguments based on the targeted historical reasoning processes: comparison or continuity and change over time. While causation is not asked specifically by the prompt, including causes or effects will greatly strengthen your response and is a step toward demonstrating historical complexity that will be discussed further in Period 6. Feel free to finish this chart or create a different one based on how you want to answer this question.

Historical Reasoning Claim	Description of the Main Point	Supporting Documents and Outside Evidence	Causes or Effects
Racism toward Blacks in the North was a continuity between 1855 and 1877.	Even with growing abolitionism in the North before the war and Lincoln eventually shifting the focus of the war to emancipation, many Northerners remained prejudiced toward Blacks and opposed racial equality throughout the time period.	- Document 1: Republican Party was not opposed to slavery in the South in the 1850s. - Document 3: Some Northern whites believed that Blacks were lazy and needed vagrancy laws. - Document 7: Many Northerners grew tired of supporting Reconstruction. - Crittenden Plan would have extended slavery westward below the 36°30′ line. - Black Union soldiers were initially paid less than white Union soldiers. - Liberal Republicans emphasized the corruption in some Reconstruction programs.	- Fear that Blacks might compete with them for low-wage jobs contributed to racism and draft riots by Irish immigrants. - The failure to redistribute land in the South to formerly enslaved persons after the Civil War led to a system of sharecropping and long-term economic inequality in the South.

Step 5 ▶ Set the context and write a thesis

After you have organized your essay, it's time to write the thesis. Just like an LEQ, you have to include both a **claim** where you respond to the *extent* of change in regional attitudes toward civil rights for Blacks, and a **line of reasoning** that describes the specific sub-arguments that you will use to support your overall claim. If you use the graphic organizer from above, or something similar, you can borrow information from the second column for your line of reasoning. Be sure to save any specific outside evidence and the documents for use in your body paragraphs.

Once you've created your thesis, it's time to develop a context. We recommend that you create a **preceding context** in the introduction to set up your thesis and, if time allows, an **immediate context** in one of your body paragraphs or a **concluding context** in your conclusion. For a preceding context, you should make a connection between your argument and a significant prior historical development such as abolitionism, immigration trends, or the market revolution. Remember, it's best to develop your context using **Claim, Support, Explain (CSE)**.

(continued)

Step 6 ▶ **Write the essay**

The final step is to compose the remainder of your essay. Each body paragraph should be devoted to one of the main points in your essay that supports your thesis. The first sentence of each paragraph should begin with a **sub-argument** that relates to a portion of your thesis. Much of each paragraph should focus on the evidence from and beyond the documents and your analysis of how that evidence supports or furthers your sub-argument. Make sure to historically source some of the documents as you explain and use them. Don't forget that you can **CSE** your **outside evidence**, **document evidence**, and **document sourcing**.

ACTIVITY

Write a five to six paragraph essay in response to the prompt, following the provided steps. Do your best to accomplish the bulleted criteria (page 493) as you follow the step-by-step process. The following outline has been provided to guide your response.

> Evaluate the extent of change in regional attitudes regarding civil rights between 1855 and 1877.

I. Introductory Paragraph (approximately five or six sentences)
   (A) Preceding Contextualization Using CSE
   (B) Thesis Claim and Line of Reasoning
II. Body Paragraphs (approximately seven to nine sentences each)
   (A) Sub-Argument
   (B) Claim, Support, Explain Documents with Sourcing
   (C) Claim, Support, Explain Outside Information
   (D) Summary of Sub-Argument
III. Conclusion (approximately five sentences)
   (A) Restatement of Thesis Claim and Line of Reasoning
   (B) Concluding Contextualization Using CSE

Period 5 Review 1844–1877

KEY CONCEPTS AND EVENTS

American Equal Rights Association, *475*
American Party, *417*
Battle of Antietam, *438*
Battle of Gettysburg, *450*
Battle of Shiloh, *436*
Black codes, *471*
Bleeding Kansas, *418*
California gold rush, *387*
Californio, *387*
carpetbagger, *482*
Civil Rights Act of 1875, *488*
Compromise of 1850, *404*
Compromise of 1877, *488*
Confederate States of America (Confederacy), *427*
Confiscation Acts, *436*
contraband, *435*
Copperhead, *445*
Crittenden Plan, *429*
Dred Scott v. Sandford, *421*
Emancipation Proclamation, *438*
Enrollment Act, *444*
Exodusters, *484*
Field Order Number 15, *455*
Fifteenth Amendment, *475*
filibuster, *412*
First Battle of Bull Run (First Manassas), *435*
Force Acts, *486*
Fort Sumter, *430*
Fourteenth Amendment, *472*
Freedmen's Bureau, *464*
Fugitive Slave Act of 1793, *404*
Fugitive Slave Act of 1850, *408*
Gettysburg Address, *451*
Great Railway Strike, *487*
hard war, *454*
John Brown's raid, *423*
Kansas-Nebraska Act, *416*
Knights of the Ku Klux Klan (KKK), *485*
Liberty Party, *389*
Lincoln-Douglas debates, *422*
manifest destiny, *390*
martial law, *444*
Mexican-American War, *395*
Military Reconstruction Acts, *473*
National Woman Suffrage Association, *475*
overland trail, *386*
Oregon Trail, *386*
Ostend Manifesto, *412*
Panic of 1873, *487*
Proclamation of Amnesty and Reconstruction, *469*
Radical Republican, *469*
Reconstruction, *463*
Redeemers, *485*
Republican Party, *417*
Sand Creek Massacre, *455*
scalawag, *482*
Second Battle of Bull Run (Second Manassas), *436*
sharecropping, *483*
Sherman's March to the Sea, *454*
Siege of Vicksburg, *451*
Slaughterhouse Cases, *487*
Tenure of Office Act, *473*
Thirteenth Amendment, *456*
transcontinental railroad, *416*
Treaty of Guadalupe Hidalgo, *398*
Uncle Tom's Cabin, *412*
United States v. Cruikshank, *488*
Underground Railroad, *408*
Wade-Davis bill, *469*
Wilmot Proviso, *402*
Women's National Loyal League, *443*

KEY PEOPLE

Susan B. Anthony, *443*
Clara Barton, *443*
John Wilkes Booth, *458*
John Brown, *418*
James Buchanan, *412*
Anthony Burns, *413*
John C. Calhoun, *405*
Henry Clay, *389*
John Crittenden, *429*
Jefferson Davis, *426*
Stephen Douglas, *416*
Frederick Douglass, *409*
Millard Fillmore, *403*
Nathan Bedford Forrest, *485*
John Frémont, *397*
William Lloyd Garrison, *409*
Ulysses S. Grant, *436*
Horace Greeley, *430*
John Hale, *411*
Rutherford B. Hayes, *488*
Stonewall Jackson, *434*
Andrew Johnson, *463*
Robert E. Lee, *423*
Abraham Lincoln, *383*
George A. Meade, *450*
George B. McClellan, *436*
John L. O'Sullivan, *389*
Franklin Pierce, *408*
James K. Polk, *389*
Dred Scott, *421*
Winfield Scott, *395*
William H. Seward, *405*
Horatio Seymour, *474*
Philip Sheridan, *454*
William Tecumseh Sherman, *452*
Edwin Stanton, *455*
Elizabeth Cady Stanton, *443*
Thaddeus Stevens, *470*
Lucy Stone, *443*
Harriet Beecher Stowe, *412*
Charles Sumner, *418*
Roger Taney, *421*
Zachary Taylor, *395*
Sojourner Truth, *475*
Harriet Tubman, *408*
Daniel Webster, *405*
David Wilmot, *402*

CHRONOLOGY

1830s	Economic opportunity leads to an increase in westward settlement
1837	Panic of 1837
1844	James K. Polk (Democrat) elected president
1846–1848	Mexican-American War
1846	Wilmot Proviso proposed
1848	Treaty of Guadalupe Hidalgo signed Zachary Taylor (Whig) elected president California gold rush begins
1849	California applies for admission to the Union as a free state
1850	Compromise of 1850
1851	Major protests over Fugitive Slave Act
1852	Franklin Pierce (Democrat) elected president Publication of *Uncle Tom's Cabin* by Harriet Beecher Stowe
1854	Ostend Manifesto leaked Republican Party established Kansas-Nebraska Act passed
1855	Proslavery government installed in Kansas
1856	Bleeding Kansas
1858	Lincoln-Douglas debates
1859	John Brown's raid on Harpers Ferry
1860	Abraham Lincoln (Republican) elected president Crittenden Plan proposed
1861	Confederate States of America established Attack on Fort Sumter
1861–1862	U.S. Sanitary Commission established Series of Confederate victories
1862	Technological advances aid Union victory at Battles of Shiloh and Antietam
1863	Emancipation Proclamation takes effect Union victory at Gettysburg, followed by Gettysburg Address Lincoln's Proclamation of Amnesty and Reconstruction
1864	Launch of Ulysses S. Grant's "hard war" campaign Sand Creek Massacre
By 1865	Federal government is nation's largest employer
1865–1877	Reconstruction Carpetbaggers move south

CHRONOLOGY *(continued)*

1865	Sherman issues Field Order Number 15 Lee surrenders to Grant at Appomattox Lincoln assassinated Thirteenth Amendment ratified Republicans bar southern lawmakers from Congress Ku Klux Klan founded
1867	Start of Congressional Reconstruction Richmond Republican convention attracts Black voters
1868	Fourteenth Amendment ratified *Dred Scott* verdict from 1857 nullified Congress votes to impeach Andrew Johnson Ulysses S. Grant (Republican) elected president
1869	Fifteenth Amendment passed
1870s	Violence toward Black Americans widespread in the South Northern resentment toward aid to Black Southerners grows
1870–1871	Force Acts passed
1872	Grant's reelection challenged by Liberal Republicans
1873	Panic of 1873 triggers an economic depression
1873–1877	Supreme Court restricts voting rights of Black people
1874	Andrew Johnson elected to Senate Restrictions on former Confederate leaders lifted
1877	Reconstruction ends Compromise of 1877 Nationwide labor strikes
1879	Exodusters begin to move west

Period 5 AP® Exam Practice

Multiple-Choice Questions

Questions 1–3 refer to the excerpt.

"The members of the Republican party who controlled the Union during the Civil War worked consciously to create a new nation, both on the battlefields, where they insured the survival of their country, and in the halls of Congress, where they constructed the framework for the postwar era. The Republicans acted on a belief that the United States could become the wealthiest, strongest, and most egalitarian nation on earth. Surprised when they found themselves in such a bloody war, they quickly understood that the war years would both compel and enable them to pass sweeping novel legislation to bring their optimistic vision of the nation's future to life. . . .

While they had not agreed on a legislative plan for the nation, Republicans did share a world view that they had inherited from the rural antebellum world of farming and small towns from which most of them had come. Having seen their communities develop from agricultural beginnings, party members believed that God had given man the ability to create value with the labor of his hands. Every individual could thus build capital, which would accumulate faster than it was consumed. . . . In their optimistic conception of economic development, all elements in society would work together to increase individual and national wealth, so long as no one monopolized money or power."

Heather C. Richardson, *Greatest Nation of the Earth: Republican Economic Policies During the Civil War*, 1997

1. The ideas expressed in the excerpt most directly led to which of the following developments?
- (A) A visible abolitionist movement
- (B) Increased nativist sentiments in northern cities
- (C) Compromises over enslavement in western territories
- (D) Legislation that expanded western transportation

2. Which issue was most responsible for the creation of the Republican Party described in the excerpt?
- (A) The strength of abolitionism
- (B) The expansion of slavery
- (C) The belief in manifest destiny
- (D) Economic initiatives in Asia

3. Which of the following best represents an important consequence of the beliefs held by Republicans described in the excerpt?
- (A) A temporary reordering of race relations in the South after the Civil War
- (B) Northern support of southern Democrats during Reconstruction
- (C) A support for ethnic communities in northern cities
- (D) The support of women's rights in the antebellum years

Questions 4–6 refer to the excerpt.

"I make no war upon the South nor upon slavery in the South. I have no squeamish sensitiveness upon the subject of slavery, nor morbid sympathy for the slave. I plead the cause of the rights of white freemen. I would preserve for free white labor a fair country, a rich inheritance, where the sons of toil, of my own race and own color, can live without the disgrace which association with negro slavery brings upon free labor. I stand for the inviolability of free territory. It shall remain free, so far as my voice or vote can aid in the preservation of its character."

David Wilmot, *Wilmot Proviso Speech*, 1847

4. The ideas expressed in the excerpt emerged in the context of which of the following?
(A) The use of violence as a means of abolitionism
(B) An increase in Irish immigration
(C) Debates over the extension of slavery
(D) The legality of secession

5. Southerners who opposed the ideas expressed by Wilmot in the speech believed in which of the following arguments?
(A) The Supreme Court had no authority over slavery in the western territories.
(B) Decisions over slavery should be left to the U.S. Congress.
(C) Land taken by the Mexican-American War would be determined by popular sovereignty.
(D) Slavery was protected by the Constitution.

6. Which of the following best represents an important political consequence of the beliefs expressed by Wilmot?
(A) The efforts of southern Democrats to control Reconstruction
(B) The election of Abraham Lincoln on a free-soil platform
(C) A decrease in national authority over enslavement
(D) The creation of the Northern Democratic party

Questions 7–9 refer to the excerpt.

"But now, where and what are we? Our population has filled up its original seats. It has swarmed across the Alleghanies, and occupied with its industry, its powers, its principles, its civilization, the vast and fertile valley of the Mississippi. The remote Rocky Mountains have proved no barrier to its progress. It now stands upon the shores of the Pacific, with expansive energies unabated, regretful, not, like Alexander [the Great] on the limits of India, that no kingdoms remained to be conquered, but that no wildernesses are left to be reclaimed by the hand of industry from the dominion of uncultivated Nature.

Nor in the wrestle with Nature only have we shown our manhood, for science, learning, art, have also risen up and flourished under the vivifying [energizing] influences of prosperity and freedom; and in all that appertains to material as well as moral greatness, whether in the cultivation of the earth or in the advancement of mechanic art, manufacture and commerce, we, the once feeble child of England, now range side by side with our great parent, while the nations, distanced by us in the race of wealth and power, gaze on our marvelous progress, with admiration and with awe."

Caleb Cushing, speech in Newburyport, Massachusetts, July 4, 1850

7. Which of the following best represents a historical factor for the claims in the excerpt?
(A) Beliefs in the superiority of American institutions
(B) Desire to expand cotton production into western territories
(C) Effort to reform political institutions in the West
(D) Legislation to promote universal education

8. The sentiments in the excerpt most directly led to which of the following situations in the 1870s?
(A) Women's rights proponents debating education in the South during Reconstruction
(B) Advocates of big business discussing trade agreements with European nations
(C) Debates surrounding the status of American Indians in western territories
(D) Northern Democrats' waning support of Reconstruction legislation in the South

9. Which of the following represents a short-term consequence of the ideas in the excerpt?
(A) Tenant farming in the South
(B) Questions about the expansion of slavery
(C) An expansion of industrial mining in the West
(D) A strengthening of the two-party system

Questions 10–12 refer to the political cartoon.

Library of Congress, LC-USZ62-128619

Thomas Nast, "The Union as It Was, The Lost Cause, Worse than Slavery," *Harper's Weekly,* 1874

10. Which of the following historical developments best explains the historical situation of the political cartoon?
(A) Northern efforts to remake southern society
(B) New powers of the federal government after the Civil War
(C) Violent political acts by Southerners to control southern legislatures
(D) Radical Republicans passing civil rights acts

11. The economic condition of formerly enslaved persons during Reconstruction ended in
- (A) an economy primarily based on exporting staple crops.
- (B) an exploitive sharecropping system.
- (C) European encroachment on American Indian lands.
- (D) the presence of competing European empires.

12. The actions depicted in the cartoon were most directly supported by
- (A) Radical Republicans.
- (B) Moderate Republicans.
- (C) Southern Republicans.
- (D) Southern Democrats.

Questions 13–15 refer to the excerpt.

"I am naturally anti-slavery. If slavery is not wrong, nothing is wrong. I can not remember when I did not so think, and feel. And yet I have never understood that the Presidency conferred upon me an unrestricted right to act officially upon this judgment and feeling. . . . When, in March, and May, and July 1862 I made earnest, and successive appeals to the border states to favor compensated emancipation, I believed the indispensable necessity for military emancipation, and arming the blacks would come, unless averted by that measure. They declined the proposition; and I was, in my best judgment, driven to the alternative of either surrendering the Union, and with it, the Constitution, or of laying strong hand upon the colored element. I chose the latter. . . . I claim to not have controlled events, but confess plainly that events have controlled me. Now, at the end of three years struggle the nation's condition is not what either party, or any man devised, or expected. God alone can claim it. Whither it is tending seems plain. If God now wills the removal of a great wrong, and wills also that we of the North as well as you of the South, shall pay fairly for our complicity in that wrong, impartial history will find therein new cause to attest and revere the justice and goodness of God."

Abraham Lincoln, Letter to Albert Hodges, April 4, 1864

13. The statement by President Lincoln above supports the idea that
- (A) European nations wanted to recognize the Confederacy.
- (B) supporters of the Union did not agree with the Emancipation Proclamation.
- (C) Lincoln viewed emancipation as a consequence of the Civil War.
- (D) Lincoln believed the Civil War had always been about ending slavery.

14. In the immediate aftermath of the Civil War, southern resistance to the emancipation of enslaved Black Americans most directly led to
- (A) weakened state governments in the North.
- (B) constitutional changes to ensure equal protection under the law.
- (C) a retreat of Reconstruction ideas by Radical Republicans.
- (D) Supreme Court decisions to block the civil rights of Black Americans.

15. Which of the following pieces of evidence would prove Lincoln's hesitation to emancipate enslaved Black Americans at the beginning of the war?
- (A) The passage of the First Confiscation Act
- (B) Lincoln's suspension of habeas corpus
- (C) Conscription of citizens in the North
- (D) Republicans' free-soil party platform in 1860

Short-Answer Questions

"To historians writing after the dust had settled, it appeared that the emergence of the Republican party was the central development in all this complicated process of political disintegration and reintegration. . . . The antislavery party had now clearly, and somewhat unexpectedly, emerged as the dominant party in the North. Thus, as it appears in retrospect, the Know-Nothing phase of American politics had served as a kind of intermediate stage in the transition from Whiggism to Republicanism . . . nativism was intrinsically a transient phenomenon . . . the slavery issue was a more lasting one."

David M. Potter, *The Impending Crisis: America Before the Civil War, 1848–1861*, 1976

"In much historical writing on the politics of the 1850s, the formation of the Republican party and its subsequent rise to national power seem almost the fulfillment of destiny. . . . Without question, the slavery expansion issue was crucial to the formation of a northern sectional party. . . . In reality, the interaction of the slavery issue with other concerns, particularly nativism, in the 1854 state elections produced a complex and at times bewildering set of developments that represented only the first faltering steps toward the formation of the Republican party."

William E. Gienapp, *The Origins of the Republican Party: 1852–1856*, 1987

1. Using the excerpts, answer **A**, **B**, and **C**.
   (A) Briefly describe one major difference between Potter's and Gienapp's historical interpretations about the formation of the Republican party in the period before the Civil War.
   (B) Briefly explain how one historical event or development from 1848 to 1860 that is not explicitly mentioned in the excerpts could support Potter's interpretation.
   (C) Briefly explain how one historical event or development from 1848 to 1860 that is not explicitly mentioned in the excerpts could support Gienapp's interpretation.

Smithsonian American Art Museum, Bequest of Sara Carr Upton, 1931.6.1

Emmanuel Leutze, *Westward the Course of Empire Takes Its Way (study)*, 1861

2. Using the image, answer **A**, **B**, and **C**.
   (A) Briefly describe the historical situation described in the image.
   (B) Briefly explain how one specific historical event or development from 1844 to 1860 led to the historical situation depicted in the image.
   (C) Briefly explain how one specific historical event or development from 1850 to 1877 happened as a result of the historical situation depicted in the image.

3. Answer **A**, **B**, and **C**.
   (A) Briefly describe one specific historical change in the political debates over slavery in the period from 1844 to 1854.
   (B) Briefly describe one specific historical continuity in the political debates over slavery in the period from 1844 to 1854.
   (C) Briefly explain one historical consequence of the debates over slavery in the period from 1854 to 1861.

4. Answer **A**, **B**, and **C**.
   (A) Briefly explain one example of how the Civil War and its aftermath changed the power of the federal government in the period from 1861 to 1877.
   (B) Briefly explain one example of how the Civil War changed American society in the period from 1861 to 1865.
   (C) Briefly explain one example of how the Civil War changed American politics in the period from 1861 to 1865.

Document-Based Question

1. Evaluate the extent to which Reconstruction changed the lives of Black Americans in the period from 1865 to 1877.

Document 1

Source: Garrison Frazier, a Black Baptist minister, meeting with Secretary of War Edwin Stanton and Major-General William Tecumseh Sherman, Savannah, Georgia, January 12, 1865

"The way we can best take care of ourselves is to have land, and turn in and till it by our labor—that is, by the labor of women, and children, and old men—and we can soon maintain ourselves and have something to spare; and to assist the Government, the young men should enlist in the service of the Government, and serve in such manner as they may be wanted. . . . We want to be placed on land until we are able to buy it and make it our own."

Document 2

Source: *Charleston Mercury,* January 13, 1865

"It was on account of encroachments upon the institution of slavery by the sectional majority of the old Union, that South Carolina seceded from that Union. . . .

She stands upon her institutions—and there she will fall in their defen[s]e. We want no Confederate Government without our institutions. And we will have none. Sink or swim, live or die, we stand by them, and are fighting for them this day. . . . We are free men, and we chose to fight for ourselves—we want no slaves to fight for us . . . Hack at the root of the Confederacy—our institutions—our civilization—and you kill the cause as dead as a boiled crab."

Document 3

Source: Charles Rauschenberg, Freedmen's Bureau Agent, Report from Albany, Georgia, 1867

"The majority of complaints that have been made at this Office by both races have found their origin in contracts, where freedmen received as compensation for their labor a certain share in the crop. The majority of the plantations in my division were worked under such contracts. The freedman claims under such contracts frequently that he has no other work to do but to cultivate and gather the crop, that being a partner in the concern he ought to be allowed to exercise his own judgement in the management of the plantation, that he ought to be permitted to loose time, when it suits his convenience to do so and when according to his judgement his labor is not needed in the field, that he ought to have a voice in the manner of gathering and dividing the corn and cotton and in the grinning, packing and selling of the latter product—while the employer claims that the labor of the employee belongs to him for the whole year, that he must labor for him six days during the week . . . that he must have the sole and exclusive management of the plantation and that the freedman must obey his orders and do all work required."

Document 4

Source: Sharecropping Agreement, 1870

"Contract made the 3rd day of January in the year 1870 between us the free people who have signed this paper of one part, and our employer, Willis P. Bocock, of the other part. . . . We are to furnish the necessary labor . . . and are to have all proper work done, ditching, fencing, repairing, etc., as well as cultivating and saving the crops of all kinds, so as to put and keep the land we occupy and tend in good order for cropping, and to make a good crop ourselves; and to do our fair share of job work about the place. . . . We are to be responsible for the good conduct of ourselves, our hands, and families, and agree that all shall be respectful to employer, owners, and manager, honest, industrious, and careful about every thing . . . and then our employer agrees that he and his manager shall treat us kindly, and help us to study our interest and do our duty. If any hand or family proves to be of bad character, or dishonest, or lazy, or disobedient, or any way unsuitable our employer or manager has the right, and we have the right, to have such turned off. . . .

For the labor and services of ourselves and hands rendered as above stated, we are to have one third part of all the crops, or their net-proceeds, made and secured, or prepared for market by our force. . . .

We are to be furnished by our employer through his manager with provisions if we call for them . . . to be charged to us at fair market prices.

And whatever may be due by us, or our hands to our employer for provisions or any thing else, during the year, is to be a lien on our share of the crops, and is to be retained by him out of the same before we receive our part."

Document 5

Source: First Black Legislators, Forty-First and Forty-Second Congress, 1872

Library of Congress, LC-DIG-ppmsca-17564

Document 6

Source: Abram Colby, a formerly enslaved Black person and Georgia state legislator, *Testimony Taken by the Joint Select Committee to Inquire into the Condition of Affairs in the Late Insurrectionary States,* 1872

"Colby: On the 29th of October 1869, [the Klansmen] broke my door open, took me out of bed, took me to the woods and whipped me three hours or more and left me for dead. They said to me, 'Do you think you will ever vote another damned Radical [Republican] ticket?' . . . I said, 'If there was an election tomorrow, I would vote the Radical ticket.' They set in and whipped me a thousand licks more . . .

Question: What is the character of those men who were engaged in whipping you?

Colby: Some are first-class men in our town. One is a lawyer, one a doctor, and some are farmers. . . . They had their pistols and they took me in my night-clothes and carried me from home. They hit me five thousand blows. . . . About two days before they whipped me they offered me $5,000 to go with them and said they would pay me $2,502 in cash if I would let another man go to the legislature in my place. I told them that I would not do it if they would give me all the county was worth.

The worst thing was . . . my mother, wife and daughter were in the room when they came. . . . My little daughter begged them not to carry me away. They drew up a gun and actually frightened her to death. She never got over it until she died."

Document 7

Source: Representative Robert B. Elliot, Republican, South Carolina, 1874

"Sir, equality before the law is now the broad, universal, glorious rule and mandate of the Republic. No State can violate that. Kentucky and Georgia may crowd their statute-books with retrograde and barbarous legislation; they may rejoice in the odious eminence of their consistent hostility to all the great steps of human progress . . . but, if Congress that enforce the great guarantees which the Supreme Court has declared to be the one pervading purpose of all the recent amendments, then their unwise and unenlightened conduct will fall with the same weight upon the gentlemen from those States who now lend their influence to defeat this bill, as upon the poorest slave who once had no rights which the honorable gentlemen were bound to respect. . . .

The results of the war, as seen in reconstruction, have settled forever the political status of my race."

Long-Essay Questions

2. Evaluate the extent to which westward expansion changed ideas about an American identity in the period from 1844 to 1877.

3. Evaluate the extent to which different regional economic systems contributed to the causes of the Civil War.

4. Evaluate the extent to which the policies of the Lincoln administration contributed to Union victory in the Civil War in the period from 1861 to 1865.

PERIOD 6 1865–1898

A Gilded Age

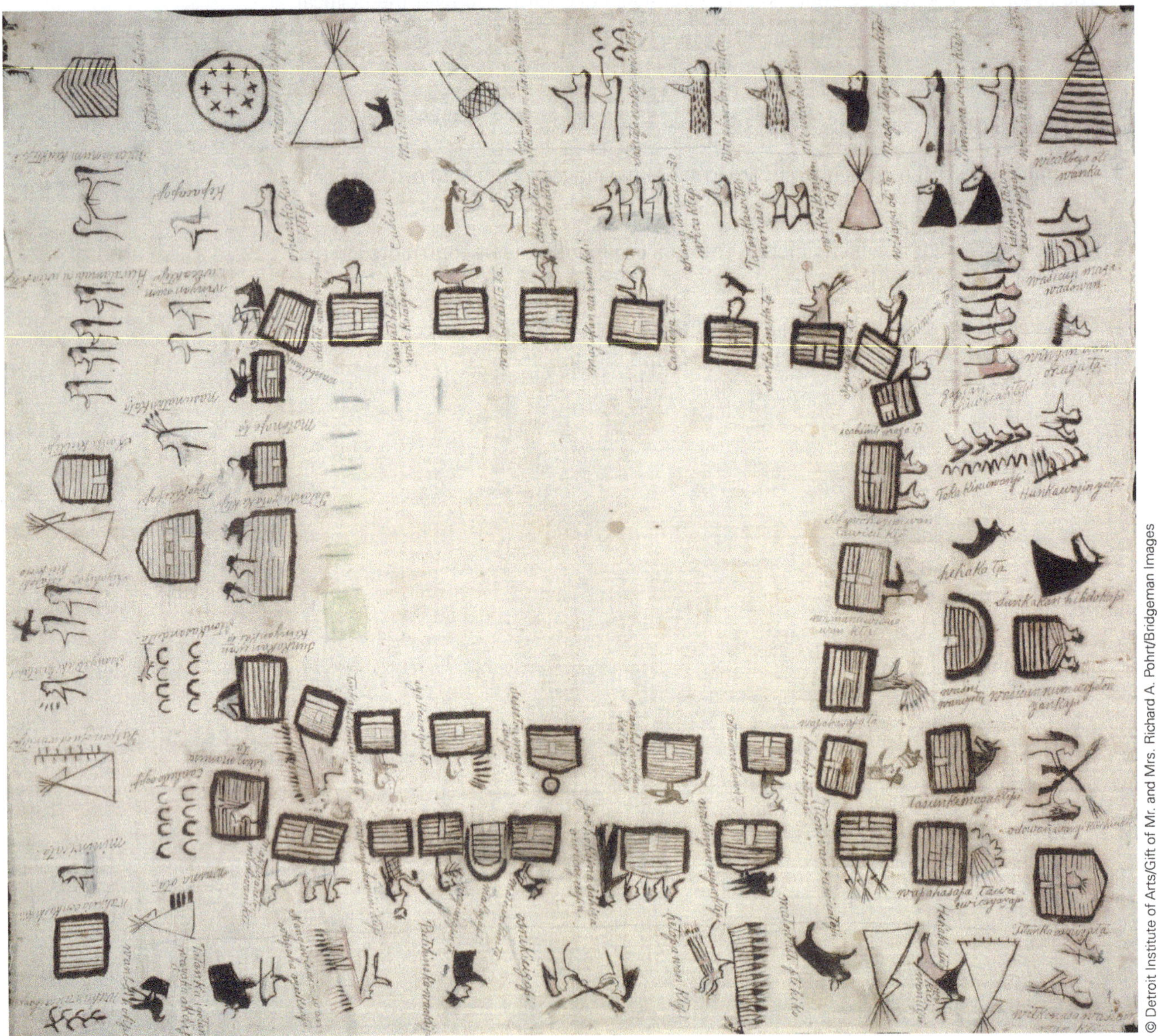

Dakota Sioux Winter Count, 1911 Plains Indians used winter counts to record major events in a tribe's history in pictographs, each of which summarized a major event in a given year. This winter count records the history of the Yanktonai tribe between 1823 and 1911. According to the translations Linea Sundstrom provided for the Buechel Memorial Lakota Museum, some of the events portrayed here include: "1823 Pictograph of white attack on earthlodge," "1827 Starvation winter. The Santees ate two of their own people," "1853 They killed a lone Crow warrior who was on a suicide charge. This was on the Powder River," and "1890 Sitting Bull was killed; also Spotted Elk."

Contextualizing Period 6

MODULE 6.1

The generation after the Civil War experienced upheavals and hardships but also opportunities and prosperity. Mark Twain called the period from the end of the Civil War through the end of the nineteenth century "The Gilded Age," a nod to the process of gilding, which can disguise something cheap by covering it with a thin layer of gold. Although Twain's term has stuck to the age, it is a satire that obscures more than it reveals.

Two broad changes—a second industrial revolution and millions of immigrants mostly from southern and eastern Europe—defined this age. As a result, many of America's towns and cities grew from ports of trade to centers of industrial production. The conditions in factories and the lives of the Americans who worked in them were often dire, and these production centers led to paradoxical results—increased wealth for most Americans as well as reform movements and worker protests. During this period, the American middle and upper classes continued building the consumer culture that began in the early nineteenth century.

Yet for many Americans, these years accelerated—or simply changed the nature of—the oppression that they experienced before the Civil War. Black Americans were relegated to second-class citizenship by the Jim Crow laws and sharecropping systems of the South; Mexican Americans struggled with growing Anglo settlements in the West; and women faced a cultural expectation of domesticity that allowed some participation in reform efforts but denied them basic rights including suffrage.

During the Gilded Age, the West was integrated into the U.S. economy through the building of transcontinental railroads, the vast and varied migration of settlers, and the conquest and forced relocation of American Indians. Many Americans assumed that the diversity present in both the West and in America's booming urban centers was temporary and that these people would merge into a "melting pot" of cultures based on the economic, social, and political structures of the predominantly white, northern European American majority. Yet many immigrants, American Indians, and Mexican Americans resisted wholesale assimilation as they sought to define their own identity.

Politically, the nation was closely divided, as government grappled with the destabilizing effects of industrialization. Americans argued over whether the government had an obligation to promote or control corporations for the sake of the common good. Workers and farmers sought relief through organizing and collective action, but labor unions and farmers' political efforts had limited success in the era. Throughout this period, reformers and civic leaders debated whether the people who were destabilized by the industrial revolution, including small businessmen and the working poor, could be better helped through government intervention or through private philanthropy.

Period 6: What's Inside 1865–1898

MODULE	AP® THEMATIC FOCUS
6.1 Contextualizing Period 6	While the Civil War devastated the South, northern manufacturers had thrived from the industrial needs of the war effort. The dependency of industrial production, and the collapse of the southern economy, shifted economic power to the North and West. The Civil War and Reconstruction also left unresolved the future rights and freedoms for the nation's new Black citizens, as well as leaving open the future of native peoples in the West. Changes in production and distribution inaugurated a second industrial revolution in the United States. Changes in the economy extended the interconnected national economy from before the Civil War and led to the transformation of cities from centers of trade to production centers which fueled immigration. Likewise, the second industrial revolution, like the first, led to new opportunities and conflicts between labor and capital and, with completion of the transcontinental railroad, encouraged new westward expansion. This expansion led to ongoing conflict with American Indians.
6.2 Westward Expansion: Economic Development	**Migration and Settlement** Completion of the transcontinental railroad and the concurrent expansion of the U.S. railroad network facilitated the large-scale migration of white American settlers to the Great Plains and Far West. Settlers in the West used hard work and technological innovations to transform their environments for their benefit.
6.3 Westward Expansion: Social and Cultural Developments	**Migration and Settlement** Despite many obstacles posed by difficult terrain, daunting climate, and unfamiliar inhabitants of the land they sought to harness, migrants were attracted to the West by new economic opportunities in mining, lumber, ranching, and commercial farming. Military conquest and oft-broken treaties resulted in the forced relocation of American Indians to reservations. American Indians struggled to maintain their cultural and tribal identities as reformers promoted a policy of assimilation.
6.4 The "New South"	**American and National Identity** Despite the expansion of the railroads and construction of textile mills, efforts to industrialize the South after the Civil War met with limited success as sharecropping and tenant farming continued to be the region's main economic activities. Black Americans in the South were denied equal rights as the Supreme Court upheld the Jim Crow laws permitting legal segregation in its 1896 *Plessy v. Ferguson* ruling.
6.5 Technological Innovation	**Work, Exchange, and Technology** Business entrepreneurs used technological innovations, new inventions, and greater extraction of natural resources to raise production to new heights. These innovations transformed the U.S. economy and the lives of many Americans.
6.6 The Rise of Industrial Capitalism	**Work, Exchange, and Technology** New corporate and financial practices emerged as businesses sought to create and consolidate large-scale corporations and control the production and distribution of goods. Consolidation allowed a few corporations to control production in several key industries.
6.7 Labor in the Gilded Age	**Work, Exchange, and Technology** While some workers benefitted from the second industrial revolution, others, in response to the growing power of large corporations, mechanization, and the loss of autonomy, created labor unions and used strikes to fight for better wages and working conditions. In most cases, states and the federal government favored business interests over workers in labor disputes, some of which became violent.
6.8 Immigration and Migration in the Gilded Age	**Migration and Settlement** During the late 1800s, immigration to the United States soared as waves of so-called "new immigrants" from southern and eastern Europe arrived alongside "old immigrants" from northern and western Europe. Most European immigrants settled in big cities along the East Coast or in the Midwest, while immigrants from East Asia settled in the West. The surge of immigration led to debates over assimilation, a nativist backlash, and passage of the first race-based federal immigration legislation, the Chinese Exclusion Act (1882).

MODULE	AP® THEMATIC FOCUS
6.9 Responses to Immigration in the Gilded Age	**Migration and Settlement** American cities grew dramatically as hundreds of thousands of Black Americans from the South and millions of Europeans came in search of economic opportunities. Urban newcomers clustered in ethnic neighborhoods as many cities struggled to cope with the challenges of rapid growth. In large cities, politics was dominated by corrupt political machines, which provided a measure of basic social services in exchange for votes. Meanwhile, elite and middle-class reformers generated different ideas about the capacities of immigrants to assimilate, and how to assist immigrants in their new country.
6.10 Development of the Middle Class	**Social Structures** Industrialization and urbanization raised the standard of living for most Americans and provided new opportunities for leisure-time pursuits, which varied by social class and gender. An emerging middle class led to an expansion of consumer culture. Certain industrialists, notably Andrew Carnegie in his "Gospel of Wealth," promoted philanthropy as some academics called for a new social order.
6.11 Reform in the Gilded Age	**Social Structures** Many reformers, including economists, artists, socialists, and champions of the "Social Gospel," proposed various reforms to help Americans who suffered from the effects of the second industrial revolution. Also during this period, women increasingly sought to influence society through social and political reform.
6.12 Controversies over the Role of Government in the Gilded Age	**Politics and Power** The ideologies of laissez-faire economics and Social Darwinism placed the burden of success or failure on the individual while restraining the federal government from intervention in the economy during the Gilded Age. U.S. policymakers increasingly looked overseas for new markets and resources to fuel the second industrial revolution.
6.13 Politics in the Gilded Age	**Politics and Power** Federal elections were closely contested during the two decades after Reconstruction as partisanship reached new heights, even though it was a time of weak federal government. Faced with falling food prices and overproduction, farmers joined new movements for cooperative self-help and political action, including the creation of the Populist Party. In the aftermath of the Panic of 1893, Republicans emerged as the majority party, while Democrats tightened their control of the South and the Populist Party faded.
6.14 Continuity and Change in Period 6	The period between 1865 and 1898 witnessed enormous social and economic change, but also persistent, and often unfortunate, continuities. In the aftermath of the Civil War, the liberation of more than four million enslaved people represented one of the largest social transformations in U.S. history, while the expansive growth of American cities was fueled by both migration from the countryside and immigration from Europe and Asia. Also during this period, transportation networks continued to connect the regions of the United States, while industrial production and innovation continued apace. Likewise, abiding racial disparities and discrimination, class conflict, and debates about the role of gender in social life continued throughout this period.
Support and Practice	• Practice writing and thinking historically in each module. • See the Period Review of key concepts, events, people, and dates after the last module. • Try the AP® Exam Practice at the end of the period.

MODULE 6.2

Westward Expansion: Economic Development

FOCUS

Federal policy, foreign investment, and expansion of the railroads were essential in transforming the West. Determined settlers, lured to the Great Plains by the appeal of cheap land and a fresh start, found it less hospitable than earlier settlers who had looked for economic opportunity beyond the Appalachians.

As you read this module, consider the historical linkages between the causes and effects of western settlement. Take note of how and why the federal government and private business interests promoted western settlement, and how western settlement shaped the lives of migratory farmers who sought to build an agricultural economy in the West.

The Great Plains

Great Plains
The territory between the Mississippi River and the Rocky Mountains characterized by flat topography and a drier climate, consisting mainly of prairie and grassland. Much of this region was acquired by the United States through the Louisiana Purchase in 1803.

In the mid-nineteenth century, the western borderlands of the United States lay in the **Great Plains**. Consisting of the wide expanse of land between the Rocky Mountains to the west and the Mississippi River to the east, the Great Plains is a semiarid region with an average yearly rainfall sufficient to sustain short grasslands but not many trees. Prospects for farmers, particularly in the drier western part of the region known as the High Plains, did not appear promising.

In 1878, geologist John Wesley Powell issued a report that questioned whether the land beyond the easternmost portion of the Great Plains could support small farming. Lack of rainfall, he argued, would make it difficult or even impossible for farmers to support themselves on family farms of 160 acres. Instead, he recommended that for the plains to prove economically sustainable, settlers would have to work much larger stretches of land, around 2,560 acres (4 square miles). This would provide ample room to raise livestock under dry conditions.

Powell's words of caution did little to diminish Americans' conviction, dating back to Thomas Jefferson, that small farmers would populate territories brought under U.S. jurisdiction and renew democratic values as they ventured forth. Charles Dana Wilber summed up the view of those who saw no barriers to the expansion of small farmers in the plains. Rejecting the idea that the Great Plains should remain a "perpetual desert," Wilber asserted that "in reality there is no desert anywhere except by man's permission or neglect." Along with millions of others, he had great faith in Americans' ability to turn the Great Plains into a place where Jefferson's republican vision could take root and prosper.

 REVIEW

- What were the basic challenges facing prospective farmers on the Great Plains?
- Why were settlers undeterred by these challenges?

Federal Policy and Foreign Investment

Despite the popular association of the West with individual initiative and self-sufficiency, the federal government played a huge role in facilitating the settlement of the West. Federal lawmakers enacted legislation offering free or cheap land to settlers and to mining, lumber, and railroad companies. The U.S. government also provided subsidies for transporting mail and military supplies, recruited soldiers to subdue the American Indians who stood in the way of expansion, and appointed officials to govern the territories. Through these efforts, the government provided a necessary measure of safety and stability for new businesses to start up and grow as well as interconnected transportation and communication systems to supply workers and promote opportunities to develop new markets across North America.

Along with federal policy, foreign investment helped fuel development of the West. Lacking sufficient funds of its own, the United States turned to Europe to finance the sale of public bonds and private securities. European firms also invested in American mines, with the British leading the way. In 1872, an Englishman wrote that mines in Nevada were "more British than American." The development of the western cattle range—the symbol of the American frontier and the heroic cowboy—was also funded by overseas financiers. At the height of the cattle boom in the 1880s, British firms supplied some $45 million to underwrite ranch operations. The largest share of money, however, that flowed from Europe to the United States came with the expansion of the railroads, the most important ingredient in opening the West.

The **transcontinental railroad** became the gateway to the West. In 1862, the Republican-led Congress appropriated vast areas of land that railroad companies could use to lay their tracks or sell to raise funds for construction. The Central

AP® EXAM TIP

Understand how government policies affected both the development of big business in the west and the divide between agricultural and commercial markets. Think of this as a way to explore how industrial combinations benefited from government policies while the agricultural sector came to think they were victims of the same system.

transcontinental railroad

A railroad linking the East and West Coasts of North America. Completed in 1869, the transcontinental railroad facilitated the flow of migrants and the development of economic connections between the West and the East.

MAP 6.1 The American West, 1860–1900 Railroads played a key role in the expansion and settlement of the American West. The network of railroads running throughout the West opened the way for extensive migration from the East and for the development of a national market. None of this would have been possible without the land grants provided to the railroads by the U.S. government.

How does this map illustrate the roles of the federal government and private enterprise in opening the American West to settlement?

Science History Images/Alamy

Railroad Construction Crew Chinese and other immigrant groups were instrumental in the construction of the transcontinental railroad and other railway lines in the West. This photo shows Chinese laborers working on the Secret Town Trestle near Sacramento around 1876. In addition to transporting people, railroads were essential to the growth of the western lumber industry, which needed railways to transport timber from forest to sawmill.

How does this photograph reflect the challenges workers faced in constructing the transcontinental railroad?

Pacific Company built from west to east, starting in Sacramento, California. The construction project attracted thousands of Chinese railroad workers. From the opposite direction, the Union Pacific Company began laying track in Council Bluffs, Iowa, and hired mainly Irish workers. In May 1869, the Central Pacific and Union Pacific crews met at Promontory Point, Utah. Workmen from the two companies drove a golden spike to complete the connection.

For many Americans recovering from four years of civil war and still embroiled in Reconstruction, the completion of the transcontinental railroad renewed their faith in the nation's ingenuity and destiny. A wagon train had once taken six to eight weeks to travel across the West. That trip could now be completed by rail in seven days. The railroad allowed both people and goods to move faster and in greater numbers than before. The West was now open not just to hardy farmers, but to anyone who could afford a railroad ticket.

The government-subsidized railroad construction boom also provided new opportunities for corruption. For example, Union Pacific promoters created a fake construction company called the Crédit Mobilier, which they used to funnel government bond and contract money into their own pockets. They also bribed congressmen to avoid investigation into their fraudulent dealings. Despite these efforts, a congressional investigation exposed this corruption in 1872.

AP® EXAM TIP

Railroads and transportation are significant elements of this module. Be sure you can move from defining the relative importance of these concepts to connecting other historical developments such as government subsidies and debates over the role of government in the economy to the overall importance of railroads.

REVIEW

- Explain some of the positive and negative effects of railroad construction in the West.

Homesteaders Farm the Great Plains

Migrant farmers to the West were often called "homesteaders," named for the agricultural "homestead" that they hoped to establish on land west of the Mississippi River. Surviving loneliness, drudgery, and bad weather still did not guarantee financial success for homesteaders.

The economic realities of farming on the plains proved formidable. Despite the image of yeomen farmers—individuals engaged in subsistence farming with the aid of wives and children—most agriculture was geared to commercial transactions. Few farmers were independent or self-reliant. Farmers depended on barter and short-term credit. They borrowed from banks to purchase the additional land necessary to make agriculture economically feasible in the semiarid climate. They also needed loans to buy machinery to help increase production and to sustain their families while they waited for the harvest.

The federal government played a major role in opening up the Great Plains to farmers. The Republican Party of Abraham Lincoln had opposed the expansion of slavery and promoted the virtues of free soil and free labor for white men and their families. During the Civil War, preoccupation with defeating the South did not stop the Republican-controlled Congress from passing the **Homestead Act**. As an incentive for western migration, the act established procedures for distributing 160-acre lots to western settlers, on condition that they develop and farm their land. What most would-be settlers did not know, however, was that lots of 160 acres were not viable in the harsh, dry climate of the Great Plains.

Homestead Act
The Homestead Act of 1862 granted free 160-acre lots to western settlers, on condition that they live on and farm their land for at least five years, as an incentive for western migration.

Innovation and technology bolstered homesteaders' dreams of success. Farmers planted hardy strains of wheat imported from Russia that survived the fluctuations of dry and wet and hot and cold weather. Machines produced by industrial laborers in northeastern factories allowed western farmers to plow tough land and harvest its yield. Steel-tipped plows, threshers, combines, and harvesters expanded production, and windmills and pumping equipment provided sources of power and access to scarce water. These improvements in mechanization led to a significant expansion in agricultural production, which helped to lower food prices for consumers.

The people who accepted the challenge of carving out a new life were a diverse lot. The Great Plains attracted a large number of immigrants from Europe, some 2 million by 1900. Minnesota and the Dakotas welcomed communities of settlers from Sweden and Norway. Nebraska housed a considerable population of Germans, Swedes, Danes, and Czechs. About one-third of the people who migrated to the northern plains came directly from a foreign country.

Railroads and land companies lured settlers to the plains with tales of the fabulous possibilities that awaited their arrival. The federal government had given railroads generous grants of public land on which to build their tracks as well as parcels surrounding the tracks that they could sell off to raise revenue for construction. Western railroads advertised in both the United States and Europe, proclaiming that migrants to the plains would find "the garden spot of the world."

Having enticed prospective settlers with exaggerated claims, railroads offered bargain rates to transport them to their new homes. Families and friends often journeyed together and rented an entire car on the train, known as "the immigrant car," in which they loaded their possessions, supplies, and even livestock. Often migrants came to the end of the rail line before reaching their destination. They completed the trip by wagon or stagecoach.

Commercial advertising alone did not account for the desire to journey westward. Settlers who had successfully made the trip wrote to relatives and neighbors back east and in the old country about the chance to start fresh. Linda Slaughter, the wife of an army doctor in the Dakotas, gushed: "The farms which have been opened in the vicinity of Bismarck have proven highly productive, the soil being kept moist by frequent rains. Vegetables of all kinds are grown with but little trouble."

Those who took the chance shared a faith in the future and a willingness to work hard and endure misfortune. They found their optimism and spirits sorely tested. Despite the company of family members and friends, settlers faced a lonely existence on the vast expanse of the plains. Homesteads were spread out, and a feeling of isolation became a routine part of daily life.

With few trees around, early settlers constructed sod houses. These structures let in little light but a good deal of moisture, keeping them gloomy and damp. A Nebraskan who lived in this kind of house jokingly remarked: "There was running water in our sod house. It ran through the roof." Bugs, insects, and rodents, like the rain, often found their way inside to make living in such shelters even more uncomfortable.

If these dwellings were bleak, the climate posed even greater challenges. The plains did experience an unusual amount of rainfall in the late 1870s and early 1880s, but severe drought quickly followed. A plague of grasshoppers ravaged the northern plains in the late 1870s, destroying fruit trees and plants. Intense heat in the summer alternated with frigid temperatures in the winter.

The Norwegian American writer O. E. Rolvaag, in *Giants in the Earth* (1927), described the extreme hardships that accompanied the fierce weather: "Blizzards from out of the northwest raged, swooped down and stirred up a greyish-white fury, impenetrable to human eyes. As soon as these monsters tired, storms from the northeast were sure to come, bringing more snow."

Farmers endured hardships to make their living in the West. They struggled to raise crops in an often-inhospitable climate in hopes that their yields would be sold for a profit. Instead of raising crops solely for their own use, farmers concentrated on the cash crops of corn and wheat. The price of these commodities depended on the vagaries of an international market that connected American farmers to growers and consumers throughout the world.

When supply expanded and demand remained relatively stable during the 1880s and 1890s, prices fell. This **deflation** made it more difficult for farmers to pay back their loans, and banks moved to foreclose. Falling crop prices led to soaring debt and forced many farmers into bankruptcy and off their land, while others were fortunate enough to survive and make a living.

Under these challenging circumstances, almost half of the homesteaders in the Great Plains picked up and moved either to another farm or to a nearby city. Large operators bought up the farms they left behind and ran them like big businesses. Therefore, farming became increasingly commercialized and consolidated over the course of the second half of the nineteenth century.

The federal government unwittingly aided this process of commercialization and consolidation, to the benefit of large companies. The government sought to make bigger plots of land available in regions where small farming had proved impractical. The Desert Land Act (1877) offered 640 acres to settlers who would irrigate the land, but it brought small relief for farmers because the land was too dry. These properties soon fell out of the hands of homesteaders and into those of cattle ranchers. The Timber and Stone Act (1878) allowed homesteaders to buy 160 acres of forestland at $2.50 an acre. Lumber companies hired "dummy entrymen" to file claims and then quickly transferred the titles and added the parcels to their growing tracts of woodland.

AP® EXAM TIP

When writing about government policies, corporations, or farmers in this era, you should move from universal statements such as, "big business benefited from government policies," to specific examples of such developments. Think about connecting an example from the textbook such as hydraulic mining or the activities of the Central Pacific or Union Pacific railroad companies.

REVIEW

- Explain the relationship between federal policies and homesteading during this period.

Women in the West

While the image of the hardy homesteader was often imagined as a male in the field, the women of the homesteading family were responsible for making homesteads more bearable. Mothers and daughters were in charge of household duties, cooking the meals, canning fruits and vegetables, and washing and ironing clothing. Despite the drudgery of this work, women contributed significantly to the economic well-being of the family by occasionally taking in boarders and selling milk, butter, and eggs.

In addition, a surprisingly large number of single women staked out homestead claims by themselves. Some were young, unmarried women seeking, like their male counterparts, economic opportunity. Others were widows attempting to take care of their children after their husband's death.

Kansas State Historical Society

Woman Homesteader in Kansas Ada McColl was among the thousands of homesteaders who moved west in the late nineteenth century. This 1893 photo shows her gathering buffalo chips (dry dung) to use for heating and cooking fuel, just as the American Indians had elsewhere on the Great Plains.

What hardships facing homesteaders are evident in this photograph?

One such widow, Anne Furnberg, settled a homestead in the Dakota Territory in 1871. Born in Norway, she had lived with her husband and son in Minnesota. After her husband's death, the thirty-four-year-old Furnberg moved with her son near Fargo and eventually settled on eighty acres of land. She farmed, raised chickens and a cow, and sold butter and eggs in town.

The majority of women who settled in the Dakotas were between the ages of twenty-one and twenty-five, had never been married, and were native-born children of immigrant parents. A sample of nine counties in the Dakotas shows that more than 4,400 women became landowners. Nora Pfundheler, a single woman, explained her motivation: "Well I was 21 and had no prospects of doing anything. The land was there, so I took it."

AP® WORKING with EVIDENCE

Source: Ida Lindgren, Swedish homesteader, Letter, August 25, 1874

> "[W]e have not had rain [on the Kansas Prairie] since the beginning of June, and then with the heat and often strong winds as well, you can imagine how everything has dried out. There has also been a general lamentation and fear for the coming year. We have gotten a fair amount of wheat, rye, and oats, for they are ready so early, but no one here will get corn or potatoes. We have a few summer potatoes, but many don't even have that, and we thought and hoped we would get a good crop of other potatoes, but will evidently get none. Instead of selling the oats and part of the rye as we had expected, we must now use them for the livestock, since there was no corn. We are glad we have the oats (for many don't have any and must feed wheat to the stock) and had hoped to have the corn leaves to add to the fodder. But then one fine day there came millions, trillions of grasshoppers in great clouds, hiding the sun, and coming down onto the fields, eating up *everything* that was still there, the leaves on the trees, peaches, grapes, cucumbers, onions, cabbage, everything,

everything. Only the peach stones still hung on the trees, showing what had once been there.

They are not the kind of grasshoppers we see in Sweden but are large, grayish ones. Now most of them have moved southward, to devastate other areas since there was nothing more to consume here. Certainly it is sad and distressing and depressing for the body and soul to find that no matter how hard one drudges and works, one still has nothing, less than nothing."

Questions for Analysis

1. Identify the difficulties Lindgren's family encountered as homesteaders in Kansas.
2. Describe Lindgren's purpose for writing an account of her daily life.
3. Explain why immigrant families settled on the Great Plains.

Once families settled in and towns began to develop, women, married and single, directed some of their energies to moral reform and extending democracy on the frontier. Because of loneliness and grueling work, some men turned to alcohol for relief. Law enforcement in newly established communities was often no match for the saloons that catered to a raucous and drunken crowd. In their roles as wives, mothers, and sisters, many women tried to remove the source of alcohol-induced violence that disrupted both family relationships and public decorum.

In Kansas in the late 1870s, women flocked to the state's Woman's Christian Temperance Union, founded by Amanda M. Way. Although they did not yet have the vote, in 1880, these women vigorously campaigned for a constitutional amendment that banned the sale of liquor.

Temperance women also threw their weight behind the issue of women's suffrage. In 1884, Kansas women established the statewide Equal Suffrage Association, which delivered to the state legislature a petition with seven thousand signatures in support of women's suffrage. Their attempt failed, but in 1887, women won the right to vote and run for office in all Kansas municipal elections. Julia Robinson, who campaigned for women's suffrage in Kansas, recalled the positive role that some men played: "My father had always said his family of girls had just as much right to help the government as if we were boys, and mother and he had always taught us to expect Woman Suffrage in our day." Kansas did not grant equal voting rights in state and national elections until 1912, but women obtained full suffrage before then in many western states, starting with the Wyoming Territory in 1869.

REVIEW

- Why did the temperance and women's suffrage movements achieve early success in the West?

Farmers Unite

From the end of the Civil War to the mid-1890s, increased production of wheat and cotton, two of the most important American crops, led to a precipitous drop in the price for these crops. Falling prices created a debt crisis for many farmers.

Most American farmers were independent businessmen who borrowed money to pay for land, seed, and equipment. When their crops were harvested and sold, they repaid their debts with the proceeds. As prices fell, farmers increased production in an effort to cover their debts. This tactic led to a greater supply of farm produce in the marketplace and even lower prices. Unable to pay back loans, many farmers lost their property in foreclosures to the banks that held their mortgages and furnished them credit.

To make matters worse, farmers lived isolated lives. Spread out across vast acres of rural territory, farmers had few social and cultural diversions. As the farm economy declined, more and more of their children left the monotony of rural America behind and headed for cities in search of new opportunities and a better life.

Early efforts to organize farmers were motivated by a desire to counteract the isolation of rural life by creating new forms of social interaction and cultural engagement. In 1867, Oliver H. Kelley founded the Patrons of Husbandry to brighten the lonely existence of rural Americans through educational and social activities. Known as the **Grange** (from the French word for "granary"), the association grew rapidly in the early 1870s, especially in the Midwest and the South. Between 1872 and 1874, approximately fourteen thousand new Grange chapters were established.

Grange
An organization founded in 1867 to meet the practical economic, social, and cultural needs of farmers. Grangers advocated the use of farm cooperatives and took an active role in the promotion of the economic and political interests of farmers during the 1870s.

Grangers also formed farm cooperatives to sell their crops at higher prices and pool their purchasing power to buy finished goods at wholesale prices. The Grangers' interest in promoting the collective economic interests of farmers led to their increasing involvement in politics. Rather than forming a separate political party, Grangers endorsed candidates who favored their cause.

Perhaps the Grangers' most important objective was the regulation of shipping and grain storage prices. In many areas, individual railroads had monopolies on both of these services and, as a result, were able to charge farmers higher-than-usual rates to store and ship their crops. By electing sympathetic state legislators, Grangers managed to obtain regulations that placed a ceiling on the prices railroads and grain elevators could charge.

The Supreme Court temporarily upheld these victories in *Munn v. Illinois* (1877). In 1886, however, in *Wabash v. Illinois*, the Supreme Court reversed itself and struck down these state regulatory laws as hindering the free flow of interstate commerce.

The Grange Movement, 1876
As the farmer's central placement in this lithograph implies, farmers were the heart of the Grange movement. The phrase at the center, "I Feed You All!" is a variation on the movement's motto, "I Pay for All." A farmer with a plow and two horses stands at the center of the scene providing food for all, while other occupational types positioned around him echo a similar refrain based on their profession.

What argument does this poster make about farmers' role in the U.S. economy?

- Explain the economic and environmental hardships western farmers faced and some of the ways they countered these hardships.

AP® Skills Workshop: Thinking Historically

Sourcing a Document to Establish Significance

As you recall from Modules 4.3 and 5.9, historians interpret primary sources by **sourcing**, in which they consider four attributes of a source:

- **Historical Situation:** What is a specific piece of historical information that connects the primary source to the broader historical context?
- **Intended Audience:** Who is supposed to be reading/seeing/hearing this source?
- **Purpose:** What is the statement/image for, according to the speaker/creator?
- **Point of View (POV):** What are the source's biases and outlook on the subject?

To better judge the usability of primary sources, historians also determine the **significance** of these attributes. Historians determine significance in light of the questions they ask, or in your case, the prompt you answer. Consider this primary source from Module 6.2 (pages 521–522):

Source: Ida Lindgren, Swedish homesteader, Letter, August 25, 1874

"[W]e have not had rain [on the Kansas Prairie] since the beginning of June, and then with the heat and often strong winds as well, you can imagine how everything has dried out. There has also been a general lamentation and fear for the coming year. We have gotten a fair amount of wheat, rye, and oats, for they are ready so early, but no one here will get corn or potatoes. We have a few summer potatoes, but many don't even have that, and we thought and hoped we would get a good crop of other potatoes, but will evidently get none. Instead of selling the oats and part of the rye as we had expected, we must now use them for the livestock, since there was no corn. We are glad we have the oats (for many don't have any and must feed wheat to the stock) and had hoped to have the corn leaves to add to the fodder. But then one fine day there came millions, trillions of grasshoppers in great clouds, hiding the sun, and coming down onto the fields, eating up *everything* that was still there, the leaves on the trees, peaches, grapes, cucumbers, onions, cabbage, everything, everything. Only the peach stones still hung on the trees, showing what had once been there.

They are not the kind of grasshoppers we see in Sweden but are large, grayish ones. Now most of them have moved southward, to devastate other areas since there was nothing more to consume here. Certainly it is sad and distressing and depressing for the body and soul to find that no matter how hard one drudges and works, one still has nothing, less than nothing."

Now, consider this prompt:

Evaluate the extent to which women in the West were offered more opportunities than women in the East after 1865.

(continued)

When you analyze this source in light of the prompt, some of the attributes of its sourcing become more significant than others. Considering a document's significance will help you decide which sourcing feature to explain when writing a DBQ. Here's a table to show you how this sourcing for significance could work:

Sourcing	Analysis	Significant for responding to prompt?	Explanation
Historical Situation	Lindgren is likely a beneficiary of opportunities like the Homestead Act.	Yes	Lindgren likely went West with her family to take advantage of inexpensive land. This speaks to the historical significance of federal efforts to promote western settlement such as the Homestead Act, which provided settlers with free land.
Intended Audience	This letter is likely for an individual who is familiar to the author. It is a private letter from a young immigrant woman to an unknown recipient.	No	While women were able to write letters in both the East and the West, and this could point to the same opportunities in both, we don't know the recipient of the letter, and therefore the intended audience is not particularly significant to consider opportunities for women in the West.
Purpose	The purpose of Lindgren's letter is likely to explain to individuals back East that economic opportunities in the West are limited, at least in agriculture.	Yes	This source is significant to the prompt because Lindgren is describing the limited opportunities for agriculturalists in the West. This implies women as well, and therefore is significant to responding to the prompt.
Point of View	Ida Lindgren is quite bitter about her situation, and depressed. The geographic realities of the West have made success in farming very difficult.	Yes	Lindgren's point of view makes clear that she has very little opportunity in the West. This point of view is significant to the prompt because it shows that her dependence on agricultural production is similar to the majority of American women during this period, who were often agriculturalists.

As you recall from Modules 5.9 and 5.10, when you source a document, you should provide a brief **document summary**, **connect that document to your argument**, and **analyze the document** according to one of the **sourcing categories** (historical situation, intended audience, purpose, or point of view). Let's try it here with Ida Lindgren's document above, and let's fit it within a thesis's line of reasoning.

(continued)

As you recall, the prompt is:

Evaluate the extent to which women in the West were offered more opportunities than women in the East after 1865.

A possible thesis statement for this prompt could be (with the portion of the line of reasoning underlined that we'll use in a sample body paragraph):

> While the West provided some opportunities for women to own land, the land they acquired offered few opportunities for economic prosperity or independence. **[claim]** <u>The climate of the West,</u> the unpredictability of the agricultural market, and the eventual overproduction of agricultural products ultimately undermined what opportunities the West offered to women in the late nineteenth century. **[line of reasoning]**

Here is a sample paragraph where sourcing is integrated into a CSE statement.

> Women had opportunities to acquire land in the West, but the land they acquired often offered little opportunity in itself because of the climate of the region. **[sub-argument]** For example, Ida Lindgren, a farmer, was quite depressed that the climate of the West proved so inhospitable to farming. **[claim summarizing Lindgren's letter]** As a farmer, Lindgren's opportunities were dependent upon climactic factors beyond her control, like temperature, rainfall, and the quality of the soil. Lindgren's opportunities were limited in this regard because of grasshoppers, the heat, and the dryness of the climate. **[support using POV as a *farmer*—note that the sourcing category "POV" has been integrated into the support for the claim ("As a farmer . . .")]** Therefore, while the federal government subsidized and encouraged people such as Lindgren to move west, the land and the climate of the West literally did not bear fruit, and their opportunities often proved limited. **[explanation connecting to sub-argument]**

ACTIVITY

Now try to complete the table below on your own using the same primary source above. Be sure to determine the source's significance in each category in light of the prompt.

Sourcing	Analysis	Significant for responding to prompt?	Explanation
Historical Situation			
Intended Audience			
Purpose			
Point of View			

Once you have completed the chart, write a **CSE** statement that sources one significant attribute of the source, either historical situation, intended audience, purpose, or point of view.

Westward Expansion: Social and Cultural Developments

MODULE 6.3

FOCUS

As you read this module, consider the causes and effects of westward migration on white and Black Americans, European and Asian immigrants, Spanish-speaking populations in the West, and American Indians. Consider specifically how migrants' actions and economic activities changed the West, and how the West was integrated into the larger economy of the United States. Take note of the causes and effects of migration for specific groups of people—farmers, prospectors, and cowboys—and how their plans for economic independence eventually became wage work for larger corporations.

The West attracted a diverse group of settlers. Miners poured into the Black Hills in the Rocky Mountains in search of gold and silver. Despite visions of instant riches, the vast majority found only backbreaking work, danger, and frustration. Miners continued to face hardship and danger as industrial mining operations took over from individual prospectors. By 1900, the mining rush had peaked, and many of the boomtowns that had sprung up around the mining industry had emptied out. Closely related to mining, the lumber industry was less demographically diverse but also followed the pattern of eventual domination by big business.

Cattle ranching and farming in the West also increasingly became controlled by big business. Cowboys worked long hours in tough but boring conditions on the open range. Similarly, commercial farmers who headed west endured great hardships in trying to raise crops in an often-inhospitable climate. Extreme weather and falling crop prices forced many ranchers and farmers out of business, and their lands and businesses were snatched up by larger, consolidated commercial ranching and agricultural enterprises.

Mormon settlers trekked into Utah in search of religious freedom, while Chinese immigrants fled war, starvation, and unemployment on their journey to the West Coast. Federal legislation targeted both groups by banning the Mormon practice of polygamy and excluding further Chinese immigration. Despite difficult conditions, western settlers of all types demonstrated grit and determination not only in surviving, but in improving their lives.

The Mining and Lumber Booms

The discovery of gold in California in 1848 had set this mining frenzy in motion. Over the next thirty years, successive waves of gold and silver strikes in Colorado, Nevada, Washington, Idaho, Montana, and the Dakotas lured individual prospectors with shovels and wash pans. One of the biggest finds came in 1859 with the **Comstock Lode** in the Sierra Nevada. All told, miners extracted around $350 million worth of silver from this source.

Comstock Lode

The Comstock Lode was the first major discovery of silver ore in the United States, and it led to a rush for silver in the West on par with the gold rush in California of 1859. Silver production from the Comstock Lode declined precipitously after the mid-1870s but continued into the early twentieth century.

Library of Congress, LC-USZ62-9889

Hydraulic Mining near French Corral, Nevada County, California, 1866 Hydraulic mining was a technique that used water from high pressure hoses to blast away rock and sediment in the search for deeper veins of gold. As individual miners exhausted surface deposits of gold, corporations brought in new and expensive equipment to continue the search.

How did the industrialization of mining affect the environment?

One of those who came to try to share in the wealth was Samuel Clemens. Like most of his fellow miners, Clemens did not find his fortune in Nevada and soon turned his attention to writing, finally achieving success as the author called Mark Twain, who called the era the Gilded Age.

Like Twain, many of those who flocked to the Comstock Lode and other mining frontiers were men. Nearly half were foreign-born, many of them coming from Mexico or China. Using pans and shovels, prospectors could find only the ore that lay near the surface of the earth and water. Once these initial discoveries were played out, individual prospectors could not afford to buy the equipment needed to dig out the vast deposits of gold and silver buried deep in the earth. As a result, western mining became dominated by big businesses with the financial resources necessary to purchase industrial mining equipment.

When mining became an industry, prospectors became wageworkers. In Virginia City, Nevada, miners labored for $4 a day, an amount that barely covered the expenses of life in a mining boomtown. Moreover, the work was extremely dangerous. Mine shafts extended down more than a thousand feet, and working temperatures regularly exceeded 100 degrees Fahrenheit. Noxious fumes, fires, and floods of scalding water flowed through the shafts, and other threats killed or disabled thousands each year.

Struggling with low pay and dangerous work, western miners sought to organize. In the mid-1860s, unions formed in the Comstock Lode areas of Virginia City and Gold Hill, Nevada. Although these unions had some success, they also provoked a violent backlash from mining companies determined to resist union demands. Companies hired private police forces to help break strikes. Such forces were often assisted by state militias deployed by elected officials with close ties to the companies. For example, in 1892, the governor of Idaho crushed an unruly strike by calling up the National Guard, a confrontation that resulted in the deaths of seven strikers.

In 1893, mine workers formed one of the most militant labor organizations in the nation, the Western Federation of Miners. Within a decade, it had attracted fifty thousand members, although membership did not extend to all ethnicities. The union excluded Chinese, Mexican, and American Indian workers from its ranks.

Men worked the mines, but women flocked to the area as well. In Storey County, Nevada, the heart of the Comstock Lode, the 1875 census showed that women made up about half the population. Most employed women worked long hours as domestic laborers in boarding houses, hotels, and private homes.

Prostitution, which was legal, accounted for the single largest segment of the female workforce. Most prostitutes were between the ages of nineteen and twenty-four, and they entered this occupation because few other well-paying jobs were available to them. The demand for their services remained high among the large population of unmarried men. Yet prostitutes faced constant danger, and many were victims of physical abuse, robbery, and murder.

As early as the 1880s, gold and silver discoveries had played out in the Comstock Lode. Boomtowns, which had sprung up almost overnight, now became ghost towns

Bill Manns/Shutterstock

Prostitution in the West
Prostitution was one of the main sources of employment for women in western mining towns. A legal enterprise at the time, it paid better than other work such as domestic service and teaching. In 1875, in the Comstock region of Nevada, 307 women worked as prostitutes in brothels and saloons similar to the saloon shown here.

What economic and social factors led many younger women to work as prostitutes in mining towns?

as gold and silver deposits dwindled. Even more substantial places like Virginia City, Nevada, experienced a severe decline as the veins of ore ran out. One revealing sign of the city's plummeting fortunes was the drop in the number of prostitutes, which declined by more than half by 1880.

The mining business then shifted from gold and silver to copper, lead, and zinc, centered in Montana and Idaho. As with the early prospectors in California and Nevada, these miners eventually became wageworkers for giant consolidated mining companies. By the end of the nineteenth century, the Amalgamated Copper Company and the American Smelting and Refining Company dominated the industry.

Mining towns that survived became only slightly less rowdy places, but they did settle into more complex patterns of urban living. At its height in the 1870s, Virginia City contained twenty-five thousand residents and was among the largest cities west of the Mississippi River. It provided schools and churches and featured such cultural amenities as theaters and opera houses. Though the population in mining towns remained mainly young and male, the young men were increasingly likely to get married and raise families.

Residents lived in neighborhoods divided by class and ethnicity. For example, in Butte, Montana, the west side of town became home to the middle and upper classes. Mine workers lived on the east side in homes subdivided into apartments and in boardinghouses. The Irish lived in one section, Finns, Swedes, Serbs, Croatians, and Slovenes in other sections. Each group formed its own social, fraternal, and religious organizations to relieve the harsh conditions of overcrowding, poor sanitation, and discrimination. Residents of the east side relied on one another for support and frowned on those who deviated from their code of solidarity. "They didn't try to outdo the other one," one neighborhood woman remarked. "If you did, you got into trouble. . . . If they thought you were a little richer than they were, they wouldn't associate with you." Although western mining towns retained distinctive qualities, in their social and ethnic divisions they came to resemble older cities east of the Mississippi River.

The mining industry created a huge demand for timber, as did the railroad lines that operated in the West. At first, small logging firms moved into the Northwest and

California, cut down all the trees they could, sent them to nearby sawmills for processing, and moved on. By 1900, a few large firms came to dominate the industry and acquired vast tracts of forests. Frederick Weyerhaeuser bought 900,000 acres of prime timberland in the Western Cascades of Oregon, largely bringing an end to the often-chaotic competition of small firms that had characterized the industry in its early days. Increasingly, the western lumber industry became part of a global market that shipped products to Hawaii, South America, and Asia.

Loggers and sawmill workers did not benefit from these changes. Exclusively male, large numbers of workers came from Scandinavia, and only a few were Asian or African American. Men died or lost limbs in cutting down the trees, transporting them on the rivers, or processing the wood in sawmills. As lumber camps and mill villages became urbanized, those who gained the most were the merchants and bankers who supplied the goods and capital.

- How did the mining and lumber industries shape the late-nineteenth-century American economy?
- How did the lives of workers in those industries change over time?

The Life of a Cowboy

There is no greater symbol of the frontier West than the cowboy. As portrayed in novels and film, the cowboy hero was the essence of manhood, an independent figure who fought for justice and defended the honor and virtue of women. Never the aggressor, he fought to protect law-abiding residents of frontier communities.

This romantic image excited generations of American readers and, later, movie and television audiences. In reality, cowboys' lives were much more routine. Rather than working as independent adventurers, they increasingly operated in an industrial setting dominated by large cattle companies.

Cowboys worked for paltry monthly wages, put in long days herding cattle, and spent part of the night guarding them on the open range. Their major task was to make the 1,500-mile **Long Drive** along the Chisholm Trail. Beginning in the late 1860s, cowboys moved cattle from ranches in Texas through Oklahoma to rail depots in Kansas towns such as Abilene and Dodge City; from there, cattle were shipped by train eastward to slaughterhouses in Chicago. Life along the trail was monotonous, and riders had to contend with bad weather, dangerous work, and disease.

Numbering around forty thousand and averaging twenty-four years of age, the cowboys who rode through the Great Plains from Texas to Kansas came from diverse backgrounds. The majority, about 66 percent, was white, mainly southerners who had fought for the South during the Civil War. Most of the rest were divided evenly between Mexicans and Black Americans, some of whom were formerly enslaved and others Union veterans of the Civil War.

Besides experiencing rugged life on the range, Black and Mexican cowboys faced racial discrimination. Jim Perry, a Black cowboy who rode for the three-million-acre XIT Ranch in Texas for more than twenty years, complained: "If it weren't for my damned old black face I'd have been boss of one of these divisions long ago." Mexican *vaqueros*, or cowboys, earned one-third to one-half the wages of white counterparts, whereas Black cowboys were usually paid on a par with white ones.

Because the cattle kingdoms first flourished during Reconstruction, racial discrimination and segregation carried over into the Southwest. On one drive along the route to Kansas, a white boss insisted that a Black cowboy eat and sleep separately from white men and shot at him when he refused to heed this order. Nevertheless, the proximity in which cowboys worked and the need for cooperation to overcome the pitfalls of the Long Drive made it difficult to enforce rigid racial divisions on the open range.

AP® EXAM TIP

The peoples in the West were not just American Indians and white settlers. Rather, the West included a rich tapestry of dynamic cultures consisting of various native peoples, white and Black American settlers, Mexican Americans, and European and Chinese immigrants. Be able to explain how those groups interacted with each other and the physical environment.

REVIEW

- How were the experiences of Black and Mexican cowboys different from and similar to those of white cowboys?
- How did the experiences of cowboys compare to those of miners and lumberjacks during the late nineteenth century?

The Rise of Commercial Ranching

Commercial ranches absorbed cowboys into their expanding operations. Spaniards had originally imported cattle into the Southwest, and by the late nineteenth century, some five million Texas longhorn steers grazed in the area. Cattle that could be purchased in Texas for $3 to $7 fetched a price of $30 to $40 in Kansas.

The extension of railroads across the West opened up a quickly growing market for beef in the East. The development of refrigerated railroad cars guaranteed that meat from slaughtered cattle could reach eastern consumers without spoiling. With money to be made, the cattle industry rose to meet the demand.

Fewer than 40 ranchers owned more than 20 million acres of land. Easterners and Europeans joined the boom and invested money in giant ranches. By the mid-1880s, approximately 7.5 million head of cattle roamed the western ranges, and large cattle ranchers became rich. Cattle ranching had become fully integrated into the national commercial economy.

Then the bubble burst. Ranchers, often already raising more cattle than the market could handle, increasingly faced competition from cattle producers in Canada and Argentina. Prices spiraled downward. Another challenge came from homesteaders who moved into the plains and fenced in their farms with barbed wire, thereby reducing the size of the open range.

Yet the greatest disaster occurred from 1885 to 1887. Two frigid winters, together with a scorching summer drought, destroyed 90 percent of the cattle on the northern plains of the Dakotas, Montana, Colorado, and Wyoming. Under these conditions, outside financial capital to support ranching diminished, and many of the great cattle barons went into bankruptcy. This economic collapse consolidated the remaining cattle industry into even fewer hands. The cowboy, never more than a hired hand, became a laborer for large corporations.

REVIEW

- What economic and environmental factors led to changes in ranching in the West?

American Indian Civilizations and Resistance to U.S. Expansion

The frontier was home to diverse peoples long before white and immigrant settlers appeared. The many native groups who inhabited the West spoke distinct languages, engaged in varied economic activities, and competed with one another for power and resources.

Additionally, the descendants of Spanish conquistadors had lived in the Southwest and California since the sixteenth century, pushing the boundaries of the Spanish empire northward from Mexico. Indeed, Spaniards established the city of Santa Fe as the territorial capital of New Mexico, around the time the English landed at Jamestown, Virginia, in 1607.

By the end of the Civil War, around 350,000 American Indians were living west of the Mississippi. They constituted the surviving remnants of the one million people who had occupied North America for thousands of years before Europeans set foot in America. Some of the tribes, such as the Cherokee, Creek, and Shawnee, had been forcibly removed from traditional homes in the East during Andrew Jackson's presidency in the 1830s.

Given the rich assortment of tribes and nations, it is difficult to generalize about American Indian culture and society. The tribes each adapted in unique ways to the geography and climate of their home territories, spoke their own languages, and had their own history and traditions. Some were hunters, others farmers; some nomadic, others sedentary, living in permanent dwellings.

In New Mexico, for example, Apache people were expert horsemen and fierce warriors, while the Pueblo people built homes out of adobe and developed a flourishing system of agriculture. They also cultivated the land through methods of irrigation that foreshadowed modern practices.

The Pawnee tribe in the Great Plains periodically set fire to the land to improve game hunting and the growth of vegetation. American Indians on the southern plains gradually became enmeshed in the market economy for bison robes, which they sold to white American traders (**Map 6.2**).

The lives of all native peoples were affected by the arrival of Europeans, but the consequences of cross-cultural contact varied considerably depending on the history and circumstances of each tribe. White people trampled on hunting grounds, polluted streams with acid runoff from mines, and introduced native peoples to liquor.

They inflicted the greatest damage through diseases for which American Indians lacked the immunity that Europeans and white Americans had acquired. By 1870, smallpox had wiped out half the population of Plains Indians, while additional waves of cholera, diphtheria, and measles caused serious but lesser harm. Traditional modes of living similarly influenced the impact of such diseases, as nomadic tribes such as the Lakota Sioux were able to flee the contagion, while more stationary agrarian tribes such as the Mandan suffered extreme losses.

As a result, the balance of power among Plains tribes shifted to the more mobile Sioux nation. American Indians were not pacifists, and they engaged in warfare with their enemies in disputes over hunting grounds, horses, and honor. However, the introduction of guns by European and American traders transformed American Indian warfare into a much more deadly affair than had existed previously. And by the mid-nineteenth century, some tribes had become so deeply engaged in the commercial fur trade with white settlers that they had depleted their own hunting grounds.

American Indians had their own approach toward nature and the land they inhabited. While most tribes recognized the concept of private property in ownership of their

MAP 6.2 The American Indian West, late 1800s Western migration posed a threat to the dozens of American Indian tribes and the immense herds of bison in the region. The tribes had signed treaties with the U.S. government recognizing the right to live on their lands. The presence of U.S. forts did not protect the American Indians from settlers who invaded their territories.

Based on this map, what conclusions can you draw about interactions between white settlers and American Indians as indicated by the bison ranges, battles, and forts?

horses, weapons, tools, and shelters, they did not accept private ownership of land, as white pioneers did. By contrast, they viewed the land as the common domain of their tribe, for use by all members. This communitarian outlook also reflected native attitudes toward the environment. American Indians considered human beings not as superior to the rest of nature's creations, but rather as part of an interconnected world of animals, plants, and natural elements. According to this view, all plants and animals were part of a larger spirit world, which flowed from the power of the sun, the sky, and the earth.

Bison (commonly known as buffalo) were central to the religion and society of many tribes. By the mid-nineteenth century, approximately 30 million bison grazed on the Great Plains. Before acquiring guns, American Indians used a variety of means to hunt their prey, including bows and arrows and spears. Some rode horses to chase bison and strategically force them to stampede over cliffs. The meat from buffalo provided food; its hide provided material to construct tepees, blankets, and clothes; bones were crafted into tools, knives, and weapons; dried bison dung served as an excellent source of fuel. It is therefore not surprising that the Plains Indians dressed up in colorful outfits, painted their bodies, and danced to evoke the almighty power of the buffalo and the spiritual presence within it.

American Indian hunting societies, such as the Lakota Sioux and Apache nations, contained gender distinctions. The task of riding horses to hunt bison became men's work; women waited for the hunters to return and then prepared the buffalo meat and hides. Nevertheless, women refused to think of their role as passive; they saw themselves as sharing in the work of providing food, shelter, and clothing for the members of their tribe. Similarly, the religious belief that the spiritual world touched every aspect of the material world gave women an opportunity to experience this transcendent power without the mediation of male leaders.

REVIEW

- Characterize the relationship between the American Indian tribes on the Great Plains and in the West, and the environments in which they lived.

Treaty of Fort Laramie

A treaty of 1851 that sought to confine American Indian tribes on the northern plains to designated areas in an attempt to keep white settlers from encroaching on their land. In 1868, the second Treaty of Fort Laramie gave northern tribes control over the "Great Reservation" in parts of present-day Montana, Wyoming, North Dakota, and South Dakota. The treaty was ineffective in keeping out white settlers and hunters.

AP® EXAM TIP

The Course and Exam Description calls for you to understand how the U.S. government violated treaties with American Indians throughout the Gilded Age. Be able to identify a specific example from the text such as one of the Treaties at Fort Laramie. When you connect this concept, think about describing the short-term and intermediate consequences of treaty violations on the lives of American Indians.

Conflict Escalates in the West

The U.S. government started out by treating western American Indians as autonomous nations, thereby recognizing their stewardship over the land they occupied. In 1851, the **Treaty of Fort Laramie** confined tribes on the northern plains to designated areas in an attempt to keep white settlers from encroaching on their land. A treaty two years later applied these terms to tribes on the southern plains. American Indians generally kept their part of the agreement, but white miners racing to strike it rich did not. They roamed through American Indian hunting grounds in search of ore and faced little government enforcement of the existing treaties.

In fact, the U.S. military made matters considerably worse. On November 29, 1864, a peaceful band of 700 Cheyennes and Arapahos under the leadership of Chief Black Kettle gathered at Sand Creek, Colorado, supposedly under guarantees of U.S. protection. Instead, Colonel John M. Chivington and his troops launched an attack, despite a white flag of surrender hoisted by the American Indians, and brutally killed some 150 American Indians, mainly women and children. A congressional investigation later determined that the victims "were mutilated in the most horrible manner." Although there was considerable public outcry over the incident, the government did nothing to increase enforcement of its treaty obligations. In almost all disputes between white settlers and American Indians, the government sided with the white settlers, regardless of the American Indians' legal rights.

In 1867, the government once again signed treaties with tribes in the southern plains, with similarly devastating results. The **Treaty of Medicine Lodge** provided reservation lands for the Comanche, Kiowa-Apache, and Southern Arapaho peoples to settle. Despite this agreement, white hunters soon invaded this territory and destroyed the buffalo herds.

The dishonesty of the U.S. government was not without consequences. The Sand Creek massacre unleashed American Indian wars throughout the central plains, where the Lakota Sioux nation led the resistance from 1865 to 1868. After two years of fierce fighting, both sides signed a second Treaty of Fort Laramie, which gave northern tribes control over the "Great Reservation" set aside in parts of present-day Montana, Wyoming, North Dakota, and South Dakota. Another treaty placed the southern tribes in a reservation carved out of western Oklahoma.

One of the tribes that wound up in Oklahoma was the Nez Percé. Originally settled in the corner where Washington, Oregon, and Idaho meet, the tribe was forced to sign a treaty ceding most of its land to the United States and to relocate to a southern reservation. In 1877, Chief Joseph led a small group of Nez Percé opposed to the treaty out of the Pacific Northwest, directing his people in a march of 1,400 miles over mountains into Montana and Wyoming as federal troops pursued them. Intending to flee to Canada, the Nez Percé were finally intercepted in the mountains of northern Montana, just thirty miles from the border. Subsequently, the government relocated these northwestern American Indians to the southwestern territory of Oklahoma. In 1879, Chief Joseph pleaded with lawmakers in Congress to return his people to their home and urged the U.S. government to live up to the original intent of the treaties. His words carried some weight, and the Nez Percé returned under armed escort to a reservation in Washington.

The treaties did not produce a lasting peace. Although most of the tribes relocated to reservations, some refused. The Apache chief Victorio explained why he would not resettle his people on a reservation. "We prefer to die in our own land under the tall cool pines," he declared. "We will leave our bones with those of our people. It is better to die fighting than to starve." General William Tecumseh Sherman, commander of the military forces against the American Indians, ordered the army to wage a war of annihilation "against all hostile Indians till they are obliterated or beg for mercy."

In November 1868, Lieutenant Colonel George Armstrong Custer took Sherman at his word and assaulted a Cheyenne village, killing more than one hundred inhabitants. Nearly a decade later, in 1876, American Indians, this time Lakota Sioux, exacted revenge by killing Custer and all of his troops at the **Battle of the Little Bighorn** in Montana. Yet this proved to be the final victory for the Lakota nation, as the army mounted an extensive and fierce offensive against them that shattered their resistance.

Battle of the Little Bighorn
A major battle in the Montana Territory in which Lieutenant Colonel George Armstrong Custer and all of his troops were killed by the Lakota Sioux in 1876. This was the last major victory of the Lakota in their attempt to defend their lands from U.S. encroachment.

Among the troops that battled the American Indians were Black Americans. Known as **buffalo soldiers**, they represented a cross section of the postwar Black population looking for new opportunities that were now available after their emancipation. Some Black people enlisted to learn how to read and write, while others sought to avoid unpleasant situations back home. Cooks, waiters, painters, bakers, and farmers

buffalo soldier
A Black cavalryman, many of whom had been formerly enslaved, who fought in the West against American Indians in the 1870s and 1880s.

The Stapleton Collection/Bridgeman Images

American Indian Drawing of Battle of Little Bighorn This ink-on-paper drawing by Amos Bad Heart Buffalo (1869–1913) depicts the June 1876 Battle of Little Bighorn, also known as Custer's Last Stand. It portrays the retreat of Major Marcus Reno's forces. The painted warrior on the white horse who is shooting a soldier from his saddle is Crazy Horse, the Sioux chieftain.

What aspects of the drawing suggest it was created by an American Indian artist?

signed up for a five-year stint in the army at $13 a month. A few gained more glory than money. In May 1880, Sergeant George Jordan of the Ninth Cavalry led troops under his command to fend off Apache raids in Tularosa, New Mexico, for which he was awarded the Congressional Medal of Honor.

By the late 1870s, American Indians had largely succumbed to U.S. military aggression. The tribes, as their many victories demonstrated, contained agile horsemen and skilled warriors, but the U.S. army was backed by the power of an increasingly industrial economy. Telegraph lines and railroads provided logistical advantages in the swift deployment of U.S. troops and the ability of the central command to communicate with field officers. Although American Indians had acquired firearms over the years, the army boasted a nearly unlimited supply of superior weapons.

The diversity of American Indians and historic rivalries among tribes also made it difficult for them to unite against their common enemy. The federal government exploited these divisions by hiring American Indians to serve as army scouts against their traditional tribal foes.

The wholesale destruction of the bison, however, was the final blow to American Indian independence. As railroads pushed their tracks beyond the Mississippi, they cleared bison from their path by sending in professional hunters with high-powered rifles to shoot the animals. At the same time, buffalo products such as shoes, coats, and hats became fashionable in the East. By the mid-1880s, hunters had killed more than 13 million bison. As a result of the relentless move of white Americans westward and conspicuous consumption back east, bison herds were almost annihilated.

Faced with elimination of the bison, broken treaties, and their opponents' superior military technology, American Indians' capacity to wage war collapsed. They had little choice but to settle on shrinking reservations that the government established for them.

The absence of war, however, did not necessarily bring them security. In the late 1870s, discoveries of gold in the Black Hills of South Dakota ignited another furious rush by miners onto lands supposedly guaranteed to the Lakota people. Rather than honoring its treaties, the U.S. government forced tribes to relinquish still more land. General Custer's Seventh Cavalry was part of the military force trying to push American Indians out of this mining region, when it was annihilated at the Little Bighorn in 1876.

Elsewhere, Congress opened up a portion of western Oklahoma to white homesteaders in 1889. Although this land had not been assigned to specific tribes relocated in Indian Territory, more than eighty thousand American Indians from various tribes lived there. This government-sanctioned **land rush** only added to the pressure from homesteaders and others to acquire more land at the expense of American Indians. A decade later, Congress officially ended American Indian control of Indian Territory.

REVIEW

- How and why did federal policy toward American Indians change between 1865 and 1880?
- What factors led to the defeat of American Indians on the Great Plains?

Reforming American Indian Policy

As reservations continued to shrink under expansionist assault and government policy, a movement arose to reform American Indian policy. Largely centered in the East, where few American Indians lived, reformers came to believe that the future well-being of American Indians lay not in sovereignty but in assimilation.

In 1881, Helen Hunt Jackson published *A Century of Dishonor*, her exposé of the unjust treatment the American Indians had received. Roused by this depiction of the American Indians' plight, groups such as the Women's National Indian Association joined with ministers and philanthropists to advocate the transformation of native peoples into "full-fledged" Americans.

These well-intentioned reformers ultimately contributed to the oppression of American Indians by generating and advocating policies that led to the eradication of indigenous cultural heritage. Even most sympathetic reformers of the period offered an approach that supported assimilation as the only alternative to extinction. Lewis Morgan, influential author of *Ancient Society* (1877), concluded that all cultures evolved through three stages: savagery, barbarism, and civilization. According to Morgan's conception, American Indians occupied the lower rungs, and by adopting white values, they could become civilized. Thus, even those who thought they were helping American Indians rejected the legitimacy of their culture.

Reformers faced opposition from white Americans who doubted that American Indian assimilation was possible. For many white people, secure in their sense of their own superiority, the decline and eventual extinction of the American Indian peoples was an inevitable consequence of what they saw as American Indians' innate inferiority. For example, a Wyoming newspaper predicted: "The same inscrutable Arbiter that decreed the downfall of Rome has pronounced the doom of extinction upon the red men of America."

Reformers found their legislative spokesman in Senator Henry Dawes of Massachusetts. As legislative director of the Boston Indian Citizenship Association, Dawes shared Christian reformers' belief that becoming a true American would save both the American Indians and the soul of the nation. A Republican who had served in Congress since the Civil War, Dawes had the same condescending attitude toward American Indians as he had toward freedpeople. He believed that if both groups worked hard and practiced thrift and individual initiative in the spirit of seventeenth-century New England Puritans, they would succeed. The key for Dawes was private ownership of land.

Passed in 1887, the **Dawes Act** attempted to promote American Indian assimilation by encouraging the division of tribal lands into 160-acre homesteads. The act allocated one parcel to each family head. The government held the lands in trust for the American Indians for twenty-five years. At the end of this period, the American Indians would receive American citizenship. In return, they had to abandon their religious and cultural rites and practices, including storytelling and the use of medicine men. Whatever lands remained after this reallocation—and the amount was considerable—would be sold on the open market, and the profits from the sales would be placed in an educational fund for American Indians.

Dawes Act
An 1887 act that ended federal recognition of tribal sovereignty and divided American Indian land into 160-acre parcels to be distributed to American Indian heads of household to promote assimilation. The act dramatically reduced the amount of American Indian-controlled land and undermined American Indian solidarity by eroding social and cultural institutions.

Like most of the policies it replaced, the Dawes Act proved detrimental to American Indians. Native families received inferior farmlands and inadequate tools to cultivate them, while speculators reaped profits from the sale of the "excess" American Indian lands. A little more than a decade after the Dawes Act went into effect, American Indians controlled 77 million acres of land, down sharply from the 155 million acres they held in 1881.

Additional legislation in 1891 forced American Indian parents to send their children to boarding schools or else face arrest. At these educational institutions, American Indian children were given "American" names, had their long hair cut, and wore uniforms in place of their native dress. The program for boys provided manual and vocational training and the program for girls taught domestic skills, so that they could emulate the gender roles of white middle-class American families. However, this schooling offered few skills of use in an economic world undergoing rapid industrial transformation.

The federal government devised its policies based on flawed cultural assumptions. Even the most sensitive white administrators of American Indian affairs considered them a degraded race, in accordance with the scientific thinking of the time. At most, white people believed that American Indians could be lifted to a higher level of civilization, which in practice meant a withering away of their traditional culture and heritage.

AP® WORKING with EVIDENCE

Source: Zitkala-Ša, *The School Days of an Indian Girl*, 1921

"There were eight in our party of bronzed children who were going East with the missionaries [in 1884]. Among us were three young braves, two tall girls, and we three little ones, Judéwin, Thowin, and I. . . .

We were placed in a line of girls who were marching into the dining room. These were Indian girls, in stiff shoes and closely clinging dresses. The small girls wore sleeved aprons and shingled hair [A hair style cut short from the back of the head to expose the nape of the neck]. As I walked noiselessly in my soft moccasins, I felt like sinking to the floor, for my blanket had been stripped from my shoulders. I looked hard at the Indian girls, who seemed not to care that they were even more immodestly dressed than I, in their tightly fitting clothes. . . .

A small bell was tapped, and each of the pupils drew a chair from under the table. Supposing this act meant they were to be seated, I pulled out mine and at once slipped into it from one side. But when I turned my head, I saw that I was the only one seated, and all the rest at our table remained standing. Just as I began to rise, looking shyly around to see how chairs were to be used, a second bell was sounded. All were seated at last, and I had to crawl back into my chair again. I heard a man's voice at one end of the hall, and I looked around to see him. But all the others hung their heads over their plates. As I glanced at the long chain of tables, I caught the eyes of a paleface woman upon me. Immediately I dropped my eyes, wondering why I was so keenly watched by the strange woman. The man ceased his mutterings, and then a third bell was tapped. Every one picked up his knife and fork and began eating. I began crying instead, for by this time I was afraid to venture anything more.

But this eating by formula was not the hardest trial in that first day. Late in the morning, my friend Judéwin gave me a terrible warning. Judéwin knew a few words of English; and she had overheard the paleface woman talk about cutting our long, heavy hair. Our mothers had taught us that only unskilled warriors who were captured had their hair shingled by the enemy. Among our people, short hair was worn by mourners, and shingled hair by cowards!

We discussed our fate some moments, and when Judéwin said, "We have to submit, because they are strong," I rebelled.

"No, I will not submit! I will struggle first!" I answered. . . .

I remember being dragged out, though I resisted by kicking and scratching wildly. In spite of myself, I was carried downstairs and tied fast in a chair.

I cried aloud, shaking my head all the while until I felt the cold blades of the scissors against my neck, and heard them gnaw off one of my thick braids. Then I lost my spirit. Since the day I was taken from my mother I had suffered extreme indignities. People had stared at me. I had been tossed about in the air like a wooden puppet. And now my long hair was shingled like a coward's! In my anguish I moaned for my mother, but no one came to comfort me.

Not a soul reasoned quietly with me, as my own mother used to do; for now I was only one of many little animals driven by a herder."

Questions for Analysis

1. Describe the methods used by the boarding school to forcibly assimilate American Indian students.
2. Explain how Zitkala-Ša's experience contrasts with the beliefs of nineteenth-century missionary reformers.
3. Evaluate the impact of American Indian boarding schools on the lives of their students and on tribal culture.

- How did the provisions of the Dawes Act affect the lives of American Indians?

American Indian Assimilation and Resistance

Not all American Indians conformed to the government's attempts at forced acculturation. Some refused to abandon their traditional social practices, and others rejected the white man's version of private property and civilization.

Even on reservations, American Indians found ways to preserve aspects of their native traditions. Through close family ties, they communicated to sons and daughters their languages, histories, and cultural practices. Parents refused to grant full control of their children to white educators and often made sure that schools were located on or near reservations where they fit into the pattern of their lives.

Many others displayed more complicated approaches to survival in a world that continued to view American Indians with prejudice. Geronimo and Sitting Bull participated in pageants and Wild West shows but refused to disavow their heritage. Ohiyesa, a Lakota also known as Charles Eastman, went to boarding school, graduated from Dartmouth College, and earned a medical degree from Boston University. He supported passage of the Dawes Act and believed in the virtues of an American education. At the same time, he spoke out against government corruption and fraud perpetrated against American Indians. Reviewing his life in his later years, Ohiyesa (Eastman) reflected: "I am an Indian and while I have learned much from civilization . . . I have never lost my Indian sense of right and justice."

Disaster loomed for those who resisted assimilation and held on too tightly to the old ways. In 1888, the prophet Wovoka, a member of the Paiute tribe in western Nevada, had a vision that American Indians would one day regain control of the world and that white people would disappear. He believed the Creator had provided him with a **Ghost Dance** that would make this happen. The dance spread to thousands of Lakota Sioux in the northern plains. Seeing the Ghost Dance as a sign of renewed American Indian resistance, the army attempted to put a stop to the revival. On December 29, 1890, the Seventh Cavalry chased three hundred ghost dancers to Wounded Knee Creek on the Pine Ridge Reservation in present-day South Dakota. In a confrontation with the Lakota leader Big Foot, a gunshot accidentally rang out during a struggle with one of his followers. The cavalry then turned the full force of their weaponry on the American Indians, killing 250 people, many of them women and children.

AP® EXAM TIP

American Indians resisted cultural assimilation even as the federal government sought policies to that end. Think of a specific example such as the Ghost Dance movement. When you describe events such as Ghost Dance, it is vital that you connect it to a broader historical development such as westward expansion.

Ghost Dance

A religious ritual performed by the American Indians in the late nineteenth century. The ritual was created following a vision received by Paiute prophet Wovoka in 1888. Wovoka believed performing the Ghost Dance would cause white people to disappear and allow American Indians to regain control of their lands.

Wounded Knee massacre
A massacre committed by the U.S. military in South Dakota, December 29, 1890. The Plains Indians, on the edge of starvation, began the "Ghost Dance," which they believed would protect them from bullets and restore their old way of life. Following one of the dances, a rifle held by an American Indian misfired. In response, U.S. soldiers invaded the encampment, killing some 250 people.

The message of the **Wounded Knee massacre** was clear for those who raised their voices against Americanization. As Black Elk, a spiritual leader of the Oglala Lakota tribe, asserted: "A people's dream died there. . . . There is no center any longer, and the sacred tree is dead." It may not have been the policy of the U.S. government to exterminate the Indians as a people, but it was certainly U.S. policy to destroy American Indian culture and society once and for all.

REVIEW

- What methods did American Indians use to resist assimilation?
- Why and how did some American Indians adapt to dominant white culture?

Mormons, Californios, and the Chinese in the West

Mormon
A follower of Joseph Smith and Brigham Young who migrated to Utah in the 1840s to escape religious persecution; the religious denomination is also known as the Church of Jesus Christ of Latter-Day Saints (LDS).

Mormons, a religious society formed in the 1840s, sought refuge in the West mainly for religious reasons almost twenty years before the Civil War. By 1870, the migration of Mormons (members of the Church of Jesus Christ of Latter-Day Saints) into the Utah Territory had attracted more than eighty-five thousand settlers, most notably in Salt Lake City.

Originally traveling to Utah under the leadership of Brigham Young in the late 1840s, Mormons had come under attack from opponents of their religion and the federal government for several reasons. Most important, Mormons practiced polygamy, the practice of having more than one wife at a time. Far from seeing the practice as immoral, Mormon doctrine held polygamy as a blessing that would guarantee both husbands and wives an exalted place in the afterlife. Non-Mormons denounced polygamy as a form of involuntary servitude. In reality, only a small minority of Mormon men had multiple wives, and most of these polygamists had only two wives.

Mormons also departed from the mainstream American belief in private property. The church considered farming a communal enterprise. To this end, church elders divided land among their followers, so that, as Brigham Young explained, "each person perform[ed] his several duties for the good of the whole more than for individual aggrandizement."

In the 1870s, the federal government took increased measures to control Mormon practices. In *Reynolds v. United States* (1879), the Supreme Court upheld the criminal conviction of a polygamist Mormon man. Previously in 1862 and 1874, Congress had banned plural marriages in the Utah Territory. Congress went further in 1882 by passing the Edmunds Act, which disfranchised men engaging in polygamy. In 1887, Congress aimed to slash the economic power of the church by limiting the Mormon Church's assets to $50,000 and seizing the rest for the federal treasury. A few years later, under this considerable pressure, the Mormons officially abandoned polygamy. With the rejection of polygamy, Congress accepted statehood for Utah in 1896.

As with the nation's other frontiers, migrants to the West Coast did not find uninhabited territory. Besides American Indians, the largest group that lived in California consisted of Spaniards and Mexicans. Since the eighteenth century, these Californios had established themselves as farmers and ranchers. The 1848 Treaty of Guadalupe Hidalgo, which ended the Mexican-American War, supposedly guaranteed the property rights of Californios and granted them U.S. citizenship, but in reality proved different.

Mexican American miners had to pay a "foreign miners tax," and Californio landowners lost their holdings to squatters, settlers, and local officials. By the end of the nineteenth century, about two-thirds of all land originally owned by Spanish-speaking residents had fallen into the hands of Euro-American settlers. By this time, many of these once-wealthy Californios had been forced into poverty and the low-wage labor force. The loss of land was matched by a diminished role in the region's government, as economic decline, ethnic bias, and the continuing influx of white migrants combined to greatly reduce the political influence of the Californio population.

Spaniards and Mexicans living in the Southwest met the same fate as the Californios. When Anglo cattle ranchers began forcing Mexican Americans off their land near Las Vegas, New Mexico, a rancher named Juan José Herrera, a former captain in the Union army, assembled a band of masked night riders known as Las Gorras Blancas (The White Caps). According to fliers that they distributed promoting their grievances, the group sought "to protect the rights and interests of the people in general and especially those of the helpless classes." Enemies "of bulldozers and tyrants," they desired a "free ballot and fair court." In 1889 and 1890, as many as seven hundred White Caps burned Anglo fences, haystacks, barns, and homes. In the end, however, Spanish-speaking inhabitants could not prevent the growing number of white settlers from pouring into their lands, further isolating them politically, economically, and culturally.

California and the far West also attracted a large number of Chinese immigrants. Migration to California and the West Coast was part of a larger movement in the nineteenth century out of Asia that brought impoverished Chinese to Australia, Hawaii, Latin America, and the United States. The Chinese migrated for several reasons in the decades after 1840. Economic dislocation related to the British Opium Wars (1839–1842 and 1856–1860), along with bloody family feuds and a decade of peasant rebellion from 1854 to 1864, propelled migration. Faced with unemployment and starvation, the Chinese sought economic opportunity overseas.

Chinese immigrants were attracted first by the 1848 gold rush and then by jobs building the transcontinental railroad. By 1880, the Chinese population in the United States had grown to 200,000, most of whom lived in the West. San Francisco became the center of the transplanted Chinese population, which congregated in the city's

Granger – Historical Picture Archive

Rock Springs Massacre This engraving depicts the Rock Springs massacre in Wyoming. On September 3, 1885, a mob of white coal miners killed at least 28 Chinese miners, injured 15, and burned 75 homes of Chinese residents. The violence came after years of anti-Chinese sentiment in the western United States.

What factors contributed to violence against the Chinese in the American West?

Chinatown. Under the leadership of a handful of businessmen, Chinese residents found jobs, lodging, and meals, along with social, cultural, and recreational outlets. Most of those who came were young unmarried men who intended to earn enough money to return to China and start anew. The relatively few women who immigrated often worked as servants or prostitutes.

For many Chinese, the West proved unwelcoming. When California's economy slumped in the mid-1870s, many white people looked to the Chinese as scapegoats. White workingmen believed that Chinese laborers in the mines and railroads undercut their demands for higher wages. They contended that Chinese would work for less because they were racially inferior people who lived degraded lives.

Anti-Chinese clubs mushroomed in California during the 1870s, and they soon became a substantial political force in the state. The Workingmen's Party advocated laws that restricted Chinese labor, and it initiated boycotts of goods made by Chinese people. Vigilantes attacked Chinese people in the streets and set fire to factories that employed Asians. The Workingmen's Party and the Democratic Party joined forces in 1879 to craft a new state constitution that blatantly discriminated against Chinese residents. In many ways, these laws resembled the Jim Crow laws passed in the South that deprived Black Americans of their freedom following Reconstruction (see Module 6.4).

Chinese Exclusion Act
A law enacted in 1882 that banned most Chinese immigration into the United States and prohibited resident Chinese from becoming naturalized American citizens.

Pressured by anti-Chinese sentiment on the West Coast, the U.S. government enacted drastic legislation to prevent any further influx of Chinese. The **Chinese Exclusion Act** of 1882 banned Chinese immigration into the United States, prohibited those Chinese already in the country from becoming naturalized American citizens, and set a precedent for a race-based immigration policy. The exclusion act, however, did not stop anti-Chinese assaults. In the mid-1880s, white mobs drove Chinese out of Eureka, California; Seattle and Tacoma, Washington; and Rock Springs, Wyoming. These attacks were often organized. In 1885, the Tacoma mayor and police led a mob that rounded up seven hundred Chinese residents and forced them to leave the city on a train bound for Portland.

REVIEW

- What factors contributed to the differences in the experiences of Mormons, Californios, and Chinese in the West?
- What experiences were common to all three groups?

AP® Skills Workshop: Thinking Historically

Tracing Developments and Processes to Create Context in an Essay Conclusion

As you recall from Module 3.2, historians interpret the past by asking questions and engaging in debates with other historians. One of the goals of interpreting the past is to construct a narrative that not only lists events in chronological order, but also explains how they fit together by analyzing causation, comparison, and continuity and change. Through this process, historians create a narrative to explain past events, and they continually revise that narrative as new information and arguments come to light.

In Module 3.2, you also practiced writing a **thesis** that established a **development** or a **process**. As you recall, your thesis included a **claim** and a **line of reasoning**,

(continued)

which established your argument about a development or process and led to your body paragraphs, which supported your thesis with evidence and analysis.

You can also establish developments or processes in your **conclusion**. A good conclusion convinces your reader of your essay's thesis, leaves them with a feeling that the essay is thoroughly argued, and gives them a sense of how the topic influenced U.S. history after the time period in question. One of the best ways to conclude an essay is through an **immediate concluding context** or a **long-term concluding context** (Module 4.10), both of which give your reader a sense of the way in which the events resonate after the time period of your topic. Tracing developments and processes can help with this.

Consider, for example, a conclusion to an essay that answers this prompt:

> Evaluate the extent to which government intervention drove westward expansion between 1877 and 1898.

A thesis with a claim and a line of reasoning might look like this:

> Throughout the late nineteenth century, individual initiative, supported by government intervention, drove westward expansion. **[claim]** In industries like farming, mining, and ranching, the federal government aided settlement at the beginning of expansion and, when individual initiatives failed, drove consolidation so that the West became an integral part of the national economy. **[line of reasoning]**

For your conclusion, you'll want to do four things:

- Revisit your **thesis**.
- Make a **claim** about an immediate or long-term concluding context *after* 1898.
- **Support** that claim with information regarding an immediate or long-term concluding context *after* 1898.
- **Explain** how that information supports your claim.

To do so, you can trace a **development** that shaped your concluding context. Below is an example. Don't worry if you're not familiar with this material; it will be covered in Period 7. Instead, notice how a development shapes the description of the concluding context.

> Both individual initiative and government intervention drove westward expansion. **[restated thesis claim]** The federal government cleared the way for settlement to pursue farming, mining, and ranching and, when individual initiatives failed, encouraged consolidation and made the West part of the nation's industrial economy. **[restated thesis line of reasoning]** The federal government continued to play this role throughout the late nineteenth and early twentieth centuries. **[immediate concluding context claim]** After westward expansion, the combination of individual and government initiative *developed* into a U.S. policy that supported efforts to invest in overseas markets in Asia and Latin America, leading to overseas conflicts undertaken by the federal government, like the Spanish-American War of 1898. **[immediate concluding context support]** In this way, the interplay of individual initiative and government intervention that settled the West became U.S. international policy in the twentieth century. **[immediate concluding context explanation]**

(continued)

Notice how this conclusion draws a connection between the restated thesis and the immediate concluding context by noting the way government policy during westward expansion **developed** into a policy used for overseas expansion after 1898.

Now try the same thing yourself with a conclusion that reveals a **process** as a way to explain concluding context. For this prompt, we'll use a topic from this module, and you can use the information here to establish your concluding context. Here's the new prompt:

> Evaluate the extent to which U.S. relations with native peoples changed between 1865 and 1887.

A two-part thesis might look like this:

> While U.S. government relations with native peoples between 1865 and 1887 continued to attempt to force native people from their land, the tactics used by the U.S. government changed over the course of this period. **[claim]** After the Civil War, the government continued its practice of establishing reservations for native peoples, yet by the late 1880s, the U.S. government also began a policy of severing American Indians from their cultural traditions in an attempt to assimilate them into the dominant American culture. **[line of reasoning]**

ACTIVITY

Now write your own conclusion. Try using the **immediate concluding context** of native peoples after the passage of the Dawes Act of 1887. Use what you have read in this module to help you find supporting information. After you restate your thesis and line of reasoning, trace the **process**, after 1887, by which native peoples were forced to assimilate to American culture.

The "New South"

MODULE 6.4

FOCUS

As you read this module, examine the extent and nature of change in the South's economy. Ask yourself why the South's industrial progress was limited during this era. Likewise, consider the changes and constants in the lives of Black people and the reasons for changes and continuity.

The industrial transformation of the U.S. economy continued in the decades after the end of the Civil War. In 1874, Henry Grady, the editor of the *Atlanta Constitution*, called for a "New South" with an economy based on textile mills, factories, and mining. Yet efforts to industrialize the South met with uneven success.

For the majority of Black people still living in the South, southern industrialization provided few benefits. Increased Black migration to cities in the South yielded limited economic opportunities for most Black Americans who relocated. In response to Black aspirations for social and economic advancement, white politicians imposed a rigid system of racial **segregation** on the South. Although white people championed the cause of individual upward mobility, they restricted opportunities to achieve success to whites only.

AP® EXAM TIP

Historians often extend Reconstruction beyond its traditional period ending in 1877 to include the events of the Gilded Age. Think about how you can use ideas such as sharecropping to explain long-term developments like the Democratic takeover of the South in the 1870s. Know how sharecropping and tenant farming shaped the lives of Blacks and whites in the South in the 1880s and 1890s.

segregation

The purposeful separation of people into ethnic or racial groups. Segregation was often actively perpetuated and enforced through "Black codes" and Jim Crow-era legislation that persisted into the latter half of the twentieth century.

"New South"

Term popularized in the 1880s by newspaper editor Henry Grady, a proponent of the modernization of the southern economy in order for a distinctively industrial "New South" to emerge.

Building a "New South"

Although the largely rural South lagged behind the North and the Midwest in manufacturing, industrial expansion did not bypass the region. Well aware of global economic trends and eager for the South to achieve its economic potential, southern business leaders and newspaper editors saw industrial development as the key to the creation of a "**New South**."

Attributing the Confederate defeat in the Civil War to the North's superior manufacturing output and railroad supply lines, "New South" proponents hoped to modernize their economy in a similar fashion. One of those boosters was Richard H. Edmonds, editor of the *Manufacturers' Record*. He extolled the virtues of the "real South" of the 1880s, characterized by "the music of progress—the whirr of the spindle, the buzz of the saw, the roar of the furnace, the throb of the locomotive." The South of Edmonds's vision would move beyond the regional separatism of the past and become fully integrated into the national economy.

Railroads were the key to achieving such economic integration, so after the Civil War new railroad tracks were laid throughout the South. The expanded railroad system created direct connections between the North and the South, and it also facilitated the growth of the southern textile industry. Seeking to take advantage of plentiful cotton, cheap labor, and the improved transportation system, investors built textile mills throughout the South. Victims of falling prices and saddled with debt, sharecroppers and tenant farmers moved into mill towns in search of better employment. Mill owners preferred to hire girls and young women, who worked for low wages, to spin cotton and weave it on the looms. To do so, however, owners had to employ their entire family, for mothers and fathers would not let their daughters relocate without their supervision.

Agricultural refugees who flocked to cotton mills in the South also faced dangerous working conditions. Working twelve-hour days breathing the lint-filled air from the processed cotton posed health hazards. Textile workers also had to place their hands into heavy machinery to disentangle threads, making them extremely vulnerable to serious injury. Wages scarcely covered necessities, and on many occasions, families did not know where their next meal was coming from. North Carolina textile worker J. W. Mehaffry complained that the mill owners "were slave drivers" who "work their employees, women, and children from 6 a.m. to 7 p.m. with a half hour for lunch." Mill workers' meals usually consisted of potatoes, cornbread, and dried beans cooked in fat. This diet, without dairy products and fresh meat, led to outbreaks of pellagra, a debilitating disease caused by niacin (vitamin B_3) deficiency.

convict lease system
The system used by southern governments to furnish mainly Black prison labor to plantation owners and industrialists. The program was designed to raise revenue for the states. In practice, convict labor replaced slavery as the means of providing a forced labor supply.

Whatever attraction the mills offered applied only to white people. The pattern of white supremacy emerging in the post-Reconstruction South kept Black Americans out of all but the most menial jobs. Black people contributed greatly to the construction of railroads in the "New South," but they did not do so as free men.

Convicts, most of whom were Black men, performed the exhausting work of laying tracks through hills and swamps. Southern states used the **convict lease system**, in which Black people, usually imprisoned for minor offenses, were hired out to private companies to serve their time or pay off their fine. The convict lease system brought additional income to the state and supplied cheap labor to the railroads and planters, but it left Black convict laborers impoverished and virtually enslaved.

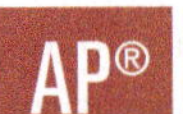

WORKING with EVIDENCE

Source: Henry Grady, *The New South*, 1886

> "What is the sum of our work? We have found out that in the general summary the free Negro counts more than he did as a slave. We have planted the schoolhouse on the hilltop and made it free to white and black. We have sowed towns and cities in the place of theories and put business above politics. We have challenged your spinners in Massachusetts and your iron-makers in Pennsylvania. We have learned that the $400,000,000 annually received from our cotton crop will make us rich, when the supplies that make it are home-raised. We have reduced the commercial rate of interest from twenty-four to six per cent, and are floating four per cent bonds. . . .
>
> The Old South rested everything on slavery and agriculture, unconscious that these could neither give nor maintain healthy growth. The New South presents a perfect democracy, the oligarchs leading in the popular movement—a social system compact and closely knitted, less splendid on the surface, but stronger at the core—a hundred farms for every plantation, fifty homes for every palace—and a diversified industry that meets the complex need of this complex age."

Questions for Analysis

1. Identify the main differences between the "Old South" and the "New South," according to Grady.
2. Describe the point of view expressed by Grady in this excerpt.
3. Evaluate the impact of southern industrialization on working-class whites and on Black Americans.

The South attracted a number of industries besides textile manufacturing. In the 1880s, James B. Duke established a cigarette manufacturing empire in Durham, North Carolina. Nearby tobacco fields provided the raw material that Black workers prepared for white workers, who then rolled the cigarettes by machine. Acres of timber pines in the Carolinas, Florida, and Alabama sustained a lucrative lumber industry. Rich supplies of coal and iron in Alabama fostered the growth of the steel industry in Birmingham (**Map 6.3**).

Plagued by poverty, sharecropping debt, and the added burden of racial oppression and violence in the post-Reconstruction period, rural Black women and men migrated to southern cities. Black American migrants found work as cooks, janitors, and domestic servants. Many found employment as manual laborers in manufacturing companies—including tobacco factories, which employed women and men; tanneries; and cottonseed oil firms—and as dockworkers. Although the overwhelming majority of Black people in cities worked as unskilled laborers for very low wages, others opened small businesses such as funeral parlors, barbershops, and construction companies or went into professions such as medicine, law, banking, and education that catered to residents of segregated Black neighborhoods. Yet by the turn of the twentieth century, and

MAP 6.3 The "New South," 1900 Although the South remained largely agricultural by 1900, it had made great strides toward building industries in the region. This so-called "New South" boasted an extensive railway network that provided a national market for its raw materials and manufactured goods, including coal, iron, steel, and textiles. Still, the southern economy in 1900 depended mainly on raising cotton and tobacco.

How does this map illustrate both the limitations and successes of the "New South"?

despite significant individual accomplishments, most Black people in the urban South had few prospects for upward economic mobility.

AP® EXAM TIP

Terms such as the "New South" are important to know, but understanding the concept itself is often not enough. Be able to explain how at least two historical events or processes limited the development of a "New South," and at how at least one historical event or process contributed to the development of a "New South."

Even with the frenzy of industrial activity and urban growth, the "New South" in many ways resembled the Old South. Southern entrepreneurs still depended on northern investors to supply much of the capital for investment. Investors were attracted by the low wages that prevailed in the South, but low wages also meant that southern workers remained poor and, in many cases, unable to buy the manufactured goods produced by industry.

Efforts to diversify agriculture beyond tobacco and cotton were constrained by a sharecropping system based on small, inefficient plots. In fact, even though industrialization did make considerable headway in the South, the economy remained overwhelmingly agricultural. This suited many white southerners who wanted to hold on to the individualistic, agrarian values they associated with the Old South. Yoked to old ideologies and a system of forced labor, modernization in the South could go only so far.

REVIEW

- To what extent were late-nineteenth-century efforts to create a "New South" successful?

Black America and Jim Crow

While wealthy, middle-class, and working-class white people experimented with new forms of social behavior, Black Americans faced greater challenges to preserving their freedom and dignity. In the South, where the overwhelming majority of Black people lived, post-Reconstruction southern governments adopted various tactics to keep them from voting.

poll tax
A common tactic in southern states to disenfranchise poor, mostly Black voters by charging a fee to cast a ballot.

Jim Crow law
Any late-nineteenth-century state or local law that established legal segregation in the South. Many Jim Crow laws were enacted in the South, helping ensure the social and economic disfranchisement of southern Black people.

Plessy v. Ferguson
A Supreme Court ruling in 1896 that upheld the legality of Jim Crow legislation. The Court ruled that as long as states provided "separate but equal" facilities for white and Black people, Jim Crow laws did not violate the equal protection clause of the Fourteenth Amendment.

To circumvent the Fifteenth Amendment, southern states devised suffrage qualifications that they claimed were racially neutral, and the Supreme Court ruled in their favor. They instituted the **poll tax**, a tax that each person had to pay to cast a ballot. Poll taxes fell hardest on the poor, a disproportionate number of whom were Black.

Disfranchisement reached its peak in the 1890s, as white southern governments managed to deny the vote to most of the Black electorate (**Map 6.4**). Literacy tests officially barred the uneducated of both races, but they were administered in a manner that discriminated against Black people while allowing illiterate whites to satisfy the requirement. Many literacy tests contained a loophole called a "grandfather clause." Under this exception, men whose father or grandfather had voted in 1860—a time when white men but not Black men, most of whom were enslaved, could vote in the South—were excused from taking the test.

In the 1890s, white southerners also imposed legally sanctioned racial segregation on the region's Black citizens. Commonly known as **Jim Crow laws** (named for a character in a minstrel show, where whites performed in blackface), these new statutes denied Black Americans equal access to public facilities and ensured that Black people lived apart from whites. In 1883, when the Supreme Court struck down the Civil Rights Act of 1875 (Module 5.11), it had given southern states the freedom to adopt measures confining Black people to separate schools, public accommodations, seats on transportation, beds in hospitals, and sections of graveyards.

In 1896, the Supreme Court sanctioned Jim Crow, constructing the constitutional rationale for legally keeping the races apart. In ***Plessy v. Ferguson***, the high

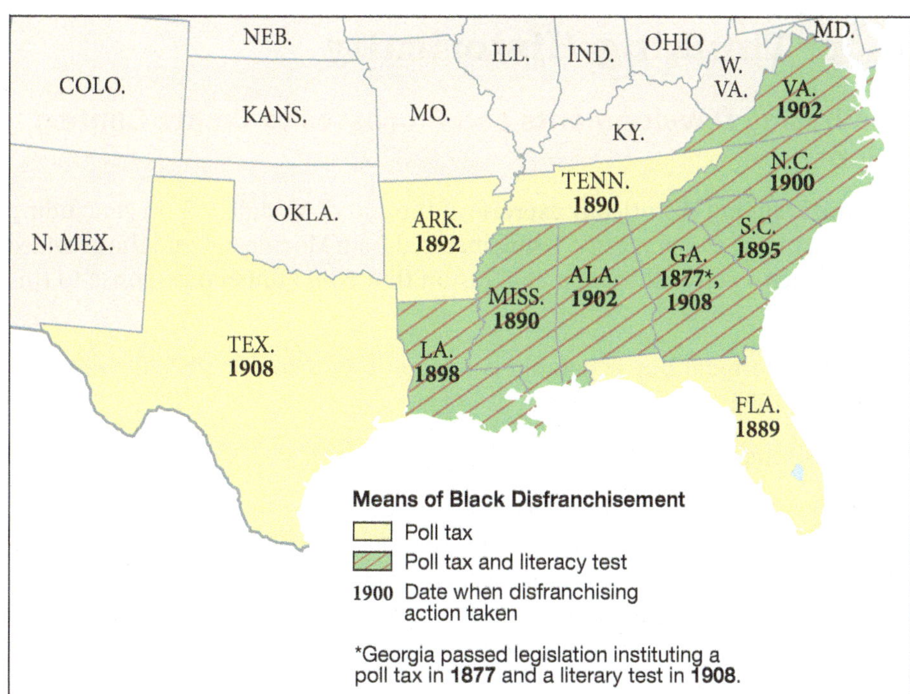

MAP 6.4 Black Disfranchisement in the South, 1889–1908 After Reconstruction, Black voters posed a threat to the ruling Democrats by occasionally joining with third-party insurgents. To repel these challenges, Democratic Party leaders made racial appeals to divide poor whites and Black people. Chiefly in the 1890s and the early twentieth century, white leaders succeeded in disfranchising Black voters (and some poor whites), mainly by adopting poll taxes and literacy requirements.

How does the process depicted by this map illustrate the challenges Black Americans faced in their struggle for equality in the South?

court ruled that a Louisiana law providing for "equal but separate" accommodations for "whites" and "coloreds" on railroad cars did not violate the equal protection clause of the Fourteenth Amendment. In its decision, the Court concluded that civil rights laws could not change racial destiny. "If one race be inferior to the other socially," the justices explained, "the Constitution of the United States cannot put them on the same plane." In practice, however, white southerners obeyed the "separate" part of the ruling but never provided equal services. If Black people tried to overstep the bounds of Jim Crow in any way that whites found unacceptable, they risked their lives. Between 1884 and 1900, nearly 1,700 Black people were lynched in the South. Victims were often subjected to brutal forms of torture before they were hanged or shot.

In everyday life, Black Americans carried on as best they could. Segregation required Black people to build their own businesses and churches; develop their own schools, staffed by Black teachers; and form their own civic associations and fraternal organizations. Segregation, though harsh and unequal, did foster a sense of Black community, promote a rising middle class, and create social networks that enhanced racial pride. Founded in 1898, the North Carolina Life Insurance Company, one of the leading Black-owned and operated businesses, employed many Black Americans in managerial and sales positions. Burial societies ensured that their members received a proper funeral when they died. As with whites, Black men joined lodges such as the Colored Masons and the Colored Odd Fellows, while women participated in the YWCA and the National Association of Colored Women. A small percentage of southern Black people resisted Jim Crow by migrating to the North, where Black people still exercised the right to vote, more jobs were open to them, and segregation was less strictly enforced, though racism against Black people was still prevalent.

AP® EXAM TIP

The Supreme Court's decision in *Plessy v. Ferguson* is specifically mentioned in the Course Framework. Be able to explain the significance of the ruling and how the decision created historical continuities in the treatment of Blacks across the South.

REVIEW

- What tactics did southern legislators use to discriminate against Black Americans during the 1880s and 1890s?

AP® Skills Workshop: Thinking Historically

Additional Practice in Tracing Developments and Processes to Create Context in an Essay Conclusion

Review the Thinking Historically exercise at the end of Module 6.3 on concluding with developments and processes. Using material from Module 6.4 and the provided thesis statement, you will write a conclusion that could finish a response to this prompt:

> Evaluate the extent of economic change in the "New South" between 1875 and 1895.

Use this thesis statement:

> While the "New South" increasingly industrialized after 1875, the old labor system of cash crop production that depended upon oppressed labor continued. **[claim]** After 1875, the textile industry expanded, and railroads increasingly connected the region to the rest of the nation; however, cotton continued to be an important export of the southern economy, and laborers on cotton farms continued to struggle under the labor system that produced this cash crop. **[line of reasoning]**

Now write a conclusion that traces a development or process that continued or arose after 1895. In your conclusion, make sure that you:

1. Rephrase your **thesis claim** and **line of reasoning**.
2. Make a **claim** about a specific **development** or **process** exhibited in the **immediate** or **long-term context** after 1895.
3. **Support** your claim with evidence.
4. **Explain** how this evidence supports your claim.

Technological Innovation

MODULE 6.5

FOCUS

As you read, consider how railroads, technological inventions, and new corporate structures led to the expansion of the industrial economy in the United States. Weigh the positive and negative effects of these changes and the responses of the federal government to these changes.

Industrialization and big business reshaped the nation. Between 1870 and 1900, the United States grew into a global industrial power. Transcontinental railroads spurred this breathtaking transformation, linking regional markets into a national market and fueling increased international trade as well. At the same time, railroads themselves served as a major new market for raw materials and new technologies. Innovations and new inventions promoted the growth of large corporations.

The New Industrial Economy

The industrial revolution of the late nineteenth century originated in Europe. Great Britain was the world's first industrial power, but by the 1870s, Germany had emerged as a major challenger for industrial dominance, increasing its steel production at a rapid rate and leading the way in the chemical and electrical industries. The dynamic economic growth and innovation stimulated by industrial competition quickly crossed the Atlantic.

Industrialization transformed the American economy. As industrialization took hold, the U.S. **gross domestic product**, the output of all goods and services produced each year, quadrupled—from $9 billion in 1860 to $37 billion in 1890. During this same period, the number of Americans employed by industry doubled. Moreover, the nature of industry itself changed, as small factories catering to local markets were displaced by large-scale firms producing for national and international markets. The midwestern cities of Chicago, Cincinnati, and St. Louis joined Boston, New York, and Philadelphia as centers of factory production, while the exploitation of natural resources in the West took on an increasingly industrial character. Trains, telegraphs, and telephones connected the country in ways never before possible.

From 1870 to 1913, the United States experienced an extraordinary rate of growth in industrial output: In 1870, American industries turned out 23.3 percent of the world's manufacturing production; by 1913, this figure had jumped to 35.8 percent. In fact, U.S. output in 1913 almost equaled the combined total for Europe's three leading industrial powers: Germany, the United Kingdom, and France. By the end of the nineteenth century, the United States was surging ahead of northern Europe as the manufacturing center of the world.

At the heart of the American industrial transformation was the railroad. Large-scale business enterprises would not have developed without a national market for raw materials and finished products. A consolidated system of railroads crisscrossing the nation facilitated the creation of such a market. In addition, railroads were direct

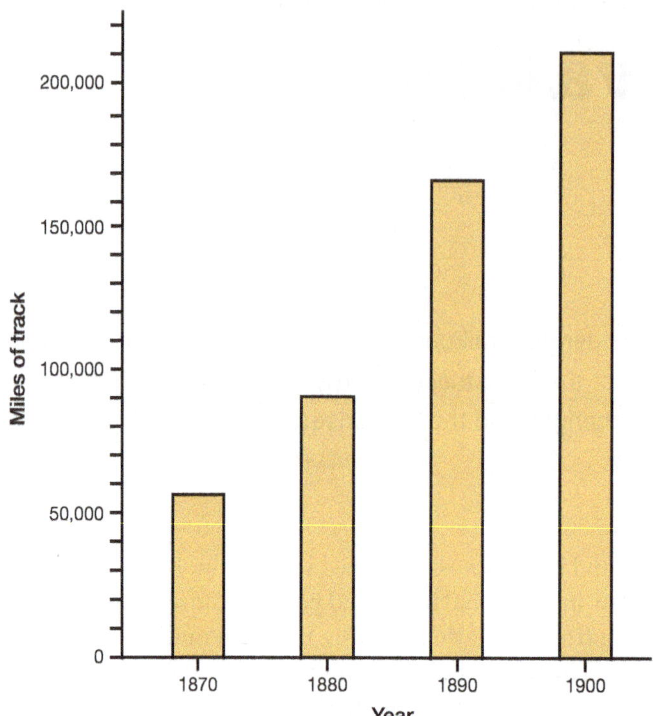

Expansion of the Railroad System, 1870–1900 The great expansion of the railroads in the late nineteenth century fueled the industrial revolution and the growth of big business. Connecting the nation from East Coast to West Coast, transcontinental railroads created a national market for natural resources and manufactured goods. The biggest surges in railroad construction occurred west of the Mississippi River and in the South.

What social and economic factors contributed to large-scale railroad expansion from 1870 to 1900?

consumers of industrial products, stimulating the growth of a number of industries through their consumption of steel, wood, coal, glass, rubber, brass, and iron. Finally, railroads contributed to economic growth by increasing the speed and efficiency with which products and materials were transported.

Before railroads could create a national market, they had to overcome several critical problems. In 1877, railroad lines were scattered haphazardly across the country. They mainly served local markets and remained unconnected at key points. This lack of coordination stemmed mainly from the fact that each railroad had its own track gauge (the width between the tracks), making shared track use impossible and long-distance travel extremely difficult.

The consolidation of railroads solved many of these problems. In 1886, railroad companies finally agreed to adopt a standard gauge. Railroads also standardized time zones, thus eliminating confusion in train schedules. During the 1870s, towns and cities had each set their own time zone, a practice that created discrepancies among them. In 1882, the time in New York City and in Boston varied by 11 minutes and 45 seconds. The following year, railroads agreed to coordinate times and divided the country into four standard time zones. Most cities soon cooperated with the new system, but not until 1918 did the federal government legislate the standard time zones that the railroads had first adopted.

AP® EXAM TIP

This module highlights technological innovations used by businesses to increase production and lower costs of goods. Use your book to record examples such as the telephone, Bessemer processes, air brakes, and electric companies, each of which is defined in the text. Select one and explain how it advanced businesses and/or urban areas.

REVIEW

- How did the expansion of railroads change life in the United States?

Innovations and Inventions

As important as railroads were, they were not the only engine of industrialization. American technological innovation created new industries, while expanding the efficiency and productivity of old ones. By 1866, a permanent transatlantic telegraph

Left: Library of Congress, LC-DIG-ggbain-23944; center: University of Minnesota Libraries, Charles Babbage Institute

New Office Machines for the Industrial Era Starting in the late nineteenth century, industrial production and the growth of corporations led to the mechanization of office work. Above are a typewriter from 1868 (left), an adding machine from 1891 (center), and a mimeograph machine for copying documents from 1913 (right).

In what ways could these office machines aid in the expansion of the industrial economy during this period?

cable connected the United States and Europe, allowing businessmen on both sides of the ocean to pursue profitable commercial ventures.

New inventions also allowed business offices to run more smoothly: Typewriters were invented in 1868, carbon paper in 1872, adding machines in 1891, and mimeograph machines in 1892. As businesses grew, they needed more space for their operations. The construction of towering skyscrapers in the 1880s in cities such as Chicago and New York was made possible by two innovations: structural steel, which had the strength to support tall buildings, and elevators.

Alexander Graham Bell's telephone revolutionized communications. By 1880, fifty-five cities offered local service and catered to a total of 50,000 subscribers, most of them business customers. In 1885, Bell established the American Telephone and Telegraph Company (AT&T), and long-distance service connected New York, Boston, and Chicago. By 1900, around 1.5 million telephones were in operation.

AP® WORKING with EVIDENCE

Source: *Chicago Tribune,* "The Telephone," December 12, 1880

"The number of telephones in use in Chicago is rapidly running up into the thousands, and the wires have literally cobwebbed the city. It is estimated that 'hello!' is said 6,461,009 times every day in the transmission of messages. . . . Merely a baby as yet in age, the telephone has nevertheless risen to a prominent place in public esteem, and is now almost an actual necessity to any one engaged in large business. By its means now a man is practically placed in the same room with every large firm in the city, to converse with its members at will and with perfect ease."

Questions for Analysis

1. Identify the evidence the article uses to prove the impact of the telephone on Chicago.
2. Describe how the telephone has transformed the city of Chicago according to the article.
3. Explain the effect on business the telephone has had, according to the article.

Perhaps the greatest technological innovations that advanced industrial development in the late nineteenth century came in steel manufacturing. In 1859 Henry Bessemer, a British inventor, designed a furnace that burned the impurities out of melted iron and converted it into steel. The open-hearth process, devised by another Englishman, William Siemens, further improved the quality of steel by removing additional impurities from the iron.

AP® EXAM TIP

Here, the textbook provides an excellent example of an innovation that led to more natural resources being used by businesses. Think about the extraction of petroleum and how that was used for oil in different areas of industry. Putting together concepts like these two is an essential part of developing historical connections.

Railroads replaced iron rails with steel because it was lighter, stronger, and more durable than iron. Steel became the major building block of industry, furnishing girders and cables to construct manufacturing plants and office structures. As production became cheaper and more efficient, steel output soared from 13,000 tons in 1860 to 28 million tons in the first decade of the twentieth century.

Factory machinery needed constant lubrication, and the growing petroleum industry made this possible. A drilling technique devised in 1859 had tapped into pools of petroleum located deep below the earth's surface. In the post–Civil War era, new distilling techniques transformed petroleum into lubricating oil for factory machinery. This process of "cracking" crude oil also generated lucrative by-products for the home, such as kerosene and paraffin for heating and lighting and salve to soothe cuts and burns. After 1900, the development of the gasoline-powered, internal-combustion engine for automobiles opened up an even richer market for the oil industry.

American Stock Archive/Getty Images

Manufacturing of Steel Tubing, 1897 This engraving appeared in the December 18, 1897, issue of *Scientific American* and illustrates the manufacture of steel tubing pipes at the National Tube Works in McKeesport, Pennsylvania. With high flames in the background, workers are welding rings on a twenty-three-inch pipe.

What aspects of the image reveal the changes in industrial production during the late nineteenth century?

Railroads also benefited from innovations in technology. Improvements included air brakes and automatic coupling devices to attach train cars to each other. Elijah McCoy, a trained engineer and the son of freedpeople, was forced because of racial discrimination to work at menial railroad jobs shoveling coal and lubricating train parts every few miles to keep the gears from overheating. This experience encouraged him to invent and patent an automatic lubricating device to improve efficiency.

Early innovations resulted from the genius of individual inventors, but by the late nineteenth century, technological progress was increasingly an organized, collaborative effort. Thomas Alva Edison and his team served as the model. In 1876, Edison set up a research laboratory in Menlo Park, New Jersey. Housed in a two-story, white frame building, Edison's "invention factory" was staffed by a team of inventors and craftsmen. In 1887, Edison opened another laboratory, ten times bigger than the one at Menlo Park, in nearby Orange, New Jersey. These facilities pioneered the research laboratories that would become a standard feature of American industrial development in the twentieth century.

Out of Edison's laboratories flowed inventions that revolutionized American business and culture. The phonograph and motion pictures changed the way people spent their leisure time. The electric light bulb illuminated people's homes and made them safer by eliminating the need for candles and gas lamps, which were fire hazards. The light bulb also brightened city streets, making them available for outdoor evening activities, and lit up factories so that they could operate all night long.

Like his contemporaries who were building America's huge industrial empires, Edison cashed in on his workers' inventions. He joined forces with the Wall Street banker J. P. Morgan to finance the Edison Electric Illuminating Company, which in 1882 provided lighting to customers in New York City. Goods produced by electric equipment jumped in value from $1.9 million in 1879 to $21.8 million in 1890. In 1892, Morgan helped Edison merge his companies with several competitors and reorganized them as the General Electric Corporation, which became the industry leader.

- What was the relationship between technological innovation and industrialization during the late nineteenth century?

AP® Skills Workshop: Thinking Historically

Making Connections across Time in an Essay Conclusion

Now that you've learned to incorporate context into your conclusions (Module 4.10), and to trace developments and processes within that context (Module 6.3), you're ready to **make connections** between the subject of your response and your concluding context. This will allow you to illuminate patterns in U.S. history and draw broader conclusions about the history of the nation as a whole.

Consider the following prompt:

> Evaluate the extent to which technological innovations in the late nineteenth century transformed U.S. society between 1865 and 1898.

A thesis that answers this prompt might look like this:

> Between 1865 and 1898, technological innovations transformed the way Americans communicated with each other, traveled, and worked, but social classes still tended to be broadly divided between the working class, the middle class, and an elite that controlled the economy. **[claim]** While the telephone, the transcontinental railroad, and the advent of national corporations changed the way Americans lived, the expansion of the working class, the middle class, and the stability of a small and powerful capitalist class followed social structures that predated the period. **[line of reasoning]**

A concluding paragraph for this thesis should include a rephrasing of the thesis statement's claim and line of reasoning, a concluding context (don't forget to **CSE**!)

(continued)

that discerns a development or process, and a **connection** to a specific trend that establishes a pattern in U.S. history. For example:

> While the way Americans communicated, traveled, and worked changed between 1865 and 1898, the nation's broad social structures remained the same. **[claim]** Innovations like the telephone, the transcontinental railroad, and national corporations had enormous social effects, but the existence of three broad classes — working, middle, and elite — continued during the second industrial revolution. **[line of reasoning]** This development likewise occurred in the twenty-first century, when technology changed Americans' lives again, but social classes remained very much the same. **[long-term concluding context claim that connects "technological change" in the nineteenth and twenty-first centuries]** Innovations like the Internet and smartphones transformed the ways in which Americans communicated with each other, yet the structure of society's lower, middle, and small upper classes remained broadly unchanged. **[long-term concluding context support]** The continuity of these class divisions points to a certain consistency in social structures in the United States in the one-hundred-odd years between the second industrial revolution and the digital revolution of our time. **[long-term concluding context explanation with connection]**

Notice how in this sample conclusion, the explanation **connects** the two time periods (1865–1898 and the twenty-first century) by pointing out the way in which the development of changing technology and static social structures **are connected** by similar attributes. Oftentimes, when you draw connections like this in your conclusion, you will do so when you **explain** how your long-term concluding context evidence **supports** your long-term concluding context **claim.**

ACTIVITY

Now try to write a concluding paragraph that traces a contextual development or process and makes a connection in your explanation of that context. So you don't have to use material from later in this book, here is a prompt based on material in Period 4. A thesis with a claim and line of reasoning is provided for you. Write a conclusion that includes a rephrasing of this thesis, establishes a concluding context from Period 6 that traces a trend or process, and connects the two time periods (Period 4 and Period 6).

> Evaluate the extent to which technological innovations in the early nineteenth century transformed U.S. society between 1800 and 1844.

> Between 1800 and 1844, Americans' lives were transformed by innovation in communication, transportation, and production, but the social structures of the period reflected earlier patterns. **[claim]** While the telegraph, the canal and steamboat system, and the advent of factory production changed the way many Americans lived, the nation remained mostly divided between a poor class of farmers and workers, a small middle class, and a few powerful landholders and early industrialists that controlled the U.S. economy. **[line of reasoning]**

The Rise of Industrial Capitalism

MODULE 6.6

FOCUS

During the second industrial revolution, business owners used new ways to organize production to increase output and distribute goods throughout the nation. Likewise, they reorganized the economy by consolidating corporations (profit-seeking companies) into national entities that had the power to control whole sectors of the economy. These corporations also sought resources and markets outside of the United States.

As you read this module, consider the way in which the growth of industrial capitalism transformed the U.S. economy, while also continuing some of the trends in American capitalism that predated the second industrial revolution.

Industrial Consolidation

In the North, South, and West, nineteenth-century industrialists strove to minimize or eliminate competition. To gain competitive advantages and increase profits, industrial entrepreneurs concentrated on reducing production costs, charging lower prices, and outselling the competition. Successful firms could then acquire rival companies that could no longer afford to compete, creating an industrial empire in the process.

Building such industrial empires was not easy, however, and posed creative challenges for business ventures. Heavy investment in machinery resulted in very high fixed costs (or overhead) that did not change much over time. Because overhead costs remained stable, manufacturers could reduce the per-unit cost of production by increasing the output of a product—what economists call "economy of scale."

Manufacturers thus aimed to raise the volume of production and find ways to cut variable costs—for labor and materials, for example. Through such savings, a factory owner could sell his product more cheaply than his competitors and gain a larger share of the market. A major organizational technique for reducing costs and underselling the competition was **vertical integration**.

"Captains of industry," as their admirers called them, did not just build a business. They created a system—a network of firms, each contributing to the final product. Men like Andrew Carnegie controlled the various phases of production from top to bottom (vertical)—extracting the raw materials, transporting them to the factories, manufacturing the finished products, and shipping them to market.

By using vertical integration, Carnegie eliminated middlemen and guaranteed regular and cheap access to supplies. He also lowered inventories and gained increased flexibility by shifting segments of the labor force to areas where they were most needed. His credo became "Watch the costs and the profits will take care of themselves."

Men like Carnegie became both the heroes and the villains of their age. They created systems of industrial organization and corporate management that altered the economic landscape of the country and changed the place of the United States in the world. They also engaged in ruthless practices that would lead some to label the new industrialists **robber barons**.

AP® EXAM TIP

Understand how to explain what the course framework describes as *management structures*. Here, your book provides useful explanations about horizontal and vertical integration, which are examples of management structures.

vertical integration

An organizational technique used by a company to gain control over all steps in the production of a product. Carnegie Steel, an example of a vertically integrated corporation, controlled the mines where iron ore was acquired and the mills where it was turned into steel.

robber baron

A negative term applied to late-nineteenth-century industrialists and capitalists who became very rich by dominating large industries while employing low-cost labor alongside new money-saving technologies.

horizontal integration
The use of mergers or acquisitions to create a company with a large enough market share to dominate an industry and control pricing. John D. Rockefeller's Standard Oil Company, a horizontally integrated corporation, controlled most oil refining in the United States and, therefore, much of the petroleum market.

Businessmen also employed another type of integration—**horizontal integration**. This approach focused on gaining greater control over the market by acquiring firms that sold the same products. John D. Rockefeller, the founder of the mammoth Standard Oil Company, specialized in this technique. In the mid-1870s, he brought a number of key oil refiners into an alliance with Standard Oil to control four-fifths of the industry. At the same time, the oil baron ruthlessly drove out of business or bought up marginal firms that could not afford to compete with him.

Horizontal integration was also a major feature in the telegraph industry. By 1861, Western Union had strung 76,000 miles of telegraph line throughout the nation. Founded in 1851, the company had thrived during the Civil War by obtaining most of the federal government's telegraph business. The firm had 12,600 offices housed in railroad depots throughout the country and strung its lines adjacent to the railroads.

Seeing an opportunity to make money, Wall Street tycoon Jay Gould set out to acquire Western Union. In the mid-1870s, Gould, who had obtained control over the Union Pacific Railway, financed companies to compete with the giant telegraph outfit. Gould did not succeed until 1881, when he engineered a takeover of Western Union by combining it with his American Union Telegraph Company. Gould made a profit of $30 million on the deal. On February 15, the day after the agreement, the *New York Herald Tribune* reported: "The country finds itself this morning at the feet of a telegraphic monopoly," a business that controlled the market and destroyed competition.

interlocking directorate
A system of corporate economic collusion accomplished by having members on multiple corporations' board of directors working in unison rather than in competition.

Bankers played a huge role in engineering industrial consolidation. No one did it more skillfully than J. P. Morgan. In the 1850s, Morgan started his career working for a prominent American-owned banking firm in London, and in 1861, he created his own investment company in New York City. Morgan played the central role in channeling funds from Britain to support the construction of major American railroads. During the 1880s and 1890s, Morgan orchestrated the refinancing of several ailing railroads. To maintain control over these enterprises, the Wall Street financier created **interlocking directorates** by placing his allies on their boards of directors and selecting the companies' chief operating officers. Morgan then turned his talents for organization to the steel industry.

AP® WORKING with EVIDENCE

Source: U.S. Workforce by Industry in 1870 and 1900

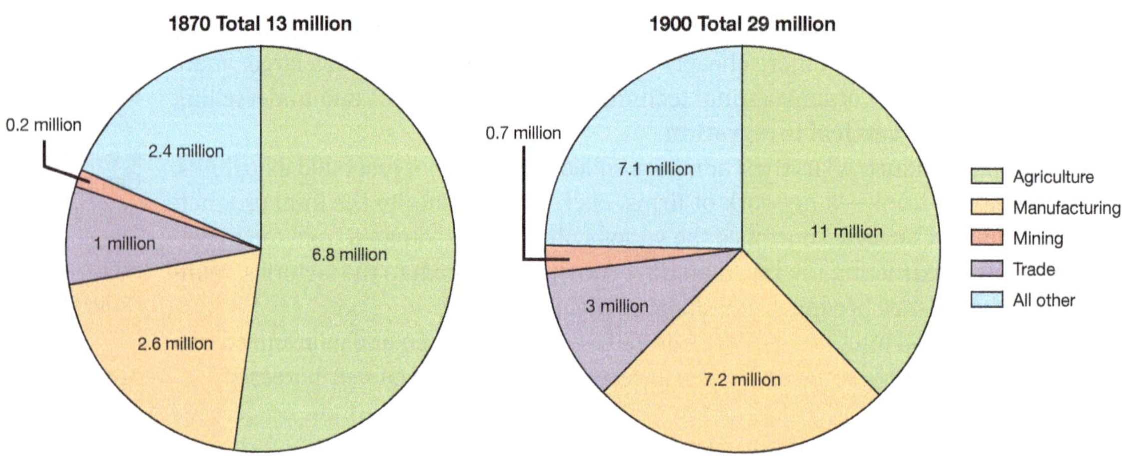

Questions for Analysis

1. Identify the changes and continuities illustrated by these charts.
2. Explain the reasons for the changes and continuities illustrated by the charts.
3. Evaluate the impact of one change and one continuity on American society.

In 1901, Morgan was instrumental in merging Carnegie's company with several competitors in which he had a financial interest. Morgan's creation, United States Steel, became the world's largest industrial corporation, worth $1.4 billion. By the end of the first decade of the twentieth century, Morgan's investment house held more than 340 directorships in 112 corporations, amounting to more than $22 billion in assets, the equivalent of $525 billion in 2015, all at a time when there was no income tax.

- How did vertical integration, horizontal integration, and the use of interlocking directorates promote industrial consolidation?

The Growth of Corporations

With economic consolidation came the expansion of corporations. Before the age of large-scale enterprise, the predominant form of business ownership was the partnership. Unlike a partnership, a **corporation** provided investors with "limited liability." This meant that if the corporation went bankrupt, shareholders could not lose more than they had invested. Limited liability encouraged investment by keeping the shareholders' investment in the corporation separate from their other assets. In addition, corporations provided "perpetual life." Partnerships dissolved on the death of a partner, whereas corporations continued to function despite the death of any single owner. This form of ownership brought stability and order to financing, building, and perpetuating what was otherwise a highly volatile and complex business endeavor.

Capitalists devised new corporate structures to gain greater control over their industries. Rockefeller's Standard Oil Company led the way by creating the **trust**, a monopoly formed by a small group of leading stockholders from several firms who manage the consolidated enterprise. To evade state laws against monopolies, Rockefeller created a petroleum trust. He combined other oil firms across the country with Standard Oil and placed their owners on a nine-member board of trustees that ran the company.

Subsequently, Rockefeller fashioned another method of bringing rival businesses together. Through a **holding company**, he obtained stock in a number of other oil companies and held them under his control.

Between 1880 and 1905, more than three hundred mergers occurred in 80 percent of the nation's manufacturing firms. Great wealth became heavily concentrated in the hands of a relatively small number of businessmen. Around two thousand businesses, a tiny fraction of the total number, dominated 40 percent of the nation's economy.

In their drive to consolidate economic power and shield themselves from risk, corporate titans generally had the courts on their side. In ***Santa Clara County v. Southern Pacific Railroad Company*** (1886), the Supreme Court decided that under the Fourteenth Amendment, which originally dealt with the issue of federal protection of African Americans' civil rights, a corporation was considered a "person." In effect, this ruling gave corporations the same right of due process that the framers of the amendment had meant to give to freedpeople. In the 1890s, a majority of the Supreme Court embraced this interpretation. The right of due process shielded corporations from prohibitive government regulation of the workplace, including the passage of legislation reducing the number of hours in the workday.

Yet there was opposition to the trusts. In 1890, Congress passed the **Sherman Antitrust Act**, which outlawed monopolies that prevented free competition in interstate commerce. The bill passed easily with bipartisan support because it merely codified legal

corporation
A legally recognized form of business ownership in which the liability, or financial risk, of shareholders in a company is limited to their individual investments. The formation of corporations in the late nineteenth century greatly stimulated investment in industry, and large corporations came to dominate certain industries.

trust
A business monopoly formed in the late nineteenth and early twentieth centuries through mergers and consolidation that inhibited competition and controlled the market.

holding company
A form of business consolidation in which one company holds controlling stock in multiple corporations, thereby giving the holding company control over those corporations simultaneously.

AP® EXAM TIP

Business consolidation is an essential part of understanding industrial capitalism in the Gilded Age. Use the information in your book about how John D. Rockefeller and Standard Oil Company established a holding company and used horizontal integration to understand this process.

Sherman Antitrust Act
A law enacted in 1890 banning monopolies and business practices that restrained free trade or fixed prices in interstate or foreign commerce. This act was the first congressional legislation to address the problems of trusts.

scientific management
Also known as Taylorism, a management style developed by Frederick W. Taylor that aimed to continually improve the efficiency of employees by reducing manual labor to its simplest components. While aiming to increase productivity and decrease cost for employers, scientific management proved more successful in accelerating the loss of worker autonomy than in cutting costs.

principles that already existed. Senator John Sherman and his colleagues never intended to stifle large corporations that had come to dominate the market through efficient business practices. Rather, the lawmakers attempted to limit underhanded actions that destroyed competition.

The judicial system further bailed out corporate leaders. In ***United States v. E. C. Knight Company*** (1895), a case against the "sugar trust," the Supreme Court rendered the Sherman Act toothless by ruling that manufacturing was a local activity within a state and that, even if it was a monopoly, it was not subject to congressional regulation. This ruling left most trusts in the manufacturing sector beyond the jurisdiction of the Sherman Antitrust Act.

The introduction of managerial specialists, already present in European firms, proved the most critical innovation for integrating industry. With many operations controlled under one roof, large-scale businesses required a corps of experts to oversee and coordinate the various steps of production. As the expanding labor force worked to produce a rapidly rising volume of goods, efficiency experts sought to cut labor costs and make the production process operate more smoothly.

Frederick W. Taylor, a Philadelphia engineer and businessman, developed the principles of **scientific management**. Based on his concept of reducing manual labor to its simplest components and eliminating independent action on the part of workers, managers introduced time-and-motion studies. Using a stopwatch, they calculated how to break down a job into simple tasks that could be performed in the least amount of time. From this perspective, workers were no different from the machines they operated. With production soaring, marketing and advertising managers were called upon to devise new techniques to gauge consumer interests and stimulate their demands.

Another vital factor in creating large-scale industry was the establishment of retail outlets that could sell the enormous volume of goods pouring out of factories. As consumer goods became less expensive, retail outlets sprang up to serve the growing market for household items. Customers could shop at department stores — such as Macy's in New York City, Filene's in Boston, Marshall Field's in Chicago, May's in Denver, Nordstrom's in Seattle, and Jacome's in Tucson — where they were waited on by a growing army of salesclerks. Or they could buy the cheaper items in Frank W. Woolworth's five-and-ten-cent stores, which opened in towns and cities nationwide.

Chain supermarkets — such as the Great Atlantic and Pacific Tea Company (A&P), founded in 1869 — sold fruits and vegetables packed in tin cans. They also sold foods from the meatpacking firms of Gustavus Swift and Philip Armour, which shipped them on refrigerated railroad cars.

Mail-order catalogs allowed Americans in all parts of the country to buy consumer goods without

Granger – Historical Picture Archive

1899 Sears, Roebuck Catalog The expansion of industrialization and completion of the transcontinental railroad created a national market for manufactured goods and led to the growth of consumer culture. The Chicago-based Sears, Roebuck used its mail-order catalog to attract customers throughout the United States and, as its cover suggests, the world. This colorful 1899 catalog offered the latest in carpets, furniture, tableware, fashion, and photographic equipment and supplies.

How did this image promote consumerism?

leaving their home. The catalogs of Montgomery Ward (established in 1872) and Sears, Roebuck (founded in 1886) offered tens of thousands of items. Rural free delivery, instituted by the U.S. Post Office in 1891, made it even easier for farmers and others living in the countryside to obtain these catalogs and buy their merchandise without having to travel miles to the nearest post office. By the end of the nineteenth century, the industrial economy had left its mark on almost all aspects of life in almost every corner of America.

AP® EXAM TIP

Making connections is a vital part of historical writing. Practice by connecting the following concepts in no more than three sentences: industrial production, labor, and technological changes. Being able to make concise, accurate connections will help you on each part of the writing sections for the AP® Exam.

REVIEW

- What historical developments led to the growth of corporations?

AP® Skills Workshop: Thinking Historically

Additional Practice in Making Connections across Time in an Essay Conclusion

Use the following Period 4 prompt and thesis statement to compose a conclusion that incorporates an immediate or long-term concluding context for a development or process and makes a connection to a different time period. For your connection, consider the information you have read about thus far in Period 6. Review the Thinking Historically exercise in Module 6.5 if you need more help in making connections in a conclusion.

> Evaluate the extent to which transportation innovations between 1800 and 1844 unified the U.S. economy.
>
> Starting in the early 1800s, the transportation network of the United States depended upon innovations that united the U.S. economy in terms of production, yet these innovations could not unify the ideological differences that continued to shape the economy overall. **[claim]** While canals, steamboats, roads, and railroads made it easier to transport goods from one region to another, the divisions between free-labor capitalism and a southern economy dependent upon enslaved labor divided the nation as to which system best represented the economic future. **[line of reasoning]**

MODULE 6.7

Labor in the Gilded Age

FOCUS

The work of many Americans was transformed by the second industrial revolution. While some workers saw their purchasing power increase when industrial output caused prices to fall, others saw declines in wages, suffered through economic depressions, and faced harsh working conditions.

As you read this module, consider how the lives of workers changed as a result of technological inventions, the rise of large corporations, and industrial production. Examine how those changes led workers to create labor unions, and evaluate the degree of success organized labor experienced during this time. Also consider how, how much, and why the role of government in the economy changed.

Just as industrialists had built powerful corporations to promote their economic interests, working men and women also saw the benefits of organizing to increase their political and economic leverage. Determined to secure decent wages and working conditions, workers joined labor unions, formed political parties, and engaged in a variety of collective actions, including strikes.

However, workers' organizations were beset by internal conflicts over occupational status, race, ethnicity, and gender. They proved no match for the powerful alliance between corporations and the federal government that stood against them, and they failed to become a lasting national political force. Workers fared better in their own communities, where family, neighbors, and local businesses were more likely to come to their aid.

The Industrialization of Labor

The industrialization of the United States transformed the workplace, bringing together large numbers of laborers under difficult conditions. In 1870, few factories employed 500 or more workers. Thirty years later, more than 1,500 companies had workforces of this size. Just after the Civil War, manufacturing employed 5.3 million workers; thirty years later, the figure soared to more than 15.1 million.

Most of these new industrial workers came from two main sources. First, farmers who could not make a decent living from the soil moved to nearby cities in search of factory jobs. Although mostly white, this group also included Black people who sought to escape the oppressive conditions of sharecropping. Between 1870 and 1890, some 80,000 Black Americans journeyed from the rural South to cities in the South and the North to search for employment. Second, the economic opportunities in America drew millions of immigrants from Europe over the course of the nineteenth century. Immigrant workers initially came from northern Europe. However, by the end of the nineteenth century, immigrants from southern and eastern European countries predominated.

Inside factories, unskilled workers, those with no particular skill or expertise, encountered a system undergoing critical changes, as small-scale manufacturing gave way to larger and more mechanized operations. Immigrants, who made up the bulk of unskilled laborers, had to adjust both to a new country and to unfamiliar, unpleasant, and often dangerous industrial work. A traveler from Hungary who visited a steel mill in Pittsburgh that employed many Hungarian immigrants compared the factories to prisons where "the heat is most insupportable, the flames most choking." Nor were any government benefits—such as workers' compensation or unemployment insurance—available to industrial laborers who were hurt in accidents or laid off from their jobs.

Skilled workers, who had particular training or abilities and were more difficult to replace, were not immune to the changes brought about by industrialization and the rise of large-scale businesses. In the early days of manufacturing, skilled laborers operated as independent craftsmen. They provided their own tools, worked at their own pace, and controlled their production output. This approach to work enhanced their sense of personal dignity, reflected their notion of themselves as free citizens, and distinguished them from the mass of unskilled laborers.

Mechanization, however, undercut their autonomy by dictating both the nature and the speed of production through practices of scientific management. Instead of producing goods, skilled workers increasingly applied their craft to servicing machinery and keeping it running smoothly. While owners reaped the benefits of the mechanization and regimentation of the industrial workplace, many skilled workers saw such "improvements" as a threat to their freedom.

Still, most workers did not oppose the technology that increased their productivity and resulted in higher wages. Compared to their mid-nineteenth-century counterparts, industrial laborers now made up a larger share of the general population, earned more money, and worked fewer hours. During the 1870s and 1880s, the average industrial worker's real wages (actual buying power) increased by 20 percent. At the same time, the average workday declined from ten and a half hours to ten hours. From 1870 to 1890, the general price index dropped 30 percent, allowing consumers to benefit from lower prices.

AP® EXAM TIP

A common error is to think that most laborers became poorer during the Gilded Age. While the gap between the wealthiest and everyone else greatly increased and wages for unskilled labor declined, the purchasing power of those same unskilled workers substantially increased as manufacturing innovations led to lower prices. Be able to explain and reconcile these developments in a short paragraph with specific examples.

AP® WORKING with EVIDENCE

Source: John Morrison, *Testimony of a Machinist before the Senate Committee on the Relations between Labor and Capital*, 1883

"**Question:** Is there any difference between the conditions under which machinery is made now and those which existed ten years ago?
Answer: A great deal of difference.

Question: State the differences as well as you can.
Answer: Well, the trade has been subdivided and those subdivisions have been again subdivided, so that a man never learns the machinist's trade now. Ten years ago he learned, not the whole of the trade, but a fair portion of it. Also, there is more machinery used in the business, which again makes machinery. The different branches of the trade are divided and subdivided so that one man may make just a particular part of a machine and may not know anything whatever about another part of the same machine. In that way machinery is produced a great deal cheaper than it used to be formerly, and in fact, through

this system of work, 100 men are able to do now what it took 300 or 400 men to do fifteen years ago. By the use of machinery and the subdivision of the trade they so simplify the work that it is made a great deal easier and put together a great deal faster. There is no system of apprenticeship, I may say, in the business. You simply go in and learn whatever branch you are put at, and you stay at that unless you are changed to another. . . .

Question: Are the machinists here generally contented, or are they in a state of discontent and unrest?
Answer: There is mostly a general feeling of discontent, and you will find among the machinists the most radical workingmen, with the most revolutionary ideas. You will find that they don't so much give their thoughts simply to trade unions and other efforts of that kind, but they go far beyond that; they only look for relief through the ballot or through a revolution, a forcible revolution."

Questions for Analysis

1. Describe the changes in working conditions stated by Morrison.
2. Explain how the document reflects the longer-term positive and negative effects of trade subdivision for skilled workers.
3. Evaluate the extent to which the process of trade subdivision described in the excerpt represented a continuity in industrial working conditions.

Yet workers were far from content, and the lives of industrial workers remained extremely difficult. Although workers as a group saw improvements in wages and hours, they did not earn enough income to support their families adequately. Also, there were widespread disparities based on job status, race, ethnicity, sex, and region. Skilled workers earned more than unskilled workers. Whites were paid more than Blacks, who were mainly shut out of better jobs. Immigrants from northern Europe, who had settled in the United States before southern Europeans, tended to hold higher-paying skilled positions. Southern factory workers, whether in textiles, steel, or armaments, earned less than their northern counterparts.

Between 1870 and 1900, the number of female wageworkers grew by 66 percent, accounting for about one-quarter of all nonfarm laborers. Women, an increasingly important component of the industrial workforce, earned, on average, only 25 percent of what men did. The majority of employed women, including those working in factories, were single and between the ages of sixteen and twenty-four. Overall, only 5 percent of married women worked outside the home, although 30 percent of Black wives were employed.

Women workers were concentrated in several areas. White and Black women continued to serve as maids and domestics. Others took over jobs that were once occupied by men. They became teachers, nurses, clerical workers, telephone operators, and department store salesclerks. Some women toiled in manufacturing jobs requiring fine eye-hand coordination, such as cigar rolling and work in the needle trades and textile industry.

Women also turned their homes into workplaces. In crowded apartments, they sewed furs onto garments, made straw hats, prepared artificial flowers, and fashioned jewelry. Earnings from piecework (work that pays at a set rate per unit) were even lower than factory wages, but they allowed married women with young children to contribute to the family income.

When sufficient space was available, families rented rooms to boarders, and women provided meals and housekeeping for the lodgers. Some female workers found other ways to balance work with the needs and constraints of family life. To gain greater autonomy in their work, Black laundresses began cleaning clothes in their own homes, rather than their white employers' homes, so that they could control their own work hours. In 1881, Black washerwomen in Atlanta conducted a two-week strike to secure higher fees from white customers.

Manufacturing also employed many child workers. By 1900, about 10 percent of girls and 20 percent of boys between the ages of ten and fifteen worked, and at least 1.7 million children under the age of sixteen held jobs. Employers often exposed children to dangerous and unsanitary conditions. Most child workers toiled long, hard hours breathing in dust and fumes as they labored in textile mills, tobacco plants, print shops, and coal mines. In Indiana, young boys worked the night shift in dark, windowless glass factories. Children under the age of ten, known as "breaker boys," climbed onto filthy coal heaps and picked out unprocessed material. Working up to twelve-hour days, these children received less than a dollar a day.

Be able to describe examples of places child laborers were more likely to work. Think about specific examples and connect that to broader developments such as industrialization or urbanization.

Women and children worked because the average male head of household could not support his family on his own pay, despite the increase in real wages. As Carroll D. Wright, director of the Massachusetts Bureau of the Statistics of Labor, reported in 1882, "A family of workers can always live well, but the man with a family of small children to support, unless his wife works also, has a small chance of living properly." For example, in 1883 in Joliet, Illinois, a railroad brakeman tried to support his wife and eight children on $360 a year. A state investigator described the way they lived: "Clothes ragged, children half dressed and dirty. They all sleep in one room regardless of sex. The house is devoid of furniture, and the entire concern is as wretched as could be imagined."

Not all laborers lived in such squalor, but many wageworkers barely lived at subsistence level. Many laborers put in more than ten hours a day on the job even though the average number of working hours dropped during this era. In the steel industry, blast-furnace operators toiled twelve hours a day, seven days a week. They received a day off every two weeks, but only if they worked a twenty-four-hour shift.

The History Collection/Alamy

Breaker Boys at a Coal Mine in Northeastern, Pennsylvania Breaker boys used their bare hands to break coal into pieces, sort pieces by size, and remove impurities. The dirty and dangerous work often led to injury and disease and was sometimes fatal. Public outrage, compulsory education requirements, technological innovations, and child labor laws eventually led to the discontinuance of the practice by the 1920s.

What does this photograph reveal about the working conditions of child laborers?

Given the long hours and backbreaking work, it is not surprising that accidents were a regular feature of industrial life. Each year tens of thousands were injured on the job, and thousands died as a result of mine cave-ins, train wrecks, explosions in industrial plants, and fires at textile mills and garment factories. Railroad employment was especially unsafe—accidents ended the careers of one in six workers.

Although wages and working hours improved slightly for some workers, employers kept the largest share of the increased profits that resulted from industrialization. In 1877, John D. Rockefeller collected dividends at the rate of at least $720 an hour, roughly double what his average employee earned in a year. Despite some success stories, prospects for upward mobility for most American workers remained limited. A manual worker might rise into the ranks of the semiskilled but would not make it into the middle class. And to achieve even this small upward mobility required putting the entire family to work and engaging in rigorous economizing, what one historian called "ruthless underconsumption." Despite their best efforts, most Americans remained part of the working class.

WORKING with EVIDENCE

Source: Bernhard Gillam, "Hopelessly Bound to the Stake," *Puck* magazine, 1883

Library of Congress, LC-DIG-ppmsca-28415

About the source: In this image, the heads at the ends of the logs on the fire include wealthy industrialists, one of whom is spewing fire labeled "MONOPOLY PRICES," a political machine boss, and the "monopoly press." The stake the man is tied to is labeled "MONOPOLY," and the belt that chains him to the stake is labeled "WORKMAN."

Questions for Analysis

1. Describe the intended audience for this image.
2. Explain how Gillam uses symbols to convey his main argument in this cartoon.
3. Explain the historical developments that led to the viewpoint expressed by the cartoonist.

REVIEW

- What effects did industrialization have on skilled versus unskilled workers?
- How were the experiences of women and children in the labor force similar to and different from the experiences of male workers?

Organizing Labor Unions

Faced with improving but inadequate wages and with hazardous working conditions, industrial laborers sought to counter the concentrated power of corporate capitalists by joining forces. They attempted to organize **labor unions**—groups of workers seeking rights and benefits from their employers through their collective efforts.

labor union
An organized group of workers, who, through power in numbers and collective efforts, seek to secure and improve the pay, benefits, and working conditions from their employers.

Union organizing was prompted by attitudes that were common among employers. Most employers were convinced that they and their employees shared identical interests, and they believed that they were morally and financially entitled to establish policies on their workers' behalf. They refused to engage in negotiations with labor unions, a process known as **collective bargaining**, where workers collectively—rather than individually—negotiated work contracts. Although owners appreciated the advantages of companies banding together to eliminate competition or to lobby for favorable regulations, similar collective efforts by workers struck them as unfair, even immoral. It was up to the men who supplied the money and the machines — rather than the workers—to determine what was a fair wage and what were satisfactory working conditions.

In 1877, William H. Vanderbilt, the son of transportation tycoon Cornelius Vanderbilt, explained this way of thinking: "Our men feel that although I . . . may have my millions and they the rewards of their daily toil, still we are about equal in the end. If they suffer, I suffer, and if I suffer they cannot escape." Needless to say, many workers disagreed.

Industrialists expected their reputation for generosity to reduce grievances among their workforce. They sponsored sports teams, set up social clubs, and offered cultural activities. The railroad magnate George Pullman built a model village to house his workers. In return, capitalists demanded unquestioned loyalty from their employees.

Yet a growing number of working people failed to see the relationship between employer and employee as mutually beneficial. Increasingly, they considered labor unions to be the best vehicle for communication and negotiation between workers and owners.

Knights of Labor
A labor union founded in 1869 that aimed to unite all workers under a single national union that would be powerful enough to challenge the power of corporate capitalists. Not limiting themselves to pay, benefits, and working conditions, the Knights of Labor became politically active and sought broader social changes.

Although not the first national workers' organization, the **Knights of Labor**, founded in 1869, initiated the most extensive and successful campaign after the Civil War to unite workers and challenge the power of corporate capitalists. "There is no mutuality of interests . . . [between] labor and capital," the Massachusetts chapter of the Knights proclaimed. "It is the iron heel of a soulless monopoly, crushing the manhood out of sovereign citizens." The central premise of the Knights was that all workers shared common interests that were much different from those of owners.

Granger – Historical Picture Archive

Women in the Labor Movement, 1884 This wood engraving shows the wives of striking coal miners jeering at Pinkerton detectives as they escort strikebreakers into the mines in Buchtel, Ohio, in 1884. It was common for the family and friends of strikers in local communities to rally support on their behalf.

How does this image illustrate a rejection of nineteenth-century gender roles?

The Knights did not enjoy immediate success and did not begin to flourish until Terence V. Powderly became the head of the organization in 1879. Powderly advocated an eight-hour workday, the abolition of child labor, and equal pay for women. Under his leadership, the Knights accepted Black Americans, immigrants, and women as members, although they excluded Chinese immigrant workers, as did other labor unions. As a result, the Knights experienced a surge in membership from nine thousand in 1879 to nearly a million in 1885, about 10 percent of the industrial workforce.

Rapid growth proved to be a mixed blessing. As membership grew, Powderly and the national organization exercised less and less control over local chapters. In fact, local chapters often defied the central organization by engaging in strikes, a tactic Powderly had officially disavowed. Members of the Knights struck successfully against the Union Pacific Railroad and the Missouri Pacific Railroad in 1885.

The following year, on May 1, 1886, local assemblies of the Knights joined a nationwide strike to press for an eight-hour workday. However, this strike was soon overshadowed by events in Chicago that would prove to be the undoing of the Knights.

For months in 1886, the McCormick Harvester plant in Chicago had been at the center of often-violent strikes over wages and work conditions. On May 3, 1886, police killed two strikers in a clash between union members and strikebreakers who tried to cross the picket lines. In response, a group of anarchists led by the German-born anarchist August Spies called for a rally in Haymarket Square to protest police violence. Consisting mainly of foreign-born activists, such anarchists believed that government represented the interests of capitalists and stifled freedom for workers. Anarchists differed among themselves, but they generally advocated tearing down government authority, restoring personal freedom, and forming worker communes to replace capitalism. To achieve their goals, anarchists like Spies advocated the violent overthrow of government.

AP® EXAM TIP

Simplify your understanding of labor unions by comparing the American Federation of Labor with the Knights of Labor. Think about who was allowed in each union and specific issues each union advocated in their battles against management.

The Haymarket rally began at 8:30 in the evening on May 4 and attracted no more than 1,500 people, who listened to a series of speeches as rain fell. By 10:30 p.m., when the crowd had dwindled to some 300 people, 180 policemen decided to break it up.

As police moved into the square, someone set off a bomb. The police fired back, and when the smoke cleared, seven policemen and four protesters lay dead. Most of the fatalities and injuries resulted from the police crossfire.

A subsequent trial convicted eight anarchists of murder, though there was no evidence that any of them had planted the bomb or used weapons. Four of them, including Spies, were executed. Although Powderly and other union leaders denounced the anarchists and the bombing, the incident greatly tarnished the labor movement. Capitalists and their allies in the press attacked labor unionists as radicals prone to violence and denounced strikes as un-American. Following this incident, which came to be known as the **Haymarket riot**, the membership rolls of the Knights plunged to below 500,000. By the mid-1890s, the Knights had fewer than 20,000 members.

Haymarket riot
A labor rally in Haymarket Square in Chicago in May 1886 that resulted in violence, including the deaths of several police officers. The carnage was blamed on the supposedly radical nature of the labor movement and contributed to the demise of the Knights of Labor.

As the fortunes of the Knights of Labor faded, the **American Federation of Labor (AFL)** grew in prominence, offering an alternative vision of unionization. Instead of one giant industrial union that included all workers, skilled and unskilled, the AFL organized only skilled craftsmen—the labor elite—into trade unions.

American Federation of Labor (AFL)
A trade union federation founded in 1886. The AFL sought to organize skilled male workers into trade-specific unions and encouraged the vigorous use of the strike in pursuit of better wages and working conditions.

In 1886, Samuel Gompers became president of the AFL. Gompers considered trade unions "the business organizations of the wage earners to attend to the business of the wage earners" and favored the use of strikes. No social reformer, the AFL president concentrated on obtaining better wages and hours for workers so that they could share in the prosperity generated by industrial capitalism. By 1900, the AFL had around a million members. It achieved these numbers by recruiting the most independent, highest-paid, and least replaceable segment of the labor force—white male skilled workers. Unlike the Knights, the AFL had little or no place for women and Black Americans in its ranks.

As impressive as the AFL's achievement was, the union movement as a whole experienced only limited success in the late nineteenth century. Only about one in fifteen industrial workers belonged to a union in 1900. Union membership was low for a variety of reasons. First, the political and economic power of corporations and the prospects of retaliation made the decision to sign up for union membership a risky venture. Second, the diversity of workers made organizing a difficult task. Foreign-born laborers came from many countries and were divided by language, religion, ethnicity, and history. Moreover, European immigrants quickly adopted native-born whites' racial prejudices against Black Americans. Third, despite severe limitations in social mobility, American workers generally retained their faith in the benefits of the capitalist system. Finally, the government used its legal and military authority to side with employers and suppress militant workers.

Southern workers were the most resistant to union organizing. The agricultural background of mill workers left them with a heightened sense of individualism and isolation. In addition, their continued connection to family and friends in the countryside offered a potential escape route from industrial labor. Moreover, employers' willingness to use racial tensions to divide working-class Black people and whites prevented them from joining together to further their common economic interests.

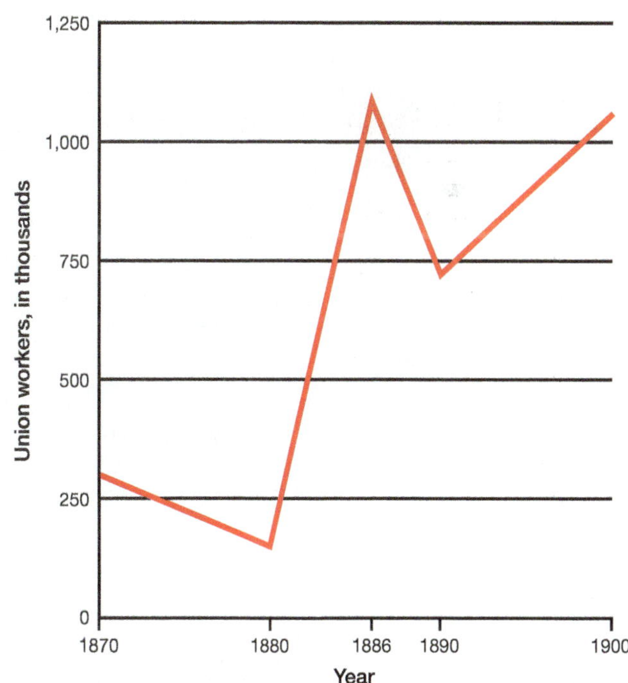

Union Membership, 1870–1900 Union membership fluctuated widely in the late nineteenth century. After reaching a low point in 1880, the number of union members rebounded. However, membership plummeted after 1886 only to soar again in the 1890s.

What developments account for the changes in union membership depicted on the graph between 1880 and 1900?

- What views did industrialists hold regarding organized labor?

Labor Clashes Escalate

Despite the difficulties of organizing workers, labor challenged some of the nation's largest industries in the late nineteenth century. Faced with owners' refusal to recognize or negotiate with unions, workers marshaled their greatest source of power: withholding their labor and going on strike. Employers in turn had powerful weapons at their command to break strikes. They could recruit strikebreakers and mobilize private and public security forces to protect their businesses. That workers went on strike against such odds testified to their desperation and courage (**Map 6.5**).

Homestead strike
The violent 1892 strike by locked-out steelworkers at Andrew Carnegie's Homestead Steel Works. The strike collapsed after the National Guard took control of the mill from workers and a failed assassination attempt on Carnegie's plant manager, Henry Clay Frick.

Labor mounted several highly publicized strikes in the 1890s in their efforts to combat industrial exploitation and secure better wages and working conditions. Perhaps the most famous was the 1892 **Homestead strike**. Steelworkers at Carnegie's Homestead, Pennsylvania, factory near Pittsburgh played an active role in local politics and civic affairs. Residents generally believed that Andrew Carnegie's corporation paid decent wages that allowed them to support their families and buy their own homes. In 1892, craftsmen earned $180 a month, and they appeared to have Carnegie's respect. Others, like John McLuckie, the twice-elected mayor of Homestead and popular union boss, earned less than half that amount, and unskilled workers made even less.

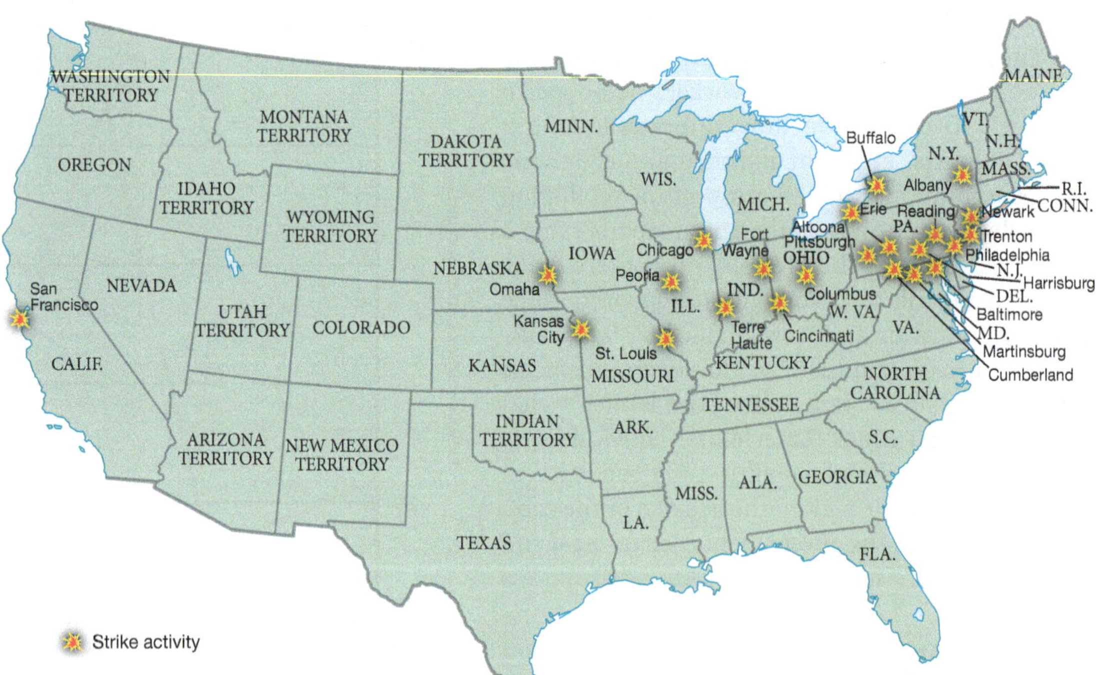

MAP 6.5 **The Great Railroad Strike** This nationwide strike, precipitated by falling wages during the Panic of 1873, started in West Virginia and Pennsylvania and spread to Chicago, St. Louis, and San Francisco. The strike brought a halt to rail traffic as over 100,000 workers and another half a million sympathizers walked off their jobs. Violence broke out in Pittsburgh, resulting in more than twenty deaths. Federal troops were eventually dispatched to end the strike. Many workers quickly recognized the need to form unions to gain the power to stand up against employers and the government.

What factors account for the fact that most of the strike activity shown on this map is concentrated in a belt from the Mid-Atlantic to the Midwest?

In 1892, with steel prices falling, Carnegie decided to replace some of his skilled craftsmen with machinery, cut wages, save on labor costs, and bust McLuckie's union, the Amalgamated Association of Iron and Steel Workers. Knowing that his actions would provoke a strike and seeking to avoid the negative publicity that would result, Carnegie left the country and went to Scotland, leaving his plant manager, Henry Clay Frick, in charge.

Fiercely anti-union, Frick prepared for the strike by building a three-mile, fifteen-foot-high fence, capped with barbed wire and equipped with searchlights, around three sides of the Homestead factory. A hated symbol of the manager's hostility, the fence became known as "Fort Frick." Along the fourth side of the factory flowed the Monongahela River. Frick had no intention of negotiating seriously with the union on a new contract, and on July 1, he ordered a lockout. Only employees who rejected the union and accepted lower wages could return to work. The small town rallied around the workers, and the union members won a temporary victory. On July 6, barge-loads of armed **Pinkerton** detectives, hired by Frick to protect the plant, set sail toward the factory entrance alongside the Monongahela. From the shore, union men shot at the barges and set fire to a boat they pushed toward the Pinkertons. When the smoke cleared, the Pinkertons surrendered and hastily retreated onshore as women and men chased after them.

Pinkerton Agency
A company of private investigators and security guards sometimes used by corporations to violently break up strikes and labor disputes, most famously at the Homestead strike of 1892.

This triumph proved costly for the union. The battle left nine strikers and three Pinkerton detectives dead. Frick persuaded the governor of Pennsylvania to send in state troops to protect the factory and the strikebreakers. Frick's efforts to end the strike spurred some radicals to action. Emma Goldman, an anarchist who advocated the violent overthrow of capitalism, declared that a blow against Frick would "strike terror in the enemy's ranks and make them realize that" America's working class "had its avengers." On July 23, Alexander Berkman, Goldman's partner, who had no connection with the union, entered Frick's office and shot the steel executive in the neck, leaving him wounded but alive. The resulting unfavorable publicity, together with the state's prosecution of the union, broke the strike. Subsequently, steel companies blacklisted the union leaders for life, and McLuckie fled Pennsylvania and wound up nearly penniless in Arizona.

Like Andrew Carnegie, George Pullman considered himself an enlightened employer, one who took good care of the men who worked in his luxury sleeping railcar factory outside Chicago. However, also like the steel titan, Pullman placed profits over personnel. In 1893, a severe economic depression prompted Pullman to cut wages without correspondingly reducing the rents that his employees paid for living in company houses.

The Homestead Steel Strike, 1892 This lithograph depicts the battle between strikers at the Carnegie Steelworks in Homestead, Pennsylvania, and Pinkerton detectives brought in to protect the mill and break the strike. The Pinkertons attempted to get to the plant by barge but were repelled by the strikers from the dock. The strike received international attention, and this illustration appeared in the British weekly newspaper *The Graphic* on July 30, 1892.

Why did each side resort to violence during the Homestead Steel Strike?

This dual blow to worker income and purchasing power led to a fierce strike the following year. The Pullman workers belonged to the American Railway Union, headed by Eugene V. Debs. After George Pullman refused to negotiate, the union voted to go on strike.

Pullman strike

A strike by workers against the Pullman railcar company in 1894, which expanded to a broader railroad strike when American Railway Union workers refused to handle any trains with Pullman cars. When the strike disrupted rail service nationwide, threatening mail delivery, the government sought an injunction against the union, which was followed by a presidential order by Grover Cleveland for federal troops to intervene.

In the end, the **Pullman strike** was broken not by the Pullman company, but by the federal government. President Grover Cleveland ordered federal troops to get the railroads operating, but the workers still refused to capitulate. Richard Olney, Cleveland's attorney general, then obtained a court injunction, an order from the federal courts, to restrain Debs and other union leaders from continuing the strike. The government used the Sherman Antitrust Act (Module 6.6) to punish unions for conspiring to restrain trade, something it had rarely done with respect to large corporations. Refusing to comply, Debs and other union officials were charged with contempt, convicted under the Sherman Antitrust Act, and sent to jail. The strike collapsed.

Debs remained unrepentant. After serving his jail sentence, he became even more radical. In 1901, he helped establish the **Socialist Party of America**, appealing for working-class support by advocating the creation of a more just and humane economic system through the ballot box, not by violent revolution. Debs favored a nonviolent, democratic brand of socialism and managed to attract a base of supporters by articulating socialist doctrines in the language of cooperation and citizenship that many Americans shared. Debsian socialism appealed not only to industrial workers but also to dispossessed farmers and miners in the Southwest and Midwest.

Western miners had a history of labor activism, and by the 1890s, they were ready to listen to radical ideas.

Shortly after the Homestead strike ended in 1892, silver miners in Coeur d'Alene, Idaho, walked out after owners slashed their wages. Employers refused to recognize any union, obtained an injunction against the strike, imported strikebreakers to run the mines, and persuaded Idaho's governor to impose martial law. The work stoppage lasted four months, resulting in the arrest of six hundred strikers. Although the workers lost, the following year they succeeded in forming the Western Federation of Miners, which continued their fight.

Industrial Workers of the World (IWW)

A socialist labor organization that grew out of the activities of the Western Federation of Miners in the 1890s and was formed by Eugene V. Debs and other prominent labor leaders. Known as the "Wobblies," the IWW attempted to unite all skilled and unskilled workers in an effort to overthrow capitalism.

The **Industrial Workers of the World (IWW)**, which emerged largely through the efforts of the Western Federation of Miners, sought to raise wages, improve working conditions, and gain union recognition for the most exploited segments of American labor. The IWW, or "Wobblies" as they were popularly known, sought to unite all skilled and unskilled workers in an effort to overthrow capitalism. The Wobblies favored strikes and direct-action protests rather than collective bargaining or mediation. At their rallies and strikes, they often encountered government force and corporation-inspired mob violence. Nevertheless, the IWW had substantial appeal among lumberjacks in the Northwest, dockworkers in port cities, miners in the West, farmers in the Great Plains, and textile workers in the Northeast.

Even though industrialists usually had state and federal governments as well as the media on their side, workers continued to press for their rights. Workers used strikes as a last resort when business owners refused to negotiate or recognize their demands to organize themselves into unions. Although most strikes in the late nineteenth century failed, striking unionists nonetheless called for collective bargaining, higher wages, shorter hours, and improved working conditions—an agenda that unions and their political allies would build on in the future.

■ How did the tactics used by management compare to those used by organized labor during the 1880s and 1890s?

AP® Skills Workshop: Writing Historically

Responding to a Long-Essay Question with Historical Complexity Using the *GEM* Approach

By this point in the course, you have had plenty of practice writing history essays. You know how to set context for your historical argument in either your introduction or conclusion, and how to craft a thesis that makes evaluative claims that take both sides of every historical reasoning process—cause and effect, continuity and change, and similarity and difference—into account. You have also learned how to support claims effectively with evidence drawn from your knowledge of historical developments and from your interpretation of multiple primary source documents. All of these skills are vital to crafting and developing an argument, and they will serve you well not just on the AP® Exam, but also in college.

Now, you're ready to add the last piece of the essay puzzle: developing complexity in your argument. While the skills you have learned in previous Periods—particularly making and supporting evaluative claims using **CSE**—lay much of the necessary groundwork for demonstrating a complex understanding of history, the strongest essays don't simply make and support historical claims in response to the topic of the prompt. Here, we'll walk you through three common strategies you can use together to deepen your historical analysis in an essay.

These approaches are abbreviated in one easy-to-remember acronym: **GEM**. You've probably heard the phrase "diamond in the rough" before. It refers to something great that's a little unfinished around the edges, and it calls to mind the method by which precious stones are mined from the earth before being cut and smoothed for the final product. Likewise, each element of the **GEM** strategy is designed to help you dig deeper into your analysis to uncover new insight to refine and polish your argument.

So, what does **GEM** stand for?

- **Generating nuance**
- **Explaining both sides**
- **Making connections** that go beyond the prompt (either within or outside of the time period it specifies)

Each of these tactics may appear difficult to carry out at first glance, but in reality, they are simply ways to build on techniques you are already using when you write essays. Let's explore how you might pre-write for a more sophisticated response to the following prompt, which asks you to draw on what you have learned in Modules 6.2–6.6.

> Evaluate the extent of change in the economies of the West, the South, and the North in the period 1865 to 1898.

Step 1 ▶ Break down the prompt

As always, carefully analyzing the prompt is the first thing you should do. This question in particular asks you to determine how much and, by extension, in what ways the economies of the West, the South, and the North changed between 1865 and 1898.

It's important always to keep in mind that each of the three main reasoning skills of the course is double-sided: a causation question is really about causes and effects, a continuity or change question is about both continuities and changes, and a comparison question is asking for similarities and differences. In this case, the phrase

(continued)

"extent of change" in the prompt is most easily answered by an essay framed around change *and* continuity.

Step 2 ▶ List and categorize your historical knowledge, then use GEM to refine your historical argument

In brainstorming and preparing to write an essay focused on continuity and change, think about the economies of the West, South, and North as they were in 1865, at the end of the Civil War, and in 1898, at the end of the nineteenth century. Consider how each economy had changed over those decades. For each major change you identify, jot down as much evidence as you can to support your claims. Remember, thinking of relevant proper nouns is a great place to start.

Here is where **GEM** comes into the picture. Incorporating this approach into your pre-writing will ensure that you can bring complex and sophisticated analysis into your historical argument. Let's unpack this strategy and consider how we can generate nuance, explain both sides, and make connections at this stage in the process.

G: Generate nuance. You can use the pre-writing strategies you're already familiar with to demonstrate nuance in three ways. First, you can examine the relationship among multiple aspects of historical developments and weigh their significance. Think of this as taking one step beyond assessing the relative significance of a given development. For instance, if you plan to claim that one change in the West's economy was its integration into the larger economic system of the United States, then you could plan to discuss the relative impact of relationships between factors such as the extension of the railroads, the growth of population in the West, the rise of commercial farming, and the advent of national corporations that were based in the Northeast.

Second, you can draw on multiple perspectives to support the argument you are developing. For this prompt, your pre-writing might examine big-picture factors such as the impact of geography, politics, or demographics on the economies of each region. For example, you could analyze how the natural resources and climate of the West fed the growth of an integrated, national economy. You can also look at more specific perspectives, such as the views of homesteaders versus American Indians toward land and economic development in the West, industrial laborers and factory owners in the North, and landholders and sharecroppers in the South.

Finally, you can qualify—that is, modify—your argument by considering evidence or perspectives that don't fully or obviously back up your position. For instance, you could plan to explain how the integration of the West into the national economy was slowed by droughts and harsh winters, which ended the Long Drive and forced hundreds of thousands of homesteaders to abandon their farms in the mid-1880s.

E: Explain both sides. This is a technique you already use to make evaluative claims in your writing. Remember, every historical reasoning process is like a coin with two sides, and just because a prompt may mention only one doesn't mean you're off the hook when it comes to the other.

For this essay question, which asks about "the extent of change," we'll need to look at continuities as well as changes. As you know, it's generally easier to focus most of your essay on the half of the skill mentioned in the prompt—changes to the West's, the North's, and South's economies between 1865 and 1898.

However, at least one paragraph ought to examine the implicit, or unspoken, side of the historical reasoning process of the prompt—in this case, continuities in the economies of all three regions. For instance, you could explain how both economies remained

(continued)

dependent on their respective geographies, as mining continued to play a vital role in the West, cotton cultivation remained a primary feature in the South, and Northern cities continued to be centers of industrial production and export. Ideally, you'll connect your explanation of both sides to a nuanced analysis. Here, you might mention how production changed as large mining companies replaced independent miners in the West, textile manufacturing arose alongside cotton farming in the South, and national corporations based in the East replaced local industrial production in the North.

M: Make connections that go beyond the prompt. These connections to historical events or developments add interest to your essay and help thread deeper insight into your historical argument. Make sure these connections are strong ones, not just passing references. Connections can be made across time periods by extending the argument chronologically, either forward or backward.

You have already practiced one way of **making connections**: creating a long-term concluding context. But connections across time don't have be in your conclusion, either; it sometimes makes sense to include them in a body paragraph. For this prompt, you could make a connection by discussing the role of the federal government in promoting economic development in the West by subsidizing the transcontinental railroad, or you could connect it to earlier federal efforts to promote transportation such as the American System in the Jacksonian era. So long as the connection is relevant and insightful, it can work. Like context, the best way to make a connection is to use **CSE**. On the AP® Exam, it will be much easier to make connections to future events such as connecting to later efforts like the building of a national highway system after World War II.

Connections can also be made within a time period to other regions or histories, but this is often more challenging than connecting your historical argument to other time periods because it often (but not always) involves bringing in knowledge you have gained through other courses, such as AP® World History. To make this type of connection, you could look at the relationship between American economic growth and the global economy, or compare the economic motives and impacts of forcibly relocating American Indians onto reservations to the removal of indigenous peoples in other countries.

The following graphic organizer shows one way to incorporate the **GEM** strategy into your pre-writing. One column has been modeled for you. For each change or continuity you add to the chart, try to provide several pieces of evidence and at least one example of nuance. Also try to think of a connection or two you can make in your essay. The first is done for you, and "change" has been chosen for this category.

Change / Continuity (The West): Integration of the West's economy into the American economy	**Change / Continuity (The South):**	**Change / Continuity (The North):**
Evidence: - Transcontinental railroad - Large-scale domestic and foreign investment in the West's economy - Homesteaders farming cash crops instead of for subsistence - Native removal	**Evidence:**	**Evidence:**

(continued)

Nuance or Qualification of Claim:	Nuance or Qualification of Claim:	Nuance or Qualification of Claim:
- Comparing the relative impact of domestic vs. foreign economic investment - Explaining the limitations of federal efforts to support the West's economic growth (for example, homesteaders needed more than 160 acres, Chinese Exclusion Act limited labor supply) - Noting that the reservation system for native peoples was based on American Indian removal policies from the 1830s		

Connection 1:	Connection 2:
- Federal subsidies for the transcontinental railroad promoted economic growth, as had federal and state efforts in the early 1800s (such as the National Road and Erie Canal).	

Step 3 ▶ Set the context, craft a thesis, and write the introduction of your essay

Now that you have constructed an outline for your essay that creates claims, lists evidence, and incorporates examples of complex reasoning, you can move on to setting the context and crafting your thesis in your opening paragraph.

Even within the introduction approach you have been practicing since Period 4, you can begin to show that your essay will demonstrate a complex historical understanding by applying the **GEM** approach. Generate nuance by carefully articulating each claim and indicating the *extent* of change in the explanation of that claim. Explain both sides by including at least one claim of continuity (the other half of the targeted historical reasoning process) alongside your claims of change in your thesis. Make connections by remembering to set the context and connect it to your argument. Once you have laid the foundation for a sophisticated response in your introduction, it's just a matter of following through in the body paragraphs and conclusion.

Step 4 ▶ Use both CSE and GEM to write the body of your essay

The most straightforward way to write this essay is to devote one or two body paragraphs to each claim of change or continuity you stated in your thesis. Those claims become your sub-argument sentences and should be supported by the evidence. As you construct your paragraphs, keep the **Claim, Support, Explain (CSE)** strategy in mind for each claim. The evidence you provide must connect to the claim in your paragraph's sub-argument, and you must explain how the evidence you've chosen to use supports your claim. Remembering CSE will keep you on track to fully support your argument throughout your essay.

Once you have explained how your evidence supports your claim, you can use **GEM** to deepen your analysis to demonstrate a complex understanding of the changes in the economies of the West, South, and North. In addition to using examples from your pre-write, look for opportunities to close each body paragraph

(continued)

by weaving the other two historical reasoning processes into your explanation of how the evidence you've chosen is relevant to each paragraph's central claim. For example, you could explain how the integration of the West into the American economy affected migration to and within the United States (causation). Or, you could examine the similarities and differences in the pace of industrialization in the West, South, and North (comparison). You could even compare the impacts of technological innovation on working conditions in all three regions (complex comparison and causation). In all cases, try to be as precise with your wording as you can.

You can also demonstrate a complex historical understanding by increasing the amount of outside evidence used in your essay, using four or more specific and relevant items (think "proper nouns") to support your argument.

Step 5 ▶ Craft your essay conclusion

The final step is to write a strong conclusion that not only summarizes but, ideally, extends your argument. Remember, you should fully restate your thesis—not word-for-word, but idea-for-idea. After all, it's one last chance to articulate a sound and complete answer to the prompt. As you first learned in Module 4.10, your final paragraph is also a logical place to set an **immediate concluding context** by connecting your argument (in this case, about the economic changes in the West, South, and North) to a significant development shortly after the time period—such as Progressive Era reforms or the domestic impact of World War I, both of which you will be familiar with by the time you take the AP® Exam.

Setting a context in your conclusion is also a final opportunity to demonstrate historical complexity by making a relevant and insightful connection between time periods (the "M" in **GEM**). You already know how to do this—it's simply a variation on the long-term concluding context you practiced at the end of Modules 6.3, 6.5, and 6.6. Finishing your essay by linking a part of your argument to a forward-looking context or making a connection to a later time period will once again demonstrate the sophistication that you have woven throughout your response.

Let's use the completed column of the table above to show how **GEM** can work in a sample body paragraph based on the underlined portion of the sample thesis statement.

> Evaluate the extent of change in the economies of the West, the South, and the North in the period 1865 to 1898.
>
> **Thesis Statement:** Between 1865 and 1898, the West, the South, and the North were all profoundly transformed by the second industrial revolution, though each changed in ways that reflected trends during the period before 1865. **[claim]** <u>The West was integrated into the national economy with help from the federal government, although this had been started through government initiatives from before 1865;</u> the South added industrial production to its economy, but continued to depend on oppressed Black labor; and the North became the seat of new and powerful corporations, but these rested upon economic innovations that began before the Civil War. **[line of reasoning]**
>
> **Body Paragraph:** During this period, the federal government helped integrate the West into the national economy. By 1865, homesteaders had come to depend upon government assistance, and the ranching, mining, and logging industries would soon follow. **[claim]** The Homestead Act of 1862 offered inexpensive federal land for farmers in the East, thereby setting the early precedent that the West would be settled with government assistance after 1865. Likewise, as prices for beef collapsed and individual ranches went bankrupt in the 1880s,

(continued)

the government aided in the consolidation of small ranches into large corporate ranches with cowboys, wage-earners, as employees. A similar trend followed the mining and logging industries as well. **[support]** In all these cases, the federal government had a hand in the integration of the West into the larger national economy by supporting large corporations and assisting with the creation of a transportation network through the transcontinental railroad. **[explanation of how evidence supports claim]** However, this was not the first time that government assistance led to westward settlement. **[Generate nuance]** While settlement west of the Mississippi River did not depend upon much government assistance before 1865, the regions between the Southeast and the Mississippi River did, specifically in terms of American Indian removal and internal improvements. **[Explain both sides]** During the 1830s, the federal government provided support for the construction of the National Road and for the forced removal of native peoples from the Southeast to the Indian (Oklahoma) Territory so as to clear the way for settlers in the Midwest. In this way, the period between 1865 and 1898 reflected trends similar to the settlement of the "old" West between the 1820s and the 1840s. **[Make connections to another time period]**

ACTIVITY

Use the five steps outlined earlier to write a full essay in response to the same prompt. Be sure to incorporate multiple examples of historical complexity and sophistication in your essay by generating nuance in your response, explaining both sides of the targeted historical reasoning process, and making relevant and insightful connections within and across time periods (**GEM**). You may use the thesis statement and information from the graphic organizer as well as the following outline to guide your response.

I. Introductory paragraph
   A. Immediate/preceding contextualization statement.
      1. Make a claim about a preceding context.
      2. Support this claim with a piece of specific evidence from the preceding context.
      3. Explain how this evidence supports your claim regarding the preceding context.
   B. Thesis statement: Answer the prompt with a historically defensible claim supported by a line of reasoning that describes the main points you will develop in your response. Be sure to include both sides of the reasoning process in your thesis.

II. Body Paragraph 1: Change 1
   A. Sub-argument from the first part of your line of reasoning.
      1. Claim 1 that supports your sub-argument.
      2. Support Claim 1 with factual information.
      3. Explain how your support proves Claim 1.
      4. (Optional) Claim 2 that supports your sub-argument.
      5. (Optional) Support Claim 2 with factual information.
      6. (Optional) Explain how your support proves Claim 2.
   B. Generate nuance by examining multiple variables, diverse perspectives, counter-evidence, or limitations of your claims.

(continued)

III. Body Paragraph 2: Change 2
   A. Sub-argument from the second part of your line of reasoning.
      1. Claim 1 that supports your sub-argument.
      2. Support Claim 1 with factual information.
      3. Explain how your support proves Claim 1.
      4. (Optional) Claim 2 that supports your sub-argument.
      5. (Optional) Support Claim 2 with factual information.
      6. (Optional) Explain how your support proves Claim 2.
   B. Generate nuance by examining multiple variables, diverse perspectives, counter-evidence, or limitations of your claims.

IV. Body Paragraph 3: Continuity 1
   A. Sub-argument from the third part of your line of reasoning.
      1. Claim 1 that supports your sub-argument.
      2. Support Claim 1 with factual information.
      3. Explain how your support proves Claim 1.
      4. (Optional) Claim 2 that supports your sub-argument.
      5. (Optional) Support Claim 2 with factual information.
      6. (Optional) Explain how your support proves Claim 2.
   B. Generate nuance by examining multiple variables, diverse perspectives, counter-evidence, or limitations of your claims.

V. (Optional) Claim 4 body paragraph: Change 3 or Continuity 2
   A. Sub-argument from the first part of your line of reasoning.
      1. Claim 1 that supports your sub-argument.
      2. Support Claim 1 with factual information.
      3. Explain how your support proves Claim 1.
      4. (Optional) Claim 2 that supports your sub-argument.
      5. (Optional) Support Claim 2 with factual information.
      6. (Optional) Explain how your support proves Claim 2.
   B. Generate nuance by examining multiple variables, diverse perspectives, counter-evidence, or limitations of your claims.

VI. Conclusion
   A. Restate thesis claim and line of reasoning.
   B. Make a claim connecting your historical argument to context immediately after the time range provided by the prompt OR make a claim connecting your historical argument to a similar phenomenon and/or a long-term contextual trend in a later time period.
   C. Support your concluding context claim with a piece of evidence.
   D. Explain how your evidence supports your concluding context/connection in a later time period.

Immigration and Migration in the Gilded Age

FOCUS

As you read this module, think about both the push factors (reasons why immigrants would leave their homeland) and pull factors (reasons why immigrants would choose to come to the United States) for migration to the United States. Also consider how immigrants changed the demographics of urban cities and the West.

A flood of immigrants entered the United States from 1880 to the outbreak of World War I in 1914. Unlike the majority of earlier immigrants, who had come from northern and western Europe, most of the more than twenty million people who arrived during this period came from southern and eastern Europe. A smaller number of immigrants came from Asia and Mexico. Most remained in cities, which grew as a result. Urban immigrants were welcomed by local politicians (see Module 6.9), who saw in them a chance to gain the allegiance of millions of new voters. At the same time, their coming upset many middle- and upper-class city dwellers who blamed these new arrivals for lowering the quality of urban life.

AP® EXAM TIP

Migration includes both internal patterns of movement within the country and external patterns of movement to the country, also known as immigration. For both internal and external migration, think about how to connect industrialization to the processes associated with the movements of people within and across borders. Be able to describe both cultural and economic reasons for this historical process.

For more than three hundred years following the settlement of the North American colonies, the majority of white immigrants were European Protestants. Unlike European immigrants who came voluntarily, Black people were brought forcibly from Africa, mainly by way of the West Indies and the Caribbean. Although Black people originally followed their own religious practices, most eventually converted to Protestantism.

By the end of the nineteenth century, however, a new pattern of immigration had emerged, one that included much greater ethnic and religious diversity. These new immigrants often encountered hostility from those whose ancestors had arrived generations earlier and faced the difficult challenge of retaining their cultural identities.

Immigrants Arrive from Many Lands

Immigration to the United States was part of a worldwide phenomenon. In addition to the United States, European immigrants also journeyed to other countries in the Western Hemisphere, Asia, and India. While most immigrants voluntarily left their homelands to find new job opportunities or to obtain land to start their own farms, some made the move bound by labor contracts that limited their movement during the terms of the agreement. Chinese, Mexican, and Italian workers made up a large portion of this group.

The late nineteenth century saw a shift in the country of origin of immigrants to the United States: Instead of coming from northern and western Europe, many now came from southern and eastern European countries, most notably Italy, Greece,

Austria-Hungary, Poland, and Russia. Most of those settling on American shores after 1880 were Catholic or Jewish and hardly knew a word of English. They tended to be even poorer than immigrants who had arrived before them, coming mainly from rural areas and lacking useful skills for a rapidly expanding industrial society.

Immigrants came from other parts of the world as well. From 1860 to 1924, some 450,000 Mexicans migrated to the U.S. Southwest. Many traveled to El Paso, Texas, near the Mexican border, and from there, they hopped aboard one of three railroad lines to jobs on farms and in mines, mills, and construction. Cubans, Spaniards, and Bahamians traveled to the Florida cities of Key West and Tampa, where they established and worked in cigar factories.

Despite the 1882 Chinese Exclusion Act (Module 6.3), Congress did not close the door to migrants from Japan. Unlike the Chinese, the Japanese had not competed with white workers for jobs on railroad and other construction projects.

Immigrants came to the United States largely for economic, political, and religious reasons. Nearly all were poor and expected to find ways to make money in America. U.S. railroads and steamship companies advertised in Europe and recruited passengers by emphasizing economic opportunities in the United States. Early immigrants wrote to relatives back home praising the opportunities they found in the United States, sometimes exaggerating their success.

The importance of economic incentives in luring immigrants is underscored by the fact that millions returned to their home countries after they had earned sufficient money. Of the more than 10 million immigrants from 1875 to 1899, 3 million returned home. Immigrants facing religious or political persecution in their homeland were the least likely to return.

AP® EXAM TIP

Immigration patterns during the late nineteenth century happened along more than one coastline. Be able to explain the historical factors that contributed to international migration on both the West and East Coasts of the United States.

AP® WORKING with EVIDENCE

Source: J. Keppler, "Welcome to All!," *Puck*, 1880

Library of Congress, LC-USZC4-954

About the source: "U.S. Ark of Refuge" is engraved above the doorway. The sign to the left of Uncle Sam reads: "Free Education. Free Land. Free Speech. Free Ballot. Free Lunch." The sign to the right reads: "No oppressive taxes. No expensive kings. No compulsory military service. No knouts [whips] or dungeons."

Questions for Analysis

1. Identify the arguments for and against immigration in this cartoon.
2. Describe one perspective about immigrants expressed in the cartoon.
3. Explain the causes of European immigration to the United States in the late 1800s.
4. Explain the context for the cartoon.

REVIEW

- In what ways was immigration from southern and eastern Europe in the late 1800s similar to immigration from northern and western Europe in the early 1800s?
- In what ways was it different?

Creating Immigrant Communities

In cities such as New York, Boston, and Chicago, immigrants occupied neighborhoods that took on the distinct ethnic characteristics of the groups that inhabited them. A mixture of different languages echoed in the streets as new residents generally communicated in their mother tongues. The neighborhoods of immigrant groups often were clustered together, so residents were as likely to learn phrases in their neighbors' languages as they were to learn English.

Peter Newark Pictures/Bridgeman Images

Polish Saloon in Chicago, 1903 The *Polska Stacya* was a saloon located in the heart of one of the Polish neighborhoods in Chicago. Saloons were a central institution of immigrant culture, where men spent a good deal of leisure time. They read newspapers written in their native languages, swapped information about job opportunities, enjoyed time away from overcrowded tenements, discussed politics, and fostered bonds of masculinity exclusive of women. However, the excessive drinking associated with saloons put a severe strain on family health and finances, especially when drunken husbands and fathers lost their tempers at home or squandered their wages on alcohol.

What does this photograph reveal about life in immigrant communities?

The formation of **ghettos**—neighborhoods dominated by a single ethnic, racial, or class group—eased immigrants' transition into American society. Living within these ethnic enclaves made it easier for immigrants to find housing, hear about jobs, buy food, and seek help from those with whom they felt most comfortable. Mutual-aid societies sprang up to provide social welfare benefits, including insurance payments and funeral rites. Group members established social centers where immigrants could play cards or dominoes, chat and gossip over tea or coffee, host dances and benefits, or just relax among people who shared a common heritage.

In San Francisco's Chinatown, the largest Chinese community in California, such organizations usually consisted of people who had come from the same towns in China. These groups performed a variety of services, including finding jobs for their members, resolving disputes, campaigning against anti-Chinese discrimination, and sponsoring parades and other cultural activities. One society member explained: "We are strangers in a strange country. We must have an organization to control our country fellows and develop our friendship."

That same impulse to band together occurred in immigrant communities throughout the nation. The establishment of clubs and cultural centers in those communities demonstrated the commitment of immigrant groups to enhance their communities.

Besides family and civic associations, churches and synagogues provided religious and social activities for urban immigrants. Between 1865 and 1900, the number of Catholic churches nationwide more than tripled. Like mutual-aid societies, churches offered food and clothing to those who were ill or unable to work and fielded sports teams to compete in recreational leagues.

Immigrants altered the religious practices and rituals in their churches to meet their own needs and expectations, many times over the objections of their clergy. German Catholics challenged Vatican policy by insisting that each ethnic group have its own priests and parishes. Other ethnic groups demanded that their parishes retain religious practices and relics that they had worshipped in the old country.

Religious worship also varied among Jews. German Jews had arrived in the United States in an earlier wave of immigration than their eastern European counterparts. By the late nineteenth century, they had embraced Reform Judaism and established a major cultural center in Cincinnati, Ohio, with the founding of the Union of American Hebrew Congregations. This brand of Judaism relaxed strict standards of worship, including absolute fidelity to kosher dietary laws, and allowed prayers to be said in English. By contrast, eastern European Jews typically observed the traditional faith, maintained a kosher diet, and prayed in Hebrew.

With few immigrants literate in English, over a thousand new foreign-language newspapers came into existence to inform their readers of local, national, and international events. These newspapers helped sustain ethnic solidarity in the New World as well as maintain ties to the Old World. Newcomers could learn about social and cultural activities in their communities and keep abreast of news from their homeland.

Like other communities with poor, unskilled populations, immigrant neighborhoods bred crime. Young men joined gangs based on ethnic heritage and battled with those of other immigrant groups to protect their turf. Adults formed underworld organizations—some of them tied to international criminal syndicates, such as the Mafia—that trafficked in prostitution, gambling, robbery, and murder. Tongs

AP® EXAM TIP

Understand how international migrant groups developed cultural ties amid the broader backdrop of urbanization. Be able to explain a specific example such as the movement of Italians to New York City and how that led to the creation of urban enclaves.

Mulberry Street, New York City, c. 1900 This colorized photograph taken by Jacob Riis depicts a vibrant scene on Mulberry Street, in the heart of New York City's Little Italy. Street vendors can be seen selling fresh produce and other goods as pedestrians and horse-drawn carriages make their way. The population of New York City swelled from fewer than one million to more than three million from 1870 to 1900, mostly due to European immigration.

What does the photograph reveal about life in New York City at the turn of the century?

(secret organizations) in New York City's and San Francisco's Chinatowns controlled the opium trade, gambling, and prostitution in their communities. New York City police and municipal court records from 1898 described the frequency "of forgery, violation of corporation ordinance, as disorderly persons (failure to support wife or family), [grand and petty] larceny, and of the lighter grade of assault."

Crime was not the only social problem that plagued immigrant communities. Newspapers and court records reported husbands abandoning wives and children, engaging in drunken and disorderly conduct, or abusing their family. Boarders whom immigrant families took into their homes for economic reasons also posed problems. Cramped spaces created a lack of privacy, and male boarders sometimes attempted to assault the woman of the house while her husband and children were out to work or in school. Finally, generational conflicts within families began to develop as American-born children of immigrants questioned their parents' values. Thus, the social organizations and mutual-aid societies that immigrant groups established were more than a simple expression of ethnic solidarity and pride. They were also a response to the very real problems that challenged the health and stability of immigrant communities.

- How did late-nineteenth-century immigrants adapt to life in America?
- What social problems did they face?

Hostility toward Recent Immigrants

On October 28, 1886, the United States held a gala celebration for the opening of the Statue of Liberty in New York Harbor, a short distance from Ellis Island. French sculptor Frédéric-Auguste Bartholdi and engineer Alexandre-Gustave Eiffel had designed the monument to appear at the Centennial Exposition in Philadelphia in 1876. Ten years overdue, the statue arrived in June 1885, but funds were still needed to finish construction of a base on which the sculpture would stand. Ordinary people dipped into their pockets for spare change, contributing to a campaign that raised $100,000 so that Lady Liberty could finally hold her uplifted torch for all to see. In 1903, the now-famous words of Emma Lazarus, a Jewish poet, were inscribed on the pedestal welcoming new generations of immigrants:

> Give me your tired, your poor,
> Your huddled masses yearning to breathe free,
> The wretched refuse of your teeming shore,
> Send these, the homeless, tempest-tost to me,
> I lift my lamp beside the golden door!

Despite the welcoming inscription on the Statue of Liberty, many Americans whose families had arrived before the 1880s considered the influx of immigrants from southern and eastern Europe, Mexico, the Caribbean, and Asia at best a necessary evil and at worst a menace. Industrialists counted on immigrants to provide cheap labor. Not surprisingly, existing industrial workers saw the newcomers as a threat to their economic livelihoods and believed that their arrival would result in greater competition for jobs and lower wages. Moreover, even though most immigrants came to the United States to find work and improve the lives of their families, a small portion antagonized and frightened capitalists and middle-class Americans with their radical calls for the reorganization of society and the overthrow of the government.

Of course, the vast majority of immigrants were not radicals, but a large proportion of radicals were recent immigrants. During times of labor-management strife, this fact made it easier for businessmen and their spokesmen in the press to associate all immigrants with anti-American radicalism.

AP® WORKING with EVIDENCE

Source: Saum Song Bo, *A Chinese View of the Statue of Liberty*, 1885

> "SIR: A paper was presented to me yesterday for inspection, and I found it to be specially drawn up for subscription among my countrymen toward the Pedestal Fund of the . . . Statue of Liberty. Seeing that the heading is an appeal to American citizens, to their love of country and liberty. . . . But the word liberty makes me think of the fact that this country is the land of liberty for men of all nations except the Chinese. I consider it as an insult to us Chinese to call on us to contribute toward building in this land a pedestal for a statue of Liberty. That statue represents Liberty holding a torch which lights the passage of those of all nations who come into this country. But are the Chinese allowed to come? As for the Chinese who are here, are they allowed to enjoy liberty as men of all other nationalities enjoy it? Are they allowed to go about everywhere free from the insults, abuse, assaults, wrongs and injuries from which men of other nationalities are free? . . .
>
> [W]hether [the Chinese Exclusion Act] or the statue to Liberty will be the more lasting monument to tell future ages of the liberty and greatness of this country, will be known only to future generations.
>
> Liberty, we Chinese do love and adore thee; but let not those who deny thee to us, make of thee a graven image [an idol or object of worship] and invite us to bow down to it."

Questions for Analysis

1. Identify the reason Saum Song Bo wrote this letter.
2. Describe Saum Song Bo's complaint.
3. Explain the reasons why Saum Song Bo is skeptical of the promise of liberty for Chinese people in the United States.

Source: United States Supreme Court, *Yick Wo v. Hopkins*, 1886

> "[I]n 1880, San Francisco passed a fire-safety ordinance that all laundries operating in wooden buildings be licensed or the owners would risk criminal penalties. After the city government refused to grant licenses to nearly all Chinese laundries while approving those run by whites, Yick Wo, the owner of one rejected establishment, refused to close his business and was prosecuted. . . .
>
> [P]etitioners have complied with every requisite, deemed by the law or by the public officers charged with its administration, necessary for the protection of neighboring property from fire, or as a precaution against injury to the public health. No reason whatever, except the will of the supervisors, is assigned why they should not be permitted to carry on, in the accustomed manner, their harmless and useful occupation, on which they depend for a livelihood. And while this consent of the supervisors is withheld from them and from two hundred others who have also petitioned, all of whom happen to be Chinese subjects, eighty others, not Chinese subjects, are permitted to carry on the same business under similar conditions. The fact of this discrimination is admitted. No reason for it is shown, and the conclusion cannot be resisted, that no reason for it exists except hostility to the race and nationality to which the petitioners

belong, and which in the eye of the law is not justified. The discrimination is, therefore, illegal, and the public administration which enforces it is a denial of the equal protection of the laws and a violation of the Fourteenth Amendment of the Constitution. The imprisonment of the petitioners is, therefore, illegal, and they must be discharged."

Questions for Analysis

1. Identify the main issue in *Yick Wo v. Hopkins* and the Supreme Court's decision in that case.
2. Explain the reasoning behind the Supreme Court's decision in *Yick Wo v. Hopkins*.

Questions for Comparison

1. Explain how each document reflects a common context.
2. Evaluate the extent to which the *Yick Wo v. Hopkins* decision undermines Saum Song Bo's argument.

Anti-immigrant fears linked to ideas about race and ethnicity had a long history in the United States. Congress enacted the Naturalization Act of 1790 restricting citizenship to those deemed white. Among those excluded from citizenship were American Indians, who were regarded as savages, and Black Americans, most of whom were enslaved at the time. In the 1857 *Dred Scott* case (Module 5.6), the Supreme Court ruled that even free Black people were not citizens. From the very beginning of the United States, largely Protestant lawmakers debated whether Catholics and Jews qualified as whites. Although lawmakers ultimately included Catholics and Jews within their definition of "white," over the next two centuries Americans viewed racial categories as not simply matters of skin color.

Ethnicity (nationality or culture of origin) and religion became absorbed into and intertwined with racial categories. A sociological study of Homestead, Pennsylvania, published in 1910, broke down the community along the following constructed racial lines: "Slav, English-speaking European, native white, and colored." Russian Jewish immigrants were often recorded as "Hebrews" rather than as Russians, suggesting that Jewishness was seen by Christian America as a racial identity.

Natural scientists and social scientists gave credence to the idea that some races and ethnic groups were superior and others were inferior. Referring to Darwin's theory of evolution, biologists and anthropologists constructed measures of racial hierarchies, placing descendants of northern Europeans with lighter complexions—Anglo-Saxons, Teutonics, and Nordics—at the top of the evolutionary scale. Those with darker skin were deemed inferior "races," with Black people and American Indians at the bottom.

Scholars attempting to make disciplines such as history more "scientific" accepted these racial classifications. The prevailing sentiment of this era reflected demeaning images of many immigrant groups: Irish as drunkards, Mexicans and Cubans as lazy, Italians as criminals, Hungarians as ignorant peasants, Jews as cheap and greedy, and Chinese as drug addicts. These characteristics supposedly resulted from inherited biological traits, rather than from extreme poverty or other environmental conditions.

Newer immigrants, marked as racially inferior, became a convenient target of hostility. Skilled craftsmen born in the United States viewed largely unskilled workers from abroad who would work for low wages as a threat to their attempts to form unions and keep wages high. Middle-class city dwellers blamed urban problems on the rising tide of foreigners. In addition, Protestant purists felt threatened by Catholics and Jews and believed these "races" incapable or unworthy of assimilation into what they considered to be the superior white, Anglo-Saxon, and Protestant culture.

Nativism—the belief that foreigners pose a serious danger to one's native society and culture—arose as a reactionary response to immigration. Nativist sentiment, directed primarily at the large numbers of Irish and German immigrants in the 1840s and 1850s, fueled the rise of the short-lived American Party (also called the Know-Nothing Party, Module 5.6).

nativism
The belief that religious or culturally diverse foreigners pose a serious danger to the nation's society and culture. Nativist sentiment rose in the United States as the size and diversity of the immigrant population grew in the nineteenth century.

In 1887, Henry F. Bowers of Clinton, Iowa, founded the American Protective Association. The group proposed restricting Catholic immigration, making English literacy a prerequisite to American citizenship, and prohibiting Catholics from teaching in public schools or holding public offices.

New England elites, such as Massachusetts senator Henry Cabot Lodge and writer John Fiske, argued that what they called "southern European, Semitic, and Slavic races" did not fit into the "community of race" that had founded the United States. In 1893, Lodge and fellow Harvard graduates established the Immigration Restriction League and lobbied for federal legislation that would exclude adult immigrants unable to read in their own language. Proposals to restrict immigration, however, did nothing to deal with the millions of foreigners already in America.

To preserve their status and power and increase the size of the native-born population, nativists embraced the idea of **eugenics**—a pseudoscience that advocated "biological engineering"—and supported the selective breeding of "desirable" races to counter the rapid population growth of "useless" races. Accordingly, eugenicists promoted the institutionalization of people deemed "unfit," sterilization of those considered mentally impaired, and the licensing and regulation of marriages to promote better breeding. In pushing for such measures, eugenicists believed that they were following the dictates of modern science and acting in a humane fashion to prevent those deemed unfit from causing further harm to themselves and to society.

Others took a less harsh approach. As had been the case with American Indians, reformers stressed the need for immigrants to assimilate into the dominant culture, embrace the values of individualism and self-help, adopt American styles of dress and grooming, and exhibit loyalty to the U.S. government. They encouraged immigrant children to attend public schools, where they would learn to speak English and adopt American cultural rituals by celebrating holidays such as Thanksgiving and Columbus Day and reciting the pledge of allegiance, introduced in 1892. Educators encouraged adult immigrants to attend night classes to learn English.

If immigrants were not completely assimilated, neither did they remain the same people who had lived on the farms and in the villages of Europe, Asia, Mexico, and the Caribbean. Some sought to become full-fledged Americans or at least see that their children did so. Writer Israel Zangwill, an English Jew, furnished the enduring image of assimilation in his play *The Melting Pot*. Zangwill portrayed people from distinct backgrounds entering the cauldron of American life, mixing together, and emerging as citizens identical to their native-born counterparts.

However, the image of America as a **melting pot** worked better as an ideal than as a mirror of reality. Immigrants during this period never fully lost the social, cultural, religious, and political identities they had brought with them. Even if all immigrants had sought full assimilation, which they did not, the anti-immigrant sentiment of many native-born Americans reinforced their status as strangers and aliens.

melting pot
A popular metaphor for immigrant assimilation into American society. According to this ideal, despite their varied cultures and differences, all immigrants underwent a similar process of Americanization that produced a homogenous society.

The same year that Zangwill's play was published, Alfred P. Schultz, a New York physician, provided a dim view of the prospects of assimilation in his book *Race or Mongrel*. Schultz dismissed the melting-pot metaphor that public schools could convert the children of all "races" into Americans.

Therefore, most immigrants faced the dilemma of assimilating while holding on to their heritage. Sociologist and civil-rights activist W. E. B. Du Bois summed up this predicament for one of the nation's earliest transported groups. In *The Souls of Black Folk*, Du Bois wrote that Black Americans felt a "two-ness," an identity carved out of their African heritage together with their lives as enslaved and free people in America. This "double-consciousness . . . two souls, two thoughts, two unreconciled strivings" also applied to immigrants at the turn of the twentieth century. Immigrants who entered the country after 1880 were more like vegetable soup—an amalgam of distinct parts within a common broth—than a melting pot.

REVIEW

- What aspects of late-nineteenth-century American life fostered hostility toward immigrants?
- In what ways was the United States a "melting pot" for immigrants? In what ways was it a "vegetable soup" for immigrants?

AP® Skills Workshop: Thinking Historically

Additional Practice in Responding to a Short-Answer Question with a Primary Source

You've been answering short-answer questions for a long time now. In fact, you answered your first way back in Period 1. Below is an SAQ to remind you of some of the skills needed to answer these kinds of questions. Review Module 1.7 to remind you how to answer an SAQ with a primary source. Then, answer the question below.

Using the image, answer **A**, **B**, and **C**.

Source: J. Keppler, "Welcome to All!" *Puck*, 1880

Library of Congress, LC-USZC4-954

About the source: "U.S. Ark of Refuge" is engraved above the doorway. The sign to the left of Uncle Sam reads: "Free Education. Free Land. Free Speech. Free Ballot. Free Lunch." The sign to the right reads: "No oppressive taxes. No expensive kings. No compulsory military service. No knouts [whips] or dungeons."

(A) Briefly describe ONE perspective about immigration expressed in the image.

(B) Briefly explain ONE specific historical event or development that led to the perspective expressed in the image.

(C) Briefly explain ONE specific historical argument that could be used to challenge the perspective expressed in the image.

Responses to Immigration in the Gilded Age

MODULE 6.9

FOCUS

As you read this module, consider the various ways that American cities and the immigrants who populated them evolved over the second half of the nineteenth century. Also consider the ways in which Americans responded to those changes. Compare the impacts of rural migration, white and Black, as well as European immigration. Make sure to understand the link between the growth of urban immigrant enclaves, reform efforts, and attempts to explain urban poverty.

In the half century after the Civil War, the population of the United States more than doubled, but the urban population soared nearly fivefold. In 1870, one in five Americans lived in cities with a population of 8,000 or more. By 1900, one in three resided in cities of this size.

In 1870, only Philadelphia and New York had populations over half a million. Twenty years later, in addition to these two cities, Chicago's population exceeded 1 million; St. Louis, Boston, and Baltimore had more than 500,000 residents; and Cleveland, Buffalo, San Francisco, and Cincinnati boasted populations over 250,000. Urbanization was not confined to the Northeast and Midwest. Denver's population jumped from 4,700 in 1870 to more than 107,000 in 1890. During that same period, Los Angeles grew nearly fivefold, from 11,000 to 50,000, and Birmingham leaped from 3,000 to 26,000. This phenomenal urban growth also brought remarkable physical changes to the cities, as tall buildings reached toward the skies, electric lights brightened the nighttime hours, and water and gas pipes, sewers, and subways snaked below the ground.

Booming cities faced formidable and at times seemingly insurmountable problems in trying to absorb millions of immigrants. From a governmental standpoint, cities had limited authority over their own affairs. They were controlled by state legislatures and needed state approval to raise revenues and pass regulations. For the most part, there were no zoning laws to regulate housing construction. Private companies owned public utilities, and competition among them often produced duplication and waste. The government services that did exist operated with an emphasis on serving wealthier neighborhoods at the expense of the city at large. Missing was a vision of the city as a whole, working as a single unit.

The New Industrial City

Although cities have long been a part of the landscape, Americans have felt ambivalent about their presence. Many Americans have shared Thomas Jefferson's idea that democratic values were rooted in the soil of small, independent farms. In contrast to the natural environment of rural life, cities have been perceived as artificial creations in which corruption and contagion flourish.

frontier thesis
The argument, made by historian Frederick Jackson Turner in the 1890s, that the conquest of the West symbolized American exceptionalism and shaped its democratic spirit and, conversely, that its closing endangered the existence of democracy.

In the 1890s, the very identity of Americans seemed threatened as the U.S. Census Bureau declared the frontier closed, since a discernible frontier line no longer existed. Some agreed with the historian Frederick Jackson Turner, who argued in his **frontier thesis** that the closing of the western frontier as it became more fully settled by white Americans endangered the existence of democracy because it removed the opportunity for the pioneer spirit that had built the country to regenerate.

Rural Americans were especially uncomfortable with the country's increasingly urban life. When the small-town lawyer Clarence Darrow moved to Chicago in the 1880s, he was horrified by the "solid, surging sea of human units, each intent upon hurrying by."

Still, like Darrow, millions of people were drawn to the new opportunities cities offered.

Urban growth in America was part of a long-term worldwide phenomenon. Between 1820 and 1920, some sixty million people globally moved from rural to urban areas. Most of them migrated after the 1870s, and as noted earlier, millions journeyed from towns and villages in Europe to American cities. Yet, the number of Europeans who migrated internally was greater than those who went overseas. As in the United States, Europeans moved from the countryside to urban areas in search of jobs. Many migrated to the city seasonally, seeking winter employment in cities and then returning to the countryside at harvest time.

Before the Civil War, commerce was the engine of growth for American cities. Ports like New York, Boston, New Orleans, and San Francisco became distribution centers for imported goods or items manufactured in small shops in the surrounding countryside. Cities in the interior of the country located on or near major bodies of water, such as Chicago, St. Louis, Cincinnati, and Detroit, served similar functions. As the extension of railroad transportation led to the development of large-scale industry, these cities and others became industrial centers as well.

Industrialization contributed to rapid urbanization in several ways. It drew those living on farms, who either could not earn a satisfactory living or were bored by the isolation of rural areas, into the city in search of better-paying jobs and excitement. One rural dweller in Massachusetts complained: "The lack of pleasant, public entertainments in this town has much to do with our young people feeling discontented with country life."

In addition, while the mechanization of farming increased efficiency, it also reduced the demand for farm labor. In 1896, one person could plant, tend, and harvest as much wheat as it had taken eighteen farmworkers to do sixty years before.

Industrial technology and other advances also made cities more attractive and livable places. Electricity extended nighttime entertainment and powered streetcars to convey people around town. Structural steel and electric elevators made it possible to construct taller and taller buildings, which gave cities such as Chicago and New York their distinctive skylines. Improved water and sewage systems provided more sanitary conditions, especially given the demands of the rapidly expanding population. Scientists and physicians made significant progress in the fight against the spread of contagious diseases, which had become serious problems in crowded cities.

Many of the same causes of urbanization in the Northeast and Midwest applied to the far West. The development of the mining industry attracted business and labor to urban settlements. Cities grew up at railroad terminals, and railroads stimulated urban growth by bringing settlers and creating markets. By 1900, the proportion of residents in western cities with a population of at least ten thousand was greater than in any other section of the country except the Northeast. More so than in the East, Asians and Hispanics inhabited western urban centers along with whites and Black Americans. In 1899, Salt Lake City boasted the publication of two Black newspapers as well as the president of the Western Negro Press Association. Western cities also took advantage of the latest technology, and in the 1880s and 1890s, electric trolleys provided mass transit in Denver and San Francisco.

Although immigrants increasingly accounted for the influx into the cities across the nation, the rise in urban population before 1890 came mainly from Americans on the move. In addition to young men, young women left the farm to seek their fortune. The female protagonist of Theodore Dreiser's novel *Sister Carrie* (1900) abandons small-town Wisconsin for the lure of Chicago. In real life, mechanization created many "Sister Carries" by making farm women less valuable in the fields. The possibility of purchasing mass-produced goods from mail-order houses such as Sears, Roebuck also left young women less essential as homemakers because they no longer had to sew their own clothes and could buy labor-saving appliances from catalogs.

REVIEW

- How did industrialization affect the growth of cities?
- How did industrialization affect the quality of life in cities?

Black Migration to Northern Cities

In 1890, although 90 percent of Black Americans lived in the South, a growing number was moving to northern cities to seek employment and greater freedom. Boll weevil infestations during the 1890s reduced cotton production and forced sharecroppers and tenants off farms.

At the same time, Black people saw significant erosion of their political and civil rights in the last decade of the nineteenth century, which was reinforced by the Supreme Court's 1896 ruling in *Plessy v. Ferguson* (Module 6.4) upholding the doctrine of legal segregation. Most Black citizens in the South were denied the right to vote and experienced rigid, legally sanctioned racial segregation in all aspects of public life.

Between 1890 and 1914, roughly 485,000 Black Americans left the South, with many headed to large cities such as New York, Chicago, and Philadelphia. A Black woman expressed her enthusiasm about the employment she found in Chicago, where she earned $3 a day working in a railroad yard. "The colored women like this work," she explained, because "we make more money . . . and we do not have to work as hard as at housework" as domestic help, which required working sixteen-hour days, six days a week.

Although many Black Americans preferred their new lives to the ones they had led in the South, the North did not turn out to be the promised land of freedom. Black newcomers encountered discrimination in housing and employment. Residential segregation confined Black Americans to racial ghettos. Black workers found it difficult to obtain skilled employment despite their qualifications, and women and men most often toiled as domestics, janitors, and part-time laborers.

Nevertheless, Black Americans in northern cities built communities that preserved and reshaped their southern culture and offered a degree of insulation from the harshness of racial discrimination. A small Black middle class appeared consisting of teachers, lawyers, and small-business owners. In 1888, Black Americans organized the Capital Savings Bank of Washington, D.C. Ten years later, two Black real estate agents in New York City were worth more than $150,000 each, and one agent in Cleveland owned $100,000 in property. The rising Black middle class provided leadership in the formation of mutual-aid societies, lodges, and women's clubs. Newspapers such as the *Chicago Defender* and *Pittsburgh Courier* furnished local news to their subscribers and reported national and international events affecting people of color.

Library of Congress, LC-USZ62-38150

Black Family, 1900 Despite the rigid racial segregation and oppression that Black people faced in the late nineteenth century, some Black families found ways to achieve economic success and upward mobility. The father is a graduate of Hampton Institute, a historically Black university founded after the Civil War to educate freedpeople.

What details in this photograph indicate the family's middle-class status?

As was the case in the South, the church was at the center of Black life in northern cities. More than just religious institutions, churches furnished space for social activities and the dissemination of political information. By the first decade of the twentieth century, more than two dozen Black churches had sprung up in Chicago alone.

AP® EXAM TIP

The course framework calls for you to understand how migrant communities negotiated cultures. Your textbook explains mutual-aid societies at length and connects this concept across multiple cultures. You can also examine how religion shaped the processes associated with negotiating cultures.

Whether housed in newly constructed buildings or in storefronts, Black churches provided worshippers freedom from white control. They also allowed members of the northern Black middle class to demonstrate what they considered to be respectability and refinement. This meant discouraging enthusiastic displays of "old-time religion," which celebrated more exuberant forms of worship. As the Reverend W. A. Blackwell of Chicago's AME Zion Church declared, "Singing, shouting, and talking [were] the most useless ways of proving Christianity."

This conflict over modes of religious expression reflected a larger process that was underway in Black communities at the turn of the twentieth century. As Black urban communities in the North grew and developed, tensions and divisions emerged within the increasingly diverse Black community, as a variety of groups competed to shape and define Black culture and identity.

REVIEW

- What opportunities and challenges did Black Americans from the South encounter as they migrated to northern cities?

Cities Expand Upward and Outward

As the urban population increased, cities expanded both up and out. Before 1860, the dominant form of brick and stone construction prevented buildings from rising more than four or five stories. However, as cities became much more populous, land

sweatshops, where spaces were configured to concentrate on production, and laborers, usually young women, worked long hours and in poor conditions, as a cheap way to produce their products.

AP® WORKING with EVIDENCE

Source: Jacob Riis, "'Knee Pants' at Forty-Five Cents a Dozen—A Ludlow Street Sweater's Shop," *How the Other Half Lives*, 1890

Granger – Historical Picture Archive

Questions for Analysis

1. Describe the conditions depicted in this photograph.
2. Explain the factors that contributed to the conditions revealed in this photograph.
3. Explain how this photograph reveals Riis's point of view about working-class life in cities.

Slums compounded the potential for disease, poor sanitation, fire, congestion, and crime. Living on poor diets, slum dwellers proved particularly vulnerable to epidemics. Cholera, yellow fever, and typhoid killed tens of thousands. Tuberculosis was even deadlier. An epidemic that began in a slum neighborhood could easily spread into more affluent areas of the city. Children suffered the most. Almost one-quarter of the children born in American cities in 1890 did not live to celebrate their first birthdays.

Contributing to the outbreak of disease was faulty sewage disposal, a problem that vexed city leaders. Until the widespread adoption of the modern indoor flush toilet in the early twentieth century, people relied on outdoor toilets, with as many as eight hundred people using a single facility. All too often, cities dumped human waste into rivers that also supplied drinking water. In 1881, the exasperated mayor of Cleveland called the Cuyahoga River "an open sewer through the center of the city."

At the same time, the great demand for water caused by the population explosion resulted in lower water pressure. Consequently, residents in the upper floors of tenements had to carry buckets of water from the lower floors. Until cities overcame their water and sanitation challenges, epidemics plagued urban dwellers.

Urban crowding created other problems as well. Traffic moved slowly through densely populated cities. Pedestrians and commuters had to navigate around throngs of people walking on sidewalks and streets, peddlers selling from pushcarts, and piles of garbage cluttering the walkways.

Streets remained in poor shape. In 1889, the majority of Cleveland's 440 miles of streets consisted of sand and gravel. Chicago did not fare much better. In 1890, many streets were paved with wooden blocks, and of the more than 2,000 miles of city streets, three-quarters remained unpaved. Rainstorms quickly made matters worse by turning manure-filled streets into foul-smelling mud.

Poverty and overcrowding contributed to increased crime. The U.S. murder rate quadrupled between 1880 and 1900, at a time when the murder rates in most European cities were declining. In New York City, crime thrived in slums with the apt names of "Bandit's Roost" and "Hell's Kitchen," and groups of young hoodlums preyed on unsuspecting citizens. Rising criminality led to the formation of urban police departments, though many law officers supplemented their incomes by collecting graft (illegal payments) for ignoring criminal activities.

Poverty forced some of the poor to turn to theft or prostitution. One twenty-year-old prostitute, who supported her sickly mother and four brothers and sisters, lamented: "Let God Almighty judge who's to blame most, I that was driven, or them that drove me to the pass I'm in."

■ What difficulties did poor urban residents face during the 1880s and 1890s?

Reformers and Elite Reaction

settlement house

A community center started by urban reformers in the late nineteenth century. Settlement house organizers resided in the institutions they created and were often female, middle-class, and college educated. More than two hundred settlement houses were established in the United States by 1905.

AP® EXAM TIP

Though many references are made to social reformers throughout Period 6, Jane Addams and her work with settlement houses are explicitly mentioned in the course framework. Be able to specifically explain how women reformers, particularly Addams, responded to urbanization, immigration, and reform efforts within each.

Another group of Americans from upper- and middle-class backgrounds put aside whatever prejudices they might have held about working-class immigrants and dealt directly with newcomers to try to solve various social problems. These reformers, like Jane Addams—mostly young people, and many of them women and college graduates—took up residence in **settlement houses** located in urban slums. Settlement houses, like Addams's Hull House in Chicago, offered a variety of services to community residents, including day care for children; cooking, sewing, and secretarial classes; neighborhood playgrounds; counseling sessions; and meeting rooms for labor unions.

Settlement house organizers understood that immigrants gravitated to the political machine or congregated in the local tavern not because they were inherently immoral, but because these institutions helped mitigate their suffering and, in some cases, offered concrete paths to advancement. Although settlement house workers wanted to Americanize immigrants, they also understood immigrants' need to hold on to remnants of their original culture. By 1900, approximately one hundred settlement houses had been established in major American cities.

However, other Americans believed that immigrant poverty was a product of nature rather than social structures. In the middle of the nineteenth century, British philosopher Herbert Spencer proposed a theory of social evolution based on this premise in his book *Social Statics* (1851). Imagining a future utopia, Spencer wrote, "Man was not created with an instinct for his own degradation, but from the lower he has risen to the higher forms. Nor is there any conceivable end to his march to perfection." In his view, those at the top of the economic ladder were closer to perfection than were those at the bottom. Any effort to aid the unfortunate would only slow the march of progress for society as a whole.

Spencer's book proved extremely popular, selling nearly 400,000 copies in the United States by 1900. Publication of Charles Darwin's landmark *On the Origin of Species* (1859) appeared to have provided some scientific legitimacy for Spencer's view. The British naturalist argued that plants, animals, and humans progressed or declined because of their ability or inability to adapt favorably to the environment and transmit these characteristics to future generations. The connection between the two men's ideas led some people decades later to label Spencer's theory **Social Darwinism**.

Doctrines of success, such as Social Darwinism, gained favor because they helped Americans explain the rapid economic changes that were disrupting their lives. Although most ordinary people would not climb out of poverty to middle-class respectability, let alone affluence, they clung to ideas that promised hope. Theories such as Spencer's that linked success with progress provided a way to explain those who did not do well in terms of supposedly innate inadequacies. At the same time, the notion that economic success derived from personal merit legitimized the fabulous wealth of those who did rise to the top. This ideology upheld the status quo during the late nineteenth century for many Americans who looked with dismay at the plight of immigrants in U.S. cities.

Social Darwinism
A belief that human society should be governed by the same principles of natural selection and survival of the fittest that Charles Darwin described in his work on evolutionary theory. Social Darwinism was often employed to justify economic inequality, racism, imperialism, and hostility to federal government regulation.

AP® EXAM TIP

Be able to define, and then connect, Social Darwinism to the processes associated with the accumulation of wealth. Think about how to use specific examples in your explanation.

- In what ways were federal and local reform efforts during the late nineteenth century similar, and in what ways did they differ?

AP® Skills Workshop: Thinking Historically

Responding to a Long-Essay Question with Historical Complexity, Revisited

Let's revisit the Long-Essay Question. Below is a table to show you where you can find our instruction for all the major elements of an LEQ. Review these AP® Skills Workshops "Thinking Historically" and "Writing Historically" exercises.

Writing Task	AP® Skills Workshop
Outlining and Thesis	3.2: The Thesis: Developments and Processes
	3.12: Combining Reasoning Processes in a Thesis
	3.6: Creating a Thesis Statement
	4.14: Outlining an Essay
	5.2: Using Course Themes to Brainstorm and Organize an Essay
Introductions	4.8: Introductions with Contextualization
	5.4: Contextualizing: Writing the Introduction
Body Paragraphs	3.5: Body Paragraphs: Argumentation
	3.13: Combining CCOT and Causation in a Body Paragraph
	4.5: Body Paragraphs: Support an Argument Using Evidence

(continued)

General Writing	5.8: Writing an LEQ 6.7: Developing Historical Complexity in a Long-Essay Question Using the GEM Approach
Conclusions	4.10: Context: Writing the Conclusion 6.3: Conclusions: Developments and Processes, a Closer Look 6.5: Conclusions: Making Connections

Now, consider the following long-essay question, which asks you to reflect on what you have learned in this module as well as earlier modules in Period 6.

> Evaluate the extent of difference in the experiences of European and Chinese immigrants to the United States in the period 1865 to 1900.

Step 1 ▶ Break down the prompt

Notice that this prompt asks you to compare the experiences of two groups of immigrants, Europeans and Chinese, during the second half of the nineteenth century. While the prompt uses the term "extent of difference," evaluating the extent of difference is a reminder that you also have to evaluate the other, implicit half of the reasoning process, the extent of similarity. Being aware that you have to do both in your essay is the first step toward demonstrating historical complexity.

Step 2 ▶ List and categorize your historical knowledge, then use GEM to refine your historical argument

Start your brainstorm by jotting down all the relevant historical information you can remember (inductive reasoning) or start with a list of topics such as the course themes and then brainstorm possible information relating to similarities or differences for those topics (deductive reasoning). Either way, organize your information under three or four categories, making sure that at least one represents a historical difference and at least one represents a historical similarity. Keep in mind both the **CSE** and **GEM** strategies as you build an outline for your response. Complete the following graphic organizer or one of your own making as you organize your thoughts to answer the prompt with a complex and well-supported argument. Strive to incorporate at least four specific and relevant pieces of outside evidence.

Difference / Similarity	**Difference / Similarity**	**Difference / Similarity**	**Difference / Similarity**
Chinese immigrants faced more discrimination than European immigrants.			
Evidence: *- Chinese workers not allowed to join major labor unions* *- Anti-Chinese violence in western states* *- Chinese Exclusion Act*	**Evidence:**	**Evidence:**	**Evidence:**

(continued)

Nuance:	**Nuance:**	**Nuance:**	**Nuance:**
- European immigrants faced discrimination and nativism, though to a lesser extent than Chinese immigrants. - *Yick Wo v. Hopkins* ruling demonstrates that the U.S. government did not always allow discrimination against the Chinese.			

Connection 1:	**Connection 2:**
Anti-Chinese sentiment was a continuation of nativist beliefs that emerged in response to Irish and German immigration in the 1840s and 1850s.	

Step 3 ▶ Set the context, craft a thesis, and write the introduction of your essay

Immigration is a major topic in American history, so when thinking about setting the context, you are going to want to think equally big. The phenomena of industrialization and urbanization are similarly large developments that could be used to provide context in the opening paragraph.

Follow the steps provided above and use **CSE** (Claim, Support, Explain) to structure your arguments in a full essay that responds to the prompt. Be sure to also use **GEM** (Generate nuance, Explain both sides, Make relevant, insightful connections beyond the prompt, either within its time period or across multiple time periods) to incorporate multiple examples of historical complexity in your essay. Here is an outline to guide your writing:

I. Introductory paragraph
   A. Immediate/preceding contextualization statement
      1. Make a claim about a preceding context.
      2. Support this claim with a piece of specific evidence from the preceding context.
      3. Explain how this evidence supports your claim regarding the preceding context.
   B. Thesis statement: Answer the prompt with a historically defensible claim supported by a line of reasoning that describes the main points you will develop in your response. Be sure to include both sides of the reasoning process in your thesis.

II. Claim 1 body paragraph: Change 1
   A. Sub-argument from the first part of your line of reasoning
      1. Claim 1 that supports your sub-argument
      2. Support Claim 1 with factual information.
      3. Explain how your support proves Claim 1.
      4. (Optional) Claim 2 that supports your sub-argument
      5. (Optional) Support Claim 2 with factual information
      6. (Optional) Explain how your support proves Claim 2.
   B. Generate nuance by examining multiple variables, diverse perspectives, counter-evidence, or limitations of your claims.

(continued)

III. Claim 2 body paragraph: Change 2
   A. Sub-argument from the second part of your line of reasoning
      1. Claim 1 that supports your sub-argument
      2. Support Claim 1 with factual information.
      3. Explain how your support proves Claim 1.
      4. (Optional) Claim 2 that supports your sub-argument
      5. (Optional) Support Claim 2 with factual information.
      6. (Optional) Explain how your support proves Claim 2.
   B. Generate nuance by examining multiple variables, diverse perspectives, counter-evidence, or limitations of your claims.

IV. Claim 3 body paragraph: Continuity 1
   A. Sub-argument from the third part of your line of reasoning
      1. Claim 1 that supports your sub-argument
      2. Support Claim 1 with factual information.
      3. Explain how your support proves Claim 1.
      4. (Optional) Claim 2 that supports your sub-argument
      5. (Optional) Support Claim 2 with factual information.
      6. (Optional) Explain how your support proves Claim 2.
   B. Generate nuance by examining multiple variables, diverse perspectives, counter-evidence, or limitations of your claims.

V. (Optional) Claim 4 body paragraph: Change 3 or Continuity 2
   A. Sub-argument from the first part of your line of reasoning
      1. Claim 1 that supports your sub-argument
      2. Support Claim 1 with factual information.
      3. Explain how your support proves Claim 1.
      4. (Optional) Claim 2 that supports your sub-argument
      5. (Optional) Support Claim 2 with factual information.
      6. (Optional) Explain how your support proves Claim 2.
   B. Generate nuance by examining multiple variables, diverse perspectives, counter-evidence, or limitations of your claims.

VI. Conclusion
   A. Restate thesis claim and line of reasoning.
   B. Claim connecting historical argument to context immediately after the time range provided by the prompt OR claim connecting historical argument to a similar phenomenon and/or a long-term contextual trend in a later time period.
   C. Support concluding context claim with a piece of evidence.
   D. Explain how your evidence supports your concluding context/connection in a later time period.

ACTIVITY

Now, it's time to complete the graphic organizer and write the essay. Answer the same prompt with a complete essay that includes an introduction with a preceding context and a thesis with a claim and line of reasoning, body paragraphs with specific evidence that support your claims, and a conclusion in which you restate your thesis and provide additional context or make a connection across time. Use **CSE** and **GEM** to aid your analysis. Feel free to incorporate the information already provided in the graphic organizer into your essay.

Development of the Middle Class

MODULE 6.10

FOCUS

As you read this module, consider how industrialization led to new forms of leisure-time activities and how it changed societal expectations for men and women. Make sure also to compare how the effects of economic changes reinforced social class divisions.

Wealthy people in the late nineteenth century used their fortunes to support lavish lifestyles. For many of them, especially those with recent wealth, opulence rather than good taste was the standard of adornment. This tendency inspired writer Mark Twain and his collaborator Charles Dudley Warner to describe this era of wealth creation as the **Gilded Age**. Glittering on the outside, the enormous riches covered up the unrestrained materialism and political rottenness that lay below the surface.

Twain and Warner had the very rich in mind when they coined the phrase, but others further down the social ladder found ways to participate in the culture of consumption. The rapidly expanding middle class enjoyed modest homes furnished with mass-produced consumer goods. Women played the central role in running the household, as most wives remained at home to raise children. Women and men often spent their free time attending meetings and other events sponsored by social, cultural, and political organizations. Despite the challenges industrial workers faced, a steady expansion of leisure time allowed greater participation in sports, visiting dance halls, and other forms of cheap entertainment.

Gilded Age
The term created by Mark Twain and Charles Dudley Warner to describe the late nineteenth century. It implies the glittering appearance of the era was a shell that covered the corruption and materialism of the superrich.

Wealthy and Middle-Class Leisure Pursuits

Industrialization and the rise of **corporate capitalism** led to the expansion of the wealthy upper class as well as the expansion of the middle class, and new lifestyles emerged. Urban elites lived lives of unparalleled material opulence. J. P. Morgan, William Vanderbilt, and John D. Rockefeller built lavish mansions in New York City. High-rise apartment buildings also catered to the wealthy. Overlooking Central Park, the nine-story Dakota Apartments boasted fifty-eight suites, a banquet hall, and a wine cellar.

Millionaire residents furnished their stately homes with an eclectic mix of priceless art objects and furniture in a jumble of diverse styles. The rich and famous established private social clubs, sent their children to exclusive prep schools and colleges, and worshipped in the most fashionable churches.

Second homes, usually for use in the summer, were no less expensively constructed and decorated. Besides residences in Manhattan and Newport, Rhode Island, the Vanderbilts constructed a "home away from home" in the mountains of Asheville, North Carolina. The Biltmore, as they named it, contained 250 rooms, 40 master bedrooms, and an indoor swimming pool.

AP® EXAM TIP

Use the description of corporate capitalism in your textbook to explain the development of a middle class. This book provides specific examples of the lifestyle of the middle class in a consumer culture. Look for specific examples to use in your explanation.

The rich also built and frequented opera houses, concert halls, museums, and historical societies as testimonies to their taste and sophistication. For example, the Vanderbilts, Rockefellers, Goulds, and Morgans financed the completion of the Metropolitan Opera House in New York City in 1883. When the facility opened, a local newspaper commented about the well-heeled audience: "The Goulds and the Vanderbilts and people of that ilk perfumed the air with the odor of crisp greenbacks." Upper-class women often traveled abroad to visit the great European cities and ancient Mediterranean sites.

Industrialization and the rise of corporate capitalism also brought an array of white-collar workers in managerial, clerical, and technical positions. These workers formed a new, expanded middle class and joined the businesspeople, doctors, lawyers, and clergy who constituted the old middle class. More than three million white-collar workers were employed in 1910, nearly three times as many as in 1870.

Middle-class families decorated their residences with mass-produced furniture, musical instruments, family photographs, books, periodicals, and a variety of memorabilia collected in their leisure time. They could relax in their parlors and browse through mass-circulation magazines and popular newspapers. Or they could read some of the era's outpouring of fiction, including romances, dime novels, westerns, humor, and social realism, an art form that depicted working-class life.

- How did life change for the middle class during the Gilded Age?

Working-Class Leisure in Industrial America

Despite the hardships industrial laborers faced in the late nineteenth century, workers carved out recreational spaces that they could control and that offered relief from their backbreaking toil. For many, Sunday became a day of rest that took on a secular flavor.

Working-class leisure patterns varied by gender, race, and region. Women did not generally attend spectator sporting events, such as baseball and boxing matches, which catered to men. Nor did they find themselves comfortable in union halls and saloons where men found solace in drink. Working-class wives preferred to gather to prepare for births, weddings, and funerals or to assist neighbors who had suffered some misfortune.

Once employed, working-class daughters found a greater measure of independence and free time by living in rooming houses on their own. Women's wages were only a small fraction of men's earnings, so workingwomen rarely made enough money to support a regular social life. Still, they found ways to enjoy their free time. Some single women went out in groups, hoping to meet men who would pay for drinks, food, or a vaudeville show. Others dated so that they knew they would be taken care of for the evening. Some of the men who "treated" on a date assumed a right to sexual favors in return, and some of these women then expected men to provide them with housing and gifts in exchange for an ongoing sexual relationship. Thus, emotional and economic relationships became intertwined.

Around the turn of the twentieth century, dance halls flourished as one of the mainstays of working-class communities. Huge dance palaces were built in the entertainment districts of most large cities. They made their money by offering music with lengthy intermissions for the sale of drinks and refreshments. Women and men also attended nightclubs, some of which were racially integrated. In so-called red-light districts of the city, prostitutes earned money entertaining their clients with a variety of sexual pleasures.

Not all forms of leisure were strictly segregated along class lines. A number of forms of cheap entertainment appealed not only to working-class women and men but also to their middle-class counterparts. By the turn of the twentieth century, most large American cities featured amusement parks. Brooklyn's Coney Island stood out as the most spectacular of these sprawling playgrounds. In 1884, the world's first roller coaster was built at Coney Island, providing thrills to those brave enough to ride it. In Chicago at the 1893 World's Columbian Exposition, residents enjoyed the new Ferris wheel, which soared 250 feet in the air.

AP® WORKING with EVIDENCE

Source: Sheet Music for Piano and Singers, "New York and Coney Island Cycle March: Two Step," 1896

From The New York Public Library

Questions for Analysis:

1. Identify some of the new leisure activities available to urban dwellers in this image.
2. Describe how this sheet music, likely to be performed at home with a family piano, formed part of these new leisure activities.
3. Explain how the growth of industrial production contributed to these new leisure activities.

photo-fox/Alamy

Vaudeville, 1897 The popular comedy team of J. Sherrie Matthews and Harry Bulger performed in vaudeville shows throughout the country. This photo, taken in the San Francisco Bay area, shows Matthews playing a traditional Chinese instrument called a *yueqin*, while Bulger dances. Notice the braid running down the front of Bulger's costume, apparently meant to impersonate the braid that Chinese men often wore in the nineteenth century. In similar fashion, in minstrel shows, the predecessor of vaudeville, whites appeared in blackface to impersonate Black Americans.

How did minstrel and vaudeville shows, such as the one in this image, reflect the social values of the era?

Vaudeville houses—with their minstrel shows (white people in blackface) and comedians, singers, and dancers—brought howls of laughter to working-class audiences. Nickelodeons charged five cents to watch short films. Live theater generally attracted more wealthy patrons, although Yiddish theater, which flourished on New York's Lower East Side, and other immigrant-oriented stage productions appealed mainly to working-class audiences.

Itinerant musicians entertained audiences throughout the South. Lumber camps, which employed mainly Black men, offered a popular destination for these musicians. Each camp contained a "barrelhouse," also called a "honky tonk" or a "juke joint." Besides showcasing music, the barrelhouse also gave workers the opportunity to "shoot craps, dice, drink whiskey, dance, every modern devilment you can do," as one musician who played there recalled.

From the Mississippi Delta emerged a new form of music—the blues. W. C. Handy, "the father of the blues," discovered this music in his travels through the delta, where he observed southern Black people performing songs of woe, accompanying themselves with anything that would make a "musical sound or rhythmical effect, anything from a harmonica to a washboard."

Meanwhile in New Orleans, an amalgam of Black musical forms evolved into jazz. Musicians such as "Jelly Roll" Morton experimented with a variety of sounds, putting together African and Caribbean rhythms with European music, mixing pianos with clarinets, trumpets, and drums. Blues and jazz spread throughout the South.

In mountain valley mill towns, southern whites preferred "old-time" music, but with a twist: they modified the lyrics of traditional ballads and folk songs, originally enjoyed by British settlers, to extol the exploits of outlaws and adventurers. Country music, which combined romantic ballads and folk tunes to the accompaniment of guitars, banjos, autoharps, dulcimers, and organs, emerged as a distinct style of music by the twentieth century.

As with Black Americans, in the late nineteenth century, working-class and rural whites found new and exciting types of music to entertain them in their leisure. Religious music also appealed to both white and Black audiences and drew crowds to evangelical revivals.

Mill workers also amused themselves by engaging in social, recreational, and religious activities. Women visited each other and exchanged confidences, gossip, advice on child rearing, and folk remedies. Men from various factories organized baseball teams that competed in leagues. Managers of a mill in Charlotte, North Carolina, admitted that they "frequently hired men better known for their batting averages than their work records."

REVIEW

- How did working-class leisure activities compare to those of the middle and upper classes during the late nineteenth century?

Skills Workshop: Thinking Historically

Additional Practice in Responding to a Long-Essay Question

Review the AP® Skills Workshops in Modules 5.8 and 6.9 and then respond to the following Long-Essay Question. Make sure you include the following in your response:

- Thesis (making a historically defensible claim with a line of reasoning)
- Contextualization (connecting to a relevant and broader historical context)
- Evidence (supporting an argument by using multiple pieces of relevant information)
- Historical reasoning (using causation, comparison, or continuity and change over time to frame an argument)
- Complexity (demonstrating a sophisticated historical understanding of the topic)

Evaluate the extent to which industrialization affected culture in the United States in the period 1865 to 1900.

MODULE 6.11

Reform in the Gilded Age

FOCUS

In reaction to social and economic changes during the Gilded Age, many Americans sought alternative ways to reform the United States. These reform efforts sometimes attracted large followings, and sometimes, they initiated reforms that came to fruition only in later time periods. Likewise, women, especially in the middle and upper classes, sought greater equality with men through social and political reform, as well as taking part in an expanded set of leisure activities.

As you read this module, trace the causes and effects of different reform efforts—their origins, justifications, means of reform, and degrees of success.

Challenges to Industrial Capitalism

laissez-faire
French for "let do." Advocates of laissez-faire believed the marketplace should be left to regulate itself, claiming that by allowing individuals to pursue their own self-interest without any government restraint or interference, the market would produce a natural balance.

Proponents of the second industrial revolution did not go unchallenged. Critics of **laissez-faire** economics, which advocated unrestrained corporate growth and little government oversight, created an alternative ideology for those who sought to organize workers and expand the role of government as way of restricting capitalists' power over labor and ordinary citizens.

Lester Frank Ward attacked laissez-faire in his book *Dynamic Sociology* (1883). Ward did not disparage individualism but viewed the main function of society as "the organization of happiness." Contradicting Herbert Spencer's Social Darwinism (Module 6.10), Ward maintained that societies progressed when government directly intervened to help citizens—even the unfortunate. Rejecting laissez-faire, he argued that what people "really need is more government in its primary sense, greater protection from the rapacity of the favored few."

Some academics supported Ward's ideas. Most notably, economist Richard T. Ely applied Christian ethics to his scholarly assessment of capital and labor. He condemned the railroads for dragging "their slimy length over our country, and every turn in their progress is marked by a progeny of evils." In his book *The Labor Movement in America* (1886), Ely suggested that the solution for social ills resulting from industrialization lay in "the union of capital and labor in the same hands, in grand, wide-reaching, co-operative enterprises."

AP® EXAM TIP

Be able to explain what is meant by alternative visions for the U.S. economy during the Gilded Age and who advocated these ideas. Reformers represented a disparate group, so select a couple to focus on and be able to describe specific ways in which they advocated reforms.

Two popular writers, Henry George and Edward Bellamy, added to the critique of materialism and greed. In *Progress and Poverty* (1879), George lamented: "Amid the greatest accumulations of wealth, men die of starvation." George blamed the problem on rent, which he viewed as an unjustifiable payment on the increase in the value of land. His remedy was to have government confiscate rent earned on land by levying a single tax on landownership. Though he advocated government intervention, he did not envision an enduring role for the state once it had imposed the single tax.

By contrast, Bellamy imagined a powerful central government. In his novel *Looking Backward, 2000–1887* (1888), Bellamy attacked industrialists who "maim and slaughter workers by thousands." In his view, the federal government should take over large-scale firms, administer them as workers' collectives, and redistribute wealth equally among all citizens.

One thing Bellamy, George, Ward, and Ely had in common was that none of them endorsed the militant socialism of Karl Marx. The German philosopher predicted that capitalism would be overthrown and replaced by a revolutionary movement of industrial workers that would control the means of economic production and establish an egalitarian society. Although Marx's ideas gained popularity among European labor leaders, they were not widely accepted in the United States during this period. Most critics believed that the U.S. political system could be reformed without resorting to the extreme solution of a socialist revolution. They favored a cooperative commonwealth of capital and labor, with the government acting as an umpire between the two.

REVIEW

- What were some common critiques of industrial capitalism among intellectuals during this period? What were some different reform solutions?

Charitable Reform

With more money and time on their hands, middle-class women and men were able to devote their efforts to charity. They joined a variety of social and professional organizations that arose to deal with the problems accompanying industrialization.

The expansion of corporations and big business stimulated a demand for clerical workers, female as well as well as male. This offered women many new opportunities to enter the job market. Along with this development, the push for women's rights, especially the right to vote, and women's increasing involvement in civic associations threatened to reduce absolute male control over the public sphere.

During the 1880s, charitable organizations such as the American Red Cross were established to provide disaster relief. In 1892, the General Federation of Women's Clubs was founded to improve women's educational and cultural lives. Four years later, the National Association of Colored Women organized to help relieve suffering among the Black poor, defend Black women, and promote the interests of the Black race.

During these swiftly changing times, adults became increasingly concerned about the nation's youth and sought to create organizations that catered to young people. Formed in England before the Civil War and later expanded to the United States, the Young Men's Christian Association (YMCA) grew briskly during the 1880s as it erected buildings where young men could socialize, build moral character, and engage in healthy physical exercise. The Young Women's Christian Association (YWCA) provided similar opportunities for women. Black Americans also participated in "Y" activities through the creation of racially separate branches.

Religiously inspired reform provided similar support for poor city dwellers. Some Protestant ministers began to argue that immigrants' problems resulted not from chronic racial or ethnic failings, but from their difficult environment. Some of them preached Christianity as a **social gospel**, which included support for civil service reform, antimonopoly regulation, income tax legislation, factory inspection laws, and workers' right to strike.

Despite the efforts of advocates of the social gospel and the charitable organizations that arose to help relieve human misery, private attempts to combat the various urban

AP® EXAM TIP

Social and political reform is a useful way to begin a categorization of women reformers. Yet those areas of reform have to be defined further. Think about specific reform efforts such as settlement houses or suffrage to build an explanation of the ways in which women sought to reform society.

social gospel
A religious movement that advocated the application of Christian teachings to social and economic problems. The ideals of the social gospel inspired many progressive reformers but were largely ineffectual, as their reforms sought to change the individual rather than larger social structures and their impact.

ills, however well-meaning, proved insufficient. The problems were structural, not personal, and one group or even several operating together did not have the resources or power to make urban institutions more efficient, equitable, and humane. If reformers were to succeed in tackling the most significant social problems and make lasting changes in American society and politics, they would have to enlist state and federal governments.

REVIEW

- Compare the charitable reform efforts during this era to the critiques of industrial capitalism by intellectuals like Richard Ely, Edward Bellamy, and Lester Frank Ward.

Changing Gender Roles

AP® EXAM TIP

The development of a middle class both challenged and supported previously held beliefs about gender roles in American society. Brainstorm how new gender roles both challenged and supported previously held beliefs. Be able to write a two- or three-sentence explanation reconciling these differences.

Economic changes led to adjustments in lifestyles and gender roles during the industrial era. Whereas in the past farmers and artisans had worked from the home, now most men and women accepted as natural the separation of the workplace and the home caused by industrialization and urbanization.

Middle-class wives generally remained at home, caring for the house and children, often with the aid of a servant. Although birth and marriage rates among the middle class dropped during the late nineteenth century, wives were still expected to care for their husbands and family first to fulfill their feminine duties. Even though daughters increasingly attended colleges reserved for women, their families viewed education as a means of providing refinement rather than a career. One physician summed up the prevailing view that women could only use their brains "but little and in trivial matters" and should concentrate on serving as "the companion or ornamental appendage to man."

Middle-class women threw themselves into the new consumer culture. Department stores, chain stores, ready-made clothes, and packaged goods, from Jell-O and Kellogg's Corn Flakes to cake mixes, competed for the money and loyalty of female consumers. Hairdressers, cosmetic companies, and department stores offered a growing and ever-changing assortment of styles.

Yet the availability of mass-produced goods to assist the housewife in her chores made her role as consumer highly visible, while making her role as worker nearly invisible. The expanding array of consumer goods did not decrease women's domestic workload. They had more furniture to dust, fancier meals to prepare, changing fashions to keep up with, higher standards of cleanliness to maintain, and occasions to entertain guests.

For more socially and economically independent young women — those who attended college or beauty and secretarial schools — new worlds of leisure opened up. Bicycling, tennis, and croquet became popular sports for women in the late nineteenth century. So, too, did playing basketball, both in colleges and through industrial leagues. Indeed, women's colleges made sports a requirement, to offset the stress of intellectual life and produce a more well-rounded graduate.

Middle-class men enjoyed new leisure pursuits, too. During the late nineteenth century, 5.5 million men (of some 19 million adult men in the United States) joined fraternal orders, such as the Odd Fellows, Masons, Knights of Pythias, and Elks. These groups offered middle-class men a network of business contacts and gave them a chance to enjoy a communal, masculine social environment otherwise lacking in their lives; they also undertook charitable work and fund-raising for community projects.

Robert Alexander/Getty Images

Women Bicyclists In the 1890s, with improvements in technology, middle-class women had both more leisure time and access to easy-to-ride bicycles. This photograph shows women at an early stage of the bicycle craze before changes in fashion allowed women to wear less-restrictive clothing that permitted exposed ankles and visible bloomers. In 1895, a Nebraska newspaper commented on the larger social implications of women bicyclists: The bicycle took "old-fashioned, slow-going notions of the gentler sex," and replaced them with "some new woman, mounted on her steed of steel."

How does this photograph illustrate both changing social norms for women and the limitations of those changes?

In fact, historians have referred to a "crisis of masculinity" afflicting a segment of middle- and upper-class men in the late nineteenth and early twentieth centuries. Middle-class occupations whittled away the sense of autonomy that men had experienced in an earlier era when they worked for themselves. The emergence of corporate capitalism had swelled the ranks of the middle class with organization men, who held salaried jobs in managerial departments. At the same time, the expansion of corporations and big business stimulated a demand for clerical workers, female as well as male. This offered women many new opportunities to enter the job market. Along with this development, the push for women's rights, especially the right to vote, and women's increasing involvement in civic associations threatened to reduce absolute male control over the public sphere.

Responding to this gender crisis, middle-class men sought ways to exert their masculinity and keep from becoming frail and effeminate. Psychologists like G. Stanley Hall warned that unless men returned to a primitive state of manhood, they risked becoming spiritually paralyzed. To avoid this, went their advice, men should build up their bodies and engage in strenuous activities to improve their physical fitness.

Men turned to sports to cultivate their masculinity. Besides playing baseball and football, they could attend various sporting events. Baseball, a game played by elites in New York City in the 1840s, soon became a commercially popular sport. It spread across the country as baseball clubs in different cities competed with each other. The sport came into its own with the creation of the professional National League in 1876 and the introduction of the World Series in 1903 between the winners of the National League and American League pennant races. Baseball became the national pastime, and men could root for their home team and establish a community with the thousands of male spectators who filled up newly constructed ballparks.

Boxing also became a popular spectator sport in the late nineteenth century. Bare-knuckle fighting — without the protection of gloves — epitomized the craze to display pure masculinity. A boxing match lasted until one of the fighters was knocked out, leaving both fighters bloody and battered.

AP® WORKING with EVIDENCE

Source: *The Delineator*, a women's magazine, 1900

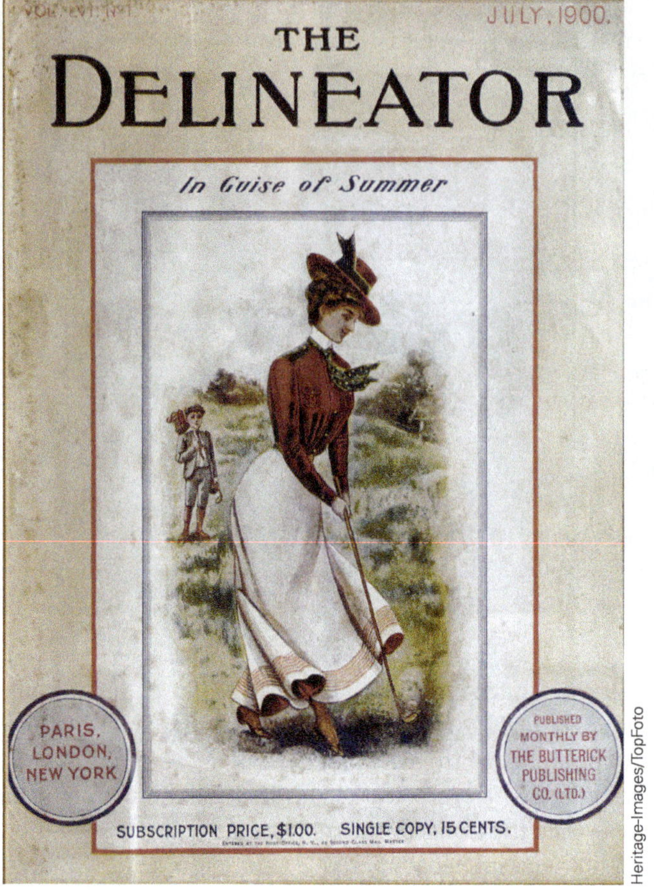

JULY, 1900.
THE
DELINEATOR
In Guise of Summer
PARIS, LONDON, NEW YORK
PUBLISHED MONTHLY BY THE BUTTERICK PUBLISHING CO. (LTD.)
SUBSCRIPTION PRICE, $1.00. SINGLE COPY, 15 CENTS.

Heritage-Images/TopFoto

Questions for Analysis

1. Identify the primary activity in the image.
2. Describe the intended audience for this image.
3. Explain how the clothing worn by the woman reflects both economic and social changes of the late nineteenth century.
4. Evaluate the extent to which this image reflects gains for women in the public sphere during the late nineteenth century.

Source: Theodore Roosevelt, *Professionalism in Sports*, 1890

> "It is hardly necessary at the present day to enter a plea for athletic exercise and manly outdoor sports. During the last twenty-five years there has been a wonderful growth of interest in and appreciation of healthy muscular amusements; and this growth can best be promoted by stimulating, within proper bounds, the spirit of rivalry on which all our games are based. The effect upon the physique of the sedentary classes, especially in the towns and cities, has already been very marked. . . . As a nation we have many tremendous problems to work out, and we need to bring every ounce of vital power possible to their solution. No people has ever yet done great and lasting work if its physical type was infirm and weak. Goodness and strength must go hand in hand if the Republic is to be preserved. The good man who is ready and able to strike a blow for the right, and to put down evil with the strong

arm, is the citizen who deserves our most hearty respect. There is a certain tendency in the civilization of our time to underestimate or overlook the need of the virile, masterful qualities of the heart and mind which have built up and alone can maintain and defend this very civilization. . . . There is no better way of counteracting this tendency than by encouraging bodily exercise, and especially the sports which develop such qualities as courage, resolution, and endurance."

Questions for Analysis

1. Describe Roosevelt's argument in this excerpt.
2. Describe Roosevelt's purpose in this excerpt.
3. Evaluate the extent to which changing middle-class social norms contributed to the argument Roosevelt makes in this excerpt.

Questions for Comparison

1. Explain how Roosevelt's ideal of manhood compares with the ideal of womanhood depicted on the *Delineator* cover.
2. Explain how each source represents a reaction to changing social norms in the late 1800s.

During the late nineteenth century, middle-class women and men also had increased opportunities to engage in different forms of sociability and sexuality. Although treated by medical experts as sexual "inverts" who might be cured by an infusion of "normal" contact with members of the opposite gender, gays and lesbians began to emerge from the shadows of restrictive social norms around the turn of the twentieth century. Gay men and lesbians could find safe havens in New York City's Greenwich Village and Chicago's North Side for their own entertainment.

"Boston marriages" constituted another form of relationship between women. The term apparently came from Henry James's book *The Bostonians* (1886), which described a female couple living together in a monogamous, long-term relationship. This association appealed to financially independent women who did not want to get married. Many of these relationships were sexual, but some were not. In either case, they offered women of a certain class an alternative to traditional, heterosexual marriage.

Skills Workshop: Thinking Historically

Additional Practice in Responding to a Short-Answer Question

Use what you have learned in Modules 6.10 and 6.11 to respond to each part of the following SAQ using CSE. Review the AP® Skills Workshop in Module 1.4 if needed.

Answer **A**, **B**, and **C**.

(A) Briefly explain ONE way industrialization changed the everyday lives of working-class Americans between 1865 and 1900.

(B) Briefly explain ONE way industrialization changed the everyday lives of middle-class American women between 1865 and 1900.

(C) Briefly explain ONE response to challenges of industrialization between 1865 and 1900.

Controversies over the Role of Government in the Gilded Age

FOCUS

The beliefs that supported the Gilded Age placed the burden of success or failure on the individual while restraining the federal government from intervention in the economy. While some industrialists promoted philanthropy, all believed their economic power represented the natural order of things.

As you read this module, consider how arguments about economic efficiency, individualism, and expansion represented changes in American ideas as well as continuities.

AP® EXAM TIP

Laissez-faire economic policies in the Gilded Age can be a misunderstood concept because its advocates benefited from government policies that furthered their hold on an industrial economy. Think about how you can explain the belief in laissez-faire with the contradiction of government policies that helped industrial capitalists. Showing contradiction can lead to a more nuanced understanding of the role of government in the economy.

American industrialization developed as rapidly as it did in large part because it was reinforced by traditional ideas and values. The notion that hard work and diligence would result in success meant that individuals felt justified, even duty-bound, to strive to achieve upward mobility and accumulate wealth. Those who succeeded believed that they had done so because they were more talented, industrious, and resourceful than others.

Therefore, prosperous businessmen regarded competition and the free market as essential to the health of an economic world they saw based on merit. Yet these same businessmen also created trusts that destroyed competition, and they depended on the government for resources and protection. This obvious contradiction, along with the profoundly unequal distribution of wealth that characterized the late-nineteenth-century economy, generated a good deal of criticism of business tycoons and their beliefs.

Doctrines of Success

Those at the top of the new industrial order justified their great wealth in a manner that most Americans could understand. The ideas of the Scottish economist Adam Smith, in *The Wealth of Nations* (1776), had gained popularity during the American Revolution. Advocating laissez-faire (Module 6.11), Smith contended that an "Invisible Hand," guided by natural law, guaranteed the greatest economic success if the government let individuals pursue their own self-interest unhindered by outside and artificial influences.

In the late nineteenth century, businessmen and their conservative allies on the Supreme Court used Smith's doctrines to argue against restrictive government regulation. They equated their right to own and manage property with the personal liberty protected by the Fourteenth Amendment. Thus, the Declaration of Independence, with its defense of "life, liberty, and the pursuit of happiness," and the Constitution, which enshrined citizens' political freedom, became instruments to guarantee unfettered economic opportunity and safeguard private property.

The view that success depended on individual initiative was reinforced in schools and churches. The McGuffey Readers, widely used to educate children, taught moral lessons of hard work, individual initiative, reliability, and thrift. The popular dime novels of Horatio Alger portrayed the story of young men who rose from "rags to riches" through a combination of "luck and pluck."

Americans could also hear success stories in houses of worship. Russell Conwell, pastor of the Grace Baptist Church in Philadelphia, delivered a widely printed sermon entitled "Acres of Diamonds," which equated godliness with riches and argued that ordinary people had an obligation to strive for material wealth. "I say that you ought to get rich, and it is your duty to get rich," Conwell declared, "because to make money honestly is to preach the gospel."

Capitalists such as Carnegie found a way to soften both the message of extreme competition and its impact on the American public. Denying that the government should help the poor, they proclaimed that men of wealth had a duty to furnish some assistance.

In his famous essay **"The Gospel of Wealth"** (1889), Carnegie argued that the rich should act as stewards of the wealth they earned. As trustees, they should administer their surplus income for the benefit of the community. Carnegie distinguished between charity (direct handouts to individuals), which he deplored, and philanthropy (building institutions that would raise educational and cultural standards), which he advocated. Carnegie was particularly generous in funding libraries (he provided the buildings, but not the books) because they allowed people to gain knowledge through their own efforts.

AP® EXAM TIP

Think about ways to explore the economic developments of the Gilded Age by comparing the social gospel, gospel of wealth, and Social Darwinism. Compare and contrast the views held by Americans about these beliefs to produce a more nuanced understanding of the economy of the Gilded Age.

"The Gospel of Wealth" An essay by Andrew Carnegie published in 1889 in which he argued the rich should act as guardians of society through the wealth they earned. Carnegie advocated that the wealthy generate programs to uplift intelligent self-starters by using their surplus income for the benefit of the community, creating public libraries or community centers, rather than engaging in charity.

AP® WORKING with EVIDENCE

Source: Andrew Carnegie, "The Gospel of Wealth," 1889

> "In bestowing charity, the main consideration should be to help those who will help themselves; to provide part of the means by which those who desire to improve may do so; to give those who desire to rise the aids by which they may rise; to assist, but rarely or never to do all. Neither the individual nor the race is improved by almsgiving [giving food or money directly to the poor]. Those worthy of assistance, except in rare cases, seldom require assistance. . . .
>
> [T]he best means of benefiting the community is to place within its reach the ladders upon which the aspiring can rise—free libraries, parks, and means of recreation, by which men are helped in body and mind; works of art, certain to give pleasure and improve the public taste; and public institutions of various kinds, which will improve the general condition of the people; in this manner returning their surplus wealth to the mass of their fellows in the forms best calculated to do them lasting good.
>
> Thus is the problem of rich and poor to be solved. The laws of accumulation will be left free, the laws of distribution free. Individualism will continue, but the millionaire will be but a trustee for the poor, intrusted for a season with a great part of the increased wealth of the community, but administering it for the community far better than it could or would have done for itself."

Questions for Analysis

1. Describe Carnegie's argument.
2. Explain how Carnegie's proposed solutions reflect his social-economic standing.
3. Evaluate the extent to which working conditions for laborers undermine Carnegie's argument.

(continued)

Source: "A Workingman's Prayer," *The Coming Nation*, 1894

> "Oh, Almighty Andrew Philanthropist Library Carnegie, who art in America when not in Europe spending the money of your slaves and serfs, thou art a good father to the people of Pittsburgh, Homestead and Beaver Falls. We bow before thee in humble obedience of slavery. . . . We have no desire but to serve thee. If you sayest black was white we believe you, and are willing, with the assistance of . . . the Pinkerton's agency, to knock the stuffin[g] out of anyone who thinks different, or to shoot down and imprison serfs who dare say you have been unjust in reducing the wages of your slaves, who call themselves citizens of the land of the free and the home of the brave. . . .
>
> Oh, lord and master, we love thee because you and other great masters of slaves favor combines and trusts to enslave and make paupers of us all. We love thee though our children are clothed in rags. We love thee though our wives . . . are so scantily dressed and look so shabby. But, oh master, thou hast given us one great enjoyment which man has never dreamed of before—a free church organ, so that we can take our shabby families to church to hear your great organ pour forth its melodious strains. . . .
>
> Oh, master, we thank thee for all the free gifts you have given the public at the expense of your slaves. . . . Oh, master, we need no protection, we need no liberty so long as we are under thy care. So we commend ourselves to thy mercy and forevermore sing thy praise."

Questions for Analysis

1. Describe the author's attitude toward wealthy industrialists.
2. Explain how specific effects of industrialization are portrayed in this excerpt.
3. Explain how the author's references to specific historical patterns and events contribute to the main argument of "A Workingman's Prayer."

Questions for Comparison

1. Explain how each document appeals to its particular audience.
2. Evaluate how effective "A Workingman's Prayer" is in rebutting Carnegie's argument.

Capitalists may have sung the praises of individualism and laissez-faire, but their actions contradicted their words. Successful industrialists in the late nineteenth century sought to destroy competition, not perpetuate it. Their efforts over the course of several decades produced giant corporations that measured the worth of individuals by calculating their value to the organization. As John D. Rockefeller, the master of consolidation, proclaimed, "The day of individual competition in large affairs is past and gone."

Nor did capitalists strictly oppose government involvement. Although industrialists did not want the federal government to take any action that *hindered* their economic efforts, they did favor the use of the government's power to *promote* their enterprises and to stimulate entrepreneurial energies. Thus, manufacturers pushed for congressional passage of high tariffs to protect goods from foreign competition and to foster development of the national marketplace. Industrialists demanded that federal and state governments dispatch troops when labor strikes threatened their businesses. They persuaded Washington to provide land grants for railroad construction and to send the army to clear American Indians and bison from their tracks. They argued for state and federal courts to interpret constitutional and statutory law in a way that shielded property rights against attacks from workers. In large measure, capitalists succeeded not in spite of governmental support, but because of it.

REVIEW

- What was the relationship between Social Darwinism (Module 6.9) and laissez-faire policies?

Seeking International Markets

Industrialization of new sectors of the U.S. economy and the growth of corporate capitalism stimulated desires in the late nineteenth century to seek markets outside the borders of the United States, often through the control or conquest of peoples in other lands.

Throughout its early history, the United States had sought overseas markets for exports. However, the importance of exports to the U.S. economy grew dramatically in the second half of the nineteenth century, as industrialization gained momentum. In 1870, U.S. exports totaled $500 million. Forty years later, the value of U.S. exports had increased threefold to $1.7 billion.

The bulk of U.S. exports went to the developed markets of Europe and Canada, which had the greatest purchasing power. And although the less economically powerful nations of Latin America and Asia did not have the same ability to buy U.S. products, businessmen still considered these regions — especially China, with its large population — as future markets for U.S. products.

The desire to expand foreign markets remained a steady feature of U.S. business interests. The fear that the domestic market for manufactured goods was shrinking gave this expansionist hunger greater urgency.

Commercial ambitions led many in the United States also to covet Hawaii. U.S. missionaries first visited the Hawaiian Islands in 1820, and as they tried to convert native islanders to Christianity, U.S. businessmen sought to establish plantations on the islands, especially to grow sugarcane. In exchange for duty-free access to the U.S. sugar market, white Hawaiians signed an agreement in 1887 that granted the United States exclusive rights to a naval base at Pearl Harbor in Honolulu.

The growing influence of white-owned sugar plantations on the islands alarmed native Hawaiians. In 1891, Queen Liliuokalani, a strong nationalist leader who voiced the slogan "Hawaii for the Hawaiians," sought to increase the power of the indigenous peoples she governed, at the expense of the sugar growers. In 1893, white plantation owners, with the cooperation of the U.S. ambassador to Hawaii and 150 U.S. marines, overthrew the queen's government. Once in command of the government, they entered into a treaty of annexation with the United States. However, President Grover Cleveland opposed annexation and withdrew the treaty. Nevertheless, planters remained in power and waited for a suitable opportunity to seek annexation.

As in Hawaii, Christian missionaries served as foot soldiers for the advancing U.S. commercial empire to the rest of the world. In fact, there was often a clear connection between religious and commercial interests. For example, in 1895, industrialists John D. Rockefeller Jr. and Cyrus McCormick created the World Student Christian Federation, which dispatched more than five thousand young missionaries throughout the world, many of them women. Likewise, it was no coincidence that China became a magnet for U.S. missionary activity. Many Americans hoped that, under missionary supervision, the Chinese would become consumers of both U.S. ideas and U.S. products.

AP® EXAM TIP

Connecting the economic processes of industrialization with the age of imperialism can lead to a sophisticated understanding of controversies surrounding the role of government in the economy. Develop one link between industrialization and imperialism to explain this idea. Be ready to expand your analysis when you read Modules 7.2 and 7.3.

REVIEW

- In what ways did the second industrial revolution fuel U.S. policymakers' desire to expand American influence overseas, for example, in Hawaii?

Skills Workshop: Thinking Historically

Additional Practice in Responding to a Short-Answer Question with a Primary Source

Read the following SAQ carefully and write a response to each part of the question using CSE. If you need extra help, review the AP® Skills Workshop in Module 1.7.

Source: Thomas Nast, "Uncle Sam," *The President's Message*, 1887

Uncle Sam, don't play with it,—be a Man. Monopolists' soap-bubbles soon burst.

Thomas Nast

About the source: In this cartoon, Uncle Sam is shown holding a bowl labeled "Soap Fat." Using a pipe, he is blowing a bubble that reads, "GUARANTEEING EQUAL TAXATION." In the background, a bubble labeled "PROTECTION OF LABOR" floats above two bubbles—"FAIRNESS" and "JUSTICE," which have already burst. A pile of soap bars by Uncle Sam's feet read (clockwise) "MONOPOLY," "FAT," "TRUST," and "INFANT SOAP." The text beneath the illustration of Uncle Sam reads, "Uncle Sam, don't play with it—, be a Man. Monopolists' soap-bubbles soon burst."

Using the image, answer **A**, **B**, and **C**.

(A) Briefly describe ONE perspective about government's role in society expressed in the image.

(B) Briefly explain ONE specific historical event or development that led to the perspective expressed in the image.

(C) Briefly explain ONE specific historical argument that could be used to support or challenge the perspective expressed in the image.

Politics in the Gilded Age

FOCUS

As you read this module, use the lens of comparison to help you better understand the political parties and movements during the Gilded Age. Compare the farm movements of the era—Granges, Farmers' Alliances, and Populists—to each other, and to politics at both the federal level, and in the cities.

Politicians played an important role in the expanding industrial economy that provided new opportunities for the wealthy and the expanding middle class. For growing companies and corporations to succeed, they needed a favorable political climate that would support their interests. During this era, the office of the president was a weak and largely administrative post, and legislators and judges were highly influenced and sometimes directly controlled by business leaders. For much of this period, the two national political parties battled to a standoff, which resulted in congressional gridlock with little accomplished. Yet, spurred by fierce partisan competition, political participation grew among the electorate.

Farmers, like industrial workers, experienced severe economic hardships and a loss of political power in the face of rapid industrialization. The introduction of new machinery, such as the combine harvester in 1878, led to substantial increases in the productivity of American farms. Soaring production, however, led to a decline in agricultural prices in the late nineteenth century, a trend that was accelerated by increased agricultural production around the world. Faced with an economic crisis caused by falling prices and escalating debt, farmers fought back, creating new organizations to champion their collective economic and political interests.

In early 1893, the bankruptcy of the Philadelphia and Reading Railroad set off a chain reaction that pushed one-quarter of American railroads into insolvency. As a result, on May 5, 1893, "Black Friday," the stock market collapsed in a panic, triggering the **Panic of 1893**. Hundreds of banks failed, which hurt the businesspeople and farmers who relied on a steady flow of bank credit. The depression became the chief political issue of the mid-1890s and resulted in a realignment of power among the various national political parties.

Panic of 1893
A severe economic downturn triggered by railroad and bank failures. The severity of the depression, combined with the failure of the federal government to offer an adequate response for half a decade, led to a realignment of American politics.

Weak Presidencies and an Inefficient Congress

James Bryce, a British observer of American politics, devoted a chapter of his book *The American Commonwealth* (1888) to "why great men are not chosen presidents." He believed that the White House attracted mediocre occupants because the president functioned mainly as an executor. The stature of the office had shrunk following the impeachment of Andrew Johnson and the reassertion of congressional power during Reconstruction (Module 5.10).

Presidents considered themselves mainly as the nation's top administrator. They did not see their roles as formulating policy or intervening on behalf of legislative objectives. With the office held in such low regard, great men became corporate leaders, not presidents.

Perhaps aware that they could expect little in the way of assistance or imagination from national leaders, voters refused to give either Democrats or Republicans solid support. No president in the two decades between Ulysses S. Grant and William McKinley won back-to-back elections or received a majority of the popular vote. The only two-time winner, the Democrat Grover Cleveland, lost his bid for reelection in 1888 before triumphing again in 1892.

Nevertheless, the presidency attracted accomplished individuals. Rutherford B. Hayes (1877–1881), James A. Garfield (1881), and Benjamin Harrison (1889–1893) all had served ably in the Union army as commanding officers during the Civil War and had prior political experience.

The nation greatly mourned Garfield following his assassination in 1881 by Charles Guiteau, a disgruntled applicant for a job in the federal government. Upon Garfield's death, Chester A. Arthur (1881–1885) became president. He had served as a quartermaster general during the Civil War, had a reputation as being sympathetic to Black civil rights, and had run the New York City Customs House effectively. Grover Cleveland (1885–1889, 1893–1897) first served as mayor of Buffalo and then as governor of New York.

All of these men, as even Bryce admitted, worked hard, possessed common sense, and were honest. However, they were uninspiring individuals who lacked qualities of leadership that would arouse others to action.

The most important factor in the weakened presidency was the structure of Congress, which prevented the president from providing vigorous leadership. Throughout most of this period, Congress remained narrowly divided. Majorities continually shifted from one party to the other.

For all but two terms, Democrats controlled the House of Representatives, while Republicans held the majority in the Senate. Divided government meant that during his term in office, no late-nineteenth-century president had a majority of his party in both houses of Congress.

Turnover among congressmen in the House of Representatives, who are elected every two years, was quite high, and there was little power of incumbency. The Senate, however, provided greater continuity and allowed senators, with six-year terms of office, to amass greater power than congressmen could.

For all the power that Congress wielded, it failed to govern effectively or efficiently. In the House, measures did not receive adequate attention on the floor because the Speaker did not have the power to control the flow of debate. Committee chairmen held a tight rein over the introduction and consideration of legislation and competed with one another for influence in the chamber. Congressmen showed little decorum as they conducted business on the House floor and often chatted with each other or read the newspaper rather than listen to the speakers at the podium.

The Senate, though more manageable in size and more stable in membership (only one-third of its membership stands for reelection every two years), did not function much more smoothly. Senators valued their own judgments and business interests more than party unity. The position of majority leader, someone who could impose discipline on his colleagues and design a coherent legislative agenda, had not yet been created. Woodrow Wilson, the author of *Congressional Government* (1885) and a future president, concluded: "Our government is defective as it parcels out power and confuses responsibility." Under these circumstances, neither the president nor Congress governed efficiently.

- What did presidents during the 1880s and 1890s have in common?
- What factors contributed to congressional inefficiency?

The Business of Politics

Many lawmakers viewed politics as a business enterprise that would line their pockets with money. One cabinet officer grumbled, "A Congressman is a hog! You must take a stick and hit him on the snout!" Senators were elected by state legislatures, and these bodies were often controlled by well-funded corporations that generously spread their money around to gain influence. In both branches of Congress, party leaders handed out patronage to supporters regardless of their qualifications for the jobs, a practice known as the spoils system, which started during the Jacksonian era (Module 4.8).

Modern-day standards of ethical conduct did not exist, nor did politicians see a conflict of interest in working closely with corporations. Indeed, there were no rules to prevent lawmakers from accepting payments from big business. Most congressmen received free passes from railroads and in turn voted on the companies' behalf. To be fair, most politicians such as Senator Sherman did not see a difference between furthering the legislative agenda of big corporations and promoting the nation's economic interests. Nevertheless, the public held politicians in very low esteem because they resented the influence of corporate money in politics.

The 1890 Congress stands out as an example of fiscal irresponsibility. Known as the **Billion Dollar Congress**, the same Republican legislative majority that passed the Sherman Antitrust Act adopted the highest tariff in U.S. history. Sponsored by Ohio congressman William McKinley, a close associate of the industrialist Mark Hanna, it lavishly protected manufacturing interests. Congress also spent enormous sums on special projects to enrich their constituents and themselves. Republicans spent so much money on extravagant enterprises that they wiped out the federal budget surplus.

Increasingly throughout the 1890s, many corporate leaders and their political allies joined together in favor of extending American influence and control over foreign markets and natural resources abroad, especially in Central America and the Pacific regions. They agreed that cyclical fluctuations in the domestic economy required overseas markets to assure high profits. To accomplish this would necessitate the building up of American military and commercial power.

Despite all the difficulties of the legislative process, political candidates eagerly pursued office and conducted extremely heated campaigns. The electorate considered politics a form of entertainment. Political parties did not stand for clearly stated issues or offer innovative solutions. Instead, campaigns took on the qualities of carefully staged performances. Candidates crafted their oratory to arouse the passions and prejudices of their audiences, and their managers handed out buttons, badges, and ceramic and glass plates stamped with the candidates' faces and slogans.

Partisanship helped fuel high political participation. During this period, voter turnout in presidential elections was much higher than at any time in the twentieth century. Region, as well as historical and cultural allegiances, replaced ideology as the key to party affiliation.

The wrenching experience of the Civil War had cemented voting loyalties for many Americans. After Reconstruction, white southerners tended to vote Democratic; northerners and newly enfranchised southern Black people generally voted Republican. However, geographic region alone did not shape political loyalties; a sizable contingent of

Democratic voters remained in the North, and southern whites and Black people periodically abandoned both the Democratic and Republican Parties to vote for third parties.

Religion played an important role in shaping party loyalties during this period of intense partisanship. The Democratic Party tended to attract Protestants of certain denominations, such as German Lutherans and Episcopalians, as well as Catholics. These faiths emphasized religious ritual and the acceptance of personal sin. They believed that the government should not interfere in matters of morality, which should remain the province of Christian supervision on earth and divine judgment in the hereafter.

By contrast, other Protestant denominations, such as Baptists, Congregationalists, Methodists, and Presbyterians, highlighted the importance of individual will and believed that the law could be shaped to eradicate ignorance and vice. These Protestants were more likely to cast their ballots for Republicans, except in the South, where regional loyalty to the Democratic Party trumped religious affiliation.

Some people went to the polls because they fiercely disliked members of the opposition party. Northern white workers in New York City or Cincinnati, Ohio, for example, might vote against the Republican Party because they viewed it as the party of Black Americans. Other voters cast their ballots against Democrats because they identified them as the party of Irish Catholics, intemperance, and secession.

Overall, the continuing strength of party loyalties produced equilibrium as voters cast their ballots mainly along strict party lines. The outcome of presidential elections depended on key "undecided" districts in several states in the Midwest and in New York and nearby states, which swung the balance of power in the electoral college.

Interstate Commerce Commission (ICC)
Created by the Interstate Commerce Act in 1887, the ICC required railroads to make their rates public and could bring lawsuits to force shippers to reduce "unreasonable" fares. The ICC had limited success in the late 1800s due to court rulings and the influence of business interests.

Despite partisanship in Congress, an apparent victory for regulation came in 1887 when Congress passed the Interstate Commerce Act, establishing the **Interstate Commerce Commission (ICC)** to regulate railroads. Although big businessmen could not prevent occasional government regulation, they managed to render it largely ineffective. In time, railroad advocates came to dominate the ICC and enforced the law in favor of the railway lines rather than the shippers.

Implementation of the Sherman Antitrust Act also favored big business. From the standpoint of most late-nineteenth-century capitalists, national regulations often turned out to be more of a help than a hindrance.

REVIEW

- How were business interests able to maintain sway over Congress?
- What factors led to the passage of the Interstate Commerce Act in 1887?

Political Machines and City Bosses

political machine
A type of urban political organization that dominated many late-nineteenth-century cities. Machines provided the organization and funding needed to provide services to the urban poor, but they also fostered corruption, crime, and inefficiency.

City government in the late nineteenth century was fragmented. Mayors usually did not have much power, and decisions involving public policies such as housing, transportation, and municipal services often rested in the hands of private developers. Bringing some order out of this chaos, the **political machine** functioned to give cities the centralized authority and services that they otherwise lacked. At the head of the machine was the **political boss**. Although the boss held some public office, his real authority came from leadership of the machine. These organizations maintained a tight network of loyalists throughout city wards (districts), each of which contained designated representatives responsible for catering to the needs of their constituents. Whether Democratic or Republican, political machines did not care about philosophical issues. They were concerned mainly with staying in power.

The strength of political machines rested in large measure on immigrants. The organization provided a kind of public welfare when private charity could not cope satisfactorily with the growing needs of the poor. Machines doled out turkeys on holidays, furnished a load of coal for the winter, provided jobs in public construction, arranged for shelter and meals if tenement houses burned down, and intervened with the police and the courts when a constituent got into trouble. Bosses sponsored baseball clubs, held barbecues and picnics, and attended christenings, bar mitzvahs, weddings, and funerals. For enterprising members of immigrant groups — and this proved especially true for the Irish during this period — the machine offered upward mobility out of poverty as they rose through its ranks.

The poor were not the only group that benefited from connections to political machines. The machine and its functionaries helped businessmen maneuver through the maze of contradictory and overlapping codes regulating building and licenses that impeded their routine course of activities. In addition to assisting legitimate businessmen, the machine facilitated the underworld commerce of vice, prostitution, and gambling by acting as an arbiter to keep this trade within established boundaries — all for a cut of the illegal profits.

AP® EXAM TIP

Be able to connect urban political machines with both immigration and social reform efforts. Explaining how political machines helped migrant populations combined with the idea of political corruption can lead to a sophisticated understanding.

In return for these services, the machine received the votes of immigrants and money from businessmen. When challenged by reformers or other political rivals, the machine readily engaged in corrupt election practices to maintain its power. Mobilizing the "graveyard vote," bosses took names from tombstones to pad lists of registered voters. They also hired "repeaters" to vote more than once under phony names and did not hesitate from dumping whole ballot boxes into the river or using hired thugs to scare opponents from the polls.

Bosses enriched themselves through graft and corruption. They secured protection money from both legitimate and illegitimate business interests in return for their services. In the 1860s and 1870s, Boss Tweed, the head of **Tammany Hall**, New York City's political machine, swindled the city out of a fortune while supervising the construction of a lavish three-story courthouse in lower Manhattan. The original budget for the building was $250,000, but the city spent more than $13 million on the structure. The building remained unfinished in 1873, when Tweed was convicted on fraud charges and sent to jail.

Tammany Hall
New York City's political machine during the nineteenth century. The term became a byword for political corruption and favoritism.

In later years, Tammany Hall's George Washington Plunkitt distinguished this kind of "dishonest graft" from the kind of "honest graft" that he practiced. If he received inside information about a future sale of city property, Plunkitt reasoned, why shouldn't he get a head start, buy it at a low price, and then sell it at a higher figure? As he delighted in saying, "I seen my opportunities and I took 'em."

The services of political machines came at a high cost. Corruption and graft led to higher taxes on middle-class residents. Moreover, the image of the political boss as a modern-day Robin Hood who stole from the rich and gave to the poor is greatly exaggerated. Much of the proceeds of machine activities went into the private coffers of machine bosses and other functionaries. Trafficking in vice might have run more smoothly under the coordination of the machine, but the safety and health of city residents hardly improved. Most important, although immigrants and the poor did benefit from an informal system of social welfare, the machine had no interest in resolving the underlying causes of their problems. As the dominant urban political party organization, the machine cared little about issues such as good housing, job safety, and sufficient wages. It remained for others to provide alternative approaches to relieving the plight of the urban poor.

The men and women who criticized the political bosses and machines — and the corruption and vice they fostered — usually came from the ranks of the upper-middle class and the wealthy. Their solutions to the urban crisis typically centered on toppling the political machine and replacing it with a civil service that would allow government to function on the basis of merit rather than influence peddling and favoritism. Both locally and nationally, they pushed for civil service reform. In 1883, Congress responded to this demand by passing the **Pendleton Civil Service Reform Act**, which required federal jobs to be awarded on the basis of merit, as determined by competitive examinations, rather than through political connections. As for the immigrants who supported machine politics, these reformers preferred to deal with them from afar and expected that through proper education, they might change their lifestyles and adopt American ways.

Pendleton Civil Service Reform Act

An act passed in 1883 that required the elimination of favoritism and nepotism in the hiring for federal jobs. The act established that positions would be awarded based on merit rather than political connections.

 REVIEW

- What tactics did political machines use to maintain control of city politics during the late nineteenth century?

The Farmers' Revolt

By the late 1880s, the Grangers (Module 6.1) had abandoned electoral politics and once again devoted themselves strictly to social and cultural activities. Several factors explain the Grangers' return to their original mission. First, prices began to rise for some crops, particularly corn, relieving the economic pressure on midwestern farmers. Second, the passage of regulatory legislation in a number of states convinced some Grangers that their political goals had been achieved. Finally, a lack of marketing and business experience led to the collapse of many agricultural collectives.

The withdrawal of the Grangers from politics did not, however, signal the end of efforts by farmers to form organizations to advance their economic interests. While farmers in the midwestern corn belt experienced some political success and an economic upturn, farmers farther west in the Great Plains and in the Lower South fell more deeply into debt, as the price of wheat and cotton on the international market continued to drop.

In both of these regions, farmers organized **Farmers' Alliances**. In the 1880s, Milton George formed the Northwestern Farmers' Alliance. At the same time, Dr. Charles W. Macune organized the much larger Southern Farmers' Alliance. Southern Black farmers, excluded from the Southern Farmers' Alliance, created a parallel Colored Farmers' Alliance. The Alliances formed a network of recruiters to sign up new members. No recruiter was more effective than Mary Elizabeth Lease, who excited farm audiences with her forceful and colorful rhetoric, delivering 160 speeches in the summer of 1890 alone.

Farmers' Alliance

A regional economic organization formed in agrarian areas in the late nineteenth century to advance the interests of farmers, many of whom were heavily indebted by the second half of the century.

The Southern Farmers' Alliance advocated a sophisticated plan to solve the farmers' problem of mounting debt. Macune devised a proposal for a **subtreasury system**. Under this plan, the federal government would locate offices near warehouses in which farmers could store nonperishable commodities. In return, farmers would receive federal loans for 80 percent of the current market value of their produce. In theory, temporarily taking crops off the market would decrease supply and, assuming demand remained stable, lead to increased prices. Once prices rose, farmers would return to the warehouses, redeem their crops, sell them at the higher price, repay the government loan, and leave with a profit.

subtreasury system

A reform proposal to use government warehouses to hold excess farm products to control supply and maintain crop values. In return, farmers would receive government loans for 80 percent of the value of the product stored.

The first step toward creating a nationwide farmers' organization came in 1889, when the Northwestern and Southern Farmers' Alliances agreed to merge. Alliance leaders, including Lease, saw workers as fellow victims of industrialization, and they invited the Knights of Labor to join them. They also attempted to lower prevailing racial barriers by bringing the Colored Farmers' Alliance into the coalition. The following year, the National Farmers' Alliance and Industrial Union held its convention in Ocala, Florida. The group adopted resolutions endorsing the subtreasury system, as well as recommendations that would promote the economic welfare of farmers and extend political democracy to "the plain people." These proposals included tariff reduction, government ownership of banks and railroads, and political reforms to extend democracy, such as direct election of U.S. senators.

AP® WORKING with EVIDENCE

Source: Mary Elizabeth Lease, "A Nation of Inconsistencies," 1891

> "This is a nation of inconsistencies. The Puritans fleeing from oppression became oppressors. We fought England for our liberty and put chains on four million of black people. We wiped out slavery and our tariff laws and national banks began a system of white wage slavery worse than the first.
>
> Wall Street owns the country. It is no longer a government of the people, by the people, and for the people, but a government of Wall Street, by Wall Street, and for Wall Street.
>
> The great common people of this country are slaves, and monopoly is the master. The West and South are bound and prostrate before the manufacturing East.
>
> Money rules, and our Vice-President is a London banker. Our laws are the output of a system which clothes rascals in robes and honesty in rags.
>
> The [political] parties lie to us and the political speakers mislead us. . . . The politicians said we suffered from overproduction. Overproduction, when 10,000 little children, so statistics tell us, starve to death every year in the United States, and over 100,000 shopgirls in New York are forced to sell their virtue for the bread their [very low] wages deny them. . . .
>
> We want money, land and transportation. We want the abolition of the National Banks, and we want the power to make loans direct from the government. We want the foreclosure system wiped out. . . . We will stand by our homes and stay by our fireside by force if necessary, and we will not pay our debts to the loan-shark companies until the government pays its debts to us. The people are at bay; let the bloodhounds of money who dogged us thus far beware."

Questions for Analysis

1. Identify Lease's complaints in this speech.
2. Describe Lease's proposed remedies for those complaints.
3. Explain the economic context surrounding Lease's speech.
4. Evaluate the extent of similarity between the arguments Lease makes in this speech and the principles embraced by other labor movements of the late nineteenth century.

Finally, the Alliance pressed the government to increase the money supply by expanding the amount of silver coinage in circulation. In the Alliance's view, such a move would have two positive, and related, consequences. First, the resulting inflation would lead to higher prices for agricultural commodities, putting more money in farmers' pockets. Second, the real value of farmers' debts would decrease, because the debts were contracted in pre-inflation dollars and would be paid back with inflated currency.

Naturally, the eastern bankers who supplied farmers with credit opposed such a policy. In fact, in 1873 under the leadership of Senator John Sherman, Congress had halted the purchase of silver by the Treasury Department, a measure that helped reduce the money supply. Later, however, under the **Sherman Silver Purchase Act** (1890), the government resumed buying silver, but the act placed limits on its purchase and did not guarantee the creation of silver coinage by the Treasury.

In the past, some members of the Alliance had favored expanding the money supply with greenbacks (paper money). However, to attract support from western silver miners, Alliance delegates emphasized the free and unlimited coinage of silver. Alliance supporters met with bitter disappointment, though, as neither the Republican nor the Democratic Party embraced their demands. Denied, farmers took an independent course and became more directly involved in national politics through the formation of the Populist Party.

AP® WORKING with EVIDENCE

Source: Bernhard Gillam, "Party of Patches: Grand Balloon Ascension—Cincinnati, May 20th, 1891," *Judge*, 1891

A PARTY OF PATCHES.
Grand Balloon Ascension—Cincinnati, May 20th, 1891.

Fotosearch/Getty Images

About the source: The patches on the balloon in this image are labeled "Anarchists," "Prohibition Party," "The People's Party: Cincinnati May 1891," "The Silver Party," "Communists," "Farmers' Alliance," "Old Greenback Party," "Socialists," "Old Granger Party," "Knights of Labor Party," and "Women's Rights." The man on the far left in the balloon basket is wearing a ribbon labeled "Powderly," and the man second from the right is wearing a ribbon labeled "Simpson." The men are dropping papers out of the balloon, which read "Free Coinage," "Government Control of R.Roads & Telegraphs," "Unlimited Greenbacks," and "Government Pawnshops." The balloon basket itself is labeled "The Platform of Lunacy."

Questions for Analysis

1. Identify Gillam's main point in this cartoon.
2. Describe the details Gillam uses to illustrate his main point.
3. Explain how, and from whom, the changes proposed by the Populist Party might prompt the kind of response illustrated in this cartoon.

▪ What goals and political proposals did the Grange and the Farmers' Alliance share?

Populists and Depression Politics

In 1892, the National Farmers' Alliance moved into the electoral arena as a third political party. The People's Party of America, known as the **Populists**, held its first nominating convention in Omaha, Nebraska, in 1892. In addition to incorporating the Alliance's Ocala planks into their platform, they adopted recommendations to broaden the party's appeal to industrial workers. Populists endorsed a graduated income tax, which would impose higher tax rates on higher income levels, the eight-hour workday, and immigration restriction, which stemmed from the unions' desire to keep unskilled workers from glutting the market and depressing wages. Reflecting the influence of women such as Mary Elizabeth Lease, the party endorsed women's suffrage. The party did not, however, offer specific proposals to prohibit racial discrimination or segregation. Rather, the party focused on remedies to relieve the economic plight of impoverished white and Black farmers in general.

Populists
Originating in the agrarian movements in the late 1800s, Populists attempted to unite farmers and laborers in a coalition promoting broad economic and political reforms.

In 1892, the Populists nominated former Union Civil War general James B. Weaver for president. Although he came in third behind the Democratic victor, Grover Cleveland, and the Republican incumbent, Benjamin Harrison, he won over one million popular votes and twenty-two electoral votes.

AP® EXAM TIP
The Populist Party is a significant development that connects the Gilded Age economy with a changing political structure. Be able to connect the Omaha Platform of 1892 with at least two economic changes that arose in the Gilded Age. Connections such as these move you from generalizations to specific analyses.

At the state level, Populists performed even better. They elected 10 congressional representatives, 5 U.S. senators, 3 governors, and 1,500 state legislators. Two years later, the party made even greater strides by increasing its total vote by 42 percent and achieving its greatest strength in the South. This electoral momentum positioned the Populists to make an even stronger run in the next presidential election. The economic depression that began in 1893 and the political discontent it generated enhanced Populist chances for success.

President Cleveland's handling of the depression, accompanied by protest marches and labor strife, only made a bad situation worse. In the spring of 1894, Jacob Coxey, a Populist reformer from Ohio, led a march on Washington, D.C., demanding that Cleveland and Congress initiate a federal public works program to provide jobs for the unemployed. Though highly critical of the favored few who dominated the federal government, Coxey had faith that if "the people . . . come in a body like this, peaceably to discuss their grievances and demanding immediate relief, Congress . . . will heed them and do it quickly."

After traveling for a month from Ohio, Coxey led a parade of some five hundred unemployed people into the nation's capital. Attracting thousands of spectators,

Coxey's army

A protest movement led by Jacob Coxey. In 1894, Coxey and five hundred supporters marched from Ohio to Washington, D.C., to protest the lack of government response to the Panic of 1893. Although the movement garnered widespread support, this and subsequent marches did little to effect change in governmental policy.

Coxey's army attempted to mount their protest on the grounds of the Capitol building. In response, police broke up the demonstration and arrested Coxey for trespassing. Cleveland turned a deaf ear to Coxey's demands for federal relief and also disregarded protesters participating in nearly twenty other marches on Washington.

In the coming months, Cleveland's political stock plummeted further. He responded to the Pullman strike in the summer of 1894 (Module 6.7) by obtaining a federal court injunction against the strikers and dispatching federal troops to Illinois to enforce it. The president's action won him high praise from the railroads and conservative business interests, but it showed millions of American workers that the Cleveland administration did not have a solution for ending the suffering caused by the depression. "While the people should patriotically and cheerfully support their Government," the president declared, "its functions do not include the support of the people."

Making matters worse, Cleveland convinced Congress to repeal the Sherman Silver Purchase Act. This angered western miners, who relied on strong silver prices, along with farmers in the South and Great Plains, who were swamped by mounting debt. At the same time, the removal of silver as a backing for currency caused private investors to withdraw their gold deposits from the U.S. Treasury.

To keep the government financially solvent, Cleveland worked out an agreement with a syndicate led by J. P. Morgan to help sell government bonds, a deal that netted the banker a huge profit. Amid economic suffering, this deal looked like a corrupt bargain between the government and the rich.

In 1894, Congress also passed the Wilson-Gorman Tariff Act, which raised tariffs on imported goods. Intended to protect American businesses by keeping the price of imported goods high, it also deprived foreigners of the necessary income with which to buy American exports. This drop in exports did not help economic recovery.

The Wilson-Gorman Act did include a provision that the Populists and other reformers endorsed: a progressive income tax of 2 percent on all annual earnings over \$4,000. No federal income tax existed at this time, so even this mild levy elicited cries of "socialism" from conservative critics, who challenged the tax in the courts. The next year, the Supreme Court declared the income tax unconstitutional and denounced it as the opening wedge in "a war of the poor against the rich; a war constantly growing in intensity and bitterness."

With Cleveland's legislative program in shambles and his inability to solve the depression abundantly clear, the Democrats suffered a crushing blow at the polls. In the congressional elections of 1894, the party lost an astonishing 120 seats in the House. This defeat offered a preview of the political shakeup that loomed ahead.

REVIEW

- How did President Cleveland respond to the Panic of 1893?
- What similarities did the Populists and Farmers' Alliance share?

Political Realignment in the Election of 1896

The presidential election of 1896 marked a turning point in the political history of the nation. Democrats nominated William Jennings Bryan of Nebraska, a farmers' advocate who favored silver coinage. When he vowed that he would not see Republicans "crucify mankind on a cross of gold," the Populists endorsed him as well.

Republicans nominated William McKinley, the governor of Ohio and a supporter of the gold standard and high tariffs on manufactured and other goods. McKinley's campaign manager, Mark Hanna, an ally of Ohio senator John Sherman, raised an unprecedented amount of money, about $16 million, mainly from wealthy industrialists who feared that the free and unlimited coinage of silver would debase the U.S. currency. Hanna saturated the country with pamphlets, leaflets, and posters, many of them written in the native languages of immigrant groups. He also hired a platoon of speakers to fan out across the country denouncing Bryan's free silver cause as financial madness. By contrast, Bryan raised about $1 million.

The outcome of the election transformed the Republicans into the majority party in the United States. McKinley won 51 percent of the popular vote and 61 percent of the electoral vote. More important than this specific contest, however, was that the election proved critical in realigning the two parties. Voting patterns shifted with the 1896 election, giving Republicans the edge in party affiliation among the electorate not only in this contest but also in presidential elections over the next three decades.

What happened to produce this critical realignment in electoral power? The main ingredient was Republicans' success in fashioning a coalition that included both corporate capitalists and their workers. Many urban dwellers and industrial workers took out their anger on Cleveland's Democratic Party, and Bryan as its standard-bearer, for failing to end the depression. In addition, Bryan, who hailed from Nebraska and reflected small-town agricultural America and its values, could not win over the swelling numbers of urban immigrants who considered Bryan's world alien to their experience. Finally, fear that Bryan's free silver policy would lead to inflation, increasing the costs of goods and services without a corresponding bump in factory wages, kept many urban workers from voting for him.

The election of 1896 broke the political stalemate of the preceding two decades. The core of Republican backing came from industrial cities of the Northeast and Midwest. Republicans won support from their traditional constituencies of Union veterans, businessmen, and Black Americans and added to it the votes of a large number of urban wageworkers. The campaign persuaded voters that the Democratic Party represented the party of depression and that Republicans stood for prosperity and

AP® EXAM TIP

Be able to explain how political parties differed over monetary policy and the historical context in which these disagreements surfaced. This is a useful way to practice the skill of historical contextualization. Select an event such as the presidential election of 1896 to examine these developments.

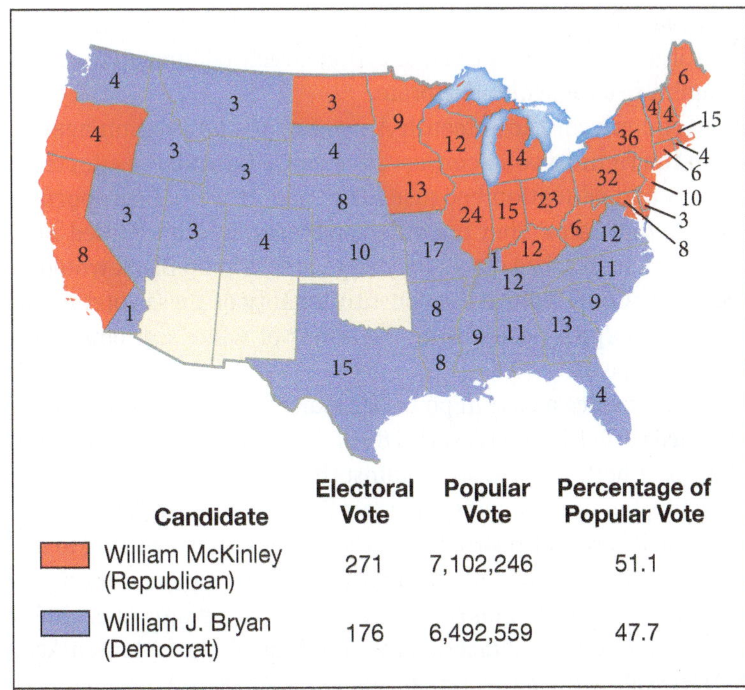

Candidate	Electoral Vote	Popular Vote	Percentage of Popular Vote
William McKinley (Republican)	271	7,102,246	51.1
William J. Bryan (Democrat)	176	6,492,559	47.7

MAP 6.6 The Election of 1896 William McKinley's election in 1896 resulted in a realignment of political power in the United States that lasted until 1932. Republicans became the nation's majority party by forging a coalition of big business and urban industrial workers from the Northeast and Midwest. Democratic strength was confined to the South and to small towns and rural areas of the Great Plains and Rocky Mountain states.

Why did Republicans decisively win the electoral vote even though each party won a similar number of states?

progress. They were soon able to take credit for ending the depression when, in 1897, gold discoveries in Alaska helped increase the money supply and foreign crop failures raised American farm prices. Democrats managed to hold on to the South as their solitary political base.

REVIEW

- What were the short-term and long-term consequences of the election of 1896?

Decline of the Populists

The year 1896 also marked the end of the Populists as a national force, as the party was torn apart by internal divisions over policy and strategy. Populist leaders such as Tom Watson of Georgia did not want the Populist Party to emphasize free silver above the rest of its reform program. Northern Populists, who either had fought on the Union side during the Civil War or had close relatives who did, could not bring themselves to join the Democrats, the party of the old Confederacy. Nevertheless, the Populist Party officially backed Bryan, but to retain its identity, the party nominated Watson for vice president on its own ticket.

After McKinley's victory, the Populist Party collapsed. Losing the presidential election alone did not account for the disintegration of the Populists. Several problems plagued the third party. The nation's recovery from the depression removed one of the Populists' prime sources of electoral attraction. Despite appealing to industrial workers, the Populists were unable to capture their support. The free-silver plank attracted silver miners in Idaho and Colorado, but the majority of workers failed to identify with a party composed mainly of farmers. As consumers of agricultural products, industrial laborers did not see any benefit in raising farm prices. Populists also failed to create a stable, biracial coalition of farmers. Most southern white Populists did not truly accept Black Americans as equal partners, even though both groups had mutual economic interests.

To eliminate Populism's insurgent political threat, southern opponents found ways to disfranchise Black and poor white voters. During the 1890s, southern states inserted into their constitutions voting requirements that largely eliminated the Black electorate and greatly diminished the white electorate.

Seeking to circumvent the Fifteenth Amendment's prohibition against racial discrimination in the right to vote, conservative white lawmakers adopted regulations based on wealth and education because Black people were disproportionately poor and had lower literacy rates. They instituted poll taxes, which imposed a fee for voting, and literacy tests, which asked questions designed to trip up Black would-be voters. In 1898, the Supreme Court upheld the constitutionality of these voter qualifications in ***Williams v. Mississippi***. Recognizing the power of white supremacy, the Populists surrendered to its appeals.

Tom Watson provides a case in point. He started out by encouraging racial unity but then switched to divisive politics. In 1896, the Populist vice presidential candidate called on citizens of both races to vote against the crushing power of corporations and railroads. By whipping up antagonism against Black people, his Democratic opponents appealed to the racial pride of poor whites to keep them from defecting to the Populists.

Embittered by the outcome of the 1896 election and learning from the tactics of his political foes, Watson embarked on a vicious campaign to exclude Black people from voting. "What does civilization owe the Negro?" he bitterly asked. "Nothing! Nothing! NOTHING!!!" Only by disfranchising Black Americans and maintaining white

Library of Congress, LC-USZ62-51942

Wilmington, North Carolina, Massacre, 1898 In 1898, Populists in alliance with the Republican Party in Wilmington, North Carolina, elected a white mayor and a biracial city council. Two days after the election, on November 10, armed members of the defeated Democratic Party, at the time, the party of white supremacy in the South, overthrew the new city government. A mob of around two thousand white men, some of whom are pictured here, set fire to the city's Black newspaper building. White terrorists killed at least fifteen people and forced more than two thousand Black people to flee the city permanently.

Why might men who committed violence willingly pose for a photograph? What does that suggest about the legal status of Black people in the South?

supremacy, Watson and other white reformers reasoned, would poor whites have the courage to vote against rich whites.

Nevertheless, even in defeat, the Populists left an enduring legacy. Many of their political and economic reforms—direct election of senators, the graduated income tax, government regulation of business and banking, and a version of the subtreasury system (called the Commodity Credit Corporation, created in the 1930s)—became features of reform in the twentieth century.

Perhaps their greatest contribution, however, came in showing farmers that their old individualist ways would not succeed in the modern industrial era. Rather than re-creating an independent political party, most farmers looked to organized interest groups, such as the Farm Bureau, to lobby on behalf of their interests.

REVIEW

- What were the major causes for the decline of the Populists?

AP® Skills Workshop: Thinking Historically

Additional Practice in Responding to a Short-Answer Question with Secondary Sources

Respond to each part of the following Short-Answer Question using **CSE**. For a review of answering SAQs with secondary sources, see Modules 2.4 and 2.8.

> "As a businessman, the farmer was appropriately hardheaded; he tried to act upon a cold and realistic strategy of self-interest. As the head of the family, however, the farmer felt that . . . when he risked the farm he risked his home—that he was, in short, a single man running a personal enterprise in

(continued)

a world of impersonal forces. It was from this aspect of his situation—seen in the hazy glow of the agrarian myth—that his political leaders in the 1890s developed their rhetoric and some of their concepts of political action.

The utopia of the Populists was in the past, not the future. According to the agrarian myth, the health of the state was proportionate to the degree to which it was dominated by the agricultural class, and this assumption pointed to the superiority of an earlier age. The Populists looked backward with longing to the lost agrarian Eden, to the Republican America of the early years of the nineteenth century in which there were few millionaires, and as they saw it, no beggars when the laborer had excellent prospects and the farmer had abundance, when the statesman still responded to the mood of the people and there was no such thing as money power. What they meant—though they did not express themselves in such terms—was that they would like to restore the conditions prevailing before the development of industrialism and the commercialization of agriculture. . . . In Populist thought the farmer is not a speculating businessman, victimized by the risk economy of which he is a part, but rather a wounded yeoman preyed upon by those who are alien to the life of folkish virtue."

Richard Hofstadter, *The Age of Reform: From Bryan to F.D.R.*, 1955

"The Populist world was too commercially and intellectually dynamic to resemble a traditional society in any meaningful sense of the term. This tells us something important about the nature of late nineteenth-century reform: the men and women of the Populist movement were modern people. The term *modern* does not mean 'good.' Nor is it a value judgment across the political spectrum from right to left. Moreover, to say that the Populists were modern does not imply that they were more modern than, say, their Republican or Democratic opponents. Nor does it imply that all rural people shared the Populists' modern sensibility. On the contrary, the Populists understood that the transformations they sought required the uprooting of ignorance, inertia, and force of habit. Populism formed a unique social movement that represented a distinctly modernizing impulse. . . .

Modernity also implied a particular kind of people with particular types of strivings . . . Modern men and women . . . 'look forward to future developments in their conditions of life and their relations with their fellow men.' The Populists were just this kind of people. They sought to improve their domestic economy and their national government. They sought renewal in local schoolhouses and federal credit systems. They sought to refashion associational ties with neighbors and commercial relations with the world. They sought new techniques, new acreage, and new avenues of spiritual expression."

Charles Postel, *The Populist Vision*, 2007

Using the excerpts, answer **A**, **B**, and **C**.

(A) Briefly explain ONE major difference between Hofstadter's and Postel's interpretations of the Populists.

(B) Briefly explain how ONE specific historical event or development that is not explicitly mentioned in the excerpts could be used to support Hofstadter's argument.

(C) Briefly explain how ONE specific historical event or development that is not explicitly mentioned in the excerpts could be used to support Postel's argument.

Continuity and Change in Period 6

MODULE 6.14

AP® Skills Workshop: Writing Historically

Responding to a Document-Based Question with Historical Complexity Using the *GEM* Approach

Now you're ready to apply the GEM approach to a Document-Based Question. Here are the relevant "Thinking Historically" and "Writing Historically" exercises to help you review for this DBQ:

	Thinking Historically
Outlining and Thesis	3.2: The Thesis: Developments and Processes 3.6: Creating a Thesis Statement 3.12: Combining Reasoning Processes in a Thesis 5.2: Using Course Themes to Brainstorm and Organize an Essay 4.14: Outlining an Essay
Introductions	4.8: Introductions with Contextualization 5.4: Contextualizing: Writing the Introduction
Body Paragraphs	3.8/3.9: Body Paragraphs: Claims and Evidence in Sources 4.5: Body Paragraphs: Support an Argument Using Evidence 5.10: Claims and Evidence in Sources: Writing DBQ Body Paragraphs
Using Primary Sources	1.2: Primary Sources: Developments and Processes 1.3: Primary Sources: Claims and Evidence in Sources 1.5: Primary Sources: Making Connections 4.3: Primary Sources: Sourcing and Situation 4.6: Linking Primary Sources: Developments and Processes 4.7: Linking Primary Sources: Making Connections 4.9: Sourcing Documents 4.12: Linking Primary Sources: Claims and Evidence 5.9: Sourcing: Using CSE for Integrated Document Analysis 6.2: Significance in Primary Sources
General Writing	5.12: Writing a DBQ 6.7: Developing Historical Complexity in a Long-Essay Question Using the GEM Approach
Conclusions	4.10: Context: Writing the Conclusion 6.3: Conclusions: Developments and Processes, a Closer Look 6.5: Conclusions: Making Connections

(continued)

As you recall, the **GEM** approach stands for **Generate nuance, Explain both sides of the historical reasoning process,** and **Make relevant, insightful connections beyond the prompt**, either within its time period or across multiple time periods.

You'll use the GEM approach as you have in LEQs, but you can also apply the GEM approach to your interpretation of primary sources too. Consider the following prompt and documents:

> Evaluate the extent of change in the lives of urban and rural residents in the United States in the period 1865 to 1900.

Document 1

Source: Charles Loring Brace, *The Dangerous Classes of New York and Twenty Years among Them*, 1872

> "The source of juvenile crime and misery in New York, which is the most formidable, and, at the same time, one of the most difficult to remove, is the overcrowding of our population. The form of the city-site is such—the majority of the dwellings being crowded into a narrow island between two water-fronts—that space near the business-portion of the city becomes of great value. These districts are necessarily sought for by the laboring and mechanic classes, as they are near the places of employment. They are avoided by the wealthy on account of the population which has already occupied so much of them. The result is, that the poor must live in certain wards; and as space is costly, the landlords supply them with (comparatively) cheap dwellings, by building very high and large houses, in which great numbers of people rent only rooms, instead of dwellings. . . .
>
> In the Seventeenth Ward, the Board of Health reports that in 1868, 4,120 houses contained 95,091 inhabitants, of whom 14,016 were children under five years. In the same report, the number of tenement-houses for the whole city is given at 18,582, with an estimate of one-half the whole population dwelling in them—say 500,000."

Document 2

Source: Ida Lindgren, Swedish homesteader, Letter, August 25, 1874

> "[W]e have not had rain [on the Kansas Prairie] since the beginning of June, and then with the heat and often strong winds as well, you can imagine how everything has dried out. There has also been a general lamentation and fear for the coming year. We have gotten a fair amount of wheat, rye, and oats, for they are ready so early, but no one here will get corn or potatoes. We have a few summer potatoes, but many don't even have that, and we thought and hoped we would get a good crop of other potatoes, but will evidently get none. Instead of selling the oats and part of the rye as we had expected, we must now use them for the livestock, since there was no corn. We are glad we have the oats (for many don't have any and must feed wheat to the stock) and had hoped to have the corn leaves to add to the fodder. But then one fine day there came millions, trillions of grasshoppers in great clouds, hiding

(continued)

the sun, and coming down onto the fields, eating up *everything* that was still there, the leaves on the trees, peaches, grapes, cucumbers, onions, cabbage, everything, everything. Only the peach stones still hung on the trees, showing what had once been there."

Document 3

Source: Mary Elizabeth Lease, "A Nation of Inconsistencies," 1891

"Wall Street owns the country. It is no longer a government of the people, by the people, and for the people, but a government of Wall Street, by Wall Street, and for Wall Street.

The great common people of this country are slaves, and monopoly is the master. The West and South are bound and prostrate before the manufacturing East.

Money rules, and our Vice-President is a London banker. Our laws are the output of a system which clothes rascals in robes and honesty in rags.

The [political] parties lie to us and the political speakers mislead us. . . . The politicians said we suffered from overproduction. Overproduction, when 10,000 little children, so statistics tell us, starve to death every year in the United States, and over 100,000 shopgirls in New York are forced to sell their virtue for the bread their [very low] wages deny them. . . .

We want money, land and transportation. We want the abolition of the National Banks, and we want the power to make loans direct from the government. We want the foreclosure system wiped out. . . . We will stand by our homes and stay by our fireside by force if necessary, and we will not pay our debts to the loan-shark companies until the government pays its debts to us. The people are at bay; let the bloodhounds of money who dogged us thus far beware."

Document 4

Source: F. J. Kingsbury, "The Tendency of Men to Live in Cities," *Journal of Social Science,* No. 33, 1895

"We must remember too that cities as places of human habitation have vastly improved within half a century. About fifty years ago, neither New York nor Boston had public water, and very few of our cities had either water or gas . . .

A few years since, the great improvement of the lift, or elevator, added 10 percent, actually, and probably much more than that theoretically, to the possibilities of population on a given ground; and now within a very recent period three new factors have been suddenly developed which promise to exert a powerful influence on the problems of city and country life. These are the trolley, the bicycle, and the telephone. . . . it adds from five to fifteen miles to the radius of every large town, bringing all this additional area into new relations to business centers. Places five or ten miles apart and all the intervening distances are rendered accessible and communicable for all purposes of life as if they were in the next street."

(continued)

Document 5

Source: Sheet Music for Piano and Singers, "New York and Coney Island Cycle March: Two Step," 1896

From The New York Public Library

Document 6

Source: Royal Melendy, *The Saloon in Chicago*, 1900

"That same instinct in man which leads those of the more resourceful classes to form such clubs as the Union League Club, or the Marquette Club; which leads the college man into the fraternity, leads the laboring men into the clubs furnished them by the saloonkeeper. . . . Here men 'shake out their hearts together.' Intercourse quickens the thought, feeling, and action. . . .

This is the workingman's school. He is both scholar and teacher. The problems of national welfare are solved here. Many as patriotic men as our country produces learn here their lessons in patriotism and brotherhood. . . . Men of all nationalities meet and mingle, and by the interchange of views and opinions their own are modified. Nothing short of travel could exert so broadening an influence upon these men. It does much to assimilate the heterogeneous crowds that are constantly pouring into our city from foreign

(continued)

shores. But here, too, they learn their lessons in corruption and vice. It is their school for good and evil."

Document 7

Source: Theodore Dreiser, *Sister Carrie,* 1900

"At that time the department store was in its earliest form of successful operation, and there were not many. The first three in the United States, established about 1884, were in Chicago. . . .

They were along the line of the most effective retail organisation, with hundreds of stores coordinated into one and laid out upon the most imposing and economic basis. They were handsome, bustling successful affairs, with a host of clerks and a swarm of patrons. Carrie passed along the busy aisles, much affected by the remarkable displays of trinkets, dress goods, stationery, and jewelry. Each separate counter was a show place of dazzling interest and attraction. . . .

Not only did Carrie feel the drag of desire for all which was new and pleasing in apparel for women, but she noticed too, with a touch at the heart, the fine ladies who elbowed and ignored her, brushing past in utter disregard of her presence, themselves eagerly enlisted in the materials which the store contained. . . . A flame of envy lighted in her heart. She realised in a dim way how much the city held—wealth, fashion, ease—every adornment for women, and she longed for dress and beauty with a whole heart."

Now we will apply the same steps from Module 6.9 in responding to this DBQ:

Step 1 ▶ Break down the prompt

Notice that this prompt asks you to evaluate the extent of change in the lives of urban and rural residents in the United States in the period 1865 to 1900. While the prompt uses the term "extent of change," evaluating the "extent of continuity" is the other, implicit half of the reasoning process, continuity and change over time. Being aware that you need to do both in your essay is the first step toward demonstrating historical complexity in your response.

Step 2 ▶ List and categorize your historical knowledge, then use GEM to refine your historical argument

Start your brainstorm by jotting down all the relevant historical information you can remember (inductive reasoning) or start with a list of topics such as the course themes and then brainstorm possible information relating to similarities or differences for those topics (deductive reasoning). Either way, organize your information under three or four categories, making sure that at least one represents a historical difference and at least one represents a historical similarity. Keep in mind both the **CSE** and **GEM** strategies as you build an outline for your response. Complete the following graphic organizer or one of your own making as you organize your thoughts to answer the prompt with a complex and well-supported argument. The first three documents have been "GEMed" for you.

(continued)

Change / Continuity **Document 1:** Charles Loring Brace, *The Dangerous Classes of New York and Twenty Years Among Them*, 1872	Change / Continuity **Document 2:** Ida Lindgren, Swedish homesteader, Letter, August 25, 1874	Change / Continuity **Document 3:** Mary Elizabeth Lease, *Monopoly Is the Master*, 1890
Evidence: After the second industrial revolution, cities became increasingly crowded with industrial workers, lowering living conditions and concentrating a poor working class in urban areas.	**Evidence:** American farmers have always been subject to changes in weather and climate, and while Lindgren's living conditions are harsh, they represent common obstacles faced by farmers before westward expansion after 1865.	**Evidence:** After 1865, the creation of a national transportation network through the railroad, the rise of stock exchanges in major cities like New York and Chicago, and the advent of large corporations presented a new target for the economic grievances of rural Americans.
Nuance or Qualification of Claim: Nevertheless, throughout the late nineteenth century, workers' wages slowly increased, making industrial work attractive for immigrants and domestic farmers, which fueled the growth of the cities.	**Nuance or Qualification of Claim:** While farmers have always had to deal with harsh weather and climate conditions, the conditions in the West were particularly unsuitable for traditional, semi-subsistence farming, which accounted for the high number of family-farm failures in the West after 1865.	**Nuance or Qualification of Claim:** Americans had targeted large economic institutions before, especially during the 1830s, when Jacksonians accused the national bank of creating a monopoly within the nation's economy.
Connection 1: Before 1865, U.S. cities experienced enormous growth, but nothing compared to after 1865, when industrialization encouraged large populations of foreign and domestic laborers to settle in urban areas.	**Connection 2:** While U.S. farmers in the countryside had suffered bad crops and blamed entities like the national bank for economic woes, after 1865, the climate of the West and the growth of large corporations and railroads elevated this anger and led to the formation of Farmers' Alliances and the Populists, who claimed to speak for rural Americans.	

Now **GEM** the last four documents on your own, adding to the table above. On the AP® Exam, you will not need to use all of the documents in a DBQ to earn full credit. However, using all seven documents to support your argument, or sourcing at least four documents, can count as a complex response.

Step 3 ▶ Set the context, craft a thesis, and write the introduction of your essay

The changes experienced by urban and rural residents during this period is a big topic. So, when thinking about setting the context, you are going to want to think equally big. Follow the steps provided above and use **CSE** (Claim, Support, Explain) to structure the context that begins your introduction and consult Modules 4.8 and 5.4 to remind yourself how to do so. Then, generate a thesis that makes an argument, and then establishes your line of reasoning. Review Modules 3.2 and 3.6 if you need a refresher on how to construct a thesis.

Step 4 ▶ Use both CSE and GEM to write the body of your essay

Remember, whether responding to a LEQ or a DBQ, the most direct way to structure an essay is to devote one or two body paragraphs to each claim of change or continuity you stated in your thesis. Use those claims to create each body paragraph's

(continued)

sub-argument (topic) sentences and then support the sub-arguments with evidence from and outside of the documents. As you construct your paragraphs, keep the **CSE** (Claim, Support, Explain) strategy in mind for each claim. The evidence you provide must connect to the claim in your paragraph's sub-argument, and you must explain how the evidence you've chosen supports your claim. Using **CSE** will keep you on track to fully support your argument throughout your essay.

In addition to using **CSE** to explain how your evidence supports your claim, you can use **GEM** to create a more sophisticated analysis that demonstrates a complex understanding of the extent of changes for rural and urban dwellers. In addition to using GEM examples from your pre-write, you can also look for opportunities to include multiple historical reasoning processes into your explanation of how the evidence you've chosen supports each paragraph's central claim. For example, you could explain how immigration shaped urban life (causation). Or you could examine the similarities and differences in the ways technology affected the lives of rural and urban Americans (comparison). You could even compare the impacts of technological innovation on working conditions for both (complex comparison and causation). In all of your analysis, try to be as accurate and specific with your wording as you can.

Here's how a portion of a body paragraph might look for a DBQ using **CSE** and **GEM** to create a sophisticated response.

> Urban residents experienced enormous changes during this time period. **[sub-argument]** First, the cities became extremely crowded because laborers were needed to work in urban factories. **[claim]** Charles Loring Brace noted that juvenile crime was rising, and that housing was very crowded and dangerous (Doc 1). **[support]** The juvenile crime and dangerous housing were entirely a product of poor working-class residents who had relocated to the cities for factory work, even though in this time period, working-class income continued to rise. **[explanation with nuance and Historical Situation]** These changes were not, however, the first time the United States experienced growing cities and the dangers they caused. Between the 1830s and 1860s, growing cities like New York and Philadelphia saw increased urban violence, like the draft riots of 1863, and urban crime, publicized by the spread of cheap newspapers and the telegraph. **[making a connection across time]**

Let's take a closer look at how the paragraph weaves together several skills. Notice that the "E" sentence, for the **CSE** in the sample paragraph, not only *explains* the supporting evidence but it does so in a *nuanced* way, providing the "G" in **GEM**. Further, by making clear connections between crime, migration, and industrialization, this sentence also provides a **Historical Situation** for this document, fulfilling an element of the DBQ's sourcing requirement. Review Modules 4.3, 4.9, and 5.10 if you need a refresher on document sourcing and how to incorporate it into your DBQ response.

Step 5 ▶ **Craft your essay conclusion**

The final step is to write a strong conclusion that not only summarizes but, ideally, extends your argument. Remember, you should fully restate your thesis—not word-for-word, but idea-for-idea. After all, it's one last chance to articulate a sound and complete answer to the prompt. As you first learned in Module 4.10, your final paragraph is also a logical place to set an **immediate concluding context** by connecting your argument (in this case, about the urban and rural residents between 1856 and 1900) to a significant development that continues beyond the time period—such as

(continued)

Progressive Era reforms or the domestic impact of World War I, which you will be familiar with by the time you take the AP® Exam.

Setting a context in your conclusion is also a final opportunity to demonstrate historical complexity by making a relevant and insightful connection between time periods (the "M" in **GEM**). You already know how to do this—it's simply a variation on the long-term concluding context you practiced at the end of Modules 6.3, 6.5, and 6.6. Finishing your essay by linking a part of your argument to a forward-looking context or making a connection to a later time period will once again demonstrate the sophistication that you have woven throughout your response. You practiced this already in Modules 6.5 and 6.6.

ACTIVITY

Use the steps provided to write a full essay in response to the prompt at the beginning of this Writing Historically feature. Be sure to Claim, Support, and Explain (**CSE**) your argument. Also, strive to incorporate multiple examples of historical complexity and sophistication in your essay by generating nuance in your response, explaining both sides of the targeted historical reasoning process, and making relevant and insightful connections within and across time periods (**GEM**). Feel free to use the example claims, evidence, and analysis in the graphic organizer as well as the following outline to guide your response.

I. Introductory paragraph
   A. Immediate/preceding contextualization statement
      1. Make a claim about a preceding context.
      2. Support this claim with a piece of specific evidence from the preceding context.
      3. Explain how this evidence supports your claim regarding the preceding context.
   B. Thesis statement: Answer the prompt with a historically defensible claim supported by a line of reasoning that describes the main points you will develop in your response. Be sure to include both sides of the reasoning process in your thesis.

II. Body Paragraph 1: Extent of Change or Continuity 1
   A. Sub-argument from the first part of your line of reasoning
      1. Claim 1 that supports your sub-argument
      2. Support Claim 1 with factual information and one document.
      3. Explain how your support proves Claim 1.
      4. Claim 2 that supports your sub-argument
      5. Support Claim 2 with factual information and a second document.
      6. Explain how your support proves Claim 2.
   B. Generate nuance by examining multiple variables, diverse perspectives, counter-evidence, or limitations of your claims.

III. Body Paragraph 2: Extent of Change or Continuity 2
   A. Sub-argument from the second part of your line of reasoning
      1. Claim 1 that supports your sub-argument
      2. Support Claim 1 with factual information and a third document.
      3. Explain how your support proves Claim 1.
      4. Claim 2 that supports your sub-argument
      5. Support Claim 2 with factual information and a fourth document.
      6. Explain how your support proves Claim 2.

(continued)

B. Generate nuance by examining multiple variables, diverse perspectives, counter-evidence, or limitations of your claims.

IV. Body Paragraph 3: Extent of Change or Continuity 3
   A. Sub-argument from the third part of your line of reasoning
      1. Claim 1 that supports your sub-argument
      2. Support Claim 1 with factual information and a <u>fifth document</u>.
      3. Explain how your support proves Claim 1.
      4. Claim 2 that supports your sub-argument
      5. Support Claim 2 with factual information and a <u>sixth document</u>.
      6. Explain how your support proves Claim 2.
   B. Generate nuance by examining multiple variables, diverse perspectives, counter-evidence, or limitations of your claims.

V. Body Paragraph 4: Extent of Change or Continuity 4
   A. Sub-argument from the first part of your line of reasoning.
      1. Claim 1 that supports your sub-argument
      2. Support Claim 1 with factual information and a <u>seventh document</u>.
      3. Explain how your support proves Claim 1.
      4. (Optional) Claim 2 that supports your sub-argument
      5. (Optional) Support Claim 2 with factual information.
      6. (Optional) Explain how your support proves Claim 2.
   B. Generate nuance by examining multiple variables, diverse perspectives, counter-evidence, or limitations of your claims.

VI. Conclusion
   A. Restate thesis claim and line of reasoning.
   B. Claim connecting historical argument to context immediately after the time range provided by the prompt OR claim connecting historical argument to a similar phenomenon and/or a long-term contextual trend in a later time period.
   C. Support concluding context claim with a piece of evidence.
   D. Explain how your evidence supports your concluding context/connection in a later time period.

Period 6 Review 1865–1898

KEY CONCEPTS AND EVENTS

American Federation of Labor (AFL), *569*
Battle of the Little Bighorn, *535*
Billion Dollar Congress, *619*
buffalo soldier, *535*
Chinese Exclusion Act, *542*
collective bargaining, *567*
Comstock Lode, *527*
convict lease system, *546*
corporate capitalism, *601*
corporation, *559*
Coxey's army, *626*
Dawes Act, *537*
deflation, *520*
eugenics, *587*
Farmers' Alliance, *622*
frontier thesis, *590*
ghetto, *582*
Ghost Dance, *539*
Gilded Age, *601*
"The Gospel of Wealth," *613*
Grange, *523*
Great Plains, *516*
gross domestic product, *551*
Haymarket riot, *569*
holding company, *559*
Homestead Act, *519*
Homestead strike, *570*
horizontal integration, *558*
Industrial Workers of the World (IWW), *572*
interlocking directorate, *558*
Interstate Commerce Commission (ICC), *620*
Jim Crow law, *548*
Knights of Labor, *567*
labor union, *567*
laissez-faire, *606*
land rush, *536*
Long Drive, *530*
melting pot, *587*
Mormon, *540*
nativism, *587*
"New South," *545*
Panic of 1893, *617*
Pendleton Civil Service Reform Act, *622*
Pinkerton Agency, *571*
Plessy v. Ferguson, *548*
political boss, *620*
political machine, *620*
poll tax, *548*
Populists, *625*
Pullman strike, *572*
robber baron, *557*
Santa Clara County v. Southern Pacific Railroad Company, *559*
scientific management, *560*
segregation, *545*
settlement house, *596*
Sherman Antitrust Act, *559*
Sherman Silver Purchase Act, *624*
Social Darwinism, *597*
social gospel, *607*
Socialist Party of America, *572*
subtreasury system, *622*
sweatshop, *595*
Tammany Hall, *621*
tenement, *594*
transcontinental railroad, *517*
Treaty of Fort Laramie, *534*
Treaty of Medicine Lodge, *534*
trust, *559*
United States v. E. C. Knight Company, *560*
vertical integration, *557*
Williams v. Mississippi, *628*
Wounded Knee massacre, *540*

KEY PEOPLE

Alexander Graham Bell, *553*
Henry Bessemer, *554*
William Jennings Bryan, *626*
Andrew Carnegie, *557*
Grover Cleveland, *572*
Jacob Coxey, *625*
George Armstrong Custer, *535*
Eugene V. Debs, *572*
W. E. B. Du Bois, *587*
Thomas Alva Edison, *554*
Geronimo, *539*
Samuel Gompers, *569*
Jay Gould, *558*
Henry Grady, *545*
Chief Joseph, *535*
William McKinley, *618*
J. P. Morgan, *555*
Terence V. Powderly, *568*
George Pullman, *567*
Jacob Riis, *594*
John D. Rockefeller, *558*
William Tecumseh Sherman, *535*
Sitting Bull, *539*
Frederick W. Taylor, *560*
Frederick Jackson Turner, *590*
Boss Tweed, *621*

CHRONOLOGY

1850s	Tenements began to be built in cities
1851	Herbert Spencer proposes theory of social evolution in *Social Statistics*
1859	Invention of Bessemer converter Publication of Charles Darwin's landmark text *On the Origin of Species*
By 1861	Western Union runs 76,000 miles of telegraph line
1864	Sand Creek massacre
1866	Transatlantic telegraph cable connects the United States and Europe
1867	Treaty of Medicine Lodge
1869	Central Pacific and Union Pacific Railroad crews meet in Utah Founding of the Knights of Labor
1870s	Gold discovered in the Black Hills
1871	Great Chicago Fire, in which much of the city burned to the ground
1873	Congress halts purchase of silver by the Treasury Department, reducing the money supply
By 1874	Establishment of approximately 14,000 new Grange chapters
1874	Henry Grady calls for a "New South"
1875–1899	Ten million people immigrate to the United States
1876	Battle of the Little Bighorn
1877	Passage of the Desert Land Act
1879	Henry George critiques materialism and greed in *Progress and Poverty*
By 1880	Chinese population in United States reaches 200,000
1880s	Height of the cattle boom Development of new industry throughout the South Skyscrapers constructed due to invention of structural steel and elevators Establishment of many charitable organizations such as the American Red Cross Exodus of Black Americans from the South begins
1881	Black washerwomen strike in Atlanta
1882	Chinese Exclusion Act of 1882 Beginning of widespread electric lighting in New York City Homestead strike and collapse of steel prices
1883	The 1875 Civil Rights Act struck down by Supreme Court Construction is completed on the Brooklyn Bridge Passage of Pendleton Civil Service Reform Act *Dynamic Sociology*, by Lester Frank Ward, attacks laissez-faire policy
1885	Establishment of American Telephone and Telegraph Company (AT&T) Successful strike against the Union Pacific and Missouri Pacific Railroads
1886	Samuel Gompers becomes president of AFL Nationwide strikes for eight-hour workday Opening of the Statue of Liberty

CHRONOLOGY *(continued)*

1887	Passage of the Dawes Act Establishment of the American Protective Association
1889	Publication of "The Gospel of Wealth," an essay by Andrew Carnegie Northwestern and Southern Farmers' Alliances merge
1890s	Jim Crow laws become prevalent in the South
1890	Frontier declared closed by U.S. Census Bureau Passage of the Sherman Antitrust Act Jacob Riis publishes *How the Other Half Lives* Sherman Silver Purchase Act resumes government purchase of silver
1892	National Guard called in to end strikes in Idaho National Farmers' Alliance becomes a political party, the Populists
1893	Establishment of the Immigration Restriction League Bankruptcy of the Philadelphia and Reading Railroads signals a nationwide economic depression
1894	Federal troops dispatched to Illinois in Pullman strike
1896	*Plessy v. Ferguson* upholds Jim Crow segregation William McKinley wins presidential election Populist Party dissolves
1897	First subway opens, in Boston
By 1900	Peak of the mining rush 200,000 miles of railroad track laid throughout the United States

Period 6 AP® Exam Practice

Multiple-Choice Questions

Questions 1–3 refer to the photograph.

Pictures From History/AGE Fotostock

"East and West Shaking Hands at Laying of Last Rail," Promontory Point, Utah, May 10, 1869.

1. During the late nineteenth century, the U.S. government facilitated the historical event depicted in the image in all of the following ways EXCEPT
   (A) by proving rail companies with financial loans.
   (B) by granting rail companies cheap or free land.
   (C) by creating political safety and stability.
   (D) by passing high protective tariffs.

2. Which significant source of laborers on the transcontinental railroad is most notably absent from the image?
   (A) Chinese
   (B) American Indians
   (C) Freedmen
   (D) Germans

3. What effect did the railroad construction boom in the late nineteenth century have on American Indian societies?
   (A) More efficient transportation improved American Indian lifestyles because they could buy goods from mail-order catalogs and have them shipped via railroad to them in the west.
   (B) Railroad construction provided American Indians with economic prosperity as workers for the railroad companies.
   (C) The mass destruction of the bison, spurred in part by railroad construction, devastated American Indian society and culture.
   (D) Cheaper forms of travel allowed American Indians to move to eastern cities and enjoy a much higher standard of living.

Questions 4–6 refer to the excerpt.

"Notwithstanding our great losses by war, substantially all that we had before is here. . . . [White men have] . . . filled the earth with the most beneficent and utilitarian civilization it has ever witnessed, and strewed the shores of its oceans with mighty cities, reticulated [marked] its surface with steam roads, covered the wild seas with the white wings of commerce, and even invaded their unknown depths with the iron-shod pathways of lightning, for these men to acknowledge that the wheels of their progress are stopped because the negroes won't work and keep contracts is a sorry spectacle indeed! Shame to us, if it be so!"

Zebulon Vance, prior governor of North Carolina, "Vance on Capital and Labor," *The Southern Watchman*, 1875

4. Why did proponents of the "New South," as exemplified in the excerpt, hope to modernize and industrialize their economy?
   (A) They believed the Confederacy lost the Civil War because of the North's superior manufacturing output and railroad supply lines.
   (B) They saw this as a way to segregate the two races, with whites in factories and Blacks in agricultural fields.
   (C) Southern states had weaker labor unions and lower state minimum wage laws.
   (D) They supported Southern industrialization in preparation for another attempt at secession.

5. Which industry became dominant in the South during the Gilded Age?
   (A) Steel production
   (B) Textiles
   (C) Oil industry
   (D) Lumber

6. Based on the sentiments expressed in the excerpt, Vance would have most likely supported which of the following post–Civil War developments in the South?
   (A) Black codes enforcing sharecropping contracts
   (B) Voting rights for Blacks being added to state constitutions
   (C) Jim Crow laws segregating whites and Blacks in public places
   (D) The exodus of Black migrants out of the South

Questions 7–9 refer to the cartoon.

Joseph Keppler, "Looking Backward," *Puck,* 1893

About the source: The caption at the bottom says, "They Would Close To The New-Comer The Bridge That Carried Them And Their Fathers Over."

7. The sentiments expressed in the cartoon were most directly a response to immigration in the 1880s and 1890s from which country?

(A) China
(B) England
(C) Italy
(D) Mexico

8. What was the main economic impact of immigrants to the U.S. such as those depicted in the image in the period 1865 to 1900?

(A) Strengthening labor unions, which increased the average worker's income
(B) Growing agricultural products, because most became homesteaders
(C) Providing cheap labor in U.S. factories, keeping the cost of manufacturing low
(D) Creating a larger market for luxury goods, stimulating economic demand for manufacturing

9. What emerged in the United States as a reactionary response to immigrants in the late 1880s?

(A) Nativism, the belief that foreigners pose a serious danger to one's native society and culture
(B) Mass migration of farmers from the countryside to the cities to enjoy a multicultural society
(C) Political parties, such as the Know-Nothings, formed to promote social reforms targeting the immigrants
(D) Personal liberty laws to promote immigrants' assimilation into American society

Questions 10–12 refer to the excerpt.

"It is the issue of 1776 over again. Our ancestors, when but three millions in number, had the courage to declare their political independence of every other nation; shall we, their descendants, when we have grown to seventy millions, declare that we are less independent than our forefathers?

No, my friends, that will never be the verdict of our people. Therefore, we care not upon what lines the battle is fought. If they say bimetallism is good. . . we will restore bimetallism. . . . If they dare to come out in the open field and defend the gold standard as a good thing, we will fight them to the uttermost. Having behind us the producing masses of this nation and the world, supported by the commercial interests, the laboring interests and the toilers everywhere, we will answer their demand for a gold standard by saying to them: You shall not press down upon the brow of labor this crown of thorns, you shall not crucify mankind upon a cross of gold."

William Jennings Bryan, Cross of Gold Speech, 1896

10. In the excerpt, William Jennings Bryan makes an argument to
(A) replace gold coinage with silver coinage.
(B) increase the coinage of gold.
(C) unlink U.S. currency from gold or silver.
(D) allow for silver coinage alongside gold coinage.

11. Which popular third party most agreed with the argument Bryan made in the excerpt?
(A) Greenback Party
(B) Populist Party
(C) Progressive Party
(D) Know-Nothing Party

12. What major event in the United States provides the most relevant historical context for Bryan's argument in his Cross of Gold Speech?
(A) U.S. imperialism across Pacific islands
(B) A railroad construction boom
(C) An economic depression
(D) An increase in leisure and entertainment activities

Questions 13–15 refer to the excerpt.

"The old nations of the earth creep on at a snail's pace; the Republic thunders past with the rush of the express. The United States, the growth of a single century, has already reached the foremost rank among nations, and is destined soon to out-distance all others in the race. In population, in wealth, in annual savings, and in public credit; in freedom from debt, in agriculture, and in manufactures, America already leads the civilized world. . . .

Into the distant future of this giant nation we need not seek to peer; but if we cast a glance forward, as we have done backward, for only fifty years, and assume that in that short interval no serious change will occur, the astounding fact startles us that in 1935, fifty years from now, when many in manhood will still be living, one hundred and eighty millions of English-speaking republicans will exist under one flag and possess more than two hundred and fifty thousand millions of dollars, or fifty thousand millions sterling of national wealth."

Andrew Carnegie, "The Triumph of America," 1885

13. Which of the following historical developments would Carnegie most likely credit for the "rush of express" he describes in the excerpt?
    (A) High levels of European immigration
    (B) The philanthropy of businessmen like himself
    (C) Technological and manufacturing innovations
    (D) Mercantilist efforts to promote economic growth

14. Carnegie's reference to America having "reached the foremost rank among nations" could best be supported by which of the following?
    (A) The many colonization attempts made by the U.S. in South America
    (B) The unprecedented importation of manufactured products from Asia
    (C) The unrivaled dominance of the U.S. military
    (D) The emergence of the U.S. as a world economic power

15. How did Carnegie most directly contradict the ideas he expressed in the excerpt?
    (A) Encouraging philanthropic giving by wealthy industrialists
    (B) Working himself up from a poor immigrant to the head of U.S. Steel
    (C) Innovating via the Bessemer process and vertical integration
    (D) Locking out strikers to lower labor costs at the Homestead Steel Works

Short-Answer Questions

"The parlor was the front room of the middle-class home where friends, acquaintances, and carefully screened strangers met formally 'in society.' Geographically, it lay between the urban street where strangers freely mingled and the back regions of the house where only family members were permitted to enter uninvited. . . . [T]he parlor provided the woman of the house with a 'cultural podium' from which she was to exert her moral influence over American society. There she ruled as a kind of constitutional monarch whose responsibility was to enforce the hundreds of rules governing polite social intercourse."

Karen Halttunen, *Confidence Men and Pained Women: A Study of Middle-Class Culture in America, 1830–1870*, 1982.

"The design of middle-class womanhood in relation to the . . . space of the parlor created . . . a form of tension. As . . . individualism began to define personhood, . . . the . . . woman . . . was . . . deprived of full personhood. Since the parlor was, by definition a permeable [open], performative space that brought men and women together, the parlor woman literally had no room of her own at the precise moment when having such a room became a prerequisite for personal liberty."

Milette Shamir, *Inexpressible Privacy: The Interior Life of Antebellum American Literature*, 2006.

1. Using the excerpts, answer **A**, **B**, and **C**.
    (A) Briefly describe ONE major difference between Halttunen's and Shamir's historical interpretations regarding the Victorian home during the late nineteenth century.
    (B) Briefly explain how ONE specific historical event, development, or circumstance in the period 1865 to 1900 that is not explicitly mentioned in the excerpts could be used to support Halttunen's argument.
    (C) Briefly explain how ONE specific historical event, development, or circumstance in the period 1865 to 1900 that is not explicitly mentioned in the excerpts could be used to support Shamir's argument.

THE BALLOT
IN COUNTING THERE IS STRENGTH
"THAT'S WHAT'S THE MATTER."
Boss Tweed. "As long as I count the Votes, what are you going to do about it? say?"
Library of Congress, LC-DIG-ds-12564

Thomas Nast, "That's What's the Matter," *Harper's Weekly*, October 7, 1871

About the source: The bottom line reads "Boss Tweed. 'As long as I count the Votes, what are you going to do about it? say?'"

2. Using the political cartoon, answer **A**, **B**, and **C**.
   (A) Briefly describe ONE historical perspective expressed by the artist in the image regarding the American political system.
   (B) Briefly explain ONE specific event or development in the period 1840 to 1890 that contributed to the development depicted in the image.
   (C) Briefly explain ONE specific historical effect in the period from 1865 to 1900 that resulted from the development depicted in the image.

3. Answer **A**, **B**, and **C**.
   (A) Briefly explain ONE important way in which the second industrial revolution (1865–1900) transformed the relationship of the United States with the rest of the world.
   (B) Briefly explain ONE important way in which the second industrial revolution (1865–1900) transformed U.S. society.
   (C) Briefly explain ANOTHER important way in which the second industrial revolution (1865–1900) transformed U.S. society.

4. Answer **A**, **B**, and **C**.
   (A) Briefly describe ONE specific historical change in the lives of women in the United States between 1865 and 1900.
   (B) Briefly describe ONE specific historical continuity in the lives of women in the United States between 1865 and 1900.
   (C) Briefly explain how ONE specific historical development between 1800 and 1865 led to a continuity or change in the lives of women in the United States in the period 1865 to 1900.

Document-Based Question

1. Evaluate the extent to which technological developments and governmental policies shaped the settlement of the western United States from 1865 to 1900.

Document 1

Source: President Chester A. Arthur, State of the Union Address, 1881

"We have to deal with the appalling fact that though thousands of lives have been sacrificed and hundreds of millions of dollars expended in the attempt to solve the Indian problem, it has until within the past few years seemed scarcely nearer a solution than it was half a century ago. But the Government has of late been cautiously but steadily feeling its way to the adoption of a policy which has already produced gratifying results, and which, in my judgment, is likely, if Congress and the Executive accord in its support, to relieve us ere long from the difficulties which have hitherto beset us.

For the success of the efforts [we are] now making to introduce among the Indians the customs and pursuits of civilized life and gradually to absorb them into the mass of our citizens, sharing their rights and holden to their responsibilities, there is imperative need for legislative action."

Document 2

Source: Chief Joseph of the Nez-Percé, message sent to U.S. General Howard, 1877

"I am tired of fighting. Our chiefs are killed. . . . The old men are all dead. It is the young men, now, who say 'yes' or 'no.' He who led on the young men is dead. It is cold, and we have no blankets. The little children are freezing to death. My people—some of them—have run away to the hills, and have no blankets, no food. No one knows where they are— perhaps freezing to death. I want to have time to look for my children, and see how many of them I can find; may be I shall find them among the dead. Hear me, my chiefs; my heart is sick and sad. From where the sun *now* stands, I will fight no more forever!"

Document 3

Source: Frederick Jackson Turner, "The Significance of the Frontier in American History," 1893

"Up to our own day American history has been in a large degree the history of the colonization of the Great West. The existence of an area of free land, its continuous recession, and the advance of American settlement westward, explain American development.

Behind institutions, behind constitutional forms and modifications, lie the vital forces that call these organs into life and shape them to meet changing conditions. The peculiarity of American institutions is, the fact that they have been compelled to adapt themselves to the changes of an expanding people—to the changes involved in crossing a continent, in winning a wilderness, and in developing at each area of this progress out of the primitive economic and political conditions of the frontier into the complexity of city life. . . .

Thus American development has exhibited not merely advance along a single line, but a return to primitive conditions on a continually advancing frontier line, and a new development for that area. American social development has been continually beginning over again on the frontier. This perennial rebirth, this fluidity of American life, this expansion westward with its new opportunities, its continuous touch with the simplicity of primitive society, furnish the forces dominating American character. The true point of view in the history of this nation is not the Atlantic coast, it is the great West."

Document 4

Source: U.S. Bureau of the Census, Railroad Mileage Laid by Year, 1865–1900

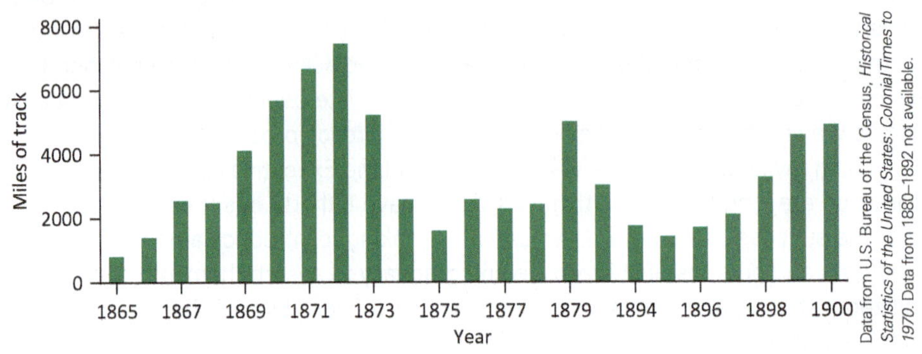

Document 5

Source: W. Skelton Glenn, "The Recollections of W.S. Glenn, Buffalo Hunter," *Panhandle-Plains Historical Review,* 1875

"We will now describe a camp outfit. They would range from six to a dozen men, there being one hunter who killed the buffalo and took out the tongues, also the tallow [animal fat]. As the tallow was of an oily nature, it was equal to butter; [it was used] for lubricating our guns and we loaded our own shells, each shell had to be lubricated and [it] was used also for greasing wagons and also for lights in camp. . . .

A remarkable good hunter would kill seventy-five to a hundred a day, an average hunter about fifty, and a common one twenty-five, some hardly enough to run a camp. It was just like in any other business. A good skinner would skin from sixty to seventy-five, an average man from thirty to forty, and a common one from fifteen to twenty-five. These skinners were also paid by the hide about five cents less than the hunter was getting for killing, being furnished with some kind of a gun, not as valuable as Sharp's rifle, to kill cripples with, also kips [young animals] and calves that were standing around."

Document 6

Source: Walt Whitman, "Specimen Days and Collect," 1879

"Speaking generally as to the capacity and sure future destiny of that plain and prairie area (larger than any European kingdom), it is the inexhaustible land of wheat, maize, wool, flax, coal, iron, beef and pork, butter and cheese, apples and grapes—land of ten million virgin farms—to the eye at present wild and unproductive—yet experts say that upon it when irrigated may easily be grown enough wheat to feed the world. . . . I am not so sure but the Prairies and the Plains, while less stunning at first sight, last longer, fill the esthetic sense fuller, precede all the rest, and make North America's characteristic landscape."

Document 7

Source: Horse-drawn harvester-thresher, Moro, Oregon, 1890

Library of Congress, LC-USZ62-39863

Long-Essay Questions

2. Evaluate the extent to which the rise in leisure time activities for middle- and upper-class Americans during the late 1800s changed American culture.

3. Evaluate the relative effects of organized labor in American society in the period 1865 to 1900.

4. Evaluate the extent of similarity in the response of Americans to immigrants in the period 1870 to 1900 and earlier immigrants in the period 1830 to 1860.

PERIOD 7 1890–1945

New Imperialism and Global Conflicts

Prohibition and Popular Opinion During the first decades of the twentieth century, the United States experimented with reforms that pursued economic justice, greater democracy, gender equality in terms of suffrage, and the prohibition of alcohol. The Eighteenth Amendment, which prohibited the sale and production of alcoholic beverages in 1918, was unpopular — and, by the 1930s, it had become increasingly clear that the amendment was unenforceable. Peck and Peck, a New York clothing retailer founded in 1888, produced this patriotically themed handkerchief in 1933. It provides a window into what everyday people thought of the Eighteenth Amendment and how they expressed those opinions.

Contextualizing Period 7

MODULE 7.1

By the 1890s, the second industrial revolution had been in motion for nearly twenty-five years, It was the second period in U.S. history where industry and transportation transformed U.S. society and the economy. Middle-class Americans reacted with misgivings to the rise of big business and urban political machines that seemingly undermined democracy. While many in the United States celebrated the economic changes of this period, others saw the rising inequality and corruption as threats to traditional American republicanism and free-market ideology.

From these concerns arose an organized and activist reform movement, progressivism, that sought government regulation of elements of the economy and greater democracy in the political arena. Although laboring Americans continued to do often backbreaking and underpaid work, they also began to desire consumer goods and leisure activities that were available to the middle class. Immigrants and their descendants, especially, began to imagine themselves as taking part in what came to be known as the "American Dream."

During the first decades of the twentieth century, consumption continued to rise, a middle class of consumers grew, and the national transportation infrastructure expanded. At the same time, many Americans protested against consumerism, persistent racism, and growing class divisions. These conflicts were temporarily eased by strict government controls on dissent and U.S. involvement in the First World War in 1917 and 1918.

By the 1920s and into the 1930s, challenges to the status quo came from diverse quarters—young Americans who inaugurated a so-called Jazz Age, Black people who migrated to northern cities and initiated a cultural renaissance based mainly in Harlem in New York City, and young Latinos who struggled for social and cultural space in California. In the midst of this flux, the Great Depression shook the nation to its foundations and inaugurated the creation of a limited welfare state through President Franklin Delano Roosevelt's New Deal.

The role played by the United States in world affairs also shifted significantly during this period. The era began with the proclaimed closing of the American frontier west of the Mississippi and ended as the United States stood as one of two superpowers able to exert global power. Between these two events, Americans debated the role of their overseas military ventures within the context of traditional American ideals. The tensions between Americans who held isolationist views and those who held expansionist sentiments continued throughout the twentieth century, and both sides used the rights-based rhetoric of the American Revolution to justify their positions. This created a dynamic and high-stakes argument around American conceptions of liberty and equality.

AP® EXAM TIP

The United States underwent historic transformations between 1890 and 1945. Immigration, urbanization, and continued industrialization reshaped how Americans lived, while wars, progressive reforms, and the New Deal strengthened and expanded the role of government. On the AP® Exam, be able to explain the causes and effects of these transformations and how they interacted with each other.

Period 7: What's Inside 1890–1945

MODULE	AP® THEMATIC FOCUS
7.1 Contextualizing Period 7	During the Gilded Age, the United States became a growing industrial and military power. By the late 1800s, labor upheaval, government corruption, immigration, urbanization, and swift industrialization had transformed the lives of many Americans. Between 1890 and 1945, the United States experienced profound changes as it participated in three global conflicts, faced a Great Depression, and expanded the size and role of government in response to these challenges and reform movements. With the victory in World War II in 1945, the United States emerged as a global economic and military superpower.
7.2 Imperialism: Debates	**America in the World** Beginning in the second half of the nineteenth century, policymakers in the United States increasingly began to imagine the nation projecting its power outside the continental United States. From Secretary of State Seward's acquisition of Alaska from Russia in 1867 to the domination of the Hawaiian economy in the 1880s, the United States pursued its interests overseas.
7.3 The Spanish-American War	**America in the World** Starting in the 1890s, American officials ramped up efforts to compete with older imperial powers in Europe. U.S. territorial annexations during and after the Spanish-American War and a more aggressive foreign policy expanded U.S. influence and might in the Pacific and the Caribbean despite the vocal concerns of some anti-imperialists at home.
7.4 The Progressives	**Politics and Power ■ Geography and the Environment** Many Americans pursued reform measures to relieve the problems raised by a quickly modernizing economy and society. To this end, some middle-class Americans envisioned a society that promoted social reform through philanthropy and investigative journalism, while others turned to government to pass legislation to bring change. By the late nineteenth and early twentieth centuries, progressive reform shaped local activism and government legislation throughout the United States and included new efforts to protect the environment and better manage the use of natural resources.
7.5 World War I: Military and Diplomacy	**America in the World** As the United States increasingly exercised its power beyond its borders, the major powers of Europe descended into conflict over regional borders and colonial holdings. Starting in the summer of 1914, the coalitions of Allied and Central Powers marched into what would be called the First World War. While the United States proclaimed its neutrality in the conflict, American policymakers and the public debated the proper response to the conflict until 1917, when the Senate declared war on Germany and the rest of the Central Powers. Soon after the declaration, President Woodrow Wilson claimed that the United States fought not for victory, but to "make the world safe for democracy." However, his broad vision for a remade postwar world inspired opposition at home, which left a mixed legacy of successes and failures for both the United States and the world.
7.6 World War I: Home Front	**Migration and Settlement** Though the United States was involved in World War I only during the its last year, the war's effects reverberated through American society and the economy during that year and in the years following. New wartime opportunities led to a Great Migration of Blacks out of the South, while the Russian Revolution and labor unrest sparked a Red Scare.
7.7 1920s: Innovations in Communication and Technology	**Work, Exchange, and Technology** The U.S. economy experienced significant and sustained growth through the 1920s with low unemployment and a rise in real wages. Pro-business government policies fueled the economic growth but also contributed to the growing inequality in wealth that accompanied it. Mass production and electrification led to a burst of consumption as credit and advertising eased ways of buying cars and appliances.

MODULE	AP® THEMATIC FOCUS
7.8 1920s: Cultural and Political Controversies	**Migration and Settlement ▪ American and Regional Culture** During the 1920s, American culture and society seemed to be in a state of flux. Many women, Black people, and middle-class youth experimented with new forms of self-identification and leisure. However, during this same period, conservative trends in American society revived reactionary organizations like the Ku Klux Klan and political ideologies like nativism. Culture and society in the United States during this period appeared to be growing increasingly modern, while at the same time seeking to restore perceived traditions from the past.
7.9 The Great Depression	**Work, Exchange, and Technology** The seeming prosperity of the 1920s was built on credit, consumerism, and an ever-rising stock market. As in other eras in U.S. history, the economic boom was followed by an economic bust. The Great Depression of the 1930s shook many Americans' confidence in the ability of capitalism to maintain economic prosperity and led to financial strains that cut across American society.
7.10 The New Deal	**Politics and Power** Franklin Roosevelt, elected president in 1932, promised to counteract the effects of the Great Depression. Although Roosevelt's New Deal gave many Americans hope and reshaped the government's role in society, critics saw it as wasteful and un-American.
7.11 Interwar Foreign Policy	**America in the World** While the United States experienced the trauma of the Great Depression and tried to counteract its effects with the New Deal, other industrialized nations suffered a similar economic collapse but turned to other, less idealistic, solutions. In Europe, nations like Italy, Spain, and Germany adopted fascism, a hyper-nationalistic ideology that promoted racial superiority and a strong, centralized government. In Asia, Japan embraced militarism and tried to create a European-style empire of colonies under Japanese economic and political control. In the United States, citizens and policymakers debated a proper response to this aggressive turn.
7.12 World War II: Mobilization	**Social Structures** During the Second World War, the United States marshaled the power of the economy and society in the war effort. The enhanced power of the federal government during the New Deal era had laid the foundation for the war effort. While the domestic economy during the war offered opportunities for many Americans who had been left out of the industrial economy, not all of these opportunities were shared equally.
7.13 World War II: Military	**America in the World** In 1941, the United States had entered its second world war in a generation. During the First World War, the United States had fought mainly in Europe, but during World War II, the United States was at war on two fronts, across the Atlantic and in the Pacific. Though the United States did not bear the brunt of the war (that bitter distinction fell to the people on whose soil the most devastating battles took place), the U.S. effort proved central to victory for the Allied forces.
7.14 Postwar Diplomacy	**America in the World** By the end of the war, it became clear that the United States had an enormous role in world affairs, and that the so-called isolationism of the 1920s and 1930s could not hold. Wartime conferences at Tehran and Yalta and the agreement to create the United Nations showed promise to create a postwar framework for peace, but mistrust and ideological differences would prove challenging in the immediate aftermath of World War II.
7.15 Comparison in Period 7	Period 7 provides rich opportunities to compare major historical developments, including the ways innovations in manufacturing and new technologies shaped society, how reformers changed government's role in society, U.S. foreign policy approaches in Europe and elsewhere, and the causes and consequences of U.S. involvement in wars.
Support and Practice	• Practice thinking and writing historically in each module. • See the Period Review of key concepts, events, people, and dates after the last module. • Try the AP® Exam Practice at the end of the period.

MODULE

7.2 Imperialism: Debates

FOCUS

While reading this module, consider the similarities and differences in attitudes about the nation's proper role in the world. What economic, political, and ideological factors accounted for the similarities and differences?

The United States became a modern imperial power relatively late. In the decades following the Civil War, the U.S. government concentrated most of its energies on settling the western territories, pushing American Indians aside, and extracting the region's resources.

In many ways, westward expansion in the nineteenth century foreshadowed international expansion. The conquest of the American Indians reflected a broader imperialistic impulse within the country. Arguments based on racial superiority and the nation's duty to expand became justifications for expansion in North America and overseas.

By the end of the nineteenth century, sweeping economic, cultural, and social changes led many in the United States to conclude that the time had come for the country to assert its power beyond its borders. This goal became particularly important as Americans came to believe that their internal frontier was rapidly closing because of western expansion and settlement and that they needed room for further development. In fact, the 1890 census of the nation's population announced that the frontier had disappeared. Based on these data, three years later, the influential U.S. historian Frederick Jackson Turner argued that the ending of the frontier would require a "wider field" for the "exercise [of] American energy" and reinvigorating the nation's political, economic, and cultural strengths.

AP® EXAM TIP

The results of the second industrial revolution and corporate capitalism fueled desire for overseas markets. Consequently, the United States secured islands to serve as "steppingstones" to markets in Latin America and especially Asia. You should be able to identify and explain the arguments for and against imperialism.

Convinced of the argument for empire advanced by imperialists, U.S. officials led the nation in a burst of overseas expansion from 1898 to 1904, in which the United States acquired Guam, Hawaii, the Philippines, and Puerto Rico; established a protectorate (a region under the control of a more powerful nation, though not considered a colony) in Cuba; and exercised force to build a canal through Panama. These gains paved the way for subsequent U.S. intervention in Haiti, the Dominican Republic, and Nicaragua.

The Economics of Expansion

The industrialization of the United States and the growth of corporate capitalism stimulated imperialist desires in the late nineteenth century. Throughout its early history, the United States had sought overseas markets for exports. However, the importance of exports to the U.S. economy increased dramatically in the second half of the nineteenth century, as industrialization gained momentum. In 1870, U.S. exports totaled \$500 million. By 1910, the value of U.S. exports had increased threefold to \$1.7 billion. (The figure shows the growth over time.)

The fluctuating business cycle of boom and bust that characterized the economy in the 1870s and 1880s culminated in the depression of the 1890s. The social unrest that accompanied this depression worried business and political leaders about the stability

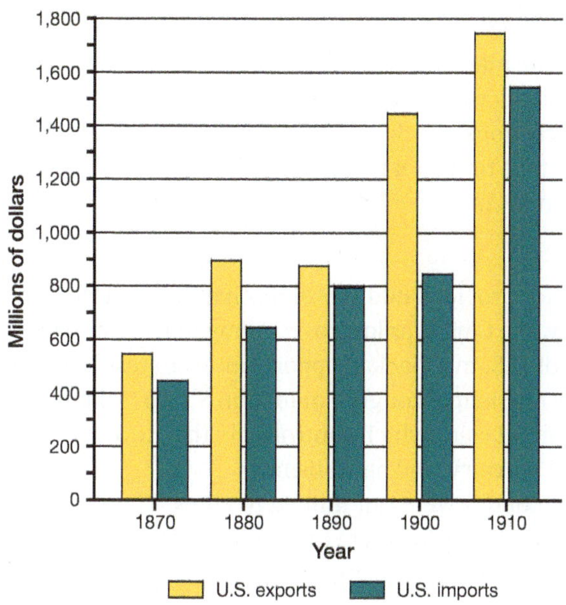

U.S. Exports and Imports, 1870–1910 As U.S. industrial power expanded at the end of the nineteenth century, exports increased dramatically. Between 1870 and 1910, U.S. exports more than tripled. Imports rose as well but were restrained by protective tariffs.
How did the desire for overseas trade influence U.S. expansion overseas?

of the country. The way to sustain prosperity and contain radicalism, many businessmen agreed, was to find foreign markets for U.S. goods. Senator William Frye of Maine argued, "We must have the market [of China] or we shall have revolution."

Cultural Justifications for Imperialism

Imperialists linked overseas expansion to practical, economic considerations, but race was also a key component in their arguments for empire. Many in the United States and western Europe declared themselves superior to nonwhite peoples of Latin America, Asia, and Africa. Buttressing their arguments with racist studies claiming to show scientifically the "racial" superiority of white Protestants, imperialists asserted a "natural right" of conquest and world domination.

Imperialists added an ethical dimension to this ideology by contending that "higher civilizations" had a duty to uplift inferior nations. In *Our Country* (1885), the Congregationalist minister Josiah Strong proclaimed the superiority of the Anglo-Saxon and other white northern European peoples, and the responsibility of the United States to spread the "blessings" of its Christian way of life throughout the world. Secular intellectuals, such as historian John Fiske, praised the English race for settling the United States and predicted that English society and culture would become "predominant" in the less civilized parts of the globe.

WORKING with EVIDENCE

Source: Rudyard Kipling, British author, "The White Man's Burden" (poem), 1899

"Take up the White Man's burden—
Send forth the best ye breed—
Go send your sons to exile
To serve your captives' need;
To wait in heavy harness
On fluttered folk and wild—
Your new-caught, sullen peoples,
Half devil and half child."

Questions for Analysis

1. Identify the "white man's burden" in this poem.
2. Describe the obligations the poem places on the "white man."
3. Explain the perceptions of colonized peoples portrayed in this poem.
4. Evaluate the extent to which the poem reflects previous conceptions of nonwhite peoples common in American history.

Gender anxieties provided additional motivation for U.S. imperialism. In the late nineteenth century, the Civil War long over, many in the United States worried that the rising generation of U.S. men lacked opportunities to test and strengthen their manhood. For example, Mississippi congressman John Sharp Williams in 1897 lamented the fading of "the dominant spirit which controlled in this Republic [from 1776 to 1865] . . . one of honor, glory, chivalry, and patriotism."

Such gender anxieties were not limited to elites. The depression of the 1890s hit working-class men hard, causing them to question their self-worth as they lost the ability to support their families. By embracing imperialist ideals, they would regain their manly honor.

The growing presence of women as political activists in campaigns for suffrage and moral, humanitarian, and governmental reforms challenged traditional notions of male identity. Some men warned that dire consequences would result if women succeeded in feminizing politics. Many prominent imperialists believed that women's suffrage would undermine the nation's military security because women lacked the will to use physical force. Military historian Alfred Thayer Mahan asserted that giving the vote to women would destroy the "constant practice of the past ages by which to men are assigned the outdoor rough action of life and to women that indoor sphere which we call the family." For such men, calling U.S. men to action was often paired with a call for U.S. women to leave the public arena and return to the home.

jingoist
An extremely patriotic supporter of the expansion and use of military power. Jingoists such as Theodore Roosevelt longed for a war to demonstrate America's strength and prove their own masculinity.

Males in the United States could reassert their manhood by adopting a militant spirit. Known as **jingoists**, war enthusiasts such as Theodore Roosevelt saw war as necessary to the development of a generation of men who could meet the challenges of the modern age. "No greater danger could befall civilization than the disappearance of the warlike spirit (I dare say war) among civilized men," military historian Alfred Thayer Mahan asserted. "There are too many barbarians still in the world."

Mahan and Roosevelt promoted naval power, and by 1900, the U.S. fleet contained seventeen battleships and six armored cruisers, making it the third-most powerful navy in the world, up from twelfth place in 1880. Having built a powerful navy, the United States would soon find opportunities to use it.

AP® WORKING with EVIDENCE

Source: Albert Beveridge, *The March of the Flag*, 1898

"The Opposition tells us that we ought not to govern a people without their consent. I answer, the rule of liberty that all just government derives its authority from the consent of the governed, applies only to those who are capable of self-government. We govern the Indians without their consent, we govern our territories without their consent, we govern our children without their consent. How do they know [what] our government would be without their consent? . . .

If England can govern foreign lands, so can America. If Germany can govern foreign lands, so can America. If they can supervise protectorates, so can America. Why is it more difficult to administer Hawaii than New Mexico or California? Both had a savage and an alien population; both were more remote from the seat of government when they came under our dominion than the Philippines are today. . . .

The march of the flag! In 1789 the flag of the Republic waved over 4,000,000 souls in thirteen states, and their savage territory which stretched to the Mississippi, to Canada, to the Floridas. The timid minds of that day said that no new territory was needed, and, for the hour, they were right. But Jefferson, through whose intellect the centuries marched; Jefferson, who dreamed of Cuba as an American state; Jefferson, the first Imperialist of the Republic—Jefferson acquired that imperial territory which swept from the Mississippi to the mountains, from Texas to the British possessions, and the march of the flag began!

The ocean does not separate us from lands of our duty and desire. . . . Steam joins us; electricity joins us—the very elements are in league with our destiny. Cuba not contiguous! Porto Rico not contiguous! Hawaii and the Philippines not contiguous! The oceans make them contiguous. And our navy will make them contiguous."

Questions for Analysis

1. Identify Beveridge's justification for imperialism.
2. Explain how Beveridge uses history to justify American imperialism.
3. Explain how Beveridge unites technology and the future of American power.

Questions for Comparison

Rudyard Kipling, "The White Man's Burden," 1898

1. Explain how these two documents were shaped by a common historical situation.
2. Evaluate the extent of similarity in the position each document takes on imperialism.

▪ How did American citizens and policymakers justify imperialism?

Skills Workshop: Writing Historically

Additional Practice in Responding to a Long-Essay Question

Evaluate the extent of difference in the causes for U.S. expansionism in the period 1800 to 1850 and U.S. expansionism in the period 1865 to 1900.

MODULE 7.3

The Spanish-American War

FOCUS

As you read this module, think about the effects of U.S. victory in its war against Spain. How did the conflict expand the territory under U.S. control? How were the people in newly conquered or annexed lands affected? How did overseas expansion change U.S. foreign policy and its role in the world?

In 1898, the United States went to war with Spain over Cuba not to defend itself from attack but because U.S. policymakers decided that Cuban independence from Spain was in the economic and strategic interests of the United States. Victory over Spain, however, brought the United States much more than control over Cuba. In the peace negotiations following the war, the United States acquired a significant portion of Spain's overseas empire, turning the United States into a major imperial power. After the war, the United States extended its influence into the Caribbean and parts of Asia.

The War with Spain

AP® EXAM TIP

The United States went to war with Spain over Cuba, not only supposedly for the benefit of the Cubans, but because Cuba would strengthen U.S. economic and security interests. The outcome of the war gave access to much of Spain's possessions around the world and transformed America into a major imperialist nation. You should be able to explain U.S. imperialist ambitions and outcomes. The AP® Exam may ask you to explain the causes and effects of imperialism on U.S. society, as well as to compare imperialism with the earlier movement of manifest destiny.

The Cuban War for Independence began in 1895 around the concept of *Cubanidad*—pride of nation. José Martí envisioned that this war of national liberation from Spain would provide land to impoverished peasants and offer genuine racial equality for the large Afro-Cuban population that had been liberated from slavery less than a decade earlier, in 1886. "Our goal," the revolutionary leader declared in 1892, "is not so much a mere political change as a good, sound, and just and equitable system." Black Cubans flocked to the revolutionary cause and constituted a significant portion of the senior ranks in the rebel army.

The insurgents fought a brilliant guerrilla war. Facing some 200,000 Spanish troops, 50,000 rebels ground them down in a war of attrition. Within eighteen months, the rebellion had spread across the island and garnered the support of all segments of the Cuban population. The Spanish government's brutal attempts to crack down on the rebels only stiffened their resistance.

By the end of 1897, the Spanish government recognized that the war was going poorly and offered the rebels a series of reforms that would give the island home rule within the empire but not independence. Sensing victory, the insurgents held out for total separation to realize their vision of **Cuba Libre**, an independent Cuba with social and racial equality.

The revolutionaries had every reason to feel confident as they wore down Spanish troops. First, they had help from the climate. A fourth of Spanish soldiers had contracted yellow fever, malaria, and other tropical illnesses and remained confined to hospitals. Second, mounting a successful counterinsurgency would have required far more troops than Spain could spare. Its forces were spread too thin around the globe to keep the empire intact. Finally, antiwar sentiment was mounting in Spain, and on January 12, 1898,

Granger – Historical Picture Archive

Cuban Revolutionary Soldiers Under the command of General Maximo Gómez, these Cuban soldiers, many of them of mixed Afro-Cuban descent, fought against Spanish forces in 1898. Gómez waged guerrilla warfare for Cuban independence from Spain before the United States entered the war.

What does the image suggest about the nature of the resistance to Spanish rule in Cuba?

Spanish troops mutinied in Havana. Speaking for many, a former president of Spain asserted: "Spain is exhausted. She must withdraw her troops and recognize Cuban independence before it is too late."

With the Cuban insurgents on the verge of victory, President William McKinley came to favor military intervention as a way to increase U.S. control of postwar Cuba. By intervening before the Cubans won on their own, the United States staked its claim for determining the postwar relationship between the two countries and protecting its vital interests in the Caribbean, including the private property rights of U.S. landowners in Cuba.

The U.S. press, however, helped build support for U.S. intervention by framing the war as a matter of U.S. honor rather than focusing on economic interests and geopolitics. William Randolph Hearst's *New York Journal* competed with Joseph Pulitzer's *New York World* for readership by seeing which could provide the most shocking coverage of Spanish atrocities. Known disparagingly as **yellow journalism**, these sensationalist newspaper accounts aroused jingoistic outrage against Spain.

On February 15, 1898, the battleship *Maine*, anchored in Havana harbor in a display of American military might, exploded, killing 266 U.S. sailors. Newspapers in the United States blamed Spain. The *World* shouted the rallying cry "Remember the *Maine*! To hell with Spain!" Assistant Secretary of the Navy Theodore Roosevelt seconded this sentiment by denouncing the explosion as a Spanish "act of treachery" after a naval investigation improbably blamed the explosion on an underwater mine. Why the Spaniards would choose to blow up the *Maine* and provoke war with the United States while already losing to Cuban revolutionaries remained unanswered, but the incident was enough to turn U.S. opinion toward war.

On April 11, 1898, McKinley asked Congress to declare war against Spain. The declaration included an amendment proposed by Senator Henry M. Teller of Colorado declaring that Cuba "ought to be free and independent." Yet the **Teller Amendment** left enough room for U.S. maneuvering to satisfy the imperial ambitions of the McKinley administration. In endorsing independence, the war proclamation asserted the right of the United States to remain involved in Cuban affairs until it had achieved "pacification."

On April 21, the United States officially went to war with Spain. In the United States., the war has traditionally been called the **Spanish–American War**, but this

yellow journalism
Sensationalist news accounts meant to sell newspapers by provoking an emotional response in readers. Yellow journalism contributed to the growth of public support for American intervention in Cuba in 1898.

Teller Amendment
An amendment to the 1898 declaration of war against Spain stipulating that Cuba should be free and independent. The amendment was largely ignored in the aftermath of the U.S. victory.

Spanish–American War
The war the United States declared against Spain to aid Cuban revolutionaries in their ongoing war for independence. The war was also fought in the Philippines, and U.S. victory led to annexation of the Philippines, Puerto Rico, and Guam from Spain as well as influence in Cuban affairs. It is also sometimes called the War of 1898.

term fails to take into account the significant role played by the Cuban people and subsequently by the Filipinos who were also under Spanish rule.

In going to war, McKinley embarked on an imperialistic course that had been building since the early 1890s. The president signaled the broader expansionist concerns behind the war when, shortly after it began, he successfully steered a Hawaiian annexation treaty through Congress. Businessmen joined imperialists in seizing the moment to create a commercial empire that would catch up to their European rivals.

It was fortunate for the United States that the Cuban insurgents had seriously weakened Spanish forces before the U.S. fighters arrived. The U.S. army lacked sufficient strength to conquer Cuba on its own, and McKinley had to mobilize some 200,000 National Guard troops and assorted volunteers. Theodore Roosevelt resigned from his post as assistant secretary of the navy and organized his own regiment, called the **Rough Riders**. U.S. forces faced several problems: They lacked battle experience; supplies were inadequate; their uniforms were not suited for the hot, humid climate of a Cuban summer; and the soldiers did not have immunity to tropical diseases.

Rough Riders
The nickname of Theodore Roosevelt's regiment of the First United States Volunteer Cavalry, which fought in Cuba during the Spanish-American War in 1898. Roosevelt's popularity and political career were boosted by his fame as a Rough Rider.

Black soldiers, who made up about one-quarter of the U.S. troops, encountered additional difficulties. As more and more Black troops arrived in southern ports for deployment to Cuba, they faced increasingly hostile crowds, angered at the presence of armed Black men in uniform. In Tampa, Florida, where troops gathered from all over the country to be transported to Cuba, racial tensions exploded on the afternoon of June 8. Intoxicated white soldiers from Ohio grabbed a two-year-old Black boy from his mother and used him for target practice, shooting a bullet through his shirtsleeve.

Philippine Theater

Cuban Theater

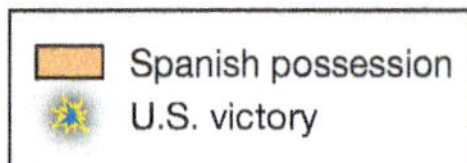

MAP 7.1 The Spanish-American War The United States and Spain fought the Spanish-American War in two theaters of operation — the Philippines and Cuba. Naval forces led by Admiral George Dewey made the difference in the U.S. victory by defeating the Spaniards first in Manila Bay and then off the coast of Cuba. In Cuba, rebels had seriously weakened the Spanish military before U.S. ground troops secured victory.

What similarities and differences between the two theaters of operation are evident from the map?

In retaliation, Black soldiers stormed into the streets and exchanged gunfire with white people, leaving three of them, along with twenty-seven Black soldiers, wounded.

Despite military inexperience, logistical problems, and racial tensions, the United States quickly defeated the weakened Spanish military, and the war was over four months after it began. During this war, 460 U.S. soldiers died in combat, far fewer than the more than 5,000 who lost their lives to disease.

The subsequent peace treaty ended Spanish rule in Cuba, ceded Puerto Rico and the Pacific island of Guam to the United States, and recognized U.S. occupation of the Philippines until the two countries could arrange a final settlement. As a result of the territorial gains in the war, U.S. foreign-policy strategists could now begin to construct an empire.

Although Congress had adopted the Teller Amendment in 1898 pledging Cuba's independence from Spain, President McKinley and his supporters insisted that Cuban self-rule would come only after pacification. Racial and cultural prejudice blinded Americans to the contributions Cubans had made to defeat Spain. One U.S. officer reported to the *New York Times*: "The typical Cuban I encountered was a treacherous, lying, cowardly, thieving, worthless half-breed mongrel, born of a mongrel spawn of [Spain], crossed upon the fetches of darkest Africa and aboriginal America." José Martí may have been fighting for racial equality, but the U.S. government certainly was not.

Because U.S. officials presumed that Cuba was unfit for immediate freedom, the island remained under U.S. military occupation until 1902. The highlight of Cuba's transition to self-rule came with the adoption of a governing document based on the U.S. Constitution. However, the Cuban constitution came with strings attached. In March 1901, Congress passed the **Platt Amendment**, introduced by Senator Orville Platt of Connecticut, which limited Cuban sovereignty. The amendment prohibited the Cuban government from signing treaties with other nations without U.S. consent, permitted the United States to intervene in Cuba to preserve independence and remove threats to economic stability, and perpetually leased Guantánamo Bay to the United States as a naval base. U.S. officials pressured Cuban leaders to incorporate the Platt Amendment into their constitution, and as a result, when U.S. occupation ended in 1902, Cuba was not fully independent.

Platt Amendment
A 1901 act of Congress limiting Cuban sovereignty. U.S. officials pressured Cuban leaders to incorporate the amendment into the Cuban constitution.

REVIEW

- What arguments did the United States use to justify war with Spain in 1898?

The Philippine War

Even before invading Cuba, the United States had won a significant battle against Spain on the other side of the world. At the outset of the war, the U.S. Pacific Fleet, under the command of Commodore George Dewey, attacked Spanish forces in their colony of the Philippines. Dewey defeated the Spanish flotilla in Manila Bay on May 1, 1898. Two and a half months later, U.S. troops followed up with an invasion of Manila, and Spanish forces promptly surrendered.

While pacifying Cuba, the U.S. government had to decide what to do with the Philippines. Imperialists viewed U.S. control of the islands as an important step forward in the quest for entry into the China market. The Philippines could serve as a naval station for the merchant marine and the navy to safeguard potential trade with the Asian mainland. Moreover, President McKinley believed that if the United States did not act, another European power would take Spain's place, something he thought would be "bad business and discreditable."

With this in mind, McKinley decided to annex the Philippines. As with Cuba, McKinley and most U.S. citizens believed that nonwhite Filipinos were not yet capable of self-government. Thus, McKinley set out "to educate the Filipinos, and uplift and Christianize them," even though many Filipinos had been Catholic for centuries. As was often the case with imperialism, assumptions of racial and cultural superiority provided a handy justification for the pursuit of economic and strategic advantage.

AP® WORKING with EVIDENCE

Source: President William McKinley, *Remarks to a Methodist Delegation*, 1899

> "When I next realized that the Philippines had dropped into our laps I confess I did not know what to do with them. . . . And one night late it came to me this way . . . 1) That we could not give them back to Spain—that would be cowardly and dishonorable; 2) that we could not turn them over to France and Germany—our commercial rivals in the Orient—that would be bad business and discreditable; 3) that we [could] not leave them to themselves—they are unfit for self-government—and they would soon have anarchy and misrule over there worse than Spain's wars; and 4) that there was nothing left for us to do but to take them all, and to educate the Filipinos, and uplift and civilize and Christianize them, and by God's grace do the very best we could by them, as our fellow-men for whom Christ also died."

Questions for Analysis

1. Describe McKinley's perspective on acquiring the Philippines.
2. Explain how the first three of McKinley's ideas about "how to deal with" the Philippines served U.S. interests.
3. Explain how McKinley's fourth idea about "how to deal with" the Philippines implies that the acquisition of these islands was for reasons other than imperialism.

Questions for Comparison

Albert Beveridge, *The March of the Flag*, 1898 (Module 7.2)

1. Identify the similarities between the arguments of Beveridge and McKinley.
2. Identify the differences between the arguments of each.
3. Evaluate the relative appeal of each source to U.S. policymakers during this period.

The president's plans, however, ran into vigorous opposition. Anti-imperialists in Congress took a strong stand against annexing the Philippines. Their cause drew support from such prominent Americans as industrialist Andrew Carnegie, social reformer Jane Addams, writer Mark Twain, and labor organizer Samuel Gompers, all of whom joined the **Anti-Imperialist League**, founded in November 1898.

Anti-Imperialist League
An organization founded in 1898 to oppose annexation of the Philippines. Some feared the annexation would bring competition from cheap labor; others considered Filipinos racially inferior and the Philippines unsuitable as an American territory.

Progressives like Addams who were committed to humanitarian reforms at home questioned whether the United States should exploit colonial people overseas. Some argued that the United States would violate its anticolonialist heritage by acquiring the islands. Labor union leaders feared that annexation would prompt the migration of cheap laborers into the country and undercut wages. Others worried about the financial costs of supporting military forces across the Pacific.

Most anti-imperialists also had racial reasons for rejecting the treaty. Like imperialists, they considered Asians to be inferior to Europeans. In fact, many anti-imperialists held an even dimmer view of the capabilities of people of color than did their opponents, rejecting the notion that Filipinos could be "civilized" under U.S. supervision.

WORKING with EVIDENCE

Source: Platform of the American Anti-Imperialist League, *The Commons*, 1899

> "We hold that the policy known as imperialism is hostile to liberty and tends towards militarism, an evil from which it has been our glory to be free. We regret that it has become necessary in the land of Washington and Lincoln to reaffirm that all men, of whatever race or color, are entitled to life, liberty and the pursuit of happiness. We maintain that governments derive their just powers from the consent of the governed. We insist that the subjugation of any people is 'criminal aggression' and open disloyalty to the distinctive principles of our government.
>
> We earnestly condemn the policy of the present national administration in the Philippines. It seeks to extinguish the spirit of 1776 in those islands. We deplore the sacrifice of our soldiers and sailors, whose bravery deserves admiration even in an unjust war. We denounce the slaughter of the Filipinos as a needless horror. We protest against the extension of American sovereignty by Spanish methods.
>
> We demand the immediate cessation of the war against liberty, begun by Spain and continued by us. We urge that congress be promptly convened to announce to the Filipinos our purpose to concede to them the independence for which they have so long fought and which of right is theirs."

Questions for Analysis

1. Identify the rationale the Anti-Imperialist League provides for the United States to leave these islands.
2. Explain how the document uses an appeal to American history to support its argument.
3. Evaluate the extent to which U.S. control over these protectorates during the late 1800s and early 1900s was like British control over the American colonies before the American Revolution.

Despite this opposition, imperialists won out. Approval of the treaty annexing the Philippines in 1898 marked the beginning of problems for the United States. As in Cuba, rebellion against Spain had preceded U.S. occupation. At first, the rebels welcomed the Americans as liberators, but once it became clear that U.S. rule would replace Spanish rule, the mood changed. Led by Emilio Aguinaldo, insurgent forces fought back against the 70,000 U.S. troops using the same guerrilla tactics they had wielded against the Spanish.

U.S. forces responded with harsh methods to suppress the uprising. General Jacob H. Smith ordered his troops to "kill and burn, and the more you kill and burn, the better you will please me." Racist sentiments inflamed passions against the dark-skinned Filipino insurgents. U.S. counterinsurgency efforts, which indiscriminately targeted combatants and civilians alike, extracted a heavy toll on the native population. An estimated 200,000 Filipino civilians died between 1899 and 1902.

U.S. public support for the war in the Philippines quickly faded, as nearly five thousand Americans died in the Philippine war, far more combat deaths than in Cuba. Dissenters turned imperialist arguments of manly U.S. honor upside down. Anti-imperialists claimed that the war had done nothing to affirm U.S. manhood. Rather, they charged, the United States acted as a bully, taking the position of "a strong man" fighting against "a weak and puny child."

Despite mounting casualties on the battlefield and antiwar sentiment at home, the conflict ended with a U.S. military victory. In March 1901, U.S. forces captured Aguinaldo and broke the back of the rebellion. Exhausted, the Filipino leader asked his

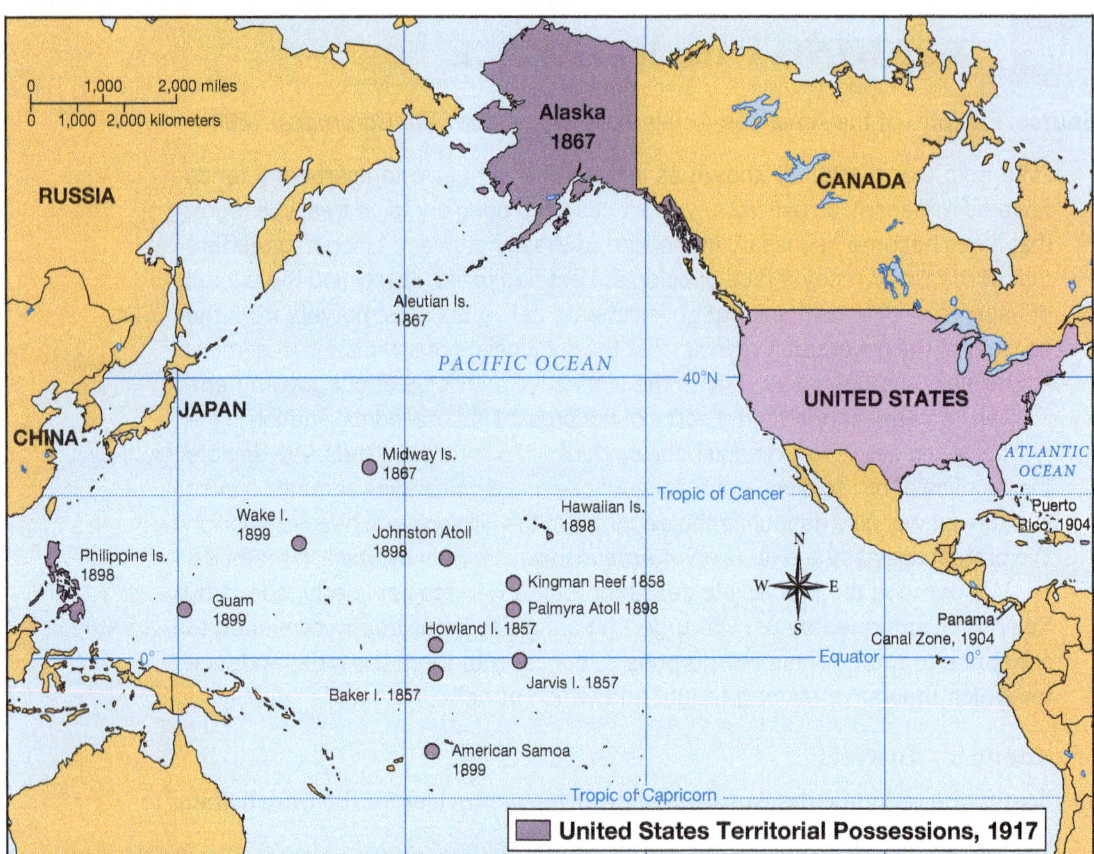

MAP 7.2 U.S. Expansionism in the Pacific During the second half of the nineteenth century, the United States expanded its presence in the Pacific. While the purchase of Alaska and annexations of Hawaii and the Philippines significantly increased the land area and population under U.S. control, most of the new U.S. possessions consisted of smaller and less populated islands, ideally suited as refueling stations for the U.S. navy and merchant shipping.

How was U.S. expansion in the Pacific similar to and different from previous U.S. expansion across the North American continent?

comrades to lay down their arms. In July 1901, President McKinley appointed Judge William Howard Taft of Ohio as the first civilian governor to oversee the government of the Philippines. For the next forty-five years, except for a brief period of Japanese rule during World War II, the United States remained in control of the islands.

- What were the main arguments against U.S. occupation of the Philippines?

Extending U.S. Imperialism, 1899–1913

The Spanish–American War turned the United States into an imperial nation. Once the war was over, and with its newly acquired empire in place, the United States sought to extend its influence, competing with its European rivals for even greater global power.

Theodore Roosevelt and his successors achieved imperialists' dreams of building a Central American canal and wielded U.S. military and financial might in the Caribbean with little restraint. At the same time, the United States took a more active role in Asian affairs.

After President McKinley was assassinated in 1901, Vice President Theodore Roosevelt succeeded him as president. A progressive reformer at home, Roosevelt believed that the national government must intervene in economic and social affairs to maintain stability and avoid class warfare. Likewise, he advocated using military power to protect U.S. commercial and strategic interests as well as to preserve international order. A Progressive Era interventionist, Roosevelt welcomed his nation's new role as an international policeman. "It is contemptible, for a nation, as for an individual," Roosevelt instructed Congress, "[to] proclaim its purposes, or to take positions which are ridiculous if unsupported by potential force, and then to refuse to provide this force."

To fulfill his international agenda, Roosevelt sought to demonstrate U.S. might and preserve order in the Caribbean and Central and South America. The building of the Panama Canal provides a case in point. Some considered a canal across Central America as vital because it would provide faster access to Asian markets by allowing ships to cross from the Atlantic to the Pacific without sailing around South America as well as improve the U.S. navy's ability to patrol two oceans effectively. The United States took a step toward realizing this goal in 1901, when it signed the **Hay-Pauncefote Treaty** with Britain, granting the United States the right to construct such a canal. After first considering Nicaragua, Roosevelt settled on Panama as the prime location. A French company had already begun construction at this site and had completed two-fifths of the operation. However, when it ran out of money, it sold its holdings to the United States.

Before the United States could build, it had to negotiate with the South American country of Colombia, which controlled Panama. Secretary of State John Hay and Colombian representatives reached an agreement highly favorable to the United States, which the Colombian government refused to ratify. When Colombia held out for a higher price, Roosevelt accused the Colombians of being "utterly incapable of keeping order" in Panama and declared that transit across Panama was vital to world commerce. In 1903, the president supported a pro-U.S. uprising by sending warships into the harbor of Panama City, an action that prevented the Colombians from quashing the Panamanian revolt. Roosevelt signed a treaty with the new government of Panama granting the United States the right to build the canal and exercise perpetual "power and authority" over it. After eight years of construction and at the cost of thousands of lives and hundreds of millions of dollars, the Panama Canal opened to sea traffic in 1914.

Kharbine-Tapabor/Shutterstock

Boxer Rebellion In 1900, the Society of Righteous and Harmonious Fists, a Chinese militia and secret society known as the Boxers, attacked foreign diplomatic offices in Beijing to expel outsiders. This illustration from Hunan Province portrays the Boxers killing foreigners and burning Christian books.

What themes are emphasized in this image of the Boxer Rebellion?

With the United States controlling Cuba, the Panama Canal, and Puerto Rico, President Roosevelt intended to deter any threats to U.S. power in the region. The economic instability of Central American and Caribbean nations provided Roosevelt with the opportunity to brandish what he called a **"big stick"** to keep these countries in check and prevent intervention by European powers also interested in the area.

"big stick" diplomacy
Aggressive foreign diplomacy backed by the threat of force. Its name comes from a proverb quoted by Theodore Roosevelt: "Speak softly and carry a big stick."

In 1904, when the government of the Dominican Republic was teetering on the edge of bankruptcy and threatened to default on $22 million in European loans, Roosevelt sprang into action. He announced U.S. opposition to any foreign intervention to reclaim debts, a position that echoed the principles of the Monroe Doctrine, which in 1823 proclaimed that the United States would not tolerate outside intervention in the Western Hemisphere (see Module 4.4). Moreover, Roosevelt added his own corollary to the Monroe Doctrine by affirming the right of the United States to intervene in the internal affairs of any country in Latin America or the Caribbean that displayed "chronic wrong-doing" and could not preserve order and manage its own affairs. The **Roosevelt Corollary** proclaimed that the countries of Central America and the Caribbean had to behave according to U.S. wishes or face American military invasion. Accordingly, the president acknowledged that this region was part of the U.S. sphere of influence.

Roosevelt Corollary
A modification to the Monroe Doctrine made in 1904 that affirmed the right of the United States to intervene in the internal affairs of Caribbean and Latin American countries to preserve order and protect American interests.

- How did the United States expand its influence in the Western hemisphere after the Spanish-American War?

Opening the Door in China

Roosevelt displayed U.S. power in other parts of the world, too. His major concern was protecting the **Open Door policy** in China that his predecessor McKinley had engineered to secure naval access to the Chinese market. By 1900 European powers had already dominated foreign access to Chinese markets, leaving little room for newcomers. When the United States sent 2,100 troops to China in August 1900 to help quell a nationalist rebellion against foreign involvement known as the Boxer Rebellion, European competitors in return were compelled to allow the United States free trade access to China.

Open Door policy
An 1899 policy in which Secretary of State John Hay informed the nations occupying China that the United States had the right of equal trade in China.

In 1904, the Russian invasion of the northern Chinese province of Manchuria prompted the Japanese to attack the Russian fleet. Roosevelt admired Japanese military prowess, but he worried that if Japan succeeded in driving the Russians out of the area, it would cause "a real shifting of equilibrium as far as the White races are concerned." To prevent that from happening, Roosevelt convened a peace conference in Portsmouth, New Hampshire, in 1905. Under the agreement reached at the conference, Japan received control over Korea and parts of Manchuria but pledged to support the U.S. Open Door policy of equal (in effect, European and American) access to the Chinese market. In 1906, the president sent sixteen U.S. battleships on a trip around the globe in a show of force meant to demonstrate that the United States was serious about taking its place as a premier world power.

When Roosevelt's secretary of war, William Howard Taft, became president (1909–1913), he continued his predecessor's foreign policy with slight modification. Proclaiming that he would rather substitute "dollars for bullets," Taft encouraged private bankers to invest money in the Caribbean and Central America, a policy known as **dollar diplomacy**. Yet Taft did not rely on financial influence alone. He dispatched more than two thousand U.S. troops to the region to guarantee economic stability.

dollar diplomacy
The term used by President Taft to describe the economic focus of his foreign policy. Taft hoped to use economic policies and the control of foreign assets by American companies to expand U.S. influence in Latin America and Asia.

Taft's diplomacy also led to extensive intervention in Nicaragua. In 1909, U.S. fruit and mining companies in Nicaragua helped install a regime sympathetic to their interests. When a group of rebels threatened this pro-U.S. government, Taft invoked the Roosevelt

Corollary and sent in U.S. marines to police the country and deter further uprisings. They remained there for another twenty-five years. Under this occupation, U.S. bankers took control of Nicaragua's customs houses and paid off debts owed to foreign investors, a move meant to prevent outside intervention in a nation that was now under U.S. "protection."

REVIEW

- How did U.S. policies in Asia mirror U.S. policies in Latin America during the late nineteenth and early twentieth centuries?

AP® Skills Workshop: Writing Historically

Additional Practice in Responding to a Short-Answer Question with a Primary Source

Library of Congress, LC-DIG-ppmsca-25887

Source: Grant Hamilton, "I Rather Like That Imported Affair," *Puck*, 1904

About the source: From left to right, the three hats in the background are labeled "U.S. Grant Style," "A. Lincoln Hat," and "G. Washington Hat." Theodore Roosevelt is shown wearing a ribbon labeled "The Colonel" and says, "I rather like that imported affair."

Using the 1904 political cartoon depicting President Theodore Roosevelt, answer parts **A**, **B**, and **C**.

A. Briefly explain ONE perspective expressed in the image.

B. Briefly explain ONE specific historical event or development from the period 1890 to 1904 that led to the situation depicted in the image.

C. Briefly explain ONE specific historical event or development from the period 1904 to 1914 that resulted from the situation depicted in the image.

MODULE

7.4a The Progressives: Social Reform

FOCUS

While reading this module, compare the varied problems facing the nation according to reform-minded Americans and the solutions they recommended.

From roughly 1900 to 1917, many Americans sought to bring some order out of the chaos accompanying rapid industrialization and urbanization. Despite the magnitude of the issues, those who believed in the need to combat the problems of industrial America possessed an optimistic faith—sometimes derived from religious principles, sometimes from a secular outlook—that they could relieve the stresses and strains that modern life brought. Such people were not bound together by a single, rigid ideology. Instead, they were united by faith in the notion that if people joined together and applied human intelligence to the task of improving the nation, progress was inevitable. So widespread was this hopeful conviction that we call this period the Progressive Era.

In pursuit of progress and stability, some reformers tried to control the behavior of groups they considered a threat to the social order. Equating difference with disorder, many progressives tried to impose white middle-class standards of behavior on immigrant populations. Some sought to eliminate the "problem" altogether by curtailing further immigration from southern and eastern Europe. Others advocated birth control as a means to preserve the lives of childbearing women, but also to promote ethnic and racial engineering. In addition, progressives fought for women's suffrage, consumer protection, regulation of business, and good government reform.

Many white progressives, particularly in the South, favored racial segregation and disfranchisement of Black people. At the same time, however, Black progressives and their white allies created organizations dedicated to securing racial equality. Despite their disparate and sometimes conflicting aims, progressives remained committed to change as a means of improving the nation.

Reformers focused on the plight of urban immigrants, Black Americans, and the underprivileged. They tried mainly to improve housing and working conditions for impoverished city dwellers. Their motives were not always purely altruistic. Unless living standards improved, many reformers reasoned, immigrants and racial minorities would contaminate the cities' middle-class inhabitants with communicable diseases, escalating crime, and threats to traditional cultural norms. These reformers also supported suffrage for women, whose votes, they believed, would help purify electoral politics and elect candidates committed to social and moral reform.

The Roots of Progressivism

At the turn of the twentieth century, many Americans believed that the nation was in dire need of reform. Two decades of westward expansion, industrialization, urbanization, and skyrocketing immigration had transformed the country in unsettling ways. In the aftermath of the social and economic turmoil that accompanied the depression of the 1890s, many members of the middle and upper classes were convinced that unless they took corrective measures, the country would collapse under the weight of class conflict.

Progressives contended that old ways of governing and doing business did not address modern conditions. In one sense, supporters of **progressivism** inherited the legacy of the Populist movement of the 1890s. Progressives attacked laissez-faire capitalism, and by regulating monopolies they aimed to limit the power of corporate trusts. Like the Populists, progressives advocated instituting an income tax as well as a variety of initiatives designed to give citizens a greater say in government. However, progressives differed from Populists in fundamental ways. Perhaps most important, progressives were interested mainly in urban and industrial America and were typically middle class, while the Populist movement had emerged in direct response to the problems that plagued rural America, and its proponents were often connected to the agricultural economy.

progressivism
A movement that emerged during the late nineteenth century whose adherents were united by the belief that if people joined together and applied human intelligence to the task of improving the nation, progress was inevitable. Progressives advocated governmental intervention yet sought change without radically altering capitalism or the political system.

Progressives were heirs to the intellectual critics of the late nineteenth century who challenged laissez-faire and rejected Herbert Spencer's doctrine of the "survival of the fittest." **Pragmatism** greatly influenced progressives. Pragmatists contended that the meaning of truth did not reside in some absolute doctrine but could be discovered only through experience. Ideas had to be measured by their practical consequences. From these critics, progressives derived a skepticism toward rigid principles and instead relied on human experience to guide social action.

pragmatism
A philosophy that holds that truth can be discovered only through experience and that the value of ideas should be measured by their practical consequences. Pragmatism had a significant influence on progressives.

Reformers also drew inspiration from the religious ideals of the social gospel (see Module 6.11). In *Christianity and the Social Crisis* (1907), Walter Rauschenbusch urged Christians to embrace the teachings of Jesus on the ethical obligations for social justice and to put these teachings into action by working among the urban poor. Washington Gladden argued that unregulated private enterprise was "inequitable" and compared financial speculators to vampires "sucking the life-blood of our commerce." Progressive leaders combined the moral fervor of the social gospel with the rationalism of the gospel of scientific efficiency.

AP® EXAM TIP

A significant reform movement developed in the late nineteenth and early twentieth centuries, known as progressivism. You will have to know the participants in the progressive movement, their philosophies regarding the potential of U.S. society that motivated their actions, and their accomplishments. The AP® Exam regularly asks questions about the causes and effects of the progressive movement, or questions that compare it to other reform movements in U.S. history.

Pragmatism and the social gospel appealed to members of the new middle class. Before the Civil War, the middle class had consisted largely of ministers, lawyers, physicians, and small proprietors. The growth of large-scale businesses during the second half of the nineteenth century expanded the middle class, which now included men whose professions grew out of industrialization, such as engineering, corporate management, and social work. Progressivism drew many of its most devoted adherents from this new middle class.

The growing desire for reform at the turn of the century also received a boost from investigative journalists known as **muckrakers**. Popular magazines such as *McClure's* and *Collier's* sought to increase their readership by publishing exposés of corruption in government and the shady operations of big business. Filled with details uncovered through intensive research, these articles had a sensationalist appeal that both informed and aroused their mainly middle-class readers. In 1902, journalist Ida Tarbell lambasted the ruthless and dishonest business practices of the Rockefeller family's Standard Oil Company, the model of corporate greed. Lincoln Steffens wrote about machine bosses' shameful rule in many American cities. Ida B. Wells was born enslaved in Holly Springs, Mississippi, and rose to become a teacher, writer, editor, and civil rights activist. She wrote scathing articles and pamphlets condemning the lynching of Black people. Other muckrakers exposed fraudulent practices in insurance companies, child labor, drug abuse, and prostitution.

muckrakers
Investigative journalists during the late nineteenth and early twentieth centuries who specialized in exposing corruption, scandal, and vice. Muckrakers helped build public support for progressive causes.

AP® WORKING with EVIDENCE

Source: Lincoln Steffens, *The Shame of the Cities*, 1904

> "There is hardly an office from United States Senator down to Alderman in any part of the country to which the business man has not been elected; yet politics remains corrupt, government pretty bad. . . .
>
> The commercial spirit is the spirit of profit, not patriotism; of credit, not honor; of individual gain, not national prosperity; of trade and dickering, not principle. 'My business is sacred,' says the business man in his heart. 'Whatever prospers my business, is good; it must be. Whatever hinders it, is wrong; it must be. A bribe is bad, that is, it is a bad thing to take; but it is not so bad to give one, not if it is necessary to my business.'. . .
>
> If our political leaders are to be always a lot of political merchants, they will supply any demand we may create. All we have to do is to establish a steady demand for good government. . . . Why? Because if the honest voter cared no more for his party than the politician and the grafter, then the honest vote would govern, and that would be bad—for [corruption]. . . . If we would vote in mass on the more promising ticket, or, if the two are equally bad, would throw out the party that is in, and wait till the next election and then throw out the other party that is in—then, I say, the commercial politician would feel a demand for good government and he would supply it."

Questions for Analysis

1. Identify the problem that Steffens believes lies at the heart of American politics.
2. Describe the solution Steffens proposes to address this problem.
3. Evaluate the extent to which Steffens's reform plan would represent a change in American politics.

REVIEW

- What factors contributed to the rise of progressivism?
- How did the Muckrakers help further progressive reforms?

Female Progressives and the Poor

Women played the leading role in efforts to improve the lives of the impoverished. Jane Addams had toured Europe after graduating from a women's college in Illinois. The Toynbee Hall settlement house in London impressed her for its work in helping poor residents of the area. After returning home to Chicago in 1889, Addams and her friend Ellen Starr established **Hull House** as a center for social reform. Hull House inspired a generation of young women to work directly in immigrant communities. Many were college-educated, professionally trained women who were shut out of jobs in male-dominated professions.

Hull House
The settlement house established by Jane Addams and Ellen Starr in Chicago in 1889. It served as a center of social reform, provided educational and social opportunities for working-class poor and immigrant women and their children, and inspired the creation of other settlement houses in major U.S. cities.

Staffed mainly by women, settlement houses became all-purpose urban support centers providing recreational facilities, social activities, and educational classes for neighborhood residents (see Module 6.9). Calling on women to take up **civic housekeeping**, Addams maintained that women could protect their individual households from the chaos of industrialization and urbanization only by attacking the sources of that chaos in the community at large.

Settlement houses and social workers led humanitarian reform, but they found considerable support from women's clubs. Formed after the Civil War, these local groups provided middle-class women places to meet, share ideas, and work on common projects. By 1900, these clubs counted 160,000 members.

Initially devoted to discussions of religion, culture, and science, club women began to help the needy and lobby for social justice legislation. "Since men are more or less closely absorbed in business," one club woman remarked about this civic awakening, "it has come to pass that the initiative in civic matters has devolved largely upon women." Starting out in towns and cities, club women carried their message to state and federal governments and campaigned for legislation that would establish social welfare programs for working women and their children.

In an age of strict racial segregation, Black women formed their own clubs. They sponsored day care centers, kindergartens, and work and home training projects. The activities of Black club women, like those of white club women, reflected a class bias, and they tried to lift up poorer Black people to ideals of middle-class womanhood. Yet in doing so, they challenged racist notions that Black women and men were incapable of raising healthy and strong families. By 1916, the **National Association of Colored Women (NACW)**, whose motto was "lifting as we climb," boasted 1,000 clubs and 50,000 members.

National Association of Colored Women (NACW)
An organization that became the largest federation of Black local women's clubs in 1896. The group was designed to relieve suffering among poor Black people, defend Black women, and promote the interests of all Black people.

White working-class women also organized, but because of employment discrimination, there were few, if any, Black female industrial workers to join them. Building on the settlement house movement and together with middle-class and wealthy women, working-class women founded the Women's Trade Union League (WTUL) in 1903. Recognizing that many women needed to earn an income to help support their families, the WTUL was dedicated to securing higher wages, an eight-hour day, and improved working conditions. Believing women to be physically weaker than men, most female reformers advocated special legislation to protect women in the workplace. They campaigned for state laws prescribing the maximum number of hours women could work, and they succeeded in 1908 when they won a landmark victory in the Supreme Court

Library of Congress, LC-DIG-ppmsca-18483

Mary Crane Nursery at Hull House, Chicago, Illinois, early 1900s Hull House and other settlement houses offered a range of services for immigrants and the working class in inner cities such as daycare, kindergarten, English and citizenship classes, and job placement services. In this image, hooded students are receiving instruction in an open-air setting at wooden desks.

How does the image convey both the need for settlement houses and the role settlement houses played in urban communities?

Muller v. Oregon
U.S. Supreme Court ruling in 1908 that upheld an Oregon law establishing a ten-hour workday for women.

in ***Muller v. Oregon***, which upheld an Oregon law establishing a ten-hour workday for women. These reformers also convinced lawmakers in forty states to establish pensions for mothers and widows.

In 1912, their focus shifted to the federal government with the founding of the Children's Bureau in the Department of Commerce and Labor. Headed by Julia Lathrop, the bureau collected sociological data and devised a variety of publicly funded social welfare measures. In 1916, Congress enacted a law banning child labor under the age of fourteen (it was declared unconstitutional in 1918). In 1921, Congress passed the **Sheppard-Towner Act**, which allowed nurses to offer maternal and infant health care information to mothers.

Not all women believed in the idea of protective legislation for women. In 1898, Charlotte Perkins Gilman published *Women and Economics*, in which she argued against the notion that women were ideally suited for domesticity. She contended that women's reliance on men was unnatural: "We are the only animal species in which the female depends on the male for food." Emphasizing the need for economic independence, Gilman advocated the establishment of communal kitchens that would free women from household chores and allow them to compete on equal terms with men in the workplace. Emma Goldman, an anarchist critic of capitalism and middle-class sexual morality, also spoke out against the kind of marriage that made women "keep their mouths shut and their wombs open." These women considered themselves as **feminists**—women who aspire to reach their full potential and gain access to the same opportunities as men.

REVIEW

- In what ways did women progressives challenge traditional conceptions of women's roles in society?

Fighting for Women's Suffrage

As late as 1910, women had the right to vote in only a handful of western states. Although the Fourteenth and Fifteenth Amendments extended citizenship to Black Americans and protected the voting rights of Black men, they left women, both white and Black, ineligible to vote. Following Reconstruction, the two major organizations campaigning for women's suffrage at the state and national levels—Susan B. Anthony and Elizabeth Cady Stanton's National Woman Suffrage Association and Lucy Stone and Julia Ward Howe's American Woman Suffrage Association—failed to achieve major victories. In 1890, the two groups combined to form the **National American Woman Suffrage Association**, and in part due to their efforts, by 1918 women could vote in fifteen states and the territory of Alaska.

National American Woman Suffrage Association
A national organization created in 1890 that contributed to the ratification of the Nineteenth Amendment in 1920, which guaranteed women's right to vote in the United States.

Suffragists included a broad coalition of supporters and based their campaign on a variety of arguments. Reformers such as Jane Addams attributed corruption in politics to the absence of women's maternal influence. In this way, mainstream suffragists couched their arguments within traditional views of women as family nurturers and claimed that men should see women's vote as an expansion of traditional household duties into the public sphere.

By contrast, suffragists such as Alice Paul rejected such arguments, asserting that women deserved the vote on the basis of their equality with men as citizens. She founded the **National Woman's Party** and, in 1923, proposed that Congress adopt an Equal Rights Amendment to provide full legal equality to women.

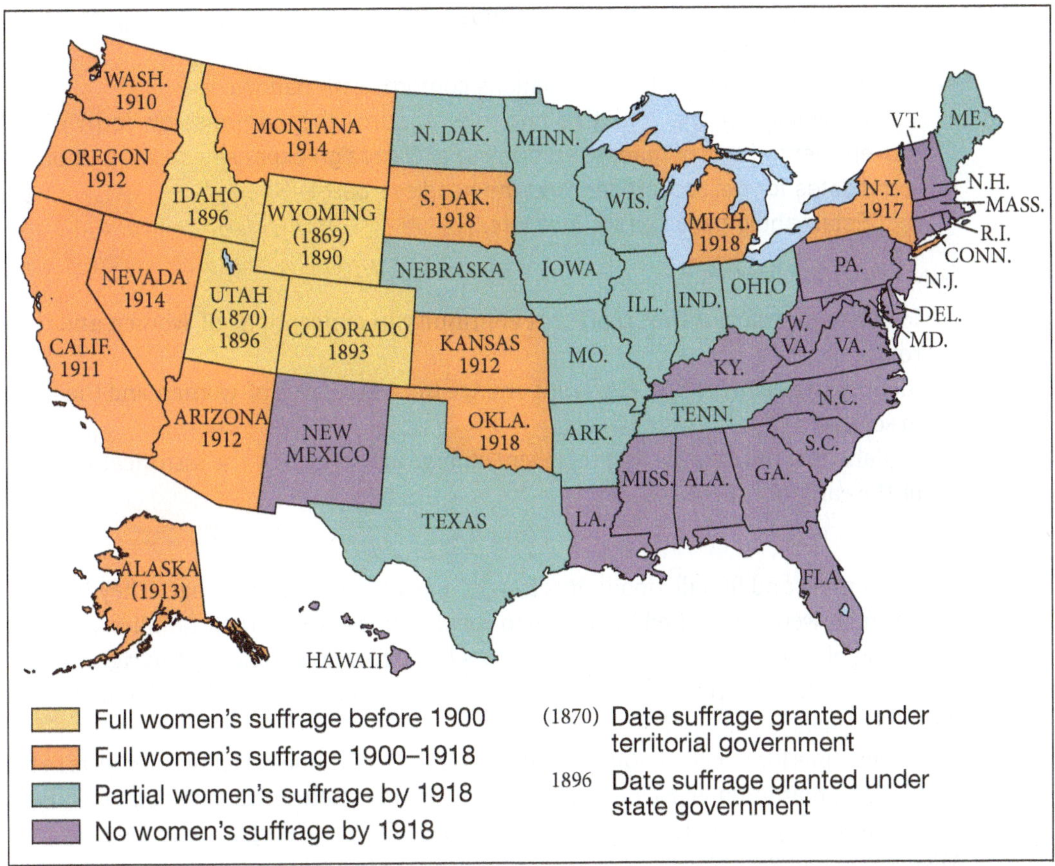

MAP 7.3 Women's Suffrage Western states and territories were the first to approve women's suffrage. Yet even as western states enfranchised women, most placed restrictions on or excluded Black, American Indian, Mexican American, and Asian American women. States granting partial suffrage allowed women to vote only in certain contests, such as municipal or school board, primary, or presidential elections.

How did popular views of women and minorities justify these restrictions?

AP® WORKING with EVIDENCE

Source: National American Woman Suffrage Association, "Where Women Vote—Wyoming," *Woman Suffrage: History, Arguments, Results*, 1917

"Despite the lack of effective organization, due to frontier conditions of life, the women have been able to exert considerable influence upon legislation. They have helped secure the following important measures:

Making gambling illegal.

Giving women absolute rights over their own property.

Making exactly equal inheritance by husband and wife, father and mother; giving the mother equal rights with the father over the children; limiting the hours of labor of women to ten a day.

Providing that men and women teachers shall receive equal pay for equal work.

Raising the age of protection of young girls to 18.

Providing penalties for child neglect, abuse or cruelty.

Forbidding the employment of children in certain industries.

Making it unlawful to give or sell liquor or tobacco to children.

Establishing kindergartens and a State industrial school.

Providing for the care of dependent children and infirm, indigent or incompetent persons.

Making State pure food regulations conform with national law.

Providing for the initiative and referendum, the commission form of government, direct primaries, accounting of campaign expenses on the part of candidates for political offices, and the headless ballot.

Establishing pensions for mothers."

Questions for Analysis

1. Identify two reforms that represent continuity in conceptions of women and their role in society.
2. Identify two reforms that represent change in conceptions of women and their role in society.
3. Explain how the reforms that represent change are shaped by the historical situation of the early twentieth century.

Both male and female opponents fought against women's suffrage. They believed that women were best suited by nature to devote themselves to their families and leave the world of politics to men. Suffrage critics insisted that extending the right to vote to women would destroy the home, lead to the moral degeneracy of children, and tear down the social fabric of the country.

Campaigns for women's suffrage did not apply to all women. White suffragists in the South often manipulated racial prejudice to support female enfranchisement. Outspoken white suffragists such as Rebecca Latimer Felton from Georgia, Belle Kearney from Mississippi, and Kate Gordon from Louisiana contended that as long as even a fraction of Black men voted and the Fifteenth Amendment continued to exist, allowing southern white women to vote would preserve white supremacy by offsetting Black men's votes. These arguments also had a class component, because poll taxes disfranchised poor white people. Extending the vote to white women would benefit mainly those in the middle class who had enough family income to satisfy restrictive poll tax requirements.

Suffrage Campaign, 1913
During the Progressive Era, women mounted a determined campaign to gain suffrage from state and federal governments. They employed a variety of tactics, from persuasion through education to direct confrontation and getting arrested. On August 10, 1913, New York women suffragists took the opportunity to promote their cause at the New York Fair held in Yonkers, a suburb of New York City. Women won the right to vote in New York in 1917 and finally succeeded nationally with ratification of the Nineteenth Amendment in 1920.

What tactics did white women use to gain mainstream support for their suffrage?

Many middle-class women outside the South used similar reasoning, but they targeted newly arrived immigrants instead of Black Americans. Many Protestant women and men viewed Catholics and Jews from southern and eastern Europe as racially inferior and spiritually dangerous. They blamed such immigrants for the ills of the cities in which they congregated, and some suffragists believed that the vote of middle-class Protestant women would help clean up the mess the immigrants created.

Black women challenged these racist arguments and mounted their own drive for universal female suffrage. They had an additional incentive to press for enfranchisement. As the target of white sexual predators during slavery and its aftermath, some Black women saw the vote as a way to address this problem. "The ballot," Nannie Helen Burroughs, the founder of the NACW remarked, is the Black woman's "weapon of moral defense." Although they did not gain much support from white suffragists, by 1916 Black women worked through the NACW and formed suffrage clubs throughout the nation.

The campaign for women's suffrage in the United States was part of an international movement. Victories in New Zealand (1893), Australia (1902), and Norway (1913) spurred on American suffragists. In the 1910s, radical American activists found inspiration in the militant tactics employed by some in the British suffrage movement. Activists such as Alice Paul conducted wide-ranging demonstrations in Washington, D.C., including chaining themselves to the gates of the White House. Although mainstream suffrage leaders denounced these new tactics, they gained much-needed publicity for the movement, which in turn aided the lobbying efforts of more moderate activists. In 1919, Congress passed the **Nineteenth Amendment**, granting women the vote. The following year, the amendment was ratified by the states.

Nineteenth Amendment
The amendment to the Constitution granting women the right to vote, passed in 1919 and ratified into law in 1920.

- In what ways did the pursuit of suffrage for women fit within the broader ideals of progressivism?

Progressivism and the Fight for Racial Equality

As with suffrage, social justice progressives faced huge barriers in the fight for racial equality. By 1900, white supremacists in the South had disfranchised most Black voters and imposed a rigid system of segregation in education and all aspects of public life, which they enforced with violence. From 1884 to 1900, approximately 2,500 people were lynched, most of them Black Americans.

Antiblack violence also took the form of race riots that erupted in southern cities. Farther north, in Springfield, Illinois, a riot broke out in 1908 when the local sheriff tried to protect two Black prisoners from a would-be lynch mob. This confrontation triggered two days of white violence against Black people, some of whom fought back, leaving twenty-four businesses and forty homes destroyed and seven people (two Black and five white) dead.

As the situation for Black Americans deteriorated, Black leaders responded in several ways. Booker T. Washington promoted an approach that his critics called accommodation but that he defended as practical. Born enslaved and emancipated at age nine, Washington attended Hampton Institute, run by sympathetic white people in his home state of Virginia. Such school officials believed that Black Americans would first have to build up their character and accept the virtues of abstinence, thrift, and industriousness

Tuskegee Institute
An educational institute for southern Blacks founded in 1881 by Booker T. Washington. Following Washington's philosophy, the institute focused on teaching industrious habits and practical job skills.

before seeking a more intellectual education. In 1881, Washington founded **Tuskegee Institute** in Alabama, which he modeled on Hampton. In 1895, he received an enthusiastic reception from white business and civic leaders in Atlanta for his message urging Black people to remain in the South, accept racial segregation, concentrate on moral and economic development, and avoid politics. At the same time, he called on white leaders to protect Black people from the growing violence directed at them.

White leaders in both the South and the North embraced Washington, and he became the most powerful Black man of his generation. Although he discouraged public protests against segregation, he emphasized racial pride and solidarity among Black people. Yet Washington was a complex figure who secretly financed and supported court challenges to electoral disfranchisement and other forms of racial discrimination.

Washington's enormous power did not discourage opposing views among Black people. Ida B. Wells, like Washington, had been born enslaved. In 1878, she took a job in Memphis as a teacher. Six years later, Wells sued the Chesapeake & Ohio Railroad for moving her from the first-class "Ladies Coach" to the segregated smoking car because she was Black. She won her case in the lower court, but her victory was reversed by the Tennessee Supreme Court. Undeterred, she began writing for the newspaper *Free Speech*, and when her articles exposing injustices in the Memphis school system got her fired from teaching, she took up journalism full-time.

Unlike Washington, Wells believed that Black leaders had to speak out vigorously against racial inequality and lynching. On March 9, 1892, three Black men in Memphis were murdered by a white mob. The victims had operated a grocery store that became the target of hostility from white competitors. The Black businessmen fought back and shot three armed attackers in self-defense. In support of their actions, Wells wrote, "When the white man . . . knows he runs as great a risk of biting the dust every time his Afro-American victim does, he will have greater respect for Afro-American life." Subsequently arrested for their armed resistance, the three men were snatched from jail and lynched.

In response to Wells's articles about the Memphis lynching, a white mob burned down her newspaper's building. She fled to Chicago, where she published a report refuting the myth that the rape of white women by Black men was the leading cause of lynching. She concluded that racists used this brand of violence to ensure that Blacks would not challenge white supremacy. Wells waged her campaign throughout the North and in Europe. She also joined the drive for women's suffrage, which she hoped would give Black women a chance to use their votes to help combat racial injustice.

W. E. B. Du Bois also rejected Washington's accommodating stance and urged Black people to demand first-class citizenship. In contrast to Washington's and Wells's families, Du Bois's ancestors were free, and he grew up in Great Barrington, Massachusetts. He earned a doctorate in history from Harvard. Du Bois agreed with Washington about advocating self-help as a means for advancement, but he did not believe this effort would succeed without a proper education and equal voting rights.

In *The Souls of Black Folk* (1903), Du Bois argued that Black Americans needed a liberal-arts education. Du Bois contended that a classical, humanistic education would produce a cadre of leaders, the "Talented Tenth," who would guide Black Americans to the next stage of their development. Rather than forgoing immediate political rights, Black leaders should demand the universal right to vote. Only then, Du Bois contended, would Black people gain equality, self-respect, and dignity as a race.

Du Bois was an intellectual who put his ideas into action. In 1905, he spearheaded the creation of the Niagara Movement, a group that first met on the Canadian side of Niagara Falls. The all-Black organization demanded the vote and equal access to public facilities for Black Americans. By 1909, internal squabbling and a shortage of funds had crippled the group. That same year, however, Du Bois became involved in the creation of an organization that would shape the fight for racial equality throughout the twentieth century: the **National Association for the Advancement of Colored People (NAACP)**. In addition to Du Bois, Ida B. Wells and veterans of the Niagara Movement, and white activists such as Jane Addams joined in forming the organization.

National Association for the Advancement of Colored People (NAACP) An organization founded by W. E. B. Du Bois, Ida B. Wells, Jane Addams, and others in 1909 to fight for racial equality. The NAACP strategy focused on fighting discrimination through the courts, and it became the leading civil rights organization for Black Americans in the twentieth century.

Beginning in 1910, the NAACP initiated court cases challenging racially discriminatory voting practices and other forms of bias in housing and criminal justice. Its first victory came in 1915, when its lawyers convinced the Supreme Court to strike down the grandfather clause that discriminated against Black voters (*Guinn v. United States*).

AP® WORKING with EVIDENCE

Source: Committee on the Negro "Call" for a National Conference, *Founding Document of the National Association for the Advancement of Colored People (NAACP)*, 1909

> "If Mr. Lincoln could revisit this country in the flesh, he would be disheartened and discouraged. He would learn that on January 1st, 1909, Georgia had rounded out a new confederacy by disenfranchising the negro after the manner of all other Southern states. He would learn that the Supreme Court of the United States, supposedly a bulwark of American liberties, had dodged every opportunity to pass squarely upon this disfranchisement of millions, by laws avowedly discriminatory and openly enforced in such manner that the white men may vote and black men be without a vote in their government; he would discover, therefore, that taxation without representation is the lot of millions of wealth-producing American citizens, in whose hands rests the progress and welfare of an entire section of the country. . . . In many States Lincoln would find justice enforced, if at all, by judges elected by one element in a community to pass upon the liberties and lives of another. He would see black men and women, for whose freedom a hundred thousand of soldiers gave their lives, set apart in trains, in which they pay first-class fares for third-class service, in railway stations and in places of entertainment, while State after State declines to do its elementary duty in preparing the negro through education for the best exercise of citizenship."

Questions for Analysis

1. Identify three examples of discrimination against Black people stated in the excerpt.
2. Describe the context for this document.
3. Explain how repeatedly invoking Lincoln was meant to support the argument expressed in the excerpt.

Black Americans also pursued social justice initiatives outside the realm of politics. In the South, they remained committed to securing a high-quality education for their children after white people failed to live up to their responsibilities under *Plessy v. Ferguson* (Module 6.4). Black schools remained inferior to white schools, and Black Americans did not receive a fair return from their tax dollars. In fact, a large portion of their payments helped subsidize white schools.

Hanna Holborn Gray Special Collections Research Center, University of Chicago Library

Ida B. Wells Born into slavery in Mississippi, Ida B. Wells rose to become a teacher, writer, editor, and civil rights activist. As a muckraker, she wrote about and campaigned against lynching. This photograph from 1910 shows Wells around the age of forty-eight, the same year she joined in the founding of the NAACP. Three years later, Wells founded the Alpha Suffrage Club, a Black female suffrage organization in Chicago, Illinois.

How do Wells's life experiences illustrate both the goals and challenges faced by progressive reformers?

Black women played a prominent role in promoting education. For example, in 1901, Charlotte Hawkins Brown set up the Palmer Memorial Institute outside Greensboro, North Carolina. In these endeavors, Black educators received financial assistance from northern philanthropists, white club women interested in moral uplift of the Black race, and religious missionaries seeking converts in the South. By 1910, more than 1.5 million Black children went to school in the South, most of them taught by the region's 28,560 Black teachers. Thirty-four Black colleges existed, and more than 2,000 Black people held college degrees.

Like Black Americans, American Indians struggled against injustice. American Indian muckrakers criticized government policies and anti-American Indian attitudes, but the magazines that exposed the evils of industrialization often ignored their plight. Instead, American Indian reformers turned to the *Quarterly Journal*, published by the Society of American Indians, to air their grievances.

Carlos Montezuma was the most outspoken critic of U.S. government policy toward American Indians. A Yavapai tribe member from Arizona, he called for the abolition of the Indian Office as an impediment to the welfare of American Indians. Arthur C. Parker, an anthropologist from the Seneca tribe of New York, challenged the notion that American Indians suffered mainly because of their own backwardness. In scathing articles, he condemned the United States for robbing American Indians of their cultural and economic independence. One American Indian who wrote for magazines with mainly white audiences, such as *Harper's Weekly*, was Zitkala-Ša, a Dakota woman whose essays exposed the practices of boarding schools designed to forcibly assimilate American Indians. Non–American Indian anthropologists such as Franz Boas and Ruth Benedict added their voices to those of American Indian journalists in attacking traditional views of them as inferior and uncivilized.

American Indian reformers, however, did not succeed in persuading state and federal governments to pass legislation to address their concerns. Nevertheless, activists did succeed in filing thirty-one complaints with the U.S. Court of Claims for monetary compensation for federal payments to which they were entitled but had not received. Like other exploited groups during the Progressive Era, American Indians created organizations, such as the Black Hills Treaty Council and others, to pressure the federal government and to publicize their demands.

REVIEW

- How did Black Americans and American Indians work to bring about progressive reforms?
- How successful were these efforts?

Morality, Prohibition, and Social Control

In many cases, progressive initiatives crossed over from social reform to social control. Convinced that the "immorality" of the poor was the cause of social disorder, some reformers sought to impose middle-class standards of behavior and morality on the lower classes. As with other forms of progressivism, reformers interested in social control were driven by a variety of motives. However, regardless of their motives, efforts to prohibit alcohol, fight prostitution, and combat juvenile delinquency often involved attempts to repress and control the poor. So, too, did protective health measures such as birth control. Some social control progressives went even further in their efforts to impose their own morality, calling for restrictions on immigration, which they saw as a cultural threat.

Prohibition campaigns began long before the Civil War but scored few important successes until 1881, when Kansas became the first state whose constitution banned the consumption of alcohol. Women spearheaded the prohibition movement by forming the **Woman's Christian Temperance Union (WCTU)** in 1874 under the leadership of Frances Willard. Willard built the temperance movement around the need to protect the home. Husbands and fathers who drank excessively were also likely to abuse their wives and children and to drain the family finances. Prohibiting the consumption of alcohol would therefore help combat these evils. At the same time, the quality of family and public life would be improved if women received the right to vote and young children completed their education without having to go to work.

Woman's Christian Temperance Union (WCTU)
An organization founded in 1874 to campaign for a ban on the sale and consumption of alcohol. In the late nineteenth century, under Frances Willard's leadership, the WCTU supported a broad social reform agenda.

After Willard's death in 1898, the Anti-Saloon League (ASL) became the dominant force in the prohibition movement. Established in 1893, the league grew out of evangelical Protestantism. The group had particular appeal in the rural South, where Protestant fundamentalism flourished. Between 1906 and 1917, twenty-one states, mostly in the South and West, banned liquor sales.

Concern over alcohol was not confined to the South. Middle-class progressives in northern cities, who identified much of urban decay with the influx of immigrants, saw the tavern as a breeding ground for immoral activities. In 1913, the ASL persuaded Congress to pass the Webb-Kenyon Act, which banned the transportation of alcoholic beverages into dry states. After the United States entered World War I in 1917, reformers argued that prohibition would help win the war by conserving grain used to make liquor and by saving soldiers from intoxication. The **Eighteenth Amendment**, ratified in 1919, made prohibition the law of the land until it was repealed in 1933.

Eighteenth Amendment
The 1918 amendment to the Constitution banning the production and sale of alcoholic beverages. It was repealed in 1933 by the Twenty-First Amendment.

Alarmed by the increased number of brothels and "streetwalkers" that accompanied the growth of cities, progressives sought to eliminate prostitution. Some framed the issue in terms of public health, linking prostitution to the spread of sexually transmitted diseases. Others presented it as an effort to protect female virtue. Such reformers were generally interested only in white women, who, unlike Black and Asian women in similar circumstances, were considered sexual innocents coerced into prostitution. Still others claimed that prostitutes themselves were to blame, seeing women who sold their sexual favors as inherently immoral.

Mann Act
An act passed in 1910 that banned the transportation of women across state lines for immoral purposes. In practice, this legislation was used to enforce codes of racial segregation and standards of moral behavior that enforced traditional social roles for women.

Reformers offered two different approaches to the problem. Taking the moralistic solution, Representative James R. Mann of Chicago steered through Congress the White-Slave Traffic Act (known as the **Mann Act**) in 1910, banning the transportation of women across state lines for immoral purposes. By contrast, the American Social Hygiene Association, founded in 1914, subsidized scientific research into sexually transmitted diseases, funded investigations to gather more information, and drafted

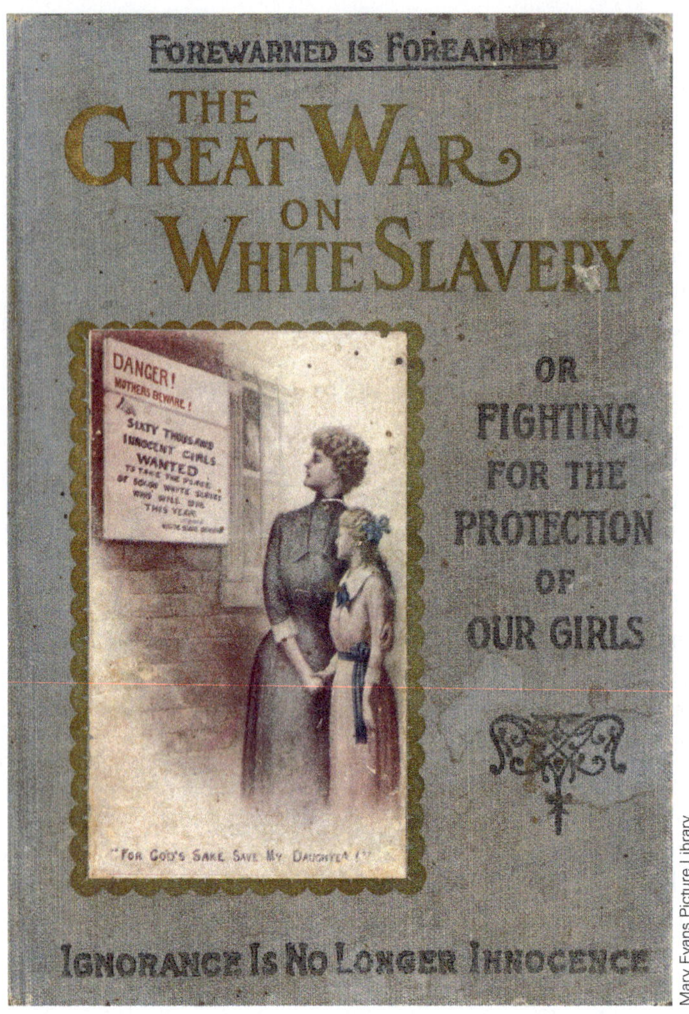

Mary Evans Picture Library

The Crusade against White Slavery Published by Clifford B. Roe and B. S. Steadwell in 1911, *The Great War on White Slavery* campaigned against prostitution and the criminals who lured impoverished young women into what they called "the human stockyards . . . for girls." As an assistant state's attorney in Chicago, Roe prosecuted more than 150 cases against sex traffickers.

How does this cover illustrate the kind of moral reform that progressives attempted to bring about?

model ordinances for cities to curb prostitution. By 1915, every state had laws making sexual solicitation a crime.

Prosecutors used the Mann Act to enforce codes of traditional racial as well as sexual behavior by using the act to criminalize interracial relationships and consensual sexual relationships outside of marriage. In 1910, Jack Johnson, a Black boxer, defeated the white heavyweight champion, Jim Jeffries. His victory upset some white men who were obsessed with preserving their racial dominance and masculine integrity. Johnson's relationships with white women further angered some white people, who eventually succeeded in bringing down the outspoken Black champion by prosecuting him on morals charges in 1913.

Moral crusaders also sought to eliminate the use and sale of narcotics. By 1900, approximately 250,000 people in the United States were addicted to opium, morphine, or cocaine—far fewer, however, than those who abused alcohol. On the West Coast, immigration opponents associated opium smoking with the Chinese and tried to eliminate its use as part of their wider anti-Asian campaign. In alliance with the American Medical Association, reformers convinced Congress to pass the Harrison Narcotics Control Act of 1914, prohibiting the sale of narcotics except by a doctor's prescription.

Progressives also tried to combat juvenile delinquency. Led by women, these reformers lobbied for a juvenile court system that focused on rehabilitation rather than punishment for youthful offenders. Despite progressives' sincerity, many youthful offenders doubted their intentions. Young women often appeared before a magistrate because their parents did not like their choice of friends, their sexual conduct, or their frequenting of dance halls and saloons. These activities, which violated middle-class social norms, had now become criminalized, even if in a less coercive and punitive manner than that applied to adults.

The health of women and families occupied reformers such as Margaret Sanger, the leading advocate of birth control. Working as a nurse mainly among poor immigrant women in New York City, she witnessed the damage that unrestrained childbearing produced on women's health. According to Sanger, contraception—the use of artificial means to prevent pregnancy—would save the lives of mothers by preventing unwanted childbearing and avoiding unsafe and illegal abortions, and would keep families from having large numbers of children they could not afford. Moreover, Sanger believed that if women were freed from the anxieties of becoming pregnant, they would experience more sexual enjoyment and make better companions for their spouses. Her arguments for birth control also had a connection to eugenics. Contraception, she believed, would raise the quality of the white race by reducing the chances of immigrant and minority women reproducing so-called unfit children.

Sanger and her supporters encountered enormous opposition. It was illegal to sell contraceptive devices or furnish information about them. Nevertheless, Sanger opened up the nation's first birth control clinic in an immigrant section of Brooklyn in 1916. The police quickly closed down the facility and arrested Sanger. Undeterred, she continued to agitate for her cause and push to change attitudes toward women's health and reproductive rights.

- In what ways did progressives connect social and economic reform to moral reform?

AP® Skills Workshop: Writing Historically

Additional Practice in Responding to a Short-Answer Question with Secondary Sources

"Southern progressivism was essentially urban and middle class in nature, and the typical leader was a city professional man or businessman, rather than a farmer. Under the growing pressure of monopoly, the small businessmen and urban middle-class overcame their fear of reform and joined hands with the discontented farmers. They envisaged as a common enemy the plutocracy [wealthy, ruling class] of the Northeast, together with its agents, banks, insurance companies, public utilities, oil companies, pipelines, and railroads. . . .

The direct primary system of nominating party candidates was not invented in Wisconsin in 1903 . . . for by that time a majority of the Southern states were already practicing the system. . . . The joker [hitch] in the Southern primaries was the fact that they were *white* primaries. Southern progressivism generally was progressivism for white men only. . . . The paradoxical combination of white supremacy and progressivism was not new to the region, but it never ceased to be a cause of puzzlement and confusion above the Potomac—and not a little, below. The paradox nevertheless had its counterpart in the North, where it was not uncommon for one man to champion both progressivism and imperialism. In such instances it was a matter of white supremacy over browns instead of blacks."

C. Vann Woodward, *Origins of the New South, 1877–1913*, 1971

"From the debris of disfranchisement, black women discovered fresh approaches to serving their communities and crafted new tactics to dull the blade of white supremacy. . . . After disfranchisement . . . the political culture black women had created through thirty years of work in temperance organization, Republican Party aid societies, and churches furnished both an ideological basis and an organization structure from which black women could take on those tasks. After black men's banishment from politics, North Carolina's black women added a network of women's groups that

(continued)

crossed denominational [religious]—and later party—lines and took a multi-issue approach to civic action. In a nonpolitical guise, black women became the black community's diplomats to the white community. Black women might not be voters, but they could be clients, and in that role they could become spokespeople for and motivators of black citizens. They could claim a distinctly female moral authority and pretend to eschew [avoid] any political motivation. The deep camouflage of their leadership style—their womanhood—helped them remain invisible as they worked toward political ends. At the same time, they could deliver not votes but hands and hearts through community organization: willing workers in city clean up campaigns, orderly children who complied with state educational requirements and hookworm-infested people eager for treatment at public health fairs. . . .

As much as southern whites plotted to reserve progressivism for themselves, and as much as they schemed to alter the ill-fitting northern version accordingly, they failed. African American women embraced southern white progressivism, reshaped it, and sent back a new model that included black power brokers and grass roots activists. . . . Southern black women initiated every progressive reform that southern white women initiated, a feat they accomplished without financial resources, without the civic protection of their husbands, and without publicity."

Glenda Elizabeth Gilmore, *Gender and Jim Crow: Women and the Politics of White Supremacy in North Carolina: 1896–1920*, 1996

Using the excerpts, answer **A**, **B**, and **C**.

(A) Briefly describe ONE major difference between Woodward's and Gilmore's historical interpretations.

(B) Briefly explain ONE specific piece of historical information not mentioned in the excerpts that could be used to support Woodward's argument.

(C) Briefly explain ONE specific piece of historical information not mentioned in the excerpts that could be used to support Gilmore's argument.

The Progressives: Political Reform

MODULE

7.4b

FOCUS

While reading this module, compare the goal, strategies, and successes of various progressive reform efforts. Also consider the ways progressivism represented a continuation of prior reform efforts.

In an effort to diminish the power of corrupt urban political machines and unregulated corporations, progressives pushed for good-government reforms, promoting initiatives they claimed would produce greater efficiency, openness, and accountability in government. Many of the progressives' proposed reforms appeared, at least on the surface, to give citizens more direct say in their government. Yet a closer look reveals a more complicated picture.

Progressives advocated governmental intervention, yet they sought change without radically altering capitalism or the political system. Not everyone endorsed progressives' goals, however. Conservatives continued to support individualism and the free market as legitimate means to political and economic power, and radicals pressed for the socialist reorganization of the economy and the democratization of politics. Nevertheless, the public showed widespread support for progressivism by electing the reformers Theodore Roosevelt and Woodrow Wilson as president.

New Immigrants and New Challenges

The late-nineteenth-century wave of immigration had already changed the composition of the American population by the turn of the twentieth century, and the inflow continued unabated until the start of World War I in 1914. From 1900 to 1914, an average of almost 900,000 immigrants arrived every year in the United States, and almost 70 percent of those newcomers hailed from eastern, southern, and central Europe. As a result, foreigners and their children made up more than three-quarters

Year	Arrivals	Departures	Percentage of Departures to Arrivals
1900–1904	3,575,000	1,454,000	41%
1905–1909	5,533,000	2,653,000	48%
1910–1914	6,075,000	2,759,000	45%

Percentage of Immigrant Departures versus Arrivals, 1900–1914 The late nineteenth and early twentieth centuries saw one of the largest influxes of immigration in U.S. history. However, not all immigrants remained in the United States permanently.

What factors pulled immigrants to the United States during these years, and what factors might have compelled them to leave?

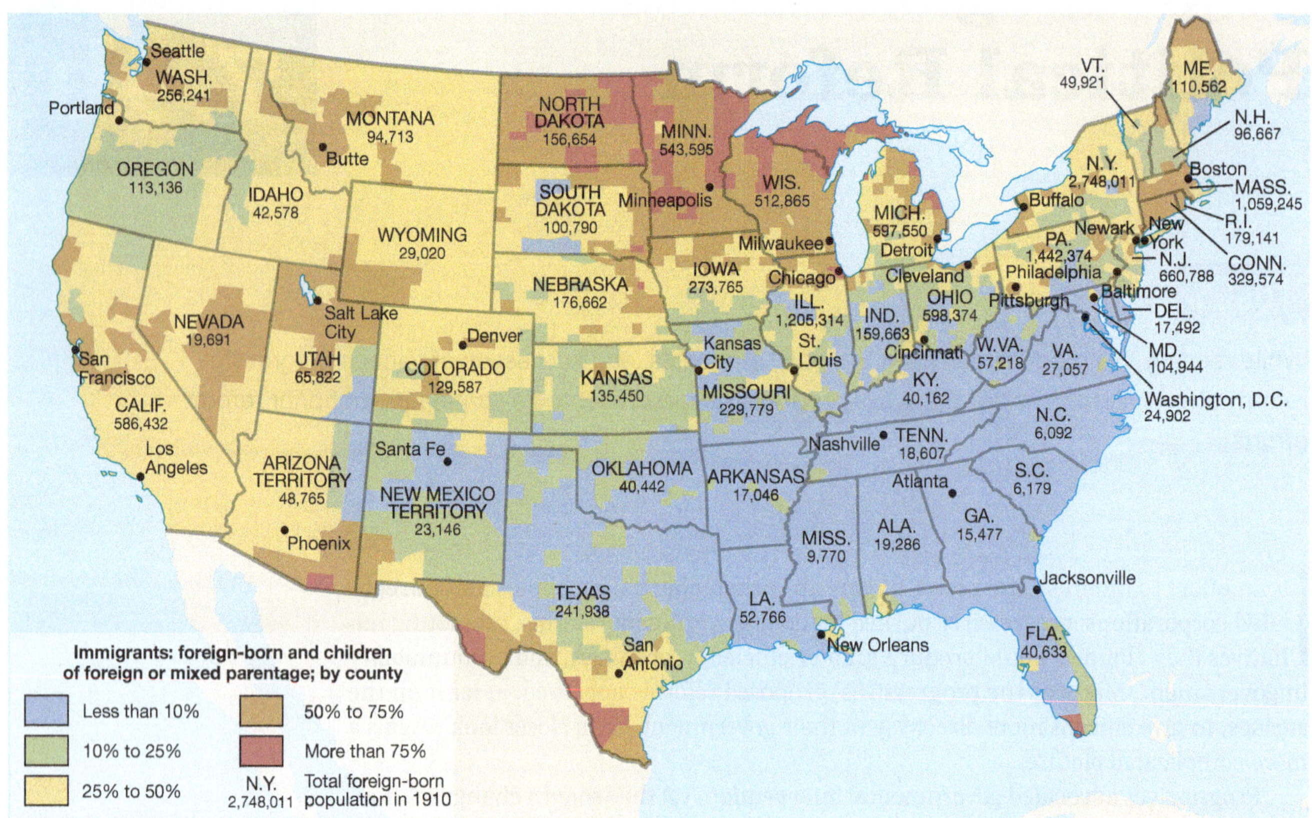

MAP 7.4 Immigrants in the United States, 1910 By 1910, many immigrants had come to the United States mainly from Europe, East Asia, Mexico, and Latin America. They tended to settle near their ports of entry in cities, where they usually joined people from their own country who had settled previously. The pattern of settlement varied widely among regions of the country, as the map shows.

What common settlement patterns do you notice here? What explains these settlement patterns?

of the population of New York City, Detroit, Chicago, Milwaukee, Cleveland, Minneapolis, and San Francisco.

Immigration, although not as extensive in the South as in the North, also altered the character of southern cities. About one-third of the population of Tampa, Miami, and New Orleans consisted of foreigners and their immediate descendants. The border states of Texas, New Mexico, and Arizona, as well as southern California, contained similar percentages of immigrants, most of whom came from Mexico.

On the West Coast, the government established an immigration station at Angel Island in San Francisco Bay in 1910. In contrast to Ellis Island, Angel Island served mainly as a detention center where Chinese immigrants were imprisoned for months, even years, while they sought to prove their eligibility to enter the United States. Nevertheless, over the next thirty years, some 50,000 Chinese immigrants successfully passed through Angel Island.

Some 260,000 Japanese immigrants also arrived in the United States during the first two decades of the twentieth century. Many of them settled on the West Coast, where they worked as farm laborers and gardeners and established businesses catering to a Japanese clientele. Although Japan was a major world power in the late nineteenth century and earned American respect by defeating Russia in the Russo-Japanese War of 1904–1905, Japanese immigrants were still considered part

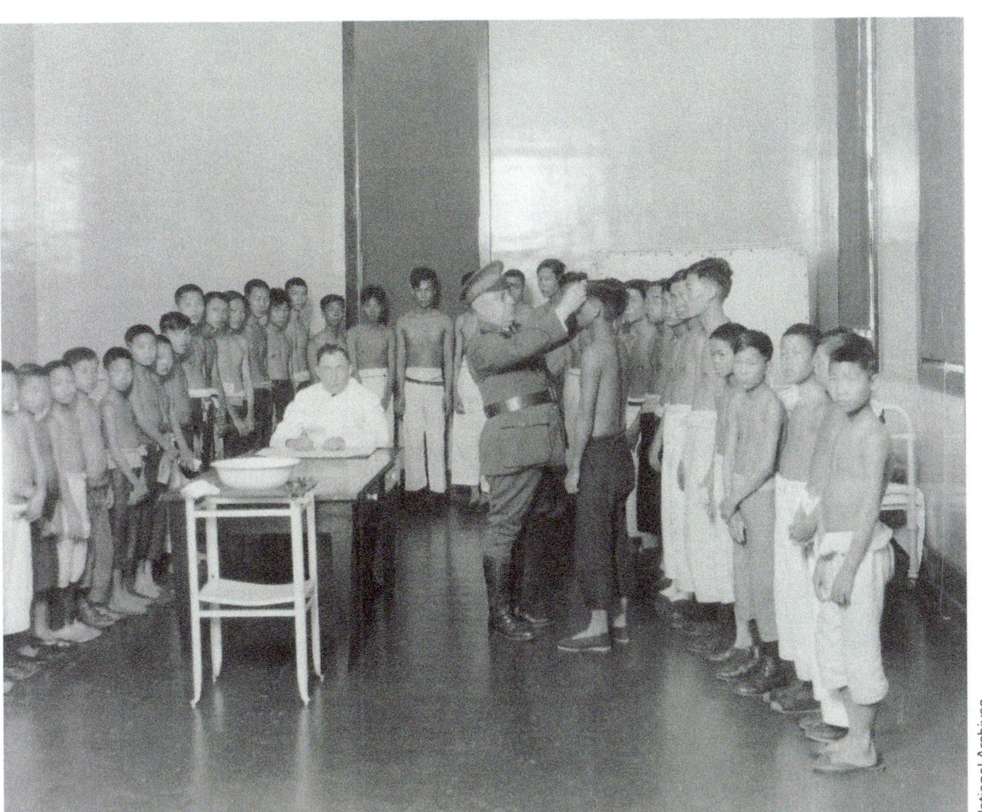

National Archives

Angel Island Physical Exam Beginning in 1910, tens of thousands of Chinese who tried to immigrate to the United States were processed by authorities at Angel Island in San Francisco Bay. Thousands were detained for long periods until they could prove their identities and demonstrate they had relatives in the country. One of the hurdles they had to overcome was the medical examination. In this photo taken in 1923, a group of Chinese boys waits to see the doctor while a military official inspects one of them.

How did the treatment of immigrants at Angel Island reflect popular attitudes toward Chinese immigrants?

of an inferior "yellow race" and encountered discrimination in their West Coast settlements.

Immigrants who left piecework in apartments and went to work in sweatshop factories during the early twentieth century continued to face exploitation regardless of the city they called home. For example, the Jewish and Italian clothing workers who toiled in the Triangle Shirtwaist Company, located in the Greenwich Village neighborhood of New York City, worked long hours for little pay.

In 1911, a fire broke out on the eighth story of the factory and quickly spread to the ninth and tenth floors. The fire engines' ladders could not reach that high, and one of the exits on the ninth floor was locked to keep workers from stealing material. More than 140 people died in the **Triangle Shirtwaist fire**—some by jumping out the windows, but most by getting trapped behind the closed exit door.

Triangle Shirtwaist fire
An infamous industrial fire at the Triangle Shirtwaist factory in New York City in 1911. Inadequate fire safety provisions led to the deaths of 146 workers, mostly young women and girls, and spurred efforts to regulate occupational safety.

Following public outrage over the fire and through the efforts of reformers, New York City established a Bureau of Fire Protection, required safety devices in buildings, and prohibited smoking in factories. Furthermore, this tragedy spearheaded legislative efforts to improve working conditions in general, protect women workers, and abolish child labor.

REVIEW

- What challenges did immigrants face when coming to the United States during this period?

The Triangle Shirtwaist Company Fire, 1911 On March 25, 1911, fire broke out in the Triangle Shirtwaist factory in lower Manhattan. Most of the company's six hundred garment workers were immigrant women. The building had inadequate fire escapes and blocked exits, which resulted in the high death toll of 146 workers. In this photograph, people are viewing the bodies of victims to identify them. This catastrophe aroused many New Yorkers to rally around factory reforms. Within a year, New York began factory inspections and passed more than two dozen new labor laws.

What factors surrounding this particular industrial disaster led to reform?

Municipal and State Reform

The expanding economy and rising immigration placed American cities at the forefront of government reform during the Progressive Era. Municipal governments had failed to keep up with the problems ushered in by accelerated urban growth, and political machines filled these needs by distributing city services—largely to immigrants—within a system bloated by corruption and graft (Module 6.13). Upper-middle-class businessmen and professionals fed up with wasteful and inefficient political machines sought to institute new forms of government that functioned more rationally and cost less.

The adoption of the commission form of government was a hallmark of urban reform. Commission governments replaced the old form of a mayor and city council with elected commissioners, each of whom ran a municipal department as if it were a business. By 1917, commissions had spread to more than four hundred cities throughout the country. Governments with a mayor and city council also began to appoint city managers, who functioned as chief operating officers, to foster businesslike efficiency. The head of the National Cash Register Company, who helped bring the city manager system to Dayton, Ohio, praised it for resembling "a great business enterprise whose stockholders are the people."

Reformers also adopted direct primaries so that voters could select candidates rather than allowing a handful of machine politicians to decide elections behind closed doors. To reverse the influence of immigrants clustered in ghettos who supported their own ethnic candidates and to topple the machines that catered to them, municipal reformers replaced district elections with citywide "at-large" elections. Ethnic enclaves lost not only their ward representatives but also a good deal of their influence because citywide election campaigns were expensive, shifting power to those who could afford to run. Working- and lower-class residents of cities still retained the right to vote, but their power was diluted.

In the South, where fewer immigrants lived, white supremacists employed these tactics to further efforts taken in the late nineteenth century to disenfranchise Black Americans. Southern lawmakers diminished whatever Black political power remained by adopting at-large elections and commission governments. Throughout the South, direct primary contests (or "white primaries") were closed to Black people.

While urban progressivism limited the impact of immigrant and Black voting, it did produce a number of mayors who carried out genuine reforms. Elected in 1901, Cleveland mayor Tom L. Johnson implemented measures to assess taxes more equitably, regulate utility companies, and reduce public transportation fares. Samuel "Golden Rule" Jones, who served as mayor of Toledo, Ohio, from 1897 to 1903, supported social justice measures by establishing an eight-hour workday for municipal employees, granting them paid vacations, and prohibiting child labor. Under Mayor Hazen Pingree, who served from 1889 to 1896, Detroit built additional schools and recreational facilities and put the unemployed to work on municipal projects during economic hard times.

Progressives also took action at the state level. Robert M. La Follette, Republican governor of Wisconsin from 1901 to 1906, led the way by initiating a range of reforms to improve the performance of state government and increase its accountability to constituents. During his tenure as governor, La Follette dismantled the statewide political machine by instituting direct party primaries, an expanded civil service, a law forbidding direct corporate contributions to political parties, a strengthened railroad regulatory commission, and a graduated income tax. In 1906, La Follette entered the U.S. Senate, where he battled for further reform.

Other states picked up and expanded La Follette's progressive agenda. In 1913, three-quarters of the states ratified the Seventeenth Amendment, which mandated that U.S. senators would be elected by popular vote instead of being chosen by state legislatures. This constituted another effort to remove the influence of money from politics.

- How did municipal reform during the Progressive Era shape the lives of city dwellers across America?

Conservation and Preservation of the Environment

The fondness for efficiency that characterized good-government progressivism also shaped progressive efforts to conserve natural resources. As chief forester in the Department of Agriculture, Gifford Pinchot emphasized the efficient use of resources and sought ways to reconcile the public interest with private profit motives. His **conservationism** often won support from large lumber companies, which had a long-term interest in sustainable forests. Large companies also saw conservationism as a way to drive their smaller competitors out of business, because large companies could better afford the additional costs associated with managing healthy forests.

conservationism A Progressive Era political and social movement whose supporters worked to protect the environment by balancing demand for natural resources against calls to preserve the nation's wildlife and natural lands. Conservationists believed in intelligent management and sustainable use of natural resources, while preservationists sought to preserve the beauty of the environment above all else.

This gospel of efficiency faced a stiff test in California. On April 18, 1906, a devastating earthquake in San Francisco set the city ablaze, causing about 1,500 deaths. San Francisco officials, coping with water and power shortages, asked the federal government to approve construction of a hydroelectric dam and reservoir

Theodore Roosevelt and John Muir, 1903 This photograph pictures President Theodore Roosevelt and his associates standing in front of the "Grizzly Giant," a towering sequoia tree more than two hundred feet in height in Yosemite National Park, California. Roosevelt is in the center, and standing to his left is bearded John Muir, the founder of the Sierra Club, who persuaded Roosevelt to remove Yosemite Valley and the Mariposa Grove of Giant Sequoias from state control and add them to the Yosemite National Park, which had been established in 1890.

Why did conservation grow as a movement during the late 1800s and early 1900s in the United States?

in **Hetch Hetchy Valley**, located in Yosemite National Park. Pinchot supported the project because he saw it as the best use of the land for the greatest number of people. The famed naturalist John Muir strongly disagreed. He campaigned to save Hetch Hetchy from "ravaging commercialism" and warned against choosing economic gains over spiritual values. After a bruising seven-year battle, Pinchot (by this time a private citizen) triumphed. Still, this incursion into a national park helped spur the development of environmentalism as a political movement.

Besides the clash with preservationists, the Hetch Hetchy Dam project reveals another aspect of the progressive conservation movement. Like progressives who focused on urban and political issues, progressive conservationists had a racial bias. Conservationists such as Pinchot may have seen themselves as acting in the public interest, but their definition of "the public" did not include all Americans. In planning for the Hetch Hetchy Dam, progressives did not consult with the Mono Lake Paiutes who lived in Yosemite and who were most directly affected by the project. Conservation was meant to serve the interests of white San Franciscans and not those of the American Indian inhabitants of Yosemite.

MAP 7.5 National Parks and Forests In 1872, the federal government created the first national park at Yellowstone, which spread over portions of the future states of Wyoming, Montana, and Idaho. President Theodore Roosevelt designated six sites — Crater Lake, Wind Cave, Petrified Forest, Lassen Volcanic, Mesa Verde, and Zion — to the park system, proposing the addition of 125 million acres of land to the national park and forest system. The expansion of protected lands during the Progressive Era marks one of the most enduring reforms of the movement.

How does this map illustrate the role of Roosevelt and other Progressive Era reformers in expanding the system of national parks and forests?

REVIEW

- In what ways did conservation during the Progressive Era benefit some groups at the expense of others?

Theodore Roosevelt and the Square Deal

The problems created by industrialization and the growth of big business were national in scope. Recognizing this fact, prominent progressives sought national leadership positions, and two of them, Presidents Theodore Roosevelt and Woodrow Wilson, instituted progressive reforms during their terms. In the process, they reinvigorated the presidency, an office that had declined in power and importance during the late nineteenth century.

Born into a moderately wealthy New York family, Theodore Roosevelt graduated from Harvard in 1880 and entered government service. In 1898, Roosevelt formed a regiment of soldiers — the Rough Riders — and fought in Cuba against Spanish forces during the Spanish-American War. That same year he was elected governor of New York.

Elected as McKinley's vice president in 1900, Roosevelt became president after McKinley's assassination a year later. Roosevelt brought an activist style and youthful vigor to the presidency, taking the oath of office at forty-two years old, the youngest president thus far in American history. He considered his office a **bully pulpit** — a

bully pulpit
The term used by Theodore Roosevelt to describe the office of the presidency. Roosevelt believed that the president should use his office as a platform to promote his programs and rally public opinion.

platform from which to promote his programs and from which he could rally public opinion. To this end, he used his energetic and extroverted personality to establish an unprecedented rapport with the American people.

For all his exuberance and energy, President Roosevelt pursued a moderate domestic course. Like his progressive colleagues, he opposed ideological extremism in any form. Roosevelt believed that as head of state, he could serve as an impartial referee among competing factions and determine what was best for the public. To him, reform was the best defense against revolution.

Square Deal
Theodore Roosevelt's plan to provide economic and political stability to the nation by guaranteeing the rights of everyday workers and protecting business interests.

As president, Roosevelt sought to provide economic and political stability, what he referred to as a **Square Deal**. The coal strike that began in Pennsylvania in 1902 gave Roosevelt an opportunity to play the role of impartial mediator and defender of the public good. Miners had gone on strike for an eight-hour workday, a pay increase of 20 percent, and recognition of their union. Union representatives agreed to have the president create a panel to settle the dispute, but George F. Baer, president of the Reading Railroad, which also owned the mines, pledged that he would never agree to the workers' demands. Disturbed by what he considered the owners' "arrogant stupidity," Roosevelt threatened to dispatch federal troops to take over and run the mines. When the owners backed down, the president established a commission that hammered out a compromise, which raised wages and reduced working hours but did not recognize the union.

At the same time, Roosevelt tackled the problems caused by giant business trusts. In February 1902, the president instructed the Justice Department to sue the Northern Securities Company under the Sherman Antitrust Act (see Module 6.6). Financed by J. P. Morgan, Northern Securities held monopoly control of the northernmost transcontinental railway lines. In 1904, the Supreme Court ordered that the Northern Securities Company be dissolved, ruling that the firm had restricted competition. With this victory, Roosevelt affirmed the federal government's power to regulate business trusts that violated the public interest. Overall, Roosevelt initiated twenty-five suits under the Sherman Antitrust Act, including litigation against the tobacco and beef trusts and the Standard Oil Company, actions that earned him the title of "trustbuster."

Elkins Act
An act outlawing railroad rebates passed in 1903. The act was designed to protect smaller businesses and shippers who were paying higher rates than large, favored customers, such as Standard Oil.

While Roosevelt believed that trusts were a natural outcome in a capitalist economy, he distinguished between "good" trusts, which he argued acted responsibly, and "bad" trusts, which abused their power. Railroads had earned an especially bad reputation with the public for charging higher rates to small shippers and those in remote regions while granting rebates to favored customers, such as Standard Oil. In 1903, Roosevelt helped persuade Congress to pass the **Elkins Act**, which outlawed railroad rebates. Three years later, the president increased the power of the Interstate Commerce Commission to set maximum railroad freight rates. Also in 1903, Roosevelt secured passage of legislation that established the **Department of Commerce and Labor**. Within this cabinet agency, the Bureau of Corporations gathered information about large companies in an effort to promote fair business practices.

Soaring in popularity, Roosevelt easily won reelection in 1904. During the next four years, the president applied antitrust laws even more vigorously than before. He steered through Congress various reforms concerning the railroads, such as the Hepburn Act (1906), which standardized shipping rates.

The Jungle
A novel by muckraker Upton Sinclair published in 1906 that portrayed the poor working and living conditions in the Chicago meatpacking district, as well as the unsanitary practices in the unregulated meat production industry, leading to public demand for government regulation of food safety.

Roosevelt took a strong stand for conservation of public lands, charting a middle course between preservationists and conservationists. He reserved 150 million acres of timberland as part of the national forests, but he authorized the expenditure of more than $80 million in federal funds to construct dams, reservoirs, and canals largely in the West.

Not all reform came from Roosevelt's initiative. Congress passed two notable consumer laws in 1906 that reflected the many, sometimes contradictory, forces that shaped progressivism. That year, Upton Sinclair published ***The Jungle***, a muckraking novel that portrayed the impoverished lives of immigrant workers in Packingtown (Chicago) and

Library of Congress, LC-USZ62-50217

Making Link Sausages, Swift & Co. Packing House, Chicago Upton Sinclair's 1906 novel *The Jungle* exposed unsanitary conditions in the meatpacking industry and led to passage of the Meat Inspection Act. In this photo taken around 1905, workers at the Swift company process sausages as they roll off machines at ten feet per second.

What aspects of this image reflect the issues highlighted in *The Jungle* and addressed by the Meat Inspection Act?

the deplorable working conditions they endured. Outraged readers responded to the vivid description of the shoddy and filthy ways the meatpacking industry slaughtered animals and prepared beef for sale.

Yet the largest and most efficient meatpacking firms had financial reasons to support reform as well. They were losing money because European importers refused to purchase tainted meat, which was a widespread and dangerous problem. Congress responded by passing the **Meat Inspection Act**, which benefited consumers and provided a way for large corporations to eliminate competition from smaller, marginal firms that could not afford to raise standards to meet the new federal meat-processing requirements.

AP® WORKING with EVIDENCE

Source: Upton Sinclair, *The Jungle*, 1906

"A full hour before the party reached the city they had begun to note the perplexing changes in the atmosphere. It grew darker all the time, and upon the earth the grass seemed to grow less green. Every minute, as the train sped on, the colors of things became dingier; the fields were grown parched and yellow, the landscape hideous and bare. And along with the thickening smoke they began to notice another circumstance, a strange, pungent odor. . . . The new emigrants were still tasting it, lost in wonder, when suddenly the car came to a halt, and the door was flung open, and a voice shouted — 'Stockyards!' . . .

[T]hey were left standing upon the corner, staring; down a side street there were two rows of brick houses, and between them a vista: half a dozen chimneys, tall as the tallest of buildings, touching the very sky—and leaping from them half a dozen columns of smoke, thick, oily, and black as night. . . . It was inexhaustible; one stared, waiting to see it stop, but still the great streams rolled out. They spread in vast clouds overhead, writhing, curling; then, uniting in one giant river, they streamed away down the sky, stretching a black pall as far as the eye could reach.

Then the party became aware of another strange thing. This, too, like the odor, was a thing elemental; it was a sound, a sound made up of ten thousand little sounds. You scarcely noticed it at first—it sunk into your consciousness, a vague disturbance, a trouble. It was like the murmuring of the bees in the spring, the whisperings of the forest; it suggested endless activity, the rumblings of a world in motion. It was only by an effort that one could realize that it was made by animals, that it was the distant lowing of ten thousand cattle, the distant grunting of ten thousand swine."

Questions for Analysis

1. Identify the reasons for the smoke and sounds that Sinclair describes.
2. Describe the effect of this factory on the environment, as portrayed by Sinclair.
3. Explain Sinclair's perspective on these effects.

Questions for Comparison

Lincoln Steffens, *The Shame of the Cities*, 1904 (Module 7.4a)

1. Explain how both Sinclair's and Steffens's accounts reflect progressive ideals.
2. Evaluate the extent of similarity between Sinclair's portrayal of the stockyards and Steffens's description of corrupt politics.

Pure Food and Drug Act
A law passed in 1906 to prevent the manufacturing, sale, and transportation of harmful "foods, drugs, medicines, and liquors."

In 1906, Congress also passed the **Pure Food and Drug Act**, which prohibited the sale of adulterated and fraudulently labeled food and drugs. The push for this law came from consumer groups, medical professionals, and government scientists. Dr. Harvey Wiley, a chemist in the Department of Agriculture, drove efforts for reform from within the government. He considered it part of his professional duty to eliminate harmful products.

Roosevelt initially gave Black people reason to believe that they, too, would get a square deal. In October 1901, at the outset of his first term, Roosevelt invited Booker T. Washington to a dinner at the White House, outraging white supremacists in the South. Although Roosevelt dismissed this criticism, he never invited another Black guest. Also in his first term, Roosevelt supported the appointment of a few Black Republicans to federal posts in the South.

Nevertheless, Roosevelt lacked a full commitment to Black equality and espoused the racist ideas of eugenics that were then in fashion. He deplored the declining birthrate of native-born white Americans compared with that of eastern and southern European newcomers and Black Americans, whom he considered inferior stock. He argued that unless Anglo-Saxon women produced more children, white people would end up committing "race suicide." "If the women flinch from breeding," Roosevelt worried, "the . . . death of the race takes place even quicker."

Once he won reelection in 1904, Roosevelt had less political incentive to defy the white South. He stopped cooperating with southern Black officeholders and maneuvered to build the Republican Party in the region with all-white support. One example illustrating his change in approach involved an incident that occurred in Brownsville, Texas, in 1906. White residents of the town charged that Black soldiers stationed at Fort Brown shot and killed one man and wounded another. Roosevelt ordered that unless the alleged perpetrators stepped forward, the entire regiment would receive dishonorable discharges without a court-martial. Roosevelt never doubted the guilt of the Black soldiers, and when no one admitted responsibility, he summarily dismissed 167 men from the military.

- What progressive reforms did Roosevelt undertake during his presidency?
- Who benefited most from these reforms?

Taft's Limited Progressivism

When Roosevelt decided not to seek another term as president in 1908, choosing instead to back William Howard Taft as his successor, he thought he was leaving his reform legacy in capable hands. A Roosevelt loyalist, Taft easily defeated the Democratic candidate, William Jennings Bryan, who was running for the presidency for the third and final time.

Taft's presidency did not proceed as Roosevelt and his progressive followers had hoped. Taft did not have the charisma or energy of his predecessor and appeared to move in slow motion compared with Roosevelt. Taft proved a weak leader and frequently took stands opposite those of progressives. After convening a special session of Congress in March 1909 to support lower tariffs, the president retreated in the face of conservative Republican opposition in the Senate. That year, when lawmakers passed the **Payne-Aldrich tariff**, which raised duties on imports, Taft signed it into law, thereby alienating key progressive legislators.

The situation deteriorated even further in the field of conservation. When Pinchot criticized Taft's secretary of the interior, Richard Ballinger, for returning restricted Alaskan coal mines to private mining companies in 1910, Taft fired Pinchot. Taft did not oppose conservation—he transferred more land from private to public control than did Roosevelt—but his dismissal of Pinchot angered conservationists.

Even more harmful to Taft's political fortunes, Roosevelt turned against his handpicked successor. After returning from overseas in 1910, Roosevelt, who had regretted a rash promise in 1904 not to seek a third term in office, became increasingly troubled by Taft's missteps. The loss of the House of Representatives to the Democrats in the 1910 elections highlighted the split among Republicans that had developed under Taft.

A year later, relations between the ex-president and the incumbent further deteriorated when Roosevelt attacked Taft for filing antitrust litigation against U.S. Steel for a deal that the Roosevelt administration had approved in 1907. Ironically, Roosevelt, known as a trustbuster, believed that filing more lawsuits under the Sherman Antitrust Act yielded diminishing returns, whereas Taft, the conservative, initiated more antitrust litigation than did Roosevelt.

Convinced that only he could heal the party breach, and desperate to reenter the political arena, Roosevelt announced his candidacy for the 1912 Republican presidential nomination. However, despite Roosevelt's widespread popularity among rank-and-file Republicans, Taft still controlled the party machinery and the majority of convention delegates. Losing to Taft on the first ballot, an embittered but optimistic Roosevelt formed a third party to sponsor his run for the presidency. Roosevelt excitedly told thousands of supporters gathered in Chicago that he felt "as strong as a BULL MOOSE," which became the nickname for Roosevelt's new **Progressive Party**.

In accepting the nomination, Roosevelt articulated the philosophy of **New Nationalism**. He argued that the federal government should use its power to fight

Progressive Party
A political party formed by Theodore Roosevelt in 1912 to facilitate his candidacy for president. Nicknamed the "Bull Moose Party," the Progressive Party split the Republican vote, allowing Democrat Woodrow Wilson to win the election. The party promoted an income tax, an eight-hour workday, labor unions, women's suffrage, and an end to child labor.

New Nationalism
The agenda put forward by Theodore Roosevelt in his 1912 presidential campaign. Roosevelt called for increased regulation of large corporations, a more active role for the president, and the extension of social justice using the power of the federal government.

against the forces of special privilege and for social justice for the majority of Americans. To this end, the Progressive Party platform advocated income and inheritance taxes, an eight-hour workday, the abolition of child labor, workers' compensation, fewer restrictions on labor unions, and women's suffrage.

Roosevelt was not the only progressive candidate in the contest. The Democrats nominated Woodrow Wilson, the reform governor of New Jersey. As an alternative to Roosevelt's New Nationalism, Wilson offered his **New Freedom**. As a Democrat and a southerner born in Virginia, Wilson had a more limited view of government than did Roosevelt. Wilson envisioned a society of small businesses, with the government's role confined to ensuring open competition among businesses and freedom for individuals to make the best use of their opportunities. Unlike Roosevelt's New Nationalism, Wilson's New Freedom did not embrace social reform and rejected federal action in support of women's suffrage and the elimination of child labor.

New Freedom
Term used by Woodrow Wilson to describe his limited-government, progressive agenda. Wilson's New Freedom was offered as an alternative to Theodore Roosevelt's New Nationalism.

AP® WORKING with EVIDENCE

Source: Woodrow Wilson, *The New Freedom: A Call for the Emancipation of the Generous Energies of a People,* 1913

> "Gentlemen say, they have been saying for a long time, and, therefore, I assume that they believe, that trusts are inevitable. They don't say that big business is inevitable. They don't say merely that the elaboration of business upon a great co-operative scale is characteristic of our time and has come about by the natural operation of modern civilization. We would admit that. But they say that the particular kind of combinations that are now controlling our economic development came into existence naturally and were inevitable; and that, therefore, we have to accept them as unavoidable and administer our development through them. . . .
>
> I answer . . . that this attitude rests upon a confusion of thought. Big business is no doubt to a large extent necessary and natural. The development of business upon a great scale, upon a great scale of co-operation, is inevitable, and, let me add, is probably desirable. But that is a very different matter from the development of trusts, because the trusts have not grown. They have been artificially created; they have been put together, not by natural processes, but by the will, the deliberate planning will, of men who were more powerful than their neighbors in the business world, and who wished to make their power secure against competition."

Questions for Analysis

1. Identify the position Wilson takes regarding the rise of big business in the United States.
2. Describe what Wilson is unwilling to agree with when it comes to the rise of trusts.
3. Evaluate the extent to which Wilson's arguments were shaped by previous progressive reforms.

If voters considered either Roosevelt's or Wilson's brand of reform too mainstream, they could cast their ballots for Eugene V. Debs, the Socialist Party candidate who had been once imprisoned for his leadership in the Pullman strike. He favored overthrowing capitalism through peaceful, democratic methods and replacing it with government ownership of business and industry for the benefit of the working class.

The splintering of the Republican Party decided the outcome of the election. The final results gave Roosevelt 27 percent of the popular vote and Taft 23 percent. Together they had a majority, but because they were divided, Wilson became president, with 42 percent of the popular vote and 435 electoral votes. Finishing fourth, Debs did not win any electoral votes, but he garnered around a million popular votes (6 percent). With the most moderate candidate, incumbent President Taft, finishing third, the American public clearly indicated its appetite for continued progressive policies.

National Progressive Legislation	
1903	Department of Labor and Commerce (established to promote fair business practices)
	Elkins Act
1906	Pure Food and Drug Act
	Meat Inspection Act
	Hepburn Act
1910	White Slave Trade Act (Mann Act)
1912	Children's Bureau (created in the Department of Commerce and Labor)
1913	Underwood Tariff Act (reduced tariffs to benefit farmers)
	Sixteenth Amendment (graduated income tax)
	Seventeenth Amendment (election of senators by popular vote)
	Federal Reserve System
1914	Harrison Narcotics Control Act
	Federal Trade Commission
	Clayton Antitrust Act
1916	Adamson Act (provided eight-hour workday for railroad workers)
	Keating-Owen Act (outlawed child labor in firms engaged in interstate commerce)
	Workmen's Compensation Act
1919	Eighteenth Amendment (prohibition)
1920	Nineteenth Amendment (women's suffrage)

- In what ways did President Taft retreat from and expand on progressivism during his administration?

Woodrow Wilson and the New Freedom Agenda

Once in office, Wilson hurried to fulfill his New Freedom agenda. Even though he differed from Roosevelt about the scope of federal intervention, both men believed in a strong presidency. An admirer of the British parliamentary system, Wilson viewed the president as an active and strong leader whose job was to provide his party with a legislative program. The 1912 elections had given the Democrats control over Congress, and Wilson expected his party to support his New Freedom measures.

National Archives, ARC identifier 306143

Woodrow Wilson Priming the Pump, 1914 In this political cartoon, President Wilson is shown priming the pump of business prosperity with antitrust legislation. Wilson's New Freedom assailed the "triple wall of privilege": the tariff, banks, and trusts. In response, Congress passed the Federal Reserve Act, Underwood Tariff Act, and Clayton Antitrust Act.

Why did progressives believe that increased regulation would create economic growth?

Tariff reduction came first. The **Underwood Tariff Act** of 1913 reduced import duties, a measure that appealed to southern and midwestern farmers who sought lower prices on the manufactured goods they bought that were subject to the tariff. The law also incorporated a reform that progressives had adopted from the Populists: the graduated income tax (tax rates that increase at higher levels of income).

The ratification of the **Sixteenth Amendment** in 1913 provided the legal basis for the income tax after the Supreme Court had previously declared such a levy unconstitutional. The graduated income tax was meant to advance the cause of social justice by moderating income inequality. The need to recover revenues lost from lower tariffs provided an additional practical impetus for imposing the tax. Because the law exempted people earning less than $4,000 a year from paying the income tax, more than 90 percent of Americans owed no tax. Those with incomes exceeding this amount paid rates ranging from 1 percent to 6 percent on $500,000 or more.

Wilson also pressed Congress in 1913 to consider banking reform. Farmers favored a system supervised by the government that afforded them an ample supply of credit at low interest rates. Eastern bankers wanted reforms that would stabilize a system plagued by cyclical financial panics, the most recent in 1907, while keeping the banking system under the private control of bankers.

The resulting compromise created the Federal Reserve System. The act established twelve regional banks. These banks lent cash reserves to member banks in their districts at a "discount rate," a rate that could be adjusted according to the fluctuating demand for credit. Federal Reserve notes became the foundation for a uniform currency. The Federal Reserve Board, appointed by the president and headquartered in Washington, D.C., supervises the system.

Sixteenth Amendment

An amendment ratified in 1913 providing a legal basis for a graduated income tax, which had been previously deemed unconstitutional.

Clayton Antitrust Act

An act that strengthened the Sherman Antitrust Act by banning certain corporate operations, such as price discrimination and overlapping membership on company boards, and by protecting labor unions. The 1914 act was designed to encourage economic competition.

Nevertheless, as with other progressive agencies, the experts selected to oversee the new banking system came from within the banking industry itself. Although farmers won a more rational and flexible credit supply, Wall Street bankers retained considerable power over the operation of the Federal Reserve System.

Next, President Wilson took two steps designed to help resolve the problem of economic concentration. First, in 1914, he persuaded Congress to create the Federal Trade Commission. The commission had the power to investigate corporate activities and prohibit "unfair" practices (which the law left undefined).

Wilson's second measure directly attacked monopolies. Enacted in 1914, the **Clayton Antitrust Act** strengthened the Sherman Antitrust Act by banning certain corporate operations, such as price discrimination and overlapping membership on company boards, which undermined economic competition. The statute also exempted labor unions from prosecution under antitrust legislation, reversing the policy initiated by the federal government in the wake of the Pullman strike (see Module 6.7).

By the end of his second year in office, Wilson had achieved most of his New Freedom objectives. Political considerations, however, soon forced him to widen his progressive agenda and support measures he had previously rejected.

With the Republican Party once again united after the electoral fiasco of 1912, Wilson, looking ahead to reelection in 1916, resumed the campaign for progressive legislation. Wilson appealed to Roosevelt's constituency by supporting New Nationalism social justice measures. In 1916, he signed into law the **Adamson Act**, which provided an eight-hour workday and overtime pay for railroad workers; the **Keating-Owen Act**, outlawing child labor in firms that engaged in interstate commerce; and the **Workmen's Compensation Act**, which provided insurance for federal employees in case of injury.

Adamson Act
A 1916 act establishing an eight-hour workday and overtime for workers in private industry—in this case, railroad workers.

Keating-Owen Act
An act preventing the interstate sale of goods made by children under the age of 14, among other protections for children, passed in 1916. The Supreme Court ruled it unconstitutional in 1918.

Workmen's Compensation Act
Regulation guaranteeing the rights of federal employees to receive financial compensation or pursue legal action for any injury occurring on the job.

In supporting programs that required greater intervention by the federal government, Wilson had placed political expediency ahead of his professed principles. He would later show a similar flexibility when he lent his support to a women's suffrage amendment, a cause he had long opposed.

Despite facing a challenge from a united Republican Party, Wilson won the 1916 election against former New York governor Charles Evans Hughes with slightly less than 50 percent of the vote. Wilson's reelection received little support from Black Americans. W. E. B. Du Bois, who backed Wilson in 1912 for pledging to "assist in advancing the interest of [the Black] race," had become disillusioned with the president. Born in the South and with deep southern roots, Wilson surrounded himself with white appointees from the South.

Despite Black protests, Wilson held a screening in the White House of the film *Birth of a Nation*, which glorified the Ku Klux Klan and denigrated Black people. Making the situation worse, Wilson introduced racial segregation into government offices and dining facilities in the nation's capital, and Black people lost jobs in post offices and other federal agencies throughout the South. In Wilson's view, segregation and discrimination were in the "best interests" of Blacks.

Still, President Wilson achieved much of the progressive agenda—more, in fact, than he had intended to when he first came to office. By the beginning of his second term, the federal government had further extended regulation over the activities of corporations and banks. Big business and finance still wielded substantial power, but Wilson had steered the government on a course that also benefited ordinary citizens, including passage of social justice measures he had originally opposed.

- What reforms did the Wilson administration pursue?
- To what extent did these reforms reflect a progressive political agenda?

The Progressive Legacy

By the end of the Progressive Era, Americans had come to expect more from their government. They were more confident that their food and medicine were safe, that children would not have to sacrifice their health and education by going to work, that women laborers would not be exploited, and that political officials would be more responsive to their wishes. As a result of the efforts of environmentalists, the nation expanded its efforts both to conserve and to preserve its natural resources. These and other reforms accomplished what Theodore Roosevelt, Woodrow Wilson, and their fellow progressives wanted: to bring order out of chaos.

In challenging laissez-faire and championing governmental intervention, progressives sought to balance individualism with social justice and social control. Despite cloaking many of their political reforms in democratic garb, middle- and upper-class progressives generally were more interested in enhancing their ability to advance their own agenda than in expanding opportunities for political participation for all Americans. Confident that they spoke for the "interests of the people," progressives had little doubt that increasing their own political power would be good for the nation as a whole.

Racial boundaries shaped the progressive movement. American Indians campaigned and organized to get the federal government to repair its broken promises of justice. Black Americans were active participants in progressivism, whether through extending educational opportunities, working in settlement houses, campaigning for women's suffrage, or establishing the NAACP.

Nevertheless, racism was also a characteristic of progressivism. White southern reformers generally favored disenfranchisement and segregation. Northern white people did not prove much more sympathetic. Immigrants also found themselves unwelcome targets of moral outrage as progressives forced these newcomers to conform to middle-class standards of social behavior. Campaigns for temperance, moral reform, and birth control all shared a desire to mold people deemed inferior into proper citizens, uncontaminated by chronic vice and corruption.

Progressivism was not monolithic and included a range of disparate and overlapping efforts to reorder political, social, moral, and physical environments. Except for the brief existence of the Progressive Party in 1912, reformers did not have a tightly knit organization or a fixed agenda. Leaders were more likely to come from the middle class, but support came from the rich as well as the poor, depending on the issue. Of course, many Americans did not embrace progressive principles, as conservative opponents continued to hold power and to fight against reform.

Nevertheless, by 1917, a combination of voluntary changes and government intervention had cleared the way to regulate corporations, increase governmental efficiency, and promote social justice. Progressives succeeded in improving conditions that might otherwise have produced disorder or even violence. In time, they would bring their ideas to reordering international affairs.

REVIEW

- Who benefited most from progressive reforms?
- Who was left out and why?

AP® Skills Workshop: Writing Historically

Additional Practice in Responding to a Long-Essay Question

Evaluate the extent of difference between Progressive-led social reform efforts and political reform efforts in the period 1900 to 1920.

World War I: Military and Diplomacy

MODULE **7.5**

FOCUS

As you read this module, pay close attention to the causes of the First World War, the U.S. part in this conflict, and the results of the war. Consider the ways in which this war transformed the politics and national identity of Americans, while also fostering change in the U.S. conception of its place in the world.

When Woodrow Wilson became president in 1913, he pledged to open a new chapter in U.S. relations with Latin America and the rest of the world. Dismissing power politics and the use of force, Wilson vowed to place diplomacy and moral persuasion at the center of U.S. foreign policy. Diplomacy, however, proved less effective than he had hoped. Despite Wilson's stated commitment to the peaceful resolution of international issues, during his presidency, the U.S. military intervened repeatedly in Latin America, and U.S. troops fought on European soil in the global conflict that contemporaries called the Great War.

Wilson and U.S. Foreign Policy, 1912–1917

While he claimed a preference for moral diplomacy, Wilson preserved the U.S. sphere of influence in the Caribbean using much the same methods as had Roosevelt and Taft. To protect U.S. investments, the president sent marines to Haiti in 1915, to the Dominican Republic in 1916, and to Cuba in 1917.

The most serious challenge to Wilson's diplomacy came in Mexico. The **Mexican Revolution** in 1911 spawned a civil war among various factions. The resulting instability threatened U.S. economic interests in Mexico, particularly oil. When Mexicans refused to accept Wilson's demands to install leaders he considered "good men," Wilson withdrew diplomatic recognition from Mexico.

In a disastrous attempt to influence Mexican politics, Wilson sent the U.S. navy to seize the port of Veracruz on April 22, 1914, leading to a bloody clash that killed 19 Americans and 126 Mexicans. U.S. forces ended their occupation six months later after international mediation. The situation worsened after Wilson first supported and then turned against one of the rebel competitors for power in Mexico, General Francisco "Pancho" Villa. In response, Villa and 1,500 troops rode across the border and attacked the town of Columbus, New Mexico.

In July 1916, Wilson ordered General John Pershing to send 10,000 army troops into Mexico in an attempt to capture Villa, the second U.S. military incursion into Mexico in two years. This operation was a complete failure, as Villa and his forces eluded capture. The presence of the U.S. army in northern Mexico for over a year only further

Central Powers
Political allies during World War I consisting mainly of Austria-Hungary, Germany, and the Ottoman Empire.

Allies
Political allies during World War I consisting mainly of Great Britain, France, and Russia. Italy joined in 1915 and the United States in 1917.

World War I
The 1914–1918 world war, also known as the Great War, fought between the Central Powers and the Allies. The United States entered the war in 1917.

angered Mexican leaders and confirmed their sense that Wilson had no respect for Mexican sovereignty.

At the same time as the situation in Mexico was deteriorating, a much more serious problem was developing in Europe. On June 28, 1914, a Serbian nationalist named Gavrilo Princip, intending to strike a blow against Austria-Hungary, assassinated the Austrian archduke Franz Ferdinand in Sarajevo, the capital of the province of Bosnia. This terrorist attack plunged Europe into what would become a world war. On August 4, 1914, the **Central Powers**—Germany, the Ottoman Empire, and Austria-Hungary—officially declared war against the **Allies**—Great Britain, France, and Russia. (Italy joined the Allies in 1915.)

For the first three years of **World War I**, also known as the Great War, Wilson kept the United States neutral, though privately he supported the British. Nevertheless, the president urged Americans to remain "impartial in thought as well as action." Peace activists sought to keep Wilson to his word. In 1915, women reformers and suffragists such as Jane Addams and Carrie Chapman Catt organized the Women's Peace Party to keep the United States out of the war.

Wilson faced two key problems in maintaining neutrality. First, the United States had closer and more important economic ties with the Allies than with the Central Powers, a disparity that would only grow as the war went on. The Allies purchased more

MAP 7.6 European Alliances, 1914 Prewar alliances helped precipitate World War I. The assassination of Archduke Ferdinand of Austria-Hungry by a Serbian revolutionary in Sarajevo set the countries in the Austro-Hungarian- and German-led Central Alliance against the British-French-Russian Allied Powers on the map.

In what ways would its diverse population pose a problem for the United States in choosing a side in this conflict?

than $750 million in U.S. goods in 1914, a figure that quadrupled over the next three years. By contrast, the Germans bought approximately $350 million worth of U.S. products in 1914; by 1917, the figure had shrunk to $30 million.

Moreover, when the Allies did not have the funds to pay for U.S. goods, they sought loans from private bankers. Initially, the Wilson administration resisted such requests. In 1915, however, Wilson reversed course. Concerned that failure to keep up the prewar level of commerce with the Allies would hurt the country economically, the president authorized private loans. The gap in financial transactions with the rival war powers grew even wider; by 1917, U.S. bankers had lent the Allies $2.2 billion, compared with just $27 million to Germany.

The second problem facing Wilson arose from Great Britain's and Germany's differing war strategies. As the superior naval power, Britain established a blockade of the North Sea to quarantine Germany and starve it into submission. The British navy violated international law by mining the waters to bottle up the German fleet and keep foreign ships from supplying Germany with food and medicines. Although Wilson protested this treatment, he did so weakly. He believed that the British could pay compensation for such violations of international law after the war.

Confronting a strangling blockade, Germany depended on the newly developed U-boat (*Unterseeboot*, or submarine) to counter the British navy. In February 1915, Germany declared they would attack any ship within a zone around the British Isles. Citizens of neutral nations were warned to stay off British ships in the area. U-boats, which were slower and less resistant to damage than British warships, relied on surprise attacks. This tactic violated the rules of engagement under international maritime law, which required warships from belligerent nations, countries at war, to allow civilians to leave passenger liners and cargo ships before firing. The British complicated the situation for the Germans by flying flags of neutral countries on merchant vessels and arming them with small "defensive" weapons. If U-boats played by the rules and surfaced before inspecting merchant ships, they risked being blown out of the water by disguised enemy guns.

Under these circumstances, U.S. neutrality could not last long. On May 15, 1915, catastrophe struck. Without surfacing and identifying itself, a German submarine off the Irish coast attacked the British luxury liner ***Lusitania***, which had departed from New York City en route to England. Although the ship's stated objective was to provide passengers with transport, its cargo contained a large supply of ammunition for British weapons. The U-boat's torpedoes rapidly sank the ship, killing 1,198 people, including 128 Americans.

Lusitania
A British passenger liner struck by German submarine torpedoes off the coast of Ireland on May 15, 1915. The U-boat's torpedoes sank the ship, killing 1,198 people, including 128 Americans.

Outraged Americans called on the president to respond; some, including Theodore Roosevelt, advocated the immediate use of military force. Despite his pro-British sentiments, Wilson resisted going to war. Instead, he held the Germans in "strict accountability" for their action. Wilson demanded that Germany refrain from further attacks against passenger liners and offer a financial settlement to the *Lusitania*'s survivors. Unwilling to risk war with the United States, the Germans consented.

Wilson had only delayed U.S. entry into the war. By pursuing a policy of neutrality that treated the combatants unequally and by insisting that Americans had a right to travel on the ships of belligerent nations, the president made it less likely that the United States could stay out of the war.

Throughout 1916, Wilson pursued two separate but interrelated policies that embodied the ambivalence that he and the U.S. people shared about the war. On the one hand, with Germany alternating between continued U-boat attacks and apologies, the president sought to build the country's military preparedness in the event of war. He signed into law the National Defense Act, which increased the size of the army, navy,

Library of Congress, LC-DIG-ds-09934

German Submarine Attack This 1916 painting depicts a German submarine (U-boat) attacking an armed British trawler. Unlike surface vessels, German U-boats made surprise attacks and sank an estimated 5,000 ships during the conflict. To counter the threat, the Allies used convoys guarded by destroyers, aircraft patrols, and sea mines.

What advantages and disadvantages of using submarines in naval combat are evident in the image?

and National Guard. On the other hand, Wilson stressed his desire to remain neutral and stay out of the war.

With U.S. public opinion divided on the Great War, Wilson chose to run for reelection as a peace candidate. The Democrats adopted the slogan "He kept us out of war" and also emphasized the president's substantial record of progressive reform. Wilson won a narrow victory against Charles Evans Hughes, the former Republican governor of New York, who wavered between advocating peace and criticizing Wilson for not sufficiently supporting the Allies.

- How did President Wilson justify neutrality during the first three years of World War I?

Making the World Safe for Democracy

As 1917 dawned, the war headed toward its third bloody year. Neither side wanted a negotiated peace because each counted on victory to gain sufficient territory and financial compensation to justify the great sacrifices in human lives and materiel caused by the conflict. Nevertheless, Wilson tried to persuade the belligerents to abandon the battlefield for the bargaining table. On January 22, 1917, he declared that the world needed a "peace without victory," one based on self-determination, freedom of the seas, respect for international law, and the end of hostile alliances. It was a generous vision from a nation that had made few sacrifices.

AP® WORKING with EVIDENCE

Source: Woodrow Wilson, *Remarks to the Senate*, 1917

> "On the eighteenth of December last I addressed [a] . . . note to the governments of the nations now at war requesting them to state, more definitely than they had yet been stated by either group of belligerents, the terms upon which they would deem it possible to make peace. I spoke on behalf of humanity and of the rights of all neutral nations like our own, many of whose most vital interests the war puts in constant jeopardy. . . . We are . . . nearer a definite discussion of the peace which shall end the present war. We are . . . nearer the discussion of the international concert which must thereafter hold the world at peace. In every discussion of the peace that must end this war it is taken for granted that that peace must be followed by some definite concert of power which will make it virtually impossible that any such catastrophe should ever overwhelm us again. . . .
>
> It is inconceivable that the people of the United States should play no part in that great enterprise. To take part in such a peace will be the opportunity for which they have sought to prepare themselves . . . ever since the days when they set up a new nation in the high and honourable hope that it might in all that it was and did show mankind the way to liberty. . . .
>
> No covenant of cooperative peace that does not include the peoples of the New World can suffice to keep the future safe against war. . . . The elements of that peace must be elements that engage the confidence and satisfy the principles of the American governments, elements consistent with their political faith and with the practical convictions which the peoples of America have once for all embraced and undertaken to defend."

Questions for Analysis

1. Identify what Wilson says is "inconceivable" about the war.
2. Explain how Wilson's reference to a "covenant of cooperative peace" revealed a shift in his approach to U.S. foreign policy.
3. Evaluate the extent to which the position Wilson takes in this speech marked a change in U.S. foreign policy.

Germany quickly rejected Wilson's proposal. The United States had never been truly neutral, and Germany's increasingly desperate leaders saw no reason to believe that the situation would change. In 1915 and again in 1916, to prevent the United States from entering the war, Germany had pledged to refrain from using its U-boats against passenger and merchant ships. However, on February 1, 1917, the Germans chose to change course and resume unrestricted submarine warfare, calculating that they could defeat the Allies before the United States declared war and its troops could make a substantial difference. In response, Wilson used his executive power to arm merchant ships, bringing the United States one step closer to war.

The country moved even closer to war after the **Zimmermann telegram** became public. On February 24, the British turned over to Wilson an intercepted message from Arthur Zimmermann, the German foreign minister, to the Mexican government. The note revealed that Germany had offered Mexico an alliance in the event that the United States joined the Allies. If the Central Powers won, Mexico would receive the territory it had lost to the United States in the mid-nineteenth century—Texas, New Mexico, and Arizona. When U.S. newspapers broke the story several days later, it inflamed public

Zimmermann telegram
A secret 1917 telegram in which Germany offered Mexico an alliance in the event that the United States entered World War I and promised to help Mexico reclaim lands ceded to the United States after the Mexican-American War in 1848. The telegram's publication in U.S. newspapers helped build public support for war.

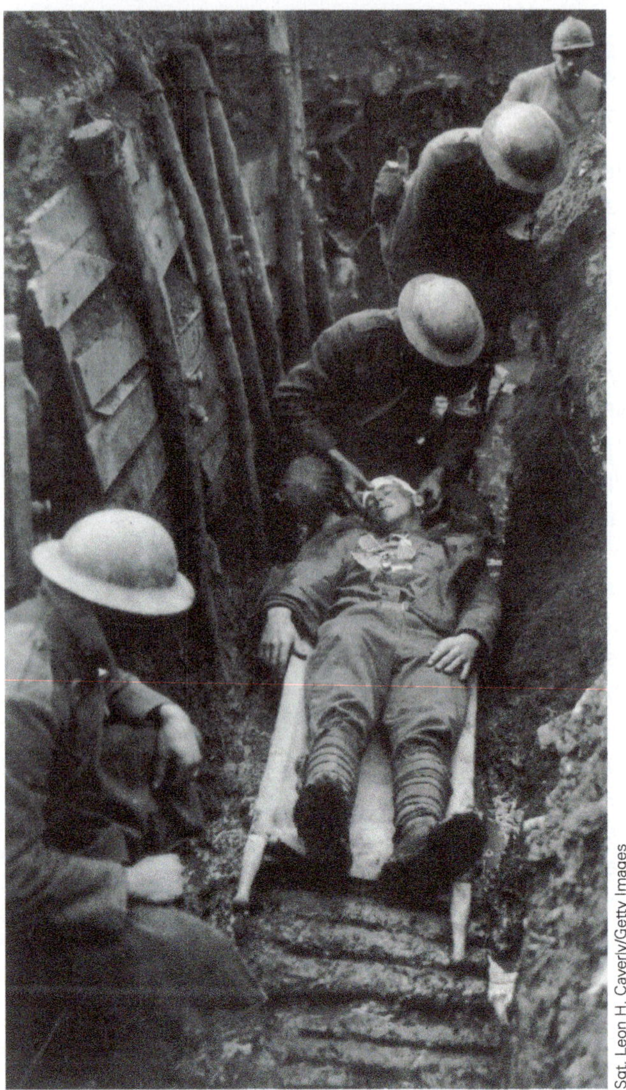

Sgt. Leon H. Caverly/Getty Images

Trench Warfare Trench warfare was at the center of the fighting in World War I on the western front. This photograph snapped by Sergeant Leon H. Caverly on March 22, 1918, shows Red Cross workers in a trench caring for a wounded American soldier.

How does this photograph illustrate the hardships soldiers faced during World War I?

opinion and provided the Wilson administration another reason to fear a German victory.

In late February and March, German U-boats sank several armed U.S. merchant ships, and on April 2, 1917, President Wilson asked Congress to declare war against Germany and the other Central Powers. After four days of vigorous debate led by opponents of the war—including Senator Robert M. La Follette of Wisconsin and the first female elected representative, Jeanette P. Rankin from Montana—Congress voted to approve the war resolution.

President Wilson had not reached his decision quickly. For three years, he resisted calls for war. In the end, however, Wilson believed that only by going to war would he be able to ensure that the United States played a role in shaping the peace. For the president, the security of the nation rested on respect for law, human rights, and extension of free governments. "The world must be made safe for democracy," he informed Congress in his war message, and he had concluded that the only way to guarantee this outcome was by helping to defeat Germany.

This need became even more urgent when in November 1917 the **Russian Revolution** installed a Bolshevik (Communist) regime that negotiated a separate peace with the Central Powers. This development allowed Germany to focus solely on fighting along the western front in France.

It would take a while for Americans to make their presence felt in Europe. First, the United States needed a large army, which it created through the draft. The **Selective Service Act** of 1917 conscripted three million men by war's end. Unlike drafts during the Civil War, there was relatively little protest against conscription during World War I because most Americans now accepted the federal government's power to draft soldiers.

Mobilizing such a large force required substantial time, and the **American Expeditionary Forces (AEF)**, established in 1917 under General Pershing, did not make much of an impact until 1918. Before then, the U.S. navy made the greatest contribution. U.S. warships joined the British in escorting merchant vessels, combating German submarines, and laying mines in the North Sea. The United States also provided crucial funding and supplies to the Allies as their reserves became depleted.

Selective Service Act
The act authorizing a nationwide draft to support U.S. participation in World War I that went into effect in 1917.

The AEF finally began to make an impact in Europe in May 1918. From May through September, more than one million U.S. troops helped the Allies repel German offensives in northern France near the Belgian border. One momentous battle in the Argonne Forest lasted two months until the Allies broke through enemy lines and pushed toward Germany. Nearly 50,000 U.S. troops died in the fierce fighting, and another 230,000 were injured.

Like their European counterparts, who suffered a staggering 8 to 10 million casualties, Americans experienced the horrors of war magnified by new technology. Dug into filthy trenches, soldiers dodged rapid machine-gun fire, heavy artillery explosions, and shells spewing poison gas. In the end, however, the AEF succeeded in tipping the balance in favor of the Allies. On November 11, 1918, an exhausted Germany surrendered.

REVIEW

- Why did President Wilson find it so difficult to keep the United States out of World War I?

Waging Peace after World War I

In January 1918, ten months before the war ended, President Wilson presented Congress with his plan for peace. Wilson consolidated his ideas in the **Fourteen Points**, principles that he hoped would prevent future wars. Based on his assessment of the causes of the Great War, Wilson envisioned a generous peace treaty that included freedom of the seas, open diplomacy and the abolition of secret treaties, free trade, self-determination for colonial subjects, and a reduction in military spending. More important than any specific measure, Wilson's proposal hinged on the creation of the **League of Nations**, an organization of large and small nations that would guarantee peaceful resolution of disputes and back up decisions through collective action, including the use of military force as a last resort.

Following the armistice that ended the war on November 11, 1918, Wilson took his message to the Paris Peace Conference, the postwar meeting of the victorious Allied nations that would set the terms of the peace. The first sitting president to travel overseas, Wilson was greeted in Paris by joyous crowds.

For nearly six months, Wilson tried to convince reluctant Allied leaders to accept the central components of his plan. Having exhausted themselves financially and having suffered the loss of a generation of young men, the Allies expected to collect the spoils of victory and make the Central Powers pay dearly. The European Allies intended to hold on to their respective colonies regardless of Wilson's call for self-determination, and as a nation that depended on a strong navy, Britain refused to limit its options by discussing freedom of the seas.

Perhaps Georges Clemenceau, France's prime minister, best expressed the skepticism of Wilson's colleagues about his idealistic vision: "President Wilson and his Fourteen Points bore me. Even God Almighty has only ten commandments!"

During the conference, Wilson was forced to compromise on a number of his principles to retain the cornerstone of his diplomacy—the establishment of the League of Nations. He abandoned his hope for peace without bitterness by agreeing to a "war guilt" clause that levied huge economic reparations on Germany for starting the war. He was willing to sacrifice some of his ideals because the league took on even greater importance in the wake of the 1917 Communist revolution in Russia. The president believed that capitalism, as regulated and reformed during the Progressive Era, would raise living conditions throughout the world as it had done in the United States, would prevent the spread of **communism**, and would benefit U.S. commerce. Wilson needed the league to keep the peace so that war-ravaged and recovering nations had the opportunity to practice economic freedom and political democracy. In the end, the president won agreement for the establishment of his cherished League of Nations. The **Treaty of Versailles**, signed at the royal palace just outside Paris, authorized the league to combat aggression against any member nation through collective military action.

In July 1919, after enduring bruising battles in Paris, Wilson returned to Washington, D.C., only to face another wrenching struggle in the Senate over ratification of the Treaty of Versailles. The odds were stacked against Wilson from the start. The Republicans held a majority in the Senate, and Wilson needed the support of two-thirds of the Senate to secure ratification.

Fourteen Points

The core principles President Woodrow Wilson saw as the basis for lasting peace after World War I, including freedom of the seas, open diplomacy, the establishment of the League of Nations, and the right to self-determination.

League of Nations

The international organization proposed by Woodrow Wilson after the end of World War I to ensure world peace and security in the future through mutual agreement. The United States failed to join the league because Wilson and his opponents in Congress could not work out a compromise.

AP® EXAM TIP

The United States went from a long-held isolationist position in European affairs to outright intervention. Be able to describe the events that pulled America into World War I and why President Woodrow Wilson's moral diplomacy failed. Also, be able to explain why the Treaty of Versailles was not ratified by the Senate. The AP® Exam may ask a question about causes of U.S. involvement in World War I, or a question comparing U.S. foreign policy during World War I to an earlier or later time period.

Treaty of Versailles

The treaty officially ending World War I and creating the League of Nations, signed in 1919. The treaty imposed a "war guilt" clause on Germany, required the payment of billions of dollars in reparations to the Allies, stripped Germany of its colonies and some of its territory, and placed strict limits on the German military. The United States never ratified the treaty.

Moreover, Henry Cabot Lodge, the Republican chairman of the Senate Foreign Relations Committee, opposed Article X of the League of Nations covenant, which sanctioned collective security arrangements against military aggression. Lodge argued that such an alliance compromised U.S. independence in conducting its own foreign relations. Lodge had at least thirty-nine senators behind him, more than enough to block ratification.

Conceding the need to protect the country's national self-interest, the president agreed to modifications to the treaty so that the Monroe Doctrine and U.S. obligations in the Caribbean and Central America were kept intact. Lodge, however, was not satisfied and insisted on adding fourteen "reservations" limiting compliance with the treaty, including strong language affirming Congress's right to declare war before agreeing to a League of Nations military action.

Wilson's stubbornness more than equaled Lodge's, and the president refused to compromise further over the League. Insisting that he was morally bound to honor the treaty he had negotiated in good faith, Wilson rejected additional changes. Making matters worse, Wilson faced resistance from sixteen lawmakers dubbed "irreconcilables," who opposed the league under any circumstances. Mainly Republicans from the Midwest and West, they voiced the traditional U.S. rejection of entangling alliances.

To break the logjam, the president attempted to rally public opinion behind him. In September 1919, he embarked on a nationwide speaking tour to carry his message directly to the American people. Over a three-week period, he traveled eight thousand miles by train, keeping a grueling schedule that exhausted him. After a stop in Pueblo, Colorado, on September 25, Wilson collapsed and canceled the rest of his trip. On October 2, Wilson suffered a debilitating stroke that nearly killed him. The effects of the stroke, which left him partially paralyzed, emotionally unstable, and mentally impaired, dimmed any remaining hopes of compromise. The full extent of his illness was kept from the public.

On November 19, 1919, the Senate rejected the amended treaty. The following year, Wilson had a final chance to obtain ratification, but he still refused to accept changes to the treaty despite members of his own party urging compromise. In March 1920, treaty ratification failed one last time, falling just seven votes short of the required two-thirds majority.

Had Wilson shown the same willingness to compromise that he had in Paris, the outcome might have been different. In the end, however, the United States never signed the Treaty of Versailles or joined the League of Nations, weakening the league and diminishing the prospects for long-term peace.

AP® WORKING with EVIDENCE

Source: Woodrow Wilson, *Address at Pueblo, Colorado*, 1919

> "[R]eflect, my fellow citizens, that the membership of [the League of Nations] is going to include all the great fighting nations of the world, as well as the weak ones. . . . They enter into a solemn promise to one another that they will never use their power against one another for aggression; . . . and that no matter what differences arise amongst them they will never resort to war without first having done one or other of two things—either submitted the matter of controversy to arbitration, in which case they agree to abide by the result without question, or submitted it to the consideration of the council of the league of nations, laying before that council all the documents, all the facts, agreeing that the council can publish the documents and the facts to the

whole world, agreeing that there shall be six months allowed for the mature consideration of those facts by the council, and agreeing that at the expiration of the six months, even if they are not then ready to accept the advice of the council with regard to the settlement of the dispute, they will still not go to war for another three months. In other words, they consent, no matter what happens, to submit every matter of difference between them to the judgment of mankind, and just so certainly as they do that, my fellow citizens, war will be in the far background, war will be pushed out of that foreground of terror in which it has kept the world for generation after generation, and men will know that there will be a calm time of deliberate counsel."

Questions for Analysis

1. Identify Wilson's main argument in this speech.
2. Describe the process nations would follow under this plan instead of declaring war.
3. Explain what Wilson states will give the League of Nations its authority.

- How did the League of Nations reflect progressive ideals?

The Creation of a U.S. Empire

In the final decade of the nineteenth century, the United States transformed itself into an imperial power. Presidents McKinley and Roosevelt carried out the strategy outlined by Captain Alfred Thayer Mahan to enlarge the navy, construct a canal linking the Atlantic and Pacific Oceans, and acquire coaling stations and bases in the Pacific to service the fleet.

U.S. officials disregarded the nationalistic aspirations of freedom fighters such as José Martí in Cuba and Emilio Aguinaldo in the Philippines in favor of the imperial spoils gained from winning the War of 1898. The United States justified intervention on moral grounds imbued with racist beliefs, much as it had in conquering the Indians during westward expansion.

As a fit and manly nation, the United States had the responsibility to uplift inferior peoples to "civilized" standards and make them capable of self-government. This justification quickly wore thin. To crush the rebellion in the Philippines, the military engaged in atrocities that called into question the honor and virtue of the United States.

Once it achieved victory in the Philippines, the nation concentrated its efforts on maintaining territories mainly for commercial purposes. Within the few short years from 1898 to 1904, this commercial empire had fallen into place.

The Progressive Era presidents, Roosevelt and Wilson, created and sustained a U.S. empire. They disagreed significantly in approach—Roosevelt favoring force, Wilson preferring negotiations—but in practice they shared a willingness to use military power to protect national interests. These two presidents helped construct the modern American state, an expanded federal government that officially sanctioned cooperation with responsible corporate leaders. This relationship reached its peak during World War I. In mobilizing the home front, the Wilson administration blurred the line between public and private business by expanding the reach of government over the economy and curtailing personal liberty.

In 1917, because of its heavy reliance on trade with foreign countries, especially in Europe, the United States confronted its first major international crisis of the twentieth century. Wilson reluctantly led the country into war to guarantee a world order in which reasonable governments attempted to resolve controversies through negotiation, not violence. The failure of the United States to join the League of Nations, for which the president was largely responsible, shattered that idealistic dream.

The United States retreated from joining an international body offering collective security, but it did not isolate itself from participation in the world. The country emerged from the war in excellent financial shape. It had become the leading foreign creditor, and its industrial capacity had greatly expanded. Tending its commercial empire in the Caribbean and Central America, the United States probed for new markets in Asia and the Middle East. It would take another two decades for policymakers to realize that the country's refusal to support a strong collective response to expansionist aggression posed serious dangers for U.S. commerce and values.

- How and why did the United States become a global empire between 1890 and 1920?

AP® Skills Workshop: Writing Historically

Additional Practice in Responding to a Short-Answer Question with Secondary Sources

"In the final analysis, American policy was determined by the President and public opinion, which had a great, if unconscious, influence upon him. It was Wilson who decided to accept the British maritime system in the first instance, who set the American government against unrestricted use of the submarine, and who made the final decision for war instead of a continuance of armed neutrality. . . .

[I]f the German leaders had at any time desired a genuinely reasonable settlement and evidenced a willingness to help build a peaceful and orderly postwar world, they would have found a friend in the White House eager to join them in accomplishing these high goals.

The German decision to gamble on all-out victory or complete ruin . . . alone compelled Wilson to break diplomatic relations, to adopt a policy of armed neutrality, and finally to ask for a declaration of war—because American ships were being sunk and American citizens were being killed on the high seas, and because armed neutrality seemed no longer possible. Considerations of America's alleged economic stake in an Allied victory did not influence Wilson's thought during the critical weeks from February 1 to April 2, 1917. Nor did considerations of national interest, or of the great ideological issues at stake in the conflict."

Arthur S. Link, *Woodrow Wilson and the Progressive Era, 1910–1917*, 1963

(continued)

"Although the president emphasized German violation of neutral rights, neither American tradition nor law nor economic necessity required him to guarantee the right of Americans to travel on armed belligerent ships. Though he couched his policies in terms of international law and principle, Wilson was responsible for defining the growth of trade with Britain as a legitimate and profitable expression of neutral rights. He rejected definitions of other neutrals—Spain, the Netherlands, and the Scandinavian countries—that banned such passenger travel and embargoed guns and ammunition. In addition, he refused to consider the German and British blockades similarly or to hold Germany to a postwar accounting, as he did in the case of Britain. Thus by 1917 Wilson found himself constrained by the framework created by his earlier decisions about American rights. . . .

Wilson's policies reflected the traditional American belief that the ideals of America were the ideals of all humankind and that the other nations must conform to American prescriptions and ideals. . . . This global interventionism was new, but it drew on an attitude of superiority that had much earlier become a part of American culture. Germany had to be restrained because it had broken America's rules, disputed its ideals, threatened the rights and property of American citizens, and even challenged its security and hegemony through the proposed military alliance with Mexico."

John Whiteclay Chambers II, *The Tyranny of Change: America in the Progressive Era*, 1890–1920, 2000

Using the excerpts, answer **A**, **B**, and **C**.

(A) Briefly describe ONE major difference between Link's and Chambers's historical interpretations of causes of U.S. entry into the First World War.

(B) Briefly explain how ONE specific historical event or development during the period 1914 to 1917 that is not explicitly mentioned in the excerpts could be used to support Link's interpretation.

(C) Briefly explain how ONE specific historical event or development during the period 1914 to 1917 that is not explicitly mentioned in the excerpts could be used to support Chambers's interpretation.

MODULE

7.6 World War I: The Home Front

FOCUS

While reading this module about the economic and social changes during and shortly after World War I, consider which of these changes were results of the war itself and which changes were caused by other historical trends or events. Think about the impact of the war on international and internal migration patterns.

Modern global warfare required full mobilization at home. In preparing to support the war effort, the country drew on recent experience. The progressives' passion for organization, expertise, efficiency, and moralistic control was harnessed to the effort of placing the economy on a wartime footing and rallying the American people behind the war. In the process, the government gained unprecedented control over American life. The war effort also produced unforeseen economic and political opportunities.

At the same time, government efforts to suppress opposition to U.S. involvement in World War I fostered an atmosphere of fear and repression. An influenza epidemic in 1918, which killed hundreds of thousands of Americans and millions of people around the world, heightened the climate of anxiety. Finally, while the end of the war was widely celebrated, the abrupt transition away from a wartime economy produced inflation, labor unrest, and escalating racial tensions.

Fighting the War at Home

Progressives had relied on government commissions to regulate business practices as well as health and safety standards. In July 1917, the Wilson administration followed suit by establishing the **War Industries Board (WIB)** to supervise the purchase of military supplies and to gear up private enterprise to meet demand. However, the WIB was largely ineffective until March 1918, when the president found the right man to lead it. He chose Wall Street financier Bernard Baruch, who recruited staff from business enterprises that the board regulated. Baruch prodded businesses into compliance mainly by offering lucrative contracts rather than by coercion. By doing so, the WIB created a government partnership with the corporate sector that would last beyond the war.

Labor also experienced significant gains through government regulation. Shortages of workers and an outbreak of strikes hampered the war effort. In April 1918, Wilson created the **National War Labor Board (NWLB)** to settle labor disputes. The agency consisted of representatives from unions, corporations, and the public. In exchange for obtaining a "no strike pledge" from organized labor, the NWLB supported an eight-hour workday with time-and-a-half pay for overtime, labor's right to collective bargaining, and equal pay for equal work by women.

The NWLB fell short of reaching this last goal, but the war employed more than a million women who had not held jobs before. As military and government services expanded, women found greater opportunities as telephone operators, nurses, and clerical workers. At the same time, the number of women employed as domestic servants declined. Women temporarily took over formerly male jobs driving streetcars, delivering ice, assembling airplane motors, operating drill presses, oiling railroad engines, and welding parts. Yet women's incomes continued to lag significantly behind those of men performing the same tasks.

Americans probably experienced the expanding scope of government intervention most directly through the efforts of three new agencies that regulated consumption and travel. Wilson appointed Herbert Hoover to head the **Food Administration**. Hoover sought to increase the military and civilian food supply mainly through voluntary conservation measures. He generated a major publicity campaign urging Americans to adopt "wheatless Mondays," "meatless Tuesdays," and "porkless Thursdays and Saturdays." The government also mobilized schoolchildren to plant vegetable gardens to increase food production for the home front.

Consumers saved gas and oil under the prodding of the **Fuel Administration**. The agency encouraged fuel "holidays" along the line of Hoover's voluntary restrictions and created daylight saving time to conserve fuel by adding an extra hour of sunlight to the end of the workday. The Fuel Administration also offered higher prices to coal companies to increase productivity. Patterns of consumer travel changed under government regulation. The **Railroad Administration** acted more forcefully than most other agencies. Troop and supply shipments depended on the efficient operation of the railways.

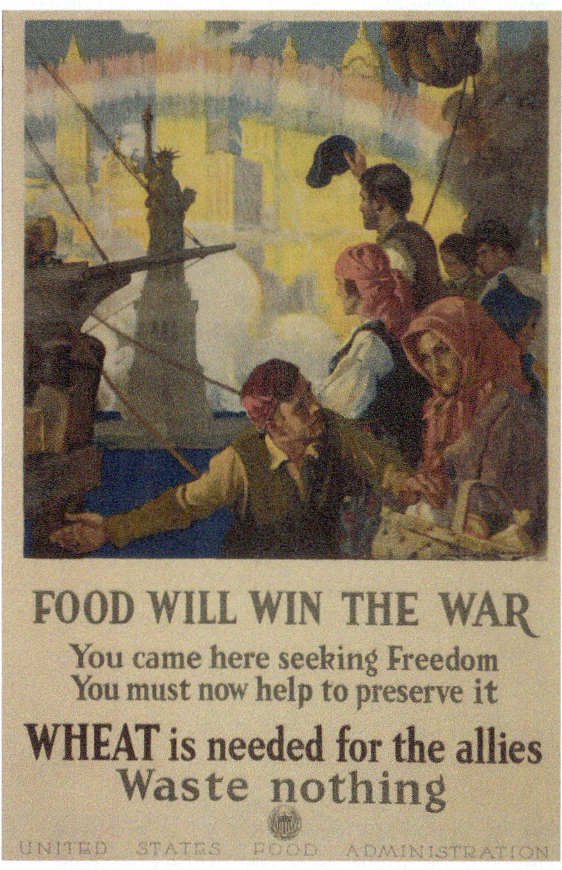

Left: Venimages/Alamy; right: Library of Congress, LC-USZC4-8890

World War I Posters Thousands of posters in the United States were printed and distributed by the Committee on Public Information and various governmental agencies to generate public support for the war effort. The poster on the left was put out by the Food Administration and translated into several languages. Twenty-five thousand copies of the one on the right were posted by the U.S. navy in recruiting stations across the country.

How does each image appeal to patriotism and self-sacrifice?

The administration controlled the railroads during the war, coordinating train schedules, overseeing terminals, regulating ticket prices, upgrading tracks, and raising workers' wages.

America's entry into the Great War did not immediately end the significant antiwar sentiment. Consequently, Wilson waged a campaign to rally support for his aims and to stimulate patriotic enthusiasm. To generate enthusiasm and ensure loyalty, the president appointed journalist George Creel to head the **Committee on Public Information (CPI)**, which focused on generating propaganda. Creel recruited a vast network of lecturers to speak throughout the country and spread patriotic messages. The committee coordinated rallies to sell bonds and raise money to fund the war. The CPI persuaded reporters to censor their war coverage, and most agreed in order to avoid government intervention. The agency helped produce films depicting the Allies as heroic saviors of humanity and the Central Powers as savage beasts. The CPI also distributed colorful and sometimes lurid posters emphasizing the depravity of the enemy and the nation's moral responsibility to defeat the Central Powers.

Committee on Public Information (CPI)

A government organization established in 1917 to create and promote pro–World War I propaganda and censor dissenting voices.

Propaganda did not prove sufficient, however, and Americans remained deeply divided about the war. To suppress dissent, Congress passed the Espionage Act in 1917 and the Sedition Act a year later. Both limited freedom of speech by criminalizing certain forms of expression. The **Espionage Act** prohibited antiwar activities, including interfering with the draft. It also banned the mailing of publications advocating forcible interference with any laws. The **Sedition Act** punished individuals who expressed beliefs disloyal or abusive to the U.S. government, flag, or military uniform.

Espionage Act

An act that prohibited antiwar activities, including opposing the military draft, passed in 1917. It banned subversive mailings as well as deliberate actions of sabotage and spying.

Sedition Act

An act limiting free speech by punishing individuals for expressing opinions deemed hostile to the U.S. government, flag, or military, passed in 1918.

Of the slightly more than two thousand prosecutions under these laws, only a handful concerned charges of actual sabotage or espionage. Most defendants brought to trial were critics who merely spoke out against the war. In 1918, for telling a crowd that the military draft was a form of slavery, the Socialist Party's Eugene V. Debs was tried, convicted, and sentenced to ten years in prison under the Espionage Act. (President Warren G. Harding later pardoned Debs in 1921.) The Justice Department also went after the Industrial Workers of the World (IWW), which continued to initiate labor strikes during the war. The government broke into the offices of the IWW, ransacked the group's files for evidence of disloyalty, and arrested more than 130 members.

AP® WORKING with EVIDENCE

Source: Eugene V. Debs, *Antiwar Speech in Canton, Ohio*, 1918

> "I realize that, in speaking to you this afternoon, there are certain limitations placed upon the right of free speech. I must be exceedingly careful, prudent, as to what I say, and even more careful and prudent as to how I say it. I may not be able to say all I think; but I am not going to say anything that I do not think. I would rather a thousand times be a free soul in jail than to be a sycophant [lackey to those in power] and coward in the streets. They . . . can not put the Socialist movement in jail. . . .
>
> Socialism is a growing idea; an expanding philosophy. It is spreading over the entire face of the earth: It is as vain to resist it as it would be to arrest the sunrise. . .
>
> When we unite and act together on the industrial field and when we vote together on election day we shall develop the supreme power of the one class that can and will bring permanent peace to the world. We shall then have the intelligence, the courage and the power for our great task. In due time industry will be organized on a cooperative basis. We shall conquer the public power. . . . We shall then have industrial democracy. We shall be a free nation whose government is of and by and for the people. . . .

In due time the hour will strike and this great cause triumphant—the greatest in history—will proclaim the emancipation of the working class and the brotherhood of all mankind."

Questions for Analysis

1. Describe Debs's vision when he says, "When we unite and act together on the industrial field and when we vote together on election day we shall develop the supreme power of the one class that can and will bring permanent peace to the world."
2. Explain how the historical situation shaped Debs's message to his audience.
3. Evaluate the extent of similarity between Debs's argument in this speech and progressive reform policies.

Government efforts to promote national unity and punish those who did not conform prompted local communities to enforce "one hundred percent Americanism." Civic groups banned the playing of German music and operas from concert halls, and schools prohibited teaching the German language. Foods with German origins were renamed—sauerkraut became "liberty cabbage," and hamburgers became "liberty sandwiches." Such sentiments were expressed in a more sinister fashion when mobs assaulted German Americans.

Prejudice toward German Americans was further inflamed by the formation of the **American Protective League (APL)**, a quasi-official association endorsed by the Justice Department. Consisting of 200,000 chapters throughout the country, the APL employed individuals to spy on German residents suspected of disloyal behavior. Most often, APL agents found little more than German immigrants who merely retained attachments to family and friends in their homeland. Gossip and rumor fueled many of the league's loyalty probes.

The repressive side of progressivism came to the fore in other ways as well. Anti-immigrant bias, shared by many reformers, flourished. The effort to conserve manpower and grain supplies bolstered the impulse to control standards of moral behavior, particularly those associated with immigrants, such as drinking. This anti-immigrant prejudice in part explains the ratification of the Eighteenth Amendment in 1919, prohibiting the sale of all alcoholic beverages.

Yet not all the moral indignation unleashed by the war resulted in restriction of freedom. After considerable wartime protest and lobbying, women suffragists succeeded in securing the right to vote.

President Wilson's goal "to make the world safe for democracy" appealed to oppressed minorities. They hoped the war would push the United States to live up to its rhetoric and extend freedom at home. Nearly 400,000 Black Americans served in the war and more than 40,000 saw combat, but most were assigned to service units and worked in menial jobs. The army remained segregated, and few Black officers commanded troops. Despite this discrimination, W. E. B. Du Bois echoed Black people's hope that their patriotism would be rewarded at the war's end: "We of the colored race have no ordinary interest in the outcome."

The same held true for American Indians. More than ten thousand American Indians participated in the war. Recruited from Arizona, Montana, and New York, they fought in the major battles in France and Belgium. Unlike Black Americans, they did not fight in segregated units and saw action as scouts and combat soldiers. They gained recognition by communicating messages in their native languages to confuse the Germans listening in. Aware of the contradiction between their troubling treatment historically by the U.S. government and the nation's democratic war aims, they expected that their wartime patriotism would bring them a greater measure of justice. However, like Black Americans, they would be disappointed.

REVIEW

- How did progressive policies and programs shape the U.S. economy and society during World War I?
- How did policymakers attempt to generate and sustain public support for U.S. involvement in World War I?

Postwar Social Turmoil

The success of the Bolshevik Revolution in Russia in 1917 and the subsequent creation of the Union of Soviet Socialist Republics terrified officials of capitalist countries in western Europe and the United States. This fear intensified further in 1919 with the creation of the Comintern, an association of communists who pledged to incite revolution in capitalist countries around the world. This sparked a panic over communist-inspired radicalism known as the **Red Scare**, which set the stage for the suppression of dissent.

Red Scare

The fear of communist-inspired radicalism in the wake of the Russian Revolution. The Red Scare culminated in the Palmer raids on suspected radicals.

Schenck v. United States

The Supreme Court ruling in 1919 limiting free speech that creates a "clear and present danger." The ruling upheld a conviction under the Espionage Act for mailing leaflets opposed to the draft.

In this atmosphere of anxiety, on March 3, 1919, in ***Schenck v. United States***, the Supreme Court invoked the Espionage Act to uphold the conviction of Charles Schenck, the general secretary of the Socialist Party, for mailing thousands of leaflets opposing the military draft. Delivering the Court's unanimous opinion, Justice Oliver Wendell Holmes argued that during wartime, Congress has the authority to prohibit individuals from using words that create "a clear and present danger" to the safety of the country, using the example of someone falsely yelling "fire" in a crowded theater to illustrate how speech could create a public danger. Although the trial record failed to show that Schenck's leaflets had convinced any young men to resist conscription, the Court upheld his conviction under Holmes's doctrine. Later that year, in ***Abrams v. United States***, the Court further limited free speech by sustaining the guilty verdict of five anarchists who distributed leaflets denouncing U.S. military efforts to overthrow the Bolshevik regime.

Immediate postwar economic problems further increased the anxiety of American citizens, reinforcing the position of officials who sought to restore order by suppressing radicals. Industries were slow to convert their plants from military to civilian production, and consumer goods therefore remained in short supply. The war had brought jobs and higher wages on the home front, and consumers who had been restrained by wartime rationing were eager to spend their savings. With demand greatly exceeding supply, however, prices soared by 77 percent, frustrating consumers. At the same time, farmers, who had benefited from wartime conditions, faced falling crop prices as European nations resumed agricultural production and the federal government ended price supports.

AP® EXAM TIP

World War I and its aftermath unleashed a new wave of nativism, as well as a renewed fear of perceived radicalism. A Red Scare occurred, along with the passage of several immigration laws that targeted individuals from eastern European countries and Asia. Be able to explain the causes and effects of the first Red Scare and be able to compare the restriction of civil liberties during World War I to the restrictions of civil liberties during other conflicts.

A series of widespread strikes launched by labor unions in 1919 contributed to the fear that the United States was under assault by sinister, radical forces. As skyrocketing inflation undercut wages and employers launched a new round of union-busting efforts, labor went on the offensive. In 1919, more than four million workers went on strike nationwide. In February, a general strike in Seattle brought the entire city to a halt for six days. In September, striking Boston policemen left the city unguarded, resulting in widespread looting and violence. Massachusetts governor Calvin Coolidge sent in the National Guard to break the strike and restore order. Coolidge later refused to rehire the striking officers at the higher wages offered to their replacements, earning a national following.

Public officials and newspapers decried the violence, but they also greatly exaggerated the peril of the Red Scare. Communists and socialists did support some union activities. Yet few of the millions of workers who struck for higher wages and better working conditions had ties to extremists. The major prewar radical organization, the Industrial

Workers of the World, never recovered from the government harassment that had crippled it during World War I.

Scattered acts of violence allowed government and business leaders to stir up anxieties about the communist threat. On May 1, 1919, radicals sent more than thirty incendiary devices through the mail to prominent Americans, though authorities defused the bombs before they reached their targets. The following month, bombs exploded in eight cities, including one at the doorstep of the home of A. Mitchell Palmer, the attorney general of the United States.

After the attack on his home, Palmer launched a government crusade to root out and prosecute communists. Palmer believed that recent immigrants, mainly those from Russia and eastern and southern Europe, were the source of dangerous radicalism. To track down suspected radicals, Palmer selected J. Edgar Hoover to head the General Intelligence Division in the Department of Justice. In November 1919, based on Hoover's research and undercover activities, government agents in twelve cities rounded up and arrested hundreds of foreigners, including the anarchist and feminist Emma Goldman. Goldman, and some 250 other people caught in the government dragnet, were soon deported to Russia. Over the next few months, the **Palmer raids** continued in more than thirty cities. Authorities seized approximately six thousand suspected radicals, took them to police stations, interrogated them without the benefit of legal counsel, and held them incommunicado without stipulating the charges against them. Of the thousands arrested, the government found reason to deport 556. The raids did not uncover any extensive plots to overthrow the U.S. government, nor did they lead to the arrest of the bombers.

Palmer raids
The government roundup of some 6,000 suspected alien radicals in 1919–1920, ordered by Attorney General A. Mitchell Palmer and his assistant J. Edgar Hoover. The raids reflected the fears of foreign radicalism present during the first Red Scare and resulted in the deportation of 556 immigrants.

WORKING with EVIDENCE

Source: A. Mitchell Palmer, "The Case against the Reds," *Forum*, 1920

> "Like a prairie-fire, the blaze of revolution was sweeping over every American institution of law and order a year ago. It was eating its way into the homes of the American workman, its sharp tongues of revolutionary heat were licking the altars of the churches, leaping into the belfry of the school bell, crawling into the sacred corners of American homes, seeking to replace marriage vows with libertine laws, burning up the foundations of society.
>
> Robbery, not war, is the ideal of communism. This has been demonstrated in Russia, Germany, and in America. As a foe, the anarchist is fearless of his own life, for his creed is a fanaticism that admits no respect of any other creed. Obviously it is the creed of any criminal mind, which reasons always from motives impossible to clean thought. Crime is the degenerate factor in society."

Questions for Analysis

1. Identify the metaphor Palmer uses to describe revolution in this excerpt.
2. Explain how this metaphor supports Palmer's argument.
3. Explain how the comparison between communism and anarchism in this speech serves Palmer's purpose.
4. Evaluate the extent to which Palmer's argument in the second paragraph reflects progressive ideals.

Americans' initial support of the Palmer raids quickly faded in the face of civil liberty violations that accompanied the raids. In 1920, a group of pacifists, progressives, and constitutional lawyers formed the **American Civil Liberties Union (ACLU)** to monitor government abridgments of the Bill of Rights. Although the Palmer raids ended, the Red Scare extended throughout the 1920s. After J. Edgar Hoover became director of the Bureau of Investigation (later renamed the **Federal Bureau of Investigation**) in 1921, he continued spying and collecting information on suspected radicals and increasing his power over the next several decades.

influenza pandemic
A worldwide flu pandemic, also known as the "Spanish Flu," following the end of World War I. It killed an estimated 50 million individuals, including approximately 675,000 Americans.

Compounding Americans' anxieties, in late 1918, an **influenza pandemic** struck the United States. Part of a worldwide contagion, the disease infected nearly 20 percent of the U.S. population and killed more than 675,000 people. As the death toll mounted over the course of 1919, terror gripped the nation. Susanna Turner, a volunteer at an emergency hospital in Philadelphia, recalled: "The fear in the hearts of people just withered them. They were afraid to go out, afraid to do anything. . . . It was a horror-stricken time." A staggering 50 million people worldwide are estimated to have died from the flu before it subsided in 1920.

Racial strife also heightened postwar anxieties. Drawn by the promise of wartime industrial jobs, more than 400,000 Black people left the South beginning in 1917 and 1918 and headed north, hoping to escape poverty, racial discrimination, and violence. (By 1930, another 800,000 Black people had left the South.) This exodus became known as the **Great Migration**.

Great Migration
The population shift of more than 400,000 Black people who left the South beginning in 1917–1918 and headed north and west to escape poverty and racial discrimination. During the 1920s, another 800,000 Black people left the South.

During World War I, many Black people found work in steel production, meatpacking, shipbuilding, and other heavy industries, but most were relegated to low-paying jobs. Still, as a carpenter earning $95 a month wrote from Chicago to a friend back in Hattiesburg, Mississippi: "I should have been here 20 years ago. I just begin to feel like a man." Most Black women remained employed as domestic workers, but more than 100,000 obtained manufacturing jobs.

For many Black people, however, the North was not the "promised land" they expected. Instead, they encountered bitter opposition from white migrants from the

Hulton Archive/Getty Images

The Influenza Epidemic, Lawrence, Massachusetts, 1918 Nurses take care of patients suffering from the Spanish influenza pandemic in Lawrence, Massachusetts. This textile town had experienced an influx of immigrants from southern and eastern Europe around the turn of the twentieth century and was the scene of major union organizing and labor strife just before the pandemic struck.

How does the historical situation of the influenza outbreak help explain anti-immigrant sentiment during this era?

South competing for employment and scarce housing. As Black and white veterans returned from the war, racial hostilities exploded.

In 1919, race riots erupted in twenty-five cities throughout the country, including one in Washington, D.C. The previous year, W. E. B. Du Bois of the NAACP had urged the Black community to "close ranks" to fight Germany, but the racial violence against Black people in 1919 embittered him. "By the God of Heaven," Du Bois wrote, "we are cowards and jackasses if now that that war is over, we do not marshal every ounce of our brain and brawn to fight a sterner, longer, more unbending battle against the forces of hell in our own land."

The worst of these disturbances occurred in Chicago. On a hot July day, a Black youth swimming at a Lake Michigan beach inadvertently crossed over into an area of water customarily reserved for white people. In response, white bathers shouted at the swimmer to return to the Black section of the beach and hurled stones at him. The Black swimmer drowned, and word of the incident quickly spread through white and Black neighborhoods in Chicago. For thirteen days, mobs of Black and white people attacked each other, ransacked businesses, and torched homes. Over the course of the riots, at least 38 people (23 Black and 15 white) died, 520 people (342 Black and 178 white) were injured, and more than 1,000 Black families were left homeless.

REVIEW

- In what ways was the social turmoil after World War I a result of the war itself?
- To what extent did the Great Migration lead to greater freedom for Black people in the United States after World War I?

AP® Skills Workshop: Writing Historically

Additional Practice in Responding to a Short-Answer Question

Answer **A**, **B**, and **C**.

(A) Briefly explain ONE historical event or development that led to the first Red Scare.

(B) Briefly explain ANOTHER historical event or development that led to the first Red Scare.

(C) Briefly explain ONE historical event or development that resulted from the first Red Scare.

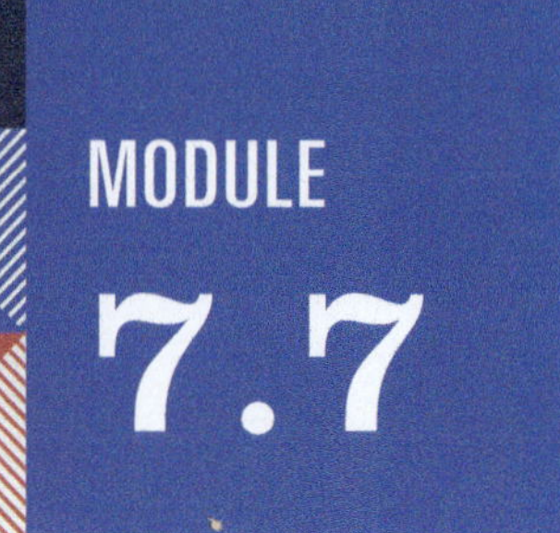

MODULE 7.7

1920s: Innovations in Communication and Technology

FOCUS

As you read this module, think about the effects of economic and technological innovations. What factors contributed to the creation of a consumer economy, and how did that affect American society? What role did federal policy play in the economic boom of the 1920s?

AP® EXAM TIP

The decade following World War I was a time of great economic growth and urbanization. Mass production of consumer goods reached new heights. Average Americans had the disposable income to buy the commodities produced and to enjoy the new forms of entertainment that became prevalent in the Roaring Twenties. Who did not enjoy this unparalleled wealth? The AP® Exam often asks questions about causes and effects of the economic success of the 1920s as well as its limitations.

Despite the turbulence of the immediate postwar period and the persistence of underlying social and racial tensions, the 1920s were a time of vigorous economic growth and urbanization. Between 1922 and 1927, the economy grew by 7 percent a year. Unemployment rates remained low, as producers added new workers in an effort to keep up with increasing consumer demand. Aligning themselves with big business, government officials took an active role in stimulating industrial and economic growth. The average purchasing power of wage earners soared, although many Americans still did not share in this new abundance.

Government's Role in the Economy

The general prosperity of the 1920s owed a great deal to backing by the federal government. Republicans controlled the presidency and Congress. Although they claimed to stand for principles of laissez-faire and opposed various economic and social reforms, they were willing to use governmental power to support large corporations and the wealthy.

Senator Warren G. Harding of Ohio, who was elected president in 1920, declared that he and his party wanted "less government in business and more business in government." Harding's cabinet appointments reflected this goal. Treasury Secretary Andrew Mellon, a banker and an aluminum company titan, believed that the government should stimulate economic growth by reducing taxes on the rich, raising tariffs to protect manufacturers from foreign competition, and trimming the budget.

The Republican Congress enacted much of this agenda. During the Harding administration, tax rates for the wealthy, which had skyrocketed during World War I, plummeted from 66 percent to 20 percent. Mellon believed that those on the lower rungs of the economic ladder would prosper once business people invested the extra money they received from tax breaks into expanding production. In theory, the wealth would trickle down through increased jobs and purchasing power. At the same time, Republicans turned Progressive Era regulatory agencies such as the Federal Trade Commission and the Federal Reserve Board into boosters for major corporations and financial institutions by weakening enforcement.

Secretary of Commerce Herbert Hoover had an even greater impact than Mellon in cementing the government-business partnership during the 1920s. Hoover believed that the federal government had a role to play in the economy and in lessening economic suffering. Rejecting government control of business activities, however, he insisted on voluntary cooperation between the public and private sectors. Hoover favored the creation of trade associations in which businesses would collaborate to stabilize production levels, prices, and wages. In turn, the Commerce Department would provide helpful data and information to improve productivity and trade.

Hoover's vision fit into a larger Republican effort to weaken unions by promoting voluntary business-sponsored worker welfare initiatives. For example, under the **American Plan**, some firms established health insurance and pension plans for their workers. As early as 1914, Henry Ford provided his autoworkers over twenty-two years of age "a share in the profits of the house" equal to a minimum wage of $5 a day, and he cut the workday from nine hours to eight. Already under pressure from such tactics, unions were further damaged by a series of Supreme Court rulings that restricted strikes and overturned hard-won victories such as child labor legislation and minimum wage laws. By 1929, union membership had dropped from approximately five million to three million, or about 10 percent of the industrial labor market.

Scandals during the presidency of Warren G. Harding diminished its luster but did not tarnish the shine of Republican economic policy. The **Teapot Dome scandal** grabbed the most headlines. In 1921, Interior Secretary Albert Fall collaborated with Navy Secretary Edwin Denby to transfer potential oil fields to the Interior Department. Fall then secretly parceled out these properties to private companies. As a result, Harry F. Sinclair's Mammoth Oil Company received a lease to develop the Teapot Dome section in Wyoming. In return for this handout, Sinclair delivered more than $300,000 to Fall. In the wake of congressional hearings, Fall and Sinclair were convicted on a number of criminal charges and sent to jail.

Teapot Dome scandal
An oil and land scandal that highlighted the close ties between big business and the federal government in the early 1920s.

Harding's sudden death from a heart attack in August 1923 brought Vice President Calvin Coolidge to the presidency. Coolidge distanced himself from the scandals of his

Granger – Historical Picture Archive

Teapot Dome Scandal Clifford K. Berryman, the political cartoonist for the Washington *Evening Star*, illustrates the Teapot Dome scandal, which damaged the Harding administration. Captioned "Juggernaut," this image shows Secretary of the Navy Edwin Denby on the left and Secretary of the Interior Albert Fall on the right fleeing from charges of bribery and corruption that a Senate committee brought to light.

In what ways is this image a reflection of its historical situation?

predecessor's administration but reaffirmed Harding's economic policies. "The chief business of the American people is business," President Coolidge remarked succinctly.

Americans Become Consumers

Despite the political scandals, the 1920s marked a period of economic expansion and general prosperity. National income rose from approximately $63 billion to $88 billion, and per capita income jumped from $641 to $847, an increase of 32 percent. The purchasing power of wage earners climbed approximately 20 percent.

This great spurt of economic growth in the 1920s resulted from the application of technological innovation and scientific management techniques to industrial production. Perhaps the greatest innovation came with the widespread use of the assembly line. Used in the automobile industry even before World War I, the assembly line moved the product to a worker who performed a specific task before sending it along to the next worker. This deceptively simple system, perfected by Henry Ford after the war, saved enormous time and energy by emphasizing repetition, accuracy, and standardization. Streamlined production lowered costs, which, in turn, allowed Ford to lower prices and make automobiles affordable for a growing middle class.

Besides the automobile, the economy of the 1920s focused on the production of consumer-oriented goods previously considered luxuries. The electrification of urban homes created demand for a wealth of new labor-saving appliances. Refrigerators, washing machines, toasters, and vacuum cleaners appealed to middle-class housewives whose husbands could afford to purchase them. Wristwatches replaced bulkier pocket watches. Radios became the chief source of home entertainment.

These new household items changed the lives of many Americans. Appliances lightened the housework of many married, middle-class women while also raising living standards and expectations of household cleanliness. However, no single product had as profound an effect on American life in the 1920s as the automobile. Auto sales soared

ullstein bild via Getty Images

Ford Assembly Line Henry Ford perfected the mass production of low-cost, easy-to-repair automobiles in the early twentieth century and put them within the economic reach of many Americans. This photograph shows the body of an automobile being attached to the frame on an assembly line at one of Ford Motor Company's plants in the 1920s.

What elements of mass production are evident in this photograph?

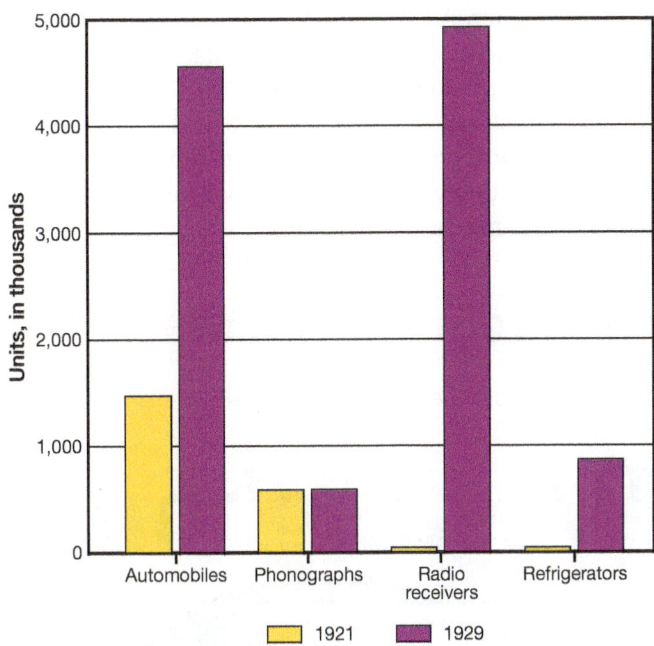

Production of Consumer Goods, 1921 and 1929 Rising per capita income, lower manufacturing costs, urban electrification, and advertising spurred the production of consumer goods in the 1920s.

How did the mass production of the goods shown in the figure bring Americans from all regions together?

in the 1920s from 1.5 million to 5 million, fueling the growth of related industries such as steel, rubber, petroleum, and glass. In 1929, Ford and his competitors at General Motors, Chevrolet, and Oldsmobile employed nearly 4 million workers, and around one in eight American workers toiled in factories connected to automobile production.

The automobile also changed day-to-day living patterns. Although most roads and highways consisted of dirt and contained rocks and ruts, enough were paved to extend the boundaries of suburbs farther from the city. By the end of the 1920s, around 17 percent of Americans lived in suburbia.

Cars allowed families to travel to vacation destinations and visit relatives at greater distances from their homes. Even the roadside landscape changed, as gas stations, diners, and motels sprang up to serve motorists. Each year, vacation resorts on the east and west coasts of Florida attracted thousands of tourists who drove south to enjoy the state's beautiful beaches. Motorists also flocked to national parks in the Rocky Mountains and on the West Coast.

The automobile also provided new dating opportunities for young men and women. At the turn of the twentieth century, a young man courted a woman by going to her home and sitting with her on the sofa or out on the porch under the watchful eyes of her parents and family members. With the arrival of the automobile, couples could move from the couch in the parlor to the backseat of a car, away from adult supervision. Driving to a "lover's lane," the young couple could express their feelings with greater physicality than before.

Although Ford and his fellow manufacturers succeeded in lowering prices, they still had to persuade Americans to spend hard-earned money to buy their products. Turning for help to the fledgling advertising industry, manufacturers nearly tripled their spending on advertising over the course of the 1920s. Firms pitched their products around price and quality, but they directed their efforts more than ever to the personal psychology of the consumer. Advertisers played on consumers' unexpressed fears, unfulfilled desires, hopes for success, and sexual fantasies. The producers of Listerine mouthwash transformed a product previously used to disinfect hospitals into one that fought the dreaded but made-up disease of halitosis (bad breath). Advertisers told people that they could measure success through consumption. Purchasing a General Electric all-steel refrigerator not only would preserve food longer, but also would enhance the owners' reputation among their neighbors.

AP® WORKING with EVIDENCE

Source: Westinghouse Appliance Advertisement, 1924

Granger – Historical Picture Archive

About the source: This magazine advertisement reads: "Isn't my new Turnover Toaster a beauty? I just bought it. During February, you know, one thinks about adding to the home furnishings, and these handy electrical appliances make housekeeping so much easier! My Westinghouse Iron and Percolator Set have really become indispensable, they're so useful and attractive. Next we're going to get the Waffle Iron. Thousands of women are choosing Westinghouse appliances, both for their reliability and their good looks. Pictures don't half tell the story, but you can see them at any of the stores handling the Westinghouse line. Now is a good time to buy them." At the bottom of the advertisement are the following electric appliances, from left to right: waffle iron, light bulbs, table stove, iron, warming pad, small motor, battery charger, electric range, percolator, and bell ringer.

Questions for Analysis

1. Identify at least five types of electric appliances depicted in the advertisement that are still in use today.
2. Describe how this advertisement was meant to appeal to 1920s consumers.
3. Explain the effects of advertisements such as this one on American society in the 1920s.

Although average wages and incomes rose during the 1920s, the majority of Americans did not have the disposable income to afford the bounty of new consumer goods. To resolve this problem, companies extended credit in dizzying amounts. By 1929, consumers were buying 60 percent of their cars and 80 percent of their radios and furniture on credit—mainly through the installment plan. "Buy now and pay later" became the motto of corporate America.

REVIEW

- How did American economic policy change during the 1920s?
- What factors contributed to the rise of the consumer economy during the 1920s?

AP® Skills Workshop: Writing Historically

Additional Practice in Responding to a Long-Essay Question

Evaluate the extent to which government policies enacted during World War I shaped the U.S. consumer economy of the 1920s.

MODULE 7.8

1920s: Cultural and Political Controversies

FOCUS

As you read this module, consider the factors that contributed to social and cultural trends during the 1920s in the United States and how those changes affected American society.

Although the general prosperity of the period masked the tensions lying beneath the surface, it did not eliminate them. The consumerism of the 1920s led to the emergence of new, distinctly modern cultural patterns. Advertising and credit, two of the mainstays of modern capitalism, sought to bypass the time-honored virtues of saving and living within one's means. Conventional sexual standards came under assault from the growth of the film and automobile industries, which influenced clothing styles and dating practices.

In addition to moral and social behavior, traditional racial assumptions came under attack. Black American writers and artists condemned racism, drew on their own rich legacies, and produced a cultural renaissance. Other Black people, led by the Jamaican immigrant Marcus Garvey, rejected the integrationist strategy of the NAACP in favor of Black nationalism. Attacks on traditional cultural and racial values did not go uncontested.

During this era when technological innovations overturned traditional economic values, when modes of social behavior were in a state of flux, and when white supremacy came under assault, it is not surprising that many segments of the population resisted these changes. Rallying around ethnic and racial purity, Protestant fundamentalism, and family values, defenders of an older America attempted to roll back the tide of modernity. The enactment of prohibition was their greatest victory.

Urban Growth and Perilous Prosperity

The growth of cities helped promote the spread of the consumer-oriented economy. Increasingly clustered in urban areas, people had more convenient access to department stores and chain stores. Advertisers targeted city residents because they were easier to reach. Although cities contained plenty of poor people who could not afford to buy items they considered luxuries, a large middle class of shoppers provided a growing market.

The census of 1920 reported that for the first time in U.S. history, a majority of Americans lived in cities. In 1910, just over 54 percent of the nation lived in small towns and villages with fewer than 2,500 people. A decade later, only 49 percent inhabited these areas. The end of World War I brought a decline in demand for American agricultural goods as European farmers raised their output, and about six million residents left their farms and villages and moved to cities. By 1930, the percentage of those living in rural America further dropped to 44 percent. The war had pushed large numbers of Black Americans out of the rural South for jobs in the cities. Also, with war's end, immigration from southern and eastern Europe resumed.

The West grew faster than any other region of the country, and its cities boomed. From 1910 to 1930, the population of the United States increased by 33.5 percent; at the same time, the population of the West soared by nearly 59 percent. In northern California, the Bay Area cities of San Francisco, Oakland, and Berkeley nearly doubled in population. Seattle, Portland, Denver, and Salt Lake City also rose in prominence. After the war, western city leaders boasted of the business and employment opportunities and beautiful landscapes that awaited migrants to their urban communities.

Los Angeles stood out for its growth, which skyrocketed from 319,000 residents in 1910 to over 1.2 million in 1930. The mild, sunny climate of southern California attracted midwesterners and northeasterners who were tired of rugged winters. Los Angeles was surrounded by beautiful mountains, and promoters enticed new residents to buy up real estate, which could be purchased cheaply and sold for a big profit. The city offered a dependable public transit system with streetcars that connected Los Angeles and neighboring counties. During the 1920s, the motion picture industry settled there, and its movies delighted audiences throughout the nation. This urban boom boosted economic growth and, along with it, consumer spending.

Prosperity in the 1920s was real enough, but behind the impressive financial indicators flashed warnings that profound danger loomed ahead. Perhaps most important, the boom was accompanied by growing income inequality. A majority of workers lived below the poverty line, and farmers plunged deeper into hard times. Corporate profits increased much faster than wages, resulting in a disproportionate share of the wealth going to the rich. The combined income of the top 1 percent of families was greater than that of the 42 percent at the bottom; 66 percent lived below the income level necessary to maintain an adequate standard of living.

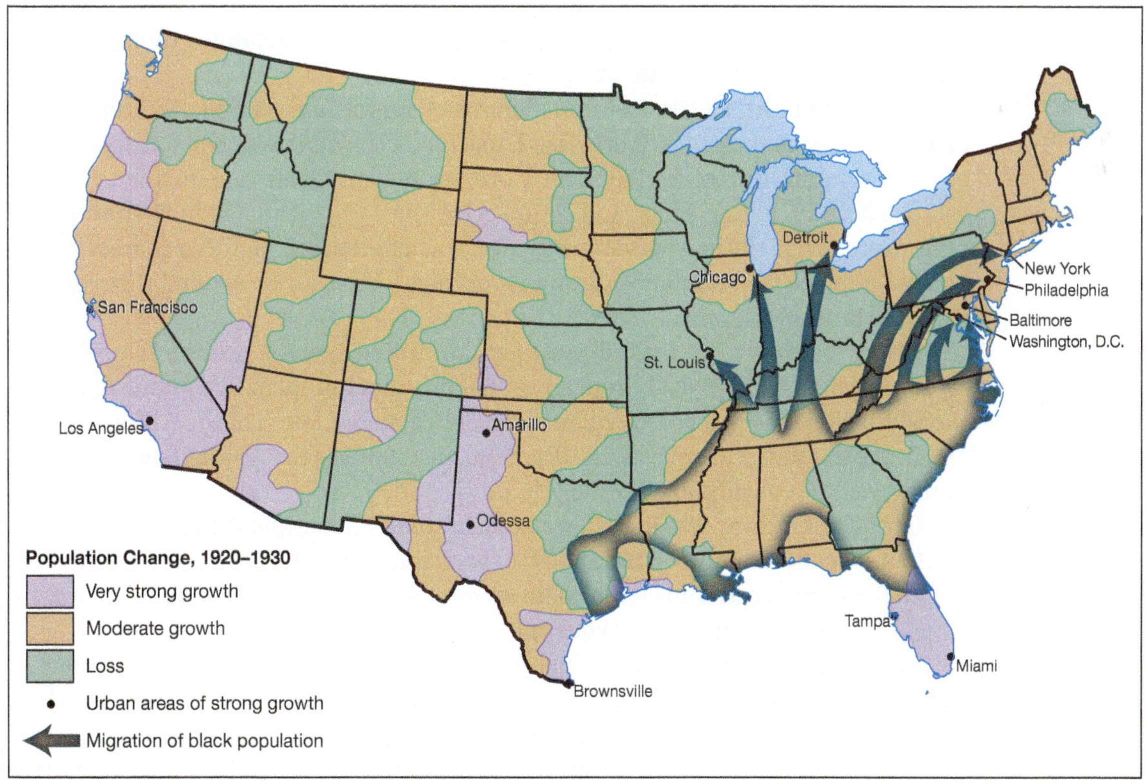

MAP 7.7 The Shift from Rural to Urban Population, 1920–1930 During the late nineteenth and early twentieth centuries, the population of the nation shifted from rural to urban areas. In the 1920s, migration continued, especially among Black Americans in the South and Latinos in the Southwest and West. Many of these migrants from rural to urban landscapes stayed in the same region, particularly Latinos.

What historical trends fueled this migration?

Income inequality was a critical problem because America's new mass-production economy depended on ever-increasing consumption. The groups with higher income could consume only so much, no matter how much of the nation's wealth they controlled. While the expansion of consumer credit helped hide this fundamental weakness, the low wages earned by most Americans drove down demand over time. Cutbacks in demand forced manufacturers to reduce production, thereby reducing jobs and increasing unemployment, which in turn dragged down the demand for consumer goods even further. As a result, by 1926, the growth of automobile sales had begun to slow, as did new housing construction—signs of an economy heading for trouble.

At the same time, the wealthy few used their disproportionate wealth to speculate in the stock market and risky real estate ventures. To encourage investments, brokers promoted buying stocks on margin (credit) and required down payments of only a fraction of the market price. Without vigilant governmental oversight, banks and lending agencies extended credit without taking into account what would happen if a financial panic occurred and they were suddenly required to call in all of their loans.

To make matters worse, many banks engaged in speculative lending operations, putting the savings of ordinary depositors at risk if a panic suddenly occurred. With minimal interference from the Federal Trade Commission, business people often managed firms in a reckless way that created a high level of interdependence among them. This interlocking system of corporate ownership and control meant that the collapse of one company could bring down many others, while also imperiling the banks and other lenders that had financed them too generously.

Rampant real estate speculation in Florida foreshadowed these dangers. Speculators and unscrupulous agents worked under the assumption that land values in Florida would continue to increase forever. At the height of the bubble, investors bought properties sight unseen. However, severe storms in 1926 and 1928 abruptly halted the rise in land values. Land prices spiraled downward, speculators defaulted on bank loans, and financial institutions tottered.

Throughout the 1920s, fortunes plummeted for farmers as well. Declining world demand following the end of World War I, together with increased productivity because of the mechanization of agriculture, drove down farm prices and income. Between 1925 and 1929, falling wheat and cotton prices cut farm income in half. The collapse of farm prices had the most devastating effects on tenants and southern sharecroppers, who were forced off their lands through mortgage foreclosures. Around three million displaced farmers migrated to cities.

Internationally, the United States encountered serious economic obstacles. World War I had destroyed European economies, leaving them ill equipped to repay the $11 billion they had borrowed from the United States. Much of the Allied recovery, and hence the ability to repay debts, depended on obtaining the reparations imposed on Germany at the conclusion of World War I.

Germany, however, was in even worse shape than France and Britain and could not meet its obligations. Consequently, the U.S. government negotiated a deal by which the United States provided loans to Germany to pay its reparations and Britain and France reduced the size of Germany's payments.

The result was a series of circular payments. American banks loaned money to Germany, which used the money to pay reparations to Britain and France, which in turn used Germany's reparations payments to repay debts owed to U.S. banks. What seemed a satisfactory resolution at the time proved a calamity. In undertaking this revolving-door solution, U.S. bankers added to the cycle of spiraling credit and placed themselves at the mercy of unstable European economies.

Compounding the problem, Republican administrations in the 1920s supported high tariffs on imports, reducing foreign manufacturers' revenues and therefore their nations' tax receipts, making it more difficult for these countries to pay off their debts. However, most of the nation ignored growing evidence of the fragility of American prosperity, as Americans fixated on the social and cultural consequences of mass consumption.

- What factors account for the growth in urban areas during the 1920s?
- What were the main weaknesses of the U.S. economy during the 1920s?

Challenges to Social Conventions

Challenges to the virtues of thrift and sacrifice were accompanied by a transformation of the moral codes of late-nineteenth-century America, especially those relating to sex. The entertainment industry played a large role in promoting relaxed attitudes toward sexual relations to a mass audience throughout the nation. The motion picture business attracted women and men to movie palaces where they could see swashbuckling heroes and glamorous heroines.

Originally shown as short films for five cents in nickelodeons, movies appealed to a national audience. By the 1920s, films had expanded into feature-length pictures, Hollywood film studios had blossomed into major corporations, and movies were shown in ornate theaters in cities and towns across the country. The star system was born, and matinee idols influenced fashions and hairstyles. Female stars dressed as **flappers** and wooed audiences. Representing the liberated **new woman**, flappers wore short skirts, used ample makeup (formerly associated with prostitutes), smoked cigarettes in public, drank illegal alcoholic beverages, and gyrated to jazz tunes on the dance floor.

Even as Americans enjoyed new entertainment opportunities, most remained faithful to traditional values. By 1929, approximately 40 percent of households owned a radio. Shows such as *The General Motors Family* and *The Maxwell House Hour* blended product advertising with family entertainment. *Amos 'n' Andy* garnered large audiences by satirizing Black working-class life, which, intentionally or not, reinforced racist stereotypes. In cities like New York and Chicago, immigrants could tune in to foreign-language radio programs aimed at non-English-speaking ethnic groups, which offered listeners an outlet for preserving their identity in the face of the increasing homogeneity fostered by the national consumer culture.

The most spirited challenge to both traditional values and the modern consumer culture came from a diverse group of intellectuals known as the **Lost Generation**. Author Gertrude Stein coined the term to describe the disillusionment that many of her fellow writers and artists felt after the ravages of World War I. Already concerned about the impact of mass culture and corporate capitalism on individualism and free thought, they focused their talents on criticizing what they saw as the hypocrisy of old values and the conformity ushered in by the new.

In the novel *This Side of Paradise* (1920), F. Scott Fitzgerald complained that his generation had "grown up to find all Gods dead, all wars fought, all faith in man shaken." In a series of novels, including *Main Street* (1920), *Babbitt* (1922), and *Elmer Gantry* (1927), Sinclair Lewis ridiculed the narrow-mindedness of small-town life, the empty materialism of businessmen, and the insincerity of evangelical preachers. Journalist Henry Louis (H. L.) Mencken picked up these subjects in the pages of his magazine, *The American Mercury*. From his vantage point in Baltimore, Maryland, he lampooned the beliefs and behavior of Middle America.

AP® EXAM TIP

While the economy prospered during the 1920s, conflicts emerged over how to address controversial topics: gender roles, urban vs. rural values, religion vs. science, immigration restrictions, and race relations. Be prepared to explain the causes and consequences of social and cultural tensions during the 1920s on the AP® Exam.

flapper

A term for the modern, sexually liberated woman popularized in movies and magazines in the 1920s. Flappers defied traditional, conservative views of women by wearing short hair and short skirts, smoking, drinking, and acting more independently.

Lost Generation

A term coined by the writer Gertrude Stein to describe the writers and artists disillusioned with the consumer culture of the 1920s.

Everett Collection, Inc.

Hollywood Hollywood's silent movies provided audiences with graphic images of changing sexual values during the 1920s before the emergence of "talkies" near the end of the decade. Rudolph Valentino, pictured in this advertisement for *Blood and Sand* (1922), was the leading male heartthrob of the era.

How does this poster both uphold and challenge the gender norms of the early twentieth century?

Scholars joined literary and social critics in challenging conventional ideas. Sigmund Freud, an Austrian psychoanalyst, shifted emphasis in psychology away from culture to individual consciousness. His disciples stressed the role of the unconscious mind and the power of the sex drive in shaping human behavior, ideas that had influence not only in university education but also in advertising appeals.

Scholars also discredited conventional wisdom about race. Challenging studies that purported to demonstrate the intellectual superiority of white people over Black people, Columbia University anthropologist Franz Boas argued that any apparent intelligence gap between the races resulted from environmental factors and not heredity. His student Ruth Benedict further argued that the culture of so-called primitive tribes, such as the Pueblo Indians, produced a less stressful and more emotionally connected lifestyle than that of more advanced societies.

REVIEW

- How did the economic and cultural changes that took place during the 1920s challenge early twentieth-century American social norms?

The Harlem Renaissance and Black Nationalism

The greatest challenge to conventional notions about race came from Black Americans. The influx of southern Black migrants to the North during and after World War I created a Black cultural renaissance, with New York City's Harlem and the South Side of Chicago leading the way. Gathered in Harlem—with a population of more than 120,000 Black Americans in 1920 and growing every day—a group of Black writers paid homage to the **New Negro**, the second generation born after emancipation. These New Negro intellectuals refused to accept white supremacy. They expressed pride in their race, sought to perpetuate Black racial identity, and demanded full citizenship and participation in American society. Black writers and poets drew on themes from Black American life and history for inspiration in their literary works.

New Negro
The 1920s term for the second generation of Black Americans born after emancipation, who stood up for their rights.

AP® WORKING with EVIDENCE

Source: A. Philip Randolph and Chandler Owen, *The New Negro—What Is He?*, 1919

> "In politics, the New Negro, unlike the Old Negro, cannot be lulled into a false sense of security with political spoils and patronage. . . . The New Negro demands political equality. He recognizes the necessity of selective as well as elective representation. He realizes that so long as the Negro votes for the Republican or Democratic party, he will have only the right and privilege to elect but not to select his representatives. And he who selects the representatives controls the representative. The New Negro stands for universal suffrage. . . .
>
> Here, as a worker, he demands the full product of his toil. His immediate aim is more wages, shorter hours and better working conditions. As a consumer, he seeks to buy in the market, commodities at the lowest possible price.
>
> The social aims of the New Negro are decidedly different from those of the Old Negro. Here he stands for absolute and unequivocal '*social equality*.' . . . He insists that a society which is based upon justice can only be a society composed of *social equals*. . . . He realizes that the acceptance of laws against intermarriage is tantamount to the acceptance of the stigma of inferiority. Besides, laws against intermarriage expose Negro women to sexual exploitation, and deprive their offspring, by White men, of the right to inherit the property of their father."

Questions for Analysis

1. Identify the aims and demands of the "New Negro," according to Randolph and Owen.
2. Explain how Randolph and Owen support their argument for addressing the aims of the "New Negro."
3. Evaluate the extent of continuity between Randolph and Owen's arguments and earlier efforts to obtain civil rights for Black Americans.

The poets, novelists, and artists of the **Harlem Renaissance** captured the imagination of Black and white people alike. Many of these artists increasingly rejected white standards of taste as well as staid middle-class Black values. Writers Langston Hughes and Zora Neale Hurston in particular drew inspiration from the vernacular of Black folk life. In 1926, Hughes defiantly asserted: "We younger Negro artists who create now

Harlem Renaissance
The work of Harlem-based Black writers, artists, and musicians who flourished following World War I through the 1920s.

intend to express our dark-skinned selves without fear or shame. If white people are pleased, we are glad. If they are not, it doesn't matter."

Black music became a vibrant part of mainstream American popular culture in the 1920s. Musicians such as Ferdinand "Jelly Roll" Morton, Louis Armstrong, Edward "Duke" Ellington, and singer Bessie Smith developed and popularized two of America's most original forms of music—jazz and the blues. These unique compositions grew out of the everyday experiences of Black life and expressed the thumping rhythms of work, pleasure, and pain. Such music did not remain confined to dance halls and clubs in Black communities. It soon spread to white musicians and audiences for whom the hot beat of jazz rhythms meant emotional freedom and the expression of sexuality.

Universal Negro Improvement Association (UNIA)
Organization founded by Marcus Garvey in 1914 to promote Black self-help, pan-Africanism, and racial separatism.

In addition to providing a fertile ground for Black intellectuals, Harlem became the headquarters of the most significant alternative Black political vision of the 1920s. In 1916, Jamaican-born Marcus Mosiah Garvey settled in Harlem and became the leading exponent of Black nationalism. In 1914, Garvey had set up the **Universal Negro Improvement Association (UNIA)** in Jamaica, an organization through which he promoted racial separation and pride as well as economic self-help through Black business ownership.

New York Daily News Archive/Getty Images

Marcus Garvey Dressed in military regalia, Jamaican immigrant Marcus Garvey embodied the spirit of Black nationalism after World War I. His Universal Negro Improvement Association, headquartered in Harlem, attracted a sizable following in the United States, the Caribbean, Central America, Canada, and Africa. Garvey advocated Black political and economic independence and a "Back to Africa" movement.

To what extent were the aims of Garvey's civil rights movement like those of the NAACP?

Unlike the leaders of the NAACP, who sought equal access to American institutions and cooperation with white people, Garvey favored a "Back to Africa" movement that would ultimately repatriate many Black Americans to their ancestral homelands on the African continent. His recently acquired Black Star Line steamship company planned to transport passengers between the United States, the West Indies, and Africa. Together with the indigenous Black African majority, transplanted Black Americans would help overthrow colonial rule and use their power to assist Black people throughout the world.

In addition to offering a revival of Black cultural heritage and providing an outlet for dreams of economic advancement, Garvey tapped into the racial discontent of Black Americans for whom living in the United States had proved so difficult. He denounced what he saw as the accommodationist efforts of the NAACP and declared, "To be a Negro is no disgrace, but an honor, and we of the UNIA do not want to become white." Ironically, the UNIA and the Ku Klux Klan agreed on the necessity of racial segregation, though Garvey never accepted the premise that Black people were inferior. Garvey's appeals to Black manhood were accompanied by a celebration of Black womanhood. He set up the Black Cross Nurses, and his wife, Amy Jacques Garvey, went beyond her husband's traditional notions of femininity to extol the accomplishments of Black women in politics and culture.

Garveyism became the first mass Black American movement in U.S. history and was especially effective in recruiting working-class Black people. UNIA branches were established in thirty-eight states throughout the North and South and attracted some 500,000 members.

Given his ideas and outspokenness, Garvey soon made powerful enemies. Du Bois and fellow members of the NAACP despised him. The Black socialist labor leader A. Philip Randolph, who saw the UNIA program as just another form of exploitative capitalism, labeled Garvey an "unquestioned fool and ignoramus." Yet Garvey's downfall came from his own business practices. Convicted in 1925 of mail fraud related to his Black Star Line, Garvey served two years in federal prison until President Coolidge commuted his sentence and had the Jamaican citizen deported.

 REVIEW

- In what ways did the Harlem Renaissance challenge early twentieth-century social and cultural norms?

Prohibition, Fundamentalism, and Modern American Life

After decades of efforts to combat the use of alcohol, the Eighteenth Amendment, banning its manufacture and sale, was ratified in 1919. That same year, Congress passed the Volstead Act, which set up the legal machinery to enforce the amendment. Supporters claimed that prohibition would promote family stability, improve morals, and prevent crime. They took aim at the ethnic culture of saloons associated with urban immigrants.

Enforcing this attempt to promote traditional values proved to be the problem. In rural areas, "moonshiners" took grain and processed it into liquor. In big cities, clubs known as speakeasies offered illegal alcohol and the entertainment to keep their customers satisfied. Treasury Department agents roamed the country destroying stills and raiding speakeasies, but liquor continued to flow.

Even though prohibition did reduce alcohol consumption, crime flourished. Gangsters paid off police, bribed judges, and turned cities into battlegrounds between rival criminal gangs, reinforcing the notion among small-town and rural dwellers that urban life eroded American values. By the end of the decade, most Americans welcomed an end to prohibition.

Protestant fundamentalists also fought to uphold long-established values against modern-day intrusions. Around 1910, two rich Los Angeles churchgoers had subsidized and distributed a series of booklets called *The Fundamentals*, informing readers that the Bible offered a true account of the origin and development of humankind and the world and that its words had to be taken literally. After 1920, believers of this approach to interpreting the Bible became known as "fundamentalists." Their preachers spread the message of old-time religion through carnival-like revivals, and ministers used the new medium of radio to broadcast their sermons.

Fundamentalism's appeal was strongest in the Midwest and the South—the so-called Bible belt—where residents felt deeply threatened by the secular aspects of modern life that left their conventional religious teachings open to skepticism and scorn.

Nothing bothered fundamentalist Protestants as much as Charles Darwin's theory of evolution. In *On the Origin of Species* (1859), Darwin replaced the biblical story of creation with a scientific theory of the emergence and development of life that centered on evolution and natural selection. Fundamentalists rejected this explanation and repudiated the views of other Protestants who attempted to reconcile Darwinian evolution with God's Word by reading the Bible as a symbolic representation of what might have happened.

To combat any other interpretation of the beginnings of human life but the biblical one, in 1925, lawmakers in Arkansas, Florida, Mississippi, Oklahoma, and Tennessee made it illegal to teach in public schools and colleges "any theory that denies the story of the Divine Creation of man as taught in the Bible." Shortly after the anti-evolution law passed, the town of Dayton, Tennessee, decided to challenge it to draw attention and attract new investment to the area. The townspeople recruited John Scopes, a high school teacher of general science, to defy the law by lecturing from a biology textbook that presented Darwin's theory. With help from the ACLU, which wanted to challenge the restrictive state statute on the grounds of free speech and academic freedom, Dayton turned an ordinary judicial hearing into the "trial of the century."

The resulting trial brought Dayton more fame, much of it negative, than the planners had bargained for. When the court convened in July 1925, millions of people listened over the radio to the first trial ever broadcast. Reporters from all over the country descended on Dayton to keep their readers informed of the proceedings.

Clarence Darrow headed the defense team. A controversial criminal lawyer from Chicago, Darrow doubted the existence of God. On the other side, William Jennings Bryan, three-time Democratic candidate for president and secretary of state under Woodrow Wilson, assisted the prosecution. As a Protestant fundamentalist, Bryan believed that accepting scientific evolution would undermine the moral basis of politics and that communities should have the right to determine their children's school curriculum. A minister summed up what the fundamentalists considered to be at stake: "[Darwin's theory] breeds corruption, lust, immorality, greed, and such acts of criminal depravity as drug addiction, war, and atrocious acts of genocide."

The presiding judge, John T. Raulston, ruled that scientists could not take the stand to defend evolution because he considered their testimony "hearsay," given that they had not been present at the creation. The jury took only eight minutes to declare Scopes guilty, but his conviction was overturned by an appeals court on a technicality. Yet fundamentalists remained as certain as ever in their beliefs, and anti-evolution laws stayed in force in some Bible-belt states until the 1970s. The trial had not "settled" anything. Rather, it served to highlight a cultural division over the place of religion in American society that persists to the present day.

AP® WORKING with EVIDENCE

Source: Clarence Darrow and William Jennings Bryan, Transcript from *The State of Tennessee v. John Thomas Scopes,* 1925

"Q. [Mr. Darrow]. You have given considerable study to the Bible, haven't you, Mr. Bryan?

A. [Mr. Bryan]. Yes, sir, I have tried to.

Q. Then you have made a general study of it.

A. Yes, I have; I have studied the Bible for about fifty years, or sometime more than that. . . .

Q. You claim that everything in the Bible should be literally interpreted?

A. I believe everything in the Bible should be accepted as it is given there; some of the Bible is given illustratively. For instance: 'Ye are the salt of the earth.' I would not insist that man was actually salt, or that he had flesh of salt, but it is used in the sense of salt as saving God's people. . . .

Q. But when you read that Jonah swallowed the whale—or that the whale swallowed Jonah—excuse me please—how do you literally interpret that?

A. When I read that a big fish swallowed Jonah—it does not say whale.

Q. Doesn't it? Are you sure?

A. That is my recollection of it. A big fish, and I believe it, and I believe in a God who can make a whale and can make a man and can make both do what He pleases. . . .

Q. Now, you say, the big fish swallowed Jonah, and he there remained how long—three days—and then he spewed him upon the land. You believe that the big fish was made to swallow Jonah?

A. I am not prepared to say that; the Bible merely says it was done.

Q. You don't know whether it was the ordinary run of fish, or made for that purpose?

A. You may guess; you evolutionists guess. . . .

Q. You are not prepared to say whether that fish was made especially to swallow a man or not?

A. The Bible doesn't say, so I am not prepared to say. . . .

Q. But do you believe He made them—that He made such a fish and that it was big enough to swallow Jonah?

A. Yes sir. Let me add: One miracle is just as easy to believe as another. . . .

Q. Just as hard?

A. It is hard to believe for you, but easy for me. A miracle is a thing performed beyond what man can perform. When you get beyond what man can do, you get within the realm of miracles; and it is just as easy to believe the miracle of Jonah as any other miracle in the Bible."

Questions for Analysis

1. Identify Darrow's and Bryan's main arguments.
2. Describe how each supports his argument.
3. Explain how Darrow and Bryan represent different beliefs among Americans in the early twentieth century.

REVIEW

- What factors contributed to the rise of fundamentalism in the 1910s and 1920s?

Restriction of Immigration

Before the 1920s, anti-immigrant sentiment often reflected racial and religious bigotry, as reformers concentrated on preventing Catholics, Jews, and all non-Europeans from entering the United States. Social scientists validated these prejudices by categorizing darker-skinned immigrants as inferior races.

The harshest treatment was reserved for Asians. In 1908, President Theodore Roosevelt entered into a "Gentlemen's Agreement" with Japan that reduced Japanese immigration to the United States. In 1913, the California legislature passed a statute barring Japanese immigrants from buying land, a law that twelve other states subsequently enacted.

In 1917, reformers succeeded in further restricting immigration. Congress passed legislation to ban people who could not read English or their native language from entering the country. The act also denied entry to other undesirables: "alcoholics," "feeble-minded persons," "epileptics," "people mentally or physically defective," "professional beggars," "anarchists," and "polygamists." In barring people considered unfit to enter the country, lawmakers intended to keep out those who could not support themselves and might become public wards of the state and, in the case of anarchists and polygamists, those who threatened the nation's political and religious values.

Prohibition reflected the surge in nativist (anti-immigrant) and racist thinking that in many ways revealed long-standing fears. In the past, temperance reform was aimed at immigrants. The end of World War I brought a new wave of Catholic and Jewish emigration from eastern and southern Europe, triggering religious prejudice among Protestants. Just as immigrants had been linked to socialism and anarchism in the 1880s and 1890s, old-stock Americans associated these immigrants with immoral behavior and political radicalism and saw them as a threat to traditional U.S. culture and values. Moreover, as in the late nineteenth century, native-born workers saw immigrants as a source of cheap labor that threatened their jobs and wages.

Sacco and Vanzetti case
The 1920 case in which Nicola Sacco and Bartolomeo Vanzetti were convicted of robbery and murder. The trial centered on the defendants' foreign birth and political views, rather than the facts pertaining to their guilt or innocence, and drew worldwide criticism.

The **Sacco and Vanzetti case** provides the most dramatic evidence of this nativism. In 1920, a botched robbery in South Braintree, Massachusetts, resulted in the murder of two employees. Police charged Nicola Sacco and Bartolomeo Vanzetti with the crime. These two Italian immigrants shared radical political views as anarchists and World War I draft evaders. The subsequent trial revolved around their foreign birth and ideology more than the facts pertaining to their guilt or innocence. The presiding judge at the trial referred to the accused as "anarchistic bastards" and "damned dagos" (a derogatory term for Italians). Convicted and sentenced to death, Sacco and Vanzetti lost their appeals for a new trial. Criticism of the verdict came from all over the world. Workers in Mexico, Argentina, Uruguay, France, and Morocco organized vigils and held rallies in solidarity with the condemned men. Despite such support, the two men were executed in the electric chair in 1927.

The Sacco and Vanzetti case provides an extreme example of 1920s nativism, but the anti-immigrant views that contributed to the two men's conviction and execution were commonplace during the period and shared by Americans across the social spectrum. For example, Henry Ford saw immigrants as a threat to cherished traditions. Ford believed that immigrants were the cause of a decline in U.S. morality. He contended that aliens did not understand "the principles which have made our [native] civilization," and he blamed the influx of foreigners for society's "marked deterioration" during the 1920s.

National Origins Act
An act passed in 1924 establishing immigration quotas by national origin. It was intended to severely limit immigration from southern and eastern Europe as well as halt all immigration from East Asia.

Ford stirred up anti-immigrant prejudices mainly by targeting Jews. Believing that an international Jewish conspiracy was attempting to subvert non-Jewish societies, Ford serialized in his company newspaper the so-called *Protocols of the Elders of Zion*, an antisemitic text concocted in czarist Russia to justify pogroms—ethnically and religiously motivated attacks—against Jews. Ford continued to publish it even after the document was proved a fake.

Ford joined other nativists in supporting legislation to restrict immigration. In 1924, Congress passed the **National Origins Act**, a quota system on future immigration. The measure limited entry by any foreign group to 2 percent of the number

AP Photo/William B. Plowman

Sacco and Vanzetti Demonstration, Boston, March 1, 1925 Nicola Sacco and Bartolomeo Vanzetti were two Italian immigrants convicted of murder. Many courtroom observers believed their prosecution was due to their anarchist views and Italian heritage. Their convictions drew protests in major U.S. cities and even outside the country. The pair were executed by electric chair in 1927.

How does this photograph demonstrate the breadth of support for Sacco and Vanzetti?

of people of that nationality who resided in the United States in 1890. The statute's authors were interested mainly in curbing immigration from eastern and southern Europe. They chose 1890 as the benchmark for immigration because most newcomers from those two regions entered the United States after that year.

Quotas established for northern Europe went unfilled, while those for southern and eastern Europe could not accommodate the vast number of people who sought admission. The law continued to bar East Asian immigration altogether.

Immigration from Mexico and elsewhere in the Western Hemisphere, however, was exempted from the quotas of the National Origins Act because farmers in the Southwest needed Mexican laborers to tend their crops and pressured the government to excuse them from coverage. In a related measure, in 1924, Congress established the Border Patrol to control the flow of undocumented immigration from Mexico. Nevertheless, *legal* immigration to the United States from Mexico increased during the 1920s.

With immigration of those considered "undesirable" severely if not completely curtailed, some nativist reformers shifted their attention to Americanization, which developed into one of the largest social and political movements in American history. Speaking about immigrants, educator E. P. Cubberley said, "Our task is to break up their groups and settlements, to assimilate and amalgamate these people as a part of our American race, to implant in their children the northern-European conception of righteousness, law and order, and popular government." Business corporations conducted Americanization and naturalization classes on factory floors. Schools, patriotic societies, fraternal organizations, women's groups, and labor unions launched citizenship classes.

In the Southwest and on the West Coast, white people aimed their Americanization efforts at the growing population of Mexican Americans. Subject to segregated education, Mexican Americans were expected to speak English in their classes. Anglo school administrators and teachers generally believed that Mexican Americans were suited only for farmwork and manual trades. For Mexican Americans, therefore, Americanization meant vocational training and preparation for low-status, low-wage jobs.

American Indians fared little better. During World War I, to save money, the federal government had ceased appropriating funds for public health programs aimed at benefiting American Indians living on reservations. With the war over, the government failed to restore the funds. Throughout the 1920s, rates of tuberculosis, eye infections, and infant mortality spiked among the American Indian population. Boarding schools continued to promote menial service jobs for American Indian students. On the brighter side, in 1924, Congress passed the **Indian Citizenship Act**, granting citizenship and the right to vote to all American Indians. Nevertheless, most remained outside the economic and political mainstream of American society with meager government help.

Chinese residents also continued to face discrimination and segregation. The Chinese Exclusion Act remained in operation, making it difficult for nurturing family life. By 1920, Chinese men outnumbered Chinese women by seven to one. Furthermore, immigration restrictions prohibited Chinese workingmen from bringing their wives into the country. The 1924 Immigration Act made matters worse by banning all Asian women from entering the country. That same year, the Supreme Court upheld the segregation of Chinese children in public schools.

Chinese communities faced problems like those experienced by other ethnic groups. Tensions over assimilation developed between those born in China and their American-born children. One Chinese American who grew up in San Francisco noted, "There was endless discussion about what to do about the dilemma of being *caught in between*." Many Chinese parents prohibited their children from speaking English at home and sent them to Chinese-language schools after public school. Chinese American children found cultural preservation efforts burdensome as they increasingly partook in America's growing consumer culture.

Despite attempts at Americanization, ethnic groups did not dissolve into a melting pot and lose their cultural identities. First-generation Americans—the children of immigrants—learned English, enjoyed American popular culture, and dressed in fashions of the day. Yet in cities around the country where immigrants had settled, ethnic enclaves remained intact and preserved the religious practices and social customs of their residents.

- What was the connection between anti-immigrant sentiment and the defense of tradition during the 1920s?

The Resurrection of the Ku Klux Klan

Nativism received its most spectacular boost from the reemergence of the Ku Klux Klan in 1915. Originally an organization dedicated to terrorizing emancipated Black Americans and their white Republican allies in the South during Reconstruction, the KKK branched out during the 1920s to the North, Midwest, and West. In addition to Black people, the new Klan targeted Catholics and Jews, and immigrants, as well as anyone who was alleged to have violated community moral values or supported the teaching of evolutionary theory.

The organization consisted of a cross section of native-born Protestants mainly from the middle and working classes who sought to reverse a perceived decline in their social and economic power. Revived by W. J. Simmons, a former Methodist minister, the new Klan celebrated its founding at Stone Mountain, Georgia, near Atlanta. There, Klansmen bowed to the twin symbols of their cause, the American flag and a burning cross that represented their fiery determination to stand up for their vision of Christian morality and against all those considered "un-American."

People flocked to the new KKK, and by the mid-1920s, Klan membership totaled more than three million men and women. Not confined to rural areas, the revived Klan counted a significant following in cities such as Indianapolis, Detroit, Chicago, Denver, Portland, and Seattle. Many rural dwellers who had moved into cities with large numbers of Black migrants and recent immigrants found solace in Klan vows to preserve "Native, white, Protestant supremacy."

The phenomenal growth of the KKK in the 1920s resulted from the desire to reestablish traditional values as well as sheer hostility toward Black people and immigrants. In the face of challenges to conventional values, a changing sexual morality, and the flouting of prohibition, wives joined their husbands as devoted followers. Some Protestant women appreciated the Klan's message condemning abusive husbands and fathers and the group's affirmation of the status of white Protestant women as the embodiment of virtue.

Ku Klux Klan March in Washington, D.C., September 13, 1926 Tens of thousands of members of the Ku Klux Klan marched in the nation's capital in 1925 and 1926, as seen in this photograph. At the height of its political power, the Klan had an estimated three million dues-paying members and had elected officials to political office in several states to further their anti-Black, anti-Jew, anti-Catholic, anti-evolution, anti–women's rights agenda.

Why was the Klan able to temporarily broaden its appeal in the 1920s?

Nevertheless, the dominant principles of the resurgent KKK remained explicitly aggressive toward minority groups. Like the original Klan, the 1920s version employed terror tactics. Acting under cover of darkness and concealed in robes and hoods, Klansmen burned crosses to scare their victims, many of whom they beat, kidnapped, tortured, and murdered.

To gain greater legitimacy and to appeal to a wider audience, the Klan also participated in electoral politics. The KKK succeeded in electing governors in Georgia and Oregon, a U.S. senator from Texas, many state legislators, and other officials in California, Indiana, Michigan, Ohio, and Oklahoma. Politicians routinely joined the Klan to advance their careers, whether they shared its views or not.

In 1925, however, the KKK's self-proclaimed role as guardians of morality was undermined by a scandal. David Curtis Stephenson, who had been Grand Dragon of the Indiana KKK since 1923, was accused of kidnapping, raping, and torturing Madge Oberholtzer, a representative of the Young People's Reading Circle, an office in the state's Department of Public Instruction that promoted literacy. Oberholtzer died of wounds she received from Stephenson's assault on her. After Stephenson was convicted of second-degree murder in Oberholtzer's death, he hoped for a pardon from the governor of Indiana, Edward L. Jackson, who had expressed sympathy for the KKK. However, when no pardon was forthcoming from the governor, Stephenson began to provide the Indiana press with salacious details of bribes the KKK had offered to Indiana state officials, including Governor Jackson, which led to further arrests and convictions of both state officials and members of the KKK. Needless to say, these events made the Klan's claims to moral integrity suspect, and they helped cause membership to decline through the late 1920s.

AP® WORKING with EVIDENCE

Source: Gerald W. Johnson, "The Ku Kluxer," *American Mercury*, 1924

"The Ku Klux Klan was swept beyond the racial boundaries of the Negro and flourishes now in the Middle West because it is a perfect expression of the American idea that the voice of the people is the voice of God. The belief that the average klansman is consciously affected by an appeal to his baser self is altogether erroneous. In the voice of the organizer he hears a clarion call to knightly and selfless service. It strikes him as in no wise strange that he should be so summoned; is he not, as an American citizen, of the nobility? Politics has been democratized. Social usage has been democratized. Religion has been most astoundingly democratized. Why, then, not democratize chivalry?

The klansman has already been made, in his own estimation, politically a monarch, socially a peer of the realm, spiritually a high priest. Now the Ku Klux Klan calls him to step up and for the trifling consideration of ten dollars he is made a Roland, a Lancelot, a knight-errant vowed to the succor of the oppressed, the destruction of ogres and magicians, the defense of the faith. Bursting with noble ideals and lofty aspirations, he accepts the nomination. The trouble is that this incantation doesn't work, as none of the others has worked, except in his imagination. King, aristocrat, high priest as he believes himself to be, he is neither royal, noble, nor holy. So, under his white robe and pointed hood he becomes not a Chevalier Bayard* but a thug."

*A French knight who lived during the late fifteenth and early sixteenth centuries. He was known for being virtuous and fearless.

Questions for Analysis

1. Describe how the article characterizes the Klansman in the first paragraph.
2. Describe how the article critiques this characterization in the second paragraph.
3. Explain how this article mocks the Ku Klux Klan.

REVIEW

- How did nativism foster the reemergence of the Ku Klux Klan during the 1920s?

Politics and the Fading of Prosperity

The 1924 presidential election exposed serious fault lines within the Democratic Party. Since Reconstruction, Democrats had dominated the South, and Republicans ceased to compete for office in the region. Southern Democrats shared fundamentalist religious beliefs and support for prohibition that usually placed them at odds with big-city Democrats. The northern urban wing of the party also represented immigrants who rejected prohibition as contrary to their cultural practices. These distinctions, however, were not absolute—some rural dwellers opposed prohibition, and some urbanites supported temperance.

Delegates to the 1924 Democratic convention in New York City disagreed over a party platform and a presidential candidate. When northeastern urban delegates

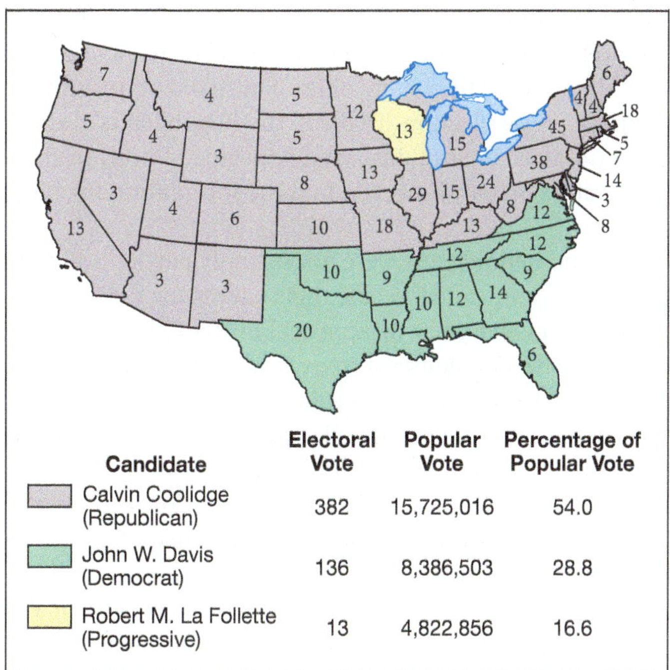

Candidate	Electoral Vote	Popular Vote	Percentage of Popular Vote
Calvin Coolidge (Republican)	382	15,725,016	54.0
John W. Davis (Democrat)	136	8,386,503	28.8
Robert M. La Follette (Progressive)	13	4,822,856	16.6

MAP 7.8 The Election of 1924 Republican Calvin Coolidge, who became president in August 1923 on the death of Warren Harding, continued Harding's policies of limited government regulation and corporate tax cuts. Coolidge easily defeated Democrat John Davis, whose strength was confined to the South. Running as the Progressive Party candidate, Senator Robert La Follette won 16 percent of the popular vote but carried only his home state of Wisconsin, with 13 electoral votes.

What do these election results reveal about public support for progressive reform in the 1920s?

attempted to insert a plank condemning the Ku Klux Klan for its intolerance, they lost by a thin margin. The sizable number of convention delegates who either belonged to or had been backed by the Klan ensured the proposal's defeat.

The selection of the presidential ticket proved even more divisive. Urban Democrats favored New York governor Alfred E. Smith. Smith came from an Irish Catholic immigrant family, had grown up on New York City's Lower East Side, and was sponsored by the Tammany Hall machine. The epitome of everything that rural Democrats despised, Smith also denounced prohibition. After a fierce contest, Smith lost the nomination to John W. Davis, a West Virginia Protestant and a defender of prohibition. Left deeply divided going into the general election, Davis lost to Calvin Coolidge in a landslide as a majority of Americans approved of the economic prosperity (**Map 7.8**).

In 1928, however, when the Democrats met in Houston, Texas, the delicate cultural equilibrium within the Democratic Party had shifted in favor of the urban forces. With Stephenson and the Klan discredited and no longer a force in Democratic politics, the delegates nominated Al Smith as their presidential candidate.

The Republicans selected Herbert Hoover, one of the most popular men in the United States. Affectionately called "the Great Humanitarian" for his European relief efforts after World War I, Hoover served as secretary of commerce during the Harding and Coolidge administrations. His name became synonymous with the Republican prosperity of the 1920s. In accepting his party's nomination for president in 1928, Hoover optimistically declared: "We in America today are nearer to the final triumph over poverty than ever before in the history of the land." A Protestant supporter of prohibition from a small town, Hoover was everything Smith was not.

The outcome of the election proved predictable. Hoover trounced Smith with 58 percent of the popular vote and more than 80 percent of the electoral vote. Despite the weakening economy, Smith lost usually reliable Democratic votes to religious and ethnic prejudices. The New Yorker prevailed only in Massachusetts, Rhode Island, and six southern states, failing to win his home state.

A closer look at the election returns showed a significant party realignment under way. Smith succeeded in identifying the Democratic Party with urban, ethnic-minority voters and attracting them to the polls. Despite the landslide loss, he captured the twelve largest cities in the nation, all of which had gone Republican four years earlier. In another fifteen big cities, Smith did better than the Democratic ticket had done in the 1924 election. To break the Republicans' national dominance, the Democrats would need a candidate who appealed to both traditional and modern Americans. Smith's defeat, however, laid the foundation for future Democratic political success.

The Democrats and Republicans were not the only parties that attracted voters in the 1920s. Some voters continued to cast their ballots for the Socialist Party. Others took the opportunity to voice their disapproval of Republican policies by voting for the remaining progressive candidates. Progressives did manage to hold on to seats in Congress, and in 1921, they helped pass the Sheppard-Towner Act, which appropriated federal funds to establish maternal and child centers. Senator Thomas J. Walsh of Montana, a progressive Democrat, led the investigation into the Teapot Dome scandal. But their efforts to restrict the power of the Supreme Court, reduce tax cuts for the wealthy, nationalize railroads, and extend agricultural relief to farmers were rebuffed by conservative legislative majorities.

In 1924, reformers nominated Senator Robert M. La Follette of Wisconsin to run for president on a revived Progressive Party ticket, but he came in a distant third. The Progressive Party collapsed soon after La Follette died in 1925.

Still, progressivism managed to stay alive on the local and state levels. Gifford Pinchot, a Roosevelt ally and a champion of conservation, twice won election as governor of Pennsylvania, starting in 1922. Social workers continued their efforts to alleviate urban poverty and lobby for government assistance to the poor. Even at the national level, women in the Children's Bureau maintained the progressive legacy by supporting assistance to families and devising social welfare proposals. Progressivism did not disappear during the 1920s, but it did fight an uphill and often losing battle during an age of conservative political ascendancy. Its weakness contributed to the government's failure to check the worst corporate and financial practices, a failure that would play a role in the nation's economic collapse.

REVIEW

- How did divisions within the Democratic Party contribute to Republican victories in the 1920s?
- In what ways did progressive reforms continue to influence American politics during the 1920s?

The Transitional Twenties

The 1920s signaled the tense transition of the United States from a rural, small-town society to an urban, industrial one. Factories roared with the noise of new products aimed at the mass of American consumers. Automobiles, fueled by gasoline, traveled up and down streets and highways. Electricity powered household appliances and ran movie projectors in theaters throughout the nation. People living throughout the country had similar opportunities to buy consumer products and partake in a mass culture made possible by movies and radio.

Producing for a mass market, industrial giants like Henry Ford transformed the nature of work and pleasure. The assembly line revolutionized the pace of labor and turned it into a standardized routine. The automobile transformed dating patterns and opened up new opportunities for the exploration of romance and sex.

Yet the roar of consumption and the excitement of breaking the ties of social and cultural conventions proved fleeting. Most Americans lived at or below the poverty line and earned just enough for bare necessities. They could live beyond their means through an ample supply of credit, but their poverty contrasted with the increasing concentration of wealth in the hands of the richest Americans. The shortcomings of the corporate business world, inadequate oversight by the federal government, and an overreliance on the private sector to look after the nation's economic health would soon result in a stock market crash and a Great Depression.

The weaknesses of the economy were often overshadowed by the clash over cultural differences. Guardians of traditional morality and values worried about the effects of more than fifty years of industrialization, immigration, and urbanization. Issues such as the enforcement of prohibition, the teaching of evolution in the schools, and the debate about whether a Catholic should be elected president dominated political discussion, while efforts to assist farmers and workers were unsuccessful.

These battles marked a turning point in U.S. history—the transition from a traditional, rural, Protestant society to an urban, ethnically and religiously diverse one. The widespread popularity of the revived Ku Klux Klan throughout the South and the North demonstrated that the older America of white, northern European Protestants did not intend to give up political or cultural power without a struggle. At the same time, ethnic minorities represented by Al Smith had no intention of backing down. Neither did millions of Black Americans, whether they joined the NAACP or supported Marcus Garvey's UNIA. During the next decade, Americans from all backgrounds would battle more than cultural threats. They would fight for their economic survival.

- How did technological innovations change the lives of Americans in the 1920s?
- What cultural conflicts divided Americans in the 1920s?

Skills Workshop: Writing Historically

Additional Practice in Responding to a Document-Based Question

Evaluate the extent of change in American society during the 1920s.

Document 1

Source: Marcus Garvey, *Address to the Second United Negro Improvement Association (UNIA) Convention,* 1921

"Just take your idea from the last bloody war, wherein a race was pitted against itself (for the whole white races united as one from a common origin), the members of which, on both sides, fought so tenaciously that they killed off each other in frightful, staggering numbers. If a race pitted against itself could fight so tenaciously to kill itself without mercy, can you

(continued)

imagine the fury, can you imagine the mercilessness, the terribleness of the war that will come when all the races of the world will be on the battlefield, engaged in deadly combat for the destruction or overthrow of the one or the other, when beneath it and as a cause of it lies prejudice and hatred? Truly, it will be an ocean of blood; that is all it will be. So that if I can sound a note of warning now that will echo and reverberate around the world and thus prevent such conflict, God help me to do it; for Africa, like Europe, like Asia, is preparing for the day."

Document 2

Source: *Blood and Sand* (film advertisement), 1922

Everett Collection, Inc.

Document 3

Source: Sinclair Lewis, *Babbitt*, 1922

"Just as he was an Elk, a Booster, a member of the Chamber of Commerce, just as the priests of the Presbyterian Church determined his every religious belief, and the senators who controlled the Republican Party decided in little smoky rooms in Washington what he should think about disarmament, tariff, and Germany, so did the large national advertisers fix the surface of his life, fix what he believed to be his individuality. These standard advertised wares — toothpastes, socks, tires, cameras, instantaneous hot-water-heaters — were his symbols and proofs of excellence; at first the signs, then the substitutes, for joy and passion and wisdom."

(continued)

Document 4

Source: Edythe Turnham and Her Dixie Aces, Club Alabam, Dunbar Hotel, Los Angeles, c.1931

Hogan Jazz Archive, Special Collections, Howard-Tilton Memorial Library, Tulane University

Document 5

Source: Clarence Darrow and William Jennings Bryan, Transcript from *The State of Tennessee v. John Thomas Scopes*, 1925

"Q. [Mr. Darrow]. You have given considerable study to the Bible, haven't you, Mr. Bryan?

A. [Mr. Bryan]. Yes, sir, I have tried to.

Q. Then you have made a general study of it.

A. Yes, I have; I have studied the Bible for about fifty years, or sometime more than that, but, of course, I have studied it more as I have become older than when I was but a boy.

Q. You claim that everything in the Bible should be literally interpreted?

A. I believe everything in the Bible should be accepted as it is given there; some of the Bible is given illustratively. For instance: 'Ye are the salt of the earth.' I would not insist that man was actually salt, or that he had flesh of salt, but it is used in the sense of salt as saving God's people. . . .

(continued)

Q. But when you read that Jonah swallowed the whale—or that the whale swallowed Jonah—excuse me please—how do you literally interpret that?

A. When I read that a big fish swallowed Jonah—it does not say whale.

Q. Doesn't it? Are you sure?

A. That is my recollection of it. A big fish, and I believe it, and I believe in a God who can make a whale and can make a man and can make both do what He pleases. . . .

Q. Now, you say, the big fish swallowed Jonah, and he there remained how long—three days—and then he spewed him upon the land. You believe that the big fish was made to swallow Jonah?

A. I am not prepared to say that; the Bible merely says it was done.

Q. You don't know whether it was the ordinary run of fish, or made for that purpose?

A. You may guess; you evolutionists guess.

Q. But when we do guess, we have a sense to guess right.

A. But do not do it often.

Q. You are not prepared to say whether that fish was made especially to swallow a man or not?

A. The Bible doesn't say, so I am not prepared to say. . . .

Q. But do you believe He made them—that He made such a fish and that it was big enough to swallow Jonah?

A. Yes sir. Let me add: One miracle is just as easy to believe as another. . . .

Q. Just as hard?

A. It is hard to believe for you, but easy for me. A miracle is a thing performed beyond what man can perform. When you get beyond what man can do, you get within the realm of miracles; and it is just as easy to believe the miracle of Jonah as any other miracle in the Bible.

Q. Perfectly easy to believe that Jonah swallowed the whale?

A. If the Bible said so; the Bible doesn't make as extreme statements as evolutionists do.

Q. That may be a question, Mr. Bryan, about some of those you have known?

A. The only thing is, you have a definition of fact that includes imagination.

Q. And you have a definition that excludes everything but imagination?

Gen. Stewart [attorney general]. I object to that as argumentative. . . .

Mr. Darrow. The Witness must not argue with me, either."

(continued)

Document 6

Source: The Brox Sisters Listening to the Radio, c. 1925

Library of Congress, LC-DIG-ggbain-37038

Document 7

Source: *Women of the Ku Klux Klan,* 1927

"Objects and Purposes

> **SECTION 1.** The objects of this Order shall be to unite white female persons, native-born Gentile citizens of the United States of America, who owe no allegiance of any nature or degree to any foreign government, nation, institution, sect, ruler, person, or people; whose morals are good; whose reputations and vocations are respectable; whose habits are exemplary; who are of sound minds and 18 years or more of age, under a common oath into a Sisterhood of strict regulation, to cultivate and promote patriotism toward our Civil Government; to practice an honorable clannishness toward each other; to exemplify a practical benevolence; to shield the sanctity of the home and the chastity of womanhood; to maintain forever white supremacy; to teach and faithfully inculcate a high spiritual philosophy through an exalted ritualism, and by a practical devotion to conserve, protect, and maintain the distinctive institutions, rights, privileges, principles, traditions, and ideals of a pure Americanism.
>
> **SEC. 2.** To create and maintain an institution by which the present and succeeding generations shall commemorate the great sacrifice, chivalric service, and imperishable achievements of the Ku Klux Klan and the Women of the Reconstruction period of American History, to the end that justice and honor be done the sacred memory of those who wrought through our mystic society during that period, and that their valiant accomplishments be not lost to posterity; to perpetuate their faithful courage, noble spirit, peerless principles, and faultless ideals; to hold sacred and make effective their spiritual purpose in this and future generations, that they be rightly vindicated before the world by a revelation of the whole truth."

MODULE 7.9

The Great Depression

FOCUS

While reading this section, consider the causes of the Great Depression, its effects, and attempts by local and federal officials to counteract those effects.

Black Tuesday
The name given to the October 29, 1929, crash of the U.S. stock market. This event marked the beginning of the Great Depression, although it was not the depression's root cause.

On October 29, 1929, a day that became known as **Black Tuesday**, stock market prices tumbled. Over the previous five years, the rising market, bolstered by optimistic buyers, earned huge profits for investors, and the value of stocks nearly doubled. In late October, panicked sellers sent stock prices into free fall. Although only 2.5 percent of Americans owned stock, the stock market collapse had an enormous impact on the economy and the rest of the world.

Because so much of the stock boom was fueled by lenient margin requirements (buying stock with a down payment of only 5 to 10 percent and borrowing money for the rest of the purchase), when investors who borrowed got caught short by falling prices, they could not repay the financial institutions that had facilitated their margin buying. Banks and lending agencies, with their interlocking managements and overextension of credit, had difficulty surviving the collapse in stock market prices by the crash.

Newly elected, Herbert Hoover had the unenviable task of assuming the presidency in 1929 as the economy crumbled. Given his long history of public service, he seemed the right man for the job. Even before the Great Depression, most Americans lived at or near the poverty level, surviving month to month. By 1933, millions of Americans had lost even this tenuous hold on economic security, as unemployment reached a record 25 percent.

Hoover, however, was unwilling to make a fundamental break with conventional economic approaches and proved unable to effectively communicate his genuine concern for the plight of the poor. Despite his sincere but limited efforts, Hoover's reliance on private charity and voluntary efforts to meet the needs of downtrodden Americans fell short of the vast need that grew during the depression. As this happened, many frustrated Americans, made desperate by their economic plight and angered by the inadequate response of their government, ultimately took to the streets in protest.

Financial Crash and Depression

Great Depression
Worldwide economic collapse caused by overproduction and financial speculation. It affected the United States from October 1929 until the start of World War II in 1939.

The 1929 crash did not cause the decade-long **Great Depression** that followed. The seeds for the greatest economic catastrophe in U.S. history had been planted earlier. The causes stemmed from flaws in an economic system that produced a great disparity of wealth, inadequate consumption, overextension of credit both at home and abroad, and the government's unwillingness to provide assistance to struggling farmers. Republican presidential administrations made matters worse by lowering taxes on the rich and raising tariffs to benefit manufacturers, creating greater economic inequality. The Federal Reserve Board also worsened the situation by keeping interest rates high, thereby making it difficult for people and businesses to get loans and repay debts.

The failure was not that of the United States alone. The depression affected capitalist nations throughout the world. The stock market collapse crushed the American public's confidence that the unfettered law of supply and demand and laissez-faire economics could ensure prosperity.

The Great Depression had many causes. You should know the factors that led to the Great Depression because the AP® Exam often asks causation questions about this event. Likewise, the AP® Exam may ask you to consider the political, economic, and social effects of the Great Depression on American society.

National prosperity was at its apparent peak when the Republican Hoover entered the White House in March 1929. Hoover brought to the presidency a blend of traditional and progressive ideas. He believed that government and business should form voluntary partnerships to work toward common goals. Rejecting the principle of absolute laissez-faire, he nonetheless argued that the government should extend its influence lightly over the economy — to encourage and persuade sensible behavior, but not to impose itself on the private sector. In a notable exception, Hoover championed the 1929 **Agricultural Marketing Act**, a measure that aimed to raise prices for long-suffering farmers by having the government buy up farm surpluses.

The Great Depression sorely tested Hoover's beliefs. Having placed his faith more in cooperation rather than coercion, the president relied on voluntarism to get the nation through hard economic times. Hoover hoped that management and labor, through gentle persuasion, would hold steady on prices and wages. In the meantime, for those in dire need, the president turned to local communities and private charities. Hoover expected municipal and state governments to shoulder the burden of providing relief to the needy, just as they had during previous economic downturns.

Hoover's remedies failed to end or even significantly lessen the devastating impacts of the depression. Initially, business people responded positively to the president's request to maintain the status quo on wages and prices, but when the economy did not

National Archives, photo no. 306-NT-165319c

Soup Kitchen, 1931 At the height of the Great Depression, these unemployed men stand in a long line outside a Chicago soup kitchen waiting for a meal. Without major governmental relief efforts for the unemployed during the Hoover administration, such men depended mainly on the efforts of charity. In this instance, the notorious gangster Al Capone set up this establishment before going to federal prison for tax evasion in 1932.

How does this photograph reflect the dire situation faced by many Americans during the depression?

bounce back, they lost confidence and defected. Nor did local governments and private agencies have the funds to provide relief to all those who needed it. With tax revenues in decline, some 1,300 municipalities across the country had gone bankrupt by 1933. Benevolent societies and religious groups could handle short-term misfortunes, but they could not cope with the ongoing disaster of mass unemployment.

Smoot-Hawley Act

A 1930 tariff act that significantly raised taxes on imported agricultural and manufactured goods to aid struggling farmers and businesses during the beginning of the Great Depression. In response, other countries greatly increased their duties on American goods, contributing to a sharp decline in global trade.

The **Smoot-Hawley Act**, passed by Congress in 1930, made matters worse. In an effort to replenish federal revenues and protect American farmers and companies from foreign competition, the act increased tariffs on agricultural and industrial imports to one of the highest levels in American history. However, other countries retaliated by lifting their import duties, which hurt American companies because it diminished demand for American exports.

As confidence in recovery fell and the economy sank deeper into depression, President Hoover shifted direction. He persuaded Congress to lower income tax rates and to allocate an unprecedented $423 million for federal public works projects.

Hoover's recovery efforts fell short, however. He refused to consider greater spending because he feared government debt more than mass unemployment. With the federal government's deficit rising, Hoover reversed course in 1932 and joined with Congress in sharply raising income, estate, and corporate taxes on the wealthy. This effectively slowed down investment and new production, throwing millions more American workers out of jobs.

Reconstruction Finance Corporation (RFC)

A government corporation endorsed by Herbert Hoover and created by Congress. It provided federal support through loans to troubled banks, railroads, and insurance companies and, later, states and municipalities in an attempt to stimulate economic growth and job creation.

Although unwilling to help citizens directly, Hoover was willing to provide financial assistance to certain companies, even with his aversion to spending, Hoover lobbied Congress to create the **Reconstruction Finance Corporation (RFC)** to supply loans to troubled banks, railroads, and insurance companies in 1932. By injecting federal dollars into these critical enterprises, the president and lawmakers expected to stimulate overall economic activity that would trickle down from the top of the economic structure to the workers at the bottom. Congress gave the RFC a budget of $1.5 billion in its first year to lend to corporations, states, and municipalities to employ people in public works projects, a significant yet insufficient allocation of funds to combat the effects of the depression.

This notable departure from Republican economic philosophy failed to reach its goal. The RFC spent its budget too cautiously, and its funds reached mainly those institutions that could best afford to repay the loans, ignoring the companies in the greatest difficulty. Wealth never trickled down. Although Hoover was not indifferent to the plight of others, he was incapable of breaking away from his ideological preconceptions. He refused to support expenditures for direct relief (cash payments) and hesitated to extend assistance for work relief (government-created jobs) because he believed that it would ruin individual initiative and character.

Hoover and the United States did not suffer the Great Depression alone. It was a worldwide calamity. By 1933, Germany, France, and Great Britain were all facing mass unemployment. In this climate of extreme social and economic unrest, authoritarian dictators came to power in a number of European countries. Each claimed that his country's social and economic problems could be solved only by placing power in the hands of a single, all-powerful leader.

REVIEW

- How did Herbert Hoover attempt to combat the effects of the Great Depression?
- How successful were these attempts?

Hoovervilles and Dust Storms

The depression hit all areas of the United States hard. In large cities, families crowded into apartments with no gas or electricity and little food to put on the table. In Los Angeles, people cooked their meals over wood fires in backyards. In many cities, unhoused people constructed makeshift housing consisting of cartons, old newspapers, and cloth — what journalists derisively dubbed Hoovervilles. Thousands of hungry citizens wound up living under bridges in Portland, Oregon; in wrecked autos in city dumps in Brooklyn, New York, and Stockton, California; and in abandoned coal furnaces in Pittsburgh.

Workers in rural areas fared no better. Landlords in West Virginia and Kentucky evicted coal miners and their families from their homes in the dead of winter, forcing them to live in tents. Farmers in the Great Plains, who were already experiencing foreclosures, were little prepared for the even greater natural disaster that laid waste to their farms. In the early 1930s, enormous dust storms swept through western Kansas, eastern Colorado, western Oklahoma, the Texas Panhandle, and eastern New Mexico, in an area that came to be known as the **Dust Bowl**, destroying crops and plant and animal life (**Map 7.9**).

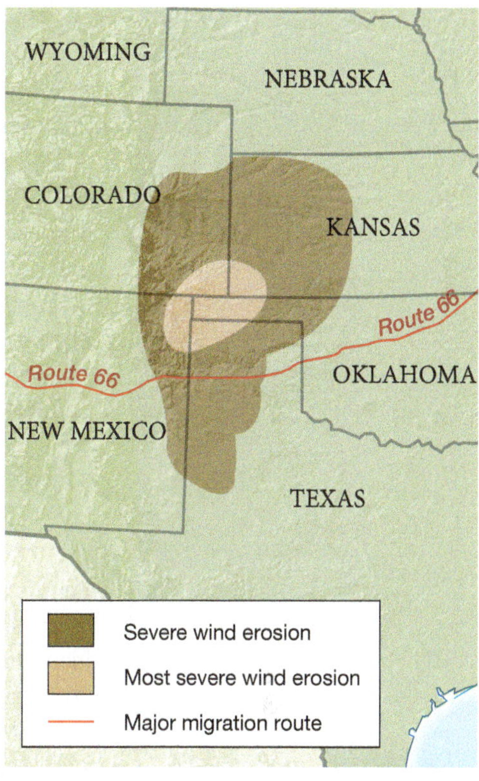

MAP 7.9 The Dust Bowl Although "Okies" was the term used for the migrants escaping the Dust Bowl and heading to California, many of those who fled the terrible windstorms also journeyed from their homes in Kansas, Texas, and Colorado.

How was the Dust Bowl a product of human actions?

The storms resulted from both climatological and human causes. A series of droughts had destroyed crops and turned the topsoil into sand, which gusts of wind carried and deposited on everything that lay in their path. Although they did not realize it at the time, plains farmers, by focusing on growing wheat for income, had neglected planting trees and grasses that would have kept the topsoil from eroding and turning into dust. As the storms continued through the 1930s, most residents — approximately 75 percent — remained on the plains.

Millions, however, headed for California looking for relief from the plague of swirling dust and hoping to find jobs in the state's fruit and vegetable fields. Although they came from several states besides Oklahoma, these migrants came to be known as "Okies," a derogatory term used by those who resented and looked down on the poverty-stricken newcomers to their communities. John Steinbeck's novel *The Grapes of Wrath* (1939) portrayed the plight of the fictional Joad family as storms and a bank foreclosure destroyed their Oklahoma farm and sent them on the road to California.

Dust Bowl
Name for the southern plains of the United States during the Great Depression, when the region experienced devastating dust storms due to soil erosion caused by poor farming practices and drought.

AP® WORKING with EVIDENCE

Source: Ann Marie Low, *Dust Bowl Diary*, 1934

"May 21, 1934, Monday

[S]aturday Dad, Bud, and I planted an acre of potatoes. There was so much dirt in the air I couldn't see Bud only a few feet in front of me. Even the air in the house was just a haze. In the evening the wind died down, and Cap came to take me to the movie. We joked about how hard it is to get cleaned up enough to go anywhere.

The newspapers report that on May 10 there was such a strong wind the experts in Chicago estimated 12,000,000 tons of Plains soil was dumped on that city. By the next day the sun was obscured in Washington, D.C., and ships 300 miles out at sea reported dust settling on their decks.

May 30, 1934, Wednesday

The mess was incredible! Dirt had blown into the house all week and lay inches deep on everything. Every towel and curtain was just black. There wasn't a clean dish or cooking utensil. There was no food. Oh, there were eggs and milk and one loaf left of the bread I baked the weekend before. . . .

Mama couldn't make bread until I carried water to wash the bread mixer. I couldn't churn until the churn was washed and scalded. We just couldn't do anything until something was washed first. Every room had to have dirt almost shoveled out of it before we could wash floors and furniture."

Questions for Analysis

1. Identify the ways in which the Dust Bowl disrupted farm life in this document.
2. Describe the impact of the Dust Bowl beyond the farms on the Great Plains in this document.
3. Explain the different ways men and women in the household were affected by the Dust Bowl in this document.

- What factors contributed to the Dust Bowl?

Challenges for Minorities

Most Americans who lost their jobs were white men, given that a majority of the population was white. Yet racial and ethnic minorities, including Black Americans, Latinos, and Asian Americans, suffered even greater hardships. Racial discrimination had kept these groups from achieving economic and political equality, and the Great Depression added to their woes.

Traditionally the last hired and the first fired, Black people occupied the lowest positions in the industrial and agricultural sectors. "The depression brought everybody down a peg or two," the Black poet Langston Hughes wryly commented. "And the Negroes had but few pegs to fall."

Despite the Great Migration to the North during and after World War I, three-quarters of the Black population still lived in the South. Mainly sharecroppers and tenant farmers, Black southerners were trapped in debt that they could not repay as crop prices plunged to record lows during the 1920s. As white landowners struggled to save their farms by introducing machinery to cut labor costs, they forced Black sharecroppers off the land and into even greater poverty.

Nor was the situation better for Black workers employed at the lowest-paying jobs as janitors, menial laborers, maids, and laundresses. On average, Black Americans earned $200 a year, less than one-quarter of the average wage of white factory workers.

AP® WORKING with EVIDENCE

Source: John Vachon, *Picket Line*, Chicago, 1941

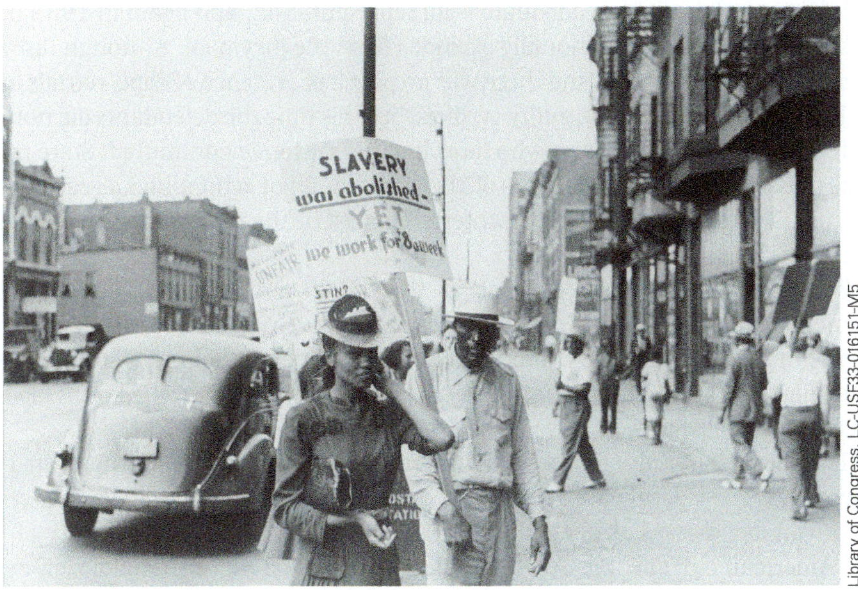

Library of Congress, LC-USF33-016151-M5

About the source: This photograph shows Black protesters as they picket a realty company in Chicago in 1941. The sign in the foreground says, "SLAVERY was abolished—yet we work for $8 a week."

Questions for Analysis

1. Identify these demonstrators' concerns.
2. Explain the ways in which this protest is a product of the legacy of the migration of Black people to cities during and after World War I.
3. Evaluate the extent to which Black Americans had achieved the civil rights enjoyed by white Americans by the 1930s.

The economic misfortune that Black people experienced was compounded by the fact that they lived in a society rigidly constructed to preserve white supremacy. The 25 percent of Black people living in the North faced racial discrimination in employment, housing, and the criminal justice system, but at least they could express their opinions and desires by voting. By contrast, Black southerners remained segregated and disfranchised by law. The depression also worsened racial tensions, as white and Black people competed for the shrinking number of jobs. Lynching surged upward during the Great Depression—in 1933, twenty-four Black people lost their lives to this form of terrorism.

Events in Scottsboro, Alabama, reflected the special misery Black Americans faced during the Great Depression. Trouble erupted in 1931 when two young, unemployed white women, Ruby Bates and Victoria Price, snuck onto a freight train. Before the train reached its final destination, a fight broke out between Black and white men on top of the freight car occupied by the two women. Nine Black youths between the ages of twelve and nineteen were arrested. Charges of assault quickly escalated into rape, when the women told authorities that the Black men in custody had molested them on board the train.

The defendants' court-appointed attorney had little time to prepare his clients' cases and the all-white male jury swiftly convicted the accused and sentenced all but the youngest defendant to death. The U.S. Supreme Court spared the lives of the **Scottsboro Nine** by overturning their guilty verdicts in 1932 on the grounds that the defendants did not have adequate legal representation, and again in 1935 because Black people had been intentionally excluded from the jury pool. Although Ruby Bates had recanted her testimony and there was no physical evidence of rape, retrials in 1936 and 1937 produced the same guilty verdicts, but this time the defendants did not receive the death penalty, save for one who later had his sentence commuted. State prosecutors dismissed charges against four of the accused, all of whom had already spent six years in jail. Despite international protests, the last of the remaining five did not leave jail until 1950.

Scottsboro Nine Nine Black youths convicted of raping two white women in Scottsboro, Alabama, in 1931. Their death penalty sentences were later overturned by the U.S. Supreme Court in the case, which drew national and international attention to ongoing racial inequalities in the U.S. criminal system.

Racism also worsened the impact of the Great Depression on Spanish-speaking Americans. Mexicans and Mexican Americans made up the largest segment of the Latino population living in the United States. Concentrated in the Southwest and California, they worked in a variety of low-wage factory jobs and as migrant laborers in fruit and vegetable fields.

The depression reduced the Mexican-born population living in the United States in two ways. The federal government, in cooperation with state and local governments and private businesses, deported around one million Mexicans, a majority of whom were American citizens. Los Angeles officials organized more than a dozen deportation trains transporting thousands of Mexicans to the border. Many others returned to Mexico voluntarily when demand for labor in the United States dried up. By 1933, the number of repatriations had begun to decline. Fewer migrants came over the border

Granger – Historical Picture Archive

Scottsboro Nine, 1933 Two years after their original conviction, the Scottsboro defendants discuss their new trial with their attorney Samuel Leibowitz in 1933 while still in prison. Flanked by two guards, they are from the left, Olen Montgomery, Clarence Norris, Willie Roberson, Andy Wright, Ozie Powell, Eugene Williams, Charlie Weems, and Roy Wright. Haywood Patterson is seated next to Leibowitz. Known as the "Scottsboro Boys," at the time of their arrest, they ranged in age from twelve to nineteen.

How does this photo reveal the impact of racism during the Great Depression?

after the depression began in 1929, thereby lessening competition for jobs. In addition, the Roosevelt administration adopted more humane policies, attempting not to break up families.

Those who remained endured growing hardships. Relief agencies refused to provide them with the same benefits as white people. Like Black Americans, they encountered discrimination in public schools, in public accommodations, and at the ballot box. Conditions remained harshest for migrant workers toiling long hours for little pay and living in overcrowded and poorly constructed housing. In both fields and factories, employers had little incentive to improve the situation because there were plenty of white migrant workers to fill their positions.

The transient nature of agricultural work and the vulnerability of Mexican laborers made it difficult for workers to organize, but Mexican American laborers engaged in dozens of strikes in California and Texas in the early 1930s. Most ended in defeat, but a few, such as a strike of pecan shellers in San Antonio, Texas, led by Luisa Moreno, won better working conditions and higher wages. Despite these hard-fought victories, the condition of Latinos remained precarious.

On the West Coast, Asian Americans also remained economically and politically marginalized. Japanese immigrants eked out livings as small farmers, grocers, and gardeners, despite California laws preventing them from owning land. Many of their college-educated U.S.-born children found few professional opportunities available to them, and they often returned to work in family businesses. The depression magnified the problem. Like other racial and ethnic minorities, the Japanese found it harder to find even the lowest-wage jobs now that unemployed white people were willing to take them. As a result, about one-fifth of Japanese immigrants returned to Japan during the 1930s.

The Chinese suffered a similar fate. Although some 45 percent of Chinese Americans had been born in the United States and were citizens, people of Chinese ancestry remained isolated in ethnic communities along the West Coast. Discriminated against in schools and most occupations, many operated restaurants and laundries.

Mexican Migrant Worker, 1937 This photograph by Dorothea Lange shows a Mexican field worker on the edge of a frozen pea field in the Imperial Valley, California. Demand for Mexican labor declined during the Great Depression as displaced farmers from the Dust Bowl moved west to take jobs formerly held by Mexicans. Government deportations further decreased the number of undocumented Mexican laborers in the United States.

In what ways did the Great Depression affect lower-income minority workers differently from middle-class white Americans?

During the depression, those Chinese who did not obtain assistance through governmental relief turned instead to their own community organizations and to extended families to help them through the hard times.

Filipino immigrants had arrived on the West Coast after the Philippines became a territory of the United States in 1901. Working as low-wage agricultural laborers, they were subject to the same kind of racial animosity as other dark-skinned minorities. Filipino farmworkers organized agricultural labor unions and conducted many strikes in California, but like their Mexican counterparts, they were brutally repressed. In 1934, anti-Filipino hostility reached its height when Congress passed the **Tydings-McDuffie Act**. The measure accomplished two aims at once: The act promised independence to the Philippines after ten years (eventually granted in 1946), and it restricted Filipino immigration into the United States.

- Why did the Great Depression hit minorities in the United States especially hard?

Financial Strain and Organized Protest

With millions of men unemployed, women faced increased family responsibilities. Stay-at-home wives had to care for their children and provide emotional support for out-of-work husbands who had lost their role as the family breadwinner. Despite the loss of income, homemakers continued their daily routines of shopping, cooking, cleaning, and child rearing.

Widespread male unemployment led to an increase in the importance of women's income. The depression hit male-dominated industries like steel mills and automakers the hardest. As a result, men were more likely to lose their jobs than women. Although more women held on to their jobs, their often meager wages had to go further because many now had to support unemployed fathers and husbands. During the 1930s, federal and local governments sought to increase male employment by passing laws to keep married women from holding civil service and teaching positions. Nonetheless, more and more married women entered the workplace, and by 1940, the proportion of women in the job force had grown by about 25 percent.

As had been the case in previous decades, a higher proportion of Black women than white women worked outside the home in the 1930s. By 1940, about 40 percent of Black women held jobs, compared to about 25 percent of white women. Racial discrimination played a key role in establishing this pattern. Black men faced higher unemployment rates than did their white counterparts, and what work was available was often limited to the lowest-paying jobs. As a result, Black women faced great pressure to supplement family incomes. Still, unemployment rates for Black women reached as high as 50 percent during the 1930s.

Despite increased burdens, most American families of all races remained intact and discovered ways to survive the economic crisis. They pared down household budgets, made do without telephones and new clothes, and held on to their automobiles for longer periods of time.

What money they managed to save, they often spent on movies. Comedies, gangster movies, fantasy tales, and uplifting films helped viewers forget their troubles, if only for a few hours. Radio remained the chief source of entertainment, and radio sales doubled in the 1930s as listeners tuned in to soap operas, comedy and adventure shows, news reports, and musical programs.

As the depression deepened, angry citizens found ways to express their discontent. Farmers had suffered economic hardship longer than any other group. Even before 1929, they had seen prices spiral downward, but in the early 1930s, agricultural income plummeted by 60 percent, and one-third of farmers lost their land. Some farmers decided that the time had come for drastic action.

In the summer of 1932, Milo Reno, an Iowa farmer, created the Farmers' Holiday Association to organize farmers to keep their produce from going to market and thereby raise prices. Strikers from the association blocked roads and kept reluctant farmers in line by smashing their truck windshields and headlights and slashing their tires. When law enforcement officials arrested fifty-five demonstrators in Council Bluffs, thousands of farmers marched on the jail and forced their release. Despite armed attempts to prevent foreclosures and the intentional destruction of vast quantities of farm produce, the Farmers' Holiday Association failed to achieve its goal of raising prices.

Disgruntled urban residents also resorted to protest. Although the Communist Party remained a tiny group of just over 10,000 members in 1932, it played a large role in organizing the dispossessed. In major cities such as New York, Communists set up unemployment councils and led marches and rallies demanding jobs and food. In Harlem, the party endorsed rent strikes by Black apartment residents against their landlords. Party members did not confine their activities to the urban Northeast. They also went south to defend the Scottsboro Nine and to organize industrial workers in the steel mills of Birmingham and sharecroppers in the surrounding rural areas of Alabama. On the West Coast, Communists unionized seamen and waterfront workers and led strikes. They also recruited writers, directors, and actors in Hollywood.

One of the most visible protests of the early 1930s centered on the Ford factory in Dearborn, Michigan. As the depression worsened after 1930, Henry Ford, who had initially pledged to keep employee wages steady, changed his mind and reduced wages. On March 7, 1932, spearheaded by Communists, three thousand autoworkers marched from Detroit to Ford's River Rouge plant in nearby Dearborn. When the demonstrators reached the factory town, policemen indiscriminately fired bullets and tear gas at the crowd, which killed four workers. The attack provoked great outrage. Around forty thousand mourners attended the funeral of the four protesters; sang the Communist anthem, the *Internationale*; and surrounded the coffins, which were draped in a red banner emblazoned with a picture of Bolshevik leader Vladimir Lenin.

Protests spread. The federal government faced an uprising by some of the nation's most patriotic and loyal citizens—World War I veterans. Scheduled to receive a $1,000 bonus for their service, unemployed veterans could not wait until the payment date arrived in 1945. Instead, in the spring of 1932, a group of ex-soldiers from Portland, Oregon, set off on a march on Washington, D.C., to demand immediate payment of the bonus by the federal government. By the time they reached the nation's capital, the ranks of this **Bonus Army** had swelled to around twenty thousand veterans. They camped in the Anacostia Flats section of the city, constructed ramshackle shelters, and in many cases moved their families in with them.

Bonus Army
World War I veterans who marched on Washington, D.C., in 1932 to demand immediate payment of their service bonuses. President Hoover refused to negotiate and instructed the U.S. army to clear the capital of protesters, leading to a violent clash.

Although many veterans returned home after Congress refused their request for an early bonus payout, the rest of the Bonus Army remained in place until late July. When President Hoover decided to clear the capital of the protesters, violence ensued. Rather than engaging in a measured and orderly removal, General Douglas MacArthur overstepped presidential orders and used excessive force to disperse the veterans and their families. The Third Cavalry, commanded by George S. Patton, torched tents and sent their residents fleeing from the city.

Everett Collection, Inc.

Bonus Army Clashes with Police, July 1932 About 20,000 World War I veterans joined a march on Washington, D.C., in 1932 to demand immediate payment of their bonus checks at the height of the Great Depression. After several months, Hoover ordered the remaining protesters removed, which led to a series of clashes and the burning of the protesters' encampments. Hoover's popularity further plunged after widespread coverage of the treatment of the Bonus Army.

How did the march of the Bonus Army and the government's response to protests reflect divisions within American society?

In this one-sided battle, the biggest loser was President Hoover. Photographs and reports of the violent displacement of the Bonus Army shocked many Americans. Through four years of the country's worst depression, Hoover had lost touch with the American people. His cheerful words of encouragement fell increasingly on deaf ears. As workers, farmers, and veterans stirred in protest, Hoover appeared aloof, standoffish, and insensitive.

REVIEW

- How did the Great Depression shape the lives of families in the United States during the 1930s?
- What were the results of organized protest during the Great Depression?

AP® Skills Workshop: Writing Historically

Additional Practice in Responding to a Long-Essay Question

Evaluate the relative importance of different causes for the Hoover administration's ineffective response to the Great Depression.

The New Deal

FOCUS

In this module, consider the extent to which the New Deal represented a change in the relationship between the federal government and citizens, and to what extent it represented a continuation of older trends.

The nation was ready for a change. On election day 1932, with hard times showing no sign of letting up, Democratic presidential candidate Franklin Delano Roosevelt defeated Hoover easily. Democrats also won control of both houses of Congress. Roosevelt's sizable victory provided him with a mandate to take the country in a bold new direction. However, few Americans, including Roosevelt himself, knew exactly what the new president meant to do or what his pledge of a "new deal" would mean for the country.

Steps toward Relief

As a presidential candidate, Roosevelt presented no clear, coherent policy. He did not spell out how his plans for the country would differ from Hoover's, but he did refer broadly to providing a "new deal" and bringing to the White House "persistent experimentation." Roosevelt's appeal derived more from the genuine compassion he was able to convey than from the specificity of his promises.

In this context, Eleanor Roosevelt's evident concern for people's suffering and her history of activism made her husband Franklin even more attractive. She was an outspoken advocate of the rights of women, minorities, workers, and the poor. Behind the scenes, she pushed her husband further to the political left. Her proximity to power provided her with a unique position from which to confront the problems of the day, and her husband's disability from polio made her an invaluable set of "eyes and ears" for him.

Instead of any fixed ideology, Roosevelt followed what one historian has called "pragmatic humanism." A seasoned politician who understood the need for flexibility, Roosevelt blended principle and practicality. "It is common sense," Roosevelt explained, "to take a method and try it. If it fails, admit it frankly and try another. But above all, try something."

More than any president before him, FDR, as he became known, created an expectation among Americans that the federal government would take concrete action to improve their lives. A Colorado woman expressed her appreciation to Eleanor Roosevelt: "Your husband is great. He seems lovable even tho' he is a 'politician.'" The policies supported by his administration would take twists and turns, but Roosevelt never lost the support of the majority of Americans.

Franklin D. Roosevelt Library

Franklin D. Roosevelt Campaigning in Kansas, 1932 New York governor Franklin Roosevelt promises a "new deal" to farmers in Topeka, Kansas, as he campaigns for president in 1932 as the Democratic candidate. Photographers were careful not to show that Roosevelt was unable to use his legs, which were paralyzed after he contracted polio in 1921. Roosevelt forged a coalition of farmers and urban workers and easily defeated the incumbent Hoover.

Why would both farmers and urban workers find Roosevelt's message particularly compelling in 1932?

New Deal
The policies and programs that Franklin Roosevelt initiated to combat the Great Depression. The New Deal represented a dramatic expansion of the role of government in American society, and its provisions were often categorized as either relief, recovery, or reform efforts (the 3 Rs).

Emergency Banking Act
An act passed in 1933 with the goal of stabilizing the banking system to calm widespread public panic over the safety of bank deposits. The act required banks to pass a federal audit before reopening after the "bank holiday," reassuring depositors that they were solvent.

Glass-Steagall Act
New Deal legislation passed in 1933 that sought to reform and strengthen the banking system. The act created the Federal Deposit Insurance Corporation (FDIC) to insure bank deposits. It also prohibited institutions from participating in both commercial and investment banking (the prohibition was repealed in 1999).

Starting with his inaugural address, in which he declared that "the only thing we have to fear is fear itself," Roosevelt took on the task of rallying the American people and restoring their confidence in the future. Using the power of radio to communicate directly, Roosevelt delivered regular fireside chats (informal radio addresses) in which he boosted morale and informed his audience of the steps the government was taking to help solve their problems. Not limited to rhetoric, Roosevelt's **New Deal** would provide relief, put millions of people to work, raise prices for farmers, extend conservation projects, revitalize America's financial system, and rescue capitalism.

President Roosevelt took swift action on entering office. In March 1933, he issued an executive order shutting down banks for several days to calm the panic that gripped many Americans in the wake of bank failures and the loss of their life's savings. Mere days after this "bank holiday," Congress passed the administration's **Emergency Banking Act**, which subjected banks to Treasury Department inspection before they reopened, reorganized the banking system, and provided federal funds to bail out banks on the brink of closing. This assertion of federal power allowed solvent banks to reopen. Together, these actions helped stop the wave of "bank runs" by panicked depositors which often led to the sudden collapse of a bank. Instead, Americans increased their bank deposits.

Boosting confidence further, Congress passed the **Glass-Steagall Act** in June 1933. The measure created the **Federal Deposit Insurance Corporation (FDIC)**, insuring personal savings accounts up to $5,000 (currently $250,000 in 2023), and separated commercial and investment banking activities to avoid risky speculation.

The president also sought tighter supervision of the stock market. By June 1934, Roosevelt had signed into law measures setting up the **Securities and Exchange Commission (SEC)** to regulate the stock market and ensure that corporations gave investors accurate information about investments.

The regulation of banks and the stock exchange did not mean that Roosevelt was antibusiness. He affirmed his belief in a balanced budget and sought to avoid a $1 billion deficit by cutting government workers' salaries and lowering veterans' pensions.

Roosevelt also tried to boost government revenues by ending prohibition, which would allow the government to tax alcohol sales and eliminate the cost of enforcement. The **Twenty-first Amendment**, ratified in 1933, ended the more-than-decade-long experiment with prohibition.

As important as these measures were, the Roosevelt administration had much more to accomplish before those hardest hit by the depression felt some relief. Roosevelt viewed the Great Depression as a crisis analogous to war and adapted many of the bureaus and commissions used during World War I to ensure productivity and mobilize popular support to fit the current economic emergency. Many former progressives lined up behind Roosevelt, including women reformers and social workers who had worked in government and private agencies during the 1920s. At Eleanor Roosevelt's urging, he appointed one of them, Frances Perkins, as the first woman to head a cabinet agency—the Department of Labor.

Rehabilitating agriculture and industry stood at the top of the New Deal's priority list. Farmers came first. In May 1933, Congress passed the **Agricultural Adjustment Act (AAA)**, aimed at raising prices by reducing production. The Agricultural Adjustment Administration paid farmers subsidies to produce less in the future, and for farmers who had already planted their crops and raised livestock, the agency paid them to plow under a portion of their harvest, slaughter hogs, and destroy dairy products.

By 1935, the program succeeded in raising farm income by 50 percent. Large farmers were the chief beneficiaries of the AAA because they could more easily afford to cut back production. In doing so, especially in the South, they forced off the land sharecroppers who no longer had plots to farm. Even when sharecroppers managed to retain a parcel of their acreage, AAA subsidies went to the landowners, who did not always distribute the designated funds owed to the sharecroppers. Though poor white farmers felt the sting of this injustice, the system of white supremacy existing in the South guaranteed that Black people suffered most.

Twenty-first Amendment
The constitutional amendment ratified in 1933 to repeal the Eighteenth Amendment and prohibition.

Agricultural Adjustment Act (AAA)
A New Deal act passed in 1933 that raised prices for farm produce by paying farmers subsidies to reduce production. Large farmers reaped most of the benefits from the act. It was declared unconstitutional by the Supreme Court in 1936.

AP® EXAM TIP

President Roosevelt's New Deal agenda consisted of many government programs to end the Depression. Yet the New Deal legislative measures offered limited relief to minority groups. In spite of the apparent lack of government assistance, these groups overwhelmingly shifted their political alliance to the Democratic Party. You should know to what extent and in what ways the New Deal did and did not help people. The AP® Exam also sometimes asks for a comparison of the New Deal to Progressivism or the Great Society in the 1960s.

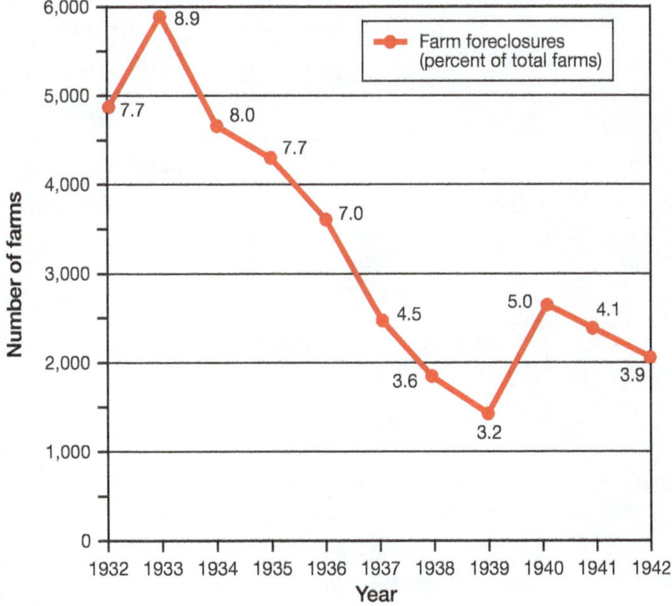

Farm Foreclosures, 1932–1942
A drop of 60 percent in prices led to a wave of farm foreclosures and rural protests in the early 1930s. From 1934 on, federal programs that promoted rural electrification, crop allotments, commodity loans, and mortgage credits allowed many farmers to retain their land.

To what extent does this figure accurately reflect the success of New Deal programs for all farmers, including tenant farmers and sharecroppers?

Tennessee Valley Authority (TVA)
A New Deal agency that brought low-cost electricity to rural Americans and redeveloped the Tennessee River valley through flood-control projects. The agency built, owned, and supervised a number of power plants and dams.

The Roosevelt administration exhibited its boldest initiative in creating the **Tennessee Valley Authority (TVA)** in 1933 to bring low-cost electric power to rural areas and help redevelop the entire Tennessee River valley region through flood-control projects. In contrast to the AAA and other farm programs in which control stayed in private hands, the TVA owned and supervised the building and operation of public power plants.

Outside the Tennessee River valley, the Rural Electrification Administration helped farmers obtain cheap electric power starting in 1935. For the first time, tens of thousands of farmers experienced the modern conveniences that electricity brought. Between 1935 and 1940, the number of farmers who had electricity quadrupled, from 10 percent to 40 percent, although most farmers would not get electric power until after World War II.

Roosevelt and Congress also acted to deal with the soil erosion problem behind the dust storms. In 1933, the Department of the Interior established a Soil Erosion Service, and two years later, Congress created a permanent Soil Conservation Service in the Department of Agriculture. Although these measures would prove beneficial in the long run, they did nothing to prevent even more severe storms from rolling through the Dust Bowl in 1935 and 1936.

At the same time, Roosevelt concentrated on industrial recovery. In 1933, Congress passed the **National Industrial Recovery Act (NIRA)**, which established the **National Recovery Administration (NRA)**. This agency allowed business, labor, and the public (represented by government officials) to create codes to regulate production, prices, wages, hours, and collective bargaining. Designers of the NRA expected that if wages rose and prices remained stable, consumer purchasing power would climb, demand would grow, and businesses would put people back to work. For this plan to work, business people had to keep prices steady by absorbing some of the costs of higher wages. Businesses that joined the NRA displayed the symbol of the blue eagle to signal their patriotic participation.

Alpha Stock/Alamy

National Recovery Act Blue Eagle Poster on Display
President Roosevelt initiated the National Recovery Administration (NRA) in 1933 as the centerpiece of his New Deal to stimulate economic growth. In this image, a woman hangs a Blue Eagle NRA poster in a restaurant window to show how the business participates in and supports the government program.

Why would businesses such as this restaurant choose to publicize their support for the National Recovery Act?

However, the NRA did not function as planned, nor did it bring the desired recovery. Businesses did not exercise the necessary restraint to keep prices steady. Large manufacturers dominated the code-making committees, and because Roosevelt had suspended enforcement of antitrust laws, those businesses often worked together to force smaller firms out of business. The NRA legislation guaranteed labor the right to unionize, but the agency did not vigorously enforce collective bargaining. The government failed to intervene to restore the imbalance of power between labor and management because Roosevelt depended mainly on big business to generate economic improvement. Moreover, the NRA had created codes for too many businesses, and government officials could not properly oversee them all. In 1935, the Supreme Court delivered the final blow to the NRA by declaring it an unconstitutional delegation of legislative power to the president.

Economic recovery programs were important, but they took time to take effect, and many Americans needed immediate help. Therefore, relief efforts and direct job creation were critical parts of the New Deal. Created in the early months of Roosevelt's term, the Federal Emergency Relief Administration (FERA) provided cash grants to states to revive their bankrupt relief efforts. Roosevelt chose Harry Hopkins, the chief of New York's relief agency, to head the FERA and distribute its initial \$500 million appropriation. On the job for two hours, Hopkins had already spent \$5 million. He did not calculate whether a particular plan "would work out in the long run," because, as he remarked, "people don't eat in the long run—they eat every day."

Harold Ickes, secretary of the interior and director of the **Public Works Administration (PWA)**, oversaw efforts to rebuild the nation's infrastructure. Funding architects, engineers, and skilled workers, the PWA built the Grand Coulee, Boulder, and Bonneville dams in the West; the Triborough Bridge in New York City; 70 percent of all new schools constructed between 1933 and 1939; and a variety of municipal buildings, sewage plants, port facilities, and hospitals.

Public Works Administration (PWA)
A New Deal administration created in 1933 to provide jobs relief through the construction of infrastructure, such as roads, schools, hospitals, dams, and libraries.

Yet neither the FERA nor the PWA provided enough relief to the millions who faced the winter of 1933–1934 without jobs or the money to heat their homes. In response, Hopkins persuaded Roosevelt to launch a temporary program to help needy Americans get through this difficult period. Both men favored "work relief"—giving people jobs rather than direct welfare payments whenever practical. The **Civil Works Administration (CWA)** lasted four months, but in that brief time it employed more than 4 million people on about 400,000 projects that built 500,000 miles of roads, 40,000 schools, 3,500 playgrounds, and 1,000 airports.

One of Roosevelt's most successful relief programs was the **Civilian Conservation Corps (CCC)**, created shortly after he entered the White House. The CCC recruited unmarried young men between the ages of eighteen and twenty-five for a two-year stint, putting them to work planting forests; cleaning up beaches, rivers, and parks; and building bridges and dams. Participants received \$1 per day, and the government sent \$25 of the \$30 in monthly wages directly to their families, helping make this the most popular of all New Deal programs. The CCC employed around 2.5 million men and lasted until 1942.

Civilian Conservation Corps (CCC)
A New Deal work program that hired young, unmarried men to work on conservation projects. It employed about 2.5 million men and lasted until 1942.

AP® WORKING with EVIDENCE

Source: President Franklin Roosevelt, *Message to Congress on Making the Civilian Conservation Corps a Permanent Agency,* 1937

> "On March 21, 1933, I addressed a message to the Congress in which I stated:
>
> 'I propose to create a civilian conservation corps to be used in simple work, not interfering with normal employment, and confining itself to forestry, the prevention of soil erosion, flood control and similar projects. . . .'

It is not necessary to go into detail regarding the accomplishments of the Corps. You are acquainted with the physical improvements that have taken place in our forests and parks as a result of the activities of the Corps and with the wealth that is being added to our natural resources for the benefit of future generations. More important than the material gain, however, is the improvement we find in the moral and physical well-being of our citizens who have been enrolled in the Corps and of their families who have been assisted by monthly allotments of pay. The functions of the Corps expire under authority of present law on June 30, 1937.

In my Budget Message to Congress on January 5 of this year I indicated that the Corps should be continued and recommended that legislation be enacted during the present session to establish the Corps as a permanent agency of the Government. . . .

I am convinced that there is ample useful work in the protection, restoration and development of our national resources, upon which the services of the Corps may be employed advantageously for an extended future period. It should be noted that this program will not in any respect reduce normal employment opportunities for our adult workers; in fact, the purchase of simple materials, of food and clothing and of other supplies required for the operations of the Corps tends to increase employment in industry.

I recommend, therefore, that provision be made for a permanent Corps of 300,000 youths (and war veterans), together with 10,000 Indians and 5,000 enrollees in our territories and insular possessions."

Questions for Analysis

1. Identify Roosevelt's reasons for making the Civilian Conservation Corps a permanent program.
2. Explain how the Civilian Conservation Corps compares with other jobs programs created during the New Deal.
3. Evaluate the extent to which the Civilian Conservation Corps represents continuity with previous government legislation regarding the environment.

- What steps did Roosevelt take to restore economic confidence early in his administration?
- Who were the main targets of Roosevelt's relief measures? Who was overlooked?

Critics of the New Deal

Despite the unprecedented efforts of the Roosevelt administration to spark recovery, provide relief, and encourage reform between 1933 and 1935, the country remained in depression. Unemployment still hovered around 20 percent. Roosevelt found himself under attack from both the left and the right. On the right, conservatives questioned New Deal spending and the growth of big government. On the left, the president's critics argued that he had not done enough to topple wealthy corporate leaders from power and relieve the plight of the downtrodden.

In 1934, officials of the Du Pont Corporation and General Motors formed the American Liberty League. From the point of view of the league's founders, the New Deal was little more than a vehicle for the spread of socialism and communism. The organization spent $1 million attacking what it considered to be Roosevelt's "dictatorial" policies and his assaults on free enterprise. The league, however, failed to attract support beyond a small group of northern industrialists, Wall Street bankers, and frustrated Democrats.

Corporate leaders also harnessed Christian ministers to promote their pro-capitalism, anti–New Deal message. The United States Chamber of Commerce and the National Association of Manufacturers allied with clergymen to challenge "creeping socialism." In 1935, the Reverend James W. Fifield founded Spiritual Mobilization and, from the pulpit of his wealthy First Congregational Church in Los Angeles, praised capitalism as a pillar of Christianity and attacked the "pagan statism" of the New Deal.

Roosevelt also faced criticism from the left. Communist Party membership reached its peak of around 75,000 in 1938. Although the party remained relatively small in numbers, it attracted intellectuals and artists whose voices could reach the larger public. Party members led unionizing drives in both the North and the South and displayed great talent and energy in organizing workers where resistance to unions was greatest. In the mid-1930s, the party followed the Soviet Union's antifascist foreign policy and joined with left-leaning, non-communist groups, such as unions and civil rights organizations, to oppose the growing menace of fascism in Europe, particularly in Germany and Italy. By the end of the decade, however, the party had lost many members after the Soviet Union reversed its anti-Nazi foreign policy.

The greatest challenge to Roosevelt came from a trio of talented men who reflected diverse beliefs. Francis Townsend, a retired California physician, proposed a "Cure for Depressions." In 1934, he formed the Old-Age Revolving Pensions Corporation, whose title summed up the doctor's idea. Townsend would have the government give all Americans over the age of sixty a monthly pension of $200 if they retired and spent the entire stipend each month. Retirements would open up jobs for younger workers, and the income these workers received, along with the pension for the elderly, would pump ample funds into the economy to promote recovery. The government would fund the Townsend plan with a 2 percent "transaction," or sales tax. By 1936, Townsend Clubs had attracted about 3.5 million members throughout the country, and one-fifth of all adults in the United States signed a petition endorsing the Townsend plan.

While Townsend appealed mainly to the elderly, Charles E. Coughlin, a priest from the Detroit area, attracted Catholics and a lower-middle-class following. Father Coughlin used his popular national radio broadcasts to talk about economic and political issues. Originally a Roosevelt supporter, by 1934, Coughlin had begun criticizing the New Deal for catering to greedy bankers. He spoke to millions of radio listeners about the evils of the Roosevelt administration, the godless communists who had allegedly infested it, and international bankers—coded language referring to Jews—who supposedly manipulated it. As the decade wore on, his vocal antisemitism and his growing fondness for fascist dictatorships abroad overshadowed his message of economic justice, and Catholic officials ordered him to stop broadcasting.

Huey Long of Louisiana posed the greatest political threat to Roosevelt. Unlike Townsend and Coughlin, Long had built and operated a successful political machine,

Bettmann/Getty Images

Father Charles E. Coughlin Father Charles E. Coughlin spoke at Cleveland Stadium in 1936 on behalf of Ohio congressional candidates who had been endorsed by his National Union for Social Justice. Coughlin, a Catholic priest and a stern critic of President Roosevelt, advocated the nationalization of banks and other industries, protection of worker rights, and monetary reform. Coughlin also spread conspiracy theories that the Great Depression was caused by international Jewish bankers, who were working with President Roosevelt to destroy the United States. **Why would Coughlin's message be attractive to some Americans in the mid-1930s?**

first as governor and then as U.S. senator, taking on the special interests of oil and railroad corporations in his home state. Early on, he had backed Roosevelt, but Long found the New Deal wanting. In 1934, Long established the **Share Our Wealth society**, promising to make "every man a king" by presenting families with a $5,000 homestead and a guaranteed annual income of $2,000. To accomplish this, Long proposed levying large income and inheritance taxes on the wealthy. Although the financial calculations behind his bold plan did not add up, Share Our Wealth clubs attracted some seven million members. The swaggering senator departed from most of his segregationist southern colleagues by appealing to a coalition of disgruntled farmers, industrial workers, and Black Americans. Before Long could help lead a third-party campaign for president, he was shot and killed in 1935.

AP® WORKING with EVIDENCE

Source: Huey Long, *Every Man a King*, 1934

"Now, we have organized a society, and we call it 'Share Our Wealth Society,' a society with the motto 'Every Man a King.'

Every man a king, so there would be no such thing as a man or woman who did not have the necessities of life, who would not be dependent upon the whims and caprices . . . of the financial barons for a living. . . .

We do not propose a division of wealth, but we propose to limit poverty that we will allow to be inflicted upon any man's family. We will not say we are going to try to guarantee any equality, or $15,000 to a family. No; but we do say that one third of the average is low enough for any one family to hold, that there should be a guarantee of a family wealth of around $5,000; enough for a home, an automobile, a radio, and the ordinary conveniences, and the opportunity to educate their children; a fair share of the income of this land thereafter to that family so there will be no such thing as merely the select to have those things, and so there will be no such thing as a family living in poverty and distress.

We have to limit fortunes. Our present plan is that we will allow no one man to own more than $50,000,000. . . .

Another thing we propose is old-age pension of $30 a month for everyone that is 60 years old. Now, we do not give this pension to a man making $1,000 a year, and we do not give it to him if he has $10,000 in property, but outside of that we do.

We will limit hours of work. There is not any necessity of having overproduction. I think all you have got to do, ladies and gentlemen, is just limit the hours of work to such an extent as people will work only so long as it is necessary to produce enough for all of the people to have what they need. . . . [A]nd then we will have 5 hours a day and 5 days a week, or even less than that, and we might give a man a whole month off during a year, or give him 2 months; and we might do what other countries have seen fit to do, and what I did in Louisiana, by having schools by which adults could go back and learn the things that have been discovered since they went to school."

Questions for Analysis

1. Identify three reforms proposed by Long.
2. Explain how these reforms draw on the ideas of the New Deal.
3. Evaluate the extent to which these ideas go beyond the reforms of the New Deal.

- What criticisms did opponents of the New Deal raise?

The New Deal Moves to the Left

Facing criticism from within his own party about the pace and effectiveness of the New Deal, and with the 1936 election looming, Roosevelt moved to the left. He adopted harsher rhetoric against uncooperative corporate leaders; beefed up economic and social programs for the unemployed, the elderly, and the infirm; and revived measures to redress the power imbalance between management and labor. In doing so, he fashioned a New Deal political coalition that would deliver a landslide victory in 1936 and allow the Democratic Party to dominate electoral politics for the next three decades.

Even though the New Deal had helped millions of people, millions of others still felt left out, as the popularity of Townsend, Coughlin, and Long indicated. "We the people voted for you," a Columbus, Ohio, worker wrote the president in disgust, "but it is a different story now. You have faded out on the masses of hungry, idle people. . . . The very rich is the only one who has benefited from your new deal."

In 1935, the president seized the opportunity to win his way back into the hearts of impoverished "forgotten Americans." Although Roosevelt favored a balanced budget, political necessity forced him to embark on deficit spending to expand the New Deal. Federal government expenditures would now exceed tax revenues, but New Dealers argued that additional spending would stimulate job creation and economic growth, which would replenish government funds.

Works Progress Administration (WPA)
A New Deal agency established in 1935 to put unemployed Americans to work on public projects ranging from construction to the arts. The WPA was the largest jobs program during the New Deal, employing more than eight million people.

Based on the highly successful but short-lived Civil Works Administration, the **Works Progress Administration (WPA)** provided jobs for the unemployed with a far larger budget, starting out with $5 billion. To ensure that the money would be spent, Roosevelt appointed Harry Hopkins to head the agency. Although critics condemned the WPA for employing people on unproductive "make-work" jobs—a criticism not entirely unfounded—the WPA overall did a good deal of work. The agency constructed or repaired more than 100,000 public buildings, 600 airports, 500,000 miles of roads, and 100,000 bridges. The WPA employed about 8.5 million workers during its eight years of operation.

The WPA also helped artists, writers, and musicians. With its support, the Federal Writers Project, the Federal Art Project, the Federal Music Project, and the Federal Theater Project encouraged the production of cultural works and helped bring them to communities and audiences throughout the country. Writers Richard Wright, Ralph Ellison, Clifford Odets, Saul Bellow, John Cheever, Margaret Walker, and many others nourished both their works and their stomachs while employed by the WPA. Some painters, such as Jacob Lawrence, worked in the "easel division." Others created elaborate murals on the walls of post offices and other government buildings. Historians and folklorists researched and prepared city and state guides and interviewed formerly enslaved Black Americans whose narratives of the system of bondage would otherwise have been lost.

In addition to the WPA, the National Youth Administration (NYA) employed millions of young people. Their work ranged from clerical assignments and repairing automobiles to building tuberculosis isolation units and renovating schools. Heading the NYA in Texas, the young Lyndon B. Johnson worked hard to expand educational and construction projects to unemployed white and Black people. The Division of Negro Affairs, headed by the Florida educator Mary McLeod Bethune and the only minority group subsection in the NYA, ensured that Black youths would benefit from the programs sponsored by the agency.

New Deal Art The Works Progress Administration, established by the Roosevelt administration in 1935, put Americans to work amid the ongoing depression. The WPA's Federal Art Project employed artists such as Ingrid E. Edwards of Minnesota, whose painting *Communications* features a newspaper boy, a telephone operator, a radio announcer, and a railroad train. Many of these works adorned public buildings.

How does this painting depict New Deal relief efforts?

Despite their many successes, these relief programs had a number of limitations. The WPA paid participants relatively low wages. The $660 in annual income earned by the average worker fell short of the $1,200 that a family needed to survive. In addition, the WPA limited participation to one family member. In most cases, this meant the male head of the household. As a result, women made up only about 14 percent of WPA workers, and even in the peak year of 1938, the WPA hired only 60 percent of eligible women. With the exception of the program for artists, most women hired by the WPA worked in lower-paying jobs than men.

The elderly required immediate relief and insurance in a country that lagged behind the rest of the industrialized world in helping the aged in its workforce. In August 1935, the president remedied this shortcoming and signed into law the **Social Security Act**. The measure provided that at age sixty-five, eligible workers would receive retirement payments funded by payroll taxes on employees and employers. The law also extended beyond the elderly by providing unemployment insurance for those temporarily laid off from work and welfare payments for the disabled who were permanently out of a job as well as for destitute, dependent children of single parents.

Social Security Act
The landmark 1935 act that created retirement pensions for most Americans funded by payroll taxes. It also provided unemployment insurance and assistance for the disabled.

The Social Security program had significant limitations. The act excluded farm, domestic, and laundry workers, who were among the neediest Americans and were disproportionately Black. The reasons for these exclusions were largely political. The president needed southern Democrats to support this measure, and as a Mississippi newspaper observed: "The average Mississippian can't imagine himself chipping in to pay pensions for able bodied Negroes to sit around in idleness." The system of financing Social Security payments differed from traditional taxation. The payroll tax, which imposed the same fixed percentage on all incomes, was a regressive tax, one that fell hardest on those with lower incomes. Nor did Social Security take into account the unpaid labor of women who remained in the home to take care of their children. Social Security also did not provide benefits for widows or children who were not part of the labor force.

Even with its flaws, Social Security revolutionized the expectations of American workers. It created a compact between the federal government and its citizens, and workers insisted that their political leaders fulfill their moral responsibilities to keep the system going. President Roosevelt recognized that the tax formula might not be economically sound, but he had a higher political objective in mind. He believed that payroll taxes would give contributors the right to collect their benefits and that "with those taxes in there, no damn politician can ever scrap my social security program."

AP® EXAM TIP

President Franklin Roosevelt's New Deal consisted of many federal initiatives to end the Great Depression. This shifted responsibility for economic recovery and welfare directly to the national government, which led to new debates about the role of the federal government. You should know the progress of events that led to the national government taking responsibility to provide relief, recovery, and reform, as well as why the New Deal did not end the depression.

REVIEW

- Why and how did the New Deal shift to the left in 1934 and 1935?
- How did mid-1930s programs such as the WPA, Social Security, and the NYA differ from earlier New Deal programs?

Organized Labor Strikes Back

In 1935, Congress passed the **National Labor Relations Act**, also known as the Wagner Act for its leading sponsor, Senator Robert F. Wagner Sr. of New York. The law created the **National Labor Relations Board (NLRB)**, which protected workers' right to organize labor unions without owner interference and bargain collectively. During the 1930s, union membership soared from fewer than 4 million workers to more than 10 million, including more than 800,000 women. At the outset of the

National Labor Relations Act
A 1935 act (also known as the Wagner Act) that created the National Labor Relations Board (NLRB). The NLRB protected workers' right to organize labor unions without business owner interference and engage in collective bargaining.

depression, barely 6 percent of the labor force belonged to unions, compared with 33 percent in 1940.

Government efforts boosted this growth, but these spectacular gains were due mainly to workers' grassroots efforts set in motion by economic hard times. Organizers traveled the country to bring as many people as possible into the union movement. The number of striking workers during the first year of the Roosevelt administration soared from nearly 325,000 to more than 1.5 million.

The most important development within the labor movement occurred in 1935, with the creation of the Congress of Industrial Organizations (CIO). After the American Federation of Labor (AFL), which consisted mainly of craft unions, rejected a proposal by John L. Lewis of the United Mine Workers to incorporate industrial workers under its umbrella, Lewis and representatives of seven other AFL unions defected and formed the CIO. Unlike the AFL, the new union sought to recruit a wide variety of workers without respect to race, gender, or region.

In 1937, the CIO mounted a full-scale organizing campaign. More than 4.5 million workers participated in some 4,700 strikes. Unions found new ways to protest poor working conditions and arbitrary layoffs. Members of the United Auto Workers (UAW), a CIO affiliate, launched a **sit-down strike** against General Motors (GM) in Flint, Michigan, to win union recognition, higher wages, and better working conditions. Strikers refused to work but remained in the plants, shutting them down from the inside. When the company sent in local police forces to evict the strikers on January 11, 1937, the barricaded workers bombarded the police with spare machine parts and anything that was not bolted down. The community rallied around the strikers, and wives and daughters called "union maids" formed the Women's Emergency Brigade, which supplied sit-downers with food and water and kept up their morale. Neither the state nor the federal government interfered with the work stoppage, and after six weeks GM acknowledged defeat and recognized the UAW.

AP Images

Women's Emergency Brigade, 1937 After the United Auto Workers initiated a sit-down strike against General Motors in Flint, Michigan, for union recognition, better working conditions, and higher wages, a group of their women relatives, friends, and coworkers formed the Women's Emergency Brigade. In this February 1937 demonstration, they held the clubs that they had used to smash windows at the Chevrolet plant occupied by the strikers.

To what extent did New Deal policies align with the goals of unions such as the United Auto Workers?

The following year, the New Deal added a final piece of legislation sought by organized labor. The **Fair Labor Standards Act** (1938) established minimum wages at forty cents an hour and maximum working hours at forty per week. By the end of the decade, "big labor," as the AFL and CIO unions were known, had become a significant force in American politics and a leading backer of the New Deal.

Fair Labor Standards Act
A law passed in 1938 that provided a minimum wage of forty cents an hour and a forty-hour workweek for employees in businesses engaged in interstate commerce.

Major New Deal Measures, 1933–1938

Year	Legislation	Purpose
1933	National Industrial Recovery Act	Government, business, labor cooperation to set prices, wages, and production codes
	Agricultural Adjustment Act	Paid farmers to reduce production to raise prices
	Civilian Conservation Corps	Jobs for young men in conservation
	Public Works Administration	Construction jobs for the unemployed
	Federal Emergency Relief Act	Relief funds for the poor
	Tennessee Valley Authority	Electric power and flood control to rural areas
	Glass-Steagall Act	Insured bank deposits and separated commercial from investment banking
1934	Securities and Exchange Commission	Regulated the stock market
1935	Social Security Act	Provided retirement pensions, unemployment insurance, aid to the disabled, and payments to women with dependent children
	National Labor Relations Act (Wagner Act)	Protected labor unions and their right to bargain collectively
	Works Progress Administration	Provided jobs to eight million unemployed
1938	Fair Labor Standards Act	Established minimum hourly wage and maximum weekly working hours

- How did the New Deal benefit the labor movement?

A Half Deal for Minorities

President Roosevelt made significant gestures on behalf of Black Americans. He appointed Mary McLeod Bethune and Robert Weaver to staff New Deal agencies and gathered an informal "Black Cabinet" in the nation's capital to advise him on matters pertaining to race. The Roosevelt administration also established the Civil Liberties Unit (later renamed Civil Rights Section) in the Department of Justice, which investigated racial discrimination. Eleanor Roosevelt acted as a visible symbol of the White House's concern with the plight of Black Americans. In 1939, Eleanor Roosevelt quit the Daughters of the American Revolution, a women's organization, when it refused to allow black singer Marian Anderson to hold a concert in Constitution Hall in Washington, D.C. Instead, the First Lady brought Anderson to sing on the steps of the Lincoln Memorial.

Perhaps the greatest measure of Franklin Roosevelt's impact on Black Americans came when large numbers of Black voters switched from the Republican to the Democratic Party in 1936, a pattern that has lasted to the present day. "Go turn Lincoln's picture to the wall," a Black observer commented after the election. "That debt has been paid in full."

Yet overall, the New Deal did little to break down racial inequality. President Roosevelt believed that the plight of Black Americans would improve, along with that of all downtrodden Americans, as New Deal measures restored the nation's economic health. Black leaders disagreed. They argued that the NRA's initials stood for "Negroes Ruined Again" because the agency displaced Black workers and approved lower wages for them than for their white counterparts. The AAA dislodged Black sharecroppers. New Deal programs such as the CCC and those for building public housing maintained existing patterns of segregation. Both the Social Security Act and the Fair Labor Standards Act omitted from coverage jobs that Black Americans were most likely to hold. In fact, the New Deal's big labor/big government alliance left out non-unionized industrial and agricultural workers, many of whom were Black and lacked bargaining power.

This pattern of halfway reform persisted for other minorities. Since the 1890s, American Indians had lived in poverty, forced onto reservations where they were offered few economic opportunities and where white people carried out a relentless assault on their culture. By the early 1930s, American Indians earned an average income of less than $50 a year—compared with $800 for whites—and their unemployment rate was three times higher than that of white Americans. For the most part, they lived on lands that whites had given up on as unsuitable for farming or mining. The policy of assimilation established by the Dawes Act of 1887 (see Module 6.3) had worsened the problem by depriving American Indians of their cultural identities as well as their economic livelihoods.

In 1934, the federal government reversed its course. Spurred on by John Collier, the commissioner of Indian affairs, Congress passed the **Indian Reorganization Act (IRA)**, which terminated the Dawes Act, authorized self-government for those living on reservations, extended tribal landholdings, and pledged to uphold native customs and language.

Indian Reorganization Act (IRA)
An act from 1934 that ended the Dawes Act, authorized self-government for those living on reservations, extended tribal landholdings, and pledged to uphold native customs and languages.

Although the Indian Reorganization Act brought economic and social improvements for American Indians, many problems remained. Despite his considerable efforts, Collier approached his role as commissioner of Indian affairs from the top down. One historian remarked that Collier had "the zeal of a crusader who knew better than the Indians what was good for them." Collier failed to appreciate the diversity of native tribes and administered laws that contradicted American Indian political and economic practices. For example, the IRA required the tribes to operate by majority rule, whereas many of them reached decisions through consensus, which respected the views of the minority. Although 174 tribes accepted the IRA, 78 tribes, including the Seneca, Crow, and Navajo, rejected it.

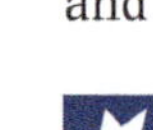

REVIEW

- In what ways did the New Deal assist minorities in the United States? In what ways did it fall short?

Decline of the New Deal

Roosevelt's shift to the left paid political dividends, and in 1936, the president won reelection by a landslide. His sweeping victory proved to be one of the rare critical elections that meant a fundamental political realignment. Democrats replaced Republicans as the majority party in the United States, overturning thirty-six years of Republican rule. While Roosevelt had won convincingly in 1932, not until 1936 did the president put together a stable coalition that could sustain Democratic dominance for many years to come.

In the 1936 election, Roosevelt trounced Alfred M. Landon, the Republican governor of Kansas, and Democrats increased their congressional majorities by staggering margins. The vote broke down along class lines. Roosevelt won the votes of 80 percent of union members, 81 percent of unskilled workers, and 84 percent of people on relief, compared with only 42 percent of high-income voters. Millions of new voters turned out at the polls, and most of them supported Roosevelt's New Deal coalition of the poor, farmers, urban ethnic minorities, unionists, white southerners, and Blacks.

The euphoria of his triumph, however, proved short-lived. An overconfident Roosevelt soon reached beyond his electoral mandate and within two years found himself unable to extend the New Deal. In response to fears that the conservative Supreme Court would continue to rule key New Deal legislation unconstitutional, as it had recently decreed with the National Industrial Recovery Act and Agricultural Adjustment Act, FDR attempted to reshape the nation's highest court.

In 1937, Roosevelt introduced a **court-packing plan** asking Congress to increase the size of the Supreme Court which would allow him to appoint new lifetime justices. He justified this as a matter of reform, claiming that the present nine-member Court could not handle its workload because six of the nine justices were over seventy years old. Under his proposal, the president would make one new appointment for each judge over the age of seventy who did not retire so long as the bench did not exceed fifteen members. In reality, Roosevelt schemed to "pack" the Court with supporters to prevent it from declaring New Deal legislation such as Social Security and the National Labor Relations Act unconstitutional.

court-packing plan
A proposal made by Franklin Roosevelt in 1937 to increase the number of members of the U.S. Supreme Court and reduce its opposition to New Deal legislation. Congress failed to pass the measure, and the scheme undermined Roosevelt's popular support.

The plan backfired. Conservatives charged Roosevelt with seeking to destroy the separation of powers among the executive, legislative, and judicial branches set out in the Constitution. In the end, the president failed to expand the Supreme Court, but he preserved his legislative accomplishments. In a series of rulings, the chastened Supreme Court approved Social Security, the National Labor Relations Act, and other New Deal legislation.

Nevertheless, the political fallout from the court-packing fight damaged the president and his plans for further legislative reform. Roosevelt's court-packing plan alienated many southern Democratic members of Congress who previously had sided with the president. Traditionally suspicious of the power of the federal government, southern lawmakers worried that Roosevelt was going too far toward centralizing power in Washington at the expense of states' rights.

Southern Democrats formed a coalition with conservative northern Republicans who shared their concerns about the expansion of federal power and excessive spending on social welfare programs. Their antipathy toward labor unions further bound them. Although they held a minority of seats in Congress, this conservative coalition could block unwanted legislation by using the filibuster in the Senate (unlimited debate that could be shut down only with a two-thirds vote). After 1938, these conservatives made sure that no further New Deal legislation passed.

Roosevelt also lost support for New Deal initiatives because of the recession of 1937, which FDR's policies had triggered. When federal spending soared after passage of the WPA and other relief measures adopted in 1935, the president lost his economic nerve for deficit spending. He called for reduced spending, which increased unemployment and slowed economic recovery. In addition, as the Social Security payroll tax took effect, it reduced the purchasing power of workers, thereby worsening the impact of reduced government spending. Making the situation worse, pension payments were not scheduled to begin for several years. The "Roosevelt Recession" further eroded congressional support for the New Deal.

AP® WORKING with EVIDENCE

Source: Clifford K. Berryman, *Old Reliable*, 1938

Granger – Historical Picture Archive

Questions for Analysis

1. Identify the Roosevelt administration policies that are critiqued in this cartoon.
2. Describe the arguments that support this critique of the New Deal.
3. Explain how this portrayal of Roosevelt is designed to undermine confidence in New Deal economic policy.

The country was still deep in depression in 1939. Unemployment was at 17 percent, with more than 11 million people out of work. Most of those who were poor at the start of the Great Depression remained poor. Recovery came mainly to those who were temporarily impoverished as a result of the economic crisis. The distribution of wealth remained skewed toward the top. In 1933, the richest 5 percent of the population controlled 31 percent of disposable income; in 1939, that figure stood at 26 percent.

Against this backdrop of persistent difficult economic times and political miscalculations, the president's popularity began to fade. In the midterm elections of 1938, Roosevelt campaigned against Democratic conservatives in the primaries in an attempt to reinvigorate his New Deal coalition. His efforts failed and upset many ordinary citizens who associated the tactic with that used by European dictators who had recently risen to power. As the decade came to a close, Roosevelt turned his attention away from the New Deal and increasingly toward a new war in Europe that threatened to engulf the entire world.

- Who benefited most from Roosevelt's New Deal reforms after 1934?
- How successful were these reforms in bringing about the end of the Great Depression?

New Deal Liberalism Appraised

The Great Depression produced enormous economic hardships that the Hoover administration fell far short of relieving. Although Hoover's successor, Franklin Roosevelt, also failed to end the depression, in contrast he provided unprecedented economic assistance to the poor as well as the rich. The New Deal expanded the size of the federal government from 605,000 employees to more than 1 million during the 1930s.

Moreover, the New Deal rescued the capitalist system, doing little to alter the fundamental structure of the American economy. Despite subjecting businesses to greater regulation, it left corporations, the stock market, farms, and banks in the hands of private enterprise. Indeed, by the end of the 1930s, large corporations had more power over markets than ever before. Income and wealth remained unequally distributed, nearly to the same extent as they had been before Roosevelt took office in 1933.

Roosevelt forged a middle path between reactionaries and revolutionaries at a time when totalitarian leaders in Germany, Italy, and the Soviet Union had seized or were consolidating power. By contrast, the American president expanded democratic capitalism, bringing a broader cross section of society to the decision-making table. Roosevelt's "broker state" of multiple competing interests provided greater democracy than a government dominated exclusively by business elites.

This system did not benefit those who remained unorganized and wielded little power, but marginalized groups — Black Americans, Latinos, and American Indians — did receive greater recognition and self-determination from the federal government. Indeed, these and other groups helped shape the New Deal.

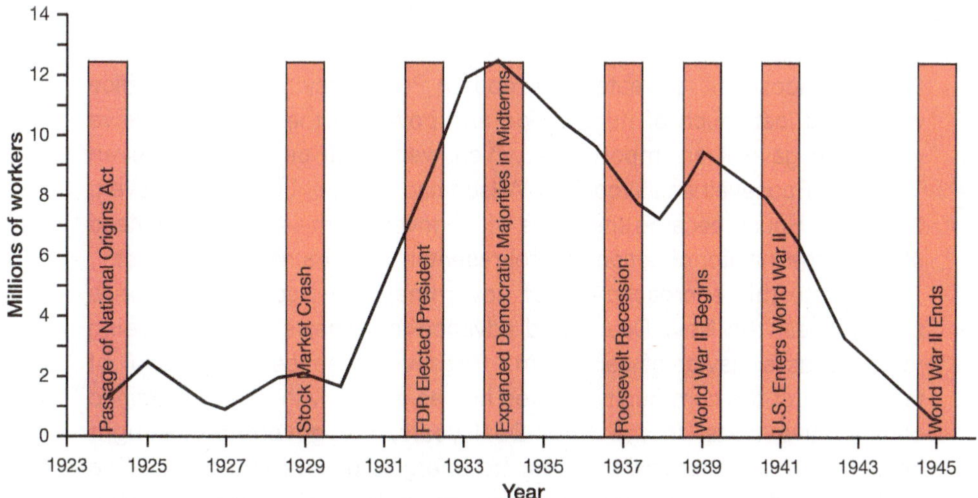

Unemployment Numbers and Major Historical Events, 1920–1945 Business prosperity and restriction of immigration ensured low unemployment during most of the 1920s. When unemployment rose dramatically in the late 1920s, President Hoover failed to solve the crisis. During the 1930s, President Roosevelt's New Deal created many initiatives to lower unemployment.

What do these data indicate about the effectiveness of New Deal programs on unemployment?

As Eleanor Roosevelt's history shows, women played key roles in campaigning for social welfare legislation. Others, like Luisa Moreno, helped organize workers and promoted ethnic pride among Latinos in the face of deportations. Blacks challenged racism and pressured the federal government to distribute services more equitably. American Indians won important democratic and cultural reforms, and though Asian Americans continued to encounter considerable discrimination on the West Coast, they joined to help each other.

President Roosevelt also solidified the institution of the presidency as the focal point for public leadership. His cheerfulness, hopefulness, and pragmatism rallied millions of individuals behind him. Even after Roosevelt died in 1945, the public retained its expectation that leadership would come from the White House.

Through his programs and his force of personality, Franklin Roosevelt convinced Americans that he cared about their welfare and that the federal government would not ignore their suffering. However, he was not universally beloved: Millions of Americans despised him because they thought he was leading the country toward socialism, and he did not solve all the problems the country faced—it would take government spending for World War II to end the depression. Still, together with his wife, Eleanor, Franklin Roosevelt conveyed a sense that the American people belonged to a single community, capable of banding together to solve the country's problems, no matter how serious they were or how intractable they might seem.

- In what ways did the New Deal achieve its goals?
- What goals did the New Deal fail to achieve?

AP® Skills Workshop: Writing Historically

Additional Practice in Responding to a Short-Answer Question with Secondary Sources

"Franklin Roosevelt re-created the modern Presidency. He took an office which had lost much of its prestige and power in the previous twelve years and gave it an importance which went well beyond what even Theodore Roosevelt and Woodrow Wilson had done. . . . Under Roosevelt, the White House became the focus of all government—the fountainhead of ideas, the initiator of action, the representative of the national interest.

Despite this encroachment of government on traditional business prerogatives, the New Deal could advance impressive claims to being regarded as a 'savior of capitalism.' Roosevelt's sense of the land, of family, and of the community marked him as a man with deeply ingrained conservative traits. In the New Deal years, the government sought deliberately, in Roosevelt's words, 'to energize private enterprise.' The RFC financed business, housing agencies underwrote home financing, and public works spending aimed to revive the construction industry. . . . Yet such considerations should not obscure the more important point: that the New Deal, however conservative it was in some respects and however much it owed to the past, marked a radically new departure. . . .

(*continued*)

The New Deal achieved a more just society by recognizing groups which had been largely unrepresented—staple farmers, industrial workers, particular ethnic groups, and a new intellectual-administrative class. Yet this was still a halfway revolution; it swelled the ranks of the bourgeoisie but left many Americans—sharecroppers, slum dwellers, most Negroes—outside of the new equilibrium."

William E. Leuchtenburg, *Franklin D. Roosevelt and the New Deal, 1932–1940*, 1963

"The liberal reforms of the New Deal did not transform the American system; they conserved and protected American corporate capitalism, occasionally by absorbing parts of threatening programs. There was no significant redistribution of power in American society, only limited recognition of other organized groups, seldom of unorganized peoples. Neither the bolder programs advanced by New Dealers nor the final legislation greatly extended the beneficence of government beyond the middle classes or drew upon the wealth of the few for the needs of the many. Designed to maintain the American system, liberal activity was directed toward essentially conservative goals. Experimentalism was most frequently limited to means; seldom did it extend to ends. Never questioning private enterprise, it operated within safe channels, far short of Marxism or even of [older] American radicalisms that offered structural critiques and structural solutions.

The New Deal was [not] . . . 'a half-way revolution,' as William Leuchtenburg concludes. Not only was the extension of representation to new groups less than full-fledged partnership, but the New Deal neglected many Americans—sharecroppers, tenant farmers, migratory workers and farm laborers, slum dwellers, unskilled workers, and unemployed Negroes. They were left outside the new order. . . . Yet by the power of rhetoric and through the appeals of political organization, the Roosevelt government managed to win or retain the allegiance of these people. Perhaps this is one of the crueler ironies of liberal politics, that the marginal men trapped in hopelessness were seduced by rhetoric, by the style and movement, of efforts seldom reaching beyond words."

Barton J. Bernstein, "The New Deal: The Conservative Achievements of Liberal Reform," *Towards a New Past: Dissenting Essays in American History*, 1968

Using the excerpts, answer **A**, **B**, and **C**.

(A) Briefly describe ONE major difference between Leuchtenburg's and Bernstein's historical interpretations of the period 1933–1939.

(B) Briefly explain how ONE specific historical event or development during the period 1933–1939 that is not explicitly mentioned in the excerpts could be used to support Leuchtenburg's interpretation.

(C) Briefly explain how ONE specific historical event or development during the period 1933–1939 that is not explicitly mentioned in the excerpts could be used to support Bernstein's interpretation.

MODULE 7.11

Interwar Foreign Policy

FOCUS

While you read this module, consider the similarities and differences in U.S. foreign policy in the years before World War I and the years between World War I and World War II. Note the effects of international crises on U.S. citizens and policymakers and the debates these effects inspired.

The end of World War I did not bring peace and prosperity to Europe. The harsh peace terms imposed on the Central Powers in 1919 left the losers, especially Germany, deeply resentful. The war saddled both sides with a huge financial debt and produced economic instability, which ultimately contributed to the Great Depression in the 1930s. The failure of the United States to join the League of Nations after the Great War dramatically reduced the organization's ability to maintain peace and stability. In Asia, Japanese invasions of the Chinese province of Manchuria in 1931, China proper in 1937, and Southeast Asia in 1940 threatened America's Open Door policy. While German expansionism in Europe in the late 1930s moved President Roosevelt and the nation toward war, it took the Japanese attack on Pearl Harbor in 1941 to bring the United States into the global conflict.

The Road to War

Despite its failure to join the League of Nations, the United States did not withdraw from international affairs in the 1920s. It participated in arms control negotiations; signed the **Kellogg-Briand Pact**, which outlawed war as an instrument of national policy but proved unenforceable; and expanded its foreign investments in Central and Latin America, Asia, the Middle East, and western Europe. In 1933, a new possibility for trade emerged when the Roosevelt administration extended diplomatic recognition to the Soviet Union (USSR).

Kellogg-Briand Pact
An international arms-control agreement that outlawed war as an instrument of national policy following World War I. The policy reflected isolationist sentiments that opposed collective security agreements, and the pact proved unenforceable.

isolationism
The informal policy stemming from the belief that the United States should not become involved in the affairs of other nations. This mindset was especially popular following World War I.

Overall, the country did not retreat from foreign affairs so much as it refused to enter into collective security agreements that would restrain its freedom of action. To the extent that American leaders practiced **isolationism**, they did so mainly in the political sense of rejecting internationalist organizations such as the League of Nations, institutions that might require the United States to use military force to implement their decisions.

The experience of World War I had reinforced this brand of political isolationism, which was reflected in an outpouring of antiwar sentiments in the late 1920s and early 1930s. Best-selling novels like Ernest Hemingway's *A Farewell to Arms* (1929), Erich Maria Remarque's *All Quiet on the Western Front* (1929), and Dalton Trumbo's *Johnny Got His Gun* (1939) presented vivid depictions of the horror and futility of war.

Beginning in 1934, Senate investigations chaired by Gerald Nye of North Dakota inaccurately concluded that bankers and munitions makers—"merchants of death," as one contemporary writer labeled them—had conspired to push the United States into the Great War in 1917. Nye's hearings appealed to popular antibusiness sentiment in Depression-era America.

Following the **Nye Committee** hearings, Congress passed a series of **Neutrality Acts**, each designed to make it more difficult for the United States to become entangled in future European armed hostilities. In 1935, Congress prohibited the sale of munitions to either warring side and authorized the president to warn Americans against traveling on passenger liners of belligerent nations. The following year, lawmakers added private loans to the ban, and in 1937, they required belligerents to pay cash for nonmilitary purchases and ship them on their own vessels—so-called cash-and-carry provisions. Each of these provisions was based on preventing a repeat of the factors that were believed to have pulled the United States into World War I.

Neutrality Acts
Legislation passed between 1935 and 1937 to make it more difficult for the United States to become entangled in overseas conflicts. The Neutrality Acts reflected the strength of isolationist sentiment in 1930s America.

Events in Europe, however, made U.S. neutrality ever more difficult to maintain. After rising to power as chancellor of Germany in 1933, Adolf Hitler revived Germany's economic and military strength despite the Great Depression. Hitler installed National Socialism (**Nazism**) at home and established the empire of the **Third Reich** abroad. The *Führer* (leader) whipped up patriotic fervor by scapegoating and persecuting communists and Jews. To garner support for his actions, Hitler manipulated German feelings of humiliation for losing World War I and having been forced to sign the "war guilt" clause and pointed to the disastrous effects of the country's inflation-ridden economy. In 1936, Hitler sent troops to occupy the Rhineland between Germany and France in blatant violation of the Treaty of Versailles and without reprisal from the League of Nations or from Great Britain and France.

Hitler did not stop there. Citing the need for more space for the Germanic people to live, he pushed for German expansion into eastern Europe. In March 1938, he forced Austria to unite with Germany. German troops were greeted as heroes by many Austrians as they marched unopposed into Austria. After falsely claiming that German people were being mistreated in the Sudetenland, the mainly German-speaking, western region of Czechoslovakia, Hitler signed the **Munich Accord** with Great Britain and France, allowing Germany to annex the territory in September of that year. Hitler still wanted more land and was convinced that his western European rivals would not stop him, so in March 1939, he sent German troops to invade and occupy what remained of Czechoslovakia. Hitler proved correct; Britain and France did nothing in response. The policy critics called **appeasement,** making concessions to avoid conflict, had failed to stop Nazi Germany's aggressive expansion in Europe.

appeasement
The policy exercised by Great Britain and France of making concessions to Nazi Germany in the hopes of avoiding a larger conflict. After Hitler's invasion of Czechoslovakia, in violation of the recently signed Munich Accord, the policy was abandoned, setting the stage for the start of a new war.

Hitler's Italian ally, Benito Mussolini, joined him in war and conquest. In 1935, Italian troops invaded Ethiopia with the support of Germany. The following year, both Germany and Italy intervened in the Spanish civil war, providing military support for General Francisco Franco in his effort to overthrow the democratically elected, socialist government of Spain. While the United States and Great Britain remained on the sidelines, only the Soviet Union officially assisted the Loyalist defenders of the Spanish republic. In violation of American law, private citizens, many of whom were communists, volunteered to serve on the side of the Spanish Loyalists and fought on the battlefield as the Abraham Lincoln Brigade. Other sympathetic Americans, such as J. Robert Oppenheimer, provided financial assistance for the anti-Franco government. Despite these efforts, Franco's forces seized control of Spain in early 1939, another victory for Hitler and Mussolini.

REVIEW

- What major factors threatened the post–World War I order during the 1930s?

The Challenge to Isolationism

AP® EXAM TIP

Following World War I, the U.S. government pursued an isolationist foreign policy that sought to prevent conflict through treaties such as the Kellogg-Briand Pact and prevent U.S. participation in any European wars by measures like the Neutrality Acts. These efforts ended with the Japanese attack on Pearl Harbor. Be able to describe how the failures of World War I led to World War II. The AP® Exam may ask a question about comparing the causes and effects of these two wars.

As Europe drifted toward war, public opinion polls revealed that most Americans wanted to stay out of any European conflict. The president, however, thought it likely that, to protect its own economic and political interests, the United States would eventually need to assist the Western democracies. Still, Roosevelt had to tread lightly in the face of the Neutrality Acts that Congress had passed between 1935 and 1937 and overwhelming public opposition to American involvement in Europe.

Germany's aggression in Europe eventually led to full-scale war. When Germany invaded Poland in September 1939, Britain and France declared war on Germany. Just before the invasion, the Soviet Union had signed a nonaggression agreement with Germany, which carved up Poland between the two nations and permitted the U.S.S.R. to occupy the neighboring Baltic states of Latvia, Lithuania, and Estonia. Soviet leader Joseph Stalin had few illusions about Hitler's design on his own nation, but he concluded that by signing this pact, he could secure his country's western borders and buy additional time. In June 1940, Italy declared war on France and Britain. (The next year, Germans broke the pact and invaded the Soviet Union.)

Roosevelt responded to the outbreak of war by reaffirming U.S. neutrality. Despite his sympathy for the Allies (mainly Great Britain and France), which most Americans had come to share, the president stated his hope that the United States could stay out of the war: "Let no man or woman thoughtlessly or falsely talk of America sending its armies to European fields."

America First Committee
An isolationist organization founded by Senator Gerald Nye in 1940 to keep the United States out of World War II.

With the United States on the sidelines, German forces marched toward victory. By the spring of 1940, German armies had launched a *Blitzkrieg* (lightning war) across Europe, defeating and occupying Denmark, Norway, the Netherlands, Belgium, and Luxembourg. With German victories mounting, committed opponents of American involvement in foreign wars organized the **America First Committee**. America First tapped into the feeling of isolationism and concern among a diverse group of Americans who did not want to get dragged into another foreign war.

AP® WORKING with EVIDENCE

Source: Charles Lindbergh, *Who Are the War Agitators?*, September 1941

"National polls showed that when England and France declared war on Germany, in 1939, less than 10 percent of our population favored a similar course for America. But there were various groups of people, here and abroad, whose interests and beliefs necessitated the involvement of the United States in the war. I shall point out some of these groups tonight, and outline their methods of procedure. In doing this, I must speak with the utmost frankness, for in order to counteract their efforts, we must know exactly who they are.

The three most important groups who have been pressing this country toward war are the British, the Jewish and the Roosevelt administration.

Behind these groups, but of lesser importance, are a number of capitalists, Anglophiles, and intellectuals who believe that the future of mankind depends upon the domination of the British empire. Add to these the Communistic groups who were opposed to intervention until a few weeks ago, and I believe I have named the major war agitators in this country.

I am speaking here only of war agitators, not of those sincere but misguided men and women who, confused by misinformation and frightened by propaganda, follow the lead of the war agitators.

As I have said, these war agitators comprise only a small minority of our people; but they control a tremendous influence. Against the determination of the American people to stay out of war, they have marshaled the power of their propaganda, their money, their patronage."

Questions for Analysis

1. Identify the people and groups agitating for U.S. entry into the war according to Lindbergh.
2. Describe, according to Lindbergh, the rationale behind these perpetrators' actions.
3. Evaluate the extent of similarity between the ideas expressed by Lindbergh and the ideas expressed by supporters and members of the KKK in the 1920s.

The greatest challenge to isolationism occurred in June 1940, when France fell to the German onslaught and Nazi troops marched into Paris. Britain now stood virtually alone, and its position seemed tenuous. The British had barely succeeded in evacuating their forces from France by sea when the German *Luftwaffe* (air force) began bombing London and other targets in the Battle of Britain.

The surrender of France and the Battle of Britain drastically changed Americans' attitude toward entering the war. Before Germany invaded France, 82 percent of Americans thought that the United States should not aid the Allies. After France's defeat, in a complete turnaround, some 80 percent of Americans favored assisting Great Britain in some way. However, four of five Americans polled still opposed immediate entry into the war. As a result, the politically astute Roosevelt portrayed all U.S. assistance to Britain as a way to prevent American military intervention by allowing Great Britain to defeat the Germans on its own.

Everett Collection, Inc.

America First Committee Rally, 1941 Organized in 1940, the America First Committee campaigned against U.S. entry into World War II. One of its leaders, the popular aviator Charles Lindbergh, addressed a rally of three thousand people in Fort Wayne, Indiana, on October 5, 1941. The isolationist group blamed eastern bankers, British sympathizers, and Jewish leaders for promoting war fever. The committee dissolved four days after the attack by Japan on Pearl Harbor.

How did these arguments echo isolationist sentiments from the mid-1930s?

Nevertheless, the Roosevelt administration found acceptable ways of helping Britain. On September 2, 1940, the president sent fifty obsolete destroyers to the British in return for leases on British naval bases in Newfoundland, Bermuda, and the British West Indies. Two weeks later, on September 16, Roosevelt persuaded Congress to pass the **Selective Training and Service Act of 1940**, the first peacetime military draft in U.S. history, which quickly registered more than 16 million men.

Selective Training and Service Act of 1940
Legislation requiring men between the ages of 18 and 35 to register for the draft, later expanded to age 45. It was the first peacetime draft in U.S. history.

This political maneuvering came as Roosevelt campaigned for an unprecedented third term in 1940. He defeated the Republican Wendell Willkie, a Wall Street lawyer who shared Roosevelt's anti-isolationist views, although by a smaller margin than in his previous two electoral victories. However, both candidates accommodated voters' desire to stay out of the European war. Roosevelt went so far as to promise American parents: "Your boys are not going to be sent into any foreign war."

Roosevelt's campaign promises did not halt the march to war. Roosevelt succeeded in pushing Congress to pass the **Lend-Lease Act** in March 1941. With Britain running out of money and its shipping devastated by German submarine attacks, this measure circumvented the cash-and-carry provisions of the Neutrality Acts. The United States would lend or lease equipment, but no one expected the recipients to return the used weapons and other commodities. To protect British ships carrying American supplies, the president extended naval and air patrols in the North Atlantic. In response, German submarines began sinking U.S. ships. By May 1941, Germany and the United States were engaged in an undeclared naval war.

Lend-Lease Act
A law permitting the United States to lend or lease military equipment and other commodities to Great Britain and its allies. Its passage in March 1941 marked the end of U.S. neutrality before the United States entered World War II.

REVIEW

- How did many Americans justify isolationism during the late 1930s?
- What factors undermined isolationist sentiments?

The United States Enters the War

Financially, militarily, and ideologically, the United States had aligned itself with Britain, and Roosevelt expected that the nation would soon be formally at war. As Germany and Italy successfully expanded their empires, they endangered U.S. economic interests and democratic values. President Roosevelt believed that American security abroad was threatened by the German Nazis and Italian fascists.

After passage of the Lend-Lease Act, American and British military planners agreed that defeating Germany would become the top priority if the United States entered the war. In August 1941, Roosevelt and British prime minister Winston Churchill met in Newfoundland, where they signed the **Atlantic Charter**, a lofty statement of war aims that included principles of freedom of the seas, self-determination, free trade, and "freedom from fear and want"—ideals that laid the groundwork for the establishment of a postwar United Nations.

At the same meeting, Roosevelt promised Churchill that the United States would protect British convoys in the North Atlantic as far as Iceland while the nation waited for a confrontation with Germany that would rally the American public in support of war. The president got what he wanted. After several attacks on American ships by German submarines in September and October, the president persuaded Congress to repeal the neutrality legislation of the 1930s and allow American ships to sail across the Atlantic to supply Great Britain. By December, the nation was close to open war with Germany.

AP Images

Roosevelt, Churchill, and the Atlantic Charter, 1941 U.S. president Franklin D. Roosevelt and British prime minister Winston Churchill converse aboard the British battleship *Prince of Wales* off the coast of Newfoundland on August 10, 1941. The five-day secret meeting produced the Atlantic Charter, a declaration that shaped the Anglo-American alliance of World War II.

What common interests did the United States and Great Britain have in this conflict?

The event that finally prompted the United States to enter the war, however, occurred not in the Atlantic but in the Pacific Ocean. For nearly a decade, U.S. relations with Japan had deteriorated over the issue of China's independence and maintaining the Open Door to Chinese markets. The United States did little to challenge the Japanese invasion and occupation of Manchuria in 1931, but after Japanese armed forces moved farther into China in 1937, the United States supplied arms to China.

Relations worsened in 1940 when the Japanese government signed the **Tripartite Pact** with Germany and Italy, which created a mutual defense agreement among the three. That same year, Japanese troops invaded northern Indochina, and Roosevelt responded by embargoing sales of products that Japan needed for war. This embargo did not deter the Japanese. In July, they occupied the remainder of Indochina to gain access to the region's natural resources. The Roosevelt administration retaliated by freezing Japanese assets and cutting off all trade with Japan.

Tripartite Pact
A 1940 mutual defense agreement between Japan, Germany, and Italy meant to deter U.S. military action against those countries.

On the quiet Sunday morning of December 7, 1941, Japan attacked the U.S. Pacific Fleet stationed at Pearl Harbor near Honolulu, Hawaii. This surprise air and naval assault killed more than 2,400 Americans and badly damaged or destroyed 300 aircraft and 19 U.S. warships, including all eight battleships stationed there. The **attack on Pearl Harbor** abruptly ended isolationism and rallied the American public behind President Roosevelt, who pronounced December 7 "a date which will live in infamy." The next day, Congress overwhelmingly voted to go to war with Japan, and on December 11, Germany and Italy, upholding the Tripartite Pact, declared war on the United States in response.

attack on Pearl Harbor
The Japanese surprise attack on the U.S. Pacific Fleet stationed at Pearl Harbor near Honolulu, Hawaii, on December 7, 1941. The attack killed more than 2,400 Americans, seriously damaged ships and aircraft, and abruptly ended isolationism by prompting U.S. entry into World War II.

In little more than a year after his reelection pledge to keep the country out of war, Roosevelt sent American men to fight overseas. Still, an overwhelming majority of Americans now considered entry into the war as necessary to preserve freedom and democracy against assaults from fascist and militaristic nations.

REVIEW

- What events in Europe and the Pacific brought the United States into World War II?

AP® Skills Workshop: Writing Historically

Additional Practice in Responding to a Short-Answer Question with a Primary Source

Winsor McCay, *Let Sam Do It*, 1931

Bettmann/Getty Images

Using the image, answer **A**, **B**, and **C**.

(A) Briefly describe ONE perspective expressed by the artist about the role of the United States during the international conflicts of the 1930s.

(B) Briefly explain how ONE event or development led to the historical situation depicted in the image.

(C) Briefly explain ONE specific outcome of debates during the 1930s about the role of the United States during these crises.

World War II: Mobilization

MODULE 7.12

FOCUS

In this module, consider the economic and social effects of World War II on different groups in American society. To what extent did those effects resemble the effects of World War I?

The global conflict had profound effects on the American home front. World War II ended the Great Depression, restored economic prosperity, and increased membership in labor unions. At the same time, it smoothed the way for a closer relationship between government and private defense contractors, later referred to as the military-industrial complex. The war extended U.S. influence in the world and offered new economic opportunities at home. Despite fierce and bloody military battles throughout the world, Americans kept up morale by rallying around family and community.

The war also had a significant impact on race relations. The fight to defeat Nazism, a doctrine based on racial prejudice and white supremacy, offered Black Americans a chance to press for equal opportunity at home. By contrast, Japanese Americans experienced intensified discrimination and oppression as wartime anti-Japanese hysteria led to the internment of Japanese Americans, an abuse of their civil rights. They were freed toward the end of the war, but their incarceration left scars. Finally, Mexican Americans and American Indians benefited from wartime jobs and military service but continued to experience ethnic prejudice.

Managing the Home-Front Economy

To mobilize for war, President Roosevelt increased federal spending to unprecedented levels. Federal government employment during the war expanded to an all-time high of 3.8 million workers, setting the foundation for a large, permanent Washington bureaucracy. War orders fueled economic growth, productivity, and employment. The gross domestic product increased by over 50 percent, industrial productivity soared 96 percent, union membership rose by two-thirds, and unemployment dropped from 8 million to less than 1 million. The armed forces helped reduce unemployment significantly by enlisting 12 million men and women, 7 million of whom had been unemployed.

Prosperity was not limited to any one region. The industrial areas of the Northeast and Midwest once again boomed, as automobile factories converted to building tanks and other military vehicles, oil refineries processed gasoline to fuel them, steel and rubber companies manufactured parts to construct these vehicles and the weapons they carried, and textile and shoe plants furnished uniforms and boots for soldiers to wear. As farmers provided food for the nation and its allies, farm production soared.

The economy diversified geographically. Fifteen million Americans—11 percent of the entire population—migrated between 1941 and 1945. The war transformed the agricultural South into a budding industrial region. The federal government poured more than $4 billion in contracts into the South to operate military camps, contract with textile factories to clothe the military, and use its ports to build and launch warships. The availability of jobs in southern cities attracted sharecroppers and tenant farmers, Black and white, away from the countryside and promoted urbanization while reducing the region's dependency on the plantation economy.

No region was changed more by the war than the West. The West Coast prospered because it was the gateway to the Pacific war against Japan. The federal government established aircraft plants and shipbuilding yards in California, Oregon, and Washington, resulting in extraordinary population growth in Los Angeles, San Diego, San Francisco, Portland, and Seattle. The West's population grew three times as fast as the rest of the nation. Los Angeles led the way in attracting defense contracts, because its balmy climate proved ideal for test-flying the aircraft that rolled off its assembly lines.

War Powers Acts

Two acts passed after the attack on Pearl Harbor that greatly expanded the power of the president during World War II. The acts allowed the president to reorganize federal agencies, expedite wartime production, censor international mail, and provide census data to the FBI.

Following the attack on Pearl Harbor, Congress passed two **War Powers Acts**, which authorized the president to reorganize federal agencies any way he thought necessary to win the war. In 1942, the president established the **War Production Board** to oversee the economy. The agency encouraged business corporations to meet ever-increasing government orders by negotiating lucrative contracts that helped underwrite their costs, lower their taxes, and guarantee large profits. The government also suspended antitrust enforcement, giving private companies great leeway in running their enterprises.

Much of the antibusiness hostility generated by the Great Depression evaporated as the Roosevelt administration recruited business executives to supervise government agencies. Indeed, the close relationship between the federal government and business that emerged during the war also produced a close relationship between the military and industry, which would have a vast influence on the future development of the economy.

In the first three years of the war, the United States increased military production by some 800 percent. American factories accounted for more than half of worldwide manufacturing output. By 1945, the United States had produced 86,000 tanks, nearly 300,000 airplanes, 15 million rifles and machine guns, and 6,500 ships to fulfill Roosevelt's pledge that the United States would become the "great arsenal of democracy."

Financing this enormous enterprise took considerable effort. The federal government spent more than $320 billion, ten times the cost of World War I. To pay for the war, the federal government sold $100 billion in bonds, only about half of what was needed. The rest came from increased income tax rates, which for the first time affected low- and middle-income workers, who had paid little or no tax before. At the same time, the tax rate for the wealthy was boosted to 94 percent. The urgency of collecting tax revenues prompted the Treasury Department to implement a system of tax withholding from paychecks, which has endured. Besides paying higher taxes and paying more often, American consumers shouldered the burden of shortages and high prices.

Building up the armed forces was the final ingredient in the mobilization for war. In 1940, about 250,000 soldiers were serving in the U.S. military. By 1945, American forces had grown to more than 12 million men and women through voluntary enlistments and a draft of men between the ages of eighteen and forty-five. The military reflected the diversity of the U.S. population. The sons of immigrants fought alongside the sons of older-stock Americans. Although the military tried to exclude homosexuals, many managed to join the fighting forces. Some 700,000 Black men served in the armed forces, but civilian and military officials confined them to segregated units in the army, assigned them to menial work in the navy, and excluded them from the U.S. Marine Corps.

Tuskegee airmen

Black pilots and airmen who served in segregated units during World War II. They earned fame escorting U.S. bomber aircraft in Europe and North Africa.

The Army Air Corps created segregated air combat units that trained at Tuskegee Institute in Alabama. These **Tuskegee airmen**, like their counterparts among the ground forces, distinguished themselves in battle.

Courtesy National Park Service, Museum Management Program and Tuskegee Airmen National Historic Site, TUAI 31

Tuskegee Airmen Twenty Black pilots, among those known as the Tuskegee airmen, line up for a photograph, which they signed. The Army Air Corps created segregated bombardment and pursuit squadrons of Black airmen. The latter flew combat missions in Europe. The success of the Tuskegee airmen, who white bomber pilots regularly requested to provide air protection, contributed to the postwar desegregation of the armed forces.

How might the motivations of the Tuskegee airmen differ from other U.S. military pilots in World War II?

AP® WORKING with EVIDENCE

Source: Anonymous, "The Case of the Negro Officer in the United States Army," to Carl Murphy, Publisher of the Baltimore *Afro-American*, 1943

"[I], a commissioned officer of the United States Army, am denied the rights and privileges of an officer. I am excluded by members of my own rank and station in the Army. I am denied the privilege to use the Officer's Club. Although members of my race are used as waiters and general help around the club, I am denied the privilege of using it. It has been a source of embarrassment for a Negro soldier working there to ask me if I am denied the privilege of the club. I ask you, gentlemen, what would you say or do if a soldier, who respected you as an officer of the Army, knew that you, an officer sworn to uphold and defend the principles of this democracy, were being denied the very thing you are and asking them to lay down their life for. How can we demand the respect of men under our command when we are not respected by members of our own rank.

They see a great Federal government built on the principle of 'Liberty and justice for all' being swayed by . . . customs and traditions that were defeated in a war seventy-five years ago. . . .

These type of conditions seriously injure the morale of the Negro soldier and tend to give him an air of indifference that he is sure to carry with him to civilian life. I have heard it expressed openly, hundreds of times by Negro soldiers that they would just as soon give their life fighting the injustices inflicted upon him right here in the United States than to fight to correct the injustices of other people they know nothing about on foreign soil. This state of mind has been brought about by the reluctance of the federal government to uphold firmly the rights of all men."

Questions for Analysis

1. Identify the three injustices described in this document.
2. Describe what the author expected of the federal government, according to this letter.
3. Evaluate the extent to which the letter's appeal was based on recent historical trends.

Women could not fight in combat, but 140,000 joined the **Women's Army Corps (WACs)**, and 100,000 joined the navy's **Women Accepted for Voluntary Emergency Service (WAVES)**. In these and other service branches, women contributed mainly as nurses and performed transport and clerical duties. Women also played an important but secret role in bolstering Allied military efforts. The navy and army recruited thousands of women college students and small-town school teachers to Washington, D.C., where they worked on deciphering German and Japanese diplomatic and military codes. These young, unmarried women worked very long, tedious hours during the week as well as on weekends and succeeded in providing the U.S. military with information about enemy planning. In this way, they joined the efforts already begun by British female codebreakers operating at Bletchley Park, England.

WORKING with EVIDENCE

Source: President Franklin Roosevelt, *State of the Union Address*, 1944

"Let us remember the lessons of 1918. In the summer of that year the tide turned in favor of the Allies. But this government did not relax, nor did the American people. In fact, our national effort was stepped up. In August 1918, the draft age limits were broadened from twenty-one to thirty-one, all the way to eighteen to forty-five. The president called for 'force to the utmost,' and his call was heeded. And in November, only three months later, Germany surrendered.

That is the way to fight and win a war—all out—and not with half an eye on the battlefronts abroad and the other eye and a half on personal, selfish, or political interests here at home.

Therefore, in order to concentrate all of our energies, all of our resources on winning this war, and to maintain a fair and stable economy at home, I recommend that the Congress adopt:

First, a realistic and simplified tax law—which will tax all unreasonable profits, both individual and corporate, and reduce the ultimate cost of the war to our sons and our daughters. The tax bill now under consideration by the Congress does not begin to meet this test.

Secondly, a continuation of the law for the renegotiation of war contracts — which will prevent exorbitant profits and assure fair prices to the government. For two long years I have pleaded with the Congress to take undue profits out of war.

Third, a cost of food law—which will enable the government to place a reasonable floor under the prices the farmer may expect for his production; and to place a ceiling on the prices a consumer will have to pay for the necessary food he buys. This should apply, as I have intimated, to necessities only and this will require public funds to carry it out. It will cost in appropriations about 1 percent of the present annual cost of the war. . . .

And [finally], a national service law—which, for the duration of the war, will prevent strikes, and, with certain appropriate exceptions, will make available for war production or for any other essential services every able-bodied adult in this whole nation."

Questions for Analysis

1. Identify Roosevelt's reasons for taking these steps to ensure a stable economy.
2. Explain how the war allowed Roosevelt to impose greater controls over the free market.
3. Evaluate the ways in which Roosevelt's requests to Congress were a product of historical situation.

The government relied on corporate executives to manage wartime economic conversion, but without the sacrifice and dedication of American workers, their efforts would have failed. The demands for wartime production combined with the departure of millions of American workers to the military created a labor shortage that gave unions increased leverage. By 1945, the membership rolls of organized labor had grown from 9 million to nearly 14 million. In 1942, the Roosevelt administration established the National War Labor Board, repeating what Wilson had done during World War I (see Module 7.6), which regulated wages, hours, and working conditions and authorized the government to take over plants that refused to abide by its decisions.

Labor unions at first refrained from striking, but later in the war, they organized strikes to protest the disparity between workers' wages and corporate profits. In 1943, Congress responded by passing the Smith-Connally Act, which prohibited walkouts in defense industries and set a thirty-day "cooling-off" period before unions could go out on strike.

REVIEW

- How did the wartime economy of World War II compare to that of World War I?

New Opportunities for Women

World War II opened up new opportunities for women in the paid workforce. Between 1940 and the peak of wartime employment in 1944, the number of employed women rose by more than 50 percent, to six million. Given severe labor shortages caused by increased production and the exodus of male workers into the armed forces, for the first time in U.S. history, married working women outnumbered single working women.

At the start of the war, about half of women employees held poorly paid clerical, sales, and service jobs. Women in manufacturing labored mainly in low-wage textile and clothing factories. During the war, however, the overall number of women in manufacturing grew by 141 percent; in industries producing directly for war purposes, the figure jumped by 463 percent. By contrast, the number of women in domestic service dropped by 20 percent. As women moved into defense-related jobs, their incomes also improved.

As impressive as these figures are, they do not tell the whole story. First, although married women entered the job market in record numbers, most of these workers were older and without young children. Women over the age of thirty-five accounted for 60 percent of those entering the workforce. The government did little to encourage young mothers to work, and few efforts were made to provide assistance for child care for those who did. In contrast to this situation, in Great Britain, child care programs were widely available. Second, openings for women in manufacturing jobs did

AP® EXAM TIP

U.S. entry into World War II created a high demand for industrial goods, thereby ending the Great Depression. As men and some women filled military ranks, opportunities opened for other women and minority groups to find work in factories. Wartime contributions of women and minority groups earned them newfound respect, which in turn generated debates regarding their position in society. Be sure you understand the political, economic, and social effects of World War II on American society.

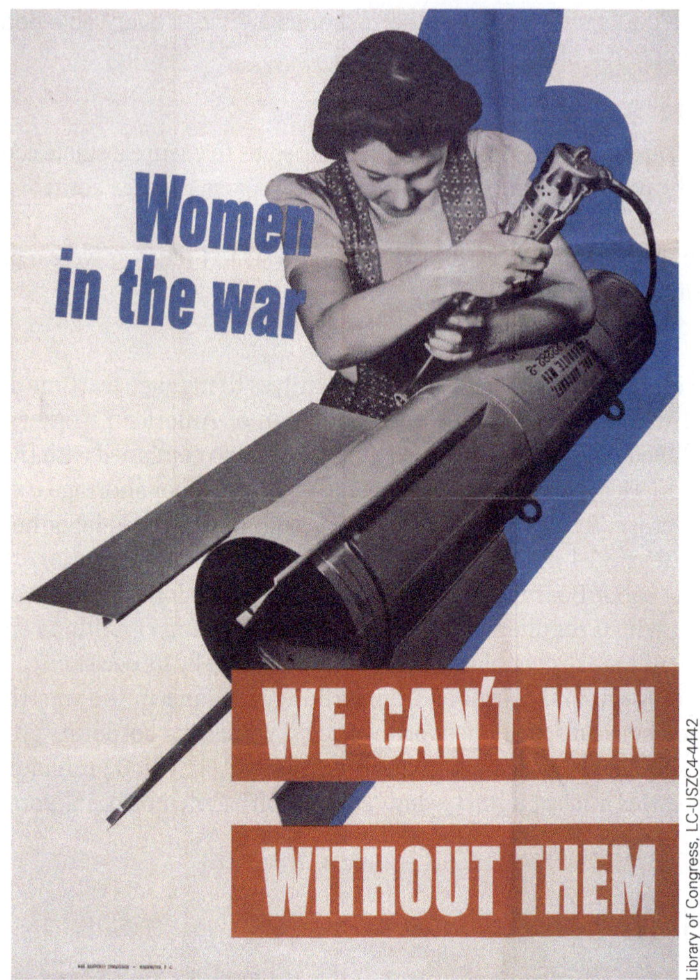

Library of Congress, LC-USZC4-4442

Women Workers during the War During the war, women worked in industrial jobs in unprecedented numbers. Corporations and the federal government actively recruited women through posters and advertisements and promised women that factory work was something that would benefit them, their families, and their nation. As the Allies neared victory, however, the message changed, and women were urged to prepare to return to the home to open up jobs for returning soldiers.

To what extent was this a change in the roles women played in previous American conflicts?

not guarantee equality. Women received lower wages for labor comparable to the work that men performed, and women did not have the same chances for advancement. Typical union benefits, such as seniority, hurt women, who were generally the most recent hires. In fact, some contracts stipulated that women's tenure in jobs previously held by men would last only for the duration of the war.

Gender stereotypes continued to dominate the workforce and society in general. Magazine covers with the image of "Rosie the Riveter," a woman with her sleeves rolled up and her biceps bulging, became a symbol for the recruitment of women, but reality proved different. Women who took war jobs were viewed not so much as war workers but as women temporarily occupying "men's jobs" during the emergency. As the war drew to a close, public relations campaigns shifted gears and encouraged the same women they had recently recruited to prepare to return home. This included nearly all of the brilliant women codebreakers secretly at work in Washington, D.C., who were ordered to go back home.

REVIEW

- What opportunities were available to women during World War II?
- To what extent were these opportunities different from those available to women during previous wars?

Everyday Life on the Home Front

Morale on the home front remained generally high during the war, as prosperity returned and American casualties proved relatively light compared with those of other allied nations. As in World War I, the government set up an agency, the **Office of War Information**, to promote patriotism and urge Americans to contribute to the war effort any way they could.

Schoolchildren collected scrap metal and rubber to donate to the production of military vehicles and weapons. With rationing in effect and food in short supply, the government encouraged families in towns and cities to grow "victory gardens" for their own fruits and vegetables. Mothers and daughters helped staff USO (United Service Organizations) dances and recreational activities for soldiers stationed in the United States. Americans also contributed to the war effort by adhering to restrictions on the consumption of consumer goods. Rationing cards restricted purchases of gasoline for cars and for food such as meat, butter, and sugar.

Hollywood kept the American public entertained, and movie attendance reached a record high of more than 100 million viewers. Films portrayed the heroism of soldiers on battlefields in Guadalcanal and Bataan. They celebrated the courage of Russian allies in propaganda epics such as *Mission to Moscow* (1943) and explored the depth of personal and political loyalties in classics such as *Casablanca* (1943). Hollywood stars such as Betty Grable kept up servicemen's spirits by posing for photos that GIs pinned up in their lockers, tents, and equipment.

For many Americans, life went on, but not quite in the same way. Around 15 million Americans moved during the war, with more than half of them relocating out of state. With husbands at war and wives at work, many children became "latchkey kids" who stayed home alone after school until their mothers or fathers returned from their jobs. With less parental supervision, juvenile delinquency rose, resulting in increased teenage arrests for robbery, vandalism, and loitering.

In contrast, with the end of the Great Depression and with more young people working, marriage rates increased, and couples wed at a younger age. By 1945, the winding down of the war and the rapidly increasing number of marriages produced the first signs of a "baby boom." At the same time, the stresses of life during wartime, including long separations of husbands and wives, also resulted in higher divorce rates.

- How did the war affect life on the home front for the average American?

Fighting for Equality at Home

In 1941, A. Philip Randolph, the head of the Brotherhood of Sleeping Car Porters, applied his labor union experience to the struggle for civil rights. He announced that he planned to lead a 100,000-person march on Washington, D.C., in June 1941 to protest racial discrimination in government and war-related employment as well as segregation in the military. Although Randolph believed in an interracial alliance of working people, he insisted that the march should be all-Black to show that Black Americans could lead their own movement.

Inching the country toward war, but not yet engaged militarily, President Roosevelt wanted to avoid any embarrassment the proposed march would bring to the forces supporting democracy and freedom. Eleanor Roosevelt served as go-between, and the president agreed to meet with Randolph to work out a compromise.

Randolph called off the march, and in return, on June 25, 1941, the president issued **Executive Order 8802**, creating the Fair Employment Practice Committee (FEPC). Roosevelt refused to order the desegregation of the military, but he set up a committee to investigate inequality in the armed forces. Although the FEPC helped Black people gain a greater share of jobs in key industries than they had before, the effect was limited because the agency did not have enforcement power.

Executive Order 8802

An executive order signed by Franklin Roosevelt in 1941 banning racial discrimination in the defense industry and creating the Fair Employment Practice Committee (FEPC). The order was issued in part as a compromise to avert a planned civil rights march on Washington, D.C.

The movement toward a march on Washington was emblematic of rising civil rights activity. Black leaders proclaimed their own "two-front war" with the symbol of the **Double V** to represent victory against racist enemies both abroad and at home.

Double V

The slogan Black Americans used during World War II to state their twin aims to fight for victory over fascism abroad and victory over racism at home.

In 1942, early civil rights activists also founded the interracial **Congress of Racial Equality (CORE)** in Chicago. CORE protested directly against racial inequality in public accommodations. Its members organized "sit-ins" at restaurants and bowling alleys that refused to serve Black people. Students at Howard University in Washington, D.C., used the same tactics, with some success, to protest racial exclusion from restaurants and cafeterias in the nation's capital.

Although these demonstrations did not get the national attention that postwar protests would, they constituted the prelude to the civil rights movement. The National Association for the Advancement of Colored People continued its policy of fighting racial discrimination in the courts. In 1944, the organization won a significant victory in a case from Texas, *Smith v. Allwright*, which outlawed all-white Democratic primary elections in the traditionally one-party South. As a result of the decision, the percentage of Black Americans registered to vote in the South doubled between 1944 and 1948.

Population shifts on the home front during World War II worsened racial tensions, resulting in violence. As jobs opened up throughout the country at military installations and defense plants, hundreds of thousands of Blacks moved from the rural South to the urban South, the North, and the West. Cities could not handle this rapid influx of people and failed to provide sufficient housing to accommodate those who migrated in search of employment.

Competition among white and Black workers for scarce housing spilled over into tensions in crowded transportation and recreational facilities. In 1943, the stress caused by close wartime contact between the races exploded in more than 240 riots. The most serious one occurred in Detroit, where thirty-four people were killed. Federal troops had to restore order after white and Black people fought with each other following a dispute at a popular amusement park.

Immigration from Mexico increased significantly during the war. To address labor shortages in the Southwest and on the Pacific coast, and departing from the deportation policies of the 1930s, the United States negotiated an agreement in 1942 with Mexico for contract laborers, known as ***braceros***, to enter the country for a limited time to work as farm laborers and in factories. *Braceros* had little or no control over their living spaces or working conditions. Not surprisingly, they conducted numerous strikes for higher wages in the agricultural fields of the Southwest and Northwest. Most U.S. residents of Mexican ancestry were, however, American citizens. Like other Americans, they settled into jobs to help fight the war, while more than 300,000 Mexican Americans served in the armed forces.

bracero

A Spanish term meaning "manual laborer," *braceros* were initially brought in from Mexico to work on U.S. farms, railroads, and factories during World War II. Bilateral agreements extended the program through 1964. Over 4.6 million guest contracts were signed before its termination.

The war heightened Mexican Americans' consciousness of their civil rights. As one Mexican American World War II veteran recalled: "We were Americans, not 'spics' or 'greasers.' Because when you fight for your country in a World War, against an alien philosophy, fascism, you are an American and proud to be in America." In southern California, newspaper publisher Ignacio Lutero Lopez campaigned against segregation in movie theaters, swimming pools, and other public accommodations. He organized boycotts against businesses that discriminated against or excluded Mexican Americans.

Wartime organizing led to the creation of the Unity Leagues, a coalition of Mexican American business owners, college students, civic leaders, and GIs that pressed for racial equality. In Texas, Mexican Americans joined the **League of United Latin American Citizens (LULAC)**, a largely middle-class group that challenged racial discrimination and segregation in public accommodations. Members of the organization emphasized the use of negotiations to redress their grievances, but when they ran into opposition, they resorted to economic boycotts and litigation. The war encouraged LULAC to expand its operations throughout the Southwest.

Mexican American citizens encountered racial prejudice and hostility from recently transplanted white people and longtime residents. Tensions were greatest in Los Angeles. Zoot suits—colorful, long, loose-fitting jackets with padded shoulders and baggy pants tapered at the bottom—had become a popular fashion among Mexican American youth, including a small group of Mexican American teenagers who had joined gangs. Not all zoot-suiters were gang members, but many outside their communities failed to make this distinction and found the zoot-suiters' dress and swagger provocative. Additionally, zoot suits were seen as unpatriotic, as the excessive amount of cloth used to create zoot suits violated wartime rationing restrictions.

zoot suit riots
A series of violent attacks by white servicemen and citizens against Mexican American teenagers wearing zoot suits in 1943 in Los Angeles, California.

On the night of June 4, 1943, squads of sailors stationed in Long Beach invaded Mexican American neighborhoods in East Los Angeles and indiscriminately attacked both zoot-suiters and those not dressed in this garb, setting off four days of violence. Mexican American youths who tried to fight back were often arrested even as servicemen and citizens who attacked them were not. The **zoot suit riots** ended when servicemen were ordered to remain in their barracks, enforced by military police street patrols. In response, the Los Angeles city council banned the wearing of zoot suits in public.

Some twenty-five thousand American Indians served in the military during the war. Although the Haudenosaunee (Iroquois) nation challenged the right of the United States to draft American Indians, it separately declared war against the Axis powers in 1942. The armed forces used Navajo and other American Indian soldiers in the Pacific theater to confuse the Japanese by sending coded messages in their tribal language. In addition to those serving the military, another forty thousand American Indians worked in defense-related industries. Their migration off reservations opened up new opportunities and fostered increased pride in the part they played in winning the war. Nevertheless, for most American Indians, the war did not improve their living conditions or remove hostility to their tribal identities.

PhotoQuest/Getty Images

Navajo Code Talkers, 1943 Private First Class Preston Toledo and Private First Class Frank Toledo, cousins and Navajo Indians, attached to a marine artillery regiment in the South Pacific, relay orders over a field radio in a code based on their native language on July 7, 1943. More than 400 bilingual Navajo "code talkers" were successfully used by the military to relay battlefield information quickly and accurately, as their code remained unbroken by the Japanese during the war.

What interests could American Indians have had in the results of World War II?

REVIEW

- How did activists further the cause of civil rights at home during World War II?
- What effects did World War II have on the lives of Mexican Americans and American Indians?

The Ordeal of Japanese Americans

World War II marked a significant crossroads for the protection of civil liberties. In general, the federal government did not repress civil liberties as harshly as it had during World War I, mainly because opposition to World War II was not nearly as great. The chief potential for radical dissent came from the Communist Party, but after the Germans attacked the Soviet Union in June 1941, communists and their sympathizers rallied behind the war effort and did whatever they could to stifle any protest that threatened the goal of defeating Germany. On the other side of the political spectrum, after the attack on Pearl Harbor, conservative isolationists in the America First Movement quickly threw their support behind the war.

Of the three ethnic groups associated with the Axis enemy—Japanese, Germans, and Italians—Japanese Americans received by far the worst treatment from the civilian population and state and federal officials. Germans had experienced some animosity and repression on the home front during World War I but, like Italian immigrants, had generally assimilated into the wider population. In addition, German Americans and Italian Americans had spread out across the country, while Japanese Americans remained concentrated in distinct geographical pockets along the West Coast. Although German Americans and Italian Americans experienced prejudice, they had come to be considered racially white, unlike Japanese Americans. Nevertheless, the government arrested about 1,500 Italians considered "enemy aliens" and placed around 250 of them in internment camps. It also arrested more than 11,000 Germans, some of them American citizens, who were considered a danger.

internment
The forced relocation of persons seen as a threat to national security to isolated camps. During World War II, nearly all people of Japanese descent living on the West Coast, approximately 120,000, were forced to quickly sell or abandon their possessions and relocate to detention camps.

The **internment**, or forced relocation and detainment, of Italians and Germans in the United States paled in comparison with that of the Japanese. On March 21, 1942, President Roosevelt issued **Executive Order 9066** authorizing military commanders to remove all persons deemed a threat to national security from specified zones on the West Coast. Nearly all people of Japanese descent lived along the West Coast or in Hawaii. Government officials forcibly and quickly relocated all of those living there—citizens and noncitizens alike—to camps in Arizona, Arkansas, California, Colorado, Idaho, Texas, Utah, and Wyoming. In Hawaii, the site of the Japanese attack on Pearl Harbor, the Japanese population, nearly one-third of the territory's population, was too large to transfer and instead lived under martial law. Approximately 120,000 Japanese people, two-thirds of them U.S. citizens, were sent to camps. The few thousand Japanese Americans living elsewhere in the continental United States remained in their homes.

On May 9, 1942, the military ordered the Korematsu family to report to Tanforan Racetrack in San Mateo, from which they would be transported to internment camps throughout the West. Although the rest of his family complied with the order, Fred, a first-generation American who worked on the Oakland docks as a welder, refused. Three weeks later, he was arrested and then transferred to the Topaz internment camp in south central Utah.

Found guilty of violating the original evacuation order, Korematsu received a sentence of five years of probation. It did not matter that Fred Korematsu had been born in

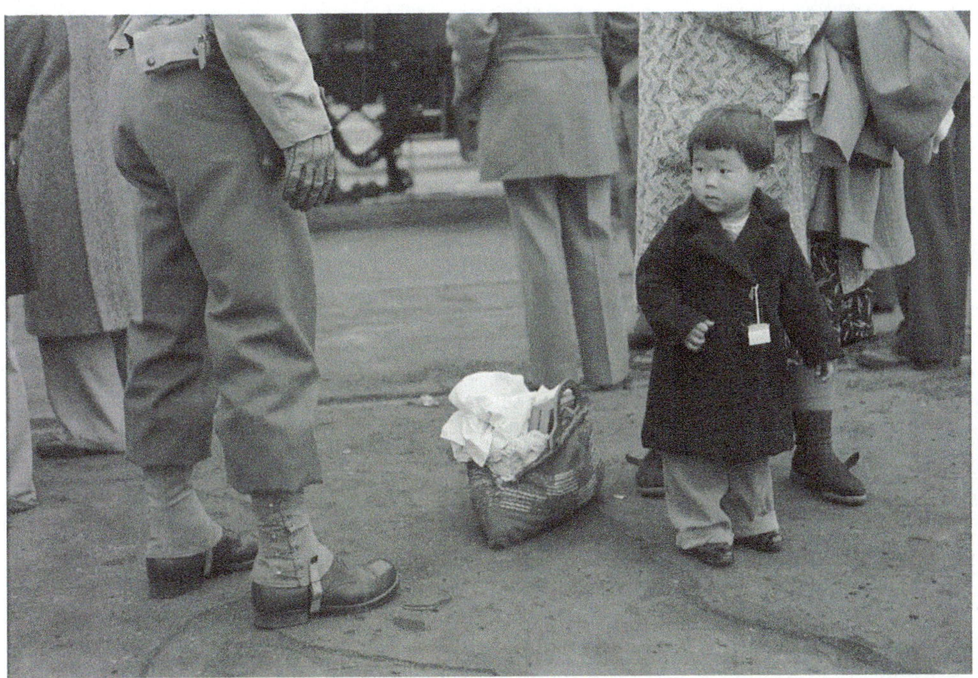

Library of Congress, LC-USF33-013290-M1

Japanese American Child on the Way to an Internment Camp, 1942 In this 1942 photograph, a Japanese American child is waiting with their family for a train to take them to the Manzanar internment camp in Owens Valley, California.

How does the picture attempt to generate sympathy for interned people?

the United States, had a white girlfriend of Italian heritage, and counted white people among his best friends. His parents had come from Japan, and for much of the American public, his racial heritage meant that he was not viewed as a true American. As one American general put it early in the war, "A Jap's a Jap. It makes no difference whether he is an American citizen or not."

Korematsu spent most of the war in an internment camp. Unlike Nazi concentration camps, these facilities did not starve or work inmates to death or execute them. Yet Japanese Americans lost their freedom and protection under the Bill of Rights and the Fourteenth Amendment. Without evidence that Japanese Americans were disloyal or harbored spies or saboteurs, U.S. officials chose to believe that as a group, they threatened national security.

The government established a system that questioned German Americans and Italian Americans individually if their loyalty came under suspicion. By contrast, U.S. officials identified all Japanese Americans and Japanese resident aliens with the nation that had attacked Pearl Harbor and incarcerated them. In this respect, the United States was not unique. Following the U.S. lead, Canada interned its Japanese population, more than 75 percent of whom held Canadian citizenship.

AP® WORKING with EVIDENCE

Source: Charles Kikuchi, Diary Entry, 1942

"There was a terrific rainstorm last night and we have had to wade through the 'slush alleys' again. Everyone sinks up to the ankles in mud. Some trucks came in today with lumber to build new barracks, but the earth was so soft that the truck sank over the hubs and they had a hell of a time pulling it out. The Army certainly is rushing things. About half of the Japanese have already been evacuated from the restricted areas in this state. Manzanar, Santa Anita, and Tanforan will be the three biggest centers. Now that [San Francisco] has been almost cleared the American Legion, the Native Sons of the Golden West, and the California Joint Immigration Committee are filing charges that the Nisei* should be disfranchised because we have obtained citizenship under false pretenses and that "we are loyal subjects of Japan" and therefore never should have been allowed to obtain citizenship. This sort of thing will gain momentum and we are not in a very advantageous position to combat it. I get fearful sometimes because this sort of hysteria will gain momentum.

The [San Francisco] Registrar has made a statement that we will be sent absentee ballots to which Mr. James Fisk of the Joint Immigration Committee protests greatly. Tomorrow I am going to carry a petition around to protest against their protests. I think that they are stabbing us in the back and that there should be a separate concentration camp for these so-called Americans. They are a lot more dangerous than the Japanese in the U.S. ever will or have been."

*Children born in the United States to Japanese parents.

Questions for Analysis

1. Describe the ways in which internees were denied their rights as Americans in Kikuchi's account.
2. Explain the arguments for the denial of these rights.
3. Explain the implicit counterarguments Kikuchi makes in this account.

Source: Justice Hugo Black, *Korematsu v. United States*, 1944

"Our task would be simple, our duty clear, were this a case involving the imprisonment of a loyal citizen in a concentration camp because of racial prejudice. Regardless of the true nature of the assembly and relocation centers—and we deem it unjustifiable to call them concentration camps with all the ugly connotations that term implies—we are dealing specifically with nothing but an exclusion order. To cast this case into outlines of racial prejudice, without reference to the real military dangers which were presented, merely confuses the issue. Korematsu was not excluded from the Military Area because of hostility to him or his race. He was excluded because we are at war with the Japanese Empire, because the properly constituted military authorities feared an invasion of our West Coast and felt constrained to take proper security measures, because they decided that the military urgency of the situation demanded that all citizens of Japanese ancestry be segregated from the West Coast temporarily, and finally, because Congress, reposing its confidence in this time of war in our military leaders—as inevitably it must—determined that they should have the power to do just this. There was evidence of disloyalty on the part of some, the military authorities considered that the need for action was great, and time was short."

Questions for Analysis

1. Identify the main argument Black makes to support Japanese internment.
2. Describe the roles Black assigns to the military and Congress regarding internment.
3. Explain how Black's decision reflected public sentiments during the war.

Questions for Comparison

1. Explain what each author argues is the true danger facing the United States.
2. Evaluate the extent of similarity between the debate over Japanese internment and the debate over the Espionage and Sedition Acts during World War I.

For their part, Japanese Americans made the best they could out of this situation. They had been forced to dispose of their homes, possessions, and businesses quickly, either selling or renting them at very low prices or simply abandoning them. They left their neighborhoods with only the possessions they could carry. They lived in wooden barracks divided into one-room apartments and shared communal toilets, showers, laundries, and dining facilities. The camps provided schools, recreational activities, and opportunities for religious worship, except for Shinto, the official religion of Japan. Some internees attempted to farm, but the arid land on which the camps were located made this nearly impossible. Inmates who worked at jobs within the camp earned monthly wages of $12 to $19, far less than they would have received outside the camps.

Japanese Americans responded to their internment in a variety of ways. Many formed community groups, and some expressed their reactions to the emotional upheaval by writing of their experiences or displaying their feelings through artwork. Contradicting beliefs that their ancestry made them disloyal or not real Americans, some 18,000 men joined the army, and many fought gallantly in some of the war's fiercest battles on the European front with the 442nd Regiment, one of the most decorated units in the military. Nisei soldiers were among the first, along with Black troops, to liberate Jews from German concentration camps.

Others, like Fred Korematsu, remained in the camps and challenged the legality of President Roosevelt's executive order, which had allowed military officials to exclude Japanese Americans from certain areas and evacuate them from their homes. However, the Supreme Court ruled against him and others. Finally, in December 1944, shortly after he won election to his fourth term as president, Roosevelt rescinded Executive Order 9066.

In contrast to the treatment of Japanese Americans, the status of Chinese Americans improved markedly during the war. With China under Japanese occupation, Congress repealed the Chinese Exclusion Act in 1943, making the Chinese the first Asians who could become naturalized citizens. Chinese American men also fought in integrated military units like their Filipino peers. For the first time, the war opened up jobs to Chinese American men and women outside their ethnic economy.

Despite the violation of the civil liberties of Japanese American citizens, the majority did not become embittered against the United States. Rather, most of the internees returned to their communities after the war and resumed their lives, still intent on pursuing the American dream from which they had been so harshly excluded; however, some eight thousand Japanese Americans renounced their U.S. citizenship and repatriated to Japan in 1945. In the name of national security, the government had established the precedent of incarcerating groups deemed "suspect." It took four decades for the U.S. government to admit its mistake and apologize, and in 1988 Congress awarded reparations of $20,000 to each of the 60,000 living internees.

REVIEW

- Why were Japanese Americans singled out as a particular threat to national security during World War II?

AP® Skills Workshop: Writing Historically

Additional Practice in Responding to a Long-Essay Question

Evaluate the extent of similarity between the social and cultural changes that took place during the 1920s and those that occurred during World War II.

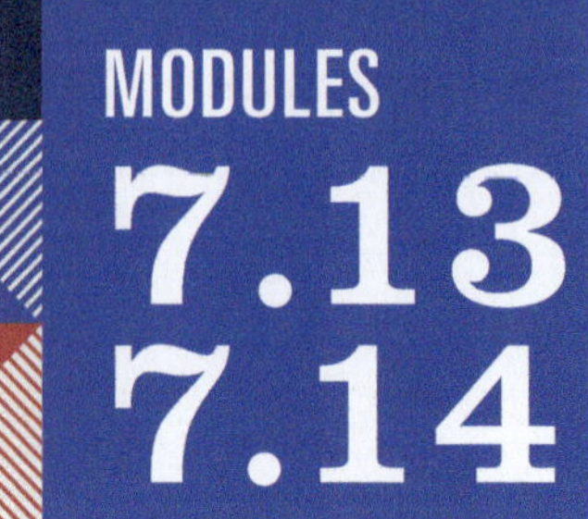

World War II: Military & Postwar Diplomacy

FOCUS

While you read these two modules, consider the reasons for Allied victory in general, and American success in particular, in the Second World War. Also, consider the effects of this victory on the United States both domestically and internationally.

World War II pitted the "Grand Alliance" of Great Britain, the Soviet Union, the French government in exile, and the United States against the Axis powers of Germany, Japan, and Italy. From the outset, the United States deployed military forces to contain Japanese aggression, but its most immediate concern was to defeat Germany. Before battles in Europe, Asia, and four other continents ended, more than 60 million people perished, including 405,000 Americans. Six million Jewish civilians died in the Holocaust, the Nazi regime's genocidal effort to eradicate Europe's Jewish population. Millions of other civilians—Slavic peoples, Romani, Jehovah's Witnesses, homosexuals, the disabled, and communists—also were systematically murdered by the Nazis. The Soviet Union experienced the greatest losses—nearly 27 million soldiers and civilians, more than two-fifths of all those killed.

Global War Erupts

United against Hitler, the Grand Alliance divided over how quickly to mount a counterattack directly on Germany. The Soviet Union, which bore the brunt of the fighting in trying to repel the German army's invasion, demanded the opening of a **second front** through France and into Germany to take the pressure off its forces. The British wanted to fight first in northern Africa and southern Europe, in part to remove Axis forces from territory that endangered their economic interests in the Mediterranean and the Middle East and in part to buy time to rebuild their depleted fighting strength.

President Roosevelt understood the Soviet position but worried about losing public support early in the war if the United States experienced heavy casualties. He approved his military advisers' plans for an invasion of France from England in 1943, but in the meantime, he agreed with Churchill to fight the Germans and Italians on the periphery of Europe.

From a military standpoint, this circuitous approach proved successful. In October 1942, British forces in North Africa overpowered the Germans at El Alamein, pushing them out of Egypt and removing their threat to the Suez Canal. The following month, British and American troops landed in Algeria and Morocco. After some early defeats, the combined strength of British and American ground, air, and naval forces drove the Germans out of Africa in May 1943.

These military victories failed to relieve political tensions among the Allies. Although the Soviets had managed to stop the German offensive against Stalingrad at great cost, the deepest penetration of enemy troops into their country, Stalin expected the second front to begin as promised in the spring of 1943. He was bitterly disappointed when Roosevelt postponed the cross–English Channel invasion of France until 1944. To Stalin, it appeared as if his allies were looking to gain a double triumph by letting the communists and Nazis slaughter each other into submission.

Instead of opening a second front in France, British, American, and Canadian troops invaded Sicily in July 1943 and then the Italian mainland. Their initial victories quickly led to the removal of Mussolini and his retreat to northern Italy, where he lived under German protection (**Map 7.10**). Not until June 4, 1944, did the Allies occupy Rome in central Italy and force the Germans to retreat.

To overcome Stalin's dissatisfaction with the postponement of opening a western front, President Roosevelt issued orders to give the Soviets unlimited access to Lend-Lease

MAP 7.10 World War II in Europe, 1941–1945 By late 1941, the Axis powers had brought most of Europe and the Mediterranean region under their control. But between 1942 and 1945, the Allied powers drove them back. Critical victories at Leningrad and Stalingrad, in North Africa, and on the beaches of Normandy forced the retreat, and then the defeat, of the Axis powers.

What does this map reveal about the relationship between the conflict in Europe and the countries of Africa and Asia?

supplies to sustain their war efforts and to care for their citizens. In November 1943, Roosevelt, Churchill, and Stalin met in Tehran, Iran. Roosevelt and Stalin seemed to get along well. Stalin agreed to deploy troops against Japan after the war in Europe ended, and Roosevelt agreed to open the second front within six months. Churchill joined Roosevelt and Stalin in supporting the creation of an international organization to ensure postwar peace.

D-Day
The invasion of German-occupied France by Allied forces on June 6, 1944. The D-Day landings opened up a western front in Europe and marked a major turning point in World War II.

This time, the Americans and British kept their word, and the Allies finally embarked on the western-front invasion. On June 6, 1944—called **D-Day**—about 150,000 American, British, and Canadian troops crossed the English Channel in nearly 5,000 ships and landed on the beaches of Normandy, France. Despite deadly machine-gun fire from German troops placed on higher ground, the Allied forces managed to establish a beachhead. The bravery and discipline of the troops, along with their superior numbers, overcame the Germans and opened the way for the Allies to liberate Paris in August 1944. By the end of the year, the Allies had regained control of the rest of France and most of Belgium.

Amid these Allied victories, Roosevelt won a fourth term against Republican challenger Thomas E. Dewey, governor of New York. He dumped from the campaign ticket his vice president, Henry A. Wallace, a liberal on economic and racial issues, and replaced him with Senator Harry S. Truman of Missouri, who was more acceptable to southern voters. Despite his declining health, Roosevelt won easily.

REVIEW

- Why did the Soviet Union want the Allies to open a western front early in the war?
- Why did the Allies wait until later in the conflict to do so?

War in the Pacific

With the Soviet Union bearing the brunt of the fighting in eastern Europe, the United States shouldered the burden of fighting Japan. U.S. military commanders began a two-pronged counterattack in the Pacific in 1942. General Douglas MacArthur, whose troops had escaped from the Philippines as Japanese forces overran the islands in May 1942, planned to regroup in Australia, head north through New Guinea, and return to the Philippines. At the same time, Admiral Chester Nimitz directed the U.S. Pacific Fleet from Hawaii toward Japanese-occupied islands in the western Pacific. If all went well, MacArthur's ground troops and Nimitz's naval forces would combine with General Curtis LeMay's air forces to overwhelm Japan.

island-hopping
This tactic, employed in the Pacific by U.S. forces in World War II, directed American and Allied forces to cut off and pass over some heavily fortified Japanese islands to speed their drive toward the Japanese mainland.

To speed their advance, the U.S. military implemented a tactic known as **island-hopping**. American and allied forces would leapfrog over some heavily fortified Japanese positions and concentrate their resources on lightly defended Japanese islands that would provide bases capable of sustaining the campaign to attack the nation of Japan. By isolating and skipping some Japanese-held islands, U.S. forces could make quicker progress on their drive toward the Japanese mainland.

All went according to plan in 1942. Shortly after the Philippines had fallen to the Japanese, the Allies won a major victory in May in the Battle of the Coral Sea, off the northeast coast of Australia, halting the Japanese naval advance toward Australia. The following month, the U.S. navy achieved an even greater victory when it defeated

Official Marine Corps Photo #50515

Fighting on Guadalcanal From August 1942 to February 1943, U.S. marines and Allied forces fought fierce battles against the Japanese on Guadalcanal, part of the Solomon Islands in the South Pacific. Operating in this tropical environment, the marines had captured this field gun position from the Japanese and camouflaged it. The victory on Guadalcanal sparked the Allied offensive in the Pacific theater.

What does this photograph reveal about fighting conditions in the Pacific during World War II?

the Japanese in the **Battle of Midway Island**, northwest of Hawaii. Having cracked the Japanese codes to learn of an impending attack against Midway, U.S. naval forces counterattacked. In the battle, four Japanese aircraft carriers were sunk, the planned invasion was repelled, and the threat of further Japanese expansion in the Pacific was halted.

In August 1942, the fighting moved to the Solomon Islands, east of New Guinea, where U.S. forces waged fierce battles at Guadalcanal Island. After six months of heavy casualties on both sides, the Americans finally dislodged the Japanese. By late 1944, American, Australian, and New Zealand troops had put the Japanese on the defensive and had begun to close in on islands of Japan.

In 1945, the United States mounted its final offensive against Japan. In preparation for an invasion of the Japanese home islands, American marines won important battles on **Iwo Jima** and **Okinawa**, two strategic islands off the coast of Japan. The fighting proved costly—on Iwo Jima alone, the Japanese fought and died nearly to the last man while killing 6,000 Americans and wounding 20,000 others.

At the same time, the U.S. Army Air Corps conducted firebomb raids over Tokyo and other major cities, killing some 330,000 Japanese civilians. These attacks were made by newly developed B-29 bombers, which could fly more than 3,000 miles and could be dispatched from Pacific island bases captured by the U.S. military. The purpose of this bombing was to destroy Japan's economic capability to sustain the war rather than to destroy their military forces. In addition, the navy blockaded Japan, further crippling its

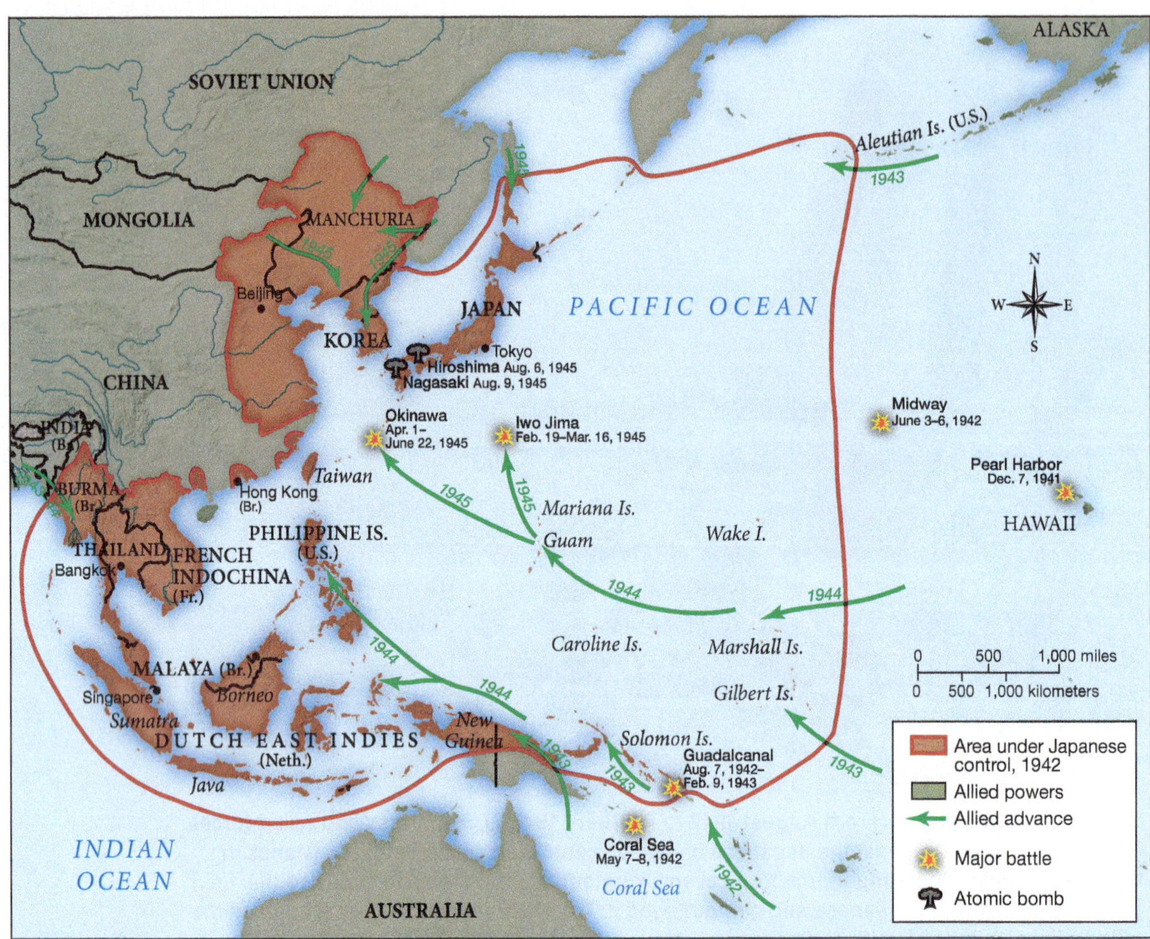

MAP 7.11 World War II in the Pacific, 1941–1945 After bombing Pearl Harbor on December 7, 1941, Japan captured the Philippines and seized control of Asian colonies from the British, French, and Dutch. The Allied powers, led by U.S. forces, eventually defeated Japan by winning a series of hard-fought victories on Central Pacific islands and by the atomic bombings of Hiroshima and Nagasaki.

How did "island-hopping" contribute to U.S. victory in the Pacific?

economy and reducing supplies of food, medicine, and raw materials (**Map 7.11**). Still, the Japanese government refused to surrender and indicated its determination to resist by launching *kamikaze* attacks (suicidal airplane crashes) on American warships and airplanes as well as encouraging civilians to sacrifice their lives rather than surrender to the United States.

- How was the United States able to turn the tide in the Pacific theater of World War II?

Ending the War

In the European theater, the Germans had launched one last offensive in mid-December 1944. Mobilizing troops from remaining outposts in Belgium, they attacked Allied forces in the **Battle of the Bulge**. After an initial German drive into enemy lines that caused the defensive lines to bulge but not break, by late January 1945, American and

British fighting men had recovered and repelled the German assault. The Allies then began to push across the Rhine River into the German heartland as an exhausted Germany hovered on the edge of collapse.

With victory in sight in both Europe and the Pacific, the Allies discussed problems of postwar relations. In February 1945, Roosevelt and Churchill met with Stalin in the resort city of Yalta in Crimea. There they clashed over the question of the postwar government of Poland and whether to recognize the claim of the Polish government in exile in London, which the United States and Great Britain supported, or that of the pro-Soviet government, which had spent the war in the U.S.S.R. The loosely worded **Yalta Agreement**, which resulted from the conference, called for the establishment of permanent governments in Poland and the rest of eastern Europe through free elections.

Yalta Agreement

An agreement negotiated at the 1945 Yalta Conference by Roosevelt, Churchill, and Stalin about the fate of postwar Eastern Europe, promising free elections. The Yalta Agreement did little to ease growing tensions between the Soviet Union and its Western Allies.

Despite this controversy, the Allies left Yalta united over other issues. They renewed their commitment to establishing the United Nations, and the Soviets reaffirmed their intention to join the war against Japan three months after Germany's surrender. The Allies also reached a tentative agreement on postwar Germany. The United States, Great Britain, the Soviet Union, and France would divide the country into four zones, each occupied by one of the powers. They would further subdivide Berlin into four sectors because the capital city fell within the Soviet occupation area. As with the accord over Poland, the agreement concerning Germany created tension after the war.

The Yalta Conference concluded just as the final assault against Germany got underway. Pushing from the west, American general Dwight D. Eisenhower stopped at the Elbe River, where he had agreed to meet up with Red Army troops who were charging from the east to Berlin. After an intense assault by the Soviets, the German capital of Berlin fell, and on April 25 Russian and American forces linked up in Torgau on the Elbe River. They achieved this triumph two weeks after Franklin Roosevelt died at the age of sixty-three from a cerebral hemorrhage. On April 30, 1945, with Berlin shattered, Hitler committed suicide in his bunker. A few days earlier, Italian antifascist partisans had captured and executed Mussolini in northern Italy. On May 2, German troops surrendered in Italy, and on May 7, the remnants of the German government formally surrendered. The war in Europe ended the next day.

With the war over in Europe, the United States made its final push against Japan. Since 1942, J. Robert Oppenheimer and his team of scientists and engineers had labored feverishly to construct an atomic bomb, in part out of fear that Nazi Germany was working on its own nuclear weapon. Few people knew about the top-secret **Manhattan Project**, and Congress appropriated $2 billion without knowing its true purpose. The program was a major undertaking, employing thousands of workers at sites in Chicago; Berkeley, California; Oak Ridge, Tennessee; Hanford, Washington; and, most famously, at the scientific laboratory in Los Alamos, New Mexico.

Manhattan Project

The code name for the secret program to develop an atomic bomb amid fears of a nuclear weapons project in Germany. The top-secret project was launched in 1942 and resulted in the first successful test of an atomic bomb in the New Mexico desert in July 1945.

Vice President Harry S. Truman did not learn about the details of the Manhattan Project until Roosevelt's death on April 12, and in July, he found out about the first atomic test while en route to a conference in Potsdam, Germany, with Stalin and Churchill. He ordered the State Department to issue a vaguely worded ultimatum to the Japanese government demanding immediate surrender or else face annihilation. When Japan indicated that it would surrender if the United States allowed the country to retain its emperor, Hirohito, the Truman administration refused and demanded unconditional surrender. As a further blow to Japan, Stalin was ready to send the Soviet military to attack Japanese troops in Manchuria on August 8, which would seriously weaken Japan's ability to hold out.

AP® EXAM TIP

The Allied nations emerged victorious from World War II due to cooperating strategies, extensive manpower (Soviet Union), and U.S. industrial production and technological supremacy. Although a major contributor in the Atlantic theater, the United States had sole responsibility in the Pacific theater, where eventually it adopted a tactic of island-hopping. Be able to explain how the Allies prevailed in World War II in both theaters of combat.

On August 6, the *Enola Gay*, an American B-29 bomber, dropped an atomic bomb on Hiroshima. The weapon immediately killed as many as 80,000 civilians, and tens of thousands later died slowly from radiation poisoning. Two days later, Stalin fulfilled his pledge at the Tehran and Yalta conferences and declared war against Japan by invading

AP Images/Stanley Troutman

The Aftermath of Hiroshima The dropping of the atomic bomb on Hiroshima devastated most of the city and killed 70,000 to 80,000 people in the blast and immediate aftermath. It was the first use of an atomic bomb and was followed by the atomic bombing of Nagasaki three days later. **In what ways did the use of this weapon change how the United States waged war?**

occupied Manchuria with 1.6 million troops. The next day, on August 9, Japan still had not surrendered, and the Army Air Corps dropped another atomic bomb on Nagasaki, killing more than 100,000 civilians. The **bombings of Hiroshima and Nagasaki** flattened more than 80 percent of the buildings and left permanent shadows on the walls and pavement in each city. Five days later, on August 14, Japan announced that it would surrender. The formal surrender was completed on September 2.

At the time, and for many years afterward, very few Americans questioned the decision to drop atomic bombs on Japan. Truman believed that had Roosevelt been alive, he would have authorized use of the bombs. Newly on the job, Truman hesitated to reverse a decision already reached by his predecessor. He reasoned that his action would save American lives because the U.S. military would not have to launch a costly invasion of Japan's home islands. He also felt justified in giving the order because he sought retaliation for the surprise attack on Pearl Harbor and for Japanese atrocities against American soldiers, especially in the Philippines.

AP® WORKING with EVIDENCE

Source: Father Johannes Siemes, *Eyewitness Account of the Hiroshima Bombing*, 1945

> "More than thirty hours had gone by until the first official rescue party had appeared on the scene. We find both children and take them out of the park: a six-year old girl who was uninjured, and a twelve-year old girl who had been burned about the head, hands, and legs, and who had lain for thirty hours without care in the park. The left side of her face and the left eye were completely covered with blood and pus, so that we thought that she had lost the eye. When the wound was later washed, we noted that the eye was intact

and that the lids had just become stuck together. On the way home, we took another group of three refugees with us. The first wanted to know, however, of what nationality we were. They, too, feared that we might be Americans who had parachuted in. When we arrived in Nagatsuka [a Jesuit monastery in Hiroshima], it had just become dark. . . .

Thousands of wounded who died later could doubtless have been rescued had they received proper treatment and care, but rescue work in a catastrophe of this magnitude had not been envisioned; since the whole city had been knocked out at a blow, everything which had been prepared for emergency work was lost, and no preparation had been made for rescue work in the outlying districts. Many of the wounded also died because they had been weakened by under-nourishment and consequently lacked in strength to recover. Those who had their normal strength and who received good care slowly healed the burns which had been occasioned by the bomb. There were also cases, however, whose prognosis seemed good who died suddenly. There were also some who had only small external wounds who died within a week or later, after an inflammation of the pharynx and oral cavity had taken place. . . .

Up to this time small incised wounds had healed normally, but thereafter the wounds which were still unhealed became worse and are to date (in September) still incompletely healed. The attending physician diagnosed it as leucopenia [a decrease in white blood cells]. There thus seems to be some truth in the statement that the radiation had some effect on the blood. . . . It was noised about that the ruins of the city emitted deadly rays and that workers who went there to aid in the clearing died, and that the central district would be uninhabitable for some time to come."

Questions for Analysis

1. Identify the immediate and long-term results of the bombing of Hiroshima detailed in this account.
2. Describe some of the effects of the bombing of Hiroshima, as detailed in this account.
3. Evaluate the extent to which the bombing of Hiroshima represented a change in the U.S. approach to international warfare.

- How did President Truman justify dropping atomic bombs on Hiroshima and Nagasaki?

Evidence of the Holocaust

The end of the war revealed the full extent and horror of the **Holocaust**—Germany's calculated and methodical slaughter of certain religious, ethnic, and political groups. As Allied troops liberated Germany and Poland, they saw for themselves the brutality of the Nazi concentration camps that Hitler had set up to execute or work to death six million Jews and millions of other "undesirables"—Slavs, Romani, homosexuals, the physically and mentally disabled, and communists. At Buchenwald and Dachau in Germany and at Auschwitz in Poland, the Allies encountered the skeletal remains of inmates tossed into mass graves, dead from starvation, illness, and executions. Crematoria on the premises contained the ashes of inmates first poisoned and then incinerated. Troops also freed the "living dead," those still alive but seriously ill and undernourished.

Holocaust
The Nazi regime's genocidal effort to eradicate Europe's Jewish population during World War II, which resulted in the death of six million Jews and millions of other "undesirables"—Slavs, Romani, homosexuals, the physically and mentally disabled, and communists.

H. Miller/Getty Images

Holocaust Survivors When American troops of the 80th Army Division liberated the Buchenwald concentration camp in Germany, they found these emaciated victims of the Holocaust. Elie Wiesel (seventh from the left on the middle bunk next to the vertical post) went on to become an internationally famous writer who wrote about his wartime experiences and won the Nobel Peace Prize.

In what ways might this image reinforce the American public's perceptions about the war?

These horrific discoveries shocked the public, but evidence of what was happening had appeared early in the war. Journalists like Varian Fry had outlined the Nazi atrocities against the Jews several years before. "Letters, reports, tables all fit together. They add up to the most appalling picture of mass murder in all human history," Fry wrote in the *New Republic* magazine in 1942.

The Roosevelt administration did little in response, despite receiving evidence of the Nazi death camps beginning in 1942. It chose not to send planes to bomb the concentration camps or the railroad lines leading to them, deeming it too risky militarily and too dangerous for the inmates. "The War Department," its assistant secretary John J. McCloy wrote to the director of the War Refugee Board in defending this decision, "is of the opinion that the suggested air operation is impracticable. It could be executed only by the diversion of considerable air support essential to the success of our forces now engaged in decisive operations and would in any case be of such very doubtful efficacy that it would not amount to a practical project."

In a less defensible decision, the Roosevelt administration refused to relax immigration laws to allow Jews and other persecuted minorities to take refuge in the United States, and only 21,000 managed to find asylum. The State Department, which could have modified these policies, was staffed with antisemitic officials, and though President Roosevelt expressed sympathy for the plight of Hitler's victims, he believed that winning the war as quickly as possible was the best way to help them.

Nevertheless, even when it had been possible to rescue Jews, the United States balked. In 1939, a German liner, the SS *St. Louis*, embarked from Hamburg with 937 Jewish refugees aboard and set sail for Cuba. Blocked from entry by the Cuban government, the ship sailed for the coast of Florida, hoping to gain permission to enter the United States. However, the United States refused, maintaining that the passengers did not have the proper documents required under the Immigration Act of 1924. The ship then headed back to Europe, where the United Kingdom, Belgium, the Netherlands, and France took in the passengers. Unfortunately, in 1940, when the Nazis invaded Belgium, the Netherlands, and France and sent their Jewish residents to concentration camps, an estimated 254 of the *St. Louis* passengers died along with countless others.

Although not nearly to the same extent as in the Holocaust, the Japanese committed many war atrocities. Around 50,000 U.S. soldiers and civilians became prisoners of war, and about half of them were forced to work as enslaved laborers. From June 1942 to October 1943, the Japanese constructed a 300-mile railroad between Burma (Myanmar) and Thailand using 60,000 Allied prisoners of war and 200,000 Asian conscripts. Working under inhumane conditions, approximately 13,000 Allied workers and 80,000 Asian laborers died before the railway was completed.

About 40 percent of American POWs died in Japanese captivity (in contrast, only 1 percent died in Nazi camps). One reason why POWs were treated so poorly was because the Japanese believed that surrender was a cowardly act and that those who did so were beneath contempt. Far more than the Americans and their allies, Chinese civilians and native residents of such countries as Burma and the Dutch East Indies (Indonesia) were brutalized, systematically raped, tortured, and killed by the Japanese occupying forces.

- Why did U.S. policymakers fail to provide meaningful assistance to European Jews during World War II?

The Impact of World War II

At first, Franklin Roosevelt charted a course of neutrality before the United States entered World War II. Yet Roosevelt believed that the rise of European dictatorships and their expansionist pursuits throughout the world threatened American national security. He saw signs of trouble early, but responding to antiwar sentiment from lawmakers and the American public, Roosevelt waited for a blatant enemy attack before declaring war. The Japanese attack on Pearl Harbor in 1941 provided that justification.

On the domestic front, World War II accomplished what Roosevelt's New Deal could not. Prosperity and nearly full employment returned only after the nation's factories began supplying the Allies and the United States joined in the fight against the Axis powers.

Mobilization for war also furthered the tremendous growth and centralization of power in the federal government that had begun under the New Deal. Washington, D.C., became the chief source of authority to which Americans looked for solutions to problems concerning economic security and financial development.

The federal government showed that it would use its authority to expand equal rights for Black Americans. The war swung national power against racial discrimination, and various civil rights victories during the war served as precursors to the civil rights movement of subsequent decades. The war also heightened Mexican Americans' consciousness of oppression and led them to organize for civil rights. However, in neither case, nor that of American Indians, did the war erase white prejudice.

At the same time, the federal government did not hesitate to trample on the civil liberties of Japanese Americans. The president succumbed to wartime antagonism against Japanese immigrants and their children and authorized their internment in camps for most of the war. With China a wartime ally, Chinese Americans escaped a similar fate. Yet, like white and Black Americans, the Nisei displayed their patriotism by distinguishing themselves as soldiers on the battlefields of Europe.

AP® EXAM TIP

The period from 1890 to 1945 contains many events worthy of comparison: Progressive reforms vs. the New Deal; the Panic of 1893 vs. the Great Depression; World War I vs. World War II; imperialism vs. isolation; isolationism vs. intervention; the role of women and minorities in the 1920s vs. in the 1940s; political party alliances before the Great Depression vs. such alliances after the Great Depression; urban vs. rural attitudes in the 1920s, and state vs. federal government power. Make sure you understand the key concepts on both sides of each issue to answer a comparison question comprehensively.

The war brought women into the workforce as never before, providing a measure of independence and distancing them from their traditional roles as wives and mothers. Nevertheless, the government and private employers made it clear that they expected most female workers to give up their jobs to returning servicemen and to become homemakers once the war ended.

Finally, the war thrust the United States onto the world stage as one of the world's two major superpowers alongside the Soviet Union. This position posed new challenges. In sole possession of the atomic bomb, the most powerful weapon on the planet, and fortified by a robust economy, the United States filled the international power vacuum created by the weakening and eventual collapse of the European colonial empires. The fragile alliance that had held together the United States and the Soviet Union shattered soon after the end of World War II. The Atomic Age, which J. Robert Oppenheimer helped usher in with a powerful weapon of mass destruction, and the government oppression that Fred Korematsu endured in the name of national security did not disappear. Rather, they expanded in new directions and shaped the lives of all Americans for decades to come.

AP® EXAM TIP

World War II resulted in the United States emerging as one of two global superpowers due to the wartime devastation in Europe and the eventual collapse of the European colonial empires. In response to the failure of post–World War I isolationism and the perceived threat of communist aggression, the United States ended its policy of non-entanglement advocated by George Washington in his Farewell Address. Be able to explain the events and circumstances that led to this change. Also, be able to compare U.S. foreign policy after World War I with that following World War II.

REVIEW

- How did World War II affect American policies at home and overseas?

AP® Skills Workshop: Writing Historically

Additional Practice in Responding to a Short-Answer Question

Answer **A**, **B**, and **C**.

(A) Briefly explain ONE specific historical event or development initiated by the United States that contributed to Allied victory in World War II.

(B) Briefly explain ONE specific debate or controversy in the United States that resulted from participation in World War II.

(C) Briefly explain ONE specific effect of World War II on American society.

Comparison in Period 7

MODULE **7.15**

AP® Skills Workshop: Writing Historically

Additional Practice in Responding to a Document-Based Question

Evaluate the extent of similarity between the impacts of World War I (1914–1919) and World War II (1939–1945) on the American home front.

Document 1

Source: "War Autos Only Now," *Stars and Stripes,* August 15, 1918

"The War Industries Board strongly counsels all manufacturers of passenger automobiles to get themselves on a hundred per cent war work basis as quickly as possible, and not later than January 1.

The manufacturers had already voluntarily agreed to curtail the production of passenger cars 50 per cent, but the board tells them that they must go to the limit."

Document 2

Source: W. E. B. Du Bois, "Returning Soldiers," *The Crisis,* May 1919

"We are returning from war! *The Crisis* and tens of thousands of black men were drafted into a great struggle. For bleeding France and what she means and has meant and will mean to us and humanity and against the threat of German race arrogance, we fought gladly and to the last drop of blood; for America and her highest ideals, we fought in far-off hope; for the dominant southern oligarchy entrenched in Washington, we fought in bitter resignation. For the America that represents and gloats in lynching, disfranchisement, caste, brutality and devilish insult—for this, in the hateful upturning and mixing of things, we were forced by vindictive fate to fight also.

But today we return! We return from the slavery of uniform which the world's madness demanded us to don to the freedom of civil garb. We stand again to look America squarely in the face and call a spade a spade. We sing: This country of ours, despite all its better souls have done and dreamed, is yet a shameful land. . . .

Make way for Democracy! We saved it in France, and by the Great Jehovah, we will save it in the United States of America, or know the reason why.

Document 3

Source: George Creel, *How We Advertised America*, 1920

"The Committee on Public Information was called into existence to make this fight for the 'verdict of mankind,' the voice created to plead the justice of America's cause before the jury of Public Opinion. . . .

(continued)

In all things from first to last, without halt or change, it was a plain publicity proposition, a vast enterprise in salesmanship, the world's greatest adventure in advertising.

Under the pressure of tremendous necessities an organization grew that not only reached deep into every American community, but that carried to every corner of the civilized globe the full message of America's idealism, unselfishness, and indomitable purpose."

Document 4

Source: Magazine Advertisement, 1944

Document 5

Source: *Korematsu v. United States*, 1944

"We uphold the exclusion order as of the time it was made and when the petitioner violated it. . . . In doing so, we are not unmindful of the hardships imposed by it upon a large group of American citizens. . . . But hardships are part of war, and war is an aggregation of hardships. All citizens alike, both in and out of uniform, feel the impact of war in greater or lesser measure. Citizenship has its responsibilities as well as its privileges, and in time of war the burden is always heavier. Compulsory exclusion of large groups of citizens from their homes, except under circumstances of direst emergency and peril, is inconsistent with our basic governmental institutions. But when under conditions of modern warfare our shores are threatened by hostile forces, the power to protect must be commensurate with the threatened danger."

(continued)

Document 6

Source: Unemployment Rate, 1915–1945

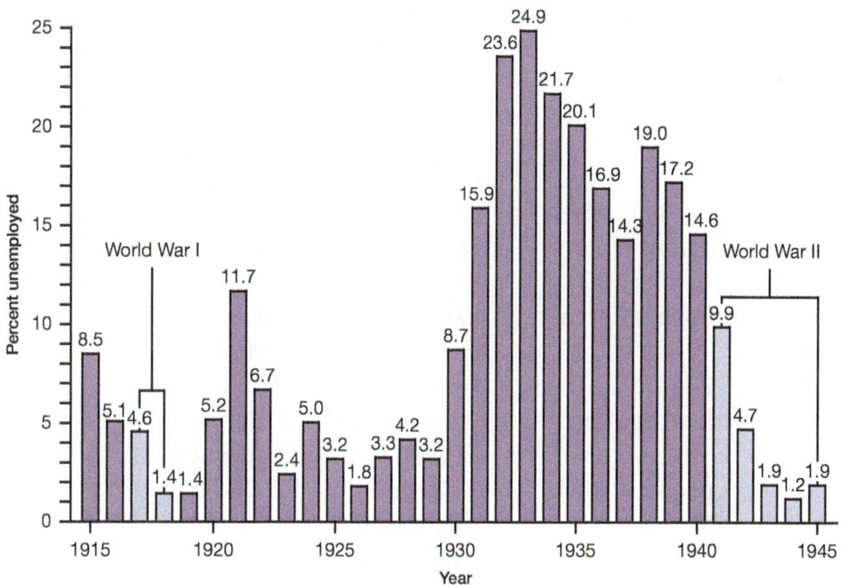

Document 7

Source: Mary Anne Read, oral interview about her childhood during World War II, June 2012

> "We would gather any scrap metal we could find; in fact; we'd walk along the railroad track picking it up. We would save any aluminum foil or any type of metallic paper that we could find. And everyone saved rubber bands; everyone had a big ball of rubber bands because rubber was in short supply and rubber was very much in demand, of course, for tires and other things in the war.
>
> Certain foods were rationed: butter, but margarine came to be (laughs) during those years. . . .
>
> And meat was rationed so Mother would try to cook strange things that we had never eaten before. . . .
>
> Gasoline and tires were rationed. I remember one time that the family was driving to Austin in our 1936 Chevrolet. You couldn't buy new cars during that time. . . . and one of the tires blew out, so my dad got out and put the spare on and we went several more miles and it blew out. And you couldn't just go to a store and buy a tire. You had to have a special certificate to get one. So we drove into Austin on the rim. We just—we didn't have any choice because there was no other way to get there."

Period 7 Review 1890–1945

KEY CONCEPTS AND EVENTS

Abrams v. United States, 716
Adamson Act, 699
Agricultural Adjustment Act (AAA), 761
Agricultural Marketing Act, 749
Allies, 702
America First Committee, 780
American Civil Liberties Union (ACLU), 718
American Expeditionary Forces (AEF), 706
American Plan, 721
American Protective League (APL), 715
Anti-Imperialist League, 664
appeasement, 779
Atlantic Charter, 782
attack on Pearl Harbor, 783
Battle of the Bulge, 802
Battle of Iwo Jima, 801
Battle of Midway Island, 801
Battle of Okinawa, 801
"big stick" diplomacy, 667
Black Tuesday, 748
bombings of Hiroshima and Nagasaki, 804
Bonus Army, 757
bracero, 792
bully pulpit, 691
Central Powers, 702
civic housekeeping, 672
Civil Works Administration (CWA), 763
Civilian Conservation Corps (CCC), 763
Clayton Antitrust Act, 698
Committee on Public Information (CPI), 714
communism, 707
Congress of Racial Equality (CORE), 792
conservationism, 689
court-packing plan, 773
Cuba Libre, 660
D-Day, 800
Department of Commerce and Labor, 692
dollar diplomacy, 668
Double V, 792
Dust Bowl, 751
Eighteenth Amendment, 681
Elkins Act, 692
Emergency Banking Act, 760
Espionage Act, 714
Executive Order 8802, 792
Executive Order 9066, 794
Fair Labor Standards Act, 771
Federal Bureau of Investigation, 718
Federal Deposit Insurance Corporation (FDIC), 760
feminist, 674
flapper, 729
Food Administration, 713
Fourteen Points, 707
Fuel Administration, 713
Glass-Steagall Act, 760
Great Depression, 748
Great Migration, 718
Harlem Renaissance, 731
Hay-Pauncefote Treaty, 667
Hetch Hetchy Valley, 690
Holocaust, 805
Hull House, 672
Indian Citizenship Act, 738
Indian Reorganization Act (IRA), 772
influenza pandemic, 718
internment, 794
island-hopping, 800
isolationism, 778
jingoist, 658
The Jungle, 692
Keating-Owen Act, 699
Kellogg-Briand Pact, 778
League of Nations, 707
League of United Latin American Citizens (LULAC), 793
Lend-Lease Act, 782
Lost Generation, 729
Lusitania, 703
Manhattan Project, 803
Mann Act, 681
Meat Inspection Act, 693
Mexican Revolution, 701
muckrakers, 671
Muller v. Oregon, 674
Munich Accord, 779
National American Woman Suffrage Association, 674
National Association for the Advancement of Colored People (NAACP), 679
National Association of Colored Women (NACW), 673
National Industrial Recovery Act (NIRA), 762
National Labor Relations Act, 769
National Labor Relations Board (NLRB), 769
National Origins Act, 736
National Recovery Administration (NRA), 762
National War Labor Board (NWLB), 712
National Woman's Party, 674
Nazism, 779
Neutrality Acts, 779
New Deal, 760
New Freedom, 696
New Nationalism, 695
New Negro, 731
new woman, 729
Nineteenth Amendment, 677
Nye Committee, 779
Office of War Information, 791
Open Door policy, 668
Palmer raids, 717
Payne-Aldrich tariff, 695
Platt Amendment, 663
pragmatism, 671
Progressive Party, 695
progressivism, 671
Public Works Administration (PWA), 763
Pure Food and Drug Act, 694
Railroad Administration, 713

KEY PEOPLE

CHRONOLOGY

1890	Creation of National American Woman Suffrage Association
1893–1897	Panic of 1893
1893	White plantation owners overthrow Hawaiian government
1898	Spanish-American War Foundation of the Anti-Imperialist League
1901	President McKinley assassinated Roosevelt launches Square Deal and becomes "bully pulpit" president
1902	Ida Tarbell exposes Standard Oil Company corruption
1903	Creation of National Women's Trade Union League to improve workplace conditions Department of Labor and Commerce established
1904	Lincoln Steffens publishes *The Shame of the Cities* Announcement of Roosevelt Corollary to extend the U.S. sphere of influence in the Western hemisphere
1906	Pure Food and Drug Act passed Meat Inspection Act passed Hepburn Act strengthens federal regulation of railroads
1907	Publication of *Christianity and the Social Crisis* inspires the social gospel movement
1909	Taft becomes president, instituting foreign policy of "dollar diplomacy" Foundation of National Association for the Advancement of Colored People (NAACP)
1911	Triangle Shirtwaist Company factory fire inspires government regulation
1912	Presidential election of Woodrow Wilson on New Freedom platform
1913	Sixteenth Amendment introduces a graduated income tax Seventeenth Amendment establishes election of senators by popular vote Federal Reserve System created
1914	World War I begins in Europe Marcus Garvey establishes Universal Negro Improvement Association Panama Canal opens Federal Trade Commission created Clayton Antitrust Act passed
1915	Sinking of passenger liner *Lusitania* by German U-Boat
1916	Adamson Act establishes eight-hour workday for railroad workers
1917–1945	Beginning of the Great Migration of Black people from the South to the North, culminating during World War II, but continuing to a lesser extent through the 1960s
1917	Germany resumes unrestricted submarine warfare Publication of Zimmerman Telegram turns public opinion toward war Wilson asks Congress for declaration of war against Central Powers Russian Revolution establishes Bolshevik regime Reformers succeed in series of immigration restrictions to ban "undesirables"
1918	End of World War I following armistice Influenza pandemic kills 50 million worldwide

CHRONOLOGY *(continued)*

1919	Supreme Court limits free speech in *Schenck* and *Abrams* rulings League of Nations is established, but United States does not join Red Scare escalates in United States Labor strikes take place across the nation Eighteenth Amendment prohibits the sale and consumption of alcohol United States deports hundreds of immigrants and radicals
by 1920	More Americans live in urban than rural areas for the first time in American history
1920s	KKK membership temporarily surges above three million people and is politically active across the United States
1920	American Civil Liberties Union (ACLU) is established Sacco and Vanzetti found guilty of murder Passage of Nineteenth Amendment grants women the right to vote
1921	Teapot Dome scandal tarnishes Harding administration
1923	Harding dies and Calvin Coolidge assumes the presidency
1924	Indian Citizenship Act grants citizenship to all native-born American Indians National Origins Act places restrictive quotas on European immigration
1925	Scopes trial over teaching evolution in high school illustrates cultural divide between religion and science
1928	Presidential election of Herbert Hoover
1929	Ford factories employ more than four million workers Stock market crashes on Black Tuesday
1930	Congress passes Smoot-Hawley Act, substantially raising tariff rates
1932	Reconstruction Finance Corporation supplies loans to troubled banks, railroads, and insurance companies in effort to stimulate the economy Bonus Army of World War I veterans marches on Washington, D.C. Presidential election of Franklin Roosevelt
by 1933	Economic depression worldwide
1933	Adolf Hitler becomes chancellor of Germany Roosevelt's "bank holiday" and Emergency Banking Act restore public confidence in the banking system Congress passes fifteen pieces of legislation during Roosevelt's first hundred days in office
1933–1945	The Holocaust
1934	American Liberty League launched to oppose New Deal policies
1935	Creation of Works Progress Administration (WPA) provides jobs for more than eight million people Passage of the Social Security Act provides pension payments for seniors Italy invades Ethiopia National Labor Relations Act organized labor
1936	Hitler sends troops to occupy the Rhineland
1937	Roosevelt unsuccessfully attempts Supreme Court packing plan

CHRONOLOGY *(continued)*

1938	Munich Accord allows Germany to annex the Sudetenland Minimum wage established by Fair Labor Standards Act
1939	Hitler, unchallenged, sends troops to occupy the rest of the Czech lands Germany invades Poland, leading Great Britain and France to declare war
1940	Germany occupies Paris
1941	Germany and the United States engaged in an undeclared naval war Creation of Fair Employment Practice Committee Japan attacks Pearl Harbor, prompting a U.S. declaration of war
1941–1942	Passage of the War Powers Acts
1942	Roosevelt establishes War Production Board Japanese living on West Coast forcibly relocated to internment camps
1944	Wartime employment reaches its peak Launch of D-Day invasion, opening a western front in Europe
1945	Roosevelt, Churchill, and Stalin make Yalta Agreement Roosevelt dies suddenly and Harry S. Truman becomes president Germany surrenders following Hitler's suicide United States drops atomic bombs on Hiroshima and Nagasaki Japan surrenders, marking the end of World War II

Period 7 AP® Exam Practice

Multiple-Choice Questions

Questions 1–3 refer to the excerpt.

"I am interested in the Panama Canal because I started it. If I had followed traditional conservative methods, I would have submitted a dignified state paper of 200 pages to Congress and the debate on it would have been going on yet; but I took the Canal Zone and let Congress debate; and while the debate goes on the Canal does also."

Theodore Roosevelt, Speech at Berkeley, California, 1911

1. Concern over which of the following most directly led to the events described in the excerpt?
   (A) Creation of a more just world order
   (B) Protecting Latin American countries from European colonization
   (C) Securing freedom of the seas for all countries
   (D) Speeding the passage of naval warships between oceans

2. The actions described in the excerpt best exemplify which early twentieth-century U.S. foreign policy approach?
   (A) The Open Door policy
   (B) Big stick diplomacy
   (C) Dollar diplomacy
   (D) The Fourteen Points

3. U.S. foreign policy actions such as those described in the excerpt most commonly resulted in which of the following responses in Latin America?
   (A) Resentment, because they felt the United States treated them as inferior nations.
   (B) Gratitude, because they viewed the United States as their protector against European countries, thereby guaranteeing Latin American economic and political independence.
   (C) Hope, because they believed the United States would help them achieve an industrial revolution similar to that taking place in America.
   (D) Respect, because they considered that the United States was treating them as equals in the western hemisphere.

Questions 4–6 refer to the photograph.

Bettmann/Getty Images

Bonus Army men, Washington, D.C., June 6, 1932

4. How did the U.S. government initially respond to this and similar demonstrations?
- (A) Jobs programs were created to provide employment opportunities for the protesters.
- (B) Protesters were arrested, beaten, jailed, and often held without bond.
- (C) Veterans who protested were offered the opportunity to re-enlist in the U.S. military.
- (D) The requests were refused and eventually force was used to end the protest.

5. Protests such as the one in the image most directly led to the
- (A) Great Depression.
- (B) reform efforts of the New Deal.
- (C) passage of high tariffs to protect American businesses.
- (D) construction of low-income housing for the poor.

6. The actions depicted in the image are the most similar to which earlier historical event?
- (A) The Boston Tea Party in 1773, where people protested the government's allowance of British tea to be sold on the streets of Boston.
- (B) Coxey's Army, which demanded that the government hire unemployed workers as government employees during the Panic of 1893.
- (C) The New York City draft riots during the summer of 1863, where people protested the Union's implementation of the draft to increase the number of soldiers in the army.
- (D) The Whiskey Rebellion in western Pennsylvania during 1794, where citizens argued against the national government's constitutional right to tax them.

Questions 7–9 refer to the excerpt.

"[W]e are raising more than we can consume. To-day, we are making more than we can use. To-day our industrial society is congested; there are more workers than there is work; there is more capital than there is investment. We do not need more money—we need more circulation, more employment. Therefore we must find new markets for our produce, new occupation for our capital, new work for our labor. And so, while we did not need the territory taken during the past century at the time it was acquired, we do need what we have taken in 1898, and we need it now. . . .

Ah! As our commerce spreads, the flag of liberty will circle the globe and the highways of the ocean—carrying trade to all mankind—be guarded by the guns of the Republic. And, as their thunders salute the flag, benighted [less advanced] peoples will know that the voice of liberty is speaking, at last, for them; that civilization is dawning, at last, for them . . ."

Albert J. Beveridge, "March of the Flag," September 16, 1898

7. Beveridge and other imperialists justified their position using all of the following arguments EXCEPT
- (A) improving the economic conditions of foreign countries would decrease the number of immigrants coming to the United States from those countries.
- (B) the United States had a responsibility to spread the blessings of its Christian way of life throughout the world.
- (C) the way to sustain prosperity and contain radicalism in the United States was to find foreign markets for U.S. industrial goods.
- (D) superior civilizations had a responsibility to uplift inferior nations.

8. Imperialists such as Beveridge believed that America's industrial and economic future depended mainly on access to which foreign market?
- (A) Cuba
- (B) The Philippines
- (C) Russia
- (D) China

9. Beveridge's statement that, "while we did not need the territory taken during the past century at the time it was acquired, we do need what we have taken in 1898" most directly links the Spanish-American War with which prior conflict?
- (A) The Revolutionary War
- (B) The War of 1812
- (C) The Mexican-American War
- (D) The Civil War

Questions 10–12 refer to the excerpt.

"For the trust reposed in me I will return the courage and the devotion that befit the time. I can do no less.

We face the arduous days that lie before us in the warm courage of national unity; with the clear consciousness of seeking old and precious moral values; with the clean satisfaction that comes from the stern performance of duty by old and young alike. We aim at the assurance of a rounded and permanent national life.

We do not distrust the future of essential democracy. The people of the United States have not failed. In their need they have registered a mandate that they want direct, vigorous action. They have asked for discipline and direction under leadership. They have made me the present instrument of their wishes. In the spirit of the gift I take it."

Franklin D. Roosevelt, Inaugural Address, March 4, 1933

10. In his address, Roosevelt sought to counter which common approach of the U.S. government to previous economic crises?
    (A) The national government considered it their responsibility to take control of the economy during an economic downturn, in order to lead the country out of a depression.
    (B) The national government sought to stimulate economic activity during a downturn by lowering taxes and providing loans to businesses.
    (C) The national government used economic downturns as opportunities to promote policies favoring economic equality among all citizens.
    (D) The national government generally avoided intervention during a downturn, instead preferring to maintain a laissez-faire approach.

11. Which of the following resulted from Roosevelt taking "direct, vigorous action"?
    (A) Economic prosperity returned to the country, and the Great Depression ended.
    (B) Women switched to the Democratic Party, but Black Americans remained loyal to the Republican Party since that was the party that ended slavery.
    (C) Political party affiliation changed as minorities and working-class people moved to the Democratic Party.
    (D) Roosevelt's actions worsened the Great Depression and led to increasing despair among Americans.

12. Which of the following groups was most opposed to Roosevelt's claim to a "mandate" for economic change?
    (A) Labor unions
    (B) Congress
    (C) Supreme Court
    (D) State governments

Questions 13–15 refer to the poster.

Boston Public Library, Arts Department

Women's Land Army of America poster, U.S. Government Printing Office, 1944

13. Women who joined organizations such as the Women's Land Army during World War II were different from women who previously worked outside the home in that these women were generally

(A) married.
(B) single.
(C) widowed.
(D) college educated.

14. Large-scale propaganda efforts to target and recruit women's participation, such as this poster, were most similar to efforts made during

(A) the temperance movement.
(B) World War I.
(C) the first Red Scare.
(D) the Great Depression.

15. Women who heeded the call in the poster generally encountered which of the following in their wartime jobs?

(A) Equal wages for equal work with men
(B) New avenues for advancement in the workplace
(C) Opportunities to work in traditionally male jobs
(D) Child care provided by the employer

Short-Answer Questions

"The sixth winter of the Great Depression was much like those that had preceded it and those that would follow. Conditions were better early in 1935 than they had been two years before. . . . But conditions were not good. National income remained more than 40 percent lower than six years earlier. Farm prices continued to languish far beneath their 1929 levels, which had themselves been uncomfortably low. Ten million people, 20 percent of the workforce, remained unemployed. The Depression was not over, and there was no end in sight. So it had been for over four years. So it would continue for four years more. . . . Now, however, the New Deal seemed to be losing both its spirits and its strength. It had been months since the President had proposed any major new initiative. He had concentrated instead on shoring up existing programs, many of which remained in disarray."

Alan Brinkley, *Voices of Protest: Huey Long, Father Coughlin and The Great Depression*, 1982

"Roosevelt had good reason for optimism. By almost any measure the economic surge since 1932 had been remarkable. National income had risen by more than 50 percent, 6 million new jobs had been created, and unemployment had dropped by more than a third. . . . The banking system had been rescued, depositors enjoyed a federal guarantee of their savings, most farm mortgages had been refinanced, and the Home Owners' Loan Corporation had bailed out more than 3 million debt-ridden home owners. Social Security, rural electrification, and the massive public works program now under way were changing the face of the nation. A *Fortune* magazine poll in June 1936 indicated that 53 percent of the nation thought the Depression was over and that 60 percent or more supported the president."

Jean Edward Smith, *FDR*, 2008

1. Using the excerpts, answer **A**, **B**, and **C**.
   (A) Briefly describe ONE major difference between Brinkley's and Smith's historical interpretations of the New Deal.
   (B) Briefly explain how ONE specific historical event or development from 1933 to 1939 not directly mentioned in the excerpts could be used to support Brinkley's argument.
   (C) Briefly explain how ONE specific historical event or development from 1933 to 1939 not directly mentioned in the excerpts could be used to support Smith's argument.

Image Courtesy of The Advertising Archives

2. Using the 1920s magazine advertisement, answer **A**, **B**, and **C**.
   (A) Briefly describe ONE perspective about the impact of technology on American society from 1900 to 1930.
   (B) Briefly explain ONE specific historical development from 1900 to 1930 that led to the changes in technology depicted in the image.
   (C) Briefly explain ONE specific impact of technology on American consumerism during the 1920s.

3. Answer **A**, **B**, and **C**.
   (A) Briefly describe ONE historical event or development that improved the status of Black people in U.S. society from 1900 to 1940.
   (B) Briefly describe ONE historical event or development that worsened the status of Black people in U.S. society from 1900 to 1940.
   (C) Briefly describe ONE specific response by Black people to the challenges they faced in U.S. society from 1900 to 1940.

4. Answer **A**, **B**, and **C**.
   (A) Briefly describe ONE similarity between U.S. foreign policy in period 1890 to 1917 and U.S. foreign policy in the period 1920 to 1941.
   (B) Briefly describe ONE difference between U.S. foreign policy in the period 1890 to 1917 and U.S. foreign policy in the period 1920 to 1941.
   (C) Briefly explain ONE reason for a difference between U.S. foreign policy in the period 1890 to 1917 and U.S. foreign policy in the period 1920 to 1941.

Document-Based Question

1. Evaluate the extent to which U.S. participation in World War I changed American society. Confine your answer to the period 1914 to 1929.

Document 1

Source: Woodrow Wilson, speech asking Congress for a declaration of war, 1917

"Our object . . . is to vindicate the principles of peace and justice in the life of the world as against selfish and autocratic power and to set up among the really free and self-governed peoples of the world such a concert of purpose and of action as will henceforth ensure the observance of those principles. . . . The world must be made safe for democracy. Its peace must be planted upon the tested foundations of political liberty. We have no selfish ends to serve. We desire no conquest, no dominion. We seek no indemnities for ourselves, no material compensation for the sacrifices we shall freely make. We are but one of the champions of the rights of mankind. We shall be satisfied when those rights have been made as secure as the faith and freedom of nations can make them."

Document 2

Source: Eugene V. Debs, speech to the jury during his trial for violating the Espionage Act, 1918

"[M]y purpose was to have the people understand something about the social system in which we live and to prepare them to change this system by perfectly peaceable and orderly means into what I, as a Socialist, conceive to be a real democracy.

From what you heard in the address of the counsel for the prosecution, you might naturally infer that I am an advocate of force and violence. It is not true. I have never advocated violence in any form. . . . I have always made my appeal to the reason and to the conscience of the people.

I admit being opposed to the present social system. I am doing what little I can, and have been for many years, to bring about a change that shall do away with the rule of the great body of the people by a relatively small class and establish in this country an industrial and social democracy."

Document 3

Source: W. E. B. DuBois, "Returning Soldiers," *The Crisis*, May 1919

"We are returning from war! *The Crisis* and tens of thousands of black men were drafted into a great struggle. . . .

This is the country to which we Soldiers of Democracy return. This is the fatherland for which we fought! But it is *our* fatherland. It was right for us to fight. The faults of *our* country are *our* faults. Under similar circumstances, we would fight again. But by the God of Heaven, we are cowards and jackasses if now that that war is over, we do not marshal every ounce of our brain and brawn to fight a sterner, longer, more unbending battle against the forces of hell in our own land. . . .

Make way for Democracy! We saved it in France, and by the Great Jehovah, we will save it in the United States of America, or know the reason why."

Document 4

Source: Edwin Marcus, "The Cheerful Giver—Or, Do Your Christmas Shipping Early," *New York Times*, December 21, 1919

About the source: "Merry Christmas to Messrs Lenin & Trotsky, Russia" is being painted on the side of the crate in the image. On the sleeves of three of the crated people are the words "Anarchists," "Bolsheviks," and "I.W.W."

Document 5

Source: Ernest Ludlow Bogart, *Direct and Indirect Costs of the Great World War*, 1920

"A few years ago pamphleteers and men in public life were declaring that there could not be another great war because of the tremendous costs that would be involved. Saner students of history pointed out that cost was relative and that no nation had ever been prevented from going into war from fear of expense. The judgement of the latter has been vindicated by recent history. The war that has just come to an end shows that anticipated costs, however, great, are not a preventative. A recital of the tremendous costs of the great war cannot therefore be regarded as worth while if the purpose of the recital is to warn against further wars. Nevertheless, it is well that the world should know as fully as possible the monetary and other costs of its bloody debauch [immoral act]."

Document 6

Source: Representative Lucien W. Parrish, a Democrat from Texas, 1921

"We should stop immigration entirely until such a time as we can amend our immigration laws and so write them that hereafter no one shall be admitted except he be in full sympathy with our Constitution and laws, willing to declare himself obedient to our flag, and willing to release himself from any obligations he may owe to the flag of the country from which he came.

It is time that we act now, because within a few short years the damage will have been done. The endless tide of immigration will have filled our country with a foreign and unsympathetic element. Those who are out of sympathy with our Constitution and the spirit of our Government will be here in large numbers, and the true spirit of Americanism left us by our fathers will gradually become poisoned by this uncertain element."

Document 7

Source: Ernest Hemingway, *A Farewell to Arms*, 1929

"I was always embarrassed by the words sacred, glorious, and sacrifice and the expression in vain. We had heard them, sometimes standing in the rain almost out of earshot, so that only the shouted words came through, and had read them, on proclamations that were slapped up by billposters over other proclamations, now for a long time, and I had seen nothing sacred, and the things that were glorious had no glory and the sacrifices were like the stockyards of Chicago if nothing was done with the meat except to bury it. There were many words that you could not stand to hear and finally only the names of places had dignity. . . . Abstract words such as glory, honor, courage, or hallow were obscene beside the concrete names of villages, the numbers of roads, the names of rivers, the numbers of regiments and the dates."

Long-Essay Questions

2. Evaluate the extent to which the Great Depression altered the role of the federal government.

3. Evaluate the extent of similarity between Progressive Era reform efforts and the reforms of the New Deal.

4. Evaluate the extent of change in American party politics between 1900 and 1940.

PERIOD 8 1945–1980

Cold War America

Paul Fusco/Magnum Photos

Hard Hat Riot, May 8, 1970 Four days after the shooting of four students at Kent State University in Ohio during an antiwar protest, approximately 1,000 antiwar protesters gathered in New York City to denounce the killings. Approximately 250 construction workers, under the direction of the state AFL-CIO, attacked the protesters in what became known as the "Hard Hat Riot." Many of the counterprotesters carried American flags.

Contextualizing Period 8

MODULE 8.1

The postwar period promised an expansion of American interests and ideals. Once the United States, the Soviet Union, and the other Allied Powers defeated the Axis Powers of Europe and Asia, they set in motion an international order grounded in the new United Nations and in declarations that protected universal human rights. However, in the final days of the Second World War, the United States and the U.S.S.R. began to engage in a global conflict that lasted for nearly fifty years.

The Cold War was waged between people living in two fundamentally different political and economic systems and reflected a precarious balance between the two world powers left standing in the aftermath of 1945. The destructive capabilities of modern warfare, especially after the invention of nuclear weaponry, made direct conflict between these two "superpowers" unthinkable for most leaders. Instead, in Europe, Asia, and the Caribbean, a series of conflicts on the fringes of each nation's sphere of influence broke out regularly throughout this period. These conflicts inspired a culture of preparedness and anxiety domestically, including debates about the power of the federal government over individuals in an age of constant fear of war.

By the early 1960s, protests against the Vietnam War (a war within the Cold War) and the civil rights movement dominated newspaper headlines in the United States and inspired movements for gender and sexual equality and for the civil rights of Blacks, Latinos, and American Indians. These movements especially influenced millions of young Americans who were coming of age in high schools and colleges. By the end of the decade, the assassinations of Martin Luther King Jr., Malcolm X, and Robert F. Kennedy and riots in the poor and predominately Black neighborhoods of large American cities ignited widespread calls for reform.

These revolutionary sentiments produced a countermovement of self-proclaimed conservatives like Ronald Reagan and Phyllis Schlafly who took inspiration from the presidential candidacy of Barry Goldwater in 1964 and looked back to an unspecified time when American society was at peace and the American economy was prosperous. For many Americans, the first decades after the Second World War represented a time when all that had gone smoothly before seemed suddenly to have become jagged and out of alignment. Already anxious from the Cold War and the threat of global nuclear destruction, many Americans felt further threatened by new value systems that challenged old conventions, by the emergence of new interest groups that demanded recognition and respect, and by the arrival of new immigrants from locations outside Europe. These sentiments seeded a revitalized conservatism in the 1970s and 1980s, breaking through on the federal level with the election of Ronald Reagan as president in 1980.

AP® EXAM TIP

The roots of the Cold War are important to understand to make historical connections throughout Period 8. Think about how you can link ideological differences between the United States and the Soviet Union in three different decades. Using a line of reasoning, such as ideological underpinnings, can be helpful when developing a historical argument.

Period 8: What's Inside 1945–1980

MODULE	AP® THEMATIC FOCUS
8.1 Contextualizing Period 8	The Second World War transformed social norms while mobilizing the economy to fight both in the Pacific and Europe. While an alliance with the Soviet Union proved convenient during the Second World War, longstanding animosity toward radicals remained. And even as the military was desegregated in 1948, Black Americans still faced long-standing social structures that undermined their equal rights. After World War II, the United States remained actively involved in world affairs, especially because of a perceived threat from the Soviet Union and China. This had far-reaching effects for U.S. domestic policy and international relations, causing anxiety about the spread of communism both at home and abroad. Likewise, during this period, Blacks began to demand an end to the Jim Crow system in the South and repressive economic structures in the North, which led other marginalized groups to also seek equal rights and opportunities. This period also saw enormous economic and cultural changes and reform, which transformed the way Americans worked and interacted with each other, causing new kinds of living arrangements, as well as social division.
8.2 The Cold War from 1945 to 1980	**America in the World** In the aftermath of World War II, fundamental differences between the United States and the Soviet Union over ideology and the fate of Europe led to the ending of the wartime alliance and the beginning of the Cold War. The United States pursued a policy of containment to limit the expansion of communism and committed itself to preserving the security of Western Europe and the free world through the investment of billions of dollars and permanent military alliances.
8.3 The Red Scare	**American and National Identity** As the Cold War solidified and Europe was divided by an iron curtain, Americans faced the threat of devastating war with a nuclear-armed Soviet Union. Efforts to uncover potential domestic communist activity took on new urgency. Investigations by the House Un-American Activities Committee, Federal Employee Loyalty review boards, and Senator Joseph McCarthy resulted in renewed debates over the balance between civil liberties and public safety.
8.4 The Economy after 1945	**Work, Exchange, and Technology ■ Migration and Settlement** After an initial postwar transition, the U.S. economy experienced a remarkable period of growth, significantly expanding the ranks of the middle class and noticeably lessening income inequality. The application of mass production techniques to home construction and federal subsidies for mortgages led to a sharp increase in home ownership and the construction of new communities on the outskirts of cities. Likewise, during this period, the public university system expanded to accommodate returning veterans and, later, their children, greatly broadening the opportunities for higher education for many Americans.
8.5 Culture after 1945	**American and Regional Culture** The rise of television reinforced a homogenous popular culture by depicting white, middle-class families in wholesome situations. At the same time, a distinctly teenage culture began to form with the emergence of rock 'n' roll music and Hollywood movies aimed at teenagers' sense of rebellion. Church attendance soared to record heights as millions of Americans sought personal connections in a changing world and comfort from the threat of nuclear annihilation. Despite mainstream expectations of conformity, writers and intellectuals challenged the cultural homogeneity of postwar American society.
8.6 Early Steps in the Civil Rights Movement (1940s and 1950s)	**Social Structures** After fighting for a double victory in World War II against fascism abroad and racism at home, Black veterans returned to a country in which they faced discrimination in the North and legal segregation in the South. In response, civil rights organizations initiated lawsuits, boycotts, and sit-ins, resulting in the Supreme Court overturning school segregation in *Brown v. Board of Education*, the desegregation of Montgomery's buses, and the integration of lunch counters in the South. White segregationists resisted civil rights by blocking passage of civil rights legislation, using threats and intimidation, and sometimes through violence and terror.

MODULE	AP® THEMATIC FOCUS
8.7 America as a World Power	**America in the World** President Eisenhower oversaw a shift in U.S. military spending as his administration emphasized the production of nuclear weapons over conventional forces. After the development of the hydrogen bomb in the early 1950s, an arms race ensued with the Soviet Union and a policy of deterrence based on mutually assured destruction took hold. Domestically, Eisenhower increased federal spending on highways to speed mobilization of U.S. military forces in wartime and education funding to counter Soviet advances in rocket technology. In 1961, President Kennedy promised to take a hard line against communism. Two years later, the Cuban Missile Crisis brought the United States and U.S.S.R. to the brink of war before it was peacefully resolved. To prevent communist gains in Latin America, Asia, and Africa, the United States often supported repressive regimes and sometimes engineered CIA-supported coups to install friendlier governments.
8.8 The Vietnam War	**America in the World** Despite the thousands of U.S. military advisors sent to South Vietnam by the Eisenhower and Kennedy administrations, the anticommunist regime in South Vietnam struggled against a determined communist insurgency. In 1964, President Lyndon Johnson escalated the conflict into a full-scale war, drafting hundreds of thousands of U.S. soldiers into the fight. Four years later, as public opinion on the war soured, Nixon was elected on a promise of "peace with honor." Even as U.S. forces withdrew, Nixon expanded the conflict into neighboring countries in an unsuccessful effort to secure better terms at the peace negotiations. The withdrawal of U.S. military forces from South Vietnam in 1973 led to its defeat two years later, and Vietnam became a communist country.
8.9 The Great Society	**Politics and Power ▪ Migration and Settlement** Promising to create a Great Society, Johnson's legislative successes rivaled the New Deal with reforms aimed at civil rights, immigration, poverty, education, health care, and environmental protection. These reforms proved to be the height of twentieth-century American liberalism, and they set the stage for a conservative backlash in the second half of the century. During this period, Americans moved from cities to suburbs and from north and east to west and south, fostering a wide-ranging shift in the ways and places Americans lived. Likewise, in the mid-1960s, the federal government lifted restrictions on immigration based on region of origin, allowing for expanded immigration from outside Europe.
8.10 The African American Civil Rights Movement (1960s)	**Social Structures ▪ Politics and Power** As the 1960s began, civil rights leaders looked to build upon their postwar successes through continued nonviolent protests, voter registration drives, and political pressure. Yet new voices challenged the approach of Martin Luther King and others as young urban Blacks in the North and West expressed their frustration with the lack of meaningful change in American cities. As the focus of the civil rights movement shifted toward racial integration and equal opportunity outside the South, policies such as court-ordered busing and affirmative action generated controversy and were eventually limited by court rulings.
8.11 The Civil Rights Movement Expands	**Social Structures** Inspired by the ideals of the civil rights movement, women, American Indians, Latinos, Asian Americans, and gay and lesbian activists demanded equal rights and opportunities on par with other Americans. These movements, like the earlier civil rights movement, challenged Americans' conception of their country as a place of equality and opportunity and led to debates about underlying social structures that perpetuated inequality.
8.12 Youth Culture of the 1960s	**American and Regional Culture** The "baby boom" generation, born in the late 1940s and 1950s, was one of the largest in U.S. history. Throughout the 1960s, this generation grew up watching scenes from the Vietnam War and the civil rights movement on their televisions. During the 1960s, some members of this generation, later called the "New Left," engaged in antiwar protests that rejected the Cold War liberalism of the Johnson administration. A smaller, but also influential portion of this generation, which came to be broadly known as the counterculture, experimented with alternative lifestyles, including communal living and experimentation with drugs and hallucinogens. Both elements of this youth culture challenged postwar culture during and after the 1960s.

MODULE	AP® THEMATIC FOCUS
8.13 The Environment and Natural Resources from 1968 to 1980	**Geography and the Environment** In the 1970s, environmentalists won new protections for air and water quality as well as endangered species. Yet a growing conservative movement opposed to the expansion of government regulations challenged advances in environmental and resource conservation. During the same period, an oil embargo led by Middle Eastern nations focused Americans' attention on the nation's need for natural resources that were often dwindling or controlled by other nations.
8.14 Society in Transition	**Politics and Power ▪ American and Regional Culture** Having won the presidency in 1968 amid the turmoil of antiwar protests, high-profile assassinations, urban riots, and political demonstrations, Nixon's victory and reelection signaled a rightward shift in American politics. However, the Watergate scandal temporarily reversed this trend and led to Carter's election in 1976. Rising prices, unemployment, and overseas competition disrupted American economic growth as workers, businesses, and politicians struggled to adapt to new conditions. After a period of détente, relations with the Soviet Union deteriorated because of its invasion of Afghanistan in 1979.
8.15 Continuity and Change in Period 8	Between 1945 and 1980, the United States maintained its tradition of projecting American power beyond its borders, but increasingly embraced a global approach in light of the Cold War. Likewise, during this period, Americans continued to debate topics regarding civil rights, government power, and economic policies.
Support and Practice	• Practice thinking and writing historically in each module. • See the Period Review of key concepts, events, people, and dates after the last module. • Try the AP® Exam Practice at the end of the period.

The Cold War

FOCUS

As you read this module, consider how U.S. foreign policy changed in the period after World War II. Ask yourself what accounts for the changes, whether the changes were unavoidable, and how the changes affected American politics.

The wartime partnership between the United States and the Soviet Union (U.S.S.R.) was an alliance of necessity. Putting aside ideological differences and a history of mutual distrust, the two nations joined forces to combat Nazi aggression. As long as the Nazi threat existed, the alliance held, but as the war ended and attention turned to the postwar world, the allies became adversaries. The two nations did not engage directly in war, but they entered into a prolonged struggle for political, economic, and military dominance known as the Cold War.

After 1947, the Cold War intensified. Both sides increased military spending and took measures to enhance their military presence around the world. Fueled by growing distrust, the Soviet Union and the United States engaged in inflammatory rhetoric that added to the danger the conflict posed to world peace. In 1950, the United States, in cooperation with the United Nations, sent troops to South Korea to turn back an invasion from the communist North. President Truman took advantage of Cold War hostilities to expand presidential power through increased military spending and the creation of a vast national intelligence network. While the Korean conflict ended in an unresolved stalemate, conflict between the United States and the Soviet Union ebbed and flowed during the next twenty-five years.

Mutual Misunderstandings

The roots of the **Cold War** stretched back several decades. After the Bolshevik Revolution of 1917, the United States refused to grant diplomatic recognition to the Soviet Union and sent troops to Russia to support anti-Bolshevik forces seeking to overturn the revolution, an effort that failed. At the same time, the American government, fearing communist efforts to overthrow capitalist governments, sought to wipe out communism in the United States by deporting immigrant radicals during the first Red Scare (see Module 7.6). The United States continued to deny diplomatic recognition to the U.S.S.R. until 1933, when President Roosevelt reversed this policy. Nevertheless, relations between the two countries remained uneasy.

Cold War
The political, economic, and military conflict, short of direct war, between the United States and the Soviet Union between 1945 and 1991.

World War II brought a thaw in tensions. President Roosevelt went a long way toward defusing Joseph Stalin's concerns at the Yalta Conference in 1945. The Soviet leader viewed the Eastern European countries that the U.S.S.R. had liberated from the Germans, especially Poland, as a buffer to protect his nation from future attacks by Germany. Roosevelt understood Stalin's reasoning and recognized political realities: The Soviet military already occupied Eastern Europe, a state of affairs that increased Stalin's bargaining position. Still, the president attempted to balance

Soviet influence by insisting that the Yalta Agreement include a guarantee of free elections in Eastern Europe.

By contrast, Roosevelt's successor, Harry S. Truman, took a much less nuanced approach to U.S.-Soviet relations. Stalin's ruthless purges within the Soviet Union in the 1930s and 1940s had convinced Truman that the Soviet dictator was paranoid and extremely dangerous. He believed that the Soviets threatened "a barbarian invasion of Europe," and he intended to deter it.

In his first meeting with Soviet foreign minister Vyacheslav Molotov in April 1945, Truman rebuked the Russians for failing to support free elections in Poland. Molotov, recoiling from the sharp tone of Truman's remarks, replied: "I have never been talked to like that in my life."

Despite this rough start, Truman did not immediately abandon the idea of cooperation with the Soviet Union. At the **Potsdam Conference** in Germany in July 1945, Truman and Stalin agreed on several issues. The two leaders reaffirmed the concept of free elections in Eastern Europe; Soviet troop withdrawal from the oil fields of northern Iran, which bordered the U.S.S.R.; and the partition of Germany (and Berlin itself) into four Allied occupation zones.

Within six months of the war's end, however, relations between the two countries soured. The United States was the only nation in the world with the atomic bomb and boasted the only economy reinvigorated by the war. As a result, the Truman administration believed that it held the upper hand against the Soviets. With this in mind, the State Department offered the Soviets a $6 billion loan, which the country needed to help rebuild its war-ravaged economy. But when the Soviets undermined free elections in Poland in 1946 and established a compliant government, the United States withdrew the offer. Soviet troops also remained in northern Iran, closing off the oil fields to potential capitalist enterprises. The failure to reach agreement over international control of atomic energy proved the last straw. The United States wanted to make sure it would keep its atomic weapons, while the Soviets wanted the United States to destroy its nuclear arsenal. Clearly, the former World War II allies did not trust each other.

Truman had significantly underestimated the strength of the Soviet position. The Soviets were well on their way toward building their own atomic bomb, negating the Americans' nuclear advantage. The Soviets could also ignore the enticement of U.S. economic aid by taking resources from East Germany and mobilizing the Russian people to rebuild their country's industry and military. Indeed, on February 9, 1946, Stalin delivered a tough speech to rally Russians to make sacrifices to enhance national security. By asserting that communism was "a better form of organization than any non-Soviet social system," according to George Kennan, a U.S. diplomat stationed in the Soviet Union, Stalin implied that capitalist nations could not coexist with communism and that future wars were unavoidable unless communism triumphed over capitalism.

Whether or not Stalin meant this speech as an unofficial declaration of a third world war, U.S. leaders interpreted it this way. A few days after Stalin spoke, Kennan sent an 8,000-word telegram from the U.S. Embassy in Moscow to Washington, blaming the Soviets for stirring up international tensions and confirming that Stalin could not be trusted. Kennan warned that Stalin was committed to expanding communism throughout the world and advised President Harry S. Truman to adopt a policy of **containment**. In Kennan's view, all Soviet efforts at expansion should be met with firm resistance. At the same time, the United States should take an active role in rebuilding the economies of war-torn Western European countries, thereby reducing the appeal of communism to their populations. Kennan's concept of containment would become the basis for President Truman's Cold War foreign policy.

containment

The U.S. strategy to prevent the spread of communism and Soviet influence around the world. First outlined by U.S. diplomat George Kennan in 1946, containment became a key element of U.S. Cold War policy.

The following month, on March 5, former British prime minister Winston Churchill gave a speech in Truman's home state of Missouri. Declaring that "an **iron curtain** has descended across the Continent" of Europe, Churchill observed that "there is nothing [the Russians] admire so much as strength, and there is nothing for which they have less respect than for weakness, especially military weakness." This comment reaffirmed Truman's sentiments expressed the previous year: "Unless Russia is faced with an iron fist and strong language another war is in the making." The message was clear: Unyielding resistance to the Soviet Union was the only way to avoid another world war.

iron curtain
A term coined by Winston Churchill in a 1946 speech to describe the ideological and political divide between the communist Soviet Union and the non-communist Western world.

Not all Americans agreed with this view. Led by Roosevelt's former vice president Henry Wallace, who served as Truman's secretary of commerce, critics voiced

MAP 8.1 The Cold War in Europe, 1945–1955 In 1946, the four major victorious wartime allies divided Germany and Berlin into distinct sectors, leading to increasing tension. Between 1949 and 1955, the descent of what Winston Churchill called the "iron curtain" that divided Europe into rival security pacts headed by the United States and the Soviet Union hardened postwar arrangements into the Cold War.

What short-term effects of World War II does this map reveal?

concern about taking a "hard line" against the Soviet Union. Stalin was pursuing a policy of expansion, they agreed, but for limited reasons. Wallace claimed that the Soviets merely wanted to protect their borders by surrounding themselves with friendly countries, just as the United States had done by establishing spheres of influence in the Caribbean.

Except for Poland and Romania, Stalin had at first accepted an array of governments in Eastern Europe, allowing free elections in Czechoslovakia, Hungary, and, to a lesser extent, Bulgaria. Only as Cold War tensions escalated did the Soviets tighten control over all of Eastern Europe. Critics such as Wallace considered this outcome the result of a self-fulfilling prophecy. By misinterpreting Soviet motives, the Truman administration pushed Stalin to counter the American hard line with a hard line of his own.

Thus, after World War II, the United States came to believe that the Soviet Union desired world revolution to spread communism, a doctrine hostile to free-market individualism. At the same time, the Soviet Union viewed the United States as seeking to make the world safe for capitalism, thereby reducing Soviet chances to obtain economic resources and rebuild its war-shattered economy. Each country tended to see the other's actions in the most negative light and to view global developments as a zero-sum game, one in which every victory for one side was a defeat for the other.

- How and why did the United States and Soviet Union interpret relations with each other before 1947 in dramatically different ways?

The Truman Doctrine, the Marshall Plan, and Economic Containment

By 1947, U.S.-Soviet relations had reached a new low. International arms control had proved futile, the United States had gone to the United Nations to pressure the Soviets to withdraw from Iran, and the rhetoric from both sides had become warlike. From the American vantage point, Soviet actions to expand communism in Eastern Europe appeared to threaten democracies in Western Europe. By contrast, the Soviets viewed the United States as seeking to extend economic control over nations close to their borders and to weaken communism in the Soviet Union.

Events in Greece allowed Truman to take the offensive and apply Kennan's policy of containment. To maintain access to the Middle East and its Asian colonies, the United Kingdom considered it vitally important to keep Greece within its sphere of influence. In 1946, a civil war broke out in Greece between the right-wing monarchy and a coalition of insurgents consisting of members of the wartime anti-Nazi resistance, communists, and non-communist opponents of the repressive government. Exhausted by the war and in desperate financial shape, the British turned to the United States for help.

The Truman administration believed that the presence of communists among the Greek rebels meant that Moscow was behind the insurgency. In fact, Stalin was not aiding the revolutionaries. Assistance came from the communist leader of Yugoslavia, Josip Broz (known as Marshall Tito), who acted independently of the Soviets and would soon break with them. Following Kennan's lead in advocating containment, Truman incorrectly believed that all communists around the world were controlled by the Kremlin.

While Truman was convinced that the United States had to intervene in Greece to contain the spread of communism, he still had to convince the Republican-controlled

Congress and the American people to go along. To overcome potential opposition to its plans, the Truman administration exaggerated the danger of communist influence in Greece. Truman sent Undersecretary of State Dean Acheson to testify before a congressional committee that "like apples in a barrel infected by one rotten one, the corruption of Greece would infect Iran and all to the east."

The administration's presentation of the issues to the American public was even more dramatic. On March 12, 1947, Truman gave a speech to a joint session of Congress that was broadcast over national radio to millions of listeners. He interpreted the civil war in Greece as a titanic struggle between freedom and **totalitarianism** that threatened the free world. "I believe," the president declared, "that it must be the policy of the United States to support free peoples who are resisting attempted subjugation by armed minorities or by outside pressures." Truman's rhetoric stretched the truth on many counts—the armed minorities to which the president referred had fought Nazi totalitarianism; the Soviets did not supply the insurgents; and the right-wing monarchy, propped up by the military, was hardly democratic. Nevertheless, Truman achieved his goal of frightening both lawmakers and the public, and Congress appropriated $400 million in military aid to fortify the existing governments of Greece and neighboring Turkey.

totalitarianism
A form of government in which all aspects of political, economic, social, and cultural life are controlled by the state, typically in the hands of a single political party. During the Cold War, the United States often described its communist rivals as inflicting a totalitarian system on the countries where they held power.

The **Truman Doctrine**, which pledged to protect democratic countries and contain the expansion of communism, was the cornerstone of American foreign policy throughout the Cold War. The United States committed itself to shoring up governments, whether democratic or dictatorial, as long as they were avowedly anticommunist. Americans believed that the rest of the world's nations wanted to be like the United States and therefore would not willingly accept communism, which they thought could be imposed only from the outside by the Soviet Union and never reasonably chosen from within.

Truman Doctrine
The U.S. pledge during the Truman administration to provide political, military, and economic aid to all democratic countries under threat of communism from internal or external sources. Truman issued the doctrine in response to perceived communist threats to Greece and Turkey.

Although Truman misread Soviet intentions with respect to Greece, Stalin's regime had given him cause for worry. Soviet actions that imposed communism in Poland, along with the U.S.S.R.'s refusal to withdraw troops from the Baltic states of Latvia, Lithuania, and Estonia, reinforced the president's concerns about Soviet expansionism and convinced many in the U.S. government that Stalin had no intention of abiding by his wartime agreements. Difficulties in negotiating with the Soviets about international control of atomic energy further worried U.S. foreign-policy makers about Russian designs for obtaining the atomic bomb.

George Kennan's version of containment called for economic and political aid to check communist expansion. In this context, to prevent communist inroads and offer humanitarian assistance to Europeans facing homelessness and starvation, the Truman administration offered economic assistance to the war-torn continent. In doing so, the United States also hoped to guarantee increased trade with Europe.

In a June 1947 speech that drew heavily on Kennan's ideas, Secretary of State George Marshall sketched out a plan to provide financial assistance to Europe. Although he invited any country, including the Soviet Union, that experienced "hunger, poverty, desperation, and chaos" to apply for aid, Marshall did not expect Stalin to ask for assistance. To do so would require the Soviets to supply information to the United States concerning the internal operations of their economy and to admit to the failure of communism.

Following Marshall's speech, Truman asked Congress in December 1947 to authorize $17 billion for European recovery. With conservative-minded Republicans still in control of Congress, the president's spending request faced steep opposition. The Soviet Union inadvertently came to Truman's political rescue. Stalin interpreted the proposed **Marshall Plan** of economic assistance as a hostile attempt by the United States to gain influence in Eastern Europe. To prevent this possibility, in late February 1948, the Soviets extinguished the remaining democracy in Eastern Europe by engineering a communist coup in Czechoslovakia. Congressional lawmakers viewed this action as further proof of Soviet aggression. In April 1948, they approved the Marshall Plan, providing $13 billion in economic assistance to sixteen European countries over the next five years.

Marshall Plan
A package of economic aid developed by U.S. Secretary of State George Marshall. The plan helped to rebuild Western Europe physically and economically, buffering it from communist influence and serving U.S. political and economic interests in the process.

REVIEW

- How did the Truman Doctrine and the Marshall Plan each support the policy of containment?

Military Containment

AP® EXAM TIP

Collective security and containment can be considered simultaneously. Think about two examples of containment through collective security and show change over time in your explanation.

The New Deal and World War II had increased the power of the president and his ability to manage economic and military crises. The Cold War further strengthened the presidency and shifted the balance of governmental power to the executive branch, creating what has been called the imperial presidency.

As the Cold War intensified, Congress granted the president enormous authority over foreign affairs and internal security. The National Security Act, passed in 1947, created the Department of Defense as a cabinet agency (replacing the Department of War), consolidated control of the various military services under its authority, and established the Joint Chiefs of Staff, composed of the heads of the army, navy, air force, and marines. To advise the president on military and foreign affairs, the act set up the **National Security Council (NSC)**, a group presided over by the national security adviser and consisting of the secretaries of state, defense, the army, the navy, and the air force as well as any others the president might appoint.

In addition to this panel, the National Security Act established the **Central Intelligence Agency (CIA)** as part of the executive branch. The CIA was given the responsibility of coordinating intelligence gathering and conducting espionage abroad to counter Soviet spying operations. Another new intelligence agency, the National Security Agency, created in 1949, monitored overseas communications through the latest technological devices. Together, these agencies enhanced the president's ability to conduct foreign affairs with little congressional oversight and out of public view.

By 1948, the Truman administration had decided that an economically healthy Germany, with its great industrial potential, provided the key to a prosperous Europe and consequently a depression-proof United States. Rebuilding postwar Germany would also fortify the eastern boundary of Europe against Soviet expansion. In mid-1948, the United States, the United Kingdom, and France consolidated their occupation zones, created the Federal Republic of Germany (West Germany), and initiated economic reforms to stimulate a speedy recovery.

The Soviet Union saw a strong Germany as a threat to its national security and responded by closing the access roads from the border of West Germany to Berlin, located in the Soviet zone of East Germany, which effectively cut off the city from the West. The Soviet blockade of West Berlin turned the Cold War even colder.

Berlin Airlift

The large-scale transport of food and supplies to West Berlin by the U.S. and British governments during the Soviet blockade of Berlin from 1948 to 1949. The Berlin Airlift was responsible for breaking the Soviet blockade of West Berlin.

Without food, fuel, and other provisions from the United States and its allies in West Germany, West Berliners could not survive. In an effort to break the blockade, Truman ordered a major airlift, during which U.S. and British planes transported more than 2.5 million tons of supplies to West Berlin. After nearly a year of these flights, the **Berlin Airlift** ended in the spring of 1949 when the Russians lifted the blockade.

Meanwhile, Truman won election in November 1948 for a second term. He drew opposition from critics on his left and right for his handling of the Cold War, challenging both his aggressiveness toward the Soviets and his increased spending for containment.

Walter Sanders/The LIFE Picture Collection/Getty Images

The Berlin Airlift This group of West Berliners anxiously waits as an American C-47 cargo plane prepares to land at Tempelhof Airfield to deliver food in July 1948. The Soviets had blockaded ground transportation to the Allied sector of West Berlin, prompting President Truman to airlift supplies. At the height of the Berlin Airlift, planes landed every 45 seconds, bringing desperately needed supplies for the two and a half million residents of West Berlin.

What does the scene in the photograph reveal about the conditions in West Berlin in 1948?

Nevertheless, most Americans stood behind his anticommunist foreign policy as the Cold War continued.

The two superpowers sustained the conflict when each fashioned military alliances to keep the other at bay. In April 1949, prompted in part by the Berlin crisis, the United States joined eleven European countries in the **North Atlantic Treaty Organization (NATO)**. A peacetime military alliance, NATO established a collective security pact in which an attack on one member was viewed as an attack on all (Map 8.1). In 1949, the Russians followed suit by organizing the Council for Mutual Economic Assistance to help their "satellite" nations rebuild and, six years later, by creating the **Warsaw Pact** military alliance, the respective counterparts in Eastern Europe to the Marshall Plan and NATO.

Amid the growing militarization of the Cold War, the United States and its allies received two new shocks in 1949. First, the Soviets successfully tested an atomic bomb in September. Second, communist forces within China led by Mao Zedong and Zhou Enlai succeeded in overthrowing the U.S.-backed nationalist government of Jiang Jieshi (Chiang Kai-shek) and creating the People's Republic of China. These two events convinced many in the United States that the threat posed by communism was escalating rapidly.

In response, the National Security Council met to reevaluate U.S. strategy in fighting the Cold War. In April 1950, the NSC recommended to Truman that the United States intensify its containment policy both abroad and at home. The document it handed

North Atlantic Treaty Organization (NATO)
A Cold War military alliance and security pact intended to enhance the collective security of the United States and Western Europe. Originally consisting of twelve nations in 1949, as of 2023, thirty-one NATO member nations operate under the principle of "an attack against one member is considered as an attack against all."

Warsaw Pact
A military alliance of the Soviet Union with its seven satellite nations in response to the U.S. Marshall Plan and establishment of NATO. The pact, formed in 1955, was dissolved in 1991 at the end of the Cold War.

NSC-68

A document issued by the National Security Council in 1950 that advocated intensification of the policy of containment both at home and abroad and a massive buildup of the U.S. military. NSC-68 defined U.S. nuclear policy, peacetime military spending, and a policy of anti-Soviet propaganda overseas and vigilance against the communist threat at home.

over to the president, entitled **NSC-68**, spelled out the need for action in ominous language. "The Soviet Union, unlike previous aspirants to hegemony," NSC-68 warned, "is animated by a new fanatic faith, antithetical to our own, and seeks to impose its absolute authority over the rest of the world. It is in this context that this Republic and its citizens . . . stand in their deepest peril." NSC-68 proposed that the United States develop an even more powerful nuclear weapon, the hydrogen bomb; increase military spending; and continue to negotiate NATO-style alliances around the globe. Departing from the original guidelines for the CIA, the president's advisers proposed that the United States engage in "covert means" to stir up support for "unrest and revolt in selected strategic [Soviet] satellite countries." At home, they added, the government should prepare Americans for the communist danger by enhancing internal security and civil defense programs.

Truman agreed with many of the principles behind NSC-68 but worried about the cost of funding it. The problem remained a political one. Though the Democrats once again controlled both houses of Congress, there was little sentiment to raise taxes and slash the economic programs established during the New Deal. However, circumstances abruptly changed when, in June 1950, shortly after the president received the NSC report, communist North Korea invaded U.S.-backed South Korea. In response to this attack, Truman took the opportunity to put into practice key recommendations of NSC-68.

REVIEW

- How did passage of the National Security Act of 1947 and NSC-68 change American foreign policy?

The Korean War

Korea emerged from World War II divided between U.S. and Soviet spheres of influence. North of the 38th parallel, the communist leader Kim Il Sung ruled North Korea with support from the Soviet Union. South of that latitude, the anticommunist leader Syngman Rhee governed South Korea. The United States supported Rhee, but in January 1950, Secretary of State Dean Acheson commented that he did not regard South Korea as part of the vital Asian "defense perimeter" protected by the United States against communist aggression. Truman had already removed remaining American troops from the country the previous year. On June 25, 1950, an emboldened Kim Il Sung sent military forces to invade South Korea, seeking to unite the country under his leadership.

Korean War

A three-year conflict (1950–1953) that began when communist North Korea, supported by the U.S.S.R. and China, launched an invasion of anticommunist South Korea, supported by the United States and the United Nations. Despite enormous destruction, large loss of civilian lives, and involvement of both U.S. and Chinese troops, fighting stopped with a cease-fire rather than a peace treaty at a similar border between the two countries.

Following the invasion, the **Korean War** took on new importance to American policymakers. If South Korea fell, the president believed, communist leaders would be "emboldened to override nations closer to our own shores." Therefore, the Truman Doctrine was now applied to Asia as it had previously been applied to Europe. This time, however, American financial aid would not be enough. It would take the U.S. military to contain the communist threat.

Truman did not seek a declaration of war from Congress. Instead, he chose a multinational course of action. Because the Soviet Union was boycotting the United Nations over its refusal to admit the communist People's Republic of China, the United States obtained authorization from the UN Security Council on June 27, 1950, to send a peacekeeping force to Korea. Fifteen other countries joined UN forces, but the

United States supplied the bulk of the troops, as well as their commanding officer, General Douglas MacArthur. In reality, MacArthur reported to the president, not the United Nations.

Before MacArthur could mobilize his forces, the North Koreans had penetrated most of South Korea, except for the port of Pusan on the southeast coast of the peninsula. In a daring counterattack, on September 15, 1950, MacArthur dispatched land and sea forces to capture Inchon on the opposite coast, just west of Seoul, the capital, which cut off North Korean supply lines. Joined by UN forces pushing out of Pusan, MacArthur's troops chased the enemy northward back over the 38th parallel.

Now Truman had to make a key decision. MacArthur wanted to invade North Korea, defeat the communists, and unify the country. Instead of sticking to his original goal of containing communist aggression against South Korea, Truman succumbed to the lure of liberating all of Korea from the communists. MacArthur received permission to proceed, and on October 9, his forces crossed into North Korea. Within three weeks, UN troops marched through the country until they reached the Yalu River, which borders China. With the U.S. military massed along their southern perimeter, the Chinese warned that they would send troops to repel the invaders if the Americans crossed the Yalu. Both General MacArthur and Secretary of State Acheson, guided by CIA intelligence, discounted this threat. The intelligence, however, was faulty.

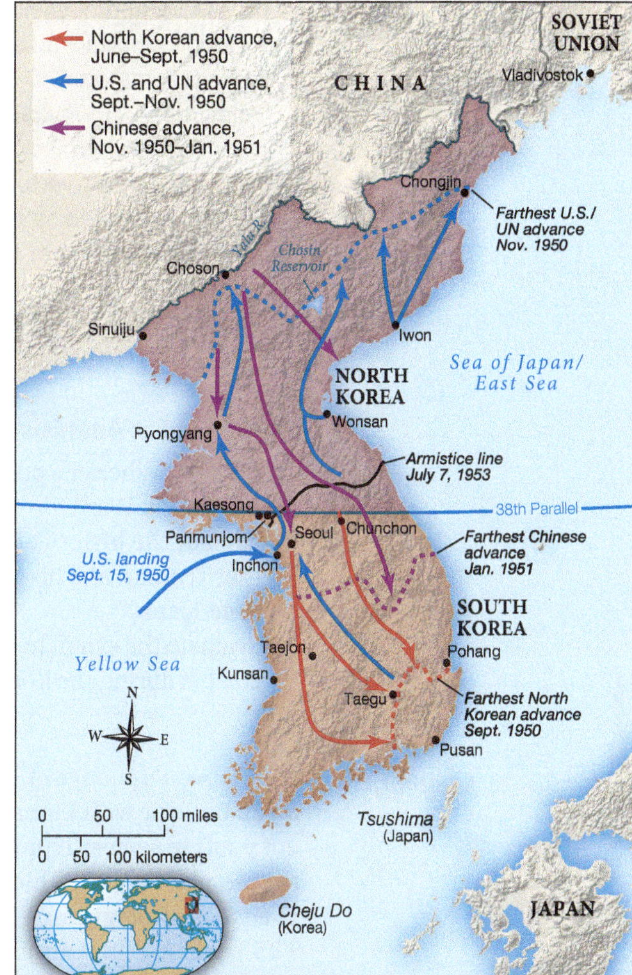

MAP 8.2 The Korean War, 1950–1953 Considered a "police action" by the United Nations, the Korean War cost the lives of nearly 37,000 U.S. troops. Approximately two million to four million Koreans were killed, wounded, or went missing. Each side pushed deep into enemy territory, but neither could achieve victory. When hostilities ceased in 1953, a demilitarized zone near the original boundary line separated North and South Korea.

What do the dotted lines and the final armistice line on this map reveal about the successes and failures of each side in the Korean War?

Truman approved MacArthur's plan to cross the Yalu, and on November 27, 1950, China sent more than 300,000 troops south into North Korea. Within two months, communist troops regained control of North Korea, allowing them once again to invade South Korea. On January 4, 1951, Seoul fell to Chinese and North Korean troops.

By the spring of 1951, the war had degenerated into a stalemate. UN forces succeeded in recapturing Seoul and repelling the communists north of the 38th parallel. This time, with the American public eager to end the war and with the presence of the Chinese promising an endless, bloody predicament, the president sought to replace combat with diplomacy. The American objective would be containment, not Korean unification.

AP® WORKING with EVIDENCE

Source: John N. Wheeler, Letter Home from the Korean War, 1950

"Can't say as I blame you, Dad, for your opinions of Mr. Truman and his administration. However, you must remember that his opinions as well as his actions represent the vast majority of the 'Soft-bellied Americans' who, for the life of them, couldn't see giving up a few of the needless luxuries of life to support a military machine big enough to protect the peace and liberty that they take for granted. Only those who have visited foreign countries can realize what they mean. It would be a good lesson to the Americans if they had to fight a war on their own soil, and had to lie for a short time under the sadistic rule of this band of perverted sadists who call themselves communists. They claim that they want to help the 'worker'—all they want to do is to help themselves. Mass murder, rape, torture, and starvation is the rule and not the exception with them. They have proved it here as well as everywhere else. I could see nothing more fitting for a young man to do then [*sic*] to devote his entire life to killing everyone of them."

Questions for Analysis

1. Describe Wheeler's point of view toward those critical of American involvement in the Korean War.
2. Explain the historical developments that provide context for Wheeler's assertion that Truman and his administration were part of the "vast majority of 'Soft-bellied Americans.'"
3. Evaluate the extent to which Wheeler's perspective is influenced by his experience in combat during the Korean War.

Truman's change of heart infuriated General MacArthur, who was willing to risk an all-out war with China and to use nuclear weapons to win. After MacArthur spoke out publicly against Truman's policy by remarking, "There is no substitute for victory," the president removed him from command on April 11, 1951. However, even with the change in strategy and leadership, the war dragged on for two more years, until July 1953, when a final armistice agreement was reached. By that time, the Korean War had cost the United States close to 37,000 lives and $54 billion.

The Korean War boosted the imperial presidency by allowing the president to bypass Congress and the Constitution to initiate wars in the name of "police actions." The war permitted Truman to expand his powers as commander in chief and augmented the strength of the national security state over which he presided. As a result of the Korean conflict, the military draft became a regular feature of American life for young men over the next two decades. The expanded peacetime military was active around the globe, operating bases in Europe, Asia, and the Middle East. During the war, the military budget rose from $13.5 billion to $50 billion, strengthening the connection between economic growth and permanent mobilization to fight the Cold War.

The Korean War also permitted President Truman to reshape foreign policy along the lines sketched in NSC-68, including the extension of U.S. influence in Southeast Asia. Consequently, he authorized economic aid to support the French against communist revolutionaries in Vietnam.

Yet the power of the imperial presidency did not go unchecked. Congress deferred to Truman on key issues of military policy, but on one important occasion, the Supreme Court stepped in to restrain him. The central issue grew out of a labor dispute in the steel industry. In 1952, the United Steel Workers of America threatened to go on strike for higher wages, which would have had a serious impact on war production as well as the economy in general. On May 2, after the steel companies refused the union's demands, Truman announced the government seizure and operation of the steel mills to keep them running. He argued that as president, he had the "inherent right" to take over the steel plants.

The steel companies objected and brought the matter before the Supreme Court. On June 2, 1952, the Court ruled against Truman. It held that the president did not have the intrinsic authority to seize private property, even during wartime. For the time being, the Supreme Court affirmed some limitations on the unbridled use of presidential power even during periods of war.

- How did the Korean War fit within the broader context of America's Cold War strategy?
- How did the Korean War expand the powers of the presidency?

The Cold War Thaws

After the Korean War, tensions between the United States and the Soviet Union rose and fell for the next twenty-five years. During President Eisenhower's administration (1953–1961), the United States accepted the stalemate on the Korean Peninsula, but expanded its nuclear arsenal to include intercontinental ballistic missiles. U.S. intervention in Latin America and the Middle East (Module 8.7), as well as in Vietnam (Module 8.8), also expanded.

President Kennedy's administration (1961–1963) built upon Eisenhower's Cold War policies and further involved the United States in anticommunist efforts in Latin America and Southeast Asia (Modules 8.7 and 8.8), which President Johnson (1963–1969) furthered into a protracted conflict in Vietnam (Module 8.8).

During President Richard M. Nixon's administration (1969–1974), though, a policy of **détente** eased Cold War tensions by supporting communist China's admission and entry to the United Nations. Nixon likewise negotiated a nuclear arms treaty with the Soviet Union. This cautious renewal of relations with China opened up possibilities of mutually beneficial trade between the two countries.

The closer relations between China and the United States worried the U.S.S.R. Although both were communist nations, the Soviet Union and China had pursued their own ideological and national interests. To check growing Chinese influence with the United States, Soviet premier Leonid Brezhnev invited President Nixon to Moscow in May 1972, the first time an American president had visited the Soviet Union since the end of World War II. The main topic of discussion concerned arms control, and with the Soviet Union eager to make a deal in the aftermath of Nixon's trip to China, the two sides worked out the historic **Strategic Arms Limitation Treaty (SALT I)**, the first treaty to curtail nuclear arms production during the Cold War. The pact froze the number of intercontinental ballistic missiles and submarine-based missiles for five years and restricted the number of antiballistic missiles that each nation could deploy.

AP® EXAM TIP

The military conflicts in Korea and Vietnam are specifically mentioned in the course framework. Be able to explain how these conflicts were bolstered by the concept of containment and the issues associated with fighting a limited war on the home front.

détente

The easing of tensions during the mid-1970s between the Soviet Union and China and the United States. Détente resulted in the first arms-limitation treaty between the Soviet Union and the United States in 1972.

Strategic Arms Limitation Treaty (SALT I)

An agreement between the United States and Soviet Union in 1972 to curtail nuclear arms production. The pact froze for five years the number of antiballistic missiles (ABMs), intercontinental ballistic missiles (ICBMs), and submarine-based missiles that each nation could deploy.

AP® Skills Workshop: Writing Historically

Additional Practice in Responding to a Short-Answer Question with Secondary Sources

"The leaders who succeeded [Franklin] Roosevelt understood neither the dilemma nor the need to alter their outlook. A handful of them thought briefly of stabilizing relations with the Soviet Union on the basis of economic and political agreements, but even that tiny minority saw the future in terms of continued [free trade]. The great majority rapidly embarked upon a program to force the Soviet Union to accept America's traditional conception of itself and the world. This decision represented the final stage in the transformation of the policy of the open door from a utopian idea into an ideology, from an intellectual outlook for changing the world into one concerned with preserving it in the traditional mold.

American leaders had internalized, and had come to *believe*, the theory and the morality of open-door expansion. Hence they seldom thought it necessary to explain or defend the approach. Instead, they *assumed* the premises and concerned themselves with exercising their apparent freedom to deal with the necessities defined by such an outlook. As far as American leaders were concerned, the philosophy and practice of open-door expansion had become, in both its missionary and economic aspects, *the* view of the world. Those who did not recognize and accept that fact were not only wrong, but they were incapable of thinking correctly."

William Appleman Williams,
The Tragedy of American Diplomacy, 1959

"Moscow's position would not have seemed so alarming to American officials . . . had it not been for the Soviet Union's continued commitment to an ideology dedicated to the overthrow of capitalism throughout the world. Hopes that the United States might cooperate successfully with the USSR after the war had been based on the belief, encouraged by Stalin himself, that the Kremlin had given up its former goal of exporting Communism. . . . It seems likely that Washington policy makers mistook Stalin's determination to ensure Russian security through spheres of influence for a renewed effort to spread communism outside the borders of the Soviet Union . . . But [Stalin] failed to make the limited nature of his objectives clear.

Revisionists are correct in emphasizing the importance of internal constraints, but they have defined them too narrowly: by focusing so heavily on economics, they neglect the profound impact of the domestic political system on the conduct of American foreign policy. . . . The delay in opening the second front, nonrecognition of Moscow's sphere of influence in Eastern Europe, and the decision to retain control of the atomic bomb can all be explained far more plausibly by citing the Administration's need to maintain popular support for its policies rather than by dwelling upon requirement of the economic order. . . . Stalin's paranoia, together with the bureaucracy of institutionalized suspicion with which he surrounded himself, made the situation much worse."

John Lewis Gaddis, *The United States and the Origins of the Cold War*, 1972

(continued)

Using the excerpts, answer **A**, **B**, and **C**.

(A) Briefly explain ONE major difference between Williams's and Gaddis's interpretations of the origins of the Cold War.

(B) Briefly explain how ONE specific historical event or development from the period that is not explicitly mentioned in the excerpts could be used to support Williams's argument.

(C) Briefly explain how ONE specific historical event or development from the period that is not explicitly mentioned in the excerpts could be used to support Gaddis's argument.

MODULE 8.3

The Red Scare

FOCUS

As you read this module, consider how events in Europe and Asia as well as revelations of spying in the United States led to creation of a climate of fear resulting in the Second Red Scare. Ask yourself how the actions of Congress and the Truman administration contributed to those fears, and examine the impact of those actions on American society.

AP® EXAM TIP

Be able to explain how the Red Scare was not a strictly partisan issue. Use at least one historical example to explain how both Republicans and Democrats actively sought to expose communism as a threat to the United States.

The Korean War heightened fear of the threat of communist infiltration in American society. In one striking example, the presiding judge in an espionage trial for two American citizens, Julius and Ethel Rosenberg, sentenced them to death in 1951 because he believed their actions "caused . . . the Communist aggression in Korea, with the resultant casualties exceeding 50,000."

For most of Truman's second administration, fear of communist subversion within the United States consumed domestic politics. Increasing evidence of Soviet espionage fueled this anticommunist obsession. Yet in an atmosphere of fear, lawmakers and judges blurred the distinction between actual Soviet spies and political radicals who were merely attracted to communist beliefs. In the process, these officials sometimes trampled on individual constitutional freedoms.

House Un-American Activities Committee (HUAC)

A committee in the U.S. House of Representatives established in 1938 to investigate and combat domestic communism. After World War II, HUAC conducted highly publicized investigations of communist influence in government and the entertainment industry.

Second Red Scare

Mass fears of communist influence infiltrating the United States and threatening national security from the late 1930s through the 1950s. Such fears resulted in the creation of government-controlled programs and entities such as the House Un-American Activities Committee and the Federal Employee Loyalty Program.

Loyalty and the Second Red Scare

The postwar fear of communism echoed earlier anticommunist sentiments. The government had initiated the Palmer raids during the First Red Scare following World War I, which led to the deportation of hundreds of immigrants suspected of holding communist, socialist, or anarchist views (see Module 7.6).

In 1938, conservative congressional opponents of the New Deal established the **House Un-American Activities Committee (HUAC)** to investigate domestic communism, which they tied to the Roosevelt administration. Much of anticommunism, however, was bipartisan. In 1940, Roosevelt signed into law the **Smith Act**, which prohibited teaching or advocating the "duty, necessity, desirability, or propriety of overthrowing or destroying any government in the United States by force or violence" or belonging to any group with that aim. At the same time, President Roosevelt secretly authorized the FBI to monitor and wiretap individuals suspected of violating the act.

The Cold War produced the **Second Red Scare**. Unlike the First Red Scare following World War I, which was based on a general fear of foreign radicalism, including communism, the Second Red Scare was directly caused by a fear that communist influence was infiltrating the United States and threatening national security.

Just two weeks after his speech announcing the Truman Doctrine in March 1947, the president signed an executive order creating the **Federal Employee Loyalty Program**. Under this program, a board investigated the approximately two and a half million federal employees to see if "reasonable grounds [existed] to suspect disloyalty." Soviet espionage was, in fact, a cause for legitimate concern. Spies operated in both Canada and the United States during and after World War II, and they had infiltrated the Manhattan Project.

Federal Employee Loyalty Program

A program established by President Truman in 1947, via executive order, to investigate federal employees suspected of disloyalty, communist ties, suspicious personal behaviors, and homosexuality. Hundreds of employees were terminated from their positions as a result of the investigations.

The loyalty board, however, did not focus on espionage. Rather, it concentrated its attention on individuals who espoused dissenting views on a variety of issues. It failed to uncover a single verifiable case of espionage or find any communists in public service. Yet the board dismissed hundreds of government employees for their political beliefs and personal behavior. Some employees were fired because they were homosexuals and considered susceptible to blackmail by foreign agents. (Heterosexual men and women who were having extramarital affairs were not treated in the same manner.)

The accused seldom faced their accusers and at times did not learn the nature of the charges against them. As loyalty boards spread to state and municipal governments, labor unions, and the private sector, Americans from all walks of life were questioned, required to sign loyalty oaths, and sometimes fired for suspected disloyalty.

Congress also investigated communism in the private sector, especially in industries that shaped public opinion. In 1947, HUAC broadened the anti-Red probe from Washington to Hollywood. Convinced that the film industry had come under communist influence and threatened to poison the minds of millions of moviegoers, HUAC conducted hearings that attracted much publicity. HUAC cited for contempt ten witnesses, among them directors and screenwriters, for refusing to answer questions about their political beliefs and associations. These and subsequent hearings assumed the form of a ritual. The committee already had information from the FBI about the witnesses. HUAC really wanted the accused to confess their communist sympathy publicly and to show remorse by naming their associates. Those who did not comply were considered "unfriendly" witnesses and were put on an industry blacklist that deprived them of employment.

HUAC grabbed even bigger headlines in 1948. With Republicans in charge of the committee, they launched a probe of Alger Hiss, a former State Department official in the Roosevelt administration who had accompanied the president to the Yalta Conference. The hearings resulted from charges brought by former Soviet spy Whittaker Chambers that Hiss had passed him classified documents. Hiss denied the allegations, and President Truman dismissed them as a distraction. In fact, Democrats viewed the charges as a politically motivated attempt by Republicans to characterize the Roosevelt and Truman administrations as having been riddled with communists.

Following Truman's victory in the 1948 presidential election, first-term Republican congressman Richard M. Nixon kept the Hiss affair alive. A member of HUAC, Nixon went to Chambers's farm and discovered a cache of State Department documents that Chambers had stored for safekeeping. Armed with this evidence, Nixon reopened the case. Although the statute of limitations for espionage from the 1930s had expired, the federal government had enough evidence to prosecute Hiss for perjury — lying under oath about passing documents to Chambers. One trial produced a hung jury, but a second convicted Hiss, who was sentenced to five years in prison.

AP® EXAM TIP

The Course and Exam Description calls for you to understand how Americans debated the methods used during the Second Red Scare. Choose one historical example from the textbook and explain the debates Americans had about the best means to combat communism on the home front.

Hiss's downfall tarnished the Democrats, as Republicans charged them with being "soft on communism." It did not matter that Truman was a cold warrior who had advanced the doctrine of containment to stop Soviet expansionism or that he had instituted the federal loyalty program to remove any communists from government. In fact, Truman tried to demonstrate his cold warrior credentials in 1949 by authorizing the Justice Department to prosecute twelve high-ranking officials of the Communist Party for violating the Smith Act. In the 1951 decision in ***Dennis v. United States***, the Supreme Court upheld the conviction of the communist leaders on the grounds that they posed a "clear and present danger" to the United States by advocating the violent overthrow of the government. Despite lacking evidence of an immediate danger of a communist uprising, the justices decided that "the gravity of the [communist] evil" was enough to warrant conviction.

WORKING with EVIDENCE

Source: Paul Robeson, Statement on the Un-American Activities Committee, 1949

"Quite clearly America faces a crisis in race relations. The Un-American Activities Committee moves now to transform the Government's cold war policy against the Negro people into a hot war. Its action incites the Ku Klux Klan, that openly terrorist organization, to [a] reign of mob violence against my people in Florida and elsewhere. This Committee attempts to divide the Negro people from one another in order to prevent us from winning jobs, security and justice under the banner of peace.

The loyalty of the Negro people is not a subject for debate. I challenge the loyalty of the Un-American Activities Committee. This committee maintains an ominous silence in the face of the lynchings . . . and the violence and unpunished murders of scores of Negro veterans by white supremacists since V-J Day. . . . Every pro-war fascist-minded group in the country regards the Committee's silence as license to proceed against my people, unchecked by Government authorities and unchallenged by the courts.

Our fight for peace in America is a fight for human dignity, and an end to ghetto life. It is the fight for constitutional liberties, the civil and human rights of every American. This struggle is the decisive struggle with which my people are today concerned. This fight is of vital concern to all progressive Americans, white as well as Negro. . . .

It is not the Soviet Union that threatens the life, liberty and the property and citizenship rights of Negro Americans. The threat comes from within. To destroy this threat our people need the aid of every honest American, Communist and non-Communist alike. Those who menace our lives proceed unchallenged by the Un-American Activities Committee."

Questions for Analysis

1. Identify the real threats to Black Americans, according to Robeson.
2. Describe Robeson's point of view toward the House Un-American Activities Committee.
3. Explain why Robeson does not view communism as a threat to Black Americans.

When the Soviets successfully tested an atomic bomb in 1949, many believed that they must have received assistance from communist spies, and anyone accused of helping them obtain this weapon fell under suspicion. The following year, the Truman administration prosecuted Julius and Ethel Rosenberg in a sensational court case for passing atomic secrets to the Soviets. Unlike the *Dennis* case, which involved political beliefs, the Rosenbergs were charged with espionage. The outbreak of the Korean War, within weeks of their arrests, heightened fears of communism throughout the country. After a lengthy trial in 1951, the Rosenbergs were convicted and received the death penalty. Julius and Ethel Rosenberg became the first spies executed in American history during peacetime.

By 1950, the anticommunist crusade included Democrats and Republicans, liberals and conservatives. Liberals had the most to lose because conservatives could easily brand them as ideologically tainted. In his successful campaign to become a U.S. senator from California in 1950, Richard Nixon had accused his opponent, the liberal Democrat Helen Gahagan Douglas, of being "pink down to her underwear," not quite a Red but close enough.

Liberal civil rights and civil liberties groups as well as labor unions were particularly vulnerable to such charges and rushed to rid their organizations of suspected communists. Such efforts did nothing, however, to slow down conservative attacks.

In 1950, Republicans supported legislation proposed by Senator Pat McCarran, a conservative Democrat from Nevada, which required communist organizations to register with the federal government, established detention camps to incarcerate radicals during national emergencies, and denied passports to U.S. citizens suspected of communist affiliations. The severity of the **McCarran Internal Security Act** proved too much for President Truman, and he vetoed it. Reflecting the bipartisan consensus on the issue, the Democratic-controlled Congress overrode the veto.

- How did President Truman and Congress respond to the fears of communist influence in American society?

McCarthyism

Joseph McCarthy, the junior Republican senator from Wisconsin, did not create the phenomenon of postwar anticommunism, which was already in full swing from 1947 to 1950, but he served as its most public and feared voice from 1950 until 1954. Although McCarthy bullied people, exaggerated his military service, drank too much, and did not pull his punches in making speeches, his anticommunist tirades fit into mainstream Cold War politics for a time.

Aware of the drawing power of the issue of communists in government, and with the support of many fellow Republicans such as Ohio senator Robert A. Taft, McCarthy gave a speech in February 1950 in Wheeling, West Virginia. Waving sheets of paper in his hand, the senator announced that he had "the names of 205 men known to the Secretary of State as being members of the

Communist Party and who nevertheless are still working and shaping the policy of the State Department." As he campaigned for Republican congressional candidates across the country, he kept changing the number of alleged communists in the government. When Senator Millard Tydings of Maryland, a Democrat who headed the Senate Foreign Relations Committee, launched an investigation of McCarthy's charges, he concluded that the allegations were irresponsible and unfounded.

This finding did not stop McCarthy. If anything, it emboldened him to go further. He accused Tydings of being "soft on communism" and campaigned against his reelection in 1952. Tydings's defeat in the election scared off many critics from openly confronting McCarthy. McCarthy won reelection to the Senate the same year and became chair of the Permanent Investigations Subcommittee on Government Operations. Senator McCarthy used his position to harass current and former government officials and employees who, he claimed, collaborated with the communist conspiracy. Not only did he make false accusations and smear witnesses with anticommunist allegations, but he also dispatched two aides to travel to Europe and purge what they considered disreputable books from the shelves of overseas libraries sponsored by the State Department.

McCarthyism

A term used to describe the harassment and persecution of suspected communists and other political radicals during the Cold War. Named after Senator Joseph McCarthy, a prominent government figure who helped incite anticommunist panic in the early 1950s.

McCarthy stood out among anticommunists not for his beliefs but for his tactics. **McCarthyism** became synonymous with anticommunism as well as with manipulating the truth. McCarthy publicly hurled charges so astounding, especially coming from a U.S. senator, that people thought there must be something to them. By the time the accusations could be discredited, the damage was already done. The senator bullied and badgered witnesses, called them names, and if necessary furnished phony documents and doctored photographs linking them to known communists.

AP® EXAM TIP

When making a sound historical argument, it is necessary to categorize and weigh your argument. Think of at least three historical categories that could be used to explain the causes of the Red Scare and then weigh the relative importance of each.

In 1954, McCarthy finally went too far. After one of his aides was drafted and the army refused to give him a special commission, McCarthy accused the army of harboring communists. To sort out these charges and to see whether the army had acted appropriately, McCarthy's own Senate subcommittee conducted an investigation, with the Wisconsin senator stepping down as chair. For two months, the relatively new medium of television broadcast live the army-McCarthy hearings, during which the cameras showed many viewers for the first time how reckless McCarthy had become.

As McCarthy's public approval declined, the Senate decided that it could no longer tolerate his outrageous behavior. The famous television journalist Edward R. Murrow ran an unflattering documentary on McCarthy on his evening program on CBS, which further cast doubt on the senator's character and honesty. In December 1954, the Senate voted to censure McCarthy for conduct unbecoming a senator, having violated senatorial etiquette by insulting colleagues who criticized him. McCarthy retained his seat on the subcommittee, but he never again wielded substantial power. In 1957, he died from acute hepatitis, a disease related to alcoholism.

The anticommunist consensus did not end with the execution of the Rosenbergs in 1953 or the censure of Joseph McCarthy in 1954. Even J. Robert Oppenheimer, "the father of the atomic bomb," came under scrutiny. In 1954, the Atomic Energy Commission revoked Oppenheimer's security clearance for suspected, though unproven, communist affiliations.

Getty Images

Army-McCarthy Hearings Wisconsin Republican senator Joseph McCarthy gestures in front of a map depicting alleged Communist Party organization in the United States. The army-McCarthy hearings in 1954 were carried live on television and watched by millions of Americans. McCarthy's bullying tactics and unsubstantiated allegations against U.S. army personnel led to his political downfall. **How does the map in this photograph reinforce McCarthy's allegations of communist influence in the United States?**

Also in 1954, Congress passed the Communist Control Act, which required "communist-infiltrated" groups to register with the federal government. Federal, state, and municipal governments required employees to take a loyalty oath affirming their allegiance to the United States and disavowing support for any organization that advocated the overthrow of the government. In addition, the blacklist continued in Hollywood throughout the rest of the decade.

After the Supreme Court declared racial segregation in public schools unconstitutional in 1954, a number of southern states, including Florida and Louisiana, set up committees to investigate communist influence in the civil rights movement. In a case concerning civil liberties, the Supreme Court upheld HUAC's authority to investigate communism and to require witnesses who came before it to answer questions about their affiliations. Yet the Court did put a stop to the anticommunist momentum. In 1957, the high court dealt a severe blow to enforcement of the Smith Act by ruling in ***Yates v. United States*** that the Justice Department could not prosecute someone for merely advocating an abstract doctrine favoring the violent overthrow of the government. In response, Congress tried, but failed, to limit the Supreme Court's jurisdiction in cases of this sort.

REVIEW

- How did McCarthy's tactics fuel the Second Red Scare? In what ways were McCarthy's actions shaped by the Cold War?

AP® Skills Workshop: Writing Historically

Additional Practice in Responding to a Short-Answer Question with a Primary Source

Source: Herblock, "Fire," *The Washington Post*, June 1949

Using the image, answer **A**, **B**, and **C**.

(A) Briefly describe ONE historical perspective expressed in the image.

(B) Briefly explain how ONE event or development in the period 1940 to 1955 led to the historical situation depicted in the image.

(C) Briefly explain ONE specific outcome of the historical situation in the period 1940 to 1955 depicted in the image.

The Economy after 1945

MODULE 8.4

FOCUS

As you read this module, consider the sustained economic growth in the United States between 1945 and 1960. Ask yourself, what caused this economic boom, and how did it affect American families and where they lived? Think about the impact of technological and scientific innovations in American society.

Although the nation struggled with economic and social challenges immediately after the Second World War, Americans by 1950 had more disposable income than they had enjoyed in decades. While President Truman struggled to hold together the New Deal coalition, consumers responded enthusiastically to the wide range of products that advertisers promised would improve their lives. The search for the good life propelled middle-class families from cities to the suburbs. At the same time, a postwar baby boom added millions of children to the population and created a market to supply them with goods from infancy and childhood to adolescence.

AP® EXAM TIP

As you study the causes of economic prosperity in the postwar years, think about how to use the factors of growth in multiple ways. For instance, be able to explain how federal spending at once led to growth and opportunity and to economic dislocation. Pay special attention to how this often landed on the fault lines of race and gender.

Economic and Political Challenges, 1945–1948

Before Americans could work their way toward prosperity, they faced major challenges. Immediately after the war, consumers experienced shortages and high prices, businesses complained about tight regulations, and labor unions sought higher wages and a greater voice in companies' decision making. The return to peace also occasioned debates about whether married women should continue to work outside the home.

By mid-1946, nine million American soldiers had returned to a changed world. The war had exerted pressures on traditional family life as millions of women had left home to work jobs that men had vacated. Most of the 350,000 women who served in the military received their discharge, and like their male counterparts, they hoped to obtain employment. Many other women who had experienced the benefits of wartime employment also wanted to keep working and were reluctant to give up their positions to men.

The war disrupted other aspects of family life as well. During the war, husbands and wives spent long periods apart, resulting in marital tensions and an increased divorce rate. The relaxation of parental authority during the war led to a rise in juvenile delinquency, which added to the anxieties of adults. In 1948, the noted psychiatrist William C. Menninger observed, "While we alarm ourselves with talk of . . . atom bombs, we are complacently watching the disintegration of our family life." Some observers worried that the very existence of the traditional American family was in jeopardy.

Even before the war ended, the U.S. government took some steps to meet postwar economic challenges. In 1944, for example, Congress passed the **Servicemen's Readjustment Act**, commonly known as the **GI Bill**, which offered veterans

Servicemen's Readjustment Act (GI Bill) An act that provided college and vocational tuition, low-interest mortgage loans, and unemployment insurance to World War II veterans. Known as the GI Bill, the 1944 law spurred college enrollment, home ownership, and overall economic growth.

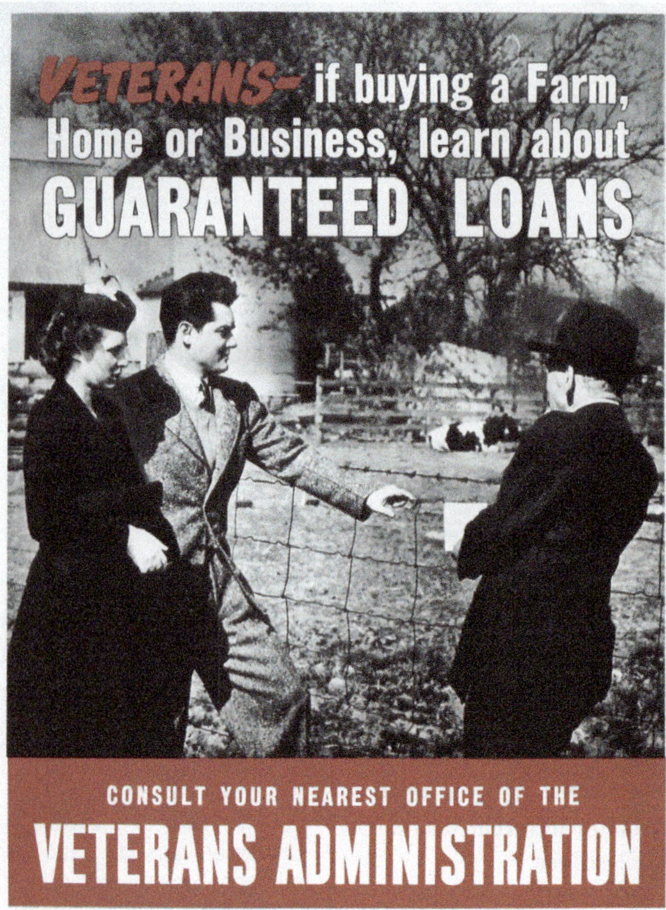

VETERANS– if buying a Farm, Home or Business, learn about
GUARANTEED LOANS
CONSULT YOUR NEAREST OFFICE OF THE
VETERANS ADMINISTRATION

Granger – Historical Picture Archive

The GI Bill of Rights The GI Bill provided a variety of benefits for World War II veterans. Not only did it pay for veterans to get a high school, vocational, or college degree, but it also offered low-cost home mortgages and low-interest loans for business and farm ventures. The government distributed this 1945 poster to make GIs aware of some of these benefits.

How did the GI Bill help veterans adjust to life after World War II and set the stage for future economic growth in the United States?

educational opportunities and financial aid as they adjusted to civilian life. Nevertheless, veterans, like other Americans, faced shortages in the supply of housing and consumer goods and high prices for available commodities.

President Harry Truman ran into serious difficulty handling these and other problems. In the years immediately following the war, real incomes fell, undermined by inflation and reduced overtime hours. As corporate profits rose, workers in the steel, automobile, and fuel industries went on strike for higher wages and a greater voice in company policies.

Truman responded harshly. Labor had been one of Franklin Roosevelt's strongest allies, but his successor put that relationship in jeopardy. In 1946, the federal government took over railroads and threatened to draft workers into the military until they stopped striking. Truman took a tough stance, but in the end union workers received a pay raise, though it did little to relieve inflation.

Political developments forced Truman to change course with the labor unions. In the 1946 midterm elections, Republicans won control of Congress. Stung by this defeat, Truman sought to repair the damage his anti-union policies had done to the Democratic Party coalition. In 1947, Congress passed the **Taft-Hartley Act**, which hampered the ability of unions to organize and limited their power to strike if larger national interests were seen to be at stake. Seeking to regain labor's support, Truman vetoed the measure. Congress, however, overrode the president's veto, and the Taft-Hartley Act became law.

AP® WORKING with EVIDENCE

Source: Representative Homer D. Angell, Speech Supporting the Taft-Hartley Bill, April 1947

1. "The right to join with his fellow workers to select as their bargaining agent the union that they want not the union that is forced upon them.

2. The right to get a job without joining any union.

3. The right to vote by secret ballot in a fair and free election. On whether his employer and the union can make him join the union to keep his job.

4. The right to require the union that is his bargaining agent to represent him without discriminating against him in anyway or for any reason even if he's not a member of the union. . . .

15. The right to settle his own grievances with his employer.

16. The right without fear of reprisal to support any candidate for public office that he chooses and to decide for himself whether or not his money will be spent for political purposes."

Questions for Analysis

1. Identify the labor issues addressed in the excerpt.
2. Describe the context surrounding the passage of the Taft-Hartley Bill.
3. Explain why Angell frames his argument in terms of workers' "rights."
4. Explain why organized labor opposed the "rights" supported by Angell.

Truman's handling of domestic and foreign affairs brought out several challengers for the 1948 election. Much of the opposition came from his own party. From the left, former Democratic vice president Henry Wallace ran on the Progressive Party ticket, backed by disgruntled liberals who opposed Truman's hardline Cold War policies. From the right, Democratic governor Strom Thurmond of South Carolina campaigned mainly on preserving racial segregation in the South and headed up the States' Rights Democratic Party, known as the **Dixiecrats**.

Dixiecrats
The nickname of Southern Democrats who created a segregationist political party in 1948, the States' Rights Democratic Party, as a response to federal extensions of civil rights. Dixiecrats advocated a state's right to legislate segregation. They ran Strom Thurmond in an unsuccessful bid for the presidency in 1948 against Truman.

Both Wallace and Thurmond threatened to take Democratic votes from the president. However, Truman's strongest challenge came from the popular Republican governor of New York, Thomas E. Dewey. Indeed, political pundits and public opinion polls predicted that Truman would lose the 1948 presidential election.

Truman confounded expectations by winning the presidency. Truman traveled across the country, delivering dozens of fiery "give 'em hell, Harry" speeches and railing against a "do-nothing" Republican Congress. His victory resulted from his vigorous campaign style and the complacency of his Republican opponent, who placed too much faith in opinion polls. In addition, Wallace and Thurmond failed to draw significant numbers of votes away from Truman, demonstrating the continuing power of the New Deal coalition.

Truman succeeded in holding together the coalition of labor, minorities, farmers, and liberals and winning enough votes in the South to come out ahead. Truman's electoral victory showed that most voters in 1948 favored a strong anticommunist policy abroad and supported a brand of reform capitalism at home that encouraged economic growth rather than a redistribution of wealth to lift Americans into the middle class.

REVIEW

- How did Truman respond to the economic challenges after World War II?
- How was Truman able to win reelection in 1948 despite facing a popular Republican challenger and challengers from within his own party?

The Boom Years

While the United States faced political challenges, the economy flourished in the decade and a half after the Second World War. Between 1945 and 1960, the gross domestic product (GDP) more than doubled, while per capita income (total income divided by the population) grew by 35 percent. During this fifteen-year period, the average real income (actual purchasing power) for American workers increased by as much as it had during the fifty years preceding World War II.

Equally striking, 60 percent of Americans achieved middle-class status, and the number of salaried office workers rose by 61 percent. Factory workers also experienced gains. Union membership leaped to the highest level in U.S. history, reaching nearly 17 million.

The affluence of the 1950s was much more equally distributed than the prosperity of the 1920s had been. As the middle class grew, the percentage of total income earned by the top 5 percent of wealthy families dropped from 21.3 percent to 19 percent. Though poverty remained a persistent problem, the rate of poverty decreased, falling from 34 percent in 1947 to 22.1 percent in 1960.

A college education served as a critical marker of middle-class status. Traditionally, colleges and universities had been accessible only to the upper class. That began to change between 1940 and 1960 as the number of high school students who entered college more than doubled, due in part to the GI Bill's college benefits for veterans.

The market for consumer goods skyrocketed. TV sets became a household staple in the 1950s, and by 1960, 87 percent of Americans owned a television. Americans also continued to buy automobiles—over 75 percent owned a car by 1960. With gas supplies plentiful and the price per gallon less than 30 cents, automakers concentrated on size, power, and style to compete for buyers. With more cars on the road, motel chains such as Holiday Inn sprang up along the highways. Fast-food establishments proliferated to feed motorists and their families.

During the postwar years, traditional gender roles were largely reinstated, as wartime factories shifted to peacetime production and laid off many female workers. With the economy booming, nuclear families began to grow. In 1955, Illinois governor Adlai Stevenson told the women graduates at Smith College that they could do their part to maintain a free society as wives and mothers. Educated women had an important role to play in maintaining households that boosted their husbands' morale. The mothers of these female college graduates had suffered through the Great

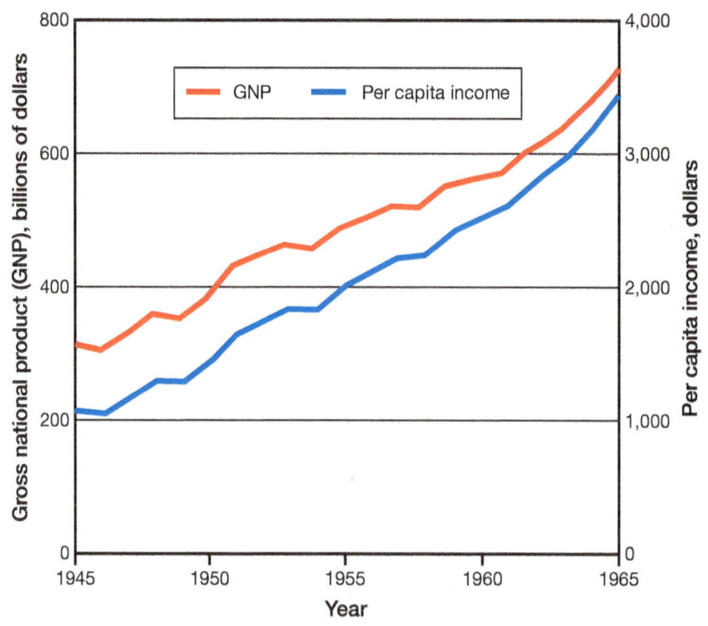

Economic Growth, 1945–1965
As industries shifted from war equipment to consumer goods, productivity remained high. More Americans entered the middle class in the two decades following World War II, while rising union membership ensured higher incomes for the working class. As a result, the purchasing power of most Americans increased in the immediate postwar period.

What factors promoted the growth of the middle class in the 1950s?

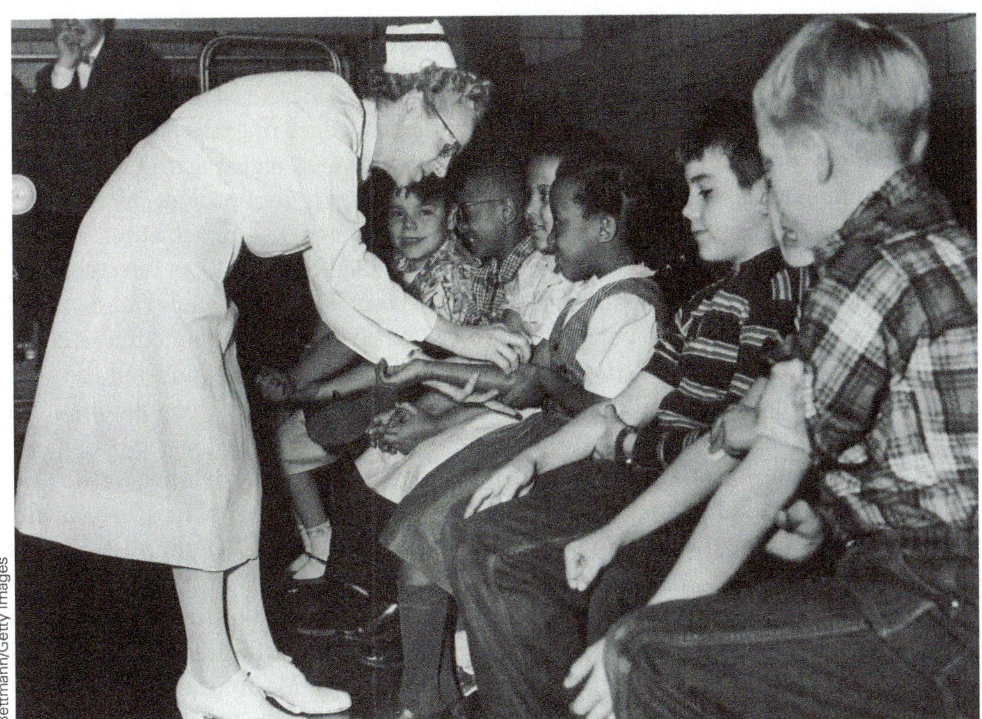

Bettmann/Getty Images

Children Receiving the Polio Vaccine, 1954 These children participated in a successful trial of the polio vaccine created by Dr. Jonas Salk in 1954. Before introduction of the polio vaccine, polio crippled 15,000 Americans yearly and infected three times as many. Within a decade, fewer than 1,000 Americans contracted the disease, and fewer than 100 were paralyzed from it. In 1979, polio was deemed officially eradicated in the United States.

What does this image suggest about public confidence in science and medicine?

Depression, when keeping the birthrate low was one way to assist the family. That was about to change.

Between 1946 and 1964, a **baby boom** occurred in the United States that caused a dramatic increase in the population. Economic prosperity made it easier to support large families, women's early age at marriage contributed to high fertility, and improved health care led to the survival of more children. In the 1940s and 1950s on average, men married for the first time at the age of just under twenty-three, and 49 percent of women married by age nineteen. Couples produced children at such an astonishing pace that in the 1950s, the growth rate in the U.S. population approached that of India.

baby boom
A term that refers to the sharp U.S. population increase between 1946 and 1964 resulting from the end of World War II, postwar economic prosperity, improvements in health care, and a trend toward marriage at a younger age.

Marriage and parenthood reflected a culture spurred by the Cold War. Public officials and the media urged young men and women to build nuclear families in which the father held a paying job and the mother stayed at home and raised her growing family. Doing so would, they implied, strengthen the moral fiber of the United States in its battle against Soviet communism.

Parents could also look forward to their children surviving diseases that had resulted in many childhood deaths in the past. In the 1950s, children received vaccinations against diphtheria, whooping cough, and tetanus before they entered school. The most serious illness affecting young children remained the crippling disease of polio, or infantile paralysis. On April 12, 1955, news bulletins interrupted scheduled television programs to announce that Dr. Jonas Salk had developed a successful injectable vaccine against the disease. As one writer recalled, "citizens rushed to ring church bells and fire sirens, shouted, clapped, sang, and made every kind of joyous noise they could." By the mid-1960s, polio was no longer a public-health menace in the United States.

REVIEW

- Why did a baby boom occur in the years after World War II?
- How was family life shaped by the context of the Cold War?

Changes in Living Patterns

AP® EXAM TIP

Be aware of the internal migration patterns after World War II. Think about selecting a pattern of migration and explaining whether or not the development represents a historical continuity or change. Remember: It is not enough just to know the facts. You have to connect specific facts to larger historical developments through a historical-reasoning skill like continuity and change.

With larger families and larger family incomes came an increased demand for better housing. The economic and demographic booms encouraged migration out of the cities so that growing families could have their own homes, greater space, and a healthier environment. To meet this demand, the federal government provided Americans opportunities to buy their own homes. The Federal Housing Administration, created in the 1930s, provided long-term mortgages to qualified buyers at low interest rates. After the war, the Veterans Administration offered even lower mortgage rates and did not require substantial down payments for ex-GIs. The federal government also cooperated by building highways that allowed drivers to commute to and from the suburbs. By 1960, nearly 60 million people, one-third of the nation's population, lived in suburbs.

Levittown The first mass-produced suburban housing developments, Levittowns were widely emulated by other developers and provided affordable housing for middle-class families, even as they used racially restrictive covenants to exclude Blacks.

William Levitt, a thirty-eight-year-old veteran from Long Island, New York, devised the formula for attracting home buyers to the suburbs. In 1948, Levitt remarked: "No man who owns his own house and lot can be a communist. He has too much to do." After World War II, Levitt, his father, and his brother saw opportunity in the housing crunch and pioneered the idea of adapting Henry Ford's mass-production principles to the housing industry. To build his subdivision of **Levittown** in Hempstead, Long Island, twenty miles from Manhattan, he bulldozed 4,000 acres of potato fields and brought in trucks that dumped piles of building materials at exact intervals of sixty feet. Specialized crews then moved from pile to pile, each performing their assigned job. In July 1948, Levitt's workers constructed 180 houses a week, or 36 a day, in two shifts. Mass-production methods kept prices low, and Levitt quickly sold his initial 17,000 houses and soon built other subdivisions in Pennsylvania and New Jersey. With Levitt leading the way, the production of new single-family homes nearly doubled, from 937,000 in 1946 to 1.7 million in 1950.

AP Images/Sam Myers

William and Daisy Myers Integrate Levittown, 1957 Daisy Myers serves coffee to her husband William in their new $12,150 ranch-style house in Levittown, Pennsylvania. The first Black family to move into this all-white community, in August 1957, the Myerses braved two weeks of threatening protests by their new neighbors and proclaimed: "We're here to stay," and they did.

What tactics were commonly used to exclude Blacks from white suburbs in the 1940s and 1950s?

Although millions of Americans took advantage of opportunities to move to the suburbs, Levitt closed his subdivisions to Black Americans. He was supported by the Federal Housing Administration, which guaranteed financing for sales of housing in all-white communities. Many whites moved out of the cities to distance themselves from the growing number of southern Black people who migrated north during World War II and the influx of Puerto Ricans who came to the United States after the war, and they did not welcome these minorities to their new communities. Many communities in the North adopted restrictive covenants, which prohibited resale of homes to Black people and members of other minority groups, including Hispanics, Jews, and Asian Americans.

Although the Supreme Court outlawed restrictive covenants in *Shelley v. Kraemer* (1948), housing discrimination remained prevalent in urban and suburban neighborhoods. Real estate brokers steered minority buyers away from white communities, and banks refused to lend money to Black purchasers who sought to move into white locales, an illegal policy called **redlining**.

redlining
A discriminatory practice in which residents of certain neighborhoods are denied financial services. The term originated when the federal Homeowner's Loan Corporation in the 1930s created maps outlining the riskiest areas to lend in red, making it difficult for the predominately minority residents in redlined urban communities to obtain mortgages.

WORKING with EVIDENCE

Source: Restrictive Housing Covenant for Labadie Avenue between Taylor Avenue and Core Avenue in St. Louis, Missouri, 1911.

> "[T]he said property is hereby restricted to the use and occupancy for the term of Fifty (50) years from this date, so that it shall be a condition all the time and whether recited and referred to as [*sic*] not in subsequent conveyances and shall attach to the land as a condition precedent to sale of the same, that hereafter no part of said property or any portion thereof shall be, for said term of Fifty-years, occupied by any person not of the Caucasian race, it being intended hereby to restrict the use of said property for said period of time against the occupancy as owners or tenants of any portion of said property for resident or other purpose by people of the Negro or Mongolian Race."

Questions for Analysis

1. Identify the year this restrictive covenant expired and the groups it targeted.
2. Describe the residential patterns that this covenant seeks to establish.
3. Evaluate the impact of restrictive covenants on housing policy and homeowner demographics post–World War II.

Nevertheless, a few Black Americans succeeded in cracking suburban racial barriers, but at great risk. In August 1957, a Black couple, William Myers, an electrical engineer, and his wife Daisy, managed to buy a new $12,500 ranch-style house in Levittown, Pennsylvania. However, once the couple moved in, they faced two weeks of intimidation and assaults from mobs of disapproving white community residents. When local police refused to protect them, the governor dispatched state troopers to keep them safe. Although they succeeded in remaining in Levittown, having proclaimed "We're here to stay," their experience underscored the racially discriminatory housing practices that existed in the North.

AP® EXAM TIP

Think about how to connect the growth of the Sun Belt's economy with the political changes in that region over the time period. Connecting economic gain, on the one hand, with political changes, on the other, advances a complex historical argument.

The baby boom and mass-produced, cheap housing led to sustained growth. No sections of the nation expanded faster than the West and the South. Attracted by the warmer climate and jobs in the defense, petroleum, and chemical industries, many Americans moved to California, Texas, and Florida. The advent of air conditioning made it feasible for these new residents to live and work in hotter parts of the country. California's population increased the most, adding nearly six million new residents between 1940 and 1960, including a large influx of Asians and Latinos. In 1957, in a sign of the times, New York City lost two of its baseball teams, the New York Giants and the Brooklyn Dodgers, to San Francisco and Los Angeles, respectively. This migration to the **Sun Belt**, as the southern and western states would be called, transformed the political and social landscapes of the nation.

Sun Belt
The southern and western parts of the United States, to which millions of Americans moved after World War II. Migrants were drawn by the region's climate and jobs in the defense, petroleum, and chemical industries.

REVIEW

- What factors led to the creation of the new suburbs?
- How did the new suburbs change U.S. society?

AP® Skills Workshop: Writing Historically

Additional Practice in Responding to a Long-Essay Question

Evaluate the relative importance of different causes for economic growth in the United States between 1945 and 1960.

Culture after 1945

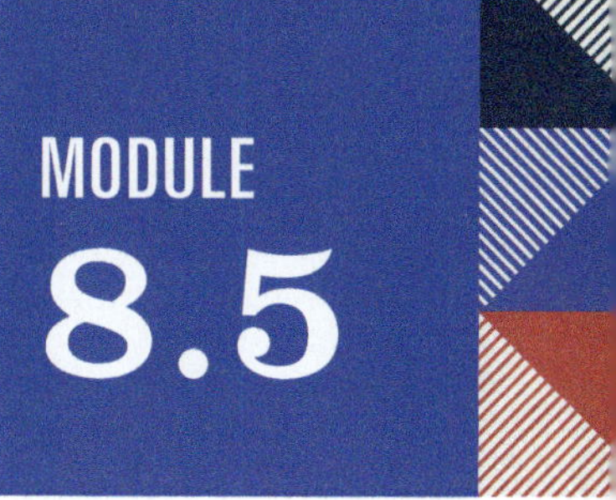

FOCUS

As you read this module, consider the changes and continuities in American society during the late 1940s and the 1950s. Ask yourself how popular culture reflected both changes and continuities in the lives of Americans in the 1940s and 1950s. Think about the reasons why some groups challenged accepted cultural values.

In the late 1940s and the 1950s, new forms of popular culture developed as the United States confronted difficult political, diplomatic, and social issues. Amid this turmoil, television played a large role in shaping people's lives, reflecting their desire for success and depicting the era as a time of innocence. The rise of teenage culture as a powerful economic force also influenced this portrayal of the 1950s. Teenage tastes and consumption patterns reinforced the impression of a simpler and more carefree time. Religion painted a similar picture, as attendance at houses of worship rose. Still, the era held a more complex social reality. Women did not always act the suburban parts that television and society assigned them, and cultural rebels—writers, actors, and musicians—emerged to challenge mainstream values.

The Rise of Television and a New Teenage Culture

Few postwar developments had a greater impact on American society and politics than the advent of television. The three major television networks—the Columbia Broadcasting System (CBS), the National Broadcasting Company (NBC), and the American Broadcasting Company (ABC)—offered programs nationwide that appealed to mainstream tastes while occasionally challenging the public with serious drama, music, and documentaries. During the 1950s, television networks began to feature presidential campaign coverage, from the national nominating conventions to election-day vote tallies, and political advertisements began to fill the airwaves.

If many Americans recall the 1950s as a time of innocence, they have in mind television programs aimed at children, such as *Howdy Doody*, *Superman*, *Hopalong Cassidy*, *The Cisco Kid*, and *The Lone Ranger*, which showcased a simple world of moral absolutes. In the course of a half hour, these shows pitted good versus evil. Honesty and decency inevitably triumphed.

Similarly, adults enjoyed evening television shows that depicted old-fashioned families entertaining themselves, mediating quarrels peacefully, and relying on the wisdom of parents. In *The Adventures of Ozzie and Harriet*, the Nelsons raised two clean-cut sons. In *Father Knows Best*, the Andersons—a father and mother and their three children—lived a tranquil life in the suburbs, and the father solved whatever dilemmas arose. The same held true for the Cleaver family on *Leave It to Beaver*.

AP® EXAM TIP

Your textbook details several examples of mass media that furthered a culture of conformity. Select an example from the book and explain how it either maintained or changed a culture of conformity.

Television portrayed working-class families in grittier fashion on shows such as *The Life of Riley*, whose lead character worked at a factory, and *The Honeymooners*, whose male protagonists were a bus driver and a sewer worker. Nevertheless, like their middle-class counterparts, these families stayed together and worked out their problems despite their more challenging financial circumstances.

By contrast, Black American families received little attention on television. Black female actors usually appeared as maids, and the one show that featured an all-Black cast, *The Amos 'n' Andy Show*, highlighted the racial stereotypes of the period. American Indians faced similar difficulties. Few appeared on television, and those who did served mainly as targets for "heroic" cowboys defending the West from "savage" American Indians. One exception was Tonto, the Lone Ranger's sidekick. Played by Jay Silverheels, a Canadian Mohawk, he challenged the image of the hostile American Indian by showing his loyalty to his white partner and his commitment to the code of "civilized" justice.

If parents expected young people to behave like Ozzie and Harriet Nelson's sons, the popular-culture industry provided teenagers with alternative role models. In *Rebel without a Cause* (1955), actor James Dean portrayed a seventeen-year-old filled with anguish about his life. A sensitive but misunderstood young man, he muses that he wants "just one day when I wasn't all confused . . . [when] I wasn't ashamed of everything . . . [when] I felt I belonged some place." *The Wild One* (1954), which starred Marlon Brando, also popularized youthful angst. The leather-outfitted leader of a motorcycle gang, Brando rides into a small town, hoping to shake it up. When asked by a local resident, "What are you rebelling against?" he coolly replies, "Whaddya got?"

Real gangs did exist on the streets of New York and other major cities. Composed of working-class youth from various ethnic and racial backgrounds, these gangs were highly organized, controlled their neighborhood turfs, and engaged in "rumbles" (fights) with intruders. A romanticized version of these battles appeared on Broadway with the production of *West Side Story* (1957), which pitted a white gang against a Puerto Rican gang in a musical rendering of *Romeo and Juliet*.

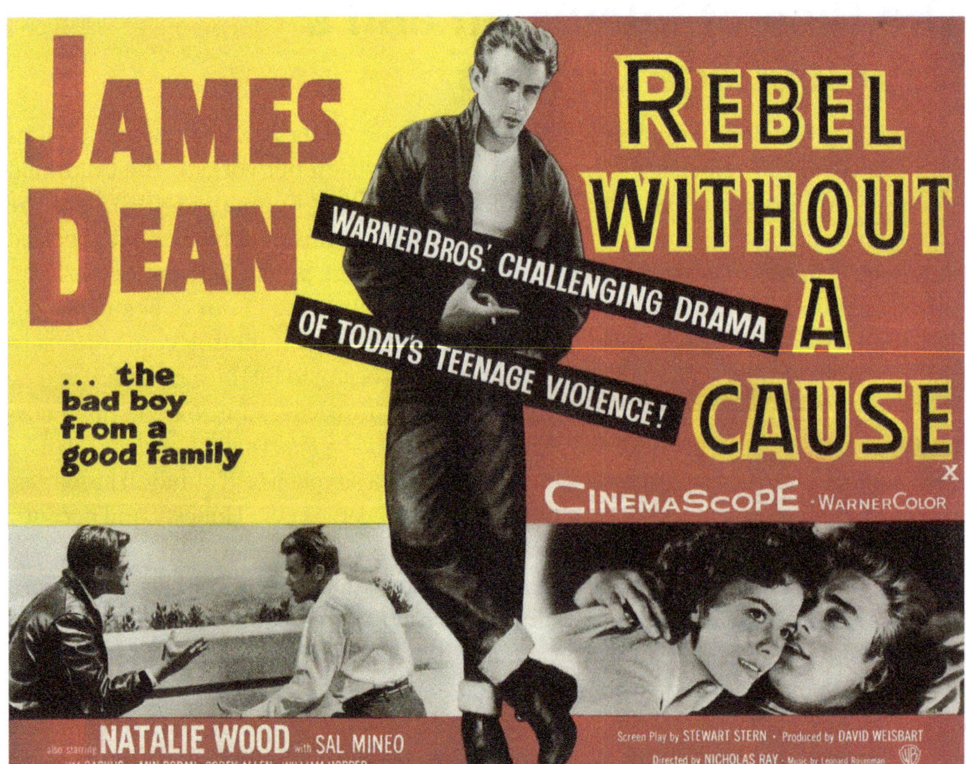

Everett Collection

***Rebel without a Cause*, 1955** James Dean starred in the movie *Rebel without a Cause*, playing Jim Stark, a troubled teenager struggling with his middle-class life in post–World War II Los Angeles. The movie explored the conflict between parents and teenagers, what we call today "the generation gap." Dean's outfit of leather jacket and blue jeans and his anguished demeanor both reflected and shaped teenage culture.

What elements from the movie poster reflect the notion of teenage angst and rebellion?

In the 1950s, Hollywood rarely portrayed women as rebels, but instead as mothers, understanding girlfriends, and dutiful wives. If they sought a career, like many of the women played by actor Doris Day, they pursued it only as long as necessary to meet the right man. Yet the film industry did offer a more tantalizing woman, a sexual being who displayed her attributes to seduce and outwit men. Marilyn Monroe in *The Seven Year Itch* (1955) and Elizabeth Taylor in *Cat on a Hot Tin Roof* (1958) revealed that women also had a powerful libido, though in the end they became domesticated or paid a terrible price.

In 1941, *Popular Science* magazine coined the term *teenager*, and by the middle of the next decade, members of this age group viewed themselves not as prospective adults but as a distinct group with its own identity, patterns of behavior, and tastes. Postwar prosperity provided teenagers with money to support their own choices and styles. In 1959, *Life* magazine found that teenagers had $10 billion at their disposal, "a billion more than the total sales of GM [General Motors]."

Teenagers owned 10 million record players, more than 1 million TV sets, and 13 million cameras. They spent 16 percent of their disposable income on entertainment, particularly the purchase of rock 'n' roll records. The comic book industry also attracted a huge audience among teenagers by selling inexpensive, illustrated, and easy-to-read pulp fiction geared toward romance and action adventure.

AP® WORKING with EVIDENCE

Source: Senate Subcommittee to Investigate Juvenile Delinquency, *Interim Report on Comic Books and Juvenile Delinquency*, 1955

> "[O]ver a period of several months the subcommittee has received a vast amount of mail from parents expressing concern regarding the possible deleterious effect upon their children of certain of the media of mass communication. . . .
>
> [I]t was the consensus that the need existed for a thorough, objective investigation to determine whether, as has been alleged, certain types of mass communication media are to be reckoned with as contributing to the country's alarming rise in juvenile delinquency. These include: 'crime and horror' comic books and other types of printed matter; the radio, television, and motion pictures. . . .
>
> Delinquency is the product of many related causal factors. But it can scarcely be questioned that the impact of these media does constitute a significant factor in the total problem. . . .
>
> One of the most significant changes of the past quarter century has been the wide diffusion of the printed word, particularly in certain periodicals, plus the phenomenal growth of radio and television audiences.
>
> The child today in the process of growing up is constantly exposed to sights and sounds of a kind and quality undreamed of in previous generations. As these sights and sounds can be a powerful force for good, so too can they be a powerful counterpoise working evil."

Questions for Analysis

1. Identify the purpose for the committee's report.
2. Describe the concerns expressed in the report.
3. Explain how the report reflects cultural changes in the 1950s.
4. Evaluate the extent of similarity between the concerns outlined by the report and concerns commonly expressed about young people in the 1920s.

Public high schools reinforced teenage identity. Following World War II, high school attendance exploded. In 1930, 50 percent of working-class children attended high school; thirty years later, the figure had jumped to 90 percent. The percentage of Black youths attending high school also grew, doubling from 1940 to 1960. For the first time, many white middle-class teenagers saw the fashions and heard the language of working-class youths close up and both emulated and feared what they encountered.

More than anything else, rock 'n' roll music set teenagers apart from their elders. The pop singers of the 1940s and early 1950s—such as Frank Sinatra, Perry Como, Rosemary Clooney, and Patti Page, who had appealed to both adolescents and parents—lost much of their teenage audience after 1954 to rock 'n' roll, with its heavy downbeat and lyrics evoking teenage passion and sexuality. Black artists such as Chuck Berry, Little Richard, and Antoine "Fats" Domino popularized the sound of classic, up-tempo rock.

Although Black people pioneered the sound, the music entered the mainstream largely through white artists who added rural flavor to rhythm and blues. Born in Tupelo, Mississippi, and living in Memphis, Tennessee, Elvis Presley adapted the fashion and sensuality of Black performers to his own style. Elvis's snarling singing and pelvic gyrations excited young people, both Black and white, while upsetting their parents. In an era when matters of sex remained private or were not discussed at all, and when Black Americans were still treated as second-class citizens, a white man singing "Black" music and shaking his body to its frenetic tempo caused alarm. When Elvis sang on the popular *Ed Sullivan Show* in 1956, cameras were allowed to show him only from the waist up to uphold standards of decency.

- How did television shape — and in what ways was it shaped by — American culture in the 1950s?
- What factors drove the development of American teenage culture during the 1950s?

Social Changes of the 1940s and 1950s

Throughout the 1950s, movies, women's magazines, mainstream newspapers, and medical and psychological experts informed women that only by embracing domesticity could they achieve personal fulfillment. Dr. Benjamin Spock's best-selling *Common Sense Book of Baby and Child Care* (1946) advised mothers that their children would reach their full potential only if wives stayed at home and watched over their offspring. In another best seller, *Modern Women: The Lost Sex* (1947), Ferdinand Lundberg and Marynia Farnham called the independent woman "a contradiction in terms." A 1951 study of corporate executives found that most businessmen viewed the ideal wife as one who devoted herself to her husband's career. College newspapers described female undergraduates who were not engaged by their senior year as distraught.

Certainly, many women professed to find domestic lives fulfilling, but not all women were so content. Many experienced anxiety and depression. Far from satisfied, these women suffered from what the social critic Betty Friedan would later call "a problem that has no name," a malady that derived not from any personal failing but from the unrewarding roles women were expected to play.

AP® WORKING with EVIDENCE

Source: Betty Friedan, *The Feminine Mystique*, 1963

> "The suburban housewife—she was the dream image of the young American woman and the envy, it was said, of women all over the world. The American housewife—freed by science and labor-saving appliances from the drudgery, the dangers of childbirth, and the illnesses of her grandmother. She was healthy, beautiful, educated, concerned only about her husband, her children, her home. She had found true feminine fulfillment. . . .
>
> In the fifteen years after World War II, this mystique of feminine fulfillment became the cherished and self-perpetuating core of contemporary American culture. Millions of women lived their lives in the image of those pretty pictures of the American suburban housewife, kissing their husbands goodbye in front of the picture window, depositing their stationwagonsful of children at school, and smiling as they ran the new electric waxer over the spotless kitchen floor. . . .
>
> If a woman had a problem in the 1950's and 1960's, she knew that something must be wrong with her marriage, or with herself. Other women were satisfied with their lives, she thought. What kind of woman did not feel this mysterious fulfillment waxing the kitchen floor? She was so ashamed to admit her dissatisfaction that she never knew how many other women shared it."

Questions for Analysis

1. Identify the reasons suburban housewives should be content, according to the excerpt.
2. Describe the 1950s ideal of womanhood expressed in the excerpt.
3. Explain why, according to Friedan, many women experienced depression and anxiety during the 1950s.
4. Evaluate how social, cultural, and economic developments in the 1950s shaped the ideals of womanhood described in the excerpt.

Not all women fit the stereotype. Although most married women with families did not work during the 1950s, the proportion of working wives doubled from 15 percent in 1940 to 30 percent in 1960, with the greatest increase coming among women over the age of thirty-five. Married women were more likely to work if they were Black or came from working-class immigrant families.

Moreover, women's magazines offered readers a more complex message than domesticity. Alongside articles about and advertisements directed at stay-at-home mothers, these periodicals profiled career women, such as Maine senator Margaret Chase Smith, the Black American educator Mary McLeod Bethune, and sports figures such as the golf and tennis great Babe (Mildred) Didrikson Zaharias. At the same time, working women played significant roles in labor unions, where they fought to reduce disparities between men's and women's income and provide a wage for housewives, recognizing the importance of their unpaid work to maintaining families.

Many other women joined clubs and organizations like the Young Women's Christian Association (YWCA), where they engaged in charitable and public service activities. Some participated in political organizations, such as Henry Wallace's Progressive Party, and peace groups, such as the Women's International League for Peace and Freedom, to campaign against the violence caused by racial discrimination at home and Cold War rivalries abroad.

Along with marriage and the family, religion experienced a revival in the postwar United States. The arms race between the United States and the Soviet Union heightened

Left: George Marks/Retrofile/Getty Images; right: Robert W. Kelley/The LIFE Picture Collection/Getty Images

Women in the Home and in the Workplace In the 1950s, married women were encouraged to stay at home. Modern appliances like this refrigerator (left) supposedly made housework less difficult, but wives had to spend a great deal of time keeping it fully stocked and attending to other household chores. With all the new devices at their disposal, wives were expected to keep the home neat and spotless, while caring for their children. But not all married women stayed at home and tended the family. Margaret Chase Smith (right) was an influential Republican senator from Maine who took on Senator Joseph McCarthy in Congress and challenged his harsh anticommunist methods. Here she is engaged in serious deliberations with Democratic majority leader Lyndon B. Johnson at a Senate hearing in 1957.

How did these images send mixed signals to American women during the 1950s?

the dangers of international conflict for ordinary citizens as the possibility of nuclear annihilation loomed like a shadow over everyday life. Social and economic changes that accompanied the Cold War intensified personal anxiety. Churchgoing underscored the contrast between the United States, a religious nation, and the "godless" communism of the Soviet Union. The link between religion and Americanism prompted Congress in 1954 to add "under God" to the pledge of allegiance and to make "In God We Trust" the national motto in 1956.

Americans worshipped in growing numbers. Between 1940 and 1950, church and synagogue membership rose by 78 percent, and more than 95 percent of the population professed a belief in God. Yet religious affiliation appeared to reflect a greater emphasis on togetherness than on specific doctrinal beliefs. It offered a way to overcome isolation and embrace community in an increasingly alienating world. "The people in the suburbs want to feel psychologically secure, adjusted, at home in their environment," theologian Will Herberg explained. "Being religious and joining a church is . . . a fundamental way of 'adjusting' and 'belonging.' "

Television spread religiosity into millions of homes. The Catholic bishop Fulton J. Sheen spoke to a weekly television audience of ten million and alternated his message of "a life worth living" with attacks on atheistic communists. The Methodist minister Norman Vincent Peale, also a popular TV figure, combined traditional religious faith with self-help remedies prescribed in his best-selling book *The Power of Positive Thinking* (1952). The Reverend Billy Graham, from Charlotte, North Carolina, preached about the unhappiness caused by personal sin at huge outdoor crusades in baseball parks and large arenas, which were broadcast on television. Americans derived a variety of meanings from their religious experiences, but many embraced Americanism as their national religion. A good American, one magazine proclaimed, could not be "un-religious."

As many Americans migrated to the suburbs, spent money on leisure and entertainment, and cultivated religion, a small group of young poets, writers, intellectuals, musicians, and artists attacked mainstream politics and culture. Known as **Beats** (derived from "beaten down"), they offered stinging critiques of what they considered the sterility and conformity of white middle-class society. In 1956, Allen Ginsberg began his epic poem *Howl* with the line "I saw the best minds of my generation destroyed by madness, starving hysterical naked." In his novel *On the Road* (1957), Jack Kerouac praised the individual who pursued authentic experiences and mind-expanding consciousness through drugs, sexual experimentation, and living in the moment. At a time when whiteness was not just a skin color but a standard of beauty and virtue, the Beats and authors such as Norman Mailer looked to Black Americans as cultural icons, embracing the spontaneity and coolness they attributed to inner-city Black people. The Beats formed their own artistic enclaves in New York City's Greenwich Village and San Francisco's North Beach and Haight-Ashbury districts.

Beats
A small group of young poets, writers, intellectuals, musicians, and artists who challenged mainstream American politics and culture in the 1950s.

The Beat writers frequently read their poems and prose to the rhythms of jazz, reflecting both their affinity with Black culture and the innovative explorations taking place in music. From the big bands of the 1930s and 1940s, postwar jazz musicians formed smaller trios, quartets, and quintets and experimented with sounds more suitable for serious listening than for dancing. The bebop rhythms of trumpeter Dizzy Gillespie and alto saxophonist Charlie Parker revolutionized jazz, as did trumpeter Miles Davis and tenor saxophonist John Coltrane, who experimented with more complex and textured forms of this music and took it to new heights. Like rock 'n' roll musicians, these Black artists broke down racial barriers as their music attracted white audiences.

Homosexuals also attempted to live nonconformist lifestyles, albeit secretly. According to studies by researcher Dr. Alfred Kinsey of Indiana University, homosexuals made up approximately 10 percent of the adult population. Despite growing gay and lesbian communities during World War II, homosexuality remained taboo, and states outlawed gay and lesbian sexual relations. In 1951, politically radical gay men formed the country's first gay rights organization, the Mattachine Society, which was followed three years later by the founding of the country's first lesbian civil rights organization, the Daughters of Bilitis. Because of police harassment and public prejudice, most homosexuals refused to reveal their sexual orientation, which made sense practically but reduced their ability to counter anti-homosexual discrimination.

Dr. Kinsey also shattered myths about conformity among heterosexuals. In two landmark publications examining sexual behavior, he revealed that 85 percent of men and 50 percent of the women he interviewed had had sexual intercourse before marriage, and 25 percent of women had had extramarital affairs. Kinsey's findings were supported by other data. Between 1940 and 1960, the frequency of out-of-wedlock births among all women rose from 7.1 newborns to 21.6 newborns per thousand women of childbearing age. The sexual experiences that Kinsey documented reflected what many Americans practiced but did not talk about.

AP® EXAM TIP
Consumerism and conformity represented larger cultural patterns throughout the decade of the 1950s. Select a person, event, or development that represents a challenge to the pattern of conformity.

The brewing sexual revolution went public in 1953 with the publication of *Playboy* magazine, founded by Hugh Hefner. Through a combination of serious articles and photographs of nude women, the controversial magazine provided its chiefly male readers with a guide to pursuing sexual pleasure and a sophisticated lifestyle.

Many writers denounced the conformity and shallowness they found in suburban America. Novelist Sloan Wilson wrote about the alienating experience of suburban life in *The Man in the Gray Flannel Suit* (1955). In J. D. Salinger's novel *Catcher in the Rye* (1951), the young protagonist, Holden Caulfield, mocks the phoniness of the adult world while ending up in a mental institution. Journalists and scholars joined

Allen Ginsberg/Corbis/Getty Images

The Beat Generation The literary rebels of the Beat Generation questioned the dominant values of the 1950s. They attacked materialism and conventional sexual morality. They explored Eastern religions as an alternative to Christianity and Judaism, and they experimented with psychedelic drugs to reach a higher consciousness. This photograph captures the rebels-to-be as they attended Columbia University in the mid-1940s. From left to right are Hal Chase, Jack Kerouac, Allen Ginsberg, and William S. Burroughs, who attended Harvard, but had settled in New York after.

What characteristics of the Beat movement are evident in the photograph?

in the criticism. Such critics often overstated the conformity that characterized the suburbs by minimizing the ethnic, religious, and political diversity of their residents. Yet they tapped into a growing feeling, especially among a new generation of young people, of the dangers of a mass culture based on standardization, compliance, and bureaucratization.

REVIEW

- In what ways did American culture offer examples for women that differed from traditional notions of suburban domesticity in the 1950s?
- How did nonconformists challenge American society in the 1950s?

AP® Skills Workshop: Writing Historically

Additional Practice in Responding to a Long-Essay Question

Evaluate the extent to which economic growth and technological innovations fostered cultural change in the United States in the period 1945 to 1960.

Early Steps in the Civil Rights Movement (1940s and 1950s)

MODULE 8.6

FOCUS

As you read this module, analyze the factors that led to the early successes of the civil rights movement in the 1940s and 1950s. Consider the relative importance of grass-roots activism versus governmental intervention. Make sure to think about not only the effects of the civil rights movement on the lives of Black Americans but also the reactions to the movement by various white Americans and the ways the movement influenced the pursuit of civil rights by other ethnic groups in the 1950s.

Black people wanted what most other Americans desired after World War II—the opportunity to make a decent living, buy a nice home, raise a healthy family, and get the best education for their children. Yet Black people faced much greater obstacles in obtaining these dreams than white people did, particularly in the Jim Crow South. Determined to eliminate racial injustices, Black Americans mounted a campaign against white supremacy in the decades after World War II. Black Americans increasingly viewed their struggle as part of an international freedom movement of Black people in Africa and other nonwhites in the Middle East and Asia to obtain their freedom from Western colonial rulers. Embracing similar hopes, Asian Americans and Latinos pursued their own struggles for equality.

The Rise of the Southern Civil Rights Movement

With the war against Nazi racism over, Black Americans continued their fight for full citizenship rights in the United States. During World War II, Black people waged successful campaigns to pressure the federal government to tackle discrimination, and organizations such as the Congress of Racial Equality (CORE) and the NAACP attacked racial injustice (see Module 7.12). Black American veterans returned home to the South determined to build on these victories, especially by extending the right to vote. Yet Black Americans found that most whites resisted demands for racial equality.

AP® EXAM TIP

Return to the modules about Reconstruction (Modules 5.10 and 5.11) and select an example of a large-scale historical change such as any of the Reconstruction amendments or a civil rights bill. Connect your selected example to the attempt by civil rights leaders in the 1940s and 1950s to secure those constitutional guarantees.

In 1946, violence surfaced as the most visible evidence of many white people's determination to preserve the traditional racial order. A race riot erupted in Columbia, Tennessee, in which Black people were killed and Black businesses were torched. In South Carolina, Isaac Woodard, a Black veteran still in uniform and on his way home on a bus, got into an argument with the white bus driver. When the local sheriff arrived, he pounded Woodard's face with a club, permanently blinding the ex-GI. In Mississippi, Senator Theodore Bilbo, running for reelection in the Democratic primary, told white audiences that they could keep Black people from voting "by seeing them

Corbis/Getty Images

U.S. Racial Integration of the Military in Korea, 1950
In 1948, President Truman issued an executive order to desegregate the armed forces. During the Korean War, Black American soldiers served in integrated combat units. On the top left of this November 20, 1950, photo, Sergeant First Class Major Cleveland, the Black American squad leader of this racially integrated unit fighting with the Second Infantry Division, points out a North Korean position to his machine gun crew.

In what ways would a desegregated military help the United States in fighting the Cold War?

the night before" the election. Groups such as the NAACP and the National Association of Colored Women demanded that the president take action to combat this reign of terror.

In December 1946, President Truman responded by issuing an executive order creating the President's Committee on Civil Rights. While the committee conducted its investigation, in April 1947, Jackie Robinson became the first Black baseball player to enter the major leagues. This accomplishment proved to be a sign of changes to come.

After extensive deliberations, the committee, which consisted of both Black and white people, as well as northerners and southerners, issued its report, ***To Secure These Rights***, on October 29, 1947. Placing the problem of "civil rights shortcomings" within the context of the Cold War, the report argued that racial inequality and unrest could only aid the Soviets in their global anti-American propaganda efforts. "The United States is not so strong," the committee asserted, "the final triumph of the democratic ideal not so inevitable that we can ignore what the world thinks of us or our record." A far-reaching document, the report called for racial desegregation in the military, interstate transportation, and education, as well as extension of the right to vote. The following year, under pressure from Black American activists, the president signed an executive order to desegregate the armed forces.

REVIEW

- What factors shaped the struggle for Black American civil rights during the late 1940s?

School Segregation and the Montgomery Bus Boycott

Led by the NAACP, Black Americans also launched a prolonged legal assault on school segregation. First, the association filed lawsuits against states that excluded Black people from publicly funded law schools and universities. After victories in Missouri and Maryland, the group's chief lawyer, Thurgood Marshall, persuaded the Supreme Court in 1950 to require the integration of the University of Texas Law School. At the same time, the Court eliminated separate facilities for Black students at the University of Oklahoma graduate school and ruled against segregation in interstate rail transportation.

Brown v. Board of Education of Topeka
A landmark 1954 Supreme Court decision that overturned the "separate but equal" principle established by *Plessy v. Ferguson* in 1896. Although the *Brown* ruling banned school segregation, few schools in the South were racially desegregated for more than a decade.

Before Black Americans could attend college, they had to obtain a first-class education in public schools. All-Black schools typically lacked the resources provided to white schools, and the NAACP understood that southern officials would never live up to the "separate but equal doctrine" asserted in *Plessy v. Ferguson* (1896). Black Americans sought to integrate schools not only because they wanted the freedom to have their children attend their local public schools, but because they also believed that integration offered the best and quickest way to secure a high-quality education.

On May 17, 1954, in ***Brown v. Board of Education of Topeka***, the Supreme Court overturned *Plessy*. In a unanimous decision read by Chief Justice Earl Warren, the Court concluded that "in the field of public education the doctrine of 'separate but equal' has no place. Separate educational facilities are inherently unequal." This ruling undercut the legal foundation for segregation and officially placed the law on the side of those who sought racial equality.

Nevertheless, the *Brown* ruling did not end the controversy. In fact, it led to more battles over segregation. In 1955, the Court issued a follow-up opinion calling for implementation with "all deliberate speed." But it left enforcement of *Brown* to federal district courts in the South, which consisted mainly of white southerners who espoused segregationist views. As a result, southern officials emphasized "deliberate" rather than "speed" and slowed the implementation of the *Brown* decision.

The *Brown* decision encouraged Black Americans to protest against other forms of racial discrimination. In 1955, in Montgomery, Alabama, the Women's Political Council, a group of middle-class and professional Black women, petitioned the city commission to improve bus service for Black passengers. Among other things, they wanted Black people not to have to give up their seats to white passengers who boarded the bus after Black passengers did. Their requests went unheeded until December 1, 1955, when Rosa Parks, a Black seamstress and an NAACP activist, refused to give up her seat to a white man.

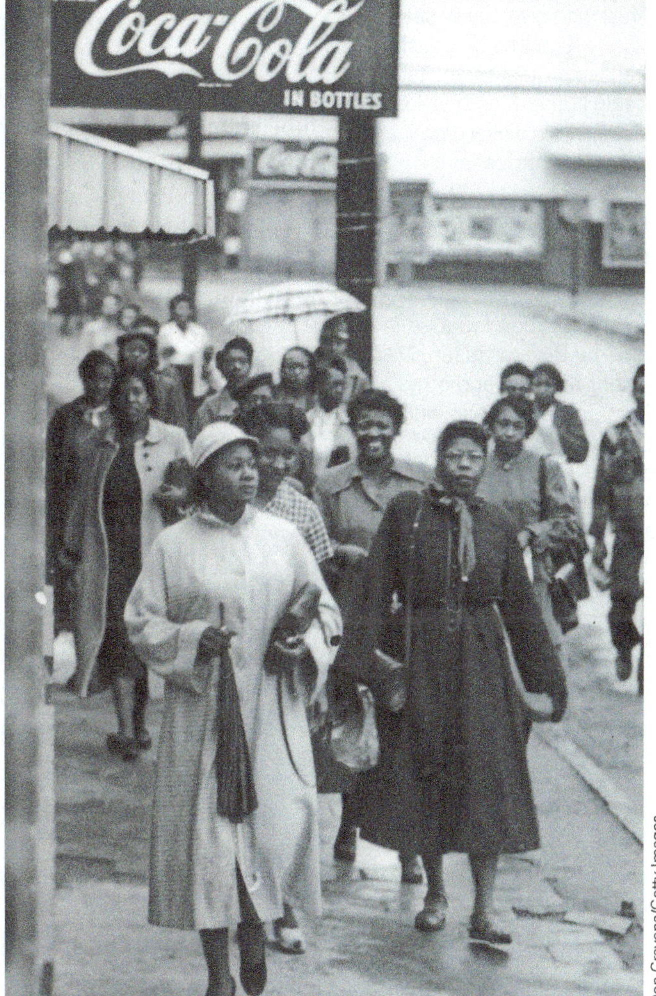

Don Cravens/Getty Images

Montgomery Bus Boycott, 1956 Two months after Black American residents of Montgomery, Alabama, began their boycott of the city buses to protest segregation and mistreatment, the Black community kept up its boycott despite violence and intimidation. Black women had made up the majority of bus riders, and this photograph, taken on February 1, 1956, shows many of them walking to work or to stores for shopping.

What does this photograph reveal about the goals of and participants in the civil rights movement in the mid-1950s?

AP® EXAM TIP

Brown v. Board of Education is another Supreme Court decision you have to understand. Explain how the *Brown* decision represented a success in the civil rights movement and how some groups fought against the decision.

Parks's arrest rallied civic, labor, and religious groups and sparked a bus boycott that involved nearly the entire Black community. Instead of riding buses, Black commuters walked to work or joined car pools. White officials refused to capitulate and fought back by arresting leaders of the Montgomery Improvement Association, the organization that coordinated the protest. Other whites hurled insults at Black people and engaged in violence. After more than a year of conflict, the Supreme Court ruled in favor of the complete desegregation of Montgomery's buses.

Out of this landmark struggle, Martin Luther King Jr. emerged as the civil rights movement's most charismatic leader. His personal courage and power of oratory could inspire nearly all segments of the Black American community. Twenty-six years old at the time of Parks's arrest, King was the pastor of the prestigious Dexter Avenue Baptist Church.

Montgomery bus boycott
A thirteen-month bus boycott in Montgomery, Alabama, that began in December 1955 with the arrest of Rosa Parks for refusing to give up her seat to a white man. The successful yearlong protest catapulted Martin Luther King Jr., a local pastor, into national prominence as a civil rights leader.

Though familiar with the nonviolent methods of the Indian revolutionary Mohandas Gandhi and the civil disobedience of the nineteenth-century writer Henry David Thoreau, King mainly drew his inspiration and commitment to these principles from the Black church and secular leaders such as A. Philip Randolph and Bayard Rustin. King understood how to convey the goals of the civil rights movement to sympathetic white Americans, but his vision and passion grew out of Black communities.

At the outset of the **Montgomery bus boycott**, King noted proudly of the boycott: "When the history books are written in future generations, the historians will have to pause and say 'There lived a great people — a Black people — who injected new meaning and dignity into the veins of civilization.' "

Southern Christian Leadership Conference (SCLC)
An organization founded in 1957 by Bayard Rustin, Martin Luther King Jr., and other Black ministers following the successful Montgomery bus boycott to encourage more nonviolent protests against racial segregation and disfranchisement in the South. It was instrumental in organizing major civil rights protests through the 1960s.

The Montgomery bus boycott made King a national civil rights leader, but it did not guarantee him further success. In 1957, King and a like-minded group of southern Black ministers formed the **Southern Christian Leadership Conference (SCLC)** to spread nonviolent protest throughout the region, but except in a few cities, such as Tallahassee, Florida, additional bus boycotts did not take hold.

REVIEW

- In what ways did the *Brown* ruling change racial segregation in the South, and in what ways did it fall short?
- How did bus boycotts show both the strength and limitations of the civil rights movement during the 1950s?

Combatting White Resistance to Desegregation

Segregationists responded forcefully to halt Black efforts to eliminate Jim Crow. In 1956, 101 southern congressmen issued a manifesto denouncing the 1954 *Brown* opinion and pledging to resist it through "lawful means." Other southerners went beyond the law.

In 1957, a federal court approved a plan submitted by the Little Rock, Arkansas, school board to integrate Central High School. However, the state's governor, Orval Faubus, obstructed the court ruling by sending the state National Guard to keep out nine Black students chosen to attend Central High. Faced with blatant state

The Desegregation of Central High School, 1957 In 1957, nine Black teenagers attempted to desegregate Central High School in Little Rock, Arkansas, pursuant to a federal court order. This photograph captures fifteen-year-old Elizabeth Eckford, one of the Little Rock Nine, surrounded by an angry white crowd on the first day of school. The photo also shows an enraged white student, Hazel Bryan, shouting at her to go home. Neither Eckford nor the other Black students managed to attend school that day, but they entered Central High after President Eisenhower sent in federal troops to protect them. **What role did students play in the battle to desegregate schools?**

resistance to federal authority, President Eisenhower placed the National Guard under federal control and sent in the 101st Airborne Division to restore order after a mob blocked the students from entering the school. These Black pioneers, who became known as the **Little Rock Nine**, attended classes for the year under the protection of the National Guard but still encountered considerable harassment from white students.

In defiance of the high court, other school districts, such as Prince Edward County, Virginia, chose to close their public schools rather than desegregate. By the end of the decade, public schools in the South remained mostly segregated.

Little Rock Nine
Nine students who, in 1957, became the first Black people to attend Central High School in Little Rock, Arkansas. Federal troops were required to overcome the resistance of white officials and the verbal and physical violence of white protesters.

AP® WORKING with EVIDENCE

Source: *The Southern Manifesto*, 1956

"We regard the decision of the Supreme Court in the school cases as a clear abuse of judicial power. It climaxes a trend in the Federal Judiciary undertaking to legislate, in derogation of the authority of Congress, and to encroach upon the reserved rights of the states and the people. . . .

This unwarranted exercise of power by the Court, contrary to the Constitution, is creating chaos and confusion in the States principally affected. It is destroying the amicable relations between the white and Negro races that have been created through ninety years of patient effort by the good people of both races. It has planted hatred and suspicion where there has been heretofore friendship and understanding.

Without regard to the consent of the governed, outside agitators are threatening immediate and revolutionary changes in our public-school systems. If done, this is certain to destroy the system of public education in some of the States. . . .

We pledge ourselves to use all lawful means to bring about a reversal of this decision which is contrary to the Constitution and to prevent the use of force in its implementation."

Questions for Analysis

1. Identify the main argument in the *Southern Manifesto*.
2. Describe the tactics used to resist desegregation in the South that would have been supported by the signers of the *Southern Manifesto*.
3. Evaluate the extent of similarity in the rhetoric used to defend segregation in the *Southern Manifesto* and that used to defend slavery before the Civil War.

The white South used other forms of violence and intimidation to preserve segregation. The third incarnation of the Ku Klux Klan (KKK) appeared after World War II to strike back at growing Black American challenges to white supremacy. This terrorist group threatened, injured, and killed Black people they considered "uppity."

Following the *Brown* decision, segregationists also formed the **White Citizens' Council (WCC)**. The WCC drew members largely from businessmen and professionals. Rather than condoning violence, the WCC generally intimidated Black people by threatening to fire them from jobs or denying them credit from banks. In Alabama, WCC members launched a campaign against radio stations playing the kind of rock 'n' roll music because they believed that it fostered close interracial contact.

The WCC and the KKK created a racial climate in the deep South that encouraged whites to believe they could get away with murder to defend white supremacy. In the summer of 1955, Emmett Till, a fourteen-year-old from Chicago who was visiting his great-uncle in Mississippi, was kidnapped and brutally beaten to death because he allegedly flirted with a white woman in a country store. Till's mother insisted on a funeral with an open coffin. The horrifying photographs of his badly mutilated body shocked Black Americans across the country and brought widespread attention to the injustice of white supremacist violence.

Although the two accused killers were quickly brought to trial, an all-white jury acquitted them. The following year, the acquitted killers admitted their guilt in a paid magazine interview, knowing they could not be tried again because of legal protections against double jeopardy. In 2007, Till's accuser confessed that she had lied under oath about Till's behavior toward her.

With boycotts petering out and white violence rising, Black Americans, especially high school and college students, developed new techniques to confront discrimination, including sit-ins, in which protesters seat themselves in a strategic spot and refuse to move until their demands are met or they are forcibly evicted. These mass protests did not really get off the ground until February 1960, when four students at North Carolina A&T University in Greensboro initiated sit-ins at the whites-only lunch counters in Woolworth and Kress department stores. Their demonstrations sparked similar efforts throughout the Southeast, leading to fifty-eight sit-ins within three months.

Student Nonviolent Coordinating Committee (SNCC)
A student-led civil rights organization that grew out of the sit-ins of 1960. The organization originally focused on taking nonviolent direct action and political organizing to achieve its goals.

A few months after the sit-ins began, a number of participants formed the **Student Nonviolent Coordinating Committee (SNCC)**. The organization's young members sought not only to challenge racial segregation in the South, but also to create interracial communities based on economic equality and political democracy. This generation

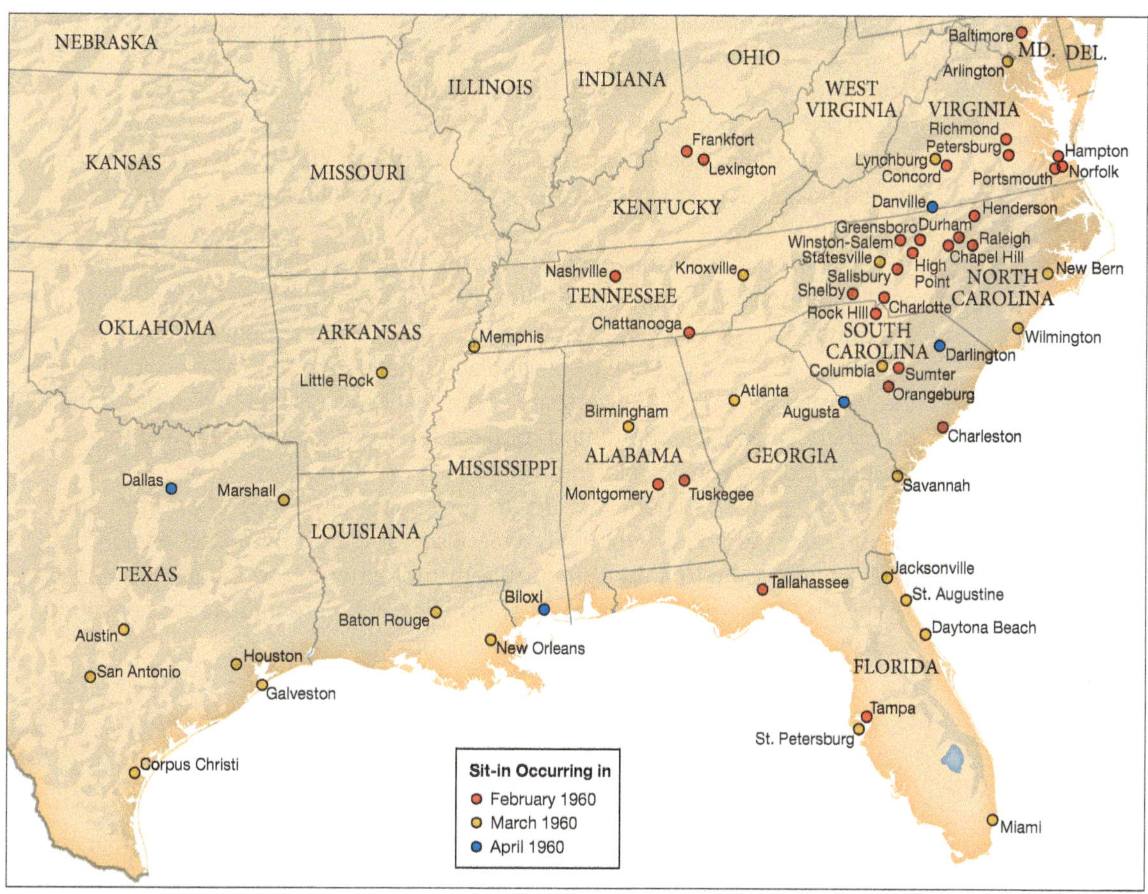

MAP 8.3 Lunch Counter Sit-Ins, February–April 1960 After starting slowly in the late 1950s, lunch counter sit-ins exploded in 1960 following a sit-in by college students in Greensboro, North Carolina. Within three months, sit-ins erupted in fifty-eight cities across the South. The participation of high school and college students revitalized the civil rights movement and led to the formation of the Student Nonviolent Coordinating Committee in April 1960.

How did the sit-in movement differ from prominent civil rights protests in the 1950s?

of Black and white sit-in veterans came of age in the 1950s at a time when Cold War democratic rhetoric and the Supreme Court's *Brown* decision raised their expectations for racial equality. Yet these young activists often saw their hopes dashed by southern segregationist resistance, including the murder of Emmett Till, which both horrified and helped mobilize them to fight for Black equality.

AP® WORKING with EVIDENCE

Source: Ella Baker, "Bigger Than a Hamburger," *Southern Patriot*, June 1960

"The Student Leadership Conference* made it crystal clear that current sit-ins and other demonstrations are concerned with something much bigger than a hamburger or even a giant-sized Coke.

Whatever may be the difference in approach to their goal, the Negro and white students, North and South, are seeking to rid America of the scourge of racial segregation and discrimination—not only at lunch counters, but in every aspect of life.

In reports, casual conversations, discussion groups, and speeches, the sense and the spirit of the following statement that appeared in the initial newsletter of the students at Barber-Scotia College, Concord, N.C., were re-echoed time and again: 'We want the world to know that we no longer accept the inferior position of second-class citizenship. We are willing to go to jail, be ridiculed, spat upon, and even suffer physical violence to obtain First Class Citizenship.'

By and large, this feeling that they have a destined date with freedom, was not limited to a drive for personal freedom, or even freedom for the Negro in the South. Repeatedly it was emphasized that the movement was concerned with the moral implications of racial discrimination for the 'whole world' and the 'Human Race.' This universality of approach was linked with a perceptive recognition that 'it is important to keep the movement democratic and to avoid struggles for personal leadership.'

It was further evident that desire for supportive cooperation from adult leaders and the adult community was also tempered by apprehension that adults might try to 'capture' the student movement. The students showed willingness to be met on the basis of equality, but were intolerant of anything that smacked of manipulation or domination."

---

*A meeting of students sponsored by the Southern Christian Leadership Conference.

Questions for Analysis

1. Identify the main goal of the Student Leadership Conference, according to Baker.
2. Describe the similarities and differences in tactics discussed in the excerpt.
3. Explain why Baker believes the movement is "bigger than a hamburger."

Questions for Comparison

The Southern Manifesto, 1956 (page 871)

1. Explain how the context surrounding each document informs the central argument it makes.
2. Explain how Baker defines "rights" differently from the signers of the *Southern Manifesto.*
3. Evaluate the extent to which the new generation of civil rights activists challenged both southern segregationists and older civil rights advocates.

World War II also sparked a continuation of the migration of Black Americans to the West, part of the Great Migration (see Module 7.6), and part of the larger population movement to the Sun Belt. From 1940 to 1960, the Black population in the region jumped from 4.9 to 5.4 percent of the total population and numbered more than 1.2 million. Encountering various forms of racial discrimination, Black Americans waged boycotts and sit-ins of businesses that refused Black people equal service in Lawrence, Kansas, and Albuquerque, New Mexico.

Perhaps the most significant protest occurred in Oklahoma City. In August 1958, the teenagers of the NAACP Youth Council and their adult adviser, Clara M. Luper, led sit-ins to desegregate lunch counters in downtown stores. Having succeeded in integrating a dozen facilities, the movement waged a six-year struggle to end discrimination in public accommodations throughout the city.

REVIEW

- What accounts for the similarities and differences between the Student Nonviolent Coordinating Committee (SNCC) and the Southern Christian Leadership Conference (SCLC)?
- What similarities and what differences characterize the civil rights movement in the South and the West?

AP® Skills Workshop: Writing Historically

Additional Practice in Responding to a Short-Answer Question with Secondary Sources

"Another force also rose from the caldron of the Great Depression and crested in the 1940s: a powerful social movement sparked by the alchemy of laborites, civil rights activists, progressive New Dealers, and Black and white radicals, some of whom were associated with the Communist party. . . . [T]he movement's commitment to building coalitions, the expansiveness of its social democratic vision, and the importance of its Black radical and laborite leadership. A national movement with a vital southern wing, civil rights unionism was not just a precursor of the modern civil rights movement. It was its decisive first phase.

The link between race and class lay at the heart of the movement's political imagination. . . . [C]ivil rights unionists sought to combine protection from discrimination with universalistic social welfare policies and individual rights with labor rights. For them, workplace democracy, union wages, and fair and full employment went hand in hand with open, affordable housing, political enfranchisement, educational equity, and an enhanced safety net, including health care for all. . . . Extending the New Deal and reforming the South were two sides of the same coin. . . . To challenge the southern Democrats' congressional stranglehold, the movement had to enfranchise Black and white southern workers and bring them into the house of labor, thus creating a constituency on which the region's emerging pro-civil rights, pro-labor politicians could rely."

Jacquelyn Dowd Hall, "The Long Civil Rights Movement and the Political Uses of the Past," *Journal of American History*, 2005

"There was a genuine movement for social change in the South during the New Deal era, but it took on a different shape from the civil rights movement that followed in the next two decades. Civil rights unions . . . performed the work of extending civil rights and laid the groundwork for what followed, but this remained distinct from the civil rights movement. . . . Class mattered more than race, and critics targeted capitalism as the source of Black oppression. . . . [O]nly through a restructuring of corporate capitalism would

(continued)

genuine economic democracy emerge and white supremacy collapse. Although Black American progressives actively participated in unions . . . the leadership and membership of these organizations in the South consisted mainly of whites. . . . These activists were courageous, visionary, and essential, but they composed only a tiny fraction of the southern population. Their influence should be neither ignored nor exaggerated. . . .

[B]y the time of the *Brown* decision and [Emmett] Till's murder, Black Americans possessed the institutional structures necessary to mobilize to close the gap between their expectations of change and the brutal reality of white supremacy. At the national level, the NAACP led the way, followed by the SCLC, CORE, and SNCC. Indeed, after *Brown*, state-led efforts to destroy the NAACP, considered the most radical of Black organizations by southern white authorities, spurred the creation of new protest organizations locally and throughout the South. Black churches, civic associations, and informal community networks added organizational muscle to the demands for racial equality during the 1950s and 1960s. Without these structures . . . the yearning for civil rights would not have grown into a movement, and people would not have taken action against the power of state-supported white supremacy."

Steven F. Lawson, "Long Origins of the Short Civil Rights Movement, 1954–1968," in *Freedom Rights: New Perspectives on the Civil Rights Movement*, 2011

Using the excerpts, answer **A**, **B**, and **C**.

(A) Briefly explain ONE major difference between Hall's and Lawson's interpretations of the origins of the civil rights movement.
(B) Briefly explain how ONE specific historical event or development from the period that is not explicitly mentioned in the excerpts could be used to support Hall's argument.
(C) Briefly explain how ONE specific historical event or development from the period that is not explicitly mentioned in the excerpts could be used to support Lawson's argument.

America as a World Power

MODULE 8.7

FOCUS

As you read this module, consider the Cold War developments in the 1950s and early 1960s. Compare the responses of Truman (see Module 8.2), Eisenhower, and Kennedy. Analyze how American politics and society were impacted by Cold War events during each presidential administration.

With the end of the Korean War in 1953, the United States and the Soviet Union each spent huge sums of money and manpower building up their arsenal of nuclear weapons and military forces. They did not engage directly on the battlefield, but they attempted to spread their influence around the world while protecting their spheres of influence closer to their borders. The growing presence of nuclear weapons hung over diplomatic crises wherever they emerged, occasionally prompting the leaders of the two most powerful nations to seek an accommodation.

Despite the existence of civil rights protesters, rock 'n' roll upstarts, intellectual dissenters, and sexual revolutionaries, the 1950s seemed to many a tranquil, even dull period. This impression owes a great deal to the leadership of President Dwight D. Eisenhower. Serving two terms from 1953 to 1961, Eisenhower, or "Ike" as he was affectionately called, convinced the majority of Americans that their country was in good hands regardless of political turbulence at home and heated international conflicts abroad.

By 1960, however, the nation was ready for a new generation of leadership. In a close election, John F. Kennedy defeated Eisenhower's vice president, Richard Nixon, becoming the youngest person ever elected to the White House. In office, Kennedy faced a series of Cold War challenges in Cuba, Vietnam, and Berlin that threatened to draw the United States into conflict overseas.

Nuclear Weapons and Containment

In foreign affairs, President Dwight D. Eisenhower perpetuated Truman's containment doctrine while at the same time espousing the contradictory principle of "rolling back" communism in Eastern Europe. However, when Hungarians rose up against their Soviet-backed regime in 1956, the U.S. government did little in response. Rather than pushing back communism, the Eisenhower administration expanded the doctrine of containment around the world by entering into treaties to establish regional defense pacts.

Eisenhower's commitment to fiscal discipline had a profound effect on his foreign policy. The president worried that the alliance among government, defense contractors, and research universities—which he dubbed the **military-industrial complex**—would bankrupt the economy and undermine individual freedom. With this in mind, he implemented the **New Look** strategy, which placed a higher priority

military-industrial complex The phrase used by President Eisenhower in his 1961 farewell address in which he warned the nation against the close relationship developing between the government and the defense industry and the threat this posed to American democracy.

on building a nuclear arsenal and delivery system than on the more expensive task of maintaining and deploying armed forces on the ground throughout the world. Nuclear missiles launched from the air by U.S. air force bombers or fired from submarines would give the United States, as Secretary of Defense Charles Wilson asserted, "a bigger bang for the buck." With the nation now armed with nuclear weapons, the Eisenhower administration threatened "massive retaliation" in the event of communist aggression.

The New Look may have saved money and slowed the rate of defense spending, but it had serious flaws. First, it placed a premium on "brinksmanship," taking communist enemies to the precipice of nuclear destruction, risking the death of millions, and hoping the other side would back down. Second, massive retaliation did not work for small-scale conflicts. For instance, in the event of a confrontation in Berlin, would the United States launch nuclear missiles toward Germany and expose its European allies in West Germany and France to nuclear contamination? Third, the buildup of nuclear warheads provoked an arms race by encouraging the Soviet Union to do the same.

mutually assured destruction (MAD) The Cold War defense strategy adopted by the United States and the U.S.S.R. to deter a nuclear attack from the other country by threatening to retaliate with a massive nuclear strike in response. MAD fueled the arms race as both sides worked to convince the other of their ongoing ability to retaliate if attacked.

Peace depended on the superpowers terrifying each other with the threat of nuclear annihilation — that is, if one country attacked the other, retaliation was guaranteed to result in shared obliteration. This strategy was known as **mutually assured destruction**, and its acronym — **MAD** — summed up its nightmarish qualities. As each nuclear power increased its capacity to destroy the other many times over, the potential for mistakes and errors in judgment increased, threatening a nuclear holocaust that would leave little to rebuild.

National security concerns occupied a good deal of the president's time. Fearing that a Soviet nuclear attack could wipe out nearly a third of the population before the

Bomb Shelter, 1954 The successful test of an atomic bomb by the Soviets in 1949 followed by the Korean War (1950–1953) prompted many Americans to begin preparing for a possible nuclear attack. This Houston, Texas, family, including their dog, poses in their bomb shelter stocked with food, first aid supplies, weapons, and ammunition. **What does this photograph suggest about the values and anxieties of middle-class American families in the 1950s?**

John Dominis/The LIFE Picture Collection/Getty Images

United States could retaliate, the Eisenhower administration stepped up civil defense efforts. Schoolchildren took part in "duck and cover" drills, in which teachers shouted, "take cover" and students hid under their desks. In the meantime, both the United States and the Soviet Union began producing intercontinental ballistic missiles armed with nuclear warheads. They also stepped up aboveground tests of nuclear weapons, which contaminated the atmosphere with dangerous radioactive particles.

Despite doomsday rhetoric of retaliation, Eisenhower relied more on diplomacy than on military action. Stalin's death in 1953 and his eventual replacement by Nikita Khrushchev in 1955 permitted a relaxation of tensions between the two superpowers. In July 1955, Eisenhower and Khrushchev, together with British and French leaders, gathered in Geneva to discuss arms control, though nothing concrete came out of this summit.

In a speech to communist officials two years later, Khrushchev denounced the excesses of Stalin's totalitarian rule and reinforced hopes for a new era of peaceful coexistence between the Cold War antagonists. In 1958, Vice President Richard Nixon visited the Soviet Union, the first top elected official to do so since the onset of the Cold War, as a sign of warming relations between the two nations. Nixon and Khrushchev attended a U.S. exhibition in Moscow on July 24, 1959, where the two leaders debated the relative merits of capitalism and communism, while looking at an American kitchen that displayed the latest household appliances. This so-called "**Kitchen Debate**" did not dissuade Khrushchev from making a twelve-day visit to the United States later that year.

Yet peaceful coexistence remained precarious. Just as President Eisenhower was about to begin his own tour of the Soviet Union in 1960, the Soviets shot down an American U-2 spy plane flying over their country. Eisenhower canceled his trip, and tensions resumed.

- In what ways did Eisenhower's foreign policy toward the U.S.S.R. differ from Truman's approach?

Interventions in the Middle East, Latin America, and Africa

While relations between the Soviet Union and the United States thawed and then cooled during the Eisenhower era, the Cold War advanced into new regions. The efforts of Iranian, Guatemalan, and Cuban leaders to seize control of their countries' resources mirrored the surge of nationalism that swept through former European colonies in the 1950s. Following World War II, revolutionary nationalists in the Middle East, Africa, and Southeast Asia toppled colonial governments and wielded the power of their newly liberated regimes to take charge of their own development. Postwar decolonization and the rise of militant nationalism collided with U.S. Cold War policy, as these nonwhite nations remained neutral.

At the **Bandung Conference** in Indonesia in 1955, twenty-nine Asian and African nations, many of them recently liberated, condemned continued colonization, particularly control in North Africa by France, a close U.S. ally, and asserted their intention to remain nonaligned with either side in the Cold War. The U.S. government took a dim view of the Bandung Conference and refused to send representatives. Especially worrisome to the United States, the communist Chinese government made serious overtures to form closer relations with these nations.

The United States often took a heavy-handed approach when it suspected newly decolonized nations were edging to the side of the Soviets. In a manner first suggested in NSC-68, the Eisenhower administration deployed the CIA to help topple governments considered pro-communist as well as to promote U.S. economic interests. For example, after Prime Minister Mohammed Mossadegh of Iran nationalized foreign oil corporations in 1953, the CIA engineered a successful coup that ousted his government and installed the pro-American shah Mohammad Reza Pahlavi in his place. Mossadegh was not a communist, but by overthrowing him, American oil companies obtained 40 percent of Iran's oil revenue.

In 1954, the economics of fruit and shipping replaced oil as the catalyst for U.S. intervention into a developing nation within its own sphere of influence. The elected socialist regime of Jacobo Arbenz Guzmán in Guatemala had seized 225,000 acres of land held by the United Fruit Company, a powerful U.S. company in which Secretary of State John Foster Dulles and his brother, CIA director Allen Dulles, held stock. According to the Dulles brothers, the land's seizure by the Guatemalan government posed a threat to the nearby Panama Canal. Eisenhower allowed the CIA to hatch a plot that resulted in a coup d'état, or government overthrow, that installed a right-wing military regime in Guatemala, which safeguarded both the Panama Canal and the United Fruit Company.

AP® EXAM TIP

Explain how the United States supported leaders in Latin America whose governments put restraints on democratic principles. How did the United States reconcile the lack of democratic reforms with the ongoing support of these anticommunist regimes?

The success of the CIA's covert efforts in Guatemala prompted the Eisenhower administration to plan a similar action in Cuba, ninety miles off the coast of Florida. In 1959, Fidel Castro led an uprising and came to power in Cuba after overthrowing the American-backed dictator Fulgencio Batista. A Cuban nationalist in the tradition of José Martí, Castro sought to regain full control over his country's economic resources, including those owned by U.S. corporations. He appropriated $1 billion worth of American property and signed a trade agreement with the Soviet Union. To consolidate his political rule, Castro jailed opponents and installed a communist regime. In 1960, President Eisenhower authorized the CIA to design a clandestine operation to overthrow the Castro government, but he left office before the invasion could occur.

The United States and the Soviet Union each tried to gain influence over emerging nations. Many newly independent countries sought neutrality in foreign affairs, accepting aid from both of the Cold War protagonists. Nonetheless, they were often drawn into East-West conflicts.

Such was the case in Egypt, which gained formal sovereignty in 1952 from British control over its military and foreign relations. Two years later, under General Gamal Abdel Nasser, the country sought to modernize its economy by building the hydroelectric Aswan Dam on the Nile River. Nasser welcomed financial backing from the United States and the Soviet Union, but the Eisenhower administration refused to contribute so long as the Egyptians accepted Soviet assistance.

In 1956, Nasser, falling short of funds, sent troops to take over the Suez Canal, the waterway run by Great Britain and through which the bulk of Western Europe's oil was shipped. He intended to pay for the dam by collecting tolls from canal users. In retaliation, Britain and France, the two European powers most affected by the seizure, invaded Egypt on October 29, 1956. Locked in a struggle with Egypt and other Arab nations since its creation in 1948, Israel joined in the attack.

The invading forces — all U.S. allies — had not warned the Eisenhower administration of their plans. Coming at the same time as the Soviet crackdown against the Hungarian revolution, the British-French-Israeli assault placed the United States in the difficult position of condemning the Soviets for intervening in Hungary while its anticommunist partners waged war in Suez. Instead, Eisenhower cooperated with the United Nations to negotiate a cease-fire and engineer a pullout of the invading forces in Egypt. Ultimately, the Soviets proved the winners in this Cold War skirmish. The Suez invasion revived memories of European imperialism and fueled anti-Western sentiments and pan-Arab nationalism (a sense of unity among Arabs across national boundaries), which worked to the Soviets' advantage.

The Eisenhower administration soon moved to counter growing Soviet power in the region. In 1957, to throttle increasing communist influence in the Middle East, Congress approved the **Eisenhower Doctrine**, which gave the president a free hand to use U.S. military forces in the Middle East "against overt armed aggression from any nation controlled by International Communism." In actuality, the Eisenhower administration proved more concerned with protecting access to oil fields from hostile Arab nationalist leaders than with any communist incursion. In 1958, when an anti-American, non-communist regime came to power in Iraq, the president sent 14,000 marines to neighboring Lebanon to prevent a similar outcome there.

Eisenhower Doctrine

An Eisenhower administration policy that promised economic and/or military assistance to a Middle Eastern country threatened by communist aggression. The strategy was meant to bolster containment and protect U.S. oil interests and pro-American governments.

Just before Eisenhower left office in January 1961, his administration intervened in a civil war in the newly independent Congo. This former colony of Belgium held valuable mineral resources, which Belgium and the United States coveted. After the Congo's first prime minister, Patrice Lumumba, stated his intentions to remain neutral in the Cold War, President Eisenhower and CIA director Allen Dulles declared him unreliable in the conflict with the Soviet Union. With the support of Belgian military troops and encouragement from the United States, the resource-rich province of Katanga seceded from the Congo in 1960. After the Congolese military, under the leadership of Joseph Mobutu, overthrew Lumumba's government, the CIA launched an operation that culminated in the execution of Lumumba on January 17, 1961. Several years later, Mobutu became president of the country and allied with the West.

AP® WORKING with EVIDENCE

Source: President Dwight D. Eisenhower, Farewell Address, 1961

> "Our military organization today bears little relation to that known by any of my predecessors in peacetime, or indeed by the fighting men of World War II or Korea.
>
> Until the latest of our world conflicts, the United States had no armaments industry.
>
> American makers of plowshares could, with time and as required, make swords as well.
>
> But now we can no longer risk emergency improvisation of national defense; we have been compelled to create a permanent armaments industry of vast proportions.
>
> Added to this, three and a half million men and women are directly engaged in the defense establishment.
>
> We annually spend on military security more than the net income of all United States Corporations.
>
> This conjunction of an immense military establishment and a large arms industry is new in the American experience.
>
> The total influence—economic, political, even spiritual—is felt in every city, every State house, every office of the Federal government. . . .

AP® EXAM TIP

Streamline your understanding of the military-industrial complex by examining a more specific task. Think about exploring at least two specific ideas President Eisenhower chose to examine in his farewell address that connect to the military-industrial complex. Use those two examples to describe how Americans debated the meaning of his warning to the nation about the necessity and dangers associated with such a development.

In the councils of government, we must guard against the acquisition of unwarranted influence, whether sought or unsought, by the military-industrial complex.

The potential for the disastrous rise of misplaced power exists and will persist.

We must never let the weight of this combination endanger our liberties or democratic processes.

We should take nothing for granted.

Only an alert and knowledgeable citizenry can compel the proper meshing of the huge industrial and military machinery of defense with our peaceful methods and goals, so that security and liberty may prosper together."

Questions for Analysis

1. Identify the main concern Eisenhower expresses in the excerpt.
2. Describe the change in the American military establishment after World War II reflected in this excerpt.
3. Explain the context for Eisenhower's address and the concerns he expresses in it.
4. Evaluate the extent to which the Eisenhower administration's foreign policy contributed to the development of the U.S. military-industrial complex.

REVIEW

- How did the Cold War shape U.S. foreign policy toward Latin American, African, and Middle Eastern nations during the mid-twentieth century?

Modern Republicanism and the Election of 1960

Modern Republicanism The political approach of President Dwight Eisenhower that tried to fit traditional Republican Party ideals of fiscal conservatism and individualism alongside more progressive social policies within the broad framework of the New Deal. In conjunction with his military record, the platform gave Eisenhower broad cross-party appeal.

President Eisenhower, a World War II hero, radiated strength and trust, qualities the American people found very attractive as they rebuilt their lives and established families in the 1950s. In November 1952, Eisenhower coasted to victory over the Democratic candidate Adlai Stevenson, winning 55 percent of the popular vote and 83 percent of the electoral vote. The Republicans managed to win slim majorities in the Senate and the House, but within two years, the Democrats regained control of Congress.

Eisenhower adopted what one of his speechwriters called **Modern Republicanism**, which tried to fit the traditional Republican Party ideals of individualism and fiscal restraint within the broad framework of Franklin Roosevelt's New Deal. As Eisenhower wrote to his brother, "Should any political party attempt to abolish social security, unemployment insurance, and eliminate labor laws and farm programs, you would not hear of that party again in our political history."

With Democrats in control of Congress after 1954, Republicans agreed to raise Social Security benefits and to include coverage for some ten million additional workers.

Congress and the president retained another New Deal mainstay, the minimum wage, and increased it from 75 cents to $1 an hour.

Departing from traditional Republican criticism of big government, the Eisenhower administration added the Department of Health, Education, and Welfare to the cabinet in 1953. In 1956, the Eisenhower administration sponsored the **National Interstate and Defense Highway Act**, which provided funds for the construction of 42,500 miles of roads throughout the country, boosting both suburbanization and national defense.

National Interstate and Defense Highway Act
An act passed in 1956 that provided federal funds for the construction of a national highway system to link major cities and facilitate future wartime mobilization. As the largest public works project in American history, the act spurred economic growth, suburbanization, and the automobile as the main method of transportation for most Americans.

In addition, in 1958 Eisenhower signed into law the **National Defense Education Act**, which provided funding for instruction in science, math, and foreign languages and graduate fellowships and loans for college students. He portrayed the new law as a way to catch up with the Soviets, who the previous year had successfully launched the first artificial satellite, called ***Sputnik***, into Earth orbit.

Sputnik
The first artificial satellite, launched in 1957 by the Soviet Union. The launch prompted a major increase in U.S. spending on the space race as well as scientific research and development.

For six of Eisenhower's eight years in office, the president had to work with Democratic majorities in Congress. Overall, he managed to forge bipartisan support for his proposals. Nowhere was this more significant than with civil rights legislation. Under his administration's leadership, Republicans joined with Democrats, led by Senate Majority Leader Lyndon B. Johnson, to pass the first pieces of civil rights legislation since Reconstruction. In 1957 and 1960, Eisenhower signed into law two bills that extended the authority of the federal government to file court challenges against southern election officials who blocked Black Americans from registering to vote. However, southern Democratic senators thwarted Congress from passing even stronger voting measures or acts that would have enforced school desegregation.

Eisenhower administration policy, however, did not work to the benefit of American Indians. The federal government reversed many of the reforms instituted during the New Deal. In the 1950s, the **Bureau of Indian Affairs (BIA)** adopted the policy of termination and relocation of American Indian tribes. Those tribes deemed to have achieved the most "progress," such as the Flathead of Montana, the Klamath of Oregon, and the Hupa of northern California, were treated as ordinary American citizens, which resulted in termination of their federal benefits and transfer of their tribal lands to state and local governments. The National Congress of American Indians fought unsuccessfully against this program.

The government also relocated American Indians to urban areas. Between 1952 and 1960, the BIA encouraged more than 30,000 American Indians to move from their reservations to cities. The American Indian population of Los Angeles grew to 25,000, including members of the Navajo, Sioux, and Cherokee nations. Although thousands of American Indians took advantage of the relocation program, many had difficulty adjusting to urban life and fell into poverty.

The Eisenhower administration also repatriated undocumented Mexican laborers. The *bracero* program instituted in 1942 (see Module 7.12) had not eliminated illegal immigration from Mexico into the United States, as large agricultural growers sought more cheap labor. Although some who came legally through the program stayed beyond the period allowed, far more Mexicans simply crossed the border illegally, seeking work. Mexico complained about these illegal immigrants because it needed a larger supply of agricultural workers, and American labor groups protested that illegal immigrants took jobs away from Americans. In 1954, Eisenhower's Immigration and Naturalization Service rounded up undocumented Mexicans, mainly in Texas and California, and returned them to Mexico. Those deported often suffered harsh conditions, and seven deportees drowned after they jumped ship. "**Operation Wetback**," as the program was dubbed using a derogatory term for Mexicans, forced an estimated 250,000 to 1.3 million Mexicans to leave the United States.

After winning a second term in 1956, Eisenhower clashed with the Democratic majority in Congress over spending. He vetoed bills that increased expenditures for public housing, public works projects, and urban renewal in an attempt to keep the budget balanced. Yet under Eisenhower, the country overcame two recessions, the middle class grew in size, and inflation remained low. However, for forty million Americans, poverty, not prosperity, remained the reality.

Even after serving two terms in office, Eisenhower remained popular. However, he could not run for a third term, barred by the Twenty-second Amendment (1951). Vice President Richard M. Nixon ran as the Republican candidate for president in 1960. Unlike Eisenhower, Nixon was not universally liked or respected. His reputation for unsavory political combat drew the scorn of Democrats, especially liberals. Moreover, Nixon had to fend off charges that Republicans, as embodied in the seventy-year-old Eisenhower, were out of date and out of new ideas.

Running as the Democratic candidate for president in 1960, Senator John F. Kennedy of Massachusetts promised to instill renewed "vigor" in the White House and get the country moving again. Yet Kennedy did not differ much from his Republican rival on domestic and foreign-policy issues. While Kennedy employed a rhetoric of high-minded change, he had not compiled a distinguished or courageous record in the Senate. Moreover, his family's fortune had paved the way for his political career, and he had earned a well-justified reputation in Washington as a playboy and womanizer.

The outcome of the 1960 election turned on several factors. The country was experiencing a slight economic recession, reviving memories in older voters of the Great Depression, which had begun with the Republican Herbert Hoover in power. In addition, presidential candidates faced off on television for the first time, participating in four televised debates. TV emphasized visual style and presentation. In the first debate, with Nixon having just recovered from a stay in the hospital and looking haggard, Kennedy convinced a majority of viewers that he possessed the presidential bearing for the job. Nixon performed better in the next three debates, but the damage had been done. Still, Kennedy had to overcome considerable religious prejudice to win the election. No Catholic had ever won the presidency, and the prejudices of Protestants, especially in the South, threatened to divert critical votes from Kennedy's Democratic base. While many southern Democrats did support Nixon, Kennedy balanced out these defections by gaining votes from the nation's Catholics, especially in northern states rich in electoral votes.

Race also exerted a critical influence. Nixon and Kennedy had similar records on civil rights, and if anything, Nixon's was slightly stronger. However, on October 19, 1960, when Atlanta police arrested Martin Luther King Jr. for participating in a restaurant sit-in, Kennedy sprang to his defense, whereas Nixon kept his distance. Kennedy telephoned the civil rights leader's wife to offer his sympathy and used his influence to get King released from jail.

As a result, King's father, a Protestant minister who had intended to vote against the Catholic Kennedy, now endorsed the Democrat. In addition to the elder King, Kennedy won back for Democrats 7 percent of Black voters who had supported Eisenhower in 1956. Kennedy triumphed by a margin of less than 1 percent of the popular vote, underscoring the importance of the Black American electorate.

Time Life Pictures/Getty Images

Watching the 1960 Presidential Debate
A family watches Democratic nominee John F. Kennedy during a televised presidential debate against Republican nominee Richard M. Nixon. The 1960 presidential election featured the first televised debates, which were watched by tens of millions of Americans.

How does this image show the ways in which TV and radio had a similar effect on politics? How does it show the ways in which they had different effects?

REVIEW

- How did Eisenhower attempt to redefine Republicanism, and to what extent was he successful?
- What factors contributed to Kennedy's narrow victory in the 1960 presidential election?

Kennedy, the Cold War, and Cuba

The Kennedy administration showed great interest in fighting the Cold War abroad. The president believed that reform capitalism, which worked well in the United States, should become a global model. Communism, like fascism before it, posed a fundamental threat to American interests and to other countries' ability to copy the economic miracle of the United States. The faith of liberals in U.S. ingenuity, willpower, technological superiority, and moral righteousness encouraged them to reshape the "free world" in America's image.

President Kennedy's first Cold War battle took place in Cuba. Before his election, Kennedy learned of a secret CIA plan, devised by the Eisenhower administration, to topple Fidel Castro from power. After becoming president, Kennedy approved the scheme that Eisenhower had set in motion.

MAP 8.4 The Bay of Pigs Invasion, 1961 President Kennedy launched the Bay of Pigs invasion on April 17, 1961, to topple the communist regime of Fidel Castro. The CIA secretly trained Cuban exiles in locations in the southern United States, Central America, and the Caribbean. After three days of fighting, the invasion failed and turned Castro into a national hero, thereby strengthening his leadership. Fearing further U.S. aggression, Castro turned to the Soviet Union to install missiles in Cuba for protection.

Why were the Eisenhower and Kennedy administrations so worried about the Castro-led government in Cuba?

Bay of Pigs invasion
An unsuccessful attempt under the Kennedy administration to overthrow Cuban leader Fidel Castro by sending 1,400 armed Cuban exiles to invade the island in 1961. Castro's troops contained the poorly trained invaders, and the failed invasion proved to be an international embarrassment for the United States.

The operation ended disastrously. On April 17, 1961, an invasion force trained by the CIA of between 1,400 and 1,500 Cuban exiles who had fled the island during Castro's overthrow of the Batista regime landed by boat on Cuba's southwest coast, launching the **Bay of Pigs invasion**. Kennedy refused to provide backup military forces for fear of revealing the U.S. role in the attack. Castro's troops defeated the insurgents in three days. CIA planners had underestimated Cuban popular support for Castro, falsely believing that the invasion would inspire a national uprising against the communist regime. The Kennedy administration had blundered into a bitter foreign policy defeat.

WORKING with EVIDENCE

Source: President John F. Kennedy, Address before the American Society of Newspaper Editors, April 20, 1961

"The message of Cuba, of Laos, of the rising din of Communist voices in Asia and Latin America—these messages are all the same. The complacent, the self-indulgent, the soft societies are about to be swept away with the debris of history. Only the strong, only the industrious, only the determined, only the courageous, only the visionary who determine the real nature of our struggle can possibly survive.

No greater task faces this country or this administration. No other challenge is more deserving of our every effort and energy. Too long we have fixed our eyes on traditional military needs, on armies prepared to cross borders, on missiles poised for flight. Now it should be clear that this is no longer enough—that our security may be lost piece by piece, country by country, without the bringing of a single missile or the crossing of a single border.

We intend to profit from this lesson. We intend to reexamine and reorient our forces of all kinds—our tactics and our institutions here in this community. We intend to intensify our efforts for a struggle in many ways more difficult than war, where disappointment will often accompany us.

For I am convinced that we in this country and in the free world possess the necessary resource, and the skill, and the added strength that comes from a belief in the freedom of man. And I am equally convinced that history will record the fact that this bitter struggle reached its climax in the late 1950's and the early 1960's. Let me then make clear as the President of the United States that I am determined upon our system's survival and success, regardless of the cost and regardless of the peril!"

Questions for Analysis

1. Identify the "lesson" Kennedy shares in his speech.
2. Describe the immediate context for Kennedy's speech.
3. Explain why Kennedy claims the "struggle" is "in many ways more difficult than war."
4. Evaluate the validity of Kennedy's claim that "this bitter struggle reached its climax in the late 1950's and early 1960's."

Two months later, Kennedy met Soviet leader Nikita Khrushchev at a summit meeting in Vienna. Khrushchev took advantage of the president's embarrassing defeat in Cuba to press his own demands. After the confrontational summit meeting increased tensions between the superpowers, Kennedy persuaded Congress to increase the defense budget, dispatch additional troops to Europe, and bolster civil defense. In August, the Soviets responded by constructing the **Berlin Wall**, making it more difficult for refugees fleeing poverty and oppression in East Berlin to escape to West Berlin.

Berlin Wall
A wall built by the Soviet Union in 1961 to keep East Berliners from escaping to West Berlin. The Berlin Wall quickly became a Cold War symbol of the "iron curtain" that Winston Churchill described in a 1946 address in Missouri. The destruction of the Berlin Wall in 1989 symbolized the end of the Cold War.

Despite the Bay of Pigs disaster, the United States continued its efforts to topple the Castro regime. Such attempts were unsuccessful. In response, Castro invited the Soviet Union to install short- and intermediate-range nuclear missiles in Cuba to protect the country against any U.S. incursion. After their discovery by American U-2 spy planes, Kennedy went on national television on October 22, 1962, to inform the American people that the Soviets had placed missiles in Cuba. The Kennedy administration decided to blockade Cuba to prevent Soviet ships from supplying the deadly warheads that would make the missiles fully operational. If Soviet ships defied the blockade, the president would order air strikes and an invasion to destroy the missiles and overthrow Castro. Ordinary Americans nervously contemplated the very real possibility of nuclear destruction as Soviet ships sailed toward the blockade.

On the brink of nuclear war, both sides chose compromise. Khrushchev agreed to remove the missiles, and Kennedy pledged not to invade Cuba and secretly promised to dismantle U.S. missile sites in Turkey aimed at the Soviet Union. The world breathed a sigh of relief, and Kennedy and Khrushchev, having stepped back from the edge of nuclear holocaust, worked to ease tensions further. In 1963, they signed a Partial Nuclear Test Ban Treaty—which prohibited atmospheric but not underground testing—and installed an electronic "hot line" to ensure swift communications between Washington and Moscow.

Kennedy sought to balance his hardline, anticommunist policies with new outreach efforts to inspire developing nations to follow a democratic path. The Peace Corps program sent thousands of volunteers to teach and advise developing nations, and Kennedy's Alliance for Progress supplied economic aid to emerging democracies in Latin America.

REVIEW

- How did Kennedy's Cold War policies almost lead to open conflict in Cuba during the early 1960s?

AP® Skills Workshop: Writing Historically

Additional Practice in Responding to a Short-Answer Question with a Primary Source

Source: Edward Valtman, "This hurts me more than it hurts you!" *Hartford Times*, October 1962

Library of Congress, Prints & Photographs Division, drawing by Edmund S. Valtman [DIG-ppmsc-07978]

About the source: This cartoon depicts Cuban president Fidel Castro (left) and Soviet premier Nikita Khrushchev (right).

Using the image, answer **A**, **B**, and **C**.

(A) Briefly describe ONE perspective expressed by the artist about the Cold War.

(B) Briefly explain how ONE development led to the historical situation shown in the image.

(C) Briefly explain ONE specific outcome of Cold War era debates about U.S. foreign policy.

The Vietnam War

MODULE 8.8

FOCUS

As you read this module, consider the short- and long-term causes of the Vietnam War and the impact of the war on American society. Be sure to weigh the relative importance of foreign-policy concerns (e.g., containment) and domestic political concerns (e.g., not appearing soft on communism). Assess the reasons why America lost the Vietnam War and the effectiveness of Nixon's foreign policy.

While substantial progress was made on civil rights and liberal reforms at home, the Eisenhower, Kennedy, and Johnson administrations enjoyed far less success in fighting communism abroad. Following the overthrow of French colonial rule in Vietnam in 1954, the Cold War spread to Southeast Asia, where the United States applied the doctrine of containment. Believing that the situation in Vietnam posed a threat to the whole of Southeast Asia and American credibility abroad, the United States deployed hundreds of thousands of troops to fight the spread of communist rule to South Vietnam in what was, instead, a civil war.

AP® EXAM TIP

The United States was involved in Vietnam—to varying levels of commitment—from the time of President Truman until President Ford. Select moments of inflection and explain how each represented a historical continuity or change in U.S. foreign policy. Aside from the specific administration, think about connecting a specific event or development that explains the historical change or continuity.

Early Intervention in Vietnam, 1954–1963

One offshoot of the Korean War was increased U.S. intervention in Vietnam, resulting in profound, long-term consequences. By the 1950s, Vietnamese revolutionaries (the Vietminh) had been fighting for independence from the French for decades. They were led by Ho Chi Minh, a revolutionary who had studied communist theory in the Soviet Union but was not controlled by the Soviets. In fact, he modeled his 1945 Vietnamese Declaration of Independence on that of the United States. Despite sizable U.S. economic assistance for the French military effort, the Vietminh defeated the French at the Battle of Dien Bien Phu in 1954. With the backing of the United States, the Soviet Union, and China, both sides agreed to divide Vietnam at the seventeenth parallel and hold free elections to unite the country in 1956.

President Dwight Eisenhower, who had brought the Korean War to a close in 1953, believed that if Vietnam fell to the Communists, the rest of Southeast Asia and Japan would "go over very quickly" like "a row of dominoes," threatening American strategic power in East Asia as well as free access to Asian markets. Convinced that Ho Chi Minh and his followers would win free elections, in 1955, the Eisenhower administration supported the anti-French, anticommunist Ngo Dinh Diem to lead South Vietnam and then backed his regime's refusal to hold national elections in 1956. The anticommunist fears of the United States had trumped its democratic promises.

With the country now permanently divided, Eisenhower funneled economic aid to Diem to undertake needed land reforms that would strengthen his government and weaken the appeal of Ho Chi Minh. The president also dispatched hundreds of military advisers to support the South Vietnamese government. However, Diem used most of the money to consolidate his power rather than implement reforms, which only widened opposition to his regime from communists and non-communists alike. This prompted Ho Chi Minh in 1959 to support the creation in the South of the National Liberation Front, or **Vietcong**, to wage a military insurgency against Diem. By the end of the decade, the Eisenhower administration faced a major diplomatic problem with no clear plan for its resolution.

Vietcong

The popular name for the National Liberation Front, formed in 1959 in South Vietnam. The Vietcong waged a military insurgency against the U.S.-backed president, Ngo Dinh Diem, and received support from Ho Chi Minh, the leader of North Vietnam.

domino theory

The prevalent belief during the Cold War, maintaining that if one country fell under the influence of communism, other surrounding countries would soon similarly fall under the influence of communism, like a row of falling dominoes.

Like Eisenhower, President Kennedy believed in the **domino theory**, that if communists toppled one regime in Asia, one country after another would fall like dominoes to the communists. Kennedy, a World War II veteran, also believed that aggressive nations that attacked weaker ones threatened world peace unless they were challenged. The domino theory justified the policy of containment (Module 8.2) in East Asia.

Kennedy's containment efforts in Vietnam ran into difficulty because the United States did not control the situation on the ground. By 1961, Diem had spent more than $1 billion of U.S. aid on building up military and personal security forces to suppress political opposition rather than implement the land reform that he had promised. That year, Kennedy sent additional U.S. military special forces to train the South Vietnamese military in counterinsurgency. But the situation deteriorated in 1963 when the Catholic Diem prohibited the country's Buddhist majority from holding religious celebrations. In protest, Buddhist monks committed suicide by setting themselves on fire, a grisly display captured on television news programs in the United States.

With political opposition mounting against Diem and with the war going poorly, the Kennedy administration endorsed a military coup to replace the Diem government with one more capable of fighting communists. On November 1, 1963, the coup leaders removed Diem from office, assassinating him and key members of his regime within days, and installed a military government.

Diem's death, however, did little to improve the worsening war against the communists. The Vietcong had more support in the rural countryside than did the South Vietnamese government. The rebels promised land reform and recruited local peasants opposed to the corruption and ruthlessness of the Diem regime. The Kennedy administration committed itself to supporting Diem's successor, but by late November 1963, Kennedy seemed torn between sending more U.S. troops and finding a way to negotiate a peace.

REVIEW

- Why did the Eisenhower administration become involved in Vietnam, and why were its efforts unsuccessful?
- How did the Kennedy administration's involvement in Vietnam compare to that of Eisenhower?

AP® EXAM TIP

The Vietnam War is a complex historical event. Be able to explain at least three causes for U.S. involvement in the war and explain the extent to which each cause related to a commitment to contain communism. If one of your causes does not explain containment, you should explain why this is the case, because this type of thinking can show a complex understanding of a historical topic.

Johnson Escalates the War in Vietnam

When Lyndon Johnson took office after Kennedy's assassination on November 22, 1963, there were 16,000 American military advisers in Vietnam. Although Johnson privately harbored reservations about fighting in Vietnam, he feared appearing soft on communism and was concerned that a demonstration of weakness would jeopardize congressional support for his domestic plans. Although Johnson eventually concluded that more U.S. forces had to be sent to Vietnam, he waited for the right moment to rally Congress and the American public behind an escalation of the war.

That moment came in August 1964. On August 2, North Vietnamese gunboats attacked a U.S. navy destroyer sixty miles off the North Vietnamese coast in the Gulf of Tonkin in response to South Vietnamese naval raids along the coast. Two days later, another U.S. destroyer reported coming under torpedo attack, but because of stormy weather, the second ship was not certain that it had been fired on. Despite the considerable uncertainty about what had happened and the lack of damage, Johnson seized the opportunity to urge Congress to authorize military action. On August 7, 1964, Congress passed the **Gulf of Tonkin Resolution**, which provided the president with unlimited power to make military decisions regarding Vietnam.

Gulf of Tonkin Resolution A 1964 congressional resolution giving President Johnson wide discretion to use U.S. forces in Vietnam without an official declaration of war by Congress. The resolution allowed Johnson to escalate U.S. troop presence in Vietnam from tens of thousands to hundreds of thousands.

AP® WORKING with EVIDENCE

Source: *Gulf of Tonkin Resolution*, 1964

"To promote the maintenance of international peace and security in southeast Asia.

Whereas naval units of the Communist regime in Vietnam, in violation of the principles of the Charter of the United Nations and of international law, have deliberately and repeatedly attacked United States naval vessels lawfully present in international waters, and have thereby created a serious threat to international peace; and

Whereas these attackers are part of deliberate and systematic campaign of aggression that the Communist regime in North Vietnam has been waging against its neighbors and the nations joined with them in the collective defense of their freedom; and

Whereas the United States is assisting the peoples of southeast Asia to protest their freedom and has no territorial, military or political ambitions in that area, but desires only that these people should be left in peace to work out their destinies in their own way:

Now, therefore be it

Resolved by the Senate and House of Representatives of the United States of America in Congress assembled, That the Congress approves and supports the determination of the President, as Commander in Chief, to take all necessary measures to repel any armed attack against the forces of the United States and to prevent further aggression."

Questions for Analysis

1. Identify the goal of the Gulf of Tonkin Resolution.
2. Describe the reasons for the Gulf of Tonkin Resolution expressed in this excerpt.
3. Explain how the Gulf of Tonkin Resolution would allow the president to expand the conflict in Vietnam into a war.
4. Evaluate the extent to which U.S. military involvement in the Vietnam War represents a continuation of U.S. Cold War policy in the late 1940s and 1950s.

After winning election in 1964, President Johnson stepped up U.S. military action. In March 1965, with North Vietnamese forces flooding into the South, the president initiated a major bombing campaign called Operation Rolling Thunder. For more than three years, American planes dropped nearly a million tons of bombs on North Vietnam, more than the total amount the United States used in World War II. Despite this enormous firepower, the operation proved ineffective. A largely agricultural country, North Vietnam did not have the type of industrial targets best suited for air attacks.

escalation
A policy of the Johnson administration of continuously increasing the numbers of ground troops in Vietnam from 1964 to 1968 in hopes of securing victory in the war.

Vietnam War
Conflict between the communist nationalist government in North Vietnam, backed by the Soviet Union and China, against the United Nations and U.S.-backed South Vietnam government. The war is seen as part of a series of proxy wars as a result of Cold War tensions between the United States and the Soviet Union from 1954 to 1975.

It stored its vital military resources underground and was able to reconstruct rudimentary bridges and roads to maintain the flow of troops into the South within hours after U.S. bombers had pounded them.

Responding to the need to protect American air bases and the persistent ineffectiveness of the South Vietnamese military, Johnson deployed ever-increasing numbers of ground troops to Vietnam, a continuation of the U.S. policy of **escalation** that transformed the conflict into the **Vietnam War**. Troop levels rose from 16,000 in 1963 to 380,000 in 1966, 485,000 in 1967, and 536,000 in 1968. The U.S. military also deployed napalm bombs, which spewed burning jellied gasoline, and Agent Orange, a chemical that defoliated the Vietnamese countryside and produced long-term adverse health effects for those who came in contact with it, including American soldiers. These attacks added to the resentment of South Vietnamese peasants and helped the Vietcong gain new recruits.

The United States confronted a challenging guerrilla war in Vietnam. The Vietcong often fought at night and blended in during the day as ordinary residents of cities and villages. They did not provide a visible target, and they recruited women and men of all ages, making it difficult for U.S. ground forces to distinguish friend from foe. Although U.S. military commanders realized the necessity of "winning hearts and minds" in Vietnam, in the end, the U.S. military effort alienated the population it was designed to safeguard.

AP® WORKING with EVIDENCE

Source: Philip Caputo, *A Rumor of War,* 1977

"On March 8, 1965, as a young infantry officer, I landed at Danang with a battalion of the 9th Marine Expeditionary Brigade, the first U.S. combat unit sent to Indochina. . . .

For Americans who did not come of age in the early sixties, it may be hard to grasp what those years were like—the pride and overpowering self-assurance that prevailed. Most of the thirty-five hundred men in our brigade, born during or immediately after World War II, were shaped by that era, the age of Kennedy's Camelot. We went overseas full of illusions, for which the intoxicating atmosphere of those years was as much to blame as our youth.

War is always attractive to young men who know nothing about it, but we had also been seduced into uniform by Kennedy's challenge to 'ask what you can do for your country' and by the missionary idealism he had awakened in us. America seemed omnipotent then: the country could still claim it had never lost a war, and we believed we were ordained to play cop to the Communists' robber and spread our own political faith around the world. Like the French soldiers of the late eighteenth century, we saw ourselves as the champions of 'a cause that was destined to triumph.' So, when we marched into the rice paddies on that damp March afternoon, we carried, along with our packs and rifles, the implicit convictions that the Viet Cong would be quickly beaten and that we were doing something altogether noble and good. We kept the packs and rifles; the convictions, we lost.

The discovery that the men we had scorned as peasant guerrillas were, in fact, a lethal, determined enemy and the casualty lists that lengthened each week with nothing to show for the blood being spilled broke our early confidence. By autumn, what had begun as an adventurous expedition had turned into an exhausting, indecisive war of attrition in which we fought for no cause other than our own survival."

Questions for Analysis

1. Identify the reasons for Caputo's initial confidence as a soldier in Vietnam.
2. Describe the change in Caputo's perspective during the Vietnam War.
3. Explain how "peasant guerrillas" were able to outlast the U.S. military in Vietnam.
4. Evaluate the extent to which Caputo's account rejects the idea of American exceptionalism.

On the ground, frustration grew as many conscripted American soldiers realized that war was not winnable and that public support for it was flagging back home. Frustrated by rising casualties from an enemy they could not see, an American platoon killed several hundred unarmed Vietnamese civilians in March 1968 in an event that came to be known as the **My Lai massacre**. Although dozens of U.S. military personnel participated in the massacre and subsequent coverup attempt, only one soldier was ever convicted of a crime.

My Lai massacre
A massacre by U.S. troops on March 16, 1968, of nearly 500 elderly, women, and children in the South Vietnam area of My Lai. The massacre shocked the American public, diminished support for the Vietnam War among many Americans, and fueled growing anti-U.S. sentiment worldwide.

The My Lai carnage came in the aftermath of the **Tet Offensive**. On January 31, 1968, the lunar New Year of Tet, some 67,000 communist troops mounted a surprise offensive throughout South Vietnam that targeted major population centers and even included a dramatic attack on the U.S. Embassy in Saigon (Map 8.4). U.S. forces finally repelled the Tet Offensive, but the battle proved psychologically costly to the United States. Following it, the most revered television news anchor of the era, Walter Cronkite of CBS, turned against the war and expressed the doubts of a growing number of viewers when he announced: "To say that we are mired in stalemate seems the only reasonable, yet unsatisfactory conclusion." His report heralded a growing change in public sentiment against the war, demonstrating the impact of the Tet Offensive in the United States.

Tet Offensive
A widescale offensive mounted by Vietcong and North Vietnamese forces specifically targeting population centers across South Vietnam in January 1968. The offensive was turned back, but its initial success surprised many Americans and increased public opposition to the war.

Tet marked the beginning of the end of the war's escalation. On March 31, 1968, President Johnson ordered a halt to the bombing campaign and called for peace negotiations. He also stunned the nation by announcing that he would not seek reelection. By the time Johnson left the White House in January 1969, peace negotiations had stalled and some 36,000 Americans had died in combat, along with 52,000 South Vietnamese troops.

AP Images/Horst Faas

American and South Vietnamese Forces Assault Vietcong Camp, 1965
South Vietnamese soldiers move toward a Vietcong camp near the Cambodian border as U.S. army helicopters provide covering fire and reconnaissance.

How does this photograph illustrate both the advantages possessed by the U.S. military in Vietnam as well as the challenges it faced?

MAP 8.5 The Vietnam War, 1968 The United States wielded more military personnel and weaponry than the Vietcong and North Vietnamese but faced a formidable challenge in fighting a guerrilla war in a foreign country. American bombing campaigns failed to defeat the North Vietnamese or stop their troop movements and supply lines along the Ho Chi Minh Trail. The 1968 Tet Offensive demonstrated the shortcomings in the U.S. strategy.

What does this map reveal about the scope of the Tet Offensive?

The escalation of the war had exacted another high price as well: It created a crisis of public confidence in government and turned many ordinary Americans into dissenters against the political establishment.

REVIEW

- How did the Johnson administration transform the conflict in Vietnam into the Vietnam War?
- Why were Johnson's policies in Vietnam unsuccessful?

AP® EXAM TIP

In no more than a few sentences, briefly explain the extent to which the conflict in Vietnam represented a civil war. Next, connect that understanding to why the United States was involved and how it affected the internal disputes among the Vietnamese. These kinds of connections can be useful to establish historical context or develop an argument.

Nixon and the Failure of Vietnamization

After Richard Nixon won the 1968 presidential election, Vietnam plagued him as it had his Democratic predecessor. In 1968, Nixon won the presidential election in part by promising "an honorable end to the war in Vietnam." Despite hinting during the campaign that he had a secret plan to end the war, Nixon's approach to Vietnam turned out to look much the same as Johnson's.

Henry Kissinger, who served first as national security adviser and then as secretary of state, continued peace talks with the North Vietnamese, which had been initiated by Johnson. Over the next four years, Nixon and Kissinger devised a strategy that removed U.S. ground forces and turned over greater responsibility for the fighting to the South Vietnamese army, a process called **Vietnamization**.

Vietnamization did not mean an end to U.S. military involvement in the region, however. In fact, Nixon widened the conflict before bringing it to an end. In 1969, at the same time that American troop levels were being drawn down, the president ordered secret bombing raids in Cambodia, a neutral country bordering South Vietnam that contained enemy forces and parts of the Ho Chi Minh Trail. Meant to pressure the North Vietnamese into accepting U.S. peace terms, the bombing accomplished little. In April 1970, Nixon ordered an invasion of eastern Cambodia to destroy enemy bases, which destabilized the country and eventually brought to power the communist organization Khmer Rouge, which later slaughtered two million Cambodians. In 1971, the United States sponsored the South Vietnamese invasion of Laos, a neighboring country that harbored North Vietnamese troops and supply lines, which again yielded no battlefield gains. Finally, in December 1972, shortly before Christmas, the United States carried out an eleven-day bombing campaign of targets in North Vietnam meant to force the North Vietnamese government to come to a peace accord.

The intense bombing of North Vietnam did end formal U.S. involvement in the war. An agreement signed on January 27, 1973, stipulated that the United States would remove all American troops, the North Vietnamese would return captured U.S. soldiers, and North and South Vietnam would strive for peaceful national unification. Crucially, the agreement did not require the withdrawal of North Vietnamese troops from South Vietnam.

Despite this agreement, peace had clearly not been achieved. The war in Vietnam continued, now without the participation of the U.S. military. In April 1975, North Vietnamese and Vietcong forces captured Saigon, resulting in a communist victory. In the end, the Vietnam War extracted a terrible cost. Some 58,000 American soldiers, 215,000 South Vietnamese soldiers, 1 million North Vietnamese and Vietcong soldiers, and an estimated 4 million South and North Vietnamese civilians were killed in the conflict.

The Fall of Saigon, 1975 On April 29, 1975, the day before communist troops took control of Saigon, crowds of South Vietnamese, many of whom had supported the United States, scramble to climb the wall of the U.S. Embassy. They were making a desperate attempt to get to evacuation helicopters, but with space limited on available aircraft, many of these people were left behind.

What does the photograph suggest about conditions in South Vietnam right before the communist victory?

The Nixon administration's war efforts generated great controversy at home. The invasion of Cambodia in April 1970 touched off widespread campus demonstrations. At Kent State University in Ohio, four student protesters were shot and killed on May 4, 1970, by the National Guard in an incident that became known as the **Kent State shootings**. Large crowds of antiwar demonstrators descended on Washington in 1969 and 1971, though the president refused to heed their message. Nevertheless, a majority of the American public, not just radicals, had turned against the war. By 1972, more than 70 percent of those polled believed that the Vietnam War was a mistake. Growing numbers of Vietnam veterans also spoke out against the war.

Contributing to this disillusionment, in 1971, the *New York Times* and the *Washington Post* published a classified report known as the ***Pentagon Papers***. This document confirmed that the Kennedy and Johnson administrations had misled the public about the origins and nature of the Vietnam War.

War Powers Resolution

An act that limited the ability of the president to wage war without the approval of Congress. The 1973 resolution required the president to consult with Congress within forty-eight hours of deploying military forces and required a declaration of war from Congress if troops remained on foreign soil beyond sixty days.

Congress reflected growing disapproval for the war by repealing the Gulf of Tonkin Resolution in 1970 after the Cambodian invasion. In 1973, Congress passed the **War Powers Resolution**, which required the president to consult with Congress within forty-eight hours of deploying military forces and to obtain a declaration of war from Congress if troops remained on foreign soil beyond sixty days. Although Nixon oversaw the winding down of U.S. military involvement in Vietnam, his handling of the Vietnam War remained controversial throughout his time in office.

REVIEW

- How did Nixon change American tactics in Vietnam?
- Why was Nixon's approach also unsuccessful?

AP® Skills Workshop: Writing Historically

Additional Practice in Responding to a Short-Answer Question

Answer **A**, **B**, and **C**.

(A) Briefly explain ONE specific historical factor that contributed to U.S. involvement in the Vietnam War.

(B) Briefly explain ONE specific historical factor that contributed to the failure of the United States to win the Vietnam War.

(C) Briefly explain ONE specific historical effect of U.S. involvement in the Vietnam War on American society.

The Great Society

MODULE 8.9

FOCUS

As you read this module, consider the ways in which the events or trends led to the reforms that came to be known as the Great Society. Consider the continued trends in liberal policies from before 1945, as well as the ways in which Great Society programs represented new reforms.

Hoping to build on the legacy of the New Deal, liberals sought to increase the role of the federal government in the economy, education, and health care. Most liberals supported a staunchly anticommunist foreign policy, differing with Republicans more over means than over ends. Indeed, when Democrats recaptured the White House in 1960, Presidents Kennedy and Johnson seized opportunities in Cuba and Southeast Asia to vigorously challenge the expansion of Soviet influence.

President Johnson's liberal accomplishments reached beyond civil rights to include an ambitious expansion of social welfare policies, the Great Society. At the heart of Johnson's agenda was a war on poverty, which included expanding health care coverage and educational opportunities for the young, old, and sick. While Johnson pressed ahead in the legislative arena, Chief Justice Earl Warren's Supreme Court issued rulings that extended social justice to minorities and the economically oppressed and favored those who believed in a firm separation of church and state, free speech, and a right to privacy.

Federal Efforts toward Social Reform, 1960–1968

With victory in World War II and the revival of economic prosperity, liberal thinkers regained confidence in capitalism. Many saw the postwar American free-enterprise system as different from the old-style capitalism that had existed before Franklin Roosevelt's New Deal. In their view, this new "reform capitalism," or democratic capitalism, created abundance for all and not just for the elites. Rather than pushing for the redistribution of wealth, liberals now called on the government to help create conditions conducive to economic growth and increased productivity. The liberal economist John Kenneth Galbraith thus argued in *The Affluent Society* (1958) that increased public investments in education, research, and development were the key to American prosperity and progress.

These ideas guided the thinking of Democratic politicians such as Senator John F. Kennedy of Massachusetts. Elected president in 1960, the forty-three-year-old Kennedy brought good looks, charm, a beautiful wife, and young children to the White House. Kennedy pledged a **New Frontier** to battle "tyranny, poverty, disease, and war," but lacking strong majorities in Congress, he contented himself with making small gains on the New Deal's foundation. Congress expanded unemployment benefits, increased the minimum wage, extended Social Security benefits, and raised appropriations for public housing, but Kennedy's caution disappointed many liberals.

AP® EXAM TIP

Define liberalism and explain why some historians think of the Great Society as a turning point for liberal views of government influence. Instead of using several historical examples, try to limit your selected evidence so that you can develop your explanation and ability to make historical connections.

Tragically, Kennedy was assassinated on November 22, 1963, by Lee Harvey Oswald as Kennedy and his wife rode in an open motorcade in Dallas, Texas, during a campaign event. Days later, Oswald was shot to death by nightclub owner Jack Ruby. The assassination shocked the nation. Millions of grieving Americans watched the elaborate televised funeral modeled after President Lincoln's funeral proceedings. In death, Kennedy achieved immense popularity, yet his legislative agenda remained unfulfilled.

Great Society
President Lyndon Johnson's legislative reform program that called for an expansion of social welfare programs, medical care for the elderly, support for civil rights, protection of the environment, alleviation of poverty, and greater funding to education, especially for marginalized communities.

For newly inaugurated president Lyndon Johnson, a product of modest upbringing in rural Texas, urban and rural poverty were issues that required action. Awareness of social and economic inequality had increased with the publication of *The Other America* (1962), in which socialist author Michael Harrington exposed the invisibility of the poor in America. In an address at the University of Michigan on May 22, 1964, President Johnson sketched out his dream for the **Great Society**, one that "rests on abundance and liberty for all. It demands an end to poverty and racial injustice, to which we are totally committed in our time. But that is just the beginning."

AP® WORKING with EVIDENCE

Source: Michael Harrington, *The Other America*, 1962

"There is a familiar America. It is celebrated in speeches and advertised on television and in the magazines. It has the highest mass standard of living the world has ever known.

In the 1950s this America worried about itself, yet even its anxieties were products of abundance. The title of a brilliant book was widely misinterpreted, and the familiar America began to call itself 'the affluent society. . . .'

While this discussion was carried on, there existed another America. In it dwelt somewhere between 40,000,000 and 50,000,000 citizens of this land. They were poor. They still are. . . .

The millions who are poor in the United States tend to become increasingly invisible. Here is a great mass of people, yet it takes an effort of the intellect and will even to see them. . . .

Now the American city has been transformed. The poor still inhabit the miserable housing in the central area, but they are increasingly isolated from contact with, or sight of, anybody else. Middle-class women coming in from Suburbia on a rare trip may catch the merest glimpse of other America on the way to an evening at the theater, but the children are segregated in suburban schools. The business or professional man may drive along the fringes of slums in a car or bus, but it is not an important experience to him. The failure, the unskilled, the disabled, the aged, and the minorities are right there, across the tracks, where they have always been. But hardly anyone else is.

In short, the very development of the American city has removed poverty from the living, emotional experience of millions upon millions of middle-class Americans. . . .

That the poor are invisible is one of the most important things about them. They are not simply neglected and forgotten as in the old rhetoric of reform; what is much worse, they are not seen."

Questions for Analysis

1. Identify the fundamental contradiction Harrington highlights in the excerpt.
2. Describe how the poor have become invisible to the middle class, according to Harrington.
3. Explain why Harrington argues that poverty is worse than it used to be.
4. Evaluate the extent of similarity between Harrington's argument and the arguments of progressives about urban poverty at the turn of the twentieth century.

Besides poverty and race, Johnson outlined three broad areas in need of reform: education, the environment, and cities. Toward this end, the Elementary and Secondary Education Act (1965) provided federal funds directly to public schools to improve their quality. The Model Cities program (1966) set up the Department of Housing and Urban Affairs, which coordinated efforts at urban planning and rebuilding neighborhoods in decaying cities. The Department of Transportation sought to ensure a fast, safe, and convenient transportation system. In addition, the president pushed Congress to pass hundreds of environmental protection laws, including those dealing with air and water pollution, waste disposal, the use of natural resources, and the preservation of wildlife and wilderness areas.

LBJ Library photo

President Johnson Signs Medicare into Law, 1965 On July 30, 1965, President Johnson signed the Medicare bill, the health insurance program for elderly Americans, and Medicaid, which provided medical assistance for the poor. The ceremony took place at the Truman Library in Independence, Missouri, and former president Harry S. Truman received the first Medicare card. In 1945, Truman had first proposed national health insurance, but Congress rejected it. Standing to the right immediately behind Johnson (seated on the left) and Truman (seated on the right) are (from left to right) Claudia "Lady Bird" Johnson, the president's wife; Vice President Hubert Humphrey; and Bess Truman, the former president's wife.

In what ways was Medicare an extension of Truman's Fair Deal and Franklin Roosevelt's New Deal?

Still, it was the War on Poverty that garnered the most attention. The opening battle of the War on Poverty came with passage of the Economic Opportunity Act of 1964. Through this measure, Johnson wanted to offer the poor "a hand up, not a handout." Among its major components, the law provided job training, food stamps, rent supplements, redevelopment of depressed rural areas, remedial education (later to include the preschool program Head Start), a domestic Peace Corps called Volunteers in Service to America (VISTA), and a Community Action Program that empowered the poor to shape policies affecting their own communities.

Between 1965 and 1968, expenditures targeted for the poor doubled, from $6 billion to $12 billion. The antipoverty program helped reduce the proportion of poor people from 20 percent in 1963 to 13 percent five years later, and it helped reduce the rate of Black poverty from 40 percent to 20 percent during this same period.

Johnson intended to fight the War on Poverty through the engine of economic growth, which would create new jobs for the unemployed without redistributing wealth. With this in mind, he persuaded Congress to enact significant tax cuts. Johnson's tax cut, which applied across the board, stimulated the economy and sent the gross national product soaring from $591 billion in 1963 to $977 billion by the end of the decade.

AP® EXAM TIP

Be able to explain at least one historical example of how the Great Society sought to address racial discrimination and issues related to poverty. After you have outlined an explanation, provide an example of how the Great Society led to limited changes for some groups of Americans.

Despite the gains made, many liberals believed that Johnson's spending on the War on Poverty did not go far enough. Whatever the shortcomings, Johnson campaigned on his antipoverty and civil rights record in his bid to recapture the White House in 1964. His Republican opponent, Senator Barry Goldwater of Arizona, personified the conservative right wing of the Republican Party. The Arizona senator condemned big government, supported states' rights, and accused liberals of not waging the Cold War forcefully enough. His aggressive conservatism appealed to his grassroots base in small-town America, especially in southern California, the Southwest, and the South. His tough rhetoric, however, scared off moderate Republicans, resulting on election day in a landslide for Johnson as well as considerable Democratic majorities in Congress.

Flush with victory, Johnson pushed Congress to move quickly. Working together, they achieved remarkable results. To cite only a few examples, the Eighty-ninth Congress (1965–1967) subsidized health care for the elderly and the poor by creating Medicare and Medicaid, expanded voting rights for Black Americans in the South, raised the minimum wage, and created national endowments for the fine arts and the humanities. The 1965 Immigration Act repealed discriminatory national origins quotas established in 1924, resulting in a shift of immigration from Europe to Asia and Central and South America.

The Warren Court reflected this high tide of liberalism. The Court affirmed the constitutionality of the Voting Rights Act. In 1967, the justices overturned state laws prohibiting interracial marriages. A year later, fourteen years after the *Brown* decision, they ruled that school districts in the South could no longer maintain racially exclusive schools and must desegregate immediately. In a series of cases, the Warren Court ensured fairer legislative representation for both Black and white people by removing the disproportionate power that rural districts had held over urban districts.

The Supreme Court's most controversial rulings dealt with the criminal justice system, religion, and private sexual practices. Strengthening the rights of criminal defendants, the justices ruled in *Gideon v. Wainwright* (1963) that states had to provide poor people accused of felonies with an attorney, and in *Miranda v. Arizona* (1966), they ordered the police to advise suspects of their constitutional rights.

The Warren Court also moved into new, controversial territory concerning school prayer, contraception, and pornography. In 1962, the Court outlawed a nondenominational Christian prayer recited in New York State schools as a violation of the separation of church and state guaranteed by the First Amendment. Three years later, in *Griswold v. Connecticut*, the justices struck down a state law that banned the sale of contraceptives

Major Great Society Measures, 1964–1968		
Year	**Legislation or Order**	**Purpose**
1964	Civil Rights Act	Prohibited discrimination in public accommodations, education, and employment
	Economic Opportunity Act	Established War on Poverty agencies: Head Start, VISTA, Job Corps, and Community Action Program
1965	Elementary and Secondary Education Act	Federal funding for elementary and secondary schools
	Medical Care Act	Provided Medicare health insurance for citizens sixty-five years and older and Medicaid health benefits for the poor
	Voting Rights Act	Banned literacy tests for voting, authorized federal registrars to be sent into seven southern states, and monitored voting changes in these states
	Executive Order 11246	Required employers to take affirmative action to promote equal opportunity and remedy the effects of past discrimination
	Immigration and Nationality Act	Abolished quotas on immigration that reduced immigration from non-Western and southern and eastern European nations
	Water Quality Act	Established and enforced federal water-quality standards
	Air Quality Act	Established air pollution standards for motor vehicles
	National Arts and Humanities Act	Established National Endowment for the Humanities and National Endowment for the Arts to support the work of scholars, writers, artists, and musicians
1966	Model Cities Act	Approved funding for the rehabilitation of inner cities
1967	Executive Order 11375	Expanded affirmative action regulations to include women
1968	Civil Rights Act	Outlawed discrimination in housing

Between 1964 and 1968, Lyndon Johnson's proposed legislation, known collectively as the "Great Society," attempted to improve Americans' lives through federal programs modeled on Johnson's experience with the New Deal (Period 7).

What similarities and differences do you see between the legislation of the Great Society of the 1960s and the New Deal of the 1930s?

because such laws, they contended, infringed on an individual's right to privacy. In a 1966 case, the justices ruled that states could not prohibit what they deemed pornographic material unless it was "utterly without redeeming social value," a standard that opened the door for the dissemination of sexually explicit books, magazines, and films. These verdicts unleashed a firestorm of criticism, especially from religious groups that accused the Warren Court of undermining traditional values of faith and decency.

AP® EXAM TIP

Think about ways to illustrate historical change and/or continuity. The course framework specifically cites the changes brought on by immigration laws in 1965. Explain how these represented changes from the immigration quota laws from the 1920s by citing what specifically changed.

- How did Johnson's Great Society attempt to address issues of poverty, race, education, health care, and the environment?

AP® Skills Workshop: Writing Historically

Additional Practice in Responding to a Short-Answer Question with a Primary Source

"We are going to assemble the best thought and the broadest knowledge from all over the world to find those answers for America. I intend to establish working groups to prepare a series of White House conferences and meetings—on the cities, on natural beauty, on the quality of education, and on other emerging challenges. And from these meetings and from this inspiration and from these studies we will begin to set our course toward the Great Society.

The solution to these problems does not rest on a massive program in Washington, nor can it rely solely on the strained resources of local authority. They require us to create new concepts of cooperation, a creative federalism, between the National Capital and the leaders of local communities."

President Lyndon Johnson, Remarks at the University of Michigan, 1964

Using the excerpt, answer **A**, **B**, and **C**.

(A) Briefly describe the point of view expressed by Johnson in the excerpt.

(B) Briefly explain how ONE specific event or development led to the historical situation described in the excerpt.

(C) Briefly explain how ONE specific event or historical development resulted from the historical situation in the excerpt.

The African American Civil Rights Movement (1960s)

MODULE 8.10

FOCUS

As you read this module, consider how the goals, strategies, and support of the civil rights movement of the late 1940s and 1950s (Module 8.6) fostered an expansion of civil rights activism in the 1960s and 1970s. Consider the reasons for the similarities and differences between the movement in each time period. Think about the how the civil rights movement both changed and remained the same between 1945 and 1970.

At home, the most critical issue facing the nation in the early 1960s was the intensification of the civil rights movement. As a candidate, Kennedy had promised vigorous action on civil rights, but as president he did little to follow through on his promises. With southern Democrats occupying key positions in Congress and threatening to block any civil rights proposals, Kennedy sought to appease this critical component of his political base.

Following Kennedy's death in 1963, President Johnson succeeded in breaking the legislative logjam and signed into law three major pieces of civil rights legislation. He did so under considerable pressure from the civil rights movement. At the height of their triumphs, however, many civil rights activists became increasingly skeptical of nonviolence and integration and turned to the racial nationalism and self-determination of Black power.

Freedom Rides

The Congress of Racial Equality took the offensive on May 4, 1961. Much like Bayard Rustin's efforts in the 1940s, CORE mounted racially integrated **Freedom Rides** to test whether facilities in the South were complying with the 1960 Supreme Court ruling that outlawed segregated bus and train stations serving passengers who were traveling interstate. CORE alerted the Justice Department and the FBI of its plans, but the riders received no protection when Ku Klux Klan–dominated mobs in Anniston and Birmingham, Alabama, attacked two of its buses, seriously wounding several activists.

Freedom Rides
Integrated bus rides through the South in 1961 to test southern compliance with Supreme Court rulings on segregation. After Freedom Riders were attacked in Montgomery, Alabama, the Kennedy administration sent federal marshals to protect the riders.

After safety concerns forced CORE to forgo the rest of the trip, members of the Student Nonviolent Coordinating Committee (SNCC) rushed to Birmingham to continue the bus rides. The Kennedy administration urged them to reconsider, but Diane Nash, an SNCC founder, explained that although the group realized the peril of resuming the journey, "we can't let them stop us with violence. If we do, the movement is dead."

When the replenished busload of riders reached Montgomery on May 20, they were brutally assaulted by a mob. Dr. Martin Luther King Jr. subsequently held a rally in a

AP® EXAM TIP

Because you have to know several examples of civil rights leaders, strategies, and tactics, think about creating a chart for this information. Remember, you do not have to know all the examples from your reading. Instead, think about developing an understanding of one or two historical examples that can advance an argument about the leaders, strategies, and tactics associated with the civil rights movement.

Montgomery church, where white mobs threatened the lives of King and the Freedom Riders inside the building. Faced with the prospect of serious bloodshed, the Kennedy administration dispatched federal marshals to the scene and persuaded the governor to call out the Alabama National Guard to ensure the safety of everyone in the church.

The president and his brother, Attorney General Robert F. Kennedy, worked out a compromise to let the rides continue with minimal violence, and with minimal publicity. The Cold War worked in favor of the protesters. With the Soviet Union publicizing the violence against Freedom Riders in the South, the Kennedy administration attempted to preserve America's image abroad by persuading the Interstate Commerce Commission to issue an order prohibiting segregated transportation facilities. Still, southern whites resisted. When Freedom Riders encountered opposition in Albany, Georgia, in the fall of 1961, SNCC workers remained in Albany and helped local leaders organize residents against segregation and other forms of racial discrimination. But even with the assistance of Dr. King and the Southern Christian Leadership Conference (SCLC), the Albany movement stalled.

REVIEW

- How did Freedom Riders confront continued segregation in the South?
- How successful were they in challenging systematic racial discrimination?

Kennedy Supports Civil Rights

Despite the setback in Albany, the civil rights movement kept up pressure on other fronts. In September 1962, Mississippi governor Ross Barnett tried to block the registration of James Meredith as an undergraduate at the University of Mississippi. Barnett's obstruction led to a riot on campus, and President Kennedy dispatched army troops and federalized the Mississippi National Guard to restore order, but not before two bystanders were killed.

The following year, King and the SCLC joined the Reverend Fred Shuttlesworth's movement in Birmingham, Alabama, in its battle against discrimination, segregation, and police brutality. With the white supremacist Eugene "Bull" Connor in charge of law enforcement, civil rights protesters, including children from age six to sixteen, encountered violent resistance, vicious police dogs, and high-powered water hoses. Connor ordered mass arrests, including Dr. King's, prompting the minister to write his famous "Letter from Birmingham Jail," in which he justified the use of nonviolent direct action. Seeking to defuse the crisis, President Kennedy sent an emissary in early May 1963 to negotiate a peaceful solution that granted concessions to Black residents of Birmingham and ended the demonstrations.

WORKING with EVIDENCE

Source: Martin Luther King Jr., "Letter from Birmingham Jail," April 1963

> "We know through painful experience that freedom is never voluntarily given by the oppressor; it must be demanded by the oppressed. Frankly, I have never yet engaged in a direct-action movement that was 'well timed' according to the timetable of those who have not suffered unduly from the disease of

segregation. For years now I have heard the word 'wait.' It rings in the ear of every Negro with a piercing familiarity. This 'wait' has almost always meant 'never.' . . . But when you have seen vicious mobs lynch your mothers and fathers at will and drown your sisters and brothers at whim; when you have seen hate-filled policemen curse, kick, brutalize, and even kill your black brothers and sisters with impunity; when you see the vast majority of your twenty million Negro brothers smothering in an airtight cage of poverty in the midst of an affluent society; when you have to concoct an answer for a five-year-old son asking in agonizing pathos, 'Daddy, why do white people treat colored people so mean?'; . . . when you are humiliated day in and day out by nagging signs reading 'white' and 'colored'; . . . when you are forever fighting a degenerating sense of 'nobodyness'—then you will understand why we find it difficult to wait. . . .

I must confess that over the last few years I have been gravely disappointed with the white moderate. I have almost reached the regrettable conclusion that the Negro's great stumbling block in the stride toward freedom is not the White Citizens Councillor or the Ku Klux Klanner but the white moderate who is more devoted to order than to justice; who prefers a negative peace which is the absence of tension to a positive peace which is the presence of justice; who constantly says, 'I agree with you in the goal you seek, but I can't agree with your methods of direct action'; who paternalistically feels that he can set the timetable for another man's freedom; who lives by the myth of time; and who constantly advises the Negro to wait until a 'more convenient season.' Shallow understanding from people of good will is more frustrating than absolute misunderstanding from people of ill will."

Questions for Analysis

1. Identify the immediate context for King's letter.
2. Describe King's disappointment with sympathetic white moderates.
3. Explain how King appeals to readers in his letter.
4. Explain why King is unwilling to "wait" until a "more convenient season" for civil rights.

Angered by the events in Birmingham and King's imprisonment, Kennedy finally embraced the nation's duty to guarantee equal rights regardless of race. On June 11, 1963, shortly after negotiating the Birmingham agreement, Kennedy delivered a nationally televised address. He acknowledged that the country faced a "moral crisis" heightened by the events in Birmingham, and he noted the difficulty of preaching "freedom around the world" while "this is a land of the free except for Negroes." He proposed congressional legislation to end segregation in public accommodations, increase federal power to promote school desegregation, and broaden the right to vote.

Events on the day Kennedy delivered his powerful speech reinforced the need for swift action. Earlier that morning, Alabama governor George C. Wallace stood in front of the administration building at the University of Alabama to block the entrance of two Black undergraduates. To uphold the federal court decree ordering their admission, Kennedy deployed federal marshals and the Alabama National Guard. Wallace, having dramatized his point, stepped aside. However, victory soon turned into tragedy. That evening Medgar Evers, the head of the NAACP in Mississippi, was shot and killed in the driveway of his home by the white supremacist Byron de la Beckwith. (Following two trials that resulted in hung juries, de la Beckwith remained free until 1994, when he was retried and convicted for Evers's murder.)

Wally McNamee/Corbis/Getty Images

Women and the March on Washington for Jobs and Freedom, 1963 Although Black women played central roles in grassroots organizing within the civil rights movement, they received far less attention on the national stage than did male leaders, such as Martin Luther King Jr. and A. Philip Randolph. At the historic 1963 March on Washington, women, Black and white, turned out in large numbers, as this photograph shows, but they were not chosen to give any of the major speeches or march at the front of the line with the leading men.

What does this photograph reveal about the marchers?

Nonetheless, Congress was still unwilling to act. To increase pressure on lawmakers, civil rights organizations held the **March on Washington for Jobs and Freedom** on August 28, 1963, carrying out an idea first proposed by A. Philip Randolph in 1941 (see Module 7.12). With Randolph as honorary chair, his associate Bayard Rustin directed the proceedings as 250,000 Black and white peaceful protesters rallied in front of the Lincoln Memorial.

Two speakers in particular caught the attention of the crowd. John Lewis, the chairman of SNCC, expressed the frustration of militant Black people with both the Kennedy administration and Congress. "The revolution is at hand. . . . We will not wait for the President, nor the Justice Department, nor Congress," Lewis asserted. "But we will take matters into our own hands." In a more conciliatory tone, King delivered an impassioned speech expressing his hope for racial reconciliation: "I have a dream today that my four little children will one day live in a nation where they will not be judged by the color of their skin but by the content of their character." Still, King issued a stern warning to "those who hope that the Negro needed to blow off steam and will now be content. . . . There will be neither rest nor tranquility in America until the Negro is granted his citizenship rights."

Weeks later, the Ku Klux Klan dynamited Birmingham's Sixteenth Street Baptist Church, a freedom movement staging ground. The blast killed four young girls attending services on Sunday, September 15, 1963. After the assassination of President Kennedy in November, it was up to Vice President Lyndon Johnson to step into the breach.

REVIEW

- What efforts to advance civil rights were made in 1963?
- What responses did those efforts receive?

Freedom Summer and Voting Rights

Following Kennedy's death, President Johnson took charge of the pending civil rights legislation. Capitalizing on public sympathy over Kennedy's assassination and his own skills in backroom deal-making honed as the former Senate majority leader, Johnson marshalled a bipartisan coalition to pass the **Civil Rights Act of 1964**. The law prohibited discrimination in public accommodations, increased federal enforcement of school desegregation and the right to vote, and created the Community Relations Service, a federal agency authorized to help resolve racial conflicts. The act also contained a final measure to combat employment discrimination on the basis of race and sex.

Civil Rights Act of 1964
A landmark act signed into law in 1964 by President Lyndon Johnson that prohibited discrimination in public accommodations and employment and increased federal enforcement of school desegregation and voting access.

Yet even as President Johnson signed the Civil Rights Act into law on July 2, Black freedom forces launched a new offensive to secure the right to vote in the South. The 1964 act contained a voting rights provision but did little to address the main problems of the discriminatory use of literacy tests and poll taxes and the biased administration of registration procedures that kept the majority of southern Black people from registering.

Beatings, killings, acts of arson, and arrests became a routine response to voting rights efforts. Although the Justice Department filed lawsuits against uncooperative voter registrars and police officers, the government refused to send in federal personnel or instruct the FBI to safeguard vulnerable civil rights workers.

Freedom Summer
A 1964 civil rights effort in Mississippi sponsored by a national coalition of civil rights organizations following the passage of the Civil Rights Act of 1964. During the Freedom Summer, some eight hundred volunteers, mainly white college students, worked on voter registration drives and in freedom schools to improve education for rural Black youngsters.

To focus national attention on this problem, SNCC, CORE, the NAACP, and the SCLC launched the **Freedom Summer** project in Mississippi. They assigned eight hundred volunteers from around the nation, mainly white college students, to work on voter registration drives and in "freedom schools" to improve education for rural Black youngsters. White supremacists fought back against what they perceived as an enemy invasion. In the summer of 1964, the Ku Klux Klan, sometimes in collusion with local law enforcement officials, killed three civil rights workers and attacked more than thirty Black churches. These tragedies focused national attention and energized civil rights workers, who continued to encounter white violence and harassment throughout Freedom Summer.

AP® WORKING with EVIDENCE

Source: *Prospectus for the Mississippi Freedom Summer,* 1964

"[A] program is planned for this summer which will involve the massive participation of Americans dedicated to the elimination of racial oppression. Scores of college students, law students, medical students, teachers, professors, ministers, technicians, folk artists, and lawyers from all over the country have already volunteered to work in Mississippi this summer—and hundreds more are being recruited. . . .

Mississippi at this juncture in the movement has received too little attention—that is, attention to what the state's attitude really is. . . . Either the civil rights struggle has to continue, as it has for the past few years, with small projects in selected communities with no real progress on any fronts, or [there must be a] task force of such a size as to force either the state and the municipal governments to change their social and legal structures, or the Federal Government to intervene on behalf of the constitutional rights of its citizens.

Since 1964 is an election year, the clear-cut issue of voting rights should be brought out in the open. Many SNCC and CORE workers in Mississippi hold the view that Negroes will never vote in large numbers until Federal marshals intervene. . . . [M]any Americans must be made to realize that the voting rights they so often take for granted involve considerable risk for Negroes in the South. . . . Major victories in Mississippi, recognized as the stronghold of racial intolerance in the South, would speed immeasurably the breaking down of legal and social discrimination in both North and South."

Questions for Analysis

1. Identify the goals expressed in the prospectus.
2. Describe the context surrounding the Mississippi Freedom Summer.
3. Explain the rationale for the Mississippi Freedom Summer expressed in this excerpt.
4. Explain the relationship between grassroots protests such as the Mississippi Freedom Summer and federal legislation such as the Civil Rights Act of 1964.

One outcome of the Freedom Summer project was the creation of the **Mississippi Freedom Democratic Party (MFDP)**. Because the regular state Democratic Party excluded Black people, the civil rights coalition formed an alternate Democratic Party open to everyone. In August 1964, the mostly Black MFDP sent a delegation to the Democratic National Convention, meeting in Atlantic City, New Jersey, to challenge the seating of the all-white delegation from Mississippi. One MFDP delegate, Fannie Lou Hamer, who had lost her job for her voter registration activities, offered passionate testimony that was broadcast on television. Johnson then hammered out a compromise that gave the MFDP two at-large seats, seated members of the regular delegation who took a loyalty oath, and prohibited racial discrimination in the future by any state Democratic Party. While both sides rejected the deal, four years later an integrated delegation, which included Hamer, represented Mississippi at the Democratic National Convention in Chicago.

Freedom Summer highlighted the problem of disfranchisement, but it took further demonstrations in Selma, Alabama, to resolve it. After state troopers shot and killed a Black voting-rights demonstrator in February 1965, Dr. King called for a march from Selma to the capital, Montgomery, to petition Governor Wallace to end the violence and allow Black people to vote. On Sunday, March 7, as Black and white marchers left Selma, the sheriff's forces sprayed them with tear gas, beat them, and sent them running for their lives. A few days later, a white pastor who had joined the protesters was killed by a group of white thugs. On March 21, following another failed attempt to march to Montgomery, King finally led protesters on the fifty-mile hike to the state capital, where they arrived safely four days later. Still, after the march, the Ku Klux Klan murdered a white female marcher from Michigan.

Events in Selma prompted President Johnson to take action. On March 15, he addressed a joint session of Congress and told lawmakers and a nationally televised audience that the Black "cause must be our cause too" and "we shall overcome." On August 6, 1965, the president signed

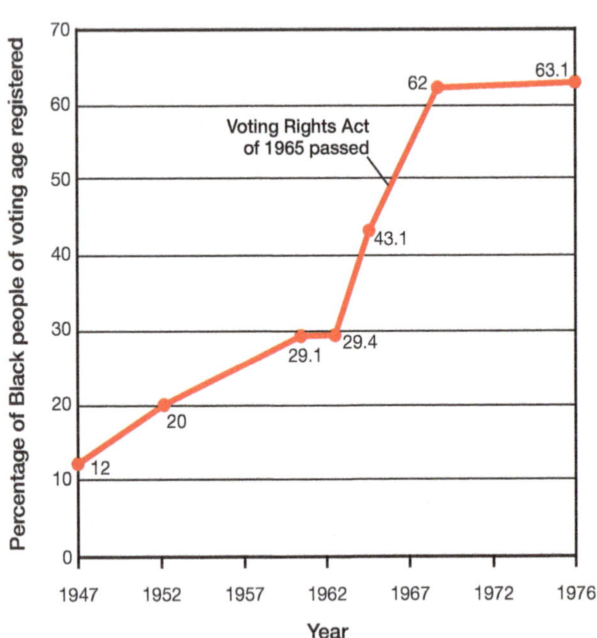

Black Voter Registration in the South, 1947–1976 After World War II, the percentage of Black adults registered to vote in the South slowly but steadily increased, largely as a result of grassroots voting drives. Despite the Kennedy administration's support for voter registration drives, a majority of southern Black people still could not vote in 1964. The passage of the 1965 Voting Rights Act outlawed literacy tests, strengthened the federal government's enforcement powers, and enabled more than 60 percent of southern Black people to vote by the late 1960s.

What historical developments contributed to the steeper rise in Black voter registration during the Johnson administration (1963–1968) than in the years before and after his presidency?

the **Voting Rights Act**, which banned the use of literacy tests for voter registration, authorized a federal lawsuit against the poll tax (which succeeded in 1966), empowered federal officials to register disfranchised voters, and required seven southern states to submit any changes in voting rules to Washington, D.C., before they went into effect. With strong federal enforcement of the law, by 1968, a majority of Black southerners and nearly two-thirds of Black Mississippians could vote.

Voting Rights Act A 1965 act that eliminated literacy tests and other measures commonly used at the time in southern states to prevent Black Americans from voting. The act resulted in dramatic increases in Black voter participation.

However, these civil rights victories had exacted a huge toll on the movement. SNCC and CORE had come to distrust Presidents Kennedy and Johnson for failing to provide protection for voter registration workers. Furthermore, Johnson's attempt to broker a compromise at the 1964 Atlantic City Democratic Convention convinced MFDP supporters that the liberal president had sold them out. The once-united movement showed signs of cracking.

REVIEW

- In what ways did the Johnson administration support the civil rights movement in 1964 and 1965?
- In what ways did the Johnson administration fail to support the civil rights movement in 1964 and 1965?

From Civil Rights to Black Power

Increasingly after 1964, SNCC and CORE began exploring new ways of seeking freedom through strategies of Black self-determination and self-defense. They were greatly influenced by Malcolm X. Born Malcolm Little, he had engaged in a life of crime, which landed him in prison. Inside jail, he converted to the Nation of Islam, a religious sect based partly on Muslim teachings and partly on the belief that white people were devils (not a doctrine associated with orthodox Islam). After his release from jail, Malcolm rejected his "slave name" and substituted the letter X to symbolize his unknown African forebears. Minister Malcolm helped convert thousands of disciples in Black ghettos by denouncing whites and encouraging Black people to embrace their African heritage and beauty as a people. Favoring self-defense over nonviolence, he criticized civil rights leaders for failing to protect their communities.

After 1963, Malcolm X broke away from the Nation of Islam, visited the Middle East and Africa, and accepted the teachings of traditional Islam. He moderated his anti-white rhetoric but remained committed to Black self-determination. He had already influenced the growing number of disillusioned young Black activists when, in 1965, he was murdered. Two members of the Nation of Islam were arrested for the murder on the suspicion that they sought vengeance for Malcolm X's break with the Nation of Islam. Both were convicted, but their convictions were overturned in 2021.

Black militants, echoing Malcolm X's ideas, challenged racial liberalism. They renounced the principles of integration and nonviolence in favor of Black power and self-defense. Instead of welcoming whites within their organizations, Black radicals believed that Black Americans had to assert their independence from white America. In 1966, SNCC expelled white members and created an all-Black organization. Stokely Carmichael, SNCC's chairman, proclaimed "Black power" as the central goal of the freedom struggle and linked the cause of Black American freedom to revolutionary conflicts in Cuba, Africa, and Vietnam.

AP Photo

Malcolm X, 1963 While civil rights leaders campaigned for racial integration and equality through nonviolent protests in the South, Malcolm X questioned their tactics and goals. A charismatic minister in the Nation of Islam, he preached a fiery message of Black nationalism and self-defense, ideas that later merged into the ideology of Black power. Although his message drew criticism from liberal whites and Black civil rights leaders, Malcolm X appealed to many Black Americans, as demonstrated here at a rally in Harlem in New York City on June 29, 1963.

What was the appeal of Malcolm X to many Black people in northern cities?

Black power emerged against a backdrop of riots in Black ghettos, which erupted across the nation starting in the mid-1960s: in Harlem and Rochester, New York, in 1964; in Los Angeles in 1965; and in Cleveland, Chicago, Detroit, Newark, and Tampa in the following two years. While the civil rights movement had lifted the hopes of Black Americans throughout the country by dismantling segregation in public facilities and impediments to voting, urban Black people, many in the North and West, faced problems of high unemployment, broken-down housing, and police mistreatment that civil rights legislation had done nothing to correct. Many whites perceived the ghetto uprisings solely as an exercise in criminal behavior, while many Black people viewed the violence as an expression of political discontent—as rebellions, not riots. The Kerner Commission, appointed by President Johnson to assess urban disorders, concluded in 1968 that white racism remained at the heart of the problem: "Our nation is moving toward two societies, one black, one white—separate and unequal."

New groups emerged to take up the cause of Black power. In 1966, Huey P. Newton and Bobby Seale, college students in Oakland, California, formed the **Black Panther Party**. Dressed in black leather, sporting black berets, and carrying guns, the Black Panthers appealed mainly to Black men. They did not, however, rely on armed confrontation and bravado alone. The Black Panthers established day care centers and health facilities, often run by women, which gained the admiration of many in their communities. Much of this good work was overshadowed by violent confrontations with the police, which led to the deaths of Black Panthers in shootouts and the imprisonment of key party officials. By the early 1970s, government crackdowns on the Black Panthers had destabilized the organization and reduced its influence.

Black Panther Party
A radical Black power group founded by Huey P. Newton and Bobby Seale in 1966 to promote Black empowerment and armed self-resistance in Black communities. The group's influence waned by the early 1970s largely due to repression by law enforcement.

The assassination of Martin Luther King Jr. in 1968 furthered Black disillusionment. King was shot and killed by James Earl Ray in Memphis, where he was supporting demonstrations by striking sanitation workers while preparing to launch a Poor People's Campaign to fight for economic justice for poor people, both Black and white.

In the wake of his murder, riots erupted in hundreds of cities throughout the country. Little noticed amid the fiery turbulence, President Johnson signed into law the 1968 Fair Housing Act, the final piece of civil rights legislation of his term.

■ Why did elements of the civil rights movement embrace Black power during the mid-1960s?

Racial Struggles Continue

The civil rights struggle did not end with the 1960s. The civil rights coalition of organizations that banded together in the 1960s had disintegrated, but the National Association for the Advancement of Colored People (NAACP) remained active, as did local organizations in communities nationwide.

Following passage of the 1965 Voting Rights Act, electoral politics became the new form of activism. By 1992, there were more than 7,500 Black elected officials in the United States. Many of them had participated in the civil rights movement and subsequently worked to gain for their constituents the economic benefits that integration and **affirmative action** had not yet achieved. During this time, the number of Latino American and Asian American elected officials also increased.

affirmative action
Policies that first emerged from the civil rights movement of the 1960s meant to overcome historical patterns of discrimination against Blacks, women, and other minorities in education and employment. Affirmative action guidelines controversially established limited preferences in hiring and college admissions to favor groups that had been historically discriminated against.

The issue of **school busing** highlighted the persistence of racial discrimination. In the fifteen years following the landmark 1954 decision in *Brown v. Board of Education of Topeka*, few schools had been integrated. Starting in 1969, the U.S. Supreme Court ruled that genuine racial integration of the public schools must no longer be delayed. In 1971, the Court went even further in *Swann v. Charlotte-Mecklenburg Board of Education* by requiring school districts to bus pupils to achieve integration. Cities such as Charlotte, North Carolina; Lexington, Kentucky; and Tampa, Florida, embraced the ruling and carefully planned for it to succeed.

school busing
The transporting of students to schools within and across school districts to accelerate school desegregation. The practice of school busing was often controversial and continued well into the 1990s.

The decision, however, was more controversial in other municipalities around the nation, and it exposed racism as a national problem. In many northern communities, racially discriminatory housing policies created segregated neighborhoods and, thus, segregated schools. When white parents in the Detroit suburbs objected to busing their children to inner-city, predominantly Black schools, the Supreme Court in 1974 departed from the *Swann* case and prohibited busing across school-district boundaries. This ruling created a serious problem for integration efforts because many whites were fleeing the cities and moving to the suburbs where few Black people lived.

As the conflict over school integration intensified, violence broke out in communities throughout the country. In Boston, Massachusetts, busing opponents led by Louise Day Hicks tapped into the racial and class resentments of the largely white working-class population of South Boston, which was paired with the Black community of Roxbury for busing, leaving mainly middle- and upper-class white communities unaffected. In the fall of 1974, battles broke out inside and outside the schools. Despite the violence, schools stayed open, and for the next three decades Boston remained under court order to continue busing.

From 1970 to 1977, with the acceleration of affirmative action programs, the number of Black Americans attending college doubled, constituting nearly 10 percent of the student body, a few percentage points lower than the proportion of Black people in the national population. Though Black Americans still earned lower incomes than the average white family, Black family income as a percentage of white family income had grown from 55.1 percent in 1965 to 61.5 percent ten years later. Black Americans,

Spencer Grant/Getty Images

Boston Anti-Busing March, 1975 Boston City Council member Louise Day Hicks (in center) arrives to address a large demonstration in South Boston's Columbus Park to protest busing of Black students to all-white neighborhood schools ordered by the federal court. Joining her were some men dressed in Revolutionary War–era outfits. In 1976, Hicks was elected as the first woman president of the City Council.

What do the costumes and American flags shown in this photograph suggest about the arguments of opponents of school busing?

however, still had a long way to go to catch up with whites. The situation was even worse for those who did not reach middle-class status: About 30 percent of Black Americans slid deeper into poverty during the decade.

Along with busing, affirmative action generated fierce controversy, as the case of Alan Bakke showed. Bakke, a white male in his thirties, was twice denied admission to the medical program at the University of California at Davis in the early 1970s. Bakke sued the university after learning it awarded sixteen of its one hundred spots to minorities, as part of its affirmative action policy to recruit a more racially and ethnically diverse student body. In court, he contended that the policy violated his constitutional rights of equal protection under the Fourteenth Amendment and amounted to "reverse discrimination." He provided evidence that he had higher qualifications than some of the minority students accepted into the medical school. "I realize that the rationale for these quotas is that they attempt to atone for past racial discrimination," Bakke stated. "But insisting on a new racial bias in favor of minorities is not a just situation." In 1978, in *Regents of the University of California v. Bakke*, the U.S. Supreme Court struck down the use of strict racial quotas in college admissions but allowed for the continued consideration of race as one of many factors.

AP® EXAM TIP

The course framework calls for you to understand how each branch of the federal government promoted civil rights. Be able to cite and explain at least one example for each branch of government.

Despite the persistence of economic inequality, many whites believed that affirmative action placed them at a disadvantage with Black people in the educational and economic marketplaces. In particular, many white men condemned policies that they thought recruited Black people at their expense. Polls showed that although most white people favored equal treatment of Black Americans, they disapproved of affirmative action as a form of "reverse discrimination." Over the next three decades, opponents of affirmative action succeeded in narrowing the use of racial consideration in employment and education.

REVIEW

- Why were affirmative action and school busing so controversial during the 1960s and 1970s?

AP® Skills Workshop: Writing Historically

Additional Practice in Responding to a Document-Based Question

Evaluate the extent of change within the movement for Black civil rights in the period 1945 to 1970.

Document 1

Source: *Brown v. Board of Education of Topeka*, 1954

"Segregation of white and colored children in public schools has a detrimental effect upon the colored children. The impact is greater when it has the sanction of the law, for the policy of separating the races is usually interpreted as denoting the inferiority of the negro group. A sense of inferiority affects the motivation of a child to learn. Segregation with the sanction of law, therefore, has a tendency to [slow] the educational and mental development of negro children and to deprive them of some of the benefits they would receive in a racial[ly] integrated school system.

Whatever may have been the extent of psychological knowledge at the time of *Plessy v. Ferguson*, this finding is amply supported by modern authority. Any language in *Plessy v. Ferguson* contrary to this finding is rejected.

We conclude that, in the field of public education, the doctrine of 'separate but equal' has no place. Separate educational facilities are inherently unequal."

Document 2

Source: Martin Luther King Jr., *Speech at Holt Street Baptist Church*, December 5, 1955

"My friends, we are certainly very happy to see each of you out this evening. We are here this evening for serious business. We are here in a general sense because first and foremost we are American citizens and we are determined to apply our citizenship to the fullness of its meaning. We are here also because of our love for democracy, because of our deep-seated belief that democracy transformed from thin paper to thick action is the greatest form of government on earth.

But we are here in a specific sense, because of the bus situation in Montgomery. We are here because we are determined to get the situation corrected. This situation is not at all new. The problem has existed over endless years. For many years now Negroes in Montgomery and so many other areas have been inflicted with the paralysis of crippling fears on buses in our community. On so many occasions, Negroes have been intimidated and humiliated and impressed—oppressed—because of the sheer fact that they were Negroes. . . .

And you know, my friends, there comes a time when people get tired of being trampled over by the iron feet of oppression. There comes a time,

(continued)

my friends, when people get tired of being plunged across the abyss of humiliation, where they experience the bleakness of nagging despair. . . .

We are here, we are here this evening because we're tired now. And I want to say that we are not here advocating violence. We have never done that. I want it to be known throughout Montgomery and throughout this nation that we are Christian people. We believe in the Christian religion. We believe in the teachings of Jesus. The only weapon that we have in our hands this evening is the weapon of protest. That's all."

Document 3

Source: *Sit-in at a Woolworth's Lunch Counter*, Jackson, Mississippi, May 28, 1963

Granger – Historical Picture Archive

Document 4

Source: Malcolm X, Speech to Mississippi Youth, December 1964

"I myself would go for nonviolence if it was consistent, if everybody was going to be nonviolent all the time. I'd say, okay, let's get with it, we'll all be nonviolent. But I don't go along with any kind of nonviolence unless everybody's going to be nonviolent. If they make the Ku Klux Klan nonviolent, I'll be nonviolent. If they make the White Citizens Council nonviolent, I'll be nonviolent. But as long as you've got somebody else not being nonviolent, I don't want anybody coming to me talking any nonviolent talk. I don't think it is fair to tell our people to be nonviolent unless someone is out there making the Klan and the Citizens Council and these other groups also be nonviolent."

(continued)

Document 5

Source: Huey Newton and Bobby Seale, *Black Panther Party Platform and Program*, October 1966

1. "We want freedom. We want power to determine the destiny of our Black community. . . .
2. We want full employment for our people.

We believe that the federal government is responsible and obligated to give every man employment or a guaranteed income. . . .

3. We want an end to the robbery by the white man of our Black community. . . .
4. We want decent housing, fit for shelter of human beings. . . .
5. We want education for our people that exposes the true nature of this decadent American society. We want education that teaches us our true history and our role in the present-day society. . . .
6. We want all Black men to be exempt from military service. We believe that all Black men should not be forced to fight in the military service to defend a racist government that does not protect us. . . .
7. We want an immediate end to POLICE BRUTALITY and MURDER of Black people. . . . The Second Amendment to the Constitution of the United States gives a right to bear arms. We therefore believe that all Black people should arm themselves for self-defense.
8. We want freedom for all Black men held in federal, state, county, and city prisons and jails. . . .
9. We want all Black people when brought to trial to be tried in court by a jury of their peer group or people from their Black communities . . .
10. We want land, bread, housing, education, clothing, justice and peace."

Document 6

Source: *Chicago Student Nonviolent Coordinating Committee Leaflet*, 1967

"The black man in America is in a perpetual state of slavery no matter what the white man's propaganda tells us. . . .

We must not get hung-up in the bag of having one great leader who we depend upon to make decisions. This makes the Movement too vulnerable to those forces the white man uses to keep us enslaved, such as the draft, murder, prison or character assassination. . . .

We have got to begin to say and understand with complete assuredness what black is. Black in an inner pride that the white man's language hampers us from expressing. Black is being a complete fanatic, who white society considers insane. We have to learn that black is so much better than belonging to the white race . . .

We believe that we belong to the 90 percent majority of the people on earth that the white man oppresses and that we should not beg the white man for anything. We want what belongs to us as human beings and we intend to get it through BLACK POWER."

(continued)

Document 7

Source: *Report of the National Advisory Commission on Civil Disorders* (The Kerner Commission Report), 1967

"This is our basic conclusion: Our nation is moving toward two societies, one black, one white—separate and unequal.

Reaction to last summer's [urban riots] has quickened the movement and deepened the division. Discrimination and segregation have long permeated much of American life; they now threaten the future of every American. . . .

Segregation and poverty have created in the racial ghetto a destructive environment totally unknown to most white Americans.

What white Americans have never fully understood—but what the Negro can never forget—is that white society is deeply implicated in the ghetto. White institutions created it, white institutions maintain, and white society condones it. . . .

Our recommendations embrace three basic principles:

To mount programs on a scale equal to the dimension of the problems;

To aim these programs for high impact in the immediate future in order to close the gap between promise and performance;

To undertake new initiatives and experiments that can change the system of failure and frustration that now dominates the ghetto and weakens our society.

These programs will require unprecedented levels of funding and performance, but they neither probe deeper nor demand more than the problems which called them forth. There can be no higher priority for national action and no higher claim on the nation's conscience."

The Civil Rights Movement Expands

MODULE 8.11

FOCUS

While reading this module, consider the ways in which the civil rights movement of the 1950s and 1960s inspired other marginalized Americans to pursue equal rights and opportunities. Compare the particular needs and strategies of these different groups.

The varieties of political protest and cultural dissent arising out of the Black civil rights movement emboldened other marginalized groups to emancipate themselves. Women, Latinos, American Indians, Asian Americans, and gay and lesbian Americans all launched liberation movements during the 1960s and 1970s.

The Women's Liberation Movement

Despite passage of the Nineteenth Amendment in 1920, which gave women the right to vote, women did not have equal access to employment, wages, or education, or control over reproduction. Nor did they have sufficient political power to remove these obstacles to full equality. Yet by 1960, nearly 40 percent of all women held jobs, and women made up 35 percent of college enrollments. The social movements of the 1960s—civil rights, the New Left, and the counterculture—attracted large numbers of women. Groups like SNCC empowered female staff in community-organizing projects, and women also played central roles in antiwar efforts, leading many to demand their own movement for liberation.

The women's liberation movement also built on efforts of the federal government to address gender discrimination. In 1961, President Kennedy appointed the **Commission on the Status of Women**. The commission's report, *American Women*, issued in 1963, reaffirmed the primary role of women in raising the family but cataloged the inequities women faced in the workplace. In 1963, Congress passed the Equal Pay Act, which required employers to give men and women equal pay for equal work. The following year, the Civil Rights Act of 1964 opened up further opportunities when it prohibited sexual bias in employment and created the Equal Employment Opportunity Commission (EEOC).

In 1963, Betty Friedan published a landmark book, *The Feminine Mystique*, which questioned society's prescribed gender roles and raised the consciousness of mostly college-educated women. In *The Feminine Mystique*, she described the post-college isolation and alienation experienced by her female friends who got married and stayed home to care for their children. However, not all women saw themselves reflected in Friedan's book. Many working-class women and those from Black American and other minority families had not had the opportunity to attend college or stay home with their children, and younger college women had not yet experienced the burdens of domestic isolation.

AP® EXAM TIP

Like other civil rights movements, feminists in the 1960s and 1970s had general agreement on some issues such as reproductive rights and equal opportunity in the workplace. Yet differences among feminist leaders persisted. Choose two groups or individuals and compare the historical factors that led to their different approaches to civil rights for women.

National Organization for Women (NOW)
A feminist organization formed in 1966 by Betty Friedan, Gloria Steinem, and other like-minded activists demanding an end to sexual discrimination and full equality between the sexes.

Equal Rights Amendment (ERA)
A proposed constitutional amendment to guarantee equal rights for men and women. The amendment was not ratified because fewer than three-quarters of the states ratified it by the 1982 deadline.

Nevertheless, Friedan and like-minded women formed the **National Organization for Women (NOW)** in October 1966. With Friedan as president, NOW dedicated itself to moving society toward "true equality for all women in America, and toward a fully equal partnership of the sexes." NOW called on the EEOC to enforce women's employment rights more vigorously and favored passage of an **Equal Rights Amendment (ERA)**, paid maternity leave for working women, the establishment of child care centers, and reproductive rights.

Although NOW advocated job training programs and assistance for impoverished women, it attracted a mainly middle-class white membership. Some Black people were among its charter members, but most Black women chose to concentrate first on eliminating racial barriers that affected Black women and men alike. Some union women also continued to oppose the ERA, and advocates opposed to abortion wanted to steer clear of NOW's support for reproductive rights.

Young women, Black and white, had also faced discrimination, sometimes in unexpected places. Even within the civil rights movement, women were not always treated equally, often being assigned clerical duties. Men held a higher status within the antiwar movement because women were not eligible for the draft. As a result of these experiences, radical women formed their own, mainly local organizations. They created "consciousness-raising" groups that allowed them to share their experiences of oppression in the family, the workplace, the university, and movement organizations.

These women's liberationists went beyond NOW's emphasis on legal equality and attacked male domination, or patriarchy, as a crucial source of women's subordination. They criticized the nuclear family and cultural values that glorified women as the object of male sexual desires, and they protested creatively against discrimination.

In 1968, radical feminists picketed the popular Miss America contest in Atlantic City, New Jersey, and set up a "Freedom Trash Can" into which they threw undergarments and cosmetics. Radical groups such as the Redstockings condemned all men as oppressors and formed separate female collectives to affirm their identities as women. In contrast, other feminists attempted to build the broadest possible coalition.

In 1972, Gloria Steinem, a founder of NOW, established *Ms.* magazine in hope of attracting readers from across the feminist political spectrum. The magazine featured women's art and poetry alongside articles on sisterhood, child rearing, and abortion.

Roe v. Wade
The 1973 Supreme Court decision that women have a constitutional right to an abortion based on an implied right to privacy in the Fourteenth Amendment. The decision was overturned in the 2022 Supreme Court ruling *Dobbs v. Jackson's Women's Health Organization*, which dismantled federal *Roe v. Wade* abortion rights in favor of federal or state-by-state legislation.

In 1973, feminists won a major battle in the Supreme Court over a woman's right to control reproduction. In ***Roe v. Wade***, the high court ruled that states could not prevent a woman from obtaining an abortion in the first three months of pregnancy but could impose some limits in the next two trimesters. In furthering the constitutional right of privacy for women, the justices classified abortion as a private medical issue between a patient and her doctor. This decision marked a victory for a woman's right to choose to terminate her pregnancy, but it also stirred up a fierce reaction from women and men who considered abortion to be the murder of an unborn child. The decision was overturned in the *Dobbs v. Jackson Women's Health Organization* decision in 2022.

In the 1970s, the women's movement gained strength, but it also attracted powerful opponents. The 1973 Supreme Court victory for abortion rights in *Roe v. Wade* did not end the controversy over the legality of abortion. In 1976, Congress responded to abortion opponents by passing legislation prohibiting the use of federal funds for impoverished women seeking to terminate their pregnancies.

Feminists engaged in other debates in this decade, often clashing with more conservative women. The National Organization for Women and its allies succeeded in getting thirty-five states out of a necessary thirty-eight to ratify the Equal Rights Amendment (ERA), which prevented the abridgment of "equality of rights under law . . . by the United States or any State on the basis of sex."

AP Photo

The Miss America Pageant Protest, 1968 In fighting for gender equality, the women's movement that emerged in the 1960s challenged all aspects of the male-dominated culture that considered women as sex objects. On September 7, 1968, feminists targeted the Miss America contest in Atlantic City, New Jersey. Protesters believed the pageant degraded women by producing a sex-driven ideal of femininity. Unidentified members of the Women's Liberation Party hold protest signs reading "Welcome to the Miss America Cattle Auction" and showing a woman depicted as various cuts of steak while protesters march in the background.

What similarities existed between women's rights protests and civil rights protests?

In response, other women activists formed their own movement to block ratification. Phyllis Schlafly, a conservative activist, founded the Stop ERA organization to prevent the creation of a "unisex society." Despite the inroads made by feminists, traditional notions of femininity appealed to many women and to male-dominated legislatures. The remaining states refused to ratify the ERA, thus killing the amendment in 1982, when the ratification period expired.

AP® WORKING with EVIDENCE

Source: Gloria Steinem, Testimony before the Senate Judiciary Committee Hearing on the Equal Rights Amendment, May 6, 1970

> "During 12 years of working for a living, I have experienced much of the legal and social discrimination reserved for women in this country. I have been refused service in public restaurants, ordered out of public gathering places, and turned away from apartment rentals; all for the clearly stated, sole reason that I am a woman. And all without the legal remedies available to blacks and other minorities. I have been excluded from professional groups, writing assignments on so-called 'unfeminine' subjects such as politics, full participation in the Democratic Party, jury duty, and even from such small male privileges as discounts on airline fares. Most important to me, I have been denied a society in which women are encouraged, or even allowed to think of themselves as first-class citizens and responsible human beings. . . .
>
> The truth is that all our problems stem from the same sex based myths. . . . Like racial myths, they have been reflected in our laws. Let me list a few.

That woman are biologically inferior to men. In fact, an equally good case can be made for the reverse. Women live longer than men, even when the men are not subject to business pressures. Women survived Nazi concentration camps better . . . and are so much more durable at every stage of life that nature must conceive 20 to 50 percent more males in order to keep the balance going. . . .

Another myth, that children must have full-time mothers. American mothers spend more time with their homes and children than those of any other society we know about. In the past, joint families, servants, a prevalent system in which grandparents raised the children, or family field work in the agrarian systems—all these factors contributed more to child care than the labor-saving devices of which we are so proud.

The truth is that most American children seem to be suffering from too much mother, and too little father. Part of the program of Women's Liberation is a return of fathers to their children. If laws permit women equal work and pay opportunities, men will then be relieved of their role as sole breadwinner. Fewer ulcers, fewer hours of meaningless work, equal responsibility for his own children . . . Women's Liberation is Men's Liberation too."

Questions for Analysis

1. Identify Steinem's main argument and the reasons she uses to support her argument.
2. Describe the benefits of women's liberation for men according to Steinem.
3. Explain the strategies Steinem uses to support her argument.

Source: *The Phyllis Schlafly Report*, vol. 5, no. 7, February 1972

"Of all the classes of people who ever lived, the American woman is the most privileged. We have the most rights and rewards, and the fewest duties. . . .

1. We have the immense good fortune to live in a civilization which respects the family as the basic unit of society. This respect is part and parcel of our laws and our customs. It is based on the fact of life—which no legislation or agitation can erase—that women have babies and men don't.

If you don't like this fundamental difference, you will have to take up your complaint with God because He created us this way. The fact that women, not men, have babies is not the fault of selfish and domineering men, or of the establishment, or of any clique of conspirators who want to oppress women. It's simply the way God made us. . . .

2. [W]e are the beneficiaries of a tradition of special respect for women which dates from the Christian Age of Chivalry. The honor and respect paid to Mary, the Mother of Christ, resulted in all women, in effect, being put on a pedestal. . . .

3. [T]he great American free enterprise system has produced remarkable inventors who have lifted the backbreaking 'women's work' from our shoulders. . . .

Thus, household duties have been reduced to only a few hours a day, leaving the American woman with plenty of time to moonlight. She can take a full or part-time paying job, or she can indulge to her heart's content in a tremendous selection of interesting educational or cultural or homemaking activities. . . .

The 'women's lib' movement is *not* an honest effort to secure better jobs for women who want or need to work outside the home. This is just the superficial sweet-talk to win broad support for a radical 'movement.' Women's lib is a total assault on the role of the American woman as wife and mother, and on the family as the basic unit of society."

Questions for Analysis

1. Identify Schlafly's main argument and the reasons she uses to support her argument.
2. Describe how Schlafly dismisses the women's liberation movement.
3. Explain the strategies Schlafly uses to support her argument.

Questions for Comparison

1. Explain how each author appeals to tradition to support her argument.
2. Evaluate the extent to which each excerpt reflects 1970s politics and society.

Beyond the failure to ratify the Equal Rights Amendment, the women's movement experienced other successes and challenges. In 1972, Congress passed the Educational Amendments Act. Title IX of this law prohibited colleges and universities that received federal funds from discriminating on the basis of sex, leading to substantial advances in women's athletics. Many more women sought and received relief against job discrimination through the Equal Employment Opportunity Commission. NOW membership continued to grow, and the number of battered women's shelters and rape crisis centers multiplied in towns and cities across the country. Women saw their ranks increase on college campuses, in both undergraduate and professional schools. Women also began entering politics in greater numbers, especially at the local and state levels.

At the same time, women of color sought to broaden the definition of feminism to include struggles against race and class oppression as well as sex discrimination. In 1974, a group of Black feminists, led by author Barbara Smith, organized the Combahee River Collective and proclaimed: "We . . . often find it difficult to separate race from class from sex oppression because in our lives they are most often experienced simultaneously."

▪ What were the major successes and failures of the women's movement during the 1970s?

Latino Activism

During the 1960s, the size of the Spanish-speaking population in the United States tripled from three million to nine million. Hispanic Americans were a diverse group who hailed from many countries and backgrounds, yet many faced economic and social injustices that inspired civil rights activism.

For Mexican Americans, World War II inspired such efforts. In southern California, Unity Leagues formed to protest segregation, and they often joined with Black American groups in seeking equality. In 1947, the League of United Latin American Citizens (LULAC) won a case in federal court in *Mendez v. Westminster*, prohibiting separate public schools for Mexican American students. Spurred on by such efforts, Mexican Americans in 1949 succeeded in electing Edward Roybal to the Los Angeles City Council, the first American of Mexican descent to serve on that body since 1888. In Texas, LULAC succeeded through litigation and boycotts in desegregating movie theaters, swimming pools, restaurants, and other public accommodations. LULAC also brought an end to discrimination in jury selection.

Once Jackie Robinson integrated baseball in 1947, he opened the way for other players of color. Two years later, the Cleveland Indians baseball team (now called the Cleveland Guardians) signed Orestes "Minnie" Miñoso, an Afro-Cuban. Miñoso, Major

League Baseball's first Afro-Hispanic ballplayer, played sixteen seasons and was elected to the Hall of Fame in 1996.

In the 1950s, Cesar Chavez had emerged as the leader of oppressed Mexican farmworkers in California. In seeking the right to organize a union and gain higher wages and better working conditions, Chavez shared King's nonviolent principles. In 1962, Chavez and Dolores Huerta formed the National Farm Workers Association, and in 1965, the union called a strike against California grape growers, one that attracted national support and finally succeeded after five years.

AP® WORKING with EVIDENCE

Source: Dolores Huerta, Statement before U.S. Senate Subcommittee on Migratory Labor, 1969

> "Mr. Chairman and members of the committee, we are again glad to be here and present our long, sad story of trying to organize the farmworkers. . . .
>
> The horrible state in which farmworkers find themselves, faced with such extreme poverty and discrimination, has taught us that the only way we can change our situation is by organization of a union. . . .
>
> As you know, UFWOC [United Farm Workers Organizing Committee] has undertaken an international boycott of all California-Arizona table grapes in order to gain union recognition for striking farmworkers. We did not take up the burden of the boycott willingly. It is expensive. It is a hardship on the farmworkers' families who have left the small valley towns to travel across the country to boycott grapes.
>
> But, because of the table grape growers' refusal to bargain with their workers, the boycott is our major weapon and I might say a nonviolent weapon, and our last line of defense against the growers who use foreign labor to break our strikes.
>
> It is only through the pressure of the boycott that UFWOC has won contracts with major California wine grape growers. At this point, the major obstacles to our efforts to organize farmworkers are obstacles to our boycott.
>
> Our boycott has been met with well-organized and well-financed opposition by the growers and their sympathizers. Most recently, several major California grape growers joined with other agribusiness interests and members of the John Birch Society to form an employer-dominated "union" the Agricultural Workers Freedom To Work Association (AWFWA), for the sole purpose of destroying UFWOC. . . .
>
> In spite of this type of antiunion activity, our boycott of California-Arizona table grapes has been successful. It is being successful for the simple reason that millions of Americans are supporting the grape workers strike by not buying table grapes."

Questions for Analysis

1. Identify the tactics used by each side in the labor dispute that Huerta refers to in this statement.
2. Describe the challenges and successes of the farmworkers, according to Huerta.
3. Evaluate the extent of similarity between the UFWOC protest and other civil rights movement protests.
4. Evaluate the extent to which Huerta's activism reflects the influence of the feminist movement.

Robert Kennedy and Cesar Chavez, March 10, 1968 Robert Kennedy, a Democratic presidential candidate in 1968 (left), and Cesar Chavez, leader of the United Farm Workers (right), are seen praying together at a mass to celebrate Chavez ending a twenty-five-day hunger strike to demand better treatment of farmworkers by growers. Kennedy said he visited Chavez "out of respect for one of the heroic figures of our time." Less than two months later, Kennedy was assassinated in Los Angeles hours after winning the California and South Dakota primary elections.

How was the farmworker movement similar to and different from the Black civil rights movement?

Younger Mexican Americans, especially those in cities such as Los Angeles and other western *barrios* (ghettos), supported Chavez's economic goals but challenged older political leaders who sought cultural assimilation. Borrowing from the Black Panthers, Mexican Americans formed the Brown Berets, a self-defense organization. In 1969, some 1,500 activists gathered in Denver and declared themselves *Chicanos*, a term that expressed their cultural pride and identity.

Chicanos created a new political party, **La Raza Unida (The United Race)**, to promote their interests, and the party and its allies sponsored demonstrations to fight for jobs, bilingual education, and the creation of Chicano studies programs in colleges. Chicano and other Spanish-language communities also took advantage of the protections of the Voting Rights Act, which in 1975 was amended to include sections of the country — from New York to California to Florida and Texas — where Hispanic literacy in English and voter registration were low. Latinas also joined the feminist movement, often forming their own organizations, but they, like Black women, also joined men in struggles for racial equality and advancement.

La Raza Unida (The United Race)
A Chicano political party, formed in 1969, that advocated job opportunities for Chicanos, bilingual education, and Chicano cultural studies programs in universities. The party was especially influential in states with large Latino populations such as California and Texas.

In similar fashion, Puerto Ricans organized the Young Lords Party (YLP). Originating in Chicago in 1969, the group soon spread to New York City. Like the Black

AP® EXAM TIP

Characterize how Latino, American Indian, and Asian American movements sought civil rights during this period. Be able to describe an event or development for each group that explains the methods, strategies, and tactics used so you can explain the degree to which each movement was successful.

Panthers, the organization established inner-city breakfast programs and medical clinics. The YLP supported bilingual education in public schools, condemned U.S. imperialism, favored independence for Puerto Rico, and supported women's reproductive rights.

REVIEW

- In what ways was Latino civil rights activism similar to Black civil rights activism? In what ways was it different?

American Indian Activism

American Indians also joined the upsurge of activism and self-determination. By 1970, some 800,000 people identified themselves as American Indians, many of whom lived in poverty on reservations. They suffered from inadequate housing, high alcoholism rates, low life expectancy, staggering unemployment, and lack of education.

American Indian Movement (AIM)
An American Indian group, formed in 1968, that promoted "red power," the preservation of tribal cultural traditions, poverty relief, and improved living conditions on reservations and condemned the continued mistreatment of American Indians.

Conscious of their heritage as the first Americans, they determined to halt their deterioration by asserting "red power" and pride and established the **American Indian Movement (AIM)** in 1968. The following year, American Indians occupied the abandoned prison island of Alcatraz in San Francisco Bay, where they remained until 1971. Among their demands, they offered to buy the island for $24 in beads and cloth—a reference to the purchase of Manhattan Island in 1626—and turn it into an American Indian educational and cultural center. In 1972, AIM occupied the headquarters of the Federal Bureau of Indian Affairs in Washington, D.C. In 1973, AIM demonstrators seized the village of Wounded Knee, South Dakota, the scene of the 1890 massacre of Sioux residents by the U.S. army, to dramatize the impoverished living conditions on reservations. They held out for more than seventy days with eleven hostages until a shootout with the FBI ended the confrontation, killing one protester and wounding another.

The results of the red power movement proved mixed. Demonstrations focused media attention on the plight of American Indians but did little to halt their downward spiral. Nevertheless, courts became more sensitive to American Indian claims and protected mineral and fishing rights on reservations.

REVIEW

- In what ways did AIM's demand for reform reflect continuities and changes in the treatment of American Indians in the late nineteenth and early twentieth centuries?

Asian American Activism

Asian American college students on the West Coast engaged in their own liberation struggle. World War II had advanced civil rights for the Chinese: In 1943, Congress repealed the exclusion law and followed up by passing the War Brides Act in 1945, which resulted in the admission of 6,000 Chinese women to the United States.

However, the fall of China to the communists in 1949 and the beginning of the Korean War the next year posed new challenges to Chinese communities on the West Coast. Although organizations such as the Six Companies of San Francisco denounced communist China and pledged their loyalty to the United States, Cold War witch-hunts targeted the Chinese. With the Chinese communists fighting against the United States in Korea, some regarded Chinese people in America with suspicion. "People would look at you in the street and think," one Chinese woman recalled, " 'Well, you're one of the enemy.' "

The federal government established a "Confession Program" by which Chinese people illegally in the country would be allowed to stay if they came forward, acknowledged their loyalty to the United States, and provided information about friends and relatives. Some 10,000 Chinese in San Francisco participated in this program.

During the 1950s, Chinatowns shrank in population as their upwardly mobile residents moved to the suburbs. By 1959, Chinese Americans had a median family income of $6,207, compared with $5,660 for all Americans.

The children of newly arrived Chinese immigrants faced different problems, however, doing poorly in public schools that taught exclusively in English. Established in 1969, the Chinese for Affirmative Action filed a lawsuit against San Francisco school officials for discriminating against students with limited English-language skills. In *Lau v. Nichols* (1974), the Supreme Court upheld the group's claim, accelerating opportunities for bilingual education.

Japanese Americans also took part in civil rights activism during this era. Since the late 1940s and 1950s, Japanese Americans had attempted to rebuild their lives following their wartime evacuation and internment. Although many returned to the West Coast and found their neighborhoods occupied by other ethnic groups and their businesses in other hands, they persevered and stressed education for their children. The **McCarran-Walter Immigration Act** of 1952 made it possible for Japanese noncitizens to become U.S. citizens, although it maintained a race-based system of immigration and discriminatory quotas. In addition, California repealed its Alien Land Law of 1913, which prohibited noncitizen Japanese from purchasing land.

During the late 1950s and early 1960s, many Japanese American high school and college students learned for the first time about their parents and grandparents' internment during World War II. Like other activists, they expressed pride in their ethnic heritage and joined in efforts to publicize the injustices that earlier generations had endured. The activism of this third generation of Japanese people helped convince the moderate Japanese American Citizens League in 1970 to endorse reparations for the internees, the first step in a two-decade effort that later succeeded.

REVIEW

- Compare Asian American activism during this period to the activism of Latino Americans and American Indians. What similar grievances do all three groups share? Where do they differ?

The Gay Liberation Movement

Unlike Black Americans, Chicanos, American Indians, and Asian Americans, gay, lesbian, and transgender people are not distinguished by the color of their skin and remained largely invisible to the rest of society. In the 1950s, gay men and women created their own political and cultural organizations and frequented bars and taverns outside mainstream commercial culture, but most hid their identities.

It was not until 1969 that they took a major step toward asserting their collective grievances in a very visible fashion. Police regularly cracked down on gay bars like the Stonewall Inn in New York City's Greenwich Village. But on June 27, 1969, gay patrons battled back. The *Village Voice* called the **Stonewall riots** "a kind of liberation, as the gay brigade emerged from the bars, back rooms, and bedrooms of the Village and became street people." In the manner of Black power, the New Left, and radical feminists, homosexuals organized the Gay Liberation Front, voiced pride in being gay, and demanded equality of opportunity regardless of sexual orientation.

Stonewall riots
A series of protests in 1969 by the gay and lesbian community in New York City after a police raid at the Stonewall Inn, a gathering place for gay men, turned violent. This uprising helped launch the gay liberation movement of the 1970s.

As with other oppressed groups, gay, lesbian, and transgender people achieved victories slowly and unevenly. In the decades following the 1960s, gay, lesbian, and transgender individuals faced discrimination in employment, could not marry or receive domestic benefits, and were subject to violence for public displays of affection.

REVIEW

- What does the gay liberation movement have in common with other civil rights movements during this period? What are some important differences?

AP® Skills Workshop: Writing Historically

Additional Practice in Responding to a Long-Essay Question

Evaluate the extent to which different rights movements fostered change in American society in the 1960s.

Youth Culture of the 1960s

MODULE 8.12

FOCUS

While reading this module, consider the continuities and changes in American culture during the social turbulence of the 1960s, and consider what factors caused these changes to arise from the youth during the decade.

The civil rights movement inspired many young people to activism. Combining ideals of freedom, equality, and community with direct-action protest, civil rights activists offered a model for those seeking to address a variety of problems, including the threat of nuclear devastation, the loss of individual autonomy in a corporate society, racism, poverty, sexism, and environmental degradation.

The New Left

The formation of the Student Nonviolent Coordinating Committee (SNCC) in 1960 opened the possibilities for personal and social transformation and offered a movement founded on democracy that promised to remake the nation. One young activist, Tom Hayden, helped apply the ideals of SNCC to predominantly white college campuses. After spending the summer of 1961 registering voters in Mississippi and Georgia, the University of Michigan graduate student returned to campus eager to recruit like-minded students who questioned America's commitment to democracy.

Hayden became an influential leader of the **Students for a Democratic Society (SDS),** which advocated the formation of a "New Left." They considered the "Old Left," which revolved around communism and socialism, as autocratic and no longer relevant. "We are people of this generation," SDS proclaimed, "bred in at least modest comfort, housed now in universities, looking uncomfortably to the world we inherit."

Students for a Democratic Society (SDS) A student-led activist organization that advocated the formation of a "New Left" to overturn the social and political status quo. SDS growth on college campuses was fueled by opposition to U.S. Cold War policies, especially involvement in the Vietnam War.

In its **Port Huron Statement** (1962), SDS condemned mainstream liberal politics, Cold War foreign policy, racism, and research-oriented universities that cared little for their undergraduates. It called for the adoption of "participatory democracy," which would return power to the people. In an ironic twist, the framers of the manifesto picked up the rhetoric of the moderate Republican president, Dwight Eisenhower, in condemning the military-industrial complex (see Module 8.7). "Not only is ours the first generation to live with the possibility of world-wide cataclysm," the statement declared, "it is the first to experience the actual social preparation for cataclysm, the general militarization of American society." The attack on the military-industrial complex and the unrestrained power of the executive branch to conduct foreign and military policy would become a staple of New Left protest.

AP® WORKING with EVIDENCE

Source: Tom Hayden and others, "The Port Huron Statement," 1962

> "As we grew . . . our comfort was penetrated by events too troubling to dismiss. First, the permeating and victimizing fact of human degradation, symbolized by the Southern struggle against racial bigotry, compelled most of us from silence to activism. Second, the enclosing fact of the Cold War, symbolized by the presence of the Bomb, brought awareness that we ourselves, and our friends, and millions of abstract "others" we knew more directly because of our common peril, might die at any time. . . .
>
> We would replace power rooted in possession, privilege, or circumstance by power and uniqueness rooted in love, reflectiveness, reason, and creativity. As a social system we seek the establishment of a democracy of individual participation, governed by two central aims: that the individual share in those social decisions determining the quality and direction of his life; that society be organized to encourage independence in men and provide the media for their common participation.
>
> In social change or interchange, we find violence to be abhorrent because it requires generally the transformation of the target, be it a human being or a community of people, into a depersonalized object of hate. It is imperative that the means of violence be abolished and the institutions—local, national, international—that encourage non-violence as a condition of conflict be developed."

Questions for Analysis

1. Identify the two troubling factors that led to the writing of this statement, and the solutions it proposes.
2. Describe the vision of the "Port Huron Statement" for a new form of democracy.
3. Explain how this document is a product of the historical context in which it was written.
4. Evaluate the extent to which this vision of democracy represents a continuity or change from the way in which democracy was practiced at the time.

The New Left, however, never consisted of one central organization. After all, many protesters challenged the very idea of centralized authority. In fact, SDS did not initiate the New Left's most dramatic early protest. In 1964, the University of California at Berkeley banned political activities just outside the main campus entrance in response to Congress of Racial Equality (CORE) protests against racial bias in local hiring. When CORE defied the prohibition, campus police arrested its leader, prompting a student uprising.

Free Speech Movement (FSM)
The 1964–1965 college student-led movement using sit-in and rallies to protest policies of the University of California at Berkeley that restricted students' ability to protest for civil rights. The successful FSM protests inspired greater student activism on college campuses.

Student activists then formed the **Free Speech Movement (FSM)**, which held rallies in front of the administration building, culminating in a nonviolent, civil rights–style sit-in. When California governor Edmund "Pat" Brown dispatched state and county police to evict the demonstrators, students and faculty joined in protest and forced the university administration to yield to FSM's demands for amnesty and reform. By the end of the decade, hundreds of demonstrations had erupted on campuses throughout the nation.

AP Images/Robert Houston

The Berkeley Free Speech Movement Mario Savio, a student leader at the University of California at Berkeley and a Freedom Summer volunteer, stands among demonstrators sitting in at Sproul Hall on December 3, 1964, to protest university curbs on free speech. A day earlier, Savio had declared: "There's a time when the operation of the machine becomes so odious . . . you've got to put your bodies upon the gears . . . and you've got to make it stop."

To what extent were the free-speech sit-ins at universities like the sit-ins to desegregate public facilities in the South?

The Vietnam War accelerated student radicalism, and college campuses provided a strategic setting for antiwar activities. Like most Americans in the mid-1960s, undergraduates had only a dim awareness of U.S. activity in Vietnam. Yet all college men were eligible for the draft once they graduated and lost their student deferment. As more troops were sent to Vietnam, student concern intensified.

Protests escalated in 1966 when President Johnson authorized an additional 250,000-troop buildup in Vietnam. With induction into the military a looming possibility, student protesters launched a variety of campaigns and demonstrations. Others resisted the draft by fleeing to Canada, and still others engaged in various forms of civil disobedience. Most college students, however, were not activists—between 1965 and 1968, only 20 percent of college students attended demonstrations. Nevertheless, the activist minority received extensive media attention and helped raise awareness about the difficulty of waging the Vietnam War abroad and maintaining domestic tranquility at home.

By the end of 1967, as the number of troops in Vietnam approached half a million, protests increased. Antiwar sentiment had spread to faculty, artists, writers,

AP® EXAM TIP

Identify a peaceful and a violent protest over the Vietnam War. Identify both the causes and effects of each protest. In what ways were these protests a reflection of the context in which they took place?

businesspeople, and elected officials. In April, Martin Luther King Jr. delivered a powerful antiwar address at Riverside Church in New York City. "The world now demands," King declared, "that we admit that we have been wrong from the beginning of our adventure in Vietnam, that we have been detrimental to the life of the Vietnamese people." As protests spread and the government clamped down on dissenters, some activists substituted armed struggle for nonviolence. SDS split into factions, with the most prominent of them, the Weathermen, going underground and adopting violent tactics.

- What goals did the New Left share with progressive movements earlier in the twentieth century? What were some differences?

The Counterculture

counterculture

Young cultural rebels of the 1960s and 1970s who rejected conventional cultural and social norms. The movement began in San Francisco and was known for anti-establishment rock music, protests against the Vietnam War, drug use, and the practice of "free love."

The New Left's challenge to liberal politics attracted many students, and the **counterculture**'s rejection of conventional middle-class values of work, sexual restraint, and rationality captivated even more. Cultural rebels, overwhelmingly under thirty years old, emphasized living in the present, seeking immediate gratification, expressing authentic feelings, and reaching a higher consciousness through mind-altering drugs. Despite differences in approach, both the New Left and the counterculture expressed concerns about modern technology, bureaucratization, and the possibility of nuclear annihilation and sought new means of creating political, social, and personal liberation.

Rock 'n' roll became the soundtrack of the counterculture. In 1964, Bob Dylan's song "The Times They Are A-Changin'" became an anthem for youth rebellion. That same year, the Beatles, a British quartet influenced by Black and white rock 'n' rollers of the 1950s, toured the United States and revolutionized popular music. Originally singing melodic compositions of teenage love and angst, the Beatles embraced the counterculture and began writing songs about alienation and politics, flavoring them with the drug-inspired sounds of psychedelic music. Although most of the songs that reached the top ten on the record charts did not undermine traditional values, the music of groups like the Beatles, the Rolling Stones, the Who, the Grateful Dead, Jefferson Airplane, and the Doors spread counterculture messages.

The counterculture viewed the elimination of sexual restrictions as central to transforming personal and social behavior. The 1960s generation did not invent sexual freedom, but it did a great deal to shatter time-honored moral codes of monogamy, fidelity, and moderation. Casual sex, extramarital affairs, and public nudity all gradually became more acceptable, and the broader culture reflected these changes. The Broadway production of the musical *Hair* showed frontal nudity, the movie industry adopted ratings of X and R that made films with nudity and profane language available to a wider audience, and new television comedy shows featured sketches with risqué content.

AP® WORKING with EVIDENCE

Source: Photograph Taken Outside the Democratic National Convention in Chicago, Illinois, August 26, 1968

Library of Congress, LC-DIG-ppmsca-40810

Question for Analysis

1. Identify the groups of people in this image.
2. Describe the ways in which their clothes and stances characterize the debates over the Vietnam War in 1968.
3. Evaluate the extent to which this image represents both change and continuity in popular support for war during the first half of the twentieth century.

With sexual conduct in flux, society had difficulty maintaining the double standard of behavior that privileged men over women. In particular, the availability of birth control pills for women, introduced in 1960, made sexual freedom more possible. Although sexual liberation still carried more risks for women than for men, increased openness in discussing sexuality allowed many women to gain greater control over their bodies and their relationships.

The antiwar movement and counterculture influenced popular culture in many ways. Rock musicians such as Bruce Springsteen, Jackson Browne, and Billy Joel sang of loss, loneliness, urban decay, and adventure. The film *M*A*S*H* (1970), though dealing with the Korean War, was a thinly veiled satire of the horrors of the Vietnam War. In the late 1970s, filmmakers began producing movies specifically about Vietnam and the toll the war took on ordinary Americans who served there. The television sitcom *All in the Family* gave American viewers the character of Archie Bunker, an opinionated, white, blue-collar worker, in a comedy that dramatized the contemporary political and cultural wars as conservative Archie taunted his liberal son-in-law with politically incorrect remarks about minorities, feminists, and liberals.

Despite growing conservatism nationwide in the 1970s, political activism for civil rights, peace, and the counterculture did not die out. Many of the changes sought by youth culture during the 1960s had entered the political and cultural mainstreams in the 1970s. The counterculture, with its long hairstyles and colorful clothes, entered the mainstream, and rock continued to dominate popular music.

Some Americans experimented with recreational drugs, and the remaining sexual taboos of the 1960s fell. Many parents became resigned to seeing their daughters and sons living with boyfriends or girlfriends before getting married. And many of those same parents engaged in extramarital affairs or divorced their spouses. The divorce rate increased by 116 percent in the decade after 1965; in 1979, the rate peaked at 23 divorces per 1,000 married couples.

- In what ways did the counterculture affect broader American culture in the 1960s and 1970s?

AP® Skills Workshop: Writing Historically

Additional Practice in Responding to a Short-Answer Question

Answer **A**, **B**, and **C**.

(A) Briefly explain ONE specific historical event or development that shaped youth culture during the 1960s.

(B) Briefly explain ANOTHER specific historical event or development that shaped youth culture during the 1960s.

(C) Briefly explain ONE specific historical event or development that resulted from youth culture of the 1960s.

The Environment and Natural Resources from 1968 to 1980

MODULE 8.13

FOCUS

As you read this module, consider the factors that inspired debates about the environment and natural resources during the later years of this time period. Consider the ways debates about environmental protections and natural resources were an extension of debates earlier in the century.

An outgrowth of 1960s liberal activism that flourished in the 1970s was the effort to clean up and preserve the environment. The publication of Rachel Carson's *Silent Spring* in 1962 had renewed awareness of what Progressive Era reformers called conservation. Carson expanded the concept of conservation to include ecology, which addressed the relationships of human beings and other organisms to their environments. By exploring these connections, she offered a revealing look at the devastating effects of pesticides on birds and fish, as well as on the human food chain and water supply.

AP® EXAM TIP

Explain how the federal government's role in environmental protection and regulation changed from the beginning of Period 8 (1945) to the end of the period (1980). What specifically changed, and what caused the change you identified? Explaining historical developments through cause and effect is a good way to build historical arguments.

Environmentalism

This new environmental movement not only focused on open spaces and national parks but also sought to publicize urban environmental problems. By 1970, 53 percent of Americans considered air and water pollution to be one of the top issues facing the country, up from only 17 percent five years earlier. Responding to this shift in public opinion, in 1971, President Nixon established the **Environmental Protection Agency (EPA)** and signed the Clean Air Act, which regulated auto emissions. In this regard, Nixon departed from conservatives, who favored limited government, and strengthened federal oversight of environmental programs throughout the country.

Environmental Protection Agency (EPA)
A federal agency established by President Nixon in 1971 to regulate activities that resulted in pollution or other environmental degradation.

AP® WORKING with EVIDENCE

Source: Michael McCloskey, *Ecotactics: The Sierra Club Handbook for Environmental Activists*, 1970

> "A few years ago, our friends in law school laughed at us because we wanted to 'change the world.' Young activists in the Fifties, of course, represented the silent majority. Their laughing peers believed the lessons of the Thirties and Forties had already exposed the delusion of Grand Causes.
>
> But with the causes of the Sixties—civil rights, anti-poverty and peace—activism became a less lonely avocation. Suddenly, students discovered they could make a difference—and they did, producing some profound changes in public policy. Now, as the Seventies begin, we face a

crisis that affects everyone in ways some of the earlier crises never did. The ecology of Earth's life-support system is disintegrating.

A revolution is truly needed—in our values, outlook and economic organization. For the crisis of our environment stems from a legacy of economic and technical premises which have been pursed in the absence of ecological knowledge. That other revolution, the industrial one that is turning sour, needs to be replaced by a revolution of new attitudes toward growth, goods, space and living things."

Questions for Analysis

1. Identify the intended audience for this excerpt.
2. Describe the point of view on technology and industrialization that McCloskey expresses in this excerpt.
3. Explain the relationship between the activism of the 1960s and the environmental movement of the 1970s.
4. Evaluate the extent to which environmental activism of the 1970s represented a continuity with the conservation movement of the Progressive Era.

Not everyone embraced environmentalism. As the EPA toughened emission standards, automobile manufacturers complained that the regulations forced them to raise prices and hurt an industry that was already feeling the threat of foreign competition, especially from Japan. Workers were also affected, as declining sales forced companies to lay off employees.

Similarly, passage of the Endangered Species Act of 1973 pitted timber companies in the Northwest against environmentalists. The new law prevented the federal government from funding any projects that threatened the habitat of animals at risk of extinction.

REVIEW

- In what ways was environmental reform during this era a change from the conservation efforts from earlier in the century?
- In what ways was it similar?

Health, Safety, and Natural Resources

In 1972, the federal government increased its responsibility for protecting the health and safety of American workers through the creation of the Occupational Safety and Health Administration (OSHA). The Consumer Products Safety Commission was established also to provide added safety for the buying public. In addition, President Nixon signed a law banning cigarette advertising on radio and television because of the link between smoking and cancer.

Despite a series of environmental and occupational reforms domestically, the United States faced international shocks that threatened its access to national resources necessary for its advanced industrial economy. By the 1970s, four-fifths of the world's oil supply came from Saudi Arabia, Iran, Iraq, and Kuwait, all members of the Arab-dominated **Organization of Petroleum Exporting Countries (OPEC).** The organization had been formed in 1960 by these Persian Gulf countries together with Venezuela, and it used its control of petroleum supplies to set world prices.

In 1973, during the Nixon administration, OPEC imposed an oil embargo on the United States as punishment for its support of Israel during the Yom Kippur War with

Egypt and Syria. The price of oil skyrocketed as a result. The effect of high oil prices rippled through the economy, leading to increased inflation and unemployment. The crisis lasted until May 1974, when OPEC lifted its embargo following six months of diplomacy by the Nixon administration.

By the end of the decade, America's consumer-oriented economy depended on cheap energy, a substantial portion of which came from sources outside the United States. By 1977, the cost of a barrel of oil had jumped to around $30. American drivers who had paid 30 cents a gallon for gas in 1970 paid more than four times that amount ten years later.

Energy concerns helped reshape American industry. With energy prices rising, U.S. manufacturers sought ways to reduce costs by moving their factories to nations that offered cheaper labor and lower energy costs. This outsourcing of American manufacturing had two significant consequences. First, it weakened the American labor movement, particularly in heavy industry. In the 1970s, union membership dropped from 28 to 23 percent of the workforce and continued to decline over the next decade. Second, this process of **deindustrialization** accelerated a significant population shift that had begun during World War II from the old industrial areas of the Northeast and the Midwest (the Rust Belt) to the South and the Southwest (the Sun Belt), where cheaper costs and lower wages were enormously attractive to businesses. Only 14 percent of southern workers were unionized in a region with a long history of opposition to labor organizing. Consequently, Sun Belt cities such as Houston, Atlanta, Phoenix, and San Diego flourished, while steel and auto towns in Ohio, Michigan, and Pennsylvania decayed.

deindustrialization
The decline of manufacturing in a specific town, region, or nation. Along with increased foreign competition and a rise of overseas outsourcing, deindustrialization led to a significant decline in union membership, as populations shifted across the country away from urban centers in search of new economic opportunity in the South and West.

stagflation
A period of economic instability in the 1970s characterized by slow economic growth, high inflation, and high unemployment.

These monumental shifts in the American economy produced widespread pain. Higher gasoline prices affected all businesses that relied on energy, leading to serious inflation. To maintain their standard of living in the face of rising inflation and stagnant wages, many Americans went into debt, using a new innovation, the credit card, to borrow collectively more than $300 billion.

The American economy had gone through inflationary spirals before, but they were usually accompanied by high employment, with wages helping to drive up prices. In the 1970s, however, rising prices were accompanied by growing unemployment, a situation that economists called "**stagflation**." Traditionally, remedies to control inflation increased unemployment, yet most unemployment cures also spurred inflation. With both occurring at the same time, economists were confounded, and many Americans felt they had lost control over their economy.

President James "Jimmy" Carter tried his best to find a solution. To reduce dependency on foreign oil, in 1977, Carter devised a plan for energy self-sufficiency, which he called the "moral equivalent of war." Critics called the proposal weak and gave it a mocking acronym, MEOW. A more substantial accomplishment came on August 4, 1977, when Carter signed into law the creation of the Department of Energy, with responsibilities covering research, development, and conservation of energy. In 1978, he backed the **National Energy Act**, which set gas emission standards for automobiles and provided incentives for installing alternate energy systems, such as solar and

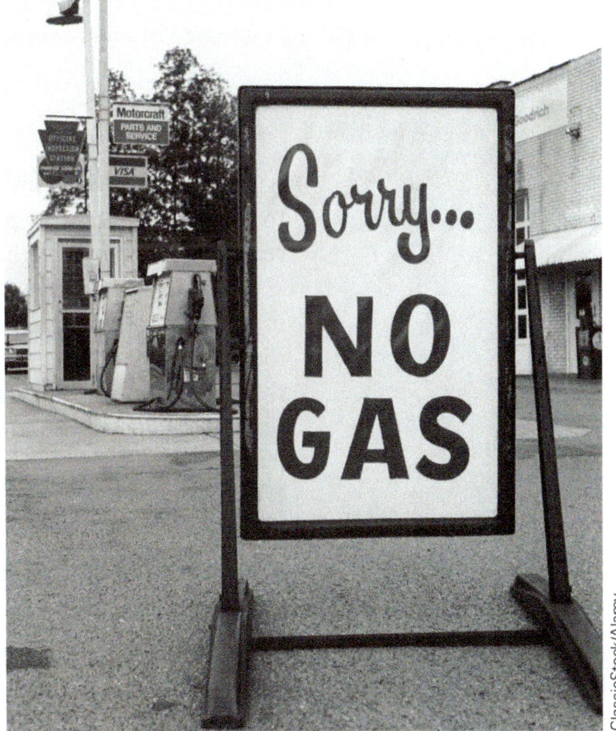

ClassicStock/Alamy

Gas Shortages, 1973 A gas station lets customers know there is no gasoline. OPEC's oil embargo started during the Yom Kippur War in 1973 and caused gas shortages and soaring prices in the United States. Motorists scrambling to find available supplies at gas stations created long lines.

How does this image reflect the ways in which the OPEC oil embargo affected American society?

MAP 8.6 The Sun and Rust Belts Dramatic economic and demographic shifts during the 1970s led to industrial development and population growth in the "Sun Belt" in the South and Southwest at the expense of the "Rust Belt" in the Northeast and Midwest. As manufacturers sought cheap, non-unionized labor, they moved factories to the South or overseas, while defense industries and agribusiness fueled growth from Texas to California.

How did the migration of Americans to the Sun Belt impact American society?

wind power, in homes and public buildings. He also supported congressional legislation to spend $14 billion for public sector jobs as well as to cut taxes by $34 billion, which reduced unemployment but only temporarily.

In many other respects, President Carter embraced conservative principles. Believing in fiscal restraint, he rejected liberal proposals for national health insurance and more expansive employment programs. Instead, he signed into law bills deregulating the airline, banking, trucking, and railroad industries, measures that appealed to conservative proponents of free-market economics.

REVIEW

- What economic and foreign policy challenges did the Carter administration face, and how were those challenges related?
- In what ways did President Carter support a conservative agenda?

AP® EXAM TIP

Several notable environmental accidents took place in the 1970s. Select one of these accidents and explain how it led to a specific environmental program or regulation by the federal government.

Several disasters also heightened public demands for stronger government oversight of the environment. In 1978, women living near Love Canal outside Niagara Falls, New York, complained about unusually high rates of illnesses and birth defects in their community. Investigations revealed that their housing development had been constructed on top of a toxic waste dump. This discovery spawned grassroots efforts to clean up this area as well as other contaminated communities.

AP Images/Barry Thumma, File

Three Mile Island Nuclear Power Plant, 1979 On March 28, 1979, the Three Mile Island nuclear power plant, outside Harrisburg, Pennsylvania, started leaking radioactive steam that contaminated the surrounding area. The governor called for a voluntary evacuation within a twenty-mile distance. The cooling tower of the nuclear plant stands behind an abandoned playground, where children had been playing only days earlier. **What does this photograph suggest about the potential consequences of a nuclear meltdown at Three Mile Island?**

In 1980, President Carter and Congress responded by passing legislation known as the EPA's **Superfund** to clean up sites contaminated with hazardous substances. Further inquiries showed that the presence of such poisonous waste dumps disproportionately affected minorities and the poor. Critics called the placement of these waste locations near Black and other minority communities "environmental racism" and launched a movement for environmental justice.

Superfund
A reserve fund established in 1980 to be used by the Environmental Protection Agency to clean up sites of industrial pollution and waste deemed particularly hazardous to public health.

The most dangerous threat came in March 1979 at the Three Mile Island nuclear power plant near Harrisburg, Pennsylvania. A broken valve at the plant leaked coolant and threatened the meltdown of the reactor's nuclear core. As officials quickly evacuated residents from the surrounding area, employees at the plant narrowly averted catastrophe by fixing the problem before an explosion occurred. Grassroots activists protested and raised public awareness against the construction of additional nuclear power facilities.

REVIEW

- How did environmental disasters help shape the environmentalist movement of the 1970s?

AP® Skills Workshop: Writing Historically

Additional Practice in Responding to a Long-Essay Question

Evaluate the extent to which U.S. domestic and international policies during the 1970s were shaped by concerns over the environment and natural resources.

MODULE 8.14

Society in Transition

FOCUS

As you read this module, consider the causes and effects of the political and economic changes in the 1960s and 1970s. Ask yourself how developments during these decades shook public confidence in the government.

The social, political, and cultural changes of the 1960s proved unsettling to many Americans. While the New Left and the counterculture captured media attention and came to define the decade, a conservative movement in reaction to these changes built upon older conservative movements that rejected the legacy of liberalism. In 1968, Richard Nixon promised to represent a "silent majority" of Americans who had misgivings about transformations around them. The 1970s proved to be an era when a rising conflict between political and cultural forces on the American Left and Right came to define the national discourse.

The Revival of Conservatism

The social movements of the 1960s and 1970s did a great deal to change the political and cultural landscapes of the United States, but they did not go unchallenged. Many Americans worried about Black militancy, opposed liberalism, and were even more dismayed by the radical offshoots they spawned. Conservatives soon attracted support from many Americans who did not see change as progress. Many believed that the political leadership of the nation did not speak for them about what constituted a great society.

The brand of conservatism that emerged in the 1960s united libertarian support for a laissez-faire political economy with opposition to social welfare policies along with moralistic concerns for defeating communism and defending what they saw as religious devotion, moral decency, and family values. Unlike earlier conservatives, the new generation believed that the United States had to escalate the struggle against the evil of godless communism anywhere it posed a threat in the world, but they opposed internationalism as represented in the United Nations.

Conservative religious activists who built grassroots organizations to combat liberalism joined forces with political and intellectual conservatives such as William F. Buckley, the founder of the *National Review*, an influential journal of conservative ideas. The Reverend Billy James Hargis's Christian Crusade and Dr. Frederick Charles Schwarz's Christian Anti-Communist Crusade, both formed in the early 1950s, promoted conspiracy theories about how the eastern liberal establishment intended to sell the country out to the communists by supporting the United Nations, foreign aid, Social Security, and civil rights. The John Birch Society packaged these ideas in periodicals and radio broadcasts throughout the country and urged readers and listeners to remain vigilant to attacks against their freedom.

In the late 1950s and early 1960s, the conservative revival grew at the grassroots level in the suburbs of southern California and the Southwest. Bolstered by the postwar economic boom that centered on military research and development, these towns in the Sun

Belt attracted college-educated engineers, technicians, managers, and other professionals from the Midwest (or Rust Belt) seeking new economic opportunities. These migrants brought with them Republican loyalties as well as traditional conservative political and moral values. Women played a large part in conservative causes, especially in protesting against public-school curricula that they perceived as un-Christian and un-American. Young housewives built an extensive network of conservative study groups.

In addition, the conservative revival, like the New Left, found fertile recruiting ground on college campuses. In October 1960, some ninety young conservatives met at William Buckley's estate in Sharon, Connecticut, to draw up a manifesto of their beliefs. "In this time of moral and political crisis," the framers of the Sharon Statement declared, "the foremost among the transcendent values is the individual's use of his God-given free will, whence derives his right to be free from the restrictions of arbitrary force." Based on this principle, the manifesto affirmed the conservative doctrines of states' rights, the free market, and anticommunism. Participants at the conference formed the **Young Americans for Freedom (YAF)**, which six months later boasted 27,000 members. In 1962, the YAF filled Madison Square Garden to listen to a speech by the politician who most excited them: Republican senator Barry M. Goldwater of Arizona.

Goldwater's book *The Conscience of a Conservative* (1960) attacked New Deal liberalism and advocated abolishing Social Security; dismantling the Tennessee Valley Authority, the government-owned public power utility; and eliminating the progressive income tax. His firm belief in states' rights put him on record against the ruling in *Brown v. Board of Education* and prompted him to vote against the Civil Rights Act of 1964, positions that won him increasing support from conservative white southerners. Nevertheless, Goldwater's advocacy of small government did not prevent him from supporting increased military spending to halt the spread of communism. The senator may have anticipated growing concerns about government excess, but his defeat in a landslide to Lyndon Johnson in the 1964 presidential election indicated that most voters perceived Goldwater's brand of conservatism as too extreme.

The election of 1964 also brought George C. Wallace onto the national stage as a leading architect of the conservative revival. As Democratic governor of Alabama, the segregationist Wallace had supported states' rights and opposed federal intervention to reshape social and political affairs. Wallace began to attract white northerners fed up with rising Black militancy, court-ordered busing to promote school integration, and open housing laws to desegregate their neighborhoods. Running in the Democratic presidential primaries in 1964, the Alabama governor garnered 34 percent of the votes in Wisconsin, 30 percent in Indiana, and 43 percent in Maryland.

More so than Goldwater, Wallace united a populist message against the political establishment with concern for white working-class Americans. Wallace voters identified with the governor as an "outsider." Many of them also backed Wallace for attacking privileged college students who, he claimed, mocked patriotism, violated sexual taboos, and looked down on hardworking, churchgoing, law-abiding Americans. How could "all those rich kids—from the fancy suburbs," one father wondered, "[avoid the draft] when my son has to go over there and maybe get his head shot off?" Each in his own way, Wallace and Goldwater waged political campaigns against liberals for undermining the economic freedom of middle- and working-class whites and coddling what they considered "racial extremists."

REVIEW

- What factors contributed to the revival of conservatism in the 1960s?
- How successful were prominent conservative politicians in promoting their ideas during the early 1960s?

The Election of 1968

The year 1968 was a turbulent one. In January, the Vietcong launched the Tet Offensive in South Vietnam, demonstrating that the war was far from over despite official prior pronouncements to the contrary. In February, police shot indiscriminately into a crowd gathered for civil rights protests at South Carolina State University in Orangeburg, killing three students. In March, student protests at Columbia University led to a violent confrontation with the New York City police. On April 4, the murder of Martin Luther King Jr. sparked an outburst of rioting by Black people in more than one hundred cities throughout the country. The assassination of the likely Democratic presidential nominee, Robert Kennedy, in June further heightened the mood of despair. Adding to the unrest, demonstrators gathered in Chicago in August at the Democratic National Convention to press for an antiwar plank in the party platform. Thousands of protesters were beaten and arrested by Chicago police officers. Many Americans watched in horror as television networks broadcast the bloody clashes, but a majority of viewers sided with the police rather than with the protesters.

WORKING with EVIDENCE

Source: Richard M. Nixon, Address Accepting the Presidential Nomination at the Republican National Convention, August 8, 1968

> "[T]o those who say that law and order is the code word for racism, there and here is a reply:
>
> Our goal is justice for every American. If we are to have respect for law in America, we must have laws that deserve respect.
>
> Just as we cannot have progress without order, we cannot have order without progress, and so, as we commit to order tonight, let us commit to progress.
>
> And this brings me to the clearest choice among the great issues of this campaign.
>
> For the past five years we have been deluged by government programs for the unemployed; programs for the cities; programs for the poor. And we have reaped from these programs an ugly harvest of frustration, violence and failure across the land.
>
> And now our opponents will be offering more of the same—more billions for government jobs, government housing, government welfare.
>
> I say it is time to quit pouring billions of dollars into programs that have failed in the United States of America. . . .
>
> But for those who are able to help themselves—what we need are not more millions on welfare rolls—but more millions on payrolls in the United States of America.
>
> Instead of government jobs, and government housing, and government welfare, let government use its tax and credit policies to enlist in this battle the greatest engine of progress ever developed in the history of man—American private enterprise.
>
> Let us enlist in this great cause the millions of Americans in volunteer organizations who will bring a dedication to this task that no amount of money could ever buy. . . .
>
> Black Americans, no more than white Americans, they do not want more government programs which perpetuate dependency.

They don't want to be a colony in a nation.

They want the pride, and the self-respect, and the dignity that can only come if they have an equal chance to own their own homes, to own their own businesses, to be managers and executives as well as workers, to have a piece of the action in the exciting ventures of private enterprise."

Questions for Analysis

1. Identify Nixon's response to accusations that his platform is racist.
2. Describe the contrast Nixon makes between his party platform and Democratic proposals.
3. Evaluate the extent to which Nixon's speech reflects conservative ideology.

Similar protests occurred around the world. In early 1968, university students in Nanterre, a suburb of Paris, protested educational policies and what they perceived as their second-class status. When students at the Sorbonne in Paris joined them in the streets, police attacked them viciously. In June, French president Charles de Gaulle sent in tanks to break up widespread student demonstrations and concurrent labor strikes but also instituted political and economic reforms.

Protests also erupted during the spring in Prague, Czechoslovakia, where Alexander Dubček vowed to reform the communist regime by initiating "socialism with a human face." In August, the Soviet Union sent its military into Czechoslovakia to crush the reforms, bringing this brief experiment in freedom remembered as the "Prague

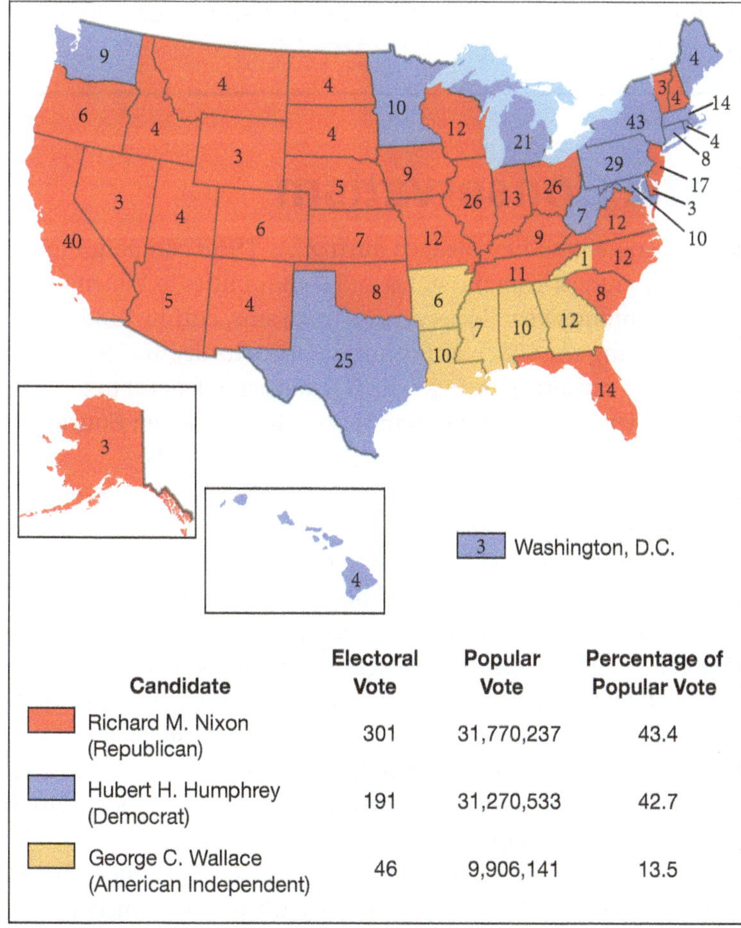

Candidate	Electoral Vote	Popular Vote	Percentage of Popular Vote
Richard M. Nixon (Republican)	301	31,770,237	43.4
Hubert H. Humphrey (Democrat)	191	31,270,533	42.7
George C. Wallace (American Independent)	46	9,906,141	13.5

MAP 8.7 The Election of 1968 Democratic presidential candidate Hubert Humphrey lost across the South as white voters turned to Republican Richard Nixon or segregationist George Wallace. Many working-class whites in the North and West also shifted their allegiance to these "law and order" candidates, rejecting the civil rights and antipoverty agendas promoted by President Johnson and blaming Democrats for the turmoil over the Vietnam War. **What do the electoral results suggest about the regional appeal of each candidate and their party?**

Spring" to a violent end. During the same year, student-led demonstrations erupted in Yugoslavia, Poland, West Germany, Italy, Spain, Japan, and Mexico.

It was against this backdrop of global unrest that Richard Nixon ran for president against the Democratic nominee Hubert H. Humphrey and the independent candidate, George C. Wallace, the segregationist governor of Alabama and a popular archconservative. To outflank Wallace on the right, Nixon declared himself the "law and order" candidate, a phrase that became a code for reining in Black militancy. To win southern supporters, he pledged to ease up on enforcing federal civil rights legislation and oppose court-ordered busing to achieve racial integration in schools. He criticized antiwar protesters and promised to end the Vietnam War with honor. Seeking to portray the Democrats as the party of social and cultural radicalism, Nixon geared his campaign message to the "silent majority" of voters — what one political analyst characterized as "the unyoung, the unpoor, and unblack." This conservative message appealed to many Americans who were fed up with domestic upheaval and war abroad.

Although Nixon won 301 electoral votes, 110 more than Humphrey, none of the three candidates received a majority of the popular vote. Yet Nixon and Wallace together garnered about 57 percent of the popular vote, a dramatic shift to the right compared with Lyndon Johnson's landslide victory just four years earlier. The New Left had given way to an assortment of old and new conservatives, overwhelmingly white, who were determined to contain, if not roll back, the Great Society.

- What factors contributed to Nixon's election in 1968?
- Why were the electoral results of 1968 so different from the results of 1964?

Pragmatic Conservatism

On the domestic front, Nixon had pledged during his 1968 campaign to "reverse the flow of power and resources from the states and communities to Washington." He kept his promise by dismantling Great Society social programs, cutting funds for the War on Poverty, and eliminating the Office of Economic Opportunity. In 1972, the president adopted a program of revenue sharing, which transferred federal tax revenues to the states to use as they wished. Hoping to rein in the liberal Warren Court, Nixon nominated conservative justices to the Supreme Court.

Nixon also applied a pragmatic approach to racial issues. In general, he supported "benign neglect" concerning the issue of race and rejected new legislative attempts to use busing to promote school desegregation. In this way, Nixon courted southern conservatives in an attempt to deter George Wallace from mounting another third-party challenge in 1972. Still, Nixon moved back to the political center with efforts that furthered civil rights. Expanding affirmative action programs begun under the Johnson administration, he adopted plans that required construction companies and unions to recruit minority workers according to their percentage in the local labor force. His support of affirmative action was part of a broader approach to encourage "black capitalism," a concept designed to convince Black Americans to seek opportunity within the free-enterprise system rather than through government handouts.

Moreover, in 1970, Nixon signed the extension of the 1965 Voting Rights Act, thereby renewing the law that had provided suffrage to the majority of Black Americans in the South.

The law also lowered the voting age from twenty-one to eighteen for national elections. Support for the measure reflected the impact of the Vietnam War: If young men could fight at eighteen, then they should be able to vote at eighteen. In 1971, the **Twenty-Sixth Amendment** was ratified to lower the voting age for state and local elections as well.

The Nixon administration also veered away from the traditional Republican free-market philosophy by resorting to wage and price controls to curb rising inflation brought on, for the most part, by increased military spending during the Vietnam War. In 1971, the president by executive order declared a ninety-day freeze on wages and prices, placed a temporary 10 percent surtax on imports, and let the value of the dollar drop on the international market, leading to increased U.S. exports. Taken together, these measures stabilized consumer prices, reduced unemployment, and boosted the gross national product. Although these proved to be only short-term gains, they improved Nixon's prospects for reelection.

Nixon's diplomatic initiatives, however, failed to resolve festering problems in the Middle East. Since its victory in the Six-Day War of 1967, Israel had occupied territory once controlled by Egypt, Jordan, and Syria as well as East Jerusalem. On October 6, 1973, during the start of the Jewish High Holidays of Yom Kippur, Egyptian and Syrian troops, fortified with Soviet arms, launched a surprise attack on Israel. An Israeli counterattack, reinforced by a shipment of $2 billion of American weapons, repelled Arab forces, and the Israeli military stood ready to destroy the Egyptian army. To avoid a complete breakdown in the balance of power, the United States and the Soviet Union agreed to broker a cease-fire that left the situation the same as before the war.

- What were the main accomplishments and failures of President Nixon's foreign policy?
- In what areas did Nixon diverge from conservative ideas?

The Nixon Landslide and Watergate Scandal, 1972–1974

By appealing to voters across the political spectrum, Nixon won a monumental victory in 1972. The president invigorated the "silent majority" by demonizing his opponents and encouraging Vice President Spiro Agnew to aggressively pursue his tactic of polarization. Agnew called protesters "kooks" and "social misfits" and attacked the media and Nixon critics with heated rhetoric. While Wallace won impressive victories in the North as well as the South, his campaign ended after an assassination attempt left him paralyzed. With Wallace out of the race, the Democrats inadvertently made Nixon look more centrist by nominating George McGovern, a liberal antiwar senator from South Dakota.

Winning in a landslide, Nixon captured more than 60 percent of the popular vote and nearly all of the electoral votes. Nonetheless, Democrats retained control of Congress. However, Nixon would have little time to savor his victory, for within the next two years his conduct in the campaign would come back to destroy his presidency.

In the early hours of June 17, 1972, five men had broken into Democratic Party headquarters in the Watergate complex in Washington, D.C. What appeared at first as a routine burglary turned into the most infamous political scandal of the twentieth century. It was eventually revealed that the break-in had been authorized by the Committee for the Re-Election of the President in an attempt to steal documents from the Democrats.

Nixon Watergate Burglars, 1973 Four of seven defendants charged with breaking into the Democratic National Committee offices at the Watergate complex take a break with their attorney during their trial. Standing outside the federal courthouse from left to right are: Virgilio Gonzales, Frank Sturgis, attorney Henry Rothblatt, Bernard Barker, and Eugenio Martinez. E. Howard Hunt, G. Gordon Liddy, and James McCord are not pictured. All were convicted.

How did the Watergate scandal undermine public trust in the government?

Wally McNamee/Corbis via Getty Images

President Nixon may not have known in advance the details of the break-in, but he did authorize a cover-up of his administration's involvement. Nixon ordered his chief of staff, H. R. Haldeman, to get the CIA and FBI to back off from a thorough investigation of the incident. To silence the burglars at their trials, the president promised them $400,000 and hinted at a presidential pardon after their conviction.

Nixon embarked on the cover-up to protect himself from revelations of his administration's other illegal activities. Several of the Watergate burglars belonged to a secret band of operatives known as "the plumbers," which had been formed in 1971 and authorized by the president to find and plug up unwelcome leaks of information from government officials. On their first secret operation, the plumbers broke into the office of the psychiatrist of military analyst Daniel Ellsberg to look for embarrassing personal information with which to discredit Ellsberg, who had leaked the *Pentagon Papers* (see Module 8.8).

The president had other unsavory matters to hide. In an effort to contain leaks about the administration's secret bombing of Cambodia in 1969, the White House had illegally wiretapped its own officials and members of the press.

Watergate
The political scandal and cover-up that forced the resignation of President Nixon in 1974. The scandal centered on a break-in at the Democratic Party headquarters in 1972 and subsequent efforts of the Nixon White House to conceal the administration's involvement in the break-in. The Watergate scandal undermined public trust in government.

Watergate did not become a major scandal until after the election. The trial judge forced one of the burglars to reveal the men's backers. This revelation led two *Washington Post* reporters, Bob Woodward and Carl Bernstein, to investigate the link between the administration and the plumbers. With the help of Mark Felt, a top FBI official whose identity long remained secret and whom the reporters called "Deep Throat," Woodward and Bernstein succeeded in exposing the true nature of the crime.

The Senate created a special committee in February 1973 to investigate the scandal. White House counsel John Dean, whom Nixon had fired, testified about discussing the cover-up with the president and his closest advisers. His testimony proved accurate after the committee learned that Nixon had secretly taped all Oval Office conversations. When the president refused to release the tapes to a special prosecutor, the Supreme Court ruled against him.

With Nixon's cover-up revealed, and impeachment and conviction likely, Nixon resigned on August 9, 1974. The scandal took a great toll on the administration: Attorney General John Mitchell and Nixon's closest advisers, H. R. Haldeman and John Ehrlichman, resigned, and twenty-five government officials went to jail. Watergate also damaged the office of the president, leaving Americans wary and distrustful.

Vice President Gerald Ford served out Nixon's remaining term. The Republican representative from Michigan had replaced Vice President Spiro Agnew after Agnew resigned in 1973 following charges that he had taken illegal kickbacks while governor of Maryland. Ford chose Nelson A. Rockefeller, the moderate Republican governor of New York, as his vice president. Thus, neither man had been elected to the office he now held.

President Ford's most controversial and defining act took place shortly after he entered the White House. Explaining to the country that he wanted to quickly end the "national nightmare" stemming from Watergate, Ford pardoned Nixon for any criminal offenses he might have committed as president. Rather than healing the nation's wounds, this preemptive pardon polarized Americans and cost Ford considerable political capital. Ford also wrestled with a troubled economy as Americans once again experienced rising prices and high unemployment.

- How did the Watergate scandal lead to Nixon's resignation?

The Carter Presidency and the World

Despite his political shortcomings, Gerald Ford received the Republican presidential nomination in 1976 and ran against James Earl (Jimmy) Carter, a little-known former governor of Georgia who used his "outsider" status to his advantage. Shaping his campaign with Watergate in mind, Carter stressed personal character over economic issues. As a moderate, post-segregationist governor of Georgia, Carter won the support of the family of Martin Luther King Jr. and other Black leaders. Carter needed all the help he could get and eked out a narrow victory.

In the area of foreign policy, Carter departed from Nixon. Whereas Nixon was a realist who considered the U.S. role in world affairs as an exercise in power politics, Carter was an idealist who made human rights a cornerstone of his foreign policy. Unlike previous presidents who had supported dictatorial governments as long as they were anticommunist, Carter intended to hold such regimes to a higher moral standard. Thus, the Carter administration cut off military and economic aid to repressive regimes in Argentina, Uruguay, and Ethiopia. Still, Carter was not entirely consistent in his application of moral standards to diplomacy. Important U.S. allies around the world such as the Philippines, South Korea, and South Africa were hardly models of democracy, but national security concerns kept the president from severing ties with them.

WORKING with EVIDENCE

Source: Warren Christopher, Deputy Secretary of State, Presidential Review Memorandum on Human Rights, May 20, 1977

> "The over-all objective of our human rights policy is to encourage the respect that governments accord to human rights. . . .
>
> First, the right to be free from governmental violations of the integrity of the person: such violations include torture; cruel, inhuman or degrading treatment and punishment; arbitrary arrest or imprisonment; denial of fair public trial; and invasion of the home ('the first group').
>
> Second, economic and social rights: the right to be free from government action or inaction which either obstructs an individual's efforts

to fulfill his vital needs for food, shelter, health care and education or fails adequately to support the individual in meeting basic needs ('the second group').

Third, the right to enjoy civil and political liberties: freedom of thought, of religion, of assembly, of speech, of the press; freedom of movement both within and outside one's own country; freedom to take part in government ('the third group'). . . .

In countries where the first group of rights is denied or threatened, the protection of those rights has obvious priority, since human life and fundamental human dignity [are] threatened. In countries where the first group of rights is generally observed, but political and civil rights are abridged or non-existent, our policy should emphasize the promotion of those rights. Promotion of economic rights is, for the U.S., primarily a matter of cooperation with and contribution to bilateral and multilateral foreign assistance efforts. We should do our share."

Questions for Analysis

1. Identify both the immediate and the broader intended audiences for Christopher's memo.
2. Explain the basic challenges in implementing an approach to foreign policy centered on human rights as recommended in the excerpt.
3. Evaluate the extent of similarity between the foreign policy framework expressed in the excerpt and the foreign policy of Nixon and Kissinger.
4. Evaluate the extent to which the foreign policy recommended in the excerpt represents a continuation of U.S. foreign policy after World War II.

One way that Carter tried to set an example of responsible moral leadership was by signing an agreement to return control of the Panama Canal Zone to Panama at the end of 1999. The treaty that President Theodore Roosevelt negotiated in 1903 gave the United States control of this 550-square-mile piece of Panamanian land forever. Panamanians resented this affront to their sovereignty, and Carter considered the occupation a vestige of colonialism.

The president's pursuit of détente, or the easing of tensions, with the Soviet Union was less successful. In 1978, the Carter administration extended full diplomatic recognition to China. After the fall of China to the communists in 1949, the United States had supported Taiwan, an island off the coast of China, as an outpost of democracy against mainland China. In abandoning Taiwan by recognizing China, Carter sought to drive a greater wedge between China and the Soviet Union.

SALT II

A strategic arms limitation treaty agreed on by President Jimmy Carter and Soviet leader Leonid Brezhnev in 1979. After the Soviet Union invaded Afghanistan, Carter persuaded the Senate not to ratify the treaty, thereby ending the period of détente.

mujahideen

Religiously inspired Afghan rebels who resisted the Soviet invasion of Afghanistan in 1979.

Nevertheless, Carter did not give up on cooperation with the Soviets. In June 1979, Carter and Soviet leader Leonid Brezhnev signed **SALT II**, a new strategic arms limitation treaty. Six months later, however, the Soviet Union invaded Afghanistan to bolster its pro-communist government. President Carter viewed this action as a violation of international law and a threat to Middle East oil supplies, so he persuaded the Senate to drop consideration of SALT II. In addition, Carter obtained from Congress a 5 percent increase in military spending, reduced grain sales to the U.S.S.R., and led a boycott of the 1980 Olympic Games in Moscow.

Of perhaps the greatest long-term importance was President Carter's decision to authorize the CIA to provide covert military and economic assistance to Afghan rebels resisting the Soviet invasion. Chief among these groups were the **mujahideen**, or warriors who wage jihad. Although portrayed as freedom fighters, these Islamic fundamentalists (including a group known as the Taliban) did not

Pascal Manoukian/Sygma/Getty Images

Afghan Mujahideen, January 1980 On December 25, 1979, Soviet troops invaded Afghanistan to suppress mujahideen guerrillas who were trying to overthrow the nation's secular, pro-Soviet regime. These rebel forces were among the guerrillas who defeated the Soviets after a decade of warfare and eventually established an Islamic theocracy.

What parallels can be drawn from the photograph between the experience of the Soviet military in Afghanistan and the experience of the U.S. military in Vietnam?

support democracy in the Western sense. Among the mujahideen who received assistance from the United States was Osama bin Laden, a Saudi Arabian Islamic fundamentalist, who later planned the 9/11 attacks against the United States. After a decade of warfare, the Soviets were defeated, leading to the eventual establishment of an Islamic theocracy.

In ordering these CIA operations, Carter ignored recent revelations about questionable intelligence practices. Responding to presidential excesses stemming from the Vietnam War and the Watergate scandal, the Senate had held hearings in 1975 into clandestine CIA and FBI activities at home and abroad. Led by Frank Church of Idaho, the Senate Select Committee to Study Governmental Operations with Respect to Intelligence Activities (known as the Church Committee) issued reports revealing that both intelligence agencies had illegally spied on Americans and that the CIA had fomented revolution abroad, contrary to the provisions of its charter. Despite the Church Committee's findings, Carter revived some of these murky practices to combat the Soviets in Afghanistan.

REVIEW

- How did the Carter administration's foreign policy differ from that of Nixon? In what ways was it similar?

Challenges in the Middle East

Before President Carter tried to restrain the Soviet Union in Afghanistan, he did have some notable diplomatic successes. Five years after the 1973 Yom Kippur War, with relations between Israel and its Arab neighbors in a deadlock, Carter invited the leaders of Israel and Egypt to the United States. Following two weeks of discussions in

September 1978 at the presidential retreat at Camp David, Maryland, Israeli prime minister Menachem Begin and Egyptian president Anwar Sadat reached an agreement on a "framework for peace." For the first time in its history, Egypt would extend diplomatic recognition to Israel in exchange for Israel's agreement to return the Sinai Peninsula to Egypt, which Israel had captured and occupied since 1967. Carter facilitated Sadat's acceptance of the **Camp David accords** by promising to extend foreign aid to Egypt. The treaty, however, left unresolved controversial issues between Israelis and Arabs concerning the establishment of a Palestinian state and control of Jerusalem.

Camp David accords

An agreement between Israel and Egypt facilitated by President Carter in 1978. The accords led to a peace treaty and normalization of relations between the two nations.

Whatever success Carter had in promoting peace in the Middle East suffered a serious setback in the Persian Gulf nation of Iran. In 1953, the CIA had helped overthrow Iran's democratically elected prime minster, replacing him with a monarch and staunch ally, Mohammad Reza Pahlavi, the shah of Iran. For more than two decades, the shah ruled Iran with U.S. support, seeking to construct a modern, secular state allied with the United States. In doing so, he used repressive measures against Islamic fundamentalists, deploying his secret police to imprison, torture, and exile dissenters.

In 1979, revolutionary forces headed by Ayatollah Ruhollah Khomeini, an Islamic fundamentalist exiled by the shah, overthrew his government. Khomeini intended to end the growing secularism in Iran and reshape the nation according to strict Islamic law.

When the deposed shah needed treatment for terminal cancer, President Carter invited him to the United States for medical assistance as a humanitarian gesture, despite warnings from the Khomeini government that it would consider this invitation a hostile action. On November 4, 1979, the ayatollah ordered fundamentalist Muslim students to seize the U.S. Embassy in Tehran and hold its fifty-two occupants hostage until the United States returned the shah to Iran to stand trial. President Carter retaliated by freezing all Iranian assets in American banks, breaking off diplomatic relations, and imposing a trade embargo.

In response, Khomeini denounced the United States as "the Great Satan." As the impasse dragged on and with the presidential election of 1980 fast approaching, Carter became desperate. After a failed U.S. rescue attempt that left one Iranian civilian and eight American soldiers dead, Khomeini's guards separated the hostages, making any more rescue efforts impossible.

AP® EXAM TIP

U.S. foreign policy in the Middle East is an important topic. Think about how you could combine a foreign policy in the Middle East, a specific oil crisis, and the environmental movement in a cohesive argument.

Carter suffered a bruising defeat at the polls in November, the revolution under Khomeini seized on its victory to consolidate power and support, and Iran and the United States would become long-term enemies, deeply complicating geopolitics in the oil-rich Middle East. Further humiliating Carter personally, Khomeini released the hostages on January 20, 1981, the inauguration day of Carter's successor, Ronald Reagan.

REVIEW

- To what extent was the Carter administration's foreign policy toward the Middle East a success?

New Forms of Conservatism

New Right

A conservative coalition of old and new conservatives, as well as disaffected Democrats, who supported strong U.S. national security initiatives, low taxes, and reduced government intervention in the economy.

As the 1970s progressed, the backlash against affirmative action and the ERA confirmed that liberal reformers were losing ground to conservatives. By the end of the decade, liberalism had become identified with special interests and elitism. At the same time, the pragmatic conservatism of Richard Nixon was being displaced by a harder-edged brand of conservatism called the **New Right**.

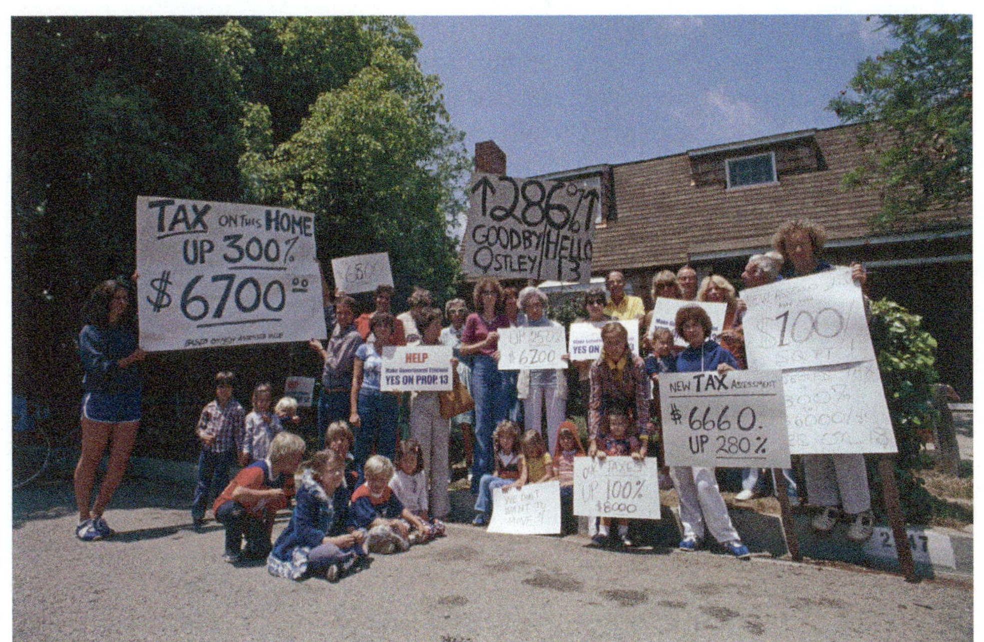

Tony Korody/Sygma/Getty Images

Tax Revolt in California, 1978 California residents gather in support of Proposition 13, a state constitutional amendment that proposed a cap on property tax rates. The amendment also required a two-thirds vote by any local or state government to increase taxes in the future. The initiative passed overwhelmingly by a statewide vote on June 6, 1978.

What do the signs held by anti-tax protesters in the photograph reveal about the reasons many Californians supported Proposition 13?

The New Right was founded on the budding conservatism of the 1960s as represented in the Sharon Statement and the presidential candidacy of Barry Goldwater. In the 1970s, it expanded for a variety of reasons: the revolt against higher taxes, the backlash against the growth of the federal government, the disillusionment of former liberal intellectuals, and the growth of the Christian Right.

In the 1970s, working- and middle-class white resentment centered on big government spending and higher taxes. During the 1970s, taxation claimed 30 percent of the gross domestic product, while the wealthiest Americans were taxed at a 70 percent marginal tax rate. Although Americans still paid far less in taxes than their counterparts in Western Europe, Americans objected to raising state and federal taxes. Leading the tax revolt was the Sun Belt state of California. In a 1978 referendum, California voters passed Proposition 13, a measure that reduced property taxes and placed strict limits on the ability of local governments to raise them in the future. In the wake of Proposition 13, a dozen states enacted similar measures.

Economic conservatives also set their sights on reducing the federal income tax. They supported cutting personal and corporate taxes by a third in the belief that reducing taxes would encourage new investment and job creation.

"Supply-side" economists argued that lowering tax rates would boost tax receipts: With lower taxes, companies and investors would have more capital to invest, leading to expanded job growth; with increased employment, more people would be paying taxes. At the same time, supply-side conservatives called for reduced government spending, especially in the social service sector, to ensure balanced budgets and to eliminate what they saw as unnecessary spending on domestic programs.

The New Right also benefited by the defection of disillusioned liberals. Labeled **neoconservatives**, intellectuals such as Irving Kristol, Norman Podhoretz, and Nathan Glazer reversed course and condemned the Great Society programs that they had originally supported. They believed that federal policies, such as affirmative action, had worsened rather than improved the problems government planners intended to solve. They considered the New Left's opposition to the Vietnam War and its disapproval of foreign intervention a threat to national security.

neoconservative A disillusioned liberal who condemned the Great Society programs they had originally supported. Neoconservatives were particularly concerned about affirmative action programs, the domination of campus activism by New Left radicals, and left-wing criticism of the use of American military and economic might to advance U.S. interests overseas.

Perhaps the greatest spark igniting the New Right came from religious and social conservatives, mainly evangelical Christians and Catholics. Evangelicals considered themselves to have been "born again"—having experienced Jesus Christ's saving presence inside of them. By the end of the 1970s, evangelical Christians numbered around 50 million, about a quarter of the population. As evangelicals became politically active, a **Christian Right** emerged that opposed abortion, gay rights, and sex education; criticized Supreme Court rulings banning prayer in the public schools; rejected Charles Darwin's theory of evolution in favor of divine creationism; supported the traditional role of women as mothers and homemakers; and backed a hard-line, anticommunist stand against the Soviet Union. Certainly not all evangelical Christians, such as President Carter, held all of these beliefs. Still, conservative Christians believed that the liberals and radicals of the 1960s had spread the secular creed of individual rights and personal fulfillment at the expense of established Christian values.

Christian Right
A coalition of evangelical Christians and Catholics that supported traditional values, laissez-faire economics, and an anticommunist foreign policy. The Christian Right, also known as the religious right, joined forces with political conservatives to form a powerful conservative voting bloc in the Republican Party.

Social conservatives worried that the traditional nuclear family was in danger, as households consisting of married couples with children declined from 30 percent in the 1970s to 23 percent thirty years later, and the divorce rate soared. The number of unmarried couples living together doubled over the last quarter of the twentieth century. In 1970, 26.4 percent of infants were born to single mothers; by 1990, the rate had risen to 43.8. This increase was part of a trend in developed countries worldwide.

Moreover, social conservatives united in fierce opposition to abortion, which the Supreme Court legalized in *Roe v. Wade* (see Module 8.11). They argued that an unborn fetus is a person and therefore has a right to life protected by the Constitution.

One direct impetus pushing conservative evangelicals into politics came when the Internal Revenue Service (IRS) removed tax-exempt status from a fundamentalist Christian college. Bob Jones University in South Carolina defended racial segregation on biblical grounds but, under pressure from the federal government, began admitting some Black American students in the mid-1970s. However, the school continued practicing discrimination by prohibiting interracial dating. In 1976, when the IRS revoked the university's tax-exempt status, conservative Christians charged that the federal government was interfering with religious freedom. This sparked a grassroots political campaign to rally Christian evangelicals around a host of grievances.

Since the 1950s, Billy Graham, a charismatic Southern Baptist evangelist from North Carolina, had used television to conduct nationwide crusades. Television became an even greater instrument in the hands of New Right Christian preachers in the 1970s and 1980s. The Reverend Pat Robertson of Virginia founded the Christian Broadcasting Network, and ministers such as Jerry Falwell used the airwaves to great effect. What distinguished Falwell and Robertson from earlier evangelists like Graham was their fusion of religion and electoral politics. In 1979, Falwell founded the Moral Majority, an organization that backed political candidates who supported a "family values" social agenda. Within two years of its creation, the Moral Majority counted four million members who were eager to organize in support of New Right politicians.

The New Right also lined up advocacy groups such as the American Enterprise Institute and the Heritage Foundation to generate and promote conservative ideals. The alliance of economic, intellectual, and religious conservatives offered a formidable challenge to liberalism.

- What factors contributed to the rise of each of the new forms of conservatism?

AP® Skills Workshop: Writing Historically

Additional Practice in Responding to a Short-Answer Question with Secondary Sources

"Historians of the American left have made much of the way in which the civil rights movement influenced the social movements of the 1960s and 1970s, inspiring, for example, the women's rights movement and the politics of sexual liberation. But the movement's counterrevolutionary effects are equally important. In the three decades following the emergence of George Wallace, the rhetoric of racial politics evolved: from the issues of public accommodations to school desegregation, busing, housing, quotas, and struggles over job discrimination, and proposals for economic affirmative action. . . .

Economic and social conservatives—particularly those who have been lifelong opponents of racial bigotry—have bridled at the attempt to link what neoconservatives have called the 'new majoritarianism' of the 1980s with the politics of race. Nevertheless, I think it is fair to say that even though the streams of racial and economic conservatism have sometimes flowed in separate channels, they ultimately joined in the political coalition that reshaped American politics from the 1970s through the mid-1990s. . . . [George] Wallace's sensitivity to being "looked down on" and his identity as a beleaguered white southerner strengthened his appeal to white ethnic minorities and working class Americans."

Dan T. Carter, *From George Wallace to Newt Gingrich: Race in the Conservative Counterrevolution*, 1963–1994, 1996

"During . . . the late 1960s, conservative Protestants succeeded not only in making alliances with Republican politicians, but in changing the agenda of the party. This time, they focused more on the culture wars than the Cold War. Conservative Protestants who mobilized against feminism, abortion, pornography, and gay rights acquired control of the Republican Party, partly because of their long-standing alliances with Republican politicians, but perhaps more important because of the united front that they presented, and because of demographic and political shifts that favored evangelicals. . . . The sexual revolution, sex education, race riots, the counterculture, increases in drug use, and the beginning of the feminist movement convinced them that the nation had lost its Christian identity and that the family was under attack.

The end of the civil rights movement facilitated the formation of the Christian political coalition, because it enabled fundamentalists and evangelicals who had disagreed over racial integration to come together. After the passage of federal civil rights legislation and the end of nationally publicized civil rights marches, fundamentalists such as Jerry Falwell accepted the reality of racial integration and began forging political alliances with mainstream Republicans who would have been embarrassed by their segregationist rhetoric only a few years earlier. At the same time, moderate evangelicals who had once cautiously supported the civil rights movement reacted in horror to the race

(continued)

riots and began taking more conservative stances on civil rights. Both fundamentalists and evangelicals embraced Richard Nixon's call for 'law and order.' "

Daniel Williams, *God's Own Party: The Making of the Christian Right*, 2010

Using the excerpts, answer **A**, **B**, and **C**.

(A) Briefly explain ONE major difference between Carter's and Williams's interpretations of the rise of the New Right.

(B) Briefly explain how ONE specific historical event or development from the period that is not explicitly mentioned in the excerpts could be used to support Carter's argument.

(C) Briefly explain how ONE specific historical event or development that is not explicitly mentioned in the excerpts could be used to support Williams's argument.

Continuity and Change in Period 8

MODULE 8.15

Skills Workshop: Writing Historically

Additional Practice in Responding to a Document-Based Question

Evaluate the extent to which the decline in public confidence in the government during the 1970s represented a continuation of Americans' distrust of government, and to what extent it represented a change.

Document 1

Source: Senator Joseph McCarthy, Speech on Communists in the State Department, 1950

"At war's end we were physically the strongest nation on Earth and, at least potentially, the most powerful intellectually and morally. Ours could have been the honor of being a beacon in the desert of destruction, a shining, living proof that civilization was not yet ready to destroy itself. Unfortunately, we have failed miserably and tragically to arise to the opportunity.

The reason why we find ourselves in a position of impotency is not because our only powerful, potential enemy has sent men to invade our shores, but rather because of the traitorous actions of those who have been treated so well by this nation. It has not been the less fortunate or members of minority groups who have been selling this nation out, but rather those who have had all the benefits that the wealthiest nation on earth has had to offer—the finest homes, the finest college education, and the finest jobs in government we can give.

This is glaringly true in the State Department. There the bright young men who are born with silver spoons in their mouths are the ones who have been worst."

Document 2

Source: Barry Goldwater, Acceptance Speech, Republican Presidential Nomination, 1964

"It has been during Democratic years that we have weakly stumbled into conflict, timidly refusing to draw our own lines against aggression, deceitfully refusing to tell even our people of our full participation, and tragically, letting our finest men die on battlefields (unmarked by purpose, unmarked by pride or the prospect of victory).

Yesterday it was Korea. Tonight it is Vietnam. Make no bones of this. Don't try to sweep this under the rug. We are at war in Vietnam. And yet the President, who is Commander-in-Chief of our forces, refuses to

(continued)

say—refuses to say, mind you, whether or not the objective over there is victory. And his Secretary of Defense continues to mislead and misinform the American people, and enough of it has gone by. . . .

Our towns and our cities, then our counties, then our states, then our regional contacts—and only then, the national government. That, let me remind you, is the ladder of liberty, built by decentralized power. On it also we must have balance between the branches of government at every level.

I would remind you that extremism in the defense of liberty is no vice. And let me remind you also that moderation in the pursuit of justice is no virtue."

Document 3

Source: U.S. Senate Committee on Government Operations, *Confidence and Concern: Citizens View American Government: A Survey of Public Attitudes*, 1973

"In the Fall of 1973, for the first time since the 1968 assassinations of Martin Luther King and Robert Kennedy, a majority of the American people (by 53–37 percent) felt 'there is something deeply wrong in America' today, that these are no ordinary times of crisis. . . .

By 45–35 percent, the public tends to believe that the quality of life in the country has deteriorated. . . .

As a young medical engineer in Del Ray, Florida, put it: 'I feel I have a permanent hand in my pocket, picking my money out every couple of hours. That isn't comfortable.' A retired man in Sarasota added: 'I thought I had worked all my life to retire comfortably. Now inflation is out of control, and I feel poor all the time.'

Still another public complaint about the quality of life is that crime has not been checked. As a 44-year old processing worker in Texarkana, Texas, put it: 'We get a lot of talk about law and order and nobody seems to do much or care much if we actually have it. That makes the quality of life worse, as far as I'm concerned.' Others talked about drug abuse, Watergate, loss of confidence in government, erosion of moral standards, shortages of food and gasoline, unrest, and high taxes."

Document 4

Source: Articles of Impeachment Adopted by the House of Representatives Committee on the Judiciary, July 27, 1974

Article I

"In his conduct of the office of President of the United States, Richard M. Nixon, in violation of his constitutional oath . . . has prevented, obstructed, and impeded the administration of justice, in that:

On June 17, 1972, and prior thereto, agents of the Committee for the Re-Election of the President committed unlawful entry of the

(continued)

headquarters of the Democratic National Committee in Washington, District of Columbia, for the purpose of securing political intelligence. Subsequent thereto, Richard M. Nixon, using the powers of his high office, engaged personally and through his close subordinates and agents, in a course of conduct or plan designed to delay, impede, and obstruct the investigation of such illegal entry; to cover up, conceal and protect those responsible; and to conceal the existence and scope of other unlawful covert activities. . . .

Article II

Using the powers of the office of President of the United States, Richard M. Nixon . . . has repeatedly engaged in conduct violating the constitutional rights of citizens, impairing the due and proper administration of justice and the conduct of lawful inquiries, or contravening the laws governing agencies of the executive branch and the purposed of these agencies. . . .

Wherefore, Richard M. Nixon, by such conduct, warrants impeachment and trial, and removal from office."

Document 5

Source: President Carter, Address to the Nation on Energy and National Goals (also known as "The Malaise Speech"), July 15, 1979

"[I] want to talk to you right now about a fundamental threat to American democracy. . . .

The threat is nearly invisible in ordinary ways. It is a crisis of confidence. It is a crisis that strikes at the very heart and soul and spirit of our national will. We can see this crisis in the growing doubt about the meaning of our own lives and in the loss of a unity of purpose for our Nation.

The erosion of our confidence in the future is threatening to destroy the social and the political fabric of America. . . .

In a nation that was proud of hard work, strong families, close-knit communities, and our faith in God, too many of us now tend to worship self-indulgence and consumption. Human identity is no longer defined by what one does, but by what one owns. But we've discovered that owning things and consuming things does not satisfy our longing for meaning. We've learned that piling up material goods cannot fill the emptiness of lives which have no confidence or purpose.

The symptoms of this crisis of the American spirit are all around us. For the first time in the history of our country a majority of our people believe that the next 5 years will be worse than the past 5 years. Two-thirds of our people do not even vote. The productivity of American workers is actually dropping, and the willingness of Americans to save for the future has fallen below that of all other people in the Western world.

As you know, there is a growing disrespect for government and for churches and for schools, the news media, and other institutions. This is not a message of happiness or reassurance, but it is the truth and it is a warning."

(continued)

Document 6

Source: U.S. Embassy Workers Being Held Hostage in Tehran, Iran, November 4, 1979

Bettmann/Getty Images

Document 7

Source: United States Unemployment Rate and Inflation Rate (the "Misery Index"), 1970–1980

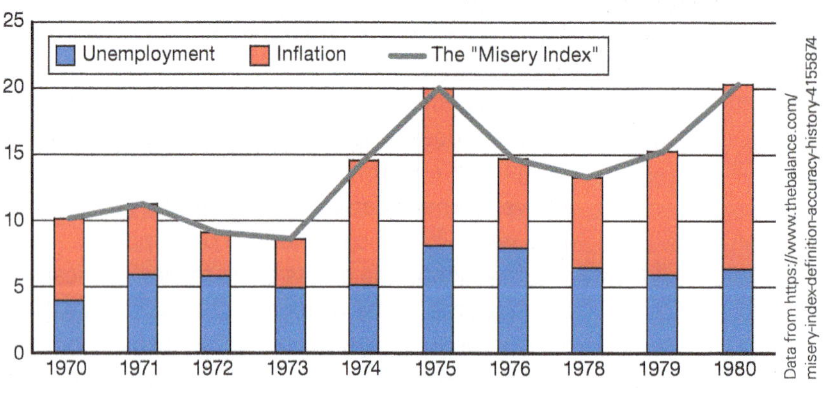

Data from https://www.thebalance.com/misery-index-definition-accuracy-history-4155874

Period 8 Review 1945–1980

KEY CONCEPTS AND EVENTS

affirmative action, *911*
American Indian Movement (AIM), *924*
baby boom, *855*
Bandung Conference, *879*
Bay of Pigs invasion, *886*
Beats, *865*
Berlin Airlift, *836*
Berlin Wall, *887*
Black Panther Party, *910*
Brown v. Board of Education of Topeka, *869*
Bureau of Indian Affairs (BIA), *883*
Camp David accords, *948*
Central Intelligence Agency (CIA), *836*
Christian Right, *950*
Civil Rights Act of 1964, *907*
Cold War, *831*
Commission on the Status of Women, *917*
containment, *832*
counterculture, *930*
deindustrialization, *935*
Dennis v. United States, *846*
détente, *841*
Dixiecrats, *853*
domino theory, *890*
Eisenhower Doctrine, *881*
Environmental Protection Agency (EPA), *933*
Equal Rights Amendment (ERA), *918*
escalation, *892*
Federal Employee Loyalty Program, *845*
Freedom Rides, *903*
Freedom Summer, *907*
Free Speech Movement (FSM), *928*
Great Society, *898*
Gulf of Tonkin Resolution, *891*
House Un-American Activities Committee (HUAC), *844*
iron curtain, *833*
Kent State shootings, *896*
Kitchen Debate, *879*
Korean War, *838*
La Raza Unida (The United Race), *923*
Levittown, *856*
Little Rock Nine, *871*
March on Washington for Jobs and Freedom, *906*
Marshall Plan, *835*
McCarran Internal Security Act, *847*
McCarran-Walter Immigration Act, *925*
McCarthyism, *848*
military-industrial complex, *877*
Mississippi Freedom Democratic Party (MFDP), *908*
Modern Republicanism, *882*
Montgomery bus boycott, *870*
mujahideen, *946*
mutually assured destruction (MAD), *878*
My Lai massacre, *893*
National Defense Education Act, *883*
National Energy Act, *935*
National Interstate and Defense Highway Act, *883*
National Organization for Women (NOW), *918*
National Security Council (NSC), *836*
neoconservative, *949*
New Frontier, *897*
New Look, *877*
New Right, *948*
North Atlantic Treaty Organization (NATO), *837*
NSC-68, *838*
Operation Wetback, *883*
Organization of Petroleum Exporting Countries (OPEC), *934*
Pentagon Papers, *896*
Port Huron Statement, *927*
Potsdam Conference, *832*
redlining, *857*
Roe v. Wade, *918*
SALT II, *946*
school busing, *911*
Second Red Scare, *844*
Servicemen's Readjustment Act (GI Bill), *851*
Smith Act, *844*
Southern Christian Leadership Conference (SCLC), *870*
Sputnik, *883*
stagflation, *935*
Stonewall riots, *926*
Strategic Arms Limitation Treaty (SALT I), *841*
Student Nonviolent Coordinating Committee (SNCC), *872*
Students for a Democratic Society (SDS), *927*
Superfund, *937*
Sun Belt, *858*
Taft-Hartley Act, *852*
Tet Offensive, *893*
To Secure These Rights, *868*
totalitarianism, *835*
Truman Doctrine, *835*
Twenty-Sixth Amendment, *943*
Vietcong, *890*
Vietnamization, *895*
Vietnam War, *892*
Voting Rights Act, *909*
War Powers Resolution, *896*
Warsaw Pact, *837*
Watergate, *944*
White Citizens' Council (WCC), *872*
Yates v. United States, *849*
Young Americans for Freedom (YAF), *939*

KEY PEOPLE

Chuck Berry, *862*
Marlon Brando, *860*
Leonid Brezhnev, *841*
William F. Buckley, *938*
Stokely Carmichael, *909*
James "Jimmy" Carter, *935*
Fidel Castro, *880*
Whittaker Chambers, *845*
Cesar Chavez, *922*
Frank Church, *947*
Winston Churchill, *833*
John Coltrane, *865*
Eugene "Bull" Connor, *904*
Miles Davis, *865*
James Dean, *860*
John Dean, *944*
Bob Dylan, *930*
Dwight D. Eisenhower, *877*
Medgar Evers, *905*
Jerry Falwell, *950*
Gerald Ford, *945*
Betty Friedan, *862*
Dizzy Gillespie, *865*
Allen Ginsberg, *865*
Barry Goldwater, *827*
Billy Graham, *864*
Fannie Lou Hamer, *908*
Tom Hayden, *927*
Alger Hiss, *845*
Ho Chi Minh, *889*
Dolores Huerta, *922*
Hubert H. Humphrey, *942*
Lyndon B. Johnson, *883*
George Kennan, *832*
John F. Kennedy, *877*
Robert F. Kennedy, *827*
Jack Kerouac, *865*
Ayatollah Ruhollah Khomeini, *948*
Nikita Khrushchev, *879*
Martin Luther King Jr., *827*
Dr. Alfred Kinsey, *865*
Henry Kissinger, *895*
William Levitt, *856*
John Lewis, *906*
Douglas MacArthur, *839*
Norman Mailer, *865*
Mao Zedong, *837*
George Marshall, *835*
Thurgood Marshall, *869*
Joseph McCarthy, *847*
George McGovern, *943*
James Meredith, *904*
John Mitchell, *944*
Marilyn Monroe, *861*
Huey P. Newton, *910*
Ngo Dinh Diem, *889*
Richard M. Nixon, *841*
Rosa Parks, *869*
Norman Vincent Peale, *864*
Elvis Presley, *862*
A. Philip Randolph, *870*
Ronald Reagan, *827*
Pat Robertson, *950*
Jackie Robinson, *868*
Ethel Rosenberg, *844*
Julius Rosenberg, *844*
Edward Roybal, *921*
Bayard Rustin, *870*
Dr. Jonas Salk, *855*
Phyllis Schlafly, *827*
Bobby Seale, *910*
Frank Sinatra, *862*
Barbara Smith, *921*
Dr. Benjamin Spock, *862*
Joseph Stalin, *831*
Gloria Steinem, *918*
Emmett Till, *872*
Harry S. Truman, *832*
George C. Wallace, *905*
Henry Wallace, *833*
Earl Warren, *869*
Bob Woodward, *944*
Malcolm X, *827*

CHRONOLOGY

1940	Smith Act bars supporting overthrow of U.S. government
1941	Term *teenager* is coined
1944	GI Bill subsidizes education, mortgages, health care for veterans
1945	Yalta Conference
1946	Churchill delivers "iron curtain" speech
1947	United States provides military aid to Greece and Turkey Marshall Plan proposed Taft-Hartley Act limits power of labor unions Truman creates Federal Employee Loyalty Program HUAC holds hearings on communist influence in Hollywood *Mendez v. Westminster* prohibits separate schools for Mexican Americans
1948	Formation of West Germany; Berlin Airlift begins Creation of Levittown Truman wins reelection President Truman orders desegregation of U.S. military

CHRONOLOGY *(continued)*

1949	Formation of NATO alliance Russia tests its first atomic bomb
1950	Korean War begins McCarran Internal Security Act passed over Truman's veto NSC-68 urges more aggressive U.S. posture toward U.S.S.R.
1951	*Dennis v. United States* labels communist leaders as dangerous
1952	McCarran-Walter Immigration Act allows Japanese noncitizens to become citizens Eisenhower wins election on Modern Republicanism platform United States tests the world's first hydrogen bomb
1953	Korean War ends with an armistice agreement Rosenbergs executed for sharing atomic bomb secrets with U.S.S.R.
1954	Army-McCarthy hearings Senate censures McCarthy "Under God" added to the pledge of allegiance Supreme Court decision in *Brown v. Board of Education* overturns "separate but equal" doctrine Mass deportation of undocumented Mexican immigrants in "Operation Wetback" Overthrow of French colonial rule in Vietnam
1955	Introduction of polio vaccine James Dean stars in *Rebel without a Cause* Arrest of Rosa Parks and start of Montgomery bus boycott
1956	Elvis Presley appears on the *Ed Sullivan Show* Publication of Allen Ginsberg's poem "Howl" "In God We Trust" becomes the official motto of the United States Eisenhower wins second term National Interstate and Defense Highway Act passed Supported by the United States, Ngo Dinh Diem rejects national elections in Vietnam
1957	*Yates v. United States* severely weakens Smith Act Crisis of integration of Central High School in Little Rock, Arkansas Formation of the Southern Christian Leadership Conference (SCLC) Eisenhower Doctrine approved by Congress Soviets launch *Sputnik* satellite into space
1958	Vice President Richard Nixon visits the Soviet Union
1959	Nixon and Khrushchev engage in "Kitchen Debate" Fidel Castro leads uprising that overthrows the Cuban government
By 1960	One-third of Americans live in suburbs 90 percent of teens attending high school
1960	Sit-in movement begins at Woolworth's lunch counter in Greensboro, North Carolina Formation of the Student Nonviolent Coordinating Committee (SNCC) American U-2 spy plane shot down by Soviet Union Birth control pills made available to American public Barry Goldwater's *The Conscience of a Conservative* published John F. Kennedy wins close presidential election

CHRONOLOGY *(continued)*

1961	Bay of Pigs invasion fails to create popular uprising against Castro Freedom Rides to integrate transportation facilities in South
1962	Soviets construct Berlin Wall Cuban Missile Crisis brings United States and U.S.S.R. to brink of war Port Huron Statement by Students for a Democratic Society *Silent Spring* by Rachel Carson increases awareness of environmental concerns
1963	Partial Nuclear Test Ban Treaty signed Publication of *The Feminine Mystique* by Betty Friedan Kennedy endorses coup to replace Diem in Vietnam Civil rights protests in Birmingham March on Washington for Jobs and Freedom KKK bombing of Sixteenth Street Baptist Church Assassination of President Kennedy
1964	Gulf of Tonkin Resolution grants president control of Vietnam conflict Johnson launches Great Society program and War on Poverty Civil Rights Act prohibits discrimination in public accommodations, education, and employment Economic Opportunity Act establishes War on Poverty agencies Freedom Summer voter registration drive in South Johnson wins reelection in a landslide
1965	Johnson launches Operation Rolling Thunder, a massive bombing campaign Civil Rights March from Selma to Montgomery Assassination of Malcolm X Elementary and Secondary Education Act provides federal funding for public schools Medicare provides health insurance for citizens sixty-five years and older Medicaid provides health benefits for the poor Voting Rights Act bans literacy tests for voting Immigration and Nationality Act abolishes quotas on immigration Water Quality Act establishes federal water quality standards Air Quality Act establishes air pollution standards for motor vehicles National Endowment for the Arts created
1966	Formation of Black Panther Party National Organization for Women (NOW) founded Model Cities Act approves funding for the rehabilitation of inner cities Antiwar protests escalate
1968	Tet Offensive My Lai Massacre American Indian Movement (AIM) established Assassination of Martin Luther King Jr. Fair Housing Act signed into law Assassination of Robert F. Kennedy Richard Nixon wins presidential election
1969	Stonewall riots signal emergence of gay liberation movement Chicanos form *La Raza Unida* political party
1970	U.S. invasion of Cambodia Kent State shootings Environmental Protection Act passed

CHRONOLOGY *(continued)*

1971	Publication of the *Pentagon Papers* further undermines public support for Vietnam War Supreme Court mandates forced busing to achieve integration in *Swann* case Twenty-Sixth Amendment lowers voting age to eighteen Environmental Protection Agency established Clean Air Act passed
1972	SALT I treaty limits nuclear arsenals and ushers in détente Nixon wins reelection Title IX greatly expands women's collegiate athletics
1973	War Powers Resolution limits presidential power to wage war without congressional approval *Roe v. Wade* affirms women's constitutional right to abortion Watergate investigations begin Vice President Spiro Agnew resigns OPEC oil embargo Endangered Species Act signed into law
1974	President Nixon resigns over Watergate scandal President Ford pardons Nixon
1975	Fall of Saigon to North Vietnam
1976	Jimmy Carter wins presidential election
1978	*Bakke* case ruling limits use of affirmative action in college admissions Camp David accords bring peace between Egypt and Israel Proposition 13 passed by California voters, launching nationwide taxpayer protests
1979	Iranian hostage crisis begins Three Mile Island nuclear reactor meltdown Jerry Falwell founds the Moral Majority
1980	United States boycotts Moscow Olympics Ronald Reagan wins presidential election
1981	Iranian hostages released on Reagan's inauguration day
1982	Effort to ratify Equal Rights Amendment (ERA) defeated

Period 8 AP® Exam Practice

Multiple-Choice Questions

Questions 1–3 refer to the excerpt.

"This brief discussion of fears and threats . . . illuminates the extent to which U.S. officials defined their national security in terms of correlations of power. American power depended on the country's magnificently productive economic machine, its technological prowess, and its capacity to use strategic air power to inflict great damage on the economy of any enemy. Adversaries would be able to threaten U.S. security only if they could undermine the American economy, attack it militarily, or develop comparable or superior industrial warmaking capabilities. These eventualities were most likely to occur if the Soviet Union gained direct or indirect control over the industrial infrastructure and skilled labor of advanced nations or if the Kremlin developed its own strategic air force, atomic bomb, and forward bases. . . . Subsequently, the most important National Security Council (NSC) papers of the Truman administration incorporated a geostrategic vision. National security was interpreted in terms of correlations of power. Power was defined in terms of the control of resources, industrial infrastructure, and overseas bases."

Melvyn P. Leffler, *A Preponderance of Power: National Security, the Truman Administration, and the Cold War*, 1992

1. The historical developments expressed in the excerpt most directly led to which of the following developments?
   (A) The creation of atomic weapons
   (B) Legislation that restricted migration to the United States
   (C) Increased efforts toward establishing collective-security organizations
   (D) A decrease in tension between the United States and the Soviet Union

2. Which of the following events can be used as historical evidence to support the ideas in the excerpt?
   (A) The establishment of the United Nations
   (B) The testing of hydrogen weapons
   (C) The decolonization of Southeast Asia
   (D) Military engagement in Korea

3. Which of the following best represents an important short-term consequence of the ideas expressed above?
   (A) The development of a military-industrial complex
   (B) Antiwar protests by the counterculture
   (C) A dependency on foreign oil
   (D) The increase in military spending under President Ronald Reagan

Questions 4–6 refer to the excerpt.

"The Student Leadership Conference made it crystal clear that current sit-ins and other demonstrations are concerned with something much bigger than a hamburger or even a giant-sized Coke.

Whatever may be the difference in approach to their goal, the Negro and white students, North and South, are seeking to rid America of the scourge of racial segregation and discrimination—not only at lunch counters, but in every aspect of life. . . .

It was further evident that desire for supportive cooperation from adult leaders and the adult community was also tempered by apprehension that adults might try to 'capture' the student movement. The students showed willingness to be met on the basis of equality, but were intolerant of anything that smacked of manipulation or domination."

Ella Baker, "Bigger Than a Hamburger,"
Southern Patriot, June 1960

4. Which of the following debates most directly contributed to the ideas expressed in the excerpt?
(A) Whether to use violence instead of nonviolence in protests
(B) The meaning of the Vietnam War as it related to civil rights
(C) Whether to focus on economic or political reform
(D) How best to employ the tactic of nonviolence in protests

5. Which of the following serves as evidence for the success of the ideas expressed in the excerpt?
(A) The Supreme Court's decision in *Brown v. Board of Education*, 1954
(B) The Civil Rights Act of 1957
(C) The ending of segregation in public places
(D) The resistance to the military draft during the Vietnam War

6. The ideas expressed in the excerpt would have been supported by which of the following groups?
(A) Northern conservatives
(B) Northern liberals
(C) Southern conservatives
(D) Southern moderates

Questions 7–9 refer to the excerpt.

"Orange County, as contemporary newspaper commentators never tired of emphasizing, was a real center and symbol of American conservatism in the 1960s. Its conservative movement was the nucleus of a broader conservative matrix evolving in the Sunbelt and the West that eventually propelled assertive and unapologetic conservatives to national prominence. . . .

These conservative activists and the movement they forged are essential to understanding the rightward shift in American politics since the 1960s. Far outside the boundaries of respectable politics in the early 1960s, the Right expanded its influence on the national scene in the late 1960s and 1970s and vaulted to national power with the Reagan landslide of 1980. . . . Conservatives' successes, to be sure, were due in no small part to liberalism's foundering on the shoals of race, economic discontent, and its own internal contradictions. But just as significantly, conservatives' ability to build a powerful movement enabled them to pick up the pieces and profit politically from liberal failures."

Lisa McGirr, *Suburban Warriors:*
The Origins of the New American Right, 2001

7. The historical argument in the excerpt most directly reflects which of the following changes in American politics during the late 1960s?
   (A) The emergence of a successful third party
   (B) A decline in the belief that the federal government could solve economic problems
   (C) A belief in liberalism that promoted the use of government intervention in the economy
   (D) The use of courts to promote civil rights

8. Which of the following historical developments would support the statements in the excerpt above?
   (A) The passage of Great Society legislation
   (B) American escalation of the war in Vietnam
   (C) An increase in civil rights legislation
   (D) A significant increase in the number of evangelical Christian churches

9. Which of the following represents an immediate consequence of the changes described in the excerpt?
   (A) An internal migration to northern cities
   (B) The economic conditions of stagflation
   (C) An increase in political clashes between liberals and conservatives
   (D) The establishment of a national energy policy

Questions 10–12 refer to the excerpt.

"During 12 years of working for a living, I have experienced much of the legal and social discrimination reserved for women in this country. I have been refused service in public restaurants, ordered out of public gathering places, and turned away from apartment rentals; all for the clearly stated, sole reason that I am a woman. And all without the legal remedies available to blacks and other minorities. I have been excluded from professional groups, writing assignments on so-called 'unfeminine' subjects such as politics, full participation in the Democratic Party, jury duty, and even from such small male privileges as discounts on airline fares. Most important to me, I have been denied a society in which women are encouraged, or even allowed to think of themselves as first-class citizens and responsible human beings. . . .

The truth is that all our problems stem from the same sex-based myths . . . Like racial myths, they have been reflected in our laws."

Gloria Steinem, "Testimony before the Senate Judiciary Committee Hearing on the Equal Rights Amendment," May 6, 1970

10. The ideas expressed in the excerpt above emerged in the context of which of the following?
   (A) The growing influence of conservatives in northern urban areas
   (B) A youth culture that rejected some of the gender expectations held by previous generations
   (C) A decrease in conservatives' commitment to the Vietnam War
   (D) The emergence of a nonviolent civil rights movement

11. The ideas expressed in the excerpt reveal which of the following historical trends in the late 1960s and early 1970s?
    (A) A rejection of political leaders' commitment to equality
    (B) A decline in the number of people who supported conservative causes
    (C) A rejection of feminist goals by civil rights leaders
    (D) A lack of federal legislation to address gender discrimination

12. The perspectives presented in the excerpt were opposed by which of the following groups?
    (A) Northern liberals
    (B) Civil rights leaders
    (C) Southern conservatives
    (D) Western liberals

Questions 13–15 refer to the cartoon.

Source: Bill Mauldin, "The Strategists," *Chicago Sun-Times,* 1966.

Pritzker Military Museum & Library

13. The cartoon above best serves as evidence of which of the following developments?
    (A) Early support for the effort to contain communism throughout the world
    (B) Popular support for the New Left criticism of U.S. involvement in Vietnam
    (C) Disagreements over U.S. policy in Vietnam
    (D) President Lyndon Johnson's Great Society legislation

14. By the early 1970s, which of the following best characterizes a major change in U.S. foreign policy in Southeast Asia?
(A) An increase in the number of troops in Vietnam
(B) A lack of support for decolonization efforts throughout the world
(C) New immigration laws that ended discriminatory quotas
(D) Increasing debates over the use of executive power in the war in Vietnam

15. Which of the following historical developments could best be used to support the point of view in the cartoon above?
(A) An increase in antiwar protests
(B) The U.S. military strategy of Vietnamization
(C) Support for the policy of détente with the Soviet Union
(D) The problems of inflation in the late 1970s

Short-Answer Questions

"This optimism was not altogether new: most Americans, living in a land of opportunity, have always had great hopes for the future. But high expectations, rooted in vibrant economic growth, ascended as never before in the 1950s and peaked in the 1960s, an extraordinarily turbulent decade during which faith in the wealth of the United States — and in the capacity of the federal government to promote progress — aroused unprecedented rights-consciousness on the home front. America's political leaders, meanwhile, managed to stimulate enormous expectations about the nation's ability to direct world affairs. More than ever before — or since — Americans came to believe that they could shape the international scene in their own image as well as fashion a more classless, equal opportunity society.

The economy, a driving force behind the rise of expectations from 1945 to the late 1960s, also developed worrisome problems by the early 1970s. These problems — which stymied economic growth in the mid- and late 1970s — did not destroy either the grand expectations or the rights-consciousness that had mushroomed since 1945. Demands for rights, sharply whetted during the previous decades, remained as enduring legacies of the postwar era. But popular uneasiness about the economy did more than any other development of the 1970s to dull the extraordinary optimism that peaked in the mid-1960s."

James T. Patterson, *Grand Expectations: The United States, 1945–1974*, 1996

"The United States at midcentury was a far more complicated and troubled place than emerges from most histories and popular accounts. The nation was at a peak of economic and global strength in the 1940s and 1950s. America's aggregate rate of economic growth was nothing short of stunning. . . . But the celebration of affluence masked significant regional variations and persistent inequality. . . .

The cities of America's industrial heartland were the bellwethers of economic change. The rusting of the Rust Belt began neither with the much-touted stagflation of oil crisis of the 1970s, nor with the rise of global economic competition and the influx of car or steel imports. It began, unheralded, in the 1950s. . . .

The problems that beset Detroit were not solely economic. The fate of Northern industrial cities was fundamentally entangled with the troubled history of race in twentieth-century America. . . . Racial ideology, a shifting and fluid popular vernacular of race, served as the backdrop to the relationship between blacks and whites in the postwar city."

Thomas J. Sugrue, *The Origins of the Urban Crisis: Race and Inequality in Postwar Detroit*, 1996

1. Using the excerpts, answer **A**, **B**, and **C**.
   (A) Briefly describe ONE major difference between Patterson's and Sugrue's historical interpretations about the economic situation in the postwar years from 1945 to 1975.
   (B) Briefly explain how ONE historical event or development from 1945 to 1975 that is not explicitly mentioned in the excerpts could support Patterson's interpretation.
   (C) Briefly explain how ONE historical event or development from 1945 to 1975 that is not explicitly mentioned in the excerpts could support Sugrue's interpretation.

"The history of life on earth has been a history of interaction between living things and their surroundings. To a large extent, the physical form and the habits of the earth's vegetation and its animal life have been molded by the environment. Considering the whole span of earthly time, the opposite effect, in which life actually modifies its surroundings, has been relatively slight. Only within the moment of time represented by the present century has one species—man—acquired significant power to alter the nature of his world.

During the past quarter century this power has not only increased to one of disturbing magnitude but it has changed in character. The most alarming of all man's assaults upon the environment is the contamination of air, earth, rivers, and sea with dangerous and even lethal materials."

Rachel Carson, *Silent Spring*, 1962

2. Using the excerpt, answer **A**, **B**, and **C**.
   (A) Briefly explain the point of view expressed in the excerpt.
   (B) Briefly explain how ONE specific historical event or development from 1945 to 1980 contributed to the point of view expressed in the excerpt above.
   (C) Briefly explain how ONE specific historical event or development from 1945 to 1980 happened as a result of the historical situation described in the excerpt above.

3. Answer **A**, **B**, and **C**.
   (A) Briefly describe ONE specific historical change in the political debates over the role of government in U.S. society in the period from 1945 to 1970.
   (B) Briefly describe ONE specific historical continuity in the political debates over the role of government in U.S. society in the period from 1945 to 1970.
   (C) Briefly explain ONE historical consequence of the debates over the role of government in U.S. society in the period from 1970 to 1980.

4. Answer **A**, **B**, and **C**.
   (A) Briefly explain ONE example of how the Vietnam War changed American culture in the period from 1964 to 1973.
   (B) Briefly explain ANOTHER example of how the Vietnam War changed American culture in the period from 1964 to 1973.
   (C) Briefly explain ONE consequence of the cultural change you identified in either part A or part B in the period from 1973 to 1980.

Document-Based Question

1. Evaluate the extent to which the debates over the power of the federal government fostered change in the lives of Americans from 1964 to 1980.

Document 1

Source: President Lyndon Johnson, Remarks at the University of Michigan, May 22, 1964.

"The challenge of the next half century is whether we have the wisdom to use that wealth to enrich and elevate our national life, and to advance the quality of our American civilization.

Your imagination, your initiative, and your indignation will determine whether we build a society where progress is the servant of our needs, or a society where old values and new visions are buried under unbridled growth. For in your time we have the opportunity to move not only toward the rich society and the powerful society, but upward to the Great Society.

The Great Society rests on abundance and liberty for all. It demands an end to poverty and racial injustice, to which we are totally committed in our time."

Document 2

Source: Daniel Patrick Moynihan, Assistant Secretary for Labor, *The Negro Family: The Case for National Action,* 1965

"In the decade that began with the school desegregation decision of the Supreme Court, and ended with the passage of the Civil Rights Act of 1964, the demand of Negro Americans for full recognition of their civil rights was finally met. . . .

In this new period the expectations of the Negro Americans will go beyond civil rights. Being Americans, they will now expect that in the near future equal opportunities for them as a group will produce roughly equal results, as compared with other groups. This is not going to happen. Nor will it happen for generations to come unless a new and special effort is made."

Document 3

Source: Herblock, "The Agony and the Ecstasy," *The Washington Post*, May 31, 1966.

Document 4

Source: Warren K. Leffler, Women's liberation march from Farragut Square to Lafayette Park, August 26, 1970.

Document 5

Source: *The Phyllis Schlafly Report*, vol. 5, no. 7, February 1972.

"Of all the classes of people who ever lived, the American woman is the most privileged. We have the most rights and rewards, and the fewest duties. . . .

1. We have the immense good fortune to live in a civilization which respects the family as the basic unit of society. This respect is part and parcel of our laws and our customs. It is based on the fact of life—which no legislation or agitation can erase—that women have babies and men don't.

If you don't like this fundamental difference, you will have to take up your complaint with God because He created us this way. The fact that women, not men, have babies is not the fault of selfish and domineering men, or of the establishment, or of any clique of conspirators who want to oppress women. It's simply the way God made us. . . .

2. [W]e are the beneficiaries of a tradition of special respect for women which dates from the Christian Age of Chivalry. The honor and respect paid to Mary, the Mother of Christ, resulted in all women, in effect, being put on a pedestal. . . .

3. [T]he great American free enterprise system has produced remarkable inventors who have lifted the backbreaking 'women's work' from our shoulders."

Document 6

Source: Ronald Reagan, Neshoba County Fair Speech, Philadelphia, Mississippi, August 3, 1980.

"[In] more recent years with the best intention, they have created a vast bureaucracy, or a bureaucratic structure—bureaus and departments and agencies—to try and solve all the problems and eliminate all the things of human misery that they can. They have forgotten that when you create a government bureaucracy, no matter how well-intentioned it is, almost always instantly its top priority becomes preservation of the bureaucracy. . . .

I believe in states' rights; I believe in people doing as much as they can for themselves at the community level and at the private level. And I believe that we've distorted the balance of our government today by giving powers that were never intended in the constitution to that federal establishment. And if I do get the job I'm looking for, I'm going to devote myself to trying to reorder those priorities and to restore to the states and local communities those functions which properly belong there."

Document 7

Source: United States Unemployment Rate and Inflation Rate (the "Misery Index"), 1970–1980.

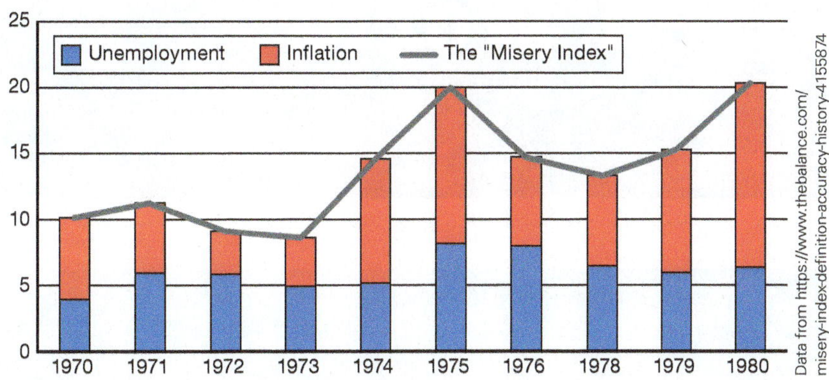

Long-Essay Questions

2. Evaluate the extent to which the Cold War contributed to changing the role of the United States in the world from 1945 to 1975.

3. Evaluate the extent to which the women's movement changed U.S. society from 1950 to 1980.

4. Evaluate the extent to which the Black civil rights movement changed tactics from 1945 to 1980.

PERIOD **9** 1980–The Present

Challenges in a Globalized World

Library of Congress, Prints & Photographs Division, photograph by Carol M. Highsmith [reproduction number LC-DIG-highsm-13502]

AIDS Quilt in Washington, D.C., 1987 The AIDS Quilt began in 1987 as a project in San Francisco to memorialize those who have died from the effects of acquired immune deficiency syndrome (AIDS). Each person who died of AIDS-related disease is represented by one three-by-six-foot panel. In this image, the AIDS Quilt is on display in Washington, D.C., in 1987, when it comprised almost 2,000 panels and covered a space larger than a football field. Since then, the AIDS Quilt has grown to comprise almost 50,000 panels.

Contextualizing Period 9

MODULE 9.1

For many Americans, after the 1960s and 1970s, society seemed jagged and out of alignment. Already anxious from the Cold War and the ongoing threat of global nuclear destruction, many in the United States felt further threatened by new value systems that challenged old conventions, by the emergence of new interest groups that demanded recognition and respect, and by the arrival of new immigrants from locations outside of Europe.

The instability of American society and culture initiated a political movement that emphasized traditional American values and interests. This conservative movement grew in intensity throughout the 1970s and came to fruition with the election of Ronald Reagan as president in 1980.

In hindsight, some Americans called the election of Ronald Reagan in 1980 the beginning of the "Reagan revolution." Although there is debate over the meaning of this phrase, most historians agree that Reagan's election represented a shift in American political rhetoric and policy. It seemed that the liberal project that began with Franklin D. Roosevelt and reached its high tide with the Great Society programs of Lyndon B. Johnson had come to an end.

Reagan's election represented the political maturity of two divergent social movements that began in the early 1960s—the New Right and the New Left. In these two ideologies, free-market economics and traditional moral beliefs collided with civil rights activism, identity politics, and environmentalism. This shift in sensibilities, especially regarding a government and society overseen by experts, bound both the New Right and the New Left to each other while raising tensions between the two throughout this period.

Despite these tensions, the United States entered the twenty-first century in the midst of economic prosperity and peace that coincided with the collapse of the Soviet Union in 1991. With the end of the Cold War, the United States selectively engaged in foreign intervention under the umbrella of peace-keeping while promoting capitalism and democracy around the world to bring about "a new world order" in the words of President George H. W. Bush.

In the aftermath of the terrorist attacks of September 11, 2001, the nation seemed to rally together in response to its worst attack since the Pearl Harbor attack, which led it to fully enter World War II. But that unified front proved short-lived. The Bush administration's response to the attacks, the administration's attempts to overhaul key New Deal legislation, and lingering anger over the contested presidential election of 2000 deepened the ideological divide and signaled the dawn of a new era of bitter political partisanship and cultural conflict.

While the election of Barack Obama in 2008 promised progress in the nation's historical struggle for racial justice, a long recession triggered by a mortgage crisis, ongoing anxiety over terrorism and immigration, a rougher political discourse fueled by the rise of social media, and the contentious elections of 2016 and 2020 caused many Americans to face the second quarter of the twenty-first century with apprehension.

AP® EXAM TIP

Understand and be able to contextualize the factors in U.S. society since 1980 that have produced significant changes. Changes happened in politics with a conservative resurgence; in economics with the impact of technology; and in international affairs with the United States once again becoming the dominant global force after the end of the Cold War. Also, new waves of immigration from Asia and Latin America entered the country. What impact did these events have on society in general, and the family in particular? How did America change from these events?

Period 9: What's Inside 1980–The Present

MODULE	AP® THEMATIC FOCUS
9.1 Contextualizing Period 9	The tumult of the 1960s reverberated throughout the remainder of the twentieth century. In response to the expansion of social welfare policies as well as changing cultural values, a new conservatism emerged, which united Americans who were ambivalent about countercultural influences with those who rejected liberal economics. This conservative turn led to the 1980 election of Ronald Reagan and marked a rightward shift in American politics. In foreign affairs, the détente of the 1970s was quickly replaced by a return to Cold War sentiment before the fall of the Berlin Wall in 1989. While deindustrialization, outsourcing, and globalization continued to challenge and remake the U.S. economy, new technological innovations reshaped American society and work.
9.2 Reagan and Conservatism	**Politics and Power** The Reagan presidency ushered in a politically more conservative era with large tax cuts, continued deregulation, and increased military spending. Supply-side economics left a mixed legacy of stock market and economic growth alongside growing inequality and soaring federal debt. The New Right also sought to restore its vision of traditional family values by opposing abortion rights, gay rights, and undocumented immigration.
9.3 The End of the Cold War	**America in the World** Reagan launched a renewed confrontation with the Soviet Union and a worldwide campaign against communism. By his second term, a thaw in relations led to arms control negotiations deals and an easing of tensions. After the collapse of the Soviet Union and the end of the Cold War, the United States increasingly faced the twin prospects of peace with its former rivals and greater instability in new regions. U.S. policymakers struggled to redefine the nation's place as the sole superpower, while also debating the role of the United States in this new era.
9.4 A Changing Economy	**Work, Exchange, and Technology** Starting in the 1990s, the United States underwent profound economic, technological, and social changes. Americans elected the first president born after World War II, Bill Clinton, who was also the first president in nearly fifty years who did not have to fight the Cold War. Throughout the decade, Americans continued to debate the legacy of the 1960s, while at the same time, they embraced new digital technologies that opened the economy to new markets.
9.5 Migration and Immigration in the 1990s and 2000s	**Migration and Settlement** Changing immigration patterns in the late twentieth and early twenty-first centuries as well as continued internal migration altered the nation's demographics and reshaped the distribution of its population. Large inflows of immigrants, mainly from the Americas and Asia, significantly contributed to the country's population growth and growing diversity while the movement of people toward the Sun Belt strengthened the economies and political power of states in the South and West.
9.6 Challenges of the Twenty-First Century	**America in the World** At the dawn of the twenty-first century, the United States stood at the center of a global economy that stretched across the world, from production centers in Asia, through regions of high consumption in Western Europe and the United States. But these economic changes, generally called "globalization," also caused unemployment among manufacturing workers in North America and Western Europe while at the same time benefiting consumers through lower prices. In the twenty-first century, Americans could no longer convince themselves that war and environmental degradation were worries for people far away. Terrorist attacks by non-state groups, both domestic and international, shook American society, and the effects of climate change became increasingly apparent throughout the world. Technological innovations, globalization, and demographic changes continue to reshape the U.S. economy and American society in the twenty-first century as heightened partisanship poses new challenges for the nation.
9.7 Causation in Period 9	During the end of the twentieth and beginning of the twenty-first centuries, a new conservative ascendancy shifted American politics to the right, while technological innovations, continued globalization, and demographic changes reshaped the U.S. economy and American society. The end of the Cold War and rise of international terrorism posed new foreign-policy challenges for the nation.
Support and Practice	• Practice thinking and writing historically in each module. • See the Period Review of key concepts, events, people, and dates after the last module. • Try the AP® Exam Practice at the end of the period.

Reagan and Conservatism

MODULE 9.2

FOCUS

While reading this section, consider the ways in which Reagan's economic policies fostered a change in the U.S. economy and the extent to which it represented a continuation of older historical trends.

The election of former California governor Ronald Reagan as president in 1980 reflected the spectacular growth in political power of the New Right. Reagan pushed the conservative economic agenda of lower taxes and business deregulation alongside the New Right's concern for traditional religious and family values. His presidency installed conservatism as the dominant political ideology for the remainder of the twentieth century.

Reagan and Reaganomics

Ronald Reagan's presidential victory in 1980 consolidated the growing New Right coalition and reshaped American politics for a generation to come. The former movie actor had transformed himself from a New Deal Democrat into a conservative Republican politician when he ran for governor of California in 1966. As governor, he implemented conservative ideas of free enterprise and small government and denounced Johnson's Great Society for threatening private property and individual liberty. His support for conservative economic and social issues carried him to the presidency.

AP Images/Walter Zeboski

Ronald Reagan Campaigns for President, 1980
During his 1980 campaign, Reagan expressed the main principle of antigovernment conservatism: "Government is like a baby, an alimentary canal [a digestive tract] with a big appetite at one end and no sense of responsibility at the other."

What events preceding Reagan's election help explain why this statement appealed to many Americans?

Reagan easily beat Jimmy Carter and John Anderson, a moderate Republican who ran as an independent candidate (**Map 9.1**). The high unemployment and inflation of the late 1970s worked in Reagan's favor. Reagan appealed to a coalition of conservative Republicans and Democrats, promising to cut taxes and reduce spending, to relax federal supervision over civil rights programs, and to end what was left of expensive Great Society measures and affirmative action. The 1980 election and subsequent presidential elections demonstrated the rising political, economic, and social influence of the American South and West, especially as these regions continued their rapid population growth by drawing migrants from other areas of the nation.

Finally, Reagan energized members of the religious right, who flocked to the polls to support Reagan's platform, which included voluntary prayer in the public schools, defeat of the Equal Rights Amendment, and a constitutional amendment to outlaw abortion. In fact, the religious right attracted its strongest supporters from the growing population of the South and West.

In his inaugural address, Reagan underscored his conservative approach to government. It's "not my intention to do away with government," the president declared. "It is rather to make it work—work with us, not over us; to stand by our side, not ride on our back. Government can and must provide opportunity, not smother it; foster productivity, not stifle it." With this in mind, his first priority was stimulating the stagnant economy.

AP® EXAM TIP

A conservative political resurgence began in 1980 with the election of Ronald Reagan. His two terms solidified the national political transition from liberalism to conservatism. Make sure you understand the appeal of Ronald Reagan's popularity, as well as the political and social debates during the time period.

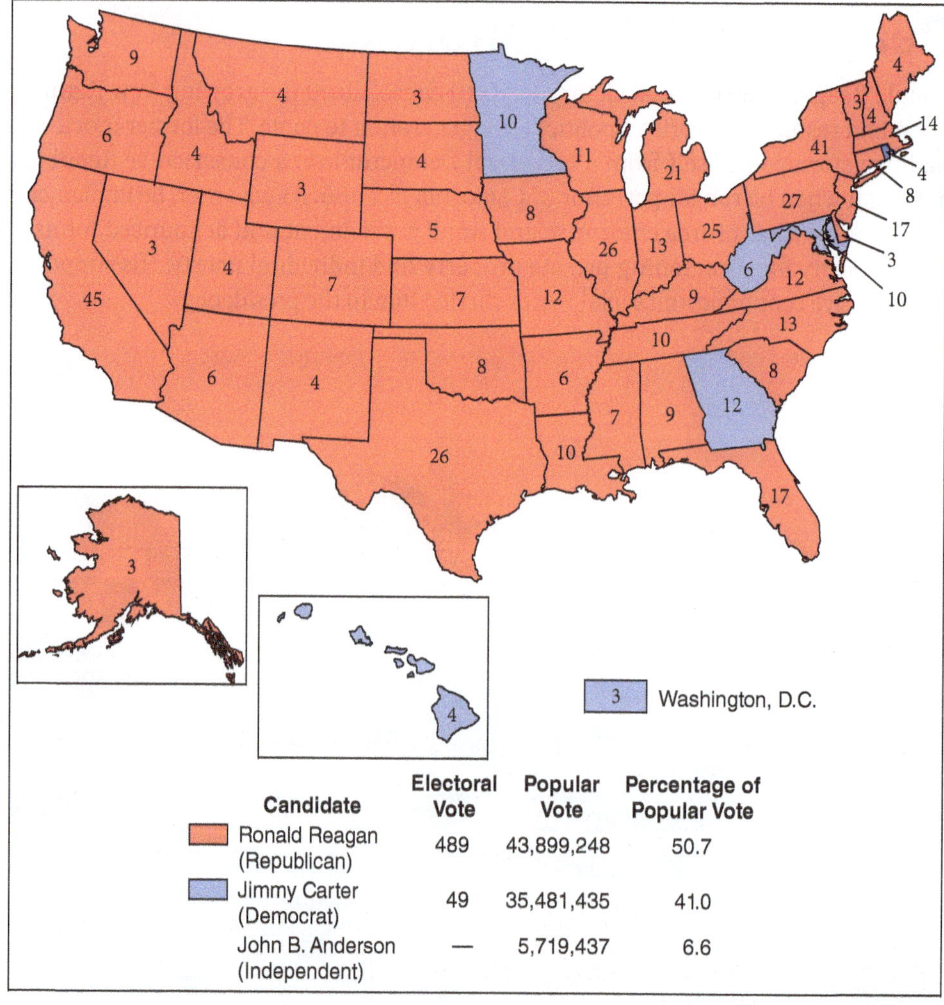

Candidate	Electoral Vote	Popular Vote	Percentage of Popular Vote
Ronald Reagan (Republican)	489	43,899,248	50.7
Jimmy Carter (Democrat)	49	35,481,435	41.0
John B. Anderson (Independent)	—	5,719,437	6.6

MAP 9.1 The Election of 1980 Ronald Reagan won 50.7 percent of the popular vote in the 1980 election, but his margin of victory over Jimmy Carter was much greater in the electoral vote. Reagan won the votes of the South and many discontented Democrats in the urban North. A third-party candidate, John Anderson of Illinois, won 6.6 percent of the popular vote, demonstrating significant disapproval of both major parties.

What does this map reveal about Americans' reaction to the cultural and social trends of the 1960s and 1970s?

The president's strategy, known as **Reaganomics**, reflected the ideas of both conservative Republicans and **supply-side economics**, which theorized that tax cuts and industry deregulation would raise incomes and lower unemployment, thereby promoting economic growth. While supply-siders believed deregulation and low corporate taxes would lead to more jobs and higher wages, opponents criticized tax breaks and other financial benefits for corporations and the wealthy as trickle-down economics which would primarily benefit the rich while only marginally helping those in greatest need.

Reaganomics
The nickname given to Reagan's economic policies based on the theories of supply-side economists and centered on tax cuts and cuts to domestic programs.

During his campaign, Reagan had stated that "in this present crisis, government is not the solution to our problem; government is the problem." After his election, he followed this up by asking Congress for an income tax cut of 30 percent over three years, a reduction in spending for domestic programs of more than $40 billion, and new monetary policies to lower rising rates for loans.

AP® WORKING with EVIDENCE

Source: President Ronald Reagan, Inaugural Address, January 20, 1981

> "The business of our nation goes forward. These United States are confronted with an economic affliction of great proportions. We suffer from the longest and one of the worst sustained inflations in our national history. It distorts our economic decisions, penalizes thrift [saving], and crushes the struggling young and the fixed-income elderly alike. It threatens to shatter the lives of millions of our people.
>
> Idle industries have cast workers into unemployment, human misery, and personal indignity. Those who do work are denied a fair return for their labor by a tax system which penalizes successful achievement and keeps us from maintaining full productivity. . . . In this present crisis, government is not the solution to our problem; government is the problem. From time to time we've been tempted to believe that society has become too complex to be managed by self-rule, that government by an elite group is superior to government for, by, and of the people. Well, if no one among us is capable of governing himself, then who among us has the capacity to govern someone else? All of us together, in and out of government, must bear the burden. The solutions we seek must be equitable, with no one group singled out to pay a higher price.
>
> It is my intention to curb the size and influence of the Federal establishment and to demand recognition of the distinction between the powers granted to the Federal Government and those reserved to the States or to the people. All of us need to be reminded that the Federal Government did not create the States; the States created the Federal Government.
>
> Now, so there will be no misunderstanding, it's not my intention to do away with government. It is rather to make it work—work with us, not over us; to stand by our side, not ride on our back. Government can and must provide opportunity, not smother it; foster productivity, not stifle it."

Questions for Analysis

1. Identify the economic challenges the nation faces according to Reagan.
2. Describe Reagan's view of the proper relationship between the federal government and the states.
3. Explain what Reagan means when he says, "government is the problem."

The president did not operate in isolation from the rest of the world. He learned a great deal from Margaret Thatcher, the British prime minister who took office two years before Reagan. Thatcher combated inflation by slashing welfare programs, selling publicly owned companies, and reducing the budgets of health and education programs. An advocate of supply-side economics, Thatcher reduced income taxes on the wealthy by more than 50 percent to encourage new investment. West Germany also moved toward the right under Chancellor Helmut Kohl, who reined in welfare spending. In the 1980s, the economic policies of Reagan, Thatcher, and Kohl set the economic agenda in their respective countries and signaled a rightward shift in the economic approach of many Western nations.

In March 1981, Reagan survived a nearly fatal assassin's bullet. More popular than ever after his recovery, the president persuaded the Democratic House and the Republican Senate to pass his economic measures in slightly modified form in the **Economic Recovery Tax Act**. These cuts in taxes and spending did not produce the immediate results Reagan sought—unemployment rose to 9.6 percent in 1983 from 7.1 percent in 1980. However, the government's tight money policies, as engineered by the Federal Reserve Board raising interest rates, reduced inflation from 14 percent in 1980 to 4 percent in 1984. By 1984, the unemployment rate had fallen to 7.5 percent, while the gross national product grew by a healthy 4.3 percent, an indication that the recession of the previous two years had ended.

The poor and the lower-middle class saw fewer of the benefits of Reaganomics than others. Spending for food stamps, school lunches, Aid to Families with Dependent Children (welfare), and Medicaid was reduced, while programs that middle-class voters relied on, such as Medicare and Social Security, were maintained. While social spending was lessened, defense spending increased, bolstering the nation's military. Large corporations in the defense industry received government military contracts and favorable tax write-offs.

As a result of the Reagan era tax cuts and deregulation, financial institutions earned huge profits and the stock market boomed. The Reagan administration relaxed antitrust regulations, allowing corporate mergers to a degree unseen since the Great Depression. Fueled by falling interest rates and soaring corporate profits, the stock market created wealth for many investors and financial companies. The number of millionaires doubled during the 1980s, as the top 1 percent of families' control of the nation's wealth reached 42 percent, which included 60 percent of corporate stock. Reflecting this phenomenal accumulation of riches, television produced nighttime soap operas depicting the lives of oil barons (such as *Dallas* and *Dynasty*), whose characters lived glamorous lives filled with intrigue and extravagance.

The gap between the rich and the poor widened. Contrary to the promises of supply-side economics, most of the new wealth did not trickle down. During the 1980s, the nation's share of poor people rose from 11.7 percent to 13.5 percent, representing 33 million Americans. The number of homeless people grew to as many as 400,000 during the 1980s. The middle class also shrank from a high of 53 percent of families in the early 1970s to 49 percent in 1985.

The Reagan administration also challenged labor unions. During the air traffic controllers strike in 1981, the president fired the strikers who refused to return to work, and in their place, he hired new controllers. Reagan's opposition to labor unions both reflected and encouraged a decline in union membership throughout the 1980s, with union membership falling to 16 percent, its lowest level since the New Deal. Because fewer workers were under union contracts, wages failed to keep up with inflation, further increasing the gap between rich and poor.

Reagan continued the business deregulation initiated under Carter. Federal agencies concerned with environmental protection, consumer product reliability, and occupational safety saw key functions shifted to the states, which often made them less effective. Reagan also extended banking deregulation, which allowed savings and loan institutions, a type of bank that primarily accepts deposits and issues mortgages, to make risky loans to real-estate ventures. When real-estate prices began to tumble, savings and loan associations faced collapse. More than one thousand failed, a third of the total sector. Congress appropriated over $100 billion to rescue them.

Reagan's landslide reelection over Democratic candidate Walter Mondale in 1984 sealed the national political transition from liberalism to conservatism. Voters responded overwhelmingly to the improving economy, Reagan's defense of traditional social values, and his boundless optimism about America's future. Despite the landslide, the election was notable for the nomination of Representative Geraldine Ferraro of New York as Mondale's Democratic running mate, the first woman to run on a major party ticket for national office.

Reagan's second term did not produce changes as significant as those of his first term. Democrats still controlled the House and, in 1986, recaptured the Senate. The Reagan administration focused on foreign affairs and the continued Cold War with the Soviet Union. With lower tax revenue as a result of large tax cuts and continued spending on the military and social programs, the federal deficit ballooned. By 1989, the nation had accumulated a $2.8 trillion debt, greatly exceeding any prior peacetime debt and generating much public concern. However, in the twenty-first century, deficit spending and the national debt has skyrocketed well past previous records.

The president further reshaped American politics through his nominations to the U.S. Supreme Court. Starting with the choice of Sandra Day O'Connor, the Court's first female justice, in 1981, Reagan's appointments moved the Court in a more conservative direction. The elevation of Associate Justice William Rehnquist to chief justice in 1986 reinforced this trend, which would have significant consequences for decades to come.

AP® EXAM TIP

The 1980 election marked a turning point from the liberal, Democratic policies of the 1960s and 1970s to the conservative, laissez-faire policies of Reagan. During this time period, the economy was making a transition from traditional industry and manufacturing to a dependence on technology. Be able to explain the causes and effects of these changes.

REVIEW

- To what extent did Reaganomics represent a change in federal economic policy in the United States since the 1950s?

Social Conservatism

Throughout his two terms, President Reagan's policies aligned with the New Right's social agenda. Conservatives blamed political liberalism for what they saw as a decline in family values. Their solution was a renewed focus on conservative Christian principles. In addition to trying to remove evolution and sex education from public school classrooms and bring in voluntary prayer, the New Right stepped up its opposition to abortion and worked to restrict access to birth control. The Reagan administration required family planning agencies seeking federal funding to notify parents of children under age eighteen before dispensing birth control, ceased financial aid to international organizations supporting abortion, and provided funds to promote sexual abstinence. While conservatives succeeded in blocking ratification of the Equal Rights Amendment when it failed to get the required two-thirds approval from the states in 1982, they were unable at the time to convince the Supreme Court to overturn *Roe v. Wade*.

AP® WORKING with EVIDENCE

Source: Senate Testimony by Susan Baker [wife of Treasury Secretary James Baker] and Tipper Gore [wife of Senator and later Vice President Al Gore], members of the Parents Music Resource Center, September 19, 1985

> "Mrs. BAKER. The Parents Music Resource Center was organized in May of this year by mothers of young children who are very concerned by the growing trend in music toward lyrics that are sexually explicit, excessively violent, or glorify the use of drugs and alcohol.
>
> Our primary purpose is to educate and inform parents about this alarming trend as well as to ask the industry to exercise self-restraint. . . .
>
> While a few outrageous recordings have always existed in the past, the proliferation of songs glorifying rape, sadomasochism, incest, the occult, and suicide by a growing number of bands illustrates this escalating trend that is alarming. . . .
>
> Some say there is no cause for concern. We believe there is. Teen pregnancies and teenage suicide rates are at epidemic proportions today. The Noedecker Report states that in the United States of America we have the highest teen pregnancy rate of any developed country: 96 out of 1,000 teenage girls become pregnant.
>
> Rape is up 7 percent in the latest statistics, and the suicide rates of youth between 16 and 24 has gone up 300 percent in the last three decades while the adult level has remained the same.
>
> There certainly are many causes for these ills in our society, but it is our contention that the pervasive messages aimed at children which promote and glorify suicide, rape, sadomasochism, and so on, have to be numbered among the contributing factors. . . .
>
> Mrs. GORE. We are asking the recording industry to voluntarily assist parents who are concerned by placing a warning label on music products inappropriate for younger children due to explicit sexual or violent lyrics. . . .
>
> We have asked the record companies to voluntarily label their own products and assume responsibility for making those judgments. We ask the record industry to appoint a one-time panel to recommend a uniform set of criteria which could serve as a policy guide for the individual companies. Those individual recording companies would then in good faith agree to adhere to this standard, and make decisions internally about which records should be labeled according to the industry criteria."

Questions for Analysis

1. Identify the effects attributed to negative music lyrics.
2. Describe how the testimony attempts to build a case for music warning labels.
3. Explain the political and social context of the document.
4. Evaluate the extent to which the proposed solution reflects the conservative ideology prevalent in the 1980s.

acquired immune deficiency syndrome (AIDS)
An immune disorder caused by the human immunodeficiency virus (HIV) that reached epidemic proportions in the United States in the 1980s, especially among gay men and drug users.

Social conservatives also opposed more tolerant views of homosexuality. The gay-rights movement, which began in the 1960s, strengthened during the 1970s as thousands of gay men and lesbians made known their sexual orientation, fought discrimination, and expressed pride in their sexual identity.

Then, in the early 1980s, physicians traced an outbreak of a deadly illness among gay men to a virus that attacked the immune system (human immunodeficiency virus, or HIV), making it vulnerable to infections that were usually fatal. This disease, called **acquired immune deficiency syndrome (AIDS)**, was

AP Images/J. Scott Applewhite

ACT UP Protest, 1988 Amid the AIDS epidemic in the gay community, the militant group AIDS Coalition to Unleash Power (ACT UP) campaigned for better funding of programs to fight the disease. This photo shows ACT UP protesters blocking the entrance to the headquarters of the Food and Drug Administration (FDA) in Rockville, Maryland, on October 11, 1988.

What reforms did these activists seek?

transmitted through bodily fluids during sexual intercourse, through blood transfusions, and by drug users sharing needles or equipment.

Scientists could not explain why the disease initially showed up among gay men in the United States. Some members of the religious right believed that AIDS was a plague visited on sexual deviants by an angry God. As the epidemic spread beyond the gay community, gay-rights organizers and their heterosexual allies raised research money and public awareness. By the early 1990s, medical advances had begun to extend the lives of AIDS patients and manage the disease.

Increased immigration also troubled social conservatives as another reflection of what they viewed as a culture undergoing troubling change. The number of immigrants to the United States rose dramatically in the 1970s and 1980s following the relaxation of quota restrictions after 1965. During these decades, immigrants came mainly from Mexico, Central America, the Caribbean, and eastern and southern Asia and tended to settle in California, Florida, Texas, New York, and New Jersey. Like those who came nearly a century before, most sought economic opportunity, political freedom, and escape from wars. By 1990, one-third of Los Angeles's

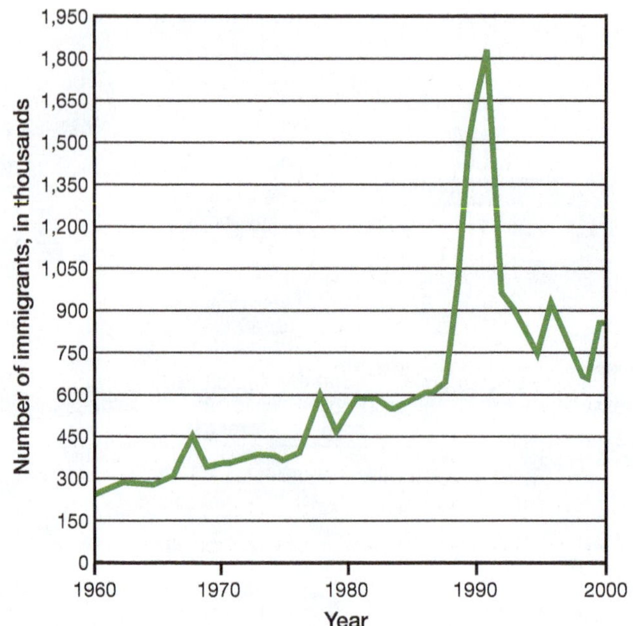

Immigrant Arrivals to the United States, 1960–2000 Immigration to the United States rose dramatically in the 1970s and 1980s, peaking in the early 1990s. Between 1970 and 2000, nearly 21 million immigrants arrived in the United States, mainly from Mexico, Central America, the Caribbean, and eastern Asia. **How do these immigration trends compare to those during the late 1800s and early 1900s?**

and New York City's populations was foreign-born, figures similar to the high numbers of European immigrants at the turn of the twentieth century.

As happened during previous immigration waves, many Americans whose ancestors had immigrated to the United States generations earlier expressed hostility toward the new immigrants. Some members in the New Right provoked traditional fears that immigrants took away jobs and depressed wages, and questioned whether these culturally diverse people could assimilate into American society, while other conservatives argued that immigration was a hallmark of American history and provided a dedicated and inexpensive workforce for the economy.

In 1986, Reagan departed from many of his conservative anti-immigrant supporters and, with bipartisan congressional support, fashioned a compromise that extended amnesty to undocumented aliens residing in the United States for a specified period and allowed them to acquire legal status. At the same time, the **Immigration Reform and Control Act** penalized employers who hired new undocumented workers. The measure allowed Reagan and the Republicans to appeal to Latino voters in the Sun Belt states while convincing the New Right that the administration intended to halt further undocumented immigration.

Immigration Reform and Control Act
A 1986 act legalizing long-term immigrants while also strengthening immigration restrictions. The law extended amnesty to most undocumented immigrants living in the United States continually since before 1982, and penalized employers who hired undocumented immigrants.

REVIEW

- What were the primary social concerns of the New Right?
- How were these concerns a reaction to cultural changes dating from the 1960s?

"Kinder and Gentler" Conservatism

After Reagan left office, his vice president, George H. W. Bush, received the Republican nomination to replace him. While sharing most of Reagan's views, Bush called for a "kinder, gentler nation" in dealing with social justice and the environment.

In his 1988 presidential campaign against Michael Dukakis, the Democratic governor of Massachusetts, Bush defended conservative principles when he promised, "Read my lips: No new taxes." The Republican candidate attacked Dukakis for his liberal positions and accused him of being soft on crime. Bush also affirmed his own opposition to abortion and support for gun rights and the death penalty, in part to convince conservative Republicans that he would be a faithful heir of the Reagan legacy. Bush easily defeated Dukakis in the general election, demonstrating the rightward electoral shift ushered in by Reagan.

Once in office, Bush had to deal with several economic challenges. Tax cuts and increased military spending had left the nation with a mounting federal budget deficit that slowed economic growth, resulting in another recession in 1990. Unemployment rose from 5.3 percent in 1989, when Bush took office, to 7.5 percent by 1992. State and local governments had difficulty paying for the educational, health, and social services that the Reagan and Bush administrations had transferred to them. In 1990, to improve economic conditions, Bush supported a deficit reduction package that included more than $130 billion in new taxes, which angered many Americans who had voted for him.

Despite opposition from some fellow conservatives, Bush signed the **Americans with Disabilities Act (ADA)** in 1990, extending a range of protections to some 40 million Americans with physical and mental disabilities. The act provided protections against discrimination similar to those in the landmark Civil Rights Act of 1964, requiring employers and municipalities to provide accommodations so as to offer disabled Americans equal opportunity under the law.

Americans with Disabilities Act (ADA)
The landmark 1990 legislation banning discrimination due to disability. The law extended legal protections and accessibility mandates for Americans with physical and mental disabilities.

Bush supported some domestic environmental legislation, while he opposed some international efforts to regulate the environment. In 1989, the oil tanker *Exxon Valdez* struck a reef off the coast of Alaska, dumping nearly 11 million gallons of oil into Prince William Sound. This disaster created pressure for stricter environmental legislation. The president signed the **Clean Air Act of 1990**, which reduced emissions from automobiles and power plants. In 1992, however, Bush opposed international efforts to limit carbon dioxide emissions, **greenhouse gases** that contribute to climate change.

Clean Air Act of 1990
An act that set new standards to reduce car and power plant emissions to address the problems of acid rain, air pollution, and ozone depletion.

greenhouse gas
Any atmospheric gas that absorbs energy from the sun and other radiant sources, which warm the Earth. The increased emissions of greenhouse gases, especially carbon dioxide and methane, by human activity is a main cause of global warming and climate change.

In 1991, Bush nominated Clarence Thomas to fill the Supreme Court vacancy left by Justice Thurgood Marshall, the first Black justice. Thomas belonged to a rising group of conservative Black Americans who shared Republican views supporting private enterprise and the free market system and opposing affirmative action. He had previously served as chief of the Equal Employment Opportunity Commission (EEOC) under President Reagan. He also opposed abortion and welfare. During the course of Thomas's Senate confirmation hearing, Anita Hill, a law professor who had worked as Thomas's assistant at the EEOC, testified before the Senate Judiciary Committee and a nationally televised audience that Thomas had made unwanted sexual advances to her on and off the job, which she quit in 1983.

Hill's charges of sexual harassment upended the hearings and riveted the nation, but the Senate ultimately confirmed Thomas's nomination to the Supreme Court. Nevertheless, membership in women's political associations — such as Emily's List, founded in 1984, and the Fund for a Feminist Majority, founded in 1987 — soared following Hill's testimony. In the 1992 midterm elections, more women were elected to the House of Representatives than in any previous election, and the number of women in the Senate increased, from two members in 1991 to eight in 1993. While this unprecedented "Year of the Woman" was a product of many long-term cultural and social trends, Hill's testimony placed women's struggle for equal rights at the forefront of public consciousness at a key moment in American history.

Shutterstock

Anita Hill Testifies against the Supreme Court Nomination of Clarence Thomas, 1991
Anita Hill is sworn in to testify before the Senate Judiciary Committee on the confirmation of Clarence Thomas to the U.S. Supreme Court by chairman Joseph Biden, a Democrat from Delaware, on October 11, 1991. Hill claimed Thomas had sexually harassed her when she worked for him in the early 1980s. There were no women serving on the Judiciary Committee at that time.

To what extent did the process and outcome of Hill's testimony reflect both continuity and change in American politics?

REVIEW

- How did President George H. W. Bush's domestic policies differ from the economic and social policies of the Reagan administration?

AP® Skills Workshop: Writing Historically

Additional Practice in Responding to a Long-Essay Question

Evaluate the extent to which debates over cultural and social values shaped U.S. politics in the 1980s.

The End of the Cold War

MODULE
9.3

FOCUS

While reading this module, analyze the factors that led to the end of the Cold War and how the end of the Cold War impacted U.S. foreign relations.

Conservatives came to power amid major changes occurring in foreign affairs, most notably the intensification and then the ending of the Cold War. President Reagan, a charismatic and determined anticommunist crusader, together with his pragmatic and influential secretary of state, George Shultz, guided the United States through a policy of heightened military preparedness to push the Soviet Union toward peace. The policy worked; diplomacy rather than armed conflict prevailed.

Reagan's Cold War strategy succeeded in part because during the 1980s, a leader amenable to peace, Mikhail Gorbachev, governed the Soviet Union. He envisioned the end of the Cold War as a means of bringing political and economic reform to his beleaguered and bankrupt nation. What Reagan and Gorbachev began, their successors, George H. W. Bush and Boris Yeltsin, completed: The Cold War came to a conclusion, and the Soviet Union dismantled its empire and incorporated a measure of democracy and capitalism into Russia.

Reagan and the Cold War, 1981–1988

As Ronald Reagan entered the White House determined to pose a direct challenge to liberalism, so too did he intend to confront the Soviets. Reagan and Secretary of State George Shultz believed that détente would become feasible only after the United States achieved military supremacy over the Soviet Union, summed up in an approach Reagan referred to as "peace through strength." Reagan also took vigorous measures to fight communism around the globe, from Central America to the Middle East.

Military superiority was not the only reason for the defeat the Soviet Union. A shift of leadership within the U.S.S.R., as well as a worldwide protest movement for nuclear disarmament, helped bring an end to the Cold War and prepare the way for the dissolution of the Soviet empire.

In running for president in 1980, Reagan wrapped his anticommunist message in the rhetoric of peace. "I've called for whatever it takes to be so strong that no other nation will dare violate the peace," he told the Veterans of Foreign Wars Convention on August 18, 1980. Once in the White House, Reagan left no doubt about his anticommunist stance. He called the Soviet Union "the evil empire," regarding it as "the focus of evil in the modern world." The president planned to confront that evil with both words and deeds, backing up his rhetoric with a massive military buildup.

In a show of moral and economic might, Reagan proposed the largest military budget in American history. The defense budget grew by about 7 percent per year, increasing from $157 billion in 1981 to around $282 billion in 1988.

AP® WORKING with EVIDENCE

Source: Ronald Reagan, *Tear Down This Wall* (speech at the Berlin Wall), 1987

> "[W]e hear much from Moscow about a new policy of reform and openness. Some political prisoners have been released. Certain foreign news broadcasts are no longer being jammed. Some economic enterprises have been permitted to operate with greater freedom from state control. Are these the beginnings of profound changes in the Soviet state? Or are they token gestures, intended to raise false hopes in the West, or to strengthen the Soviet system without changing it? We welcome change and openness; for we believe that freedom and security go together, that the advance of human liberty can only strengthen the cause of world peace.
>
> There is one sign the Soviets can make that would be unmistakable, that would advance dramatically the cause of freedom and peace. General Secretary Gorbachev, if you seek peace, if you seek prosperity for the Soviet Union and Eastern Europe, if you seek liberalization: Come here to this gate! Mr. Gorbachev, open this gate! Mr. Gorbachev, tear down this wall!"

Questions for Analysis

1. Identify the signs of a change in Soviet policy that Reagan notes in this speech.
2. Identify what conditions Reagan believes must be met to be convinced these changes are permanent.
3. Describe the significance of the "wall" that Reagan refers to.
4. Evaluate the extent to which this speech reflects a shift in American attitudes toward the Cold War and the Soviets.

Strategic Defense Initiative (SDI)

A proposal first announced by Ronald Reagan in 1983 to build a missile defense system that would use satellite lasers to protect the United States from nuclear attack by shooting down enemy missiles. The initiative was never completed.

Strategic Arms Reduction Talks (START)

Arms-control negotiations between the United States and the Soviet Union that began in 1982 with the goal of significantly reducing existing missiles and warheads rather than simply slowing the growth of nuclear stockpiles as the SALT negotiations had done in the 1970s. The Soviets abandoned the talks in 1983 after the United States deployed new, intermediate-range missiles in Europe. Talks resumed in 1985, leading to the first START agreement in 1991.

The president also sought to develop new weapons to be deployed in outer space. He proposed the **Strategic Defense Initiative (SDI)**, which in theory would use space-based lasers to shoot down enemy missiles. Critics dubbed this program "Star Wars." The SDI was never carried out, though the government spent $17 billion on research.

Reagan was unyielding in his initial dealings with the Soviet Union, and negotiations between the superpowers moved slowly and unevenly. The Reagan administration's initial "zero option" proposal called for the Soviets to dismantle all of their intermediate-range missiles in exchange for the United States agreeing to refrain from deploying any new medium-range missiles.

The administration expected the Soviets to reject the "zero option" proposal. However, in 1982, after the Soviets accepted the principle, Reagan sent negotiators to begin **Strategic Arms Reduction Talks (START)**. Influenced by antinuclear protests in Europe, which had a great impact on European governments, the Americans proposed shelving the deployment of 572 Pershing II and cruise missiles in Europe in return for the Soviets' dismantling of Eastern European–based intermediate-range ballistic missiles that were targeted at Western Europe. The Soviets viewed this offer as perpetuating American nuclear superiority and rejected it.

Relations between the two superpowers deteriorated in September 1983, when a Soviet fighter jet shot down a South Korean passenger airliner that had accidentally flown into Soviet airspace, killing 269 people. In reaction, the United States sent additional missiles to bases in West Germany, Great Britain, and Italy. In response, the Soviets abandoned the disarmament talks and replenished their nuclear arsenal in Czechoslovakia and East Germany. More symbolically, the Soviets boycotted the 1984 Olympic

Games in Los Angeles, in retaliation for the U.S. boycott of the Olympics in Moscow four years earlier. As the two adversaries swung from peace talks to threats of nuclear confrontation, one European journalist observed: "The second Cold War has begun."

REVIEW

- How did Reagan administration policies affect the relationship between the United States and the U.S.S.R.?

Human Rights and the Fight against Communism

The Reagan administration extended its firm Cold War position throughout the world. The president saw threats of Soviet intervention in Central America and the Middle East, and he aimed to contain them. During the 1980s, the United States continued its economic isolation of Cuba via a trade embargo, and it sought to prevent other communist or leftist governments from emerging in Central America and the Caribbean.

In the late 1970s, Nicaraguan revolutionaries, known as the National Liberation Front or **Sandinistas**, overthrew the government of General Anastasio Somoza Debayle, a brutal dictator. President Jimmy Carter, who had originally supported Somoza's overthrow, halted all aid to Nicaragua in 1980 after the Sandinistas began nationalizing foreign companies and drawing closer to Cuba.

Under Reagan, Secretary of State Shultz suggested a U.S. invasion of Nicaragua, reflecting the administration's belief that the revolution in Nicaragua had been sponsored by Moscow. Instead, Reagan adopted a more indirect approach. In 1982, he authorized the CIA to train approximately two thousand guerrillas outside the country, known as **Contras** (counterrevolutionaries), to overthrow the Sandinista government. The group consisted of former Somoza supporters as well as anti-Marxist democrats who blew up bridges and oil dumps, burned crops, and killed civilians.

Contras
Nicaraguan counterrevolutionaries, trained by the CIA, who fought to overthrow the new Sandinista government in Nicaragua during the 1980s. Their use of terrorism and violation of human rights led the U.S. Congress to prohibit funding the efforts of the Contras.

Boland Amendment
An amendment to a 1982 bill in Congress prohibiting direct aid to the Nicaraguan Contra forces in response to the human rights violations and terrorist activities of the Contras. In 1984 a second Boland Amendment further restricted assistance to the Contras.

Congress, unwilling to support such actions, passed the **Boland Amendment**, which prohibited direct aid to the Contras, in 1982. In the face of congressional opposition, Reagan and his advisers developed a plan that would secretly fund the efforts of the Contras. The CIA and the National Security Council (NSC) raised money from anticommunist leaders abroad and wealthy conservatives at home. This effort, called "Project Democracy," raised millions of dollars, and by 1985, the number of Contra troops had swelled from 10,000 to 20,000. In violation of federal law, CIA director William Casey also authorized his agency to continue training the Contras in assassination techniques and other methods of subversion.

Elsewhere in Central America, the Reagan administration supported a government in El Salvador that, in an effort to put down an insurgency, sanctioned military death squads and killed forty thousand people during the 1980s. In reaction, the Reagan administration maintained that communist regimes in Nicaragua and Cuba were behind the Salvadoran insurgents. The United States sent more than $5 billion in aid to El Salvador and trained its military leaders to combat guerrilla forces.

Civil wars in Central America drove many people to flee their dangerous, poverty-stricken countries and seek asylum in the United States. Between 1984 and 1990, 45,000 Salvadorans and 9,500 Guatemalans applied for asylum in the United States, but because the United States supported the regimes in those two nations, nearly all requests for refugee status were denied. Approximately five hundred American churches and synagogues established a sanctuary movement to provide safe haven for those fleeing Central American civil wars. Other Americans, especially in California and Texas, began to view the influx of refugees from Central America with alarm. This immigration, both legal and illegal, meant an increase in medical and educational costs for state and local communities, which some taxpayers considered a burden.

invasion of Grenada
A U.S. led invasion in coalition with six Caribbean governments that installed a pro-American government after a 1983 coup toppled the Caribbean island's leftist, Soviet-supported government.

In addition to providing financial support for pro-American governments in Central America, the United States sent 7,000 marines on October 25, 1983, to invade the Caribbean island-nation of Grenada. After a coup toppled the leftist government of Maurice Bishop, who had received Cuban and Soviet aid, the United States stepped in, ostensibly to protect American medical school students in Grenada from political instability following the coup and to prevent a possible hostage crisis. A pro-American government was installed, and general elections were held the next year. The brief **invasion of Grenada** boosted Reagan's popularity.

apartheid
A legal and institutionalized system of discrimination and segregation based on white supremacy and racial separation in South Africa from 1948 until 1994.

Reagan's firm stance against communism extended around the world, and his administration supported repressive, antidemocratic governments in the Middle East, Asia, Latin America, and Africa. Reagan's ambassador to the United Nations, Jeane Kirkpatrick, explained this foreign policy strategy as one that distinguished between noncommunist "authoritarian" nations, which were acceptable, and communist "totalitarian" regimes, which were not.

Comprehensive Anti-Apartheid Act
An act passed in 1986 prohibiting new trade and investment in South Africa because of apartheid. President Reagan vetoed the act, but Congress overrode his veto.

The South African government was an example of acceptable authoritarianism during the Cold War, even though it practiced **apartheid** (white supremacy and racial separation). The fact that the South African Communist Party had joined the fight against apartheid led the Reagan administration to support the racist, white-minority, anticommunist government. In response, some protesters across the United States and the world spoke out against South Africa's government and campaigned for divestment of public and corporate funds from South African companies. After years of pressure from the divestment movement on college campuses and elsewhere, Congress in 1986 passed the **Comprehensive Anti-Apartheid Act**, which prohibited new trade and investment in South Africa. President Reagan vetoed it, but Congress overrode the president's veto.

David Lyons

Anti-Apartheid Protest, Cornell University In 1986, students on college campuses such as Cornell protested apartheid in South Africa. They constructed shantytowns to highlight the poverty of nonwhite South Africans. Their immediate goal was to persuade their universities to remove their investments in companies that did business in South Africa.

Explain how these protest movements drew inspiration from the protest movements in the 1960s and 1970s.

■ How did anticommunism shape Reagan's foreign policy?

Fighting International Terrorism

Two days before the Grenada invasion in 1983, the U.S. military suffered a grievous blow halfway around the world. In the tiny country of Lebanon, wedged between Syrian occupation along its eastern border and the fight by the **Palestine Liberation Organization (PLO)** against Israel to the south, a civil war raged between Christians and Muslims. Reagan believed that stability in the region was in the U.S. national interest. With this in mind, the Reagan administration sent 800 marines in 1982, as part of a multilateral force that included French and Italian troops, to keep the peace. On October 23, 1983, a suicide bomber drove a truck into a marine barracks, killing 241 U.S. soldiers. Reagan withdrew the remaining troops the next year.

Palestine Liberation Organization (PLO)
A movement founded in 1964 with the goal of achieving Palestinian independence from Israel, through armed force if necessary. For many years, the PLO was considered a terrorist organization by the U.S. government.

terrorism
The use of violence to inspire fear in service of achieving a political goal.

The removal of troops did not end threats to Americans in the Middle East. **Terrorism**, the attempt by non-state groups or organizations to foster political change by spreading fear through violence that often targets civilians, had become an ever-present danger, especially since the Iranian hostage crisis in 1979–1980. In 1985, 17 American citizens were killed in terrorist assaults, and 154 were injured. In June 1985, Shi'ite Muslim extremists hijacked a TWA airliner in Athens with 39 Americans on board and flew it to Beirut. The hijackers beat several passengers and executed U.S. navy diver Robert Stethem. That same year, commandos of the Palestine Liberation Organization hijacked the Italian ocean liner *Achille Lauro*, which was cruising from Egypt to Israel. One of the 450 passengers, the wheelchair-bound, elderly Jewish American Leon Klinghoffer, was murdered and thrown overboard. After three days, Egyptian authorities negotiated an end to the terrorist hijacking.

In response to the 1985 PLO cruise-ship attack, the Reagan administration retaliated against the North African country of Libya by expanding sanctions against the country and freezing its assets in the United States. Its military leader, Muammar al-Qaddafi, supported the Palestinian cause and provided sanctuary for terrorists. The Reagan administration had placed a trade embargo on Libya, and Secretary of State Shultz remarked: "We have to put Qaddafi in a box and close the lid." In 1986, after the bombing of a nightclub in West Berlin killed two American servicemen and injured 230, the Reagan administration held Qaddafi responsible. In late April, the United States responded by sending planes to bomb the Libyan capital of Tripoli. Following the bombing, Qaddafi took a much lower profile against the United States. Reagan had demonstrated his nation's military might despite the retreat from Lebanon (**Map 9.2** on page 990).

In the meantime, the situation in Lebanon remained critical when strife caused by civil war led to the seizing of American hostages. By mid-1984, seven Americans in Lebanon had been kidnapped by Shi'ite Muslims financed by Iran. Since 1980, Iran, a Shi'ite nation, had been engaged in a protracted war with Iraq, which was ruled by military leader Saddam Hussein and his Sunni Muslim Ba'ath Party, the chief rival to the Shi'ites. Because relations between the United States and Iran had deteriorated badly in the aftermath of the 1979 Iranian Revolution, the Reagan administration backed Iraq in this war.

The fate of the hostages in Lebanon, however, motivated the Reagan administration to make a deal with Iran. In late 1985, Reagan's national security adviser, Robert McFarlane, negotiated secretly with an Iranian intermediary for the United States to sell antitank missiles to Iran in exchange for the Shi'ite government using its influence to induce the kidnappers to release the hostages.

MAP 9.2 The United States in the Middle East, 1978–1991 The United States has historically needed access to the rich oil reserves of the Middle East. From the 1970s to the 1990s, both Democratic and Republican administrations were committed to the security of Israel, supportive of Afghan rebels fighting Soviet invaders, and opposed to the rising power of Islamic regimes.

 **According to this map, which Middle Eastern nations stood the greatest chance of affecting U.S. policy through control of oil distribution?**

Had the matter ended there, the secret deal might never have come to light. However, National Security Council (NSC) aide Lieutenant Colonel Oliver North developed a plan to transfer the proceeds from the arms-for-hostages deal to fund the Contras in Nicaragua, a violation of the Boland Amendment, which prohibited direct aid to the rebels.

Iran-Contra affair
A scandal during the Reagan administration involving the secret funneling of funds from an illegal arms-for-hostages deal with Iran to the Nicaraguan Contras in the mid-1980s in violation of the Boland Amendment.

In 1986 information about the **Iran-Contra affair** came to light. In the summer of 1987, televised Senate hearings exposed much of the tangled, covert dealings with Iran. In 1988, an appointed independent counsel, Lawrence Walsh, indicted NSC adviser Vice Admiral John Poindexter (who had replaced McFarlane), North, and several others on charges ranging from perjury to conspiracy to obstruction of justice. Reagan took responsibility for the transfer of funds to the Contras and weathered the political crisis. His vice president and successor, George H. W. Bush, later pardoned many of those involved in the scandal.

REVIEW

- How did terrorism affect the Reagan administration's policy in the Middle East?

The Road to Nuclear De-Escalation

Rising protests against nuclear weapons in the United States and Europe in the early 1980s revealed a public increasingly anxious about the possibility of nuclear confrontation with the Soviet Union. At the end of the Carter administration, the United States had promised NATO that it would station new missiles in England, Italy, West Germany, and Belgium. Coupled with his firm stance against the Soviet Union, Reagan's decision to implement this policy sparked protests.

Activities such as the Women's Encampment for a Future of Peace and Justice were part of a larger **nuclear freeze movement** that began in 1980. Its proponents called for a "mutual freeze on the testing, production, and deployment of nuclear weapons and of missiles and aircraft designed primarily to deliver nuclear weapons." Grassroots activists also held town meetings throughout the United States to mobilize ordinary citizens to speak out against nuclear proliferation. In 1982, some 750,000 people rallied in New York City's Central Park to support a nuclear freeze resolution presented at the United Nations. Despite opposition from the United States and its NATO allies, measures favoring the freeze passed in the UN General Assembly. According to a 1982 public opinion poll, 57 percent of Americans favored an immediate nuclear freeze. While a nuclear freeze never materialized, the freeze movement inside and outside the United States pressured both sides to negotiate toward nuclear disarmament, a development which did occur by the end of the decade.

nuclear freeze movement
Protests in the 1980s calling for a halt to the testing, production, and deployment of missiles and aircraft designed primarily to deliver nuclear weapons.

Ronald Reagan won reelection in 1984 by a landslide. Following his victory, the president softened his stance and became more amenable to negotiating with the U.S.S.R. It took a president with impeccable credentials in fighting communism, like Nixon's détente with China in the 1970s, to reduce Cold War conflicts. Reagan espoused conservative principles during his presidency, but he refused to let rigid dogma interfere with more pragmatic considerations to foster peace. By the time President Reagan left office, little remained of the Cold War.

In the mid-1980s, powerful changes were sweeping through the Soviet Union, which also helped bring the Cold War to a close. In September 1985, Mikhail Gorbachev became general secretary of the Communist Party and head of the Soviet Union. Gorbachev introduced a program of economic and political reform. Through ***glasnost*** (openness) and ***perestroika*** (restructuring), the Soviet leader hoped to reduce heavy-handed state control over the declining economy and to extend democratic elections and freedom of speech and freedom of the press. Gorbachev understood that the success of his reforms depended on reducing Cold War tensions with the United States and

glasnost
A policy of political "openness" initiated by Soviet leader Mikhail Gorbachev in the 1980s. Under *glasnost*, the Soviet Union began a transition to democratic elections, freedom of speech, and freedom of the press.

perestroika
A policy of economic "restructuring" initiated by Soviet leader Mikhail Gorbachev. Gorbachev hoped that by reducing state control, he could revive the Soviet economy.

AP Images/Jim McKnight

Women's Peace Encampment Vigil On October 24, 1983, protesters from the Women's Encampment for a Future of Peace and Justice held a candlelight vigil outside the Seneca Army Depot in Romulus, New York. Originally organized by feminist women, the protests also drew men. Together, they campaigned to shut down the base, which was used as a munitions storage and disposal facility. In 1995, the military closed the depot.

In what ways did the Women's Encampment for a Future of Peace and Justice show both continuity and change from the American antiwar movement from the 1960s and 1970s?

slowing the arms race that was bankrupting the Soviet economy. Gorbachev's *glasnost* even brought the popular American musical performer Billy Joel to the Soviet Union in August 1987, staging the first rock concert in the country.

The changes that Gorbachev brought to the internal affairs of the Soviet Union carried over to the international arena. From 1986 to 1988, the Soviet leader negotiated in person with the American president, something that had not happened during Reagan's first term.

Intermediate Nuclear Forces Treaty
A 1987 treaty between the United States and the Soviet Union that required the destruction of existing intermediate-range missiles and mandated on-site inspections to ensure both countries continued to adhere to the treaty terms.

In 1986, at a summit in Reykjavik, Iceland, the two leaders agreed to cut the number of strategic nuclear missiles in half. In 1987, the two sides negotiated an **Intermediate Nuclear Forces Treaty**, which provided for the destruction of existing intermediate-range missiles and on-site inspections to ensure compliance. The height of détente came in December 1987, when Gorbachev traveled to the United States to take part in the treaty-signing ceremony and impressed Americans with his personal charm and by demonstrating the media savvy associated with American politicians. The following year, Reagan flew to the Soviet Union and hugged Gorbachev at the tomb of the founder of the U.S.S.R., Vladimir Lenin. He later told reporters, "They've changed," referring to the once and not-so-distant "evil empire." Citizens of the two adversarial nations breathed a collective sigh of relief. At long last, the icy terrain of the Cold War appeared to be melting.

REVIEW

- What factors led the Cold War to thaw during the late 1980s?

The Breakup of the Soviet Union

When George H. W. Bush became president in 1989, he encountered a Soviet Union that differed greatly from the country Ronald Reagan had faced at the start of the decade. The U.S.S.R. was undergoing an internal revolution, which allowed Bush and the United States to take on a new role in a world that was no longer divided between capitalist and communist nations and their allies.

Bush's first year in office coincided with upheavals in the Soviet-controlled communist bloc in eastern Europe, with Poland leading the way. In 1980, Polish dockworker Lech Walesa had organized **Solidarity**, a trade-union movement that conducted a series of popular strikes that forced the communist government to recognize the group. Solidarity had ten million members and attracted various opponents of the communist regime, including working-class democrats, Catholics, and nationalists who favored breaking ties with the Soviet Union.

Solidarity
Polish trade-union movement led by Lech Walesa. During the 1980s, Solidarity played a central role in ending communist rule in Poland.

The following year, Soviet leaders, disturbed by Solidarity's growing strength, had forced the Polish government to crack down on the organization, arrest Walesa, and ban Solidarity. In 1989, though, Walesa and Solidarity were still active and seized on the changes ushered in by Mikhail Gorbachev's *glasnost* in the U.S.S.R. to press their demands for democracy in Poland. This time, the Soviets refused to intervene, and Poland conducted its first free elections since the beginning of the Cold War, electing Walesa as president of the country. In July 1989, Gorbachev further broke from the past and announced that the Soviet Union would respect the national sovereignty of all the nations in the Warsaw Pact, which the Soviet Union had controlled since the late 1940s.

Gorbachev's proclamation spurred the end of communism throughout Eastern Europe. Within the next year, Soviet-sponsored regimes fell peacefully in Hungary and Czechoslovakia, replaced by elected governments. Bulgaria held free elections, which brought reformers to power. Only in Romania did Communist rulers put up a fight. There, it took a violent popular uprising to topple the brutal dictator Nicolae Ceaușescu.

The Baltic states of Latvia, Lithuania, and Estonia, which the Soviets had incorporated into the U.S.S.R. at the outset of World War II, also regained their independence, sparking the political breakup of the Soviet Union itself.

Perhaps the most striking symbolism in the dismantling of the Soviet empire came in Germany, a country that had been divided into two states since 1945. With Communist governments collapsing around them, East Germans demonstrated against the regime of Erich Honecker. With no Soviet help forthcoming, Honecker decided to open the border between East and West Germany. On November 9, 1989, East and West Germans flocked to the Berlin Wall and jubilantly joined workers in knocking down the concrete barricade that divided the city. A year later, East and West Germany were reunified under the democratic, capitalist government of West Germany, formally known as the Federal Republic of Germany.

WORKING with EVIDENCE

Source: Francis Fukuyama, *The End of History?*, 1989

> "In watching the flow of events over the past decade or so, it is hard to avoid the feeling that something very fundamental has happened in world history. The past year has seen a flood of articles commemorating the end of the Cold War, and the fact that 'peace' seems to be breaking out in many regions of the world. Most of these analyses lack any larger conceptual framework for distinguishing between what is essential and what is contingent or accidental in world history, and are predictably superficial. If Mr. Gorbachev were ousted from the Kremlin or a new Ayatollah proclaimed the millennium for a desolate Middle Eastern capital, these same commentators would scramble to announce the rebirth of a new era of conflict. . . .
>
> What we may be witnessing . . . [is] not just the end of the Cold War, or the passing of a particular period of post-war history, but the end of history as such: that is, the end point of mankind's ideological evolution and the universalization of Western liberal democracy as the final form of human government. This is not to say that there will no longer be events to fill the pages of *Foreign Affairs*'s yearly summaries of international relations, for the victory of liberalism has occurred primarily in the realm of ideas or consciousness and is as yet incomplete in the real or material world. But there are powerful reasons for believing that it is the ideal that will govern the material world in the long run."

Questions for Analysis

1. Identify the signs of change Fukuyama perceives in the world.
2. Explain the significance of these changes, according to Fukuyama.
3. Evaluate the extent to which the changes Fukuyama names were brought about by the policies of the United States.

Gorbachev also brought an end to the costly nine-year Soviet-Afghan War. When the Soviets withdrew their last troops on February 15, 1989, they left Afghanistan in shambles. One million Afghans had perished, and another five million fled the country for Pakistan and Iran, resulting in the political destabilization of Afghanistan.

Following a civil war, the **Taliban**, a group of Sunni Muslim fundamentalists, came to power in the mid-1990s and established a theocratic regime that, among other things, strictly regulated what women could wear in public and denied them educational and professional opportunities. The Taliban also provided sanctuary for many of the **mujahideen** rebels who had fought against the Soviets, including Osama bin

Taliban
A militant movement of radical Sunni Muslim fundamentalists that ruled Afghanistan in the mid-1990s. The Taliban established a strict theocracy and allowed al-Qaeda, a Sunni Muslim terrorist organization, to establish a base of operations in the country. The Taliban returned to power in Afghanistan in 2021.

al-Qaeda
An Islamic terrorist organization founded by Osama bin Laden in the late 1980s during the Soviet invasion of Afghanistan. Al-Qaeda is a loosely organized, radical religious fundamentalist organization, which opposes westernization and orchestrated the September 11, 2001, attacks on the United States.

Laden, who would use the country as a base for his **al-Qaeda** organization to promote terrorism against the United States.

Meanwhile, the Soviet Union disintegrated. Free elections were held in 1990, which ironically threatened Gorbachev's own power by bringing noncommunists to local and national political offices. Although an advocate of economic reform and political openness, Gorbachev remained a communist and was committed to preserving the U.S.S.R. Challenges to Gorbachev came from both ends of the political spectrum. Boris Yeltsin, his former protégé, led the noncommunist forces that wanted Gorbachev to move more quickly in adopting capitalism. On the other side, hard-line generals in the Soviet army disapproved of Gorbachev's reforms and his cooperation with the United States.

On August 18, 1991, a group of hard-core conspirators staged a coup against Gorbachev, placed him under house arrest, and surrounded the parliament building with troops. Yeltsin, the president of the Russian Republic, rallied fellow legislators and Muscovites against the plotters and brought the uprising to a peaceful end. Several months later, in early December, Yeltsin and the leaders of the independent republics of Belarus and Ukraine formed the Commonwealth of Independent States (CIS), consisting of the Russian Federation and eleven of fifteen former Soviet states. Shortly after, the CIS removed the hammer and sickle, the symbol of communism, from its flag.

Under these circumstances, on December 25, 1991, Gorbachev resigned. The next day, the Soviet legislative body passed a resolution dissolving the U.S.S.R. With the Soviet Union dismantled, Yeltsin, as head of the Russian Federation and the CIS, expanded the democratic and free-market reforms initiated by Gorbachev (**Map 9.3**).

MAP 9.3 The Fall of Communism in Eastern Europe and the Soviet Union, 1989–1991 The collapse of communist regimes in Eastern Europe was due in part to political and economic reforms initiated by Soviet premier Mikhail Gorbachev, including agreements with the United States to reduce nuclear arms. These changes inspired demands for free elections that were supported by popular uprisings, first in Poland and then in other former Soviet satellites.

What does this map reveal about the reasons why the uprisings happened in nations like Poland and East Germany?

Before Gorbachev left office, he completed one last agreement with the United States to curb nuclear arms. In mid-1991, just before conspirators staged their unsuccessful coup, Gorbachev met with President Bush, who had traveled to Moscow to sign a strategic-arms reduction treaty. Under this pact, each side agreed to reduce its bombers and missiles by a third and to trim its conventional military forces. This accord led to a second strategic-arms reduction treaty (START II), signed in 1993. Gorbachev's successor, Boris Yeltsin, met with Bush in January 1993, and the two agreed to ban multiple-warhead intercontinental missiles within a decade. However, later disputes over U.S. anti-ballistic missile defenses led Russia to withdraw from the treaty before it was implemented.

AP® EXAM TIP

The Reagan administration reasserted U.S. commitment to oppose communism around the world. These actions, as well as the structural weaknesses of the Soviet system and their failed efforts at economic and political reform, hastened the end of the Cold War. Be able to explain how the end of the Cold War affected American foreign policy and politics.

REVIEW

- What factors led to the collapse of the Soviet Union?

Managing Conflict after the Cold War

The end of the Cold War left the United States as the only remaining superpower. After the breakup of the Soviet Union, the question remained how the United States would use its strength to preserve world order and maintain peace.

Events in China showed the limitations of American military might. In May 1989, university students in Beijing and other major cities in China held large-scale protests to demand political and economic reforms in the country. Some 200,000 demonstrators consisting of students, intellectuals, and workers gathered in the capital city's huge **Tiananmen Square**, where they constructed a papier-mâché figure resembling the Statue of Liberty and sang songs borrowed from the American civil rights movement. Deng Xiaoping, China's ruler, cracked down on the demonstrations by declaring martial law and dispatching the army to disperse the protesters. Peaceful activists were mowed down by machine guns and crushed by tanks. In response, President Bush issued a temporary ban on sales of weapons and nonmilitary items to China. When outrage over the Tiananmen Square massacre subsided, normal trade relations resumed.

Tiananmen Square
The location of the 1989 pro-democracy protests by Chinese university students who wanted political and economic reforms. China's leader, Deng Xiaoping, dispatched the military to break up the protests, killing thousands and crushing the uprising.

Flexing military muscle in Panama was more feasible for the Bush administration than doing so in China. During the 1980s, the United States had developed a precarious relationship with Panamanian general Manuel Noriega. Although Noriega channeled aid to the Contras with the approval and support of the CIA, he worsened relations with the Reagan administration by maintaining close ties with Cuba. Noriega also cooperated with the U.S. Drug Enforcement Agency in halting shipments of cocaine from Latin America headed for the United States at the same time that he helped Latin American drug kingpins launder their profits. In 1988, two Florida grand juries had indicted the Panamanian leader on charges of drug smuggling and bribery. As a result, the Reagan administration cut off aid to Panama and the U.S. Senate passed a resolution asking Noriega to resign. Not only did Noriega refuse to step down, but he also nullified the results of the 1989 presidential election in Panama and declared himself the nation's "maximum leader."

invasion of Panama
The U.S. invasion of Panama in 1989, resulting in the capture, extradition, and incarceration of its leader, Manuel Noriega, after he rejected the results of a democratic election and claimed he was the "maximum leader" of Panama.

After the United States tried unsuccessfully to bring about an internal coup against Noriega, the Panamanian leader proclaimed a "state of war" between the United States and his country. On December 20, 1989, President Bush launched an **invasion of Panama**, sending some 27,000 marines into the country. The Bush administration justified the conflict as necessary to protect the Panama Canal and the lives of American citizens, as well as to halt the drug traffic promoted by Noriega. In reality, the main purpose of the mission was to overthrow and capture the Panamanian dictator. In the military operation, the United States easily defeated the much weaker Panamanian military. The U.S. government installed a new regime, and the marines captured Noriega and sent him back to Florida to stand trial on the drug charges. In 1992, he was found guilty and sentenced to forty years in prison.

The Bush administration deployed much greater military force against Iraq. Maintaining a steady flow of oil from the Persian Gulf was vital to U.S. strategic interests. During the prolonged Iraq-Iran War in the 1980s, the Reagan administration had taken steps to ensure that neither side emerged as too powerful. Though the administration had orchestrated the arms-for-hostages deal with Iran, it had also courted the Iraqi dictator Saddam Hussein. U.S. support for Hussein abruptly ended in 1990, after Iraq sent 100,000 troops to invade the small oil-producing nation of Kuwait, on the southern border of Iraq.

President Bush responded by warning the Iraqis that their invasion "will not stand." Hussein sought to revitalize the Iraqi economy, which was devastated after a decade of war with Iran. Bush feared that the Iraqi dictator would also attempt to overrun Kuwait's neighbor Saudi Arabia, a U.S. ally, thereby giving Iraq control of half of the world's oil supply. Bush was also concerned that an emboldened Saddam Hussein would then upset the delicate balance of power in the Middle East and pose a threat to Israel by supporting the Palestinians. The Iraqis were rumored to be quickly developing nuclear weapons, which Hussein could use against Israel or as a deterrent against a U.S. military response.

Rather than act unilaterally, President Bush organized a multilateral coalition against Iraqi aggression. Secretary of State James Baker persuaded the United Nations to adopt a resolution calling for Iraqi withdrawal from Kuwait and imposing economic sanctions. Thirty-eight other nations, including the Arab countries of Egypt, Saudi Arabia, Syria, and Kuwait, contributed 160,000 troops, roughly 24 percent of the 700,000 allied forces that were deployed in Saudi Arabia in preparation for an invasion if Iraq did not comply.

With military forces stationed in Saudi Arabia, Bush gave Hussein a deadline of January 15, 1991, to withdraw from Kuwait or risk attack. However, the president faced serious opposition at home against waging a war. Demonstrations occurred throughout the nation, and most Americans supported the continued implementation of economic sanctions, which were already causing serious hardships for the Iraqi people. In the face of widespread opposition, the president requested congressional authorization for military operations against Iraq. After a long debate, Congress narrowly approved Bush's request.

Operation Desert Storm
The code name of the 1991 allied air and ground military offensive that pushed Iraqi forces out of Kuwait.

Gulf War
The 1990–1991 military conflict authorized by the United Nations in response to Iraq's invasion of Kuwait. A 39-nation coalition, led by the United States, liberated Kuwait after weeks of bombing and a brief land invasion.

Saddam Hussein let the deadline pass. On January 17, **Operation Desert Storm** began when the United States launched air attacks on Baghdad and other key targets in Iraq. After a month of bombing, Hussein still refused to back down, so a ground offensive was launched on February 24, 1991. More than 500,000 allied troops moved into Kuwait and easily drove Iraqi forces out of that nation. They then moved into southern Iraq. Although Hussein had confidently promised that the U.S.-led military assault would encounter the "mother of all battles," the vastly outmatched Iraqi army, worn out from its ten-year war with Iran, was quickly defeated. Desperate for help, Hussein ordered the firing of Scud missiles on Israel to provoke it into war, which he hoped would drive a wedge between the United States and its Arab allies. Despite sustaining some casualties, Israel refrained from retaliation. The ground war ended within one hundred hours, and Iraq agreed to withdraw its remaining forces from Kuwait. An estimated 100,000 Iraqis died; by contrast, 136 Americans perished in the **Gulf War**.

With the war over quickly, President Bush resisted pressure to march to Baghdad and overthrow Saddam Hussein. Bush's stated goal had been to liberate Kuwait. He did not wish to fight a war in the heart of Iraq. The administration believed that such

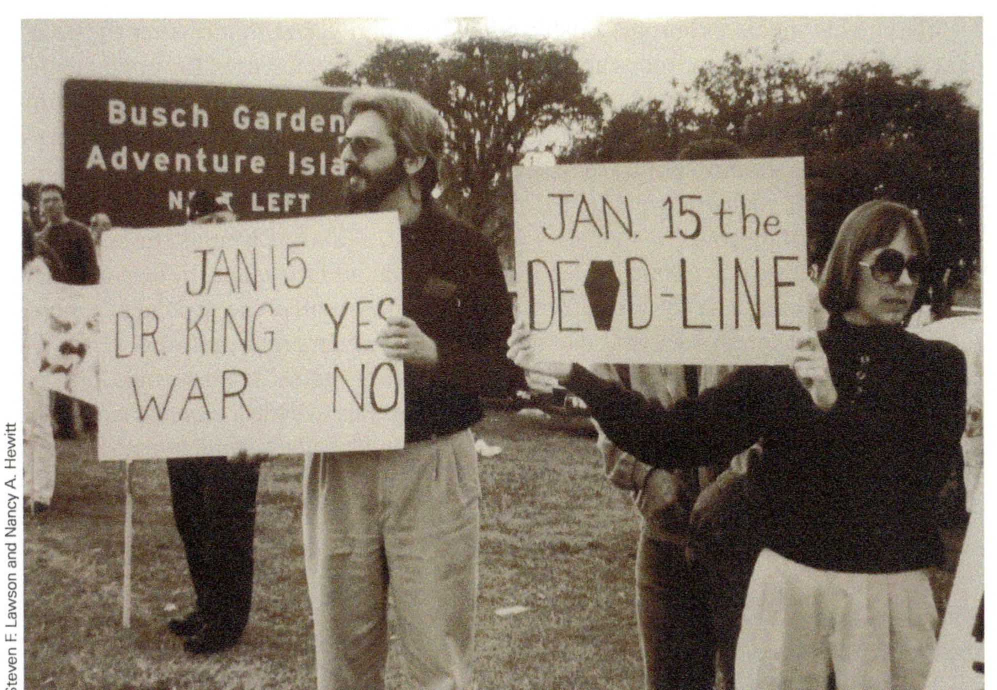

Steven F. Lawson and Nancy A. Hewitt

Gulf War Protests, 1991 The United States gave Iraq a January 15, 1991, deadline to withdraw from Kuwait or face military force. Protesters at the University of South Florida in Tampa favored continued diplomatic efforts. They carry signs that refer to the January 15 deadline, which also is the birthday of Martin Luther King Jr., a critic of U.S. militarism.

How does the choice to use Martin Luther King Jr.'s birthday as a date for Gulf War protests show continuity with social movements and conflicts of the 1960s?

an expedition would involve house-to-house, urban guerrilla warfare. Marching on Baghdad would also entail battling against Hussein's elite Republican Guard, not the weaker conscripts who had put up little resistance in Kuwait. Bush's Arab allies opposed expanding the war, and the president did not want to risk losing their support. Finally, getting rid of Hussein might make matters worse by leaving Iran and its Muslim fundamentalist rulers the dominant power in the region.

Operation Desert Storm succeeded because of its limited military objectives. President Bush and his advisers understood that the United States had triumphed because it had pieced together a genuine coalition of nations, including Arab ones, to coordinate diplomatic and military action. Military leaders had a clear and defined mission—the liberation of Kuwait—as well as adequate troops and supplies, and a technologically superior fighting force. When they carried out their purpose, the war was over. However, American withdrawal later allowed Saddam Hussein to slaughter thousands of Iraqi rebels, including Kurds and Shi'ites, to whom Bush had promised support. In effect, the Bush administration had applied the Cold War policy of limited containment in dealing with Hussein.

This successful U.S. military intervention in the Middle East provided President Bush an opportunity to address other explosive issues in the region. Following the end of the Iraq war, Bush set in motion the peace process that brought the Israelis and Palestinians together to sign a 1993 agreement providing for eventual Palestinian self-government in the Gaza Strip and the West Bank. In doing so, the United States for the first time officially recognized Yasser Arafat, the head of the PLO, whom both the Israelis and the Americans had previously labeled a terrorist.

In several areas of the globe, the move toward democracy that had begun in the late 1980s proceeded peacefully into the 1990s. The oppressive, racist system of apartheid fell in South Africa, and anti-apartheid activist Nelson Mandela was released after twenty-seven years in prison to become president of the country in 1994. In 1990, dictator Augusto Pinochet stepped down as president of Chile and ceded control to a democratically elected candidate. That same year, the procommunist Sandinista government lost at the polls in Nicaragua, and in 1992, the ruling regime in El Salvador signed a peace accord with the rebels.

Despite his successes abroad, Bush's popularity plunged at home. After the president dispatched American troops and defeated Iraqi military forces in Kuwait in 1991, his approval rating stood at a whopping 89 percent. In sharp contrast, Bush's poll numbers plummeted to 34 percent in 1992. This precipitous decline resulted mainly from the fact that the economy continued to sag.

Bush ran for reelection against Governor William Jefferson (Bill) Clinton of Arkansas. Learning from the mistakes of Michael Dukakis as well as the successes of Reagan, Clinton ran as a centrist Democrat who promised to reduce the federal deficit by raising taxes on the wealthy. Clinton supported conservative social policies such as the death penalty, tough measures against crime, and welfare reform. Although he did pledge to extend health care and opposed discrimination against homosexuals, Clinton relied on his mainstream southern Democratic credentials to deflect any claims that he was too liberal. Bush also faced a challenge from the independent candidate Ross Perot, a wealthy self-made businessman from Texas, whose campaign against rising government deficits won 19 percent of the popular vote, mostly at Bush's expense. On election day, Clinton defeated the incumbent by a two-to-one margin in the electoral college.

REVIEW

- How did Bush's efforts to manage international conflict after the end of the Cold War affect his popularity at home?

Conservative Ascendancy and the End of the Cold War

The election of President Ronald Reagan in 1980 represented the culmination of conservative ideas first set in motion by Republican Barry Goldwater's campaign for the White House in 1964. He emerged from southern California, where the movement to lower property taxes, increase community control over school curricula, rein in student protesters, disband affirmative action, and dismantle liberal programs had gained momentum in the 1960s and 1970s. First as governor of California and then as president, Reagan spearheaded the New Right movement. Although Reagan did not have a Republican-controlled Congress to work with throughout his presidency (Republicans held the Senate but not the House), he did succeed in reshaping government policies along more conservative lines.

Yet Reagan's New Right regime bestowed a mixed legacy. The Reagan and Bush administrations reduced inflation and revived economic growth, but their policies resulted in large budget deficits and swelled the national debt. Tax and spending cuts fueled the stock market, enriching corporations and the wealthy, but economic inequality widened and the social safety net for the most vulnerable Americans frayed.

The activism of ordinary people around the world also helped transform the relationship between the superpowers. Antinuclear protesters in Western Europe and the United States kept up pressure on Western leaders to make continued nuclear expansion unacceptable. In Eastern Europe, Polish shipyard electrician Lech Walesa and other fighters for democracy broke from the Soviet orbit and tore down the bricks and barbed-wire fences of the iron curtain.

The United States emerged as the winner of the Cold War, thereby gaining dominance as the world's sole superpower. Yet this did not necessarily guarantee peace. In assuming this preeminent role, the United States faced new threats to international security from governments and insurgents seeking to rebuild nations along ethnic and religious lines in the Middle East and the Persian Gulf.

Ironically, the bipolar Cold War in some ways had meant a more stable and manageable world presided over by the two superpowers. The collapse of the Soviet empire created a power vacuum that would be filled by a variety of unchecked and combustible local and regional forces intent on challenging the political and economic dominance of the United States. President Bush responded with a successful but limited war against Iraq. However, terrorism, which transcended national borders, replaced communism as the leading enemy of the United States and its allies.

REVIEW

- What foreign policy challenges emerged for the United States after the Cold War?

AP® Skills Workshop: Writing Historically

Additional Practice in Responding to a Short-Answer Question with Secondary Sources

"The rapidity of the change in the two superpowers' relationship was certainly astounding. . . . Soviet policy was at a high point in the 1970s. . . . The apparent successes of the Soviet Union were, however, deceptive. Two reasons account for what was, in fact, a flawed policy. One was the failure of the Soviet economy. The economic growth rate, 5 percent in the 1960s, and only 2 percent by the early 1970s, was standing still at virtually 0 percent a decade later. Capable of producing a plentiful supply of weapons, the Soviet economy was characterized by an absence of consumer goods and food. . . . A second reason for the Soviet turnabout was the cost of . . . [its] foreign policy. . . . The continuous arms buildup across the board and Moscow's expansionist activities in the third world produced fear and suspicion of Soviet intentions. . . . The Reagan administration's hard-line policies made Soviet foreign policy even more costly, thereby contributing to Gorbachev's awareness that the Soviet Union faced a systemic crisis.

Gorbachev therefore changed priorities and launched his program of *glasnost* (openness) and *perestroika* (restructuring) to revitalize Soviet society and the economy. . . . Opposition to Gorbachev was. . . . fueled by fear that the loosening of central controls could be harmful, if not fatal, politically. . . . In the other words, the fundamental structural reforms required by the Soviet Union might threaten not only the party's sole control of power but also Moscow's imperial control over its own vast country. . . . The Soviet Union faced the real possibility of becoming the Soviet *Dis*union. . . . the Soviet political system had become the greatest obstacle to economic modernization. That is why, preoccupied at home, Gorbachev needed to end the Cold War."

John Spanier, *American Foreign Policy Since World War II*, 1992

(*continued*)

"Washington did not merely respond to changes within the Soviet Union. In fact, the Reagan administration began seeking rapprochement with the Kremlin *before* the Soviets began to reform. The White House switched to a more conciliatory policy toward Moscow in January 1984—fifteen months before Gorbachev became leader of the Soviet Union, and more than two years before the introduction of *glasnost* and *perestroika*. . . .

[T]he Reagan administration's stated policy toward Moscow was especially hard-line through October 1983. . . . Only ten weeks later, however, Washington reversed course. On January 16, 1984, President Reagan delivered an address on superpower relations that proved to be a turning point in his administration's approach to the Kremlin. With this speech, Reagan began seeking a rapprochement. . . . Reagan warned of the dangers of war, and declared that the United States posed no threat to the security of the Soviet Union. . . .

Throughout 1984 and 1985, others within the administration echoed Reagan's calls for 'cooperation and understanding' between the superpowers, and underscored that Washington 'posed no threat' to Soviet security. . . .

The policy changes that Reagan introduced in 1984 are striking for a number of reasons. Most importantly, they are remarkable because they were implemented before the Soviets began to reform. . . . The old guard within the Kremlin was still fighting the cold war. The conventional view that Washington responded to changes within the Soviet Union is therefore inaccurate."

Beth A. Fischer, *The Reagan Reversal: Foreign Policy and the End of the Cold War,* 1997

Using the excerpts, answer **A**, **B**, and **C**.

(A) Briefly describe ONE major difference between Spanier's and Fischer's historical interpretations of the end of the Cold War.

(B) Briefly explain how ONE historical event or development from the period 1980 to 1991 that is not explicitly mentioned in the excerpts could be used to support Spanier's argument.

(C) Briefly explain how ONE historical event or development from the period 1980 to 1991 that is not explicitly mentioned in the excerpts could be used to support Fischer's argument.

A Changing Economy & Migration and Immigration in the 1990s and 2000s

MODULES 9.4 9.5

FOCUS

As you read these modules, consider the causes of the cultural and economic changes in the United States during the 1990s. Also think about the causes and effects of immigration and internal migration.

The 1990s marked a period of optimism, economic growth, and technological advancement in the United States. President Bill Clinton, the first president born after the conclusion of World War II in 1945, promised a youthful optimism in the aftermath of the Cold War. His wife, Hillary Rodham Clinton, was influenced by the ideals of 1960s feminism and aimed to be politically and socially active in the role of First Lady.

The nation also underwent a technological revolution. Computers allowed both small and large businesses to reach new markets and transform the workplace. Digital technology also altered the way individuals worked, bought goods and services, communicated, and spent leisure time.

As the Internet connected Americans to the rest of the world, corporate leaders embraced globalization as the key to economic prosperity. They put together business mergers so that their companies could operate more powerfully in the international market. Government officials generally supported their efforts by reducing regulations on business and financial practices. Globalization not only thrust American business enterprises outward but also brought a new population of immigrants to the United States.

Globalization

With the end of the Cold War, cooperation and market competition replaced economic and political rivalry between capitalist and communist nations in a new era of **globalization** — the extension of economic, political, and cultural interconnections among nations, through commerce, migration, and communication. In 1976, the major industrialized democracies had formed the Group of Seven (G7). Consisting of the United States, the United Kingdom, France, West Germany, Italy, Japan, and Canada, leaders of the G7 nations met annually to discuss common problems related to issues of global concern, such as trade, health, energy, the environment, and economic and social development. After the fall of communism, Russia joined the organization, which became known as G8. This group of countries represented only 14 percent of the globe's population but produced 60 percent of the world's economic output.

globalization
The growth of international trade and cultural exchange between peoples and countries resulting in increased economic and cultural integration, migration, and interdependence among nations.

Dave Bartruff/Getty Images

Globalization, 1980s Following the efforts of Presidents Nixon, Ford, and Carter to normalize relations with the People's Republic of China, companies established commercial enterprises there, including American fast-food chain restaurants. Here a Chinese soldier, standing beside a replica of Colonel Sanders, picks up his order at the bike ride-up window of a Kentucky Fried Chicken restaurant.

Why would American corporations be interested in investing in China during the 1980s and 1990s?

Globalization was accompanied by the extraordinary growth of multinational (or transnational) corporations — companies that operate production facilities or deliver services in more than one country. Between 1970 and 2000, the number of such firms soared from 7,000 to well over 60,000. By 2000, the 500 largest corporations in the world generated more than $11 trillion in revenues, owned more than $33 trillion in assets, and employed 35.5 million people.

American companies left their cultural and social imprint on the rest of the world. Walmart greeted shoppers in more than 1,200 stores outside the United States, and McDonald's changed global eating habits with its more than 1,000 fast-food restaurants worldwide. As American firms penetrated other countries with their products, foreign companies changed the economic landscape of the United States. For instance, by the twenty-first century, Japanese automakers, led by Toyota and Honda, captured a major share of the American market, surpassing Ford and General Motors, once the hallmark of the country's manufacturing and salesmanship.

Globalization also affected popular culture and media. In the 1990s, reality shows, many of which originated in Europe, became a staple of American television. At the same time, American programs were shown as reruns all over the world. As cable channels proliferated, American viewers of Hispanic or Asian origin could watch programs in their native languages. The Cable News Network (CNN), the British Broadcasting Corporation (BBC), and Al Jazeera, an Arabic-language television channel, competed for viewers with specially designed international broadcasts.

Globalization had some negative consequences as well. Organized labor in particular suffered a severe blow. By 2004, union membership in the United States had dropped to 12.5 percent of the industrial workforce. Fewer and fewer consumer goods bore the label "Made in America," as multinational companies shifted manufacturing jobs to low-wage workers in developing countries. Many of these foreign workers earned more than the prevailing wages in their countries, but by Western standards their pay was extremely low. There were few or no regulations governing working conditions or the use of child labor, and many foreign factories resembled the sweatshops of early twentieth-century America.

Not surprisingly, workers in the United States could not compete in this market. Furthermore, China, which by 2007 had become a prime source for American manufacturing, failed to regulate the quality of its products closely. Chinese-made toys, including the popular Thomas the Tank Engine, showed up in U.S. stores that same year with dangerous levels of lead paint and had to be returned before endangering millions of children.

Perhaps the biggest downside to globalization was the danger it posed to the world's environment. As poorer nations sought to take advantage of the West's appetite for low-cost consumer goods, they industrialized rapidly, with little concern for the uncontrolled pollution that accompanied their efforts. The desire for wood products and the expansion of large-scale farming eliminated one-third of Brazil's rain forests. The health of indigenous people often suffered where globalization-related manufacturing appeared. In Taiwan and China, chemical byproducts of factories and farms turned rivers into polluted sources of drinking water and killed the rivers' fish and plants.

The older industrialized nations added their share to the environmental damage. Besides using nuclear power, Americans consumed electricity and gas produced overwhelmingly from coal and petroleum. The burning of fossil fuels by cars and factories released greenhouse gases, raising the temperature of the atmosphere and the oceans and contributing to the phenomena known as **global warming** and **climate change**.

Most scientists believe that global warming has led to the melting of the polar ice caps and poses grave risks to human and animal life on the planet. However, after the industrialized nations of the world signed the **Kyoto Protocol** in 1998 to curtail greenhouse-gas emissions, the U.S. Senate refused to ratify it. Critics of the agreement maintained that it did not address the newly emerging industrial countries such as China and India that polluted heavily and thus was unfair to the United States. Other critics noted the enormous costs of transitioning away from fossil fuel use or questioned whether human activity caused rising temperatures.

Globalization also highlighted health problems such as the AIDS epidemic. By the outset of the twenty-first century, approximately 33.2 million people worldwide suffered from the disease, although the number of new cases diagnosed annually had dropped to 2.5 million from more than 5 million a few years earlier. Africa remained the continent with the largest number of AIDS patients and the center of the epidemic. Increased education and the development of more effective pharmaceuticals to treat the illness reduced cases and prolonged the lives of those affected by the disease. Although treatments were more widely available in prosperous countries like the United States, agencies such as the United Nations and the World Health Organization, together with nongovernmental groups such as Partners in Health, were instrumental in offering relief in developing countries.

global warming
The long-term rise in the temperature of the atmosphere and oceans caused by the increased presence of greenhouse gases in the atmosphere. Since 1880, the average global annual temperature has risen 1.9° Fahrenheit (1.1° Celsius) with most of the warming having occurred since 1975.

climate change
The climatic effect of global warming, leading to unpredictable weather conditions, severe weather events like hurricanes, draughts, flooding, and dangerous blizzards, but also ancillary effects like wild fires, declining water tables, and stresses on essential infrastructure.

REVIEW

- How did globalization affect living standards throughout the world during the 1980s and early 1990s?

The Clinton Presidency

Bill Clinton served twelve years as Democratic governor of his home state of Arkansas. As governor, Clinton supported healthcare reform, improved education, and economic development. After defeating President George H. W. Bush in 1992, Clinton entered the White House as the first Democrat to serve as president since Jimmy Carter.

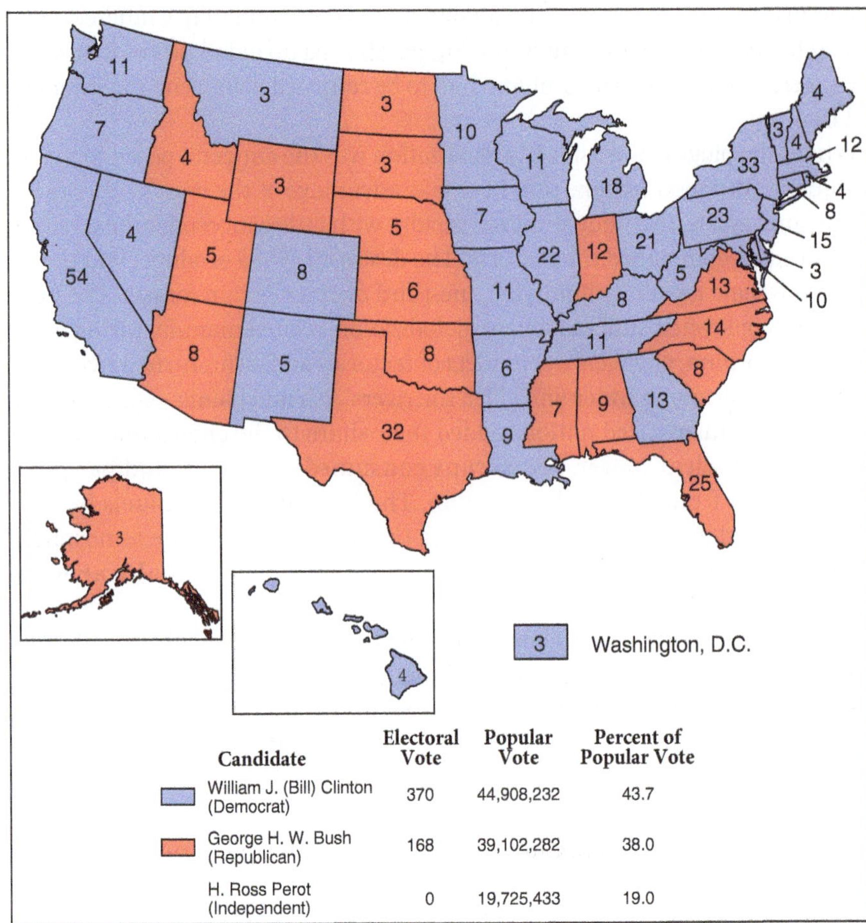

Candidate	Electoral Vote	Popular Vote	Percent of Popular Vote
William J. (Bill) Clinton (Democrat)	370	44,908,232	43.7
George H. W. Bush (Republican)	168	39,102,282	38.0
H. Ross Perot (Independent)	0	19,725,433	19.0

MAP 9.4 The Election of 1992 Bill Clinton campaigned as a moderate Democrat and won 43.7 percent of the popular vote in the 1992 election, defeating President George H. W. Bush and wealthy independent candidate Ross Perot. Clinton and his vice presidential running mate, Al Gore, were both southerners, and their ticket received more than 370 electoral votes.

How does the map illustrate both the strengths and potential weaknesses of Clinton's support?

In 1993, Clinton sought to reverse many Reagan-Bush policies. He persuaded Congress to raise taxes on wealthy individuals and corporations, while his administration reduced defense spending following the end of the Cold War. Economic growth rose to a rate of 4 percent annually, the national debt decreased, and there was a budget surplus. Clinton further departed from his Republican predecessors by signing executive orders expanding federal assistance for legal abortion. Clinton also signed the 1993 **Family and Medical Leave Act**, which allowed parents to take up to twelve weeks of unpaid leave to care for newborn children without risk of losing their jobs.

Family and Medical Leave Act
An act passed in 1993 that protects individuals' right to take up to twelve weeks of unpaid leave for medical reasons or parenthood without risk of losing their jobs.

The president had less success with some of his other initiatives. His policy of "don't ask, don't tell" permitted homosexuals to serve in the armed forces so long as they kept their sexual orientation a secret. This compromise failed to end discrimination toward those already covertly serving in the military and frustrated people on both sides of the issue. The Clinton administration's most stinging defeat came when Congress did not pass universal health care, a proposal guided by his wife, Hillary Clinton. Opposed by conservatives and the health insurance industry, the failure of Clinton's health care reform plan diminished his popularity during his first term.

AP® WORKING with EVIDENCE

Source: President Bill Clinton, *Address to Congress on Health Care Reform*, 1993

"Every one of us knows someone who's worked hard and played by the rules and still been hurt by this system that just doesn't work for too many people. . . . We have to preserve and strengthen what is right with the health care system, but we have got to fix what is wrong with it.

Now, we all know what's right. We're blessed with the best health care professionals on Earth, the finest health care institutions, the best medical research, the most sophisticated technology. My mother is a nurse. I grew up around hospitals. Doctors and nurses were the first professional people I ever knew or learned to look up to. They are what is right with this health care system. But we also know that we can no longer afford to continue to ignore what is wrong.

Millions of Americans are just a pink slip [notification of losing a job] away from losing their health insurance and one serious illness away from losing all their savings. Millions more are locked into the jobs they have now just because they or someone in their family has once been sick and they have what is called a preexisting condition. And on any given day, over 37 million Americans, most of them working people and their little children, have no health insurance at all."

Questions for Analysis

1. Identify the main strength and the main weakness of the U.S. health care system, according to Clinton.
2. Describe what Clinton broadly proposes as a solution to the health care system's weakness.
3. Evaluate the extent to which Clinton's argument in this excerpt represents a continuation of progressive ideals from the early twentieth century.

Clinton tried to appeal to voters across the political spectrum on other issues. He signed a tough anticrime law that funded the recruitment of an additional 100,000 police officers to patrol city streets. Although the prison population had been on the rise before the 1990s, Clinton's anticrime bill accelerated the rate of incarceration. Critics of the bill believed it had a disproportionately negative effect on Blacks and Latinos.

Despite opposition from the **National Rifle Association**, in 1993 Clinton signed the **Brady Handgun Violence Prevention Act** (popularly known as the Brady Bill), which imposed a five-day waiting period to check the background of gun buyers and, in 1994, a **Federal Assault Weapons Ban**, which prohibited the production and use of semi-automatic weapons by civilians.

To further expand the nation's economy, Clinton embraced the economic regional cooperation of Europe. In 1993, western European nations formed the **European Union (EU)**, which encouraged free trade and investment among member nations. In 1999, the EU introduced a common currency, the euro, which twenty-six nations have since adopted.

Clinton encouraged the formation of similar economic partnerships in North America. In 1993, together with the governments of Mexico and Canada, the U.S. Congress ratified the **North American Free Trade Agreement (NAFTA)**. The agreement removed tariffs and other obstacles to commerce and investment among the three countries to encourage trade.

Between 1994 and 2004, trade among NAFTA nations increased by nearly 130 percent. Although Mexico saw a significant drop in poverty rates and a rise in real income, NAFTA harmed many blue-collar workers in the United States. From 1994 to 2007, net manufacturing jobs dropped by 3,654,000 as U.S. companies outsourced production to Mexico, taking advantage of its low wages and benefits. In addition to the impact of NAFTA, many more manufacturing jobs were lost to automation.

Clinton also actively promoted globalization through the **World Trade Organization (WTO)**. Created in 1995, the WTO consists of more than 150 nations

Brady Handgun Violence Prevention Act

A gun-control law passed in 1993 and named after Ronald Reagan's press secretary James Brady, who was shot and nearly killed during an assassination attempt on Reagan in 1981. The Brady Bill established a five-day waiting period and background check for gun buyers until the implementation of the National Instant Criminal Background Check System in 1998.

Federal Assault Weapons Ban

A 1994 ban prohibiting the manufacturing and use of certain assault-style semi-automatic firearms and large-capacity ammunition magazines in the United States. The ban was allowed to expire in 2004.

North American Free Trade Agreement (NAFTA)

A free-trade agreement approved in 1993 by the United States, Canada, and Mexico. It was replaced in 2020 by a similar free-trade pact, the U.S.-Mexico-Canada Agreement (USMCA).

and seeks "to ensure that trade flows as smoothly, predictably, and freely as possible." The policies of the WTO generally have benefited wealthier nations, such as the United States. From 1978 to 2000, the value of U.S. exports and imports jumped from 17 percent to 25 percent of gross domestic product.

Contract with America
A Republican legislative agenda proposed in 1994 that called for reduced welfare spending, lower taxes, term limits for lawmakers, and a constitutional amendment for a balanced budget.

Personal Responsibility and Work Opportunity Reconciliation Act
An act reforming the welfare system in the United States. The 1996 law required adults receiving welfare to find work within two years or lose their welfare benefits, granted states greater flexibility in administering welfare programs, and strengthened enforcement of child support.

Defense of Marriage Act (DOMA)
An act that defined marriage as only between a man and woman and banned federal recognition of same-sex marriage. The 1996 act also allowed states to not recognize same-sex marriages legally performed in other states. DOMA was ruled unconstitutional in 2013 by the Supreme Court.

Despite his free-trade economic policies, conservatives were fiercely opposed to Clinton on several fronts, including the effort to reform health care. Many conservatives also opposed Clinton's liberal positions on issues such as feminism, abortion, affirmative action, and secularism. Opponents called attention to his and his wife's pre-presidential dealings in a controversial real estate development project known as **Whitewater**, which prompted the appointment in 1994 of a special prosecutor to investigate allegations of misconduct, though no charges were ever filed against them.

Facing conservative criticism, the president and the Democratic Party fared poorly in the 1994 congressional elections, losing control of both houses of Congress for the first time since 1952. Republicans, led by House Minority Leader Newt Gingrich of Georgia, championed the **Contract with America**. This document embraced conservative principles, including a constitutional amendment for a balanced budget, reduced welfare spending, lower taxes, and term limits for lawmakers. The election also underscored the increasing electoral influence of white evangelical Christians, who voted in large numbers for Republican candidates.

In the wake of this defeat, Clinton shifted rightward and championed welfare reform. In 1996, he signed the **Personal Responsibility and Work Opportunity Reconciliation Act**. It replaced the Aid to Families with Dependent Children provision of the Social Security law, the basis for welfare in the United States since the New Deal, with a new measure that required adult welfare recipients to find work within two years or lose the benefits provided to families earning less than $7,700 annually. The law also placed a lifetime limit of five years on these federal benefits. Also in 1996, the president approved the **Defense of Marriage Act (DOMA)**, which banned the federal government from recognizing same-sex marriage.

In adopting such positions as welfare reform, Clinton angered many of his liberal supporters, but he was reelected in 1996. Running against Republican senator Robert Dole of Kansas and the independent candidate Ross Perot, Clinton captured 49 percent of the popular vote and 379 electoral votes. Dole received 41 percent of the vote, and Perot came in a distant third.

Richard Ellis/AFP/Getty Images

The Republican "Contract with America" On April 7, 1995, Speaker of the House Newt Gingrich holds up a copy of the *Contract with America* on the steps of the U.S. Capitol. The document helped Republicans win the midterm congressional elections in 1994, the first time they controlled both houses of Congress since 1953. Gingrich is joined by some 160 House Republicans to celebrate the completion of the Republicans' 100-day promise of change. However, their legislative efforts to achieve the contract's proposals were mixed.

How did the Contract with America illustrate the growing political conservatism of the American electorate?

MAP 9.5 The Breakup of Yugoslavia, 1991–2008 With the collapse of communist control of Yugoslavia, the country splintered along ethnic and religious lines, eventually forming seven separate nations. A civil war between Serbia and Croatia ended in 1995, but Serbs then attacked Muslims in Bosnia and Kosovo.

How does the map illustrate the post–Cold War challenges faced by the United States?

During his two terms in office, Clinton faced many foreign-policy challenges, including answering questions on the future of NATO in the aftermath of the dissolution of the Soviet Union and the end of the Cold War. Although communist aggression was no longer a threat, the Clinton administration began to expand NATO into Eastern Europe, eventually incorporating the Baltic states and nations like Poland and Hungary into the alliance. NATO expansion would continue in the twenty-first century under Clinton's successors.

Yet the greatest threats to the United States in the 1990s came from the implosion of national governments into factionalism and genocide, as well as the dangers posed by violent Islamic extremists. For example, Clinton faced a long-simmering conflict in the former communist nation of Yugoslavia that erupted into a civil war, beginning in 1991. In response to the violence and slaughter of tens of thousands of Muslims, in 1995 the United States sponsored NATO bombing raids and dispatched 20,000 American troops as part of a multilateral peacekeeping force. In 1999, renewed conflict led to a new round of NATO airstrikes and troops placed on the ground.

The United States faced an even graver danger from Islamic extremists intent on waging a religious struggle (jihad) against their perceived enemies and establishing a transnational Muslim government, or caliphate. The close relationship with Israel placed the United States high on the list of terrorist targets, along with pro-American Muslim governments in Egypt, Pakistan, and Indonesia. In 1993, Islamic militants orchestrated the bombing of the World Trade Center's underground garage in New York City, killing six people and injuring more than one thousand. Five years later, terrorists blew up American embassies in Kenya and Tanzania, killing hundreds and injuring thousands of local workers and residents. In retaliation, Clinton ordered air strikes against terrorist bases in Sudan and Afghanistan. However, the danger persisted. In 2000, al-Qaeda terrorists blew a gaping hole in the side of the USS *Cole*, a U.S. destroyer anchored in Yemen, killing seventeen American sailors.

During his second term, President Clinton faced a severe domestic challenge to his presidency that led to him to be the second president in U.S. history to be impeached. Starting in 1995, Clinton, then age forty-nine, had engaged in sexual relations with Monica Lewinsky, a twenty-two-year-old White House intern. Clinton denied these charges under oath in a separate sexual-harassment lawsuit brought against him, as well as before a national television audience. But when Lewinsky testified about the details of their sexual encounters, the president recanted his earlier statements and admitted to the relationship. After an independent prosecutor concluded that Clinton had committed perjury and obstructed justice, the House voted to impeach the president on December 19, 1998. However, on February 12, 1999, the Senate failed to muster the necessary two-thirds vote to convict Clinton on the charges as he was buoyed by high public approval ratings and a booming economy.

Clinton's second term also saw economic prosperity. In 1998, the unemployment rate fell to 4.3 percent, the lowest level since the early 1970s. The rate of home ownership reached a record-setting 66 percent. As the "misery index"—a compilation of unemployment and inflation—fell, the gross domestic product grew by more than $250 billion. In 1999, the stock market's Dow Jones Industrial Average reached a then-historic high of 10,000 points. That same year, the president signed into law a measure that freed banks to merge commercial, investment, and insurance services. This reversal of the 1933 Glass-Steagall Act allowed banks to undertake profitable but sometimes risky ventures and ultimately contributed to a financial collapse in 2007. The Clinton administration boasted that its economic policies had succeeded in canceling the budget deficit, yielding a surplus for the fiscal year 2000. This boom, however, did not affect everyone equally. Blacks and Latinos lagged behind whites economically, and the gap between rich and poor widened as the wealthiest 13,000 American families earned as much income as the poorest 20 million.

REVIEW

- How did policies enacted during Clinton's administration reflect both liberal and conservative policies from earlier in the twentieth century?

The Computer Revolution

During the 1990s, computers began to revolutionize the lives of average Americans. The first working computers were developed for military purposes during World War II and the Cold War and were enormous in size and cost. Engineers began to reduce the size and cost of computers with the creation of transistors. Invented in the late 1940s, these small electronic devices came into widespread use in running computers during the 1960s. The design of integrated circuits in the 1970s led to the production of microcomputers in which a silicon chip the size of a nail head did the work once performed by huge computers.

In 1980, Microsoft, founded by Bill Gates and Paul Allen, collaborated with International Business Machines (IBM) to create a disk operating system, MS-DOS, for IBM's new line of personal computers. They were not the only ones to recognize the potential market of microcomputers for home and business use. Steve Jobs, like Gates a college dropout, founded Apple Computer, Inc. with Stephen Wozniak in 1976, turned it into a publicly traded corporation, and in 1984 pioneered the first widely used consumer computer with a mouse and a graphical operating system, the Macintosh (now known as the Mac). The following year, Microsoft released its first graphical operating system for personal computers, Microsoft Windows. Like industrial behemoths a century earlier, both companies came to dominate the personal computer and related technological industries, as each attained a market capitalization (a company's share price multiplied by the total number of outstanding shares) of over $2 trillion in 2022.

Microchips and digital technology found a market beyond home and office computers. Over the last two decades of the twentieth century, computers came to operate everything from standard appliances such as televisions and telephones, to new electronic devices such as CD players, fax machines, and mobile phones. Computers controlled traffic lights on the streets and air traffic in the skies. They also changed the leisure patterns of youth: Many young people preferred to play video games indoors than to engage in outdoor activities. Consumers purchased goods online, and later, companies such as eBay and Amazon sold merchandise through the Internet without any retail stores.

The **Internet**—an open, global series of interconnected computer networks that transmit data, information, electronic mail, and other services—grew out of military research in the 1970s, when the Department of Defense constructed a system of computer servers connected to one another throughout the United States. The main objective of this network was to preserve military communications in the event of a Soviet nuclear attack.

Internet
A worldwide, interconnected computer communication network. Originally started as a U.S. military communication system in the 1970s, the Internet has become the backbone of global commerce and communication.

At the end of the Cold War, the Internet was repurposed for nonmilitary use, linking government, academic, business, and organizational systems. In 1991, the **World Wide Web** came into existence as a way to access the Internet and connect documents and other resources to one another through hyperlinks. By 2021, about 93 percent of people in the United States used the Internet, up from 50 percent in 2000. Internet use worldwide leapt by almost 1,400 percent between 2000 and 2022, from nearly 361 million people to over 5 billion.

The astounding growth of the computer industry led to increased business consolidation, making it possible for large firms to keep control of their far-flung operations by communicating instantly within the United States and throughout the world. The federal government aided the merger process by relaxing financial regulation. Media companies took the greatest advantage of this situation. For example, in 1990 the giant Warner Communications merged with Time Life to create an entertainment empire that included a film studio (Warner Brothers), a television cable network (Home Box Office), a music company (Atlantic Records), a baseball team (the Atlanta Braves), and several magazines (*Time*, *Sports Illustrated*, and *People*).

AP® EXAM TIP
By the close of the twentieth century, the computer revolution had transformed the U.S. economy. Be able to explain the causes for this transformation and both the positive and negative effects of this change, especially for American workers. In doing so, you should be able to provide specific examples and a nuanced analysis of how technological changes both helped and hurt Americans and American businesses.

Other mergers mirrored the trend in the media: The estimated number of business mergers rose from 1,529 in 1991 to 4,500 in 1998. The market value of these transactions in 1998 was approximately $2 trillion, compared with $600 billion for 1989, the previous peak year for consolidation. Corporate consolidation also brought corporate wrongdoing, as some chief executives abused their power by expanding their companies too quickly and making risky financial deals, which put workers and stockholders in jeopardy.

REVIEW

- How did technological innovation during the 1990s change the U.S. economy and culture?

The Changing American Population

As the technological revolution transformed the U.S. economy and society, an influx of immigrants began to alter the composition of the American population. Since passage of the Immigration Act of 1965, which repealed discriminatory national origins quotas established in 1924, the country had experienced a wave of immigration comparable to that at the turn of the twentieth century. As the population of the United States grew from 202 million to 300 million between 1970 and 2006, immigrants accounted for some 28 million of the increase. They came to the United States for many of the same reasons as those arriving earlier: to seek economic opportunity and to find political and religious freedom.

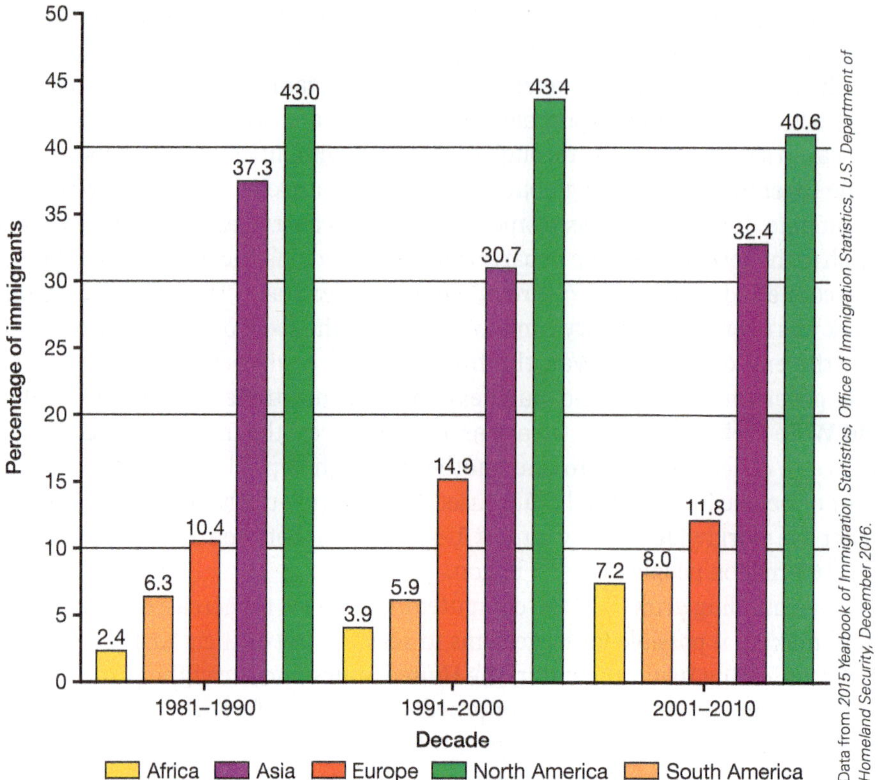

Immigrant Growth by Home Region, 1991–2010 In the late twentieth and early twenty-first centuries, immigration to the United States increased significantly, especially from North America (which in this figure includes Mexico, Central America, and the Caribbean). East and South Asia formed the second-largest group of immigrants, while Africans arrived in small but growing numbers.

What conclusions can you draw by comparing the changes in each region's percentage of immigration?

AP® EXAM TIP

In the second half of the twentieth century, migration patterns in the United States changed as immigration shifted away from Europe and more towards the Americas and Asia. Likewise, internal migration to suburbs and the Sun Belt brought population growth to the West and Southwest and challenges to large, urban cities. Understand the causes and effects mobility had on American society. Also, be able to compare migration patterns during this time period with earlier internal migration and immigration.

Most newcomers in the 1980s and 1990s arrived mainly from Latin America and South and East Asia. Relatively few Europeans (approximately 2 million) moved to the United States, although their numbers increased after the collapse of the Soviet empire in the early 1990s. Poverty and political unrest pushed migrants out of Mexico, Central America, and the Caribbean.

At the beginning of the twenty-first century, Latinos (35 million) had surpassed Black Americans (34 million) as the nation's largest minority group. However, with the arrival of Caribbean and African immigrants, Black America was also becoming more diverse.

In addition to the 16 million immigrants who came from south of the U.S. border, another 9 million headed eastward from Asia, including Chinese, South Koreans, and Filipinos, together with refugees from Vietnam and Cambodia. By 2010, roughly 3 million Indians from South Asia lived in the United States, most arriving after the 1960s. Indian Americans became the third-largest Asian American group behind Chinese and Filipinos. Another 1–2 million people came from predominantly Islamic nations such as Pakistan, Lebanon, Iraq, and Iran.

AP® WORKING with EVIDENCE

Source: Bo Yee, Interview, *Sweatshop Warriors: Immigrant Women Workers Take On the Global Factory*, 2001

"I started working at a factory a month after I got here. I immigrated to the U.S. because of my two sons. They were not going to be happy in Hong Kong after the 1997 changeover [the transfer of Hong Kong from the United Kingdom to China]. My husband did not want to come to the U.S. but he did come in 1985.

I started working at Lucky Sewing Company in June 1986. Working there was like being a prisoner in a sealed cage. All the windows were locked. They wouldn't let you go to the bathroom. They had 'No loud talking' signs posted. There were about 20 of us there working ten hours a day, seven days a week, endlessly, without rest. Most of the workers were from mainland China, although some came from Hong Kong and there were a few Latinos. The boss' wife created a tense, competitive atmosphere between the workers. She would praise some people and downgrade others. Because of my experience, I can work faster than newer workers from China who are not as skillful. They would sacrifice their lunch and break time to catch up. I hated the way the boss made us compete. There were three of us in one department who had to produce 200 pieces. They would push us to see who could finish first. They were getting people to exploit themselves. How disgusting! I hate this!

I couldn't communicate with the Latino workers, but you can have fun without speaking each other's language. You motion. You use body language and whatever method you can. The relations with Latinos were better. We were not forced to compete with each other.

I thought America was a very advanced country, but working in sweatshops here, I see that the garment industry is very backward compared to Hong Kong."

Questions for Analysis

1. Describe the conditions Bo Yee faced working in the garment factory.
2. Explain the similarities and differences between Bo Yee's account and the experiences of garment workers in the early 1900s (Period 7).
3. Evaluate the extent to which globalization shaped Bo Yee's work experience.

California displayed this change most vividly. Latinos and Asians had long settled there, and by 2016, 27 percent of the state's population was foreign-born. The majority of Californians consisted of Latinos, Asian Americans, and Black Americans, with whites in the minority. In addition to California, immigrants also flocked to the Southwest and to northeastern and midwestern cities like New York City, Jersey City, Chicago, and Detroit. Immigrants also fanned out across the Southeast, adding to the growing populations of Atlanta, Raleigh-Durham, Charlotte, Columbia, and Memphis and providing these cities with an unprecedented ethnic mixture. Like immigrants before them, they created their own businesses, spoke their own languages, and retained their own religious and cultural practices.

REVIEW

- What accounts for the changing demographics of immigrants to the United States during the 1990s?

AP® Skills Workshop: Writing Historically

Additional Practice in Responding to a Short-Answer Question

Answer **A**, **B**, and **C**.

(A) Briefly explain how ONE specific event or development contributed to the globalization of the U.S. economy in the period 1980 to 2000.

(B) Briefly explain ONE important way globalization affected American society in the period 1980 to 2000.

(C) Briefly explain ANOTHER important way globalization affected American society in the period 1980 to 2000.

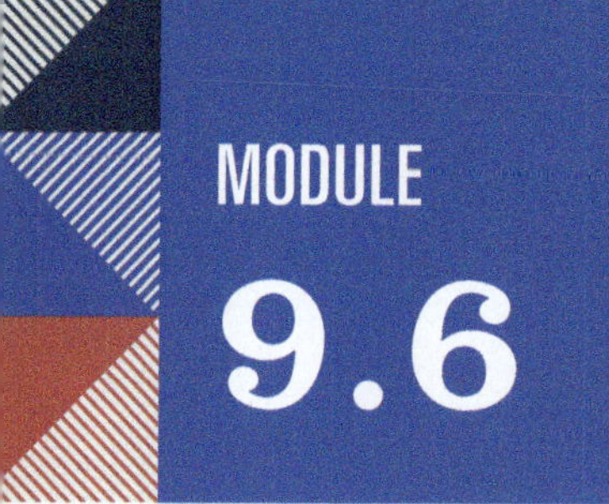

MODULE 9.6 Challenges of the Twenty-First Century

FOCUS

While reading this module, consider the causes of the economic and social changes experienced by Americans during the first quarter of the twenty-first century, and determine the effects of those changes.

At the beginning of the twenty-first century, the United States found itself the sole superpower, with peace at home and what appeared to be a future of free markets and international peace abroad.

President George W. Bush began his presidency with a call for "compassionate conservativism," including faith-based policy initiatives, which combined efforts to improve the general welfare of society with support for modern free-market capitalism. However, eight months into his presidency, the terrorist attacks on September 11, 2001, occurred, and the Bush administration was faced with its first major challenge. By 2003, the United States had established new forms of domestic and international surveillance to prevent future attacks and entered into conflicts in Afghanistan and Iraq as part of its global war on terrorism.

The new century also experienced an economic shock and long recession brought about by changes in the American economy. Barack Obama, the nation's first Black president, faced two terms with economic challenges, lingering overseas conflicts in the Middle East, and strong resistance from conservatives. Obama nevertheless saw the Great Recession end during his presidency, and his policies expanded access to health care. However, prosperity returned unevenly.

In 2016, Republican nominee Donald Trump narrowly won the presidential election against Hillary Clinton, the Democratic nominee, but lost reelection in 2020 against former vice president, Joseph Biden, a Democrat.

Bush and Compassionate Conservatism

In 2000, the Democratic candidate, Vice President Al Gore, ran against George W. Bush, the Republican governor of Texas and son of the forty-first president. Gore ran on the legacy of prosperity during the Clinton presidency, while Bush campaigned as a "compassionate conservative." Also in the race was Ralph Nader, an anti-corporate activist who ran under the banner of the Green Party, a party formed in 1991 to support grassroots democracy, environmentalism, social justice, and gender equality.

Nader's candidacy drew votes away from Gore, who won a narrow plurality of the popular vote (48.4 percent, compared with 47.8 percent for Bush and 2.7 percent for Nader). However, Bush won a slim majority of the electoral votes: 271 to 267. The key state in this Republican victory was Florida, where George W. Bush's brother, Jeb Bush, was governor, and where Bush outpolled Gore by fewer than 500 popular votes. When litigation over the mandatory recount reached the U.S. Supreme Court in December 2000, the Court halted the recount and proclaimed Bush the winner in a contentious 5–4 vote.

Despite his narrow, contested victory, George W. Bush appealed to his conservative political base by governing boldly. Republicans still controlled the House, while the

Democrats had gained a one-vote majority in the Senate. President Bush promoted the agenda of the evangelical Christian wing of the Republican Party and spoke out against same-sex marriage, abortion, and federal support for stem-cell research, a scientific procedure that used discarded embryos to research cures for diseases. Bush created the White House **Office of Faith-Based and Neighborhood Partnerships**, providing religious institutions with federal funds for social-service activities without violating the First Amendment's separation of church and state.

Sanctuary Building of the First Baptist Church in Dallas, Texas, 2014 This 2014 photograph shows the modernist sanctuary building that is part of the First Baptist Church, a megachurch with nearly 10,000 members located in Dallas, Texas. The former building that housed this church, originally built in the 1890s, can be seen in the reflection of the windows beside the doors.

How does this building convey details specific to American religious life during the twenty-first century?

These initiatives reflected a change in American religious life at the turn of the twenty-first century, when a growing number of churchgoers were joining megachurches. These Protestant congregations each contained 2,000 or more worshippers. Between 1970 and 2005, the number of megachurches jumped from 50 to more than 1,300, with California, Texas, and Florida taking the lead. The establishment of massive churches was part of a worldwide movement, with South Korea home to the largest congregation. Joel Osteen—the evangelical pastor of Lakewood Church in Houston, Texas, the largest megachurch in the United States—drew average weekly audiences of 43,000 people, with sermons available in English and Spanish. Such religious leaders, with their influential platforms, became an increasingly important constituency for Republican Party officials.

During his presidency, Bush also pursued policies that appealed to economic conservatives. In 2001, Bush signed the Economic Growth and Tax Relief Reconciliation Act, and in 2003, he signed the Jobs and Growth Tax Relief Reconciliation Act. Both of these acts provided tax cuts to most Americans by lowering most marginal tax rates. However, critics of these policies believed that increasing deficits without substantially reducing government spending would hinder economic growth and worsen income inequality.

At the same time, Bush attempted to show the compassionate side of his conservatism. His cabinet appointments reflected racial, ethnic, and gender diversity. They included Black Americans like Colin Powell, secretary of state, and the national security adviser, Condoleezza Rice, who later succeeded Powell as secretary of state.

Bush's compassionate conservatism also included educational reform, under the program **No Child Left Behind (NCLB)**, which sought to raise national standards and education opportunity, especially for those attending school in underprivileged areas, by requiring standardized tests to assess school success. In addition, in 2003 Bush signed into law the **Medicare Prescription Drug, Improvement, and Modernization Act**, which aimed to lower the cost of prescription drugs to some 40 million senior citizens enrolled in Medicare.

Office of Faith-Based and Neighborhood Partnerships

An office of the White House established by President George W. Bush to provide religious and community institutions with federal funds for social services.

No Child Left Behind (NCLB)

Legislation that aimed to raise student educational outcomes by requiring states to adopt standards-based instruction and standardized assessments to receive federal school funding. The bipartisan 2001 act significantly expanded the role of the federal government in education in an effort to close the achievement gap of underprivileged students. The law was replaced in 2015 after widespread pushback against its testing provisions.

REVIEW

- In what ways did George W. Bush's version of "compassionate conservativism" differ from his father's domestic policies, and in what ways did it show continuity with them?

Global War on Terror (GWOT) A military campaign against international terrorism launched by the George W. Bush administration after the attacks on September 11, 2001. The campaign against international terrorist organizations and governments that supported them led to long and costly conflicts in Afghanistan and Iraq.

International and Domestic Challenges

Events originating abroad vaulted President Bush into the role of wartime president. In foreign affairs, Bush relied heavily on Vice President Richard (Dick) Cheney, Secretary of Defense Donald Rumsfeld, and Condoleezza Rice. The president's closest advisers sought to reshape critical parts of the post–Cold War world through preemptive force, most notably in the Persian Gulf.

Less than a year into the Bush presidency, the United States experienced the worst terrorist attack in its history. The terrorist organization responsible for the attack was al-Qaeda, which began in the late 1980s as one of many groups who fought the Soviet Union's occupation of Afghanistan. However, starting in the 1990s, the group's leader, Osama bin Laden, increasingly aimed the organization's efforts against the United States because of its support for Israel and its occupation of bases in Saudi Arabia in the aftermath of the first Gulf War.

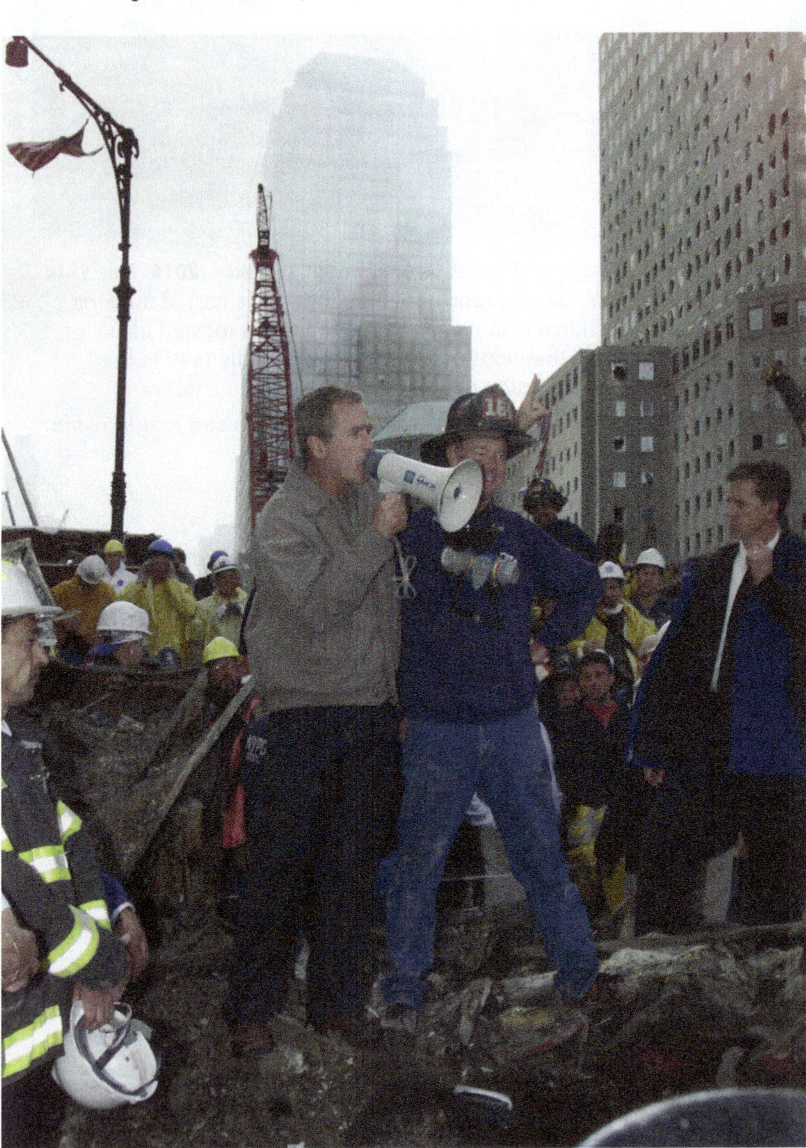

Paul J. Richards/Getty Images

President Bush at Ground Zero On September 14, 2001, President George W. Bush toured the wreckage of the destroyed World Trade Center. Standing on a pile of rubble, he heard firefighters, police officers, and other rescuers shout, "USA, USA." He responded: "I can hear you. The rest of the world hears you. And the people who knocked these buildings down will hear all of us soon."

How did the sentiments Bush expressed lead to the Global War on Terror?

On September 11, 2001, nineteen al-Qaeda terrorists hijacked four American planes from airports in Boston, Washington, D.C., and Newark, New Jersey. Two groups of these terrorists hijacked two planes departing from Boston and crashed them into the Twin Towers at the World Trade Center in New York City. A third group of terrorists hijacked and crashed a third plane into the Pentagon in Washington, D.C. While passengers on the fourth plane attempted to halt the attack by charging the cockpit, the terrorists in control of the plane crashed it in the Pennsylvania countryside. After the Twin Towers burned for over two hours, both collapsed, killing civilians and rescue workers inside. All told, almost 3,000 Americans died in the 9/11 attacks.

After the attacks on the World Trade Center and the Pentagon, Bush launched a **Global War on Terror (GWOT)** that led to protracted and costly conflicts in Afghanistan and Iraq and debates over civil liberties at home. First, the president dispatched U.S. troops to Afghanistan, whose Taliban leaders refused to turn over Osama bin

Laden and other terrorists operating training centers in the country. A combination of anti-Taliban warlords and U.S. military forces quickly toppled the Taliban regime and installed a pro-American government. However, the elusive bin Laden escaped into a remote area of Pakistan.

On the home front, the war on terror prompted passage of the **USA Patriot Act** in October 2001. The measure eased restrictions on domestic and foreign intelligence gathering and expanded the authority of law-enforcement and immigration officials in detaining and deporting immigrants suspected of terrorism-related acts. The act gave law enforcement agencies nearly unlimited authority to wiretap telephones, retrieve e-mail messages, and search the medical, financial, and library borrowing records of individuals, including U.S. citizens, suspected of involvement in terrorism overseas or at home.

The computer age had provided terrorist networks like al-Qaeda with the means to communicate quickly across national borders through electronic mail and cell phones and to raise money and launder it into safe bank accounts online. Computer technology also gave U.S. intelligence agencies ways to monitor these communications and transactions. Despite some criticism of the provisions of the Patriot Act as harsh violations of civil liberties, Congress renewed the act with only minor changes in 2006.

As part of the effort to combat terrorist threats to the United States, Congress created a cabinet-level superagency in 2002, the **Department of Homeland Security**, responsible for developing a national strategy against further terrorist threats. In 2004, Congress created the Office of the Director of National Intelligence to coordinate the work of security agencies more effectively.

Amid rising anti-Muslim sentiments in the weeks and months following September 11, some people committed acts of violence against mosques, Arab American community centers and businesses, individual Muslims, and people they thought were Muslims. Anti-Muslim hate crimes in the United States skyrocketed from 28 in 2000 to 481 in 2001, a 1,700 percent increase.

President Bush and his advisers sought to expand the war on terror beyond defeating the Taliban in Afghanistan. They envisioned a larger plan to reshape the politics of the Middle East and Persian Gulf regions along pro-American lines. By replacing authoritarian regimes with democratic governments in places like Iraq and Afghanistan, the Bush administration envisioned a cascading effect that would lead to the toppling of reactionary leaders throughout the region.

The war on terror was also designed to improve the country's energy security. Political stability and pro-Western governments in these regions would also ensure that they continued to export enough natural resources, such as oil, to meet consumer demand in the United States and its European allies. In crafting this strategy, the Bush administration departed from the post–World War II policy of containing enemies short of going to war. Instead, the **Bush Doctrine** proposed undertaking preemptive war against despotic governments deemed a threat to U.S. national security, even if that danger was not imminent.

Embracing this doctrine, President Bush declared in his State of the Union address in January 2002 that Iraq was part of an **"axis of evil,"** along with Iran and North Korea. The Bush administration considered Saddam Hussein, the Iraqi dictator, a sponsor of terrorism and sought to remove him from power. The administration believed this would also open a path to overthrowing the radical Islamic government of neighboring Iran.

USA Patriot Act

A law passed in 2001 in response to the September 11 terror attacks. The law eased restrictions on domestic and foreign intelligence gathering and expanded governmental power to deport immigrants suspected of terrorism.

Department of Homeland Security

A cabinet-level agency created in 2002 that is responsible for various aspects of public security, including counterterrorism, border security, cybersecurity, and air and sea travel.

Bush Doctrine

President George W. Bush's proposal to engage in preemptive war against tyrannical governments that were perceived as a threat to U.S. national security, even if the danger was not immediate.

axis of evil

A term used by President George W. Bush in 2002. Bush claimed Iraq, Iran, and North Korea were a part of an "axis of evil" due to their support of terrorist organizations and pursuit of chemical, biological, and nuclear weapons.

AP® EXAM TIP

September 11, 2001, marked the first major attack against the U.S. homeland since Pearl Harbor in 1941, uniting the country in the initial fight against terrorism and al-Qaeda. Yet, over time, national unity faded with the invasion of Iraq, passage of the Patriot Act, and the extended conflict in Afghanistan. Be able to explain how these and other controversies impacted U.S. politics and foreign policy.

AP® WORKING with EVIDENCE

Source: President George W. Bush, News Conference on Iraq, 2003

"This has been an important week on two fronts on our war against terror. First, thanks to the hard work of American and Pakistani officials, we captured the mastermind of the September the 11th attacks against our nation. Khalid Sheikh Mohammed conceived and planned the hijackings and directed the actions of the hijackers. We believe his capture will further disrupt the terror network and their planning for additional attacks.

Second, we have arrived at an important moment in confronting the threat posed to our nation and to peace by Saddam Hussein and his weapons of terror. In New York tomorrow, the United Nations Security Council will receive an update from the chief weapons inspector. The world needs him to answer a single question: Has the Iraqi regime fully and unconditionally disarmed, as required by Resolution 1441, or has it not? . . .

Iraqi operatives continue to hide biological and chemical agents to avoid detection by inspectors. In some cases, these materials have been moved to different locations every 12 to 24 hours, or placed in vehicles that are in residential neighborhoods. . . .

These are not the actions of a regime that is disarming. These are the actions of a regime engaged in a willful charade. These are the actions of a regime that systematically and deliberately is defying the world. If the Iraqi regime were disarming, we would know it, because we would see it. Iraq's weapons would be presented to inspectors, and the world would witness their destruction. Instead, with the world demanding disarmament, and more than 200,000 troops positioned near his country, Saddam Hussein's response is to produce a few weapons for show, while he hides the rest and builds even more."

Questions for Analysis

1. Identify the ways in which Saddam Hussein's actions raised suspicions about his willingness to disarm.
2. Explain how President Bush drew connections between the attacks on September 11, 2001, and Saddam Hussein's actions.
3. Explain how this document illustrates the Bush Doctrine.
4. Evaluate the extent of continuity in American foreign policy regarding Iraq during the presidencies of George H. W. Bush (1989–1993) and George W. Bush (2001–2009).

By late 2002, the Bush administration had convinced a majority of Congress and the American people that Iraq presented an immediate danger to the security of the United States. This was due in part to efforts to connect Saddam Hussein to the al-Qaeda terrorists of September 11. The administration also argued that Iraq was well advanced in building and stockpiling "weapons of mass destruction," such as chemical, biological, and even nuclear weapons, despite evidence to the contrary.

In March 2003, after a congressional vote of approval, U.S. military aircraft unleashed bombing attacks on Baghdad. In the 1991 Gulf War, the first President Bush had responded to the Iraqi invasion of Kuwait by leading a broad coalition of nations, including Arab countries. In 2003, the United States did not wait for an overt act of aggression and led a much smaller alliance of nations, with only Great Britain supplying significant combat troops to the **Iraq War**. Within weeks, Hussein went into hiding, prompting President Bush to declare that "major combat operations had ended in Iraq" in a speech aboard the aircraft carrier USS *Abraham Lincoln*. Several months later, Hussein was captured by U.S. military forces.

Iraq War
The invasion and occupation of Iraq by the United States and its allies from 2003 to 2011. The administration of George W. Bush started the conflict in an effort to overthrow Iraq's dictator, Saddam Hussein, and destroy its suspected weapons of mass destruction, which no longer existed in significant quantities.

Although at first it appeared to many that the military conflict would be short-lived, the war dragged on, despite the presence of 130,000 U.S. and 30,000 British troops. More American soldiers—over 4,000—died after the invasion than had died during it. The perception of the United States as an occupying power destabilized Iraq, leading to a civil war between the country's Shi'ite Muslim majority, which had been persecuted under Saddam Hussein, and its Sunni minority, which Hussein represented. In the northern part of the country, the Kurdish minority, another group brutalized by Hussein, also battled Sunnis. Moreover, al-Qaeda forces, which previously had been absent from the country, joined the fray.

At the same time, the Bush administration instituted the policy of incarcerating suspected al-Qaeda rebels in the U.S. military base at **Guantánamo Bay** in Cuba, without due process of law. The facility housed more than six hundred men classified as "enemy combatants," who were subject to torture and deprived of legal counsel.

Guantánamo Bay
The site of a U.S. military base in Cuba, where the George W. Bush administration imprisoned suspected al-Qaeda members without due process of law. Despite campaigning on promises to end this policy, the Obama administration failed to close the Guantánamo Bay prison, and it continues to operate today.

Amid a protracted war in Iraq, President Bush won reelection in 2004 by promising to stay the course and deter further terrorism. Although the Democratic presidential candidate, Senator John Kerry of Massachusetts, criticized Bush's handling of Iraq, Bush emerged victorious with 286 electoral votes and a majority of the popular vote (50.7 percent).

During his second term, President Bush's approval rating suffered. Several issues—sectarian violence in Iraq, mounting death tolls, and the failures of the U.S.-supported Iraqi government—turned the majority of Americans against the war, though American troops remained in Iraq and Afghanistan. With turmoil also continuing in the Persian Gulf, the threat of nuclear proliferation grew. Iraq did not have nuclear weapons, but Iran sought to develop nuclear capabilities. Iranian leaders claimed that they wanted nuclear technology for peaceful purposes, but the Bush administration believed that Iran's real purpose was to build nuclear devices to attack Israel and establish its supremacy in the region. Likewise, in Asia, North Korea began to refine its nuclear capabilities in hopes of maintaining its communist dictatorship.

President Bush also faced domestic challenges during his second term. On August 29, 2005, **Hurricane Katrina** slammed into the Gulf coast states of Louisiana and Mississippi. This powerful storm devastated New Orleans, a city with a population of nearly 500,000, a majority of whom was Black. The flood surge caused poorly maintained levees to break, flooding large areas of the city and trapping 50,000 residents.

Hurricane Katrina
A storm that hit the Gulf coast states of Louisiana, Mississippi, and Alabama in 2005. The hurricane caused major flooding in New Orleans after levees broke, resulting in approximately 1,800 deaths.

In the days after the storm hit, chaos plagued New Orleans. Evacuees were housed in the Superdome football stadium and a municipal auditorium without adequate food, water, and sanitary facilities. The flooding killed at least 1,800 residents of the Gulf coast, New Orleans's population dropped by around 130,000 residents, and critics blamed state and local officials, as well as the federal government, for a slower response to the crisis than they believed necessary.

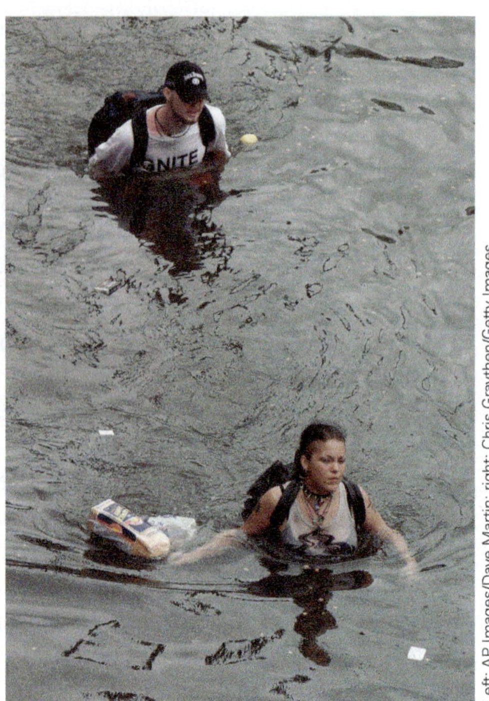

Left: AP Images/Dave Martin; right: Chris Graythen/Getty Images

Two Perceptions of New Orleans Looting Compare the two photographs taken in the aftermath of Hurricane Katrina. The original caption for the photo on the left was, "A young man walks through chest-deep floodwater after looting a grocery store in New Orleans," while the caption for the photo on the right read, "Two residents wade through chest-deep water after finding bread and soda from a local grocery store after Hurricane Katrina came through the area in New Orleans."

What would explain the discrepancy between "looting" and "finding" in the two images?

REVIEW

- How did the September 11, 2001, attacks shape George W. Bush's foreign and domestic policy?
- What domestic challenges did the Bush administration face?

The Great Recession

In 2008, the last year of his presidency, President Bush faced his greatest domestic challenge. The boom times of the previous decade came to a sudden halt. The stock market's Dow Jones Industrial Average, which had hit a high of 14,000, fell 6,000 points, the steepest percentage drop since the Great Depression. Americans who had invested their money in the stock market lost trillions of dollars. The gross domestic product fell by about 6 percent, a loss too great for the economy to absorb quickly. Millions of Americans lost their jobs as consumer spending decreased, and many forfeited their homes when they could no longer afford to pay their mortgages. Unemployment jumped from 4.9 percent in January 2008 to 7.6 percent a year later. Confronted by this spiraling disaster, President Bush approved a $700 billion bailout plan to rescue the nation's largest banks and brokerage houses.

Great Recession

The severe economic decline in the United States and throughout the world from 2007 to 2009, leading to bank failures, high unemployment, home foreclosures, and large federal deficits.

The causes of the **Great Recession** were many and had developed over a long period. Since the Reagan presidency, the federal government had relaxed regulation of the financial industry, including repeal of the Glass-Steagall Act (see Module 7.10) during the Clinton administration. Also, the Federal Reserve Bank encouraged excessive borrowing by keeping interest rates very low and relaxed its oversight of Wall Street practices that placed ordinary investors' money at risk. Investment banks developed elaborate computer models that produced new kinds of financial instruments, which went unregulated and whose complex nature few people understood. Insurance companies such as American International Group (AIG) sold credit default swaps (a contract for an investor to purchase protection against losses) for risky securities, worsening the financial crisis.

Consumers also shared some of the blame. Many took advantage of risky but easily accessible mortgage policies that appealed to borrowers with low incomes or poor credit ratings. Dubious mortgage products were pushed by banks and mortgage brokers eager to earn a quick commission, such as zero-down payment mortgages, allowing borrowers to state their income without documenting it on loan applications, and negative amortization borrowing, where the balance increases over time. In this environment, mortgages were doomed to fail as soon as property values stopped rising. When the housing market collapsed, many homeowners ended up owing banks and mortgage companies much more than their homes were worth, leading to a wave of foreclosures and destabilizing banks, brokerage houses, and insurance companies.

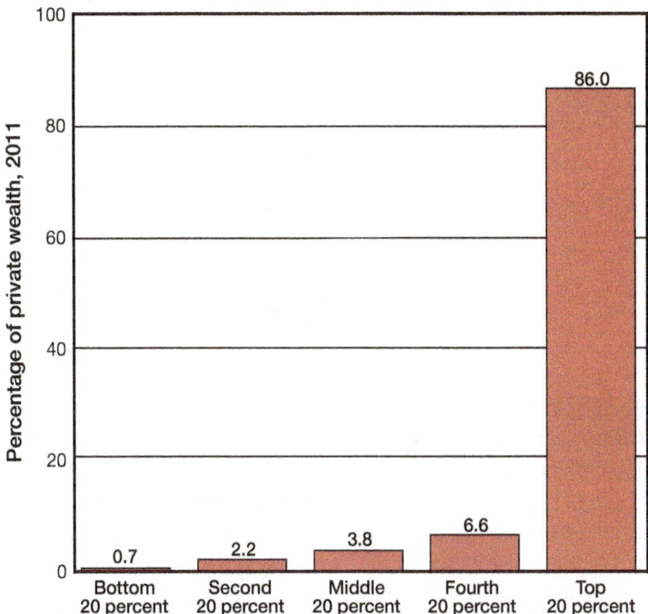

Wealth Inequality (Capital Income), 2011 The decline of American manufacturing and the expansion of the low-wage service sector, combined with the rise of high-tech industries and unregulated investment banking, led to growing disparities of wealth in the early twenty-first century. Disparities existed even within the top percentile. In 2011, the top 1 percent controlled more than half of all capital income. (Capital income includes taxable and nontaxable interest income, as well as income from dividends, capital gains, and corporate tax liability. Capital income does not include earned income in the form of salaries and wages.)

How does the distribution of wealth in the graph compare to the distribution of wealth in America in the late 1800s?

Wealth remained concentrated in relatively few hands. In 2007, the top 1 percent of households owned 34.6 percent of all privately held wealth, and the next 19 percent held 50.5 percent. The other 80 percent of Americans owned only 15 percent of the wealth, and the gap between rich and poor continued to widen. This level of wealth inequality made it extremely difficult to support an economy that required ever-expanding purchasing power and produced steadily rising personal debt.

With the interdependence of economies through globalization, the Great Recession spread rapidly throughout the world. Great Britain's banking system teetered on the edge of collapse. Other nations in the European Union (EU), most notably Greece and Spain, verged on bankruptcy and had to be rescued by stronger EU nations. In providing financial assistance to its member states, the EU required countries such as Greece to slash spending for government services and to lower minimum wages. Even in China, where the economy had boomed as a result of globalization, businesses shut down and unemployment rose as global consumer demand for its products declined.

REVIEW

- What economic changes after 1988 contributed to the Great Recession?
- What were the global effects of the Great Recession?

Obama and Domestic Politics

In the midst of the Great Recession, the United States held the 2008 presidential election. The Republican candidate, John McCain, was a Vietnam War hero and a senator from Arizona. His Democratic opponent from Illinois, Barack Obama, had served only four years in the Senate before his candidacy. For their vice presidential running mates,

McCain chose Sarah Palin, the outspoken and popular first-term governor of Alaska, and Obama selected Joseph Biden, the senior senator from Delaware.

Obama connected with voters throughout America by speaking about his background as a biracial child, the son of an immigrant from Kenya and the grandson of a World War II veteran from Kansas. As important, the former community organizer succeeded in building a nationwide, grassroots political movement through digital technology. He raised an enormous amount of campaign money from ordinary donors through the Internet and used Web sites and text messaging to mobilize his supporters.

Obama's victory was also aided by the fact that many Americans blamed the Bush administration for the recession, and Obama's campaign platform offered hope for economic recovery. Obama captured 53 percent of the popular vote, obtaining a majority of votes from Blacks, Latinos, women, and the young, who turned out in record numbers, and 365 electoral votes. The Democrats also won majorities in the House and Senate.

Patient Protection and Affordable Care Act ("Obamacare")
Passed in 2010, this law expanded health insurance to millions of Americans previously uncovered through a variety of measures including extending Medicaid, setting up health-insurance exchanges, allowing children to remain under their parents' coverage until the age of twenty-six, and preventing insurance companies from denying coverage based on preexisting conditions.

President Obama continued the Bush administration's bailout of collapsing banks and investment firms and expanded it to include American automobile companies, which within three years bounced back, became profitable again, and began paying back the government for the bailout. In 2009, the president supported passage of an economic stimulus plan that provided federal funds to state and local governments to create jobs and keep their employees, including teachers, on the public payroll.

More controversially, President Obama pushed Congress to pass the **Patient Protection and Affordable Care Act ("Obamacare")** in 2010, a measure mandating that all Americans had to obtain health insurance or face a tax penalty, that no one could be denied coverage for a preexisting condition, and that insurance companies extend coverage for dependents up to age twenty-six. Obama also signed into law the repeal of President Clinton's "don't ask, don't tell" policy, which had prevented people who are openly gay, bisexual, or lesbian from serving in the military.

A Political Cartoonist's View of the Presidential Election of Barack Obama, 2008 Published by politico.com on November 6, 2008, two days after the election of Barack Obama, this cartoon drawn by Matt Wuerker captures the joyous response of many Americans, Black and white, to the victory of the first Black president.

Why does the cartoonist include the Lincoln Memorial and the Capitol in the image? How does he convey his attitude toward the election of Barack Obama in this cartoon?

President Obama also took action to address the divisive issue of immigration. Congress had not passed the **Development, Relief, and Education for Alien Minors (DREAM) Act**, first introduced in 2001, which would have provided an opportunity for undocumented minors in the United States to gain legal residency status. To protect these so-called "Dreamers," the president instituted the **Deferred Action for Childhood Arrivals (DACA)** policy in 2012, which allows children who have entered the country illegally to receive a renewable two-year extension of their U.S. residence along with eligibility for work permits.

President Obama encountered vigorous political opposition as Republicans in Congress blocked much of Obama's agenda. In 2009, a group of conservatives and libertarians formed the **Tea Party movement**, which labeled the president as a "socialist" for what they perceived as an effort to expand federal control over the economy and diminish individual liberty with the health care act. The rise of the Tea Party reflected heightened partisanship within the country. In the 2010 midterm elections, Republicans, energized by the Tea Party movement, regained a majority in the House while the Democratic majority in the Senate narrowed.

Obama also encountered political difficulties from the left. Although the president's policies prevented a possible collapse of the financial system, unemployment remained above 8 percent (a drop from its high of 10.2 percent) at the end of 2011. With millions of people still out of work, a resurgent Wall Street rewarded its managers and employees with big financial bonuses as large corporations earned huge profits during the "jobless" economic recovery. Protesters in cities around the country launched the **Occupy Wall Street movement**, which attacked what they perceived as corporate greed, economic inequality, and government ineffectiveness by staging an extended protest and sit-in in the financial district of New York City. Many in the movement were inspired to act by declining tax revenues that they saw as responsible for state budget deficits and cuts in spending on education, social services, and infrastructure while young people faced high unemployment and crushing student loan debts.

With unemployment remaining high, economic growth moving at a slow pace, and a number of European nations unable to pay mounting debts, the economy loomed as the top issue in the 2012 presidential election. The Republican nominee, Mitt Romney, the former governor of Massachusetts, appealed to conservative voters by advocating a reduction in the role of the federal government in health care and for a general reduction in federal spending coupled with a reduction of income tax rates. Despite the slower-than-expected economic recovery, Barack Obama won reelection against Romney by holding together his coalition of Black, Latino, female, young, and lower-income voters.

During President Obama's second term, the economy showed greater improvement. The unemployment rate dropped to 4.9 percent in February 2016, the lowest figure in eight years. From 2010 to 2014, the gross domestic product grew steadily by an average of more than 2 percent, and the strengthening economy cut the budget deficit significantly.

However, as the economy recovered from recession, real wages declined and income and wealth inequality widened. The top 1 percent gained about 95 percent of the income growth since 2009, and the top 10 percent held its highest share of income since World War I.

One reason for this widening gap was that since 2000, the U.S. economy had lost five million good-paying manufacturing jobs. Many of the jobs created by the recovery were low-wage service positions. Union membership continued its long-term decline, eliminating a major means for workers to increase their wages. At the same time, the wealthiest Americans benefited from the soaring stock market and rising capital gains.

Development, Relief, and Education for Alien Minors (DREAM) Act
Legislation proposed in 2001 to provide the children of undocumented immigrants in the United States the opportunity to gain legal residency status. The proposed legislation failed to pass Congress.

Deferred Action for Childhood Arrivals (DACA)
A policy, initiated under the administration of President Obama in 2012, that allowed undocumented immigrant children to apply for renewable two-year extensions, granting them temporary residency in the United States along with eligibility for work permits.

Tea Party movement
A loose coalition of conservatives, populists, and libertarians that advocated small government, low taxes, and reduced federal deficits. The Tea Party movement became a driving force in the Republican Party and mobilized opposition to President Obama's agenda.

Occupy Wall Street movement
A loose coalition of progressive and radical forces that emerged in 2011 in New York City and around the country to protest what they perceived to be corporate greed and federal policies that benefit the wealthy.

In two other areas, equality in marriage and the environment, the Obama administration made major policy changes in its second term. Initially, Obama had supported civil unions rather than same-sex marriage, but in 2012, he changed his position in support of same-sex marriage. The following year, the Supreme Court overturned the 1996 Defense of Marriage Act, thereby extending recognition of same-sex marriage. In 2015, in ***Obergefell v. Hodges***, the Court legalized same-sex marriage nationwide. With respect to the environment, the Obama administration sought to address climate change by encouraging fuel efficiency and clean energy production and by extending protection of significant cultural and natural landmarks.

Obergefell v. Hodges
A Supreme Court decision in 2015 legalizing same-sex marriage throughout the nation on the basis of the Fourteenth Amendment's equal protection and due process clauses.

Obama's second term also saw renewed calls by activists for criminal justice and policing reforms. While many white people saw police as protectors, many Black people had long-standing grievances against the criminal-justice system and often viewed law enforcement with suspicion or as threats to their safety. A series of controversial police killings of unarmed Black people in Ferguson, Missouri; Cleveland, Ohio; Staten Island, New York; and Baltimore, Maryland, renewed these fears.

Black Lives Matter
A social movement that formed after Trayvon Martin, an unarmed Black youth, was shot by a civilian in 2012. Organized by protesters around the social media hashtag #blacklivesmatter, the movement advocated a policy agenda that mainly focused on criminal justice and police reforms.

The movement that came to be known as **Black Lives Matter** formed in the wake of the fatal shooting of Trayvon Martin, an unarmed Black teenager, by a civilian in 2012. Technology helped spread its message through social media, especially Twitter. As a result of federal investigations, the Justice Department in 2015 found a pattern of systemic racism and excessive use of force in the Ferguson and Cleveland police departments and negotiated settlements that instituted reforms, although persistent problems remained.

AP® WORKING with EVIDENCE

Source: Frederick C. Harris, *The Price of the Ticket: Barack Obama and the Rise and Decline of Black Politics*, 2012

> "[W]ith the election of Barack Obama as the forty-fourth president of the United States, one could easily draw the conclusion that black America reached the pinnacle of political empowerment—a journey that has taken blacks from one of the most marginalized groups in American history (alongside Native Americans) to a key constituency that helps to elect a man of African descent to lead the nation. . . . Far from black America gaining greater influence in American politics, Obama's ascendency to the White House actually signals a decline of a politics aimed at challenging racial inequality head on. . . .
>
> In the age of Obama . . . the majority of black voters have struck a bargain with Obama. In exchange for the president's silence on community-focused interests, black voters are content with a governing philosophy that helps 'all people' and a politics centered on preserving the symbol of a black president and family in the White House. . . . Indeed, the symbol of a black president is not a trivial matter. Yet, the grand bargain granting black pride in exchange for silence on race-specific issues and the marginalization of targeted policies by the Obama administration have left much to be desired. . . .
>
> [T]his one-dimensional approach to policymaking will not catch all the social ills facing black communities. . . . For black America—and its leaders—the dispiriting silence to this reality is the price paid for the election of the nation's first black president."

Questions for Analysis

1. Identify the "grand bargain" that Harris claims Black voters struck with Obama.
2. Describe the shortcomings of this "grand bargain," according to Harris.
3. Evaluate the extent to which the election of Barack Obama marked a change in American race relations.

REVIEW

- What major domestic challenges did Obama face during his presidency?

Obama and the World

Throughout Obama's two terms, his administration faced serious tests of its international leadership. In 2008, the president appointed Hillary Clinton, the former First Lady and a senator from New York, as his secretary of state. The U.S. military increased combat troop withdrawals from Iraq and turned over security for the country to the newly elected Iraqi government. At the same time, the Obama administration stepped up the war in Afghanistan by increasing U.S. troop levels, which led to a rise in casualties. Then, in 2011, the Obama administration achieved a dramatic success when U.S. special forces killed Osama bin Laden in his hideout in Pakistan.

By 2016, with John Kerry now his secretary of state, the president had withdrawn most combat soldiers from Afghanistan. Yet Iraq remained unstable in the absence of a strong U.S. military presence, while the Taliban in Afghanistan had regained control of large portions of the country. Despite bin Laden's death, radical jihadists continued to pose a serious danger.

Other international challenges continued as well. From 2006 to 2013, a hostile North Korea tested a series of nuclear weapons. During this period, instability in other parts of Asia, the Middle East, and the Persian Gulf also heightened U.S. security concerns and underscored the difficulties of achieving lasting peace in these regions (**Map 9.6**). In 2011, in a period known as the **Arab Spring**, great changes swept across the Middle East, as young people, armed mainly with cell phones and connected through social media networks, toppled pro-Western but despotic governments in Egypt and Tunisia and persuaded the leader of Yemen to step down. In Libya, armed rebels succeeded in overthrowing the anti-American dictator Muammar al-Qaddafi.

However, many of these changes in the Middle East did not last. The military returned to power in Egypt, and civil war consumed Libya and Syria. The Obama administration drew criticism for unsuccessful interventions in both countries, and for its lack of full support for rebels against Syrian dictator Bashar al-Assad. Even more dangerous was the rise of a new militant terrorist organization in the region known as the **Islamic State in Iraq and Syria (ISIS)**, an offshoot of al-Qaeda that grew out of the sectarian violence following the overthrow of Saddam Hussein in Iraq. ISIS took over parts of Syria and Iraq, prompting the United States and some Arab nations to launch air strikes against its forces.

The ongoing Syrian civil war had profound effects on the rest of the world. Starting in 2010, millions of Syrians fled their homes, and tens of thousands sought refuge in Western Europe and the United States. This movement of refugees, which is greater than at any time since World War II, overwhelmed those European countries to which they first came—Greece, Hungary, and the Czech Republic. Hungary constructed fences to stop the flow of migrants, while the EU split over how to manage the crisis.

Arab Spring
A series of pro-democracy protests and rebellions in the Middle East in 2011, which led to the toppling of pro-Western but despotic governments in Egypt, Tunisia, Yemen, and Libya. Street protests that did not result in regime changes also took place in several other Arab countries during this time.

Islamic State in Iraq and Syria (ISIS)
A jihadist terrorist group originally founded in 1999, which gained strength from the sectarian violence that followed the 2003 U.S. invasion of Iraq. The group captured territory in Iraq and Syria and claimed responsibility for terrorist attacks in Paris, France, San Bernardino, California, and Lebanon. However, by 2017, ISIS had been largely driven out of the territories it formerly occupied by American, Russian, Iraqi, Kurdish, and Syrian government forces.

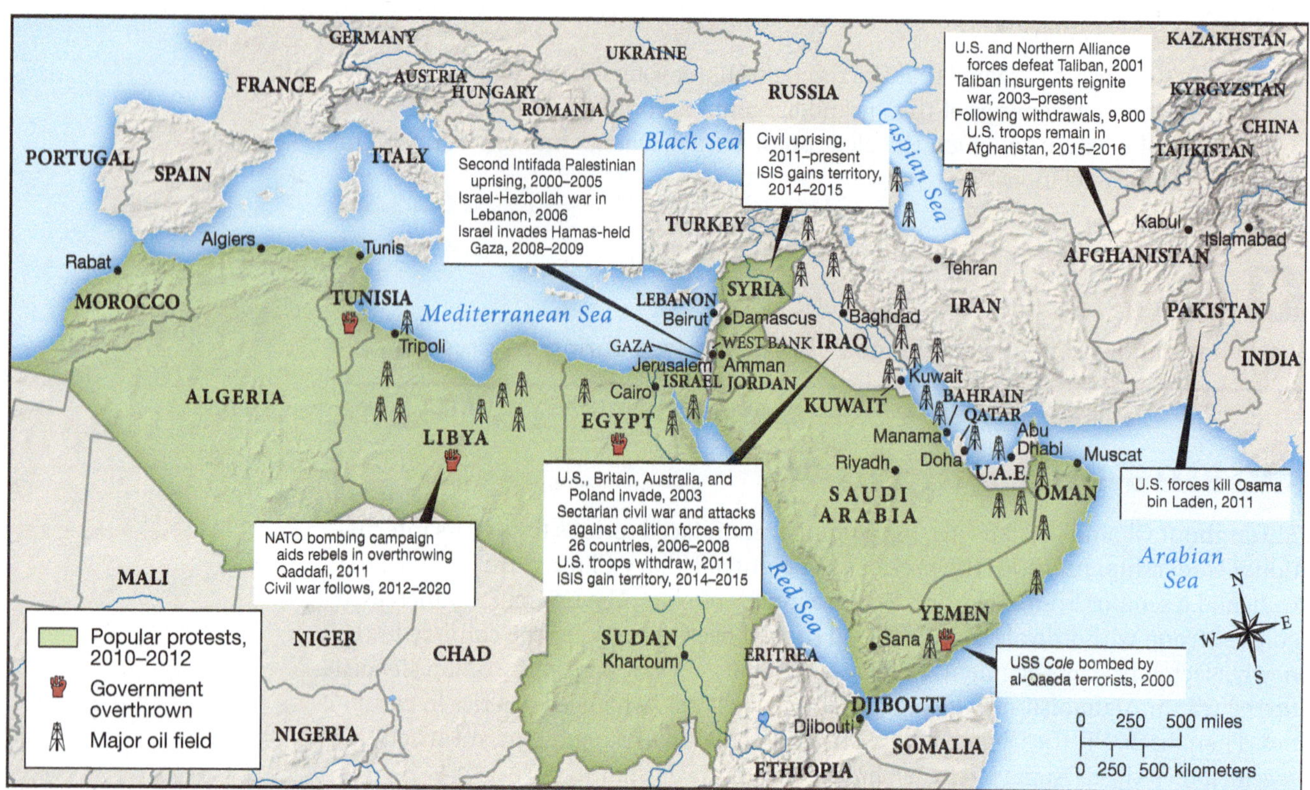

MAP 9.6 The Middle East, 2000–2020 Since 2000, the Middle East has been marked by both terrorism and democratic uprisings. After 9/11, the United States tried to transform Iraq and Afghanistan through military occupation, which led to prolonged wars. Yet popular rebellions in 2011, led by young people and fueled by new technology, created hope that change was possible. By 2016, however, the military had regained power in Egypt, and Libya had descended into civil war. Syria remained involved in a brutal civil war. The terrorist military organization ISIS captured sections of Syria as well as territory in Iraq, but in 2017, they were driven out of most of this territory by Syrian government, Russian, Iraqi, Kurdish, and American-backed military forces.

What similarities do the countries where these uprisings took place share?

From the outset of his first term in 2009, President Obama fought the war against terror by stepping up the use of remote-controlled armed drones (unmanned, aerial vehicles) against al-Qaeda and ISIS leaders in Pakistan, Afghanistan, Yemen, and Somalia. Although some top terrorist leaders were killed, drone attacks also resulted in significant civilian deaths.

At home, antiterrorist surveillance provoked growing controversy. Under the USA Patriot Act, the National Security Agency (NSA) began collecting and storing phone records of U.S. citizens. The NSA did not listen to the calls, but it drew on these bulk data to track suspected terrorists. The existence of this operation came to light in 2013, when Edward Snowden, an intelligence analyst contracted by the NSA, leaked the information to the *Guardian* newspaper before seeking refuge abroad, eventually settling in Russia. Some believed Snowden's disclosures ensured public scrutiny of the balance between national security and individual privacy, while his critics claimed that he undermined national security and endangered Americans in an age of terrorist threats. Snowden's revelations led Congress to pass legislation in 2015 curtailing the collection of intelligence data.

AP® WORKING with EVIDENCE

Source: Edward Snowden, Interview, *The Guardian*, July 18, 2014

"We constantly hear the phrase 'national security' but when the state begins . . . broadly intercepting the communications, seizing the communications by themselves, without any warrant, without any suspicion, without any judicial involvement, without any demonstration of probable cause, are they really protecting national security or are they protecting state security?

What I came to feel . . . is that a regime that is described as a national security agency has stopped representing the public interest and has instead begun to protect and promote state security interests. And the idea of western democracy as having state security bureaus, just that term, that phrase itself, 'state security bureau,' is kind of chilling. . . .

Generally, it's not the people at the working level you need to worry about. It's the senior officials, it's the policymakers who are shielded from accountability, who are shielded from oversight and who are allowed to make decisions that affect all of our lives without any public input, any public debate, or any electoral consequences because their decisions and the consequences of the decisions are never known.

Because of the advance of technology, storage becomes cheaper and cheaper year after year and when our ability to store data outpaces the expense of creating that data, we end up with things that are no longer held for short-term periods, they're held for long-term periods and then they're held for a longer term period. At the NSA for example, we store data for five years on individuals. And that's before getting a waiver to extend that even further."

Questions for Analysis

1. Identify the aspects of public surveillance that Snowden believes have increasingly "shielded [policymakers] from accountability."
2. Explain how technology fueled these surveillance measures.
3. Evaluate the extent to which the consequences of the surveillance measures Snowden describes represent a change from the U.S. government's interpretation of Americans' right to privacy and due process during the twentieth century.

On other foreign issues, President Obama departed from previous foreign policy. In 2014, he set in motion the normalization of diplomatic relations with Cuba and, the following year, along with several other world powers, negotiated the **Iran Nuclear Agreement** restricting its nuclear program. In contrast, relations with Russia deteriorated. In 2014, Russia, led by Vladimir Putin, annexed its former territory of the Crimea from Ukraine, and in 2015, it provided military support for pro-Russian separatists in eastern Ukraine. In response, the United States and the EU imposed economic sanctions on Russia but declined to take military action. Later in 2015, Russia sent military forces to Syria to support the government of the dictator Bashar al-Assad, a long-time ally, and fight his opponents, both ISIS and rebels backed by the United States.

Iran Nuclear Agreement Compliance agreement in 2015 between Iran and the United Nations Security Council, which placed restrictions on Iran's nuclear program in exchange for an easing of economic sanctions by partner nations. In 2018, President Trump withdrew the United States from the agreement.

The United States faced global economic and environmental challenges as well. As China flourished economically, American workers lost jobs, and China reached a nearly $200 billion trade surplus with the United States. In addition, the growth of manufacturing and the market economy in China resulted in the rising consumption of oil and gasoline. The increase in carbon emissions in China and other parts of Asia contributed to the problem of climate change.

According to climate scientists, emissions of greenhouse gases into the atmosphere in the twentieth and twenty-first centuries resulted in an increase in global temperatures, causing a cascade of side effects. As temperatures climbed, they caused the melting of glaciers, a rise in the sea level and ocean temperature, extreme fluctuations of weather with severely damaging storms, and famines. Disruptions in industrial and agricultural production caused by storms and the subsequent expense of rebuilding have had a negative impact on the economies worldwide. In December 2015, the United States joined 194 nations, including China and India, in signing the **Paris Climate Agreement** to reduce greenhouse gas emissions produced from fossil fuels.

Paris Climate Agreement A worldwide agreement by the United States and 194 other nations in 2015 to dramatically reduce greenhouse-gas emissions produced from fossil fuels. In 2017, President Donald Trump withdrew the U.S. commitment to the agreement, and then in 2021, President Joseph Biden rejoined the United States to the agreement.

In addition, the racial and ethnic composition of the population has been transformed in the twenty-first century through immigration and intermarriage. In 2012, the U.S. Census Bureau reported that nonwhite babies made up the majority of births for the first time. If the current trends in immigration and birthrates continue, the percentage of Latinos and Asian Americans in the nation will increase, while that of white and Black people will decline. In 2010, the Census Bureau reported that one of seven new marriages, or 14.6 percent, was interracial. In 1961, when Barack Obama was born, the figure for interracial marriages was less than 0.1 percent. Thus, in an increasingly globalized nation, debates over immigration, race, and citizenship have taken new forms and significance.

REVIEW

- To what extent did the Obama administration's foreign policies differ from those of the George W. Bush administration?

The 2016 Election

As Barack Obama's second term drew to a close in 2016, Americans elected Donald Trump to succeed him. A New York City real estate tycoon and the host of the reality television show *The Apprentice*, Trump was a celebrity and political outsider who had never held political office before running for the presidency. His opponent, Hillary Clinton, was a political insider who had served as First Lady, a U.S. senator, and secretary of state.

After waging hard-fought primaries, Donald Trump and Hillary Clinton faced each other in the general election. Clinton ran on a progressive platform that focused on addressing growing wealth inequality. Her platform included proposals for campaign finance reform, affordable college education, and a path to citizenship for undocumented immigrants.

Running as an antiestablishment candidate, Trump adopted the slogan "Make America Great Again" (MAGA). As part of his "America First" platform, Trump criticized international military alliances such as NATO, a major component of U.S. foreign policy since World War II, by emphasizing that not all alliance members contributed their fair share.

Trump also embraced populist opposition to immigration. On the campaign trail, he promised to temporarily limit Muslim immigration to the United States and to build a wall along the Mexican border at Mexico's expense to prevent "criminals" from entering the country. Trump also opposed free-trade agreements that he claimed shipped jobs overseas, remarking that NAFTA was "the worst trade deal in history." This stance likely appealed to many working-class Americans who had been left behind by the continued decline of U.S. manufacturing.

Trump's political appeal was part of a broader global phenomenon of voter anger toward the establishment and the political elite, notably evident in Western Europe. In June 2016, voters in the United Kingdom approved a referendum, which was given the nickname *Brexit* (British exit), to withdraw from the European Union. Trump's position aligned with the sentiment in the United Kingdom (particularly in England) opposed to trade agreements, open borders, and globalization.

Both campaigns attacked their opponent's fitness for office. Clinton's campaign charged that Trump's personal behavior was disqualifying for the nation's highest office, citing several allegations of sexual harassment and assault as well as his apparent mockery of a disabled journalist. The Clinton campaign also claimed that Trump actively encouraged the Russian government to intervene in the election.

Trump's campaign attacked Clinton's service as secretary of state and her use of a private e-mail server to conduct State Department business, claiming that Clinton had posed a threat to national security by transmitting classified material, and that she had erased the classified e-mails to cover this up. The FBI investigated and reported that although Clinton's actions were "extremely careless," she was not guilty of a crime.

After the election, two congressional committees and a special prosecutor appointed by the Justice Department, Robert Mueller, looked into Russian hacking and the allegations of coordination between members of the Trump campaign and Kremlin-sponsored operatives seeking to damage Hillary Clinton's campaign. The report documented Russian attempts to influence the outcome of the 2016 presidential election, primarily through propaganda dispersed via social media, but ultimately determined that no evidence of a criminal conspiracy existed between the Russian efforts and the Trump campaign.

Until election day, many pollsters predicted that Clinton would become the first woman president, though some polling organizations considered the race too close to call. Although Clinton won the popular vote by nearly three million ballots, she lost in the electoral college, 304–227. Trump captured six states that Obama had won in 2012, and the outcome turned on a total of 78,000 votes in Pennsylvania, Michigan, and Wisconsin. With the exception of Florida, those swing states from the Upper Midwest and Middle Atlantic were among the areas slowest to rebound from the Great Recession and were still grappling with the economic changes brought on by globalization.

The reasons for Trump's victory were varied. There has been much debate about who was a typical Trump supporter and whether a Trump coalition even existed. He ran a populist, anti-establishment campaign in the tradition of American nativism, emphasizing national identity and domestic economic interests. This appealed to an electorate fed up with politics-as-usual and gridlock in Washington, D.C. His agenda resonated especially with older whites, residents of small towns and rural areas, workers who had lost their jobs to automation and globalization, those who had not completed a college education, and evangelical Christians fearful of growing secularism. For her part, Clinton ran a campaign that struggled to connect with voters, and she was unable to retain the broad coalition of the support that Obama had garnered, especially in the swing states. Yet a supposed "working-class rebellion" does not tell the whole story—the median household income of Trump voters was higher than the median household income of Clinton voters.

And there are complexities in assessing President Trump's victory. Trump earned a majority of the vote from white women (53 percent), although Clinton won a majority of women's votes due to her overwhelming support among Black women. Trump succeeded by bringing out enough alienated Democratic and independent voters willing to take a chance on him, while retaining most traditional Republican voters. While working-class and middle-class economic anxieties and grievances certainly played a role in Trump's victory, exit polls showed that those who ranked the economy as the most important issue voted for Clinton. Instead, for many white voters, social and cultural issues determined whom they supported in the election.

REVIEW

- What major factors shaped the outcome of the 2016 presidential election?

The Trump Presidency

Once in the White House, Trump continued to disrupt the norms of American politics, and his relationship with the mainstream American media remained complicated. He claimed many mainstream media outlets promoted "fake news." Using social media to bypass the filter of conventional media, Trump often directly communicated his thoughts with the American public, using his Twitter account to criticize those who disagreed with him, including some world leaders and even fellow Republicans.

President Trump had mixed success in achieving his legislative agenda. Congress narrowly rejected his signature campaign promise to repeal and replace the Patient Protection and Affordable Care Act (Obamacare). Yet the Tax Cuts and Jobs Act of 2017, which included major changes to the tax code, successfully passed. This act substantially reduced tax rates for many businesses and individuals, lowering the maximum corporate rate from 35 percent to 21 percent and the maximum personal rate from 39.6 percent to 37 percent while limiting some deductions and exemptions.

As is typical of the modern presidency, Trump used executive orders to advance his policy agenda and undo many of his predecessor's policies. He put into effect a ban on immigrants from countries he deemed to be state sponsors of terrorism, which mainly were Muslim-majority nations. He revoked the Deferred Action for Childhood Arrivals (DACA) executive order issued by President Obama, which had allowed those who had been brought to the country as children by their undocumented immigrant parents, known as "Dreamers," to remain indefinitely. His administration also revoked the provisional residency permits of more than 200,000 immigrants from El Salvador, Haiti, and Honduras who had fled to the United States following natural disasters in their countries. During his second year in office, **U.S. Immigration and Customs Enforcement (ICE)** began to separate the children of undocumented immigrants from their parents at the U.S. border, provoking an outcry from both sides of the political spectrum. In 2018, a federal judge in California ordered the reunification of separated families and an end to forced separation.

U.S. Immigration and Customs Enforcement (ICE)
A branch of the Department of Homeland Security created in 2003 to prevent and investigate illegal immigration to the United States and cross-border crime.

Trump also promoted traditional Republican views of limited government involvement in the economy. He appointed cabinet secretaries and heads of regulatory agencies who favored limited governance and privatization of public services. His administration pushed deregulation efforts, including overturning "net neutrality" rules mandating that Internet providers treat all traffic equally, and challenging California's authority to limit auto emissions. While fewer regulations make it easier for businesses to operate and may stimulate economic growth, they can also result in lessened protections for the environment and consumers.

President Trump was successful in winning confirmation of his three appointments to the Supreme Court. The additions of Neil Gorsuch in 2017, Brett Kavanaugh in 2019, and Amy Coney Barrett in 2020 remade the Court with a clear conservative majority. Kavanaugh's confirmation proved especially controversial when a psychology professor, Dr. Christine Blasey Ford, accused Kavanaugh of sexually assaulting her at a party both attended when in high school. He strongly denied the charges. Perhaps the greatest impact of the new conservative "super majority" (where one vote could no longer swing a divided Court) was the *Dobbs v. Jackson Women's Health Organization* decision in June 2022. In the *Dobbs* case, the Court deemed the rationale for abortion rights established in the 1973 *Roe v. Wade* ruling (Module 8.11) was flawed and overturned the decision. Thereafter, legislation regarding abortion access was returned to state legislatures.

Trump also achieved some of his foreign-policy goals. He withdrew the United States from the Paris Climate Agreement, rolled back Obama-initiated trade and travel relations with Cuba, and decertified the Iran Nuclear Agreement. Trump met with North Korean dictator Kim Jong-un in a bid to reduce nuclear weapons on the Korean peninsula, despite earlier verbal clashes between the two leaders.

The relationship between China (now the world's biggest economy) and the United States was strained during the Trump administration, as the United States levied tariffs on Chinese goods and China retaliated with duties on American products. Underlying the tensions were disagreements over equitable access to markets, protection of U.S. intellectual property, economic competition, and concerns over human-rights abuses in China.

In 2019, President Trump was impeached by the Democratic-majority House of Representatives for abuse of power and obstruction of Congress. The charges were based on the claim that the executive branch withheld funds intended for the nation of Ukraine in its defense against Russia, which had invaded Ukraine in 2014 and annexed part of its territory. According to the charges, Trump withheld these funds in an attempt to force Ukrainian president Volodymyr Zelenskyy to open an investigation into the prospective 2020 Democratic nominee and former U.S. Vice President Joseph Biden, and his son, Hunter Biden, for their business arrangements in Ukraine. A 2020 Senate investigation found Hunter Biden had "cashed in" on his status as the son of Vice President Biden, but it found no "massive smoking guns," in the words of one of its committee chairpersons, Republican Senator Ron Johnson. After Congress opened its impeachment investigation, the president ordered his staff and cabinet members to refuse to respond to congressional subpoenas, which led to a charge of obstruction of Congress. At the trial in the Republican-led Senate, no witnesses were called, and no documents entered into evidence. On February 5, 2020, Trump was acquitted of the charges with 51 senators voting against conviction and 49 in favor, well short of the required two-thirds majority of senators needed to remove a president from office.

REVIEW

- What domestic and foreign policies did the Trump administration pursue, and what were the results of those efforts?

Polarization Persists

The election of Donald Trump and his defeat of the first female, major-party, candidate for president sparked the largest single day of protest in American history to date: the Women's March. On January 21, 2017, the day after President Trump's inauguration, approximately four million people marched in Washington, D.C., and major cities around the nation and the world to affirm that "women's rights are human rights." His election also inspired many women to run for political office.

Social media provided another place for movement-building. Originated by Tarana Burke, a Black social activist and sexual assault survivor, the **#MeToo movement** linked tens of millions of women on Twitter and Facebook. Many of them shared their stories of rape, sexual harassment, and sexual assault. The movement gained momentum after allegations by more than 80 women against movie mogul Harvey Weinstein led to his arrest and conviction. As a result, by the end of 2018, many women had come forward with complaints of sexual misconduct by media, entertainment, and sports celebrities, corporate executives, and politicians of both parties, leading in many cases to the swift firing or resignation of these men.

#MeToo movement The social movement linking tens of millions of women through social media networks in opposition to sexual harassment and abuse.

Mario Tama/Getty Images

Women's March on Washington, D.C., 2017 About 500,000 demonstrators gather in the nation's capital on January 21, 2017, a day after President Trump's inauguration, to attend the Women's March on Washington. Marchers supported a wide range of goals, including gender equality, racial equality, worker rights, immigration reform, health care expansion, and environmental protection. **What does this photograph reveal about American politics at the beginning of Trump's presidency?**

Social unrest, particularly over the issue of race, continued to increase during Trump's presidency. At a 2017 Unite the Right rally in Charlottesville, Virginia, a group that included Nazis and Ku Klux Klan members marched across the University of Virginia campus, chanting slogans against Jewish people and other minoritized groups. They were there to oppose the removal of a Confederate monument from the university campus. Many Confederate monument removals have become sites of protest in recent years: they offend those who view them as symbols of oppression celebrating those who fought to maintain slavery, while others see these monuments as representations of American history that should be kept in place. The following day, the protests in Charlottesville escalated, leading to tragedy. A white supremacist intentionally rammed his car into a counter-protest of the Unite the Right rally, killing one and injuring 35 other people.

The United States also continued to experience a growing trend in mass shootings that began just before the start of the twenty-first century, with the attack by two students on Columbine High School in Colorado in 1999. While there is no single definition of a mass shooting, some examples from George W. Bush's and Barack Obama's presidencies include the murder of thirty-two students and faculty members at Virginia Polytechnic Institute and State University in 2007; twenty children and six adults at Sandy Hook Elementary School in Newton, Connecticut in 2012; nine Black worshippers by a white supremacist at the Emanuel African Methodist Episcopal Church in Charleston, South Carolina, in 2015; and fifty patrons at the Pulse nightclub in Orlando, Florida, in 2016.

This trend continued during Trump's presidency. On October 1, 2017, outdoor concert attendees in Las Vegas, Nevada, were victims of the deadliest mass shooting in American history to date. Fifty-nine people were murdered when a gunman used a high-powered, long-range rifle to shoot into the crowd from the thirty-ninth floor of a nearby hotel. The following year, on February 14, 2018, a gunman murdered seventeen people at Marjory Stoneman Douglas High School in Parkland, Florida. In the aftermath of the Parkland attack, national protests calling for background checks and gun control measures, led largely by Marjory Stoneman Douglas High School students, inspired Florida legislators to raise the minimum age for gun ownership and institute background checks before purchasing. The state legislation also allowed for the arming of properly trained teachers. However, despite President Trump calling for more "powerful" background checks and issuing an executive order banning bump stocks, no additional federal gun measures were implemented. These tragedies raised the question of whether the United States had entered an era in which mass violence seemed to be an everyday occurrence broadcast by the media.

Pandemic and Protest

In late 2019, the COVID-19 pandemic began in Wuhan, China, and spread quickly to the rest of the world in 2020. It was the worst global pandemic since the 1918 influenza pandemic. In mid-March 2020, most of the schools and public facilities in the United States closed to prevent the spread of the disease. Eventually, many businesses required their workers to remain at home and continue to work remotely, while essential workers, including those in the health care industry, continued to operate with mask protocols and social distancing to mitigate the spread of the virus. Nevertheless, within two years of the appearance of COVID-19, more than 10 million Americans caught the virus, and over 1 million died. By 2023, more than 600 million cases had been confirmed worldwide, resulting in more than 6 million deaths.

For a short time in spring and summer 2020, the Trump administration experienced bipartisan support for its advocacy of the mitigation measures, directed by the White House Coronavirus Task Force, whose spokesperson, Dr. Anthony Fauci, became the face of American efforts to combat the virus. Likewise, the Trump administration supported Operation Warp Speed, an effort to accelerate development of a vaccine for the disease, which was accomplished in late 2020. However, by late summer and early fall, some state and local governments, along with a growing number of Americans, rejected the masking measures, and face masks soon became a political flashpoint that broadly divided Americans. President Trump often appeared in public without a mask and, in October 2020, caught the disease. He was airlifted to the Walter Reed Medical Center for treatment, where he recovered.

The nation was engulfed in another crisis during the summer of 2020 after George Floyd, a Black resident of Minneapolis, Minnesota, was strangled by a city police officer who was attempting to arrest him for paying with a counterfeit $20 bill at a convenience store. Floyd's murder was captured by residents on cell-phone video. The image of a police officer kneeling on Floyd's neck for over nine minutes shocked the nation and sparked widespread protests against police brutality under the banner of the Black Lives Matter movement. These protests also further divided the nation along political and cultural lines, although the 2020 protests initially had broader support than previous ones. While some protesters argued that the best solution to police brutality was to "defund the police," others expressed their support for the "Blue Lives Matter" movement through social media campaigns and public events. These protests gave rise to a renewed national discussion about policing, with some people on both sides of the political divide advocating some degree of reform. Others—also on both sides of the political divide—expressed criticism of the 2020 protests, advocating increased investment in and support for law enforcement.

REVIEW

- How did the pandemic and social protests demonstrate the social and political tensions in the United States?

The 2020 Election and the Biden Presidency

These ongoing conflicts and a sharp economic downturn, resulting from the COVID-19 pandemic and efforts to control it, made the election of 2020 especially heated. In response to the pandemic, many states extended the opportunities for voting by mail during the election, which had the effect of delaying the results of the election for a number of days. Because in-person and mail-in balloting also tended to divide along party lines, Donald Trump's early lead on election night faded as mail-in ballots were counted over the following days. Ultimately, Democratic candidate Joseph Biden won both the popular vote (by nearly 7 million votes) and the electoral college (306 to 232), having taken the states of Arizona and Georgia, as well as states like Pennsylvania, Wisconsin, and Michigan, which Trump won in 2016.

After the results of the election became clear, Trump and many of his supporters claimed that local partisans in closely contested states had committed electoral fraud and rigged the election. The Trump campaign raised legal challenges to the outcome in an effort referred to as "stop the steal." In the end, all of these legal challenges failed in the courts, including an attempt to bring the issue to the Supreme Court in *Texas v. Pennsylvania* on December 8, which the Court refused to hear. During this same period, Trump and his lawyers encouraged Vice President Mike Pence to reject the electoral college votes during the official count. Despite substantial pressure, Pence refused to do so.

In the weeks that followed, Trump partisans, and the president himself, encouraged a protest of Biden's inauguration in a "Save America" rally outside of the White House. On the day the electoral votes were officially tallied, January 6, 2021, tens of thousands of Trump supporters attended the rally, and acted on Trump's invitation to take the protest to the Capitol to demand Congress reject the electoral college vote. In the hours following the rally, thousands stormed the Capitol steps, and hundreds broke into the Capitol building, ransacked offices, raided the floor of the House of Representatives, and had to be removed from the building by force. One protester was killed in the **Capitol Riot**, and more than 140 police officers were injured during the attack. Late in the evening of January 6, after protesters were removed from the Capitol, Congress reconvened for the official counting of the electoral college votes, which certified Biden's election as president of the United States. Vice President Pence, who had sheltered in a Capitol garage rather than leave the building during the riot, oversaw the official count.

Capitol Riot
The storming of the U.S. Capitol building on January 6, 2021, by supporters of President Trump in an attempt to stop the official certification of Joseph Biden's electoral college victory by Congress. Rioters marched from an earlier "Save America" rally, assaulted and overwhelmed police officers, and ransacked the Capitol for several hours before order was restored.

On January 13, 2021, the House of Representatives impeached Donald Trump for a second time on the charge of inciting an insurrection. Trump, who was out of office by the time the trial was held, was acquitted by the Senate. Fifty-seven senators, including 7 Republicans, voted to convict, falling short of the two-thirds threshold for conviction.

Upon his inauguration on January 20, 2021, President Joseph Biden faced a nation still in the grips of a global pandemic, torn by the aftermath of the murder of George Floyd, and recovering from the violence at the Capitol earlier that month. The streets of Washington, D.C. were heavily patrolled by law enforcement during the inauguration festivities, and the mall in front of the Capitol was empty and fortified. The new president and Vice President Kamala Harris, the first woman of African and South Asian descent elected to national office, were sworn in without incident.

Within six weeks of taking office, Biden signed the American Rescue Plan Act of 2021, which injected $1.9 trillion into the American economy in an attempt to

Roberto Schmidt/AFP/Getty Images

Trump Supporters Clash with Capitol Police, January 6, 2021 On January 6, 2022, thousands of Trump supporters marched from the "Save America" rally led by President Trump near the White House to the Capitol building on the day Congress met to certify Joseph Biden's victory in the 2020 presidential election. After overwhelming law enforcement, hundreds of rioters breached the building, injuring scores of police officers and causing substantial damage, in an effort to halt the official tally and overturn the results. After several hours, the rioters were removed from the building, and Congress certified Biden's victory that evening.

What factors contributed to the events of January 6, 2021?

overcome the economic effects of the COVID-19 pandemic. While the measure was intended to help the nation recover from the recession caused by the closing of the economy, it likely contributed to a rise in inflation during 2022 and 2023.

Biden's presidency continued some policies enacted under Trump but ceased others. Until 2023, Biden maintained COVID-era restrictions on immigration at the Mexican border, and extended the Trump administration's economic restrictions on trade with China, and reaffirmed U.S. support for "peace and stability across the Taiwan Strait as an . . . element of security and prosperity in the international community." On the other hand, he quickly repealed the ban on immigration from majority-Muslim countries and signed an Executive Order to rejoin the Paris Climate Accord.

As with other twenty-first century presidencies, mass shootings continued to afflict the country. On May 14, 2022, an eighteen-year-old white supremacist shooter killed 10 Black people in a grocery store in Buffalo, New York. Just weeks later, another eighteen-year-old gunman attacked Robb Elementary School in Uvalde, Texas, murdering 19 children and two adults and injuring 17 others. In the wake of these tragedies, the Bipartisan Safer Communities Act was passed. It was the first federal gun safety legislation passed since 1994. Provisions of the bill included extended background checks for gun purchasers under the age of 21, federal funding for mental health and school security programs, and stronger laws against arms trafficking.

The Biden administration also faced international crises. Since 2014, Russia has occupied Crimea, a formerly autonomous region of Ukraine with a majority ethnically Russian population, and supported pro-Russian militias in eastern Ukraine who eventually gained control of about one-third of the Donbas region. On February 24, 2022, Russia launched a large-scale invasion of Ukraine. In response, the Biden administration helped coordinate a coalition of nations, largely centered on NATO, to provide financial and military support for Ukraine. After one year of warfare, Russia controlled 18 percent of Ukraine's territory, down from 27 percent in the weeks following the invasion. As the war in Ukraine continued, Russian attacks on civilians in Ukrainian cities resulted in heavy casualties on both sides.

Starting in the summer of 2022, the United States largely ceased all COVID-19 mitigation efforts. Schools opened to regular schedules, masking was largely discontinued, and businesses increasingly returned to normal operations. However, various strains of COVID-19 continued to evolve, although the new vaccines and an increase in natural immunity due to prior infections prevented the high mortality rates seen early in the pandemic. While the debates over COVID-19 mitigation efforts cooled, the nation continued to be firmly divided along partisan and cultural lines. On November 22, 2022, Donald Trump, age 76, announced his intention to run again for president in 2024 and on April 25, 2023, President Biden, age 80, announced his reelection bid.

- What issues did the Biden administration face in the early 2020s?

An Era of Anxiety and Hope

Since the 1980s, Americans have faced new forms of globalization, new technologies, and new modes of warfare. The computer revolution begun by Bill Gates, Steve Jobs, and others helped change the way Americans gather information, communicate ideas, purchase goods, and conduct business. It has also shaped national and international conflicts.

The September 11, 2001, attacks on the World Trade Center and the Pentagon demonstrated that terrorists could use technology to organize and wreak havoc on the most powerful nation in the world. Barack Obama's 2008 presidential campaign, protesters demonstrating against various Middle East dictatorships, and the leaders of the Tea Party and Occupy Wall Street movements also used technology to promote their causes. In the interest of combating terrorism, the U.S. government has also used this technology to monitor the activities of citizens it considers a threat to national security, thereby raising concerns about civil liberties.

The Bush administration responded to the 9/11 terrorist attacks by fighting wars in Iraq and Afghanistan. The Obama administration ended the Iraq War and steadily withdrew troops from Afghanistan, but neither administration was able to build stable governments in these countries. In 2021, the Taliban quickly retook control of Afghanistan when President Biden moved to withdraw the remaining U.S. troops ahead of the twentieth anniversary of the 9/11 attacks. The rise of ISIS, which grew out of sectarian violence in Iraq, posed an even greater danger than had al-Qaeda to stability in the Middle East and contributed to the spread of terrorism throughout the world. At the same time, the United States and its allies faced a militarily revitalized Russia seeking to extend its influence in Ukraine and Syria, once again heightening the prospect of confrontation between the world's major nuclear powers.

Along with the computer revolution, globalization has encouraged vast economic transformations throughout the world. Presidents as politically different as Bill Clinton and George W. Bush supported deregulation, free trade, and other policies that fostered corporate mergers and allowed businesses to reach beyond U.S. borders for cheap labor, raw materials, and new markets. While the 1990s witnessed the benefits of the new global economy, the dangers of financial speculation and intertwined national economies became strikingly clear in 2008 with the onset of the Great Recession. This economic collapse underscored the inequalities of wealth that continue to widen, aggravated by racial, ethnic, and gender disparities.

Policies passed by the Obama administration mitigated the impacts of the recession and extended health care coverage to some of the country's most vulnerable citizens. During his time in office, the Supreme Court extended marriage equality nationwide. Yet Obama faced increased partisan congressional gridlock that made other aspects of his political agenda difficult to achieve.

The election of Donald Trump to the presidency in 2016 demonstrated that many Americans felt that career politicians did not prioritize the issues they faced and that the economic recovery begun in the Obama era was uneven. Trump waged a populist political campaign based on economic and cultural grievances that appealed to voters who wanted to disrupt politics as usual. Trump's election, and his subsequent defeat in 2020, reflected an increased political polarization in America's electorate that remains sharper than at any time since the turbulent 1960s and is heightened by social media.

Biden took office in the midst of a global pandemic and in the wake of a riot at the Capitol that underscored how difficult it would be to bring Americans together and bridge the political divide. Domestically, the Biden administration supported policies to reduce racism and poverty, though little meaningful legislation passed the closely divided Congress. Likewise, while President Biden hoped to provide debt relief for college graduates, the plan could not pass Congress. Nevertheless, a trillion-dollar infrastructure bill became law with bipartisan support in 2021, along with a plan to bring semi-conductor production back to the United States. After March 2022, the Biden administration coordinated international support for Ukraine in the face of a Russian invasion.

Throughout its history, the United States has shown great strength in finding solutions to its problems. The nation has incorporated diverse populations into its midst, redefined old cultural identities and created new ones, expanded civil rights and civil liberties, extended economic opportunities, and joined other nations to fight military aggression and address other international concerns. As the twenty-first century continues to progress, the United States will have to draw on these strengths and continue to innovate and adapt to new challenges to maintain its global leadership and unique legacy in an ever-changing world.

REVIEW

- What major challenges has the United States faced in the twenty-first century?
- How has the nation responded to those challenges?

Skills Workshop: Writing Historically

Additional Practice in Responding to a Short-Answer Question with a Primary Source

Ted Rall/CartoonStock

Using the image, answer **A**, **B**, and **C**.

(A) Briefly describe ONE perspective expressed by the artist in the image.

(B) Briefly explain how ONE historical event or development led to the historical situation depicted in the image.

(C) Briefly explain how ONE historical event or development resulted from the situation depicted in the image.

Causation in Period 9

MODULE 9.7

AP® Skills Workshop: Writing Historically

Additional Practice in Responding to a Document-Based Question

Evaluate the extent to which the end of the Cold War transformed U.S. foreign policy from 1989 to 2020.

Document 1

Source: President George H. W. Bush, Address to the Nation Announcing Allied Military Action in the Persian Gulf, January 16, 1991

"This is an historic moment. We have in this past year made great progress in ending the long era of conflict and cold war. We have before us the opportunity to forge for ourselves and for future generations a new world order—a world where the rule of law, not the law of the jungle, governs the conduct of nations. When we are successful—and we will be—we have a real chance at this new world order, an order in which a credible United Nations can use its peacekeeping role to fulfill the promise and vision of the U.N.'s founders.

We have no argument with the people of Iraq. Indeed, for the innocents caught in this conflict, I pray for their safety. Our goal is not the conquest of Iraq. It is the liberation of Kuwait. . . .

I am convinced not only that we will prevail but that out of the horror of combat will come the recognition that no nation can stand against a world united, no nation will be permitted to brutally assault its neighbor."

Document 2

Source: Anthony Lake, National Security Advisor to President Clinton, "From Containment to Enlargement," September 21, 1993

"The expansion of market-based economics abroad helps expand our exports and create American jobs, while it also improves living conditions and fuels demands for political liberalization abroad. The addition of new democracies makes us more secure because democracies tend not to wage war on each other or sponsor terrorism. They are more trustworthy in diplomacy and do a better job of respecting the human rights of their people.

These dynamics lay at the heart of Woodrow Wilson's most profound insights; although his moralism sometimes weakened his argument, he understood that our own security is shaped by the character of foreign regimes. Indeed, most Presidents who followed, Republicans and Democrats alike, understood we must promote democracy and market economics in

(continued)

the world—because it protects our interests and security; and because it reflects values that are both American and universal.

Throughout the Cold War, we contained a global threat to market democracies; now we should seek to enlarge their reach, particularly in places of special significance to us.

The successor to a doctrine of containment must be a strategy of enlargement—enlargement of the world's free community of market democracies."

Document 3

Source: Stephen M. Walt, "Two Cheers for Clinton's Foreign Policy," *Foreign Affairs*, March/April 2000

"President Clinton's handling of international institutions and multilateralism illustrates the central irony in his handling of foreign policy, namely, the degree to which he departed from his initial idealism and embraced realpolitik. In 1992, candidate Clinton declared that 'the cynical calculus of pure power politics is ill-suited to a new era,' but his policies as president have shown an ample appreciation of the realities of power. Under Clinton, the United States consolidated its Cold War victory by bringing three former Warsaw Pact members into its own alliance. It shored up its alliances in East Asia and readied itself for a possible competition with a rising China while encouraging Beijing to accept a status quo that favored the United States. It rejected the land-mines treaty and opposed the creation of an international criminal court while moving steadily closer to the construction of NMD [National Missile Defense]. It forced its allies to bear a greater share of the burden in Europe and East Asia while insisting on leading both alliances. And, together with its NATO allies, it asserted the right to intervene in the sovereign territory of other states, even without Security Council authorization. Clinton may cloak U.S. policy in the rhetoric of 'world order' and general global interests, but its defining essence remains the unilateral exercise of sovereign power."

Document 4

Source: Senator Robert Byrd, Speech on the floor of the U.S. Senate, February 12, 2003

"This nation is about to embark upon the first test of a revolutionary doctrine applied in an extraordinary way at an unfortunate time. The doctrine of preemption—the idea that the United States or any other nation can legitimately attack a nation that is not imminently threatening but may be threatening in the future—is a radical new twist on the traditional idea of self-defense. It appears to be in contravention of international law and the U.N. Charter. And it is being tested at a time of world-wide terrorism, making many countries around the globe wonder if they will soon be on our—or some other nation's—hit list. . . . There are huge cracks emerging in our time-honored alliances, and U.S. intentions are suddenly subject to damaging worldwide speculation. Anti-Americanism

(continued)

based on mistrust, misinformation, suspicion, and alarming rhetoric from U.S. leaders is fracturing the once solid alliance against global terrorism which existed after September 11."

Document 5

Source: President Barack Obama, Remarks at the Department of State, May 19, 2011

"[F]or six months, we have witnessed an extraordinary change taking place in the Middle East and North Africa. Square by square, town by town, country by country, the people have risen up to demand their basic human rights. . . . And though these countries may be a great distance from our shores, we know that our own future is bound to this region by the forces of economics and security, by history and by faith. . . .

[A]lready, we've done much to shift our foreign policy following a decade defined by two costly conflicts. After years of war in Iraq, we've removed 100,000 American troops and ended our combat mission there. In Afghanistan, we've broken the Taliban's momentum, and this July we will begin to bring our troops home and continue a transition to Afghan lead. And after years of war against al-Qaeda and its affiliates, we have dealt al-Qaeda a huge blow by killing its leader, Osama bin Laden. . . .

So we face a historic opportunity. We have the chance to show that America values the dignity of the street vendor in Tunisia more than the raw power of the dictator. There must be no doubt that the United States of America welcomes change that advances self-determination and opportunity. Yes, there will be perils that accompany this moment of promise. But after decades of accepting the world as it is in the region, we have a chance to pursue the world as it should be."

Document 6

Source: Donald Trump, Republican presidential candidate, foreign policy speech, April 27, 2016

"It's time to shake the rust off America's foreign policy. It's time to invite new voices and new visions into the fold, something we have to do. The direction I will outline today will also return us to a timeless principle. My foreign policy will always put the interests of the American people and American security above all else. Has to be first, has to be.

That will be the foundation of every single decision that I will make. America—thank you.

America First will be the major and overriding theme of my administration. . . .

We're getting out of the nation-building business and instead focusing on creating stability in the world. . . .

Finally, I will work with our allies to reinvigorate Western values and institutions. Instead of trying to spread universal values that not everybody shares or wants, we should understand that strengthening and promoting Western civilization and its accomplishments will do more to inspire positive reforms around the world than military interventions."

(continued)

Document 7

Source: U.S. Counterterrorism Operations 2018–2020 Infographic, Watson Institute for International and Public Affairs at Brown University, 2021

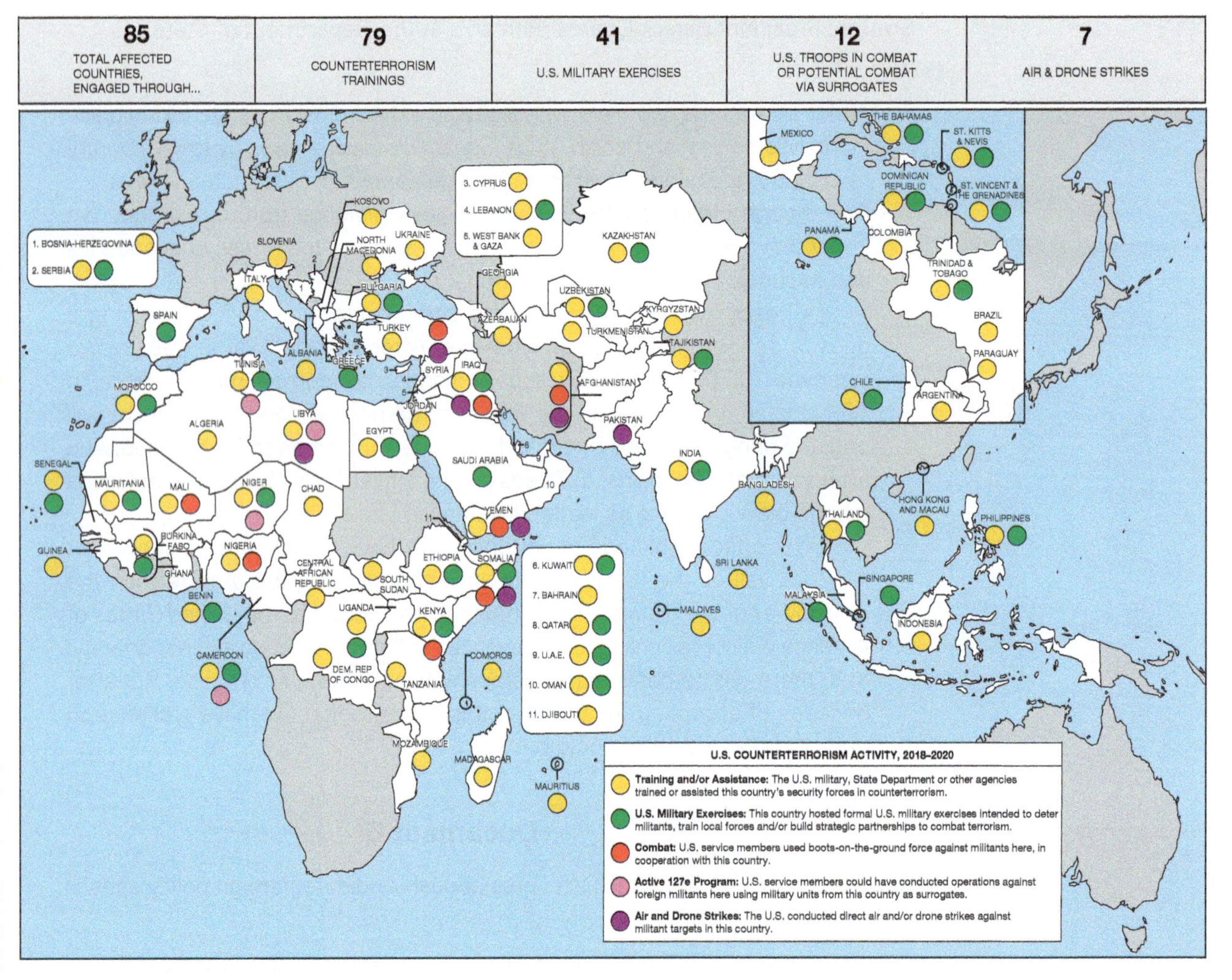

Period 9 Review 1980–The Present

KEY CONCEPTS AND EVENTS

acquired immune deficiency syndrome (AIDS), *980*
Americans with Disabilities Act (ADA), *983*
apartheid, *988*
Arab Spring, *1023*
axis of evil, *1015*
Black Lives Matter, *1022*
Boland Amendment, *987*
Brady Handgun Violence Prevention Act, *1005*
Bush Doctrine, *1015*
Capitol Riot, *1032*
Clean Air Act of 1990, *983*
climate change, *1003*
Comprehensive Anti-Apartheid Act, *988*
Contract with America, *1006*
Contras, *987*
Defense of Marriage Act (DOMA), *1006*
Deferred Action for Childhood Arrivals (DACA), *1021*
Department of Homeland Security, *1015*
Development, Relief, and Education for Alien Minors (DREAM) Act, *1021*
Economic Recovery Tax Act, *978*
European Union (EU), *1005*
Family and Medical Leave Act, *1004*
Federal Assault Weapons Ban, *1005*
glasnost, *991*
globalization, *1001*
global warming, *1003*
Global War on Terror (GWOT), *1014*
Great Recession, *1018*
greenhouse gas, *983*
Guantánamo Bay, *1017*
Gulf War, *996*
Hurricane Katrina, *1017*
Immigration Reform and Control Act, *982*
Intermediate Nuclear Forces Treaty, *992*
Internet, *1009*
invasion of Grenada, *988*
invasion of Panama, *995*
Iran-Contra affair, *990*
Iran Nuclear Agreement, *1025*
Iraq War, *1017*
Islamic State in Iraq and Syria (ISIS), *1023*
Kyoto Protocol, *1003*
Medicare Prescription Drug, Improvement, and Modernization Act, *1013*
#MeToo movement, *1029*
mujahideen, *993*
National Rifle Association, *1005*
No Child Left Behind (NCLB), *1013*
North American Free Trade Agreement (NAFTA), *1005*
nuclear freeze movement, *991*
Obergefell v. Hodges, *1022*
Occupy Wall Street movement, *1021*
Office of Faith-Based and Neighborhood Partnerships, *1013*
Operation Desert Storm, *996*
Palestine Liberation Organization (PLO), *989*
Paris Climate Agreement, *1025*
Patient Protection and Affordable Care Act ("Obamacare"), *1020*
perestroika, *991*
Personal Responsibility and Work Opportunity Reconciliation Act, *1006*
al-Qaeda, *994*
Reaganomics, *977*
Sandinista, *987*
Solidarity, *992*
Strategic Arms Reduction Talks (START), *986*
Strategic Defense Initiative (SDI), *986*
supply-side economics, *977*
Taliban, *993*
Tea Party movement, *1021*
terrorism, *989*
Tiananmen Square, *995*
U.S. Immigration and Customs Enforcement (ICE), *1028*
USA Patriot Act, *1015*
Whitewater, *1006*
World Trade Organization (WTO), *1005*
World Wide Web, *1009*

KEY PEOPLE

Yasser Arafat, *997*
Bashar al-Assad, *1023*
Amy Coney Barrett, *1028*
Tarana Burke, *1029*
George H. W. Bush, *973*
George W. Bush, *1012*
Richard (Dick) Cheney, *1014*
William (Bill) Clinton, *998*
Hillary Clinton, *1004*
Deng Xiaoping, *995*
Geraldine Ferraro, *979*
Christine Blasey Ford, *1028*
Bill Gates, *1008*
Mikhail Gorbachev, *985*
Neil Gorsuch, *1028*
Kamala Harris, *1032*
Anita Hill, *983*
Saddam Hussein, *989*
Steve Jobs, *1008*
Kim Jong-un, *1029*
Brett Kavanaugh, *1028*
Osama bin Laden, *993*
Monica Lewinsky, *1007*
Nelson Mandela, *997*
Trayvon Martin, *1022*
Robert Mueller, *1027*
Manuel Noriega, *995*
Barack Obama, *973*
Sandra Day O'Connor, *979*
Ross Perot, *998*

Colin Powell, *1013*
Vladimir Putin, *1025*
Muammar al-Qaddafi, *989*
Ronald Reagan, *973*
William Rehnquist, *979*
Condoleezza Rice, *1013*
Donald Rumsfeld, *1014*
Edward Snowden, *1024*
Clarence Thomas, *983*
Donald Trump, *1012*
Lech Walesa, *992*
Stephen Wozniak, *1008*
Boris Yeltsin, *985*

CHRONOLOGY

1980s	AIDS epidemic spreads Rise of the nuclear freeze movement
1980s–1990s	Immigration surges from Mexico, Central America, the Caribbean, and South and East Asia
1980	Ronald Reagan (Republican) wins presidential election on conservative, anticommunist platform
1981	Assassination attempt on Reagan Passage of the Economic Recovery Tax Act Air traffic controllers strike
1982	Strategic Arms Reduction Talks with Soviet Union Boland Amendment passed Ratification period expires for Equal Rights Amendment
1983	U.S. invasion of Grenada U.S.S.R. shoots down a South Korean passenger airliner
1984	President Reagan wins re-election
1986	Passage of Immigration Reform and Control Act
1987	Senate hearings on Iran-Contra affair Intermediate Nuclear Forces Treaty signed
1988	George H. W. Bush (Republican) wins presidential election
1989	Tiananmen Square protests Fall of the Berlin Wall
1990	Americans with Disabilities Act passed Clean Air Act passed Passage of the Omnibus Budget Reconciliation Act
1991	Operation Desert Storm begins; United States pushes Iraq out of Kuwait Further strategic arms reduction talks with Soviet Union World Wide Web created Collapse of the Soviet Union
1992	Bill Clinton (Democrat) wins presidential election
1993	Second strategic-arms reduction treaty (START II) signed North American Free Trade Agreement (NAFTA) ratified
1994	Whitewater investigation Contract with America announced
c. 1995	Taliban comes to power in Afghanistan
1995	Creation of World Trade Organization

CHRONOLOGY *(continued)*

1996	Clinton wins reelection Personal Responsibility and Work Opportunity Reconciliation Act passed Defense of Marriage Act passed
1998	United States refuses to ratify Kyoto Protocol to reduce greenhouse emissions U.S. House of Representatives votes to impeach Clinton
1999	Stock market reaches a then historic high U.S. Senate votes against convicting Clinton in impeachment hearing
2000	George W. Bush (Republican) wins presidential election after Supreme Court halts Florida recount
2001	September 11 attacks on World Trade Center and Pentagon Bush launches Global War on Terror U.S. troops invade Afghanistan Patriot Act passed
2002	Department of Homeland Security created
2003–2011	War in Iraq
2005	Hurricane Katrina
2008	Great Recession begins Barack Obama (Democrat) wins presidential election
c. 2009	Tea Party movement formed
2010	Patient Protection and Affordable Care Act ("Obamacare") passed
2011	Arab Spring protests Occupy Wall Street movement formed
2012	Obama wins re-election Deferred Action for Childhood Arrivals (DACA) policy enacted
c. 2013	Black Lives Matter movement formed
2015	Supreme Court legalizes same-sex marriage nationwide
2016	Donald Trump (Republican) wins presidential election
2019	Special Prosecutor Robert Mueller submits report on Russian interference in the 2016 election
2020	Joseph Biden (Democrat) wins presidential election
2021	Capitol Riot by Trump supporters attempting to halt certification of electoral college vote on January 6

Period 9 AP® Exam Practice

Multiple-Choice Questions

Questions 1–3 refer to the 1984 cartoon.

"STRANGE HOW SOME CHOOSE TO LIVE LIKE THAT INSTEAD OF CHOOSING TO BE RICH LIKE US"
©1984 HERBLOCK

"A 1967 Herblock Cartoon, © The Herb Block Foundation," image courtesy of the Prints & Photographs Division, Library of Congress, LC-DIG-ppmsca-21953

1. The image was created most directly in response to
   (A) intense political debates over immigration policy.
   (B) U.S. opposition to communism.
   (C) policy debates over the scope of the government social safety net.
   (D) reductions in defense spending.

2. Which of the following most directly led to the circumstances illustrated by the image?
   (A) Conservative efforts to reduce the size of the government
   (B) The deregulation of many industries
   (C) Conservative beliefs regarding the need for traditional social values
   (D) Tax increases that were passed by the Reagan administration

3. Which of the following would have the most in common with the ideas expressed by the automobile passengers in the image?
   (A) The programs of the New Deal
   (B) The philosophy of Social Darwinism
   (C) The ideals of the Social Gospel
   (D) The presidency of Lyndon Johnson

Questions 4–6 refer to the excerpt.

"The States have contributed to the fundamental character of the marriage right by placing that institution at the center of so many facets of the legal and social order.

There is no difference between same- and opposite-sex couples with respect to this principle. Yet by virtue of their exclusion from that institution, same-sex couples are denied the constellation of benefits that the States have linked to marriage. This harm results in more than just material burdens. Same-sex couples are consigned to an instability many opposite-sex couples would deem intolerable in their own lives. As the State itself makes marriage all the more precious by the significance it attaches to it, exclusion from that status has the effect of teaching that gays and lesbians are unequal in important respects. It demeans gays and lesbians for the State to lock them out of a central institution of the Nation's society. . . .

The limitation of marriage to opposite-sex couples may long have seemed natural and just, but its inconsistency with the central meaning of the fundamental right to marry is now manifest. With that knowledge must come the recognition that laws excluding same-sex couples from the marriage right impose stigma and injury of the kind prohibited by our basic charter."

U.S. Supreme Court, *Obergefell v. Hodges*, 2015

4. Which of the following Supreme Court decisions was consistent with the legal reasoning expressed in the excerpt?
   (A) *Cherokee Nation v. Georgia*, 1831
   (B) *Plessy v. Ferguson*, 1896
   (C) *Korematsu v. United States*, 1944
   (D) *Brown v. Board of Education*, 1954

5. The excerpt is best understood in the context of
   (A) questions raised about the protection of human rights.
   (B) the growing political and cultural influence of the American South and West.
   (C) declines in immigration.
   (D) the popularity of many government social programs with voters.

6. Which of the following groups would have been most likely to oppose the sentiments expressed in the excerpt?
   (A) Americans under the age of thirty
   (B) Conservative activists such as the Moral Majority
   (C) The liberal wing of the Democratic Party
   (D) Urban voters in large U.S. cities

Questions 7–9 refer to the graph.

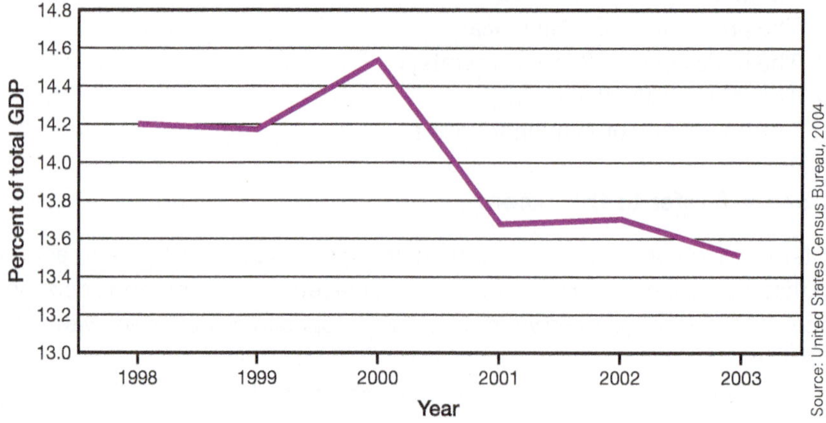

Manufacturing as a Percent of Total Gross Domestic Product (GDP), 1998–2003

7. Which of the following most directly contributed to the economic trend depicted in the graph?
- (A) The end of the Cold War
- (B) Growth in the service sector of the economy
- (C) Reforms of the U.S. financial system
- (D) Conservative beliefs regarding the need for traditional social values

8. The graph is best understood in the context of
- (A) the increase in real wages for the working class.
- (B) a decline in union membership.
- (C) federal efforts to deregulate the economy.
- (D) the decreasing productivity of American workers.

9. Which of the following trends represents a culmination of the process depicted in the graph?
- (A) Increased American participation in the global economy
- (B) Intensifying debates over the impact of economic consumption on the environment
- (C) Immigrants supplying the economy with an important labor force
- (D) A sharp reduction in economic inequality

Questions 10–12 refer to the excerpt.

"My hope is that all nations will heed our call and eliminate the terrorist parasites who threaten their countries and our own. . . . But some governments will be timid in the face of terror. And make no mistake about it: If they do not act, America will . . . to prevent regimes that sponsor terror from threatening America or our friends and allies with weapons of mass destruction . . .

States like these and their terrorist allies constitute an axis of evil, arming to threaten the peace of the world. By seeking weapons of mass destruction, these regimes pose a grave and growing danger."

George W. Bush, State of the Union Address,
January 29, 2002

10. The excerpt best supports the conclusion that in the 2000s, the U.S. government
   (A) sought to contain the expansion of communism globally.
   (B) rejected international alliances.
   (C) found itself in a renewed Cold War.
   (D) continued as the world's leading superpower.

11. Which of the following was a long-term result of the developments described in the excerpt?
   (A) A lengthy and controversial conflict with Russia over Eastern Europe
   (B) An increase in the protection of civil liberties and human rights
   (C) Continued debates over the appropriate use of U.S. power in the world
   (D) U.S. policies to pursue arms reduction

12. The foreign-policy outcomes for the United States that came about from the ideas expressed in the excerpt had the most in common with the aftermath of which of the following?
   (A) World War II
   (B) The Vietnam War
   (C) The Korean War
   (D) The Civil War

Questions 13–15 refer to the excerpt.

"I rise today and ask you to consider where we were before the Affordable Care Act. Premiums were rising three times faster than wages—and eating up more of Americans' hard earned paychecks. Millions more families were drowning in medical debt. Americans had to pay for critical preventive services like flu shots, yearly check-ups, and birth control. Many young twenty-somethings went without insurance. Your suffering child could be denied coverage due to preexisting conditions . . .

Thankfully, in the six years since the ACA was enacted, 20 million Americans have insurance for the first time in their lives, and the uninsured rate is the lowest it has been in American history, currently at 8.6 percent. The ACA has helped 105 million Americans, including 39.5 million women and nearly 28 million children, by preventing health care plans from capping benefits . . .

Unfortunately, over the past few years, it has been popular around here to say that the ACA is a failure. That it has socialized medicine and that it is driving down the quality of American healthcare. That we need to "repeal and replace" it because Obamacare isn't working. This mindset is all wrong because I'm happy to report that the ACA is working. However, faster progress has been prevented due to obstruction and politics. . . .

It is time once and for all for Congress to accept the ACA as the law of the land and begin working to improve the law, not repeal it."

Rep. Michael Quigley of Illinois, Speech before
the House of Representatives, September 22, 2016

13. The ideas expressed in the excerpt were most consistent with which of the following domestic-policy agendas after 1980?
   (A) Support for deregulation due to its perceived positive effects on the American economy
   (B) The reduction of the membership in and influence of organized labor
   (C) Liberal opposition to efforts to reduce the scope of government
   (D) Support for tax cuts and reduced deficit spending

14. Based upon the excerpt, Quigley would have been most likely to support which of the following in the 2000s?

(A) Stricter immigration policies and the denial of amnesty

(B) Legislative actions to improve real wages for the working and middle classes

(C) Resistance to change in cultural debates over family structures

(D) Greater political and social activism on the part of religious conservatives

15. Which president would have been most opposed to the ideas expressed in the excerpt?

(A) Franklin Roosevelt

(B) Lyndon Johnson

(C) Ronald Reagan

(D) Bill Clinton

Short-Answer Questions

"These reverberations of the 1980's opposition attest to the idea that a given decade contains a far more complex array of forces than media shorthand and popular history can neatly encompass. The 1980's are thus more than simply the decade of Reagan's America or the triumph of a nostalgic, flag-wrapped conservativism. Beneath the surface, there were countless individuals, activists, and organizations that rejected the attitude of supine [total] surrender, opting instead to fight against the grain for what they believed was right, their sense of justice cutting in a fundamentally different direction from those who held the reins of power."

Bradford Martin, *The Other Eighties; A Secret History of America in the Age of Reagan*, 2011

"It was perhaps inevitable that some of Reagan's former advisers would begin to rewrite his legacy using their hardline script. Back in the 80's, however, this script produced nothing but new cold war crises, an accelerated arms race, and a huge budget deficit. . . . It is not clear how much vision regarding the end of Soviet communism Reagan had. What Reagan certainly had in abundance was luck and instinct. He was lucky that a new reformist leadership came to power in Moscow . . . He sensed a historic opportunity in his relationship with Gorbachev and finally seized upon it. It was Reagan, the peacemaker . . . who made the greatest contribution to history."

Vladislav M. Zubok, "Soft Power: Reagan the Dove," *The New Republic*, June 21, 2004

1. Using the excerpts, answer **A**, **B**, and **C**.

(A) Briefly describe ONE major difference between Martin's and Zubok's historical interpretations of American politics in the 1980s.

(B) Briefly explain how ONE historical event or development from 1980 to 1990 that is not explicitly mentioned in the excerpts could support Martin's interpretation.

(C) Briefly explain how ONE historical event or development from 1980 to 1990 that is not explicitly mentioned in the excerpts could support Zubok's interpretation.

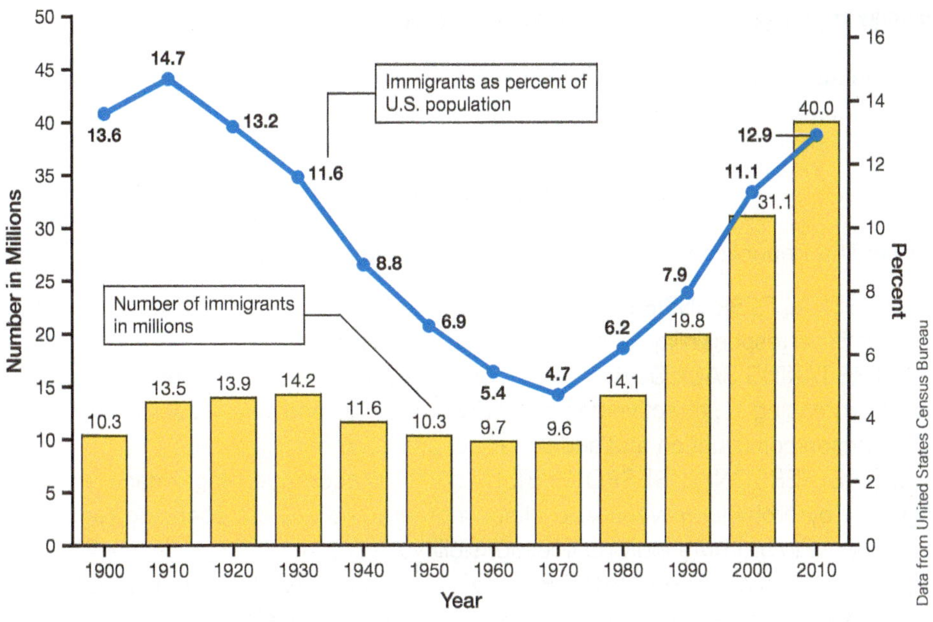

Number and Percent of Immigrants in the United States, 1900–2010

2. Using the image, answer **A**, **B**, and **C**.
   (A) Briefly explain ONE specific historical event or development that accounts for a change depicted in the graph.
   (B) Briefly explain ONE specific historical effect of a change depicted in the graph.
   (C) Briefly explain ANOTHER specific historical effect of a change depicted in the graph.

3. Answer **A**, **B**, and **C**.
   (A) Briefly describe ONE similarity between the U.S. economy in the 1950s and the U.S. economy in the 2000s.
   (B) Briefly describe ONE difference between the U.S. economy in the 1950s and the U.S. economy in the 2000s
   (C) Briefly explain ONE reason for a difference between the U.S. economy in the 1950s and the U.S. economy in the 2000s.

4. Answer **A**, **B**, and **C**.
   (A) Briefly describe ONE specific historical similarity between reasons for U.S. military involvement in Iraq and reasons for U.S. military involvement in Afghanistan.
   (B) Briefly describe ONE specific historical difference between the U.S. experience in Iraq and the U.S. experience in Afghanistan.
   (C) Briefly explain ONE specific historical effect of either the involvement in Iraq or the involvement in Afghanistan on U.S. society.

Document-Based Question

1. Evaluate the extent to which the conservative movement in the United States achieved its national policy aims from 1992 to 2022.

Document 1

Source: The Republican Party, "Contract with America," 1994

"1. THE FISCAL RESPONSIBILITY ACT: A balanced budget/tax limitation amendment . . . to restore fiscal responsibility to an out-of-control Congress . . .

2. THE TAKING BACK OUR STREETS ACT: An anti-crime package including stronger truth in sentencing . . . effective death penalty provisions, and cuts in social spending . . . to fund prison construction and additional law enforcement . . .

3. THE PERSONAL RESPONSIBILITY ACT: Discourage illegitimacy and teen pregnancy by prohibiting welfare to minor mothers and . . . cut spending for welfare programs . . . to promote individual responsibility . . .

6. THE NATIONAL SECURITY RESTORATION ACT: No U.S. troops under U.N. command and restoration of the essential parts of our national security . . .

8. THE JOB CREATION AND WAGE ENHANCEMENT ACT: Small business incentives, capital gains cut and indexation . . . to create jobs and raise worker wages. . . .

10. THE CITIZEN LEGISLATURE ACT: A first-ever vote on term limits to replace career politicians . . ."

Document 2

Source: California Ballot Initiative, Proposition 187, 1994

"The People of California find and declare as follows:

That they have suffered and are suffering economic hardship caused by the presence of illegal aliens in this state.

That they have suffered and are suffering personal injury and damage caused by the criminal conduct of illegal aliens in this state.

That they have a right to the protection of their government from any person or persons entering this country unlawfully.

Therefore, the People of California declare their intention to provide for cooperation between their agencies of state and local government with the federal government, and to establish a system of required notification by and between such agencies to prevent illegal aliens in the United States from receiving benefits or public services in the State of California."

Document 3

Source: President Clinton, President Clinton's Announcement on Welfare Legislation, July 31, 1996

"When I ran for President four years ago, I pledged to end welfare as we know it. I have worked very hard for four years to do just that.

Today the Congress will vote on legislation that gives us a chance to live up to that promise, to transform a broken system that traps too many people in a cycle of dependence to one that emphasizes work and independence, to give people on welfare a chance to draw a paycheck, not a welfare check. It gives us a better chance to give those on welfare what we want for all families in America, the opportunity to succeed at home and at work. . . .

I made my principles for real welfare reform very clear from the beginning. First and foremost, it should be about moving people from welfare to work. It should impose time limits on welfare. It should give people the child care and the health care they need to move from welfare to work without hurting their children. It should crack down on child-support enforcement, and it should protect our children."

Document 4

Source: Presidential Press Release, Office of the Press Secretary, June 9, 2016

"FACT SHEET: Obama Administration's Record and the LGBT Community

Since taking office, President Obama and his Administration have made historic strides to expand opportunities and advance equality and justice for all Americans, including Lesbian, Gay, Bisexual, and Transgender (LGBT) Americans. From major legislative achievements to historic court victories to important policy changes, the President has fought to promote the equal rights of all Americans—no matter who they are or who they love. That commitment to leveling the playing field and ensuring equal protection under the law is the bedrock principle this nation was founded on and has guided the President's actions in support of all Americans. And the progress the Administration has made mirrors the changing views of the American people, who recognize that fairness and justice demand equality for all, including LGBT Americans."

Document 5

Source: Office of the United States Trade Representative, Executive Office of the President, September 18, 2018

"As part of the United States' continuing response to China's theft of American intellectual property and forced transfer of American technology, the Office of the United States Trade Representative (USTR) today released a list of approximately $200 billion worth of Chinese imports that will be subject to additional tariffs. In accordance with the direction of President Trump, the additional tariffs will be effective starting September 24, 2018, and initially will be in the amount of 10 percent. Starting January 1, 2019, the level of the additional tariffs will increase to 25 percent. . . .

After separate notice and comment proceedings, in June and August USTR released two lists of Chinese imports, with a combined annual trade value of approximately $50 billion, with the goal of obtaining the elimination of China's harmful acts, policies, and practices. Unfortunately, China has been unwilling to change its policies involving the unfair acquisition of U.S. technology and intellectual property. Instead, China responded to the United States' tariff action by taking further steps to harm U.S. workers and businesses. In these circumstances, the President has directed the U.S. Trade Representative to increase the level of trade covered by the additional duties in order to obtain elimination of China's unfair policies. The Administration will continue to encourage China to allow for fair trade with the United States."

Document 6

Source: Testimony of Chye-Ching Huang, Director of Federal Fiscal Policy, Tax Policy Center, Before the House Budget Committee, February 27, 2019

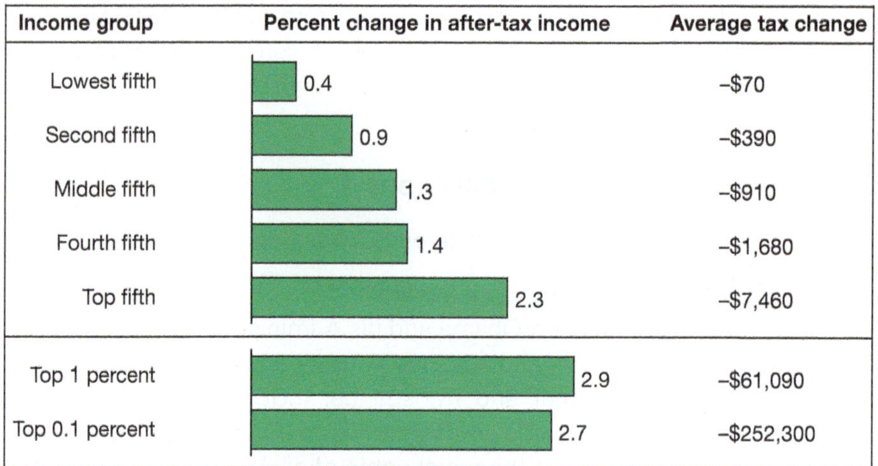

Income group
Percent change in after-tax income
Average tax change
Lowest fifth
0.4
–$70
Second fifth
0.9
–$390
Middle fifth
1.3
–$910
Fourth fifth
1.4
–$1,680
Top fifth
2.3
–$7,460
Top 1 percent
2.9
–$61,090
Top 0.1 percent
2.7
–$252,300

Projected 2025 Distribution of Taxation Changes as a Result of the Tax Cuts and Jobs Act of 2017

Note: Excludes effect of repeal of health reform's individual mandate, which required most people to buy health insurance or pay a penalty.

Document 7

Source: United States Supreme Court, *Dobbs v. Jackson Women's Health Organization*, June 2022

"Finally, the Court considers whether a right to obtain an abortion is part of a broader entrenched right that is supported by other precedents. The Court concludes the right to obtain an abortion cannot be justified as a component of such a right. Attempts to justify abortion through appeals to a broader right to autonomy and to define one's 'concept of existence' prove too much. . . . Those criteria, at a high level of generality, could license fundamental rights to illicit drug use, prostitution, and the like. What sharply distinguishes the abortion right from the rights recognized in the cases on which *Roe* and *Casey* rely is something that both those decisions acknowledged: Abortion is different because it destroys what *Roe* termed 'potential life' and what the law challenged in this case calls an 'unborn human being.' None of the other decisions cited by *Roe* and *Casey* involved the critical moral question posed by abortion. Accordingly, those cases do not support the right to obtain an abortion, and the Court's conclusion that the Constitution does not confer such a right [to abortion] . . ."

Long-Essay Questions

2. Analyze the ways in which U.S. involvement in the Middle East fostered change in the foreign and domestic policies of the United States in the period from 1990 to the present.

3. Analyze the ways in which the presidency of Ronald Reagan (1981–1989) fostered change in the foreign and domestic policies of the United States.

4. Analyze the ways in which globalization fostered change in the economy of the United States in the period from 1980 to the present.

Practice AP® Exam

SECTION I Multiple-Choice Questions

Questions 1–3 refer to the image.

Theodor de Bry, "Columbus Landing on Hispaniola," 1594

1. The image most directly supports which of the following beliefs held by European powers in the sixteenth century?

(A) The desire to spread Christianity to Native Americans
(B) The European belief in private land ownership
(C) The divine right of kings to rule with absolute power
(D) The racial and cultural superiority of Europeans

2. The image was created with the purpose of

(A) highlighting the cultural differences between Natives and Europeans.
(B) illustrating the commonalities held by Natives and Europeans.
(C) facilitating the financing of joint-stock companies.
(D) showing the futility of military resistance to European armies.

3. Which of the following most directly resulted from the situation depicted in the image?
   (A) European efforts to establish mutually beneficial trade networks with Native Americans
   (B) European attempts to conquer Native Americans and claim their lands
   (C) Differences between the English and the Spanish in their approach to colonization
   (D) The development of plantation-based agricultural systems

Questions 4–6 refer to the excerpt.

"In letters, diaries, and chronicles, Englishmen and -women in New England expressed their agonies, mourned their losses, and, most of all, defended their conduct. Not all colonists agreed about the causes of [Metacom's] war, or about how it should be waged, but most agreed about what was at stake: their lives, their land, and their sense of themselves. And, in the end, their writings proved to be pivotal to their victory, a victory that drew new, firmer boundaries between English and Indian people, between English and Indian land, and between what it meant to be 'English' and what it meant to be 'Indian.'

Yet those boundaries were never stable, either before or after the war. Seventeenth-century New England was, after all, a frontier, at once a dividing line and a middle ground between at least two cultures."

Jill Lepore, *The Name of War: King Philip's War and the Origins of American Identity*, 1998

4. The events described in the excerpt occurred in the context of what historical situation?
   (A) Failed attempts by the British at assimilating Native American populations
   (B) A decrease in imperial competition over a transatlantic economy
   (C) British confrontations with Native Americans over land claims
   (D) Attempts by the Spanish to arm Native Americans hostile to the British

5. British settlement in North America during the second half of the seventeenth century most differed from French and Dutch settlement in that the British
   (A) came in comparatively large numbers.
   (B) often intermarried with Native Americans.
   (C) relied on the fur trade to support their settlements.
   (D) emphasized the conversion of native peoples to Christianity.

6. The creation of "firmer boundaries between English and Indian people, between English and Indian land" most directly contributed to which of the following developments in the early eighteenth century?
   (A) Decades of peaceful coexistence between Native Americans and British settlers
   (B) Continued expansion by the British into the interior of North America
   (C) The relocation of Native Americans to reservations
   (D) Attempts by the British to halt colonial movement westward

Questions 7–9 refer to the image.

The Rise and Decline of the Slave Trade

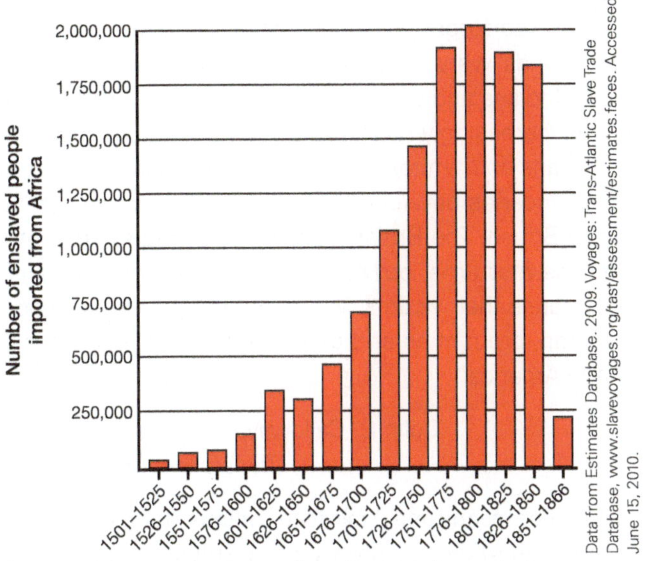

Graph of the number of enslaved people imported from Africa to the Western Hemisphere per twenty-five-year time periods

7. The trend depicted on the chart from 1676 to 1800 was most directly caused by
(A) demand for cash crops produced for European markets.
(B) the large numbers of enslaved laborers in the middle colonies.
(C) imperial wars over land in North America.
(D) an abundance of indentured servants.

8. Despite the growth of slavery throughout the colonial period, enslaved Africans in the Chesapeake and the Carolinas responded by
(A) engaging in large-scale rebellions.
(B) creating and maintaining cultural and religious practices.
(C) accepting the chattel system of southern colonies.
(D) working as indentured servants in northern colonies.

9. One of the long-term consequences of the trend depicted on the chart from 1676 to 1850 was
(A) a decline in the production of cash crops in the middle colonies.
(B) a decrease in the number of enslaved Africans sent to the West Indies.
(C) a codification of slavery based on race in the southern colonies.
(D) a lack of enslaved laborers in port cities.

Questions 10–12 refer to the excerpt.

"The year 1763 was ostensibly one of peace, but for Indians and whites peace proved more elusive than ever. Indians and colonists had clashed in conflict virtually from first contact, but they also forged alliances and built patterns of coexistence. Such negotiated 'middle grounds' were breaking down by the early 1760s. . . . Despite efforts to preserve harmony, Indians and whites fell on each other with renewed fury in 1763 and the violence was increasingly racial. As European nations drew new boundaries in North America, Indians and whites built increasingly rigid, and increasingly bloody, ethnic and cultural boundaries between themselves. Indians went to war to try to rid Indian country of the British. The British government tried to clear Indian country of settlers . . . Not for the first time, but more than ever before, Indians and whites in 1763 killed people because their victims were, respectively, whites and Indians. . . .

The year 1763, then, brought an end to an era of world war but initiated an era of upheaval that remade America."

Colin G. Calloway, *The Scratch of a Pen: 1763 and the Transformation of North America*, 2006

10. Examples of when Europeans and American Indians "forged alliances and built patterns of coexistence" most often happened as a result of
- (A) colonial respect for cultural practices of American Indians.
- (B) the sharing of religious practices.
- (C) efforts to promote trade.
- (D) agreement over the use of land.

11. Which of the following developments supports Calloway's argument that 1763 was a historical turning point?
- (A) Attempts by the British to limit colonial expansion into western territories
- (B) Imperial conflicts over power in North America
- (C) An increase in Anglicization by British colonists
- (D) Continued confrontations between British colonists and the British Parliament

12. The idea that the events of 1763 "initiated an era of upheaval that remade America" can be explained by
- (A) a continuation of French-Indian alliances.
- (B) alliances between Native Americans and British colonists.
- (C) the French maintaining control over trade in North America.
- (D) imperial efforts to consolidate political power over the colonists.

Questions 13–15 refer to the excerpt.

"[O]ne of these conclusions must necessarily follow, either that justice is not the same in America as in Britain, or else that the British parliament pay less regard to it here than there. But that we do not point out to his majesty the injustice of these acts, with intent to rest on that principle the cause of their nullity; but to show that experience confirms the propriety of those political principles which exempt us from the jurisdiction of the British parliament. The true ground on which we declare these acts void is, that the British parliament has no right to exercise authority over us."

Thomas Jefferson, *A Summary View of the Rights of British North America*, 1774

13. Which of the following pieces of evidence best supports the assertions in the source above?
   (A) A belief in the ideas of the Enlightenment
   (B) The mobilization of the patriot movement
   (C) The formation of a military alliance between the breakaway colonies and France
   (D) Economic shortages caused by the British blockade of American ports

14. The ideas described in the excerpt most directly led to which of the following?
   (A) Efforts by political leaders to emphasize Anglicization
   (B) American political beliefs in republican forms of government
   (C) A decline in the value placed on individual talent
   (D) A movement to reconcile differences between Americans and the British Parliament

15. Which of the following would most likely have supported the ideas expressed in the excerpt?
   (A) An Anglican minister in Philadelphia
   (B) A royal governor
   (C) A southern plantation holder with Loyalist sentiments
   (D) A laborer who believed in traditional self-rule

Questions 16–18 refer to the excerpt.

"We hold these truths to be self-evident: that all men and women are created equal; that they are endowed by their Creator with certain inalienable rights; that among these are life, liberty, and the pursuit of happiness. . . .

The history of mankind is a history of repeated injuries and usurpations on the part of man toward woman, having in direct object the establishment of an absolute tyranny over her. . . .

He has never permitted her to exercise her inalienable right to the elective franchise.

He has compelled her to submit to laws, in the formation of which she had no voice. . . .

He has taken from her all right in property, even to the wages she earns."

Elizabeth Cady Stanton, *Declaration of Sentiments*, 1848

16. The ideas expressed by Stanton in the excerpt occurred in the context of what historical situation?
   (A) The emergence of a national culture that encouraged independent female thinking
   (B) The growth of individualistic beliefs during the Second Great Awakening
   (C) A market revolution that privileged the work of female laborers
   (D) Greater social mobility for southern working-class women

17. Which of the following is an example of a historical consequence in the mid-1800s of the debates caused by the ideas in the excerpt?
   (A) The passage of legislation limiting the daily working hours of women in factories
   (B) A rapid increase in public support for women's suffrage
   (C) A women's movement that sought greater equality and opportunity for women
   (D) The emergence of prominent movements to protect the rights of other groups of Americans

18. Which of the following represents a historical continuity to the ideas expressed in the excerpt?
    (A) Antebellum women who embraced ideas such as separate spheres
    (B) Female reformers during the Progressive Era
    (C) Fundamentalist women in the 1920s
    (D) Conservative leaders in the 1970s

Questions 19–21 refer to the map.

Map of major roads, navigable rivers, and major canals in the United States to 1837

19. The map reflects which of the following historical developments?
    (A) A significant growth in southern infrastructure
    (B) An increase in migration from southern Europe
    (C) An attempt to promote regional economic interdependence
    (D) New industrial management techniques such as vertical integration

20. The historical developments depicted in the map most directly led to
(A) sectional disputes over slavery.
(B) the emergence of the second political party system in the United States.
(C) the creation of a national banking system.
(D) legislation that promoted the development of transportation systems.

21. Which of the following groups would have been most likely to support the developments depicted in the image?
(A) Jacksonian Democrats opposed to a national banking system
(B) Whig politicians who embraced the American System
(C) Tobacco and rice plantation owners in the South
(D) Subsistence farmers living along the borderlands

Questions 22–24 refer to the excerpt.

"It is impossible to say how many slaves escaped to freedom in the decades before the Civil War. Contemporary sources are often of little help. . . . Estimates—guesses, really—suggest somewhere between 1,000 and 5,000 per year between 1830 and 1860. . . . It is impossible to think of fugitive slaves without also thinking of the underground railroad. . . . The term, in fact, did not yet exist when [Frederick] Douglass reached the North, and it remains unclear exactly when it originated. . . . Whatever its origin, the phrase soon became ubiquitous. . . .

During the 1850s, journalists throughout the country credited the underground railroad with far more organization and impact than it actually enjoyed. The southern press attributed escapes of all kinds—by land and sea, to the North, Canada, or southern cities—to the underground railroad. In 1860, the *New York Herald*, a fierce opponent of abolitionism, described the underground railroad as essentially a fund-raising racket that preyed on the misplaced sympathy of well-meaning whites."

Eric Foner, *Gateway to Freedom: The Hidden History of the Underground Railroad*, 2015

22. The description of the Underground Railroad in the excerpt is best explained by which of the following developments?
(A) The gradual growth of abolitionist and antislavery movements in the North
(B) The efforts of state governments to restrict the movement of Black Americans
(C) The attempt by the federal government to manage slavery in the western territories
(D) The construction of privately funded railroads linking the Northeast and Midwest

23. Even southerners who did not enslave people often opposed antislavery efforts such as the Underground Railroad because they
(A) hoped to one day own a plantation.
(B) benefited from a system of indentured servitude.
(C) argued slavery was a way of life.
(D) feared the success of large-scale slave rebellions.

24. Which of the following historical situations best explains the development of the Underground Railroad?
(A) The Enlightenment
(B) The market revolution
(C) The temperance movement
(D) The Second Great Awakening

Questions 25–27 refer to the excerpt.

"Nor can we justifiably withhold this, on any ground save our conviction that slavery is wrong. If slavery is right, all words, acts, laws, and constitutions against it, are themselves wrong, and should be silenced, and swept away. If it is right, we cannot justly object to its nationality—its universality; if it is wrong, they cannot justly insist upon its extension—its enlargement. . . .

Wrong as we think slavery is, we can yet afford to let it alone where it is, because that much is due to the necessity arising from its actual presence in the nation; but can we, while our votes will prevent it, allow it to spread into the National Territories, and to overrun us here in these Free States? If our sense of duty forbids this, then let us stand by our duty, fearlessly and effectively."

Abraham Lincoln, Cooper Union Speech, February 27, 1860

25. The argument made by Lincoln to encourage northerners "to let it alone where it is" best explains which of the following?
(A) The abolitionist movement
(B) The Mexican-American War
(C) The free-soil movement
(D) The argument for states' rights

26. Southerners who opposed the arguments made by Lincoln relied on which of the following arguments?
(A) The supremacy of the national government over state governments
(B) The view that slavery was a positive social good
(C) The Supreme Court's ruling in the *Dred Scott* case
(D) The dependence of northern industrialization on southern enslaved labor

27. Which of the following most directly contributed to the national debates over slavery during the 1850s?
(A) Attempted political compromises over western territories
(B) U.S. efforts to expand trade with Asia
(C) The increase in migration from western Europe
(D) The emergence of the American Party (Know-Nothing Party)

Questions 28–30 refer to the excerpt.

"Here is where secession was born and Nurtured. Here is where we have toiled nearly all Our lives as slaves and were treated like dumb Driven cattle, This is our home, we have made These lands what they are. we were the only true and Loyal people that were found in possession of these Lands. we have been always ready to strike for Liberty and humanity yea to fight if needs be To preserve this glorious union. Shall not we who Are freedman and have been always true to this Union have the same rights as are enjoyed by Others? Have we broken any Law of these United States? Have we forfieted our rights of property in Land?—If not then! are not our rights as A free people and good citizens of these United States To be considered before the rights of those who were Found in rebellion against this good and just Government . . ."

Letter from the Freedmen of Edisto Island, South Carolina, to President Andrew Johnson, October 28, 1865

28. Which of the following best explains how freedmen gained "rights as A free people and good citizens" during Reconstruction?
(A) The Emancipation Proclamation banning slavery in the Confederate states
(B) The ratification of the Fourteenth Amendment
(C) The efforts of northern states to expand suffrage to all Black people
(D) The large-scale redistribution of southern plantation lands to formerly enslaved workers

29. Which of the following groups would have been most likely to support the ideas in the excerpt?
(A) Moderate Republicans
(B) Northern Democrats
(C) Southern Democrats
(D) Radical Republicans

30. Which of the following resulted from opposition to the ideas expressed in the excerpt in the late nineteenth century?
(A) The mass migration movement of freedmen to California and other western territories
(B) The use of political and racial violence in the South against Black people
(C) The establishment of the Freedmen's Bureau to provide assistance to formerly enslaved Black people
(D) The failure to create a "New South" with an industrialized economy

Questions 31–33 refer to the excerpt.

"What made anti-Chinese violence distinct was its principal intent, together with its method and result.

The intent was exclusion. At the local level, anti-Chinese advocates fought to prohibit Chinese from entering spaces and working in occupations deemed the sole entitlement of white citizens. At the national level, they fought to bar Chinese migrants from entering the United States and to deny citizenship to those already in the country. At the international level, they fought to exclude China from the conversation about immigration, hoping to turn a bilateral policy into a unilateral one. . . .

At the time, national exclusion was a particularly radical objective. Although border control may seem natural and inevitable today, the United States began with a policy of open immigration for all. In the early nineteenth century, the federal government was more concerned with attracting 'desirable' immigrants than prohibiting 'undesirable' ones. . . . This meant that there was no need for passports, no concept of an 'illegal alien,' and no consensus that the United States should determine the makeup of its citizenry by closing its gates.

Anti-Chinese advocates demanded that the federal government change all of this."

Beth Lew-Williams, *The Chinese Must Go: Violence, Exclusion, and the Making of the Alien in America*, 2018

31. Despite the response of many Americans to Chinese immigration described in the excerpt, many policymakers sought to
(A) expand U.S. economic influence in Asia.
(B) promote a laissez-faire approach to immigration.
(C) embrace existing migration patterns from Asia and Europe.
(D) champion the goals of the Social Gospel movement.

32. Williams's argument that in the early 1800s, "the federal government was more concerned with attracting 'desirable' immigrants than prohibiting 'undesirable' ones" best supports the idea of which of the following historical continuities?
(A) The belief in Social Darwinism held by industrial leaders
(B) The lack of social mobility for all migrant populations
(C) The expansion and diversification of the industrial workforce
(D) The lack of urban ethnic neighborhoods

33. The changes in immigration attitudes toward Chinese immigrants described in the excerpt are most similar to
(A) the emergence of anti-Catholic nativist groups in the 1850s.
(B) segregation policies in the South after Reconstruction.
(C) internal migration patterns in the early twentieth century.
(D) restrictions on European immigration after World War I.

Questions 34–37 refer to the excerpt.

"To those of my race who depend on bettering their condition in a foreign land or who underestimate the importance of cultivating friendly relations with the Southern white man, who is their next-door neighbor, I would say: 'Cast down your bucket where you are'—cast it down in making friends in every manly way of the people of all races by whom we are surrounded.

Cast it down in agriculture, mechanics, in commerce, in domestic service, and in the professions. And in this connection it is well to bear in mind that whatever other sins the South may be called to bear, when it comes to business, pure and simple, it is in the South that the Negro is given a man's chance in the commercial world, and in nothing is this Exposition more eloquent than in emphasizing this chance. Our greatest danger is that in the great leap from slavery to freedom we may overlook the fact that the masses of us are to live by the productions of our hands, and fail to keep in mind that we shall prosper in proportion as we learn to dignify and glorify common labor, and put brains and skill into the common occupations of life; . . . No race can prosper till it learns that there is as much dignity in tilling a field as in writing a poem. It is at the bottom of life we must begin, and not at the top."

Booker T. Washington, "Speech Before the Atlanta Cotton States and International Exposition," Atlanta, Georgia, September 18, 1895

34. Which historical development was most closely associated with Washington's observation that "the masses of us are to live by the productions of our hands"?
(A) Industrial capitalism
(B) Tenant farming
(C) Interchangeable parts
(D) Declining prices

35. The ideas expressed in the excerpt could be used as evidence by historians to study which of the following developments?
(A) Imperialist attitudes
(B) The Populist movement
(C) Debates over Reconstruction policies
(D) The limitations of the "New South"

36. The significance of the ideas expressed in the excerpt is best understood as an example of how Black reformers
   (A) sought to promote Black economic improvement.
   (B) fought for full social equality with whites.
   (C) tried to promote industrialization in southern states.
   (D) resisted the system of Jim Crow laws in the South.

37. The historical issues facing Black Americans referenced in the excerpt are best explained by
   (A) the failure of Reconstruction policies to secure Black self-sufficiency.
   (B) the corruption in urban politics resulting from political machines.
   (C) the consolidation of wealth by large corporations and trusts.
   (D) the ways technological innovation decreased the need for factory labor.

Questions 38–40 refer to the image.

Sarin Images/Granger – Historical Picture Archive

Clifford Berryman, "The President's Dream of a Successful Hunt," 1907

About the Source: The bear on left is labeled "good trusts" and has a leash with the word "restraint" on it, while the bear in the center is labeled "bad trusts." The sign in the back reads "White House."

38. Which group would have most likely supported the actions depicted in the image?
   (A) Wealthy industrialists
   (B) Progressive reformers
   (C) Political machine bosses
   (D) Conservationists

39. The image best illustrates which of the following developments?
(A) An increasing amount of leisure time for the middle class
(B) The spread of conservationist ideals
(C) Popular support for efforts to regulate the economy
(D) The growing popularity of American art depicting nature

40. Which of the following most directly led to the problem depicted in the image?
(A) The efforts of muckrakers to expose corruption and abuses of power
(B) The decimation of the buffalo population in the West
(C) An expansion of the industrial workforce
(D) A persistent belief in laissez-faire policies

Questions 41–44 refer to the image.

Venimages/Alamy

Committee on Public Information, a U.S. government agency, 1918

41. The ideas expressed in the image are best understood in the context of
(A) deficit spending by the federal government during and after World War I.
(B) discrimination encountered by Black people as they moved out of the South.
(C) record levels of immigration from Europe and attacks on immigrant culture.
(D) the fear of foreign radicalism infiltrating labor movements.

42. Which of the following represents a direct consequence of the ideas depicted in the image?
(A) The failure of the United States to join the League of Nations
(B) Restrictions on freedom of speech
(C) The emergence of new forms of mass media
(D) Increased U.S. manufacturing to meet wartime demands

43. In the decade after the war, which of the following is most directly related to the ideas expressed in the image?
(A) Nativist campaigns to restrict immigration
(B) The emergence of radical movements to change the U.S. economic system
(C) New forms of art that expressed ethnic identities
(D) American support for the punitive provisions of the Treaty of Versailles

44. Despite the messages in the image above, what was a central argument the U.S. government made for entry in World War I?
(A) To increase trade with allies
(B) To lead the peace process after the war
(C) To create collective security organizations with European nations
(D) To defend democratic systems of government

Questions 45–47 refer to the excerpt.

"Detroit's journey from urban heyday to urban crisis has been mirrored in other cities across the nation. Scenes of devastation and poverty are disturbingly familiar to anyone who has traveled through the streets of America's Rust Belt, the northeastern and midwestern cities that formed the backbone of American industrial might a half-century ago. . . . Rates of poverty among black residents of these cities all range from 25 to 40 percent. . . . Almost all of these cities . . . 'have large ghettos characterized by extreme segregation and spatial isolation.' The faces that appear in the rundown houses, homeless shelters, and social agencies in these urban wastelands are predictably familiar. Almost all are people of color. . . .

No one social program or policy, no single force, whether housing segregation, social welfare programs, or deindustrialization, could have driven Detroit and other cities like it from their positions of economic and political dominance; there is no simple explanation for the inequality and marginality that beset the urban poor. It is only through the complex and interwoven histories of race, residence, and work in the postwar era that the state of today's cities and their impoverished residents can be fully understood and confronted"

Thomas J. Sugrue, *The Origins of the Urban Crisis: Race and Inequality in Postwar Detroit*, 1996

45. Which of the following most directly resulted from the "journey from urban heyday to urban crisis" in the late 1960s?
(A) Peaceful demonstrations such as sit-ins
(B) Rulings by the Supreme Court to desegregate schools
(C) Social unrest in urban areas
(D) An embrace of Black power by civil rights advocates

46. Which of the following developments in the 1970s represents a historical consequence of the urban realities described by Sugrue?
(A) The weakening of the tax base in American cities
(B) Debates over busing as a means to integrate urban schools
(C) A decline in the numbers of urban riots
(D) A reversal of fair housing mandates in northern suburbs

47. Which of the following best represents a major historical trend in the 1970s whose effects are implied in this excerpt?
(A) Manufacturing jobs in northern cities declined.
(B) Court rulings increasingly promoted civil rights.
(C) Black power activists increasingly drove the civil rights movement.
(D) Redlining of neighborhoods by the federal government increased.

Questions 48–50 refer to the excerpt.

"During 12 years of working for a living, I've experienced much of the legal and social discrimination reserved for women in this country. I have been refused service in public restaurants, ordered out of public gathering places, and turned away from apartment rentals; all for the clearly stated, sole reason that I am a woman. And all without the legal remedies available to blacks and other minorities. I have been excluded from professional groups, writing assignments on so-called 'unfeminine' subjects such as politics, full participation in the Democratic Party, jury duty, and even from such small male privileges as discounts on airline fares. Most important to me, I have been denied a society in which women are encouraged, or even allowed, to think of themselves as first-class citizens and responsible human beings."

Gloria Steinem, Testimony before the Senate Judiciary Committee
Hearing on the Equal Rights Amendment, May 6, 1970

48. The purpose of Steinem's testimony was to advocate
(A) the elevation of women's rights above other rights movements.
(B) trust in the government's ability to solve social problems.
(C) separate spheres for men and women.
(D) changes to society's gendered expectations.

49. The "legal and social discrimination" Steinem spoke of in the excerpt would have been most visible in
(A) the ability to exercise suffrage.
(B) the economic opportunities afforded to women.
(C) the power of anti-feminist movements among other women.
(D) the suburbs of middle-class families.

50. Which of the following groups would have most likely opposed the arguments made by Steinem?
(A) College-educated liberals
(B) Young members of the counterculture
(C) Sun Belt conservatives
(D) Black civil rights leaders

Questions 51–53 refer to the graph.

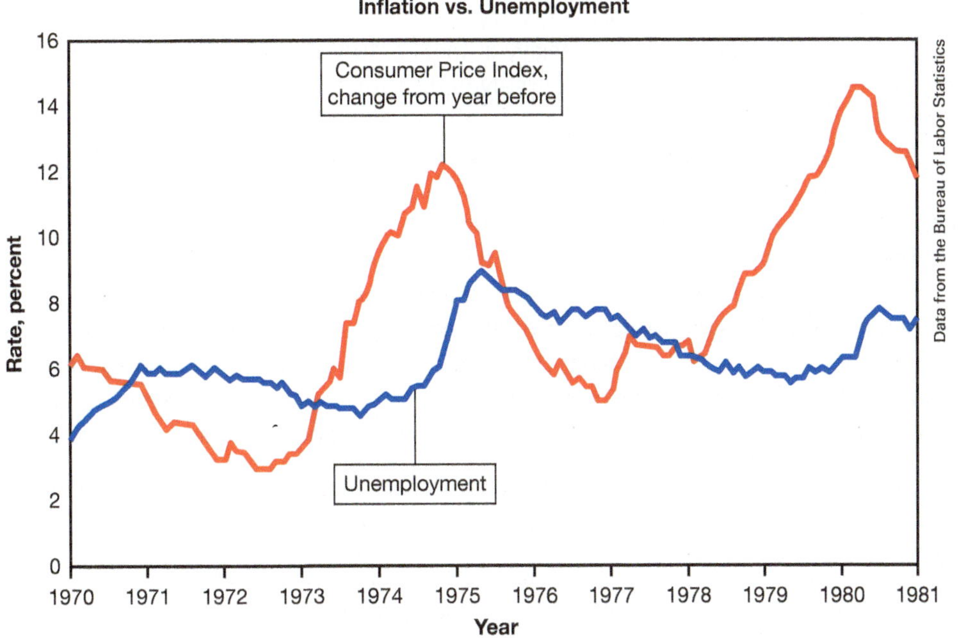

U.S. Unemployment Rate and Inflation Rate, 1970–1981

51. The economic circumstances depicted in the graph were most directly caused by which of the following?
(A) Generational differences over gender norms
(B) Liberal Supreme Court rulings
(C) Foreign-policy crises
(D) Political scandals of the decade

52. The economic downturn depicted in the graph most directly led to
(A) extensive tax cuts in the mid-1970s.
(B) economic recovery in the late 1970s.
(C) conservative economic programs in the 1980s.
(D) an end to the Cold War in the late 1980s.

53. The trend depicted in the graph happened in the context of
(A) a lack of public confidence in government.
(B) successful peace processes in the Middle East.
(C) increased economic productivity due to globalization.
(D) rapid changes in migration patterns to the United States.

Questions 54 and 55 refer to the excerpt.

"But whatever sad episodes exist in our past, any objective observer must hold a positive view of American history, a history that has been the story of hopes fulfilled and dreams made into reality. Especially in this century, America has kept alight the torch of freedom, but not just for ourselves, but for millions of others around the world. . . .

At the same time, however, they [the Soviets] must be made to understand: we will never compromise our principles and standards. We will never give away our freedom. We will never abandon our belief in God. . . .

The reality is that we must find peace through strength. . . .

So, in your discussions of the nuclear freeze proposals, I urge you to beware the temptation of pride—the temptation of blithely . . . declaring yourselves above it all and label both sides equally at fault, to ignore the facts of history and the aggressive impulses of an evil empire, to simply call the arms race a giant misunderstanding and thereby remove yourself from the struggle between right and wrong and good and evil."

President Ronald Reagan, Address to the National Association of Evangelicals, March 8, 1983

54. The argument expressed by Reagan most directly illustrated his desire to
- (A) stimulate economic growth through spending on defense.
- (B) reduce the power of the federal government through deregulation.
- (C) return to more traditional social values and repeal liberal policies.
- (D) oppose communism through the buildup of nuclear weapons.

55. The tone of the speech marked an important historical change because
- (A) it immediately led to arms control talks and a renewed period of peace.
- (B) Reagan was more assertive in his anticommunism than previous administrations.
- (C) it furthered U.S. peacekeeping missions in southern Europe and Africa.
- (D) the government enacted strict measures to expose suspected communists.

Short-Answer Questions

"The period of mass European immigration, from the 1840s to the restrictive legislation of 1924, witnessed a fracturing of whiteness into a hierarchy of plural and scientifically determined white races. Vigorous debate ensued over which of these was truly 'fit for self-government' in the good old Anglo-Saxon sense. Finally, in the 1920s and after, partly because the crisis of over-inclusive whiteness had been solved by restrictive legislation and partly in response to a new racial alchemy generated by African-American migrations to the North and West, whiteness was reconsolidated: the late nineteenth century's probationary white groups were now remade and granted the scientific stamp of authenticity as the unitary Caucasian race—an earlier era's Celts, Slavs, Hebrews, Iberics, and Saracens, among others, had become the Caucasians so familiar to our own visual economy and racial lexicon."

Matthew Frye Jacobson, *Whiteness of a Different Color: European Immigrants and the Alchemy of Race*, 1998

"Most important, the cutoff of immigration created conditions for the second generation of those immigrants who had come to the United States from the 1890s to World War I to more readily assimilate into American society. . . . Immigration restriction produced the illegal alien as a *new legal and political subject*, whose inclusion within the nation was simultaneously a social reality and a legal impossibility—a subject barred from citizenship and without rights. Moreover, the need of state authorities to identify and distinguish between citizens, lawfully resident immigrants, and illegal aliens posed enforcement, political, and constitutional problems for the modern state. The illegal alien is thus an 'impossible subject,' a person who cannot be and a problem that cannot be solved."

Mae M. Ngai, *Impossible Subjects: Illegal Aliens and the Making of Modern America*, 2004

1. Using the excerpts, answer **A**, **B**, and **C**.
   (A) Briefly describe ONE major difference between Jacobson's and Ngai's historical interpretations about the effects of the restrictive immigration legislation passed in the 1920s.
   (B) Briefly explain how ONE historical event or development that is not explicitly mentioned in the excerpts could support Jacobson's interpretation.
   (C) Briefly explain how ONE historical event or development that is not explicitly mentioned in the excerpts could support Ngai's interpretation.

"Ask Maryland, with her tens of thousands of slaves if she is not prepared for freedom, and hear her answer: 'I helped supply the coffle-gangs [groups of shackled enslaved persons] to the South.' Ask Virginia with her hundreds of thousands of slaves if she is not weary with her merchandise of blood and anxious to shake the gory traffic from her hands and hear her reply: 'Though fertility has covered my soul, though a genial sky bends over my hills and vales [valleys], though I hold in my hand a wealth of water power enough to turn the spindles to clothe the world, yet with all these advantages, one of my chief staples has been the sons and daughters I send to the human market and human shambles [slaughterhouse].' Ask farther South and all the cotton-growing States chime in, 'We have need of fresh supplies to fill the ranks of those whose lives have gone out in unrequited toil [unpaid labor] on our distant plantations.'

A hundred-thousand new-born babes are annually added to the victims of slavery; twenty thousand lives are annually sacrificed on the plantations of the South. Such a sight should send a thrill of horror through the nerves of civilization and impel the heart of humanity to lofty deeds. So it might, if men had not found out a fearful alchemy by which this blood can be transformed into gold. Instead of listening to the cry of agony, they listen to the ring of dollars and stoop down and pick up the coin."

Frances Ellen Watkins Harper, Speech to the New York Anti-Slavery Society, May 13, 1857

2. Using the excerpt, answer **A**, **B**, and **C**.
   (A) Briefly describe the historical situation described in the excerpt.
   (B) Briefly explain how ONE specific historical event or development between 1800 and 1854 led to the historical situation depicted in the excerpt.
   (C) Briefly explain how ONE specific historical event or development between 1855 and 1877 happened as a result of the historical situation depicted in the excerpt.

3. Answer **A**, **B**, and **C**.
   (A) Briefly describe ONE important historical factor that shaped relations between Native Americans and the French in the period from 1607 to 1754.
   (B) Briefly describe ONE important historical factor that shaped relations between Native Americans and the British in the period from 1607 to 1754.
   (C) Briefly explain ONE important outcome of relations between Native Americans and either the British or the French in the period from 1700 to 1776.

4. Answer **A**, **B**, and **C**.
   (A) Briefly explain ONE important historical factor that shaped relations between the Soviet Union and the United States from 1941 to 1950.
   (B) Briefly explain ONE important historical factor that shaped relations between the Soviet Union and the United States from 1950 to 1972.
   (C) Briefly explain ONE important historical outcome of relations between the Soviet Union and the United States from 1972 to 1991.

SECTION II Document-Based Question

1. Evaluate the extent to which the civil rights movement for Black people changed American society in the period from 1940 to 1970.

Document 1

Source: *The Pittsburgh Courier*, February 7, 1942

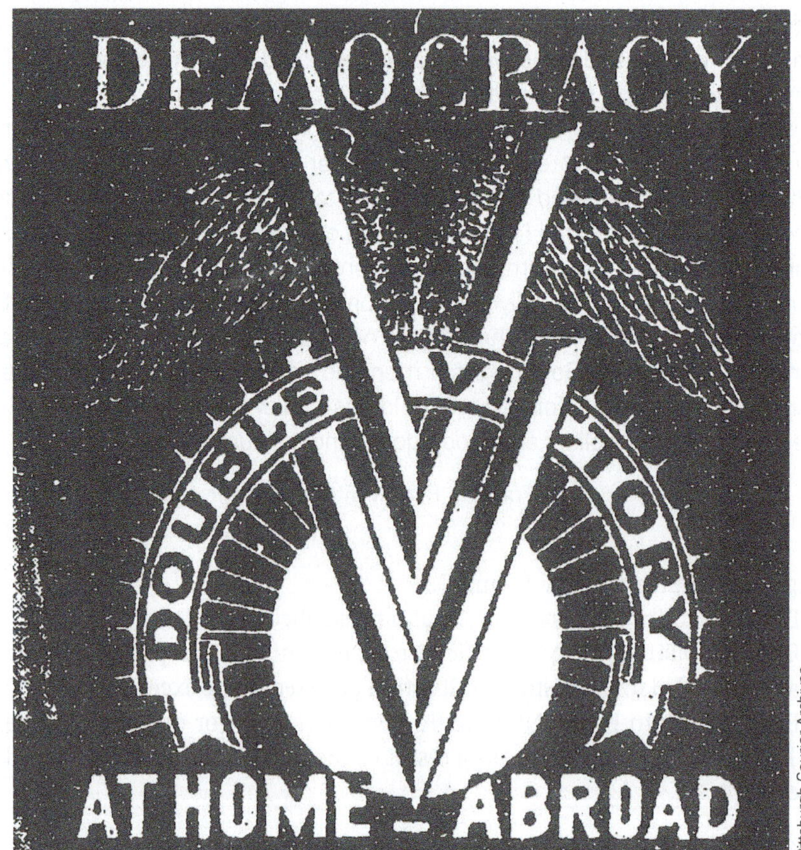

Pittsburgh Courier Archives

Document 2

Source: U.S. Supreme Court Decision, *Shelley v. Kraemer*, 1948

"Whether the equal protection clause of the Fourteenth Amendment inhibits judicial enforcement by state courts of restrictive covenants based on race or color is a question which this Court has not heretofore been called upon to consider. . . .

It cannot be doubted that among the civil rights intended to be protected from discriminatory state action by the Fourteenth Amendment are the rights to acquire, enjoy, own and dispose of property. Equality in the enjoyment of property rights was regarded by the framers of that Amendment as an essential pre-condition to the realization of other basic civil rights and liberties which the Amendment was intended to guarantee. . . .

We hold that, in granting judicial enforcement of the restrictive agreements in these cases, the States have denied petitioners the equal protection of the laws, and that, therefore, the action of the state courts cannot stand."

Document 3

Source: The "Declaration of Constitutional Principles" (The "Southern Manifesto") signed by 77 Representatives and 19 Senators from the South, March 12, 1956

"The unwarranted decision of the Supreme Court in the public school cases is now bearing the fruit always produced when men substitute naked power for established law. . . .

The original Constitution does not mention education. Neither does the 14th Amendment nor any other amendment. The debates preceding the submission of the 14th Amendment clearly show that there was no intent that it should affect the systems of education maintained by the states. . . .

We pledge ourselves to use all lawful means to bring about a reversal of this decision which is contrary to the Constitution and to prevent the use of force in its implementation."

Document 4

Source: Paul Robeson, Testimony before the House Un-American Activities Committee (HUAC), 1956

"Mr. Arens: Are you now a member of the Communist Party?

Mr. Robeson: Would you like to come to the ballot box when I vote and take out the ballot and see? . . .

Mr. Robeson: Gentlemen, in the first place, wherever I have been in the world, Scandinavia, England, and many places, the first to die in the struggle against Fascism were the Communists and I laid many wreaths upon graves of Communists. It is not criminal, and the Fifth Amendment has nothing to do with criminality. The Chief Justice of the Supreme Court, Warren, has been very clear on that in many speeches, that the Fifth Amendment does not have anything to do with the inference of criminality. I invoke the Fifth Amendment. . . .

Mr. Robeson: In Russia I felt for the first time like a full human being. No color prejudice like in Mississippi, no color prejudice like in Washington. It was the first time I felt like a human being. Where I did not feel the pressure of color as I feel [it] in this Committee today.

Mr. Scherer: Why do you not stay in Russia?

Mr. Robeson: Because my father was a slave, and my people died to build this country, and I am going to stay here, and have a part of it just like you. And no Fascist-minded people will drive me from it. Is that clear? I am for peace with the Soviet Union, and I am for peace with China, and I am not for peace or friendship with the Fascist Franco, and I am not for peace with Fascist Nazi Germans. I am for peace with decent people.

Mr. Scherer: You are here because you are promoting the Communist cause.

Mr. Robeson: I am here because I am opposing the neo-Fascist cause which I see arising in these committees. You are like the Alien [and] Sedition Act, and Jefferson could be sitting here, and Frederick Douglass could be sitting here, and Eugene Debs could be here."

Document 5

Source: Civil Rights March, Birmingham, Alabama, May 3, 1963

Afro Newspaper/Gado/Getty Images

Document 6

Source: Civil Rights Act of 1964

"An Act

To enforce the constitutional right to vote, to confer jurisdiction upon the district courts of the United States to provide injunctive relief against discrimination in public accommodations, to authorize the Attorney General to institute suits to protect constitutional rights in public facilities and public education, to extend the Commission on Civil Rights, to prevent discrimination in federally assisted programs, to establish a Commission on Equal Employment Opportunity, and for other purposes."

Document 7

Source: *Report of the National Advisory Commission on Civil Disorders* (The Kerner Commission Report), 1967

"In addressing the question 'Why did it happen?' we shift our focus from the local to the national scene, from particular events of the summer of 1967 to the factors within the society at large that created a mood of violence among many urban Negroes.

These factors are complex and interacting; they vary significantly in their effect from city to city and from year to year; and the consequences of one disorder, generating new grievances and new demands, become the causes of the next. . . .

Despite these complexities, certain fundamental matters are clear. Of these, the most fundamental is the racial attitude and behavior of white Americans toward black Americans.

Race prejudice has shaped our history decisively; it now threatens to affect our future.

White racism is essentially responsible for the explosive mixture which has been accumulating in our cities since the end of World War II."

Long-Essay Questions

2. Evaluate the extent to which the emergence of a transatlantic economy shaped disputes between Great Britain and the British North American colonists in the period from 1754 to 1776.

3. Evaluate the extent to which the rise of democratic beliefs changed American society in the period from 1800 to 1848.

4. Evaluate the extent to which the ideas about the federal government's power changed American politics in the period from 1972 to 2000.

Glossary / Glosario

English	Español
A	
abolitionist (p. 345) Member of the movement seeking to end the system of slavery.	**abolicionista (pág. 345)** Miembro del movimiento que pretendía acabar con el sistema de esclavitud.
Abrams v. United States **(p. 716)** Supreme Court ruling in 1919 limiting free speech by sustaining a guilty verdict of five anarchists who distributed leaflets denouncing U.S. military efforts to overthrow the Bolshevik regime.	***Abrams contra Estados Unidos*** **(pág. 716)** Sentencia del Tribunal Supremo de 1919 que limita la libertad de expresión al confirmar la condena de cinco anarquistas que distribuyeron panfletos denunciando los esfuerzos militares estadounidenses para derrocar el régimen bolchevique.
acquired immune deficiency syndrome (AIDS) (p. 980) An immune disorder caused by the human immunodeficiency virus (HIV) that reached epidemic proportions in the United States in the 1980s, especially among gay men and drug users.	**síndrome de inmunodeficiencia adquirida (SIDA) (pág. 980)** Trastorno inmunitario causado por el virus de la inmunodeficiencia humana (VIH) que alcanzó proporciones epidémicas en Estados Unidos en la década de 1980, especialmente entre hombres homosexuales y consumidores de drogas.
Act of Religious Toleration (p. 72) Act passed in 1649 by the Maryland Assembly granting religious freedom to all Christians, including Catholics.	**Ley de Tolerancia Religiosa (pág. 72)** Ley aprobada en 1649 por la Asamblea de Maryland que concede la libertad religiosa a todos los cristianos, incluidos los católicos.
Adams–Onís Treaty (p. 284) Treaty negotiated by John Quincy Adams and signed in 1819 by which Spain ceded all of its lands east of the Mississippi River to the United States.	**Tratado Adams-Onís (pág. 284)** Tratado negociado por John Quincy Adams y firmado en 1819 por el que España cedía a Estados Unidos todas sus tierras al este del río Misisipi.
Adamson Act (p. 699) A 1916 act establishing an eight-hour workday and overtime for workers in private industry—in this case, railroad workers.	**Ley Adamson (pág. 699)** Ley de 1916 por la que se establece la jornada laboral de ocho horas y las horas extraordinarias para los trabajadores de la industria privada, en este caso, los ferroviarios.
affirmative action (p. 911) Policies that first emerged from the civil rights movement of the 1960s meant to overcome historical patterns of discrimination against Blacks, women, and other minorities in education and employment. Affirmative action guidelines controversially established limited preferences in hiring and college admissions to favor groups that had been historically discriminated against.	**acción afirmativa (pág. 911)** Políticas surgidas a raíz del movimiento por los derechos civiles de la década de 1960, destinadas a superar los patrones históricos de discriminación contra los negros, las mujeres y otras minorías en la educación y el empleo. Las directrices de discriminación positiva establecieron polémicamente preferencias limitadas en la contratación y la admisión universitaria para favorecer a grupos históricamente discriminados.
Agricultural Adjustment Act (AAA) (p. 761) A New Deal act passed in 1933 that raised prices for farm produce by paying farmers subsidies to reduce production. Large farmers reaped most of the benefits from the act. It was declared unconstitutional by the Supreme Court in 1936.	**Ley de Ajuste Agrícola (AAA) (pág. 761)** Ley del *New Deal* aprobada en 1933 que elevaba los precios de los productos agrícolas mediante el pago a los agricultores de subvenciones para reducir la producción. Los grandes agricultores cosecharon la mayor parte de los beneficios de la ley. El Tribunal Supremo la declaró inconstitucional en 1936.
Agricultural Marketing Act (p. 749) A 1929 act aimed at raising prices for goods created by farmers to alleviate their financial suffering.	**Ley de Comercialización Agrícola (pág. 749)** Ley de 1929 destinada a elevar los precios de los bienes creados por los agricultores para aliviar su sufrimiento financiero.
air traffic controllers strike (p. 978) A strike by air traffic controllers for better working conditions and pay in 1981. President Reagan responded by firing employees who did not return to work within 48 hours, signifying the beginning of a more hostile environment for organized labor in the 1980s.	**huelga de controladores aéreos (pág. 978)** Huelga de controladores aéreos en 1981 para exigir mejores condiciones laborales y salariales. El presidente Reagan respondió despidiendo a los empleados que no volvían al trabajo en 48 horas, lo que significó el comienzo de un entorno más hostil para los sindicatos en la década de 1980.
Al Jazeera (p. 1002) Arabic-language television channel, specifically designed for international broadcasts. Al Jazeera was established in 1996 and rose in prominence after its live coverage of the war in Afghanistan.	**Al Jazeera (pág. 1002)** Canal de televisión en lengua árabe, especialmente concebido para emisiones internacionales. Al Jazeera se fundó en 1996 y adquirió notoriedad tras su cobertura en directo de la guerra de Afganistán.
al-Qaeda (p. 994) An Islamic terrorist organization founded by Osama bin Laden in the late 1980s during the Soviet invasion of Afghanistan. Al-Qaeda is a loosely organized, radical religious fundamentalist organization, which opposes westernization and orchestrated the September 11, 2001, attacks on the United States.	**al-Qaeda (pág. 994)** Organización terrorista islámica fundada por Osama bin Laden a finales de la década de 1980 durante la invasión soviética de Afganistán. Al Qaeda es una organización fundamentalista religiosa radical, poco organizada, que se opone a la occidentalización y orquestó los atentados del 11 de septiembre de 2001 contra los Estados Unidos.

Alamo (p. 320) A Texas fort captured by General Santa Anna from rebel defenders on March 6, 1836. Sensationalist accounts of the siege of the Alamo increased popular support in the United States for Texas independence.

Álamo (pág. 320) Fuerte de Texas capturado por el general Santa Anna a los defensores rebeldes el 6 de marzo de 1836. Los relatos sensacionalistas del asedio de El Álamo aumentaron el apoyo popular en Estados Unidos a la independencia de Texas.

Albany Plan of Union (p. 150) A plan put together in 1754 by Benjamin Franklin to create a more centralized colonial government that would establish policies regarding defense, trade, and territorial expansion, as well as aim to facilitate better relations between colonists and American Indians.

Plan de Unión de Albany (pág. 150) Plan elaborado en 1754 por Benjamin Franklin para crear un gobierno colonial más centralizado que estableciera políticas en materia de defensa, comercio y expansión territorial, así como para facilitar unas mejores relaciones entre los colonos y los indios americanos.

Alien and Sedition Acts (p. 225) Two security acts passed in 1798 by the Federalist- controlled Congress. The Alien Act allowed the president, then John Adams, to imprison or deport noncitizens. The Sedition Act outlawed certain public criticisms of the federal government.

Leyes de Extranjería y Sedición (pág. 225) Dos leyes de seguridad aprobadas en 1798 por el Congreso controlado por los federalistas. La Ley de Extranjería permitía al presidente, entonces John Adams, encarcelar o deportar a los no ciudadanos. La Ley de Sedición ilegalizaba ciertas críticas públicas al gobierno federal.

Allies (p. 702) Political allies during World War I consisting mainly of Great Britain, France, and Russia. Italy joined in 1915 and the United States in 1917.

Aliados (pág. 702) Aliados políticos durante la Primera Guerra Mundial formados principalmente por Gran Bretaña, Francia y Rusia. Italia se adhirió en 1915 y Estados Unidos en 1917.

America First Committee (p. 780) An isolationist organization founded by Senator Gerald Nye in 1940 to keep the United States out of World War II.

***America First Committee* (pág. 780)** Organización aislacionista fundada por el senador Gerald Nye en 1940 para mantener a Estados Unidos fuera de la Segunda Guerra Mundial.

American Anti-Slavery Society (AASS) (p. 345) An abolitionist society founded by William Lloyd Garrison in 1833 that became the most important northern abolitionist organization of the period. The society featured prominent orators and activists such as Frederick Douglass. Members argued slavery was neither economically nor morally viable. The group often met with violence.

Sociedad Antiesclavista Estadounidense (AASS) (pág. 345) Sociedad abolicionista fundada por William Lloyd Garrison en 1833 que se convirtió en la organización abolicionista norteña más importante de la época. La sociedad contó con destacados oradores y activistas como Frederick Douglass. Los miembros argumentaron que la esclavitud no era viable ni económica ni moralmente. El grupo se enfrentaba a menudo a la violencia.

American Civil Liberties Union (ACLU) (p. 718) Founded as the National Civil Liberties Bureau in 1917, the ACLU (renamed in 1920) defends civil liberties through civil litigation. The ACLU was the first such organization to defend civil liberties for all individuals, rather than specific groups.

Unión Estadounidense de Libertades Civiles (ACLU) (pág. 718) Fundada como *National Civil Liberties Bureau* en 1917, la ACLU (rebautizada en 1920) defiende las libertades civiles a través de litigios civiles. La ACLU fue la primera organización de este tipo en defender las libertades civiles de todos los individuos, en lugar de grupos específicos.

American Equal Rights Association (p. 475) A group of Black and white women and men formed in 1866 to promote gender and racial equality. The organization split in 1869 over divided support for the Fifteenth Amendment. Prominent members included Frederick Douglass, Susan B. Anthony, and Elizabeth Cady Stanton.

***American Equal Rights Association* (pág. 475)** Grupo de hombres y mujeres blancos y negros creado en 1866 para promover la igualdad racial y de género. La organización se dividió en 1869 por el apoyo dividido a la Decimoquinta Enmienda. Entre sus miembros destacados se encontraban Frederick Douglass, Susan B. Anthony y Elizabeth Cady Stanton.

American Expeditionary Forces (AEF) (p. 706) Established in 1917 after the United States entered World War I. These army troops served in Europe under the command of General John J. Pershing.

Fuerzas Expedicionarias Americanas (AEF) (pág. 706) Creadas en 1917 tras la entrada de Estados Unidos en la Primera Guerra Mundial. Estas tropas del ejército sirvieron en Europa bajo el mando del General John J. Pershing.

American Federation of Labor (AFL) (p. 569) A trade-union federation founded in 1886. The AFL sought to organize skilled male workers into trade-specific unions and encouraged the vigorous use of the strike in pursuit of better wages and working conditions.

Federación Estadounidense del Trabajo (AFL) (pág. 569) Federación sindical fundada en 1886. La AFL pretendía organizar a los trabajadores masculinos cualificados en sindicatos de oficios específicos y fomentaba el uso enérgico de la huelga en busca de mejores salarios y condiciones de trabajo.

American Indian Movement (AIM) (p. 924) An American Indian group, formed in 1968, that promoted "red power," the preservation of tribal cultural traditions, poverty relief, and improved living conditions on reservations and condemned the continued mistreatment of American Indians.

Movimiento Indio Americano (AIM) (pág. 924) Grupo indio americano, formado en 1968, que promovía el "poder rojo", la preservación de las tradiciones culturales tribales, el alivio de la pobreza y la mejora de las condiciones de vida en las reservas y condenaba el continuo maltrato de los indios americanos.

American Party (p. 417) Also known as the Know-Nothing Party, a political party that arose in the Northeast during the 1840s. The party was anti-Catholic and anti-immigration. It also supported workers' rights against business owners, who were perceived to support immigration as a way to keep wages low.

Partido Americano (pág. 417) También conocido como Partido *Know-Nothing*, partido político que surgió en el noreste durante la década de 1840. El partido era anticatólico y se oponía a la inmigración. También apoyó los derechos de los trabajadores frente a los empresarios, a quienes se consideraba partidarios de la inmigración como forma de mantener bajos los salarios.

American Plan (p. 721) A voluntary program initiated by businesses in the early twentieth century to protect worker welfare. The American Plan was meant to undermine the appeal of labor unions.

Plan Americano (pág. 721) Programa voluntario iniciado por las empresas a principios del siglo XX para proteger el bienestar de los trabajadores. El Plan Americano pretendía socavar el atractivo de los sindicatos.

American Protective League (APL) (p. 715) An organization of private citizens that cooperated with the Justice Department and the Bureau of Investigation during World War I to spy on German residents suspected of disloyal behavior.

***American Protective League* (APL) (pág. 715)** Organización de ciudadanos particulares que cooperó con el Departamento de Justicia y la Oficina de Investigación durante la Primera Guerra Mundial para espiar a residentes alemanes sospechosos de comportamiento desleal.

American System (p. 270) A national economic plan proposed by Henry Clay in the 1810s and 1820s to promote the U.S. economy by combining federally funded internal improvements to aid farmers while protecting American manufacturers by placing high tariffs on imported goods.

Sistema Americano (pág. 270) Plan económico nacional propuesto por Henry Clay en las décadas de 1810 y 1820 para promover la economía estadounidense combinando mejoras internas financiadas con fondos federales para ayudar a los agricultores y protegiendo al mismo tiempo a los fabricantes estadounidenses mediante la imposición de elevados aranceles a los productos importados.

American system of manufacturing (p. 289) Manufacturing methods that emphasized mechanization, waterpower, division of labor, and the use of interchangeable parts. The introduction of the American system in the early nineteenth century greatly reduced the number of artisans and small shops but, through standardization, increased the productivity of American manufacturing.

Sistema americano de fabricación (pág. 289) Métodos de fabricación que hacían hincapié en la mecanización, la fuerza hidráulica, la división del trabajo y el uso de piezas intercambiables. La introducción del sistema estadounidense a principios del siglo XIX redujo enormemente el número de artesanos y pequeños comercios, pero, gracias a la normalización, aumentó la productividad de la industria manufacturera estadounidense.

Americans with Disabilities Act (ADA) (p. 983) The landmark 1990 legislation banning discrimination due to disability. The law extended legal protections and accessibility mandates for Americans with physical and mental disabilities.

Ley de Estadounidenses con Discapacidades (ADA) (pág. 983) Legislación histórica de 1990 que prohibió la discriminación debido a la discapacidad. La ley amplió las protecciones legales y los mandatos de accesibilidad para los estadounidenses con discapacidades físicas y mentales.

***Amistad* (p. 360)** A slave ship on which a slave rebellion took place in 1839 while the ship was headed for Cuba. The mutineers were captured two months later, and their ship was towed to Connecticut, still technically a slave state. There, the mutineers sued for their freedom, and in 1841, the U.S. Supreme Court declared them to be free because it was illegal to import enslaved people from Africa to America.

***Amistad* (pág. 360)** Barco negrero en el que se produjo una rebelión de esclavos en 1839 cuando el barco se dirigía a Cuba. Los amotinados fueron capturados dos meses después, y su barco fue remolcado a Connecticut, todavía técnicamente un estado esclavista. Allí, los amotinados demandaron su libertad y, en 1841, el Tribunal Supremo de Estados Unidos los declaró libres porque era ilegal importar personas esclavizadas de África a América.

Anglo-Powhatan Wars (p. 107) Series of conflicts in the 1620s between the Powhatan Confederacy and English settlers in Virginia and Maryland.

Guerras Anglo-Powhatan (pág. 107) Serie de conflictos en la década de 1620 entre la Confederación Powhatan y los colonos ingleses de Virginia y Maryland.

Anti-Imperialist League (p. 664) An organization founded in 1898 to oppose annexation of the Philippines. Some feared the annexation would bring competition from cheap labor; others considered Filipinos racially inferior and the Philippines unsuitable as an American territory.

Liga Antiimperialista (pág. 664) Organización fundada en 1898 para oponerse a la anexión de Filipinas. Algunos temían que la anexión supusiera la competencia de mano de obra barata; otros consideraban a los filipinos racialmente inferiores y a Filipinas inadecuada como territorio estadounidense.

Antifederalist (p. 212) An opponent of ratification of the Constitution of 1787. Antifederalists were generally from more rural and less wealthy backgrounds than the Federalists and opposed increasing the powers of the central government.

Antifederalista (pág. 212) Opositor a la ratificación de la Constitución de 1787. Los antifederalistas procedían generalmente de entornos más rurales y menos ricos que los federalistas y se oponían a aumentar los poderes del gobierno central.

apartheid (p. 988) A legal and institutionalized system of discrimination and segregation based on white supremacy and racial separation in South Africa from 1948 until 1994.

apartheid (pág. 988) Sistema legal e institucionalizado de discriminación y segregación basado en la supremacía blanca y la separación racial en Sudáfrica desde 1948 hasta 1994.

appeasement (p. 779) The policy exercised by Great Britain and France of making concessions to Nazi Germany in the hopes of avoiding a larger conflict. After Hitler's invasion of Czechoslovakia, in violation of the recently signed Munich Accord, the policy was abandoned, setting the stage for the start of a new war.

apaciguamiento (pág. 779) Política ejercida por Gran Bretaña y Francia de hacer concesiones a la Alemania nazi con la esperanza de evitar un conflicto mayor. Tras la invasión de Checoslovaquia por Hitler, en violación del recién firmado Acuerdo de Múnich, se abandonó la política, preparando el terreno para el inicio de una nueva guerra.

Arab Spring (p. 1023) A series of pro-democracy protests and rebellions in the Middle East in 2011, which led to the toppling of pro-Western but despotic governments in Egypt, Tunisia, Yemen, and Libya. Street protests that did not result in regime changes also took place in several other Arab countries during this time.

Primavera Árabe (pág. 1023) Serie de protestas y rebeliones prodemocráticas en Oriente Medio en 2011, que llevaron al derrocamiento de gobiernos prooccidentales pero despóticos en Egipto, Túnez, Yemen y Libia. En otros países árabes también se produjeron protestas callejeras que no desembocaron en cambios de régimen.

aristocrat (p. 25) Member of the highest class of society, typically nobility who inherited their ranks and titles.

aristócrata (pág. 25) Miembro de la clase más alta de la sociedad, normalmente la nobleza que hereda sus rangos y títulos.

Articles of Confederation (p. 202) Plan for national government with limited powers proposed by the Continental Congress of 1777 and ratified in March 1781. The Articles were replaced by the Constitution in 1789.

Artículos de la Confederación (pág. 202) Plan de gobierno nacional con poderes limitados propuesto por el Congreso Continental de 1777 y ratificado en marzo de 1781. Los Artículos fueron sustituidos por la Constitución en 1789.

astrolabe (p. 16) A tool originally invented by Greek astronomers and sailors for navigation or astronomical calculations that allowed sailors to identify distance and time based on the location of the sun and stars in relation to the horizon.

astrolabio (pág. 16) Herramienta inventada originalmente por los astrónomos y marineros griegos para la navegación o los cálculos astronómicos que permitía a los navegantes identificar la distancia y el tiempo en función de la ubicación del sol y las estrellas en relación con el horizonte.

Atlantic Charter (p. 782) The August 1941 agreement between Franklin Roosevelt and Winston Churchill that outlined potential war aims and cemented the relationship between the United States and Britain.

Carta del Atlántico (pág. 782) Acuerdo de agosto de 1941 entre Franklin Roosevelt y Winston Churchill que esbozaba los posibles objetivos de guerra y cimentaba la relación entre Estados Unidos y Gran Bretaña.

Atlantic World (p. 22) The social, intellectual, economic, and biological interactions among the peoples, plants, and animals bordering the Atlantic Ocean, mainly Africa, the Americas, and Western Europe, beginning in the late fifteenth century.

Mundo atlántico (pág. 22) Interacciones sociales, intelectuales, económicas y biológicas entre los pueblos, plantas y animales ribereños del océano Atlántico, principalmente África, América y Europa occidental, a partir de finales del siglo XV.

attack on Pearl Harbor (p. 783) The Japanese surprise attack on the U.S. Pacific Fleet stationed at Pearl Harbor near Honolulu, Hawaii, on December 7, 1941. The attack killed more than 2,400 Americans, seriously damaged ships and aircraft, and abruptly ended isolationism by prompting U.S. entry into World War II.

ataque a Pearl Harbor (pág. 783) Ataque por sorpresa japonés a la Flota del Pacífico estadounidense estacionada en Pearl Harbor, cerca de Honolulu, Hawái, el 7 de diciembre de 1941. El ataque mató a más de 2,400 estadounidenses, dañó gravemente barcos y aviones y acabó abruptamente con el aislacionismo al provocar la entrada de Estados Unidos en la Segunda Guerra Mundial.

axis of evil (p. 1015) A term used by President George W. Bush in 2002. Bush claimed Iraq, Iran, and North Korea were a part of an "axis of evil" due to their support of terrorist organizations and pursuit of chemical, biological, and nuclear weapons.

eje del mal (pág. 1015) Término utilizado por el presidente George W. Bush en 2002. Bush afirmó que Irak, Irán y Corea del Norte formaban parte de un "eje del mal" debido a su apoyo a organizaciones terroristas y a la búsqueda de armas químicas, biológicas y nucleares.

Aztecs (p. 8) Spanish term for the Mexica, an indigenous people and empire of the same name, comprised of a network of city-states in present-day Mexico between the fourteenth and sixteenth centuries. The empire collapsed following the arrival of the Spaniards.

Aztecas (pág. 8) Término español para designar a los mexicas, pueblo indígena e imperio del mismo nombre, formado por una red de ciudades-estado en el actual México entre los siglos XIV y XVI. El imperio se derrumbó tras la llegada de los españoles.

B

baby boom (p. 855) A term that refers to the sharp U.S. population increase between 1946 and 1964 resulting from the end of World War II, postwar economic prosperity, improvements in health care, and a trend toward marriage at a younger age.

***baby boom* (pág. 855)** Término que hace referencia al fuerte aumento de la población estadounidense entre 1946 y 1964 como consecuencia del final de la Segunda Guerra Mundial, la prosperidad económica de la posguerra, las mejoras en la atención sanitaria y la tendencia a contraer matrimonio a una edad más temprana.

Bacon's Rebellion (p. 75) An uprising in Virginia led by Nathaniel Bacon in 1676. Bacon and his followers were upset by the Virginia governor's unwillingness to send troops to intervene in conflicts between settlers and American Indians and by the lack of representation of western settlers in the House of Burgesses.

Rebelión de Bacon (pág. 75) Levantamiento en Virginia liderado por Nathaniel Bacon en 1676. Bacon y sus seguidores estaban molestos por la falta de voluntad del gobernador de Virginia de enviar tropas para intervenir en los conflictos entre colonos e indios americanos y por la falta de representación de los colonos occidentales en la Cámara de los Burgueses.

Bandung Conference (p. 879) A conference of twenty-nine Asian and African nations held in Indonesia in 1955, which declared their neutrality in the Cold War struggle between the United States and the Soviet Union and condemned colonialism.

Conferencia de Bandung (pág. 879) Conferencia de veintinueve naciones asiáticas y africanas celebrada en Indonesia en 1955, en la que declararon su neutralidad en la lucha de la Guerra Fría entre Estados Unidos y la Unión Soviética y condenaron el colonialismo.

Bank of the United States (p. 219) A national bank established in 1791. The bank was responsible for holding large portions of federal funds, distributing loans and currency, and funding the national debt.

Banco de los Estados Unidos (pág. 219) Banco nacional creado en 1791. El banco era responsable de mantener grandes porciones de fondos federales, distribuir préstamos y moneda, y financiar la deuda nacional.

Barbary States (p. 260) Coastal states in North Africa that sanctioned piracy to gain wealth from other weaker nations in the Atlantic world. The pirates would often seize American ships and hold the sailors for ransom in the eighteenth and early nineteenth centuries.

Estados Berberiscos (pág. 260) Estados costeros del norte de África que sancionaron la piratería para obtener riquezas de otras naciones más débiles del mundo atlántico. Los piratas solían apresar barcos estadounidenses y pedir rescate por sus marineros en el siglo XVIII y principios del XIX.

Battle of Antietam (p. 438) The fiercely fought battle at Sharpsburg, Maryland, in September 1862, resulting in more than 22,000 deaths, the single bloodiest day in U.S. military history. After repelling the Confederate invasion of Maryland, Lincoln declared it a great victory and announced a preliminary Emancipation Proclamation.

Batalla de Antietam (pág. 438) La feroz batalla de Sharpsburg, Maryland, en septiembre de 1862, que causó más de 22,000 muertos, el día más sangriento de la historia militar de Estados Unidos. Tras repeler la invasión confederada de Maryland, Lincoln declaró que había sido una gran victoria y anunció una Proclamación de Emancipación preliminar.

Battle of Bunker Hill (p. 172) A 1775 American Revolution battle in which British troops narrowly defeated patriot militias, emboldening patriot forces.

Batalla de Bunker Hill (pág. 172) Batalla de la Revolución Americana de 1775 en la que las tropas británicas derrotaron por un estrecho margen a las milicias patriotas, lo que envalentonó a las fuerzas patriotas.

Battle of Fallen Timbers (p. 240) Battle at which U.S. General Anthony Wayne won a major victory over a multi-tribe coalition of American Indians in the Northwest Territory in 1794.

Batalla de Fallen Timbers (pág. 240) Batalla en la que el general estadounidense Anthony Wayne obtuvo una importante victoria sobre una coalición multitribal de indios americanos en el Territorio del Noroeste en 1794.

Battle of Gettysburg (p. 450) A three-day battle in July 1863, the deadliest of the entire war, that halted the invasion of Pennsylvania by Lee's forces. The Confederate defeat, combined with the near-simultaneous Union victory at Vicksburg, turned the tide of the war and ended the threat of European intervention.

Batalla de Gettysburg (pág. 450) Batalla de tres días en julio de 1863, la más mortífera de toda la guerra, que detuvo la invasión de Pensilvania por las fuerzas de Lee. La derrota confederada, combinada con la victoria casi simultánea de la Unión en Vicksburg, cambió el curso de la guerra y puso fin a la amenaza de una intervención europea.

Battle of Horseshoe Bend (p. 281) An 1814 battle in which Tennessee militia led by Andrew Jackson fought alongside Cherokee warriors to defeat Creek forces allied with Britain during the War of 1812.

Batalla de Horseshoe Bend (pág. 281) Batalla de 1814 en la que la milicia de Tennessee dirigida por Andrew Jackson luchó junto a guerreros cheroquis para derrotar a las fuerzas creek aliadas con Gran Bretaña durante la Guerra de 1812.

Battle of Iwo Jima (p. 801) The March 1945 battle in which the United States captured Iwo Jima, a heavily fortified Japanese island.

Batalla de Iwo Jima (pág. 801) Batalla de marzo de 1945 en la que Estados Unidos capturó Iwo Jima, una isla japonesa fuertemente fortificada.

Battle of Midway Island (p. 801) The first engagement between Japanese and U.S. Navy six months after the Japanese attack on Pearl Harbor in June 1942. The battle resulted in a U.S. victory.

Batalla de la isla de Midway (pág. 801) Primer enfrentamiento entre la Armada japonesa y la estadounidense seis meses después del ataque japonés a Pearl Harbor en junio de 1942. La batalla se saldó con una victoria estadounidense.

Battle of New Orleans (p. 283) Battle in the War of 1812 that ended a British attempt to invade the United States through the city of New Orleans. While the Battle of New Orleans took place after the Treaty of Ghent officially ended the war, the British and U.S. forces in the American southwest had not yet received word of the cessation of hostilities. General Andrew Jackson's victory in the Battle of New Orleans led to a rush of nationalism in the United States and launched his political career.

Batalla de Nueva Orleans (pág. 283) Batalla de la Guerra de 1812 que puso fin a un intento británico de invadir Estados Unidos a través de la ciudad de Nueva Orleans. Aunque la batalla de Nueva Orleans tuvo lugar después de que el Tratado de Gante pusiera fin oficialmente a la guerra, las fuerzas británicas y estadounidenses en el suroeste de Estados Unidos aún no habían recibido la noticia del cese de las hostilidades. La victoria del general Andrew Jackson en la batalla de Nueva Orleans provocó un auge del nacionalismo en Estados Unidos y lanzó su carrera política.

Battle of Okinawa (p. 801) The last major battle and amphibious assault in the Pacific theater of World War II. It was one of the costliest battles of the war for the United States, resulting in 6,000 American casualties.

Batalla de Okinawa (pág. 801) La última gran batalla y asalto anfibio en el teatro del Pacífico de la Segunda Guerra Mundial. Fue una de las batallas más costosas de la guerra para Estados Unidos, con 6,000 bajas estadounidenses.

Battle of Saratoga (p. 183) Key Revolutionary War battle fought at Saratoga, New York, resulting in the surrender of British General John Burgoyne's forces. The Patriot victory at Saratoga in October 1777 provided hope that the colonists could triumph and increased the chances that the French would formally join the patriot side.

Batalla de Saratoga (pág. 183) Batalla clave de la Guerra de la Independencia librada en Saratoga, Nueva York, que tuvo como resultado la rendición de las fuerzas del general británico John Burgoyne. La victoria patriota en Saratoga en octubre de 1777 proporcionó la esperanza de que los colonos pudieran triunfar y aumentó las posibilidades de que los franceses se unieran formalmente al bando patriota.

Battle of Shiloh (p. 436) The April 1862 battle in Tennessee that provided the Union entrance to the Mississippi valley. Shiloh was the bloodiest battle in American history to that point.

Batalla de Shiloh (pág. 436) Batalla de abril de 1862 en Tennessee que supuso la entrada de la Unión en el valle del Misisipi. Shiloh fue la batalla más sangrienta de la historia americana hasta ese momento.

Battle of the Bulge (p. 802) The last German offensive of World War II, launched in mid-December 1944, which resulted in a German retreat across the Rhine River back into Germany.

Batalla de las Ardenas (pág. 802) Última ofensiva alemana de la Segunda Guerra Mundial, lanzada a mediados de diciembre de 1944, que provocó la retirada alemana a través del río Rin hacia el interior de Alemania.

Battle of the Little Bighorn (p. 535) A major battle in the Montana Territory in which Lieutenant Colonel George Armstrong Custer and all of his troops were killed by the Lakota Sioux in 1876. This was the last major victory of the Lakota in their attempt to defend their lands from U.S. encroachment.

Batalla de Little Bighorn (pág. 535) Importante batalla en la que los sioux lakota mataron al teniente coronel George Armstrong Custer y todas sus tropas en 1876. Esta fue la última gran victoria de los lakota en su intento de defender sus tierras de la invasión estadounidense.

Battle of Yorktown (p. 188) Decisive battle in which French naval forces forced the surrender of British forces on October 19, 1781, at Yorktown, Virginia. The joint French and American victory led to the withdrawal of the British in the American Revolution.

Batalla de Yorktown (pág. 188) Batalla decisiva en la que las fuerzas navales francesas forzaron la rendición de las fuerzas británicas el 19 de octubre de 1781, en Yorktown, Virginia. La victoria conjunta de franceses y estadounidenses provocó la retirada de los británicos en la Revolución Americana.

Bay of Pigs invasion (p. 886) An unsuccessful attempt under the Kennedy administration to overthrow Cuban leader Fidel Castro by sending 1,400 armed Cuban exiles to invade the island in 1961. Castro's troops contained the poorly trained invaders, and the failed invasion proved to be an international embarrassment for the United States.

Invasión de Bahía de Cochinos (pág. 886) Intento fallido de la administración Kennedy de derrocar al líder cubano Fidel Castro enviando a 1,400 exiliados cubanos armados a invadir la isla en 1961. Las tropas de Castro contuvieron a los invasores mal entrenados, y la invasión fallida resultó ser una vergüenza internacional para Estados Unidos.

Beats (p. 865) A small group of young poets, writers, intellectuals, musicians, and artists who challenged mainstream American politics and culture in the 1950s.

***Beats* (pág. 865)** Pequeño grupo de jóvenes poetas, escritores, intelectuales, músicos y artistas que desafiaron la política y la cultura dominantes en Estados Unidos en la década de 1950.

Berlin Airlift (p. 836) The large-scale transport of food and supplies to West Berlin by the U.S. and British governments during the Soviet blockade of Berlin from 1948 to 1949. The Berlin Airlift was responsible for breaking the Soviet blockade of West Berlin.

Puente aéreo de Berlín (pág. 836) Transporte a gran escala de alimentos y suministros a Berlín Occidental por parte de los gobiernos estadounidense y británico durante el bloqueo soviético de Berlín de 1948 a 1949. El puente aéreo de Berlín fue el responsable de romper el bloqueo soviético de Berlín Occidental.

Berlin Wall (p. 887) A wall built by the Soviet Union in 1961 to keep East Berliners from escaping to West Berlin. The Berlin Wall quickly became a Cold War symbol of the "iron curtain" that Winston Churchill described in a 1946 address in Missouri. The destruction of the Berlin Wall in 1989 symbolized the end of the Cold War.

Muro de Berlín (pág. 887) Muro construido por la Unión Soviética en 1961 para impedir que los berlineses del Este escaparan a Berlín Occidental. El Muro de Berlín se convirtió rápidamente en un símbolo de la Guerra Fría del "telón de acero" que Winston Churchill describió en un discurso pronunciado en 1946 en Misuri. La destrucción del Muro de Berlín en 1989 simbolizó el final de la Guerra Fría.

"big stick" diplomacy (p. 668) Aggressive foreign diplomacy backed by the threat of force. Its name comes from a proverb quoted by Theodore Roosevelt: "Speak softly and carry a big stick."

diplomacia del "gran garrote" (pág. 668) Diplomacia exterior agresiva respaldada por la amenaza de la fuerza. Su nombre procede de un proverbio citado por Theodore Roosevelt: "Habla bajo y lleva un garrote grande."

Bill of Rights (p. 217) The first ten amendments to the Constitution explicitly guaranteeing all Americans basic rights. These amendments, promised by Federalists during the ratification debates, helped reassure Americans who feared that the federal government established under the Constitution would infringe on the rights of individuals and states.

Declaración de Derechos (pág. 217) Las diez primeras enmiendas de la Constitución garantizan explícitamente los derechos básicos de todos los estadounidenses. Estas enmiendas, prometidas por los federalistas durante los debates de ratificación, ayudaron a tranquilizar a los estadounidenses que temían que el gobierno federal establecido bajo la Constitución infringiera los derechos de los individuos y los estados.

Billion Dollar Congress (p. 619) The Republican-controlled Congress of 1890 that spent huge sums of money to promote business and other interests.

Congreso del Billón de dólares (pág. 619) El Congreso de 1890, controlado por los republicanos, que gastaba enormes sumas de dinero para promover los negocios y otros intereses.

Black codes (p. 471) Racial laws passed by southern legislatures in the immediate aftermath of the Civil War that aimed to keep freedpeople in a condition as close to slavery as possible.

Códigos negros (pág. 471) Leyes raciales aprobadas por las asambleas legislativas del sur inmediatamente después de la Guerra Civil con el objetivo de mantener a los libertos en una condición lo más parecida posible a la esclavitud.

Black Lives Matter (p. 1022) A social movement that formed after Trayvon Martin, an unarmed Black youth, was shot by a civilian in 2012. Organized by protesters around the social media hashtag #blacklivesmatter, the movement advocated a policy agenda that mainly focused on criminal justice and police reforms.

***Black Lives Matter* (pág. 1022)** Movimiento social que se formó después de que Trayvon Martin, un joven negro desarmado, fuera tiroteado por un civil en 2012. Organizado por manifestantes en torno a la etiqueta *#blacklivesmatter*, el movimiento defendía una agenda política centrada principalmente en la justicia penal y las reformas policiales.

Black Panther Party (p. 910) A radical Black power group founded by Huey P. Newton and Bobby Seale in 1966 to promote Black empowerment and armed self-resistance in Black communities. The group's influence waned by the early 1970s largely due to repression by law enforcement.

Partido Pantera Negra (pág. 910) Grupo radical de poder negro fundado por Huey Newton y Bobby Seale en 1966 para promover la autonomía de los negros y la autorresistencia armada en las comunidades negras. La influencia del grupo disminuyó a principios de la década de 1970, en gran parte debido a la represión de las fuerzas del orden.

Black Tuesday (p. 748) The name given to the October 29, 1929, crash of the U.S. stock market. This event marked the beginning of the Great Depression, although it was not the depression's root cause.

Martes negro (pág. 748) Nombre dado al desplome de la bolsa estadounidense el 29 de octubre de 1929. Este acontecimiento marcó el inicio de la Gran Depresión, aunque no fue su causa fundamental.

Bleeding Kansas (p. 418) The nickname given to the Kansas Territory as a result of a series of violent conflicts over the fate of slavery in Kansas in the mid-1850s. Violence continued in Kansas until the Civil War.

Sangrado de Kansas (pág. 418) Apodo dado al Territorio de Kansas como resultado de una serie de violentos conflictos sobre el destino de la esclavitud en Kansas a mediados de la década de 1850. La violencia continuó en Kansas hasta la Guerra Civil.

Boland Amendment (p. 987) An amendment to a 1982 bill in Congress prohibiting direct aid to the Nicaraguan Contra forces in response to the human rights violations and terrorist activities of the Contras. In 1984, a second Boland Amendment further restricted assistance to the Contras.

Enmienda Boland (pág. 987) Enmienda a un proyecto de ley de 1982 en el Congreso que prohibía la ayuda directa a las fuerzas de la Contra nicaragüense en respuesta a las violaciones de los derechos humanos y las actividades terroristas de los Contras. En 1984, una segunda Enmienda Boland restringió aún más la ayuda a los Contras.

bombings of Hiroshima and Nagasaki (p. 804) Atomic bombs dropped by the United States on the Japanese cities of Hiroshima on August 6, 1945, and Nagasaki on August 9. Each bombing likely resulted in more than 100,000 deaths. Five days after the second bomb was dropped, Japan announced its surrender. Many survivors of the bombings later developed health issues due to the radiation exposure.

bombardeos de Hiroshima y Nagasaki (pág. 804) Bombas atómicas lanzadas por Estados Unidos sobre las ciudades japonesas de Hiroshima, el 6 de agosto de 1945, y Nagasaki, el 9 de agosto. Cada bombardeo causó probablemente más de 100,000 muertos. Cinco días después del lanzamiento de la segunda bomba, Japón anunció su rendición. Muchos supervivientes de los bombardeos desarrollaron problemas de salud debido a la exposición a la radiación.

Bonus Army (p. 757) World War I veterans who marched on Washington, D.C., in 1932 to demand immediate payment of their service bonuses. President Hoover refused to negotiate and instructed the U.S. army to clear the capital of protesters, leading to a violent clash.

***Bonus Army* (pág. 757)** Veteranos de la Primera Guerra Mundial que marcharon sobre Washington, D.C., en 1932 para exigir el pago inmediato de sus primas de servicio. El presidente Hoover se negó a negociar y ordenó al ejército estadounidense que despejara a los manifestantes de la capital, lo que provocó un violento enfrentamiento.

boom–bust cycle (p. 296) An economic cycle where strong national economic growth is often ended by a sudden fall in prices, often called a "panic," and followed by a long economic contraction and high unemployment. Boom–bust cycles continued throughout the nineteenth and twentieth centuries in the United States.

ciclo de auge y caída (pág. 296) Ciclo económico en el que el fuerte crecimiento económico nacional suele terminar con una caída repentina de los precios, a menudo denominada "pánico", y al que sigue una larga contracción económica y un elevado desempleo. Los ciclos de auge y caída continuaron a lo largo de los siglos XIX y XX en Estados Unidos.

Boston Massacre (p. 166) A clash in Boston in March 1770 between colonial protesters and British soldiers that led to the death of five colonists. The bloody incident was used as evidence of English aggressions and to promote the patriot cause. In contrast, the British referred to the event as a "riot."

Masacre de Boston (pág. 166) Enfrentamiento en Boston en marzo de 1770 entre manifestantes coloniales y soldados británicos que se saldó con la muerte de cinco colonos. El sangriento incidente se utilizó como prueba de las agresiones inglesas y para promover la causa patriota. En cambio, los británicos se refirieron al suceso como un "motín"

Boston Tea Party (p. 167) A protest against British tax policy organized by the Sons of Liberty on December 16, 1773, consisting of about fifty men disguised as American Indians who boarded British ships and dumped about forty-five tons of monopolized tea belonging to the British East India Company into Boston Harbor.

Motín del té (pág. 167) Protesta contra la política fiscal británica organizada por los Hijos de la Libertad el 16 de diciembre de 1773, consistente en unos cincuenta hombres disfrazados de indios americanos que abordaron barcos británicos y arrojaron al puerto de Boston unas cuarenta y cinco toneladas de té monopolizado perteneciente a la Compañía Británica de las Indias Orientales.

***bracero* (p. 792)** A Spanish term meaning "manual laborer," *braceros* were initially brought in from Mexico to work on U.S. farms, railroads, and factories during World War II. Bilateral agreements extended the program through 1964. Over 4.6 million guest contracts were signed before its termination.

***bracero* (pág. 792)** Término español que significa "trabajador manual", *los braceros* fueron traídos inicialmente de México para trabajar en granjas, ferrocarriles y fábricas estadounidenses durante la Segunda Guerra Mundial. Los acuerdos bilaterales prorrogaron el programa hasta 1964. Antes de su finalización se firmaron más de 4.6 millones de contratos con huéspedes.

Brady Handgun Violence Prevention Act (p. 1005) A gun-control law passed in 1993 and named after Ronald Reagan's press secretary James Brady, who was shot and nearly killed during an assassination attempt on Reagan in 1981. The Brady Bill established a five-day waiting period and background check for gun buyers until the implementation of the National Instant Criminal Background Check System in 1998.

Ley Brady de Prevención de la Violencia con Armas de Fuego (pág. 1005) Ley de control de armas aprobada en 1993 y que lleva el nombre del secretario de prensa de Ronald Reagan, James Brady, que recibió un disparo y estuvo a punto de morir durante un atentado contra Reagan en 1981. La Ley Brady estableció un periodo de espera de cinco días y una comprobación de antecedentes para los compradores de armas hasta la implantación del Sistema Nacional de Comprobación Instantánea de Antecedentes Penales en 1998.

***Brown v. Board of Education of Topeka* (p. 869)** A landmark 1954 Supreme Court decision that overturned the "separate but equal" principle established by *Plessy v. Ferguson* in 1896. Although the *Brown* ruling banned school segregation, few schools in the South were racially desegregated for more than a decade.

***Brown contra Consejo de Educación de Topeka* (pág. 869)** Sentencia histórica del Tribunal Supremo de 1954 que anuló el principio de "separados pero iguales" establecido por *Plessy contra Ferguson* en 1896. Aunque la sentencia Brown prohibió la segregación escolar, pocas escuelas del Sur estuvieron racialmente desegregadas durante más de una década.

buffalo soldier (p. 535) A Black cavalryman, many of whom had been formerly enslaved, who fought in the West against American Indians in the 1870s and 1880s.

soldado búfalo (pág. 535) Soldado de caballería negro, muchos de los cuales habían sido esclavos, que luchó en el Oeste contra los indios americanos en las décadas de 1870 y 1880.

bully pulpit (p. 691) The term used by Theodore Roosevelt to describe the office of the presidency. Roosevelt believed that the president should use his office as a platform to promote his programs and rally public opinion.

***bully pulpit* (pág. 691)** Término utilizado por Theodore Roosevelt para describir el cargo de la presidencia. Roosevelt creía que el presidente debía utilizar su cargo como plataforma para promover sus programas y movilizar a la opinión pública.

Bureau of Indian Affairs (BIA) (p. 883) Established in 1824, the BIA is responsible for management of American Indian lands and implementation of federal policy toward American Indian nations.

Oficina de Asuntos Indios (BIA) (pág. 883) Creada en 1824, la BIA es responsable de la gestión de las tierras de los indios americanos y de la aplicación de la política federal hacia las naciones indias americanas.

Bush Doctrine (p. 1015) President George W. Bush's proposal to engage in preemptive war against tyrannical governments that were perceived as a threat to U.S. national security, even if the danger was not immediate.

Doctrina Bush (pág. 1015) Propuesta del presidente George W. Bush de emprender una guerra preventiva contra gobiernos tiránicos que fueran percibidos como una amenaza para la seguridad nacional de Estados Unidos, aunque el peligro no fuera inmediato.

C

California gold rush (p. 387) The rapid influx of migrants from across the world into California seeking riches after the discovery of gold in 1848.

Fiebre del oro de California (pág. 387) Rápida afluencia de emigrantes de todo el mundo a California en busca de riquezas tras el descubrimiento de oro en 1848.

Californio (p. 387) A Spanish or Mexican resident of California. Before the nineteenth century, Californios made up California's economic and political elite. Their position, however, deteriorated after California became a part of the United States in 1848.

Californio (pág. 387) Español o mexicano residente en California. Antes del siglo XIX, los californios formaban la élite económica y política de California. Su posición, sin embargo, se deterioró después de que California pasara a formar parte de Estados Unidos en 1848.

Calvinism (p. 58) A branch of Protestantism developed by John Calvin that influenced Protestants in France, England, and Switzerland in the seventeenth and eighteenth centuries.

Calvinismo (pág. 58) Rama del protestantismo desarrollada por Juan Calvino que influyó en los protestantes de Francia, Inglaterra y Suiza en los siglos XVII y XVIII.

Camp David accords (p. 948) An agreement between Israel and Egypt facilitated by President Carter in 1978. The accords led to a peace treaty and normalization of relations between the two nations.

Acuerdos de Camp David (pág. 948) Acuerdo entre Israel y Egipto facilitado por el presidente Carter en 1978. Los acuerdos condujeron a un tratado de paz y a la normalización de las relaciones entre ambas naciones.

capitalism (p. 25) An economic system based on private business, ownership of property, and the open exchange of goods between property holders.

capitalismo (pág. 25) Sistema económico basado en la empresa privada, la propiedad y el intercambio abierto de bienes entre los titulares de la propiedad.

Capitol Riot (p. 1032) The storming of the U.S. Capitol building on January 6, 2021, by supporters of President Trump in an attempt to stop the official certification of Joseph Biden's electoral college victory by Congress. Rioters marched from an earlier "Save America" rally, assaulted and overwhelmed police officers, and ransacked the Capitol for several hours before order was restored.

Disturbios en el Capitolio (pág. 1032) Asalto al edificio del Capitolio de Estados Unidos el 6 de enero de 2021 por partidarios del presidente Trump en un intento de impedir la certificación oficial de la victoria de Joseph Biden en el colegio electoral por parte del Congreso. Los alborotadores salieron de una concentración anterior de "*Save America*", agredieron y arrollaron a los agentes de policía y saquearon el Capitolio durante varias horas antes de que se restableciera el orden.

caravel (p. 16) A narrow, small, and swift sailing ship invented by the Portuguese during the fifteenth century, particularly useful because it allowed sailors to sail into the wind much faster than traditional vessels.

carabela (pág. 16) Barco de vela estrecho, pequeño y veloz inventado por los portugueses durante el siglo XV, especialmente útil porque permitía a los marineros navegar contra el viento mucho más rápido que las embarcaciones tradicionales.

carpetbagger (p. 482) A derogatory term in the South for white Northerners who moved to the South in the years following the Civil War. Many white Southerners believed such migrants were intent on exploiting their suffering.

***carpetbagger* (pág. 482)** Término despectivo en el Sur para referirse a los norteños blancos que se trasladaron al Sur en los años posteriores a la Guerra Civil. Muchos sureños blancos creían que esos emigrantes pretendían explotar su sufrimiento.

cash crop (p. 69) A crop produced for profit rather than for subsistence. Tobacco was the main cash crop in the Chesapeake region in the 1600s and 1700s, and sugar was most commonly grown in the Caribbean colonies.

cultivo comercial (pág. 69) Cultivo producido con fines lucrativos y no de subsistencia. El tabaco era el principal cultivo comercial de la región de Chesapeake en los años 1600 y 1700, y el azúcar se cultivaba sobre todo en las colonias caribeñas.

Central Intelligence Agency (CIA) (p. 836) The intelligence organization established by the 1947 National Security Act. The CIA is part of the executive branch and is responsible for gathering information and conducting espionage in foreign nations. It was originally created to counter Soviet spying operations.

Agencia Central de Inteligencia (CIA) (pág. 836) Organización de inteligencia creada por la Ley de Seguridad Nacional de 1947. La CIA forma parte del poder ejecutivo y se encarga de reunir información y llevar a cabo actividades de espionaje en naciones extranjeras. Se creó originalmente para contrarrestar las operaciones de espionaje soviético.

Central Powers (p. 702) Political allies during World War I consisting mainly of Austria-Hungary, Germany, and the Ottoman Empire.

Potencias Centrales (pág. 702) Aliados políticos durante la Primera Guerra Mundial formados principalmente por Austria-Hungría, Alemania y el Imperio Otomano.

checks and balances (p. 211) The specific ways a branch of government can limit or modify the behavior of other branches. The system of checks and balances in the U.S. Constitution was designed to keep any one branch from exercising too much power.

controles y equilibrios (pág. 211) Formas específicas en que un poder del Estado puede limitar o modificar el comportamiento de otros poderes. El sistema de frenos y contrapesos de la Constitución de EE. UU. se diseñó para evitar que una sola rama ejerciera demasiado poder.

Cherokee Nation v. Georgia **(p. 323)** A Supreme Court ruling in 1831 that denied the Cherokee claim to be a separate sovereign and independent nation, ruling that all American Indian nations were "domestic dependent nations" rather than fully sovereign governments.

Nación Cheroqui contra Georgia **(pág. 323)** Sentencia del Tribunal Supremo de 1831 que denegó la pretensión de los cheroquis de ser una nación soberana e independiente, dictaminando que todas las naciones indígenas americanas eran "naciones dependientes domésticas" y no gobiernos plenamente soberanos.

Chinese Exclusion Act (p. 542) A law enacted in 1882 that banned most Chinese immigration into the United States and prohibited resident Chinese from becoming naturalized American citizens.

Ley de Exclusión China (pág. 542) Ley promulgada en 1882 que prohibía la mayor parte de la inmigración china a Estados Unidos y prohibía a los chinos residentes naturalizarse ciudadanos estadounidenses.

Christian Right (p. 950) A coalition of evangelical Christians and Catholics that supported traditional values, laissez-faire economics, and an anticommunist foreign policy. The Christian Right, also known as the religious right, joined forces with political conservatives to form a powerful conservative voting bloc in the Republican Party.

Derecha cristiana (pág. 950) Coalición de cristianos evangélicos y católicos que apoyaba los valores tradicionales, la economía del laissez-faire y una política exterior anticomunista. La derecha cristiana, también conocida como derecha religiosa, unió fuerzas con los conservadores políticos para formar un poderoso bloque de voto conservador en el Partido Republicano.

Church of England (p. 71) National English Protestant faith with King Henry VIII as head of the church. Created after England split with the Catholic Church in 1534.

Iglesia de Inglaterra (pág. 71) Fe protestante nacional inglesa con el rey Enrique VIII como cabeza de la iglesia. Creada tras la ruptura de Inglaterra con la Iglesia Católica.

civic housekeeping (p. 672) The idea promoted by Jane Addams for urban reform using women's traditional skills as domestic managers; caregivers for children, the elderly, and the needy; and community builders.

civic housekeeping **(pág. 672)** La idea promovida por Jane Addams para la reforma urbana utilizando las habilidades tradicionales de las mujeres como administradoras domésticas; cuidadoras de niños, ancianos y necesitados; y constructoras de la comunidad.

Civil Rights Act of 1875 (p. 488) An act extending "full and equal treatment" for all races in public accommodations, jury service, and public transportation. However, in 1883, the Supreme Court ruled that the act was unconstitutional.

Ley de Derechos Civiles de 1875 (pág. 488) Ley por la que se extiende el "trato pleno e igualitario" a todas las razas en los alojamientos públicos, el servicio de jurado y el transporte público. Sin embargo, en 1883, el Tribunal Supremo dictaminó que la ley era inconstitucional.

Civil Rights Act of 1964 (p. 907) A landmark act signed into law in 1964 by President Lyndon Johnson that prohibited discrimination in public accommodations and employment and increased federal enforcement of school desegregation and voting access.

Ley de Derechos Civiles de 1964 (pág. 907) Ley histórica promulgada en 1964 por el presidente Lyndon Johnson, que prohibía la discriminación en los alojamientos públicos y en el empleo y reforzaba la aplicación federal de las leyes de segregación escolar y acceso al voto.

Civil Works Administration (CWA) (p. 763) A 1933 New Deal program that lasted only four months but employed more than four million people on 400,000 projects, such as building schools, roads, playgrounds, and airports.

Administración de Obras Civiles (CWA) (pág. 763) Programa del Nuevo Trato de 1933 que duró sólo cuatro meses, pero empleó a más de cuatro millones de personas en 400,000 proyectos, como la construcción de escuelas, carreteras, parques infantiles y aeropuertos.

Civilian Conservation Corps (CCC) (p. 763) A New Deal work program that hired young, unmarried men to work on conservation projects. It employed about 2.5 million men and lasted until 1942.

Cuerpo Civil de Conservación (CCC) (pág. 763) Programa de trabajo del Nuevo Trato que contrataba a hombres jóvenes solteros para trabajar en proyectos de conservación. Empleó a unos 2.5 millones de hombres y duró hasta 1942.

Clayton Antitrust Act (p. 698) An act that strengthened the Sherman Antitrust Act by banning certain corporate operations, such as price discrimination and overlapping membership on company boards, and by protecting labor unions. The 1914 act was designed to encourage economic competition.

Ley antimonopolio Clayton (pág. 698) Ley que reforzó la Ley antimonopolio Sherman al prohibir determinadas operaciones corporativas, como la discriminación de precios y el solapamiento de miembros en los consejos de administración de las empresas, y al proteger a los sindicatos. La ley de 1914 tenía por objeto fomentar la competencia económica.

Clean Air Act of 1990 (p. 983) An act that set new standards to reduce car and power plant emissions to address the problems of acid rain, air pollution, and ozone depletion.

Ley de Aire Limpio de 1990 (pág. 983) Ley que establece nuevas normas para reducir las emisiones de los automóviles y las centrales eléctricas con el fin de hacer frente a los problemas de la lluvia ácida, la contaminación atmosférica y el agotamiento de la capa de ozono.

climate change (p. 1003) The climatic effect of global warming, leading to unpredictable weather conditions, severe weather events like hurricanes, draughts, flooding, and dangerous blizzards, but also ancillary effects like wild fires, declining water tables, and stresses on essential infrastructure.

cambio climático (pág. 1003) El efecto climático del calentamiento global que provoca condiciones meteorológicas impredecibles, fenómenos metereológicos graves como huracanes, sequías, inundaciones y ventiscas peligrosas, pero también efectos secundarios como incendios forestales, descenso de las capas freáticas y tensiones en infraestructuras esenciales.

Coercive Acts (p. 168) Acts of Parliament passed in 1774 in response to the Boston Tea Party. The acts closed the port of Boston until residents paid for the damaged property and moved Massachusetts court cases against royal officials back to England in a bid to weaken colonial authority. Colonists referred to these acts as the Intolerable Acts.

Leyes coercitivas (pág. 168) Leyes del Parlamento aprobadas en 1774 en respuesta al Motín del Té de Boston. Las leyes cerraron el puerto de Boston hasta que los residentes pagaran por los bienes dañados y trasladaron los casos judiciales de Massachusetts contra funcionarios reales de vuelta a Inglaterra en un intento de debilitar la autoridad colonial. Los colonos se referían a estas leyes como las Leyes Intolerables.

Cold War (p. 831) The political, economic, and military conflict, short of direct war, between the United States and the Soviet Union between 1945 and 1991.

Guerra Fría (pág. 831) Conflicto político, económico y militar, sin llegar a la guerra directa, entre Estados Unidos y la Unión Soviética entre 1945 y 1991.

collective bargaining (p. 567) The process of negotiation between labor unions and employers.

negociación colectiva (pág. 567) Proceso de negociación entre sindicatos y empresarios.

colonization (p. 58) The process of settling and controlling an already inhabited area for the economic benefit of the settlers, or colonizers.

colonización (pág. 58) Proceso de asentamiento y control de una zona ya habitada para beneficio económico de los colonos o colonizadores.

Columbian Exchange (p. 22) The biological exchange of people, plants, animals, and diseases between the Americas and the rest of the world between 1492 and the end of the sixteenth century. Although its initial impact was strongest in the Americas and Europe, it was soon felt globally.

Intercambio colombino (pág. 22) Intercambio biológico de personas, plantas, animales y enfermedades entre América y el resto del mundo entre 1492 y finales del siglo XVI. Aunque su impacto inicial fue mayor en América y Europa, pronto se dejó sentir en todo el mundo.

"come outer" movement (p. 348) A protest movement whose members would often abstain from political office, activity, or voting to protest the government and other organizations' complicity in slavery.

movimiento "*come outer*" (pág. 348) Movimiento de protesta cuyos miembros solían abstenerse de ocupar cargos políticos, realizar actividades o votar para protestar contra la complicidad del gobierno y otras organizaciones en la esclavitud.

Commission on the Status of Women (p. 917) A commission appointed by President Kennedy in 1961. Its 1963 report, *American Women*, highlighted employment discrimination against women and recommended legislation requiring equal pay for equal work regardless of sex.

Comisión de la Condición Jurídica y Social de la Mujer (pág. 917) Comisión nombrada por el presidente Kennedy en 1961. Su informe de 1963, *American Women*, destacaba la discriminación laboral de la mujer y recomendaba una legislación que exigiera igual salario por igual trabajo, independientemente del sexo.

committee of correspondence (p. 161) Correspondence network designed to rapidly circulate concerns and reports of protest and other political events to leaders and colonial assemblies in the aftermath of the Sugar Act. By 1774, each of the thirteen colonies except Pennsylvania had established an intercolonial committee of correspondence.

comité de correspondencia (pág. 161) Red de correspondencia destinada a hacer circular rápidamente las preocupaciones y los informes de protestas y otros acontecimientos políticos entre los dirigentes y las asambleas coloniales a raíz de la Ley del Azúcar. En 1774, cada una de las trece colonias, excepto Pensilvania, había establecido un comité intercolonial de correspondencia.

Committee on Public Information (CPI) (p. 714) A government organization established in 1917 to create and promote pro–World War I propaganda and censor dissenting voices.

Comité de Información Pública (CPI) (pág. 714) Organización gubernamental creada en 1917 para crear y promover propaganda a favor de la Primera Guerra Mundial y censurar las voces disidentes.

communism (p. 707) An economic theory and revolutionary ideology that imagines the overthrow of capitalism by the working class and the creation of an egalitarian society where the means of production are controlled by the state.

comunismo (pág. 707) Teoría económica e ideología revolucionaria que imagina el derrocamiento del capitalismo por la clase obrera y la creación de una sociedad igualitaria en la que los medios de producción estén controlados por el Estado.

Comprehensive Anti-Apartheid Act (p. 988) An act passed in 1986 prohibiting new trade and investment in South Africa because of apartheid. President Reagan vetoed the act, but Congress overrode his veto.

Ley Global Anti-Apartheid (pág. 988) Ley aprobada en 1986 que prohíbe nuevos intercambios comerciales e inversiones en Sudáfrica a causa del apartheid. El presidente Reagan vetó la ley, pero el Congreso anuló su veto.

Compromise of 1850 (p. 404) A series of acts admitting California as a free state, banning the slave trade in the District of Columbia, referring the decision of slavery in Utah and New Mexico to popular sovereignty, strengthening the Fugitive Slave Law, and resolving Texas's border and debt.

Compromiso de 1850 (pág. 404) Una serie de leyes que admiten a California como estado libre, prohíben el comercio de esclavos en el Distrito de Columbia, remiten la decisión de la esclavitud en Utah y Nuevo México a la soberanía popular, refuerzan la Ley del Esclavo Fugitivo y resuelven la frontera y la deuda de Texas.

Compromise of 1877 (p. 488) The compromise between Republicans and southern Democrats that resulted in the election of Rutherford B. Hayes. Southern Democrats agreed to support Hayes in the disputed presidential election in exchange for his promise to end Reconstruction.

Compromiso de 1877 (pág. 488) Compromiso entre republicanos y demócratas del sur que dio lugar a la elección de Rutherford B. Hayes. Los demócratas del sur aceptaron apoyar a Hayes en las disputadas elecciones presidenciales a cambio de su promesa de poner fin a la Reconstrucción.

Comstock Lode (p. 527) The Comstock Lode was the first major discovery of silver ore in the United States, and it led to a rush in 1859 for silver in the West on par with the gold rush in California. Silver production from the Comstock Lode declined precipitously after the mid-1870s but continued into the early twentieth century.

La veta de Comstock (pág. 527) La veta de Comstock fue el primer gran descubrimiento de mineral de plata en Estados Unidos, y provocó una fiebre por la plata en el Oeste en 1859 equiparable a la fiebre del oro en California. La producción de plata de Comstock Lode disminuyó precipitadamente a partir de mediados de la década de 1870, pero continuó a principios del siglo XX.

Confederate States of America (p. 427) The name of the government that seceded from the Union after the election of President Lincoln in 1860. Originally consisting of seven states, the Confederacy quickly grew to eleven states and located its capital in Richmond, Virginia.

Estados Confederados de América (pág. 427) Nombre del gobierno que se separó de la Unión tras la elección del presidente Lincoln en 1860. Originalmente formada por siete estados, la Confederación creció rápidamente a once estados y situó su capital en Richmond, Virginia.

Confiscation Acts (p. 436) Laws passed by Congress in 1861 and 1862 during the Civil War that authorized the emancipation of enslaved people as the confiscation of Confederate property. Under the first Confiscation Act, any enslaved people who were forced to work for the Confederate army would no longer be bound to their enslavers. The second act permanently freed any people enslaved by civilian or military Confederate officials.

Leyes de Confiscación (pág. 436) Leyes aprobadas por el Congreso en 1861 y 1862 durante la Guerra Civil que autorizaban la emancipación de las personas esclavizadas como la confiscación de las propiedades confederadas. En virtud de la primera Ley de Confiscación, las personas esclavizadas que se vieran obligadas a trabajar para el ejército confederado dejarían de estar vinculadas a sus esclavizadores. La segunda ley liberó de forma permanente a todas las personas esclavizadas por oficiales confederados civiles o militares.

Congress of Racial Equality (CORE) (p. 792) An interracial organization founded in 1942 that directly protested against racial inequality in public accommodations.

Congreso para la Igualdad Racial (CORE) (pág. 792) Organización interracial fundada en 1942 que protestaba directamente contra la desigualdad racial en los alojamientos públicos.

conquistador (p. 24) Spanish name for conqueror. This title was applied to Spanish and Portuguese military leaders who invaded and conquered the lands of Native Americans in Central and South America.

conquistador (pág. 24) Nombre español de conquistador. Este título se aplicó a los líderes militares españoles y portugueses que invadieron y conquistaron las tierras de los nativos americanos en América Central y del Sur.

conservationism (p. 689) A Progressive Era political and social movement whose supporters worked to protect the environment by balancing demand for natural resources against calls to preserve the nation's wildlife and natural lands. Conservationists believed in intelligent management and sustainable use of natural resources, while preservationists sought to preserve the beauty of the environment above all else.

conservacionismo (pág. 689) Movimiento político y social de la Era Progresista cuyos partidarios trabajaban para proteger el medio ambiente equilibrando la demanda de recursos naturales con los llamamientos a preservar la vida salvaje y las tierras naturales de la nación. Los conservacionistas creían en la gestión inteligente y el uso sostenible de los recursos naturales, mientras que los preservacionistas buscaban preservar la belleza del entorno por encima de todo.

Constitutional Convention (p. 209) The meeting in Philadelphia from May to September 1787 at which delegates drafted the Constitution to replace the Articles of Confederation.

Convención Constitucional (pág. 209) Reunión celebrada en Filadelfia entre mayo y septiembre de 1787, en la que los delegados redactaron la Constitución que sustituiría a los Artículos de la Confederación.

consumer revolution (p. 102) A process during the seventeenth and eighteenth centuries through which status in the colonies became more closely linked to financial success and a refined lifestyle rather than birth and family pedigree.

revolución del consumo (pág. 102) Proceso que tuvo lugar durante los siglos XVII y XVIII, a través del cual el estatus en las colonias se vinculó más estrechamente al éxito financiero y a un estilo de vida refinado que al nacimiento y al pedigrí familiar.

containment (p. 832) The U.S. strategy to prevent the spread of communism and Soviet influence around the world. First outlined by U.S. diplomat George Kennan in 1946, containment became a key element of U.S. Cold War policy.

contención (pág. 832) Estrategia de Estados Unidos para impedir la expansión del comunismo y la influencia soviética en el mundo. Esbozada por primera vez por el diplomático estadounidense George Kennan en 1946, la contención se convirtió en un elemento clave de la política estadounidense durante la Guerra Fría.

Continental Army (p. 172) Army created by the Second Continental Congress after the battles of Lexington and Concord began the Revolutionary War in 1775. George Washington was appointed as its commander in chief.

Ejército Continental (pág. 172) Ejército creado por el Segundo Congreso Continental después de que las batallas de Lexington y Concord iniciaran la Guerra de la Independencia en 1775. George Washington fue nombrado su comandante en jefe.

Continental Congress (p. 170) An assembly convened in Philadelphia in 1774 in response to the Intolerable Acts. The delegates launched a boycott against British goods and called for a halt of all colonial exports to Great Britain.

Congreso Continental (pág. 170) Asamblea convocada en Filadelfia en 1774 en respuesta a las Leyes Intolerables. Los delegados lanzaron un boicot contra los productos británicos y pidieron el cese de todas las exportaciones coloniales a Gran Bretaña.

contraband (p. 435) A term first used by Union general Benjamin Butler in May 1861 to describe enslaved people who during the Civil War had fled to Union lines to obtain freedom. By designating enslaved people as property forfeited by the act of rebellion, the Union was able to strike at slavery by allowing self-emancipated people to remain free without proclaiming a general emancipation.

contrabando (pág. 435) Término utilizado por primera vez por el general de la Unión Benjamin Butler en mayo de 1861 para describir a las personas esclavizadas que durante la Guerra Civil habían huido a las líneas de la Unión para obtener la libertad. Al designar a las personas esclavizadas como propiedad confiscada por el acto de rebelión, la Unión pudo golpear a la esclavitud permitiendo que las personas autoemancipadas siguieran siendo libres sin proclamar una emancipación general.

Contract with America (p. 1006) A Republican legislative agenda proposed in 1994 that called for reduced welfare spending, lower taxes, term limits for lawmakers, and a constitutional amendment for a balanced budget.

Contrato con América (pág. 1006) Programa legislativo republicano propuesto en 1994 que abogaba por la reducción del gasto social, la bajada de impuestos, la limitación de mandatos de los legisladores y una enmienda constitucional para lograr un presupuesto equilibrado.

Contras (p. 987) Nicaraguan counterrevolutionaries, trained by the CIA, who fought to overthrow the new Sandinista government in Nicaragua during the 1980s. Their use of terrorism and violation of human rights led the U.S. Congress to prohibit funding the efforts of the Contras.	**Contras (pág. 987)** Contrarrevolucionarios nicaragüenses, entrenados por la CIA, que lucharon para derrocar al nuevo gobierno sandinista en Nicaragua durante la década de 1980. Su uso del terrorismo y la violación de los derechos humanos llevaron al Congreso estadounidense a prohibir la financiación de los esfuerzos de los Contras.
convict lease (p. 546) The system used by southern governments to furnish mainly Black prison labor to plantation owners and industrialists. The program was designed to raise revenue for the states. In practice, convict labor replaced slavery as the means of providing a forced labor supply.	**arrendamiento de convictos (pág. 546)** Sistema utilizado por los gobiernos del Sur para proporcionar mano de obra penitenciaria, principalmente negra, a los propietarios de plantaciones y a los industriales. El programa se diseñó para recaudar ingresos para los estados. En la práctica, el trabajo de los convictos sustituyó a la esclavitud como medio de suministro de mano de obra forzada.
Copperhead (p. 445) A northern Democrat who did not support the Union war effort. Such Democrats enjoyed considerable support in eastern cities and parts of the Midwest, especially across the Ohio River valley. Originally a pejorative term, the name was later embraced by antiwar northern Democrats.	***Copperhead* (pág. 445)** Demócrata del norte que no apoyaba el esfuerzo bélico de la Unión. Estos demócratas gozaban de un apoyo considerable en las ciudades del este y en partes del Medio Oeste, especialmente a lo largo del valle del río Ohio. Originalmente un término peyorativo, el nombre fue adoptado más tarde por los demócratas del norte contrarios a la guerra.
corporate capitalism (p. 601) An industrialized, market economy that is dominated by large corporations.	**capitalismo corporativo (pág. 601)** Economía de mercado industrializada dominada por grandes empresas.
corporation (p. 559) A legally recognized form of business ownership in which the liability, or financial risk, of shareholders in a company is limited to their individual investments. The formation of corporations in the late nineteenth century greatly stimulated investment in industry, and large corporations came to dominate certain industries.	**sociedad anónima (pág. 559)** Forma de propiedad empresarial legalmente reconocida en la que la responsabilidad, o el riesgo financiero, de los accionistas de una empresa se limita a sus inversiones individuales. La formación de corporaciones a finales del siglo XIX estimuló enormemente la inversión en la industria, y las grandes corporaciones llegaron a dominar ciertas industrias.
Corps of Discovery (p. 262) The expedition organized by the U.S. government to explore the Louisiana Territory. Led by Meriwether Lewis and William Clark and aided by American Indian interpreters like Sacagawea, the expedition set out in May 1804 and journeyed to the Pacific coast and back by 1806.	**Cuerpo de descubrimiento (pág. 262)** Expedición organizada por el gobierno estadounidense para explorar el territorio de Luisiana. Dirigida por Meriwether Lewis y William Clark, y con la ayuda de intérpretes indios americanos como Sacagawea, la expedición partió en mayo de 1804 y llegó a la costa del Pacífico y regresó en 1806.
"corrupt bargain" (p. 311) An allegation by Andrew Jackson of a secret agreement between Henry Clay and John Quincy Adams in the 1824 presidential election that Clay would urge his supporters in the House of Representatives to support Adams over Jackson in exchange for an appointment in Adams's cabinet. Andrew Jackson's supporters expressed outrage over the perceived deal, while Adams and Clay denied the exchange.	**"pacto corrupto" (pág. 311)** Acusación de Andrew Jackson de un acuerdo secreto entre Henry Clay y John Quincy Adams en las elecciones presidenciales de 1824, según el cual Clay instaría a sus partidarios en la Cámara de Representantes a apoyar a Adams frente a Jackson a cambio de un nombramiento en el gabinete de Adams. Los partidarios de Andrew Jackson expresaron su indignación por el trato percibido, mientras que Adams y Clay negaron el intercambio.
cotton gin (p. 289) A machine invented by Eli Whitney in 1793 to remove seeds from short-staple cotton. The cotton gin dramatically reduced the time and labor involved in deseeding, facilitating the expansion of cotton production in the South and West.	**desmotadora de algodón (pág. 289)** Máquina inventada por Eli Whitney en 1793 para extraer las semillas del algodón de fibra corta. La desmotadora de algodón redujo drásticamente el tiempo y la mano de obra necesarios para eliminar las semillas, lo que facilitó la expansión de la producción de algodón en el Sur y el Oeste.
counterculture (p. 930) Young cultural rebels of the 1960s and 1970s who rejected conventional cultural and social norms. The movement began in San Francisco and was known for anti-establishment rock music, protests against the Vietnam War, drug use, and the practice of "free love."	**contracultura (pág. 930)** Jóvenes rebeldes culturales de los años 60 y 70 que rechazaban las normas culturales y sociales convencionales. El movimiento comenzó en San Francisco y era conocido por la música rock antisistema, las protestas contra la guerra de Vietnam, el consumo de drogas y la práctica del "amor libre"
court-packing plan (p. 773) A proposal made by Franklin Roosevelt in 1937 to increase the number of members of the U.S. Supreme Court and reduce its opposition to New Deal legislation. Congress failed to pass the measure, and the scheme undermined Roosevelt's popular support.	**plan *Court-packing* (pág. 773)** Propuesta realizada por Franklin Roosevelt en 1937 para aumentar el número de miembros del Tribunal Supremo de Estados Unidos y reducir su oposición a la legislación del New Deal. El Congreso no aprobó la medida, y el plan minó el apoyo popular de Roosevelt.
Covenant Chain (p. 89) Alliance between Iroquois and the northern colonies of British North America to maintain the fur trade and good relations in the aftermath of Metacom's War.	**Cadena de Pactos (pág. 89)** Alianza entre los iroqueses y las colonias del norte de la Norteamérica británica para mantener el comercio de pieles y las buenas relaciones tras la Guerra de Metacom.

Coxey's army (p. 626) A protest movement led by Jacob Coxey. In 1894, Coxey and five hundred supporters marched from Ohio to Washington, D.C., to protest the lack of government response to the Panic of 1893. Although the movement garnered widespread support, this and subsequent marches did little to effect change in governmental policy.

Ejército de Coxey (pág. 626) Movimiento de protesta liderado por Jacob Coxey. En 1894, Coxey y quinientos simpatizantes marcharon de Ohio a Washington, D.C., para protestar por la falta de respuesta del gobierno al Pánico de 1893. Aunque el movimiento obtuvo un amplio apoyo, ésta y otras marchas posteriores apenas lograron cambiar la política gubernamental.

Crittenden Plan (p. 429) A proposed political compromise which would have protected slavery in states where it already existed with a constitutional amendment and extended the Missouri Compromise line to the California border. Slavery would be protected in any existing or new territories below the line. Republicans rejected the compromise.

Plan Crittenden (pág. 429) Una propuesta de compromiso político que habría protegido la esclavitud en los estados donde ya existía con una enmienda constitucional y ampliado la línea del Compromiso de Misuri hasta la frontera con California. La esclavitud estaría protegida en cualquier territorio existente o nuevo por debajo de la línea. Los republicanos rechazaron el compromiso.

Cuba Libre (p. 660) The vision of Cuban independence developed by José Martí, who hoped that Cuban independence would bring with it greater social and racial equality.

Cuba Libre (pág. 660) La visión de la independencia cubana desarrollada por José Martí, que esperaba que la independencia cubana trajera consigo una mayor igualdad social y racial.

cult of domesticity (p. 302) New ideals of womanhood that emerged alongside the middle class in the 1830s and 1840s that called for women to remain within the domestic sphere and devote themselves to the care of children, the home, and hardworking husbands in part to promote the moral and spiritual development of their children.

culto a la domesticidad (pág. 302) Nuevos ideales de feminidad que surgieron junto a la clase media en las décadas de 1830 y 1840 y que instaban a las mujeres a permanecer en la esfera doméstica y dedicarse al cuidado de los hijos, el hogar y los maridos trabajadores, en parte para promover el desarrollo moral y espiritual de sus hijos.

Currency Act (p. 161) A 1764 act of Parliament preventing colonial assemblies from printing paper money. This limited colonial economic growth because the colonies exported lower-cost raw materials and imported higher-cost finished goods, resulting in a shortage of currency.

Ley de la moneda (pág. 161) Ley del Parlamento de 1764 que impide a las asambleas coloniales imprimir papel moneda. Esto limitó el crecimiento económico colonial porque las colonias exportaban materias primas de menor costo e importaban productos acabados de mayor costo, lo que provocaba una escasez de divisas.

D

D-Day (p. 800) The invasion of German-occupied France by Allied forces on June 6, 1944. The D-Day landings opened up a western front in Europe and marked a major turning point in World War II.

Día D (pág. 800) Invasión de la Francia ocupada por los alemanes por las fuerzas aliadas el 6 de junio de 1944. El desembarco del Día D abrió un frente occidental en Europa y marcó un importante punto de inflexión en la Segunda Guerra Mundial.

Daughters of Liberty (p. 162) The Daughters of Liberty worked with the Sons of Liberty to assure colonial resistance to British taxation, usually through fund-raising efforts and campaigns to encourage colonists to avoid purchasing goods produced by Great Britain.

Hijas de la libertad (pág. 162) Las Hijas de la Libertad trabajaron con los Hijos de la Libertad para asegurar la resistencia colonial a los impuestos británicos, generalmente a través de esfuerzos de recaudación de fondos y campañas para animar a los colonos a evitar la compra de bienes producidos por Gran Bretaña.

Dawes Act (p. 537) An 1887 act that ended federal recognition of tribal sovereignty and divided American Indian land into 160-acre parcels to be distributed to American Indian heads of household to promote assimilation. The act dramatically reduced the amount of American Indian-controlled land and undermined American Indian solidarity by eroding social and cultural institutions.

Ley Dawes (pág. 537) Ley de 1887 que puso fin al reconocimiento federal de la soberanía tribal y dividió las tierras de los indios americanos en parcelas de 160 acres que se distribuirían a los cabezas de familia indios americanos para promover la asimilación. La ley redujo drásticamente la cantidad de tierras controladas por los indios americanos y socavó la solidaridad de éstos al erosionar las instituciones sociales y culturales.

Declaration of Independence (p. 176) A document listing colonial grievances and outlining the philosophical foundations for declaring the independence of the colonies from Great Britain. Drafted by Thomas Jefferson, then debated and revised by the Second Continental Congress, the Declaration was made public on July 4, 1776.

Declaración de Independencia (pág. 176) Documento que enumera las quejas coloniales y esboza los fundamentos filosóficos para declarar la independencia de las colonias de Gran Bretaña. Redactada por Thomas Jefferson, luego debatida y revisada por el Segundo Congreso Continental, la Declaración se hizo pública el 4 de julio de 1776.

Declaration of Sentiments (p. 348) Penned by Elizabeth Cady Stanton, it was a call for women's rights in marriage, family, religion, politics, and law, first issued at the 1848 Seneca Falls convention. The document mirrored the language of the Declaration of Independence.

Declaración de Sentimientos (pág. 348) Redactada por Elizabeth Cady Stanton, fue un llamamiento a favor de los derechos de la mujer en el matrimonio, la familia, la religión, la política y la ley, publicado por primera vez en la convención de Seneca Falls de 1848. El documento reflejaba el lenguaje de la Declaración de Independencia.

Declaratory Act (p. 164) A 1766 act stating Parliament's authority to pass any law, including direct taxes, on its North American colonies. The declaration was passed following the repeal of the Stamp Act to demonstrate that the repeal had not lessened the imperial authority of Britain.

Ley Declaratoria (pág. 164) Ley de 1766 que establece la autoridad del Parlamento para aprobar cualquier ley, incluidos los impuestos directos, en sus colonias norteamericanas. La declaración se aprobó tras la derogación de la Ley del Timbre para demostrar que dicha derogación no había mermado la autoridad imperial de Gran Bretaña.

Defense of Marriage Act (DOMA) (p. 1006) An act that defined marriage as only between a man and woman and banned federal recognition of same-sex marriage. The 1996 act also allowed states to not recognize same-sex marriages legally performed in other states. DOMA was ruled unconstitutional in 2013 by the Supreme Court.

Ley de Defensa del Matrimonio (DOMA) (pág. 1006) Ley que definía el matrimonio únicamente entre un hombre y una mujer y prohibía el reconocimiento federal del matrimonio entre personas del mismo sexo. La ley de 1996 también permitía a los estados no reconocer los matrimonios entre personas del mismo sexo celebrados legalmente en otros estados. La DOMA fue declarada inconstitucional en 2013 por el Tribunal Supremo.

Deferred Action for Childhood Arrivals (DACA) (p. 1021) A policy, initiated under the administration of President Obama in 2012, that allowed undocumented immigrant children to apply for renewable two-year extensions, granting them temporary residency in the United States along with eligibility for work permits.

Acción Diferida para los Llegados en la Infancia (DACA) (pág. 1021) Una política, iniciada bajo la administración del presidente Obama en 2012, que permitía a los niños inmigrantes indocumentados solicitar prórrogas renovables de dos años que les concedían la residencia temporal en Estados Unidos junto con la posibilidad de obtener permisos de trabajo.

deflation (p. 520) A fall in prices caused by supply exceeding demand.

deflación (pág. 520) Caída de los precios causada por una oferta superior a la demanda.

deindustrialization (p. 935) The decline of manufacturing in a specific town, region, or nation. Along with increased foreign competition and a rise of overseas outsourcing, deindustrialization led to a significant decline in union membership, as populations shifted across the country away from urban centers in search of new economic opportunity in the South and West.

desindustrialización (pág. 935) Declive de la industria manufacturera en una ciudad, región o nación concretas. Junto con la creciente competencia extranjera y el aumento de la subcontratación en el extranjero, la desindustrialización provocó un importante descenso de la afiliación sindical, ya que la población se desplazó por todo el país alejándose de los centros urbanos en busca de nuevas oportunidades económicas en el sur y el oeste.

Democratic Party (p. 311) One of two parties that resulted from the split of the Democratic-Republicans in the early 1820s. Andrew Jackson and Martin Van Buren emerged as leaders of the Democrats.

Partido Demócrata (pág. 311) Uno de los dos partidos resultantes de la escisión de los demócratas-republicanos a principios de la década de 1820. Andrew Jackson y Martin Van Buren surgieron como líderes de los demócratas.

Democratic-Republicans (p. 224) A political party that emerged out of opposition to Federalist policies in the 1790s. The Democratic-Republicans chose Thomas Jefferson as their presidential candidate in 1796, 1800, and 1804.

Demócratas-Republicanos (pág. 224) Partido político que surgió de la oposición a las políticas federalistas en la década de 1790. Los demócratas-republicanos eligieron a Thomas Jefferson como candidato presidencial en 1796, 1800 y 1804.

***Dennis v. United States* (p. 846)** The 1951 Supreme Court decision upholding the conviction of communist leaders on the grounds they posed a "clear and present danger," despite the absence of any evidence of an immediate uprising or plot.

***Dennis contra Estados Unidos* (pág. 846)** Decisión del Tribunal Supremo de 1951 por la que se confirma la condena de dirigentes comunistas alegando que representaban un "peligro claro y actual", a pesar de la ausencia de pruebas de un levantamiento o complot inmediato.

Department of Commerce and Labor (p. 692) Government agency created in 1906 to gather information about large companies in an effort to promote fair business practices.

Departamento de Comercio y Trabajo (pág. 692) Agencia gubernamental creada en 1906 para recopilar información sobre las grandes empresas en un esfuerzo por promover prácticas comerciales justas.

Department of Homeland Security (p. 1014) A cabinet-level agency created in 2002 that is responsible for various aspects of public security, including counterterrorism, border security, cybersecurity, and air and sea travel.

Departamento de Seguridad Nacional (pág. 1014) Organismo de rango ministerial creado en 2002 y responsable de diversos aspectos de la seguridad pública, como la lucha antiterrorista, la seguridad fronteriza, la ciberseguridad y los viajes aéreos y marítimos.

deskilling (p. 295) The replacement of skilled labor with unskilled labor and machines.

descualificación (pág. 295) Sustitución de mano de obra cualificada por mano de obra no cualificada y máquinas.

détente (p. 841) The easing of tensions during the mid-1970s between the Soviet Union and China and the United States. Détente resulted in the first arms-limitation treaty between the Soviet Union and the United States in 1972.

distensión (pág. 841) Alivio de las tensiones a mediados de la década de 1970 entre la Unión Soviética y China y Estados Unidos. La distensión dio lugar al primer tratado de limitación de armamentos entre la Unión Soviética y Estados Unidos en 1972.

Development, Relief, and Education for Alien Minors (DREAM) Act (p. 1021) Legislation proposed in 2001 to provide the children of undocumented immigrants in the United States the opportunity to gain legal residency status. The proposed legislation failed to pass Congress.

Ley de fomento para el progreso, alivio y educación para menores extranjeros (DREAM) (pág. 1021) Legislación propuesta en 2001 para ofrecer a los hijos de inmigrantes indocumentados en Estados Unidos la oportunidad de obtener la residencia legal. La legislación propuesta no fue aprobada por el Congreso.

Dixiecrats (p. 853) The nickname of Southern Democrats who created a segregationist political party in 1948, the States' Rights Democratic Party, as a response to federal extensions of civil rights. Dixiecrats advocated a state's right to legislate segregation. They ran Strom Thurmond in an unsuccessful bid for the presidency in 1948 against Truman.

***Dixiecrats* (pág. 853)** Sobrenombre de los demócratas sureños que crearon un partido político segregacionista en 1948, el Partido Demócrata de los Derechos de los Estados, como respuesta a las ampliaciones federales de los derechos civiles. Los *dixiecrats* defendían el derecho de los estados a legislar la segregación. Presentaron a Strom Thurmond en una candidatura fallida a la presidencia en 1948 contra Truman.

dollar diplomacy (p. 668) The term used by President Taft to describe the economic focus of his foreign policy. Taft hoped to use economic policies and the control of foreign assets by American companies to expand U.S. influence in Latin America and Asia.

diplomacia del dólar (pág. 668) Término utilizado por el presidente Taft para describir el enfoque económico de su política exterior. Taft esperaba utilizar las políticas económicas y el control de los activos extranjeros por parte de empresas estadounidenses para ampliar la influencia de Estados Unidos en América Latina y Asia.

Dominion of New England (p. 90) The consolidation of northeastern colonies by King James II in 1686 to establish greater control over them, resulting in the banning of town meetings, new taxes, and other unpopular policies. The Dominion was dissolved during the Glorious Revolution.

Dominio de Nueva Inglaterra (pág. 90) Consolidación de las colonias del noreste por el rey Jacobo II en 1686 para establecer un mayor control sobre ellas, lo que dio lugar a la prohibición de las reuniones de los pueblos, nuevos impuestos y otras políticas impopulares. El Dominio se disolvió durante la Revolución Gloriosa.

domino theory (p. 890) The prevalent belief during the Cold War, maintaining that if one country fell under the influence of communism, other surrounding countries would soon similarly fall under the influence of communism, like a row of falling dominoes.

teoría del dominó (pág. 890) Creencia predominante durante la Guerra Fría, que sostenía que, si un país caía bajo la influencia del comunismo, otros países circundantes caerían pronto de forma similar bajo la influencia del comunismo, como una hilera de fichas de dominó que caen.

Double V (p. 792) The slogan Black Americans used during World War II to state their twin aims to fight for victory over fascism abroad and victory over racism at home.

Doble V (pág. 792) El eslogan que los negros estadounidenses utilizaron durante la Segunda Guerra Mundial para declarar su doble objetivo de luchar por la victoria sobre el fascismo en el extranjero y la victoria sobre el racismo en casa.

***Dred Scott v. Sandford* (p. 421)** *Dred Scott v. Sandford*, a Supreme Court decision, centered on the status of Dred Scott and his family. In its 1857 ruling, the Court denied the claim that Black men had any rights, ruled that the Missouri Compromise had been unconstitutional, and blocked Congress from excluding slavery from any territory.

***Dred Scott contra Sandford* (pág. 421)** *Dred Scott contra Sandford*, una decisión del Tribunal Supremo, se centró en la situación de Dred Scott y su familia. En su sentencia de 1857, el Tribunal negó que los negros tuvieran derechos, dictaminó que el Compromiso de Misuri había sido inconstitucional e impidió al Congreso excluir la esclavitud de cualquier territorio.

Dunmore's Proclamation (p. 173) A proclamation issued by the royal governor of Virginia, Lord Dunmore, in 1775, which offered freedom to all enslaved Black Americans and indentured servants held by patriots in exchange for joining the British army. Between 800 and 2,000 enslaved people joined Dunmore's army.

Proclamación de Dunmore (pág. 173) Proclamación emitida por el gobernador real de Virginia, Lord Dunmore, en 1775, que ofrecía la libertad a todos los negros americanos esclavizados y a los sirvientes contratados por los patriotas a cambio de unirse al ejército británico. Entre 800 y 2,000 esclavizados se unieron al ejército de Dunmore.

Dust Bowl (p. 751) Name for the southern plains of the United States during the Great Depression, when the region experienced devastating dust storms due to soil erosion caused by poor farming practices and drought.

***Dust Bowl* (pág. 751)** Nombre de las llanuras del sur de Estados Unidos durante la Gran Depresión, cuando la región sufrió devastadoras tormentas de polvo debido a la erosión del suelo causada por las malas prácticas agrícolas y la sequía.

E

Economic Recovery Tax Act (p. 978) An act signed into law by President Ronald Reagan in 1981 that slashed income and estate taxes, especially on those in the highest income brackets.

Ley Tributaria de Recuperación Económica (pág. 978) Ley promulgada por el presidente Ronald Reagan en 1981 que recortó drásticamente los impuestos sobre la renta y el patrimonio, especialmente en los tramos de renta más elevados.

Eighteenth Amendment (p. 681) The 1918 amendment to the Constitution banning the production and sale of alcoholic beverages. It was repealed in 1933 by the Twenty-First Amendment.

Decimoctava Enmienda (pág. 681) Enmienda de 1918 a la Constitución que prohíbe la producción y venta de bebidas alcohólicas. Fue derogada en 1933 por la Vigesimoprimera Enmienda.

Eisenhower Doctrine (p. 881) An Eisenhower administration policy that promised economic and/or military assistance to a Middle Eastern country threatened by communist aggression. The strategy was meant to bolster containment and protect U.S. oil interests and pro-American governments.

Doctrina Eisenhower (pág. 881) Política de la administración Eisenhower que prometía ayuda económica y/o militar a un país de Oriente Medio amenazado por la agresión comunista. La estrategia pretendía reforzar la contención y proteger los intereses petroleros estadounidenses y a los gobiernos proamericanos.

electoral college (p. 211) A group of electors whose vote is the formal election of the president and vice president after the general election votes are tallied. States decide how to choose their electors, and most instituted a system requiring their electors to vote in accordance with a state's popular vote, resulting in a state's vote winner receiving all of the state's electoral votes.

colegio electoral (pág. 211) Grupo de electores cuyo voto es la elección formal del presidente y el vicepresidente tras el recuento de los votos de las elecciones generales. Los estados deciden cómo elegir a sus electores, y la mayoría instituyó un sistema que obliga a sus electores a votar de acuerdo con el voto popular de un estado, lo que da como resultado que el ganador de la votación de un estado reciba todos los votos electorales del estado.

Elkins Act (p. 692) An act outlawing railroad rebates passed in 1903. The act was designed to protect smaller businesses and shippers who were paying higher rates than large, favored customers, such as Standard Oil.

Ley Elkins (pág. 692) Ley que prohíbe los descuentos ferroviarios, aprobada en 1903. La ley se concibió para proteger a las pequeñas empresas y a los transportistas que pagaban tarifas más elevadas que los grandes clientes favorecidos, como la Standard Oil.

Emancipation Proclamation (p. 438) The proclamation by President Lincoln on January 1, 1863, that declared all enslaved people in areas still in rebellion "forever free" based on his legal authority as commander in chief during wartime. While the Emancipation Proclamation did not free enslaved people in the border states, it reframed the purpose of the war from simply preserving the Union to abolishing slavery.

Proclamación de la Emancipación (pág. 438) Proclamación del presidente Lincoln el 1 de enero de 1863, que declaraba "libres para siempre" a todas las personas esclavizadas en zonas aún en rebelión, basándose en su autoridad legal como comandante en jefe en tiempos de guerra. Aunque la Proclamación de la Emancipación no liberó a los esclavos de los estados fronterizos, replanteó el objetivo de la guerra, que pasó de la mera preservación de la Unión a la abolición de la esclavitud.

Embargo Act (p. 265) An act passed in 1807 that prohibited American ships from leaving their home ports until Britain and France repealed restrictions on U.S. trade and ceased British impressment of American sailors. While the act was intended to assert U.S. neutrality between British and French trading partners, it had a devastating impact on American commerce.

Ley de Embargo (pág. 265) Ley aprobada en 1807 que prohibía a los barcos estadounidenses abandonar sus puertos de origen hasta que Gran Bretaña y Francia derogaran las restricciones al comercio estadounidense y pusieran fin a la imposición británica de marineros estadounidenses. Aunque la ley pretendía afirmar la neutralidad de Estados Unidos entre sus socios comerciales británicos y franceses, tuvo un impacto devastador en el comercio estadounidense.

Emergency Banking Act (p. 760) An act passed in 1933 with the goal of stabilizing the banking system to calm widespread public panic over the safety of bank deposits. The act required banks to pass a federal audit before reopening after the "bank holiday," reassuring depositors that they were solvent.

Ley Bancaria de Emergencia (pág. 760) Ley aprobada en 1933 con el objetivo de estabilizar el sistema bancario para calmar el pánico generalizado de la población sobre la seguridad de los depósitos bancarios. La ley exigía que los bancos pasaran una auditoría federal antes de reabrir tras las "vacaciones bancarias", lo que tranquilizaba a los depositantes en cuanto a su solvencia.

***encomienda* (p. 29)** System established by Christopher Columbus in the Caribbean by which Spanish leaders in the Americas received land and the labor of all resident Native Americans. For Native Americans, the *encomienda* system amounted to enslavement.

encomienda (pág. 29) Sistema establecido por Cristóbal Colón en el Caribe por el que los dirigentes españoles en América recibían tierras y el trabajo de todos los nativos americanos residentes. Para los nativos americanos, el sistema de encomienda equivalía a la esclavitud.

English Civil War (p. 72) Conflict (1642–1651) between parliamentary forces and the king of England over Charles I's attempt to rule without Parliament. Culminated in the execution of Charles I and the establishment of the Commonwealth under Lord Protector Oliver Cromwell, leader of Parliament's forces. Cromwell ruled as lord protector until his death in 1658. Charles I's son, Charles II, was restored as king in 1660.

Guerra Civil Inglesa (pág. 72) Conflicto (1642-1651) entre las fuerzas parlamentarias y el rey de Inglaterra por el intento de Carlos I de gobernar sin el Parlamento. Culminó con la ejecución de Carlos I y el establecimiento de la *Commonwealth* bajo el Lord Protector Oliver Cromwell, líder de las fuerzas del Parlamento. Cromwell gobernó como lord protector hasta su muerte en 1658. El hijo de Carlos I, Carlos II, fue restaurado como rey en 1660.

Enlightenment (p. 122) A European cultural movement spanning the late seventeenth century to the end of the eighteenth century, emphasizing rational and scientific thinking over traditional religion and superstition.

Ilustración (pág. 122) Movimiento cultural europeo que abarca desde finales del siglo XVII hasta finales del siglo XVIII y que hace hincapié en el pensamiento racional y científico frente a la religión y la superstición tradicionales.

Enrollment Act (p. 444) A March 1863 Union draft law that provided for draftees to be selected by an impartial lottery. A loophole in the law allowing wealthy Americans to avoid military service by paying $300 or hiring a substitute created widespread resentment.

Ley de reclutamiento (pág. 444) Ley de reclutamiento de la Unión de marzo de 1863 que disponía que los reclutas fueran seleccionados por sorteo imparcial. Una laguna legal que permitía a los estadounidenses ricos eludir el servicio militar pagando 300 dólares o contratando a un sustituto creó un resentimiento generalizado.

Environmental Protection Agency (EPA) (p. 933) A federal agency established by President Nixon in 1971 to regulate activities that resulted in pollution or other environmental degradation.

Agencia de Protección del Medio Ambiente (EPA) (pág. 933) Agencia federal creada por el presidente Nixon en 1971 para regular las actividades que provocan contaminación u otro tipo de degradación del medio ambiente.

Equal Rights Amendment (ERA) (p. 918) A proposed constitutional amendment to guarantee equal rights for men and women. The amendment was not ratified because fewer than three-quarters of the states ratified it by the 1982 deadline.

Enmienda para la Igualdad de Derechos (ERA) (pág. 918) Propuesta de enmienda constitucional para garantizar la igualdad de derechos entre hombres y mujeres. La enmienda no fue ratificada porque menos de tres cuartas partes de los estados la ratificaron antes de la fecha límite de 1982.

Erie Canal (p. 271) Completed in 1825, the Erie Canal was an important internal improvement that spanned 363 miles from Lake Erie to the Hudson River, thereby providing access, via the Great Lakes, through the canal, and down the Hudson, to trade between the Midwest and the Northeast.

Canal de Erie (pág. 271) Terminado en 1825, el Canal de Erie fue una importante mejora interna que abarcaba 363 millas desde el lago Erie hasta el río Hudson, proporcionando así acceso, a través de los Grandes Lagos, por el canal, y por el Hudson, al comercio entre el Medio Oeste y el Noreste.

escalation (p. 892) A policy of the Johnson administration of continuously increasing the numbers of ground troops in Vietnam from 1964 to 1968 in hopes of securing victory in the war.

escalada (pág. 892) Política de la administración Johnson de aumentar continuamente el número de tropas terrestres en Vietnam de 1964 a 1968 con la esperanza de asegurar la victoria en la guerra.

Espionage Act (p. 714) An act that prohibited antiwar activities, including opposing the military draft, passed in 1917. It banned subversive mailings as well as deliberate actions of sabotage and spying.

Ley de Espionaje (pág. 714) Ley que prohibía las actividades contra la guerra, incluida la oposición al servicio militar obligatorio, aprobada en 1917. Prohibía los envíos subversivos, así como las acciones deliberadas de sabotaje y espionaje.

eugenics (p. 587) The pseudoscience of producing genetic improvement in the human population through selective breeding. Supporters of eugenics often saw ethnic and racial minorities as genetically "undesirable" and inferior.

eugenesia (pág. 587) Seudociencia consistente en producir mejoras genéticas en la población humana mediante la cría selectiva. Los partidarios de la eugenesia solían considerar a las minorías étnicas y raciales como genéticamente "indeseables" e inferiores.

European Union (EU) (p. 1005) Founded in 1993, a coalition of European nations that engage in free trade and investment with member nations. The EU introduced a common currency, the euro, in 1999.

Unión Europea (UE) (pág. 1005) Fundada en 1993, coalición de naciones europeas que practican el libre comercio y la inversión con los países miembros. La UE introdujo una moneda común, el euro, en 1999.

Executive Order 8802 (p. 792) An executive order signed by Franklin Roosevelt in 1941 banning racial discrimination in the defense industry and creating the Fair Employment Practice Committee (FEPC). The order was issued in part as a compromise to avert a planned civil rights march on Washington, D.C.

Orden ejecutiva 8802 (pág. 792) Orden ejecutiva firmada por Franklin Roosevelt en 1941 por la que se prohíbe la discriminación racial en la industria de defensa y se crea el Comité de Prácticas Laborales Justas (FEPC). La orden se emitió en parte como compromiso para evitar una marcha por los derechos civiles prevista en Washington, D.C.

Executive Order 9066 (p. 794) A 1942 executive order issued by President Franklin Roosevelt requiring all people of Japanese descent living on the West Coast to be relocated to internment camps.

Orden ejecutiva 9066 (pág. 794) Orden ejecutiva de 1942 emitida por el presidente Franklin Roosevelt por la que se exigía el traslado a campos de internamiento de todas las personas de ascendencia japonesa que vivían en la costa oeste.

Exodusters (p. 484) Black Americans who migrated from the South to Kansas in 1879 seeking land, economic opportunity, and a better way of life.

***Exodusters* (pág. 484)** Negros estadounidenses que emigraron del Sur a Kansas en 1879 en busca de tierras, oportunidades económicas y un modo de vida mejor.

F

Fair Labor Standards Act (p. 771) A law passed in 1938 that provided a minimum wage of forty cents an hour and a forty-hour workweek for employees in businesses engaged in interstate commerce.

Ley de Normas Laborales Justas (pág. 771) Ley aprobada en 1938 que establecía un salario mínimo de cuarenta centavos la hora y una semana laboral de cuarenta horas para los empleados de empresas dedicadas al comercio interestatal.

Family and Medical Leave Act (p. 1004) An act passed in 1993 that protects individuals' right to take up to twelve weeks of unpaid leave for medical reasons or parenthood without risk of losing their jobs.

Ley de baja médica y familiar (pág. 1004) Ley aprobada en 1993 que protege el derecho de las personas a disfrutar de hasta doce semanas de baja no retribuida por motivos médicos o paternidad sin riesgo de perder el empleo.

Farmers' Alliance (p. 622) A regional economic organization formed in agrarian areas in the late nineteenth century to advance the interests of farmers, many of whom were heavily indebted by the second half of the century.

Alianza de Agricultores (pág. 622) Organización económica regional formada en zonas agrarias a finales del siglo XIX para defender los intereses de los agricultores, muchos de los cuales estaban muy endeudados en la segunda mitad del siglo.

Federal Assault Weapons Ban (p. 1005) A 1994 ban prohibiting the manufacturing and use of certain assault-style semi-automatic firearms and large-capacity ammunition magazines in the United States. The ban was allowed to expire in 2004.

Prohibición federal de armas de asalto (pág. 1005) Prohibición de 1994 que prohíbe la fabricación y el uso de determinadas armas de fuego semiautomáticas de asalto y cargadores de munición de gran capacidad en Estados Unidos. La prohibición expiró en 2004.

Federal Bureau of Investigation (FBI) (p. 718) Domestic investigative branch of the U.S. Department of Justice originally headed by J. Edgar Hoover. The organization was originally named the Bureau of Investigation.

Oficina Federal de Investigación (FBI) (pág. 718) Subdivisión de investigación nacional del Departamento de Justicia de EE.UU. dirigida originalmente por J. Edgar Hoover. La organización se denominó originalmente Oficina de Investigación.

Federal Deposit Insurance Corporation (FDIC) (p. 760) A federal agency created under the New Deal in 1933. It insured bank deposits up to $5,000, a figure that would substantially rise over the years.

Corporación Federal de Seguro de Depósitos (FDIC) (pág. 760) Agencia federal creada bajo el New Deal en 1933. Aseguraba los depósitos bancarios hasta 5,000 dólares, cifra que aumentaría sustancialmente con el paso de los años.

Federal Employee Loyalty Program (p. 845) A program established by President Truman in 1947, via executive order, to investigate federal employees suspected of disloyalty, communist ties, suspicious personal behaviors, and homosexuality. Hundreds of employees were terminated from their positions as a result of the investigations.

***Federal Employee Loyalty Program* (pág. 845)** Programa establecido por el presidente Truman en 1947, mediante una orden ejecutiva, para investigar a los empleados federales sospechosos de deslealtad, vínculos comunistas, comportamientos personales sospechosos y homosexualidad. Cientos de empleados fueron despedidos de sus puestos a raíz de las investigaciones.

Federalist (p. 212) A supporter of ratification of the Constitution of 1787, many of whom came from urban and commercial backgrounds. Federalists supported a strong central government with vigorous powers.

Federalista (pág. 212) Partidario de la ratificación de la Constitución de 1787, muchos de los cuales procedían de entornos urbanos y comerciales. Los federalistas apoyaban un gobierno central fuerte con poderes vigorosos.

The *Federalist Papers* (p. 213) A series of eighty-five essays by Federalists Alexander Hamilton, James Madison, and John Jay. Published in newspapers throughout the country, the *Federalist Papers* promoted the ratification of the Constitution.

Los documentos federalistas (pág. 213) Serie de ochenta y cinco ensayos de los federalistas Alexander Hamilton, James Madison y John Jay. Publicados en periódicos de todo el país, los papeles federalistas promovían la ratificación de la Constitución.

feminist (p. 674) Someone who believes that women should have access to the same opportunities as men.

feminista (pág. 674) Alguien que cree que las mujeres deben tener acceso a las mismas oportunidades que los hombres.

feudalism (p. 25) A social and economic system organized by a hierarchy of hereditary classes, in which lower social orders owed loyalty to the social classes above them and, in return, those who worked the land, vassals, received from the nobility a guarantee of protection.

feudalismo (pág. 25) Sistema social y económico organizado por una jerarquía de clases hereditarias, en el que los órdenes sociales inferiores debían lealtad a las clases sociales superiores y, a cambio, los que trabajaban la tierra, vasallos, recibían de la nobleza una garantía de protección.

Field Order Number 15 (p. 455) Order issued by General William Sherman in January 1865 setting aside more than 400,000 acres of Confederate land to be divided into plots for freedpeople. Sherman's order came in response to pressure from Black American leaders.

***Field Order Number 15* (pág. 455)** Orden emitida por el general William Sherman en enero de 1865 por la que se reservaban más de 400,000 acres de tierras confederadas para dividirlas en parcelas para libertos. La orden de Sherman se produjo en respuesta a la presión de los líderes negros estadounidenses.

Fifteenth Amendment (p. 475) An amendment to the Constitution ratified in 1870 that forbids state voting restrictions based on "race, color, or previous condition of servitude." After Reconstruction ended, southern states devised many tactics for disenfranchising Black voters.

Decimoquinta Enmienda (pág. 475) Enmienda a la Constitución ratificada en 1870 que prohíbe las restricciones estatales al voto basadas en "raza, color o condición previa de servidumbre". Una vez finalizada la Reconstrucción, los estados del sur idearon muchas tácticas para privar del derecho al voto a los votantes negros.

filibuster (p. 412) Unauthorized military expeditions launched by U.S. adventurers to gain control of Cuba, Nicaragua, and other Spanish territories in the 1850s.

filibustero (pág. 412) Expediciones militares no autorizadas lanzadas por aventureros estadounidenses para hacerse con el control de Cuba, Nicaragua y otros territorios españoles en la década de 1850.

First Battle of Bull Run (First Manassas) (p. 435) The first major battle of the Civil War, at which Confederate troops defeated Union forces in July 1861.

Primera Batalla de Bull Run (First Manassas) (pág. 435) La primera gran batalla de la Guerra Civil, en la que las tropas confederadas derrotaron a las fuerzas de la Unión en julio de 1861.

First Great Awakening (p. 124) Series of religious revivals in colonial America that began in 1720 and lasted until about 1750.

Primer Gran Despertar (pág. 124) Serie de avivamientos religiosos en la América colonial que comenzó en 1720 y duró hasta aproximadamente 1750.

flapper (p. 729) A term for the modern, sexually liberated woman popularized in movies and magazines in the 1920s. Flappers defied traditional, conservative views of women by wearing short hair and short skirts, smoking, drinking, and acting more independently.

***flapper* (pág. 729)** Término para referirse a la mujer moderna y sexualmente liberada que se popularizó en las películas y revistas de los años veinte. Las *flappers* desafiaron la visión tradicional y conservadora de la mujer llevando el pelo corto y faldas cortas, fumando, bebiendo y actuando de forma más independiente.

Food Administration (p. 713) A government agency created during World War I to regulate food production and consumption. Its head, Herbert Hoover, sought to increase the military and civilian food supply through a major public campaign of voluntary conservation measures such as family gardens and "meatless Mondays."

Administración de alimentos (pág. 713) Agencia gubernamental creada durante la Primera Guerra Mundial para regular la producción y el consumo de alimentos. Su jefe, Herbert Hoover, intentó aumentar el suministro de alimentos militares y civiles mediante una gran campaña pública de medidas voluntarias de conservación, como los huertos familiares y los "lunes sin carne".

Force Acts (p. 486) Three acts passed by Congress in 1870 and 1871 in response to vigilante attacks on southern people. The acts were designed to protect political rights and end violence by the Ku Klux Klan and similar organizations.

***Force Acts* (pág. 486)** Tres leyes aprobadas por el Congreso en 1870 y 1871 en respuesta a los ataques de los vigilantes contra la población sureña. Estas leyes tenían por objeto proteger los derechos políticos y poner fin a la violencia del Ku Klux Klan y organizaciones similares.

Force Bill (p. 319) A bill passed by Congress in 1833 in response to South Carolina's Ordinance of Nullification. It gave the president the authority to use military force to enforce national laws—in particular the Tariff of 1832.

***Force Bill* (pág. 319)** Proyecto de ley aprobado por el Congreso en 1833 en respuesta a la Ordenanza de Nulificación de Carolina del Sur. Otorgaba al presidente la autoridad de utilizar la fuerza militar para hacer cumplir las leyes nacionales, en particular el Arancel de 1832.

Fort Sumter (p. 430) The Union fort that guarded the harbor in Charleston, South Carolina. The Confederacy's decision to fire on the fort and block resupply in April 1861 marked the beginning of the Civil War.

Fuerte Sumter (pág. 430) Fuerte de la Unión que protegía el puerto de Charleston, Carolina del Sur. La decisión de la Confederación de disparar contra el fuerte y bloquear el reabastecimiento en abril de 1861 marcó el comienzo de la Guerra Civil.

Fourteen Points (p. 707) The core principles President Woodrow Wilson saw as the basis for lasting peace after World War I, including freedom of the seas, open diplomacy, the establishment of the League of Nations, and the right to self-determination.

Catorce Puntos (pág. 707) Los principios fundamentales que el presidente Woodrow Wilson consideraba la base para una paz duradera tras la Primera Guerra Mundial, incluida la libertad de los mares, la diplomacia abierta, el establecimiento de la Sociedad de Naciones y el derecho a la autodeterminación.

Fourteenth Amendment (p. 472) A constitutional amendment ratified in 1868 granting citizenship, due process, and equal protection under the law to all persons born in the United States. This amendment overturned the *Dred Scott* ruling and was aimed at protecting the rights of freedpeople.

Decimocuarta Enmienda (pág. 472) Enmienda constitucional ratificada en 1868 que concede la ciudadanía, el debido proceso y la igualdad de protección ante la ley a todas las personas nacidas en Estados Unidos. Esta enmienda anuló la sentencia Dred Scott y tenía como objetivo proteger los derechos de los libertos.

Free Speech Movement (FSM) (p. 928) The 1964–1965 college student-led movement using sit-in and rallies to protest policies of the University of California at Berkeley that restricted students' ability to protest for civil rights. The successful FSM protests inspired greater student activism on college campuses.

Movimiento por la Libertad de Expresión (FSM) (pág. 928) Movimiento liderado por estudiantes universitarios entre 1964 y 1965 que utilizó sentadas y concentraciones para protestar contra las políticas de la Universidad de California en Berkeley que restringían la capacidad de los estudiantes para protestar por los derechos civiles. El éxito de las protestas de la FSM inspiró un mayor activismo estudiantil en los campus universitarios.

Free-Soil Party (p. 350) A party founded by political abolitionists in 1848 to expand the appeal of the Liberty Party by focusing less on the moral wrongs of slavery and more on the benefits of providing economic opportunities for northern white people in western territories.

Partido de Suelo Libre (pág. 350) Partido fundado por abolicionistas políticos en 1848 para ampliar el atractivo del Partido de la Libertad centrándose menos en los males morales de la esclavitud y más en los beneficios de proporcionar oportunidades económicas a los blancos del norte en los territorios occidentales.

Freedmen's Bureau (p. 464) Federal agency created in 1865 to provide freedpeople with economic, educational, and legal resources. The Freedmen's Bureau played an active role in shaping Black life in the postwar South through the 1870s.

Agencia de Los Libertos (pág. 464) Agencia federal creada en 1865 para proporcionar a los libertos recursos económicos, educativos y legales. El *Freedmen's Bureau* desempeñó un papel activo en la configuración de la vida de los negros en el Sur de posguerra hasta la década de 1870.

Freedom Rides (p. 903) Integrated bus rides through the South in 1961 to test southern compliance with Supreme Court rulings on segregation. After Freedom Riders were attacked in Montgomery, Alabama, the Kennedy administration sent federal marshals to protect the riders.

Viajeros de la libertad (pág. 903) Viajes integrados en autobús por el Sur en 1961 para poner a prueba el cumplimiento por parte del Sur de las sentencias del Tribunal Supremo sobre segregación. Después de que los Viajeros de la libertad fueran atacados en Montgomery, Alabama, la administración Kennedy envió alguaciles federales para proteger a los pasajeros.

Freedom Summer (p. 907) A 1964 civil rights effort in Mississippi sponsored by a national coalition of civil rights organizations following the passage of the Civil Rights Act of 1964. During the Freedom Summer, some eight hundred volunteers, mainly white college students, worked on voter registration drives and in freedom schools to improve education for rural Black youngsters.

Verano de la Libertad (pág. 907) Esfuerzo por los derechos civiles realizado en 1964 en Misisipi, patrocinado por una coalición nacional de organizaciones de derechos civiles tras la aprobación de la Ley de Derechos Civiles de 1964. Durante el Verano de la Libertad, unos ochocientos voluntarios, en su mayoría estudiantes universitarios blancos, trabajaron en campañas de registro de votantes y en escuelas de la libertad para mejorar la educación de los jóvenes negros de las zonas rurales.

French and Indian War (Seven Years' War) (p. 149) A global conflict from 1754–1763 among European nations, mainly Britain and France, that began in North America over disputed territorial rights to the Ohio River Valley in 1754, with further conflict erupting in Europe in 1756. France ultimately ceded all its North American territories to Britain and Spain, but the enormous cost of the war also severely damaged the British and French economies.

Guerra Francesa e India (Guerra de los Siete Años) (pág. 149) Conflicto mundial entre 1754 y 1763 entre naciones europeas, principalmente Gran Bretaña y Francia, que comenzó en América del Norte por la disputa de los derechos territoriales sobre el valle del río Ohio en 1754, y que estalló en Europa en 1756. Francia cedió finalmente todos sus territorios norteamericanos a Gran Bretaña y España, pero el enorme coste de la guerra también dañó gravemente las economías británica y francesa.

French Revolution (p. 220) A revolution between 1789 and 1799 in which the French people, inspired by the ideals of the American Declaration of Independence, overthrew King Louis XVI (reigned 1774–1792). The uprising disrupted French agriculture among other aspects of life, increasing demand for American wheat, while the efforts of French revolutionaries to institute an egalitarian republic gained support from many Americans. However, in late 1792, as French revolutionary leaders began executing thousands of their opponents in the Reign of Terror and declared war against Prussia, Austria, and finally Great Britain, merchants worried about the impact on trade. In response, President Washington proclaimed U.S. neutrality in April 1793, prohibiting Americans from providing support or war materials to any belligerent nations.

Revolución Francesa (pág. 220) Revolución entre 1789 y 1799 en la que el pueblo francés, inspirado por los ideales de la Declaración de Independencia de Estados Unidos, derrocó al rey Luis XVI (reinó entre 1774 y 1792). El levantamiento perturbó la agricultura francesa entre otros aspectos de la vida, aumentando la demanda de trigo estadounidense, mientras que los esfuerzos de los revolucionarios franceses por instaurar una república igualitaria ganaron el apoyo de muchos estadounidenses. Sin embargo, a finales de 1792, cuando los líderes revolucionarios franceses comenzaron a ejecutar a miles de sus oponentes en el Reinado del Terror y declararon la guerra a Prusia, Austria y, finalmente, Gran Bretaña, los comerciantes se preocuparon por el impacto en el comercio. En respuesta, el presidente Washington proclamó la neutralidad de Estados Unidos en abril de 1793, prohibiendo a los estadounidenses proporcionar apoyo o material bélico a cualquier nación beligerante.

frontier thesis (p. 590) The argument, made by historian Frederick Jackson Turner in the 1890s, that the conquest of the West symbolized American exceptionalism and shaped its democratic spirit and, conversely, that its closing endangered the existence of democracy.

tesis de la frontera (pág. 590) Argumento, esgrimido por el historiador Frederick Jackson Turner en la década de 1890, según el cual la conquista del Oeste simbolizaba el excepcionalismo estadounidense y conformaba su espíritu democrático y, a la inversa, su cierre ponía en peligro la existencia de la democracia.

Fuel Administration (p. 712) Government agency created during World War I to manage the production and distribution of fuel such as coal and oil.

Fuel Administration **(pág. 712)** Agencia gubernamental creada durante la Primera Guerra Mundial para gestionar la producción y distribución de combustibles como el carbón y el petróleo.

Fugitive Slave Act of 1793 (p. 404) An Act that allowed enslavers to capture enslaved people who had fled from a slave state by mandating that local governments, even in free states, seize and return them. However, the act was largely ignored by Northerners.

Ley de Esclavos Fugitivos de 1793 (pág. 404) Ley que permitía a los esclavistas capturar a las personas esclavizadas que habían huido de un estado esclavista, obligando a los gobiernos locales, incluso en los estados libres, a incautarlos y devolverlos. Sin embargo, la ley fue ignorada en gran medida por los norteños.

Fugitive Slave Act of 1850 (p. 408) An act that strengthened earlier fugitive slave laws, passed as part of the Compromise of 1850. The act required northern citizens to help catch runaways and made it difficult for alleged runaways to receive a fair trial. The act provoked widespread anger in the North, and the backlash against it enraged Southerners.

Ley de Esclavos Fugitivos de 1850 (pág. 408) Ley que reforzaba las leyes anteriores sobre esclavos fugitivos, aprobada como parte del Compromiso de 1850. La ley obligaba a los ciudadanos del norte a ayudar a capturar a los fugitivos y dificultaba que los presuntos fugitivos recibieran un juicio justo. La ley provocó la ira generalizada en el Norte, y la reacción en su contra enfureció a los sureños.

G

gag rule (p. 320) A rule passed by the House of Representatives in 1836 to postpone action on all antislavery petitions without hearing them read to prevent congressional debate over slavery. It was renewed annually until 1844.

ley mordaza (pág. 320) Regla aprobada por la Cámara de Representantes en 1836 para posponer la acción sobre todas las peticiones antiesclavistas sin escuchar su lectura, con el fin de evitar el debate en el Congreso sobre la esclavitud. Se renovó anualmente hasta 1844.

gang labor (p. 117) A system to produce cash crops based on dividing a work force into "gangs" who work at a consistent pace at a designated task. This labor system was used to produce cash crops in the eighteenth century mainly in the southern colonies, where enslaved people were forced to work long hours in harsh conditions in a highly regulated manner.

trabajo en cuadrilla (pág. 117) Sistema para producir cultivos comerciales basado en la división de la mano de obra en "cuadrillas" que trabajan a un ritmo constante en una tarea designada. Este sistema laboral se utilizó para producir cultivos comerciales en el siglo XVIII, principalmente en las colonias del sur, donde se obligaba a los esclavizados a trabajar largas jornadas en duras condiciones y de forma muy reglamentada.

General Assembly of Virginia (p. 70) Local governing body in Virginia established by the English crown in 1619. Later, the assembly was known as the House of Burgesses.

Asamblea General de Virginia (pág. 70) Órgano de gobierno local de Virginia establecido por la corona inglesa en 1619. Más tarde, la asamblea pasó a denominarse Cámara de Burgueses.

Gettysburg Address (p. 451) A speech given by President Lincoln to inaugurate the federal cemetery at Gettysburg, Pennsylvania, in November 1863. In this speech, Lincoln expressed his belief that the war was a struggle for a "new birth of freedom" and likened the Union efforts in the Civil War to the principles of the American Revolution.

Discurso de Gettysburg (pág. 451) Discurso pronunciado por el presidente Lincoln para inaugurar el cementerio federal de Gettysburg, Pensilvania, en noviembre de 1863. En este discurso, Lincoln expresó su creencia de que la guerra era una lucha por un "nuevo nacimiento de la libertad" y comparó los esfuerzos de la Unión en la Guerra Civil con los principios de la Revolución Americana.

ghettos (p. 582) Neighborhoods dominated by a single ethnic, racial, or class group.

guetos (pág. 582) Barrios dominados por un único grupo étnico, racial o de clase.

Ghost Dance (p. 539) A religious ritual performed by the American Indians in the late nineteenth century. The ritual was created following a vision received by Paiute prophet Wovoka in 1888. Wovoka believed performing the Ghost Dance would cause white people to disappear and allow American Indians to regain control of their lands.

Danza de los fantasmas (pág. 539) Ritual religioso practicado por los indios americanos a finales del siglo XIX. El ritual se creó a raíz de una visión recibida por el profeta paiute Wovoka en 1888. Wovoka creía que la Danza de los Fantasmas haría desaparecer a los blancos y permitiría a los indios recuperar el control de sus tierras.

Gilded Age (p. 601) The term created by Mark Twain and Charles Dudley Warner to describe the late nineteenth century. It implies the glittering appearance of the era was a shell that covered the corruption and materialism of the superrich.

Edad dorada (pág. 601) Término creado por Mark Twain y Charles Dudley Warner para describir el final del siglo XIX. Implica que la brillante apariencia de la época era una cáscara que cubría la corrupción y el materialismo de los superricos.

glasnost **(p. 991)** A policy of political "openness" initiated by Soviet leader Mikhail Gorbachev in the 1980s. Under glasnost, the Soviet Union began a transition to democratic elections, freedom of speech, and freedom of the press.

glasnost **(pág. 991)** Política de "apertura" política iniciada por el líder soviético Mijaíl Gorbachov en la década de 1980. Bajo la glasnost, la Unión Soviética extendió las elecciones democráticas, la libertad de expresión y la libertad de prensa.

Glass-Steagall Act (p. 760) New Deal legislation passed in 1933 that sought to reform and strengthen the banking system. The act created the Federal Deposit Insurance Corporation (FDIC) to insure bank deposits. It also prohibited institutions from participating in both commercial and investment banking (the prohibition was repealed in 1999).

Ley Glass-Steagall (pág. 760) Legislación del New Deal aprobada en 1933 que pretendía reformar y reforzar el sistema bancario. La ley creó la Corporación Federal de Seguro de Depósitos (FDIC) para asegurar los depósitos bancarios. También prohibía a las entidades participar tanto en la banca comercial como en la de inversión (la prohibición se derogó en 1999).

Global War on Terror (GWOT) (p. 1014) A military campaign against international terrorism launched by the George W. Bush administration after the attacks on September 11, 2001. The campaign against international terrorist organizations and governments that supported them led to long and costly conflicts in Afghanistan and Iraq.

Guerra Global contra el Terrorismo (GWOT) (pág. 1014) Campaña militar contra el terrorismo internacional lanzada por la administración de George W. Bush tras los atentados del 11 de septiembre de 2001. La campaña contra las organizaciones terroristas internacionales y los gobiernos que las apoyaban condujo a largos y costosos conflictos en Afganistán e Irak.

global warming (p. 1003) The long-term rise in the temperature of the atmosphere and oceans caused by the increased presence of greenhouse gases in the atmosphere. Since 1880, the average global annual temperature has risen 1.9° Fahrenheit (1.1° Celsius) with most of the warming having occurred since 1975.

calentamiento global (pág. 1003) Aumento a largo plazo de la temperatura de la atmósfera y los océanos causado por la mayor presencia de gases de efecto invernadero en la atmósfera. Desde 1880, la temperatura media anual del planeta ha aumentado 1,1° Celsius (1.9° Fahrenheit), y la mayor parte del calentamiento se ha producido desde 1975.

globalization (p. 1001) The growth of international trade and cultural exchange between peoples and countries resulting in increased economic and cultural integration, migration, and interdependence among nations.

globalización (pág. 1001) Crecimiento del comercio internacional y del intercambio cultural entre pueblos y países que da lugar a una mayor integración económica y cultural, migración e interdependencia entre las naciones.

Glorious Revolution (p. 90) The 1688 rebellion that forced James II from the English throne and replaced him with William and Mary. The Glorious Revolution led to greater political and commercial autonomy for the British colonies.

Revolución Gloriosa (pág. 90) Rebelión de 1688 que obligó a Jacobo II a abandonar el trono inglés y lo sustituyó por Guillermo y María. La Revolución Gloriosa condujo a una mayor autonomía política y comercial de las colonias británicas.

"The Gospel of Wealth" (p. 613) An essay by Andrew Carnegie published in 1889 in which he argued the rich should act as guardians of society through the wealth they earned. Carnegie advocated that the wealthy generate programs to uplift intelligent self-starters by using their surplus income for the benefit of the community, creating public libraries or community centers, rather than engaging in charity.

"El Evangelio de la Riqueza" (pág. 613) Ensayo de Andrew Carnegie publicado en 1889 en el que argumentaba que los ricos debían actuar como guardianes de la sociedad gracias a la riqueza que ganaban. Carnegie abogaba por que los ricos generaran programas para elevar la autoestima inteligente utilizando sus excedentes de ingresos en beneficio de la comunidad, creando bibliotecas públicas o centros comunitarios, en lugar de dedicarse a la caridad.

Grange (p. 523) An organization founded in 1867 to meet the practical economic, social, and cultural needs of farmers. Grangers advocated the use of farm cooperatives and took an active role in the promotion of the economic and political interests of farmers during the 1870s.

***Grange* (pág. 523)** Organización fundada en 1867 para satisfacer las necesidades prácticas económicas, sociales y culturales de los agricultores. *Grangers* abogó por el uso de cooperativas agrícolas y desempeñó un papel activo en la promoción de los intereses económicos y políticos de los agricultores durante la década de 1870.

Great Depression (p. 748) Worldwide economic collapse caused by overproduction and financial speculation. It affected the United States from October 1929 until the start of World War II in 1939.

Gran Depresión (pág. 748) Colapso económico mundial causado por la sobreproducción y la especulación financiera. Afectó a Estados Unidos desde octubre de 1929 hasta el inicio de la Segunda Guerra Mundial en 1939.

Great Migration (p. 718) The population shift of more than 400,000 Black people who left the South beginning in 1917–1918 and headed north and west to escape poverty and racial discrimination. During the 1920s, another 800,000 Black people left the South.

Gran Migración (pág. 718) El desplazamiento de población de más de 400,000 negros que abandonaron el Sur a partir de 1917-1918 y se dirigieron hacia el Norte y el Oeste para escapar de la pobreza y la discriminación racial. Durante la década de 1920, otros 800,000 negros abandonaron el Sur.

Great Plains (p. 516) The territory between the Mississippi River and the Rocky Mountains characterized by flat topography and a drier climate, consisting mainly of prairie and grassland. Much of this region was acquired by the United States through the Louisiana Purchase in 1803.

Grandes Llanuras (pág. 516) Territorio entre el río Misisipi y las Montañas Rocosas caracterizado por una topografía llana y un clima más seco, formado principalmente por praderas y pastizales. Gran parte de esta región fue adquirida por Estados Unidos mediante la Compra de Luisiana en 1803.

Great Railway Strike (p. 487) A series of nationwide railway worker strikes in 1877 following the collapse of several railroads and wage cuts at others. In response to these strikes, U.S. troops were removed from the South and sent north and west to contain the strikes.

Gran Huelga Ferroviaria (pág. 487) Serie de huelgas nacionales de trabajadores ferroviarios en 1877 tras la quiebra de varios ferrocarriles y los recortes salariales en otros. En respuesta a estos ataques, las tropas estadounidenses fueron retiradas del sur y enviadas al norte y al oeste para contenerlos.

Great Recession (p. 1018) The severe economic decline in the United States and throughout the world from 2007 to 2009, leading to bank failures, high unemployment, home foreclosures, and large federal deficits.

Gran Recesión (pág. 1018) Grave declive económico en Estados Unidos y en todo el mundo entre 2007 y 2009, que provocó quiebras bancarias, altas tasas de desempleo, ejecuciones hipotecarias y grandes déficits federales.

Great Society (p. 898) President Lyndon Johnson's legislative reform program that called for an expansion of social welfare programs, medical care for the elderly, support for civil rights, protection of the environment, alleviation of poverty, and greater funding to education, especially for marginalized communities.

Gran Sociedad (pág. 898) Programa de reforma legislativa del presidente Lyndon Johnson que abogaba por ampliar los programas de bienestar social, la atención médica a los ancianos, el apoyo a los derechos civiles, la protección del medio ambiente, la mitigación de la pobreza y una mayor financiación de la educación, especialmente para las comunidades marginadas.

greenhouse gas (p. 1003) Any atmospheric gas that absorbs energy from the sun and other radiant sources, which warm the Earth. The increased emissions of greenhouse gases, especially carbon dioxide and methane, by human activity is a main cause of global warming and climate change.

gas de efecto invernadero (pág. 1003) Cualquier gas atmosférico que absorbe energía del sol y de otras fuentes radiantes, que calientan la Tierra. El aumento de las emisiones de gases de efecto invernadero, especialmente dióxido de carbono y metano, por la actividad humana es una de las principales causas del calentamiento global y el cambio climático.

gross domestic product (p. 551) The yearly output of all of a nation's goods and services.

producto interior bruto (pág. 551) Producción anual de todos los bienes y servicios de una nación.

Guantánamo Bay (p. 1017) The site of a U.S. military base in Cuba, where the George W. Bush administration imprisoned suspected al-Qaeda members without due process of law. Despite campaigning on promises to end this policy, the Obama administration failed to close the Guantánamo Bay prison, and it continues to operate today.

Guantánamo (pág. 1017) Emplazamiento de una base militar estadounidense en Cuba, donde el gobierno de George W. Bush encarceló a presuntos miembros de Al Qaeda sin las debidas garantías procesales. A pesar de hacer campaña prometiendo poner fin a esta política, el gobierno de Obama no cerró la prisión de Guantánamo, que sigue funcionando en la actualidad.

guerilla tactics (p. 151) Tactics deployed by irregular forces in a conflict, usually dependent on surprise attack, raids on supply lines, assassinations, and attacks on civilian supporters of an enemy.

tácticas de guerrilla (pág. 151) Tácticas desplegadas por fuerzas irregulares en un conflicto, que suelen depender del ataque por sorpresa, las incursiones en las líneas de suministro, los asesinatos y los ataques a civiles partidarios de un enemigo.

Gulf of Tonkin Resolution (p. 891) A 1964 congressional resolution giving President Johnson wide discretion to use U.S. forces in Vietnam without an official declaration of war by Congress. The resolution allowed Johnson to escalate U.S. troop presence in Vietnam from tens of thousands to hundreds of thousands.

Resolución del Golfo de Tonkín (pág. 891) Resolución del Congreso de 1964 que otorga al presidente Johnson amplia discreción para utilizar las fuerzas estadounidenses en Vietnam sin una declaración oficial de guerra por parte del Congreso. La resolución permitió a Johnson aumentar la presencia de tropas estadounidenses en Vietnam de decenas de miles a cientos de miles.

H

Haitian Revolution (p. 261) Revolt against a racialized social hierarchy and French rule by free and enslaved Black people between 1791 and 1804 in the French colony of Saint Domingue on the island of Hispaniola. The revolution led to the establishment of the Republic of Haiti, the first independent Black-led nation in the Americas, in 1803.

Revolución haitiana (pág. 261) Revuelta contra una jerarquía social racializada y el dominio francés por parte de negros libres y esclavizados entre 1791 y 1804 en la colonia francesa de Santo Domingo, en la isla de La Española. La revolución condujo al establecimiento de la República de Haití, la primera nación independiente dirigida por negros en las Américas, en 1803.

hard war (p. 454) The strategy promoted by General Ulysses S. Grant in which Union forces destroyed civilian crops, livestock, fields, property, and infrastructure to undermine Confederate morale and supply chains.

guerra dura (pág. 454) Estrategia promovida por el general Ulysses S. Grant en la que las fuerzas de la Unión destruían cosechas, ganado, campos, propiedades e infraestructuras civiles para minar la moral confederada y las cadenas de suministro.

Harlem Renaissance (p. 731) The work of Harlem-based Black writers, artists, and musicians who flourished following World War I through the 1920s.

Renacimiento de Harlem (pág. 731) Obra de escritores, artistas y músicos negros afincados en Harlem que florecieron tras la Primera Guerra Mundial hasta la década de 1920.

Hartford Convention (p. 282) A secret convention in 1814 of Federalists opposed to the War of 1812. Delegates to the convention considered a number of constitutional amendments, as well as the possibility of secession. After news of the convention spread, public sentiment turned against the Federalists, and the party never fully recovered.

Convención de Hartford (pág. 282) Convención secreta en 1814 de federalistas opuestos a la Guerra de 1812. Los delegados de la convención consideraron una serie de enmiendas constitucionales, así como la posibilidad de la secesión. Tras la noticia de la convención, la opinión pública se volvió contra los federalistas y el partido nunca se recuperó del todo.

Haudenosaunee (Iroquois) Confederacy (p. 60) A group of allied American Indian nations that included the Mohawk, Oneida, Onondaga, Cayuga, Seneca, and later the Tuscarora. The Confederacy had largely dissolved by the final decade of the 1700s.

Confederación Haudenosaunee (Iroquesa) (pág. 60) Grupo de naciones indias americanas aliadas que incluía a los mohawk, oneida, onondaga, cayuga, seneca y, más tarde, los tuscarora. La Confederación se había disuelto en gran medida en la última década del siglo XVIII.

Hay-Pauncefote Treaty (p. 667) A 1901 treaty between the United States and Great Britain granting the United States the right to construct the Panama Canal.

Tratado Hay-Pauncefote (pág. 667) Tratado de 1901 entre Estados Unidos y Gran Bretaña por el que se concede a Estados Unidos el derecho a construir el Canal de Panamá.

Haymarket riot (p. 569) A labor rally in Haymarket Square in Chicago in May 1886 that resulted in violence, including the deaths of several police officers. The carnage was blamed on the supposedly radical nature of the labor movement and contributed to the demise of the Knights of Labor.

Disturbios en Haymarket (pág. 569) Manifestación obrera en la plaza Haymarket de Chicago en mayo de 1886 que desembocó en actos violentos, entre ellos la muerte de varios policías. La matanza se achacó a la supuesta radicalidad del movimiento obrero y contribuyó a la desaparición de los Caballeros del Trabajo.

headright system (p. 69) Created in Virginia in 1618, it rewarded those who imported indentured laborers and settlers with land.

sistema de derechos de propiedad (pág. 69) Creado en Virginia en 1618, recompensaba con tierras a quienes importaban trabajadores contratados y colonos.

Hetch Hetchy Valley (p. 690) Site of a controversial dam built to supply San Francisco with water and power in the aftermath of the 1906 earthquake. The dam was built over the objections of preservationists such as John Muir.

***Hetch Hetchy Valley* (pág. 690)** Emplazamiento de una polémica presa construida para abastecer de agua y energía a San Francisco tras el terremoto de 1906. La presa se construyó a pesar de las objeciones de conservacionistas como John Muir.

holding company (p. 559) A form of business consolidation in which one company holds controlling stock in multiple corporations, thereby giving the holding company control over those corporations simultaneously.

***holding* (pág. 559)** Forma de consolidación empresarial en la que una empresa posee acciones de control de varias sociedades, lo que le confiere el control de esas sociedades simultáneamente.

Holocaust (p. 805) The Nazi regime's genocidal effort to eradicate Europe's Jewish population during World War II, which resulted in the death of six million Jews and millions of other "undesirables" — Slavs, Romani, homosexuals, the physically and mentally disabled, and communists.

Holocausto (pág. 805) Esfuerzo genocida del régimen nazi para erradicar a la población judía de Europa durante la Segunda Guerra Mundial, que se saldó con la muerte de seis millones de judíos y millones de otros "indeseables": eslavos, romaníes, homosexuales, discapacitados físicos y mentales y comunistas.

Homestead Act (p. 519) The Homestead Act of 1862 granted free 160-acre lots to western settlers, on condition that they live on and farm their land for at least five years, as an incentive for western migration.

Ley de Asentamientos Rurales (pág. 519) La Ley de Asentamientos Rurales de 1862 concedió lotes gratuitos de 160 acres a los colonos del oeste, con la condición de que vivieran y cultivaran sus tierras durante al menos cinco años, como incentivo para la migración hacia el oeste.

Homestead strike (p. 570) The violent 1892 strike by locked-out steelworkers at Andrew Carnegie's Homestead Steel Works. The strike collapsed after the National Guard took control of the mill from workers and a failed assassination attempt on Carnegie's plant manager, Henry Clay Frick.

Huelga de Homestead (pág. 570) La violenta huelga de 1892 de los trabajadores de la acería Homestead de Andrew Carnegie. La huelga fracasó después de que la Guardia Nacional arrebatara el control de la fábrica a los trabajadores y de un intento fallido de asesinato del director de la planta de Carnegie, Henry Clay Frick.

horizontal integration (p. 558) The use of mergers or acquisitions to create a company with a large enough market share to dominate an industry and control pricing. John D. Rockefeller's Standard Oil Company, a horizontally integrated corporation, controlled most oil refining in the United States and, therefore, much of the petroleum market.

integración horizontal (pág. 558) Utilización de fusiones o adquisiciones para crear una empresa con una cuota de mercado lo suficientemente grande como para dominar un sector y controlar los precios. La Standard Oil Company de John D. Rockefeller, una empresa integrada horizontalmente, controlaba la mayor parte del refinado de petróleo en Estados Unidos y, por tanto, gran parte del mercado del petróleo.

horticulture (p. 6) A form of agriculture in which people work small plots of land with simple tools.

horticultura (pág. 6) Forma de agricultura en la que la gente trabaja pequeñas parcelas de tierra con herramientas sencillas.

House of Burgesses (p. 70) Elected assembly within the General Assembly of Virginia formed in 1643 when the assembly was split into two houses. The second house in the assembly was called the Council of State and was appointed by British crown.

Cámara de los Burgueses (pág. 70) Asamblea electa dentro de la Asamblea General de Virginia formada en 1643 cuando la asamblea se dividió en dos cámaras. La segunda cámara de la asamblea se denominaba Consejo de Estado y era nombrada por corona británica.

House Un-American Activities Committee (HUAC) (p. 844) A committee in the U.S. House of Representatives established in 1938 to investigate and combat domestic communism. After World War II, HUAC conducted highly publicized investigations of communist influence in government and the entertainment industry.

Comité de Actividades Antiamericanas de la Cámara de Representantes (HUAC) (pág. 844) Comité de la Cámara de Representantes de Estados Unidos creado en 1938 para investigar y combatir el comunismo interno. Tras la Segunda Guerra Mundial, el HUAC llevó a cabo investigaciones muy publicitadas sobre la influencia comunista en el gobierno y la industria del entretenimiento.

Hudson River School (p. 338) A mid-nineteenth century American artistic movement in which artists painted romanticized landscapes, mainly of New York's Catskill and Adirondack Mountains.

Escuela del río Hudson (pág. 338) Movimiento artístico estadounidense de mediados del siglo XIX en el que los artistas pintaban paisajes románticos, principalmente de las montañas Catskill y Adirondack de Nueva York.

Huguenot (p. 57) A French Protestant who subscribed to the theology of John Calvin. Huguenots were persecuted by the French crown, which considered Catholicism the official faith of the kingdom.

Hugonote (pág. 57) Protestante francés que suscribía la teología de Juan Calvino. Los hugonotes fueron perseguidos por la corona francesa, que consideraba el catolicismo la fe oficial del reino.

Hull House (p. 672) The settlement house established by Jane Addams and Ellen Starr in Chicago in 1889. It served as a center of social reform, provided educational and social opportunities for working- class poor and immigrant women and their children, and inspired the creation of other settlement houses in major U.S. cities.

***Hull House* (pág. 672)** Casa de acogida creada por Jane Addams y Ellen Starr en Chicago en 1889. Sirvió como centro de reforma social, ofreció oportunidades educativas y sociales a mujeres pobres e inmigrantes de clase trabajadora y a sus hijos, e inspiró la creación de otros asentamientos en las principales ciudades de Estados Unidos.

Hurricane Katrina (p. 1017) A storm that hit the Gulf coast states of Louisiana, Mississippi, and Alabama in 2005. The hurricane caused major flooding in New Orleans after levees broke, resulting in approximately 1,800 deaths.

Huracán Katrina (pág. 1017) Tormenta que azotó los estados de Luisiana, Misisipi y Alabama, en la costa del Golfo, en 2005. El huracán provocó grandes inundaciones en Nueva Orleans tras la rotura de los diques, lo que causó aproximadamente 1,800 muertos.

I

Immigration Reform and Control Act (p. 982) A 1986 act legalizing long-term immigrants while also strengthening immigration restrictions. The law extended amnesty to most undocumented immigrants living in the United States continually since before 1982, and penalized employers who hired undocumented immigrants.

Ley de Reforma y Control de la Inmigración (pág. 982) Ley de 1986 que legaliza a los inmigrantes de larga duración al tiempo que refuerza las restricciones a la inmigración. La ley ampliaba la amnistía a la mayoría de los inmigrantes indocumentados que vivían en Estados Unidos de forma continuada desde antes de 1982, y penalizaba a los empresarios que contrataran a inmigrantes indocumentados.

imperialism (p. 78) A policy of expanding the border and increasing the global power of a nation, typically via military force.

imperialismo (pág. 78) Política de expansión de la frontera y aumento del poder global de una nación, normalmente mediante la fuerza militar.

impressment (p. 127) The forced enlistment of civilians into the army or navy. The impressment of residents of colonial seaports into the British navy was a major source of complaint in the eighteenth century.

imposición (pág. 127) Alistamiento forzoso de civiles en el ejército o la armada. El reclutamiento de residentes de los puertos coloniales en la armada británica fue una de las principales fuentes de quejas en el siglo XVIII.

Incas (p. 9) Andean people who built a complex bureaucratic empire ruled by aristocrats in the centuries before the arrival of the Spaniards amid the fertile land of the Andes Mountains along the Pacific coast. The Inca relied on a variety of domesticated animals and diverse farming techniques to survive. They reached the height of their power in the fifteenth century, controlling some 16 million people.

Incas (pág. 9) Pueblo andino que construyó un complejo imperio burocrático gobernado por aristócratas en los siglos anteriores a la llegada de los españoles en medio de las fértiles tierras de la cordillera de los Andes a lo largo de la costa del Pacífico. Para sobrevivir, los incas recurrían a diversos animales domesticados y a diversas técnicas agrícolas. Alcanzaron el apogeo de su poder en el siglo XV, controlando a unas 16 millones de personas.

indentured servitude (p. 66) Condition of being contracted to work for a set period of time without pay.

servidumbre por contrato (pág. 66) Condición de ser contratado para trabajar durante un periodo de tiempo determinado sin remuneración.

Indian Citizenship Act (p. 738) A 1924 act extending citizenship and the right to vote to all American Indians.

Ley de Ciudadanía Indígena (pág. 738) Ley de 1924 por la que se extiende la ciudadanía y el derecho de voto a todos los indios americanos.

Indian Removal Act (p. 321) An 1830 act, supported by President Andrew Jackson, by which American Indian peoples in the East were forced to exchange their lands for territory west of the Mississippi River. The act also voided all prior land treaties.

Ley de Traslado Forzoso de los Indios (pág. 321) Ley de 1830, apoyada por el presidente Andrew Jackson, por la que se obligó a los pueblos indígenas americanos del Este a cambiar sus tierras por territorio al oeste del río Misisipi. La ley también anulaba todos los tratados anteriores sobre tierras.

Indian Reorganization Act (IRA) (p. 772) An act from 1934 that ended the Dawes Act, authorized self-government for those living on reservations, extended tribal landholdings, and pledged to uphold native customs and languages.

Ley de Reorganización Indígena (IRA) (pág. 772) Ley de 1934 que ponía fin a la Ley Dawes, autorizaba el autogobierno de quienes vivían en reservas, ampliaba las tierras tribales y se comprometía a mantener las costumbres y lenguas nativas.

Indian Trade and Intercourse Act (p. 240) A 1790 act to regulate and maintain fair trade between American Indian and white settlers. The act was widely ignored, and relations between the two groups continued to worsen.

Indian Trade and Intercourse Act **(pág. 240)** Ley de 1790 para regular y mantener un comercio justo entre los indios americanos y los colonos blancos. El acto fue ampliamente ignorado, y las relaciones entre ambos grupos siguieron empeorando.

Industrial Workers of the World (IWW) (p. 572) A socialist labor organization that grew out of the activities of the Western Federation of Miners in the 1890s and was formed by Eugene V. Debs and other prominent labor leaders. Known as the "Wobblies," the IWW attempted to unite all skilled and unskilled workers in an effort to overthrow capitalism.

Trabajadores Industriales del Mundo (IWW) (pág. 572) Organización obrera socialista que surgió de las actividades de la *Western Federation of Miners* en la década de 1890 y fue creada por Eugene V. Debs y otros destacados líderes obreros. Conocidos como los "*Wobblies*", la IWW intentó unir a todos los trabajadores cualificados y no cualificados en un esfuerzo por derrocar al capitalismo.

inflation (p. 65) When prices rise because of a decline in the value of money because of its overabundance.

inflación (pág. 65) Cuando los precios suben debido a una disminución del valor del dinero por su sobreabundancia.

influenza pandemic (p. 718) A worldwide flu pandemic, also known as the "Spanish Flu," following the end of World War I. It killed an estimated 50 million individuals, including approximately 675,000 Americans.

pandemia de gripe (pág. 718) Pandemia mundial de gripe, también conocida como "gripe española", que siguió al final de la Primera Guerra Mundial. Se calcula que mató a 50 millones de personas, entre ellas unos 675,000 estadounidenses.

Inquisition (p. 16) A religious judicial institution established by Pope Gregory IX in 1232, designed to find and eliminate heretical beliefs that did not align with official Catholic practices. The Spanish Inquisition was first established in 1478.

Inquisición (pág. 16) Institución judicial religiosa establecida por el Papa Gregorio IX en 1232, diseñada para encontrar y eliminar creencias heréticas que no se alineaban con las prácticas católicas oficiales. La Inquisición española se estableció por primera vez en 1478.

interlocking directorate (p. 558) A system of corporate economic collusion accomplished by having members on multiple corporations' board of directors working in unison rather than in competition.

directorio entrelazado (pág. 558) Sistema de colusión económica empresarial que se consigue haciendo que los miembros de los consejos de administración de varias empresas trabajen al unísono en lugar de en competencia.

Intermediate Nuclear Forces Treaty (p. 992) A 1987 treaty between the United States and the Soviet Union that required the destruction of existing intermediate-range missiles and mandated on-site inspections to ensure both countries continued to adhere to the treaty terms.

Tratado sobre Fuerzas Nucleares Intermedias (pág. 992) Tratado de 1987 entre Estados Unidos y la Unión Soviética que exigía la destrucción de los misiles de alcance intermedio existentes y ordenaba inspecciones in situ para garantizar que ambos países siguieran cumpliendo los términos del tratado.

Internet (p. 1009) A worldwide, interconnected computer communication network. Originally started as a U.S. military communication system in the 1970s, the Internet has become the backbone of global commerce and communication.

Internet (pág. 1009) Red mundial de comunicación informática interconectada. Internet, que nació como un sistema de comunicación militar estadounidense en los años 70, se ha convertido en la espina dorsal del comercio y la comunicación mundiales.

internment (p. 794) The forced relocation of persons seen as a threat to national security to isolated camps. During World War II, nearly all people of Japanese descent living on the West Coast, approximately 120,000, were forced to quickly sell or abandon their possessions and relocate to detention camps.

internamiento (pág. 794) Reubicación forzosa en campos aislados de personas consideradas una amenaza para la seguridad nacional. Durante la Segunda Guerra Mundial, casi todas las personas de ascendencia japonesa que vivían en la costa oeste, aproximadamente 120,000, se vieron obligadas a vender o abandonar rápidamente sus posesiones y trasladarse a campos de detención.

Interstate Commerce Commission (ICC) (p. 620) Created by the Interstate Commerce Act in 1887, the ICC required railroads to make their rates public and could bring lawsuits to force shippers to reduce "unreasonable" fares. The ICC had limited success in the late 1800s due to court rulings and the influence of business interests.

Comisión de Comercio Interestatal (ICC) (pág. 620) Creada por la Ley de Comercio Interestatal en 1887, la ICC obligaba a los ferrocarriles a hacer públicas sus tarifas y podía interponer demandas para obligar a los cargadores a reducir las tarifas "no razonables". La ICC tuvo un éxito limitado a finales del siglo XIX debido a las sentencias judiciales y a la influencia de los intereses empresariales.

Intolerable Acts (p. 168) The name by which the colonial patriots referred to the Coercive Acts and the Quebec Act.

Leyes intolerables (pág. 168) Nombre con el que los patriotas coloniales se referían a las Leyes Coercitivas y a la Ley de Quebec.

invasion of Grenada (p. 988) A U.S. led invasion in coalition with six Caribbean governments that installed a pro-American government after a 1983 coup toppled the Caribbean island's leftist, Soviet-supported government.

invasión de Granada (pág. 988) Invasión encabezada por los Estados Unidos en coalición con seis gobiernos caribeños que instaló un gobierno proestadounidense después de que un golpe de estado en 1983 derrocara al gobierno izquierdista de la isla caribeña, apoyado por la Unión Soviética.

invasion of Panama (p. 995) The U.S. invasion of Panama in 1989, resulting in the capture, extradition, and incarceration of its leader, Manuel Noriega, after he rejected the results of a democratic election and claimed he was the "maximum leader" of Panama.

invasión de Panamá (pág. 995) Invasión estadounidense de Panamá en 1989, que tuvo como resultado la captura, extradición y encarcelamiento de su líder, Manuel Noriega, después de que éste rechazara los resultados de unas elecciones democráticas y se proclamara "líder máximo" de Panamá.

Iran Nuclear Agreement (p. 1025) Compliance agreement in 2015 between Iran and the United Nations Security Council, which placed restrictions on Iran's nuclear program in exchange for an easing of economic sanctions by partner nations. In 2018, President Trump withdrew the United States from the agreement.

Acuerdo nuclear con Irán (pág. 1025) Acuerdo de cumplimiento en 2015 entre Irán y el Consejo de Seguridad de las Naciones Unidas, que impuso restricciones al programa nuclear iraní a cambio de un alivio de las sanciones económicas por parte de las naciones asociadas. En 2018, el presidente Trump retiró a Estados Unidos del acuerdo.

Iran-Contra affair (p. 990) A scandal during the Reagan administration involving the secret funneling of funds from an illegal arms-for-hostages deal with Iran to the Nicaraguan Contras in the mid-1980s in violation of the Boland Amendment.

Escándalo Irán-Contra (pág. 990) Escándalo durante la administración Reagan relacionado con la canalización secreta de fondos procedentes de un acuerdo ilegal de armas por rehenes con Irán a los Contras nicaragüenses a mediados de la década de 1980, violando la Enmienda Boland.

Iraq War (p. 1017) The invasion and occupation of Iraq by the United States and its allies from 2003 to 2011. The administration of George W. Bush started the conflict in an effort to overthrow Iraq's dictator, Saddam Hussein, and destroy its suspected weapons of mass destruction, which no longer existed in significant quantities.

Guerra de Irak (pág. 1017) Invasión y ocupación de Irak por Estados Unidos y sus aliados de 2003 a 2011. El gobierno de George W. Bush inició el conflicto para derrocar al dictador iraquí Saddam Hussein y destruir sus supuestas armas de destrucción masiva, que ya no existían en cantidades significativas.

iron curtain (p. 832) A term coined by Winston Churchill in a 1946 speech to describe the ideological and political divide between the communist Soviet Union and the non-communist Western world.

telón de acero (pág. 832) Término acuñado por Winston Churchill en un discurso de 1946 para describir la división ideológica y política entre la Unión Soviética comunista y el mundo occidental no comunista.

Islamic State in Iraq and Syria (ISIS) (p. 1023) A jihadist terrorist group originally founded in 1999, which gained strength from the sectarian violence that followed the 2003 U.S. invasion of Iraq. The group captured territory in Iraq and Syria and claimed responsibility for terrorist attacks in Paris, France, San Bernardino, California, and Lebanon. However, by 2017, ISIS had been largely driven out of the territories it formerly occupied by American, Russian, Iraqi, Kurdish, and Syrian government forces.

Estado Islámico en Irak y Siria (ISIS) (pág. 1023) Grupo terrorista yihadista fundado originalmente en 1999, que cobró fuerza a raíz de la violencia sectaria que siguió a la invasión estadounidense de Irak en 2003. El grupo se hizo con territorio en Irak y Siria y reivindicó atentados terroristas en París (Francia), San Bernardino (California) y Líbano. Sin embargo, en 2017, el ISIS había sido expulsado en gran medida de los territorios que ocupaba anteriormente por las fuerzas gubernamentales estadounidenses, rusas, iraquíes y kurdas y sirias.

island-hopping (p. 800) This tactic, employed in the Pacific by U.S. forces in World War II, directed American and Allied forces to cut off and pass over some heavily fortified Japanese islands to speed their drive toward the Japanese mainland.

***island-hopping* (pág. 800)** Esta táctica, empleada en el Pacífico por las fuerzas estadounidenses en la Segunda Guerra Mundial, dirigía a las fuerzas estadounidenses y aliadas a cortar y pasar por encima de algunas islas japonesas fuertemente fortificadas para acelerar su avance hacia el territorio continental japonés.

isolationism (p. 778) The informal policy stemming from the belief that the United States should not become involved in the affairs of other nations. This mindset was especially popular following World War I.

aislacionismo (pág. 778) Política informal derivada de la creencia de que Estados Unidos no debe involucrarse en los asuntos de otras naciones. Esta mentalidad fue especialmente popular tras la Primera Guerra Mundial.

J

Jay Treaty (p. 221) Controversial 1796 treaty between the United States and Great Britain negotiated by John Jay that required British forces to withdraw from U.S. soil, required American repayment of debts to British firms, limited U.S. trade with the British West Indies, and permitted Britain to continue to stop neutral vessels.

Tratado de Jay (pág. 221) Polémico tratado de 1796 entre Estados Unidos y Gran Bretaña negociado por John Jay que exigía la retirada de las fuerzas británicas de suelo estadounidense, exigía el reembolso estadounidense de las deudas contraídas con empresas británicas, limitaba el comercio estadounidense con las Indias Occidentales británicas y permitía a Gran Bretaña seguir deteniendo buques neutrales.

Jim Crow law (p. 548) Any late-nineteenth-century state or local law that established legal segregation in the South. Many Jim Crow laws were enacted in the South, helping ensure the social and economic disfranchisement of southern Black people.

Ley Jim Crow (pág. 548) Cualquier ley estatal o local de finales del siglo XIX que establecía la segregación legal en el Sur. En el Sur se promulgaron muchas leyes Jim Crow, que contribuyeron a garantizar la privación de derechos sociales y económicos de los negros sureños.

jingoist (p. 658) An extremely patriotic supporter of the expansion and use of military power. Jingoists such as Theodore Roosevelt longed for a war to demonstrate America's strength and prove their own masculinity.

Jingoísmo (pág. 658) Partidario extremadamente patriótico de la expansión y el uso del poder militar. Jingoístas como Theodore Roosevelt ansiaban una guerra para demostrar la fuerza de Estados Unidos y probar su propia masculinidad.

John Brown's raid (p. 423) An attack on the federal arsenal at Harper's Ferry, Virginia, in 1859 led by John Brown, who hoped to inspire a slave uprising and arm enslaved Black Americans with the weapons taken from the arsenal. No uprising happened, and Brown was captured and eventually executed for treason.

Incursión de John Brown (pág. 423) Ataque al arsenal federal de Harper's Ferry, Virginia, en 1859, dirigido por John Brown, que esperaba inspirar un levantamiento de esclavos y armar a los negros estadounidenses esclavizados con las armas tomadas del arsenal. No se produjo ningún levantamiento y Brown fue capturado y finalmente ejecutado por traición.

joint-stock company (p. 66) A company in which large numbers of investors own stock. Such a company could quickly raise large amounts of money and share risk and reward equally among investors.

sociedad anónima (pág. 66) Sociedad en la que un gran número de inversores poseen acciones. Una empresa de este tipo podría recaudar rápidamente grandes cantidades de dinero y compartir el riesgo y la recompensa a partes iguales entre los inversores.

judicial review (p. 265) The Supreme Court's ability to rule on the constitutionality of cases at both the federal and state levels. The policy had the effect of solidifying a more federalist interpretation of the constitution and the powers of the government.

revisión judicial (pág. 265) La capacidad del Tribunal Supremo para pronunciarse sobre la constitucionalidad de los casos tanto a nivel federal como estatal. La política tuvo el efecto de consolidar una interpretación más federalista de la constitución y de los poderes del gobierno.

Judiciary Act (p. 264) Act passed in 1801 by the Federalist-controlled Congress to expand the federal court system by creating sixteen circuit (regional) courts, with new judges appointed for each, just before Democratic-Republicans took control of the presidency and Congress.

Ley Judicial (pág. 264) Ley aprobada en 1801 por el Congreso controlado por los federalistas para ampliar el sistema judicial federal mediante la creación de dieciséis tribunales de circuito (regionales), con nuevos jueces nombrados para cada uno, justo antes de que los demócratas-republicanos tomaran el control de la presidencia y el Congreso.

***The Jungle* (p. 692)** A novel by muckraker Upton Sinclair published in 1906 that portrayed the poor working and living conditions in the Chicago meatpacking district, as well as the unsanitary practices in the unregulated meat production industry, leading to public demand for government regulation of food safety.

***La Jungla* (pág. 692)** Novela del periodista Upton Sinclair publicada en 1906 que describe las malas condiciones de trabajo y de vida en el distrito de envasado de carne de Chicago, así como las prácticas insalubres en la industria de producción de carne no regulada, lo que llevó a la demanda pública de regulación gubernamental de la seguridad alimentaria.

K

Kansas-Nebraska Act (p. 416) A 1854 act creating the territories of Kansas and Nebraska out of what was then American Indian land. The act repealed the Missouri Compromise and allowed the issue of slavery to be settled by a popular referendum in each territory. Its passage led to widespread violence in Kansas and the demise of the Whig Party.

Ley Kansas-Nebraska (pág. 416) Ley de 1854 por la que se crean los territorios de Kansas y Nebraska a partir de lo que entonces eran tierras de los indios americanos. La ley revocaba el Compromiso de Missouri y permitía que la cuestión de la esclavitud se resolviera mediante referéndum popular en cada territorio. Su aprobación provocó una violencia generalizada en Kansas y la desaparición del Partido Whig.

Keating-Owen Act (p. 699) An act preventing the interstate sale of goods made by children under the age of 14, among other protections for children, passed in 1916. The Supreme Court ruled it unconstitutional in 1918.

Ley Keating-Owen (pág. 699) Ley que impide la venta interestatal de productos fabricados por menores de 14 años, entre otras protecciones para los niños, aprobada en 1916. El Tribunal Supremo la declaró inconstitucional en 1918.

Kellogg-Briand Pact (p. 778) An international arms-control agreement that outlawed war as an instrument of national policy following World War I. The policy reflected isolationist sentiments that opposed collective security agreements, and the pact proved unenforceable.

Pacto Kellogg-Briand (pág. 778) Acuerdo internacional de control de armamentos que prohibía la guerra como instrumento de política nacional tras la Primera Guerra Mundial. La política reflejaba sentimientos aislacionistas que se oponían a los acuerdos de seguridad colectiva, y el pacto resultó inaplicable.

Kent State Shootings (p. 896) The killing of four students and wounding of nine others by the National Guard during a 1970 Kent State campus protest about the U.S. invasion of Cambodia as part of the Vietnam War. The incident sparked further antiwar sentiment and large protests.

Tiroteo de Kent State (pág. 896) La Guardia Nacional mata a cuatro estudiantes y hiere a otros nueve durante una protesta en el campus de Kent State en 1970 contra la invasión estadounidense de Camboya como parte de la guerra de Vietnam. El incidente provocó un mayor sentimiento antibelicista y grandes protestas.

King George's War (p. 110) A war from 1739 to 1748 between France, Spain, and England fought in North America. King George's War secured Georgia for the English, although Louisbourg was ceded to the French in return.

Guerra del Rey Jorge (pág. 110) Guerra de 1739 a 1748 entre Francia, España e Inglaterra librada en Norteamérica. La Guerra del Rey Jorge aseguró Georgia para los ingleses, aunque a cambio se cedió Louisbourg a los franceses.

King William's War (p. 91) A war from 1689 to 1697 that began as a conflict over competing French and English interests on the European continent but soon spread to the American frontier. Both sides pulled American Indian allies into the war.

Guerra del Rey Guillermo (pág. 91) Guerra de 1689 a 1697 que comenzó como un conflicto por los intereses opuestos de franceses e ingleses en el continente europeo, pero que pronto se extendió a la frontera americana. Ambos bandos arrastraron a aliados indios americanos a la guerra.

Kitchen Debate (p. 879) A July 24, 1959, impromptu debate during the Cold War at the American National Exhibition in Moscow in front of a display of an American kitchen between Vice President Richard Nixon and the Soviet Union's First Secretary Nikita Khrushchev about the merits of capitalism and communism.

Debate de la cocina (Kitchen Debate) (pág. 879) Debate improvisado del 24 de julio de 1959, durante la Guerra Fría, en la Exposición Nacional Estadounidense de Moscú, ante una muestra de una cocina estadounidense, entre el vicepresidente Richard Nixon y el Primer Secretario de la Unión Soviética, Nikita Jrushchov, sobre los méritos del capitalismo y el comunismo.

Knights of Labor (p. 567) A labor union founded in 1869 that aimed to unite all workers under a single national union that would be powerful enough to challenge the power of corporate capitalists. Not limiting themselves to pay, benefits, and working conditions, the Knights of Labor became politically active and sought broader social changes.

Caballeros del Trabajo (pág. 567) Sindicato fundado en 1869 que pretendía unir a todos los trabajadores bajo un único sindicato nacional lo suficientemente poderoso como para desafiar el poder de los capitalistas corporativos. Sin limitarse a los salarios, las prestaciones y las condiciones de trabajo, los Caballeros del Trabajo se volvieron políticamente activos y buscaron cambios sociales más amplios.

Knights of the Ku Klux Klan (KKK) (p. 485) A secret organization formed in 1865 to restore white supremacy in the South. KKK members used threats and violence to terrorize freed Black people and their white allies in the South.

Caballeros del Ku Klux Klan (KKK) (pág. 485) Organización secreta creada en 1865 para restaurar la supremacía blanca en el Sur. Los miembros del KKK utilizaron las amenazas y la violencia para aterrorizar a los negros liberados y a sus aliados blancos en el Sur.

Korean War (p. 838) A three-year conflict (1950–1953) that began when communist North Korea, supported by the U.S.S.R. and China, launched an invasion of anticommunist South Korea, supported by the United States and the United Nations. Despite enormous destruction, large loss of civilian lives, and involvement of both U.S. and Chinese troops, fighting stopped with a cease-fire rather than a peace treaty at a similar border between the two countries.

Guerra de Corea (pág. 838) Conflicto de tres años (1950-1953) que comenzó cuando la comunista Corea del Norte, apoyada por la URSS y China, lanzó una invasión contra la anticomunista Corea del Sur, apoyada por Estados Unidos y las Naciones Unidas. A pesar de la enorme destrucción, la gran pérdida de vidas civiles y la participación de tropas estadounidenses y chinas, los combates cesaron con un alto el fuego en lugar de un tratado de paz en una frontera similar entre ambos países.

Kyoto Protocol (p. 1003) A 1998 agreement among many nations to curtail greenhouse gas emissions in an effort to curb global warming. The U.S. Senate refused to ratify it.

Protocolo de Kioto (pág. 1003) Acuerdo de 1998 entre muchos países para reducir las emisiones de gases de efecto invernadero con el fin de frenar el calentamiento global. El Senado estadounidense se negó a ratificarlo.

L

La Raza Unida (The United Race) (p. 923) A Chicano political party, formed in 1969, that advocated job opportunities for Chicanos, bilingual education, and Chicano cultural studies programs in universities. The party was especially influential in states with large Latino populations such as California and Texas.

La Raza Unida (pág. 923) Partido político chicano, formado en 1969, que abogaba por las oportunidades laborales para los chicanos, la educación bilingüe y los programas de estudios culturales chicanos en las universidades. El partido era especialmente influyente en estados con grandes poblaciones latinas, como California y Texas.

labor union (p. 567) An organized group of workers, who, through power in numbers and collective efforts, seek to secure and improve the pay, benefits, and working conditions from their employers. Union movements rose in prominence in the United States at the end of the nineteenth century, although they were countered by business and government efforts.

sindicato (pág. 567) Grupo organizado de trabajadores que, mediante el poder y los esfuerzos colectivos, tratan de obtener y mejorar el salario, las prestaciones y las condiciones de trabajo de sus empleadores. Los movimientos sindicales cobraron importancia en Estados Unidos a finales del siglo XIX, aunque fueron contrarrestados por esfuerzos empresariales y gubernamentales.

laissez-faire (p. 606) French for "let do." Advocates of laissez-faire believed the marketplace should be left to regulate itself, claiming that by allowing individuals to pursue their own self-interest without any government restraint or interference, the market would produce a natural balance.

***laissez-faire* (pág. 606)** Francés para "dejar hacer" Los defensores del *laissez-faire* creían que había que dejar que el mercado se regulara a sí mismo, alegando que permitiendo a los individuos perseguir su propio interés sin restricción o interferencia del gobierno, el mercado produciría un equilibrio natural.

land rush (p. 536) The 1889 government-sanctioned race to acquire land in formerly American Indian territory in Oklahoma.

fiebre de la tierra (pág. 536) Carrera de 1889 sancionada por el gobierno para adquirir tierras en Oklahoma, antiguo territorio indio americano.

League of Nations (p. 707) The international organization proposed by Woodrow Wilson after the end of World War I to ensure world peace and security in the future through mutual agreement. The United States failed to join the league because Wilson and his opponents in Congress could not work out a compromise.

Sociedad de Naciones (pág. 707) Organización internacional propuesta por Woodrow Wilson tras el final de la Primera Guerra Mundial para garantizar la paz y la seguridad mundiales en el futuro mediante el acuerdo mutuo. Estados Unidos no se unió a la liga porque Wilson y sus oponentes en el Congreso no pudieron llegar a un compromiso.

League of United Latin American Citizens (LULAC) (p. 793) A Mexican American group consisting largely of middle-class members that challenged racial discrimination and segregation in public accommodations, engaging in economic boycotts and litigation.

Liga de Ciudadanos Latinoamericanos Unidos (LULAC) (pág. 793) Grupo mexicano-estadounidense formado principalmente por miembros de clase media que desafiaba la discriminación racial y la segregación en los alojamientos públicos, participando en boicots económicos y litigios.

Leisler's Rebellion (p. 94) A class revolt in New York in 1689 led by merchant Jacob Leisler. Urban artisans and landless renters rebelled against new taxes and centralized rule.

Rebelión de Leisler (pág. 94) Revuelta de clases en Nueva York en 1689 liderada por el comerciante Jacob Leisler. Los artesanos urbanos y los arrendatarios sin tierra se rebelaron contra los nuevos impuestos y el gobierno centralizado.

Lend-Lease Act (p. 782) A law permitting the United States to lend or lease military equipment and other commodities to Great Britain and its allies. Its passage in March 1941 marked the end of U.S. neutrality before the United States entered World War II.

Ley de Préstamo y Arriendo (pág. 782) Ley que permite a Estados Unidos prestar o arrendar material militar y otros productos a Gran Bretaña y sus aliados. Su aprobación en marzo de 1941 marcó el fin de la neutralidad estadounidense antes de que Estados Unidos entrara en la Segunda Guerra Mundial.

Levittown (p. 856) The first mass-produced suburban housing developments, Levittowns were widely emulated by other developers and provided affordable housing for middle-class families, even as they used racially restrictive covenants to exclude Blacks.

Levittown (pág. 856) Los Levittown, las primeras urbanizaciones suburbanas de producción masiva, fueron ampliamente emulados por otros promotores y proporcionaron viviendas asequibles a familias de clase media, incluso cuando utilizaban pactos racialmente restrictivos para excluir a los negros.

libel (p. 128) A false written statement designed to damage the reputation of its subject.

difamación (pág. 128) Declaración escrita falsa destinada a dañar la reputación de su sujeto.

***Liberator* (p. 345)** Radical abolitionist newspaper launched by William Lloyd Garrison in 1831. Through the *Liberator*, Garrison called for immediate, uncompensated emancipation of enslaved people.

***Liberator* (pág. 345)** Periódico abolicionista radical fundado por William Lloyd Garrison en 1831. A través del *Liberator*, Garrison reclamó la emancipación inmediata y sin indemnización de los esclavizados.

Liberty Party (p. 350) An antislavery political party formed in 1840. The Liberty Party, along with the Free-Soil Party, helped place slavery at the center of national political debates.

Partido de la Libertad (pág. 350) Partido político antiesclavista formado en 1840. El Partido de la Libertad, junto con el Partido de Suelo Libre, contribuyó a situar la esclavitud en el centro de los debates políticos nacionales.

Lincoln-Douglas debates (p. 422) A series of debates between Abraham Lincoln and Stephen Douglas during the 1859 Illinois Senate race that mainly focused on the expansion of slavery in the territories.

Debates Lincoln-Douglas (pág. 422) Serie de debates entre Abraham Lincoln y Stephen Douglas durante las elecciones al Senado por Illinois de 1859, centrados principalmente en la expansión de la esclavitud en los territorios.

Little Rock Nine (p. 871) Nine students who, in 1957, became the first Black people to attend Central High School in Little Rock, Arkansas. Federal troops were required to overcome the resistance of white officials and the verbal and physical violence of white protesters.

Los nueve de Little Rock (pág. 871) Nueve estudiantes que, en 1957, se convirtieron en los primeros negros en asistir al Central High School de Little Rock, Arkansas. Se necesitaron tropas federales para vencer la resistencia de los funcionarios blancos y la violencia verbal y física de los manifestantes blancos.

Long Drive (p. 530) Cattle drive from the grazing lands of Texas to rail depots in Kansas. Once in Kansas, the cattle were shipped eastward to slaughterhouses in Chicago.

***Long Drive* (pág. 530)** Transporte de ganado desde las tierras de pastoreo de Texas hasta los depósitos ferroviarios de Kansas. Una vez en Kansas, el ganado era enviado hacia el este, a los mataderos de Chicago.

Lost Generation (p. 729) A term coined by the writer Gertrude Stein to describe the writers and artists disillusioned with the consumer culture of the 1920s.

Generación perdida (pág. 729) Término acuñado por la escritora Gertrude Stein para describir a los escritores y artistas desilusionados con la cultura consumista de los años veinte.

Louisiana Purchase (p. 261) The U.S. government's 1803 purchase from France of the vast territory stretching from the Mississippi River to the Rocky Mountains and from New Orleans to present-day Montana, doubling the size of the nation.

Compra de Luisiana (pág. 261) Compra del gobierno estadounidense a Francia en 1803 del vasto territorio que se extiende desde el río Misisipi hasta las Montañas Rocallosas y desde Nueva Orleans hasta la actual Montana, duplicando el tamaño de la nación.

loyalist (p. 178) A colonial supporter of the British during the American Revolution.

lealista (pág. 178) Colonial partidario de los británicos durante la Revolución Americana.

***Lusitania* (p. 703)** A British passenger liner struck by German submarine torpedoes off the coast of Ireland on May 15, 1915. The U-boat's torpedoes sank the ship, killing 1,198 people, including 128 Americans.

***Lusitania* (pág. 703)** Transatlántico británico de pasajeros alcanzado por torpedos submarinos alemanes frente a las costas de Irlanda el 15 de mayo de 1915. Los torpedos del submarino hundieron el barco, matando a 1,198 personas, entre ellas 128 estadounidenses.

M

Manhattan Project (p. 803) The code name for the secret program to develop an atomic bomb amid fears of a nuclear weapons project in Germany. The top-secret project was launched in 1942 and resulted in the first successful test of an atomic bomb in the New Mexico desert in July 1945.

Proyecto Manhattan (pág. 803) Nombre en clave del programa secreto para desarrollar una bomba atómica ante el temor de un proyecto de armamento nuclear en Alemania. El proyecto de alto secreto se puso en marcha en 1942 y dio lugar a la primera prueba con éxito de una bomba atómica en el desierto de Nuevo México en julio de 1945.

manifest destiny (p. 390) The term coined by John L. O'Sullivan in 1845 to describe what he saw as the nation's God-given right to expand its borders across the North American continent. Throughout the nineteenth century, the concept of manifest destiny was used to justify U.S. territorial and cultural expansion.

destino manifiesto (pág. 390) Término acuñado por John L. O' Sullivan en 1845 para describir lo que él consideraba el derecho de la nación, otorgado por Dios, a expandir sus fronteras por el continente norteamericano. A lo largo del siglo XIX, el concepto de destino manifiesto se utilizó para justificar la expansión territorial y cultural de Estados Unidos.

Mann Act (p. 681) An act passed in 1910 that banned the transportation of women across state lines for immoral purposes. In practice, this legislation was used to enforce codes of racial segregation and standards of moral behavior that enforced traditional social roles for women.

Ley Mann (pág. 681) Ley aprobada en 1910 que prohibía el transporte de mujeres a través de las fronteras estatales con fines inmorales. En la práctica, esta legislación se utilizó para imponer códigos de segregación racial y normas de comportamiento moral que reforzaban los roles sociales tradicionales de la mujer.

***Marbury v. Madison* (p. 264)** A Supreme Court decision in 1803 penned by Chief Justice John Marshall that established the authority of the Supreme Court to rule on the constitutionality of federal laws, also known as judicial review.

***Marbury contra Madison* (pág. 264)** Decisión del Tribunal Supremo en 1803, redactada por el presidente del Tribunal Supremo John Marshall, que estableció la autoridad del Tribunal Supremo para decidir sobre la constitucionalidad de las leyes federales, también conocida como revisión judicial.

March on Washington for Jobs and Freedom (p. 906) An August 28, 1963, rally by civil rights organizations in Washington, D.C., that brought increased national attention to the civil rights movement.

Marcha sobre Washington por el Trabajo y la Libertad (pág. 906) Manifestación celebrada el 28 de agosto de 1963 en Washington D.C. por organizaciones de derechos civiles, que atrajo una mayor atención nacional hacia el movimiento de derechos civiles.

market revolution (p. 287) Innovations in agriculture, industry, communication, and transportation in the early 1800s that increased efficiency and productivity and linked local producers to distant markets. It also solidified the connections of northern industry with western farms and southern plantations and eliminated independent shops and artisans in favor of factory mass production.

revolución del mercado (pág. 287) Innovaciones en la agricultura, la industria, las comunicaciones y el transporte a principios del siglo XIX que aumentaron la eficiencia y la productividad y pusieron en contacto a los productores locales con mercados lejanos. También consolidó las conexiones de la industria del norte con las granjas del oeste y las plantaciones del sur y eliminó las tiendas independientes y los artesanos en favor de la producción en masa de las fábricas.

Marshall Plan (p. 835) A package of economic aid developed by U.S. Secretary of State George Marshall. The plan helped to rebuild Western Europe physically and economically, buffering it from communist influence and serving U.S. political and economic interests in the process.

Plan Marshall (pág. 835) Paquete de ayuda económica desarrollado por el secretario de Estado estadounidense George Marshall. El plan ayudó a reconstruir física y económicamente Europa Occidental, protegiéndola de la influencia comunista y sirviendo a los intereses políticos y económicos de Estados Unidos en el proceso.

martial law (p. 444) The temporary suspension of civil law in favor of military rule during a war, rebellion, or major emergency.

ley marcial (pág. 444) Suspensión temporal de la ley civil en favor de un gobierno militar durante una guerra, rebelión o emergencia grave.

Maya (p. 8) A people and civilization that established large cities on the Yucatán peninsula with strong irrigation and agricultural techniques, astronomical knowledge, and mathematical and writing systems. While the Maya first emerged in 1500 B.C.E., they peaked between 300 and 800 C.E. before swiftly declining.

Maya (pág. 8) Pueblo y civilización que estableció grandes ciudades en la península de Yucatán con sólidas técnicas de irrigación y agricultura, conocimientos astronómicos y sistemas matemáticos y de escritura. Los mayas surgieron en el año 1500 a.C. y alcanzaron su máximo esplendor entre el 300 y el 800 a.C., antes de declinar rápidamente.

Mayflower Compact (p. 84) Written agreement created by the Pilgrims upon their arrival in Plymouth. It was the first written constitution adopted in North America.

Pacto del Mayflower (pág. 84) Acuerdo escrito creado por los peregrinos a su llegada a Plymouth. Fue la primera constitución escrita aprobada en Norteamérica.

McCarran Internal Security Act (p. 847) The 1950 act that required communist organizations to register with the federal government, established detention camps for radicals, and denied passports to American citizens who had communist affiliations.

Ley McCarran de Seguridad Interna (pág. 847) Ley de 1950 que obligaba a las organizaciones comunistas a registrarse ante el gobierno federal, establecía campos de detención para radicales y denegaba el pasaporte a los ciudadanos estadounidenses con afiliaciones comunistas.

McCarran-Walter Immigration Act (p. 925) The 1952 legislation that made it possible for Japanese noncitizens to become U.S. citizens. However, the act still maintained a race-based system of discriminatory national-origin quotas. Also known as the Immigration and Nationality Act of 1952.

Ley de Inmigración McCarran-Walter (pág. 925) La legislación de 1952 que hizo posible que los no ciudadanos japoneses se convirtieran en ciudadanos estadounidenses. Sin embargo, la ley seguía manteniendo un sistema basado en la raza de cuotas discriminatorias por origen nacional. También conocida como Ley de Inmigración y Nacionalidad de 1952.

McCarthyism (p. 848) A term used to describe the harassment and persecution of suspected communists and other political radicals during the Cold War. Named after Senator Joseph McCarthy, a prominent government figure who helped incite anticommunist panic in the early 1950s.

McCarthismo (pág. 848) Término utilizado para describir el acoso y la persecución de presuntos comunistas y otros radicales políticos durante la Guerra Fría. Debe su nombre al senador Joseph McCarthy, destacada figura gubernamental que contribuyó a incitar el pánico anticomunista a principios de los años cincuenta.

***McCulloch v. Maryland* (p. 264)** A Supreme Court decision in 1819 that reinforced the federal government's ability to employ an expansive understanding of the implied powers clause of the Constitution. The court ruled that the state of Maryland was unable to tax the Second Bank of the United States, allowing the federal government the right to establish a federal bank while rejecting the ability of states to tax it.

***McCulloch contra Maryland* (pág. 264)** Decisión del Tribunal Supremo de 1819 que reforzó la capacidad del gobierno federal para emplear una interpretación expansiva de la cláusula de poderes implícitos de la Constitución. El tribunal dictaminó que el estado de Maryland no podía gravar el Segundo Banco de los Estados Unidos, permitiendo al gobierno federal el derecho a establecer un banco federal y rechazando la capacidad de los estados para gravarlo.

Meat Inspection Act (p. 693) Regulatory standards passed by Congress in 1906, raising meatpacking standards through federal requirements. The act inadvertently hurt smaller businesses that could not afford new equipment to meet the new standards.

Ley de Inspección de la Carne (pág. 693) Normas reguladoras aprobadas por el Congreso en 1906, que elevan los estándares de envasado de la carne mediante requisitos federales. La ley perjudicó inadvertidamente a las empresas más pequeñas que no podían permitirse nuevos equipos para cumplir las nuevas normas.

Medicare Prescription Drug, Improvement, and Modernization Act (p. 1013) Also known as the Medicare Modernization Act, a 2003 act that dramatically expanded Medicare benefits and reduced costs associated with prescriptions.

Ley de Modernización y Mejoras en el Beneficio de Medicinas Recetadas de Medicare (pág. 1013) También conocida como Ley de Modernización de Medicare, una ley de 2003 que amplió drásticamente las prestaciones de Medicare y redujo los costes asociados a las recetas.

#MeToo movement (p. 1029) The social movement linking tens of millions of women through social media networks in opposition to sexual harassment and abuse.

movimiento #MeToo (pág. 1029) Movimiento social que une a decenas de millones de mujeres a través de las redes sociales en oposición al acoso y los abusos sexuales.

melting pot (p. 587) A popular metaphor for immigrant assimilation into American society. According to this ideal, despite their varied cultures and differences, all immigrants underwent a similar process of Americanization that produced a homogenous society.

crisol de culturas (pág. 587) Metáfora popular de la asimilación de los inmigrantes a la sociedad estadounidense. Según este ideal, a pesar de sus variadas culturas y diferencias, todos los inmigrantes se sometieron a un proceso similar de americanización que produjo una sociedad homogénea.

mercantilism (p. 100) An economic system centered on maintaining a favorable balance of trade for the home country, with more gold and silver flowing into that country than flowed out. Seventeenth- and eighteenth-century British colonial policy was largely shaped by mercantilism.

mercantilismo (pág. 100) Sistema económico centrado en mantener un equilibrio comercial favorable para el país de origen, con más oro y plata entrando en ese país de lo que salía. La política colonial británica de los siglos XVII y XVIII estuvo marcada en gran medida por el mercantilismo.

Metacom's War (p. 89) Also known as King Philip's War, a conflict between English settlers and an alliance of Native Americans led by the Wampanoag tribe, in 1675–1676. The settlers were the eventual victors, but fighting was fierce and casualties on both sides were high.

Guerra de Metacom (pág. 89) También conocida como Guerra del Rey Felipe, conflicto entre colonos ingleses y una alianza de nativos americanos liderada por la tribu Wampanoag, en 1675-1676. Los colonos fueron los vencedores finales, pero los combates fueron encarnizados y hubo muchas bajas en ambos bandos.

Mexican Revolution (p. 701) The 1911 revolution in Mexico, which led to nearly a decade of bloodshed and civil war.

Revolución Mexicana (pág. 701) La revolución de 1911 en México, que condujo a casi una década de derramamiento de sangre y guerra civil.

Mexican-American War (p. 395) The 1846–1848 war between the United States and Mexico, resulting in the transfer of approximately one million square miles of land to the United States, including the present-day states of California, Nevada, New Mexico, Arizona, Utah, and Texas. Debates over the status of slavery in these territories reignited the national debate about the expansion of slavery.

Guerra mexicano-estadounidense (pág. 395) Guerra de 1846-1848 entre Estados Unidos y México, que tuvo como resultado la transferencia de aproximadamente un millón de millas cuadradas de tierra a Estados Unidos, incluidos los actuales estados de California, Nevada, Nuevo México, Arizona, Utah y Texas. Los debates sobre el estatus de la esclavitud en estos territorios reavivaron el debate nacional sobre la expansión de la esclavitud.

Middle Passage (p. 114) The brutal transatlantic portion of the forced journey of enslaved Africans from Africa to the Americas. Historians estimate that millions of enslaved Africans died before they arrived in the Americas.

Pasaje Medio (pág. 114) La brutal parte transatlántica del viaje forzado de los africanos esclavizados desde África hasta América. Los historiadores calculan que millones de africanos esclavizados murieron antes de llegar a América.

Military Reconstruction Acts (p. 473) Three acts passed in 1867 dividing southern states into military districts and requiring those states to grant Black male suffrage and ratify the Fourteenth Amendment.

Leyes de Reconstrucción Militar (pág. 473) Tres leyes aprobadas en 1867 que dividen los estados del sur en distritos militares y obligan a esos estados a conceder el sufragio masculino a los negros y a ratificar la Decimocuarta Enmienda.

military-industrial complex (p. 877) The phrase used by President Eisenhower in his 1961 farewell address in which he warned the nation against the close relationship developing between the government and the defense industry and the threat this posed to American democracy.

complejo militar-industrial (pág. 877) Frase utilizada por el presidente Eisenhower en su discurso de despedida de 1961, en el que advertía a la nación contra la estrecha relación que se estaba desarrollando entre el gobierno y la industria de defensa y la amenaza que esto suponía para la democracia estadounidense.

minuteman (p. 172) A member of a colonial militia group, consisting mainly of farmers, trained for local defense in case of British attack. A "minuteman" supposedly could be ready on a minute's notice.

minuteman (pág. 172) Miembro de una milicia colonial, formada principalmente por granjeros, entrenado para la defensa local en caso de ataque británico. Un "minuteman" supuestamente podría estar listo en un minuto.

mission system (p. 40) Organizational system established by the Spanish in 1573 in which Catholic missionaries, rather than soldiers, directed all new settlements in the Americas.

sistema de misiones (pág. 40) Sistema organizativo establecido por los españoles en 1573 en el que los misioneros católicos, en lugar de los soldados, dirigían todos los nuevos asentamientos en América.

missionary (p. 15) A religious person who travels to foreign lands with the goal of converting those they meet to a new religion.

misionero (pág. 15) Persona religiosa que viaja a tierras extranjeras con el objetivo de convertir a los que encuentra a una nueva religión.

Mississippi Freedom Democratic Party (MFDP) (p. 908) A political party formed in 1964 to challenge the all-white state Democratic Party for seats at the 1964 Democratic presidential convention and run candidates for public office. Although unsuccessful in 1964, MFDP efforts led to subsequent reform of the Democratic Party and the seating of an interracial convention delegation from Mississippi in 1968.

Partido Demócrata por la Libertad de Misisipi (MFDP) (pág. 908) Partido político creado en 1964 para competir con el Partido Demócrata estatal, integrado exclusivamente por blancos, por los puestos en la convención presidencial demócrata de 1964 y presentar candidatos a cargos públicos. Aunque no tuvieron éxito en 1964, los esfuerzos del MFDP condujeron a la posterior reforma del Partido Demócrata y a la inclusión de una delegación interracial de Misisipi en la convención de 1968.

Missouri Compromise (p. 276) A compromise generated to maintain the balance of power between slave and free states in the U.S. Senate. The 1820 act established the southern border of Missouri as the boundary between future slave and free states admitted from the Louisiana Territory.

Compromiso de Misuri (pág. 276) Compromiso generado para mantener el equilibrio de poder entre los estados esclavos y libres en el Senado de Estados Unidos. La ley de 1820 estableció la frontera sur de Misuri como límite entre los futuros estados esclavos y libres admitidos desde el Territorio de Luisiana.

Modern Republicanism (p. 882) The political approach of President Dwight Eisenhower that tried to fit traditional Republican Party ideals of fiscal conservatism and individualism alongside more progressive social policies within the broad framework of the New Deal. In conjunction with his military record, the platform gave Eisenhower broad cross-party appeal.

Republicanismo moderno (pág. 882) Enfoque político del presidente Dwight Eisenhower que intentó encajar los ideales tradicionales del Partido Republicano de conservadurismo fiscal e individualismo junto con políticas sociales más progresistas dentro del amplio marco del New Deal. Junto con su historial militar, la plataforma dio a Eisenhower un amplio atractivo entre los partidos.

Monroe Doctrine (p. 284) The assertion by President James Monroe in 1823 that the Western Hemisphere was part of the U.S. sphere of influence and off limits to future European colonization. Although the United States lacked the power to back up this claim, it signaled an intention to challenge Europeans for authority in the Americas.

Doctrina Monroe (pág. 284) Afirmación del presidente James Monroe en 1823 de que el hemisferio occidental formaba parte de la esfera de influencia de Estados Unidos y estaba vedado a futuras colonizaciones europeas. Aunque Estados Unidos carecía de poder para respaldar esta reivindicación, señalaba su intención de disputar a los europeos la autoridad en América.

Montgomery bus boycott (p. 870) A thirteen-month bus boycott in Montgomery, Alabama, that began in December 1955 with the arrest of Rosa Parks for refusing to give up her seat to a white man. The successful yearlong protest catapulted Martin Luther King Jr., a local pastor, into national prominence as a civil rights leader.

Boicot a los autobuses de Montgomery (pág. 870) Boicot a los autobuses de Montgomery, Alabama, que duró trece meses y comenzó en diciembre de 1955 con la detención de Rosa Parks por negarse a ceder su asiento a un hombre blanco. El éxito de la protesta, que duró un año, catapultó a Martin Luther King Jr., un pastor local, a la fama nacional como líder de los derechos civiles.

Mormon (p. 540) A follower of Joseph Smith and Brigham Young who migrated to Utah in the 1840s to escape religious persecution; the religious denomination is also known as the Church of Jesus Christ of Latter-Day Saints (LDS).

Mormón (pág. 540) Seguidor de Joseph Smith y Brigham Young que emigró a Utah en la década de 1840 huyendo de la persecución religiosa; la confesión religiosa también se conoce como Iglesia de Jesucristo de los Santos de los Últimos Días (IJSUD).

muckrakers (p. 671) Investigative journalists during the late nineteenth and early twentieth centuries who specialized in exposing corruption, scandal, and vice. Muckrakers helped build public support for progressive causes.

Muckrakers (pág. 671) Periodistas de investigación de finales del siglo XIX y principios del XX especializados en denunciar la corrupción, el escándalo y el vicio. Los Muckrakers ayudaron a conseguir apoyo público para las causas progresistas.

mujahideen (p. 946) Religiously inspired Afghan rebels who resisted the Soviet invasion of Afghanistan in 1979.

Muyahidines (pág. 946) Rebeldes afganos de inspiración religiosa que resistieron a la invasión soviética de Afganistán en 1979.

Muller v. Oregon **(p. 674)** U.S. Supreme Court ruling in 1908 that upheld an Oregon law establishing a ten-hour workday for women.

Muller contra Oregón **(pág. 674)** Sentencia del Tribunal Supremo de EE.UU. en 1908 que confirmó una ley de Oregón que establecía una jornada laboral de diez horas para las mujeres.

multiplier effect (p. 288) The diverse changes spurred by a single invention, including other inventions it spawns and the broader economic, social, and political transformations it fuels.

efecto multiplicador (pág. 288) Cambios de diversa índole impulsados por una sola invención, incluidas otras invenciones que engendra y las transformaciones económicas, sociales y políticas más amplias que alimenta.

Munich Accord (p. 779) The 1938 agreement between Germany, Great Britain, and France that allowed Germany to annex the Sudetenland, a western region of Czechoslovakia, in exchange for Germany's promise not to acquire any more land afterwards. However, the following year, German troops occupied the rest of Czechoslovakia.

Acuerdo de Múnich (pág. 779) Acuerdo de 1938 entre Alemania, Gran Bretaña y Francia que permitió a Alemania anexionarse los Sudetes, una región occidental de Checoslovaquia, a cambio de la promesa de Alemania de no adquirir más tierras posteriormente. Sin embargo, al año siguiente, las tropas alemanas ocuparon el resto de Checoslovaquia.

mutual-aid society (p. 295) An organization formed by laborers to care for members who were unemployed, ill, or injured and unable to work. Such organizations required dues from their members, and these dues were used to care for those who could no longer work and for their families. Before unemployment insurance and health care, mutual-aid societies helped workers survive changes in the new industrial economy.

Sociedad de socorro mutuo (pág. 295) Organización formada por trabajadores para atender a los miembros desempleados, enfermos o lesionados que no podían trabajar. Estas organizaciones exigían cuotas a sus miembros, que se utilizaban para atender a quienes ya no podían trabajar y a sus familias. Antes del seguro de desempleo y la asistencia sanitaria, las mutualidades ayudaban a los trabajadores a sobrevivir a los cambios de la nueva economía industrial.

mutually assured destruction (MAD) (p. 878) The Cold War defense strategy adopted by the United States and the U.S.S.R. to deter a nuclear attack from the other country by threatening to retaliate with a massive nuclear strike in response. MAD fueled the arms race as both sides worked to convince the other of their ongoing ability to retaliate if attacked.

Destrucción mutua asegurada (MAD) (pág. 878) Estrategia de defensa de la Guerra Fría adoptada por Estados Unidos y la URSS para disuadir un ataque nuclear del otro país amenazando con responder con un ataque nuclear masivo. La MAD alimentó la carrera armamentística, ya que ambas partes se esforzaban por convencer a la otra de su capacidad para tomar represalias en caso de ataque.

My Lai massacre (p. 893) A massacre by U.S. troops on March 16, 1968, of nearly 500 elderly, women, and children in the South Vietnam area of My Lai. The massacre shocked the American public, diminished support for the Vietnam War among many Americans, and fueled growing anti-U.S. sentiment worldwide.

Masacre de My Lai (pág. 893) Masacre perpetrada por tropas estadounidenses el 16 de marzo de 1968 contra casi 500 ancianos, mujeres y niños en la zona de My Lai, en Vietnam del Sur. La masacre conmocionó a la opinión pública estadounidense, disminuyó el apoyo a la guerra de Vietnam entre muchos estadounidenses y avivó el creciente sentimiento antiestadounidense en todo el mundo.

N

Nat Turner's rebellion (p. 360) A slave uprising in Virginia led by Nat Turner in 1831. Turner's rebellion generated panic among white Southerners, leading to tighter control of Black people through the passage of stricter slave codes in southern states.

Rebelión de Nat Turner (pág. 360) Levantamiento de esclavos en Virginia liderado por Nat Turner en 1831. La rebelión de Turner generó pánico entre los sureños blancos, lo que condujo a un control más estricto de los negros mediante la aprobación de códigos esclavistas más estrictos en los estados sureños.

National American Woman Suffrage Association (p. 674) A national organization created in 1890 that contributed to the ratification of the Nineteenth Amendment in 1920, which guaranteed women's right to vote in the United States.

Asociación Nacional Estadounidense para el Sufragio de la Mujer (pág. 674) Organización nacional creada en 1890 que contribuyó a la ratificación de la Decimonovena Enmienda de 1920, la cual garantizó el derecho al voto de las mujeres en los Estados Unidos.

National Association for the Advancement of Colored People (NAACP) (p. 679) An organization founded by W. E. B. Du Bois, Ida B. Wells, Jane Addams, and others in 1909 to fight for racial equality. The NAACP strategy focused on fighting discrimination through the courts, and it became the leading civil rights organization for Black Americans in the twentieth century.

Asociación Nacional para el Progreso de las Personas de Color (NAACP) (pág. 679) Organización fundada por W. E. B. Du Bois, Ida B. Wells, Jane Addams y otros en 1909 para luchar por la igualdad racial. La estrategia de la NAACP se centró en luchar contra la discriminación a través de los tribunales, y se convirtió en la principal organización de derechos civiles de los negros estadounidenses en el siglo XX.

National Association of Colored Women (NACW) (p. 673) An organization that became the largest federation of Black local women's clubs in 1896. The group was designed to relieve suffering among poor Black people, defend Black women, and promote the interests of all Black people.

Asociación Nacional de Mujeres de Color (NACW) (pág. 673) Organización que se convirtió en la mayor federación de clubes locales de mujeres negras en 1896. El grupo fue concebido para aliviar el sufrimiento de los negros pobres, defender a las mujeres negras y promover los intereses de todos los negros.

National Defense Education Act (p. 883) A 1958 Cold War era act in response to the Soviet launch of *Sputnik*, which provided aid for instruction in science, math, and foreign language, and grants and fellowships for college students.

Ley de Educación para la Defensa Nacional (pág. 883) Ley de 1958 de la época de la Guerra Fría en respuesta al lanzamiento soviético *del Sputnik*, que proporcionaba ayudas para la enseñanza de ciencias, matemáticas y lenguas extranjeras, así como becas para estudiantes universitarios.

National Energy Act (p. 935) Legislation signed into law by President Jimmy Carter in 1978, which set gas emissions standards for automobiles and provided incentives for installing alternative energy systems, such as wind and solar power.

Ley Nacional de la Energía (pág. 935) Legislación promulgada por el presidente Jimmy Carter en 1978, que establecía normas de emisión de gases para los automóviles e incentivaba la instalación de sistemas de energía alternativa, como la eólica y la solar.

National Industrial Recovery Act (NIRA) (p. 762) The 1933 New Deal legislation establishing the National Recovery Administration to work with businesses and the public to regulate prices, wages, and production.

Ley de Recuperación Industrial Nacional (National Industrial Recovery Act, NIRA) (pág. 762) Legislación del New Deal de 1933 por la que se creaba la Administración de Recuperación Nacional para trabajar con las empresas y el público con el fin de regular los precios, los salarios y la producción.

National Interstate and Defense Highway Act (p. 883) An act passed in 1956 that provided federal funds for the construction of a national highway system to link major cities and facilitate future wartime mobilization. As the largest public works project in American history, the act spurred economic growth, suburbanization, and the automobile as the main method of transportation for most Americans.

Ley Nacional de Carreteras Interestatales y de Defensa (National Interstate and Defense Highway Act) (pág. 883) Ley aprobada en 1956 que proporcionaba fondos federales para la construcción de un sistema nacional de carreteras que uniera las principales ciudades y facilitara la futura movilización en tiempos de guerra. La ley, el mayor proyecto de obras públicas de la historia de Estados Unidos, impulsó el crecimiento económico, la suburbanización y el automóvil como principal medio de transporte para la mayoría de los estadounidenses.

National Labor Relations Act (p. 769) A 1935 act (also known as the Wagner Act) that created the National Labor Relations Board (NLRB). The NLRB protected workers' right to organize labor unions without business owner interference and engage in collective bargaining.

Ley Nacional de Relaciones Laborales (pág. 769) Ley de 1935 (también conocida como Ley Wagner) por la que se creó la Junta Nacional de Relaciones Laborales (NLRB). La NLRB protegió el derecho de los trabajadores a organizar sindicatos sin interferencias de los propietarios de las empresas y a participar en negociaciones colectivas.

National Labor Relations Board (NLRB) (p. 769) The agency created by the 1935 National Labor Relations Act (also known as the Wagner Act). The NLRB protected workers' right to organize labor unions without business owner interference and engage in collective bargaining.

Junta Nacional de Relaciones Laborales (NLRB) (pág. 769) Agencia creada por la Ley Nacional de Relaciones Laborales de 1935 (también conocida como Ley Wagner). La NLRB protegió el derecho de los trabajadores a organizar sindicatos sin interferencias de los propietarios de las empresas y a participar en negociaciones colectivas.

National Organization for Women (NOW) (p. 918) A feminist organization formed in 1966 by Betty Friedan, Gloria Steinem, and other like-minded activists demanding an end to sexual discrimination and full equality between the sexes.

Organización Nacional de Mujeres (NOW) (pág. 918) Organización feminista creada en 1966 por Betty Friedan, Gloria Steinem y otras activistas afines que exigen el fin de la discriminación sexual y la plena igualdad entre sexos.

National Origins Act (p. 736) An act passed in 1924 establishing immigration quotas by national origin. It was intended to severely limit immigration from southern and eastern Europe as well as halt all immigration from East Asia.

Ley de Orígenes Nacionales (pág. 736) Ley aprobada en 1924 que establece cuotas de inmigración por origen nacional. Su objetivo era limitar drásticamente la inmigración procedente del sur y el este de Europa, así como detener toda inmigración procedente del este de Asia.

National Recovery Administration (NRA) (p. 762) A New Deal agency established in 1933 to create codes to regulate production, prices, wages, hours, and collective bargaining. The NRA failed to produce the intended results and was eventually ruled unconstitutional.

Administración Nacional de Recuperación (NRA) (pág. 762) Agencia del New Deal creada en 1933 para crear códigos que regulasen la producción, los precios, los salarios, los horarios y la negociación colectiva. La NRA no obtuvo los resultados esperados y acabó siendo declarada inconstitucional.

National Republican Party (p. 311) One of two parties that resulted from the split of the Democratic-Republicans in the early 1820s. Henry Clay and John Quincy Adams emerged as leaders of the National Republicans.

Partido Nacional Republicano (pág. 311) Uno de los dos partidos resultantes de la escisión de los demócratas-republicanos a principios de la década de 1820. Henry Clay y John Quincy Adams surgieron como líderes de los Republicanos Nacionales.

National Rifle Association (p. 1005) A pro-gun rights organization founded in 1871.

Asociación Nacional del Rifle (pág. 1005) Organización pro-derechos de las armas fundada en 1871.

National Road (p. 266) A road built using federal funds that ran from western Maryland through southwestern Pennsylvania to Wheeling, West Virginia, also called the Cumberland Road. Completed in 1818, it was part of a larger effort to improve infrastructure. The road bridged the Potomac and Ohio Rivers and accelerated western settlement and commercial expansion.

Carretera nacional (pág. 266) Carretera construida con fondos federales que discurría desde el oeste de Maryland a través del suroeste de Pensilvania hasta Wheeling, Virginia Occidental, también llamada Cumberland Road. Terminado en 1818, formaba parte de un esfuerzo mayor por mejorar las infraestructuras. La carretera tendió puentes entre los ríos Potomac y Ohio y aceleró la colonización y la expansión comercial del oeste.

National Security Council (NSC) (p. 836) The council created by the 1947 National Security Act to advise the president on military and foreign affairs. The NSC consists of the national security adviser and the secretaries of state, defense, the army, the navy, and the air force.

Consejo de Seguridad Nacional (NSC) (pág. 836) Consejo creado por la Ley de Seguridad Nacional de 1947 para asesorar al presidente en asuntos milita res y exteriores. El NSC está formado por el consejero de seguridad nacional y los secretarios de Estado, Defensa, Ejército, Armada y Ejército del Aire.

National War Labor Board (NWLB) (p. 712) Government agency created in 1918 to settle labor disputes. The NWLB consisted of representatives from unions, corporations, and the public.

Junta Nacional de Relaciones Laborales (NWLB) (pág. 712) Organismo gubernamental creado en 1918 para resolver conflictos laborales. El NWLB estaba formado por representantes de sindicatos, empresas y ciudadanos.

National Woman Suffrage Association (p. 475) Organized in 1869 in the aftermath of the Civil War, the National Woman Suffrage Association sought voting rights for women. In 1890, the American Woman Suffrage Association and the National Woman Suffrage Association combined to form the National American Woman Suffrage Association.

Asociación Nacional pro Sufragio de la Mujer (pág. 475) Fundada en 1869 en el período posterior a la Guerra Civil, la Asociación Nacional para el Sufragio de la Mujer buscó los derechos de voto para las mujeres. En 1890, la Asociación Estadounidense para el Sufragio de la Mujer y la Asociación Nacional para el Sufragio de la Mujer se unieron para formar la Asociación Nacional Estadounidense para el Sufragio de la Mujer.

National Woman's Party (p. 674) A political organization created in 1916, headed by Alice Paul and Lucy Burns. The group promoted more militant tactics than the National American Woman Suffrage Association. They picketed the White House, promoted hunger strikes, and engaged in mass protests in their campaign for women's suffrage as well as an unsuccessful push for the passage of the Equal Rights Amendment of 1923.

Partido Nacional de la Mujer (pág. 674) Organización política creada en 1916, encabezada por Alice Paul y Lucy Burns. El grupo promovía tácticas más militantes que la National American Woman Suffrage Association. Formaron piquetes en la Casa Blanca, promovieron huelgas de hambre y participaron en protestas masivas en su campaña por el sufragio femenino, así como en una infructuosa campaña por la aprobación de la Enmienda por la Igualdad de Derechos de 1923.

nativism (p. 587) The belief that religious or culturally diverse foreigners pose a serious danger to the nation's society and culture. Nativist sentiment rose in the United States as the size and diversity of the immigrant population grew in the nineteenth century.

nativismo (pág. 587) Creencia de que los extranjeros religiosos o culturalmente diversos suponen un grave peligro para la sociedad y la cultura de la nación. El sentimiento nativista aumentó en Estados Unidos a medida que crecían el tamaño y la diversidad de la población inmigrante en el siglo XIX.

nativist (p. 342) An anti-immigrant American involved in public campaigns against foreigners in the 1840s. Nativism emerged as a response to increased immigration to the United States in the 1830s and 1840s, particularly the large influx of Catholic immigrants.

nativista (pág. 342) Estadounidense antiinmigrante que participó en campañas públicas contra los extranjeros en la década de 1840. El nativismo surgió como respuesta al aumento de la inmigración a Estados Unidos en las décadas de 1830 y 1840, en particular a la gran afluencia de inmigrantes católicos.

naturalization (p. 210) The process by which a noncitizen becomes a citizen of a nation.

naturalización (pág. 210) Proceso por el que un no ciudadano se convierte en ciudadano de una nación.

Naturalization Act (p. 226) An act passed in 1798 by the Federalist-controlled Congress that raised the residency requirement for citizenship from five to fourteen years. It was designed to delay the naturalization of immigrants who largely voted Democratic-Republican. The act included only free white persons, meaning that it excluded indentured servants, American Indians, free Black persons, and enslaved persons from gaining citizenship.

Ley de Naturalización (pág. 226) Ley aprobada en 1798 por el Congreso, controlado por los federalistas, que elevaba de cinco a catorce años el requisito de residencia para obtener la ciudadanía. Se diseñó para retrasar la naturalización de inmigrantes que votaban mayoritariamente a los demócratas-republicanos. La ley sólo incluía a los blancos libres, lo que significa que excluía de la ciudadanía a los sirvientes contratados, los indios americanos, los negros libres y los esclavizados.

Navigation Acts (p. 101) Acts passed by Parliament in the 1650s and 1660s that prohibited smuggling, established guidelines for legal commerce, and set duties on trade items.

Leyes de navegación (pág. 101) Leyes aprobadas por el Parlamento en las décadas de 1650 y 1660 que prohibían el contrabando, establecían directrices para el comercio legal y fijaban derechos sobre los artículos comerciales.

Nazism (p. 779) Ideology of the National Socialist German Workers' Party, which included virulent antisemitism, militarism, and autocratic state restriction of civil liberties. Adolf Hitler was the sole leader of the party when this ideology ruled Germany from 1933 to 1945. Nazism was the main cause of World War II in Europe, and the Nazis organized and carried out the Holocaust during the war.

Nazismo (pág. 779) Ideología del Partido Nacionalsocialista Obrero Alemán, que incluía un virulento antisemitismo, militarismo y una restricción estatal autocrática de las libertades civiles. Adolf Hitler fue el único líder del partido cuando esta ideología gobernó Alemania de 1933 a 1945. El nazismo fue la principal causa de la Segunda Guerra Mundial en Europa, y los nazis organizaron y llevaron a cabo el Holocausto durante la guerra.

neoconservative (p. 949) A disillusioned liberal who condemned the Great Society programs they had originally supported. Neoconservatives were particularly concerned about affirmative action programs, the domination of campus activism by New Left radicals, and left-wing criticism of the use of American military and economic might to advance U.S. interests overseas.

neoconservador (pág. 949) Liberal desilusionado que condena los programas de la Gran Sociedad que había apoyado en un principio. Los neoconservadores estaban especialmente preocupados por los programas de discriminación positiva, el dominio del activismo universitario por parte de los radicales de la Nueva Izquierda y las críticas de la izquierda al uso del poderío militar y económico estadounidense para promover los intereses de Estados Unidos en el extranjero.

Neutrality Acts (p. 779) Legislation passed between 1935 and 1937 to make it more difficult for the United States to become entangled in overseas conflicts. The Neutrality Acts reflected the strength of isolationist sentiment in 1930s America.

Leyes de Neutralidad (pág. 779) Legislación aprobada entre 1935 y 1937 para dificultar que Estados Unidos se viera envuelto en conflictos en el extranjero. Las Leyes de Neutralidad reflejaban la fuerza del sentimiento aislacionista en la América de los años treinta.

Neutrality Proclamation (p. 221) A 1793 proclamation declaring U.S. neutrality in any conflicts between other nations, including France and Great Britain, despite French aid in the Revolutionary War effort. The proclamation also warned American citizens against favoring either party. Britain largely ignored U.S. neutrality and seized American merchant vessels heading for France.

Proclamación de Neutralidad (pág. 221) Proclamación de 1793 que declara la neutralidad de Estados Unidos en cualquier conflicto entre otras naciones, incluidas Francia y Gran Bretaña, a pesar de la ayuda francesa en la Guerra de la Independencia. La proclamación también advertía a los ciudadanos estadounidenses que no favorecieran a ninguno de los dos partidos. Gran Bretaña ignoró en gran medida la neutralidad de Estados Unidos y apresó los buques mercantes estadounidenses que se dirigían a Francia.

New Deal (p. 760) The policies and programs that Franklin Roosevelt initiated to combat the Great Depression. The New Deal represented a dramatic expansion of the role of government in American society, and its provisions were often categorized as either relief, recovery, or reform efforts (the 3 Rs).

New Deal (Nuevo Trato) (pág. 760) Las políticas y programas que Franklin Roosevelt inició para combatir la Gran Depresión. El New Deal representó una expansión espectacular del papel del gobierno en la sociedad estadounidense, y sus disposiciones se clasificaron a menudo como esfuerzos de ayuda, recuperación o reforma (las 3 erres, en inglés).

New Freedom (p. 696) Term used by Woodrow Wilson to describe his limited-government, progressive agenda. Wilson's New Freedom was offered as an alternative to Theodore Roosevelt's New Nationalism.

Nueva Libertad (pág. 696) Término utilizado por Woodrow Wilson para describir su programa progresista de gobierno limitado. La Nueva Libertad de Wilson se ofrecía como alternativa al Nuevo Nacionalismo de Theodore Roosevelt.

New Frontier (p. 897) President John F. Kennedy's domestic agenda. Kennedy promised to battle "tyranny, poverty, disease, and war," but, lacking strong majorities in Congress, he achieved relatively modest results.

Nueva Frontera (pág. 897) La agenda nacional del presidente John F. Kennedy. Kennedy prometió luchar contra "la tiranía, la pobreza, la enfermedad y la guerra", pero, al carecer de mayorías fuertes en el Congreso, consiguió resultados relativamente modestos.

New Jersey Plan (p. 210) A proposal at the Constitutional Convention endorsed by small states for a one-house legislature with each state having an equal vote.

Plan de Nueva Jersey (pág. 210) Propuesta presentada en la Convención Constitucional, respaldada por los estados pequeños, para crear una asamblea legislativa unicameral en la que cada estado tenga el mismo número de votos.

New Light clergy (p. 124) Colonial religious leaders who called for religious revivals and emphasized the emotional aspects of spiritual commitment. The New Lights were leaders in the First Great Awakening.

El clero de la Nueva Luz (pág. 124) Líderes religiosos coloniales que abogaban por un renacimiento religioso y hacían hincapié en los aspectos emocionales del compromiso espiritual. Las Nuevas Luces fueron líderes del Primer Gran Despertar.

New Nationalism (p. 695) The agenda put forward by Theodore Roosevelt in his 1912 presidential campaign. Roosevelt called for increased regulation of large corporations, a more active role for the president, and the extension of social justice using the power of the federal government.	**Nuevo Nacionalismo (pág. 695)** Programa presentado por Theodore Roosevelt en su campaña presidencial de 1912. Roosevelt abogó por una mayor regulación de las grandes corporaciones, un papel más activo del presidente y la extensión de la justicia social utilizando el poder del gobierno federal.
New Negro (p. 731) The 1920s term for the second generation of Black Americans born after emancipation, who stood up for their rights.	***New Negro* (pág. 731)** Término utilizado en los años veinte para referirse a la segunda generación de negros estadounidenses nacidos después de la emancipación, que defendieron sus derechos.
New Right (p. 948) A conservative coalition of old and new conservatives, as well as disaffected Democrats, who supported strong U.S. national-security initiatives, low taxes, and reduced government intervention in the economy.	**Nueva Derecha (pág. 948)** Coalición conservadora de viejos y nuevos conservadores, así como de demócratas descontentos, que apoyaban iniciativas fuertes de seguridad nacional estadounidense, impuestos bajos y una menor intervención del gobierno en la economía.
"New South" (p. 545) Term popularized in the 1880s by newspaper editor Henry Grady, a proponent of the modernization of the southern economy in order for a distinctively industrial "New South" to emerge.	**"Nuevo Sur" (pág. 545)** Término popularizado en la década de 1880 por el editor de periódicos Henry Grady, partidario de la modernización de la economía sureña para que surgiera un "Nuevo Sur" distintivamente industrial.
new woman (p. 729) The 1920s term for the modern, liberated woman. The new woman, popularized in movies and magazines, defied traditional morality.	**nueva mujer (pág. 729)** Término de los años veinte para referirse a la mujer moderna y liberada. La nueva mujer, popularizada en películas y revistas, desafiaba la moral tradicional.
Nineteenth Amendment (p. 677) The amendment to the Constitution granting women the right to vote, passed in 1919 and ratified into law in 1920.	**Decimonovena Enmienda (pág. 677)** La enmienda a la Constitución que concede a las mujeres el derecho al voto, aprobada en 1919 y ratificada como ley en 1920.
No Child Left Behind (NCLB) (p. 1013) Legislation that aimed to raise student educational outcomes by requiring states to adopt standards-based instruction and standardized assessments to receive federal school funding. The bipartisan 2001 act significantly expanded the role of the federal government in education in an effort to close the achievement gap of underprivileged students. The law was replaced in 2015 after widespread pushback against its testing provisions.	**Que Ningún Niño se Quede Atrás (NCLB) (pág. 1013)** Legislación que pretendía mejorar los resultados educativos de los alumnos exigiendo a los estados que adoptaran una enseñanza basada en estándares y evaluaciones estandarizadas para recibir financiación federal para las escuelas. La ley bipartidista de 2001 amplió significativamente el papel del gobierno federal en la educación en un esfuerzo por cerrar la brecha de rendimiento de los estudiantes desfavorecidos. La ley fue sustituida en 2015 tras un amplio rechazo a sus disposiciones sobre pruebas.
Non-Intercourse Act (p. 279) An act passed by Congress in 1809 allowing Americans to trade with every nation except France and Britain in an effort to spur a sagging economy following the Embargo Act of 1807. The act failed to stop the seizure of American ships or to improve the economy.	**Non-Intercourse Act (pág. 279)** Ley aprobada por el Congreso en 1809 que permitía a los estadounidenses comerciar con todas las naciones excepto Francia y Gran Bretaña, en un esfuerzo por estimular una economía decaída tras la Ley de Embargo de 1807. La ley no consiguió detener el secuestro de barcos estadounidenses ni mejorar la economía.
North American Free Trade Agreement (NAFTA) (p. 1005) A free-trade agreement approved in 1993 by the United States, Canada, and Mexico. It was replaced in 2020 by a similar free-trade pact, the U.S.-Mexico-Canada Agreement (USMCA).	**Tratado de Libre Comercio de América del Norte (TLCAN) (pág. 1005)** Acuerdo de libre comercio aprobado en 1993 por Estados Unidos, Canadá y México. Fue sustituido en 2020 por un pacto de libre comercio similar, el Acuerdo Estados Unidos-México-Canadá (USMCA).
North Atlantic Treaty Organization (NATO) (p. 837) A Cold War military alliance and security pact intended to enhance the collective security of the United States and Western Europe. Originally consisting of twelve nations in 1949, as of 2023, thirty-one NATO member nations operate under the principle of "an attack against one member is considered as an attack against all."	**Organización del Tratado del Atlántico Norte (OTAN) (pág. 837)** Alianza militar y pacto de seguridad de la Guerra Fría destinada a reforzar la seguridad colectiva de Estados Unidos y Europa Occidental. Originalmente formada por doce naciones en 1949, a partir de 2023, treinta y una naciones miembros de la OTAN operan bajo el principio de "un ataque contra un miembro se considera un ataque contra todos"
***North Star* (p. 347)** The abolitionist newspaper started in 1847 by fugitive from slavery and antislavery activist Frederick Douglass.	***North Star* (pág. 347)** Periódico abolicionista fundado en 1847 por el fugitivo de la esclavitud y activista antiesclavista Frederick Douglass.
Northwest Ordinances of 1785 and 1787 (p. 205) The 1785 act of the confederation congress provided for the survey, sale, and eventual division into states of the Northwest Territory and set aside land for public schools. A 1787 act then clarified the process by which settled territories could become states and banned slavery across the Northwest Territory.	**Ordenanzas del Noroeste de 1785 y 1787 (pág. 205)** El acta de 1785 del congreso de la confederación preveía la medición, venta y eventual división en estados del Territorio del Noroeste y reservaba tierras para escuelas públicas. A continuación, una ley de 1787 aclaró el proceso por el que los territorios colonizados podían convertirse en estados y prohibió la esclavitud en todo el Territorio del Noroeste.

NSC-68 (p. 838) A document issued by the National Security Council in 1950 that advocated intensification of the policy of containment both at home and abroad and a massive buildup of the U.S. military. NSC-68 defined U.S. nuclear policy, peacetime military spending, and a policy of anti-Soviet propaganda overseas and vigilance against the communist threat at home.

NSC-68 (pág. 838) Documento publicado por el Consejo de Seguridad Nacional en 1950 que abogaba por la intensificación de la política de contención tanto en el interior como en el exterior y por un aumento masivo del ejército estadounidense. El NSC-68 definió la política nuclear estadounidense, el gasto militar en tiempos de paz y una política de propaganda antisoviética en el exterior y de vigilancia contra la amenaza comunista en el interior.

nuclear freeze movement (p. 991) Protests in the 1980s calling for a halt to the testing, production, and deployment of missiles and aircraft designed primarily to deliver nuclear weapons.

Movimiento de congelación nuclear (pág. 991) Protestas en la década de 1980 para detener las pruebas, la producción y el despliegue de misiles y aviones diseñados principalmente para transportar armas nucleares.

nullification (p. 318) The legal doctrine that individual states maintained their sovereignty despite union, because the federal union was created by the states, thus maintaining the right to declare federal laws unconstitutional and, therefore, void within their borders. South Carolina attempted to invoke the doctrine of nullification in response to the Tariff of 1832.

nulificación (pág. 318) Doctrina legal según la cual los estados individuales mantienen su soberanía a pesar de la unión, porque la unión federal fue creada por los estados, manteniendo así el derecho a declarar inconstitucionales las leyes federales y, por tanto, nulas dentro de sus fronteras. Carolina del Sur intentó invocar la doctrina de la anulación en respuesta al Arancel de 1832.

Nye Committee (p. 779) Committee chaired in 1934 by Republican senator Gerald Nye to investigate the actions of munitions manufacturers to ensure they were not pushing the country toward a second great war for financial profit. The Nye Committee blamed weapons manufacturers, arms dealers, and bankers who lent funds to the Allied Powers for the outbreak of World War I.

Comité Nye (pág. 779) Comité presidido en 1934 por el senador republicano Gerald Nye para investigar las acciones de los fabricantes de municiones y asegurarse de que no estaban empujando al país hacia una segunda gran guerra para obtener beneficios económicos. El Comité Nye culpó del estallido de la Primera Guerra Mundial a los fabricantes de armas, los traficantes de armas y los banqueros que prestaron fondos a las potencias aliadas.

O

***Obergefell v. Hodges* (p. 1022)** A Supreme Court decision in 2015 legalizing same-sex marriage throughout the nation on the basis of the Fourteenth Amendment's equal protection and due process clauses.

***Obergefell contra Hodges* (pág. 1022)** Decisión del Tribunal Supremo en 2015 que legaliza el matrimonio entre personas del mismo sexo en todo el país basándose en las cláusulas de igualdad de protección y garantías procesales de la Decimocuarta Enmienda.

Occupy Wall Street movement (p. 1021) A loose coalition of progressive and radical forces that emerged in 2011 in New York City and around the country to protest what they perceived to be corporate greed and federal policies that benefit the wealthy.

Movimiento: Toma de Wall Street (Occupy Wall Street) (pág. 1021) Coalición informal de fuerzas progresistas y radicales que surgió en 2011 en Nueva York y en todo el país para protestar contra lo que consideraban avaricia empresarial y políticas federales que benefician a los ricos.

Office of Faith-Based and Neighborhood Partnerships (p. 1013) An office of the White House established by President George W. Bush to provide religious and community institutions with federal funds for social services.

Oficina para Asociaciones Religiosas y Vecinales (pág. 1013) Oficina de la Casa Blanca creada por el presidente George W. Bush para proporcionar a las instituciones religiosas y comunitarias fondos federales para servicios sociales.

Office of War Information (p. 791) A government office set up during World War II to promote patriotism and urge Americans to contribute to the war effort any way they could.

Oficina de Información de Guerra (pág. 791) Oficina gubernamental creada durante la Segunda Guerra Mundial para promover el patriotismo e instar a los estadounidenses a contribuir al esfuerzo bélico de cualquier forma posible.

Old Light clergy (p. 124) Colonial religious leaders from established churches who supported the religious status quo in the early eighteenth century.

Clero de la Vieja Luz (pág. 124) Líderes religiosos coloniales de las iglesias establecidas que apoyaban el statu quo religioso a principios del siglo XVIII.

Open Door policy (p. 668) An 1899 policy in which Secretary of State John Hay informed the nations occupying China that the United States had the right of equal trade in China.

Política de Puertas Abiertas (pág. 668) Política de 1899 en la que el Secretario de Estado John Hay informó a las naciones que ocupaban China de que Estados Unidos tenía derecho a comerciar con China en igualdad de condiciones.

Operation Desert Storm (p. 996) The code name of the 1991 allied air and ground military offensive that pushed Iraqi forces out of Kuwait.

Operación Tormenta del Desierto (pág. 996) Nombre en clave de la ofensiva militar aérea y terrestre aliada de 1991 que expulsó a las fuerzas iraquíes de Kuwait.

Operation Wetback (p. 883) The forced deportation of 250,000 to 1.3 million undocumented Mexican immigrants during the Eisenhower administration.

Operación Wetback (pág. 883) Deportación forzosa de entre 250.000 y 1,3 millones de inmigrantes mexicanos indocumentados durante la administración Eisenhower.

Ordinance of Nullification (p. 318) A law passed in 1832 by South Carolina proclaiming several congressional tariff acts null and void within the state and threatening secession if the federal government tried to enforce the tariffs.

Ordenanza de Nulificación (pág. 318) Ley aprobada en 1832 por Carolina del Sur por la que se proclamaban nulas varias leyes arancelarias del Congreso dentro del estado y se amenazaba con la secesión si el gobierno federal intentaba hacer cumplir los aranceles.

Oregon Trail (p. 386) The route west from the Missouri River to the Oregon Territory. By 1860, some 350,000 Americans had made the three- to six-month journey along the trail.

La ruta de Oregón (pág. 386) La ruta hacia el oeste desde el río Misuri hasta el territorio de Oregón. En 1860, unos 350.000 estadounidenses habían hecho el viaje de tres a seis meses por el sendero.

Organization of Petroleum Exporting Countries (OPEC) (p. 934) An organization formed by oil-producing countries to control the price and supply of oil on the global market.

Organización de Países Exportadores de Petróleo (OPEP) (pág. 934) Organización formada por países productores de petróleo para controlar el precio y la oferta de petróleo en el mercado mundial.

Ostend Manifesto (p. 412) A letter from U.S. ambassadors and the secretary of state to President Franklin Pierce written in 1854 urging him to purchase Cuba from Spain and, if Spain refused the sale, to conquer Cuba for U.S. territorial expansion. When it was leaked to the press, Northerners voiced outrage at what they saw as a plot to use the power of the federal government to expand slave territories.

Manifiesto de Ostende (pág. 412) Una carta de los embajadores estadounidenses y del secretario de Estado al presidente Franklin Pierce escrita en 1854 instándole a comprar Cuba a España y, si España rechazaba la venta, a conquistar Cuba para la expansión territorial estadounidense. Cuando se filtró a la prensa, los norteños expresaron su indignación ante lo que consideraban un complot para utilizar el poder del gobierno federal para ampliar los territorios esclavistas.

overland trail (p. 386) Nineteenth-century wagon and stagecoach routes that began in Missouri and headed westward, carrying settlers and goods to present-day California and Oregon.

Ruta de overland (pág. 386) Rutas de carretas y diligencias del siglo XIX que comenzaban en Misuri y se dirigían hacia el oeste, llevando colonos y mercancías a las actuales California y Oregón.

P

Palestine Liberation Organization (PLO) (p. 989) A movement founded in 1964 with the goal of achieving Palestinian independence from Israel, through armed force if necessary. For many years, the PLO was considered a terrorist organization by the U.S. government.

Organización para la Liberación de Palestina (OLP) (pág. 989) Movimiento fundado en 1964 con el objetivo de lograr la independencia palestina de Israel, por la fuerza armada si fuera necesario. Durante muchos años, la OLP fue considerada una organización terrorista por el gobierno estadounidense.

Palmer raids (p. 717) The government roundup of some 6,000 suspected alien radicals in 1919–1920, ordered by Attorney General A. Mitchell Palmer and his assistant J. Edgar Hoover. The raids reflected the fears of foreign radicalism present during the first Red Scare and resulted in the deportation of 556 immigrants.

Redadas Palmer (pág. 717) Redada gubernamental de unos 6,000 presuntos radicales extranjeros en 1919-1920, ordenada por el fiscal general A. Mitchell Palmer y su ayudante J. Edgar Hoover. Las redadas reflejaron los temores al radicalismo extranjero presentes durante el primer Miedo Rojo y se saldaron con la deportación de 556 inmigrantes.

Panic of 1819 (p. 273) The nation's first severe economic depression, due largely to irresponsible banking practices and a decline in American exports such as cotton. The panic lasted four years, slowed previously rapid westward expansion, and resulted in widespread bankruptcies and mass unemployment, generating the loss of millions of acres of land and businesses in nationwide bankruptcies, and resulting in massive popular protests.

Pánico de 1819 (pág. 273) Primera depresión económica grave del país, debida en gran parte a prácticas bancarias irresponsables y a un descenso de las exportaciones estadounidenses, como el algodón. El pánico duró cuatro años, frenó la rápida expansión anterior hacia el oeste y provocó quiebras generalizadas y desempleo masivo, generando la pérdida de millones de acres de tierra y negocios en quiebras a escala nacional, y dando lugar a protestas populares masivas.

Panic of 1837 (p. 296) The Panic of 1837 started in the South and was rooted in a collapsing land and cotton market, as American cotton prices plummeted. The panic resulted in mass unemployment, bankruptcy, deflation, and discontent.

Pánico de 1837 (pág. 296) El Pánico de 1837 comenzó en el Sur y tuvo su origen en el colapso del mercado de la tierra y del algodón, al desplomarse los precios del algodón estadounidense. El pánico se tradujo en desempleo masivo, bancarrota, deflación y descontento.

Panic of 1873 (p. 487) A severe economic depression largely triggered by the collapse of the Northern Pacific Railroad.

Pánico de 1873 (pág. 487) Grave depresión económica desencadenada en gran medida por la quiebra del Ferrocarril del Pacífico Norte.

Panic of 1893 (p. 617) A severe economic downturn triggered by railroad and bank failures. The severity of the depression, combined with the failure of the federal government to offer an adequate response for half a decade, led to a realignment of American politics.

Pánico de 1893 (pág. 617) Grave recesión económica provocada por la quiebra de ferrocarriles y bancos. La gravedad de la depresión, combinada con la incapacidad del gobierno federal para ofrecer una respuesta adecuada durante media década, condujo a un realineamiento de la política estadounidense.

Paris Climate Agreement (p. 1025) A worldwide agreement by the United States and 194 other nations in 2015 to dramatically reduce greenhouse-gas emissions produced from fossil fuels. In 2017, President Donald Trump withdrew the U.S. commitment to the agreement, and then in 2021, President Joseph Biden rejoined the United States to the agreement.

Acuerdo de París sobre el clima (pág. 1025) Acuerdo mundial alcanzado por Estados Unidos y otras 194 naciones en 2015 para reducir significativamente las emisiones de gases de efecto invernadero producidas por los combustibles fósiles. En 2017, el presidente Donald Trump retiró el compromiso de Estados Unidos con el acuerdo y, posteriormente, en 2021, el presidente Joseph Biden lo reincorporó al acuerdo.

Patient Protection and Affordable Care Act ("Obamacare") (p. 1020) Passed in 2010, this law expanded health insurance to millions of Americans previously uncovered through a variety of measures including extending Medicaid, setting up health-insurance exchanges, allowing children to remain under their parents' coverage until the age of twenty-six, and preventing insurance companies from denying coverage based on preexisting conditions.

Ley de Protección al Paciente y Cuidado de Salud Asequible (*"Obamacare"*) (pág. 1020) Aprobada en 2010, esta ley amplió el seguro médico a millones de estadounidenses que antes no tenían cobertura mediante una serie de medidas como la ampliación de Medicaid, la creación de bolsas de seguros médicos, la posibilidad de que los hijos sigan cubiertos por sus padres hasta los veintiséis años y la prohibición de que las compañías de seguros denieguen la cobertura por enfermedades preexistentes.

patriots (p. 170) American colonists who favored the movement for independence during the 1770s.

patriotas (pág. 170) Colonos estadounidenses que favorecieron el movimiento independentista durante la década de 1770.

Payne-Aldrich tariff (p. 695) The 1909 legislation increasing the duties paid on imports.

Arancel Payne-Aldrich (pág. 695) Legislación de 1909 que aumenta los derechos pagados por las importaciones.

Peace of Paris (p. 155) A 1763 peace treaty ending the French and Indian War (Seven Years' War). Under its terms, France gave up all of its North American territorial rights and Britain gained control of present-day Canada and of North America east of the Mississippi River. Spain gained all of French-controlled Louisiana, including the Port of New Orleans.

Paz de París (pág. 155) Tratado de paz de 1763 que puso fin a la Guerra de los Siete Años. Según sus términos, Francia renunció a todos sus derechos territoriales en Norteamérica y Gran Bretaña obtuvo el control del actual Canadá y de Norteamérica al este del río Misisipi. España ganó toda la Luisiana controlada por los franceses, incluido el puerto de Nueva Orleans.

Pendleton Civil Service Reform Act (p. 622) An act passed in 1883 that required the elimination of favoritism and nepotism in the hiring for federal jobs. The act established that positions would be awarded based on merit rather than political connections.

Ley de Reforma del Servicio Civil de Pendleton (pág. 622) Ley aprobada en 1883 que exigía la eliminación del favoritismo y el nepotismo en la contratación para puestos federales. La ley establecía que los puestos se adjudicarían en función de los méritos y no de las conexiones políticas.

***Pentagon Papers* (p. 896)** A classified report on U.S. involvement in Vietnam leaked to the press in 1971. The report confirmed that the Kennedy and Johnson administrations had misled the public about the origins and nature of the Vietnam War.

***Pentagon Papers* (pág. 896)** Informe clasificado sobre la participación de Estados Unidos en Vietnam filtrado a la prensa en 1971. El informe confirmaba que las administraciones Kennedy y Johnson habían engañado a la opinión pública sobre los orígenes y la naturaleza de la guerra de Vietnam.

Pequot War (p. 88) A conflict between New England settlers and their Narragansett allies against the Pequot Indians in 1636–1637. The English perceived the Pequot tribe as both a threat and an obstacle to further English expansion.

Guerra Pequot (pág. 88) Conflicto entre los colonos de Nueva Inglaterra y sus aliados Narragansett contra los indios Pequot en 1636-1637. Los ingleses percibían a la tribu pequot como una amenaza y un obstáculo para la expansión inglesa.

***perestroika* (p. 991)** A policy of economic "restructuring" initiated by Soviet leader Mikhail Gorbachev. Gorbachev hoped that by reducing state control, he could revive the Soviet economy.

***Perestroika* (pág. 991)** Política de "reestructuración" económica iniciada por el líder soviético Mijaíl Gorbachov. Gorbachov esperaba que, reduciendo el control estatal, podría reactivar la economía soviética.

Personal Responsibility and Work Opportunity Reconciliation Act (p. 1006) An act reforming the welfare system in the United States. The 1996 law required adults receiving welfare to find work within two years or lose their welfare benefits, granted states greater flexibility in administering welfare programs, and strengthened enforcement of child support.

Ley sobre Oportunidad de Empleo y Responsabilidad Personal (pág. 1006) Ley de reforma del sistema de asistencia social en Estados Unidos. La ley de 1996 obligaba a los adultos que recibían asistencia social a encontrar trabajo en un plazo de dos años o perderían sus prestaciones, otorgaba a los estados una mayor flexibilidad en la administración de los programas de asistencia social y reforzaba el cumplimiento de la manutención de los hijos.

Pilgrims (p. 84) Also known as Separatists, a group of English religious dissenters who established a settlement at Plymouth, Massachusetts, in 1620.

Peregrinos (pág. 84) También conocidos como separatistas, grupo de disidentes religiosos ingleses que establecieron un asentamiento en Plymouth, Massachusetts, en 1620.

Pinckney Treaty (p. 241) A treaty between Spain and the United States ratified in 1796 that defined the boundary between U.S. and Spanish territory in the South and opened the Mississippi River and New Orleans to U.S. shipping. It allowed the free movement of goods from the far interior to the Atlantic via the Mississippi.

Tratado Pinckney (pág. 241) Tratado entre España y Estados Unidos ratificado en 1796 que definía la frontera entre el territorio estadounidense y el español en el Sur y abría el río Misisipi y Nueva Orleans a la navegación estadounidense. Permitía la libre circulación de mercancías desde el interior hasta el Atlántico a través del Mississippi.

Pinkerton Agency (p. 571) A company of private investigators and security guards sometimes used by corporations to violently break up strikes and labor disputes, most famously at the Homestead strike of 1892.

***Pinkerton Agency* (Agencia Pinkerton) (pág. 571)** Empresa de investigadores privados y guardias de seguridad utilizada a veces por las empresas para disolver violentamente huelgas y conflictos laborales con el caso destacado de la huelga de Homestead de 1892.

Planter (p. 72) One of the group of white southern slaveholders who owned the largest plantations and forged a distinct culture and economy around the institution of slavery.

Plantador (pág. 72) Uno de los grupos de esclavistas blancos del sur que poseían las mayores plantaciones y forjaron una cultura y una economía distintas en torno a la institución de la esclavitud.

Platt Amendment (p. 663) A 1901 act of Congress limiting Cuban sovereignty. U.S. officials pressured Cuban leaders to incorporate the amendment into the Cuban constitution.

Enmienda de Platt (pág. 663) Ley de 1901 del Congreso que limita la soberanía cubana. Funcionarios estadounidenses presionaron a los dirigentes cubanos para que incorporaran la enmienda a la Constitución cubana.

***Plessy v. Ferguson* (p. 548)** A Supreme Court ruling in 1896 that upheld the legality of Jim Crow legislation. The Court ruled that as long as states provided "separate but equal" facilities for white and Black people, Jim Crow laws did not violate the equal protection clause of the Fourteenth Amendment.	***Plessy contra Ferguson* (pág. 548)** Sentencia del Tribunal Supremo de 1896 que confirmó la legalidad de la legislación Jim Crow. El Tribunal dictaminó que mientras los estados ofrecieran instalaciones "separadas pero iguales" para blancos y negros, las leyes Jim Crow no violaban la cláusula de igualdad de protección de la Decimocuarta Enmienda.
political boss (p. 620) The head of the local political machine. The boss worked to maintain authority by strengthening the machine and its loyalists.	**jefe político (pág. 620)** Jefe de la maquinaria política local. El jefe trabajaba para mantener la autoridad reforzando la máquina y a sus leales.
political machine (p. 620) A type of urban political organization that dominated many late-nineteenth-century cities. Machines provided the organization and funding needed to provide services to the urban poor, but they also fostered corruption, crime, and inefficiency.	**máquina política (pág. 620)** Tipo de organización política urbana que dominó muchas ciudades de finales del siglo XIX. Las máquinas proporcionaban la organización y la financiación necesarias para prestar servicios a los pobres de las ciudades, pero también fomentaban la corrupción, la delincuencia y la ineficacia.
poll tax (p. 548) A common tactic in southern states to disenfranchise poor, mostly Black voters by charging a fee to cast a ballot.	**impuesto de capitación (pág. 548)** Táctica común en los estados del sur para privar del derecho de voto a los votantes pobres, en su mayoría negros, mediante el cobro de una tasa por votar.
Populists (p. 625) Originating in the agrarian movements in the late 1800s, Populists attempted to unite farmers and laborers in a coalition promoting broad economic and political reforms.	**Populistas (pág. 625)** Originados en los movimientos agrarios de finales del siglo XIX, los populistas intentaron unir a agricultores y obreros en una coalición que promoviera amplias reformas económicas y políticas.
Port Huron Statement (p. 927) The manifesto of the Students for a Democratic Society written in 1962 that condemned liberal politics, Cold War foreign policy, racism, and research-oriented universities. It called for the adoption of "participatory democracy."	**Declaración de Port Huron (pág. 927)** Manifiesto de los Estudiantes por una Sociedad Democrática escrito en 1962 que condenaba la política liberal, la política exterior de la Guerra Fría, el racismo y las universidades orientadas a la investigación. Pidió la adopción de la "democracia participativa".
Potsdam Conference (p. 832) The July 1945 meeting in Germany between Truman and Stalin. The two leaders agreed to free elections in Eastern Europe, Soviet withdrawal from northern Iran, and the creation of four Allied occupation zones in Germany.	**Conferencia de Potsdam (pág. 832)** La reunión de julio de 1945 en Alemania entre Truman y Stalin. Los dos líderes acordaron la celebración de elecciones libres en Europa Oriental, la retirada soviética del norte de Irán y la creación de cuatro zonas de ocupación aliadas en Alemania.
Powhatan Confederacy (p. 66) Large and powerful confederation of Algonquian-speaking Native Americans in Virginia. The Jamestown settlers had a complicated and often combative relationship with the leaders of the Powhatan Confederacy.	**Confederación de Powhatan (pág. 66)** Gran y poderosa confederación de nativos americanos de habla algonquina en Virginia. Los colonos de Jamestown mantuvieron una relación complicada y a menudo combativa con los líderes de la Confederación Powhatan.
pragmatism (p. 671) A philosophy that holds that truth can be discovered only through experience and that the value of ideas should be measured by their practical consequences. Pragmatism had a significant influence on progressives.	**pragmatismo (pág. 671)** Filosofía que sostiene que la verdad sólo puede descubrirse a través de la experiencia y que el valor de las ideas debe medirse por sus consecuencias prácticas. El pragmatismo influyó notablemente en los progresistas.
Privy Council (p. 71) Advisory council of the king of England, comprised typically of prominent aristocrats.	**Consejo Privado (pág. 71)** Consejo asesor del rey de Inglaterra, compuesto normalmente por aristócratas prominentes.
Proclamation Line of 1763 (p. 156) Act of Parliament following the end of the French and Indian War that restricted colonial settlement west of the Appalachian Mountains, generating widespread resentment in the colonies.	**Línea de Proclamación de 1763 (pág. 156)** Ley del Parlamento tras el final de la Guerra Francesa e India que restringió el asentamiento colonial al oeste de los Montes Apalaches, generando un resentimiento generalizado en las colonias.
Proclamation of Amnesty and Reconstruction (p. 469) An 1863 proclamation that established the basic parameters of President Abraham Lincoln's approach to Reconstruction. Lincoln's plan would have readmitted the South to the Union on relatively lenient terms.	**Proclamación de Amnistía y Reconstrucción (pág. 469)** Proclamación de 1863 que estableció los parámetros básicos del enfoque del presidente Abraham Lincoln para la Reconstrucción. El plan de Lincoln habría readmitido al Sur en la Unión en términos relativamente indulgentes.
Progressive Party (p. 695) A political party formed by Theodore Roosevelt in 1912 to facilitate his candidacy for president. Nicknamed the "Bull Moose Party," the Progressive Party split the Republican vote, allowing Democrat Woodrow Wilson to win the election. The party promoted an income tax, an eight-hour workday, labor unions, women's suffrage, and an end to child labor.	**Partido Progresista (pág. 695)** Partido político creado por Theodore Roosevelt en 1912 para facilitar su candidatura a la presidencia. Apodado el "Bull Moose Party", el Partido Progresista dividió el voto republicano, permitiendo al demócrata Woodrow Wilson ganar las elecciones. El partido promovía un impuesto sobre la renta, la jornada laboral de ocho horas, los sindicatos, el sufragio femenino y el fin del trabajo infantil.
progressivism (p. 671) A movement that emerged during the late nineteenth century whose adherents were united by the belief that if people joined together and applied human intelligence to the task of improving the nation, progress was inevitable. Progressives advocated governmental intervention yet sought change without radically altering capitalism or the political system.	**progresismo (pág. 671)** Movimiento surgido a finales del siglo XIX cuyos adeptos estaban unidos por la creencia de que si la gente se unía y aplicaba la inteligencia humana a la tarea de mejorar la nación, el progreso era inevitable. Los progresistas abogaban por la intervención gubernamental, pero buscaban el cambio sin alterar radicalmente el capitalismo o el sistema político.

Protestant Reformation (p. 83) A European religious movement to break with the Catholic Church.

Reforma protestante (pág. 83) Movimiento religioso europeo de ruptura con la Iglesia católica.

Public Works Administration (PWA) (p. 763) A New Deal administration created in 1933 to provide jobs relief through the construction of infrastructure, such as roads, schools, hospitals, dams, and libraries.

Administración de Obras Públicas (PWA) (pág. 763) Administración del Nuevo Trato creada en 1933 para aliviar el desempleo mediante la construcción de infraestructuras, como carreteras, escuelas, hospitales, presas y bibliotecas.

Pueblo (p. 11) Native American peoples in present-day New Mexico and Arizona who share common religious and agricultural practices. Pueblo, the Spanish word for village, was used to refer to Native Americans who built permanent multi-story adobe dwellings in the Southwest.

Pueblo (pág. 11) Pueblos nativos americanos de los actuales Nuevo México y Arizona que comparten prácticas religiosas y agrícolas comunes. Pueblo, palabra española que significa aldea, se utilizaba para referirse a los nativos americanos que construían viviendas permanentes de adobe de varios pisos en el suroeste.

Pueblo Revolt (p. 61) An uprising of Pueblo Indians in 1680 against Spanish forces in New Mexico that led to the Spaniards' temporary retreat from the area. The uprising was sparked by mistreatment and the suppression of Pueblo culture and religion.

Revuelta Pueblo (pág. 61) Levantamiento de los indios Pueblo en 1680 contra las fuerzas españolas en Nuevo México que provocó la retirada temporal de los españoles de la zona. El levantamiento fue provocado por los malos tratos y la supresión de la cultura y la religión Pueblo.

Pullman strike (p. 572) A strike by workers against the Pullman railcar company in 1894, which expanded to a broader railroad strike when American Railway Union workers refused to handle any trains with Pullman cars. When the strike disrupted rail service nationwide, threatening mail delivery, the government sought an injunction against the union, which was followed by a presidential order by Grover Cleveland for federal troops to intervene.

Huelga Pullman (pág. 572) Huelga de trabajadores contra la compañía de vagones Pullman en 1894, que se extendió a una huelga ferroviaria más amplia cuando los trabajadores de la American Railway Union se negaron a manejar ningún tren con vagones Pullman. Cuando la huelga interrumpió el servicio ferroviario en todo el país, amenazando la entrega del correo, el gobierno solicitó una orden judicial contra el sindicato, a la que siguió una orden presidencial de Grover Cleveland para que intervinieran las tropas federales.

Pure Food and Drug Act (p. 694) A law passed in 1906 to prevent the manufacturing, sale, and transportation of harmful "foods, drugs, medicines, and liquors."

Ley de Pureza de Alimentos y Medicinas (pág. 694) Ley aprobada en 1906 para impedir la fabricación, venta y transporte de "alimentos, drogas, medicinas y licores" nocivos

Puritan Migration (p. 86) The mass migration of Puritans from Europe to New England during the 1620s and 1630s.

Migración puritana (pág. 86) La migración masiva de puritanos de Europa a Nueva Inglaterra durante las décadas de 1620 y 1630.

Puritans (p. 84) Radical English Protestants who hoped to reform the Church of England. The first Puritan settlers in the Americas arrived in Massachusetts in 1630.

Puritanos (pág. 84) Protestantes ingleses radicales que esperaban reformar la Iglesia de Inglaterra. Los primeros colonos puritanos de América llegaron a Massachusetts en 1630.

Q

Quartering Act (p. 161) A 1765 act requiring colonial governments to provide food and housing for British troops in the colonies. Many colonists resented subsidizing the presence of British troops and eventually viewed those troops as occupiers rather than protectors.

Ley del Acuartelamiento o Alojamiento (pág. 161) Ley de 1765 que obligaba a los gobiernos coloniales a proporcionar alimentos y alojamiento a las tropas británicas en las colonias. A muchos colonos les molestaba subvencionar la presencia de tropas británicas y acabaron por considerarlas más ocupantes que protectoras.

Québec Act (p. 168) A 1774 act of Parliament extending the boundary of Québec to areas of the Ohio River valley that American colonists wanted to settle, thus revoking the Proclamation of 1763 and placing rule between the Ohio and Mississippi Rivers under the control of a royal governor. This act also set up a colonial government without a local representative assembly in Québec and legalized Catholicism in the territory.

Ley de Québec (pág. 168) Ley del Parlamento de 1774 por la que se amplían los límites de Québec a las zonas del valle del río Ohio que los colonos estadounidenses querían colonizar, revocando así la Proclamación de 1763 y poniendo el dominio entre los ríos Ohio y Mississippi bajo el control de un gobernador real. Esta ley también establece un gobierno colonial sin asamblea representativa local en Québec y legaliza el catolicismo en el territorio.

Queen Anne's War (p. 109) A war from 1702 to 1713 over control of Spain and its colonies; also known as the War of the Spanish Succession.

Guerra de la Reina Ana (pág. 109) Guerra de 1702 a 1713 por el control de España y sus colonias; también conocida como Guerra de Sucesión Española.

R

Radical Republicans (p. 469) Republican politicians who actively supported abolition before the Civil War and sought tighter controls over the South in the aftermath of the war. Radical Republicans repeatedly clashed with President Johnson over Reconstruction policy.

Republicanos radicales (pág. 469) Políticos republicanos que apoyaron activamente la abolición antes de la Guerra Civil y buscaron controles más estrictos sobre el Sur tras la guerra. Los republicanos radicales chocaron repetidamente con el presidente Johnson por la política de Reconstrucción.

Railroad Administration (p. 713) A government agency of the World War I era tasked with coordinating train schedules, regulating ticket prices, upgrading tracks, and raising workers' wages. The Railroad Administration acted more forcefully than most other agencies because of military reliance on the efficiency of railroads.

Administración de Ferrocarriles (pág. 713) Agencia gubernamental de la época de la Primera Guerra Mundial encargada de coordinar los horarios de los trenes, regular los precios de los billetes, modernizar las vías y aumentar los salarios de los trabajadores. La Administración de Ferrocarriles actuó con más contundencia que la mayoría de los demás organismos debido a la dependencia militar de la eficiencia de los ferrocarriles.

Reaganomics (p. 977) The nickname given to Reagan's economic policies based on the theories of supply-side economists and centered on tax cuts and cuts to domestic programs.

***Reaganomics* (pág. 977)** Sobrenombre dado a las políticas económicas de Reagan basadas en las teorías de los economistas de la oferta y centradas en recortes fiscales y de programas nacionales.

Reconstruction (p. 463) The period from 1865 to 1877, during which the eleven ex-Confederate states were subject to federal legislative and constitutional efforts to remake their societies as they were readmitted to the Union.

Reconstrucción (pág. 463) Periodo comprendido entre 1865 y 1877, durante el cual los once estados ex confederados estuvieron sometidos a los esfuerzos legislativos y constitucionales federales para rehacer sus sociedades a medida que eran readmitidos en la Unión.

Reconstruction Finance Corporation (RFC) (p. 750) A government corporation endorsed by Herbert Hoover and created by Congress. It provided federal support through loans to troubled banks, railroads, and insurance companies and, later, states and municipalities in an attempt to stimulate economic growth and job creation.

Corporación Financiera de Reconstrucción *(Reconstruction Finance Corporation)* (RFC) (pág. 750) Corporación gubernamental respaldada por Herbert Hoover y creada por el Congreso. Proporcionó ayuda federal mediante préstamos a bancos, ferrocarriles y compañías de seguros en dificultades y, más tarde, a estados y municipios, en un intento de estimular el crecimiento económico y la creación de empleo.

Red Scare (p. 716) The fear of communist-inspired radicalism in the wake of the Russian Revolution. The Red Scare culminated in the Palmer raids on suspected radicals.

Miedo a los rojos (pág. 716) Temor al radicalismo de inspiración comunista tras la Revolución Rusa. El Miedo Rojo culminó con las redadas Palmer contra presuntos radicales.

Redeemers (p. 485) White, conservative Democrats who challenged and overthrew Republican rule in the South during Reconstruction hoping to restore pre–Civil War racial norms.

Redentores (pág. 485) Demócratas blancos y conservadores que desafiaron y derrocaron el gobierno republicano en el Sur durante la Reconstrucción con la esperanza de restaurar las normas raciales anteriores a la Guerra Civil.

redlining (p. 857) A discriminatory practice in which residents of certain neighborhoods are denied financial services. The term originated when the federal Homeowner's Loan Corporation in the 1930s created maps outlining the riskiest areas to lend in red, making it difficult for the predominantly minority residents in redlined urban communities to obtain mortgages.

***Redlining* (pág. 857)** Práctica discriminatoria en la cual a los residentes de ciertos vecindarios se les niegan servicios financieros. El término se originó cuando la Corporación Federal de Préstamos para Propietarios en la década de 1930 creó mapas que delineaban las áreas más riesgosas para prestar en rojo, lo que dificultó que los residentes mayoritariamente pertenecientes a minorías en comunidades urbanas marcadas en rojo obtuvieran hipotecas.

redemptioner (p. 97) An immigrant who borrowed money from shipping agents to cover the costs of transport to America, loans that were repaid, or "redeemed," by colonial employers. A redemptioner worked for the "redeemer" for a set number of years.

***Redemptioner* (pág. 97)** Inmigrante que pedía prestado dinero a los agentes marítimos para cubrir los gastos de transporte a América, préstamos que eran devueltos, o "redimidos", por los empleadores coloniales. Un redentor trabajaba para el "redentor" durante un número determinado de años.

Renaissance (p. 15) A cultural and intellectual flowering that began in fifteenth-century Italy and then spread north throughout the late fifteenth and sixteenth centuries. During this time, European rulers pushed for greater political unification of their states. It contributed to dramatic changes in art, cultivated knowledge, and the questioning of old forms of authority.

Renacimiento (pág. 15) Florecimiento cultural e intelectual que comenzó en la Italia del siglo XV y se extendió hacia el norte a finales del siglo XV y durante el XVI. Durante esta época, los gobernantes europeos impulsaron una mayor unificación política de sus Estados. Contribuyó a cambios espectaculares en el arte, el saber culto y el cuestionamiento de las viejas formas de autoridad.

republican motherhood (p. 194) A concept proposed by some American political leaders in the 1790s, which supported women's education so that they could in turn instruct their sons in principles of republican government.

maternidad republicana (pág. 194) Concepto propuesto por algunos líderes políticos estadounidenses en la década de 1790, que apoyaba la educación de las mujeres para que pudieran a su vez instruir a sus hijos en los principios del gobierno republicano.

Republican Party (p. 417) A political party formed in 1854 that was committed to stopping the expansion of slavery and that advocated economic development and internal improvements. Although their appeal was limited to the North, the Republicans quickly became a major political force.

Partido Republicano (pág. 417) Partido político formado en 1854 que se comprometía a detener la expansión de la esclavitud y que abogaba por el desarrollo económico y las mejoras internas. Aunque su atractivo se limitaba al Norte, los republicanos se convirtieron rápidamente en una fuerza política importante.

***Requerimiento* (p. 29)** A statement read by Spanish conquerors to native peoples claiming the religious authority of the Catholic Church and the secular authority of the Spanish Crown to rule in the name of the pope. This statement was typically read in Latin and threatened that Indians who did not embrace Spanish rule and Christian conversion faced enslavement and other harsh punishments.

***Requerimiento* (pág. 29)** Declaración leída por los conquistadores españoles a los pueblos nativos en la que reclamaban la autoridad religiosa de la Iglesia católica y la autoridad secular de la corona española para gobernar en nombre del papa. Esta declaración se leía normalmente en latín y amenazaba a los indios que no aceptaran el dominio español y la conversión cristiana con la esclavitud y otros duros castigos.

robber baron (p. 557) A negative term applied to late-nineteenth-century industrialists and capitalists who became very rich by dominating large industries while employing low-cost labor alongside new money-saving technologies.

Barón ladrón (pág. 557) Término negativo aplicado a los industriales y capitalistas de finales del siglo XIX que se hicieron muy ricos dominando grandes industrias y empleando mano de obra barata junto con nuevas tecnologías que ahorraban dinero.

***Roe v. Wade* (p. 918)** The 1973 Supreme Court decision that women have a constitutional right to an abortion based on an implied right to privacy in the Fourteenth Amendment. The decision was overturned in the 2022 Supreme Court ruling *Dobbs v. Jackson's Women's Health Organization*, which dismantled federal *Roe v. Wade* abortion rights in favor of federal or state-by-state legislation.

***Roe contra Wade* (pág. 918)** La decisión del Tribunal Supremo de 1973 de que las mujeres tienen un derecho constitucional al aborto basado en un derecho implícito a la intimidad en la Decimocuarta Enmienda. La decisión fue anulada en la sentencia del Tribunal Supremo de 2022 *Dobbs contra la Organización de Salud de la Mujer de Jackson*, que desmanteló el derecho federal al aborto *de Roe contra Wade* en favor de la legislación federal o estatal.

Romantic era (p. 331) The early nineteenth-century artistic and philosophical movement that challenged Enlightenment ideas of rationality, materialism, and classicism by asserting the prominence of the subjective and emotional national world. The movement originated in Europe in the late eighteenth century and was widely expressed in the arts as the triumph of senses over rationalism.

Romanticismo (pág. 331) Movimiento artístico y filosófico de principios del siglo XIX que desafió las ideas de racionalidad, materialismo y clasicismo de la Ilustración afirmando la prominencia del mundo nacional subjetivo y emocional. El movimiento se originó en Europa a finales del siglo XVIII y se expresó ampliamente en las artes como el triunfo de los sentidos sobre el racionalismo.

Roosevelt Corollary (p. 668) A modification to the Monroe Doctrine made in 1904 that affirmed the right of the United States to intervene in the internal affairs of Caribbean and Latin American countries to preserve order and protect American interests.

Corolario Roosevelt (pág. 668) Modificación de la Doctrina Monroe realizada en 1904 que afirmaba el derecho de Estados Unidos a intervenir en los asuntos internos de los países caribeños y latinoamericanos para preservar el orden y proteger los intereses estadounidenses.

Rough Riders (p. 662) The nickname of Theodore Roosevelt's regiment of the First United States Volunteer Cavalry, which fought in Cuba during the Spanish-American War in 1898. Roosevelt's popularity and political career were boosted by his fame as a Rough Rider.

Rough Riders (pág. 662) El apodo del regimiento de Theodore Roosevelt de la Primera Caballería Voluntaria de Estados Unidos, que luchó en Cuba durante la Guerra Hispano-Americana en 1898. La popularidad y la carrera política de Roosevelt se vieron impulsadas por su fama de Rough Rider.

Russian Revolution (p. 706) Also known as the Bolshevik Revolution. Named for the working-class radicals called Bolsheviks, the Russian Revolution was led by Vladimir Lenin against the czarist government of Nicholas II. After the revolution, the Bolsheviks created the Soviet Union, a communist state.

Revolución Rusa (pág. 706) También conocida como Revolución Bolchevique. Llamada así por los radicales de la clase obrera llamados bolcheviques, la Revolución Rusa fue liderada por Vladimir Lenin contra el gobierno zarista de Nicolás II. Tras la revolución, los bolcheviques crearon la Unión Soviética, un Estado comunista.

S

Sacco and Vanzetti case (p. 736) The 1920 case in which Nicola Sacco and Bartolomeo Vanzetti were convicted of robbery and murder. The trial centered on the defendants' foreign birth and political views, rather than the facts pertaining to their guilt or innocence, and drew worldwide criticism.

Caso Sacco y Vanzetti (pág. 736) Caso de 1920 en el que Nicola Sacco y Bartolomeo Vanzetti fueron condenados por robo y asesinato. El juicio se centró en el nacimiento en el extranjero y las opiniones políticas de los acusados, más que en los hechos relativos a su culpabilidad o inocencia, y suscitó críticas en todo el mundo.

salutary (benign) neglect (p. 160) British colonial policy from around 1700 to 1760 that relaxed supervision of internal colonial affairs as long as the North American colonies produced sufficient raw materials and revenue.

negligencia benévola (pág. 160) Política colonial británica de alrededor de 1700 a 1760 que relajó la supervisión de los asuntos coloniales internos mientras las colonias norteamericanas produjeran suficientes materias primas e ingresos.

Sand Creek massacre (p. 455) A massacre and mutilation of more than 150 Cheyenne and Arapaho Indians, mostly women and children, by U.S. soldiers in southeastern Colorado Territory in November 1864. The atrocity led to decades of continued warfare on the Great Plains.

masacre de Sand Creek (pág. 455) Masacre y mutilación de más de 150 indios cheyenne y arapaho, en su mayoría mujeres y niños, a manos de soldados estadounidenses en el sureste del Territorio de Colorado en noviembre de 1864. La atrocidad provocó décadas de guerra continua en las Grandes Llanuras.

Sandinistas (p. 987) Also known as the National Liberation Front, Nicaraguan revolutionaries of the 1970s who overthrew the dictator Anastasio Somoza with the support of the U.S.S.R. As a result, the United States supported the overthrow of the Sandinista government.

Sandinistas (pág. 987) También conocidos como Frente de Liberación Nacional, revolucionarios nicaragüenses de la década de 1970 que derrocaron al dictador Anastasio Somoza con el apoyo de la URSS. En consecuencia, Estados Unidos apoyó el derrocamiento del gobierno sandinista.

***Santa Clara County v. Southern Pacific Railroad Company* (p. 559)** The 1886 Supreme Court decision that determined a corporation was considered a "person" under the Fourteenth Amendment. This ruling gave corporations the same right of due process that the framers of the amendment had meant to give to freedpeople, thus shielding corporations from government regulation of the workplace.

***Santa Clara County contra Southern Pacific Railroad Company* (pág. 559)** Decisión del Tribunal Supremo de 1886 que determinó que una corporación se consideraba una "persona" en virtud de la Decimocuarta Enmienda. Esta sentencia otorgó a las empresas el mismo derecho al debido proceso que los autores de la enmienda habían querido otorgar a los libertos, protegiendo así a las empresas de la regulación gubernamental del lugar de trabajo.

scalawag (p. 482) A derogatory term in the South for white Southerners who supported Reconstruction.

scalawag (pág. 482) Término despectivo en el Sur para referirse a los sureños blancos que apoyaron la Reconstrucción.

***Schenck v. United States* (p. 716)** The Supreme Court ruling in 1919 limiting free speech that creates a "clear and present danger." The ruling upheld a conviction under the Espionage Act for mailing leaflets opposed to the draft.

***Schenck contra Estados Unidos* (pág. 716)** Sentencia del Tribunal Supremo de 1919 que limita la libertad de expresión que crea un "peligro claro y presente" La sentencia confirmó una condena en virtud de la Ley de Espionaje por enviar folletos en contra del reclutamiento.

school busing (p. 911) The transporting of students to schools within and across school districts to accelerate school desegregation. The practice of school busing was often controversial and continued well into the 1990s.	**transporte escolar (pág. 911)** Transporte de alumnos a escuelas dentro de un mismo distrito escolar o entre distintos distritos para acelerar la segregación escolar. La práctica del transporte escolar en autobús fue a menudo controvertida y continuó hasta bien entrada la década de 1990.
scientific management (p. 560) Also known as Taylorism, a management style developed by Frederick W. Taylor that aimed to continually improve the efficiency of employees by reducing manual labor to its simplest components. While aiming to increase productivity and decrease cost for employers, scientific management proved more successful in accelerating the loss of worker autonomy than in cutting costs.	**gestión científica (pág. 560)** También conocido como taylorismo, un estilo de gestión desarrollado por Frederick W. Taylor que pretendía mejorar continuamente la eficiencia de los empleados reduciendo el trabajo manual a sus componentes más simples. Aunque su objetivo era aumentar la productividad y reducir los costos para los empresarios, la gestión científica tuvo más éxito en acelerar la pérdida de autonomía de los trabajadores que en reducir los costos.
Scottsboro Nine (p. 754) Nine Black youths convicted of raping two white women in Scottsboro, Alabama, in 1931. Their death penalty sentences were later overturned by the U.S. Supreme Court in the case, which drew national and international attention to ongoing racial inequalities in the U.S. criminal system.	**Los Nueve de Scottsboro (pág. 754)** Nueve jóvenes negros condenados por violar a dos mujeres blancas en Scottsboro, Alabama, en 1931. Sus condenas a muerte fueron anuladas posteriormente por el Tribunal Supremo de Estados Unidos en este caso, que atrajo la atención nacional e internacional sobre las desigualdades raciales existentes en el sistema penal estadounidense.
Second Bank of the United States (p. 273) Bank established in 1816 that distributed national currency and regulated state banks after the First Bank of the United States' charter expired. It ceased operation in 1836.	**Segundo Banco de los Estados Unidos (pág. 273)** Banco creado en 1816 que distribuía la moneda nacional y regulaba los bancos estatales tras la expiración de la carta del Primer Banco de los Estados Unidos. Dejó de funcionar en 1836.
Second Battle of Bull Run (Second Manassas) (p. 436) A battle that took place April 28–30, 1862, and resulted in a Union defeat, which led President Lincoln to relieve General Pope of command and replace him with George B. McClellan.	**Segunda Batalla de Bull Run (Segunda Manassas) (pág. 436)** Batalla que tuvo lugar del 28 al 30 de abril de 1862 y que se saldó con la derrota de la Unión, lo que llevó al presidente Lincoln a relevar del mando al general Pope y sustituirlo por George B. McClellan.
Second Continental Congress (p. 172) An assembly of colonial representatives that served as a national government beginning in May 1775 and lasting the duration of the American Revolution. Despite limited formal powers, the Second Continental Congress coordinated the war effort, printed currency, and conducted negotiations with outside powers.	**Segundo Congreso Continental (pág. 172)** Asamblea de representantes coloniales que actuó como gobierno nacional a partir de mayo de 1775 y mientras duró la Revolución Americana. A pesar de sus limitados poderes formales, el Segundo Congreso Continental coordinó el esfuerzo bélico, imprimió moneda y llevó a cabo negociaciones con potencias exteriores.
second front (p. 798) The desire expressed in 1942 by Joseph Stalin for an immediate invasion by U.S., British, and Canadian forces of German-occupied France to take pressure off the Soviet forces fighting the Germans on the eastern front. The attack in Western Europe did not begin until 1944, a fact Stalin resented.	**segundo frente (pág. 798)** El deseo expresado en 1942 por Joseph Stalin de una invasión inmediata por parte de las fuerzas estadounidenses, británicas y canadienses de la Francia ocupada por Alemania para aliviar la presión sobre las fuerzas soviéticas que luchaban contra los alemanes en el frente oriental. El ataque en Europa Occidental no comenzó hasta 1944, hecho que molestó a Stalin.
Second Great Awakening (p. 334) A series of Protestant revivals, larger in number than the First Great Awakening, from the 1790s to the 1830s, that spurred social-reform movements in response to the changes brought about by the market revolution. Prominent leaders of this movement were Charles Grandison Finney and Lyman Beecher.	**Segundo Gran Despertar (pág. 334)** Serie de avivamientos protestantes, más numerosos que el Primer Gran Despertar, desde la década de 1790 hasta la de 1830, que impulsaron movimientos de reforma social en respuesta a los cambios provocados por la revolución del mercado. Los líderes prominentes de este movimiento fueron Charles Grandison Finney y Lyman Beecher.
Second Red Scare (p. 844) Mass fears of communist influence infiltrating the United States and threatening national security from the late 1930s through the 1950s. Such fears resulted in the creation of government-controlled programs and entities such as the House Un-American Activities Committee and the Federal Employee Loyalty Program.	**Segundo Miedo Rojo (pág. 844)** Temor masivo a que la influencia comunista se infiltre en Estados Unidos y amenace la seguridad nacional desde finales de la década de 1930 hasta la de 1950. Estos temores dieron lugar a la creación de programas y entidades controlados por el gobierno, como el Comité de Actividades Antiamericanas de la Cámara de Representantes y el Programa de Lealtad de los Empleados Federales.
Second Seminole War (p. 322) A war between the Seminole nation, including enslaved Blacks who had escaped captivity and joined the tribe, and the U.S. government from 1835 to 1842 over whether the Seminole people would be forced to leave Florida and settle west of the Mississippi River. Despite substantial investments of men, money, and resources, it took seven years for the United States to achieve victory.	**Segunda Guerra Seminole (pág. 322)** Guerra entre la nación Seminole, incluidos los negros esclavizados que habían escapado del cautiverio y se habían unido a la tribu, y el gobierno de EE.UU. de 1835 a 1842 sobre si el pueblo Seminole se vería obligado a abandonar Florida y establecerse al oeste del río Misisipi. A pesar de las considerables inversiones de hombres, dinero y recursos, Estados Unidos tardó siete años en lograr la victoria.
Securities and Exchange Commission (SEC) (p. 760) The 1934 New Deal commission designed to regulate the stock market and ensure that corporations give investors accurate information about their investments.	**Comisión de Bolsa y Valores (SEC) (pág. 760)** Comisión creada en 1934 en el marco del New Deal para regular el mercado de valores y garantizar que las empresas proporcionen a los inversores información precisa sobre sus inversiones.

Sedition Act (p. 714) An act limiting free speech by punishing individuals for expressing opinions deemed hostile to the U.S. government, flag, or military, passed in 1918.	**Ley de Sedición (pág. 714)** Ley que limita la libertad de expresión castigando a las personas por expresar opiniones consideradas hostiles al gobierno, la bandera o el ejército de Estados Unidos, aprobada en 1918.
seditious (p. 128) Describing behavior or language aimed at starting a rebellion against a government.	**sedicioso (pág. 128)** Describe el comportamiento o el lenguaje destinado a iniciar una rebelión contra un gobierno.
segregation (p. 545) The purposeful separation of people into ethnic or racial groups. Segregation was often actively perpetuated and enforced through "Black codes" and Jim Crow-era legislation that persisted into the latter half of the twentieth century.	**segregación (pág. 545)** Separación intencionada de las personas en grupos étnicos o raciales. A menudo, la segregación se perpetuaba y se aplicaba activamente a través de los "códigos negros" y la legislación de la época de Jim Crow, que persistió hasta la segunda mitad del siglo XX.
Selective Service Act (p. 706) The act authorizing a nationwide draft to support U.S. participation in World War I that went into effect in 1917.	**Ley del Servicio Selectivo (pág. 706)** Ley que autoriza la llamada a filas en todo el país para apoyar la participación de Estados Unidos en la Primera Guerra Mundial y que entró en vigor en 1917.
Selective Training and Service Act of 1940 (p. 782) Legislation requiring men between the ages of 18 and 35 to register for the draft, later expanded to age 45. It was the first peacetime draft in U.S. history.	**Ley de Formación y Servicio Selectivos de 1940 (pág. 782)** Legislación que obliga a los hombres de entre 18 y 35 años a inscribirse en el servicio militar obligatorio, ampliada posteriormente a los 45 años. Fue el primer servicio militar obligatorio en tiempos de paz de la historia de Estados Unidos.
separate spheres (p. 302) Widespread belief in the nineteenth century that men and women had separate roles and should occupy separate places in society. According to this belief, men should occupy the social public sphere, while women belonged in the domestic private sphere.	**esferas separadas (pág. 302)** Creencia generalizada en el siglo XIX de que hombres y mujeres tenían papeles separados y debían ocupar lugares separados en la sociedad. Según esta creencia, los hombres debían ocupar la esfera pública social, mientras que las mujeres pertenecían a la esfera privada doméstica.
separation of powers (p. 211) A system of government advocated by Baron de Montesquieu dividing powers across multiple branches of government. In the U.S. Constitution, federal powers are distributed among legislative, executive, and judicial branches.	**separación de poderes (pág. 211)** Sistema de gobierno propugnado por el barón de Montesquieu que divide los poderes en varias ramas del gobierno. En la Constitución de Estados Unidos, los poderes federales se distribuyen entre los poderes legislativo, ejecutivo y judicial.
Servicemen's Readjustment Act (GI Bill) (p. 851) An act that provided college and vocational tuition, low-interest mortgage loans, and unemployment insurance to World War II veterans. Known as the GI Bill, the 1944 law spurred college enrollment, home ownership, and overall economic growth.	**Ley de Reajuste de Militares (pág. 851)** Ley que proporcionaba matrículas universitarias y de formación profesional, préstamos hipotecarios a bajo interés y seguro de desempleo a los veteranos de la Segunda Guerra Mundial. Conocida como GI Bill, la ley de 1944 estimuló la matriculación en la universidad, la compra de viviendas y el crecimiento económico general.
settlement house (p. 596) A community center started by urban reformers in the late nineteenth century. Settlement house organizers resided in the institutions they created and were often female, middle-class, and college educated. More than two hundred settlement houses were established in the United States by 1905.	***settlement house* (pág. 596)** Centro comunitario creado por reformadores urbanos a finales del siglo XIX. Los organizadores de los asentamientos residían en las instituciones que crearon y solían ser mujeres, de clase media y con estudios universitarios. En 1905 se habían establecido más de doscientas casas de colonización en Estados Unidos.
Share Our Wealth society (p. 766) Economic plan created by Huey Long in 1934. Long believed the New Deal did not go far enough and advocated a nationwide standard of living through wealth sharing.	**Sociedad Share Our Wealth (compartir nuestra riqueza) (pág. 766)** Plan económico creado por Huey Long en 1934. Long creía que el New Deal no había ido lo suficientemente lejos y abogaba por un nivel de vida a escala nacional mediante el reparto de la riqueza.
sharecropping (p. 483) A widespread form of agricultural labor in the South after the Civil War in which sharecroppers, often poor Blacks and whites, rented tools and supplies from landowners in exchange for a share of the eventual harvest. Corrupt practices and laws allowing creditors to take part of the harvest for nonpayment often left sharecroppers in permanent debt and resulted in a system of forced labor.	**aparcería (pág. 483)** Forma generalizada de trabajo agrícola en el Sur después de la Guerra Civil en la que los aparceros, a menudo negros y blancos pobres, alquilaban herramientas y suministros a los terratenientes a cambio de una parte de la eventual cosecha. Las prácticas corruptas y las leyes que permitían a los acreedores quedarse con parte de la cosecha en caso de impago a menudo dejaban a los aparceros permanentemente endeudados y daban lugar a un sistema de trabajo forzado.
Shays's Rebellion (p. 207) A rebellion in 1786–1787 by western Massachusetts farmers, many of whom were war veterans, caused mainly by economic hardships and taxation policies they saw as benefitting an eastern elite in the aftermath of the American Revolution. The rebellion encouraged political leaders to consider strengthening the Articles of Confederation.	**Rebelión de Shays (pág. 207)** Rebelión en 1786-1787 de los granjeros del oeste de Massachusetts, muchos de los cuales eran veteranos de guerra, causada principalmente por las dificultades económicas y las políticas fiscales que consideraban que beneficiaban a una élite del este tras la Revolución Americana. La rebelión animó a los líderes políticos a considerar el fortalecimiento de los Artículos de la Confederación.
Sheppard-Towner Act (p. 674) Idea promoted by Jane Addams for urban reform using women's traditional skills as domestic managers; caregivers for children, the elderly, and the needy; and community builders.	**Ley Sheppard-Towner (pág. 674)** Idea promovida por Jane Addams para la reforma urbana utilizando las habilidades tradicionales de las mujeres como administradoras domésticas; cuidadoras de niños, ancianos y necesitados; y constructoras de comunidades.

Sherman Antitrust Act (p. 559) A law enacted in 1890 banning monopolies and business practices that restrained free trade or fixed prices in interstate or foreign commerce. This act was the first congressional legislation to address the problems of trusts.	**Ley Sherman Antimonopolios (pág. 559)** Ley promulgada en 1890 que prohíbe los monopolios y las prácticas empresariales que restringen el libre comercio o fijan los precios en el comercio interestatal o exterior. Esta ley fue la primera legislación del Congreso que abordó los problemas de los fideicomisos.
Sherman Silver Purchase Act (p. 624) The 1890 act that increased the amount of silver the U.S. government was required to purchase to back production of federal dollars. The goal of this annual silver purchase was to raise inflation, and thereby raise the prices farmers were paid for their crops.	**Ley Sherman de Compra de Plata (pág. 624)** Ley de 1890 que aumentó la cantidad de plata que el gobierno de EE.UU. debía comprar para respaldar la producción de dólares federales. El objetivo de esta compra anual de plata era elevar la inflación y, con ello, los precios que se pagaban a los agricultores por sus cosechas.
Sherman's March to the Sea (p. 454) A Union military campaign lasting thirty-seven days led by General Sherman across Georgia from Atlanta on November 15, 1864, to Savannah. Employing hard-war tactics and abandoning their supply lines to speed up their progress, Union troops intentionally blazed a wide path of destruction as they tried to break the morale of Confederate troops.	**La Marcha de Sherman hacia el Mar (pág. 454)** Campaña militar de la Unión de treinta y siete días de duración dirigida por el general Sherman a través de Georgia, desde Atlanta el 15 de noviembre de 1864 hasta Savannah. Empleando tácticas de guerra dura y abandonando sus líneas de suministro para acelerar su avance, las tropas de la Unión abrieron intencionadamente un amplio camino de destrucción mientras intentaban quebrar la moral de las tropas confederadas.
Siege of Vicksburg (p. 451) After a prolonged siege, Union troops forced Confederate forces to surrender at Vicksburg, Mississippi, leading to Union control of the Mississippi River valley and cutting off Louisiana, Arkansas, and Texas from the rest of the Confederacy.	**Asedio de Vicksburg (pág. 451)** Tras un prolongado asedio, las tropas de la Unión obligaron a las fuerzas confederadas a rendirse en Vicksburg, Misisipi, lo que condujo al control de la Unión del valle del río Mississippi y aisló a Louisiana, Arkansas y Texas del resto de la Confederación.
sit-down strike (p. 770) A strike in which workers occupy their place of employment. In 1937 the United Auto Workers conducted sit-down strikes in Flint, Michigan, against General Motors to gain union recognition, higher wages, and better working conditions. The union won its demands.	**huelga de brazos caídos (pág. 770)** Huelga en la que los trabajadores ocupan su lugar de trabajo. En 1937, los United Auto Workers llevaron a cabo huelgas de brazos caídos en Flint, Michigan, contra General Motors para conseguir el reconocimiento del sindicato, salarios más altos y mejores condiciones de trabajo. El sindicato consiguió sus reivindicaciones.
Sixteenth Amendment (p. 698) An amendment ratified in 1913 providing a legal basis for a graduated income tax, which had been previously deemed unconstitutional.	**Decimosexta Enmienda (pág. 698)** Enmienda ratificada en 1913 que proporciona una base legal para un impuesto sobre la renta graduado, que anteriormente se había considerado inconstitucional.
Slaughterhouse Cases (p. 487) A 1873 Supreme Court decision that was one of the first tests of the Fourteenth Amendment when it decided that, although the Fourteenth Amendment guaranteed federal protection for Black people, that protection did not extend to civil or property rights, which were to be determined by the states.	**Slaughterhouse Cases (pág. 487)** Decisión del Tribunal Supremo de 1873 que supuso una de las primeras pruebas de la Decimocuarta Enmienda al decidir que, aunque la Decimocuarta Enmienda garantizaba la protección federal de los negros, dicha protección no se extendía a los derechos civiles o de propiedad, que debían ser determinados por los estados.
slave code (p. 73) A law restricting enslaved persons' rights, largely due to slaveholders' fears of rebellion. Slave codes also defined slavery as a distinct status based on racial identity, which passed that status on through future generations.	**código de esclavos (pág. 73)** Ley que restringía los derechos de las personas esclavizadas, en gran parte debido al temor de los esclavistas a la rebelión. Los códigos esclavistas también definían la esclavitud como un estatus distinto basado en la identidad racial, que transmitía ese estatus a las generaciones futuras.
Smith Act (p. 844) A law signed by Franklin Roosevelt in 1940, which prohibited teaching or advocating the destruction of the U.S. government.	**Ley Smith (pág. 844)** Ley firmada por Franklin Roosevelt en 1940, que prohibía enseñar o abogar por la destrucción del gobierno de Estados Unidos.
Smoot-Hawley Act (p. 750) A 1930 tariff act that significantly raised taxes on imported agricultural and manufactured goods to aid struggling farmers and businesses during the beginning of the Great Depression. In response, other countries greatly increased their duties on American goods, contributing to a sharp decline in global trade.	**Ley Smoot-Hawley (pág. 750)** Ley arancelaria de 1930 que elevó significativamente los impuestos sobre los productos agrícolas y manufacturados importados para ayudar a los agricultores y empresas en dificultades durante el comienzo de la Gran Depresión. En respuesta, otros países aumentaron considerablemente sus aranceles sobre los productos estadounidenses, lo que contribuyó a un fuerte descenso del comercio mundial.
Social Darwinism (p. 597) A belief that human society should be governed by the same principles of natural selection and survival of the fittest that Charles Darwin described in his work on evolutionary theory. Social Darwinism was often employed to justify economic inequality, racism, imperialism, and hostility to federal government regulation.	**Darwinismo social (pág. 597)** Creencia de que la sociedad humana debe regirse por los mismos principios de selección natural y supervivencia del más apto que describió Charles Darwin en su obra sobre la teoría evolutiva. El darwinismo social se empleó a menudo para justificar la desigualdad económica, el racismo, el imperialismo y la hostilidad a la regulación del gobierno federal.

social gospel (p. 607) A religious movement that advocated the application of Christian teachings to social and economic problems. The ideals of the social gospel inspired many progressive reformers but were largely ineffectual, as their reforms sought to change the individual rather than larger social structures and their impact.

evangelio social (pág. 607) Movimiento religioso que propugnaba la aplicación de las enseñanzas cristianas a los problemas sociales y económicos. Los ideales del evangelio social inspiraron a muchos reformistas progresistas, pero fueron en gran medida ineficaces, ya que sus reformas buscaban cambiar al individuo en lugar de las estructuras sociales más amplias y su impacto.

Social Security Act (p. 769) The landmark 1935 act that created retirement pensions for most Americans funded by payroll taxes. It also provided unemployment insurance and assistance for the disabled.

Ley de Seguridad Social (pág. 769) Ley histórica de 1935 que creó las pensiones de jubilación para la mayoría de los estadounidenses, financiadas mediante impuestos sobre las nóminas. También ofrecía seguro de desempleo y asistencia a los discapacitados.

Socialist Party of America (p. 572) A political party established in 1901 by Eugene V. Debs. It advocated labor interests and economic reforms, as well as public ownership of business through democratic processes.

Partido Socialista de América (pág. 572) Partido político fundado en 1901 por Eugene V. Debs. Defendía los intereses laborales y las reformas económicas, así como la propiedad pública de las empresas mediante procesos democráticos.

Solidarity (p. 992) Polish trade-union movement led by Lech Walesa. During the 1980s, Solidarity played a central role in ending communist rule in Poland.

Solidaridad (pág. 992) Movimiento sindical polaco liderado por Lech Wałęsa. Durante la década de 1980, Solidaridad desempeñó un papel fundamental en el fin del régimen comunista en Polonia.

Sons of Liberty (p. 162) A loosely organized society throughout the colonies whose goal was to assure colonial support for resistance to British taxation. The Sons of Liberty often used intimidation tactics against merchants and businesses as well as the crown's representatives.

Hijos de la Libertad (pág. 162) Sociedad poco organizada en todas las colonias cuyo objetivo era asegurar el apoyo colonial a la resistencia a los impuestos británicos. Los Hijos de la Libertad utilizaban a menudo tácticas intimidatorias contra comerciantes y empresas, así como contra los representantes de la corona.

Southern Christian Leadership Conference (SCLC) (p. 870) An organization founded in 1957 by Bayard Rustin, Martin Luther King Jr., and other Black ministers following the successful Montgomery bus boycott to encourage more nonviolent protests against racial segregation and disfranchisement in the South. It was instrumental in organizing major civil rights protests through the 1960s.

Conferencia de Liderazgo Cristiano del Sur (pág. 870) Organización fundada en 1957 por Bayard Rustin, Martin Luther King Jr. y otros ministros negros tras el éxito del boicot a los autobuses de Montgomery para fomentar más protestas no violentas contra la segregación racial y la privación de derechos en el Sur. Tuvo un papel decisivo en la organización de importantes protestas por los derechos civiles durante la década de 1960.

Spanish–American War (p. 661) The war the United States declared against Spain to aid Cuban revolutionaries in their ongoing war for independence. The war was also fought in the Philippines, and U.S. victory led to annexation of the Philippines, Puerto Rico, and Guam from Spain as well as influence in Cuban affairs. It is also sometimes called the War of 1898.

Guerra hispano-estadounidense (pág. 661) Guerra que Estados Unidos declaró contra España para ayudar a los revolucionarios cubanos en su guerra por la independencia. La guerra también se libró en Filipinas, y la victoria estadounidense supuso la anexión de Filipinas, Puerto Rico y Guam a España, así como su influencia en los asuntos cubanos. A veces también se la denomina Guerra de 1898.

Spanish caste system (p. 33) A system developed by the Spanish in the sixteenth century that defined the status of diverse populations based on a racial hierarchy that privileged Europeans.

Sistema de castas español (pág. 33) Sistema desarrollado por los españoles en el siglo XVI que definía el estatus de diversas poblaciones basándose en una jerarquía racial que privilegiaba a los europeos.

speculator (p. 156) An investor who buys large quantities of a commodity at a low price in hopes that prices will rise and produce a profit when sold. Speculation in a product tends to drive up its price.

especulador (pág. 156) Inversor que compra grandes cantidades de una mercancía a bajo precio con la esperanza de que los precios suban y produzcan beneficios al venderla. La especulación con un producto tiende a hacer subir su precio.

spoils system (p. 314) Also known as the "patronage system," introduced by Andrew Jackson, in which federal offices or "spoils" were awarded based on political loyalty. While supporters claimed it encouraged robust political participation, opponents claimed it encouraged corruption. The system remained in place until the late nineteenth century.

sistema de botín (pág. 314) También conocido como "sistema de patronazgo", introducido por Andrew Jackson, en el que los cargos federales o "botines" se concedían en función de la lealtad política. Mientras los partidarios afirmaban que fomentaba una participación política sólida, los detractores afirmaban que fomentaba la corrupción. El sistema se mantuvo hasta finales del siglo XIX.

***Sputnik* (p. 883)** The first artificial satellite, launched in 1957 by the Soviet Union. The launch prompted a major increase in U.S. spending on the space race as well as scientific research and development.

***Sputnik* (pág. 883)** Primer satélite artificial, lanzado en 1957 por la Unión Soviética. El lanzamiento provocó un importante aumento del gasto estadounidense en la carrera espacial, así como en investigación y desarrollo científicos.

Square Deal (p. 692) Theodore Roosevelt's plan to provide economic and political stability to the nation by guaranteeing the rights of everyday workers and protecting business interests.

Acuerdo Justo y Honesto (Square Deal) (pág. 692) Plan de Theodore Roosevelt para proporcionar estabilidad económica y política a la nación garantizando los derechos de los trabajadores y protegiendo los intereses empresariales.

stagflation (p. 935) A period of economic instability in the 1970s characterized by slow economic growth, high inflation, and high unemployment.

estanflación (pág. 935) Periodo de inestabilidad económica en la década de 1970 caracterizado por un lento crecimiento económico, una elevada inflación y un alto desempleo.

Stamp Act (p. 162) A 1765 act of Parliament that imposed a duty on all transactions involving paper items such as newspapers and wills. The Stamp Act prompted widespread, coordinated protests by colonists who insisted it was a direct attempt to raise revenue, and that only their representatives had the right to tax them. It was repealed in 1766.

Ley del Timbre (pág. 162) Ley del Parlamento de 1765 que imponía un impuesto a todas las transacciones con artículos de papel, como periódicos y testamentos. La Ley del Timbre provocó protestas generalizadas y coordinadas de los colonos, que insistían en que era un intento directo de recaudar ingresos y que sólo sus representantes tenían derecho a gravarlos. Fue derogada en 1766.

Stamp Act Congress (p. 164) An assembly of twenty-seven delegates from nine colonies that met in New York in 1765 to petition Parliament to repeal the Stamp Act and coordinate colonial resistance.

Congreso de la Ley del Timbre (pág. 164) Asamblea de veintisiete delegados de nueve colonias que se reunió en Nueva York en 1765 para solicitar al Parlamento la derogación de la Ley del Timbre y coordinar la resistencia colonial.

Statute of Religious Freedom (p. 202) A 1786 law passed by the Virginia Assembly that ensured the separation of church and state and largely guaranteed freedom of religion. Enactment of the statute established a legal precedent followed by other states and was later included in the Bill of Rights to the U.S. Constitution.

Estatuto de Libertad Religiosa (pág. 202) Ley de 1786 aprobada por la Asamblea de Virginia que aseguraba la separación de la Iglesia y el Estado y garantizaba en gran medida la libertad religiosa. La promulgación de la ley sentó un precedente legal que siguieron otros estados y que más tarde se incluyó en la Declaración de Derechos de la Constitución de Estados Unidos.

Stonewall riots (p. 926) A series of protests in 1969 by the gay and lesbian community in New York City after a police raid at the Stonewall Inn, a gathering place for gay men, turned violent. This uprising helped launch the gay liberation movement of the 1970s.

Disturbios de Stonewall (pág. 926) Serie de protestas en 1969 de la comunidad gay y lesbiana de Nueva York tras una redada policial en el Stonewall Inn, lugar de reunión de hombres homosexuales, que se tornó violenta. Este levantamiento contribuyó a lanzar el movimiento de liberación gay de la década de 1970.

Stono Rebellion (p. 118) A 1739 uprising by enslaved Africans and African Americans in South Carolina, which intensified white fear of slave revolts.

Rebelión de Stono (pág. 118) Levantamiento de 1739 de africanos y afroamericanos esclavizados en Carolina del Sur, que intensificó el temor de los blancos a las revueltas de esclavos.

Strategic Arms Limitation Treaty (SALT I) (p. 841) An agreement between the United States and Soviet Union in 1972 to curtail nuclear arms production. The pact froze for five years the number of antiballistic missiles (ABMs), intercontinental ballistic missiles (ICBMs), and submarine-based missiles that each nation could deploy.

Tratado de Limitación de Armas Estratégicas (SALT I) (pág. 841) Acuerdo entre Estados Unidos y la Unión Soviética en 1972 para reducir la producción de armas nucleares. El pacto congeló durante cinco años el número de misiles antibalísticos (ABM), misiles balísticos intercontinentales (ICBM) y misiles submarinos que cada nación podía desplegar.

Strategic Arms Limitation Treaty (SALT II) (p. 946) A strategic arms limitation treaty agreed on by President Jimmy Carter and Soviet leader Leonid Brezhnev in 1979. After the Soviet Union invaded Afghanistan, Carter persuaded the Senate not to ratify the treaty, thereby ending the period of détente.

Tratado de Limitación de Armas Estratégicas (SALT II) (pág. 946) Tratado de limitación de armas estratégicas acordado por el presidente Jimmy Carter y el dirigente soviético Leonid Brézhnev en 1979. Después de que la Unión Soviética invadiera Afganistán, Carter convenció al Senado para que no ratificara el tratado, poniendo fin así al periodo de distensión.

Strategic Arms Reduction Talks (START) (p. 986) Arms-control negotiations between the United States and the Soviet Union that began in 1982 with the goal of significantly reducing existing missiles and warheads rather than simply slowing the growth of nuclear stockpiles as the SALT negotiations had done in the 1970s. The Soviets abandoned the talks in 1983 after the United States deployed new, intermediate-range missiles in Europe. Talks resumed in 1985, leading to the first START agreement in 1991.

Conversaciones sobre la reducción de las armas estratégicas (START) (pág. 986) Negociaciones sobre el control de armamentos entre Estados Unidos y la Unión Soviética que comenzaron en 1982 con el objetivo de reducir significativamente los misiles y las cabezas nucleares existentes en lugar de simplemente frenar el crecimiento de los arsenales nucleares, como habían hecho las negociaciones SALT en los años setenta. Los soviéticos abandonaron las conversaciones en 1983, después de que Estados Unidos desplegara nuevos misiles de alcance intermedio en Europa. Las conversaciones se reanudaron en 1985 y desembocaron en el primer acuerdo START en 1991.

Strategic Defense Initiative (SDI) (p. 986) A proposal first announced by Ronald Reagan in 1983 to build a missile defense system that would use satellite lasers to protect the United States from nuclear attack by shooting down enemy missiles. The initiative was never completed.

Iniciativa de Defensa Estratégica (IDE) (pág. 986) Propuesta anunciada por primera vez por Ronald Reagan en 1983 para construir un sistema de defensa antimisiles que utilizaría láseres por satélite para proteger a Estados Unidos de un ataque nuclear derribando misiles enemigos. La iniciativa nunca llegó a completarse.

Student Nonviolent Coordinating Committee (SNCC) (p. 872) A student-led civil rights organization that grew out of the sit-ins of 1960. The organization originally focused on taking nonviolent direct action and political organizing to achieve its goals.

Comité Coordinador Estudiantil No Violento (SNCC) (pág. 872) Organización de derechos civiles dirigida por estudiantes que surgió a raíz de las sentadas de 1960. En un principio, la organización se centró en la acción directa no violenta y la organización política para lograr sus objetivos.

Students for a Democratic Society (SDS) (p. 927) A student-led activist organization that advocated the formation of a "New Left" to overturn the social and political status quo. SDS growth on college campuses was fueled by opposition to U.S. Cold War policies, especially involvement in the Vietnam War.

Estudiantes por una Sociedad Democrática (SDS) (pág. 927) Organización activista dirigida por estudiantes que abogaba por la formación de una "Nueva Izquierda" para acabar con el statu quo social y político. El crecimiento del SDS en los campus universitarios se vio impulsado por la oposición a las políticas estadounidenses de la Guerra Fría, especialmente a la participación en la guerra de Vietnam.

subsistence farmer (p. 81) A farmer who grows crops that can supply only the needs of the family rather than being sold for profit.

agricultor de subsistencia (pág. 81) Agricultor que cultiva productos que sólo pueden satisfacer las necesidades de la familia en lugar de venderlos para obtener beneficios.

subtreasury system (p. 622) A reform proposal to use government warehouses to hold excess farm products to control supply and maintain crop values. In return, farmers would receive government loans for 80 percent of the value of the product stored.

sistema de subtesorería (pág. 622) Propuesta de reforma consistente en utilizar los almacenes públicos para guardar los excedentes de productos agrícolas con el fin de controlar la oferta y mantener el valor de las cosechas. A cambio, los agricultores recibirían préstamos del gobierno por el 80% del valor del producto almacenado.

Sugar Act (p. 161) A 1764 act of Parliament designed to increase revenue and encourage the importation of molasses from the British West Indies by cracking down on the smuggling of French molasses into the colonies even as the tax on it was cut in half.

Ley del Azúcar (pág. 161) Ley del Parlamento de 1764 diseñada para aumentar los ingresos y fomentar la importación de melaza de las Indias Occidentales británicas mediante la represión del contrabando de melaza francesa en las colonias, incluso cuando el impuesto sobre la misma se redujo a la mitad.

Sun Belt (p. 857) The southern and western parts of the United States, to which millions of Americans moved after World War II. Migrants were drawn by the region's climate and jobs in the defense, petroleum, and chemical industries.

Cinturón del Sol (pág. 857) Las zonas sur y oeste de Estados Unidos, a las que se trasladaron millones de estadounidenses tras la II Guerra Mundial. Los emigrantes fueron atraídos por el clima de la región y los puestos de trabajo en las industrias química, petrolera y de defensa.

Superfund (p. 937) A reserve fund established in 1980 to be used by the Environmental Protection Agency to clean up sites of industrial pollution and waste deemed particularly hazardous to public health.

Superfondo (pág. 937) Fondo de reserva creado en 1980 por la Agencia de Protección del Medio Ambiente para limpiar los vertederos de contaminación industrial y residuos considerados especialmente peligrosos para la salud pública.

supply-side economics (p. 977) The economic theory that tax cuts and industry deregulation raise wages and lower unemployment, thereby promoting economic growth.

economía de la oferta (pág. 977) Teoría económica según la cual los recortes fiscales y la desregulación de la industria aumentan los salarios y reducen el desempleo, fomentando así el crecimiento económico.

sweatshops (p. 595) Small factories or shops in which workers toiled under poor conditions. Business owners, particularly in the garment industry, turned tenement apartments into sweatshops.

talleres clandestinos (pág. 595) Pequeñas fábricas o tiendas en las que los trabajadores trabajan en malas condiciones. Los empresarios, sobre todo los de la industria textil, convirtieron los pisos de vecindad en talleres clandestinos.

T

Taft-Hartley Act (p. 852) The 1947 law that curtailed unions' ability to organize. It prevented unions from barring employment to non-union members and authorized the federal government to halt a strike for eighty days if it interfered with the national interest.

Ley Taft-Hartley (pág. 852) Ley de 1947 que limitó la capacidad de organización de los sindicatos. Impedía a los sindicatos prohibir el empleo a los no afiliados y autorizaba al gobierno federal a detener una huelga durante ochenta días si interfería con el interés nacional.

Taliban (p. 993) A militant movement of radical Sunni Muslim fundamentalists that ruled Afghanistan in the mid-1990s. The Taliban established a strict theocracy and allowed al-Qaeda, a Sunni Muslim terrorist organization, to establish a base of operations in the country. The Taliban returned to power in Afghanistan in 2021.

Talibán (pág. 993) Movimiento militante de fundamentalistas musulmanes suníes radicales que gobernó Afganistán a mediados de la década de 1990. Los talibanes establecieron una estricta teocracia y permitieron a Al Qaeda, organización terrorista musulmana suní, establecer una base de operaciones en el país. Los talibanes volvieron al poder en Afganistán en 2021.

Tammany Hall (p. 621) New York City's political machine during the nineteenth century. The term became a byword for political corruption and favoritism.

Tammany Hall (pág. 621) La maquinaria política de la ciudad de Nueva York durante el siglo XIX. El término se convirtió en sinónimo de corrupción política y favoritismo.

Tariff of 1816 (p. 270) A protective tariff designed to increase the cost of imported manufactured goods to improve domestic sales.

Arancel de 1816 (pág. 270) Arancel protector destinado a aumentar el coste de los productos manufacturados importados para mejorar las ventas nacionales.

Tariff of 1828 (Tariff of Abominations) (p. 312) A protective tariff that substantially raised tariff rates and extended duties to include raw materials such as wool, hemp, and molasses. It was passed despite opposition from southeastern states.

Arancel de 1828 (Arancel de las Abominaciones) (pág. 312) Arancel protector que elevó sustancialmente los tipos arancelarios y amplió los derechos para incluir materias primas como la lana, el cáñamo y la melaza. Se aprobó a pesar de la oposición de los estados del sureste.

Tea Act (p. 167) An act of Parliament in 1773 that aimed to reduce the financial debts of Britain and the British East India Company by providing the company with a tea monopoly in the British American colonies leading to widespread colonial protests.

Ley del Té (pág. 167) Ley del Parlamento de 1773 que pretendía reducir las deudas financieras de Gran Bretaña y la Compañía Británica de las Indias Orientales proporcionando a la compañía el monopolio del té en las colonias británicas americanas, lo que provocó protestas coloniales generalizadas.

Tea Party movement (p. 1021) A loose coalition of conservatives, populists, and libertarians that advocated small government, low taxes, and reduced federal deficits. The Tea Party movement became a driving force in the Republican Party and mobilized opposition to President Obama's agenda.

Movimiento Tea Party (pág. 1021) Coalición informal de conservadores, populistas y libertarios que aboga por un gobierno pequeño, impuestos bajos y déficits federales reducidos. El movimiento Tea Party se convirtió en una fuerza impulsora del Partido Republicano y movilizó la oposición a la agenda del presidente Obama.

Teapot Dome scandal (p. 721) An oil and land scandal that highlighted the close ties between big business and the federal government in the early 1920s.

Escándalo Teapot Dome (pág. 721) Escándalo relacionado con el petróleo y la tierra que puso de manifiesto los estrechos vínculos entre las grandes empresas y el gobierno federal a principios de la década de 1920.

Tejano (p. 319) A Mexican resident of Texas. Although some Tejano elites allied themselves with American settlers, most American settlers were resistant to adopting Tejano culture.

Tejano (pág. 319) Mexicano residente en Texas. Aunque algunas élites tejanas se aliaron con los colonos estadounidenses, la mayoría de éstos se resistieron a adoptar la cultura tejana.

Teller Amendment (p. 661) An amendment to the 1898 declaration of war against Spain stipulating that Cuba should be free and independent. The amendment was largely ignored in the aftermath of the U.S. victory.

Enmienda Teller (pág. 661) Enmienda a la declaración de guerra contra España de 1898 que estipulaba que Cuba debía ser libre e independiente. La enmienda fue ignorada en gran medida tras la victoria estadounidense.

temperance (p. 336) The movement to moderate and then ban the sale and consumption of alcohol that emerged in the early nineteenth century as part of the larger push, mainly by middle-class reformers, to improve society.

templanza (pág. 336) Movimiento para moderar y luego prohibir la venta y el consumo de alcohol que surgió a principios del siglo XIX como parte de un impulso más amplio, principalmente por parte de los reformistas de clase media, para mejorar la sociedad.

tenement (p. 594) A multifamily apartment building that housed many poor urban dwellers at the turn of the twentieth century. Tenements were crowded, uncomfortable, and dangerous. Their poor living conditions and safety violations inspired government regulations regarding housing safety.

tenement (pág. 594) Edificio de apartamentos multifamiliar que albergaba a muchos habitantes urbanos pobres a principios del siglo XX. Las viviendas estaban abarrotadas, eran incómodas y peligrosas. Sus malas condiciones de vida y las infracciones de seguridad inspiraron la normativa gubernamental sobre seguridad en las viviendas.

Tennessee Valley Authority (TVA) (p. 762) A New Deal agency that brought low-cost electricity to rural Americans and redeveloped the Tennessee River valley through flood- control projects. The agency built, owned, and supervised a number of power plants and dams.

Autoridad del Valle del Tennessee (TVA) (pág. 762) Agencia del New Deal que suministró electricidad a bajo costo a las zonas rurales de Estados Unidos y remodeló el valle del río Tennessee mediante proyectos de control de inundaciones. La agencia construyó, poseyó y supervisó varias centrales eléctricas y presas.

Tenochtitlán (p. 8) Capital city of the Aztec empire beginning in the fourteenth century. It was an island city, surrounded by artificial floating gardens and canals. In 1521, the city was taken over by the Spanish. Modern Mexico City is on the ancient site of Tenochtitlán.

Tenochtitlán (pág. 8) Capital del imperio azteca a partir del siglo XIV. Era una ciudad-isla, rodeada de jardines flotantes artificiales y canales. En 1521, la ciudad fue tomada por los españoles. La actual Ciudad de México se asienta sobre el antiguo emplazamiento de Tenochtitlán.

Tenure of Office Act (p. 473) A law passed by Congress in 1867 to prevent the president from firing appointed officials confirmed by the Senate without Senate approval. President Johnson was impeached, but not convicted, for violating the act.

Tenure of Office Act (Ley de Permanencia en el Cargo) (pág. 473) Ley aprobada por el Congreso en 1867 para impedir que el presidente despidiera a funcionarios nombrados y confirmados por el Senado sin la aprobación de éste. El presidente Johnson fue procesado, pero no condenado, por violar la ley.

terrorism (p. 989) The use of violence to inspire fear in service of achieving a political goal.

terrorismo (pág. 989) Uso de la violencia para inspirar miedo al servicio de la consecución de un objetivo político.

Tet Offensive (p. 893) A widescale offensive mounted by Vietcong and North Vietnamese forces specifically targeting population centers across South Vietnam in January 1968. The offensive was turned back, but its initial success surprised many Americans and increased public opposition to the war.

Ofensiva del Tet (pág. 893) Ofensiva a gran escala llevada a cabo por el Vietcong y las fuerzas norvietnamitas contra centros de población de Vietnam del Sur en enero de 1968. La ofensiva fue rechazada, pero su éxito inicial sorprendió a muchos estadounidenses y aumentó la oposición pública a la guerra.

Third Reich (p. 779) Adolf Hitler's name for the Nazi regime in Germany (1933–1945). Accordingly, the First Reich was the Holy Roman Empire (800–1806), and the Second Reich was the German Empire (1871–1918).

Tercer Reich (pág. 779) Nombre dado por Adolf Hitler al régimen nazi en Alemania (1933-1945). En consecuencia, el Primer Reich fue el Sacro Imperio Romano Germánico (800-1806), y el Segundo Reich fue el Imperio Alemán (1871-1918).

Thirteenth Amendment (p. 456) Amendment to the Constitution abolishing slavery except as a form of criminal punishment. The first of three Reconstruction-era amendments, it was passed in January 1865.

Decimotercera Enmienda (pág. 456) Enmienda a la Constitución que abolía la esclavitud excepto como forma de castigo penal. La primera de las tres enmiendas de la era de la Reconstrucción, fue aprobada en enero de 1865.

Three Sisters (p. 6) Native American agricultural practice of beneficially planting corn, beans, and squash together, resulting in higher yields and a healthy diet.

Tres Hermanas (pág. 6) Práctica agrícola de los nativos americanos consistente en plantar maíz, judías y calabaza juntos para obtener mayores cosechas y una dieta sana.

three-fifths compromise (p. 210) The compromise between northern and southern delegates at the 1787 Constitutional Convention to count enslaved persons as three-fifths of a free person in deciding the proportion of representation in the House of Representatives and taxation by the federal government. It had the long-term effect of granting slaveholding states a larger amount of voting power.

compromiso de los tres quintos (pág. 210) Compromiso entre los delegados del norte y del sur en la Convención Constitucional de 1787 para contar a las personas esclavizadas como tres quintos de una persona libre a la hora de decidir la proporción de representación en la Cámara de Representantes y la tributación por parte del gobierno federal. Tuvo el efecto a largo plazo de otorgar a los estados esclavistas un mayor poder de voto.

Tiananmen Square (p. 995) The location of the 1989 pro-democracy protests by Chinese university students who wanted political and economic reforms. China's leader, Deng Xiaoping, dispatched the military to break up the protests, killing thousands and crushing the uprising.

Plaza de Tiananmen (pág. 995) Lugar de las protestas prodemocráticas de 1989 de estudiantes universitarios chinos que querían reformas políticas y económicas. El líder chino, Deng Xiaoping, envió al ejército a disolver las protestas, matando a miles de personas y aplastando el levantamiento.

***To Secure These Rights* (p. 868)** Report issued by the Committee on Civil Rights in 1947 that advocated extending racial equality. Among its recommendations was the desegregation of the military, which Truman instituted by executive order in 1948.

***To Secure These Rights* (pág. 868)** Informe publicado por el Comité de Derechos Civiles en 1947 que abogaba por ampliar la igualdad racial. Entre sus recomendaciones estaba la desegregación del ejército, que Truman instituyó por orden ejecutiva en 1948.

totalitarianism (p. 835) A form of government in which all aspects of political, economic, social, and cultural life are controlled by the state, typically in the hands of a single political party. During the Cold War, the United States often described its communist rivals as inflicting a totalitarian system on the countries where they held power.

totalitarismo (pág. 835) Forma de gobierno en la que todos los aspectos de la vida política, económica, social y cultural están controlados por el Estado, normalmente en manos de un único partido político. Durante la Guerra Fría, Estados Unidos decía que sus rivales comunistas impusieron un sistema totalitario en los países donde ejercían el poder.

Townshend Acts (p. 165) A series of acts of Parliament in 1767 that instituted an import tax on a broad range of items including glass, lead, paint, paper, and tea. The taxes prompted a boycott of British goods, because of a lack of colonial representation in the Parliament and the desire of the colonists to avoid increased taxes and led to increased violence between British soldiers and colonists.

Leyes Townshend (pág. 165) Una serie de leyes del Parlamento en 1767 que instituyeron un impuesto de importación sobre una amplia gama de artículos, incluyendo vidrio, plomo, pintura, papel y té. Los impuestos provocaron un boicot a los productos británicos, debido a la falta de representación colonial en el Parlamento y al deseo de los colonos de evitar el aumento de los impuestos, y condujeron a un aumento de la violencia entre soldados británicos y colonos.

Trail of Tears (p. 324) The forced march following passage of the Indian Removal Act of some 15,000 Cherokees from Georgia to areas west of the Mississippi River that were designated as Indian Territory, beginning in 1831. Inadequate planning, food, water, sanitation, and medicine led to the deaths of thousands of Cherokees.

Camino de las Lágrimas (pág. 324) Marcha forzada de unos 15,000 cherokees desde Georgia a zonas al oeste del río Misisipi, designadas Territorio Indio, a partir de 1831. La pobre planificación y la escasez de alimentación, agua, salubridad y medicinas adecuadas provocaron la muerte de miles de cherokees.

transcendentalism (p. 337) A Romantic-era movement founded in the 1830s, proposing that individuals look inside themselves and to nature for spiritual and moral guidance rather than to formal religion or organizations.

trascendentalismo (pág. 337) Movimiento de la era romántica fundado en la década de 1830, que proponía que los individuos buscaran en su interior y en la naturaleza orientación espiritual y moral en lugar de recurrir a la religión formal o a organizaciones.

transcontinental railroad (p. 416) A railroad linking the East and West Coasts of North America. Completed in 1869, the transcontinental railroad facilitated the flow of migrants and the development of economic connections between the West and the East and symbolized American industrial and economic achievement.

ferrocarril transcontinental (pág. 416) Ferrocarril que une las costas este y oeste de Norteamérica. Terminado en 1869, el ferrocarril transcontinental facilitó el flujo de emigrantes y el desarrollo de conexiones económicas entre el Oeste y el Este y simbolizó los logros industriales y económicos estadounidenses.

Treaty of Fort Laramie (p. 534) A treaty of 1851 that sought to confine American Indian tribes on the northern plains to designated areas in an attempt to keep white settlers from encroaching on their land. In 1868, the second Treaty of Fort Laramie gave northern tribes control over the "Great Reservation" in parts of present-day Montana, Wyoming, North Dakota, and South Dakota. The treaty was ineffective in keeping out white settlers and hunters.

Tratado de Fort Laramie (pág. 534) Tratado de 1851 que pretendía confinar a las tribus indias americanas de las llanuras del norte en zonas designadas en un intento de evitar que los colonos blancos invadieran sus tierras. En 1868, el segundo Tratado de Fort Laramie otorgó a las tribus del norte el control de la "Gran Reserva" en partes de los actuales Montana, Wyoming, Dakota del Norte y Dakota del Sur. El tratado fue ineficaz para mantener alejados a los colonos y cazadores blancos.

Treaty of Ghent (p. 282) The accord signed in December 1814 that ended the War of 1812 and reestablished the pre-war status quo regarding land claims between the United States and Britain.

Tratado de Gante (pág. 282) Acuerdo firmado en diciembre de 1814 que puso fin a la Guerra de 1812 y restableció el statu quo anterior a la guerra en relación con las reivindicaciones territoriales entre Estados Unidos y Gran Bretaña.

Treaty of Greenville (p. 240) A 1795 treaty signed following the Battle of Fallen Timbers. The treaty ended the Northwest Indian War and ceded vast tracts of lands claimed by American Indians in the Northwest Territory to the United States.

Tratado de Greenville (pág. 240) Tratado de 1795 firmado tras la batalla de Fallen Timbers. El tratado puso fin a la Guerra India del Noroeste y cedió a Estados Unidos vastas extensiones de tierras reclamadas por los indios americanos en el Territorio del Noroeste.

Treaty of Guadalupe Hidalgo (p. 398) The 1848 treaty ending the Mexican-American War. In exchange for $15 million and a settlement of $3 million in U.S. citizens' claims against the Mexican government, the prior U.S. annexation of Texas was officially recognized, and the California and the New Mexico territories were ceded to the United States.

Tratado de Guadalupe Hidalgo (pág. 398) Tratado de 1848 que puso fin a la guerra entre México y Estados Unidos. A cambio de 15 millones de dólares y un acuerdo de 3 millones de dólares en reclamaciones de ciudadanos estadounidenses contra el gobierno mexicano, se reconoció oficialmente la anexión previa de Texas por parte de Estados Unidos y se cedieron a Estados Unidos los territorios de California y Nuevo México.

Treaty of Medicine Lodge (p. 534) The 1867 treaty that provided reservation lands for the Comanche, Kiowa-Apache, and Southern Arapaho to settle. Despite this agreement, white hunters soon invaded this territory and destroyed the buffalo herd.

Tratado de Medicine Lodge (pág. 534) Tratado de 1867 que proporcionó tierras de reserva para que se asentaran los comanches, kiowa-apaches y arapaho del sur. A pesar de este acuerdo, los cazadores blancos pronto invadieron este territorio y destruyeron la manada de búfalos.

Treaty of New Echota (p. 323) A treaty made in 1836 in which a small group of Cherokee men agreed to exchange their land in the Southeast for money and land in Indian Territory. Although the treaty was obtained without tribal approval, it was approved by the U.S. Congress.

Tratado de Nueva Echota (pág. 323) Tratado realizado en 1836 en el que un pequeño grupo de hombres cherokee acordaron intercambiar sus tierras en el sureste por dinero y tierras en el Territorio Indio. Aunque el tratado se obtuvo sin la aprobación tribal, fue aprobado por el Congreso de Estados Unidos.

Treaty of Utrecht (p. 110) The 1713 treaty that ended Queen Anne's War. It aimed to achieve peace by balancing the interests of European powers and their colonial possessions.

Tratado de Utrecht (pág. 110) Tratado de 1713 que puso fin a la Guerra de la Reina Ana. Su objetivo era lograr la paz equilibrando los intereses de las potencias europeas y sus posesiones coloniales.

Treaty of Versailles (p. 707) The treaty officially ending World War I and creating the League of Nations, signed in 1919. The treaty imposed a "war guilt" clause on Germany, required the payment of billions of dollars in reparations to the Allies, stripped Germany of its colonies and some of its territory, and placed strict limits on the German military. The United States never ratified the treaty.

Tratado de Versalles (pág. 707) Tratado por el que se pone fin oficialmente a la Primera Guerra Mundial y se crea la Sociedad de Naciones, firmado en 1919. El tratado imponía a Alemania una cláusula de "culpabilidad de guerra", exigía el pago de miles de millones de dólares en reparaciones a los Aliados, despojaba a Alemania de sus colonias y parte de su territorio y ponía límites estrictos al ejército alemán. Estados Unidos nunca ratificó el tratado.

Treaty (Peace) of Paris (p. 189) The 1783 treaty that ended the Revolutionary War, recognized American independence, and established U.S. territory as the lands between the Mississippi River in the west, Florida in the South, and Canada to the north.

Tratado (de paz) de París (pág. 189) Tratado de 1783 que puso fin a la Guerra de la Independencia, reconoció la independencia de Estados Unidos y estableció el territorio estadounidense como las tierras comprendidas entre el río Misisipi al oeste, Florida al sur y Canadá al norte.

Triangle Shirtwaist fire (p. 687) An infamous industrial fire at the Triangle Shirtwaist factory in New York City in 1911. Inadequate fire safety provisions led to the deaths of 146 workers, mostly young women and girls, and spurred efforts to regulate occupational safety.

Incendio de Triangle Shirtwaist (pág. 687) Infame incendio industrial en la fábrica Triangle Shirtwaist de Nueva York en 1911. Las disposiciones inadecuadas en materia de seguridad contra incendios provocaron la muerte de 146 trabajadores, en su mayoría mujeres jóvenes y niñas, e impulsaron los esfuerzos para regular la seguridad en el trabajo.

Tripartite Pact (p. 783) A 1940 mutual defense agreement between Japan, Germany, and Italy meant to deter U.S. military action against those countries.

Pacto Tripartito (pág. 783) Acuerdo de defensa mutua de 1940 entre Japón, Alemania e Italia destinado a disuadir la acción militar estadounidense contra esos países.

Truman Doctrine (p. 835) The U.S. pledge during the Truman administration to provide political, military, and economic aid to all democratic countries under threat of communism from internal or external sources. Truman issued the doctrine in response to perceived communist threats to Greece and Turkey.

Doctrina Truman (pág. 835) Compromiso de Estados Unidos durante la administración Truman de proporcionar ayuda política, militar y económica a todos los países democráticos amenazados por el comunismo de origen interno o externo. Truman promulgó la doctrina en respuesta a las amenazas comunistas percibidas en Grecia y Turquía.

trust (p. 559) A business monopoly formed in the late nineteenth and early twentieth centuries through mergers and consolidation that inhibited competition and controlled the market.

trust (pág. 559) Monopolio empresarial formado a finales del siglo XIX y principios del XX mediante fusiones y consolidaciones que inhibían la competencia y controlaban el mercado.

Tuscarora War (p. 108) A war launched by Tuscarora Indians from 1711 to 1715 against European settlers in North Carolina and their allies from the Yamasee, Catawba, and Cherokee nations.

Guerra Tuscarora (pág. 108) Guerra emprendida por los indios Tuscarora entre 1711 y 1715 contra los colonos europeos de Carolina del Norte y sus aliados de las naciones Yamasee, Catawba y Cherokee.

Tuskegee airmen (p. 786) Black pilots and airmen who served in segregated units during World War II. They earned fame escorting U.S. bomber aircraft in Europe and North Africa.

Pilotos Tuskegee (pág. 786) Pilotos y aviadores negros que sirvieron en unidades segregadas durante la Segunda Guerra Mundial. Se hicieron famosos escoltando bombarderos estadounidenses en Europa y África del Norte.

Tuskegee Institute (p. 678) An educational institute for southern Blacks founded in 1881 by Booker T. Washington. Following Washington's philosophy, the institute focused on teaching industrious habits and practical job skills.

Instituto Tuskegee (pág. 678) Instituto educativo para negros del sur fundado en 1881 por Booker T. Washington. Siguiendo la filosofía de Washington, el instituto se centraba en enseñar hábitos laboriosos y habilidades prácticas para el trabajo.

Twenty-first Amendment (p. 761) The constitutional amendment ratified in 1933 to repeal the Eighteenth Amendment and prohibition.

Vigesimoprimera Enmienda (pág. 761) Enmienda constitucional ratificada en 1933 para derogar la Decimoctava Enmienda y la prohibición.

Twenty-sixth Amendment (p. 943) The 1971 constitutional amendment lowering the voting age to eighteen in federal, state, and local elections.

Vigesimosexta Enmienda (pág. 943) Enmienda constitucional de 1971 que rebaja la edad de voto a los dieciocho años en las elecciones federales, estatales y locales.

Tydings-McDuffie Act (p. 756) The 1934 act granting independence to the Philippines and restricting Filipino immigration into the United States.

Ley Tydings-McDuffie (pág. 756) Ley de 1934 que concede la independencia a Filipinas y restringe la inmigración filipina a Estados Unidos.

U

U.S. Immigration and Customs Enforcement (ICE) (p. 1028) A branch of the Department of Homeland Security created in 2003 to prevent and investigate illegal immigration to the United States and cross-border crime.

Servicio de Control de Inmigración y Aduanas de los Estados Unidos (ICE) (pág. 1028) Subdivisión del Departamento de Seguridad Nacional creada en 2003 para prevenir e investigar la inmigración ilegal en Estados Unidos y la delincuencia transfronteriza.

***Uncle Tom's Cabin* (p. 412)** A novel by abolitionist Harriet Beecher Stowe, published in 1852. Meant to publicize the evils of slavery, the novel struck an emotional chord in the North, expanding calls for the abolition of slavery, and was an international bestseller.

La *cabaña del tío* Tom (pág. 412) Una novela de la abolicionista Harriet Beecher Stowe, publicada en 1852. La novela, que pretendía dar a conocer los males de la esclavitud, tocó una fibra sensible en el Norte, extendió las peticiones de abolición de la esclavitud y se convirtió en un éxito de ventas internacional.

Underground Railroad (p. 408) A series of routes from southern plantation areas to northern free states and Canada along which abolitionist supporters, known as conductors, provided hiding places and transportation for enslaved people fleeing bondage.

Ferrocarril subterráneo (pág. 408) Una serie de rutas desde las zonas de plantaciones del sur hasta los estados libres del norte y Canadá a lo largo de las cuales los partidarios abolicionistas, conocidos como conductores, proporcionaban escondites y transporte a las personas esclavizadas que huían de la esclavitud.

Underwood Tariff Act (p. 698) A 1913 act that reduced import duties. The Underwood Act appealed to farmers and southerners who sought lower prices on manufactured goods.

Ley Arancelaria Underwood (pág. 698) Ley de 1913 que redujo los derechos de importación. La Ley Underwood atrajo a los agricultores y sureños que buscaban precios más bajos para los productos manufacturados.

union (p. 295) A group of organized allied workers seeking rights and benefits from their employers through collective efforts. By collectively bargaining, workers may negotiate with employers with more strength than the individual worker.

sindicato (pág. 295) Grupo de trabajadores aliados organizados que buscan derechos y beneficios de sus empleadores a través de esfuerzos colectivos. Mediante la negociación colectiva, los trabajadores pueden negociar con los empresarios con más fuerza que el trabajador individual.

***United States v. Cruikshank* (p. 488)** The 1876 Supreme Court ruling that further defined and limited the federal powers under the Fourteenth Amendment after the 1873 Slaughterhouse Cases ruling, which protected Black people against abuses only by state officials and agencies but exempted private groups, such as the Ku Klux Klan.

***United States contra Cruikshank* (pág. 488)** Sentencia de 1876 del Tribunal Supremo que definió y limitó aún más los poderes federales en virtud de la Decimocuarta Enmienda tras la sentencia de 1873 de los Slaughterhouse Cases, que protegía a los negros frente a los abusos cometidos únicamente por funcionarios y organismos estatales, pero eximía a grupos privados, como el Ku Klux Klan.

***United States v. E. C. Knight Company* (p. 560)** The 1895 Supreme Court ruling that manufacturing was a local activity within a state and that, even if it was a monopoly, it was not subject to congressional regulation. This ruling rendered the Sherman Antitrust Act virtually powerless, because it left most trusts in the manufacturing sector, thus beyond the act's jurisdiction.

***United States contra E. C. Knight Company* (pág. 560)** Sentencia del Tribunal Supremo de 1895 que establece que la fabricación es una actividad local dentro de un estado y que, aunque se trate de un monopolio, no está sujeta a la regulación del Congreso. Esta sentencia dejó prácticamente sin efecto la Ley Sherman de Defensa de la Competencia, ya que dejaba a la mayoría de los trusts en el sector manufacturero, por lo tanto fuera de la jurisdicción de la ley.

Universal Negro Improvement Association (UNIA) (p. 732) Organization founded by Marcus Garvey in 1914 to promote Black self-help, pan-Africanism, and racial separatism.

Asociación Universal para la Mejora del Hombre Negro (UNIA) (pág. 732) Organización fundada por Marcus Garvey en 1914 para promover la autoayuda de los negros, el panafricanismo y el separatismo racial.

USA Patriot Act (p. 1014) A law passed in 2001 in response to the September 11 terror attacks. The law eased restrictions on domestic and foreign intelligence gathering and expanded governmental power to deport immigrants suspected of terrorism.

USA Patriot Act (pág. 1014) Ley aprobada en 2001 en respuesta a los atentados terroristas del 11 de septiembre. La ley suavizó las restricciones a la recopilación de información de inteligencia nacional y extranjera y amplió las facultades del gobierno para deportar a inmigrantes sospechosos de terrorismo.

utopian society (p. 344) A community formed in the first half of the nineteenth century to embody alternative social and economic visions and to create models for society at large to follow.

sociedad utópica (pág. 344) Comunidad formada en la primera mitad del siglo XIX para encarnar visiones sociales y económicas alternativas y crear modelos a seguir por la sociedad en general.

V

Valley Forge (p. 183) The site of the winter 1778 encampment of the Continental army, at which the Continental army overcame numerous challenges.

Valley Forge (pág. 183) Lugar del campamento de invierno de 1778 del ejército continental, en el que éste superó numerosos desafíos.

vertical integration (p. 557) An organizational technique used by a company to gain control over all steps in the production of a product. Carnegie Steel, an example of a vertically integrated corporation, controlled the mines where iron ore was acquired and the mills where it was turned into steel.

integración vertical (pág. 557) Técnica organizativa utilizada por una empresa para hacerse con el control de todas las etapas de la fabricación de un producto. Carnegie Steel, ejemplo de empresa integrada verticalmente, controlaba las minas donde se adquiría el mineral de hierro y las fábricas donde se convertía en acero.

veto (p. 70) The right to block a decision made by a governing body.

veto (pág. 70) Derecho a bloquear una decisión tomada por un órgano de gobierno.

Vietcong (p. 890) The popular name for the National Liberation Front, formed in 1959 in South Vietnam. The Vietcong waged a military insurgency against the U.S.-backed president, Ngo Dinh Diem, and received support from Ho Chi Minh, the leader of North Vietnam.

Vietcong (pág. 890) Nombre popular del Frente de Liberación Nacional, formado en 1959 en Vietnam del Sur. El Vietcong llevó a cabo una insurgencia militar contra el presidente respaldado por Estados Unidos, Ngo Dinh Diem, y recibió el apoyo de Ho Chi Minh, el líder de Vietnam del Norte.

Vietnam War (p. 892) Conflict between the communist nationalist government in North Vietnam, backed by the Soviet Union and China, against the United Nations and U.S.-backed South Vietnam government. The war is seen as part of a series of proxy wars as a result of Cold War tensions between the United States and the Soviet Union from 1954 to 1975.

Guerra de Vietnam (pág. 892) Conflicto entre el gobierno nacionalista comunista de Vietnam del Norte, respaldado por la Unión Soviética y China, contra el gobierno de Vietnam del Sur, apoyado por las Naciones Unidas y Estados Unidos. La guerra se considera parte de una serie de guerras por poderes como resultado de las tensiones de la Guerra Fría entre Estados Unidos y la Unión Soviética de 1954 a 1975.

Vietnamization (p. 895) President Richard Nixon's strategy of turning over greater responsibility for the fighting of the Vietnam War to the South Vietnamese army.

Vietnamización (pág. 895) Estrategia del presidente Richard Nixon de traspasar una mayor responsabilidad en la lucha de la guerra de Vietnam al ejército survietnamita.

Virginia and Kentucky Resolutions (p. 226) Resolutions passed by legislatures in Virginia and Kentucky in protest of the Alien and Sedition Acts. The resolutions claimed the acts passed by the Federalists were unconstitutional and politically motivated, thus "void and of no force" in their states.

Resoluciones de Virginia y Kentucky (pág. 226) Resoluciones aprobadas por las asambleas legislativas de Virginia y Kentucky en protesta por las Leyes de Extranjería y Sedición. Las resoluciones afirmaban que las leyes aprobadas por los federalistas eran inconstitucionales y tenían motivaciones políticas, por lo que eran "nulas y carentes de fuerza" en sus estados.

Virginia Plan (p. 209) A plan put forth at the beginning of the Constitutional Convention that proposed a strong central government and a system of representation based on population.

Plan de Virginia (pág. 209) Plan presentado al principio de la Convención Constitucional que proponía un gobierno central fuerte y un sistema de representación basado en la población.

Virginia Resolves (p. 162) A series of statements by the Virginia legislature dedicated to resistance to British taxation without representation in Parliament or colonial control over taxation.

Resoluciones de Virginia (pág. 162) Serie de declaraciones de la legislatura de Virginia dedicadas a la resistencia a los impuestos británicos sin representación en el Parlamento ni control colonial sobre los impuestos.

virtual representation (p. 162) The British claim that every member of Parliament represented the interests of all British subjects, so that colonists did not need the right to vote for members of Parliament.

representación virtual (pág. 162) Los británicos afirman que cada miembro del Parlamento representa los intereses de todos los súbditos británicos, por lo que los colonos no necesitan tener derecho a votar a los miembros del Parlamento.

Voting Rights Act (p. 909) A 1965 act that eliminated literacy tests and other measures commonly used at the time in southern states to prevent Black Americans from voting. The act resulted in dramatic increases in Black voter participation.

Ley del Derecho al Voto (pág. 909) Ley de 1965 que eliminó las pruebas de alfabetización y otras medidas utilizadas habitualmente en aquella época en los estados del sur para impedir el voto a los estadounidenses de raza negra. La ley se tradujo en un aumento espectacular de la participación de los votantes negros.

W

Wade-Davis bill (p. 469) An 1864 bill that created higher barriers for the Confederate states to be readmitted to the Union and granted freedmen the right to vote. President Lincoln vetoed the bill.

Proyecto de ley Wade-Davis (pág. 469) Proyecto de ley de 1864 que creaba mayores barreras para que los estados confederados fueran readmitidos en la Unión y concedía a los libertos el derecho al voto. El presidente Lincoln vetó el proyecto de ley.

Walking Purchase (p. 97) A 1737 treaty that allowed Pennsylvania to expand its boundaries at the expense of the Delaware Indians. The treaty, likely a forgery, allowed the British to add territory that could be walked off in a day and a half.

Walking Purchase (pág. 97) Tratado de 1737 que permitió a Pensilvania ampliar sus fronteras a costa de los indios Delaware. El tratado, probablemente una falsificación, permitía a los británicos añadir territorio que se podía abandonar en un día y medio.

War Industries Board (WIB) (p. 712) A government commission created in 1917 to supervise the purchase of military supplies and oversee the conversion of the economy to meet wartime demands. The WIB embodied a government-business partnership that lasted beyond World War I.

Junta de Industrias Bélicas (WIB) (pág. 712) Comisión gubernamental creada en 1917 para supervisar la compra de suministros militares y supervisar la conversión de la economía para satisfacer las demandas en tiempos de guerra. El WIB encarnó una asociación entre el gobierno y las empresas que duró más allá de la Primera Guerra Mundial.

War of 1812 (p. 281) War between the United States and Great Britain from 1812 to 1815. The war was one consequence of ongoing conflict between Great Britain and France, as each nation sought to forcibly restrict U.S. trade with the other. While the war resulted in little territorial gains by either side, it solidified foreign recognition of the United States as a power and pushed the United States to create a stronger military and national economic foundation in the event of future wars.

Guerra de 1812 (pág. 281) Guerra entre Estados Unidos y Gran Bretaña de 1812 a 1815. La guerra fue una consecuencia del conflicto en curso entre Gran Bretaña y Francia, ya que cada nación trató de restringir por la fuerza el comercio de Estados Unidos con la otra. Aunque la guerra se saldó con escasas ganancias territoriales para ambos bandos, consolidó el reconocimiento extranjero de Estados Unidos como potencia y empujó a este país a crear una base militar y económica nacional más sólida en caso de futuras guerras.

War Powers Acts (p. 786) Two acts passed after the attack on Pearl Harbor that greatly expanded the power of the president during World War II. The acts allowed the president to reorganize federal agencies, expedite wartime production, censor international mail, and provide census data to the FBI.

War Powers Acts (pág. 786) Dos leyes aprobadas tras el ataque a Pearl Harbor que ampliaron enormemente el poder del presidente durante la Segunda Guerra Mundial. Las leyes permitían al presidente reorganizar las agencias federales, acelerar la producción en tiempos de guerra, censurar el correo internacional y proporcionar datos censales al FBI.

War Powers Resolution (p. 896) An act that limited the ability of the president to wage war without the approval of Congress. The 1973 resolution required the president to consult with Congress within forty-eight hours of deploying military forces and required a declaration of war from Congress if troops remained on foreign soil beyond sixty days.

Resolución sobre los Poderes de Guerra (pág. 896) Ley que limitaba la capacidad del presidente para hacer la guerra sin la aprobación del Congreso. La resolución de 1973 obligaba al presidente a consultar con el Congreso en un plazo de cuarenta y ocho horas antes de desplegar fuerzas militares y exigía una declaración de guerra del Congreso si las tropas permanecían en suelo extranjero más de sesenta días.

War Production Board (p. 786) A board established in 1942 to oversee the economy during World War II. It was part of a larger effort to convert American industry to the production of war materials.

Junta de Producción de Guerra (pág. 786) Junta creada en 1942 para supervisar la economía durante la Segunda Guerra Mundial. Formaba parte de un esfuerzo mayor para convertir la industria estadounidense a la producción de material de guerra.

Warsaw Pact (p. 837) A military alliance of the Soviet Union with its seven satellite nations in response to the U.S. Marshall Plan and establishment of NATO. The pact, formed in 1955, was dissolved in 1991 at the end of the Cold War.

Pacto de Varsovia (pág. 837) Alianza militar de la Unión Soviética con sus siete países satélites en respuesta al Plan Marshall estadounidense y a la creación de la OTAN. El pacto, formado en 1955, se disolvió en 1991 al finalizar la Guerra Fría.

Watergate (p. 944) The political scandal and cover-up that forced the resignation of President Nixon in 1974. The scandal centered on a break-in at the Democratic Party headquarters in 1972 and subsequent efforts of the Nixon White House to conceal the administration's involvement in the break-in. The Watergate scandal undermined public trust in government.

Watergate (pág. 944) Escándalo político y encubrimiento que forzó la dimisión del presidente Nixon en 1974. El escándalo se centró en un allanamiento de la sede del Partido Demócrata en 1972 y en los esfuerzos posteriores de la Casa Blanca de Nixon por ocultar la implicación de la administración en el allanamiento. El escándalo Watergate minó la confianza pública en el gobierno.

Whig Party (p. 324) Named for the British political faction that overthrew King James II in the Glorious Revolution, the Whig political party formed in the 1830s to challenge the power of the Democratic Party generally, and Andrew Jackson in particular. The Whigs attempted to forge a diverse coalition from around the country by promoting commercial interests and moral reforms.

Partido Whig (pág. 324) Llamado así por la facción política británica que derrocó al rey Jacobo II en la Revolución Gloriosa, el partido político Whig se formó en la década de 1830 para desafiar el poder del Partido Demócrata en general, y de Andrew Jackson en particular. Los whigs intentaron forjar una coalición diversa en todo el país promoviendo intereses comerciales y reformas morales.

Whiskey Rebellion (p. 222) An uprising beginning in 1791 by western Pennsylvania farmers who led protests against the excise tax on whiskey. The federal government used military force to crush the rebellion, demonstrating the increased federal powers under the new Constitution in contrast to the confederation congress's inability to respond to Shays's Rebellion in 1786.

Rebelión del whisky (pág. 222) Levantamiento iniciado en 1791 por los granjeros del oeste de Pensilvania que encabezaron las protestas contra el impuesto especial sobre el whisky. El gobierno federal utilizó la fuerza militar para aplastar la rebelión, demostrando el aumento de los poderes federales bajo la nueva Constitución en contraste con la incapacidad del congreso de la confederación para responder a la Rebelión de Shays en 1786.

White Citizens' Council (WCC) (p. 871) An organization created in protest following the *Brown v. Board of Education* decision. The WCC consisted mainly of businessmen and professionals who intimidated Black members of the community by threatening their jobs, denied bank loans to Black Americans, and rejected rock 'n' roll music.

Consejo de Ciudadanos Blancos (*White Citizens' Council, WCC*) (pág. 871) Organización creada como protesta tras la decisión del caso *Brown contra Consejo de Educación*. El CMI estaba formado principalmente por hombres de negocios y profesionales que intimidaban a los miembros negros de la comunidad amenazando con sus puestos de trabajo, denegaban préstamos bancarios a los estadounidenses de raza negra y rechazaban la música rock 'n' roll.

white supremacy (p. 364) An ideology promoted by southern planters and intellectuals that maintained that all white people, regardless of class or education, were superior to all Black people.

supremacía blanca (pág. 364) Ideología promovida por los plantadores e intelectuales sureños que sostenía que todos los blancos, independientemente de su clase o educación, eran superiores a todos los negros.

Whitewater (p. 1006) A real estate scandal involving investments made by the Clintons while Bill Clinton was governor of Arkansas. A special prosecutor was appointed in 1994 to investigate allegations of criminal misconduct.

***Whitewater* (pág. 1006)** Escándalo inmobiliario relacionado con las inversiones realizadas por los Clinton mientras Bill Clinton era gobernador de Arkansas. En 1994 se nombró un fiscal especial para investigar las acusaciones de conducta delictiva.

***Williams v. Mississippi* (p. 628)** The 1898 Supreme Court ruling that upheld Jim Crow voter qualifications, such as poll taxes and literacy tests, which disenfranchised Black Americans.

***Williams contra Mississippi* (pág. 628)** Sentencia del Tribunal Supremo de 1898 que confirmó los requisitos para votar establecidos por Jim Crow, como los impuestos de capitación y las pruebas de alfabetización, que privaban del derecho al voto a los estadounidenses de raza negra.

Wilmot Proviso (p. 402) An 1846 proposal by Democratic congressman David Wilmot of Pennsylvania to outlaw slavery in all territory acquired from Mexico. The proposal was defeated, but the fight over its adoption foreshadowed the sectional conflicts of the 1850s, especially regarding the legality of slavery in the territories.

Proviso Wilmot (pág. 402) Propuesta de 1846 del congresista demócrata David Wilmot de Pensilvania para ilegalizar la esclavitud en todo el territorio adquirido a México. La propuesta fue derrotada, pero la lucha por su aprobación prefiguró los conflictos seccionales de la década de 1850, especialmente en lo relativo a la legalidad de la esclavitud en los territorios.

Woman's Christian Temperance Union (WCTU) (p. 681) An organization founded in 1874 to campaign for a ban on the sale and consumption of alcohol. In the late nineteenth century, under Frances Willard's leadership, the WCTU supported a broad social reform agenda.

Unión Cristiana de Mujeres por la Templanza (WCTU) (pág. 681) Organización fundada en 1874 para hacer campaña a favor de la prohibición de la venta y el consumo de alcohol. A finales del siglo XIX, bajo el liderazgo de Frances Willard, el WCTU apoyó un amplio programa de reformas sociales.

Women Accepted for Voluntary Emergency Service (WAVES) (p. 788) The navy volunteer organization for women during World War II, ultimately disbanded in 1972.

Mujeres Aceptadas para Servicio Voluntario de Emergencia (WAVES) (pág. 788) Organización de voluntariado femenino de la Marina durante la Segunda Guerra Mundial, disuelta en 1972.

Women's Army Corps (WACs) (p. 788) The army volunteer organization for women during World War II.

Cuerpo de Mujeres del Ejército (WACs) (pág. 788) Organización de mujeres voluntarias del ejército durante la Segunda Guerra Mundial.

Women's National Loyal League (p. 443) An organization founded by abolitionist women during the Civil War to press Lincoln and Congress to enact universal emancipation.

Liga Nacional Leal de Mujeres (pág. 443) Organización fundada por mujeres abolicionistas durante la Guerra Civil para presionar a Lincoln y al Congreso para que promulgaran la emancipación universal.

Workmen's Compensation Act (p. 699) Regulation guaranteeing the rights of federal employees to receive financial compensation or pursue legal action for any injury occurring on the job.

Ley de Compensación de los Trabajadores (pág. 699) Reglamento que garantiza los derechos de los empleados federales a recibir una compensación económica o emprender acciones legales por cualquier lesión ocurrida en el trabajo.

Works Progress Administration (WPA) (p. 768) A New Deal agency established in 1935 to put unemployed Americans to work on public projects ranging from construction to the arts. The WPA was the largest jobs program during the New Deal, employing more than eight million people.

Agencia para el Progreso de las Obras Publicas (WPA) (pág. 768) Agencia del Nuevo Trato creada en 1935 para poner a trabajar a estadounidenses desempleados en proyectos públicos que abarcaban desde la construcción hasta las artes. La WPA fue el mayor programa de empleo durante el New Deal, dando trabajo a más de ocho millones de personas.

World Trade Organization (WTO) (p. 1005) An organization created in 1995 to promote free trade between its 150 member nations.

Organización Mundial del Comercio (OMC) (pág. 1005) Organización creada en 1995 para promover el libre comercio entre sus 150 países miembros.

World War I (p. 702) The 1914–1918 world war, also known as the Great War, fought between the Central Powers and the Allies. The United States entered the war in 1917.

Primera Guerra Mundial (pág. 702) La guerra mundial de 1914-1918, también conocida como la Gran Guerra, librada entre las Potencias Centrales y los Aliados. Estados Unidos entró en guerra en 1917.

World Wide Web (p. 1009) Established in 1991 as a way to access the Internet and connect documents and other resources to one another through hyperlinks.

World Wide Web (pág. 1009) Creada en 1991 como forma de acceder a Internet y conectar documentos y otros recursos entre sí mediante hiperenlaces.

Wounded Knee massacre (p. 540) A massacre committed by the U.S. military in South Dakota, December 29, 1890. The Plains Indians, on the edge of starvation, began the "Ghost Dance," which they believed would protect them from bullets and restore their old way of life. Following one of the dances, a rifle held by an American Indian misfired. In response, U.S. soldiers invaded the encampment, killing some 250 people.

Masacre de Wounded Knee (pág. 540) Masacre cometida por el ejército de los Estados Unidos en Dakota del Sur el 29 de diciembre de 1890. Los indígenas de las llanuras, al borde de la inanición, comenzaron la "Danza de los Espíritus" que creían los protegería de las balas y restauraría su antiguo estilo de vida. Al término de una de las danzas, un rifle sostenido por un indígena estadounidense se disparó por error. En respuesta, los soldados estadounidenses invadieron el campamento, matando a alrededor de 250 personas.

X

XYZ Affair (p. 225) A 1798 incident in which French agents demanded bribes before meeting with American diplomatic representatives.

Asunto XYZ (pág. 225) Incidente de 1798 en el que agentes franceses exigieron sobornos antes de reunirse con representantes diplomáticos estadounidenses.

Y

Yalta Agreement (p. 803) An agreement negotiated at the 1945 Yalta Conference by Roosevelt, Churchill, and Stalin about the fate of postwar Eastern Europe, promising free elections. The Yalta Agreement did little to ease growing tensions between the Soviet Union and its Western Allies.

Acuerdo de Yalta (pág. 803) Acuerdo negociado en la Conferencia de Yalta de 1945 por Roosevelt, Churchill y Stalin sobre el destino de la Europa Oriental de posguerra, en el que se prometían elecciones libres. El Acuerdo de Yalta no sirvió para aliviar las crecientes tensiones entre la Unión Soviética y sus aliados occidentales.

Yamasee War (p. 108) A war from 1715 to 1717 led by the Yamasee confederation, which intended, but failed, to oust the British from South Carolina.

Guerra Yamasee (pág. 108) Guerra de 1715 a 1717 liderada por la confederación Yamasee, que pretendía, pero fracasó, expulsar a los británicos de Carolina del Sur.

***Yates v. United States* (p. 849)** The 1957 Supreme Court ruling establishing that the Justice Department could not prosecute someone for merely advocating an abstract doctrine favoring the violent overthrow of the government. The ruling was seen as a severe blow to the enforcement of the 1940 Smith Act.

***Yates contra Estados Unidos* (pág. 849)** Sentencia del Tribunal Supremo de 1957 que establece que el Departamento de Justicia no puede procesar a alguien por el mero hecho de defender una doctrina abstracta que favorece el derrocamiento violento del gobierno. La sentencia se consideró un duro golpe para la aplicación de la Ley Smith de 1940.

yellow journalism (p. 661) Sensationalist news accounts meant to sell newspapers by provoking an emotional response in readers. Yellow journalism contributed to the growth of public support for American intervention in Cuba in 1898.

periodismo amarillo (pág. 661) Noticias sensacionalistas destinadas a vender periódicos provocando una respuesta emocional en los lectores. El periodismo amarillo contribuyó a el crecimiento del apoyo público a la intervención estadounidense en Cuba en 1898.

yeoman farmer (p. 361) A non-slaveholding independent landowner. Although southern yeomen farmers had connections to the plantation economy, many realized that their interests were not always identical to those of the planter elite.

***Yeoman farmer* (pág. 361)** Terrateniente independiente que no posee esclavos. Aunque los campesinos del sur tenían conexiones con la economía de las plantaciones, muchos se dieron cuenta de que sus intereses no siempre coincidían con los de la élite de los plantadores.

Young Americans for Freedom (YAF) (p. 939) A group of young conservatives from college campuses formed in 1960 in Sharon, Connecticut. The group favored free market principles, states' rights, and anticommunism.

Jóvenes Estadounidenses por la Libertad (YAF) (pág. 939) Grupo de jóvenes conservadores de campus universitarios formado en 1960 en Sharon, Connecticut. El grupo estaba a favor de los principios del libre mercado, los derechos de los estados y el anticomunismo.

Z

Zimmermann telegram (p. 705) A secret 1917 telegram in which Germany offered Mexico an alliance in the event that the United States entered World War I and promised to help Mexico reclaim lands ceded to the United States after the Mexican-American War in 1848. The telegram's publication in U.S. newspapers helped build public support for war.

Telegrama Zimmermann (pág. 705) Telegrama secreto de 1917 en el que Alemania ofrecía a México una alianza en caso de que Estados Unidos entrara en la Primera Guerra Mundial y prometía ayudar a México a reclamar las tierras cedidas a Estados Unidos tras la guerra mexicano-estadounidense de 1848. La publicación del telegrama en los periódicos estadounidenses contribuyó a aumentar el apoyo público a la guerra.

zoot suit riots (p. 793) A series of violent attacks by white servicemen and citizens against Mexican American teenagers wearing zoot suits in 1943 in Los Angeles, California.

Disturbios de los trajes zoot (pág. 793) Serie de ataques violentos por parte de militares y ciudadanos blancos contra adolescentes mexicano-americanos que llevaban trajes zoot en 1943 en Los Ángeles, California.

Credits

Period 1

Francisco García de Loaysa, Francisco (fl. 1540), letter to Francisco Vásquez de Coronado [in Spanish]. The Gilder Lehrman Institute of American History, GLC04883.

Period 2

Françoise Niellon, excerpt from "Québec in the Time of Champlain," *Post-Medieval Archaeology*, Volume 43, 2009, Issue 1: The Recent Archaeology of the Early Modern Period in Quebec City. Copyright © Society for Post-Medieval Archaeology 2009, reprinted by permission of Taylor & Francis Ltd, https://www.tandfonline.com on behalf of Society for Post-Medieval Archaeology.

Cara Anzilotti, excerpt from "Autonomy and the Female Planter in Colonial South Carolina," *The Journal of Southern History*, vol. 63, no. 2, May 1997. Copyright © 1997 by Southern Historical Association. Used with permission.

Elizabeth Reis, excerpt from "The Devil, the Body, and the Feminine Soul in Puritan New England," *The Journal of American History*, vol. 82, no. 1, June 1995, pp. 15–36. Copyright © 2003 by Oxford University Press. Used with permission. Permission conveyed through Copyright Clearance Center, Inc.

Richard L. Haan, "The 'Trade Do's Not Flourish as Formerly': The Ecological Origins of the Yamassee War of 1715," in *Ethnohistory*, vol. 28, no. 4, pp. 341–358. Copyright 1981, the American Society for Ethnohistory. All rights reserved. Republished by permission of the copyright holder, and the Publisher. www.dukeupress.edu.

William L. Ramsey, excerpt from " 'Something Cloudy in Their Looks': The Origins of the Yamasee War Reconsidered," *The Journal of American History*, vol. 90, no. 1, June 2003, pp. 44–75; https://doi.org/10.2307/3659791. Reprinted by permission of Oxford University Press on behalf of the Organization of American Historians. Permission conveyed through Copyright Clearance Center, Inc.

Mark M. Smith, excerpt from "Remembering Mary, Shaping Revolt: Reconsidering the Stono Rebellion," *The Journal of Southern History*, vol. 67, no. 3, Aug. 2001, p. 513. Copyright © Southern Historical Association. Used with permission.

Period 4

Daniel Walker Howe, excerpt from "The Evangelical Movement and Political Culture in the North during the Second Party System," *Journal of American History*, vol. 77, no. 4, Mar. 1991, pp. 1216–1239. Copyright © 1991 by Oxford University Press. Used by permission. Permission conveyed through Copyright Clearance Center, Inc.

Period 6

W. Skelton Glenn, excerpt from "The Recollections of W.S. Glenn, Buffalo Hunter," *Panhandle-Plains Historical Review*, vol. XXII, pp. 21–64, 1949. Copyright © 1949 by Panhandle-Plains Historical Review. Used with permission.

Period 7

Barton J. Bernstein, excerpt from *Towards a New Past* by Barton J. Bernstein, Lloyd C. Gardner, and Eugene D. Genovese, copyright © 1968 by Penguin Random House LLC. Copyright © renewed 1996 by Barton J. Bernstein, Lloyd C. Gardner, and Eugene D. Genovese. Used by permission of Pantheon Books, an imprint of the Knopf Doubleday Publishing Group, a division of Penguin Random House LLC. All rights reserved.

Father Johannes Siemes, "Hiroshima, August 6, 1945," *Bulletin of the Atomic Scientists*, vol. 1, no. 11, 1946, pp. 5–6. Copyright © Bulletin of the Atomic Scientists, reprinted by permission of Taylor & Francis Ltd, http://www.tandfonline.com on behalf of *Bulletin of the Atomic Scientists*.

Mary Anne Read, excerpt from oral interview about her childhood during World War II, June 2012. Moore Memorial Public Library.

Period 8

Jacquelyn Dowd Hall, "The Long Civil Rights Movement and the Political Uses of the Past," *Journal of American History*, vol. 91, Mar. 2005, pp. 1245–1246. Reproduced with permission of Oxford University Press — Journals. Permission conveyed through Copyright Clearance Center, Inc.

Martin Luther King Jr., excerpt from *Speech at Holt Street Baptist Church*, December 5, 1955. Reprinted by arrangement with The Heirs to the Estate of Martin Luther King Jr., c/o Writers House as agent for the proprietor New York, NY. Copyright © 1955 by Dr. Martin Luther King Jr. Renewed © 1983 by Coretta Scott King.

Martin Luther King Jr., excerpt from "Letter from Birmingham Jail," April 1963. Reprinted by arrangement with The Heirs to the Estate of Martin Luther King Jr., c/o Writers House as agent for the proprietor New York, NY. Copyright © 1963 by Dr. Martin Luther King Jr. Renewed © 1991 by Coretta Scott King.

Tom Hayden and others, excerpt from "The Port Huron Statement," 1962. Reproduced with permission of Barbara Williams Hayden.

Period 9

Alan Rusbridger and Ewen MacAskill, "Edward Snowden Interview," *Guardian*, July 18, 2014. Copyright Guardian News & Media Ltd. 2023. All rights reserved.

Stephen M. Walt, excerpt from "Two Cheers for Clinton's Foreign Policy," *Foreign Affairs*, March/April 2000. Copyright © 2000 Council on Foreign Affairs, publisher of *Foreign Affairs*. All rights reserved. Distributed by Tribune Content Agency, LLC.

Vladislav M. Zubok, "Soft Power: Reagan the Dove," *The New Republic*, June 21, 2004. Copyright © 2004 by The New Republic. All rights reserved. Used under license. https://newrepublic.com.

Index

Page numbers followed by *(f)* indicate figures, *(i)* indicate illustrations, *(m)* indicate maps, *(s)* indicate sources, and *(t)* indicate tables. Boldface indicates the name of a person.

G

L

O

Q

R

U